THE COLLECTED SCIENTIFIC PAPERS OF
PAUL A. SAMUELSON

VOLUME II

THE COLLECTED SCIENTIFIC PAPERS OF
PAUL A. SAMUELSON

Edited by Joseph E. Stiglitz

THE M.I.T. PRESS
Massachusetts Institute of Technology
Cambridge, Massachusetts, and London, England

See pages 1783–1791 for acknowledgments of previously published material.

Second Printing, June 1970

ISBN 0 262 19022 2

Library of Congress Catalog Card Number: 65-28408
Printed in the United States of America

AUTHOR'S PREFACE

Over the years it has been suggested that I bring out some collected papers. As the supply of my reprints has become more and more exhausted, I have in principle become more and more impressed with the force of this argument. But I have always felt hesitant to interrupt current new research merely in order to reassemble old research. Now the matter has been taken out of my hands. The M.I.T. Press and kind colleagues have undertaken to do the job. Mr. Joseph Stiglitz, an able young graduate student, has agreed to do the minimum editing needed for such a collection.

My own preference was for as complete and unpretentious an assemblage as possible. I could not see why anyone else's research program should be interrupted by the arduous job of proofreading completely reset mathematical symbolism. As to selection of articles, the choice has been that of Mr. Stiglitz alone. A number of previously unpublished papers, such as the widely circulated RAND Memorandum on "Market Mechanisms and Maximization," have been included. My advice on selection was: When in doubt, include — of course excluding all nonscientific writing, such as periodic financial journalism for the *London Financial Times,* the *Nihon Keizai Shimbun,* and the *Washington Post,* and excluding most book reviews.

Personally, I should have preferred a simple chronological listing, so that any continuities of thought might reveal themselves. But wise friends, such as Professors Robert M. Solow and Charles P. Kindleberger, have prevailed upon me to agree to an arrangement by subject matter. Mr. Stiglitz has alone taken the responsibility for the selection and arrangement of articles. And I think he would be the first to admit that alternative classifications might have been made with equal advantage, since topics like Welfare Economics and International Trade, and indeed all of the topics of modern economics, are so interdependent as to defy any arbitrary classification.

I must confess that I have been tempted to make an editorial change here or there. This temptation I have resisted. In several places where an outright error of substance occurred, I have added correcting paragraphs that are clearly marked to be of 1965 vintage. When tempted to omit a particular article, I was taken aback to have a colleague say, "Why I thought that one of your most interesting pieces." Only one of the items included seems to me to express some bad temper, but I decided that to exclude it would be invidious and would also deprive the reader of the opportunity to judge whether, as I have sometimes heard it said, I have mellowed over the years.

Finally, my thanks go to Joseph Stiglitz for a difficult and thankless job well done. Since I have continued to write articles at a steady pace and since he cannot expect to stay young forever, Mr. Stiglitz has wisely decided to call a halt at the arbitrary date of late 1964. And high time, says my wife and fairest critic.

PAUL A. SAMUELSON

Cambridge, Massachusetts
September 1965

EDITOR'S PREFACE

These two volumes contain virtually all of Professor Paul A. Samuelson's contributions to economic theory through mid-1964. These articles have been collected from the economic journals, *Festschrifts*, and several books on current economic problems. A few of the articles were unpublished RAND Memoranda, and others were lectures.

The arrangement by topics has not been easy; some of the articles, or chapters, properly belong in several sections; some might be put most properly in sections of their own. A few of the final decisions had to be made somewhat arbitrarily. The parts are arranged into books of closely related subjects. Within the parts, the articles are arranged chronologically, except where several articles were very closely tied together. For instance, the 1963 article on the "Gains from International Trade Once Again" immediately follows the 1939 article "The Gains from International Trade." I hope that this arrangement will make the book more useful to the reader than a strictly chronological ordering. For those who prefer the latter, however, I have included in the acknowledgments a chronological list of the articles.

Although no major changes in text have been made, a number of minor corrections have been made. After several of the articles, a 1965 postscript has been inserted in which Professor Samuelson states his present position on these topics.

On some of the topics discussed, a more recent exposition will be found in *The Foundations of Economic Analysis* (Cambridge: Harvard University Press, 1948) by Professor Samuelson, and *Linear Programming and Economic Analysis* (New York: McGraw-Hill, 1958) by Robert Dorfman, Paul A. Samuelson, and Robert M. Solow.

JOSEPH E. STIGLITZ

Cambridge, Massachusetts
July 1965

Revised Contents from *The Collected Scientific Papers of Paul A. Samuelson.* Published by The M.I.T. Press. Copyright © 1966, by The Massachusetts Institute of Technology

CONTENTS

Volume II

Book Three

Trade, Welfare, and Fiscal Policy

Contents

Book Four

Economics and Public Policy

Contents

BOOK THREE

Trade, Welfare, and Fiscal Policy

PART IX

Trade

60

WELFARE ECONOMICS AND INTERNATIONAL TRADE

International trade theory was developed by practical men interested in normative, welfare problems. By making rigorously abstract assumptions, we may consider trade between two individuals instead of between countries. For each individual the technical conditions of production can be expressed in terms of a family of substitution curves. As between individuals three types of movements are distinguished: (1) both individuals get more of every commodity with less of every productive service; (2) each individual moves higher on his preference scale, even though less of particular commodities may be received; (3) one individual moves to a higher position as the other moves to a lower. The first two are clearly beneficial to both parties. About the third nothing can be said in the absence of special and complete welfare judgments. It is demonstrable that free trade (pure competition) leads to an equilibrium in which each country is better off than in the absence of trade, and that no movements of the first or second kinds are possible. Nevertheless, this does not prove that each country is better off than under any other kind of trade; indeed, if all others are free trading, it always pays a single country not to trade freely.

Historically the development of economic theory owes much to the theory of international trade. Precisely because the classical theory of international trade arose in the thought of "practical" men, interested as *citizens* in problems of public policy, the normative and welfare aspects of the subject have received considerable attention. This is clearly seen in the agitation for and against free trade.

Since welfare economics still constitutes a vexing problem in the pure theory of value and distribution, it would perhaps be useful to examine some normative aspects of the conventional theory of international trade in order to determine the extent to which and the senses in which the conclusions reached in that field are valid.

At the outset, it is understood of course that the very discussion of welfare economics implies certain ethical assumptions. I do not propose, however, to discuss the philosophical grounds for holding or rejecting different ethical precepts or assumptions. Rather will the discussion be confined to the implications of different ethical assumptions and the necessary and sufficient presuppositions for the truth of various theorems.[1]

Since the real world presents almost infinite complexity, it is always necessary in matters of this sort to resort to ideally strong cases to bring out the essential theoretical issues. For this purpose I shall consider not trade between national countries as actually existing in the modern world, but rather have recourse to an analogous situation of trade and barter between two or more individuals. This may be regarded as trade between countries with perfect social solidarity and consensus (*e.g.,* totalitarian states); or between units each consisting of identical (representative) individuals; or better still, merely as trade between individuals which illuminates the

---

[1] To indicate the "objectivity" of our discussion, it may be remarked that the whole argument will be deductive, consisting essentially of *propositional functions* at the same level of thought as a maximum problem in the theory of calculus.

processes of international trade. In this way the problem of weighing and combining different individuals' advantages within each country is avoided. Our license for employing this convention is amply provided by innumerable examples in the classical theory of international trade.

From the consideration of the problem of bilateral monopoly it is hoped that much light will be thrown on the welfare problems of international trade, and that at least one important misconception in the conventional theory will be revealed as such.

I

Consider first a self-sufficient individual (country) engaging in no outside trade. We take as given all technological relations, *i.e.*, production functions; tastes of the individual in an ordinal—as opposed to a cardinal—sense. For generality, we include in the individual's scale of preferences the amounts of the various kinds of productive services (inputs) rendered.

Under these assumptions it is possible to reduce our technological relations to the following implicit form:

$$\varphi \ (x, \ y, \ a, \ b) = o$$

where x and y are the amounts of commodities produced per unit time, and a and b are amounts of productive services rendered per unit time. This relationship is to be interpreted as follows: for any pre-assigned amounts of y, a and b, there is a maximum amount of x which can be produced; x, a and b being held constant, a similar argument holds for y. Furthermore, for given amounts of x, y, and b, there is a minimum amount of a necessary; and likewise for b.

If we regard the amounts of a and b as fixed, the resulting relationship between x and y is the familiar *substitution* or *production indifference curve*. Contrary to the usual exposition, this curve is not a technological datum. Its derivation is essentially an economic problem and imposes certain equalities on the marginal physical productivities of non-specific factors. We shall take its derivation as having been performed and shall make the usual assumptions as to its shape, deducible from the law of variability of proportions (see Figure I). Be it noted that there is not one substitution curve, but one curve for any pre-assigned pair of values for a and b.

Taking account of this implicit relationship between our variables, the individual acting in isolation selects that combination of variables, consistent with the above relationship, which is most preferable to him, or which maximizes any index of his utility. This imposes as a condition of equilibrium the equivalence of the ratio of marginal utilities (rate of consumer substitution or indifference) to the slope of the production indifference curve, drawn up as of the optimum values of a and b. The optimum values of a and b are determined at the point where the derived utility of them, *i.e.*, utility of their marginal physical product, is equated to their marginal disutility.[2]

It will be seen from the above that the doctrine of opportunity cost, properly stated, in no way contradicts the so-called pain-cost theory of value. In fact, when stated with full qualifications, the doctrine of opportunity cost inevitably degenerates into the conditions of general equilibrium.

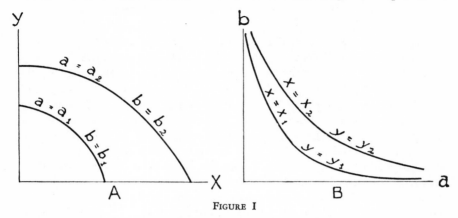

FIGURE I

It may be well to point out that the maximum conditions stated above could have been achieved by means of a system of pricing. As a matter of bookkeeping the individual might employ the fiction of setting provisional prices upon all commodities and factors of production. After a series of successive approximations, the equilibrium set of prices achieved would be such as to satisfy the various marginal conditions. Undoubtedly it is this "parametric" behavior of prices, which does yield a maximum position in a Robinson Crusoe economy, which accounts for the popularity of perfect competition with many orthodox economists, and the identification of this condition as an optimum one. That this involves the fallacy of composition will be demonstrated later.

One final point deserves emphasis. Since there exists only a scale of preference in an ordinal sense, it is impossible from the very nature of our original assumptions to evaluate numerically the magnitude of the amount of gain to an individual in moving from one position to another.[3]

[2] Although use is made of utility and disutility, only ratios of marginal utility and disutility are involved, and so all conditions could just as well have been expressed in terms of indifference directions, since the cardinal magnitude of utility is not in question.

[3] The attempt to measure gain by consumer's surplus is valid only under much more restrictive Marshallian assumptions of the existence of independent utilities with constant marginal utility of money. The use of index numbers can really only serve in this connection to determine under favorable circumstances the direction of the change—whether more or less preferred. This is not intended to be in contradiction to the use of an index number as a measure of the cost of living in different situations.

Thus, the attempt to compare the relative gains of different individuals is ruled out, entirely apart from the possibility of making inter-individual comparisons.

II

Hitherto, we have been dealing with an individual in isolation. Turning now to the consideration of two or more individuals engaged in some form of trade, the essential difficulties of the problem arise.

For simplicity let us consider only two individuals under the conditions elaborated above. It is necessary to distinguish sharply among at least three different kinds of movements which might take place as the result of the opening up of trade or of a change in the form which trade takes. (1) Both individuals may get more of every commodity while performing less of every productive service. Such a movement from almost any ethical standpoint must be regarded as an improvement and as a desirable one. (2) Each individual moves to a position higher up on his preference scale, although some of one commodity may be foregone in order to receive a more than compensating amount of another. Similarly there may be changes in the amounts of productive services rendered which are more than compensated for. Such a movement also would probably be considered desirable, although considerable knowledge of the scale of preference of each individual would be needed in order to identify such a movement. (3) One individual is moved to a lower position while the position of the other is improved. In the absence of additional ethical assumptions of a very complete kind, it would be impossible to determine whether or not such a movement would be desirable. To say that the marginal social utility of each good should be equal for every individual is to leave entirely unanswered the question as to how such a magnitude is defined. Here no attempt will be made to inquire into the various possibilities in this field.

In the case of the individual's acting in isolation, the maximum position achieved was such that a movement in any direction led to a less preferred situation, just as any movement from the top of a hill must be in a downward direction. It is precisely because of the usual assumptions of continuity that the mathematical characterization of a maximum position by certain equalities of differential coefficients (equivalences at the margin) is able to express certain inequalities for finite movements.

It would be tempting in the case of trade between two individuals to define as the equilibrium position any situation from which there is not possible any movement of the first two kinds. Clearly any tentative position reached from which both could move and be improved could not be regarded as an optimum position. However, it will be shown that there does not exist one point—or even a finite set of points—which forms the solution of these conditions. That is to say, there exists an infinite set of conceivable situations such that no movements are possible which better both parties.

This may be illustrated by the extremely simple case of barter between two individuals, each endowed with initial amounts of the various commodities.

In this case it is well known that by mutual agreement each party will finally land somewhere on the Edgeworthian contract curve. This is the locus of points (note, not a single point!) at which the ratio of the marginal utilities of the various goods are equal for both individuals. From such a locus there is no possible movement which does not injure one party. Moreover, from any point not on the contract curve, there always exist possible movements of the first two kinds. The ruling out of such movements does not serve, therefore, to pick out an optimal point of equilibrium, but rather narrows down the possibilities to a locus of points, still infinite in number. A movement along the contract curve is necessarily of the third kind concerning the desirability of which the economist, as such, has nothing to say.

Consider then the equilibrium which will result when both individuals behave like competitors, *i.e.,* each considers prices as given, but both together determine the prices at that level which will equate the amounts demanded and supplied of all commodities. This equilibrium is represented by the intersection of the familiar Marshallian offer curves.

Two things are obviously true in this case. First, in the final equilibrium established, each individual will be better off *than in the absence of any trade at all.* Second, the equilibrium point will lie somewhere on the contract curve, since the ratios of marginal utilities of all goods are equal to the ratios of the common prices, and hence equal to each other.

Thus, and this is the crux of the argument, under free trade both parties are better off than under no trade at all, but are not necessarily in *the* optimum position. There is absolutely no presumption whatsoever that this equilibrium point is superior in any sense to any other point on the contract curve; for the movement between any two such points is of the third kind, about which nothing can be said.

The very fact that any trade takes place is an indication that both individuals are better off, since each can at the very worst refuse to trade. Economists have proved this at great length in many ways under the mistaken impression that they were at the same time proving the desirability of free trade.

The free trade equilibrium point very obviously is not the most preferred point to any one country. Its maximum would occur when the other country consumes nothing, and it consumes all. Obviously the other country would not consent to this, since it need not trade at all. Under favorable circumstances of higgling, one country might be forced to a point on the contract curve at which it received an infinitesimal gain from trade, and vice versa. There is absolutely no ground for saying, or no sense in stating, that the free trade point is the point of fair compromise, since only movements of the third kind are involved. In fact, one country behaving like a competitor, it can be shown that it is always to the advantage of the other not to so behave, but rather to take account monopolistically of its own effect on price.[4]

A very similar argument holds *a fortiori* in the more general case where output in each country is variable. It could be easily shown that there exists a production locus, analogous to the contract curve, along which certain ratios of equivalence of marginal productivities hold, and from which all movements are of a kind to decrease the total potential productivities of all goods in both countries. But, as before, this is a locus and not a point. The demonstration that under free trade this locus is attained, in no way establishes a presumption in favor of the point so reached.

III

Nothing said here is in fundamental contradiction to the orthodox theory of comparative costs in international trade. But if the thesis here presented be accepted as valid, it should serve as a warning against a possible misinterpretation of the classical theory.

Furthermore, this thesis must not be construed as being necessarily contrary to the political question of free (or freer) trade. It may well be argued that modern tariff and quota restrictions are of the sort that their abolition would in many cases result in the betterment of all parties concerned. But, as a matter of scientific integrity, it would seem desirable to clarify economic theory on these issues.

PAUL A. SAMUELSON

Harvard University

[4] The monopolistic country will move the other along its offer curve up to a point of tangency of that locus with the monopolist's indifference curve.

61

THE GAINS FROM INTERNATIONAL TRADE

[1] In a recent paper[1] the thesis was advanced that while it is not possible to demonstrate rigorously that *free* trade is better (in some sense) for a country than *all* other kinds of trade, it nevertheless can be shown conclusively that (in a sense to be defined later) free trade or some trade is to be preferred to *no* trade at all. I should like here to amplify these remarks with respect to the last point, that some trade is better than no trade.

This is by no means a novel proposition. Indeed, it can be traced back to the beginnings of the Classical theory of international trade. It has become associated, however, quite unnecessarily in my opinion, with a labour theory of value, or a "real cost" theory of value, or more recently, with an opportunity cost theory of value. All of these have come in for considerable criticism in recent years as restrictive special cases of the so-called theory of general equilibrium. Those writers who have insisted on the need for a modern theory of value for a positive description of behaviour in international trade have in general ignored the normative aspects of international trade, presumably in the belief that as soon as one gives up the inadmissible special theories indicated above, nothing can be said concerning this problem.[2] It will be argued here that this is a mistake, that from the most general theories of equilibrium all valid normative propositions can be derived.

[2] It is well to indicate clearly the assumptions under which our analysis is to take place. We shall consider a single economy consisting of one or more individuals enjoying a certain unchanging amount of technological knowledge, so that we may take as data the production functions relating the output of each commodity to the amounts of inputs devoted to its production. Any number of commodities is assumed; there may also be any number of inputs or productive services. These are not necessarily fixed in amount, but may have supply functions in terms of various economic prices. Moreover, for our purposes the differentiation of the factors of production can proceed to any degree; thus, labour services of the same man in different occupations are not regarded as the same factor of production unless the provider of these services is indifferent as between these two uses. Similarly, in order that the productive services rendered by different individuals may be consid-

---

[1]P. A. Samuelson, "Welfare Economics and International Trade" (*American Economic Review*, June, 1938).

[2]A recent exception is provided by P. T. Ellsworth's *International Economics* (New York, 1938). However, the problem is posed, not settled. Professor Haberler in his *The Theory of International Trade* (London, 1936) does not employ a full general equilibrium approach.

ered the same service, it is necessary that in every use they be infinitely substitutable.

In order to ensure that perfect competition is possible, we rule out increasing returns, and assume that all production functions show constant returns with respect to proportional changes of *all* factors. Each individual acts as if he were a small part of the markets which he faces and takes prices as given parameters which he cannot influence by changes in his own supplies or demands. It is assumed that for each individual there exists an *ordinal* preference scale in which enter all commodities and productive services, and that subject to the restraints of fixed prices he always selects optimal amounts of each and every commodity and every productive service (some zero in amount). Each individual is better off if he receives more of every commodity while rendering less of every productive service. No attempt is made to render the "utilities" and "disutilities" of different persons comparable.

[3] Under these conditions, for any assumed set of prices there will correspond definite demand and supply reactions on the part of every individual. Moreover, the total outputs of each commodity will be determined, and the total amounts of productive factors necessary to produce these outputs will be determined. If the economy is isolated, it will be necessary as conditions of equilibrium that prices of commodities and factors of production be such as to equalize the amounts produced and consumed of each and every commodity, and to equalize the amounts supplied and demanded of every productive factor.

Under assumed conditions of ownership of the factors of production and assumed scales of preference for commodities and productive services on the part of every individual, there will result in general (waiving possible multiplicities of equilibrium raising problems not peculiar to international trade) unique equilibrium quantities of consumption goods and productive services for each and every individual. It is unnecessary to write down mathematically these equations to deduce the familiar fact that not enough has been assumed to be able to deduce the absolute level of commodity and factor prices, but that these are determined except for a factor of proportionality; i.e., relative commodity and factor prices are determined. Let us write as follows the equilibrium set of prices, determined to within a factor of proportionality, which will be established for our economy when isolated,

$$p_1^0, p_2^0, \ldots, p_n^0, w_1^0, w_2^0, \ldots, w_s^0,$$

with corresponding equilibrium total quantities of the respective commodities and productive services,

$$x_1^0, x_2^0, \ldots, x_n^0, a_1^0, a_2^0, \ldots, a_s^0.$$

The total amounts produced of the respective commodities will be indicated by the barred letters,

$$\bar{x}_1^0, \ \bar{x}_2^0, \ \ldots, \ \bar{x}_n^0,$$

equal respectively in the isolated state to the quantities (unbarred) consumed.

[4] Before introducing possibilities for trade into our system, it will be useful in view of the later discussion first to develop certain relations which must hold in the field of *production*. Confronted with given factor prices, firms will combine factors of production in such proportions as to produce any selected quantity of consumers' goods at the lowest total money cost. In consequence of this, certain marginal conditions of equality will be attained (or at least certain inequalities with respect to finite movements). Although the proof is not given here,[3] it can be shown that this places restrictions on the possible combinations of factors of production and commodities which can occur. Indeed, it will be found that the totals of commodities produced and the totals of productive services must obey an implicit equation of the following form:

$$\phi \, [\bar{x}_1, \bar{x}_2, \ldots, \bar{x}_n, a_1, a_2, \ldots, a_s] = 0. \tag{1}$$

This is capable of the following interpretation: for preassigned values of all productive services and all but one commodity, this equation gives the *maximum* amount of the remaining commodity which can be produced with the given state of technology. Moreover, with preassigned amounts of all commodities and all but one productive service, this shows the *minimum* amount of this one productive service which is necessary.

Utilizing the well-known law of variable proportions, the following remarkable theorem can be established. Consider any set of commodity and factor prices,

$$p_1', p_2', \ldots, p_n', w_1', w_2', \ldots, w_s'.$$

Since each entrepreneur is trying to maximize his profits, there will result an optimal set (not unique) of commodities produced and productive services used, indicated by

$$\bar{x}_1', \bar{x}_2', \ldots, \bar{x}_n', a_1', a_2', \ldots, a_s',$$

satisfying, of course, equation [1]. Our theorem says that *for such preassigned prices the resulting optimal quantities of commodities and productive services maximize for the economy as a whole the algebraic difference between total value of output and total factor cost, as compared to any other commodity and factor combinations satisfying equation* [1]. This is equivalent to the following inequality:

[3]In a forthcoming paper on the conditions of equilibrium in international trade I have gone more fully into these and other matters.

$$[p_1'\,\bar{x}_1'+p_2'\,\bar{x}_2'+\ldots+p_n'\,\bar{x}_n']-[w_1'\,a_1'+w_2'\,a_2'+\ldots+w_s'\,a_s']\geqq$$
$$[p_1'\,\bar{x}_1+p_2'\,\bar{x}_2+\ldots+p_n'\,\bar{x}_n]-[w_1'\,a_1+w_2'\,a_2+\ldots+w_s'\,a_s], \qquad [2]$$

where the unprimed x's and a's represent *any* point satisfying equation [1]. This inequality merely places certain curvature restrictions on the surface represented by equation [1], for the various ratios between respective prices correspond in a well-known manner to the respective slopes (when they exist) of this surface.[4]   In figure I are presented typical shapes for

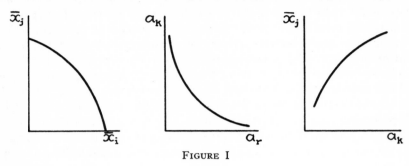

FIGURE I

various cross-sections of this surface.   In the first diagram is shown the amount that must be given up of one commodity, x_j, in order to get more of another, x_i, with all other variables held constant.   This substitution curve must be concave to the origin.   The next diagram shows the amount of one input, a_k, which must be added to compensate for withdrawals of a_r, all other variables being held constant.   The last diagram shows the amount of commodity, x_j, that can be secured with additional amounts of a_k, with constant levels for the remaining outputs and inputs.

The above inequality can be written symbolically

$$\Sigma p'\bar{x}'-\Sigma w'a'\geqq\Sigma p'\bar{x}-\Sigma w'a, \qquad [2]$$

where it is always understood that the summations are over the respective n commodities and s productive services.   Of course, a similar inequality holds for any other preassigned set of prices.

[5]   Trade can be introduced very simply into our system without explicitly dealing with any new country or countries.   This is done by the useful device of supposing that there exists an outside market in which there prevail certain arbitrarily established (relative) prices at

[4]The equality sign can hold if all the x's and a's are respectively proportional (or equal) to the primed x's and a's.   In the singular (and rare) case where the preassigned factor prices are such that all factors of production are used in equal proportions by all commodities, it is possible for the equality sign to hold.   This constant cost case does not essentially modify the analysis.

which this country can buy or sell various commodities in unlimited amounts without changing those quoted prices. It does not matter for the present purposes how, in fact, such prices would be established in this outside market or source, but rather we are interested in the effects upon this country of the existence of such quoted prices.

The fact that this outside market will both buy and sell at the new quoted prices will compel the prices of respective goods in the domestic economy to assume equivalent ratios, or else corrective arbitrage movements would take place. Obviously, therefore, we have introduced new forces to determine some of the prices. It is necessary, then, to drop some of our previous conditions. In particular, we must dispense with the condition that the amounts of commodities produced domestically and consumed domestically must be equal. Instead we have the single condition that the total value of imports must equal the total value of exports, or

$$\Sigma px = \Sigma p\bar{x}. \tag{3}$$

It is clear that for any preassigned prices of internationally tradable goods there will result certain equilibrium values for all the other variables, quantities produced and consumed, productive services supplied, and prices of non-tradable commodities and services.

For one set of prices, namely those proportional to the set $[p_1{}^0, p_2{}^0, \ldots, p_n{}^0]$ which would prevail if the economy were isolated, no trade will result.[5] For these particular prices are such as to equalize the domestic production and consumption of each and every good. For any other set of prices, some trade will result, and there will emerge new equilibrium values for all of our unknowns. By assigning appropriate values to our outside prices, we can obviously reproduce all possible conditions of trade which could conceivably arise. This is the justification for introducing a simplifying device which enables us to ignore the existence of outside economies. Of course, if we were trying to explain the *actual* prices with which our economy will be confronted, it would be necessary to consider outside conditions.

[6] I first apply our analysis of the effect of introducing relative prices, different from those which would be established if our system were isolated, to a simplified case in which all members of our economy are identical in every respect. That is, the same ordinal preference schedule relating commodities and productive services is assumed for every individual, and also the same ownership in the means of production.

---

[5] A trivial exception is provided by the constant cost case mentioned in the previous foot-note. Here at the isolated state prices there might be an unimportant possibility of neutral equilibrium as recognized in the Classical theory of international trade. I adopt the convention of defining trade to exclude this possibility.

This does not mean that the utilities of different individuals are comparable. Indeed, since all individuals are identical, if one is bettered (in an ordinal sense) by the introduction of trade, then all will be bettered, and there will be no necessity for making any welfare comparisons between individuals.

In these circumstances, the following theorem can be established: *the introduction of outside (relative) prices differing from those which would be established in our economy in isolation will result in some trade, and as a result every individual will be better off than he would be at the prices which prevailed in the isolated state.* The truth of this has been intuitively apprehended by a great many economists, but I do not believe that there exists anywhere in the literature a rigorous proof of this proposition.

To illustrate the difficulties which must be encountered in establishing this theorem I present a table showing some possible results of the introduction of trade. In the first two columns are respectively the prices and quantities consumed of three commodities; in the next two columns, the prices and quantities produced of the same three goods; in the last two columns, the prices and quantities of two factors of production. Case I gives a hypothetical set of prices which would prevail in the isolated state with equal production and consumption of all commodities. The amounts corresponding to each individual would be some constant fraction of the total quantities. Although actual prices are given to avoid the asymmetry of using any one good or service as *numéraire*, only relative prices are of importance.

If a new set of relative prices are imposed from without, new equilibrium values will be appropriate. Cases II, III, and IV indicate possible sets of equilibrium values which might emerge, depending on the particular make-up of tastes of the individuals in question.[6] In Case II after trade is established, it will be noted that more of every commodity is consumed, while less of every productive service is provided. Obviously, Case II is an instance of our theorem. But what can be said of Case III? Here, the same amounts of all productive services are provided, but not more of every commodity is consumed. More of commodities x_2 and x_3 will be consumed, but less of commodity x_1. In Case IV things appear to be still worse. Not only does the quantity of some commodity decrease, but also more of the productive service a_2 is provided. Is it possible to say in the general case that the new situation is better than the old, or is our theorem false?

It is obvious that a labour theory of value cannot be of any aid in the

[6]Cases II, III, and IV are alternative and mutually exclusive possibilities. Hence, although each is consistent with Case I, they are not necessarily consistent with each other.

analysis of this problem, since two factors of production have been assumed. The opportunity cost doctrine as presented by Professor Haberler could be applied only to Case III, where the total amounts of the various factors of production remain unchanged after trade has taken place. Contemplation of the behaviour of the terms of trade would suggest that an improvement has taken place, but it would be easy to construct examples for which this test would give a spurious result. None of the usual methods throws any light on the question as to whether Case IV represents an improvement over the condition which would

TABLE I

	p	x	p	$\bar{x}$	w	a
Case I—no trade........	1	10	1	10	4	5
	2	15	2	15	2	20
	1	20	1	20		
Case II...............	3	11	3	20	9	4
	2	17	2	15	3	18
	1	23	1	0		
Case III..............	3	8	3	20	6	5
	2	17	2	15	3	20
	1	32	1	0		
Case IV...............	3	8	3	20	6	4
	2	17	2	15	3	22
	1	32	1	0		

prevail in the absence of trade. And yet there can be no doubt that the situation represented in Case IV is the typical case when trade occurs. If we assume that in the real world there are innumerable commodities and productive services, it is scarcely conceivable that after trade takes place more of each and every commodity and less of each and every productive service will result. The introduction of trade would be expected to result in less of one or more commodities and more of one or more productive services.

Still, if the theorem given above is valid, it must follow that we can very definitely show that all the given cases in which trade takes place are better than the original situation illustrated by Case I. It remains only, therefore, to prove our theorem, after which all the illustrative examples will emerge as special instances. It will be noted that the proof to be given depends only on the elementary operations of arithmetic: addition, subtraction, equality, inequality, etc.

To ensure generality, consider any initial set of prices prevailing in the isolated state,

$$p_1{}^0, \quad p_2{}^0, \ldots, \quad p_n{}^0,$$

and the corresponding equilibrium values of the remaining variables,

$$x_1^0, x_2^0, \ldots, x_n^0, \bar{x}_1^0, \bar{x}_2^0, \ldots, \bar{x}_n^0, a_1^0, a_2^0, \ldots, a_s^0, w_1^0, w_2^0, \ldots, w_s^0.$$

Now consider any new set of prices leading to trade,

$$p_1', \quad p_2', \ldots, p_n',$$

and the corresponding new equilibrium values

$$x_1', x_2', \ldots, x_n', \bar{x}_1', \bar{x}_2', \ldots, \bar{x}_n', a_1', a_2', \ldots, a_s', w_1', w_2', \ldots, w_s'.$$

From the production inequality of equation [2] we know that

$$\Sigma p'\bar{x}' - \Sigma w'a' \geqq \Sigma p'\bar{x}^0 - \Sigma w'a^0. \qquad [4]$$

But from the condition that the total value of imports must equal exports, or that the total value of goods produced must equal the total value of goods consumed, a similar inequality will hold if we leave the bars off the x's and consider goods consumed instead of goods produced. This gives

$$\Sigma p'x' - \Sigma w'a' \geqq \Sigma p'x^0 - \Sigma w'a^0. \qquad [5]$$

I now assert that this condition (barring the unimportant case of equality sign mentioned in foot-note 4) assures us that each of our identical individuals is better off in the second case than in the first.

Imagine an individual confronted with commodity and productive service prices $[p_1', p_2', \ldots, p_n', w_1', w_2', \ldots, w_s']$. Subject to these prices, his most preferred position with respect to consumption and the providing of services is shown by his behaviour to be $[x_1', x_2', \ldots, x_n', a_1', a_2', \ldots, a_s']$. By considerations similar to the economic theory of index numbers as developed by Pigou, Haberler, Konüs, Staehle, Leontief, Frisch, *et al.*, it can be shown that this combination is preferred in an ordinal sense to $[x_1^0, x_2^0, \ldots, x_n^0, a_1^0, a_2^0, \ldots, a_s^0].$[7] If at the primed set of prices the individual would have bought the original combination of goods $[X^0]$, and provided the original amounts of productive services $[A^0]$, the total algebraic cost would have been less than that of what he actually bought and sold $[X', A']$. In addition, therefore, something more could have been bought of every commodity, and a little less of every productive service supplied. This proves that $[X', A']$ is better than $[X^0, A^0]$, for if this were not so, why did not the individual actually choose $[X^0, A^0]$, and perhaps a little more of every good and a little less of every service, in preference to $[X', A']$? If the individual was in a true maximum position at the primed prices, it must necessarily follow from

[7]For many reasons I regard the index number approach as a clumsy device for solving the problem at hand. A more convenient test as to the ordinal desirability of two situations is presented in my "Note on the Pure Theory of Consumers' Behavior" (*Economica*, March, 1938).

our inequality that $[X', A']$ is better than $[X^0, A^0]$. Thus, our theorem is proved.

To appreciate the true meaning of this theorem and its proof, the reader may make the experiment of dropping one or more of our premises to show how the proof will break down. Such an exercise is provided by the well-known Graham's Paradox.

No modification in the proof is required by the assumption that there exist domestic consumers' goods which cannot be traded under any circumstances. With slight modification transportation costs could be introduced into the analysis without affecting appreciably the results. It will be noted that the proof is still valid in the case where there exist no resources transferable between different production uses. Indeed, if the commodities are not produced at all, but fall from heaven in fixed amounts per unit time, the theorem still applies. Moreover, the introduction of discontinuities requiring modifications of the usual marginal analysis is already covered in our theorem.

[7] If, as I have shown, the introduction of outside prices different from those which would prevail in the isolated state betters all of our identical individuals, a possible generalization suggests itself. Is it possible to state that the more prices "deviate" (according to some convention) from those of the isolated state, the better off all individuals will be? The answer is in the affirmative. In order not to complicate the present exposition, I withhold the rigorous proof of this proposition until a future occasion.

[8] Before going on to consider more realistic cases where individuals are not all alike, I should like to point out two interesting special cases covered by the previous theorem. The limiting case of an economy in which all individuals are exactly alike is that of a single household or Robinson Crusoe economy consisting of but one unit. Moreover, from a formal point of view a completely unified economy under perfect control of some central authorities interested in maximizing some ordinal preference scale is like a one individual economy. For such single individual economies, pretending to play the game of perfect competition is one possible way of arriving at optimal equilibrium values. If self-sufficiency is not an end in itself, it follows from our previous theorem (and even under less stringent assumptions) that for an individual or unified economy trade is always preferable to no trade, although it is not necessarily true that free trade is the best trading policy.

[9] I now drop the assumption that all individuals are alike with respect to tastes, abilities, ownership of the means of production, etc. The introduction of changed prices leading to trade cannot, of course, be expected always to better each and every individual. After trade, the

prices of items chiefly consumed by a particular individual may have risen making him worse off than before. (It is not possible, however, for every individual to be made worse off.)

In order to evaluate the resulting situation, it would be necessary to have some scale which would take into account comparisons as between different individuals. For some type of weighting of the fortunes of different individuals, the result might be judged an improvement. For some other, such as an egocentric evaluation on the part of those rendered worse off, the resulting situation might be judged to be worse than that which prevailed in the isolated state. If nothing more than this could be said, the problem of the benefits from trade would be of limited theoretical and practical importance.

Fortunately, definite results which do *not* depend upon the comparisons of the real incomes of different people can be derived. Although it cannot be shown that every individual *is* made better off by the introduction of trade, it can be shown that through trade every individual *could* be made better off (or in the limiting case, no worse off). In other words, if a unanimous decision were required in order for trade to be permitted, it would always be possible for those who desired trade to buy off those opposed to trade, with the result that all could be made better off.[8] This can be deduced from the fact that as a result of trade larger (or in the limiting case, equal) amounts of every commodity can be secured with smaller (or equal) amounts of every productive service. Without trade the range of possible commodities which are available with preassigned amounts of all productive factors is given by the implicit equation [1]. If outside prices are introduced, it will always be desirable for production policy to be aimed at maximizing the total value of output at the outside prices, with any preassigned amounts of each and every productive factor. For this will yield a larger money sum than any other production policy, and with a larger sum of money more can be bought of every commodity than with a smaller one. As a result, each of the following three statements is true: [1] more can be had of every commodity as of the same totals of all productive services; [2] of the same preassigned quantities of all consumers' goods, less of every productive service need be rendered; [3] after trade, more of every commodity can be secured with less of every productive service. This ensures us that by Utopian co-operation everyone can be made better off as a result of trade.[9]

<hr>

[8]See Professor Viner's interesting remarks in his *Studies in the Theory of International Trade* (New York, 1937), pp. 533-4.

[9]Mathematically, subject to preassigned outside prices and with preassigned quantities of all productive services, there will result optimal production quantities

I shall make no attempt to construct a numerical index of the gains of trade. In the simplest case of a single individual, only an ordinal preference scale is assumed so that only better or worse comparisons can be made. Such constructs as consumers' surplus are in general inadmissible. Even in the singular cases where they are able to be employed, they are perfectly arbitrary and conventional, adding nothing to the analysis.

[10] In conclusion, I should like to point out that in the above exposition an attempt has been made to demonstrate rigorously with little reliance on intuition the truth of the theorems advanced. Whether or not this should be done is, of course, a matter of taste. Much more important than the carrying through of the formal steps of the argument is the realization that the theorems are true consequences of the premises, and do not rest on *presumption* or *probability*. For in pointing out the consequences of a set of abstract assumptions, one need not be committed unduly as to the relation between reality and these assumptions. On the other hand, in advancing a presumption in favour of an undeducible proposition, the suggestion is conveyed that the difficult task of interpreting reality has already been performed.

PAUL A. SAMUELSON

Society of Fellows,
Harvard University.

---

which are functions of the preassigned variables and satisfy the production limitation of equation [1]. These optimal production quantities will sell for the largest possible total in the outside market, and hence the expression $\Sigma p'x$ is maximized subject to equation [1] and fixed amounts of productive factors. The resulting money sum will be sufficient to permit consumption of goods obeying the condition that all imports must be paid for by exports, or $\Sigma p'x = \text{maximum } \Sigma p'\bar{x}$. Because production is optimal, the result is more (or equal) consumption of every good. Moreover, for sufficiently small reductions of all production services, it will still be possible to have more of every commodity, and hence the truth of the third statement follows.

62

THE GAINS FROM INTERNATIONAL TRADE
ONCE AGAIN [1]

I. Introduction

In 1939 I wrote a paper that showed how some international trade makes a society potentially better off than it would be if restricted to autarky.[2] Although this paper has received a flattering amount of notice, I had always regarded it as somewhat incomplete and had long planned to follow it with a more definite companion piece. For it was written with two purposes in mind other than to say all that can be said about the gains from international trade.

First, it was an attempt to show how the new theories of revealed preference could be used to demonstrate important theorems in welfare economics. And second, it was intended to mediate the dispute between two of my famous teachers, Jacob Viner (then of Chicago) and Gottfried Haberler (Harvard), over the doctrine of opportunity cost in international trade and value theory: my 1939 article was shaped to show how the eclectic doctrine of general equilibrium could take changes in factor supplies in its stride and by the index-number methods of revealed preference illustrate how the Haberlerian transformation curve could be generalised.

Even after the passage of twenty years, the final chapter seemed still to be lacking in the literature. And an interesting 1958 Danish criticism of my earlier paper's treatment of income distribution by Mr. Erling Olsen[3] led me to defend the argument and at long last take up the thorough completion. This time there was no need to worry about the obsolete doctrine of opportunity cost; nor to use index numbers of revealed preference, since for better or worse this approach had already won its place in the literature of economic theory. Good fortune, however, brought Dr. Murray Kemp to M.I.T. as a visiting professor in 1959–61 on his way from Canada to a chair at the University of New South Wales. For, in discussing the present paper, Professor Kemp showed that my alternative approach of 1939 could indeed be carried through all the way to achieve the same final goals.[4] In a real sense, therefore, our two papers are complementary and benefit from simultaneous publication.

[1] Grateful acknowledgement is made to the Ford Foundation for research assistance.

[2] P. A. Samuelson, " The Gains from International Trade," *Canadian Journal of Economics and Political Science*, Vol. V (May 1939), pp. 195–205. Reprinted in the *Readings in the Theory of International Trade* of the American Economic Association.

[3] Erling Olsen, " Udenrigshandelns Gevinst," *Nationaløkonomisk Tideskrift*, Haefte 1–2 (Argana, 1958), pp. 76–9. I am grateful to Mr. Olsen for sending me an English translation of his interesting paper.

[4] Murray C. Kemp, " The Gain From International Trade," pp. 803–19 above.

II. The Small Country Case

On the special assumption that our country under consideration is too small to affect its terms of trade, and on the assumption that the price ratios abroad differ from those that would prevail at home under autarky, Fig. 1's heavy line *EUF* represents our " consumption possibility frontier " with

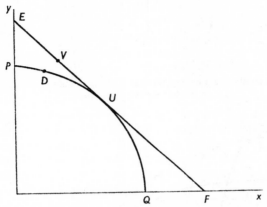

Fig. 1. With no trade, we end up at *D*. With free trade, production ends up at *U*, consumption at *V*, with *UV* the vector of algebraic imports.

some trade. With autarky the consumption possibility frontier is given by the production locus *PDUQ*. Since the trade frontier lies everywhere [1] north-east of the autarky frontier, our society can have more of all goods (and less of all irksome inputs) with some trade. It is in this sense that trade makes us potentially better off.

III. An Important Envelope

I wish to increase the generality of my 1939 argument by now dropping the assumption that our country is small. Let us be large enough to affect our terms of trade as we move along Fig. 2's Marshallian offer curve of the rest of the world for our two-goods.

[1] At *U* itself the frontiers coincide. Thus, if there were some distribution of income which brought us under autarky to *U* rather than *D*, opening up trade would at that point (1) in fact be followed by no international transactions taking place, and hence would (2) represent the limiting case where trade neither helps nor hurts us. (If individuals' tastes and endowments happen to be much alike at home there might be no redistribution of income that would, *under autarky*, get us to *U*. In such a case we would know that the *cum*-trade utility frontier of Fig. 4 does lie uniformly outside the autarky utility frontier. On the other hand, if *U* is a possible autarky point the *cum*-trade frontier will touch the autarky utility frontier at one or more points; but it must always lie north-east of the autarky point corresponding to *D*—as we shall see.)

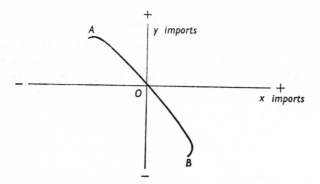

Fig. 2.   *AOB* is the familiar Marshallian offer curve of the rest of the world, but plotted in terms of our algebraic imports.

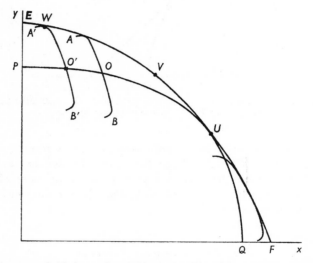

Fig. 3.   The important Baldwin envelope *EF* is generated by sliding *AOB* along *PQ* in such a way as to trace out the frontier of consumable product.   The slopes at *W* are necessarily equal to the slope at *O'*.

Now draw up the envelope frontier [1] of Fig. 3 by sliding the origin of the *AOB* offer curve along the domestic production possibility locus *PQ* in such a way as to trace out the maximal amount of each good that is available

---

[1] See R. E. Baldwin, "Equilibrium in International Trade: A Diagrammatic Analysis," *Quarterly Journal of Economics*, Vol. LXII (1948), pp. 748–62; "The New Welfare Economics and Gains in International Trade," *Quarterly Journal of Economics*, Vol. LXV (1952), pp. 91–101.   See also the valuable paper by Peter B. Kenen, "On the Geometry of Welfare Economics," *Quarterly Journal of Economics*, Vol. LXXI (1957), pp. 426–47.   Given more than two goods, we need modify the exposition only trivially.

for given amounts consumed of the other good.[1]   The resulting envelope
may be called society's *cum*-trade consumption possibility frontier.   Like
Fig. 1's *EUF*, of which it is a generalisation, the new consumption frontier
lies uniformly (save [2] for one point like *U*) outside the autarky consumption
frontier.   *Hence our society is potentially better off in the sense that there is a way
of reallocating the enlarged totals of goods so as to make every person better off.*

It may be noted that the envelope frontier could be attained by an
optimal Mill–Bickerdike tariff or by more direct means.   The Kahn–Graaff
paradox,[3] that the size of the optimal tariff depends only on foreigners'
demand elasticity and not on home consumers' demand, is easily resolved
as follows: the envelope's slope at any point like *W* is related to the slope
of *O′W* as determined by the *AOB* curve alone; but never forget that home
demand must tell us *which W* will be the equilibrium one.

IV. The Utility Possibility Frontier

Practical men and economic theorists have always known that trade
may help some people and hurt others.   Our problem is to show that trade
lovers are theoretically able to compensate trade haters for the harm done
them, thereby making everyone better off.   The ordinal utility diagram of
Fig. 4 is the natural tool to use for this purpose.[4]

The horizontal axis represents ordinal utility of one of our citizens.   The
vertical axis represents ordinal utility of a second citizen.   And for simplicity I suppose there are only two citizens, or two classes of identical
citizens in our country.   A point represents the simultaneous position of
both men: because utility need not be numerically measurable, only north
and south and east and west relationships count.

The point *d* corresponds to point *D* of Fig. 1.   The broken locus
d′dd″ represents the utility possibility frontier if the fixed goods totals of *D*
are allocated in favour of man 1 or man 2 by ideal-sum transfers so that

---

[1] It may help the reader to imagine the offer curve as being cut out from Fig. 2 with scissors
and then being carefully transposed over to Fig. 3 so as to trace out the envelope of its outlying
tangents.   At a point like *W* not only is the offer curve tangential to the envelope but in addition
if we go back to the corresponding pivot point *O′* the slope of the production possibility schedule
there will also necessarily be the same.   This follows from the geometrical properties of an envelope
and has the important economic interpretation that at an optimal point production substitution
ratios must be equal to trading substitution ratios (as well as to consumption substitution ratios).

[2] If the autarky point *D* will in fact become outmoded by the opening of trade, then *D* and *U*
cannot coincide and we know that—by going north-east from *D*—everyone can be made better
off than they were under autarky.

[3] See J. deV. Graaff, *Theoretical Welfare Economics* (Cambridge, 1957), Chapter IX.

[4] Pareto's economics would have been better understood had he explicitly used the utility
frontier concept.   I may refer the reader to my *Foundations of Economic Analysis*, Chapter 8; to
" Evaluation of Real National Income," *Oxford Economic Papers* (New Series), 2, pp. 1–29, particularly p. 6; to " Social Indifference Curves," *Quarterly Journal of Economics*, Vol. LXX (February
1956), pp. 1–22.   As Graaff points out in Chapter IV of his just-cited book, Professor M. Allais of
Paris also developed this social-utility-frontier concept.

there is no " inefficiency " or deadweight loss involved in the transfers. On the other hand, the envelope *pq* is generated by treating every point on *PQ* the way we have treated *D* and then drawing in the north-east frontier.

What is the envelope *ef*? It is the frontier traced out by *all* the points on *EF*. Thus, it is tangential at *v* to the broken locus *v'vv''* representing the

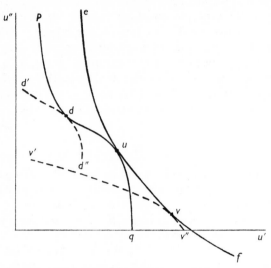

FIG. 4. The *ef* social utility frontier lies outside the autarky frontier *pq*. But the *vv'* frontier corresponding to reallocation of the actual post-trade totals may well loop inside the autarky point. (Utilities being ordinal not cardinal, the curvatures of the loci are of no definite signs.)

ideal reallocation of the goods at the post-trade point *V*. Since *EF* lies north-east of *PQ*, *ef* must obviously lie north-east of *pq*.[1]

Now let us carefully compare the pre-trade point *d* with a post-trade point *v*. Since *v* is south-east of *d*, it would be dangerous to say that trade has made the world better off: man 1 is better off, man 2 is worse off. But let us ideally reallocate the goods of *v*, moving north-west on *vv'* to compensate man 2. Can we in this way make both men better off? Mr. Olsen's reply would be: Not necessarily. If I may translate his analysis into my terminology, he argues: The *v'v* locus of reallocation may pass north-east of the autarky point *d*, or it may pass south-west of that point.

---

[1] As mentioned in footnote 1 on p. 821, *ef* might touch *pq* at one or more points (indeed in the limiting case where trade is always indifferent, at all points). It would be wrong, though, to think that *ef must* somewhere touch *pq*: as already indicated, the point *u* corresponding to *U* might never touch the *pq* frontier; and in that case *ef* would lie everywhere north-east of *pq*. If *ef* refers to a country large enough to affect its terms of trade, we can define a new frontier midway, so to speak, between the autarky frontier *pq* and the optimum-tariff frontier *ef*. I refer to the free-trade frontier that results from zero tariffs but with different lump-sum redistributions of income. This new frontier can never loop inside *pq* or outside *ef*. It corresponds to a free-trade locus that could be pencilled into Fig. 3 midway between *PQ* and *EF*.

I have no dispute with this last possibility. In fact, Fig. 4 is drawn with vv' passing below d so that the gainers from trade cannot (by reallocating the given totals) bribe the losers into acquiescing to trade.

But nothing in my 1939 [1] or present argument required that the compensation or bribing be possible out of *fixed totals*. What I was concerned to argue was that the *cum*-trade utility envelope frontier *ef*—not vv'—lay outside the autarky frontier *pq*. And this is true despite the Olsen contention.

As a matter of fact, imagine compensation beginning to take place at v and V. *This will automatically change the pattern of imports*, moving v north-westward on *ef* and moving V north-westward on *EF*. Where will the process end? If the losers are fully compensated—and my argument proves conclusively that they *can* be—the points v and V will be moved so far north-westward as to cause the Olsen effect to disappear necessarily. Thus, we end up north-east of d.

I hope no one will think that I advocate: (1) compensation, or (2) non-compensation. We need a Bergson social-welfare function to answer these questions, and I have always pointed out the illogic of those new welfare economists who used to try to reach normative conclusions on the basis of insufficient norms.

V. Scitovsky Collective Indifference Curves

In 1939, two years before Professor Tibor Scitovsky [2] introduced his collective indifference curves, I, of course, did not use them in my exposition. Nor have I yet used them here. But in that Olsen has used them, I ought to mention them briefly.

Through D in Fig. 1 (or as well in Fig. 3), Olsen would draw a Scitovsky indifference curve: this gives the minimum required totals of the goods needed to keep all men as well off as they actually were under autarky. Olsen then argues that the after-trade point V could conceivably lie *under* this Scitovsky curve, not above it. This I freely admit (as in my Fig. 4's passing of vv' below d).

But what do I need for my argument that some trade makes a society potentially better off in the sense of making it possible for all men to be made better off, the gainers being able to more than compensate the losers? Not that V lie above the D Scitovsky indifference curve. But rather the weaker, and inevitable, condition that the *EF* envelope frontier *somewhere*

[1] See Robert E. Baldwin, " A Comparison of Welfare Criteria," *Review of Economic Studies*, Vol. XXI (1953–54), p. 160, for a defence of my 1939 argument against an Olsen-like criticism.

[2] T. Scitovsky, " A Reconstruction of the Theory of Tariffs," *Review of Economic Studies*, Vol. IX (1941–42), pp. 89–110, reprinted in *Readings in the Theory of International Trade*. See, too, my cited *Quarterly Journal* article for a discussion of how these concepts all fit together.

pass above the Scitovsky indifference curve.   Fig. 5 shows how inevitable this is, and how irrelevant the crossing of the V and D Scitovsky curves is.

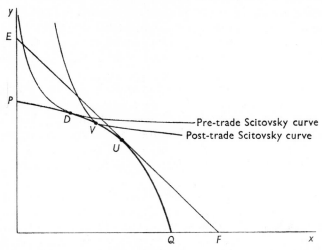

Fig. 5.   The Scitovsky community indifference curve of the actual post-trade configuration V may well pass above the community indifference curve of the actual autarky configuration D. But for the winners to be able ideally to compensate the losers requires only that UE cut somewhere above the autarky community indifference curve—as is always the case.   The fact that the post-trade community indifference curve always passes above the autarky point means that trade satisfies the 1941 Scitovsky test for an improvement—namely, the losers from trade can never afford to bribe the trade gainers into unanimously repealing all trade.

VI.   INDEX NUMBER COMPARISONS

Finally, let me review and extend the index-number type of argument used in my 1939 paper.   For simplicity, I shall revert back to Fig. 1's case where the country is too small to affect its terms of trade.[1]   In Figs. 1 and 5 the tangent line of the equilibrium point V contains U inside of it, and *a fortiori* because of the strong curvature of PQ it must contain D inside of it: in terms of index number comparisons,[2] this means

$$\sum P_V Q_V \geqslant \sum P_V Q_D$$

If only a single individual or a " representative man " standing for identical citizens were involved we could, from the familiar economic theory of index numbers,[3] deduce that the post-trade point was " better

---

[1] Since convexity of PQ makes the EF envelope convex too, I believe the argument could be extended to the general case.

[2] I have changed my 1939 notation and am neglecting changes in factor supplies.

[3] See *Foundations*, Chapter VI, for the conclusions of the Pigou, Könus, Staehle, Frisch, Haberler, Leontief, R. G. D. Allen, Lerner, Samuelson, Hicks line of reasoning.

than " the autarky point. Most of my 1939 paper dealt with this one-person case; and the remainder, to which Mr. Olsen's remarks all apply, was well advised not to use the index-number method.

What does the above index-number comparison mean when there are different men in our economy so that it must be written

$$\sum P_V(q_V' + q''_V + \ldots) \geqslant \sum P_V(q_D' + q_D'' + \ldots),$$

and when we observe only the totals in parentheses?

Professor Hicks stated in 1940 a beautiful theorem [1] that gives a partial answer. By it, the index-number comparison alone will tell us that the post-trade point v in Fig. 4 necessarily lies outside the autarky loci pq or dd''. Thus, Mr. Olsen's conclusion—which he derived in his last paragraph by perceiving that the Scitovsky collective indifference curve through V would have to lie outside the point D (and indeed outside all autarky points of PQ)—follows: Those hurt by trade are never able to bribe the trade winners into going back to autarky.

In terms of welfare economics, Mr. Olsen has proved that the post-trade situation satisfies the 1941 test [2] added by Scitovsky to supplement the Kaldor–Hicks 1939 test that the gainers from trade—or any improvement—be capable of bribing the losers. Though Mr. Olsen has proved that the Scitovsky test holds, I believe he has not thereby shown that my proof of the Kaldor–Hicks tests' holding is faulty. Actually, my proof I deem satisfactory, and by it I establish something stronger—that an *infinity* of tests or comparisons between the pre-trade and post-trade utility frontiers show the latter to be the frontier farther out. (All this is specified at a glance in Fig. 4.)

In this sense trade makes a country potentially better off.

VII. A WARNING ABOUT FEASIBILITY

What in the way of policy can we conclude from the fact that trade is a *potential* boon? As I pointed out in my 1950 paper, we can actually conclude very little.

To see this turn to Fig. 6, which is much like Fig. 4. Suppose the social welfare function, if we knew it, " favoured " the man hurt by trade, man 2 —as shown by the Bergson contours of welfare indifference. And suppose, as is the simple truth, that ideal lump-sum redistributions are never really available to us. Instead the only feasible redistributions must cause harmful substitution and other effects. Then the feasibility locus upon which we

---

[1] J. R. Hicks, " The Valuation of Social Income," *Economica*, New Series, Vol. VII (1940), pp. 105–24. See my cited *Oxford* 1950 paper, pp. 7–10, for a reformulation and proof of the Hicks theorem on group index-number comparison.

[2] T. Scitovsky, " A Note on Welfare Propositions in Economics," *Review of Economic Studies*, Vol. VIII (1941), pp. 77–88.

are free to move looks like the dotted curve in **Fig. 6**, *vg*, looping inside the *ef* frontier.   Now it is quite possible that this feasibility locus might even loop inside the autarky point *d*.   It evidently follows that, with the given Bergson contours, autarky is preferable to the post-trade situation—showing how difficult must be any rigorous interpretation of "potential" improvement.[1]

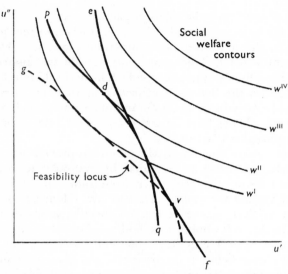

Fig. 6.   If lump-sum transfers are not feasible, so that *vg* rather than *ef* is the feasibility frontier, the highest social-welfare contour obtainable from free trade might be lower than that obtainable under autarky.

VIII. Conclusions

Rather than summarise what has been a lengthy argument, I shall simply stand by my earlier position and jot down some truths that are perhaps better understood to-day than twenty years ago.[2]

[1] Perhaps some situation very near to autarky, but involving a little trade, could be proved to give points north-east of *d*.   This is suggested by the fact that small redistributions will usually involve small deadweight distortions of a higher order of infinitesimals.   For the theory of feasibility—sometimes called the theory of the second best—and still in its infancy, see F. P. Ramsey, " A Contribution to the Theory of Taxation," ECONOMIC JOURNAL, Vol. XXXVII (1927), pp. 47–61; M. Boiteux, " Sur la question des Monopoles Publics astreints à l'équilibre budgétaire," *Econometrica*, Vol. 24 (1956), pp. 22–40; R. G. Lipsey and R. K. Lancaster, " The General Theory of the Second Best," *Review of Economic Studies*, Vol. XXIV (1956–57), pp. 11–32; I. M. D. Little, *A Critique of Welfare Economics* (Oxford, 1957), 2nd edition, Appendix IV; J. de V. Graaff, *loc. cit.*, Chapter V; P. A. Samuelson, *Oxford Economic Papers, loc. ci* ., pp. 18–19.

[2] See P. A. Samuelson, " Welfare Economics and International Trade," *American Economic Review*, Vol XXVIII (1938), pp. 261–68, for a discussion of these issues and for what appears to be the first of the modern rediscoveries of the Mill-Bickerdike theorem that some tariff is optimal.

1. If the laws of returns were appropriate for perfect competition (no external effects, indivisibilities, monopolies, dynamic uncertainties, learning processes, etc.), free trade [1] and ideal transfers could be used to give maximal *world* production in the sense of a farthest out world production possibility frontier.

2. Free trade and ideal transfers could give a similar maximal world utility frontier for all individuals.

3. Free trade will *not* necessarily maximise the real income or consumption and utility possibilities *of any one country*—even though by ideal bribes the international winning countries could bribe the losers into a unanimous vote for free trade.

4. Free trade will not necessarily maximise the income, consumption and utility possibilities of a *subset* of persons or factors within a country.

5. If all but one country will always trade freely it (almost) always pays that one country to behave monopolistically, imposing optimum Mill–Bickerdike tariffs or other interferences to take advantage of less-than-infinitely-elastic international demand.

6. Whatever the fixed pattern of tariffs abroad, it usually pays one country to introduce an optimum duty unilaterally. Some countries may then end up better off than under free trade; or perhaps none will end up better off. But never can *all* countries end up better off; and indeed, the losers from the tariff pattern can always theoretically offer the winners large enough ideal bribes to get rid of all tariffs and interferences with free trade.

7. Only at a point reachable by free trade would an international individualistic social welfare function be at its *maximum maximorum.*

8. For a given country, autarky cannot be optimal if ideal transfers are possible. Some trade is better than no trade in the sense of making the nation better off, with a farther out consumption-possibility frontier and farther out utility-possibility frontier.

If ideal lump-sum reallocations of income are not feasible the above conclusions need serious modification and qualification. The same is true when we introduce imperfections of competition, uncertainties, induced changes of an irreversible type and game-theoretic struggles for power and welfare.

P. A. SAMUELSON

Massachusetts Institute of Technology.

---

[1] Other devices, such as perfect planning or perfect discrimination, might accomplish the same result.

63

General Equilibrium Theory in International Trade. By Jacob L. Mosak. Cowles Commission monog. no. 7. (Bloomington: Principia Press. 1944. Pp. xiii, 187. $2.50.)

This is a little gem. In the modern period of ascendency of the journal article, advanced treatments in book form of fundamental economic problems are all too rare, and this one provides a masterly, compact exposition and commentary on that highest development of the neo-classical school of thought, Hicks's *Value and Capital*. It is only fair to warn the reader that part of the compactness of the book and much of its elegance stems from the fact that the author has not hesitated to treat essentially mathematical subjects mathematically.

Not more than one-third of the book is concerned with international trade, which is probably as it should be, as this subject—aside from its traditions and policy aspects—constitutes an analytical special case of general economic theory. The great advances which have been made in economic theory since Alfred Marshall are pointed up by a comparison of Mosak's treatment with the fifteen-year-old *Mathematical Reformulation of International Trade* of Theodore Yntema, a work confining itself to the application of partial equilibrium analysis to international trade. The present approach is more akin to the spirit of classical English international trade theory (which achieved its manageability not so much by making the *ceteris paribus* assumptions of partial equilibrium as by confining attention to highly simplified few-commodity-factor-country cases). And at the same time that the greater generality and comprehensiveness of the Walrasian system are achieved, skillful use of secondary maximum conditions and market stability conditions breathes formal fruitfulness into the analysis; so that the demonstration that an equilibrium is causally complete and subject to determinate economic law can be supplemented by the description of the qualitative properties of that law.

In the literature of international trade the "Transfer Problem" has enjoyed a considerable vogue ever since the famous Keynes-Ohlin controversy over the secondary reparation burden upon Germany resulting from adverse changes in her "terms of trade." Here, for once, Keynes seemed to be in the uncharacteristic position of siding with the classical camp, in that his position coincided with that of such orthodox stalwarts as Pigou and Taussig. Of course, more careful historical research revealed affinities between the self-styled "modern" approach of the Ohlin followers and that of Ricardo, Bastable, Wicksell and others. It is the more surprising that Keynes, who has recently placed so much emphasis on income effects, should have left their elucidation to Ohlin, confining himself to a purely statical Marshallian equilibrium analysis in which, erroneously, the offer curve of one country fails to shift.

Mosak subjects the statical problem to a careful reëxamination. He seems to abstain carefully from explicitly acquiescing in the prevailing opinion of Viner, Haberler, and others that, while the terms of trade *may* shift in either direction, there is an *a priori* presumption that they will shift *against* the paying country. In a statical world of exchange of two commodities between two countries with no transportation costs or tariffs, the qualitative answer is seen to be independent of price elasticities of demand and to depend only upon the relative income-elasticity shifts of demand between the goods in each country. *Absolutely no presumption in either direction seems indicated.* When he comes to taking production effects and other factors into account, Mosak indicates how the answer depends upon relative substitutability and complementarity of domestic products and factors with the import and export goods of each country. Perhaps purposely, he refrains from stating whether the "presumptions" enunciated in Viner's *Studies in International Trade* are valid, although he does qualify the conclusions found in that book on the much less important problem of absolute price levels and gold distribution. As Mosak himself is probably aware (*cf.* p. 38n.) these results are rather trivial, since the analysis proceeds upon the basis of artificial "neutral" money assumptions which, if valid, make the problem of absolute prices of little consequence.

It is this reviewer's conjecture that (1) there may be something after all in the orthodox position that terms of trade shift against the paying country; (2) that once again Keynes's intuition had run ahead of his powers of analysis; (3) that Ohlin and not Keynes was "classical," in the "bad" sense of having an inadequate theory of effective demand of the implicit Say's Law variety; and (4) that the essential condition for the orthodox presumption lies in the Keynesian "leakages" or *incomplete* income effects. Throughout Mosak is Hicksian rather than Keynesian—which is quite a difference!—so that we must wait for Lloyd Metzler's forthcoming book to throw more light on these matters.

Space precludes a detailed discussion of Mosak's felicitous exposition of modern economic theory. Suffice it to say that here is an ideal one-hundred-page textbook assignment for intermediate and advanced classes. Also, almost casually in passing, Mosak corrects the Hicksian error that extreme complementarity may make a symmetrical system unstable (p. 42); the widespread Keynesian impression that a positive rate of interest is "merely" a liquidity premium which would disappear if uncertainty and transaction friction were abolished (p. 20); two arguments of Frank Knight as to why the rate of interest could never be zero (p. 121 and p. 141); and a number of other important misunderstandings. The present reviewer is still not quite at ease with Mosak's analysis of the possibility of unemployment (*circa*

p. 154), any more than he feels that Hicks has performed a successful marriage between Walras and Keynes or between those two neutral money economists, Ricardo and Lerner.

Finally, the profession must be grateful that one of the ablest young economists should have found the time and energy in the midst of important wartime duties for the arduous task of preparing a difficult manuscript for publication.

PAUL A. SAMUELSON

Massachusetts Institute of Technology

64

DISPARITY IN
POSTWAR EXCHANGE RATES
Paul A. Samuelson

I. Introduction

There are admittedly numerous theoretical weaknesses of the purchasing power parity doctrine, as enunciated by Gustav Cassel and others. Still, something of a pragmatic case can be made for its consequences when applied to the dislocated exchange rate situation of (1) the immediate post-World War I period, and (2) the depressed 1930's.

In the hands of Cassel one of the most important functions of purchasing power parity was the defense of *de facto* postwar exchange rates against the almost unthinking demand of some economists and bankers for a return to prewar mint parities. To a first approximation, purchasing power parity's great virtue was its implicit recognition that price levels could not be easily "rolled back" to prewar levels—in short, its defense of the *status quo* as against the *status quo ante bellum*.

In the years after 1929, purchasing power parity played a minor role in economic discussions. But, generally speaking, the influence of purchasing power calculations was in the direction of causing those countries which had devalued their currencies least to depreciate their currencies. There are exceptions to this, but the Belgian case and that of the gold bloc provide important illustrations.

As a result, therefore, by the time the world had experienced considerable recovery in the middle and late 1930's, we found ourselves back at almost the same relative exchange rates as before the crash[1]—but, of course, with all currencies devalued

[1] League of Nations, *International Currency Experience*, p. 129.

in terms of gold. While no one can prove that this pattern constituted an optimal result—and certainly its time path of realization was far from ideal—still it is not a *prima facie* indefensible one.

II. Purchasing Power Parity and Present Exchange Rates

Let us grant therefore that purchasing power parity calculation did not lead to too bad results in the two major periods of international crisis prior to World War II. What then of its import for the present postwar period? What will the consequences be of neglecting its testimony, as has been done recently in setting the initial Monetary Fund exchange rates on the basis of the immediate *status quo?*

Broadly speaking, the initial exchange rates accepted by the Fund yield exchange rates for the rest of the world that are "overvalued" and a U. S. dollar that is apparently "undervalued." [2] That is to say, exchange rates abroad had not fallen by as much as their prices had risen in relation to ours. Was this neglect of purchasing power a grave mistake?

Now in a sense it is quite possible to argue that the Fund authorities had little discretion in the matter, it being necessary in terms of political expediency to accept the wishes of its member nations relative to the *status quo*. There is much to this; for example, one can immediately envisage the difficulties at the time of getting the United States to lower its buying price of gold. But let us leave these political considerations aside. Should not the member countries, if more enlightened, have desired a nearer approach to purchasing power parity?

I, for one, have not the courage to answer this question dogmatically. There is nothing sacred about the *status quo,* but the strong burden of proof must be thrown onto any doctrine that favors an extreme, and generally unpopular, departure from the prevailing state. Neither purchasing power parity nor other theoretical doctrines of international trade equilibrium

[2] See Lloyd A. Metzler's article in *International Monetary Proposals, Postwar Economic Studies* No. 7 of the Federal Reserve Board (1947), pp. 25ff. The U. K. is an apparent exception to this generalization. Her prices have been so well controlled relative to the rest of the world that her index gives a seeming picture of "undervaluation" of the pound.

have at this time, and as applied to present abnormal conditions, the theoretical or empirical validity necessary to justify strong conviction in favor of a drastic and radical gamble—which is what extensive revision of exchange rates would imply. And it is part of my diagnosis that such allegedly corrective action would have to be quantitatively fairly drastic rather than moderate. It is only reasonable to expect further revision of rates in the future; but the fulfillment of this expectation will not be proof that present rates were a mistake.

To put matters bluntly, purchasing power parity works best when *no substantive changes* in the world have taken place, but only "fictitious scale changes in price levels." One has only to look at the devastation and disorganization wrought by the war, the permanently changed pattern of international indebtedness, and the sweeping alterations in political and social structures, to realize that the essence of the present-day problem is an important substantive change in the whole international trade situation. One can hardly argue convincingly that the very real problem of "universal" dollar shortage arose primarily out of differential price level movements of the usual sort. The reverse is, in my opinion, more nearly true.

III. Elasticity of Demand?

I should go farther and argue that there are reasons to doubt the efficacy of correcting the present abnormal situation by exchange rate variations and relative price movements of the classical type. Among other things, the classical pattern of adjustment rested upon the empirical faith of very strong elasticities of reciprocal international demands. For example, if the U. S. export surplus is equal to about one-half of our total exports, minor exchange rate variations of not more than 10 per cent could only wipe out the surplus if the "net" elasticity of reciprocal[3] demand were very great indeed. A net demand elasticity of 2.0 or 3.0 would require a tremendous relative exchange rate and price change to wipe out the enormous postwar unbalances.

For an instant let me grant the extreme possibility that the

[3] As defined in section V of this paper.

dollar-shortage areas all have great net elasticities of international demand. To bring out an important element almost completely neglected in recent discussions, I shall even suppose that this elasticity is infinite, so that practically no deterioration of the terms of trade is needed to "rectify" any given import surplus. From many current discussions, one would be tempted to infer that such a rectification would then be almost completely costless!

Of course, nothing could be farther from the truth. Suppose Marshall Plan aid of, say, 5 billion dollars per annum ceases a few years from now. The loss to Europe will necessarily be a loss of at least that much worth of goods and services. She will have at least that much less of output available for domestic consumption or capital formation.

At the end of World War I, economists discussing reparations at first naïvely concentrated solely on the "primary burden" of a unilateral international payment, only gradually becoming aware of a possible "secondary" burden involved in the deterioration of terms of trade caused by the transfer. After World War II, economists have become so sophisticated as to push to the background of the discussion everything *but* the secondary burden.

Great elasticity of demand will, at best, moderate the secondary burden involved in rectifying present universal unbalance. The primary burden—which, if the optimistic classical theory were correct, would be the more important cost—would still remain. Over and beyond the real aspect of the primary burden, there is also the inflationary pressure induced by a reduction in available domestic output.

The secondary burden must now be examined. If we lump the rest of the world facing the United States into one unit, it becomes no longer a question of a single small country facing an elastic world demand. On the contrary, considering the war-induced urgency of world need for our products, the scarcity and inelasticity of foreigners' domestic supply, and the character of U. S. importing, we cannot be even sure that the net demand elasticity is greater than one. Therefore, we cannot even be sure that lowering the value of an already overvalued currency will make the situation any better at all. If the net elasticity is in a fairly wide range around the critical value of unity, no feasible exchange rate depreciation change would appreciably affect the discrepancy in the balance of U. S. trade with the rest of the world. But if the exchange rate variation is even to begin to work as envisaged by classical theory, it will succeed in turning the terms of trade substantially against Europe—for if it does not work in this direction, the classical remedy is licked to begin with. Even where a considerable net elasticity of international demand occurred, exchange depreciation would to some degree further impoverish the impoverished and increase the strain on Congressional generosity.

There remains the possibility that in the present state of trade between the United States and the rest of the world, net international demand is very inelastic. In this case the cure for so-called overvalued currencies is more overvaluation. Perhaps the United States should then be asked to raise its buying price of gold and to make the dollar cheaper to foreigners. Theoretically, a new free exchange rate might be found at which the dollar shortage would disappear. However, such an intersection of international supply and demand curves would be an "unstable" one,[4] so that any momentary departure from equilibrium would be self-aggravating and cumulative. Orthodox stabilization fund operations would encounter difficulties in maintaining exchange rate stability in free markets at such an unstable intersection, and in all probability recourse would be had to supplementary exchange control methods not unlike those now prevailing.

On the whole, therefore, the case of inelastic demand does not provide much comfort for us economists who personally favor a maximum of freedom in international trade. We cannot recommend to authorities—Go thou and adopt an equilibrium rate of exchange. At the least we must definitely tell them—depreciate your currencies; or appreciate them. And I have not yet encountered many liberal economists who are willing to stick their necks out in favor of the latter.

[4] See the discussion of Joan Robinson's analysis in section VI below.

IV. Agriculture Versus Industry

The probable elasticity of demand between the United States and the rest of the world is a difficult question of fact, concerning which it would be dangerous to make dogmatic assertions. There is some weight of theoretical authority in favor of the view of considerable elasticity; but there may be an element of wishful thinking in this position, and the extraordinary character of the postwar scene may rob customary relations of their usual validity.

On the other hand the testimony of practical observers and so-called experts seems usually to be in favor of the view that demands are rather inelastic. But the few of these whom I have interrogated on the matter have not been able to advance any very elaborate arguments in favor of their opinion, having had instead to fall back upon their best intuitive view of the situation.

Perhaps it will help bring the question into perspective if we consider the problem, not simply as one between regions, but as one between prices of agricultural foodstuffs and raw materials and prices of industrial products.[5] Agricultural staples are notoriously of short-run inelastic supply, or even in some cases of negative elasticity of supply. Their demand is usually considered to be of rather low price elasticity. When both supply and demand are rather inelastic a free price system works least well, and prices are prone to considerable amplitude of fluctuations as a result of even small shifts in the schedules. If we add to this basic fact the wartime reductions in supplies from many regions of the globe and the higher demands for food resulting from an increase in postwar money income and from equalitarian programs all over the world, the expected result can be a tremendous increase in food and raw material prices, a tremendous redistribution of real and money income as between urban and rural families, a tremendous increase in the economic rents from farming and mining.

[5] This comparison is suggestive rather than rigorous. Many agricultural countries also have their dollar shortage problems. But in part—as the case of Canada so well illustrates—this is due to the failure of multilateral convertibility of their favorable balances with such "soft currency" countries as the U. K.

Our theoretical expectations are fully matched by the quantitative revolution in the prices of staples. As compared to depression lows, the price of wheat has increased tenfold. The cost of food has more than doubled so that the percentage of disposable income spent by American families on food has significantly increased. Net farm cash incomes have more than tripled.

The end is perhaps only now coming into sight, and the wonder is that the process did not go farther than it actually did. The reason is not hard to find: throughout the war almost universal rationing and direct controls served to hold in the demand for staples so as to keep free market forces from bidding up the imputed rents of factors of production inelastic in supply. At the moment the United States has abandoned most of its direct controls; but exchange controls and internal direct controls all over much of the rest of the world are still holding in a tremendous volume of demand for basic necessities of life. One can scarcely doubt that a simultaneous release of these forces of extra demand would—other things equal—result in a further increase in basic materials' prices, in further redistribution in favor of agriculture, and a tendency toward further adverse balances of trade on the part of European countries.

If the present supply-demand situation were to be permanent, some serious problems of basic policy would be raised. Shall nations continue direct controls permanently in order to keep competitive forces from raising basic prices against them and thus reducing their real standards of living? This is not unlike the reverse problem of seemingly chronic agricultural surpluses in the years before the war. The answer rests upon considerations of administration, politics, and even ethics.

But if the problem is one simply of the next few years, the scales will be tilted more in favor of a rather gradual relaxation of exchange and direct domestic control.[6] Such a solution is by no means ideal. Leaving out the problem of over-all inflation

[6] On balance it might still be a good thing to abolish direct controls because of their detrimental effects upon productivity at a time of "suppressed inflation." Questions of fact, of economic analysis, and of political philosophy must be weighed in arriving at a decision on this question. Judgment is made all the more difficult by the fact that the cure for many of the evils of suppressed inflation may be *either more or less controls*—a halfway house being the worst possible situation.

that might result from relaxation of all controls, and concentrating only on relative prices and well-being, we can argue that the world would be better off to let the food-producing countries receive higher prices and, if desirable, make gifts to the impoverished countries to compensate them for the deterioration of the terms of trade. But I am afraid that this is utopian and irrelevant; there are very real political limitations on gifts, and already the world has probably reached its limit in this respect.

V. Technical Problem of Interpretation

I have intentionally glossed over a few technicalities. The equilibrating efficacy of exchange rate variations does not depend upon each of the two countries' having an elastic demand. The critical question is now recognized to be whether the sum of the two elasticities—the "net elasticity"—is greater or less than unity.

It is also necessary to distinguish between (1) the elasticity of real exports and imports with respect to a real change in the terms of trade, and (2) the elasticity of the trade balance with respect to exchange rate variations. Thus, suppose that real international reciprocal demands are actually very elastic with respect to the worsening of the terms of trade of a debtor nation. But suppose that exchange depreciation intensifies the inflationary spiral within the debtor country so as to cause prices and costs to rise by as much as the exchange has fallen. The terms of trade will not have fallen at all, and the resultant elasticity of the trade balance with respect to the exchange rate will give the appearance of being exactly unity, so that exchange variations will not improve the balance of payments. An omnipotent slide-rule parity theorist would keep adjusting the exchange rate downward only to find that prices move so as to make the exchange always overvalued, with the result an endless exchange spiral.[7]

This cooked-up illustration is in many ways entirely germane to the present scene. Much of the world is in the throes of ex-

---

[7] The early 1948 experience with the devaluation of the French franc may provide an illustrative case, although it is still too soon to say.

plicit or held-in inflation, and this is not simply the result of a wanton diarrhea of money on the part of Treasuries and Central Banks. People as a whole want what they cannot have in the postwar world, and, if uncontrolled, free market forces would lead to inflationary spirals. Nor does it help much to proffer smug advice concerning Spartan fiscal and monetary measures to governments already on the brink of political disaster. But to pursue this line of thought would lead us into the more remote fields of politics and sociology.

However, there does still remain one related technicality concerning some of the current interpretations of purchasing power calculations. Many writers tend to regard purchasing power parity as, under certain conditions, a truism; and, under other conditions, as definitely untrue. When a truism it is thought to be useless; but when untrue, the doctrine becomes potentially useful. This is a case of capitalizing with a vengeance on a theory's inadequacies and weaknesses; a case where the exception not only proves the rule but improves it as well.

If one has already made the error of falsely identifying purchasing power parity with a narrow theory of spatial price relationships, there is some justification for this paradoxical belief. Two wrongs can be nearer the truth than one. But even in this context possible confusion is involved.

Let me illustrate by considering the present situation where universal exchange control cloaks overvaluation of exchange rates. Prices abroad are too high compared to U. S. prices, at least in terms of free market forces. Now let us drop the crutch of exchange control. Something will have to give way. But can prices abroad and here be expected to remain constant so that it will be the exchange rate that will have to give all the way? Something like this is assumed by the usual quantitative calculation of parity.

If we still believe, as did Cassel, that Central Banks can, and do, easily control the quantity of money and, through the Quantity Theory, the level of prices, there would be something to be said for this bold assumption. But when we have come to believe that John L. Lewis has more to do with prices than does the Federal Reserve Board and that the 1948 rainfall in the wheat belt may have more lasting effects on the index of wholesale prices than interest rate policy, doubts creep in.

Even more specifically, we must realize that one-sided obstacles to trade are themselves substantive changes in international trade, and their removal is also a substantive change. Their removal will directly lower the spread between foreign and domestic prices. Any parity exchange rate calculated from data gathered while the restrictions are in force cannot be extrapolated to the restrictionless situation except with modifications and caution.[8]

To sum up by repeating the almost obvious: it is illegitimate to take price relationships as given and to assume complete passive adjustment of exchange rates. The problem is one of mutual determination, and especially complex under present abnormal conditions. Temporary controls and distortions of price relationships do not make purchasing power more valid; they simply make the exchange rate problem more significant— which is not to say less difficult.

VI. The "Dollar Shortage"

Disequilibrium in the balance of payments can arise from many reasons. Many of these are of a temporary nature and easily jibe with the simple formulations of the orthodox international trade mechanism. But the problem of the so-called chronic "dollar shortage" is something else again. Precise descriptions of what is meant by this concept are hard to find. Indeed if one interprets the classical theory of comparative advantage in a narrow sense, such a chronic unbalance will appear to be an impossibility.

[8] That most writers are at least dimly aware of this difficulty is seen by their concern with the artificial character of many official price statistics, since these represent prices of rationed commodities not freely obtainable at the stated prices. Yet sometimes it is almost argued that it is the controls and imperfections of the price series that alone make the parity theory "interesting." "Under wartime conditions calculations of purchasing power parities are, from one point of view, more useful than under normal conditions . . . Because the war has interrupted international trade, wholesale prices in the various countries can move independently. Therefore their relative change provides a better measure of comparative price level changes than in peacetime." G. Haberler, "The Choice of Exchange Rates," *American Economic Review*, vol. 35 (June 1945), p. 313.

However, from a broader view of the pure theory of international trade, such a chronic condition can certainly exist as an actual possibility. For example, it is simply not true to say that the theory of comparative cost proves that one country cannot continue to "undersell" another in every commodity. If one assumes only simple barter to be possible, then *ex definitione* goods can only be exchanged against goods. But this is a postulate, not a theorem. The question has been begged not proved.

To do justice to the pure theory of international trade, we must be willing to admit the possibility of capital movements. In this case, it is perfectly possible for one country continually to export more than its imports, the difference being made up by securities or I.O.U.'s. In this sense, one country may undersell another in every line of activity. More than that, it is possible for each country in a sense to be underselling the other *at the same time:* namely, when each is giving away exports to the other for I.O.U.'s which will later be repudiated.

There is nothing then in the pure theory of comparative cost that prevents the rest of the world from continually obligating itself to pay (in the future) for more American goods than it can pay for by barter. There is nothing in the theory from preventing such one-way borrowing from leading to periodic financial collapse—to be followed by a renewal of the same process after confidence and gullibility have been restored. Note that (1) no flow of gold need be induced by the process; (2) no exchange rate depreciation need result; and (3) no self-correcting specie-price mechanism or (4) income-multiplier mechanism need be set up by the process so as to put off the evil day of general financial collapse. The fact that the I.O.U.'s might be long-term securities rather than short-term would not alter the process, or its aftermath, even though many of the recent definitions of exchange equilibrium (à la Nurkse and Haberler)[9] would seem to regard the situation as an equilibrium one up to the moment of revealed bankruptcy.

[9] R. Nurkse, "Conditions of International Monetary Equilibrium," *Princeton Essays in International Finance,* No. 4, Spring, 1945; see also Haberler's Comments in the previously cited Federal Reserve *Postwar Economic Studies,* No. 7, pp. 99-102.

If the authorities of both the debtor or creditor countries are free to pursue any coöperative policies, and if they wish to end the chronic dollar shortage, there is much they can do about it. But they are not free. And the measures they take to "correct" the situation will have repercussions on (a) unemployment, on (b) inflation, (c) on terms of trade, (d) on available national output, and (e) on relative exchange rates. I put the word "correct" in quotation marks because there is nothing in the analytical theory of welfare economics—new or old—that assures us that the so-called equilibrium situation *sans* dollar shortage is "better" or "fairer" than the "uncorrected" situation. The equilibrium situation is perhaps in a sense more permanent and maintainable. That is all.[10]

So far I have been talking in generalities. I have shown that the possibility of a chronic dollar shortage or surplus is perfectly consistent with theory. Let me now turn to the empirical reasons for the dollar shortage both in its chronic aspects independently of the war, and also in its immediate postwar context.

The United States is the richest country in the world. Also, it is the pace-setter in technological progress, and increasingly in setting fashions of standards of life. It is natural for the poor to want to borrow from the rich. It is also natural for the rich to have the surplus income to lend to the poor. If the rich man has had trouble—however caused—in finding investment outlets for his money, the case is that much more probable.

It is also natural for the poor often to default on their obligations to the rich. And in the absence of international bailiffs who can "attach" the property of the poor, it is natural for the rich to go unpaid even when the poor are not totally devoid of assets.[11]

[10] For even this to be true, the current definition of equilibrium as involving the absence of short-term capital and gold movements needs careful reformulation, after which it will be dangerously near to a tautology incapable of empirical application.

[11] Historically within the United States, the frontier West has experienced a chronic dollar shortage in its relation with the East; but nationalism and sovereignty have not impeded the problem of creditors in receiving their due. See also P. A. Samuelson, *Economics* (McGraw-Hill, 1948), pp. 367-368.

It is not unnatural for the rich to tire of this game of "hold the bag"; when the poor country cannot find private investors who will accept I.O.U.'s, the exchange rate must fall. The debtor country offers its I.O.U.'s (currency, etc.) at lower and lower prices. So long as foreign lenders remain adamant and net commodity demands inelastic, there is no end to the process. It becomes cumulative and self-aggravating.

Recently Mrs. Robinson has argued[12] that "it can be shown that, from a formal point of view, this objection [of perverse inelasticity of demand] is not fatal to the classical analysis."[13] I do not disagree with the spirit of her remarks, but they do seem to require three modifications in their application to the present discussion.

The first qualification is within the realm of the purest formal theory and can be relegated to a footnote.[14] The second point to be noticed (as Mrs. Robinson is clearly aware) is that the existence of an elastic range of the curves beyond the prevailing region of inelasticity means that the quantitative adjustment of exchange rates and relative price levels must be very drastic indeed. The balance of trade gets worse before it gets better; therefore, the terms of trade must deteriorate to a tremendous degree. This could be elaborated upon in greater detail by the use of the concept of arc elasticity.

Thirdly, as soon as we drop the assumption of pure barter of goods against goods, the doctrine of eventual elasticity of demand sufficient to wipe out any deficit in the balance of payments not only fails to be formally true as a universal generalization, but in addition the empirical exceptions become more likely. To see this, imagine that both rich and poor countries

[12] J. Robinson, "The Pure Theory of International Trade," *Review of Economic Studies,* vol. XIV (1946-47), pp. 100-102.

[13] *Ibid.,* p. 100.

[14] From a rigorous mathematical viewpoint, her formal proposition seems to be incorrect. At the critical point in her argument she assumes as obvious what is not universally necessarily true. She says "at some point the goods become so expensive relative to world money incomes that demand turns elastic . . . and there is some level . . . at which exports fall to zero." I grant that it is customary to draw demand curves so that at high prices they touch the price axis and become elastic. Probably, this is realistic. But it is not universally necessary as a matter of logic. It is easy to specify indifference curves such that demand is *always* inelastic.

produce and consume only a single homogeneous commodity, say chocolates. Under barter assumptions, differences in (opportunity) cost are obviously meaningless since there is only one commodity, and the simplest neo-classical theory of comparative advantage tells us that trade is an absurdity. Admitting now the possibility of capital movements, suppose that the poor country has an initial amount of non-producible non-augmentable gold or an equivalent line of credit upon which it can draw over a period of time.

Is there any permanent cheapening of its relative prices that will necessarily cause it not to run an import surplus? If there were a central decision-making authority in the poor country, it would realize that regardless of the exchange rate the poor country could currently consume all of its domestic chocolates and import as well. Depending upon time preference, a deterioration of the terms of trade between gold and imported chocolates might indefinitely speed up the value of imports.

Assuming atomistic competition in both countries and more than one commodity forces us to reëxamine the above result. Consumers in either country feel that they can acquire more of either home or imported goods at going market prices. If their demands for the product of the poor and rich country are relatively elastic, then exchange rate and terms of trade changes will tend to reduce the import surplus of the poor country. But with capital movements possible, we require more than that there be elasticity of demand. There must be enough elasticity of demand of commodity balance to outweigh the previously desired capital movement. There is no geometrical or empirical reason why there should ever be that much elasticity of demand.[15]

To illustrate this argument, consider the hypothetical question: is there any permanent increase in American prices relative to England that would necessarily make the American loan to Britain last *longer?*

The above theoretical discussion of the dollar shortage is

[15] In technical terms if one or both of the Marshallian international offer curves are shifted by capital movements, then, even if they are of normal shape, they need never intersect.

meant to be suggestive rather than exhaustive. Very briefly now, I should like to point out a few reasons why the current postwar shortage of dollars is especially acute. Monetary mismanagement and clumsily suppressed inflation are certainly part of the story, but I suspect far from all.

The wartime devastation and loss of European foreign assets is of course very great. Perhaps even more important is the war-induced disorganization of production. Europe is an *off-balance* economy, full of petty shortages which spread in vicious circles. Things in themselves not important become important in such an environment. Steel is short, but it takes steel to make steel; it takes coal to make calories and it takes calories to make coal. Inept price controls are partly to blame (witness the case of Germany), but the alternative would often be open inflation of sizable proportions—and, paradoxically, in going from barely tolerable suppressed inflation to open inflation might involve in the process riots and worse.

Commodity stocks in Europe are at a low ebb. Needs and demands accumulated during the war are at a high level. Military expenditures are economically costly. Equalitarian programs add to the excess demands of those who previously were in a superior economic position and who still have considerable liquid and non-liquid assets.

All this leads to an especially acute current dollar shortage. By 1951, it may not be easy to wean Europe of American aid but conditions should be much more favorable.

VII. Conclusion

Bigger issues than those of international trade mechanics are involved in the question of free exchange rates. Many nations all over the world have forsaken the paths of liberalism in favor of governmental planning. In the Fund and International Bank, we have pledged ourselves not to force our economic doctrines on the rest of the world, much as we would recommend them. But the question of exchange control necessarily cuts across this domestic ideological problem. If a socialist government abroad wishes to supplement its income tax structure with a policy of curbing imports of luxury goods in favor of necessities or capital equipment, then we may privately disapprove. But without risking the charge of supporting imperialism and being a propagandist, we cannot raise objections. Yet that is what insisting upon free exchanges comes close to doing. Or what insisting upon financial belt-tightening measures abroad often appears like to foreign eyes.

There remains no valid alternative but to proceed cautiously, compromising, if one wishes to put it that way, with evil, but not thereby forgetting that unnecessary distortion of an efficient international division of labor does represent an evil for all parties concerned. However—fortunately or unfortunately— this does not qualify for the top rank of evils that the world faces today.

65

THEORETICAL NOTES ON TRADE PROBLEMS

Paul A. Samuelson

1. *Introduction.* One of the great pleasures in my life has been preparing chapters for various Seymour Harris symposia, and I should like nothing better than to spend the next hundred years doing the same at five-year intervals. In connection with the problem of the international balance of payments, it occurred to me to reread the 1948 theoretical essay I prepared for his *Foreign Economic Policy for the United States* (Harvard Press). It was a theoretical exercise because I didn't have the leisure to prepare an empirical one. Finding that it stands up better than I had dared hope and again lacking leisure, I venture to jot down (on the back of an envelope, so to speak) some theoretical notes relevant to present balance-of-payments problems. It will be evident that I am not aiming at comprehensiveness, rigor, documentation, or unity.

Equilibrium of Prices, Wages, and Exchange Rates

2. *Currency Overvaluation.* In 1948 I shocked at least one of my teachers by saying that the theory of comparative advantage does not guarantee a country against balance-of-payments difficulties, nor does it even keep a country from being undersold in terms of every good.[1] Then it was a question of dollar shortage rather than of American gold loss, and I am not displeased to reread what was said there. But some elucidation may be useful.

Obviously, I do not interpret the theory of comparative advantage to include the full classical apparatus of the Hume gold-flow quantity-theory price-level mechanism. I do interpret it to include the Ricardo-Torrens arithmetic concerning various factor productivities. It will be useful to consider the simplest case of a labor model.

3. *A Simplest Model.* In the United States, let the unit labor requirements for goods 1,2,3 be given by $(A_1, A_2, A_3) = (1,1,1)$ by appropriate definition of commodity units. Else-

where, call it Europe, let unit labor requirements for those goods be given by $(a_1, a_2, a_3) = (2,3,5)$. We are more efficient in every good than they; but obviously our comparative advantage is greatest in good 3 and least in good 1, by virtue of the inequalities $5/1 > 3/1 > 2/1$. The whole content of the theory of comparative advantage is this:

We can never be exporting a good i while exporting a good j if our comparative advantage is in good j rather than in good i — that is, if $a_j/A_j > a_i/A_i$.

This does *not* say that our current balance must or will balance, or that our total balance of payments will be in any kind of equilibrium. In this two-country many-good case, the money wage rates here and abroad, W and w, together with the foreign exchange rate, R (that gives the \$ price of their currency — call it the £ but think of it as the Mark), determines completely the pattern of prices and of productions.

The price of a good at any place equals the lowest cost of production anywhere translated into commensurate currency units. (Transport costs and tariff impediments are assumed away.)

Using small letters for foreign variables and large letters for ours, we have

$$P_i = \text{Min}(WA_i, Rwa_i)$$
$$p_i = \text{Min}(A_iW/R, wa_i) \qquad (i = 1,2,3)$$
$$R = P_i/p_i \qquad\qquad\qquad (1)$$

4. *Limits When Both Regions Produce.* To illustrate, suppose that each country produces something. This restricts relative *real* wages in the two regions. Thus, we in the United States must have at least twice their real wage and at most five times theirs. In terms of money wages and the exchange rate, this implies

$$\text{Min}\left[\frac{a_i}{A_i}\right] = 2 \leqq \frac{W}{Rw} \leqq 5 = \text{Max}\left[\frac{a_i}{A_i}\right] \quad (2)$$

Or given the ratio of the money wages, W in \$ and w in £, we have the obvious limit on the exchange rate if neither country is to be undersold in every good:

$$\frac{1}{5}\frac{W}{w} \leqq R \leqq \frac{1}{2}\frac{W}{w}$$

---

[1] Footnote 5 will show that rigidity of wage rates is not really basic to my assertion.

$$\frac{W}{w} \, \text{Min}\left(\frac{A_i}{a_i}\right) \leqq R \leqq \frac{W}{w} \text{Max}\left(\frac{A_i}{a_i}\right) \qquad (3)$$

Equivalent relations on $r = 1/R$, the £ price of the dollar, could be given.

5. *Superficial Equality.* Suppose instead of but three goods we had a large number of goods, so that the ratios (a_i/A_i) practically formed a continuum from the minimum, say 2, to the maximum, say 5. Then *some* critical j^{th} good will be on (or near) the borderline of indifference between being produced in either or both countries. Even if there are but few discrete goods, the well-known fact that the reciprocal demand functions form horizontal steps at each discrete $(A_i/a_i)(W/w)$ ratio, increases the probability that R will end where a jth good is *on* the borderline. Then, either as an exact equality or a good approximation, we can get the following equation for R:

$$R = \frac{W}{w}\left[\frac{A_j}{a_j}\right], \qquad (4)$$

for j the critical borderline good. Thus, if both countries are to be able to produce the $j = 2$ good at equal costs, we must have

$$R = \frac{W}{w}\frac{A_2}{a_2} = \frac{W}{w}\frac{3}{1} \qquad (4)'$$

This would permit a $3 foreign exchange rate for the £ if wages here were $3.00 per hour and there one-third of a £ (or $1).

This is a superficial equality because the identity of the borderline good will be an unknown that shifts with supply and demand changes.

6. *Deficits, Overvaluation, and Mercantilism.* It is well known that costs alone cannot determine, even in a barter system, where the real equilibrium $(W/R)/w$ ratio must fall. (This acts like a terms-of-trade parameter for us; any simple change *abroad* which raises its equilibrium level makes "us" better off.)

Tastes and demands must enter into the reciprocal-demand schedules. Even worse, once we leave barter equilibrium aside and admit capital movements and gold flows into the picture, the sky becomes the limit for R and $(W/R)/w$. If our wage levels stay high enough, we can be undersold in every good. Without transport protections, our employment could be zero. The whole of our imports would then have to be financed by capital movements or gold.

With employment less than full and Net National Product suboptimal, all the debunked mercantilistic arguments turn out to be valid. Tariffs can then reduce unemployment, can add to the NNP, and increase the *total* of real wages earned (or do the same for non-labor factors in an extended model).

Every teacher of elementary economics realizes the difficulty in selling free-trade notions when a bright student has sensed that overvaluation of the currency may be involved. That is why the new sixth edition of my *Economics* (McGraw-Hill, New York, 1964) has an appendix pointing out the genuine problems for free-trade apologetics raised by overvaluation — such as prevailed for non-dollar nations in 1948, and may have been prevailing for us in recent years.

Purchasing-Power Parity

7. *Cassel-Ricardo Neutral-Money Versions.* The above formulation can clear up confusions, old and new, in Cassel's purchasing-power parity doctrine. Originally, he and Ricardo meant no more than that money was "neutral," the absolute level of *all* prices being able to double or halve without affecting *any* price ratios or real magnitudes in a longest-run rigid classical model. Thus, in such a model the *real* ratio $(W/Rw) = Y^*$, independently of absolute $ or £ price levels.

Now, said Cassel, let a wartime government double M here and triple m there, doubling all P's and W here and tripling all p's and w there. Then, obviously, the dollar price of the pound will have to depreciate exactly by $2/3$. Using $t = 0$ for before and $t = t$ for now, we get the famous purchasing-power parity index-number formula:

$$\frac{R^t}{R^0} = \frac{P^t/P^0}{p^t/p^0} = \frac{W^t/W^0}{w^t/w^0}\frac{Y^{*t}}{Y^{*0}} \overset{?}{=} \frac{W^t/W^0}{w^t/w^0}. \qquad (5)$$

Note that this last is valid only if the real magnitude Y^* is unshiftable by the purely money changes, so that $Y_t^*/Y_0^* \equiv 1$. Cassel argued that in war inflations, the M changes were likely to be much greater than the real changes, and that hence the last formula would be a good intermediate-run approximation.

8. *Spatial Arbitrage of Prices.* Already in World War I, Keynes altered this simple doctrine, by interpreting purchasing-power parity (PPP) as simply the doctrine of spatial arbitrage for each good (in the absence of transport costs). In one domestic market wheat can have but one P_i. With an exchange rate available to all, arbitrage similarly ensures that

$$R = P_i/p_i, \qquad (6)$$

$$\frac{R^t}{R^0} = \frac{P_i^t}{P_i^0} \bigg/ \frac{p_i^t}{p_i^0} \qquad (i = 1,2,3,\ldots) \quad (6)'$$

Note that this contains no arbitrage relations for wage rates or production costs. If it holds for each good, it will hold trivially for a ratio of *any* equally-weighted price index numbers. For index numbers (written always without subscripts) generally — if the separate countries' indexes use different weights, and even if (6) always holds —

$$\frac{(P/p)^t}{(P/p)^0} \neq \frac{P^t/P^0}{p^t/p^0}, \qquad (7)$$

a fact widely overlooked. No wonder that readers of Keynes from 1915 to 1930 generally held simultaneously the view that PPP was a trivial truism of arbitrage *and* besides was quite untrue.

Actually, had Cassel tried to calculate PPP for mobile goods by $R_i^t = P_i^t/p_i^t$, he would have always found the ruling rate to be the correct one! If he calculated it in the nontruistic, historical index-number form (inclusive of domestic goods)

$$R^t = \frac{P^t/P^0}{p^t/p^0} R^0, \qquad (8)$$

we can provide the following rationale:

Suppose *each* P_i^t/P_i^0 (whether i represents a mobile good or a domestic one) will *in time* settle down toward a *common* ratio foreshadowed by the *present* index-number ratios P^t/P^0; and likewise for the foreign small p's. Then the present index-number calculation could have some long-run predictive value for the future exchange rate — the best defense I can make for Cassel.

9. *Cost-of-Living Version.* An alternative cross-space rather than cross-time PPP calculation is sometimes made.[2] It is apparently thought that

[2] H. Houthakker, "Should We Devalue the Dollar?"

$$R = \frac{\$ \text{ cost of a good}}{\pounds \text{ cost of a good}} \qquad (9)$$

$$= \frac{\$ \text{ cost-of-living-of-standard-basket-of-goods}}{\pounds \text{ cost-of-living-of-standard-basket-of-goods}}.$$

Were all trade costs and impediments zero, these would hold for each good and for every composite good. But, if the computation is made correctly, every ruling exchange rate would turn out to be the PPP equilibrium rate, bringing us back again to the trivial Keynes arbitrage version. Two mistakes by prewar writers permitted the computed result to differ from the ruling rate. First, the American and European costs of living were sometimes computed with *different* goods weightings; such index numbers should not be used together in (9).

There is a second factor. Heavy transport costs and impediments do exist. So geographical price ratios are not uniform. (That is one reason why Americans weight Bourbon heavily in our cost-of-living and Europeans weight Scotch heavily!) Hence, the instantaneous truism need not even be true.

None of this would matter in an artificial neutral-money model, for that model has no need to rule out transport costs, domestic goods, quotas, or even *ad valorem* tariffs, since it is *not* a model dependent on arbitrage.

But, at this point, Cassel nods; indeed he lies down. Suddenly he argues in the following vein, "People will pay for a currency only its *worth*, which halves when its cost-of-living index doubles. PPP exists when the exchange rate equalizes the costs-of-living of the two countries." Evidently a new, and bizarre, kind

Challenge, Vol. 11 (Oct., 1962), 11. Houthakker says: ". . . recent figures indicate that an average basket of commodities bought for $1 in the U.S. would cost only 3.11 marks in Germany, while the official exchange rate is four marks to the dollar. We may say, *therefore*, that the dollar was overvalued with respect to the mark by 22 per cent." [My emphasis.] From BLS data I find that by this reasoning the San Francisco dollar has been overvalued relative to the Houston dollar by (106.0–83.3)/83.3, or by 27 per cent. Betting these many years on a return to PPP would not have been rewarding, nor would prediction of heavier San Francisco unemployment. The change since 1948 in German p's is indeed significant but, I think, not so much for reasons connected with equation (9) as with my later equation (14). None of my criticisms in these next few sections apply to Houthakker's work, which is discussed in Section 12 and beyond.

of arbitrage is tacitly envisaged: somebody demands £'s whenever something (a market basket?) called COL can be bought more cheaply than can something called (our?) COL can be bought for $. This goes on until the $ price of the £ has been bid up to bring about equality and equilibrium.

Patently, I cannot import cheap Italian haircuts, nor can Niagara-Falls honeymoons be exported. We are left with the minute grain of truth that tourism may move in the direction of cheaper prices, thereby tending to lower in some fractional degree the net price differentials of tourists' items. It is bizarre to think that there are enough retired *rentiers*, who will move to Germany to bid up their cheap prices, and who will only cease to move in either direction when COL PPP has been achieved. What is true is that some footloose people and absentee landlords do move. Those with "American tastes" tend to move here where the things they like are relatively cheap, and those with "foreign tastes" tend to become expatriates.

Some theorists become prey to the traveller's paradox: It costs more to live away from home. Parisians complain of fantastic New York prices, while New Yorkers — who have never even visited the Waldorf-Astoria — complain about three-star restaurant prices. The female shopper is subject to the opposite paradox: everything is cheaper abroad than at home for everybody. (The rational basis for this is the inequality theorem: It can only help to be able to buy from two separate catalogues or price systems.)

Professors, particularly cultured ones, are particularly prone to infer an overvaluation of the dollar by the cheapness abroad of personal services (maids, tenors, and Doctors of Philosophy). By this reasoning, every prosperous region has a chronically overvalued currency. By it, as noted earlier, California ought to devalue its dollar relative to that of New England. They take in each other's laundry at higher price tags out there, but also wear finer linen. Somehow the cheap sunshine does not get fully into the PPP price indexes.

10. *What Chases What?* The California gold rush provides a reminder that equilibrium can be restored by changes on either side of the equation. In 1849 the dollar in California sold

for close to a dollar in Vermont, gold being cheap to ship. The wrong kind of PPP calculation would include an egg-price differential of 800 per cent and a man-day differential of 1,000 per cent; the wheat differential was 200 per cent. It might come up with the erroneous prediction of a PPP of California's $ at one-third the Vermont $. Since, as Marshall has taught, short-run price equilibrium isn't long-run price equilibrium, the proper prediction should have been in this case: wheat prices will soon fall out West to near the Eastern level; fresh egg prices, by transport-cost *addenda* to comparative advantage theory, will not fall to quite such parity; real wages, through labor mobility, will eventually come much nearer to parity. In $R < P/p$, instead of R's adjusting, it is the numerator of California's price index that primarily adjusts to restore the equilibrium.

If California were a sovereign state and could triple its nonconvertible currency, Cassel would predict that this could validate its high price level and validate the prediction that the California dollar would depreciate relative to the United States dollar. These days, when contemplating an apparently overvalued currency of a mixed economy, it is a pretty good bet that the electorate and government will not force upon itself a general deflation of the P numerator; less certain is the guess that the other sovereign country will manage its affairs well enough to prevent an inflation in the p denominator. In such a case, the odds favor either trade controls or eventual currency depreciation.

But all this chasing around assumes one has fastened on some defensible $R = P/p$ equilibrium goal. I must return to investigation of this problem.

11. *Relative Export-Price Indexes.* It was once in vogue to try to save PPP from being trivial and/or wrong by rephrasing it in terms of ratios of the export price indexes of the two countries. Thus, Bresciani-Turroni considered

$$R \text{ index} = \frac{\text{American Export Price Index}}{\text{European Export Price Index}}.$$

(10)

This unequal weighting can hardly lead to an exact relationship. Suppose we export good 3 alone, bread, and Europe exports good 1 alone, cloth. (Banish good 2 from existence.) The above equation then says, no more and no less than this:

The terms of trade between bread and cloth is a universal constant (like the speed of light, one presumes, not like the ratio of a circle's perimeter to its diameter).

Once PPP theorists had this pointed out to them, they saved face at the expense of mind by adding a codicil: "So long as there are no 'substantive' changes in real factors or supply and demand, PPP is true."

This last truism is saved from being a fatuity by the mentioned fact that in some interludes of strong inflation and dislocated exchanges, there is a likelihood that the *transient* distortions of the disturbed periods will settle back toward the previous real equilibria. This is not a reed to lean too heavily on.

Here is a good place to warn anew against a recurrent source of fallacy in international trade theory. Transport costs and *all* trade impediments aside, prices must everywhere be the same when expressed in commensurate units. So it is *not* true that classical writers like Hume expected that gold-standard disequilibria would be corrected by differential movements of prices at home and abroad. With transport costs zero, the gold points coincide as do all "goods-points," and no differentials in the prices of the same goods are ever possible. What Hume needs is differential (geographically-identical) movements in the prices of certain goods *produced* by one of the countries relative to the prices of other goods produced by other countries. (This disposes of the Laughlin fallacy that rapid telegraph and cheap transport annihilates the classical mechanism.) But precisely the above movements in relative prices are what Cassel originally had to rule out in the neutral-money version of PPP.

Obviously, a point-of-time equality like (10) is complete nonsense, since $R = P_3/p_1$ is like saying that the $2.80 price per £ must equal the ratio of the price of a California sherry to the price of a European Volkswagen. On the other hand, forgetting PPP, we should suspect that the relative rise of our export prices in the 1950's compared to those of the surplus coun-

tries did contribute to the drop in our share of world exports.

12. *Production-Cost Parities.* Each generation must rekill its phoenixes. These various issues about PPP and exchange equilibrium were discussed (one dare not say settled) in the 1920's and again in the 1940's. Now scholars [3] have again suggested use of costs instead of prices in PPP calculations. In a loose sense, one might argue that costs are more indicative of "normal long-run prices" than short-run prices are; if profits can be squeezed or bloated in the short run but must ultimately be restored to normal patterns, this way of estimating parity might be useful. But what is the exact theoretical meaning of such cost or factor-price comparisons?

Professor Houthakker in Congressional testimony, advances the following interesting ideas:

> . . . For foreign trade to be in longrun balance (still abstracting from capital movements) it is necessary, roughly speaking, that unit labor costs, converted at official exchange rates, be the same everywhere. This implies that the equilibrium exchange rate between two countries must be equal to the ratio of their unit labor costs or, more generally, unit factor costs if other inputs are taken into account. If the official value of country A's currency in terms of country B's currency is higher than the ratio of unit factor costs, A's currency is overvalued; as a result, A's balance of trade will show a long-term deficit, or its domestic economy will be depressed, or both. Countries A and B will then be in fundamental disequilibrium, except possibly for offsets from other items in the balance of payment.

The introduction of capital movements modifies the above conclusion to some extent. If these movements are unrelated to relative costs (as is the case with foreign aid or reparation payments) the capital-exporting country will have to have a surplus of

[3] H. Houthakker, op. cit.; also his "Problems of International Finance," *Agricultural Policy Review*, Vol. 3, No. 3 (July–Aug.–Sept., 1963) 12–13; "Exchange Rate Adjustment," *Factors Affecting the U.S. Balance of Payments* Joint Economic Committee compilation of studies: 87th Congress, 2d Session (Dec. 14, 1962) 289–304, particularly 293–294. Since these are non-technical writings I disclaim any right to criticize his writings from a finicky perfectionist platform: I cite them only as sources of interesting questions.

The previously cited 1948 Harris volume contains remarks by Alvin Hansen favorable to cost parities, 380 *ff.*, and by Gottfried Haberler against, 395 *ff.* See G. Haberler, *A Survey of International Trade Theory*, Special Papers in International Economics No. 1 (July, 1961), International Finance Section, Princeton University, 1961, revised and enlarged edition for discussion and bibliography of PPP.

commodity exports, and its unit factor costs, calculated in terms of foreign currency, will have to be correspondingly lower, except to the extent that the capital-importing country increases its demand for current imports from the capital-exporting countries. Conversely, if a country receives foreign aid, it may be able to afford a somewhat overvalued currency. (pp. 293–294)

. . . Information about unit factor costs in different countries is hard to obtain directly but there is an indirect and much simpler way of making the necessary comparisons. In the long run wages are equal to the marginal product of labor in terms of commodities sold locally and for export. Domestic production competes with imports, which means that prices are equalized and that marginal product can also be measured in terms of commodities consumed rather than commodities produced. The competitive position of different countries can therefore be evaluated from the relative price levels of consumption goods. For this purpose it is necessary to look not only at commodities that enter into international trade, but also at all other commodities in the proportions in which they are normally consumed in each country . . . .

. . . The theory just outlined is not new (though this particular justification apparently is). It is known as the purchasing power parity theory and was popular in the early 1920's when it was often applied uncritically; later the pendulum swung the other way, but its critics usually overlooked the relation between prices and costs which is basic to the theory. . . . If used with circumspection the PPP theory (for short) is still the only approach to a limited but important problem. It is not a general theory of international trade, nor does it give absolute prescriptions for correct exchange rates. It applies only to the long run, and in fact does not really refer to purchasing power at all but to productivity (or, to save the initials, to "production power"). (p. 296)

We must not deride commonplace notions just because they are true. From my subsequent equation (14) and irrespective of PPP terminology, the following simple conclusions seem valid.

It can hardly be disputed that a rise in our money wage rates relative to those abroad will, other things equal, tend toward overvaluation of the dollar or lessened undervaluation of it; or that superior productivity improvement abroad, unmatched by commensurate increase in money wage rates there, will tend in the same direction.

It ought not to be disputed that a spontaneous increase in United States government off-shore expenditures for defense and aid will, unless offset, conduce toward overvaluation of the dollar and require a commensurately larger current surplus on private account.

A recognition at home of improved investment opportunities abroad will also convert a previous equilibrium exchange rate into an overvalued one.

13. *Critique.* I take it that Professor Houthakker is trying to express more than these sturdy commonplaces in the above quotation. And it is those *additional* notions that raise serious questions in my mind. All my queries refer to Houthakker's interesting new theoretical formulations and not to his general position, which in consequence does not receive a balanced appraisal.

First, costs of production are not universally equalized. It is the irreducible differential in costs that leads to importing rather than producing at home. This banality is, of course, less relevant to a world of increasing cost than to my simple Ricardian model. But let me first refer back to my equations (1). In them American and European costs are definitely unequal except for the singular case of the borderline goods discussed in (4).

It is true that (4) calls for equality, or approximate equality of borderline goods. For such goods, a Houthakker equality of the exchange rate to the ratio of unit costs of production does hold, but it has been pointed out that this is both a superficial equality *and* one that involves implicit theorizing. Actually it is the wide inequalities of (3) that give the only limits on wage levels and exchange rates that are implied by the existence of some production going on in each country. It would be arbitrary to argue that, since the borderline good is likely to be "intermediate" between the broad limits, we are entitled to take an index number average of all the productivity ratios on each side and apply them to some index number of relative wages. The borderline is not guaranteed to be in the middle, and it is precisely when an exchange rate goes out of kilter that the borderline shifts so as to invalidate any simple quantitative comparison.

Thus, let the United States government increase its demand for foreign goods so much that good 1 becomes our borderline good instead of good 2; let full equilibrium be restored with the same W and w as before — which is possible in a variety of ways. Then $R = \$2$ for R is the *true* equilibrium level now. With no productivity or wage change, a simple Houthakker parity would stay unchanged at $3, giving rise to the surmise (false by hypothesis!) that the dollar is now undervalued.

Let me now leave the constant-cost case, which has been quite unfavorable to the $R =$ Cost here/Cost there approach. If labor is kept the *only* factor, or approximately the only factor — as where every good i is produced by a Cobb-Douglas production function of the form $Q_i = A_i^{-1} L^{.99}$ (capital)$^{.01}$ — we have not been able to leave this case. However, assume that there are some important unspecified factors in the background, and that our labor requirements are actually increasing functions of Q_i (and perhaps dependent on still other factors). In this case, it is marginal and not unit cost which equals price. Notationally, then, let $A_i(Q_i)$ represent MC not AC and $a_i(q_i)$ the mc abroad.

Now in equilibrium (1)–(4) can be summarized by

$$\frac{W}{w} \frac{A_k}{a_k} < R = \frac{W}{w} \frac{A_j}{a_j} < \frac{W}{w} \frac{A_q}{a_q}; \qquad (3)'$$

where goods k are those America cannot afford to produce in competition with exports, goods q are those Europe must import, and goods j are a wide array that are being produced in both countries (and possibly being shipped from one or the other country).

Since the A's and a's are now variables not constants, $(3)'$ is again a mere surface relation, one of the many needed to define equilibrium. At a point of time, transport costs aside, if Houthakker uses the ruling MC's, the existing exchange rate is always his parity rate. If he uses some pre-existing MC's, corrected by some putative changes in average wage levels and in productivity index changes, there is no necessity of his getting the correct answers. (Try our previous case where W, w, and all production functions stay the same. But now let us desire more of European exports, restoring the true equilibrium by having R go from $3 to $2. Using index numbers that record *no* change in

wages or productivity, Houthakker parity remains at $3, depicting a fictitious undervaluation.)

Thus far, I have neglected transport costs. It will not change the issue if I assume all ranges of relative transport costs (or trade impediments), from prohibitive charges for domestic goods (of all degrees of comparative advantage), to zero costs for all kinds of mobile goods, to all in-between cases for transport costs in either direction. Evidently the equalities in $(3)'$ now become widened by transport inequalities; with goods that are being actually exported being at points analogous to the familiar gold points. The reader can verify that all of the difficulties for Houthakker parity remain, and some are compounded, in this more general model.

Let me denote as a general "arbitrage" relation the competitive requirement that price anywhere equals lowest delivered cost there. Calling T_i and t_i the transport costs of American and European exports respectively expressed in $ and £ I write (1) as

$$P_i = \text{Min } (MC_i, (mc_i + t_i)R), \text{ etc.} \qquad (1)'$$

At first I thought Professor Houthakker was confusing the equalities and inequalities that result from surface arbitrage under free competition with the conditions for clearing-of-the-market of over-all balance of payments and R. But I must have been wrong. Because if that had been the case, his statement that the above holds only under zero capital movements (and is modified in the systematic direction of requiring lower United States prices than these if we are exporting capital) would lead to the fantastic conclusion that the laws of arbitrage and Gresham are abrogated by unilateral capital movements. (Example: for zero transport costs, write $R = k(P_i/p_i) = k(P/p)$, where $k = 1$ holds when capital movements balance but $k \neq 1$ holds when they don't balance. No one would continue to believe in that version of PPP.[4])

[4] An alternative interpretation occurs to me. Let our investment abroad rise, thereby increasing the amount and range of our exports. Then more goods will sell abroad at prices that exceed our prices by positive transport costs (and with the transport differential enhanced if the one-way shipping cost-supply schedule is a rising one). Thus, if capital outflow is to be matched by an equilibrium export surplus, our price level must fall a little relative to

I make one last attempt to interpret the novel PPP doctrine. Suppose *all* A_i/a_i back in (1) remain identical, so that there is never a difference in comparative advantage. Then zero capital movements with non-zero production everywhere would yield the simple wage parity form of PPP. This doctrine though would hold without any of the indicated modifications for capital movements (save for the extreme case where one nation produces nothing, living completely on the other's trade surplus). However, this rather odd defense will not really work; for great disequilibrium will be possible even when PPP holds, provided one nation is willing to take the other's proffered I.O.U.s and gold.

The case of no comparative advantage in Ricardo's model is of no empirical interest. Results like it occur, however, in my unrealistic model of complete factor price equalization between two countries with geographically similar production functions in terms of labor and "Kapital," and almost similar factor endowments. Even without capital funds flowing, such a model will equalize both the real wage and the interest rate so long as one export and one import good have uniformly different factor intensities. In that case

$$R = \frac{MC_i}{mc_i} \qquad (11)$$

for *every* good, domestic or mobile. This equality of costs does *not* destroy trade, but rather holds *at* the equilibrium pattern of specialization (which is determined, in its essentials, by demand conditions). If this is what Houthakker meant, the following observations are in order.

(a) The case is not realistic. (Even if we generalize it, from identical production functions $Q_i(x,y) \equiv q_i(x,y)$ to functions identical only in efficiency units of factors $Q_i(x,y) \equiv q_i(\alpha x, \beta y)$ where $\alpha > 1 < \beta$ in recognition of Yankee ingenuity, the result would not seem realistic enough for empirical calculations.

(b) The parity in (11) is *not* one that would have to be modified by unilateral capital movements or anything else.

(c) It would hold in disequilibrium as well as in equilibrium, so long only as trade were

theirs, a transport-cost effect which crude PPP calculations might miss.

free and even if we had mass unemployment or not-long-sustainable gold losses.

(d) Finally, if we rewrite it in the form

$$R = \left(\frac{MC_i}{W} \Big/ \frac{mc_i}{w} \right) \frac{W}{w} \qquad (12)$$

the expression cannot, I believe, be usefully approximated by index numbers of productivity changes. Any PPP calculation so arrived at may be empirically lucky in some cases, but lacks a valid theoretical basis.

(e) We are back then to the valuable commonplaces that began this section and we still lack precise numerical guidance of the PPP type.

While I have stated these matters rather dogmatically, it has been merely to avoid the awkward circumlocution of interrogation. I express doubt rather than disagreement.

14. *Equilibrium parity.* Writers such as Mill, Mangoldt, Marshall, Edgeworth, Taussig, Viner, Graham, Haberler, and G. A. Elliott have analyzed my 2-country many-good constant-labor-cost model. It is the one case where Marshall's "bales of goods" really can be used. First forbid all capital and gold movements. Then knowledge of the A's and a's, of each man's indifference contours and labor supply, will (with suitable adjustments for transport costs) enable the net current balance of America B, as expressed in any *numeraire* units, to be written as a function solely of W/Rw, the real ratio of wage rates expressed in a common currency:

$$B(W/Rw) = 0 \qquad (13)$$

A similar relation can be deduced from this for the other country. If the "normal" Marshall-Lerner elasticities prevail, raising W with R and w fixed will lead to an American deficit on current account. If non-current items N are also a decreasing function of W/Rw — as for example when a wage rise here makes wanted net investment outflow greater — equilibrium [5] can be written symbolically as

[5] I have been asked whether my argument that comparative advantage is no guarantee of balance-of-payments equilibrium depends upon an assumption of rigid wage rates. My answer is, not essentially. Of course, if we are to be outsold in terms of everything and our employment is to be zero, that does imply that our wage rates are kept rigidly so high as to prevent full (or indeed *any*) employment. But my point is a different one: even if the domestic

$$B(W/Rw) + N(W/Rw) = F(W/Rw) = 0, \quad (14)$$

and an autonomous outflow of capital or aid will call for an equilibrating drop in our relative wage level. (But recall from the Ohlin and Pigou discussions of the transfer problem that a shift in N payments may have important "income effects" on the current-payments function B.)

Naive PPP must assume that the function F is not a changing function with time. Sophisticated PPP asserts that F has not changed much or estimates how it has changed. Unless very sophisticated indeed, PPP is a misleadingly pretentious doctrine, promising us what is rare in economics, detailed numerical predictions. Few doubt that long-run wheat prices are determined by supply and demand equations rather like the one above; but who ever expects from this analysis detailed numerical predictions based upon simple historical calculations?

Finale

15. *Conclusions.* My own diagnosis of the dollar problem can be illuminated by this theoretical discussion.

(1) The dollar has been somewhat overvalued in this last decade. This does not imply that we should depreciate. It does imply that economists everywhere would prefer, if they could rerun history, that the 1949 depreciations abroad had been somewhat less sharp.

(2) The overvaluation has hampered a high-employment policy at home; it has unduly limited America's freedom to spend abroad *in an efficient manner* what our citizenry deems

money wage falls flexibly to produce full employment, there is no reason why the full-employment money wage should produce a zero "basic deficit." Spontaneous or induced capital movements may finance this algebraic deficit; or gold may flow out; or if gold payments are suspended, the exchange rate R may move to restore the equilibrium; or the Hume gold-flow price-level mechanism may work eventually to restore the equilibrium. In no case is it the comparative advantage mechanism itself which does the trick. This is really a prosaic conclusion, for its paradoxical appearance evaporates once it is understood.

Professor Bela Balassa of Yale, who has independently written a paper arriving at similar theoretical conclusions and who has presented empirical evidence to show that COL PPP tends to show a spurious overvaluation for higher-income currencies, suggests that I may be reading more sense into Cassel than is there and may be too hard on Keynes. I fear he is right.

to be desirable for our military security, altruistic and Machiavellian foreign aid, and profit-seeking investments.

(3) The productivity improvements abroad since 1949 (which represent a relative lowering of a_i/A_i ratios) have not yet been matched by commensurate rises in foreign money wages relative to ours (i.e., in w/W). As a result, we have not been able to develop the colossally large surplus on private current account needed for equilibrium offsetting of legitimate private investment and government spending on foreign-aid and security. (Note how close I come to the general spirit of Professor Houthakker's forceful writings.)

(4) Our overvaluation has had one effect that some will deem a virtue: it has kept pressure on our price levels. This anti-inflation benefit has been dearly bought in terms of unemployment, excess capacity, slow growth, and low domestic profits.

(5) Our overvaluation has helped to redistribute our disproportionate share of world gold, thus providing the miracle nations of Europe and Japan with needed secular increases in liquidity.

(6) Our overvaluation has put some upward pressure on foreign price and cost levels. By voluntary currency appreciation, the surplus countries could choose to offset this.

(7) Overvaluation pushes American capital abroad, and in turn is intensified by foreign investment. These are secondary reactions to the technological miracles of growth abroad. *The prime element in all this is the reducing of the technological gap between America and the less-than-most-affluent nations.* Their labor now has access to the best production functions. Our labor had a quasi-monopoly access to scientific management methods and to our capital. But capital and knowledge have become footloose.

If you think American capitalists will reap the reward of their foreign ownerships, our National Product may have been increased by the miracle abroad. But labor's monopoly position, and hence its *share* of the total real product, would seem to have been hurt (compared to what otherwise would have been the case). Literally, we have exported jobs and (what is not the same thing) have lowered the imputed real wage of immobile American labor needed to repatriate those jobs.

(8) Finally, has the narrowing of the technical gap hurt or helped America's total equilibrium GNP? Pollyannas say prosperity abroad swells trade volume and has to help everybody. Economists say, "It all depends." If my hypothesis is correct — that narrowing our technological gap is the prime clue to postwar international economics — the earlier theoretical models have the following implications.

Our comparative advantage (in the goods we usually specialize on for export and home production) has been narrowed down by forces originating abroad. The basic gain from international trade — its consumers surplus, so to speak — should thereby be lessened. (In my Ricardian model this would show itself in a deterioration of the equilibrium factor terms-of-trade, $Y^* = W/Rw$.) This effect may not be large, and it may be swamped by other factors making for a rising trend in United States living standards; but compared to what otherwise would be the case, an externally-caused lowering of a_i/A_i ratios which is biassed toward

our goods for which this ratio is already high, presumptively lowers our well being.[6]

If true, this is not to me a discouraging conclusion. As a man of good will, living in the most affluent country, I must cheer the material progress abroad.

[6] A balanced fall in a_i/A_i yields no easy presumptions. Note that my logic cannot be used to prove that the narrowing of comparative advantages hurts *both* regions, Europe as well as America. It does tend to lessen the consumers-surplus-from-trade of both regions; but the country in which biassed innovation originated, Europe, will presumptively gain more from domestic efficiency than she will lose in c-s-f-t (absolutely or compared to what otherwise would have been the case).

When I published the present thesis in my regular *Nihon Keizai Shimbun* column (and in other financial journalism), a New York bank economist wrote in a letter: "How can the American terms of trade deteriorate when, as you do not deny, America has been pricing herself out of the market by too-high export wages and prices (steel, etc.)?" My answer goes as follows: "It is precisely the maintenance of higher-than-equilibrium terms of trade that perpetuates trade deficits. When we restore final equilibrium by somehow bringing our relative prices down, the indicated deterioration of the terms of trade (over what they otherwise would have been) will only *then* be observable." Because we are a great continental economy, not much dependent on external trade, the indicated modest drop in terms of trade ought not to mean a great welfare loss (not nearly as great as, say, an extra 2 per cent of unemployment or 4 per cent of real GNP).

66

Protection and Real Wages

INTRODUCTION

Second only in political appeal to the argument that tariffs increase employment is the popular notion that the standard of living of the American worker must be protected against the ruinous competition of cheap foreign labour. Equally prevalent abroad is its counterpart that European industry cannot compete with the technically superior American system of production. Again and again economists have tried to show the falaciousness of this argument. Professor Taussig, for example, stated that " perhaps most familiar and most unfounded of all is the belief that complete freedom of trade would bring about an equalisation of money wages the world over. . . . There is no such tendency to equalisation."[1] And Professor Haberler classifies the argument that wages might suffer from international trade among those " that do not merit serious discussion. . . . An equalisation of wages comes about only if labour is mobile [between countries]"[2]

More recently, however, the writings of Ohlin seem to suggest that a re-examination of this accepted doctrine might be fruitful. It is the intention of the present paper to show that definitive statements are possible concerning the effects of international trade upon the relative remunerations of productive agencies, and more important, upon their absolute real incomes. That this is possible is surprising since the voluminous literature appears to contain only statements of possibilities and presumptions rather than of necessities. Indeed, in the beginning we expected to do no more than delineate factors which would indicate a likelihood in one direction or another, and only in the course of the investigation did we discover that unambiguous inferences were possible. It may be illuminating, therefore, to follow in the exposition our original sequence of thought rather than attempt the most direct derivation of theorems.

THE EFFECT OF TRADE UPON RELATIVE FACTOR PRICES

According to the train of thought associated with the name of Ohlin, differences in the proportions of the various productive factors between countries are important elements in explaining the course of international trade. A country will export those commodities which are produced with its relatively abundant factors of production, and will import those in the pro-

[1] F. W. Taussig, *International Trade*, p. 38. The statement might have been made equally well with respect to real wages, since in the classical formulation the prices of internationally traded goods cannot diverge in different countries by more than the cost of transfer. In his *Principles* there is a passage which might be interpreted in the opposite direction. " Under certain contingencies, it is conceivable that protective duties will affect the process of sharing and so will influence wages otherwise than through their effect on the total product." 4th ed., p. 517. But the phrasing is not quite clear and refers probably to the share in national income rather than to the absolute size. We have not found any similar passage either in *The Tariff History of the United States*, in *International Trade*, or in *Free Trade, the Tariff, and Reciprocity*.

[2] G. Haberler, *The Theory of International Trade*, pp. 250–251, bracketed expression ours. See also the preceding sentence on p. 251 where Haberler expressly denies that movement of goods will lead to an equalisation of factor prices. However, as will be discussed below, he does in another place introduce important qualifications to this denial.

duction of which its relatively scarce factors are important.[1] And as a result of the shift towards increased production of those goods in which the abundant factors predominate, there will be a tendency—necessarily incomplete—towards an equalisation of factor prices between the two or more trading countries.[2] It is clear that the equalisation is only partial because otherwise we would be involved in the contradiction that differences in comparative cost would disappear, and there would be no trade. Although partial, the movement in the direction of equalisation is nevertheless real and can be substantial.

Assuming, as we shall throughout, that the total amounts of the factors of production remain fixed, it is clear from the Heckscher–Ohlin theorem that the introduction of trade must lower the relative share in the real or money national income going to the scarce factor of production. For the total return to a factor equals its price times the amount employed, and since we assume full employment before and after trade, the total returns to the factors are proportional to the rates per unit. This argument seems to have relevance to the American discussion of protection versus free trade. If, as is generally thought, labour is the relatively scarce factor in the American economy, it would appear that trade would necessarily lower the relative position of the labouring class as compared to owners of other factors of production. So far we have dealt only with the relative shares of the various factors and have not gone into the effect upon absolute shares. Before entering upon this latter problem, it is of considerable interest to mention the most important currently held viewpoints.

SOME EXISTING VIEWS

Nobody, of course, ever denied that the workers employed in the particular industry which loses a tariff could be hurt in the short-run, but according to the classical theory, in the long-run there would be an increased demand for those commodities in which the country had a comparative advantage, i.e. where labour is more productive.[3] Although money wages might fall, the removal of a tariff would result in a still larger reduction in price levels so that the real wage must rise. In the words of Taussig, " The question of wages is at bottom one of productivity. The greater the productivity of industry at large, the higher will be the general level of wages."[4]

How can this argument be reconciled with the Ohlin type of discussion ? If there were only one commodity produced, then indeed the marginal productivity of labour would depend simply on the relative quantities of labour

---

[1] Professor Viner has shown that this line of reasoning was not unknown to the classical economists. See his *Studies in the Theory of International Trade*, pp. 500–507.

[2] B. Ohlin, *Interregional and International Trade*, Chapter II and elsewhere. This appears to be a novel theorem largely unknown to the classical economists, or at least completely unmentioned in Viner's masterful review of doctrine. Perhaps the earliest clear enunciation of this doctrine is that of E. Heckscher in a 1919 article in the *Ekonomisk Tidskrift*, cited by Ohlin. Heckscher apparently gives no prior references. Unfortunately, this important contribution is in Swedish, and we are indebted to Mr. Svend Laursen for a paraphrasing of its contents. Because of its extensive development at the hands of Ohlin, we shall refer to it as the Heckscher–Ohlin theorem.

[3] " The free-trader argues that if the duties were given up and the protected industries pushed out of the field by foreign competitors, the workmen engaged in them would find no less well-paid employment elsewhere." F. W. Taussig, *Principles of Economics*, 4th ed., Vol. I, p. 516.

[4] Ibid, p. 517.

and capital as a whole. And the same would be the case with more than one commodity if labour and capital were combined in the same proportions in the production of each. A movement of the factors of production from one employment to another would then leave the marginal productivities of labour and capital unchanged.

Now, while it is true that under the assumptions of pure competition, homogeneity, and perfect mobility of labour the value of the marginal product of labour (expressed in terms of any commodity) must be the same in each occupation, it nevertheless does not follow that this will depend simply on the proportion of labour and capital as a whole. For in so far as capital and labour are combined in different proportions in each occupation, any change from one production to another will change the " value marginal productivity " of labour (however expressed), even though it will, of course, still be equal in all occupations. In this sense the value marginal productivity of labour as a whole may be considered to depend upon a kind of weighted average of the effective demands for the various producible commodities. It is the essence of the argument of the previous section that international trade in accordance with the principle of comparative advantage so shifts production and the relative effective derived demands as to produce the Heckscher–Ohlin effect.

It is not surprising that the classical argument should not have touched upon the problem of relative and absolute shares since for most purposes the older economists implicitly assumed a one factor economy or an economy in which different factors of production were applied in a dose whose proportions never varied. It is to their credit as realists that again and again they relaxed these assumptions, but they were not always able to weld into a synthesis these excluded effects.[1]

Among more modern writers who are nevertheless in the classical tradition it has long been recognised that a small factor of production specialised for the production of a protected commodity might be harmed by the removal of tariffs.[2] This has received particular attention in connection with the problem of non-competing groups in the labour market. Certain sub-groups of the labouring class, e.g. highly skilled labourers, may benefit while others are harmed. Thus, Ohlin holds that it is quite possible under certain circumstances for free trade to reduce the standard of living of the manufacturing labouring class. " If manufacturing and agricultural labourers form two non-competing groups, high protection of manufacturing industries may raise the real wages of the workers in these industries at the expense of the other factors."[3] Similarly, Haberler remarks that " . . . in the short-run, specialised and immobile groups of workers, like the owners of specific material factors, may suffer

---

[1] A good case can be made out that even Ricardo did not adhere narrowly to a labour theory of value, but this is not the place to enter into controversy on this subject. See, however, John Cassels, " A Re-interpretation of Ricardo on Value," *Quarterly Journal of Economics*, Vol. 49, pp. 518 ff.

[2] " It is perfectly clear that the imposition of a prohibitive tariff on the import of raw silk into the United States would increase the rents of the owners of land suitable for the growth of mulberry trees and the earnings of workers, if there be such, completely specialised in caring for silkworms." M. C. Samuelson, " The Australian Case for Protection Re-examined," *Quarterly Journal of Economics*, November, 1939, p. 149.

[3] Ohlin, op. cit., p. 306.

heavy reductions in income when for one reason or another they are faced with more intense foreign competition."[1] Once the principle that no factor can benefit from a tariff has been broken, one is tempted to ask whether similar results are not possible for a large factor of production even if only two factors are assumed. For the logic of the case seems the same whether two classes of labour are considered to be non-competing or whether the " non-competing " factors are labelled " capital " and " labour " respectively.

In treating this problem Haberler expresses doubt that a large and mobile factor such as labour can be harmed by unrestricted international trade. " We may conclude that in the long run the working-class as a whole has nothing to fear from international trade, since, in the long run, labour is the least specific of all factors. It will gain by the general increase in productivity due to the international division of labour, and is not likely to lose at all seriously by a change in the functional distribution of the national income."[2] This is not a dogmatic necessity, but rather regarded as the most probable situation. For lower on the same page Haberler recognises explicitly a possible qualification. If labour enters more importantly in the protected industry, it might possibly be harmed by free trade.[3]

Viner criticises Haberler's conclusion maintaining that there appears to be " no *a priori* or empirical grounds for holding this to be an improbable case."[4] In this connection Viner is concerned primarily with the *relative* share of labour in the national money income. In his discussion he introduces as an element in the problem the prices which consumers must pay for commodities, particularly imports and exports with and without protection. Thus, he says, " But even if labour on the average had low occupational mobility and were employed relatively heavily in the protected industries, its real income might still rise with the removal of tariff protection . . . if it was an important consumer of the hitherto protected commodities, and if the price of these commodities fell sufficiently as a result to offset the reduction in money wages in the new situation."[5] Ohlin and other modern writers raise this problem, but it can also be found in the older literature. Bastable, for example, in good classical fashion points out that free trade may force a food exporting country " to bring worse soils into cultivation, and to raise the value of food, thus permitting of an increase in the amount of agricultural rent. In this instance, the labourers, and possibly the capitalists, may suffer while the landlords gain."[6]

We may sum up as follows : (1) In the narrowest classical version the problem of the effect of trade upon the relative and absolute shares of various productive factors could hardly arise since only one factor is assumed. (2) Outside the confines of this rigid system it has long been recognised that the relative and possibly even the absolute share of a small specific factor of production *might* be increased by protection. This received particular attention in connection with the problem of non-competing groups. (3) With reference to large

[1] Haberler, op. cit., p. 195.
[2] Haberler, ibid, p. 195.
[3] Similar views are attributed to Wicksell, Carver, Nicholson, and others.
[4] Viner, op. cit., p. 533.
[5] Viner, ibid, p. 533.
[6] C, F. Bastable, *The Theory of International Trade*, 4th ed., p. 105.

categories opinion is more divided. Almost all admit the possibility of a decline in the relative share of a large factor of production such as labour as a result of free trade ; many even admit the possibility of a decline in the real income of a large factor of production. But all writers consider highly improbable a decline in the absolute shares, and many believe the same with respect to the relative shares. Some take the position that no *a priori* presumption is possible in connection with the last problem. (4) The vast majority of writers take it as axiomatic that a calculation of effects upon real income must take into consideration the behaviour of prices of commodities entering into the consumer's budget. Thus, if the owners of a factor of production consume only the exported good (in Professor Pigou's terminology this is the wage good), a different result will be reached than if the wage good were imported. And since in the real world consumption is diversified so that the concept of a wage good is an oversimplification, a difficult index number problem would appear to be involved.

It is the purpose of the present investigation to show that under rather general assumptions definite conclusions can be derived concerning the absolute share of a factor (*a*) even when there is perfect physical mobility of factors of production and a complete absence of specificity, (*b*) even if we are dealing with as few as two large factors of production, and (*c*) without any recourse to the index number problem or to the concept of a wage good.

ASSUMPTIONS OF THE ANALYSIS

For purposes of the analysis we shall start out with rather simplified assumptions, considering subsequently the effect of more realistic modifications. In order to keep the number of variables down to manageable proportions we assume only two countries. This involves no loss of generality since the " rest of the World " may always be lumped together as Country II. For the sake of exposition and diagrammatic convenience, only two commodities are considered, labelled respectively " wheat," A, and " watches," B. To accord with the Ohlin assumptions the production functions of each commodity are made the same in both countries and involve only two factors of production identified for convenience as labour (L) and capital (C).[1]

Moreover, by means of a simple device it is possible to avoid detailed consideration of the second country since all of its effects upon the first operate via changes in the price ratio of the two traded commodities.[2] We shall call this price ratio of wheat to watches P_a/P_b. It is irrelevant for our argument just why the exchange ratio of the two commodities is different after international trade is established ; it is sufficient that it does change.[3]

[1] It might possibly give rise to less confusion if instead of capital the second factor were called land because of the ambiguities involved in the definition of capital. The reader who is bothered by this fact is invited to substitute mentally land for capital in all that follows.

[2] For an example of the use of this device see P. A. Samuelson, " The Gains from International Trade," *Canadian Journal of Economics and Political Science*, May, 1939.

[3] In the limiting P_a/P_b would be unchanged. Also, in the classical constant cost case of a large country facing a smaller one trade may take place, but to an extent insufficient to result in complete specialisation on the part of the large country, and hence P_a/P_b may be unchanged. This exception is touched upon later.

The effect of international trade upon the shares of the productive factors can now be analysed by varying P_a/P_b as a parameter from its value as determined in the absence of trade, or with a given amount of protection, to its new value after free trade is opened up. Throughout we follow the conventional method of comparative statics, disregarding the process of transition from the old to the new equilibrium. Full employment of both factors is assumed to be realised before and after the change, and each factor is assumed to have perfectly complete physical mobility.[1] Throughout pure competition is assumed. The following symbols are used :

The amount of labour used in producing A .. .. .. L_a
The amount of labour used in producing B .. .. .. L_b
The amount of capital used in producing A .. .. .. C_a
The amount of capital used in producing B .. .. .. C_b
The total amount of labour used in producing both A and B L
The total amount of capital used in producing both A and B C

It is assumed that regardless of trade the total amounts of each factor of production remain unchanged. Therefore, we have the following obvious identities :

$$L_a + L_b = L \dots\dots\dots\dots\dots\dots\dots\dots\dots\dots\dots\dots\dots\dots\dots (1)$$

$$C_a + C_b = C \dots\dots\dots\dots\dots\dots\dots\dots\dots\dots\dots\dots\dots\dots\dots (2)$$

The production functions relating each good to the inputs of the factors allocated to its production can be written respectively as :

$$A = A\ (L_a, C_a) \dots\dots\dots\dots\dots\dots\dots\dots\dots\dots\dots\dots\dots\dots (3)$$

$$B = B\ (L_b, C_b) \dots\dots\dots\dots\dots\dots\dots\dots\dots\dots\dots\dots\dots\dots (4)$$

Because we are concerned with proportions and not with the scale of the process, these functions are assumed to be homogeneous of the first order.

It is a well-known condition of equilibrium that the ratio of the marginal productivities of the two factors must be the same in each occupation, because otherwise there would be a transfer from lower to higher levels. Symbolically this can be expressed as follows :[2]

$$\frac{\dfrac{\partial A(L_a, C_a)}{\partial L_a}}{\dfrac{\partial A(L_a, C_a)}{\partial C_a}} = \frac{\dfrac{\partial B(L_b, C_b)}{\partial L_b}}{\dfrac{\partial B(L_b, C_b)}{\partial C_b}}, \dots\dots\dots\dots\dots\dots\dots\dots\dots\dots\dots\dots (5)$$

where the partial derivatives stand respectively for the marginal productivities of given factors in the production of the indicated commodity.

We are still lacking one condition to make our equilibrium complete. If we add as a known parameter the value of P_a/P_b, that is, the price ratio between the two goods, wheat and watches, all our unknowns will be completely deter-

---

[1] We should like to emphasise that in our argument there is no dependence upon imperfections in the labour market such as form the basis for the Manoilesco type for defense of a tariff. See M. Manoilesco, *The Theory of Protection and International Trade* (1931).

[2] Of course, this holds only if something of both commodities is produced, that is, if trade does not result in complete specialisation. The effect of this qualification is treated below.

mined : the amounts of each factor of production allocated to the various commodities (L_a, L_b, C_a, C_b), the amounts produced of each good (A, B), and most important for the present investigation, the marginal physical productivities of each factor in terms of each good $\left(\dfrac{\partial A}{\partial L_a}, \dfrac{\partial B}{\partial L_b}, \dfrac{\partial A}{\partial C_a}, \dfrac{\partial B}{\partial C_b}\right)$

But what is the meaning in terms of all of the above magnitudes of labour's real wage ? This is not an easy question to answer if, as is usually true, labour consumes something of both commodities. In principle it is of course possible to determine whether a given individual's real income has gone up or down if one has detailed knowledge of his (ordinal) preference field. But we cannot gather such knowledge simply from observation of the price changes which take place. Possibly an index number comparison of the type associated with the names of Pigou, Haberler, Könus, Staehle, Leontief, and others could serve to identify changes in real income. But we shall later show that this is unnecessary. At this point, purely for reasons of exposition, we shall consider the highly restrictive case where labour consumes only one of the commodities, that is, where there is a single wage good. In this case the real wage in terms of that good is an unambiguous indicator of real income[1] because of the proportionality between occupations indicated in condition (5). It is the marginal physical productivity of labour in the production of the wage good.

The effect of international trade upon the real wage (thus defined) could now be determined mathematically by varying P_a/P_b, the price ratio of the two goods, and observing how the marginal physical productivity of labour in the wage good industry is affected. One could perform this purely mathematical computation by differentiating our equilibrium equations with respect to P_a/P_b, treating as variables all the unknowns listed above. The result of this procedure, not shown here because of its purely technical character, would be found to involve a sum of terms of necessarily different sign, and without introducing further economic content into the problem, we would not be able to achieve a definite result, but would be forced, like the older writers, simply to indicate that all things are possible. However, by introducing further economic content of no less generality than theirs, we shall find that definite results can be derived.

THE ELIMINATION OF THE INDEX NUMBER PROBLEM

With the assumptions made so far it is hardly surprising that no more definite results have been reached. For no assumption has as yet been made as to which country is relatively well supplied with capital or with labour. To begin with we make two assumptions. The first is that the country in question is relatively small and has no influence on the terms of trade. Thus, any gain to the country through monopolistic or monopsonistic behaviour is excluded. Secondly, it is assumed that the removal of the duty will not destroy the formerly protected industry, but only force it to contract.

---

[1] It is true that we have been talking about the real wage rate and not about the total amount of real wages, but as we have assumed full employment before and after any change and unvarying total amounts of the factors of production, it follows that the real wage sum will always be proportional to the real wage rate.

Now in equilibrium the value marginal productivity (expressed in terms of any *numéraire*) must be the same in all occupations, and so must be the wage. Therefore, whatever wage labour receives in the wage good industry it must also receive in any other employment. Moreover, any change in the value marginal productivity and, therefore, the wage rate of labour in the wage good industry must mean a corresponding change in the wage rate in all other employments. It follows that we can tell what will happen to real wages (rates as well as sums) of labour as a whole by investigating what will happen to wages in the wage good industry. Since the relevant value marginal productivity, and hence the wage of labour in the wage good industry, is in terms of the wage good, and since labour gets the same wage in all occupations, a decline of the marginal productivity of labour in the wage good industry means a fall in the real wage rate and the real wage sum of labour as a whole.

In other words, whatever will happen to wages in the wage good industry will happen to labour as a whole. And this answer is independent of whether the wage good will be imported or exported, and can be reached without any discussion of what will happen to prices of the commodities as a consequence of international trade.[1]

Assume, for example, (a) that the country in question is relatively well supplied with capital, and (b) that the proportion of labour to capital is lower in the production of wheat than in the production of watches. There is nothing restrictive about these assumptions because in terms of our previous assumptions one of the countries must be relatively well supplied with a given factor, and through our postponement of the constant cost case for later discussion the importance of labour must be greater in the production of one of the commodities. And since the names " wheat " and " watches " are arbitrary, by re-naming the variables all possible cases could be expressed in the formulation given above.

Two alternative cases must now be considered. (1) The good in whose production capital is relatively important (wheat) is also the wage good. (2) The good in whose production labour is relatively important (watches) is the wage good. Each of these possibilities must be considered in turn.

(1) The introduction of trade will shift production in the direction of the good with " comparative advantage." According to the Ohlin analysis—even though he would not employ the previous term—this will be wheat which uses much of the abundant factor. Its production will expand, and part of it will be exported, while watch production will contract, and part of the watch consumption will be satisfied by imports. This shift in production will be accompanied by a transfer of *both* labour and capital from the watch industry to the wheat industry. But by a reduction in the production of watches more labour will be set free than can be re-employed at the same rates in the production of wheat. This is because the amount of capital released, while sufficient to employ a worker in watch production, is insufficient to employ him in wheat growing at the old wage rate. Hence wage rates have to go down in wheat growing, and

---

[1] In connection with a slightly different problem the same point is made by F. Benham, " Taxation and the Relative Prices of Factors of Production," *Economica*, N. S. Vol. 2, 1935, pp. 198–203.

it follows from the changed factor proportions that the real wage must also decline. It would be clearly incorrect to argue—as one familiar with the orthodox theory of international trade would be tempted to do—that in addition to this decline in productivity due solely to changed factor proportions, there must be added a further loss to the worker *qua* consumer resulting from the inevitable price rise of the exported wage good.

(2) We turn now to the case where watches are the wage good. On the face of it this case would seem to admit only of an ambiguous answer, since any definite conclusion in the productivity sphere would have to confront a necessary fall in the (relative) price of the wage good. Fortunately, that is not so. This case admits of no less definite an answer than the previous one.

The introduction of trade will increase the production of wheat and decrease that of watches. As shown in the previous case, this will entail a movement of both labour and capital. But just as labour has less capital to work with in wheat production than formerly, so does labour have less capital to work with in the production of watches. This is brought about by the change in relative remunerations of the factors necessary to result in the reabsorption of the otherwise redundant labour supply. Therefore, regardless of the behaviour of consumer's good prices, the lowering of the proportion of capital to labour in the production of watches must adversely affect the marginal physical productivity of labour there, and hence, along now familiar lines, the real wage.

We see, therefore, that the seemingly opposite cases lead to exactly the same result. *International trade necessarily lowers the real wage of the scarce factor expressed in terms of any good.* It follows that we are now in a position to drop the assumption of a single wage good. For if the real wage declines in terms of every good, real income must suffer regardless of the tastes and expenditure patterns of the labourers as consumers. Not only can we avoid making index number comparisons, but it is also unnecessary to make the assumption of uniform tastes of all workers which such comparisons implicitly presuppose.

DIAGRAMMATICAL TREATMENT

It may be useful to illustrate the above arguments graphically. In Fig. 1 we plot the familiar substitution curve (production indifference or transformation curve) between the two commodities in the given country. Before trade, equilibrium will have taken place at M with a price ratio corresponding to the slope of the tangent there. International trade will change the price ratio of the two goods, and a new equilibrium point may be taken as N with more wheat production, less watch production, and a higher price ratio between wheat and watches. This diagram represents the result of a fairly complicated economic process by which the given fixed amounts of productive factors are optimally allocated between the two commodities in accordance with marginal productivity conditions which guarantee a maximum amount of one commodity for preassigned given amounts of the other. For many international trade problems this " short-circuiting " is an advantage ; but it omits the essential features of the present problem, and so we must go back of the substitution curve to the underlying production relations.

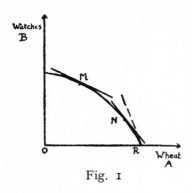

Fig. 1

This is done in Fig. 2 which consists of a modified box diagram long utilised by Edgeworth and Bowley in the study of consumers' behaviour. This rather remarkable diagram enables us to represent the relations between six variables on a two dimensional figure. On the lower horizontal axis is indicated the amount of capital used in the production of wheat. On the left-hand vertical axis is indicated the amount of labour used in the production of wheat. Because the amount of each factor which is not used in the production of wheat must be employed in the production of watches, the upper horizontal axis gives us, reading from right to left, the amount of capital used in the production of watches. Similarly, the right-hand vertical axis, reading downwards, gives us the amount of labour used in the production of watches. The dimensions of the box are, of course, simply those of the unchanging given total amounts of the two productive factors. Any point in the box represents four and capital used to things : measuring from the lower left-hand corner the amounts of labour produce wheat, and measuring from the upper right-hand corner the amounts of labour and capital used in the production of watches.

Disregarding for the moment the other commodity, watches, it is clear that every point in the box corresponds to a given production of wheat, and

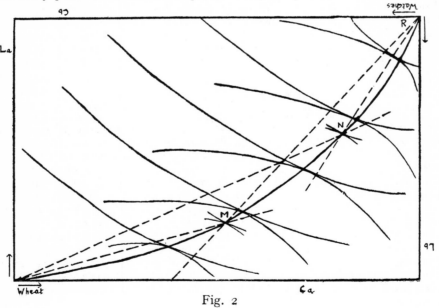

Fig. 2

hence lies on a uniquely determinable isoquant or contour line of the production surface. There is a one-parameter family of such curves with the shape as indicated by the light lines, convex to the lower left-hand corner. Turning now to the production of watches, there also exists a one-parameter family of isoquants convex to the upper right-hand corner, and indicated in the diagram by a second family of curves.

We are now in a position to derive the substitution curve. Any point in the box taken at random corresponds to given amounts of watch and wheat production, but not necessarily to a point on the substitution curve. Only those points which reflect an optimal allocation of resources according to the marginal productivity relations stated earlier correspond to points on the substitution or opportunity cost curve. The locus of points representing optimal positions is clearly given by joining all the points of tangency of the two sets of contour lines. It corresponds geometrically to Edgeworth's *contract curve*, and although the present study does not deal with bargains between contracting parties, we shall retain this descriptive title. If we hold the production of one good constant and thus move along a given isoquant, we will only stop when there is the maximum possible amount of the other good, or when we have reached the highest possible isoquant of the other family. This will be so only at a position of tangency where the ratios of the marginal productivities of the two factors are the same in each line of production.

Under the assumption of homogeneous production functions in two inputs, the contract curve must have the shape indicated in our figure. On the contract curve we have indicated points M and N corresponding to the situation before and after trade. It can now be shown graphically how the following somewhat paradoxical statement can be true: even though the proportion of total capital to total labour remains the same in both lines together, nevertheless the introduction of trade lowers the proportion of capital to labour in each line, and the prohibition of trade, as by a tariff, necessarily raises the proportion of capital to labour in each industry. Although it seems intuitively anomalous, it is graphically clear from the diagram that a movement from N to M raises the proportion of capital to labour in watches, the total proportions remaining unchanged as indicated by the box. The proportion of labour to capital in the production of wheat with trade is indicated by the slope of the angle of the dotted line going between N and the wheat origin. A similar dotted line between the same origin and M shows the proportion of labour to capital in the production of wheat after trade. Its being less steep than the other makes it clear that the ratio of capital to labour has increased. Utilising similar dotted lines between the watch origin and the points M and N, it is likewise seen that the abolition of trade increases the proportion of capital to labour in the production of watches.

How can we reconcile the graphical result with our numerical intuition which tells us that when each of two quantities goes up, an average of them cannot remain constant? An examination of the exact relationship between the proportions of capital to labour in each line and the proportions in both at once dispels the paradox. The proportion in both is found to be not a simple average but a weighted arithmetic mean of the proportions in each as indicated by the following identity :

$$\frac{L_a}{L} \frac{C_a}{L_a} + \frac{L_b}{L} \frac{C_b}{L_b} = \frac{C}{L} \dots\dots\dots\dots\dots\dots\dots\dots\dots\dots\dots\dots (6)$$

The weights are simply the proportions of the total labour supply used in the respective industries. The abolition of trade raises the proportion of capital to labour in each line, but at the same time through the reverse operation of the principle of comparative advantage automatically gives more weight to the industry which uses the lesser amount of capital to labour.

Thus, we have shown conclusively that a restriction of trade will increase the proportion of capital to labour in both lines. It follows necessarily that the real wage in terms of each commodity must increase regardless of any movements of prices of the consumer's goods. For within each industry increasing the capital which co-operates with labour raises the marginal productivity of labour expressed in physical units of that good. Not only are the labourers of that industry better off with respect to that good, but by the equivalence of real wages everywhere (expressed in terms of any good) labour in general is better off in terms of that good. If the real wage in terms of every good increases, we can definitely state that real income has increased. This is one of the few cases in economic analysis where a given change moves all relevant magnitudes in the same direction and obviates the necessity of a difficult, and often indefinite, index number comparison.

Under the assumed conditions—(a) two commodities, (b) produced by two factors of production, and (c) where trade leaves something of both commodities produced but at a new margin—it has been unequivocally demonstrated that the scarce factor must be harmed absolutely. This is in contrast to the accepted doctrine which may be fairly represented as saying that trade *might* conceivably affect adversely the relative share of a factor, but cannot be expected to harm absolutely an important factor of production. Not only is the latter possible, but under the posited conditions it follows necessarily.

THREE OR MORE COMMODITIES

If the above conclusion held only for two commodities, its interest even for theory would be limited. It is of interest to show, therefore, that the introduction of any number of commodities in no way detracts from the validity of our conclusions. Of course, no simple graphical device can be used to portray this because of the increased number of variables.

One method of approaching the problem might be to arrange the commodities in a sequence according to the relative importance of labour in each. This is not unlike the ordering of commodities long used by Mangoldt,[1] Edgeworth, and others to explain which commodities will be imported and which exported when more than two commodities are introduced into the classical theory of comparative advantage. In our case, however, costs are not constant and are not expressible in a single homogeneous unit of a factor or in a given composite factor.

For the present purpose one need not rely upon such a construction, but need only realise that the introduction of trade will increase the production of those commodities which use relatively much of the abundant factor, and will lower the production of the commodities using relatively little of the abundant factor. Accompanying this, there will be the familiar Heckscher–Ohlin tendency towards partial equalisation of factor prices in the two countries, the price of the scarce factor falling in relationship to the price of the abundant factor. By itself this tells us nothing concerning the absolute burden or benefit from trade, but deals only with the effect upon relative shares. We cannot simply infer from this anything concerning the behaviour of absolute shares. For it is not as if international trade leaves the total amount of real national income unchanged so that the more one factor receives, the less there will be left for the other. On the contrary, it has been shown elsewhere that trade must increase the national income under the conditions here postulated.

It is nevertheless true that the introduction of trade will harm absolutely the scarce factor of production. To demonstrate this we must recall the fact that at the new higher relative price of capital to labour there will inevitably be a *relative* substitution of labour for capital *in each line* of production. In exactly the same way a restriction upon trade will raise the price of the scarce factor, labour, relative to the abundant factor, capital. There is nothing paradoxical in the fact that the ratio of capital to labour can increase in every line, while the ratio of total capital to total labour remains constant. The explanation given in the two commodity case whereby the weights in the arithmetic mean change in an appropriate fashion holds without modification when there are any number of commodities.

It is now a simple matter to show that the physical marginal productivity of labour in each line must increase, and because of the equalisation of wages in all lines, expressed in terms of any commodity, it immediately follows that restriction of trade increases the real wage of workers expressed in terms of each and every commodity. This obviates the necessity for any index number comparison or for any consideration of the worsening of the terms of trade.

THE CASE OF COMPLETE SPECIALISATION

The reader of the above argument will have realised that its remarkable simplicity springs from the fact that we may infer the real wage of workers in terms of a given good from the real marginal physical productivity of those workers who produce that good. This requires that before and after trade some finite amount, however small, be produced of every good. In a world where technological conditions are conducive towards the maintenance of the state of pure competition implicit in all our previous argument, this is perhaps not too unrealistic an assumption. However, it is still desirable to see what remains of the argument when this assumption is dropped. This is even more so because in the course of the argument it will be shown that the classical theory was not so much incorrect as limited in scope.

Provided that costs are not constant, and that something of both goods was previously consumed, at first price changes brought about by international trade will shift the margin of production, but will still leave some production of

---

[1] J. Viner, op. cit., p. 458 ; G. Haberler, op. cit., pp. 136–140.

both commodities. At one crucial price ratio corresponding to the slope of the tangent at R in Fig. 1 the production of one of the commodities will cease completely, and further changes will not alter the specialisation. Up until the critical price ratio is reached, the introduction of trade worsens the position of labour according to the previous arguments. But what happens after this critical price ratio ?

There is no essential loss of generality in considering the two commodity case. For the commodity which is still produced the real wage is determined as before by the physical productivity of the workers in that line. Up until the critical price ratio at which complete specialisation takes place, the scarce labour factors have been shown to lose. Beyond this critical price ratio their physical productivities remain unchanged. It is clear, therefore, that the real wage in terms of the good using little labour is necessarily harmed by the introduction of trade.

With respect to the other commodity the matter is more complicated, and the final result is indeterminate. Up to the critical price ratio we know that the real wage in terms of this commodity must fall. But after specialisation, the level of real wages cannot be determined by the productivity of workers in this line since there are no such workers. One cannot avoid bringing into the analysis the price ratio between the two consumers' goods, that is, the terms of trade. Given this price ratio, it is possible to convert real wages in terms of one commodity into real wages in terms of the other. It becomes apparent that beyond the critical point the real wage in terms of the non-produced, imported good must begin to increase. This is to be balanced against the loss of real wages in terms of this good which took place before the critical point was reached. Whether the result will be on balance favourable or unfavourable cannot possibly be determined on *a priori* grounds, but rests upon the technological and economic features of the countries in question. Even if in a limited number of cases we could determine that the real wage in terms of the imported good would increase, there would still be involved a problem of weighing against this the demonstrated loss in real wages expressed in terms of the good in which the country has a comparative advantage. Here again the final result would be indeterminate, although in favourable cases an index number comparison might be decisive.

Applying this same line of reasoning to the constant cost case of the classical theory of international trade, it is seen that theirs is one of the special unambiguous cases. Either a single factor of production or a never varying composite dose of factors is assumed. Because of constant costs the slightest change in the price ratio of the goods will lead instantaneously to complete specialisation. There results no shifting of the proportions of the factors, and hence no deterioration of wages in terms of either good. On the contrary, in terms of the imported good there must be an improvement in real wages with a consequent increase in real income. This is made intuitively obvious from the consideration that trade necessarily increases the real income of a country, and in the classical case the proportion of income going to the respective factors cannot be changed by trade. It is the latter feature of the classical theory which constitutes one of its important short-comings.

MORE THAN TWO FACTORS

One by one we have been able to drop our various restrictive assumptions with only slight modifications of results. Still there remains the problem of introducing into the analysis more than two productive factors. Unfortunately, this entails more serious consequences.

In the first place, the definiteness of the Heckscher–Ohlin theorem begins to fade. With three or more factors of production it is certainly not necessary that the result of trade is to make the ratios of factor prices in the respective countries more closely approach unity. Some may do so, but others may diverge depending upon complicated patterns of complementarity and competitiveness.[1] Whether on balance the movement towards equalisation exceeds the tendency towards diversification is not a meaningful question until a non-arbitrary method of weighting these changes is specified. Furthermore, even the concepts of scarce and abundant factors lose their sharpness of definition.

The fact that the Heckscher–Ohlin theorem breaks down when many factors of production are involved affords an explanation of its failure to account for the facts *if the production functions in the two countries differ, or if the factors of production of different countries are not identical.* By appropriate terminological conventions it is always possible to attribute differences in the production functions to differences in amounts of some factors of production (knowledge, available free factors, etc.). Similarly, if the factors of production of different countries are regarded as non-comparable and incommensurable,[2] this can be classified as an extreme case of factor disproportionality, but there must be more than two factors. We conclude, therefore, that the Heckscher–Ohlin theorem does not necessarily hold in the case of constant costs or multiple factors of production.

It does not follow that our results stand and fall with the Heckscher–Ohlin theorem. Our analysis neglected the other country completely. If factors of production are not comparable between countries, or if production functions differ, nevertheless, so long as the country has only two factors, international trade would necessarily affect the real wage of a factor in the same direction as its relative remuneration.[3] The only loss to our analysis would be the possibility of labelling the factor which is harmed as the " scarce " (relative to the other country) one.

However, we must admit that three or more factors of production within a single country do seriously modify the inevitability of our conclusions. It is not only that the relatively scarce factor can be defined only circularly as the one whose price falls most after trade, but even if we do know the behaviour

---

[1] See Ohlin, op. cit., pp. 96–105 and parsim.

[2] If the extreme classical assumption of immobility of labour between countries were valid, then over time the working populations of the various countries would become differentiated culturally, genetically, and in the limit cease to be of the same species. But those in the narrower classical tradition are least in a position to bring this up as an argument against the Heckscher–Ohlin theory, for in expositing the comparative cost doctrine they repeatedly (and sometimes unnecessarily) compare labour (costs, productivities, hierarchies, etc.) in various countries.

[3] This is in contrast to the problem of the effect of a technological innovation to which Professor Haberler (op. cit., p. 195) has compared the effects of trade. Technological change shifts the production function, and no inferences concerning the new marginal productivity relationships are possible. As we have shown, trade leads to definite effects.

of relative factor prices, i.e. relative shares in the national income, it seems that we cannot infer unambiguously that the physical marginal productivities move in the same direction. Even though these continue to depend only upon the proportions of the factors in the respective industry, diverse patterns of complementarity and competitiveness emerge as possibilities. It is outside the scope of the present paper to attempt a catalogue of the various conceivable permutations and combinations.

This lack of definiteness in the more complex case is typical of attempts to go beyond the level of abstraction current in economic theory. We have resisted the temptation to lump together diverse factors into two composite factors and thereby achieve the appearance of versimilitude, although others may care to do so for some purpose.

CONCLUSION

We have shown that there is a grain of truth in the pauper labour type of argument for protection. Thus, in Australia, where land may perhaps be said to be abundant relative to labour, protection might possibly raise the real income of labour.[1] The same may have been true in colonial America. It does not follow that the American working man to-day would be better off if trade with, say, the tropics were cut off, because land suitable for growing coffee, rubber, and bananas is ever scarcer in America than is labour. The bearing of the many factor case will be obvious.

We are anxious to point out that even in the two factor case our argument provides no political ammunition for the protectionist. For if effects on the terms of trade can be disregarded, it has been shown that the harm which free trade inflicts upon one factor of production is necessarily less than the gain to the other. Hence, it is always possible to bribe the suffering factor by subsidy or other redistributive devices so as to leave all factors better off as a result of trade.[2]

WOLFGANG F. STOLPER.
PAUL A. SAMUELSON.

Swarthmore, Penna.
Cambridge, Mass.

---

[1] See D. B. Copland, "A Neglected Phase of Tariff Controversy," *Quarterly Journal of Economics*, 1931, pp. 289–308 ; K. L. Anderson, "Protection and the Historical Situation : Australia," *Quarterly Journal of Economics*, November, 1938, pp. 86–104 ; M. C. Samuelson, op. cit., pp. 143–149.

[2] Viner, op. cit., p. 534 ; P. A. Samuelson, op. cit., p. 204.

67

INTERNATIONAL TRADE AND THE EQUALISATION OF FACTOR PRICES

I. INTRODUCTION

CLASSICAL trade theory always took it for granted that free mobility of factors of production between different regions would tend to equalise the relative and absolute prices of productive services in the different regions. Thus, migration of labor from crowded Europe to less crowded America would result, through the law of diminishing returns, in a drop in America's wage rates relative to America's land rents and relative to commodities; at the same time, European land rents would fall and European real wages would rise. Migration of labor would cease only when absolute and relative factor prices had been finally equalised.

An important addition to this classical doctrine of factor-price equalisation has been supplied by Professor Bertil Ohlin. In his weighty *Interregional and International Trade* (1933), Ohlin has developed the highly interesting result that (1) *free mobility of commodities in international trade can serve as a partial substitute for factor mobility* and (2) *will lead to a partial equalisation of relative (and absolute) factor prices*. This important result, which we may call the Ohlin–Heckscher theorem, since Ohlin attributes it to a 1919 Swedish article by Professor E. F. Heckscher, has some foreshadowings in the literature of the last century [1]; but not until the highly original work of Ohlin was it made a central part of the theory of international trade.

II. FULL OR PARTIAL FACTOR PRICE EQUALISATION?

The present paper is concerned primarily with one aspect of this theorem—namely, the assertion that, while free factor movements *fully* equalise factor prices, nevertheless free commodity movements equalise them only *partially*. Factor prices

[1] See Ohlin's references to Longfield and Sismondi in *Interregional and International Trade* (Cambridge : Harvard University Press, 1933), pp. 31–32. All references to Ohlin hereafter will be page references to this book. See also J. Viner, *Studies in the Theory of International Trade* (New York : Harper and Brothers, 1937), pp. 500–507, for further references.

are moved in the direction of equality, but the process is believed to be necessarily an incomplete one.

Like, no doubt, many others, I have been teaching this theorem to classes in international trade for a number of years. When recently a student [1] challenged this result, I availed myself of the usual teacher's prerogative of referring him to the text-book, in this case Professor P. T. Ellsworth's excellent work, *International Economics*. But doubt once provoked is not so easily lulled; neither the class nor its instructor found the relevant passages quite satisfactory, which is not to be wondered at since an intermediate text is not the place to dwell on minute fine points of theory.

What is more surprising, careful perusal of Ohlin's treatise nowhere reveals an adequate proof of the partial equalisation theorem. Not only is the logic incomplete, but at places it seems actually to go off the track. At the least, therefore, it would seem desirable to plug a gap in the theoretical literature, to provide a rigorous proof of the theorem if it is true, or to disprove it if it is false.

III. THE OHLIN ANALYSIS

The present note attempts to throw light on the matter under the simplifying assumptions most suited to the Ohlin analysis : two regions, say Europe and Amèrica, each endowed with different proportions of two perfectly immobile factors of production, say land and labor. For convenience, we may assume but two commodities, say food and clothing, each commodity obeying common technological production functions in the two regions. We may suppose that each production function shows constant return to scale as a result of proportional increases in both land and labor; diminishing returns is involved only in the sense that as we change the proportions of one input relative to another, then the marginal productivity of factors will be affected.

So long as we stick to Ricardian or Taussigian simple-arithmetic comparative-cost examples involving only one labor factor of production, we must assume as axiomatic, and unexplained, differences in labor effectiveness in different regions. Ohlin's proportions-of-the-factors analysis, on the other hand, explains why differences in comparative advantage will exist and deduces the resulting pattern of productivities and specialisation. Thus instead of relying upon such crypto-explanations as

[1] Mr. Nathaniel Davis, formerly of the Fletcher School of Law and Diplomacy, and now of the United States Foreign Service.

" Yankee ingenuity " to explain patterns of comparative advantage, Ohlin would attribute America's comparative advantage in food production—a land-intensive industry—to the fact that each unit of American labor has relatively much land to work with. Similarly, the relative abundance of labor in Europe relative to land would result in a pattern of low wages relative to land rents and would encourage the production of clothing, which requires a greater proportion of labor to land than does food.[1]

In short, each country will tend to specialise (either partially or wholly) in the production of the commodity using much of its most abundant factor. But producing more food in America will increase the demand for land and tend to reduce its cheapness there; and producing more clothing in Europe will alleviate the demand there for land and increase the demand for labor so as to raise European wages. The pre-trade differences in the factor prices between the two countries will be partially reduced as a result of specialisation and trade according to comparative advantage. In Ohlin's words : " *Thus, the mobility of goods to some extent compensates the lack of interregional mobility of the factors* " (p. 42) . . . " [The] tendency towards equalisation also of the prices of the factors of production . . . means a better use of them and thus a reduction of the disadvantages arising from the unsuitable geographical distribution of the productive factors " (p. 49).

IV. THE ELLSWORTH PROOF

So far, so good. Something important has been added to the usual classical exposition. But why should there be only a *tendency* towards factor price equalisation? Why should the equalisation be only *partial* and *incomplete*? Why should free commodity movements be only a *partial* substitute for free factor movements? This is the crucial question now at issue.

Professor Ellsworth has more clearly addressed himself to this issue than Ohlin, and his discussion is worth reproducing at some length :

One might conclude that complete equalisation of the prices of the various productive factors would result [from

[1] When land and labor are substitutable in the production of both goods, it is a little ambiguous to say that food requires relatively more land to labor than does clothing, since there are varying possible proportions of the factors. What must be meant is that at the same ratio of wages to rent, it will be optimal to hire a greater ratio of land to labor in food production than in clothing production.

free commodity trade]. This, however, is highly improbable if not impossible. It could only occur if the demand for the various kinds of labor could be concentrated largely on those areas where each kind was most abundant, thereby raising wages there to a parity with wages in scarce-labor areas. Likewise, the demand for land would have to be concentrated on abundant, land areas, and the demand for capital on districts well supplied with capital. Such a wholesale localisation of demand is, however, quite impossible, owing to the technical requirements of production, which in the case of practically all commodities calls, not for labor, land, or capital alone, but for combinations of all three of these major groups of factors. Complete equalisation of factor prices would require an unattainably perfect adaptation of demand to the highly varying local supplies of the different agents. *Moreover, did any such price equalisation occur, it would contain the seeds of its own destruction. For when all factor prices were everywhere the same, there would no longer be any reason for trade, and with the cessation of trade, and therewith the extinction of the demands which brought about the price equalisation, the original disparities in factor equipment would immediately reassert themselves.*[1] (Italics mine.)

Until his last two sentences, the argument is a little vague and the author seems to oscillate between a belief that factor-price equalisation is (*a*) impossible, and (*b*) possible, but highly improbable under realistic technological conditions. However, we do not have to worry about which of these views he holds, because in the last two lines, which I have italicised, it is clear that Ellsworth does believe after all that factor-price equalisation involves a logical contradiction and is therefore impossible.

However, upon careful examination, I do not believe we can accept the Ellsworth proof by contradiction. Indeed, if it were logically valid, we could at each stage substitute commodity prices for factor prices, and by exactly comparable reasoning prove the absurdity of commodity-price equalisation as a result of perfectly free trade—a proposition which no one is likely to question.[2]

---

[1] P. T. Ellsworth, *International Economics* (New York : The Macmillan Company, 1938), pp. 119–20.

[2] This type of *reductio ad absurdum* indirect reasoning has been used widely by many writers other than Ellsworth. Note, for example, the following quotation from Viner dealing with a quite different topic : " When a central bank . . . raises its discount rate or engages in [open market] selling operations, the resultant rise in the market rate of interest tends to attract foreign funds. It has become the custom to say that [such] an inflow of short-term funds may offset the efforts of the central bank to bring about [monetary] contraction, but this overlooks the fact that the foreign funds will flow in only as the market rate

The flaw in the argument is not hard to find. Equalisation of factor prices would imply that *no further* profitable trade could take place. At the margin, trade would be indifferent—that being the reason why the margin is the margin ! On the intra-marginal units, trade could continue to take place indefinitely.

V. PROOFS IN OHLIN

When we turn to Ohlin's book, matters are even less satisfactory. Ellsworth at least meets the question head-on, while Ohlin—like a murderer who returns again and again to the scene of his crime—repeatedly comes back to the point only to leave it elusively hanging in air. There is almost something Freudian in the vehemence with which he asserts the proposition to be true and with which he employs the phrases " clearly," " of course," " obviously," " as a matter of fact," and similar phrases —as if subconsciously he is really a little uneasy about the proposition's validity.

At one point he even goes so far as to say, " It is not worth-while to analyse in detail why full equalisation does not occur; for, when the costs of transport and other impediments to trade have been introduced into the reasoning, such an equalisation is in any case obviously impossible " (pp. 38–39).

This is hardly cricket. The question is not whether imperfect mobility of goods leads to perfect factor-price equalisation, but whether perfect goods mobility does so.

Actually, in more than half a dozen places, primarily in Chapter II, Ohlin definitely asserts the impossibility or improbability of complete factor-price equalisation, usually as if the proposition were so obvious as to require little explanation. Only one example need be cited :

> A complete local adaptation of production through inter-regional factor movements and the resulting complete price equalisation would make prices just the same as if there were only one region and no geographical distribution of the industrial agents. These would be used and combined just as it is explained in the one-market theory. Space would be of no consequence. In such a state prices would be different from what they are, when we have a number of isolated regions. Clearly, the state of prices caused by interregional trade, under the assumptions in Part I, lies somewhere between these two extremes. The tendency is

---

becomes higher than it was previously . . . the market rate must rise *somewhat* . . ." Viner, *op. cit.*, p. 406. I do not mean to imply that such arguments are never valid, but they must be used with delicacy.

to push prices from the complete independence state to the complete equalisation state, but it is not carried through. The price differences as regards the productive factors are reduced, but they do not disappear (pp. 39–40).

Why " clearly " ?   At least to me, this argument appears as a complete *non sequitur*.   If we were to insert before Ohlin's word " clearly," the clause " which is absurd," the argument would seem to be almost identical with the already discredited Ellsworth *reductio ad absurdum*.

But even this interpreta on will not do, since on the previous page Ohlin explicitly rejects such an argument [1] in the following sentence that I have italicised.

> We have seen that trade tends to counteract the original price inequality and bring about a more uniform price formation.   One might ask if trade cannot in this way make prices in the various regions coincide exactly.   *In that situation trade would not disappear, as one might be inclined to think at first sight, for then the old price inequalities would immediately reappear.*   On the contrary, the price equality assumes a certain ad ptation of demand to the supply of factors, *i.e.*, the maintenance of a certain interregional division of labour and trade (p. 38).

Since we are thus barred from attributing to Ohlin the Ellsworth-type argument, what are we finally left with ?   As far as I can tell, only with the following line of demonstration, which Ohlin appends after the above quotation :

> Such a result is, however, almost unthinkable and certainly highly improbable.   The localisation of industry and thereby the demand for production factors cannot completely adapt themselves to the equipment with them in each region, *chiefly because the industrial demand is always the " joint demand " for several factors.*   Their combination cannot be varied at will;   on the contrary, the most economical combination is determined by the prices of the factors and the physical conditions.   Consequently, the best adaptations of production to the geographical distribution of industrial agents, which would be the result of trade under the simple assumption of these first three chapters, cannot lead to a complete interregional price equalisation; some factors will still command higher prices in one region and lower in the others, and vice versa (p. 38).

---

[1] On pp. 560–1 of the mathematical appendix, Ohlin almost seems to be endorsing the proposition that completely equal factor prices are incompatible with any trade.   But we can interpret him to mean " equal factor prices *in the pre-trade situation* is incompatible with any trade's subsequently taking place," and avoid falling into this difficulty.

The new element here is the emphasis on "jointness," in the lines that I have italicised. Unfortunately, this residual explanation upon which we are finally thrown back does not—to me at least—make sense as a proof or suggestion of a proof of the issue in question.

VI. THE TRUE THEOREM CONCERNING EQUALISATION

It would not be fruitful to stretch out further this already tedious critical exegesis. It is sufficient to note that there does not appear to be in the literature a satisfactory demonstration of the necessarily partial and incomplete character of factor-price equalisation. Having arrived at this conclusion, the present writer—still not doubting the essential truth of the proposition in question—hoped to outline a satisfactory proof. Intuitively, I suspected that the nub of the matter lay in a careful development of a line of reasoning frequently met in economic theory, according to which "secondary reactions to initial changes offset but do not wipe out those initial changes." In particular, I had in mind reasoning of the type quoted earlier from Viner, and also of the type involved in H. D. Henderson's classical exposition of the elementary beginner's error whereby a tax on a commodity appears not to lead to a rise in price.[1]

But in attempting to devise a rigorous proof of the partial character of factor-price equalisation, I made a surprising discovery : the proposition is false. It is not true that factor-price equalisation is impossible. It is not true that factor-price equalisation is highly improbable.

On the contrary, not only is factor-price equalisation possible and probable, but in a wide variety of circumstances it is inevitable. Specifically :

(1) *So long as there is partial specialisation, with each country producing something of both goods, factor prices will be equalised, absolutely and relatively, by free international trade.*

(2) *Unless initial factor endowments are too unequal, commodity mobility will always be a perfect substitute for factor mobility.*

(3) *Regardless of initial factor endowment even if factors were*

---

[1] H. D. Henderson, *Supply and Demand* (London and Cambridge : Nisbet and Cambridge University Press, 1922), p. 27. Incidentally, without detracting from the significance of Henderson's argument, we should note that in the limiting case of inelastic supply, it is not literally true that a tax will raise market prices. But to invoke such a limiting case against Henderson (or Viner) would be a mere quibble; the present criticism of the Ohlin proposition is based on something more fundamental.

mobile they would, at worst, have to migrate only up to a certain degree, after which commodity mobility would be sufficient for full price equalisation.[1]

(4) *To the extent that commodity movements are effective substitutes for factor movements, world productivity is, in a certain sense, optimal ; but at the same time, the imputed real returns of labor in one country and of land in the other will necessarily be lower, not only relatively but also absolutely, than under autarky.*[2]

Propositions (3) and (4) follow in a fairly straightforward fashion from (1) and (2). All of the propositions are essentially valid whatever the number of commodities, regions, and factors of production, but the empirical probability or improbability of price equalisation would be altered in a complex manner by such complications. I shall confine the proof of (1) and (2) to the two-region, two-commodity, two-factor case previously described.

VII. The Neo-Classical Presentation of Comparative Advantage

Figure 1a shows the now familiar production-possibility (or transformation) curve for America : *i.e.*, the maximum amounts of clothing that can be attained when land and labor resources are shifted in an optimal fashion away from food production. Knowing the production functions of the two goods and knowing the original proportions of labor and land in America, we can move out to this optimal locus only by making sure that the ratios of the marginal physical productivities of land and labor are the same in both food and clothing production, in each case being equal to the ratio of market wages to rents.[3]

[1] In his *The Economics of Control* (New York : The Macmillan Company, 1946), p. 349, Professor A. P. Lerner says, " If some of the factors cannot move, this is of no consequence provided the co-operating factors can be moved to these factors. Similarly if either the consumer goods or the consumer can move all is well. It does not matter that the mountain will not go to Mahomet as long as Mahomet is able to go to the mountain." In some cases it is more nearly right to say : it is necessary for the mountain to come some of the distance to Mahomet, after which Mahomet can go to the mountain.

[2] The real-income deterioration of these groups could theoretically be compensated out of the real-income improvements of the other groups. This is not the place to go into the intricacies of the so-called " new welfare economics." See P. A. Samuelson, *Foundations of Economic Analysis* (Cambridge : Harvard University Press, 1947), Ch. 8, for a discussion of this problem and for references to the important contribution of Professor T. Scitovsky.

[3] Geometrically, an Edgeworth box-type diagram, the respective sides of which are equal in length to the total American labor and land, can best be used to indicate the exact derivation of the optimal production-possibility curve. Any point inside the box represents, when its co-ordinates are measured from the lower

Figure 1*b* shows the corresponding production-possibility curve of Europe. Because labor—the factor used most intensively in clothing production—is plentiful in Europe, we naturally expect a relative abundance there of clothing production. This is confirmed by the relatively steep slopes of the European curve.

Where each country will end up in the absence of trade depends, of course, upon the interplay of tastes and effective

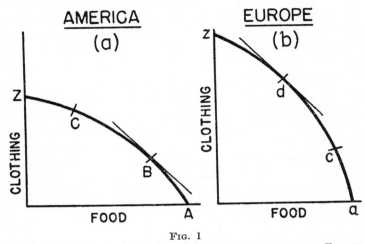

Fig. 1

DOMESTIC PRODUCTION-POSSIBILITY CURVES OF AMERICA AND EUROPE :
Without trade America is at *C* and Europe at *c*. With free trade they end up at
the points of common slope, *B*, and *d*.

demand. Unless Americans in general, or rich landlords in particular, happen to have a special liking for food rather than clothing, we should expect that the pre-trade price ratio of food to clothing would be higher in Europe and lower in America. This is shown by the pre-trade points *C* and *c* in the diagram, the respective slopes of which differ in the indicated way.[1]

___

left-hand corner, the amounts of labor and land used in food production. Similarly, from the upper right-hand corner, we measure off the factors used for clothing. For fixed food, we are forced to move along an equal food-product curve until we are tangent to the highest equal clothing-production curve. The locus of these points of equal-product tangencies is a kind of an Edgeworth " production contract curve," and along it we can read off the optimum clothing for each food, and vice versa. Any other point in the box, gives food and clothing *inside* the production-possibility curve. See W. F. Stolper and P. A. Samuelson, " Protection and Real Wages," *Review of Economic Studies*, Vol. IX, No. 1, November 1941, pp. 58–74.

[1] It is quite possible to imagine a case where the difference in tastes would more than offset the difference in factor endowments, thereby reversing our normal price expectations.

Now suppose we strip away all barriers to commodity trade, to the barter of food and clothing. There can no longer be two different food–clothing price ratios; and at any price ratio different from that under autarky, each country will no longer wish to be self-sufficient. It follows that the new world price ratio must be somewhere in between the limiting price ratios prevailing in each country under autarky. The relative price of food falls in Europe and rises in America. This causes America to move in the direction of increased food production and decreased clothing production (from C to B), and to barter food exports for clothing imports. In Europe, the opposite shift from c to d takes place. The final equilibrium price ratio settles down between the initial limits at just that level where there is a perfect quantitative meshing of international reciprocal demands. Note the equality of slopes at B and d.

So far this differs in only one important respect from John Stuart Mill's completion of the Ricardian comparative cost theory. We have dropped the assumption of *constant returns* (or of a single labor theory of value). At the new equilibrium price ratio, both countries are shown producing something of both goods. Differences of comparative advantage on the intra-marginal units have given rise to trade; when relative marginal costs in each country have become adjusted to the prevailing market price, trade has reached its equilibrium rate and further specialisation ceases.[1]

VIII. Proof of Factor-Price Equalisation

We are now face to face with the important question : Can we go behind the two production-possibility curves to show that wherever their slopes (or marginal-cost ratios) are equal then the ratio of internal factor prices must also be equal ? The answer is yes.

We might try going behind the scenes of the production-possibility curves by means of the Edgeworth box diagram discussed in footnote 3 on page 170. A better way for our purpose is to utilise Figure 2. This diagram is independent of the scale of production and can be utilised for both countries.

On the horizontal axis is measured off the ratio of labor to

---

[1] Haberler, Lerner, Leontief and Viner have elaborated upon these matters. For references, see Viner, *op. cit.*, p. 520. These results are quite consistent with Ohlin's formulations.

land.   On the vertical axis is measured off the ratio of (real) wages to (real) rents, or what is the same thing, the ratio of the marginal physical productivity of labor to the marginal physical productivity of land.   There will be a different technological dependence of this wage–rent ratio or marginal rate of substitution for each commodity, and hence we have two curves : *FF* for food, and *CC* for clothing.   In either case the physical substitution ratio depends only upon the proportions of the factors employed in each use ; this is because of our assumption of constant returns *to scale*, the only assumption possible if we are not to have to

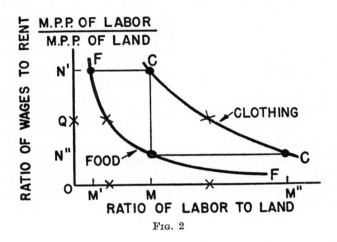

Fig. 2

investigate the composition of industry output among firms and enter upon other lengthy digressions.   Because we assume the classical law of diminishing returns (as one factor at a time varies) both curves are necessarily declining ones with wage productivity dropping relative to rent productivity as labor is more intensively applied to land.

Now let us suppose that in one of the countries the factor endowment of labor relative to total land is given by the distance *OM* on the lower axis.   Without further knowledge we can be sure of but one thing : a greater labor–land ratio than *OM* will be used in clothing production; a lesser ratio than *OM* in food production.   At uniform wages and rents, it is never proper to use the factors in the same proportions because of the basic technological differences between food and clothing production.

The ratio of total labor to total land, *OM*, is a weighted average which falls between the labor–land ratios in each industry, the exact weights being the relative proportions of total land being applied to each use.[1]   At any given wage–rent ratio, such as shown by the cross at Q, we move over horizontally to the two curves to read off the proper labor–land ratios in food and clothing.   These are indicated by crosses on the curves and also on the lower axis; and it will be noted that the total labor–land ratio, OM, always falls in between the two lower crosses.

What different factor-price ratios are possible ?   Clearly, if something of both goods is to be produced Q can only range between N'' and N'.   When the wage–rent ratio falls to as low as N'', clothing production must cease entirely if the total labor demanded is not to exceed the available supply.   With only food produced, and with unemployment always ruled out, food must be using labor and land in the ratio OM.[2]   In short, as Q falls to N'', the pair of crosses march rightward until they reach M and M'' respectively.

By the same reasoning, we establish the fact that the price ratio will never rise above N' so long as both commodities are still being produced.   As Q approaches N', less and less of food is being produced and more and more of clothing; until finally at N' itself, all factors are being used for clothing, their ratio being that of the whole community's endowment, OM.   The crosses on the horizontal axis have moved leftward to M' and M respectively.

To recapitulate :   As the factor-price ratio rises from N'' to N', the production of clothing grows and that of food declines so that in Figure 1a (or 1b) we are moving from A (or a) up to Z (or z) and the price of food is declining relative to that of clothing.   The limits N' and N'', or M' and M'' are determined by the light step-like formation around the initial community factor ratio, OM.   If this initial endowment were pushed in the direction of more labor to land, M would move rightward, and so would M' and M''; N' and N'' would move downward; the production-possibility curve would be twisted into a more vertical shape, because food production, the land-using process, would be suffering more from the relative land shortage than would clothing production.

[1] Since total land = food land + clothing land
    total labor = food labor + clothing labor,
it follows arithmetically that

$$OM = \frac{\text{total labor}}{\text{total land}} = w_1 \frac{\text{food labor}}{\text{food land}} + w_2 \frac{\text{clothing labor}}{\text{clothing land}}$$

where $w_1 = \dfrac{\text{food land}}{\text{total land}}$ and $w_2 = \dfrac{\text{clothing land}}{\text{total land}} = 1 - w_1.$

[2] No clothing is being produced, so that the labor-to-land ratio in clothing is " zero." But this is a determinate quantity in the limit, being equal to OM'' for the little unit of clothing " about to be produced."

With zero transport costs, free trade makes demand completely non-localised. The votes of European consumers have the same pull on American production as those of Americans. The final pattern of international effective demand is of no consequence for the problem of factor-price equalisation *so long as neither country is forced beyond the point of complete specialisation*. With each producing something of both goods, the common international price ratio is equal to the resulting slopes of the production possibility curves in both countries. Thus

$$\frac{\text{price of food}}{\text{price of clothing}} = \left(\frac{\text{marginal cost of food}}{\text{marginal cost of clothing}}\right)_{\text{America}} = \left(\frac{\text{marginal cost of food}}{\text{marginal cost of clothing}}\right)_{\text{Europe}}$$

= absolute slope at d = absolute slope at B.

Now, it is also true that so long as the marginal rate of factor substitution in the two industries are equal, as they must be if we are to be on the optimal production-possibility curve, the slope at any point of the production-possibility curve will be exactly equal to the ratio of labor's marginal productivity in clothing to labor's marginal productivity in food; or what will be the same thing at such an optimum point, to the corresponding ratio of the marginal physical productivities of capital.

If, as we have earlier seen, the price slopes are equal in the two countries, this can only have resulted from the fact that factor-price ratios were equal [1] and that hence the same factor proportion patterns had to emerge. Were the factor-price ratios different—say at Figure 2's Q in one country and above Q in the other—the two countries would have to use different factor proportions; and with different factor proportions, there would have had to result different relative marginal labor productivities in the two lines, and finally different price or marginal cost slopes on the production-possibility curve. Hence, equal slopes must imply equal factor prices. This completes the proof of our fundamental theorem concerning factor-price equalisation.

IX. ARITHMETIC ILLUSTRATION

An arithmetic example may help to dispel any remaining vestige of the paradox about the plausibility of complete factor-price equalisation. Let us suppose that the two continents are

---

[1] The only exception is where the FF and CC curves happened always to coincide; *i.e.*, where the two commodities had substantially identical production functions. This would imply identical straight-line production-possibility curves in both countries, and trade would never take place.

differently endowed with land and labor : suppose that America has 100 units of land and 100 units of labor, but that Europe has only 55 units of land to 100 units of labor.

Now if factors were perfectly mobile, labor would migrate from Europe to America; and after about one-third of all European labor had moved to America the factor proportions would be equal. Europe would be left with about 71 units of labor to 55 units of land, and America with about 129 units of labor to 100 units of land, and the world as a whole with about a 4 : 3 ratio of labor to land (200 : 155, to be exact).

Depending upon technology and effective demand, there would also have to emerge some definite allocation of world resources between clothing and food : let us suppose that 28 units of world labor and 112 units of world land would be used for food, and the rest (172 units of labor and 43 units of land) for clothing. The exact figures do not matter, but it is important to notice that everywhere production would be carried on in the same way and no geographical trade would be necessary. World output would be, in a certain sense, optimal. Native American laborers would have lost their pre-trade privileged positions and would have lower real incomes (measured in *either* food or clothing); the same would be true of European land-owners.

Now we must drop the assumption that factors are mobile. Can free commodity trade alone offset the fact that population is twice as dense in Europe as in America? Yes, if America allocates 20 units of labor and 80 units of land to food and the rest (80 units of labor and 20 units of land) to clothing; and if at the same time Europe were to allocate 8 units of labor and 32 units of land to food, with 92 units of labor and 23 units of land going to clothing production. The accompanying Table I summarises these figures.

Under free commodity trade it is possible for world-factor combination to be exactly the same as under perfect factor-mobility conditions. No one needs to migrate if food can be cheaply carried from America to Europe in exchange for clothing. Farmers all over the world will be using exactly the same methods and will be receiving exactly the same pay; the same is true of land or labor in clothing production. World productivity is again " optimal."

It is perhaps not so obvious, but it is none the less true that free trade has had the same harmful effects upon the vested interests of the whole laboring class in America (and land-owning class in Europe) as would the removal of all immigration barriers.

TABLE I

Comparison of Factor Mobility and Goods Mobility

	Labor.	Land.	
Original Factor Endowments of Regions			
America	100	100	
Europe	100	55	
World	200	155	
Situation if Factors were Mobile			
America	129 [1]	100	
Europe	71 [2]	55	
World	200	155	
Food Input . . .		28	112
Clothing Input . .		172	43
Situation if only Goods are Mobile			
America	100	100	
Food Input . . .		20	80
Clothing Input . . .		80	20
Europe	100	55	
Food Input . . .		8	32
Clothing Input . . .		92	23

[1] More exactly, $\frac{100}{155} \times 200 = 129\frac{5}{155}$

[2] More exactly, $\frac{55}{155} \times 200 = 70\frac{150}{155}$.

What maximises world or national output will in this case lower the absolute real returns to even so " important " and " versatile " a factor as (American) " labor." [1]   Under the broad conditions here assumed, free trade must have no less profound effects than free movements of population.

Advocates of freer trade—and I consider myself in this class —must not overstate their case.   Protection can help special groups; it can even help special large groups.   Only in the simple Ricardian labor-theory-of-value examples of comparative cost is it correct to say that " wages are not the *cause* of trade : they are the *result*." [2]   Only if labor is to receive 100% of national

---

[1] Ohlin on p. 44 incorrectly argues that relative factor-price equalisation will take place without lowering the absolute share of labor in terms of goods : " Wages are such a substantial part of the total income that it is almost unthinkable that a considerable rise of the latter could fail to raise total wages also, even if the percentage going to the laborers became somewhat reduced."   Not only is this result " thinkable "—it inevitably follows from the Ohlin–Heckscher analysis, as Professor Stolper was the first to point out.   See Stolper and Samuelson, *op. cit.*   For a position similar to Ohlin's, see G. Haberler, *Theory of International Trade* (London : W. Hodge and Co., Ltd., 1936), Ch. XII.   In his *Studies, op. cit.*, p. 533, Viner takes a more guarded position.

[2] See Lionel Robbins, " Economic Notes on Some Arguments for Protection," *Economica*, No. 31, February 1931, p. 49.

income will maximisation of income necessarily maximise real wages.   And if labor should customarily receive a large share of total income this fact itself would—in a simple Ohlin world—restrict the possible gains in income resulting from international trade and limit the explanatory value of the proportions-of-the-factors analysis.

X.   The Case of Complete Specialisation

But have we not perhaps proved too much ?   At times in the historic past tariff barriers were relatively minor, and within many regions free trade was virtually achieved.   Yet important differences in wages and other factor prices have persisted.   How shall we account for this ?

First, there is the important fact that commodities are never perfectly mobile.   Transportation costs always exist and serve as obstacles to profitable trade.   The whole theory of location of industry is based upon this basic fact.

The second reason for persisting factor-price differences in the face of commodity mobility is more difficult to describe, being rather complex and technical.   If, (a) different regions of the world are extremely different in factor endowments, or (b) the different commodities use factors of production in almost the same proportions, *complete* (rather than only partial) *geographical specialisation of production may result*.   In this case factor prices need not be equalised.

The remainder of this section will be devoted to a brief discussion of the case of complete specialisation.   The next section will discuss a third important reason why factor prices are not equalised—namely, the inadequacy of the simplified Ohlin proportions-of-the-factors analysis of the pattern of international division of labor.

So long as a country is producing something of both goods, the competitive price ratio must be equal to the ratio of domestic marginal costs.   But if one product is not being produced at all— e.g., no clothing in America—then its (relative) price may fall short of the (relative) marginal cost of producing a first unit of the product.   Thus, at the point A in Figure 1a, the price ratio of food to clothing can be anything in excess of the absolute slope of the curve at A.   Similarly, when Europe produces all clothing, the price ratio can be anything less than the absolute slope at z.

Depending upon available factor proportions, there will be in each country only a definite range of price ratios at which something of both goods will be produced.   In America this range is between the numerical slope at Z and the numerical slope at A. In Europe the slopes at z and a determine a corresponding range. These ranges are not identical unless the two countries have identical total-factor ratios.   If America has more land relative to labor, its production-possibility curve will be flatter than that of Europe and its limiting marginal-cost ratios will each be less than the corresponding limits of Europe.   But there will still be some overlapping of their ranges, unless their respective factor endowments are very far apart compared to the technological differences in factor intensities of food and clothing production.   (A visual comparison of Figures 1a and 1b will show that their production-possibility curves have about the same slopes except around Z in Figure 1a and around a in Figure 1b, where the ranges cease to overlap.[1]

So long as the final pattern of equilibrium is within the common relative price range, all of our previous analysis applies. But if the final pattern of equilibrium leads to complete specialisation on the part of one or both countries, then their production-possibility slopes need not be equal, even though market-price ratios must still coincide.   Production in the different countries may be taking place with different factor proportions, and relative factor prices will usually not be at equality.   Even in a limited sense of the word optimal, we can no longer expect world productivity to be optimal; however, in a still more limited sense —*as of a given immobile pattern of world resources*—total " productivity " cannot be made better.

The effect upon American real wages or European real rents can no longer be unambiguously ascertained.   American real wages in terms of food must certainly have deteriorated; similarly European land rents in terms of real clothing must fall. This much can be inferred from production considerations alone, *i.e.*, from the classical law of diminishing returns.   But if the final price ratio of food to clothing becomes much steeper than the critical limiting slope at A, American real wages in terms of imported clothing can begin to exceed the pre-trade real wage in clothing.   In such a case the final effect of trade upon a worker's welfare would depend upon the particular pattern of his tastes for food and clothing.

The classical constant-cost arithmetical analysis of compara-

---

[1] If the " step formations " for each country are drawn into Figure 2, the steps will partially overlap unless initial factor endowments are extremely far apart.

tive advantage happens to fall into the extreme category of complete specialisation. Almost by chance, so to speak, certain rather special relations result. Thus, as Viner has pointed out,[1] the Taussigian dictum that " productivity in the export industries sets the pace for real wages " is only half a truth (or less than 360° of a circular truism) since it ignores mutual interdependence. But, worse than that, under the partial specialisation of increasing cost it would not even be true.

The limitations upon factor-price equalisation of complete specialisation can be made more comprehensible if we revert back to the arithmetical data of Table 1. Suppose that under free labor migration the world finally settled down to the use of 100 units of labor and 77 units of land in clothing production, and to 100 units of labor and 78 units of land in food production. The relative intensities of land and labor in the two industries is now very similar. It must follow, therefore, that free commodity trade is unable to compensate for complete factor immobility. Even when the United States has specialised completely in food production and Europe in clothing production, there will still not be achieved the same methods of production as under freely mobile factor conditions. Labor in Europe will have too little land to work with, land in America too little labor.

If we superimpose on the free commodity trade situation, free factor movements, labor will begin to migrate. But it certainly will not have to migrate until full factor proportionality has been achieved in both regions. Short of that condition, the regions will become enough alike in factor endowments so that free trade can equalise factor prices—so that each country only partially specialises and by a judicious weighting of the relative importance of different industries achieves the common optimal world pattern of production.[2]

XI. Limitations of Factor-Proportions Analysis

In addition to the fact of transport cost, we have found a second impediment to complete factor-price equalisation in the

---

[1] J. Viner, " Professor Taussig's Contribution to the Theory of International Trade," *Explorations in Economics : Notes and Essays Contributed in Honor of F. W. Taussig* (New York : McGraw-Hill Book Co., Inc., 1936), p. 11.

[2] The exact conditions for partial specialisation and complete factor price equalization are as follows : the labor–land ratio in each country must lie between the labor–land ratios that would spring up in each line of production under freely mobile factors. This much can be deduced from Figure 2 or from the arithmetical consideration that the weighted average of two numbers must lie between them.

possibility of complete specialisation. There remains a third, and perhaps more fundamental, reason why factor prices need not be equalised : the Ohlin proportions-of-the-factors analysis of international trade has fundamental inadequacies and limitations.

The Ohlin analysis explains much ; but there is much that it fails to explain ; and if adhered to inflexibly, there is much that it can obscure. Its two central tenets are open to grave doubt : Is it reasonable and useful to set up the hypothesis that production functions are the same the world over ? Is it possible to find reasonably homogeneous and commensurable factors of production in diverse parts of the world, so that relative proportions can be defined and compared ?

Certainly no strong affirmative answers to these two questions can be given—as Ohlin himself has pointed out in a number of places.[1] The laws of nature may be the same " everywhere," but the laws of nature and the economically relevant production function relating maximum output obtainable from specified concrete inputs are two quite different things. Effective knowledge (" know-how ") is probably as important a variable in understanding economic history and geography as is specific factor endowment. The " same " (biological) labor working in one city of the United States with the " same " kind of equipment and other resources produces substantially different output. The " effective organisation " is different.

It would be artificial in the extreme to explain any such empirical case by saying that " knowledge " is " scarce " in the one place relative to the other. At best this is a crypto-explanation ; at worst it ignores the play on words involved in the fact that the term " factor of production " is used in two or more quite different senses : (a) as a concrete input item, such as fertiliser, purchasable in divisible units in the market place; and (b) as a condition which has a bearing upon production such as the factor of technological knowledge.[2] Knowledge is *not* an input such that the more you use of it, the less there is left.

---

[1] Ohlin recognises (p. 562) that international trade theory need not assume any commensurability of factors between regions. He also devotes a lengthy discussion (Chapter V) to qualitative differences of factors. But if one is forced ultimately to work with dozens of grades of labor, hundreds of grades of land and innumerable grades of capital equipment, the explanations become rather *ad hoc* and not very helpful.

[2] In between (a) and (b) there is a category of such non-appropriable factors of production as " humidity," which are free in the sense that nothing is paid for them, but not in the sense that they can be unlimitedly augmented.

Effective knowledge is even more important than knowledge, and it unfortunately cannot be acquired by reading a book or by editorial exhortation.

When we turn to the question of defining significantly comparable categories of productive factors, we run into similar difficulties. " A man's a man for a' that," but is a jungle pigmy to be equated to an Eskimo ? An illiterate " hill-billy " to his cousin working in the Detroit factories and " broken " to an industrial regime ? Even if we are sympathetic to the eighteenth-century view of the plasticity of human nature, so that all men (and women) are regarded as *potentially* alike, we must not overlook the important environmental differences that have conditioned their industrial effectiveness.

The commensurability of natural resources involves similar problems. No one will deny the importance of iron, coal, power, rainfall and fertile plains as localising factors. But there is little that the proportions-of-the-factor analysis can add to our understanding of the matter. We would be giving the show away if we were to descend to such fatuities as : the tropics grow tropical fruits because of the relative abundance there of tropical conditions.[1]

Space does not permit further elaboration on this important topic. We may conclude by saying that factor proportions

---

[1] In a sense, the comparison of productivities of the same factors between countries is a backward step in formal international trade analysis. To-day it is widely recognised that it is never necessary—even in the simple Ricardian examples—to make such productivity comparisons ; it is only necessary to make inter-commodity comparisons. The proudest moment in the classical analysis, when it is shown that trade is still possible between two countries where one is less " efficient " in the production of all goods, is something of an irrelevancy. These remarks do not mean that opportunity cost doctrine (where the cost of goods is only to be measured in terms of goods) is correct in the neo-Austrian form. Professor Viner has steadfastly maintained the more general equilibrium approach of Walras, Pareto and Marshall against his opponents Knight, Haberler and Robbins. And one by one they have either had to maintain an empirically gratuitous position (that all factors must be perfectly *inelastic* in total supply and indifferent between different uses) or else have had to reformulate the opportunity cost doctrine so that it becomes not only a rather awkward mumbo-jumbo, but loses all novelty and distinctiveness as well. See Viner, *Studies, op. cit.*, Ch. VIII, for references. But when Viner seems to argue that normative propositions in international trade cannot be deduced from a full general equilibrium analysis in much the same way that they can be from the inadmissably simple classical real costs comparative advantage, I part company with him. Cf. my " The Gains from International Trade," *Canadian Journal of Economics*, Vol. 5, No. 2, May 1939, pp. 195–205, and " Welfare Economics and International Trade," *American Economic Review*, Vol. XXVIII, No. 2, June 1938, pp. 261–66. Also, Viner seems unusually gentle in his criticism of the circuitous and rather feeble Taussigian real cost doctrines.

explain only part of the facts of international economics. We must still set up hypotheses of differences in international production and productivity, differences in effectiveness which are to be accepted as empirical facts even if not simply explainable. Thus, it may be a crypto-explanation to explain events of economic history by " Yankee ingenuity." But whatever we think of the explanatory value of the label, we must not deny the important fact described. Indeed, from the deeper standpoint of sound methodology, all " explanations " are really nothing but simplifying descriptive hypotheses which unify diverse facts.

XII. POLICY IMPLICATIONS CONCERNING MIGRATION

In conclusion, I should like to venture upon the dangerous task of drawing a practical moral from an abstract theoretical argument. The United Kingdom is a densely populated region. In the post-war period it has suffered from loss of overseas investment income, from high food prices and adverse terms of trade, from a certain disorganisation of production and internal division of labor.

Is widespread emigration the way out ? Perhaps it is. But despite numerous qualifications, the gist of the present discussion has been to show that relatively free commodity trade is a better substitute for mobility of factors of production than was hitherto thought to be the case.

So long as raw material can be carried to the United Kingdom by relatively cheap ocean transport, the law of diminishing returns is largely robbed of any particularly immediate local effects. The question arises : What can English industrial workers do for themselves in the remote parts of the empire that they cannot do in England ? What can they do for the present generation of Australians and Canadians after migration that they cannot do in England ?

Obviously, no simple answers can be given to such complex questions. Undoubtedly industry is in many parts of the world asleep, and new catalytic agents would contribute towards a better and more suitable long-run equilibrium. But to have asked the questions in the above form shows that the favourable effects of migration are by no means automatic and cannot be simply taken for granted.

They would be so only if it were proposed that Englishmen migrate in order to go on the land as primary food producers. This, few experts would propose on a large scale, even now when the terms of trade are abnormally favourable to agricultural production. Without venturing upon rash prophecy, one can venture scepticism that this abnormal trend of the terms of trade, counter to historical drift, will continue. And even if the trend towards relatively higher food and raw-material prices should continue to develop, it would have to go a long way before comparable labor effort on the land could anywhere in the world be expected as a matter of cold fact to yield the material real incomes of industrialised labor.

PAUL A. SAMUELSON

Massachusetts Institute of Technology,
   Cambridge, Massachusetts.

68

INTERNATIONAL FACTOR-PRICE EQUALISATION ONCE AGAIN

1. INTRODUCTION

MY recent paper [1] attempting to show that free commodity trade will, under certain specified conditions, inevitably lead to complete factor-price equalisation appears to be in need of further amplification. I propose therefore (1) to restate the principal theorem, (2) to expand upon its intuitive demonstration, (3) to settle the matter definitively by a brief but rigorous mathematical demonstration, (4) to make a few extensions to the case of many commodities and factors, and finally (5) to comment briefly upon some realistic qualifications to its simplified assumptions.

I cannot pretend to present a balanced appraisal of the bearing of this analysis upon interpreting the actual world, because my own mind is not made up on this question : on the one hand, I think it would be folly to come to any startling conclusions on the basis of so simplified a model and such abstract reasoning; but on the other hand, strong simple cases often point the way to an element of truth present in a complex situation. Still, at the least, we ought to be clear in our deductive reasoning; and the elucidation of this side of the problem plus the qualifying discussion may contribute towards an ultimate appraisal of the theorem's realism and relevance.

2. STATEMENT OF THE THEOREM

My hypotheses are as follows :—

1. There are but two countries, America and Europe.

2. They produce but two commodities, food and clothing.

3. Each commodity is produced with two factors of production, land and labour. The production functions of each commodity show " constant returns to scale," in the sense that changing all inputs in the same proportion changes output in that same proportion, leaving all " productivities "

---

[1] " International Trade and the Equalisation of Factor Prices," ECONOMIC JOURNAL, Vol. LVIII, June, 1948, pp. 163–184. I learn from Professor Lionel Robbins that A. P. Lerner, while a student at L.S.E., dealt with this problem. I have had a chance to look over Lerner's mimeographed report, dated December 1933, and it is a masterly, definitive treatment of the question, difficulties and all.

essentially unchanged. In short, all production functions are mathematically " homogeneous of the first order " and subject to Euler's theorem.

4. The law of diminishing marginal productivity holds : as any one input is increased relative to other inputs, its marginal productivity diminishes.

5. The commodities differ in their " labour and land intensities." Thus, food is relatively " land using " or " land-intensive," while clothing is relatively " labour-intensive." This means that whatever the prevailing ratio of wages to rents, the optimal proportion of labour to land is greater in clothing than in food.

6. Land and labour are assumed to be qualitatively identical inputs in the two countries and the technological production functions are assumed to be the same in the two countries.

7. All commodities move perfectly freely in international trade, without encountering tariffs or transport costs, and with competition effectively equalising the market price-ratio of food and clothing. No factors of production can move between the countries.

8. Something is being produced in both countries of both commodities with both factors of production. Each country may have moved in the direction of specialising on the commodity for which it has a comparative advantage, but it has not moved so far as to be specialising completely on one commodity.[1]

All of this constitutes the hypothesis of the theorem. The conclusion states :—

Under these conditions, real factor prices must be exactly the same in both countries (and indeed the proportion of inputs used in food production in America must equal that in Europe, and similarly for clothing production).

Our problem is from now on a purely logical one. Is " If H, then inevitably C " a correct statement? The issue is not whether C (factor-price equalisation) will actually hold; nor even whether H (the hypothesis) is a valid empirical generalisation. It is whether C can fail to be true when H is assumed true. Being a

[1] Actually we may admit the limiting case of " incipient specialisation," where nothing is being produced of one of the commodities, but where it is a matter of indifference whether an infinitesimal amount is or is not being produced, so that price and marginal costs are equal.

logical question, it admits of only one answer : either the theorem is true or it is false.

One may wonder why such a definite problem could have given rise to misunderstanding. The answer perhaps lies in the fact that even so simple a set-up as this one involves more than a dozen economic variables : at least four inputs for each country, four marginal productivities for each country (marginal productivity of American labour in food, of American land in food . . .), two outputs for each country, the prices of the two commodities, the price in each country of the two inputs, the proportions of the inputs in different lines of production, and so forth. It is not always easy for the intellect to move purposefully in a hyperspace of many dimensions.

And the problem is made worse by the fact, insufficiently realised, that constant returns to scale is a very serious limitation on the production functions. A soon as one knows a single " curve " on such a surface, all other magnitudes are frozen into exact quantitative shapes and cannot be chosen at will. Thus, if one knows the returns of total product to labour working on one acre of land, then one already knows everything : the marginal productivity schedule of land, all the iso-product curves, the marginal-rate-of-substitution schedules, etc. This means one must use a carefully graduated ruler in drawing the different economic functions, making sure that they are numerically consistent in addition to their having plausible qualitative shapes.

3. INTUITIVE PROOF

In each country there is assumed to be given totals of labour and land. If all resources are devoted to clothing, we get a certain maximum amount of clothing. If all are devoted to food production, we get a certain maximum amount of food. But what will happen if we are willing to devote only part of all land and part of total labour to the production of food, the rest being used in clothing production? Obviously, then we are in effect sacrificing some food in order to get some clothing. The iron law of scarcity tells us that we cannot have all we want of both goods, but must ultimately give up something of one good in getting some of another.

In short there is a best " production-possibility," or " transformation " curve showing us the maximum obtainable amount of one commodity for each amount of the other. Such a production-possibility schedule was drawn up for each country in Figure 1 of my earlier article.   And in each case it was made to be a curve *convex* from above, so that the more you want of any good the greater is the cost, at the margin, in terms of the other good. This convexity property is very important and is related to the law of diminishing marginal productivity.   Few readers had any qualms about accepting convexity, but perhaps some did not realise its far-reaching implications in showing why the factor-price equalisation theorem had to be true.   I propose, therefore, to show why the production-possibility curve must obviously be convex (looked at from above).[1]

To show that convexity, or increasing relative marginal costs must hold, it is sufficient for the present purpose to show that concavity, or decreasing marginal costs, involves an impossible contradiction.   Now at the very worst, it is easily shown we can move along a straight-line opportunity cost line between the

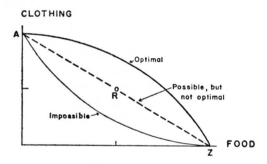

two axes.   For suppose we agree to give up half of the maximum obtainable amount of food.   How much clothing can we be sure of getting?   If we send out the crudest type of order : " Half of all labour and half of all land is to be shifted to clothing production," we will (because of the assumption of constant returns to scale) *exactly halve* food production ; and we will acquire *exactly half* of the maximum amount of clothing produceable with all resources. Therefore, we end up at a point, R, exactly half-way between the limiting points A and Z.   Similarly, if we decide to give up 10, 20, 30 or 90% of the maximum amount of food produceable, we can give out crude orders to transfer exactly 10, 20, 30 or 90% of *both* inputs from food to clothing.   Because of constant returns to scale, it follows that we can be sure of getting 90, 80, 70 or 10% of maximum clothing.

[1] I am indebted for this line of reasoning to my colleague at M.I.T., Professor Robert L. Bishop, who for some years has been using it on beginning students in economics, with no noticeable disastrous effects.   This proof is suggestive only, but it could easily be made rigorous.

In short, by giving such crude down-the-line orders that transfer both resources *always in the same proportion*, we can at worst travel along a straight line between the two limiting intercepts.   Any concave curve would necessarily lie inside such a constant-cost straight line and can therefore be ruled out : hence decreasing (marginal, opportunity) costs are incompatible with the assumption of constant returns to scale.

But of course we can usually do even better than the straight-line case.   A neophyte bureaucrat might be satisfied to give crude down-the-line orders, but there exist more efficient ways of giving up food for clothing.   This is where social-economist (or " welfare economist ") can supplement the talents of the mere technician who knows how best to use inputs in the production of any one good and nothing else.   There are an infinity of ways of giving up, say, 50% of food : we may simply give up labour, or simply give up land, or give up constant percentages of labour and land, or still other proportions.   But there will be only one best way to do so, only one best combination of labour and land that is to be transferred.   Best in what sense ?   Best in the sense of getting for us the maximum obtainable amount of clothing, compatible with our pre-assigned decision to sacrifice a given amount of food.

Intuition tells us that, qualitatively, we should transfer a larger proportion of labour than of land to clothing production. This is because clothing is the labour-intensive commodity, by our original hypothesis.   This means that the proportion of labour to land is actually declining in the food line as its produc-tion declines.   What about the proportion of labour to land in clothing production ?   At first we were able to be generous in sparing labour, which after all was not " too well adapted " for food production.   But now, when we come to give up still more food, there is less labour left in food production relative to land ; hence, we cannot contrive to be quite so generous in transferring further labour to clothing production.   As we expand clothing production further, the proportion of labour to land must also be falling in that line ; but the labour–land ratio never falls to as low as the level appropriate for food, the land-intensive commodity.[1]

---

[1] Some readers may find it paradoxical that—with a fixed ratio of total labour to total land—we nevertheless lower the ratio of labour to land *in both industries* as a result of producing more of the labour-intensive good and less of the other. Such readers find it hard to believe that men's wages and women's wages can both go up at the same time that average wages are going down.   They forget that there is an inevitable shift in the industries' weights used to compute the

Intuition tells us that by following an optimal pattern which recognises the difference in factor intensities of the two goods, we can end up on a production possibility curve that is bloated out beyond a constant-cost straight line : in short, on a production possibility curve that is convex, obeying the law of increasing marginal costs of one good as it is expanded at the expense of the other good.   Or to put the same thing in the language of the market-place : as the production of clothing expands, upward pressure is put on the price of the factor it uses most intensively, on wages relative to land rent.   An increase in the ratio of wages to rent must in a competitive market press up the price of the labour-intensive commodity relative to the land-intensive commodity.

This one-directional relationship between relative factor prices and relative commodity prices is an absolute necessity, and it is vital for the recognition of the truth in the main theorem.   Let me elaborate therefore upon the market mechanism bringing it about.   Under perfect competition, everywhere within a domestic market there will be set up a uniform ratio of wages to rents.   In the food industry, there will be one, and only one, optimal proportion of labour to land; any attempt to combine productive factors in proportions that deviate from the optimum will be penalised by losses, and there will be set up a process of corrective adaptation.   The same competitive forces will force an adaptation of the input proportion in clothing production, with equilibrium being attained only when the input proportions are such as to equate exactly the ratio of the physical marginal productivities of the factors (the " marginal rate of substitution " of labour for land in clothing production) to the ratio of factor prices prevailing in the market.   The price mechanism has an unconscious wisdom.   As if led by an invisible hand, it causes the economic system to move out to the optimal production-possibility curve.   Through the intermediary of a common market factor–price ratio, the marginal rates of substitution of the factors become the same in both industries.   And it is this marginal condition which intuition (as well as geometry and mathematics) tells us prescribes the optimal allocation of resources so as to yield maximum output.   Not only does expanding clothing production result in the earlier described

---

average-factor ratio.   Really to understand all this the reader must be referred to the Edgeworth box-diagram depicted in W. F. Stolper and P. A. Samuelson, " Protection and Real Wages," *Review of Economic Studies*, Vol. IX (1941), pp. 58–73.

qualitative pattern of dilution of the ratio of labour to land in both occupations; more than that, a price system is one way of achieving the exactly optimal quantitative degree of change in proportions.

I have established unequivocally the following facts :

> *Within any country:* (a) *an increase in the ratio of wages to rents will cause a definite decrease in the proportion of labour to land in both industries;* (b) *to each determinate state of factor proportion in the two industries there will correspond one, and only one, commodity price ratio and a unique configuration of wages and rent; and* (c) *the change in factor proportions incident to an increase in* $\dfrac{wages}{rents}$ *must be followed by a one-directional increase in clothing prices relative to food prices.*

An acute reader may try to run ahead of the argument and may be tempted to assert : " But all this holds for one country, as of a given total factor endowment. Your established chain of causation is only from factor prices (and factor proportions) to commodity prices. Are you entitled to reverse the causation and to argue that the same commodity–price ratio must—even in countries of quite different total factor endowments—lead back to a common unique factor–price ratio, a common unique way of combining the inputs in the food and clothing industries, and a common set of absolute factor prices and marginal productivities ? "

My answer is yes. This line of reasoning is absolutely rigorous. It is only proportions that matter, not scale. In such a perfectly competitive market each small association of factors (or firm, if one prefers that word) feels free to hire as many or as few extra factors as it likes. It neither knows nor cares anything about the totals for society. It is like a group of molecules in a perfect gas which is everywhere in thermal equilibrium. The molecules in any one small region behave in the same way regardless of the size of the room around them. A sample observed in the middle of a huge spherical room would act in the same way as a similar sample observed within a small rectangular room. Similarly, if we observe the behaviour of a representative firm [1] in one country it will be exactly the same in all essentials as a representative firm taken from some other country—regardless of

---

[1] The representative firm concept is in the case of homogeneous production functions not subject to the usual difficulties associated with the Marshallian concept; in this case, it should be added, the " scale " of the firm is indeterminate and, fortunately, irrelevant.

the difference in total factor amounts and relative industrial concentration—provided only that factor-price ratios are really the same in the two markets.

All this follows from the italicised conclusion reached just above, especially from (c) taken in conjunction with (a) and (b).

This really completes the intuitive demonstration of the theorem. The same international commodity–price ratio, must —so long as both commodities are being produced and priced at marginal costs—enable us to infer backwards a unique factor-price ratio, a unique set of factor proportions, and even a unique set of absolute wages and rents.

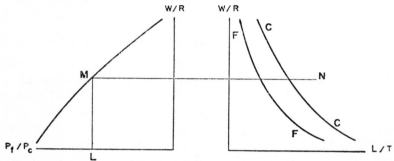

All this is summarised in the accompanying chart. On the right-hand side I have simply duplicated Figure 2 of my earlier paper. On the left-hand side I have added a chart showing the one-directional relation of commodity prices to factor prices.[1] As

[1] The left-hand curve is drawn in a qualitatively correct fashion. Actually its exact quantitative shape is determined by the two right-hand curves; but the chart is *not* exact in its quantitative details.

We may easily illustrate the importance of point (5) of our hypothesis, which insists on differences in factor intensities. Consider the depicted pathological

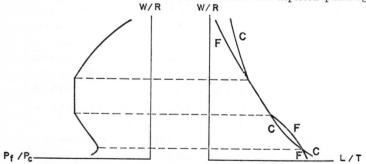

case which does not meet the requirements of our hypothesis, and in which factor intensities are for a range identical, and in still other regions food becomes the labour-intensive good. The resulting pattern of commodity prices does *not* necessarily result in factor-price equalisation. Cf. p. 175, n. 1 of my earlier article.

wages fall relative to rents the price of food is shown to rise relative to clothing in a monotonic fashion. The accompanying chart applies to either country and—so long as neither country is specialising completely—its validity is independent of their differing factor endowments. It follows that when we specify a common price ratio (say at L), we can move backward unambiguously (from M to N, etc.) to a common factor–price ratio and to a common factor proportion set-up in the two countries.

4. Mathematical Proof

Now that the theorem has been demonstrated by common-sense reasoning, let me confirm it by more rigorous mathematical proof. The condition of equilibrium can be written in a variety of ways, and can be framed so as to involve more than a dozen equations. For example, let me call America's four marginal physical productivities—of labour in food, of land in food, of labour in clothing, of land in clothing—a, b, c and d. I use Greek letters—α, β, γ, δ—to designate the corresponding marginal productivities in Europe. Then we can end up with a number of equilibrium expressions of the form

$$\frac{a}{b} = \frac{c}{d}, \frac{\alpha}{\beta} = \frac{\gamma}{\delta}, \frac{a}{c} = \frac{\alpha}{\gamma}, \ldots \text{ etc.}$$

A number of economists have tortured themselves trying to manipulate these expressions so as to result in $a = \alpha$, etc., or at least in $\frac{a}{b} = \frac{\alpha}{\beta}$, etc. No proof of this kind is possible. The essential thing is that these numerous marginal productivities are by no means independent. Because proportions rather than scale are important, knowledge of the behaviour of the marginal productivity of labour tells us exactly what to expect of the marginal-productivity schedule of land. This is because increasing the amount of labour with land held constant is equivalent to reducing land with labour held constant.[1]

[1] J. B. Clark recognised in his *Distribution of Wealth* that the " upper triangle " of his labour-marginal-productivity diagram must correspond to the " rectangle " of his other-factors diagram. But his draughtsman did *not* draw the curve accordingly ! This is a mistake that Philip Wicksteed in his *Co-ordination of the Laws of Distribution* (London School of Economics Reprint) could not have made. Clark, a believer in Providence, was unaware of the blessing—in the form of Euler's theorem on homogeneous functions—that made his theory possible. Wicksteed, a man of the cloth, appreciated and interpreted the generosity of Nature. Cf. also F. H. Knight, *Risk, Uncertainty and Profit*, ch. IV, for a partial treatment of these reciprocal relations. G. J. Stigler, *Production and Distribution Theories : the Formative Period*, gives a valuable treatment of Wicksteed's theory as exposited by Flux and others.

Mathematically, instead of writing food production, F, as any joint function of labour devoted to it, L_f, and of land, T_f, we can write it as

$$F = F(L_f, T_f) = T_f f\left(\frac{L_f}{T_f}\right) \qquad . \quad . \quad . \quad (1)$$

where the function f can be thought of as the returns of food on one unit of land, and where the number of units of land enters as a scale factor. The form of this function is the same for both countries; and there is, of course, a similar type of function holding for cloth production, C, in terms of L_c and T_c namely

$$C = C(L_c, T_c) = T_c c\left(\frac{L_c}{T_c}\right) \qquad . \quad . \quad . \quad (2)$$

It is easy to show mathematically, by simple partial differentiation of (1), the following relations among marginal physical productivities

$$\text{M.P.P. labour in food} = \frac{\partial F}{\partial L_f} = f'\left(\frac{L_f}{T_f}\right)$$

where f' represents the derivative of f and depicts the schedule of marginal product of labour (working on one unit of land). This must be a declining schedule according to our hypothesis of diminishing returns, so that we must have

$$f''\left(\frac{L_f}{T_f}\right) < 0.$$

By direct differentiation of (1), or by use of Euler's theorem, or by use of the fact that the marginal product of land can also be identified as a rent residual, we easily find that

$$\text{M.P.P. land in food} = \frac{\partial F}{\partial T_f} = f\left(\frac{L_f}{T_f}\right) - \frac{L_f}{T_f}f'\left(\frac{L_f}{T_f}\right) = g\left(\frac{L_f}{T_f}\right)$$

where g is the name for the rent residual. It is easy to show that

$$g'\left(\frac{L_f}{T_f}\right) = -\frac{L_f}{T_f}f''\left(\frac{L_f}{T_f}\right).$$

By similar reasoning, we may write the marginal productivity of land in clothing production in its proper relation to that of labour

$$\text{M.P.P. labour in clothing} = \frac{\partial C}{\partial L_c} = c'\left(\frac{L_c}{T_c}\right)$$

$$\text{M.P.P. land in clothing} = \frac{\partial C}{\partial T_c} = c\left(\frac{L_c}{T_c}\right) - \frac{L_c}{T_c}c'\left(\frac{L_c}{T_c}\right) = h\left(\frac{L_c}{T_c}\right)$$

$$h'\left(\frac{L_c}{T_c}\right) = -\frac{L_c}{T_c}c''\left(\frac{L_c}{T_c}\right).$$

The art of analysis in these problems is to select out the essential variables so as to reduce our equilibrium equations to the simplest form. Without specifying which country we are talking about, we certainly can infer from the fact that something of both goods is being produced with both factors the following conditions :—

Real wages (or labour marginal " value " productivities) must be the same in food and clothing production when expressed in terms of a common *measure*, such as clothing; the same is true of real rents (or land marginal " value " productivities). Or

(food price) (M.P.P. labour in food)
= (clothing price) (M.P.P. labour in clothing)

(food price) (M.P.P. land in food)
= (clothing price) (M.P.P. land in clothing)

which can be written in terms of previous notation [1] as

$$\left(\frac{P_f}{P_c}\right) f'\left(\frac{L_f}{T_f}\right) - c'\left(\frac{L_c}{T_c}\right) = 0$$

$$\left(\frac{P_f}{P_c}\right)\left[f\left(\frac{L_f}{T_f}\right) - \frac{L_f}{T_f}f'\left(\frac{L_f}{T_f}\right)\right] - \left[c\left(\frac{L_c}{T_c}\right) - \frac{L_c}{T_c}c'\left(\frac{L_c}{T_c}\right)\right] = 0.$$

Now these are two equations in the three variables $\frac{L_f}{T_f}$, $\frac{L_c}{T_c}$, and $\frac{P_f}{P_c}$. If we take the latter price ratio as given to us by inter-national-demand conditions, we are left with *two* equations to determine the *two* unknown factor proportions. This is a solvent situation, and we should normally expect the result to be determinate.

But a purist might still have doubts : " How do you know that these two equations or schedules might not twist around and intersect in multiple equilibria ? " Fortunately, the answer is simple and definite. On our hypothesis, any equilibrium con-figuration turns out to be absolutely unique. We may leave to a technical footnote the detailed mathematical proof of this fact.[2]

---

[1] In terms of our earlier $a, b, \ldots, \alpha, \beta \ldots$, these equations are of the form

$$\frac{P_f}{P_c}a = c, \frac{P_f}{P_c}b = d, \text{ etc.}$$

[2] The Implicit Function Theorem tells us that two suitably continuous

5. MULTIPLE COMMODITIES AND FACTORS

Adding a third or further commodities does not alter our analysis much. If anything, it increases the likelihood of complete factor–price equalisation. For all that we require is that at least *two* commodities are simultaneously being produced in both countries and then our previous conclusion follows. If we add a third commodity which is very much like either of our present commodities, we are not changing the situation materially. But if we add new commodities which are more extreme in their labour–land intensities, then we greatly increase the chance that two regions with very different factor endowments can still come into complete factor–price equalisation. A " queer " region is not penalised for being queer if there is queer work that needs doing.

I do not wish at this time to go into the technical mathematics of the n commodity, and r factor case. But it can be said that : (1) so long as the two regions are sufficiently close together in factor proportions, (2) so long as the goods differ in factor intensities, and (3) so long as the number of goods, n, is greater than the number of factors, r, we can hope to experience complete factor–price equalisation. On the other hand, if complete specialisation takes place it will do so for a whole collection of goods, the dividing line between exports and imports being a variable one depending upon reciprocal international demand (acting on factor prices) as in the classical theory of comparative advantage with multiple commodities.[1]

---

equations of the form $W_1(y_1, y_2) = 0 = W_2(y_1, y_2)$, possessing a solution $(y_1{}^0, y_2{}^0)$, cannot have any other solution provided

$$\Delta = \begin{vmatrix} \dfrac{\partial W_1}{\partial y_1} & \dfrac{\partial W_1}{\partial y_2} \\[2mm] \dfrac{\partial W_2}{\partial y_1} & \dfrac{\partial W_2}{\partial y_2} \end{vmatrix} \neq 0$$

In this case, where $y_1 = L_f/T_f$, etc., it is easy to show that

$$\Delta = \begin{vmatrix} \dfrac{P_f}{P_c} f'' & - c'' \\[3mm] - \dfrac{P_f}{P_c} \dfrac{L_f}{T_f} f'' & + \dfrac{L_c}{T_c} c'' \end{vmatrix} = \dfrac{P_f}{P_c} f'' c'' \left[\dfrac{L_c}{T_c} - \dfrac{L_f}{T_f} \right]$$

By hypothesis of diminishing returns f'' and c'' are negative, and the term in brackets (representing the respective labour intensities in food and clothing) cannot be equal to zero. Hence, the equilibrium is unique. As developed earlier, if the factor intensities become equal, or reverse themselves, the one-to-one relation between commodity and factor prices *must* be ruptured.

[1] The real wage of every resource must be the same in every place that it is used, when expressed in a common denominator. This gives us $r \ (n - 1)$

When we add a third productive factor and retain but two commodities, then the whole presumption towards factor–price equalisation disappears. Suppose American labour and American land have more capital to work with than does European labour and land. It is then quite possible that the marginal physical productivities of labour and land might be double that of Europe in both commodities. Obviously, commodity–price *ratios* would still be equal, production of both commodities will be taking place, but nonetheless absolute factor prices (or relative for that matter) need not be moved towards equality. This is our general expectation wherever the number of factors exceeds the number of commodities.

6. THE CONDITIONS OF COMPLETE SPECIALISATION

If complete specialisation takes place in one country, then our hypothesis is not fulfilled and the conclusion does not follow. How important is this empirically, and when can we expect complete specialisation to take place? As discussed earlier, the answer depends upon how disparate are the initial factor endowments of the two regions—how disparate in comparison with the differences in factor intensities of the two commodities.[1]

Unless the two commodities differ extraordinarily in factor intensities, the production-possibility curve will be by no means so convex as it is usually drawn in the neo-classical literature of international trade, where it usually resembles a quarter circle whose slope ranges the spectrum from zero to infinity. It should rather have the crescent-like shape of the new moon. Opportunity costs tend to be more nearly constant than I had previously realised. This is a step in the direction of the older classical theory of comparative advantage. But with this important difference : the same causes that tend to produce *constant* costs also tend to produce *uniform* cost ratios between nations, which

---

independent equations involving the $(n - 1)$ commodity–price ratios and the $n(r - 1)$ factor proportions. If $n = r$, we have a determinate system once the goods price ratios are given. If $n > r$, we have the same result, but now the international price ratios cannot be presented arbitrarily as there are constant-cost paths on the production-possibility locus, with one blade of Marshall's scissors doing most of the cutting, so to speak. If $n < r$, it is quite possible for free commodity trade to exist alongside continuing factor-price differentials. It is never enough simply to count equations and unknowns. In addition we must make sure that there are not multiple solutions : that factor intensities in the different commodities and the laws of returns are such as to lead to a one-to-one relationship between commodity prices and factor prices.

[1] The reader may be referred to the earlier paper's discussion of Figures 1 and 2, with respect to " step-like formations " and overlap.

is not at all in the spirit of classical theory. (Undoubtedly much
of the specialisation observed in the real world is due to something
different from all this, namely decreasing-cost indivisibilities,
tempered and counteracted by the existence of localised resources
specifically adapted to particular lines of production.)

A parable may serve the double purpose of showing the range
of factor endowment incompatible with complete specialisation
and of removing any lingering element of paradox surrounding
the view that commodity mobility may be a perfect substitute for
factor mobility.

Let us suppose that in the beginning all factors were perfectly
mobile, and nationalism had not yet reared its ugly head. Spatial
transport costs being of no importance, there would be one
world price of food and clothing, one real wage, one real rent,
and the world's land and labour would be divided between food
and clothing production in a determinate way, with uniform proportions of labour to land being used everywhere in clothing
production, and with a much smaller—but uniform—proportion
of labour to land being used in production of food.

Now suppose that an angel came down from heaven and
notified some fraction of all the labour and land units producing
clothing that they were to be called Americans, the rest to be
called Europeans; and some different fraction of the food industry
that henceforth they were to carry American passports.
Obviously, just giving people and areas national labels does not
alter anything : it does not change commodity or factor prices or
production patterns.

But now turn a recording geographer loose, and what will he
report ? Two countries with quite different factor proportions,
but with identical real wages and rents and identical modes of
commodity production (but with different relative importances
of food and clothing industries). Depending upon whether the
angel makes up America by concentrating primarily on clothing
units or on food units, the geographer will report a very high or
a very low ratio of labour to land in the newly synthesised
" country." But this he will never find : that the ratio of
labour to land should ever exceed the proportions characteristic
of the most labour-intensive industry (clothing) or ever fall short
of the proportions of the least labour-intensive industry. Both
countries *must* have factor proportions intermediate between the
proportions in the two industries.

The angel can create a country with proportions *not* intermediate between the factor intensities of food and clothing. But he cannot do so by following the above-described procedure, which was calculated to leave prices and production unchanged. If he wrests some labour in food production away from the land it has been working with, " sending " this labour to Europe and keeping it from working with the American land, then a substantive change in production and prices will have been introduced. Unless there are abnormal repercussions on the pattern of effective demand, we can expect one or both of the countries to specialise completely and real wages to fall in Europe relative to America in one or both commodities, with European real rents behaving in an opposite fashion. The extension of this parable to the many-commodities case may be left to the interested reader.

7. SOME QUALIFICATIONS

A number of qualifications to this theoretical argument are in order. In the first place, goods do not move without transport costs, and to the extent that commodity prices are not equalised it of course follows that factor prices will not tend to be fully equalised. Also, as I indicated in my earlier article, there are many reasons to doubt the usefulness of assuming identical production functions and categories of inputs in the two countries; and consequently, it is dangerous to draw sweeping practical conclusions concerning factor–price equalisation.

What about the propriety of assuming constant returns to scale ? In justice to Ohlin, it should be pointed out that he, more than almost any other writer, has followed up the lead of Adam Smith and made *increasing returns* an important cause for trade. It is true that increasing returns *may* at the same time create difficulties for the survival of perfect competition, difficulties which cannot always be sidestepped by pretending that the increasing returns are due primarily to *external* rather than internal economies. But these difficulties do not give us the right to deny or neglect the importance of scale factors.[1] Where

---

[1] Statical increasing returns is related to, but analytically distinct from, these irreversible cost economies induced by expansion and experimentation and which provide the justification for " infant industry " protection. Statical increasing returns might justify permanent judicious protection but not protection all around, since our purpose in bringing about large-scale production is to achieve profitable trade and consumption.

One other point needs stressing. For very small outputs, increasing returns to scale may take place without affecting the above analysis provided that total demand is large enough to carry production into the realm of constant returns to scale. Increasing the " extent of the market " not only increases specialisation, it also increases the possiblity of viable pure competition.

scale is important it is obviously possible for real wages to differ greatly between large free-trade areas and small ones, even with the same relative endowments of productive factors.   And while it may have been rash of me to draw a moral concerning the worth of emigration from Europe out of an abstract simplified model, I must still record the view that the more realistic deviations from constant returns to scale and the actual production functions encountered in practice are likely to reinforce rather than oppose the view that high standards of life are possible in densely populated areas such as the island of Manhattan or the United Kingdom.

There is no iron-clad a priori necessity for the law of diminishing marginal productivity to be valid for either or both commodities.[1] In such cases the usual marginal conditions of equilibrium are replaced by inequalities, and we have a boundary maximum in which we go the limit and use zero of one of the inputs in one industry. If it still could be shown that one commodity is always more labour intensive than the other, then the main theorem would probably still be true.   But it is precisely in these pathological cases that factor intensities may become alike or reverse themselves, giving rise to the difficulties discussed in my earlier footnote on p. 188.

In conclusion, some of these qualifications help us to reconcile results of abstract analysis with the obvious facts of life concerning the extreme diversity of productivity and factor prices in different regions of the world.   Men receive lower wages in some countries than in others for a variety of reasons : because they are different by birth or training ; because their effective know-how is limited and the manner of their being combined with other productive factors is not optimal ; because they are confined to areas too small to develop the full economies of scale ; because some goods and materials cannot be brought to them freely from other parts of the world, as a result of natural or man-made obstacles ; and finally because the technological diversity of commodities with respect to factor intensities is not so great in comparison with the diversity

---

[1] A " Pythagorean " production function of the form $F = \sqrt{L^2 + T^2}$ is an example of such a homogeneous function with increasing marginal productivity. So long as neither factor is to have a negative marginal productivity, *average* product must not be rising; but this is quite another thing. Surprisingly enough, the production possibility curve may still be convex with increasing marginal productivity. I have been asked whether any essential difference would be introduced by the assumption that one of the commodities, such as clothing, uses no land at all, or negligible land. Diminishing returns would still affect food as more of the transferable factor is added to the now specific factor of land ; but no essential modifications in our conclusions are introduced.

of regional factor endowments to emancipate labourers from the penalty of being confined to regions lacking in natural resources. In the face of these hard facts it would be rash to consider the existing distribution of population to be optimal in any sense, or to regard free trade as a panacea for the present geographical inequalities.

PAUL A. SAMUELSON

Massachusetts Institute of Technology.

69

A Comment on Factor Price Equalisation

All economic analysis needs careful auditing ; hence, nothing but good can come from Mr. Pearce's careful examination of the arguments bearing on factor equalisation. His important points seem to me to be the following : (1) production functions may differ in different regions ; (2) even in the two-factor two-good case of constant returns to scale and non-specialisation, the two goods may change their " relative factor intensities," food at one part of the production function being labour intensive, but clothing being labour intensive at another part ; (3) where there are more than two goods and factors, the cases where factor prices fail to be equalised increase in number and importance.

1. The first of these points seems to me to be very important on empirical grounds. By convention, we can assume identical production functions through supposing that different regions contain different proportions of such nebulous factors as " effective know-how " and so forth ; but in adopting such a convention, we are explaining nothing and possibly obscuring a great deal. At the close of my 1948 *Economic Journal* paper, I expounded on the view that the assumption of identical production functions is often a dangerous one to make, and I have nothing further to add except to re-stress the point and to refer the reader to similar statements in Viner's *Studies* and in his five Brazilian lectures (unpublished in English).

None-the-less, having admitted its inadequacies on this score, I still think the Heckscher-Ohlin factor-endowment analysis *does convey insight* into the forces shaping world trade ; and when someone like Viner goes to pains to show that similar analysis was in the minds of classical writers, I regard him as thereby reflecting credit upon our predecessors rather than implicating them as accomplices in a gigantic hoax ; and a century from now, I believe, writers will be using relative factor-proportions as an ingredient in their analysis of economic geography.

2. The third point, which is concerned with increasing the number of goods, and more importantly the number of factors relative to the number of goods, is also of unquestioned validity. Indeed, by adopting the proper conventions we can merge this with the case of non-identical production functions in the manner discussed above. Meade and Tinbergen have made important contributions to the many-factor many-goods case, as have Pearce and James. I hope myself, in an early issue of this REVIEW, to publish some of my notes on this problem.

3. In what I have termed his second point, Mr. Pearce is concerned with the problem of multiplicity of solution ; this problem was discussed in my 1949 paper, particularly in the twisty figure of p. 188, footnote 1. To me as a theorist, the problem of uniqueness or non-uniqueness of solutions is a very interesting deductive one. Around the early 1930's, Neisser, Zeuthen, Schlesinger, v. Stackelberg, v. Neumann, and Wald discussed this problem in terms of the Walrasian system of general equilibrium ; and the recent translation of Wald's paper by *Econometrica* is a valuable addition to the English literature. Anything that Mr. Pearce and Mr. James can contribute to our understanding of this phenomenon will be most welcome ; and the necessary condition of non-vanishing Jacobian, which is their last formula, is an important one.

In connection with the two-factor case, I have the impression that the phenomenon of goods that interchange their roles of being more labour intensive is much less important empirically than it is interesting theoretically. But whether or not I am correct in this, it appears to me from my re-reading of the literary arguments of Heckscher, Ohlin, Ellsworth, and my 1948 paper that they do contain in them the needed premise about factor intensities, which, if anything, they appear too willing to assume. Now I realise that one man's gnat is another man's camel, and that Mr. Pearce's standards of literary rigour may very properly be higher than my own. Therefore, in the second paragraph of Mr. Pearce's paper, where he is setting up what he regards as a fallacious literary argument, we should perhaps add the word " always " between " those goods " and " which." With this addition, the argument seems to me to be acceptable for the printed page—or for the classroom, where the whole discussion originally started.[1]

Cambridge, Massachusetts.   PAUL A. SAMUELSON.

---

[1] In a brief footnote for the interested specialist may be set down the minor changes in (1) the 1941 REVIEW OF ECONOMIC STUDIES paper with Stolper, in (2) the 1948 *Economic Journal* paper, and in (3) the 1949 *Economic Journal*, that I might be tempted to make if writing them anew. When (1) was reprinted in *Readings in Theory of International Trade* (1948), Stolper and I omitted the second complete sentence of p. 59 because we discovered that we had stubbed our toes in the manner attributed to Ellsworth in (2). The surrounding sentences we recognised to be inexact but we let them stand because they correctly portray the Ohlin-Heckscher view. The bracketed sentence added by me on p. 355 of the 1948 reprinting is too sweeping and unqualified. In (2) the third complete sentence on p. 170 is too sweeping and particularly needs qualifying in the many-factor case. In (2) the footnote on p. 175 is properly qualified by the footnote on p. 188 of (3) ; and the literary argument on p. 175 of (2) is made perfectly clear by the figures on p. 188 of (3). In (3), p. 193, the statement that almost equal factor intensities makes for uniform cost ratios and reduces the need for trade is correct ; but the possible implication, that this fails to impair the Ohlin-Heckscher point that goods mobility is an effective compensation for factor mobility, is false. To ensure that the equations on p. 188 of (3) have a single solution, the second footnote should have added to it the hypothesis that a diagonal element of $\triangle$ is one signed ; see Meade, op. cit., p. 133, fn. 1, for my restatement to meet this point. The possibility of increasing marginal productivity mentioned on (3)'s p. 196 and footnote can be ruled out if we are willing to make the " additivity assumption " of linear programming. The important empirical issue of identical production functions seems in no need of expansion ; the empirically less important, but logically interesting, case of changing factor intensities seems worthy of stress to theorists.

70

Prices of Factors and Goods in General Equilibrium

INTRODUCTION

1. The effects on factor prices of free international trade in goods is now fairly well understood in the case of few goods and factors.[1] This paper attempts to sketch briefly the general case of any number of goods and factors. At the same time a gap in the modern English literature can be partially filled by a succinct summary of the Walrasian statical model of general equilibrium in its competitive aspects. Purely technical details are briefly noted in the Mathematical Appendix, and more difficult sections of the text that can be skipped without penalty are starred.

2. I assume that each of n goods $X_1, \ldots, X_n$ is produced within a given country or region as a given function of the inputs devoted to it. Throughout I make the simplifying assumption most appropriate for viable perfect competition—namely constant-returns-to-scale or homogeneous production functions of the first order; under this strict assumption the composition of industry output among firms becomes indeterminate and of no importance, so that the factors can be thought of as hiring each other in a Darwinian process of ruthless natural selection which severely punishes any momentary deviation from the statical optimum. In the main text I limit myself to the classical case where outputs and inputs are distinct : actually, as is shown in the Mathematical Appendix, the *same results* would follow if I supposed, with Leontief and others, that each good requires in its production every *other good* as an input. Goods would then have a double function—as inputs as well as outputs, as intermediate as well as final goods. Moreover, the only way to characterise a " primary factor " in such a system would be by the fact that it cannot be produced and reproduced by a homogeneous production function.

For simplicity, then, I sharply distinguish inputs from outputs, and write the region's totals of r factors of production as $V_1, \ldots, V_r$. Each such input, such as V_j, is allocated among the n different industries, and we let V_{ij} stand for the amount of the jth input used by the ith industry. We can now write down the production functions for each industry in the following equivalent forms :

$$X^i \left(\frac{V_{i1}}{X_i}, \ldots, \frac{V_{ir}}{X_i} \right) = 1 \qquad (i = 1, 2, \ldots, n) \ldots \ldots \ldots \ldots \ldots (1)$$

$$X_i = X^i (V_{i1}, \ldots, V_{ir}), \ldots \ldots \ldots \ldots \ldots \ldots \ldots \ldots \ldots \ldots \ldots (1)'$$

---

[1] See Heckscher, E., " The Effect of Foreign Trade on the Distribution of Income," *Ekonomisk Tidskrift*, Vol. XXI, 1919, pp. 497–512, reprinted in *Readings in the Theory of International Trade*, Blakiston, Philadelphia, 1949. Ohlin, B., *Interregional and International Trade*, Harvard University Press, Cambridge, 1935. Stolper, W. F., and Samuelson, P. A., " Protection and Real Wages," REVIEW OF ECONOMIC STUDIES, Vol. IX (November, 1941), pp. 58–73. Reprinted in *Readings in the Theory of International Trade*, Blakiston, Philadelphia, 1949. Samuelson, P. A., " International Trade and the Equalisation of Factor Prices," *Economic Journal*, Vol. LVIII, June, 1948, pp. 163–84. Samuelson, P. A., " International Factor-Price Equalisation Once Again," *Economic Journal*, Vol. LIX, June, 1949, pp. 181–97. Tinbergen, J., " The Equalisation of Factor Prices between Free Trade Areas," *Metroeconomica*, Vol. I, July, 1949, pp. 40–47. Meade, J. E., " The Equalisation of Factor Prices: The Two-Country Two-Factor Three-Product Case," *Metroeconomica*, Vol. II, December, 1950, pp. 129–33. James, S. F., and Pearce, I. F., " The Factor Price Equalisation Myth," THE REVIEW OF ECONOMIC STUDIES, Vol. XIX (2), No. 49, 1951–52, pp. 111–20. See also P. A. Samuelson, " A Comment on Factor Price Equalisation," ibid., pp. 121–22. A. P. Lerner, " Factor Prices and International Trade," *Economica*, Vol. XIX, No. 73, February, 1952, pp. 1–15. See also I. F. Pearce, " A Note on Mr. Lerner's Paper," ibid., pp. 16–8.

all homogeneous functions of the first order. It will be convenient to use the usual symbols for " coefficients of production " $a_{ij} = V_{ij}/X_i$, and the reader can think of these as the input requirements for one unit of output ; (1) completely summarises the production function since it gives us the shape of one equal-product contour, and simply by changing scale we can get any other production configuration.

Some typographical errors in Walras have led to considerable confusion concerning the equivalence of (1) and (1)′, and there have been unwarranted adverse comparisons of his views with the rather confused views of Pareto relative to production and marginal productivity. I should mention explicitly that (1) makes no assumptions concerning the smoothness of the production surface : e.g. if $X^i =$ minimum of $(V_{i1}/\overline{a}_{i1} \ldots ., V_{ir}/\overline{a}_{ir})$, we have the early-Walras, Wieser, Cassel, Leontief case of fixed-proportions and so-called constant coefficients of production, the $\overline{a}$'s being the technological constants—or, strictly speaking, the constants of minimum requirement, since we may have more of an input without physical penalty.

THE LAW OF DIMINISHING RETURNS

3. If the production functions are everywhere smooth, then marginal productivities can be defined in the usual manner as partial derivatives $\partial X_i/\partial V_{ij}$. In terms of these the usual law of diminishing returns may be stated : e.g. certain curvatures or second derivatives are negative, and the same must be true for certain combinations of such terms. In common-sense terms we are assuming :

> Successive equal increments of any input or of any composite dose of inputs must *never* give rise to increasing increments of final output.

Note that this is supposed to hold *from the very beginning* and not simply after a certain stage. Note, too, that certain composite dose changes—such as varying all factors together must result in *non-increasing* returns but may result in the border-line case of constant returns rather than in strictly decreasing returns.

*4. We may simply assume that this generalised law of diminishing returns is an observed empirical hypothesis or we may try to deduce it from another empirical hypothesis that may seem more immediately plausible.

> Alternative hypothesis : We can always *independently* carry on production in two separate processes and there will not be any necessary " external " inter-action between these processes that prevents us from getting as a total *the sum* of their separate outputs.

Like the assumption of constant-returns-to-scale this is an empirical hypothesis rather than a truism ; not only are both of these hypotheses conceptually refutable, but in addition there is considerable empirical evidence, in connection with technology and the breakdown of perfect competition, that in large realms of economic life these are poor hypotheses to make. Together, our hypotheses can be expressed :

$$X^i \,(V_{i1}' + V_{i1}'', \ldots ., V_{ir}' + V_{ir}'') \geqq X^i \,(V_{i1}', \ldots ., V_{ir}') + X^i \,(V_{i1}'', \ldots ., V_{ir}''),$$

the equality sign necessarily holding if V_{ij}' and V_{ij}'' differ only in scale. This assures what the mathematician calls convexity of the production surface. In connection with some confusions in the literature between laws of diminishing *average* productivity and laws of diminishing *marginal* productivity, let me emphasise that this formulation definitely refers to the marginal version. But, because of the constant-returns-to-scale and no-over-saturation assumption, there is also implied diminishing average productivity to any composite dose that does not include *all* the really-productive inputs.

CONDITIONS OF EQUILIBRIUM FOR FACTOR ALLOCATION

5. If competition is perfect, and if factors are perfectly mobile between industries within a region, then equilibrium requires that the *value marginal productivity* of a factor (which is the good's price times $\partial X_i/\partial V_{ij}$) must be equal in every line where it is actually used, this common value being its market wage. Denoting commodity prices by $p_1, \ldots, p_n$ and factor prices by $w_1, \ldots, w_r$, we have as our conditions of equilibrium :

$$w_j \geqq p_i \partial X^i (a_{i1}, \ldots, a_{ir})/\partial V_{ij} \quad (i = 1, 2, \ldots, n) \text{ and } (j = 1, 2, \ldots, r) \ \ldots\ldots(2)$$

$$p_i \leqq a_{i1}w_1 + a_{i2}w_2 + \ldots + a_{ir}w_r \ \ldots\ldots\ldots\ldots\ldots\ldots\ldots\ldots\ldots\ldots\ldots\ldots(2)'$$

Note that the inequality signs can be disregarded if every good is actually being produced and if every factor is actually being used by every industry. However, if a good is not being produced at all, its unit cost may exceed the market price ; hence, the inequality sign can hold in (2)' only if $X_i = 0$. Similarly, the value marginal productivity of a factor may fall short of its market wage, but then it will not be used ; hence, the inequality sign in (2) can hold only where $V_{ij} = 0$. Note, too, that any marginal productivity is an intensive magnitude dependent only upon relative proportions and not upon extensive scale ; that is why we can denote it in terms of the a's rather than the V's, if we want to. Finally, note that (2)', which says that price cannot exceed unit cost of production, cannot be regarded as an additional condition to all that have gone before. Actually, if (1) holds and if (2) everywhere holds, then (2)' must assuredly hold and it is redundant to list it separately. Why ? Because the assumptions of scale about (1) imply the truth of Euler's theorem on homogeneous functions ; this in turn assures us that the separate value marginal products add up to exhaust all the revenue, so that (2)' is already implied by all the marginal conditions of (2). Alternatively, we can for one last residual factor omit the marginal conditions of (2) and deduce from (2)' what its " rent " must be, and then from Euler's theorem we would know what its marginal product must be. To put all this mathematically, for any i we can multiply each jth equality in (2) by a_{ij}, then sum them, and then from (1)'s Euler theorem deduce (2)'. It is to be emphasised that the inequalities in (2) and (2)' will never vitiate this dependence ; if a factor is not used in an industry, we lose its equation in (2), but its a also becomes zero in (2)', etc.

By themselves, equations (1) and (2) are incomplete and are clearly insufficient to determine the final position of general equilibrium. For one thing, (1) and (2) are purely intensive, never telling us anything at all about the extensive scales of any process. For another, we have said nothing about factor endowments or supply, and nothing about tastes with respect to goods and services. Even a rough count of the number of unknown X's, V's, a's, p's and w's will show : to get a determinate system we must adjoin, to the $n + nr$ independent conditions of (1) and (2), new relations—such as domestic demands for goods and supplies of factors, or international prices, etc. Depending upon what new relations we adjoin, we end up with different versions of general equilibrium or of international trade theory ; so we can consider various possibilities in turn.

FROM FACTOR PRICES TO COMMODITY PRICES : THE CLASSICAL CASE

6. Suppose we took the w's as somehow prescribed to us. Then it would be child's play to deduce what commodity prices must be. Certainly Adam Smith in Book I of the Wealth of Nations had proceeded this far and beyond, and every thinking man since antiquity must have had a roughly correct notion of the process. In the simplest

case where the a's are all constants, (2)′ alone gives us the conditions for competitive prices. In the general case of continuous or discontinuous substitutability, the conditions of minimum costs of production, as embodied in (2) or in more general inequalities, serve to determine optimal sets of a's and from this the restriction on competitive prices follow.

We can note one peculiar feature of this unilateral determination of commodity prices from factor prices : doubling all factor prices cannot make any substantive change in best factor proportions and hence must exactly double the competitive costs of producing every good. This shows the homogeneity " dualism " between prices and quantities. Just as the scale of goods is left undetermined by (1) and (2), so, too, is scale of prices left a matter of indifference.

Now one interpretation of the classical writers is to assume that they had in mind a unilateral specification of factor prices or w's. These were supposed to come from broad margins of supply or " disutility " : e.g. the minimum of subsistence or comfort determining population growth of labour ; the effective interest rate at which people cease to save, etc. However, note that if you take the w's as given in money terms, there will result money p's. Therefore, the system itself will determine your " real w's," and it is surely these that even a classical writer would want to specify in advance rather than trivial monetary levels. But, without knowing technology, you simply *cannot* specify all real w's arbitrarily : the result may simply not be feasible or may be grossly conservative.

This was dimly realised by the classical writers and explains why they had to single out a resource such as land and treat it differently from the other factors. Instead of specifying a broad margin remuneration which land must earn, Malthus and the classicists would specify its total quantity as given by nature. (The varying *qualities* of land was an empirical and analytic red-herring that both helped and hindered the classical writers' basic understanding.) In this case you can hope to specify the real remuneration of all the remaining factors : if you prescribe a higher real wage than can ever be produced by any labour-land combination, you will end up with race-suicide and a depopulated island ; if your specified real w's are simultaneously feasible at some level, then the economic process is feasible and can be expected dynamically to grow up to the point where the real w's become exactly equal to their prescribed figures. At this point of stationary equilibrium, there is no reason why the w for land, generated by equations (1) and (2) and by the adjoined real w's for all non-land factors and the adjoined inelastic supply of land, should be zero. Generally, it will be positive and there will be a *well-determined residual rent* for land. It can be proved that all this will be as true in the cases of fixed proportions or discontinuous substitutability as it will be in the case of smooth marginal productivities ! Many, perhaps most, versions of the classical theory are logically faulty, often containing too many residuals so that the system is undetermined. But it is wrong to think that there is not a valid (albeit empirically bizarre) version of the classical system.

From the standpoint of interregional trade theory, a more realistic application of the unilateral theory of w's determining p's can be found. Imagine one small firm or region imbedded in a great world, and with factors mobile between the rest of the world. Then all w's will be given, presumably in actual money terms, to this firm or region and (1) and (2) show its determinate responses : if the p's are also given, the inequalities will determine the pattern of specialisations ; if p's are not given, the equalities show the possible p's at which production can take place. This is a partial equilibrium aspect of the more general equilibrium.

SMALLNESS OF INDUCED CHANGES IN METHODS

*7. Before leaving the effects of w's on p's, I must briefly call attention to a fairly remarkable phenomenon concerning substitution in the Walras-Clark marginal productivity set-up. If the coefficients of production a_{ij} were constants, as in Walras' first edition of the *Elements* in the 1870's, then it would be very easy to predict the effects on the p's of any given change in the w's. When the a's change with the w's, we would be tempted at first glance to think that a similar prediction as to the rate at which any w_j will be inducing change in each p_i would be very difficult ; we would suspect that the resulting price changes will depend upon the substitutions that changing w_j makes mandatory. This first thought would actually be wrong—because of a fairly remarkable " envelope theorem " of what I call, in *Foundations of Economic Analysis*, the Wong-Viner type.

*8. Let us plot the relation between any p_i and any change in w_j from some previous equilibrium configuration. We may make two such plots : the first holding the a's strictly constant as in the Walras-Wieser theory, and the second letting the a's vary in an optimal way so as to keep costs down to a minimum. These curves will, of course, give the same p_i at the equilibrium point prior to any change in w_j ; but elsewhere, it is obvious that the varying a's must give us lower unit costs and a lower curve ; hence, the two curves must touch but not cross, and must, therefore, be tangential with equal slopes $\partial p_i / \partial w_j$ at the equilibrium point. This tangency means that we can always infer from the observed a's what the effects of a given small change in w will be on the p's, treating the a's as if they were constants. The substitution effects are of a higher order of smallness, influencing curvatures rather than first-order slopes.[1]

FROM COMMODITY PRICES TO FACTOR PRICES : THREE CASES

9. Returning to the quest for new conditions to complete those of (1) and (2), we consider what happens when the p's are adjoined as arbitrary prescribed constants. To go from commodity prices to factor prices is much more difficult than to go from factor to commodity prices. We must now distinguish three cases : the number of goods (i) equal to, (ii) greater than, or (iii) less than the number of factors ; i.e. $n = r$, $n > r$, and $n < r$. Also we shall first assume that the prescribed p's are not such as to cause specialisation with production of some goods becoming zero, thereby vitiating some of (2)'s equalities.

Case (i) : *Equal Goods and Factors.* Together (1) and (2) represent $nr + n$ independent relations to determine the nr unknown a's plus the r unknown w's. With $n = r$ and with the p's given to us (say, by international markets), we can hope for a determinate system in which the a's and the factor prices, $w_1, \ldots, w_r$, are uniquely determined. Of course, it is not always enough to compare the number of our equations with the number of our unknowns : the *quality* of our equations as well as their quantity is important in determining whether the relevant schedules intersect at least once and only once.

Later in connection with the discussion of factor intensities, I shall specify in detail a set of conditions sufficient to achieve uniqueness, so no more need be said here concerning the nature of the equations. But it is to be noted that the equalisation of factor prices between countries as a result of free trade between them is implied by (1) and (2) and our assumptions. This is rather a remarkable phenomenon : without mentioning factor endowments of the country or the scale of production of any good, we have uniquely determined its factor prices from knowledge of its commodity

[1] See Section 3 of the Mathematical Appendix, and *Foundations*, p. 66.

prices alone. Thus, if two different countries have the same production functions, and if they do produce in common as many different goods as there are factors, and if the goods differ in their " factor intensities," and if there are no barriers to trade to produce commodity price differentials, then the absolute returns of every factor must be fully equalised !

Case (ii) : *More Goods than Factors*. What happens if we consider the case where $n > r$? Now (1) and (2) give us $n - r$ equations *in excess* of the number of our unknowns. The situation is apparently over-determined. We seem to be imposing more conditions than the data can adjust themselves to. Something must apparently give. If the commodity prices are truly given to us in a completely arbitrary manner, it can be demonstrated that the system will then show a wisdom in deciding what commodities should *cease to be produced altogether*! Thus, the unit costs of food might turn out always to be higher than the unit costs of clothing. If, none the less, we insist upon imposing equal prices for the two goods, then by the same reasoning involved in the Ricardian theory of comparative costs it can be shown that competition will act so as to cause the more expensive commodity, food, to be not produced at all : the equality between the price of food and its domestic cost is now replaced by the inequality stating that for any good, price can be less than unit and marginal cost provided that it is not produced at all. In the case of each industry that shuts down, we, of course, lose as many marginal productivity conditions in (2) as there are zero inputs.

Generally speaking, therefore, we can expect that when more than r commodity prices are given to us perfectly arbitrarily, there will result complete specialisation in a number of industries, with the remaining number shut down completely. (Indeed, with the right factor intensities, it is possible for all but one industry to shut down completely.) However, if commodity prices are not given to us arbitrarily, but are determined by international trading between countries with the same production function as ours and with factor endowments not too different from ours, then there is a *presumption* that the international commodity prices will be such as to permit us to produce something of at least r different goods. If this should be true, then the reasoning of the previous section, where the number of goods and factors were equal, again permits us to infer complete equalisation of factor prices.

10. But with complete equalisation of factor prices here and abroad, an even stronger statement can be made : there is now no reason why in our own country we should not produce something of *every* good. What the final scales of production will be cannot, of course, be told until we say something about factor endowments. But a little reflection will suggest that whatever be the world endowment of factors, so long as factor prices have been everywhere equalised, and as long as the number of goods exceeds the number of factors, and as long as we strictly adhere to the assumption of zero transport costs—then there will be a considerable *zone of indifference* as to how production of different goods is allocated between different regions ; there are no longer *any* differences in comparative advantage, and to the extent that there exists more than one way to produce any desired world total of all goods, there will necessarily be an inessential indeterminacy of the production pattern. If we introduced ever-so-little transport costs, this indeterminacy might disappear.

11. We may summarise the case of more goods than factors by saying that an apparent over-determinacy in our equations and unknowns will resolve itself under competition by having certain industries shut down, taking with them the extra number of equations. On the other hand, if commodity prices are not given to us in a perfectly arbitrary fashion, but are determined elsewhere by cost of production, then the over-determinacy may resolve itself by virtue of the fact that the prices of

$n - r$ of the goods will already have adjusted themselves to the prices of any r goods. In this case, our country can be expected to produce at least r goods in common with the rest of the world and thus to achieve full factor price equalisation. Just how many goods we will produce in addition to these r goods cannot be determined without knowing our factor endowments. And at the world level there is an inessential indeterminacy of the exact geographical production pattern, since with equal factor prices everywhere there are no longer any differences in comparative costs, and there will usually be $n - r$ degrees of freedom in the geographical pattern of any given world totals to be produced.[1]

Case (*iii*) : *More Factors than Goods.* When $n < r$, we have in some ways the most interesting analytical case. Factor prices then will usually *not* be equalised. In fact, at first glance, it would seem that our equations are less than our unknowns by at least $r - n$ so that the equilibrium is under-determined. But our intuition tells us that something determinate must actually happen in any economy that faces given international prices for all goods. Our difficulty is resolved by the fact that although equations (1) and (2) are not sufficient to determine all our unknowns, once we go on to add the equations relating to factor endowments, the situation will then determine itself.

We could write total factor endowments for a country as a function of all prices of goods and services ; but it will be simpler for the present purpose to consider the case where all such supply functions are completely *inelastic* so that $V_1, \ldots, V_r$ can be regarded completely as constants. Our new equations are :

$$\Sigma V_{ij} = a_{1j}X_1 + a_{2j}X_2 + \ldots + a_{nj}X_n = V_j, \qquad (j = 1, 2, \ldots, r) \quad \ldots \ldots (3)$$

expressing the fact that all non-free factors must be fully employed. If a w_j becomes zero, we can replace the $=$ sign by $\leqslant$ in the jth equation.

With (3) we have added n X's as new variables, but we have also added r new equations ; so we have exactly $r - n$ surplus equations to make up for the $r - n$ deficiency of (1) and (2). Or to put the same thing in a different way : together (1), (2) and (3) are $n + nr + r$ independent relations to determine the $nr + r + n$ unknown a's, w's and X's. Hence, regardless of the relative magnitudes of n and r, the equilibrium would seem to be determinate once the p's are prescribed.

However, in the present case where $n < r$, the intensive relations of (1) and (2) do have to be taken *in conjunction* with the scale or extensive relations of (3), with this result : the equilibrium values of the w's will certainly depend upon the factor endowments or V's, so two differently-endowed regions can face the same international commodity prices and still end up with different factor prices. Within the same region as we add more of any one factor such as labour, even if the region is too small to affect world prices, we may now expect the corresponding factor price to fall. (This is in contrast to the case where $n = r$ and where an increase in any one factor does not depress its price so long as (1) commodity prices all remain unchanged and (2) all goods continue to be produced in some amount, with changes in the relative importance of the different industries providing the only needed substitutions : e.g. when $n = r$ and we add labour, the importance of labour-intensive goods increases and this absorbs all the increase in labour with no change in factor proportions within

---

[1] For those who like to think geometrically it can be said that our equations define a production-possibility or transformation locus $T(X_1, \ldots, X_n, V_1, \ldots V) = 0$, which tells us the maximum we can get of any good when all other goods and all inputs are prescribed. This locus has nice convexity properties and its partial derivatives are proportional to marginal cost-ratios and marginal productivities. Given a trading ratio from abroad, our country will be forced by competition into tangency between this locus and the trading plane. With $n > r$, there will necessarily be flat planes and straight lines on the convex locus ; and as with Ricardo, there will not be a unique tangency when the international trading ratio is exactly equal to one of these constant-cost ratios.

any industry being at all needed, and consequently there will be no diminishing returns to labour within a broad range.)

This non-equalisation of factor prices when there are more inputs than outputs is intuitively reasonable : if more capital in America made both labour and land twice as productive in the food and clothing industries as in the corresponding industries in Europe, the same food-clothing price-ratio would prevail in the two regions but with a lower American interest rate and higher wage and rent level.

OVER- AND UNDER-DETERMINACY

12. Now that we have written down the combined system (1), (2) and (3), we are able to throw additional light on the indeterminacy and apparent over-determinacy that enters when $n > r$.

In this case consider only those equations of (1) and (2) that hold for r rather than the full n of the industries. Together these are seen to be $r + r^2$ equations in $r^2 + r$ a's and w's, so that this subset can be expected to determine itself. But with *all* factor prices having been determined in this subset, the unit cost of production of every one of the remaining goods is also determined. If the prices of these goods were really prescribed at random and in an arbitrary fashion, they can hardly be expected to equal these unit costs : hence, the equations of (1) and (2) are over-determined and inconsistent, having so to speak $n - r$ *negative degrees of freedom*. It is true that (3) seems to possess $n - r$ positive degrees of freedom ; but these *cannot* be used to cancel out the over-determinacy.

13. There are different possible escapes from this simultaneous over- and under-determinacy. The first escape applies when prices are prescribed from abroad completely arbitrarily. As in the Ricardian theory of comparative advantage, the competitive system will then abandon those goods whose unit costs of production exceed the world-prescribed price. Thus $n - r$ industries will shut down, taking with them the surplus $n - r$ equations of (2).

The reader may wonder what will happen if it should turn out that the price of some one of the remaining $n - r$ goods were to be *greater* than the unit costs of production as determined from the factor prices set in the r industry subset. The answer in that case must be that we picked in the first place the *wrong set* of r goods that will actually be produced. Again, the theory of comparative advantage (or more precisely what is to-day called the mathematical theory of " linear programming ") guarantees that the *best* r goods will always be produced—best in the sense of maximising the total value of national product $p_1 X_1 + \ldots + p_n X_n$. It will then follow that for the remaining $n - r$ goods which cannot be produced, the p's must all exceed the unit costs of production.

Note that this pattern of optimal specialisation, which succeeds in getting rid of the over-determinacy in (2) does at the same time also get rid of the under-determinacy of (3). This is because in (3) we must set equal to zero the $n - r$ X's corresponding to the shut-down industries, leaving us with r equations in the remaining r unknown X's.

A still different escape from the over-determinacy dilemma applies when from r of the prescribed prices, it turns out that we are able to predict correctly the other $n - r$ in conformity with calculated costs of production. If all p's could be thought of as being drawn from an urn at random, this agreement of prediction would be a very singular case indeed. But if our country is imbedded in a world rather like itself and not differing too much in factor proportions from itself, then this singular case is likely to be the rule rather than the exception. (This can be proved rigorously by considering the full international conditions of equilibrium when factor endowments are the same abroad and at home, and then by considering the same relations as we let the factor endowments *gradually* differ from each other. Until they differ so much as to necessitate a pattern of world specialisation in which some industries in some country or countries shut down completely, the commodity prices of $n - r$ goods will be dependent upon those of r goods.)

In this singular case where $n - r$ p's are dependent upon r p's, our extra $n - r$ equations in (2) cease to be inconsistent and we are no longer plagued with over-determinacy. But this time in making our escape from over-determinacy, we have not at the same time been relieved of the concomitant indeterminacy of $n - r$ degrees of freedom in (3). But as Meade and our earlier literary discussion showed, this residual indeterminacy is intrinsic and should not disappear. For with factor prices equalised both here and abroad, we are now in the Ricardian case of strictly equal advantage, and so there is a broad zone of indifference as to the division of production between different regions. Within any country there is more than one configuration of X's that will maximise the value of the national product and also keep employment of all resources full at the well-determined equilibrium factor prices. While the division between different countries is indeterminate, the world-wide totals may be well-determined by the full conditions of equilibrium : only there are many different ways of reaching this same world-wide total.

FACTOR INTENSITIES AND STRICT DETERMINATENESS

14. I have now completed the survey of the interrelations between commodity and factor prices in the general case of any number of factors and goods. The results seem to depend in a very essential way upon the exact relation of n to r. The thoughtful reader will no doubt be somewhat worried by this result ; for after all, the number of commodities or of factors is not always such a definite thing. If we wished, we might call blue-eyed people different factors from brown-eyed ones and simply by reclassification make r go from less than to greater than n. Or we could call all autos with even-number serial listings a different good from those with odd-numbers, and thereby change the relation of n to r. Moreover, it is possible that Nature has already done one of the above things. From a production viewpoint two quite different commodities might turn out to have the same a's or to require the same proportions of inputs. Or two apparently different inputs might turn out to be perfect substitutes for each other in every line.

It is clear then that $n = r$ is not really enough to guarantee equalisation of factor prices ; and this was pointed out in some of my earlier papers. It was also shown that *differences in factor intensities of the different goods* was a crucial part of the rigorous proof in the two-input two-output case.

15. I must now examine carefully the *quality* as well as the quantity of the equilibrium equations to see if they do indeed determine a unique solution. This can be a delicate mathematical task, and I shall be content to give overly-strong sufficiency conditions for a unique equilibrium in the case of $n = r$, and where all production relations have smooth regular properties. The details of the proof may be omitted by the non-specialist and are relegated to the Mathematical Appendix, Section 3.

Theorem of Determinateness : If $n = r$, and if for all w's, we have a numbering of the goods and factors for which

$$a_{11} \neq 0, \quad \begin{vmatrix} a_{11} & a_{12} \\ a_{21} & a_{22} \end{vmatrix} \neq 0, \dots, \quad \begin{vmatrix} a_{11} & \dots & a_{1n} \\ & \cdot & \\ a_{n1} & \dots & a_{nn} \end{vmatrix} \neq 0,$$

then equations (1) and (2) have a unique solution for the w's in terms of the p's.

16. In the case of food and clothing and land and labour, this merely says that we should be able to recognise one of the goods as being always relatively labour-using and the other goods as being relatively land-using. In the case of many factors and goods the literary interpretation becomes more difficult, although in the very special case in which each factor had associated with it a single good in terms of which it was " especially important," an interpretation might be given.

It will be noted that the above conditions do rule out the case where more than one factor or more than one good are really exactly the same but hiding under different names. It also rules out more complicated cases of concealed identity between various bundles of goods or factors.

RECIPROCITY RELATIONS

*17. At this point also, two fairly interesting " reciprocity " or symmetry relations might be briefly indicated. First, there is the by-now standard case where increasing the amount of V_j, with X's and other V's held constant, will have *exactly the same effect* on w_k (as measured in any numeraire) as will a similar change in V_k on the price of V_j, w_j. A similar relation holds between two X's or between a change in an input and an output. Thus, along any country's optimum production-possibility locus, inputs and outputs are unambiguously either substitutes or complements to each other.

*18. A less well-known reciprocity relation holds when we ask for the effects on X_i or on w_j of a given change in prescribed p's or in prescribed V's. Because our equilibrium situation can always be thought of as maximising national product or of minimising its " dual," national expense, we can derive the identities :

National Product = National Expense

$$= N(p_1, \ldots, p_n, V_1, \ldots, V_r)$$

$$X_i = \partial N(p_1, \ldots, V_r)/\partial p_i \qquad , (i = 1, 2, \ldots, n)$$
$$w_j = \partial N(p_1, \ldots, V_r)/\partial V_j \qquad , (j = 1, 2, \ldots, r)$$

and

$$\partial X_i/\partial p_k = N p_i p_k = N p_k p_i = \partial X_k/\partial p_i$$
$$\partial w_j/\partial V_k = N v_j v_k = N v_k v_j = \partial w_k/\partial V_j$$
$$\partial X_i/\partial V_j = N p_i v_j = N v_j p_i = \partial w_j/\partial p_i$$

The last of these states the conclusion : If an increase in a given factor such as land will cause a good like food to be increased in production within a country facing fixed international prices, then an increase in the relative price of food can be expected to raise the rent of that kind of land. The reader may give his own interpretation of the other relations.

FULL GENERAL EQUILIBRIUM

19. It is well now to drop the assumption of p's as being given and show how the p's as well as the V's are actually determined. Assuming that we deal with a " closed economy," we must now add to (1), (2) and (3) n new equations to help determine the n p's and r new equations to help determine the r V's. These new equations we get by aggregating the demands of all households for goods and by aggregating the supplies of all factors offered by households on the market-place. Within each family or household, there can be thought to go on a balancing and weighing of the ordinal desirability of different goods purchasable for the p's, and of different services saleable in the market-

place for the w's. We may take for granted the ordinal-utility-disutility or marginal-rates-of-substitution conditions that guarantee that the family is spending the money it earns from all the productive services it sells in the way most suited to its indifference curves—so that it no longer pays anyone to substitute butter for oil, strawberries for further work, and teaching for ditch-digging. The indifference contours between the X's and V's may in many cases have corners so that the generalised tangency conditions of maximum well-being may have to be expressed in terms of inequalities rather than marginal equalities. This is of no consequence : a well-determining set of inequalities plays the same logical role as a well-determining set of equalities.

20. Just as the family demands and supplies can be expressed in terms of all the p's and w's, so too can be their sum for the whole community—Veblenesque external consumption effects being ignored. And disregarding for every individual any possibility of saving for the future, so that his total consumption of X's equals in value his total provision of V's to the market, we can know in advance that a similar identity must hold for the totals in the market-place. It will simplify our task if we do not try to go behind the total demands and supplies in the market-place and concentrate simply on the well-determined totals. These can be written as the following functions :

$$X_i = D^i\ (p_1,\ \ldots,\ p_n,\ w_1,\ \ldots,\ w_r) \qquad (i = 1,\ 2,\ \ldots,\ n) \qquad \ldots\ldots\ldots(4a)$$

$$V_j = S^j\ (p_1,\ \ldots,\ p_n,\ w_1,\ \ldots,\ w_r) \qquad (j = 1,\ 2,\ \ldots,\ r) \qquad \ldots\ldots\ldots(4b)$$

where not all of these are independent functions, by virtue of the known identity (at all p's and w's) of earnings and expenditures, or $\Sigma p_i D^i = \Sigma w_j S^j$. Also, it is clear that changing all p's and w's in the same proportion will have no effects on any individual's choices and hence no effects on any of the totals : consequently the functions in (4) like those in (2) are homogeneous of the zeroth order in the p's and w's and our system can only be solved for relative values, or for p's and w's expressed in terms of any *numeraire* good whose price is by convention set equal to unity.

21. We are now in a position to make a final audit of our complete system. Equations (1) to (4) are equivalent in number to $n + nr + r + n + r - 1$. The minus one comes in because one of the equations in our system can be shown to be dependent on the rest and, therefore, redundant. This follows from the fact that each consumer and hence all consumers spend only what they earn, and because our assumption of constant-returns-to-scale in the production sphere does through Euler's theorem lead to the same equivalence. Thus, if we wish we can drop any one equation in either (4a) or (4b) and still predict what it would have told us from the rest of the equations. Walras (and Cournot before him in a special connection) noted this very important redundancy.

When we come to count the number of our unknowns—the a's, the w's, the p's, and the X's and V's—we find they are $nr + r + n + n + r$ in all: i.e. both a price and total quantity for each input or output and in addition the unknown best proportions in which the factors should be used.[1] This total is seen to be one greater than the total of our *independent* equations. But when we recall that all of our equations depend only on ratios of p's and w's, our perplexity and despair gives way to joy and wonder : we do have just as many independent equations as there are unknowns. (If we wish to make some non-homogeneous monetary assumption, such as $p_1 = 1$, or $w_r = 1$, or $\Sigma p_i X_i =$ some constant called MV or anything else, then we have an extra equation to determine all absolute prices rather than simply price ratios.)

---

[1] In his early work, Walras replaced the least-cost marginal conditions of (2) by the simpler conditions that all the a's are fixed constants. In the second edition of the late 1880's, he indicated that the a's are to be determined by least-cost conditions, and in the third and later editions he formally included the marginal conditions. Thus Walras ended up with all that is valid in the simplified marginal productivity theory of pricing.

LOCALISATION AND INTERNATIONAL TRADE

22. The time has come to consider explicitly the interrelations between two or more separate economies. There are a variety of ways by which we can split our system up into separate parts, with a geographical division being perhaps the most common. In accordance with the classical tradition, it is often said that we must assume that factors of production are (almost by definition of what we mean by an economic region or country) perfectly mobile within the country and perfectly immobile between countries. Especially in a world of nationalism (and where national boundaries have some correspondence with geographical discontinuities) there may be some small semblance of realism in this assumption. But few would deny that there is a great divergence in reality from such a strict assumption in real life, factors within a country are to an important degree immobile, and to some degree at least some factors are mobile between countries.

Fortunately most of the apparatus of international trade theory is *not* intimately dependent upon any special mobility assumptions. The same methods can be applied to an analysis of the trading relations and changes in well-being of groups within a country (such as men and women, Negroes and whites, or right-handed and left-handed people). One of the criticisms that might be made of traditional international trade theory is that it almost completely neglects the role of space as such, and that a separate theory of location has had to grow up parallel with it.

23. For the present purpose, one might introduce international trade by postulating a geographical location initially for all resources, along with certain data on the transport costs of moving each different good and resource between geographical points. The simplest preliminary assumptions along these lines is to make the transport cost of each resource infinite and of each good zero ; but there is no reason why we should not then go on to make more complex assumptions (such as domestic finished goods that are perfectly immobile, certain categories of factors that move freely, and specified transport costs or tariff barriers for a wide range of products).

In the simplest case where we break the world into two parts, each with arbitrary factor endowments not subject to change and each producing goods that move perfectly freely in international trade, our earlier analysis shows that within a considerable range of unequal geographical endowments, the configuration of equilibrium will be *exactly the same* as if there were no space problems : factor prices are the same everywhere, and world production is exactly the same as it would be if we were dealing with a single closed economy. All this follows under ideal conditions where the production functions are everywhere the same and where there are at least as many commodities produced in both regions as there are factors, the factor intensities of the commodities being quite different in comparison with the difference in factor endowments.

But if the factor endowments become very different, there will be substantive effects of location on pricing of the inputs and on production. One or both regions will begin to shut down certain industries completely, in accordance with comparative advantage as determined by all the conditions of technology and tastes. In effect we have doubled our problem : for each country a set of a's, X's, V's, p's and w's must be determined, taking into account the trading relations between the two countries.

24. In the simplest case, equations (1) describing technology apply to each country as before. For each country we have a set of relations like (2), but with each country's w's inserted ; with zero transport costs for X's, the same international p's may be inserted. For each country, we have a set of relations like those of (3), it being understood that the variables now relate to that country alone. Each country

has a set of demand and supply relations like that of (4a) and (4b), it being understood that the w's and other variables of that country enter into the functions.

But now it is no longer true that production and consumption of each good are equal within a country. If we continue to use X_i as the symbol for production, we must introduce a new symbol, C_i, to represent our new unknown consumption variable for any good in a particular country, and in equations (4a) it is the C's and not the X's that must be inserted. Of course we must somewhere find new equations to help us determine the new unknowns : these must come from the fact that for every good, the *world's* physical total of production must just balance the world's physical total of consumption ; and from the fact that for every country, there must be a value balance between total exports and total imports—or what is the same thing, a value balance between the total value of consumption and the total value of domestic production (as measured from the $\Sigma p_i X_i$ or $\Sigma w_j V_j$ aspect).

I shall use a superscript in front of each symbol to typify country 1, 2, . . ., k, . . ., m : thus we have such things as $^2a_{15}$, meaning by this the amount of the fifth input needed in the second country to produce a unit of the first good ; the reader can supply the meaning for $^2w_5$, $^ka_{ij}$, ^kX_i, ^kC_i, ^kV_j, ^kw_j, and finally p_i without a country designation. For each country we have nr unknown a's, $2r$ unknown factor amounts and prices, $2n$ unknown amounts of production and consumption of goods— or altogether $(nr + 2r + 2n) \times m$ unknowns. In addition there are n unknown world prices, it being understood that all p's can be thought of as ratios to the price of the *numeraire* good whose price is to be set equal to unity.

25. The independent equations sufficient to determine all of our unknowns may be briefly written down for each and every country :

$$X^i\left(^ka_{i_1}, \ldots, {}^ka_{ir}\right) = 1 \qquad (i = 1, 2, \ldots, n) \text{ and } (k = 1, 2, \ldots, m) \quad \text{..(1)}$$

$$^kw_j \geqq p_i X^i{}_j\left(^ka_{i_1}, \ldots, {}^ka_{ir}\right) \qquad (i = 1, 2, \ldots, n ; \ j = 1, 2, \ldots r) \text{ and}$$
$$(k = 1, 2, \ldots, m) \quad \ldots\ldots\ldots\ldots(2)$$

$$^ka_{1j}\,{}^kX_1 + \ldots + {}^ka_{nj}\,{}^kX_n \leqq {}^kV_j \qquad (j = 1, 2, \ldots, r) \text{ and } (k = 1, 2, \ldots, m) \quad \ldots(3)$$

$$^kC_i = {}^kD^i\left(p_1, \ldots, p_n, {}^kw_1, \ldots, {}^kw_r\right) \qquad (i = 1, 2, \ldots, n) \text{ and } (k = 1, 2, \ldots, m) \quad \text{..(4a)}$$

$$^kV_j = {}^kSj\left(p_1, \ldots, p_n, {}^kw_1, \ldots, {}^kw_r\right) \qquad (j = 1, 2, \ldots, r \text{ and } k = 1, 2, \ldots, m) \quad \ldots.(4b)$$

For the world as a whole we may add the relations :

$$^1C_i + {}^2C_i + \ldots + {}^mC_i = {}^1X_i + {}^2X_i + \ldots + {}^mX_i \qquad (i = 1, 2, \ldots, n) \quad \ldots\ldots\ldots(5)$$

and also the balance of payments equations for each country :

$$p_1\,{}^kC_1 + \ldots + p_n\,{}^kC_n = p_1\,{}^kX_1 + \ldots + p_n\,{}^kX_n \qquad (k = 1, 2, \ldots, m) \quad \ldots\ldots.(6)$$

Now it is clear that for each country equations (4) are so arranged in relationship to the previous equations that equations (6) will be automatically satisfied ; hence these are dependent and redundant and may be omitted. (Incidentally, if each right-hand term in (6) is subtracted from the corresponding left-hand term, the result will show that the algebraic total of the values of all imports must be zero, which is the more familiar form in which balances of international trade are usually presented.)

Because all of our equations are homogeneous of order zero in all p's and w's, we can only hope to solve for price ratios ; and hence we may add the *numeraire* equation to pin down the representation of our system :

$$p_1 = 1 \quad \ldots\ldots\ldots\ldots\ldots\ldots\ldots\ldots\ldots\ldots\ldots\ldots\ldots\ldots\ldots\ldots\ldots\ldots\ldots\ldots(7)$$

26. Let us now count our equations and unknowns. To determine our $(nr + 2n + 2r)(m) + n$ unknowns, we have in (1) to (5) $(n + nr + r + n + r)(m) + n$ equations. If we add (7) to this, we seem to have one too many equations. Alternatively, if we decide only to work with price ratios, we have one too few unknowns. Either

way we seem to be in trouble, facing an over-determined situation. The way out of the dilemma must by now be clear. Scrutiny of our system shows that if (1) to (5) holds, and if all but one of the commodities in (5) show a balance between total world production and consumption, then the remaining commodity cannot fail to be in balance. The interested reader may verify this in the general case or in the case of a few goods, factors and countries. With one of our equations dependent and redundant, our worries over the over-determinacy of the system are at an end.

27. Of course the quality as well as the quantity of our equations must be taken into account. It is for this reason that the inequality signs were included in (2) and (3). When comparative advantage or technology decree that the amount of some input is to be zero in some industry, we lose a marginal productivity equality, replacing it by the statement that the wage must not be less than the value of marginal productivity. Similarly, if supply and demand should cause a factor to become a free-good with zero w, we would no longer in (3) require more than that its sum in all uses should not exceed the total available. Within the production sphere we could perhaps rule out all indeterminacy if the production functions all had nice regular curvature properties, with every marginal productivity running the gamut from infinity to zero.

So long as we are no longer striving to prove the geographical equalisation of factor prices, it is no longer necessary to require that there be as many goods as factors, or that the goods differ in their factor intensities ; but if we do assume inelastic supplies of the factors and fixed coefficients of production, singular cases can arise in the production sphere where inelastic supplies may overlap with inelastic demands with a resulting indeterminacy of pricing. But contrary to what some of the older writers thought, the inequalities in our equations make it quite impossible that negative prices or negative production should ever result.

28. Our equations are not complete if we do not go beyond the production sphere. The demand-supply relations of (4) were shown by Walras and Marshall to be quite capable of intersection more than once, so that multiple equilibria are possible both in the domestic and international sphere. In terms of a rudimentary theory of dynamics, or the laws of motion that govern the way a system out of equilibrium behaves, we could distinguish between locally-stable and locally-unstable equilibrium points.

CONCLUSION

37. I need scarcely add the caution that the above description is of a very idealised, statical, competitive situation, where monetary considerations scarcely raise their ugly heads. Yet, both from the standpoint of insight into the nature of pricing and into the normative aspects of *laissez-faire* not here discussed, I think that this particular set of idealised assumptions has much to be said for it—not only for quasi-aesthetic reasons, but also for the light it casts on so many of the often-confused issues of economic theory.

Cambridge, Mass. PAUL A. SAMUELSON.

MATHEMATICAL APPENDIX

1. Equations (1) and (2) are conditions for minimum unit cost for each good. Omitting the i designation, we may write for a typical good :

Subject to $X(V_1, \ldots, V_r) = X$ or $X(a_1, \ldots, a_r) = 1$, and to given w's minimise $A = \Sigma w_j V_j / X = \Sigma w_j a_j$.

This minimum unit cost must depend uniquely on the w's and can be written $A = A(w_1, \ldots, w_r)$. Intuition assures us that this must be a continuous function of the w's ; also, since doubling all w's will make no substantive difference in methods, this must be a homogeneous function of order 1 of its variables, just as the production function is homogeneous in terms of its variables. A further dualism between the A and X functions is less intuitively obvious but nonetheless true : $A(w_1, \ldots, w_r)$ can be shown to be subject to the same " generalised law of diminishing returns " in terms of its variables as was described in the text with respect to the production functions. Indeed, it is easy to verify that the equilibrium correspondences between the w's and a's, which we may write as w_a or a_w, can be defined by the following dual-minimum problem to the above original one :

Subject to $A(w_1, \ldots, w_r) = A$, and given V's or a's, pick w's so as to minimise $\Sigma w_j V_j$ or $\Sigma w_j a_j$.

It can be shown that if the X contours are flat, as in the case of infinite substitutability where many alternative configurations are indifferent, then at the corresponding places on the A contours there will be corners ; and vice versa in a perfectly dual fashion. Nonetheless, regardless of lack of uniqueness or smoothness of the relations, for all observed optimum points, we always have $\Sigma \triangle w_j \triangle V_j \leqq 0$ and $\Sigma \triangle w_j \triangle a_j \leqq 0$. It can also be shown that at all points where the functions do not have the requisite smoothness to give a unique definition to partial derivatives such as $\partial a_k / \partial w_j$ or $\partial w_k / \partial a_j$, their ranges of indeterminacy are restricted to satisfy *reciprocity* relations that represent generalisations of the *integrability* conditions holding in the regular case.

In the case of a regular smooth interior minimum, to define $(V_1, \ldots, V_r, A)$ in terms of given $(w_1, \ldots, w_r, X)$ we have :

$$A \frac{\partial X(V_1, \ldots, V_r)}{\partial V_j} = w_j, \quad \begin{bmatrix} \partial V_k/\partial w_j & \partial V_k/\partial X \\ \partial A/\partial w_j & \partial A/\partial X \end{bmatrix} = \begin{bmatrix} A\partial^2 X/\partial V_k \partial V_j & \partial X/\partial V_k \\ \partial X/\partial V_j & 0 \end{bmatrix}^{-1} (1.1)$$
$$X(V_1, \ldots, V_r) = X$$

where $(\partial V_k/\partial w_j)$ must be negative semi-definite and is seen to be symmetric. The dual relations defining $(w_1, \ldots, w_r, X)$ in terms of $(V_1, \ldots, V_r, A)$ are :

$$X \frac{\partial A(w_1, \ldots, w_r)}{\partial w_j} = V_j = X a_j, \quad \begin{bmatrix} \partial w_k/\partial V_j & \partial w_k/\partial A \\ \partial X/\partial V_j & \partial X/\partial A \end{bmatrix} = \begin{bmatrix} \partial V_k/\partial w_j & \partial V_k/\partial X \\ \partial A/\partial w_j & \partial A/\partial X \end{bmatrix}^{-1}$$
$$A(w_1, \ldots, w_1) = A, \quad = \begin{bmatrix} X\partial^2 A/\partial w_k \partial w_j & \partial A/\partial w_k \\ \partial A/\partial w_j & 0 \end{bmatrix}^{-1} \ldots \ldots \ldots (1.2)$$

where similar reciprocity and semi-definiteness conditions hold in the dual.

2. The Wong-Viner envelope type theorem, that the changes in production resulting from changes in factor prices are of a smaller order than are the direct changes in unit cost of production as of fixed a's, is already proved by (1.2), since this says that $\partial A/\partial w_j = a_j$. A general proof of the phenomenon in question is given in *Foundations*, p. 34, equation (32). To reinforce the above two proofs, calculate $\partial \Sigma w_k a_k / \partial w_j = a_j + \Sigma w_k \partial a_k / \partial w_j = a_j + \Sigma w_k \partial a_j / \partial w_k = a_j + 0$, where the last term is

seen to vanish by virtue of Euler's theorem applied to the homogeneous function of order *zero* representing a_i and where the reciprocity relations have been utilised.

3. We may use the above result to calculate the Jacobian matrix of goods prices expressed in terms of factor prices, as given in (2)'. Confining ourselves to goods actually produced, and restoring the industry superscripts, we can re-write (2)' :

$$p_i = A^i (w_1, \ldots, w_r) \text{ and } \left[\partial p_i / \partial w_j \right] = \left[a_{ij} \right], \ i = 1, 2, \ldots, n \gtreqless r \ \ldots\ldots (3.1)$$

The problem of special interest to us is the following : when $n = r$ and the goods p's are given to us and we have one resulting set of non-negative w's as a solution to (2)' or (3.1), under what conditions can we be sure that this solution is *unique* and that there exists *no other* factor price solution ?

The problem of uniqueness of solution is mathematically a delicate and rarely discussed one. In the case of $n = 2 = r$, the solution will be unique if one good is *always* more " intensive " in its use of one of the factors ; as shown in my 1949 *Economic Journal* discussion, p. 188, n. 1, if the goods should ever exchange their relative factor intensities, multiplicities of solutions *must* result. In that same discussion, I gave as a mathematical sufficiency condition for uniqueness that the Jacobian determinant of the equations to be inverted must not vanish. I am indebted to A. Turing, a mathematician friend of Professor Pigou, for pointing out that this statement was faulty and it has since been corrected in the literature. Actually, the non-vanishing Jacobian and the usual version of the Implicit Function Theorem does not guarantee uniqueness of solution *in the large*, but only that multiple solutions—if they occur—will be locally isolated. Fortunately, the economics of the situation was clearer than my mathematical analysis ; because all the elements of the Jacobian represented inputs or a's, they were essentially one-signed ; and this condition combined with the non-vanishing determinant, turns out to be sufficient to guarantee uniqueness in the large.

There appears to be a slight gap in the mathematical literature. What is needed is a slight extension of the Implicit Function Theorem that will suffice to guarantee uniqueness of solution in the large in the case of any number of implicit equations. From the nature of the case, no convenient *necessary* and sufficient conditions seem possible. But a convenient set of *sufficient* conditions can be inferred from the usual proofs of the usual Implicit Function Theorem. I presume the theorem that I am about to state is not a new result, but I have not been able to find a reference to it in the mathematical literature.

Theorem : If there exists some re-numbering of the p's and w's so that the n implicit and differentiable equations $p_i = A^i (w_1, \ldots, w_n)$ have successive principal minors that are non-vanishing *for all* w's :

$$D_1 = \left| \partial A^1 / \partial w_1 \right| \neq 0, \ D_2 = \begin{vmatrix} \partial A^1 / \partial w_1 & \partial A^1 / \partial w_2 \\ \partial A^2 / \partial w_1 & \partial A^2 / \partial w_2 \end{vmatrix} \neq 0, \ldots, D_n = \begin{vmatrix} \partial A^1 / \partial w_1 & \ldots & \partial A^1 / \partial w_n \\ \cdot & & \cdot \\ \cdot & & \cdot \\ \partial A^n / \partial w_1 & \ldots & \partial A^n / \partial w_n \end{vmatrix} \neq 0,$$

then there cannot be a second w solution for given p's.

The proof is by mathematical induction. The theorem is certainly true in the simplest case of $n = 1$, since every function possessing a one-signed derivative must always have a unique inverse. If the theorem holds for $n = k$, it is not hard to show that it must hold for $n = k + 1$. For we may always solve the first k of our $k + 1$ equations for the first k w's in terms of $(p_1, p_2, \ldots, p_k, w_{k+1})$. Then substituting into the last equation and remembering that all the p's are known, we end up with a single implicit equation in w_{k+1} alone :

$$f(w_{k+1}) = 0, \text{ with } f'(w_{k+1}) = D_{k+1}/D_k \neq 0,$$

and hence with a *unique* solution. Thus, the proof by induction proceeds smoothly.

4. We may now investigate the consequences of dropping the assumption of no intermediate goods. With Leontief we may assume that every good may be needed in the production of every other good ; however, in contrast to the simpler versions of his system, we may entertain the possibility that there are more than one " primary " or non-reproducible-at-constant-returns factors ; as before, we shall assume $r \geq 1$ such primary inputs. As before we assume statical conditions so that none of the problems of capital and interest arise.

Some revisions of notation are desirable. As before $(X_1, \ldots, X_n)$ refer to *net* production of each of the goods actually available for consumption : since something of each good may be required as intermediate inputs used up in production of other goods, it is clear that the net output, X_i, of any industry will usually be less than the *gross* output, which we may call x_i, and which is what is actually given to us by the production function. To gain the advantages of the symmetrical Leontief notations, which treat inputs simply as if they were negative outputs, we may re-write what we have called $(V_1, \ldots, V_r)$ in terms of the new symbols $(-X_{n+1}, \ldots, -X_{n+r})$. Finally, our symbol for the amount of the jth good used in the production of the ith good is x_{ij}. To test his understanding of the new notation, the reader can verify that up until now we had been assuming that $x_{ij} = 0$ for $n \geq i$; also, that what we previously called a_{ij} would now be called $x_{i,\,n+j}/x_i$ and must not be confused with what we shall now define as a_{ij}, namely x_{ij}/x_i. We may now write down the production functions of any good in terms of *all* inputs, and then write down the amount of net product left over after subtraction of all used up intermediate goods.[1]

$$x_i = x^i(x_{i_1}, \ldots, x_{in}, \ldots, x_{i,\,n+r}), \quad (i = 1, \ldots, n), \text{ with } x^i(a_{i_1}, \ldots, a_{in}, \ldots, a_{i,\,n+r}) = 1$$
$$= 0 = x_{ij} \qquad\qquad , \quad (i = n+1, \ldots, n+r) \text{ and any } j$$

$$X_i = x_i - x_{1i} - x_{2i} - \ldots - x_{ni}$$
$$= x^i(x_{i_1}, \ldots, x_{in}, \ldots x_i,\,_{n+r}) - \overset{n}{\underset{1}{\Sigma}} x_{ji}. \quad\ldots\ldots\ldots\ldots\ldots\ldots\ldots\ldots (4.1)$$

Adhering to our previous assumptions concerning scale and diminishing returns, and re-writing what we called $(p_1, \ldots, p_n, w_1, \ldots, w_r)$ as $(p_1, \ldots, p_n, \ldots, p_{n+r})$, we may write down the same competitive equalities of marginal value product in every input use, previously given in (2) and (2'), in the new form :

$$p_i \frac{\partial x_i(a_{i_1}, \ldots, a_{in}, \ldots, a_{i,\,n+r})}{\partial x_{ij}} \leq p_j \; (i = 1, \ldots, n), \, (j = 1, \ldots, n, \ldots, n+r) \;\ldots (4.2)$$

$$p_i \leq A^i(p_1, \ldots, p_n, \ldots, p_{n+r}) = \overset{n+r}{\underset{1}{\Sigma}} a_{ij} p_i \;\ldots\ldots\ldots\ldots\ldots\ldots\ldots\ldots (4.2)'$$

As before, because of our homogeneous production functions, (4.2)' is redundant being implied by (4.1) and (4.2). The inequalities have the same interpretation as before. Note, too, that the minimum cost of production A^i of the ith good now depends upon *all* market p's, including probably its own p_i. Even if the a's were technological con-

---

[1] These equations represent a generalisation to any number of primary factors of the version of the Leontief system, admitting of substitutions, given in my Chapter VII of T. C. Koopmans (ed.), *Activity Analysis of Production and Allocation* (Wiley, New York, 1951). Note that C_i there is equivalent to X_i here and my functions x^i here are written as F_i there.

stants or already determined at their optimum levels, (4.2)' would involve a set of circular simultaneous equations for the p's. Only non-negative p's are admissible, and the invisible hand will guarantee that only that subset of goods will be produced which is compatible with non-negative prices. If there exists no such set—e.g. because every good requires more than one unit of itself in production, or indirectly requires so much of other goods and they in turn require so much of it that the same exceeding of unity and violation of the so-called Hawkins-Simon conditions results—then all production will shut down.

Actually, the marginal productivity conditions of (4.2) can be given two, separate but related, " optimising " interpretations : if we are given all p's arbitrarily and told to maximise $\Sigma p_j X_j$, where both algebraic goods and services are included, then (4.2) tells us what production methods are optimal ; of course, if the best methods will result in $\Sigma p_j X_j < 0$, all production will be zero ; if $\Sigma p_j X_j = 0$, then the final scale will be indeterminate until we fix one or more of the X's ; if $\Sigma p_j X_j > 0$, the best scale would grow indefinitely—until some X were given a finite limit or until some change in the arbitrarily prescribed p's were made.

A second optimising interpretation of the marginal productivity conditions is as follows : if we arbitrarily prescribe all but one X, some being prescribed at negative levels in accordance with their interpretation as primary inputs, then (4.2), with the right p's inserted as parameters or Lagrangean undetermined multipliers, represents a necessary and sufficient condition for the algebraic maximisation of the remaining X. For the case of $r = 1$, this was proved in *Activity Analysis* just cited, and the same reasoning holds for any r.

On the assumption that we can neglect the inequalities in (4.2), we can eliminate the Lagrangean prices, and write down the logical equivalent to (4.1) and (4.2) :

$$\frac{\partial x^1}{\partial x_{1i}}\frac{\partial x^i}{\partial x_{ij}} - \frac{\partial x^1}{\partial x_{ij}} = 0 \ (i = 2, \ldots, n) \text{ and } (j = 1, 2, \ldots, n, \ldots, n+r), \frac{\partial x^1}{\partial x_{11}} = 1. \ \ldots (4.3)$$

These relations are all independent of scale and can be thought of as restrictions on the n $(n + r)$ a's. Clearly (4.3) involves $(n + r)$ $(n - 1) + 1$ restrictions, and the homogeneous production functions of (4.1) involve n more restrictions. After a little algebraic manipulation and comparison, we find that we have $(r - 1)$ more unknowns than we have restrictions. We cannot, therefore, expect (4.3) and (4.1) by themselves would determine all the unknown a's. Only in conjunction with some specified tastes or amounts of all but one of the X's will we find the missing $(r - 1)$ equations.

The Leontief case of a single primary factor can now be put in its proper perspective. The essence of the " substitutability theorem " for the Leontief system boils down in the regular smooth case to this : for $r = 1$ and $r - 1 = 0$, we can hope from the marginal conditions of social efficiency alone to deduce a unique configuration of productive methods, independently of the final specified bill-of-goods items X_i. (See *Activity Analysis*, Chapters VII, VIII, IX, X.)

When $r = 0$, we have the earlier Leontief " closed " economy with no primary factors. Here $r - 1 = - 1$, and we seem to have *negative* degrees of freedom in (4.1) and (4.3). This corresponds to an *over-determined* situation, where there are more equations than unknown a's. The only way out of this dilemma—as Leontief has already indicated in the case of fixed a's—is to assume that the technological relations are *not* arbitrarily independent. On the contrary, (1) if *all* goods and services are readily reproducible out of each other, and (2) if only a finite bill of goods is to be producible out of a finite initial supply of goods and services so that stationary equilibrium is possible, then the different x^i functions must be such as to yield, for a sub-set of X's set equal to zero, at most zero *net* outputs of the other goods. This imposes a strong restriction on the rank of the Jacobian of our implicit equations for the a's. (Cf. W. Leontief, *Structure of the American Economy* (New York, 1951), 2nd edition, for the corresponding vanishing of the determinant of Leontief's closed-system a's.) In summary, for $r = 0$, we are saved from over-determinacy by the singularity and linear dependencies that must exist between the separate equations for a's, by virtue of the assumption of the possibility of a stationary equilibrium. Incidentally, as Leontief has indicated, the resulting system is completely undetermined with respect to scale—unless or until we bring in an open-end non-homogeneous element, such as population size or Engel's laws of tastes that do *not* show unitary income elasticities for all X's.

For $r > 1$, we have a striking confirmation that the inter-industry circular whirlpools do not in any way affect the conclusions of my main text. As an example, consider the remarkable " flatnesses " of the social transformation function that must hold when there are more goods than factors, as discussed in the footnote of Section 11. Why are we never permitted to name arbitrarily the costs of production of n goods when $n > r$? This would involve our setting $n - 1$ ratios of costs or prices arbitrarily, and if a new unique configuration of a's and w's (or remaining p's) were to correspond to these $n - 1$ arbitrary parameters, we would find ourselves with more than $r - 1$ degrees of freedom—by virtue of the postulate, $n > r$. This contradicts our count of the maximum number of degrees of freedom, which is $r - 1$.[1]

5. Aside from the counting of equations and unknowns, there is another and more basic way of seeing that there are but $r - 1$ degrees of freedom possible in any general equilibrium system. (Conceptually, therefore, we might hope to determine the maximum number of primary factors in any observed systems.) Independently of all smoothness and derivatives of the production functions, we can assert the following :

Theorem : If $(p_{n+1}, \ldots, p_{n+r})$ are all given, then subject to the relations,

$$p_i = \sum_1^{n+r} a_{ij} p_j$$
$$(i = 1, 2, \ldots, n)$$
$$x^i (a_{i_1}, \ldots, a_{in}, \ldots, a_{i, n+r}) = 1.$$

there exists one or more sets of best a's that will give a minimum cost $p_k = A^k$ of any one specified k good ; this minimum cost can be written as a continuous function $A^k (p_{n+1}, \ldots, p_{n+r})$, homogeneous of the first order and subject to the " generalised law of diminishing returns." Furthermore, a set of all the a's that minimises unit costs of one good will also minimise the cost of *each* other good. Where unique partial derivatives happen to be defined, Wong-Viner considerations require :

$$\left[\partial A^i / \partial p_{n+j} \right] = \begin{vmatrix} 1-a_{11} & -a_{12} \ldots & -a_{1n} \\ -a_{21} & 1-a_{22} \ldots & -a_{2n} \\ \cdot & & \cdot \\ -a_{n1} & -a_{n2} \ldots & 1-a_{nn} \end{vmatrix}^{-1} \begin{vmatrix} a_{1, n+1} \ldots & a_{1, n+r} \\ \cdot & \cdot \\ \cdot & \cdot \\ a_{n, n+1} \ldots & a_{n, n+r} \end{vmatrix} \quad ..(5.1)$$

which will be the product of two non-negative matrices, and its rank can never exceed r.

---

[1] The *actual* number may be less than this maximum number if special linear dependencies occur between the marginal productivities and a's. For example, suppose all goods had had *identical* production functions. Then instead of there being $r - 1$ degrees of freedom, there would turn out to be only 1 : all factors could in this singular case be grouped into a single composite " dose " of factors, giving us a Ricardo-Marx one-factor world.

Thus if $n > r$, we cannot specify $n - 1$ goods prices or cost ratios arbitrarily and expect all the goods to be produced and relative factor prices to be determinable by inverting the resulting equations. If $n = r$, it *may* be possible to infer a unique set of factor prices from a given set of goods, prices and costs ; sufficient conditions would be the existence of a numbering of goods and factors for which the leading principal minors of $\left[\partial A^i/\partial p_{n+j}\right]$ are all positive, exactly as in the case without inter-industry dependencies.

Most generally, we might imagine that some factors move freely in international trade and some goods do not. Out of the total of $n + r$ goods and services, we shall not expect absolute price equalisation between regions on the basis of less than half of $n + r$ prices being equalised by trade ; if *half or more* such prices are equalised by trade, the remaining ones will also be equalised provided that certain " constant-intensity " principal minors can be found.

6. The reader can also for the case of inter-industry dependencies derive all the dual relations and reciprocity relations discussed earlier. Also, he can verify that (3) becomes :

$$\sum_{1}^{n} x_i a_{ij} = x_j - X_j \qquad\qquad j = 1, 2, \ldots, n\,$$

$$\sum_{1}^{n} x_i a_{i,\,n+j} = 0 - X_{n+j} \qquad j = 1, 2, \ldots, r \ \ldots\ldots\ldots\ldots\ldots\ldots\ldots\ldots(5.2)$$

and that all the relations of (1) through (3), can be summed up in a transformation or efficiency locus :

$$T\,(X_1, \ldots, X_n, \ldots, X_{n+r}) = 0, \text{ with } p_i \text{ proportional to } \partial T/\partial X_i$$

and with scale being of no importance, and generalised diminishing returns holding. For any set of p's being given and quantities of the remaining variables being given, there will be a maximum value for ΣpX, where the summation is over the prescribed p's. This maximum value can be written as $V\,(p\,;\,X)$ where it is understood that no good ever has both its p and X specified. V is a continuous and homogeneous function of the first order in the p variables alone and in the X variables alone. The vector $\partial V/\partial p$ is proportional to the X's and $\partial V/\partial X$ is proportional to the corresponding p's. Just as the X's maximise V as of the production relations and given p's, the p's minimise V as of given X's and competitive price relations—so here is the case of a minimax or saddlepoint, with all the implied duals of linear programming theory. Moreover, associated with this V is a similar expression ΣpX where the summation now is over the indices *not* contained in the previous definition of V ; V plus the new complementary V always add up to a constant.

7. Still other analogies can be found with the duality and saddlepoint theorem of the type met with in the fields of linear programming and game theory.

1965 Postscript

The basic sufficiency theorem for uniqueness of equilibrium solution given in Appendix 3 was shown by Professor H. Nikaido of Osaka to be not quite correct. Hence, its application to factor-price equalisation in Section 15 needs modification. I am grateful to Professor Nikaido, and to Professor David Gale of Brown University, for proving how the theorem has to be modified.

If the determinants in Appendix 3 are all non-zero, we can, by a conventional change in signs, ensure that the naturally ordered $r \times r$ principal minors are all positive, or

$$D_r = |\partial A^i/\partial W_j| > 0 \qquad\qquad (r = 1, 2, \cdots, n)$$

In 1953, I thought that such positiveness was sufficient for uniqueness of solutions in the large. But Nikaido produced counter-examples to show that I did not allow for branches whose slopes approach zero at infinity. (Nikaido proved that if $[\partial A^i/\partial W_j] = B$ is a quasi-definite matrix, so that $\frac{1}{2}[B + B']$ is positive definite, then in any convex region of $[W_i]$ any solution is unique. Later, Gale proved that it is sufficient for uniqueness in any rectangular region of $[W_i]$ that *every* principal minor of B be everywhere there positive. See D. Gale and H. Nikaido, "The Jacobian Matrix and Global Univalence of Mappings," *Mathematische Annalen*, 1965.) To repair the 1953 treatment with least loss of face, I proposed the following replacement:

THEOREM OF UNIQUENESS IN THE LARGE: If

$$P_i = A^i(W_1, \cdots, W_n) \qquad\qquad (i = 1, \cdots, n)$$

has a solution $(W_i{}^0)$ corresponding to a given $P_i{}^0$, and a naturally ordered set of principal minors are, everywhere in the Euclidean n-space, bordered by two positive numbers

$$0 < m_r < D_r = |\partial A^i/\partial W_j| < M_i < \infty \quad (r = 1, \cdots, n)$$

then the solution $(W_i{}^0)$ is a unique function of $P_i{}^0$.

Professor Nikaido has confirmed this theorem with a proof; and he and I are preparing a joint paper showing, among other things, that if

$$0 < m_r < D_r = \left|\frac{\partial \log P_i}{\partial \log W_j}\right| = \left|\frac{W_j}{A^i}\frac{\partial A^i}{\partial W_j}\right| \quad (r = 1, \cdots, n)$$

factor-price equalisation is uniquely assured. Using the logarithms of all prices, we work over the whole Euclidean space.

Since $[\partial \log A^i/\partial \log W_j]$ is a stochastic matrix whose rows have elements adding up to unity because of economic homogeneity-of-zeroth-degree properties on A^i, we can dispense with the M_r bounds. The theorem of determinateness in Section 15 should be modified accordingly.

71

EQUALIZATION BY TRADE OF THE INTEREST RATE ALONG WITH THE REAL WAGE[1]

Paul A. Samuelson

My friend and former student Professor Jagdish Bhagwati, of Delhi, wrote me the following interesting lines, and with his permission I venture to reproduce from them here:

> I have a puzzle for you. In your papers on factor price equalization, if one admits capital as a factor of production (let it take the shape of a machine), then what your theorem proves is that the *rental* on the machines is equalized between countries. However, this seems *not* the same as saying that the rate of interest has been equalized. For the rate of interest in the economy is given by [capitalizing the rental and] it seems to me perfectly possible for the rentals to be equal and yet for the interest rates to be different, depending on the time-preferences of the people in the two countries. . . . Can we incorporate growth into this system in a rigorous way unless we really begin by scrapping the Swedish-Samuelson model?

[1]This was written in early 1960 and privately circulated. It is reference 54 in the valuable bibliography of Jagdish Bhagwati, "The Pure Theory of International Trade: A Survey," *Economic Journal*, Vol. LXXIV (March 1964), pp. 1–84, a masterly and invaluable survey. Except for the final parts, which are new, I have made no substantive changes. Since this was written, other scholars, such as Mr. V. K. Ramaswami and Professors Jaroslav Vanek, Peter Kenen, and Murray Kemp, have carried on related researches. I wish to thank the Carnegie Corporation for research aids and F. H. Skidmore for assistance.

This is indeed an interesting question. Nor was it accidental that in my own work on factor-price equalization I quietly replaced the venerable pair labor and capital by labor and land, hoping thereby to sidestep some of the intricacies involved in any discussion of capital. However, the time has come to put forward some of my tentative researches that do face up to the capital problem.

At the beginning let it be stressed that I have no desire to persuade anyone to believe that the following simple models leading to factor-price equalization are realistic. Nor do I think that such simple capital models as are represented here say the last word about growth theory. My simple purpose is to examine the interesting problem posed by Bhagwati and to prove the existence of a variety of rigorous capital models in which the interest rates among countries are indeed equalized by free trade among international goods.[2]

Assumptions

I shall make the assumptions usual for this kind of analysis. Flows of food and clothing, x_1 and x_2, are respectively produced by stocks of labor and homogeneous physical capital, (L_1, K_1) and (L_2, K_2), where capital cannot move in international trade and can be supposed to be like a flexible machine. If capital goods are to be strictly homogeneous, then old and new machines must have exactly the same properties, which requires us to use the depreciation assumptions I employed in my Corfu[3] paper on capital: namely, depreciation must be a constant percentage per unit time regardless of age, although possibly varying between industries to which the capital is applied; thus, a life table involving exponential decay must hold for capital goods used in each industry, with the average length of life in the ith industry being a prescribed technological constant, $1/m_i$.

A new element added to the picture is the fact that there is an additional industry that produces a flow of gross capital formation, x_0, by using labor and capital (L_0, K_0). As is usually assumed, all neoclassical production functions are the same between countries and show constant-returns-to-scale and smoothly substitutable diminishing marginal productivities. (The assumption of smooth substitutability could be lightened without affecting most results.)

[2]Certainly models do exist in which rents become equalized but interest does not. Think only of a labor-land model, where one country has a 5 per cent time preference rate and the other a 10 per cent rate. Land will be twice as valuable in the first country even when rentals are equalized. See Murray C. Kemp, *The Pure Theory of International Trade* (Englewood Cliffs, N. J.: Prentice-Hall, 1964), p. 49. But if land can be produced, it becomes like my K.

[3]"The Evaluation of 'Social Income': Capital Formation and Wealth," Chapter 3 of *The Theory of Capital*, edited by F. A. Lutz and D. C. Hague (London, Macmillan & Co. Ltd., 1961), pp. 32–57.

Relative factor endowments of total labor and capital need not be the same in different countries. Either endowments can be assumed to differ by a little or, if certain strong factor-intensity differences for food and clothing are assumed to hold everywhere, the relative factor endowments can differ widely between countries. The usual assumption is made that something of food and clothing (and of gross capital formation) is being produced in both countries. Note that tastes for food, clothing, and saving-investment are not assumed to be the same in both countries; in particular, net capital formation, dK/dt, could be negative in one or both countries, provided its magnitude fell short of capital consumption or depreciation — which simply means that time preference need only be such that some positive gross capital formation goes on in all countries.

Finally, the absence of impediments to trade implies a common international price ratio for food and clothing. (The case of more than two internationally traded goods can be easily handled by my later general mathematical analysis.)

All the preceding assumptions and the implied equilibrium conditions can be written down symbolically:

(a) Homogeneous production functions:
$$x_i = F_i(L_i, K_i) > 0, \qquad (i = 0, 1, 2)$$

(b) Physical depreciation:
$$D = D_0 + D_1 + D_2$$
$$= m_0 K_0 + m_1 K_1 + m_2 K_2$$

(c) Net (physical) capital formation:
$$\frac{dK}{dt} = \frac{d(K_0 + K_1 + K_2)}{dt}$$
$$= x_0 - D = x_0 - \sum_0^2 m_i K_i$$

(d) Uniform money wage:
$$w = p_0 \frac{\partial F_0(L_0, K_0)}{\partial L_0} = p_1 \frac{\partial F_1(L_1, K_1)}{\partial L_1}$$
$$= p_2 \frac{\partial F_2(L_2, K_2)}{\partial L_2}$$

(e) Gross rentals of capital:
$$R_0 = p_0 \frac{\partial F_0(L_0, K_0)}{\partial K_0}, \; R_1$$
$$= p_1 \frac{\partial F_1(L_1, K_1)}{\partial K_1}, \; R_2$$
$$= p_2 \frac{\partial F_2(L_2, K_2)}{\partial K_2}$$

(f) Uniform net rental (after depreciation allowance):
$$R = R_0 - m_0 p_0 = R_1 - m_1 p_0$$
$$= R_2 - m_2 p_0$$

(g) Uniform interest rate:

$$r = \frac{R}{p_0} = \frac{\partial F_0(L_0, K_0)}{\partial K_0} - m_0$$
$$= \frac{RK_i}{p_0 K_i}$$

(h) Given (clothing-food) international price ratio:

$$\frac{p_2}{p_1} = \pi_2$$

No description of demand conditions in either country has been given, because these conditions register all their pricing effects through π_2 alone. Whatever the level of this international price ratio may be, I shall show that it alone determines a unique wage and interest imputation that must be the same for all countries satisfying our nonspecialization and factor-intensity assumptions. Before demonstrating this fact mathematically or graphically, a brief literary explanation of the model's properties is in order.

In this model, food and clothing production require direct labor in their F_1 and F_2 production functions. Their competitive unit costs involve a direct payment to labor in the form of direct wages. Since capital goods are also used, there is a direct capital cost equal to the interest on the value of the capital goods directly tied up. But these direct "value added" terms are not the whole of it. Some of the capital goods are used up in the act of production, and this depreciation also involves a cost. Even if the firm pays a gross rental that frees it from worrying about capital used up, the competitive owners of the capital goods will be able to include in their gross rentals a charge sufficient to compensate for depreciation. And if depreciation (user cost, so to speak) is different in food and clothing, we shall expect the gross rental to be that much higher in the industry with high depreciation or m_i.

All of these remarks apply also to the production and costing of the gross flow of production of capital goods, x_0. From $F_0 (L_0, K_0)$ there are incurred *direct* wage and interest costs; and, in addition, there are indirect depreciation costs whose magnitude depends on the decay factor m_0.

Factor Costs and Equilibrium Commodity Prices

These relations can be conveniently summarized in the Tableau of gross and net national product on the next page.

Since we are interested in commodity unit costs, we shall want to divide each industry row by the industry physical output. The result for each industry will be

$$p_i = \left(\frac{L_i}{x_i}\right) w + \left(\frac{K_i}{x_i}\right) rp_0 + m\left(\frac{K_i}{x_i}\right) p_0 = a_i w + b_i rp_0 + m_i b_i p_0$$
$$(i = 1, 2, 3)$$

	Money Output	Value Added		Depreciation
		Direct Labor Costs	Direct Interest Costs	
Capital Goods Industry	$p_0 x_0$	$= wL_0$	$+ \ rp_0 K_0$	$+ \ m_0 p_0 K_0$
Food Industry	$p_1 x_1$	$= wL_1$	$+ \ rp_0 K_1$	$+ \ m_1 p_0 K_1$
Clothing Industry	$p_2 x_2$	$= wL_2$	$+ \ rp_0 K_2$	$+ \ m_2 p_0 K_2$
Total	$\sum_0^2 p_i x_i$	$= w \sum_0^2 L_i$	$+ \ rp_0 \sum_0^2 K_i$	$+ \ p_0 \sum_0^2 m_i K_i$
	or			
	GNP	$=$	NNP	$+$ Depreciation

where the a's and b's are respectively the *direct* labor and capital coefficients of production for each industry, connected by the production relation along the unit isoquant

$$F_i(a_i, b_i) = 1$$

This is plotted in Figure 1. Note that the Cassel-Leontief fixed-coefficient case, as shown by the broken-line L-shaped isoquant, is perfectly admissible. In the more neoclassical case of smooth substitutability, the production coefficients are variable; but in equilibrium, they are determinate

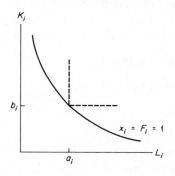

Figure 1.

The unit isoquant of an industry's production function gives us its direct coefficients of production.

functions of the ratio of w to the gross capital rental, being determined so as to minimize unit costs; and if the price of capital goods were known, so that depreciation charges were known, these coefficients would be determinate functions of the ratio of the wage to the net capital rental or to the interest rate (again they are selected so as to minimize food and clothing unit costs).

Nevertheless, the unit cost and price of capital goods, p_0, is not yet known; it is one of the unknowns of the following simultaneous equations:

(1)
$$\begin{cases} p_0 = a_0 w + b_0 r p_0 + b_0 m_0 p_0 \\ p_1 = a_1 w + b_1 r p_0 + b_1 m_1 p_0 \\ p_2 = a_2 w + b_2 r p_0 + b_2 m_2 p_0 \end{cases}$$

Let us first consider the simpler Cassel-Leontief case, where the a's and b's are fixed technological coefficients. Given the technical constants and prescribed interest rate and money wage, we have three simultaneous equations for the three unknown money prices (p_0, p_1, p_2). Can they always be solved for prices? Yes: for every system capable of generating a positive interest rate,[4] the commodity costs and prices are uniquely determined by factor prices *regardless of factor intensities of food and clothing.*

To see this, and also to deepen our insight into capital theory, it is useful to rewrite Equations (1) in the equivalent form involving the net rental of capital goods R rather than the interest rate r. (Recall that the net rental excludes from the nonuniform gross rentals the nonuniform charges for depreciation incurred as a result of using the capital good in the respective industries.) The definitional capitalization equation relating a capital good's dollar net rental per unit time R to the interest rate per unit time is, of course, $p_0 = R/r$ or $r p_0 = R$, as shown in (g) of our equilibrium equations. So our (1) becomes

(2)
$$\begin{cases} p_0 = a_0 w + b_0 R + b_0 m_0 p_0 \\ p_1 = a_1 w + b_1 R + b_1 m_1 p_0 \\ p_2 = a_2 w + b_2 R + b_2 m_2 p_0 \end{cases}$$

It is no accident that the first equation involves only the unknown p_0: we have merely, for simplicity, refused to follow Leontief's whirlpool assumption which would require food and clothing as inputs, along with labor and machine inputs, to produce machine output. Solving the first equation for p_0 gives

(3)
$$p_0 = \frac{a_0}{1 - b_0 m_0} w + \frac{b_0}{1 - b_0 m_0} R = A_0 w + B_0 R$$

[4]In my model the familiar Hawkins-Simon condition for this is merely: $1 - b_0 m_0 > 0$. This says no more than the following: the indirect amount of physical capital needed as a result of depreciation of capital goods used to make one more unit of physical capital goods must itself be less than one unit; for, otherwise, the stock of capital goods would have to run down even if *no* food and clothing were being produced!

The positive A_0 and B_0 coefficients can be interpreted as total (direct + indirect to allow for depreciation) labor and machine requirements to produce a unit of x_0. Substituting this result directly into the remaining price equations gives

$$(3)' \quad \begin{cases} p_1 = A_1 w + B_1 R \\ p_2 = A_2 w + B_2 R \end{cases}$$

where the new positive *total* coefficients of production have come from adding to the direct coefficients the indirect factor requirements needed to make good physical depreciation:

$$(4) \quad \begin{cases} A_i = a_i + b_i m_i A_0 \\ B_i = b_i + b_i m_i B_0 \end{cases} \qquad (i = 0, 1, 2)$$

All this proves that money factor prices do determine money goods prices in the fixed-coefficient case. What about the case where there is more than one technical factor combination by which goods can be produced? It is not hard to see that in such a case A_0 and B_0 will be functions of w/R and nothing else, being chosen so as to minimize p_0 for given w and R. Also, with optimal p_0 having been determined, A_i and B_i in the remaining industries become determinate functions of the ratios of (w, R, p_0) or, for that matter, of the simple ratio w/R, being chosen to minimize independently the unit costs of production p_i. So specifying w and R on the right-hand side of (3) does indeed determine the commodity p's on the left-hand side in the most general case.[5]

[5]The marginal productivity conditions of $(d) - (g)$ guarantee all the minimizations in the postulated smooth neoclassical case. In all other cases, general inequalities of nonlinear programming will achieve the same results. Note too that the fixed depreciation constants, m_i, might just as well be permitted to be technologically variable, but determinate, functions of w/R to minimize unit costs all around. Mathematically, by the methods given in my "Prices of Factors and Goods in General Equilibrium," *Review of Economic Studies*, Vol. XXI (1953), pp. 1–20, and Chapter 70 of the present volume, it can be shown that the $(3')$ equation

$$p_i = A_i(w/R)w + B_i(w/R)R \qquad (i = 1, 2)$$

have for their Jacobian $\partial(p_1, p_2)/\partial(w, R) = A_1(w/R)B_2(w/R) - A_2(w/R)B_1(w/R)$; and to be able to solve backward for w and R in terms of (p_1, p_2), or what is the same thing for w/R and r in terms of $p_2/p_1 = \pi_2$, it is sufficient that this Jacobian satisfy the strong factor-intensity assumption of being one-signed for all w/R. A similar result holds if we add more domestically produced and traded goods to food and clothing and more factors (such as land) to labor and machines. Then the crucial Jacobian matrix

$$[\partial(p_1, p_2, p_3, \cdots)/\partial(w, R, \text{land rent}, \cdots)]$$

becomes

$$\begin{bmatrix} A_1(w, R, \cdots) & B_1(w, R, \cdots) & C_1(w, R, \cdots) & \cdots \\ A_2(w, R, \cdots) & \cdots\cdots\cdots\cdots & \cdots\cdots\cdots\cdots & \cdots \\ A_3(w, R, \cdots) & \cdots\cdots\cdots\cdots & \cdots\cdots\cdots\cdots & \cdots \\ \cdots\cdots\cdots\cdots & \cdots\cdots\cdots\cdots & \cdots\cdots\cdots\cdots & \cdots \end{bmatrix}$$

Graphical Summary

All of my results can be summarized by the kind of diagram I introduced in my 1949 *Economic Journal* paper on factor-price equalization (see Figure 2). The new right-hand curves are appended to show that

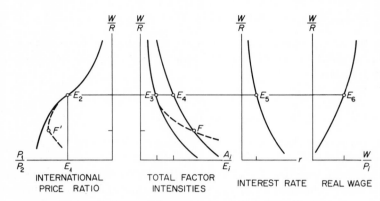

Figure 2. Factor-Price and Interest Rate Equalization.

At any internationally given clothing–food price ratio, we run up from E_1 to E_2 to read off the wage–net rent ratio, and across to E_3 and E_4, and to E_5 and E_6, which show the resulting interest and real wage. (The broken-line curves show that if factor intensities reverse, two countries with *quite different* factor endowments will *not* have the same factor prices.)

the interest rate and the real wage (expressed in *either* food or clothing) are equalized.[6] Since it is not my intention to propagandize for factor-price equalization, I have indicated with the broken curves how changing factor intensities could introduce multiple solutions for factor prices. Note, though, that whatever the factor intensities in a region may be, in the absence of technical change a rising interest rate always implies a falling real wage and a cheapening of the good that happens to be

---

and, in a correction of my theorem on determinateness (p. 9), Gale and Nikaido have shown (in as-yet-unpublished work) that it is sufficient for factor-price equalization that this matrix have all its principal minors everywhere one-signed. In the *Economic Journal*, Vol. 69 (December 1959), pp. 725–732, I. F. Pearce seems to suggest that nonsingularity will alone suffice, but Professor McKenzie has provided a counterexample to this conjecture.

[6]Here is but a brief demonstration that r is inversely related and the real wages directly related to w/R:

By definition, $r = R/p_0 = R[A_0(w/R)w + B_0(w/R)R]^{-1} = r(w/R)$.
Necessarily, $r'(w/R) < 0$ since $\partial \log r / \partial \log R = 1 - B_0 R(A_0 w + B_0 R)^{-1} > 0$.
Also, $w/p_i = w[A_i(w/R)w + B_i(w/R)R]^{-1} = f_i(w/R)$ with $f_i'(w/R) > 0$
   because $\partial \log (w/p_i)/\partial \log w = 1 - A_i w(A_i w + B_i R)^{-1} > 0$.

labor-intensive at the expense of the good that happens to be capital-intensive — in accordance with common-sense expectations.[7]

For those students of economic development who are enamored of the over-all capital output ratio $p_0(K_0 + K_1 + K_2)/(p_0x_0 + p_1x_1 + p_2x_2)$, it may be mentioned that this probably will be greater for the country with the higher $(K_0 + K_1 + K_2)/(L_0 + L_1 + L_2)$ endowment ratio — even though the capital output ratios for *every* industry (p_0K_i/p_ix_i) are *exactly* the same between countries. The difference, of course, comes from the fact that the country generously endowed with capital will give greater production weight to goods that are more capital-intensive, and it will export food and import the labor-intensive clothing.[8]

The "Local" Factor-Price Equalization Theorem

Now that capital has been admitted in a rigorous way into an international trade model, let me revert to the conclusion I had originally in mind when writing my first 1948 *Economic Journal* paper on the subject:

> Commodity movement is almost certainly a substitute for factor movements in this sense: if trade does not originally equalize factor prices and this causes factors to migrate so as to wipe out the difference, none the less *before* migration has proceeded far enough to equalize factor proportions, factor migration will come to a stop as commodity trade will have either equalized factor returns or will have so reduced the differential as to make the cost of transporting another unit of the factor greater than the present discounted value of the higher earnings it can hope to secure abroad.

This point does not, like the complete factor-price equalization theorem, require that the two goods be *everywhere* of the same factor intensity. It requires only that the complete migration of factors would lead to a situation in which the goods will not be of *exactly* the same

---

[7]If factor endowments in two regions are very far apart, then the total labor and capital available for direct and indirect food and clothing production after net capital formation has been taken care of are likely to be so different in proportion as to make it impossible to find a common pair of points like E_3 and E_4 which bracket these available domestic factor supply ratios. In such a case we know that at least one of the countries will produce nothing of one of the traded goods, and we cannot expect factor-price equalization. Along with this familiar possibility, our capital model introduces a new possibility: suppose in one or both countries gross capital formation is zero because time preference makes desired net capital formation be more negative than depreciation; then w/R may still be equalized between countries, but r may exceed the equalized values of $R(A_0w + B_0R)^{-1}$ and by different degrees in the two countries depending upon their different time preferences — in complete agreement with Mr. Bhagwati's quoted passage. The case becomes like that of unproducible land, mentioned earlier.

[8]The result is "probable" rather than "certain" because if x_0 production were itself especially labor-intensive (capital-intensive) and if the country had an especially strong (weak) demand for this domestic good's production, then the presumption about aggregate capital output ratios might be reversed. As always, we must take note of demand differences between countries.

factor intensities, even though they might exchange factor intensities elsewhere. (That is, the local theorem holds everywhere in Figure 2 except at point F.) Properly stated, this "local" factor-price equalization theorem holds wherever there are as many traded goods as factors even if that number is much greater than two.[9]

Even if the over-all factor-price equalization theorem were inapplicable because of changing factor intensities, this local theorem may be of more economic interest than has been brought out in the literature. To take a fantastic case, suppose that two factors could explain the trade pattern of the world. Now Arrow, Chenery, Minhas, and Solow[10] have done geographical studies of production of the same goods in different countries and have come up with the interesting finding that production functions involving constant fractional elasticities of substitution are suggested by the cross-sectional statistics. As they point out, the fact that these constants differ by industry means that relative factor intensities of goods are likely to become reversed in different geographical regions — a phenomenon that would be quite impossible in the case of two goods obeying different Cobb-Douglas production functions. Although the authors are modest in their claims as to the applicability of their research, their result is interesting in itself, and they have for once offered a cross-sectional study of production functions that is not internally contradictory and nonsensical. Moreover, despite all the theoretical discussion of the possibility of factor-intensity reversal, this is the first instance I have heard about that goes beyond the speculative and anecdotal stage.

For the sake of the argument, let us suppose this finding implies that India and Australia will *not* be able to achieve factor-price equalization through trade alone because their factor endowments are so far apart as to put them on different branches of the curve in Figure 2, one being above and the other below F.[11] Then we must face the fact that the world will not end up with a single pattern of factor prices. The failure of this global theorem must not distract us from noting what may still be true: trade might still equalize factor prices for Australia, New Zealand, Canada, the United States, and other countries falling on the same branch of the functions; and it might equalize factor prices for all the labor-rich countries such as India, China, Pakistan, and so forth —

[9]If free factor mobility would lead to a position where the Jacobian matrix $[\partial(P_1, \cdots, P_n)/\partial(W, R, \cdots)]$ is nonsingular, factor migration will stop *before* endowment ratios are equalized, because goods mobility will provide an adequate substitute for the *final* movement of factors.

[10]K. J. Arrow, H. B. Chenery, B. Minhas, R. M. Solow, "Capital-Labor Substitution and Economic Efficiency," *Review of Economics and Statistics*, Vol. XLIII (August 1961), pp. 225–250.

[11]To say nothing of the fact that assuming the same two-variable production functions for such countries might seem a naïve and fruitless hypothesis.

which fall on another branch. In short, the "local" version of the factor-price equalization theorem says that, in the absence of complete specialization and other specifiable phenomena, there will be only as many factor-price patterns as there are distinct branches of the curve and not as many as there are countries.[12]

The Case of Any Number of Heterogeneous Capital Goods[13]

The previous analysis rests on the nonsubstitution theorem involving the interest rate, which, as developed in my articles on Marx and Ricardo and subsequently in the Johan Akerman *Festschrift*, generalizes the 1949 nonsubstitution theorem of Georgescu-Roegen and Samuelson.[14] Nonsubstitution theorems of this type generally rest on the assumption of Leontief and neoclassical writers that there is *no joint production*. (For example, it takes demand conditions to determine relative wool and mutton prices even in a timeless world where labor is the sole input.) Simple circulating capital models fit in well with nonjointness of production. But durable capital, such as K in the previous models, intrinsically involves the joint production by labor and machines of current consumption goods *and* of older machines.

Fortunately, as indicated in my Ricardo papers, jointness of production of nonfinal goods can be tolerated in some models that still obey nonsubstitution theorems. This we have, in effect, just seen in the previous discussion of interest rate equalization with durable K. Here I shall show how one can handle the case of n heterogeneous durable capital goods $(K_1, \cdots, K_n)$ that with one primary (labor) factor L can

[12]If factor-intensity curves coincide over a finite range, there could result an infinity of different-factor-price patterns for certain π_2 ratios, and the chances of keeping food *and* clothing production going in all countries might become very slim. If we include under "complete specialization" the concept of "incipient specialization," which is the case where the two goods have identical two-factor intensities and hence straight-line transformation curves, the singular cases (like F) are swept under the carpet, and the theorem can be more easily stated.

[13]A brief fragment on the Leontief Paradox has been omitted to make room for this extension.

[14]P. A. Samuelson, "Wages and Interest: A Modern Dissection of Marxian Economic Models," *The American Economic Review*, Vol. XLVII, No. 6 (December 1957). P. A. Samuelson, "A Modern Treatment of the Ricardian Economy: I. The Pricing of Goods and of Labor and Land Services," *Quarterly Journal of Economics*, Vol. LXXIII, No. 1 (February 1959), pp. 1–35; "A Modern Treatment of the Ricardian Economy: II. Capital and Interest Aspects of the Pricing Process," *Quarterly Journal of Economics*, Vol. LXXIII, No. 2 (May 1959), pp. 217–231. On the 1949 theorem, see T. C. Koopmans, ed., *Activity Analysis of Production and Allocation* (New York: John Wiley & Sons, 1951), Chapters 7 and 10 by P. A. Samuelson and Nicholas Georgescu-Roegen, respectively; and Chapters 8 and 9 by T. C. Koopmans and Kenneth J. Arrow, respectively. P. A. Samuelson, "A New Theorem on Non-Substitution," *Money, Growth and Methodology*, published in honor of Johan Akerman, Vol. 20, Lund Social Science Studies (Lund, Sweden: CWK Gleerup, March 1961), pp. 407–423.

produce their own net capital formations $(\dot{K}_1, \cdots, \dot{K}_n)$ and r consumption goods $(C_1, \cdots, C_r)$, by the neoclassical production functions

$$(5) \quad \begin{cases} \dot{K}_j = F_j(L_j, K_{1j}, \cdots, K_{nj}) - m_j K_j & (j = 1, \cdots, n) \\ C_j = F_{n+j}(L_{n+j}, K_{1,n+j}, \cdots, K_{n,n+j}) & (j = 1, \cdots, r) \end{cases}$$

where K_{ij} = the amount of the ith machine used in the jth industry and m_j is the depreciation coefficient for the jth K (and not, as before, for the jth industry, since now m_j is assumed independent of industry use). Note, too, that what was previously p_1 and p_2 will now be P_{c1} and P_{c2}. Define $a_{0j} = L_j/F_j$, $a_{ij} = K_{ij}/F_j$. Then

$$(6) \quad F_j(a_{0j}, a_{1j}, \cdots, a_{nj}) = 1 \quad (j = 1, \cdots, n, n+1, \cdots, n+r)$$

and the least-cost a_{ij} will depend on money rental rates for labor (that is, the money wage W_0) and money (gross) rentals for all capital goods $(W_1, \cdots, W_n)$. Or

$$(7) \quad a_{ij} = a_{ij}(W_0, W_1, \cdots, W_n) = a_{ij}(1, w_1, \cdots, w_n)$$

where $w_j = W_j/W_0$, the (gross) rental of the jth machine relative to the labor wage.

The cost-of-production price for each machine is equal to the sum of the costs of the per-unit requirements of each input:

$$(8) \quad \begin{cases} P_1 = W_0 a_{01} + W_1 a_{12} + \cdots + W_n a_{n1} \\ \\ \\ \\ P_n = W_0 a_{0n} + W_1 a_{1n} + \cdots + W_n a_{nn} \end{cases}$$

For simplicity, I have made exponential-decay depreciation independent of the use to which any K_j is put. Hence, the gross rental of the jth good has been made the same W_j to every user. And this rental is merely equal to interest on capitalized value plus value of capital depreciated:

$$(9) \quad W_j = (r + m_j)P_j \quad (j = 1, \cdots, n)$$

But now we can substitute (9) into (8) and get implicit equations ot determine $(W_1/W_0, \cdots, W_n/W_0) = (w_1, \cdots, w_n)$:

$$(10) \quad w_j - \sum_{i=1}^{n} w_i a_{ij}(1, w_1, \cdots, w_n) = a_{0j}(1, w_1, \cdots, w_n) \; .$$
$$(j = 1, 2, \cdots, n)$$

Evidently, the $(r + m_j)a_{ij}$ are to be treated just like new a_{ij} in a timeless Walras-Leontief system; and r must be small enough relative to

(m_j, a_{ij}) that

$$\begin{bmatrix} 1 & 0 & \cdots & 0 \\ \cdot & & \cdots & \cdot \\ \cdot & & \cdots & \cdot \\ \cdot & & \cdots & \cdot \\ 0 & \cdots & \cdots & 1 \end{bmatrix} - \begin{bmatrix} & & \\ & (r + m_j)a_{ij} & \\ & & \end{bmatrix} = I - \bar{a}$$

have a nonnegative inverse, which is the Hawkins-Simon set of conditions for a viable system. If we rule out uninteresting decomposable cases, Equations (10) will determine positive unique $(w_1{}^*, \cdots, w_n{}^*)$ and optimal $a_{ij}{}^*$ corresponding to them. And then we find for each consumption industry

$$(11) \qquad \frac{P_{cj}}{W_0} = a_{0,n+j}{}^* + \sum_{i=1}^{n} w_i{}^* a_{i,n+j} = p_j(r)$$

with $p_j{}'(r) > 0$, so that the higher the interest rate, the lower will be *every* real wage.

Now suppose there are uniform differences in factor intensity, so that for some two goods that are simultaneously produced in both countries — say goods 1 and 2 — $p_1(r)/p_2(r) = p_{12}(r)$ is a monotone strictly increasing (or decreasing) function of r. *Then, the interest rate will be equalized by positive trade in those goods alone.*

To put the matter as strongly as I have elsewhere: (1) if effective knowledge of production were the same everywhere (so that the same F_j functions prevailed), (2) if the real rate of interest were the same everywhere, (3) if the only primary factor is labor, which in its "raw" untrained state is the same everywhere, then the real wages and *all* real price ratios would be the same everywhere, and there would be no need for any trade at all; or, more accurately, there would be need only for that amount of intramarginal trade required to keep interest rates equalized.

Suppose, for once, we let capital goods or loan funds move internationally along with consumption goods. Then we find that only differences in (*a*) effective knowledge, (*b*) endowments of *primary* factors, and (*c*) interest rates can permit differences in living standards and productivities. Anticlimactically, the curse of the poor is their poverty — their poverty in knowledge (as distinct from training, unless knowledge of how to train is lacking), their poverty in primary factors, and their poverty in having access to low-interest capital funds (and all that implies for real machinery and training in an equilibrium model).

Of course, all the preceding refers to long-enough-run equilibrium of constant-returns-to-scale systems and presupposes enough time for the system to have utilized its access to low-interest resources over time. If a developing economy can import machines themselves, it will be able, starting from capital stock appropriate to a higher interest rate, to speed up the pace at which it achieves the new long-run equilibrium appropriate to a lower interest rate.

Handling All Kinds of Intermediate Goods: A Sweeping Theorem

McKenzie, Vanek, and I have discussed how intermediate goods influence factor-price equalization problems.[15] The case considered here, where machines that work with primary factors must themselves be produced by primary factors and machines, is merely a durable-goods instance of this. The whole problem can be handled by a beautifully simple device, which enables one to sweep all the intermediate-goods relations under the carpet.

So long as *all* the F_j functions involve no jointness of production — and even if they involve intermediate flows with positive coefficients of the form $(a_{n+j,1}, \cdots, a_{n+j,n+r})$ — we can always define new Net Production Functions which give the maximum amount of any net final product (be it an investment dK_j/dt or a consumption C_K) in terms of the primary factors devoted to its net production alone (which means all the primary factors needed to produce *all* the gross outputs needed to provide the intermediate inputs that such net output of the one good requires).

To help understand this somewhat complicated description, consider an economy that produces food and clothing and other final goods by means of primary factors like labor and land. By definition of what we mean by a primary factor, labor and land cannot themselves be produced within the system. But suppose that a final good like food also requires for its production a certain amount of intermediate clothing and food itself; and suppose it requires machines, which can themselves be reproduced out of primary factors and intermediate flows and machines themselves.

Imagine putting this economy inside a black box. We observe only primary factors going into the box as inputs. And we observe only final net products coming out of the box as outputs. We do not see the intermediate inputs and gross flows within the box itself. Call final outputs $X_1, X_2, \cdots$ whether they are consumption goods or net capital formations. Call primary inputs $Y_1, Y_2, \cdots$ whether they are many kinds of

[15]Jaroslav Vanek, "Variable Factor Proportions and Interindustry Flows in the Theory of International Trade," *Quarterly Journal of Economics*, Vol. 77 (1963), pp. 129–142. L. W. McKenzie, "Specialization and Efficiency in World Production," *The Review of Economic Studies*, June 1954, pp. 165–180; "Specialization in Production and the Production Possibility Locus," *The Review of Economic Studies*, Vol. XXIII, No. 60 (1955–1956), pp. 56–64; "Equality of Factor Prices in World Trade," *Econometrica*, Vol. 23, No. 3 (July 1955), pp. 239–257.

raw labor or land. There still results a Production-Possibility Frontier relating these ultimate outputs and inputs of the form

$$(12) \qquad 0 \equiv T(X_1, X_2, \cdots; Y_1, Y_2, \cdots)$$
$$\underset{\lambda}{\equiv} T(\lambda X_1, \lambda X_2, \cdots; \lambda Y_1, \lambda Y_2, \cdots)$$

where λ can be any positive scalar because of our constant-returns-to-scale assumptions.

So far, nothing remarkable has been said. But suppose that every production function inside the box has the $F_j(\cdots)$ property of *never involving joint production of any outputs.* (Joint use of inputs is, of course, to be expected.) Then by concentrating on one X_i alone, setting all others equal to zero, we can define the Net Production Function of X_i producible from given totals of all primary inputs. Call this

$$(13) \qquad X_i = N_i(Y_1, Y_2, \cdots) \quad \text{or}$$
$$T(0, \cdots, 0, X_i, 0, \cdots; Y_1, Y_2, \cdots) = 0$$

and note that it is equivalent to putting all other X's equal to zero in Equation (12) and solving explicitly for X_i. This production function will have all the homogeneity and concavity properties of any gross F_j function met anywhere in neoclassical theory. That is what the present theorem asserts. But more than that is asserted.

If society actually wants something positive of both X_1 and X_2, *it cannot do better* than to produce all the X_1 by its independent N_1 function and X_2 by its independent N_2 function. So to speak, we could organize the X_1 food industry so that in its corner of the black box it produces *for itself* all the unseen intermediate clothing, machine, and food flows needed to enable it to produce the *net* food output to come out of the box. The same goes for the X_2 industry given the task of producing net clothing. I realize that this sounds as if the division of labor is being abrogated; but remember, as Adam Smith insisted, that much of the division of labor is required only because of *divergences* from the constant-returns-to-scale assumptions of neoclassical analysis.

Perhaps the theorem will seem obvious. But at one time, to me, it seemed wrong. I feared that there might inevitably be interactions between the X_1 and X_2 productions. But further reflection on the strong nonjointness assumptions reveals that this apprehension is misguided.[16] In equilibrium, primary factor prices and all other prices will be uniform within the black box, and there can never be any inefficiency or penalty if one industry "integrates" itself to produce *all* its nonprimary requirements. (Needless to say, turnover taxes or other impediments between sectors would require modification of these statements.)

[16]Conversation with Professors Vanek and McKenzie helped clarify my mind on these points.

The conclusion from this last analysis can now be drawn. To discuss the role of intermediate goods and durable machinery in factor-price equalization, we can often employ the Net Production Function giving each Final Good in terms of *Total* Primary Inputs needed for it alone. We thus sweep all complications into the background and concern ourselves only with the crucial factor intensities (and generalized Jacobian matrices) of these standard Net Functions.

A Trading World without Geography

We are now in a position to uncover a striking idealized case. Suppose that natural resources are not limiting factors and that (raw, untrained) labor is the only primary factor. Of course, in some general Austrian sense, "time" is also a bottleneck factor since it is technically feasible for an economy to go from one high-interest (or profit) state to another more productive low-interest state only by *consuming* less final outputs than the system is capable of permanently producing in each intermediate state.

But now suppose that the rate of interest does get equalized by free trade in some two goods that are being simultaneously produced. (Warning: This is not an innocent assumption.) Then with r the same everywhere, the Net Production Functions involve only raw labor. And on the assumption that "a man is genetically a man, for aw' of that," these identical Net Functions are the simple linear ones of the Ricardian, labor theory-of-value constant-cost case. This is a case of Equal Absolute Advantage everywhere! Enough trade must take place to keep r equalized, but no further trade need take place. As the world saves and invests, it matters not where the capital goods are placed just so long as every worker has access to enough credit and the implied $(K_1, \cdots, K_n)$ to enable him to produce something worth producing at the common interest rate.

Ironically, when I push the Heckscher-Ohlin axioms all the way, we come full circle back to a *uniform* Ricardian world. To break the circle and return to the real world, which does involve geography, we must, as Bertil Ohlin long ago insisted, study the uneven endowment of primary factors that does characterize the only globe we yet know.

72

SPATIAL PRICE EQUILIBRIUM AND LINEAR PROGRAMMING

By PAUL A. SAMUELSON*

I.—*Introduction*

Increasingly, modern economic theorists are going beyond the formulation of equilibrium in terms of such marginal equalities as marginal revenue equal to marginal costs or wage rate equal to marginal value product. Instead they are reverting to an earlier and more fundamental aspect of a maximum position: namely, that from the top of a hill, whether or not it is locally flat, all movements are downward. Therefore, the real import of marginalism is embodied in the following type of statement: for any produced units of output, extra revenues exceed extra costs; but for any further producible units, extra revenue would fall short of extra costs. These marginal inequalities—which need not apply to small local movements alone—do, in well-behaved cases with smooth slopes, imply the usual marginal equalities. But they are more general, in that from them we can derive most of what is potentially useful in marginal analysis, a point which has been missed by both the defenders and attackers of "marginalism." And more than that, the marginal inequalities can apply to cases (like simple comparative advantage) where the marginal equalities fail.

In recent years economists have begun to hear about a new type of theory called *linear programming*. Developed by such mathematicians as G. B. Dantzig, J. v. Neumann, A. W. Tucker, and G. W. Brown, and by such economists as R. Dorfman, T. C. Koopmans, W. Leontief, and others, this field admirably illustrates the failure of marginal equalization as a rule for defining equilibrium. A number of books and articles on this subject are beginning to appear. It is the modest purpose of the following discussion to present a classical economics problem which illustrates many of the characteristics of linear programming. However, the problem is of economic interest for its own sake and because of its ancient heritage.

The first explicit statement that competitive market price is determined by the intersection of supply and demand functions seems to have been given by A. A. Cournot in 1838 in connection, curiously enough, with the more complicated problem of price relations between

* The author is professor of economics at the Massachusetts Institute of Technology and consultant to the Rand Corporation, whose help in this research is acknowledged.

two spatially separate markets—such as Liverpool and New York.[1] The latter problem, that of "communication of markets," has itself a long history, involving many of the great names of theoretical economics.[2] Dr. Stephen Enke in a recent interesting paper generalized the problem of interspatial markets and gave it an elegant solution.[3]

Proceeding from the Enke formulation, I propose in this paper (1) to show how this purely descriptive problem in non-normative economics can be cast mathematically into a *maximum* problem; and (2) to relate the Enke problem to a standard problem in linear programming, the so-called Koopmans-Hitchcock minimum-transport-cost problem.[4]

Spatial problems have been so neglected in economic theory that the field is of interest for its own sake. In addition, this provides a reasonably easy-to-understand example in the new field of linear programming. But, most important, insight into the fundamental nature of economic pricing is provided by the present discussion.

II.—*Formulation of the Two Problems*

In the Cournot-Enke problem, we are given at each of two or more localities a domestic demand and supply curve for a given product (*e.g.*, wheat) in terms of its market price at that locality. We are also given constant transport costs (shipping, insurance, duties, etc.) for carrying one unit of the product between any two of the specified localities. What then will be the final competitive equilibrium of prices in all the markets, of amounts supplied and demanded at each place, and of exports and imports?

From the description of the above problem, an economist would be tempted to guess that it includes inside it the following Koopmans problem, which I slightly reword to bring out the similarity: A specified total number of (empty or ballast) ships is to be sent out from each of a number of ports. They are to be allocated among a number of other receiving ports, with the total sent in to each such port being specified. If we are given the unit costs of shipment between every two ports, how can we minimize the total costs of the program?

---

[1] A. A. Cournot, *Mathematical Principles of the Theory of Wealth* (1838), Chap. X.

[2] J. Viner, *Studies in International Trade*, New York, 1937, pp. 589–91 gives references to Cunyngham (1904), Barone (1908), Pigou (1904), and H. Schultz (1935); for a non-graphic literary exposition, see F. W. Taussig, *Some Aspects of the Tariff Question*, Cambridge, Mass. (1915 and 1931), Chap. I.

[3] S. Enke, "Equilibrium Among Spatially Separated Markets: Solution by Electric Analogue," *Econometrica*, Vol. 19 (Jan., 1951), pp. 40–47.

[4] See T. Koopmans, *Activity Analysis of Production and Allocation* (Monograph 13 of the Cowles Commission, published by John Wiley, 1951) for references. The special transport problem itself is dealt with in Chapters XIV and XXIII and independently deals with a problem considered in 1941 by F. L. Hitchcock and in 1942 by a Russian mathematician, L. Kantorovitch. For a readable account, see T. C. Koopmans, "Optimum Utilization of the Transportation System," *Econometrica*, Vol. 17, Suppl. (July, 1949), pp. 136–46.

Note that total shipments in or out of any one place are an unknown in the first problem, whereas they are given in the second. In this sense the first problem is the more general one and includes the second inside itself. Note, too, that, as it stands, the first problem is one of decentralized price-mechanics: innumerable atomistic competitors operate in the background, pursuing their private interests and taking no account of any centralized magnitude that is to be maximized. Yet, even without Adam Smith's "as-if" principle of the Invisible Hand, our teleological faith in the pricing mechanism is such that we should be surprised if the resulting allocations resulted in costly cross-haulages: we instinctively feel that arbitragers could make money getting rid of any such inefficiencies.

A final hint suggests that the first problem, which is definitely not a maximum problem to begin with, might be convertible into a maximum problem. Enke provides a simple ingenious electric circuit for its solution in the case of linear market functions. At least since the work of Clerk Maxwell and Kirchhoff a century ago it has been realized that the equilibrium of simple passive electric networks can be described in terms of an extremum principle—the minimization of "total power-loss."[5]

It is not surprising, therefore, that the Enke problem can be artificially converted into a maximum problem, from which we may hope for the following specific advantages: (1) This viewpoint might aid in the choice of convergent numerical iterations to a solution. (2) From the extensive theory of maxima, it enables us immediately to evaluate the sign of various comparative-statics changes. (*E.g.*, an increase in net supply at any point can never in a stable system *decrease* the region's exports.) (3) By establishing an equivalence between the Enke problem and a maximum problem, we may be able to use the known electric devices for solving the former to solve still other maximum problems, and perhaps some of the linear programming type. (4) The maximum problem under consideration is of interest because of its unusual type: it involves in an essential way such non-analytic functions as absolute value of X, which has a discontinuous derivative and a *corner;* this makes it different from the conventionally studied types and somewhat similar to the inequality problems met with in linear programming. (5) Finally, there is general methodological and mathematical interest in

[5] In its simplest form, such a minimum problem is of conventional interior differentiable ("Weierstrassian") type, and it does not involve the quasi-linear boundaries, inequalities, and vertexes encountered in linear programming. Nonetheless, A. W. Tucker in an unpublished Office of Naval Research memorandum "Analogues of Kirchhoff's Laws" (Stanford, 1950) noted the similarity of the Kirchhoff-Maxwell problem to the linear programming problem of the Koopmans type. Moreover, I gathered from personal conversation with Professor Tjalling Koopmans that when he first solved the transportation problem years ago, before linear programming had been explicitly formulated, the analogy with the network problem readily occurred to him and helped guide his explorations toward a solution. See *Activity Analysis, op. cit.* pp. 258–59.

the question of the conditions under which a given equilibrium problem can be significantly related to a maximum or minimum principle.

III.—*The Two-Locality Case Graphically Treated*

The two-variable case provides a convenient introduction to the principles involved. The general n variable case then follows without much difficulty. Figure 1 shows the usual textbook back-to-back diagram determining the equilibrium flow of exports from market 1 to 2.

EQUILIBRIUM OF EXPORTS AND IMPORTS

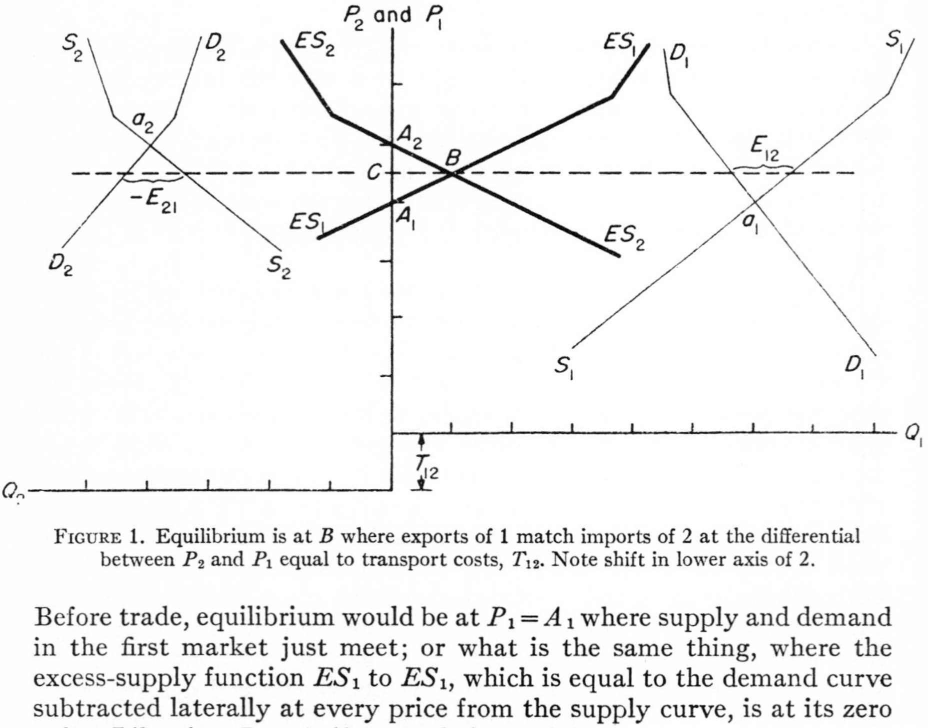

FIGURE 1. Equilibrium is at B where exports of 1 match imports of 2 at the differential between P_2 and P_1 equal to transport costs, T_{12}. Note shift in lower axis of 2.

Before trade, equilibrium would be at $P_1 = A_1$ where supply and demand in the first market just meet; or what is the same thing, where the excess-supply function ES_1 to ES_1, which is equal to the demand curve subtracted laterally at every price from the supply curve, is at its zero point. Likewise, $P_2 = A_2$ if no trade is possible.

But now suppose that goods can move from 1 to 2 for T_{12} dollars per unit, and from 2 to 1 for T_{21} dollars per unit. Since the pretrade price is lower in 1 than 2, trade will obviously never flow from 2 to 1 and so only the T_{12} figure is relevant. Because the initial differential in prices exceeds the transport costs, there will be a positive flow of exports from 1 to 2, and P_2 will come to exceed P_1 by exactly T_{12}. For this reason the axes of market 1 have been displaced relative to those of market 2 by the distance T_{12}.

The new equilibrium is shown at B, where the excess supply or exports of market 1 exactly equal the algebraically negative excess supply or imports of market 2. The bracketed distances E_{12}, and $-E_{21}$, and CB are all exactly equivalent depictions of these flows.

Of course, if A_1 and A_2 had been closer together than T_{12} (or T_{21}), then the markets would have split-up and the separate equilibria would be at (A_1, A_2). Had A_2 been less than A_1 by more than T_{21}, then the flow of exports would have automatically reversed directions so that E_{21} would be positive and E_{12} negative. What makes the problem interesting is its complicated non-linear equilibrium conditions:

(1)a   If $P_2 = P_1 + T_{12}$,

any non-negative E_{12} may flow; $E_{12} > 0$ implies $P_2 = P_1 + T_{12}$.

(1)b   If $P_2 < P_1 + T_{12}$ and if $P_1 < P_2 + T_{21}$,

then $E_{12} = 0$ and $E_{21} = 0$.

(1)c   If $P_1 = P_2 + T_{21}$,

then $E_{21} \geqq 0$, depending upon total world supply and demand, etc.; $E_{21} > 0$ implies $P_1 = P_2 + T_{21}$.

Figure 2 provides a new graphical restatement of what is shown in Figure 1. The same excess-supply curves are shown but this time the prices in the two countries are measured *from the same level* rather than with one axis shifted by the amount of transportation cost. However, the transport costs do enter into the problem. Look first at the two upper curves of the figure only. Now the final equilibrium is determined at JK where the two excess-supply curves differ vertically by T_{12}, as shown by the bracket.

This same equilibrium determination of exports and imports (E_{12} and $-E_{21}$) is shown in the lower part of the figure by the heavy NN curve which represents the *vertical* difference between the two excess supply curves. The final equilibrium is at F where the net excess-supply curve hits the curve of discontinuous transport costs $WXYZ$.

Figure 2 has the merit of suggesting how a shift in one or both of the excess-supply curves could cause the equilibrium intersection to be shifted over to the WX interval, with 2 exporting to 1 as in equation (1)c. It also suggests how the intersection *might* be on the XY interval, with exports and imports zero, and with prices related as in (1)b.

IV.—*Defining Social Pay-off*

Figure 2 paves the way toward a maximum or minimum formulation of the problem. An economist looking at these figures would naturally think of some kind of consumers surplus concept. The area A_1JKA_2, and $OMFG$, its equivalent, cry out to be compared with the area under the transport curve, $OMFY$. However, the name consumers surplus has all kinds of strange connotations in economics. To avoid these and to underline the completely artificial nature of my procedure, I shall simply define a "net social pay-off" function, with three components:[5a]

NSP = Social Pay-off in 1 + Social Pay-off in 2 — Transport Cost.

The social pay-off of any region is defined as the algebraic area under its excess-*demand* curve. This is equal in magnitude to the area under

EQUIVALENT DEPICTION OF SPATIAL EQUILIBRIUM

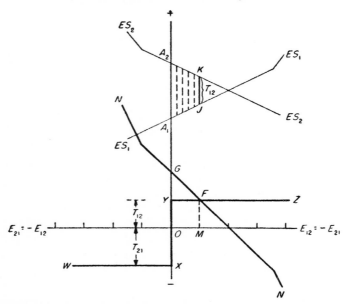

FIGURE 2. The same excess-supply curves appear as in figure 1, but now lower axes are evenly aligned. Transport costs enter through the discontinuous curve $WXYZ$. Equilibrium is where the *net* excess-supply curve for the two markets—NN = vertical subtraction of ES_1 from ES_2 —intersects $WXYZ$ at F. (Alternatively, equilibrium is where JK vertical distance equals T_{12}.)

its excess-supply curve but opposite in algebraic sign. However, since the second market has been put back-to-back to the first, the area under the second market's excess-supply curve in Figure 2 does measure the second market's pay-off; and from it we must *subtract* the area under the first country's excess-supply curve. *Hence, the area under the net curve NN in Figure 2 does perfectly measure the combined social pay-off of both markets.*

[5a] This magnitude is artificial in the sense that no competitor in the market will be aware of or concerned with it. It is artificial in the sense that after an Invisible Hand has led us to its maximization, we need not necessarily attach any social welfare significance to the result.

In Figure 3 the curve NON indicates how the combined payoff of the two markets varies with algebraic exports from 1 to 2. From this we subtract the curve of total transport cost UOU. Total transport cost has a corner at the origin because of the discontinuity between T_{12} and T_{21} as shown in $WXYZ$ of Figure 2; the algebraic integral of this discontinuous function leads to the V-shaped total function UOU.[6] We

MAXIMIZING NET SOCIAL PAY-OFF

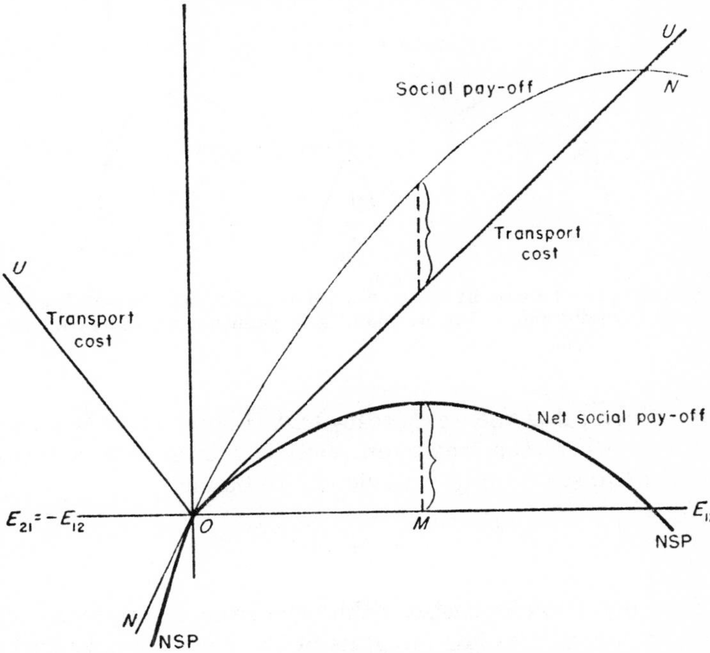

FIGURE 3. Same equilibrium as in previous figures is shown as the maximum of net social pay-off or maximum vertical difference between upper two curves.

find our equilibrium where the vertical distance between the two upper curves is at a maximum. This same optimal level of exports (E_{12}) or imports $(-E_{21})$ is also shown at the maximum point of the net social pay-off curve, the third curve which measures the vertical distance between the upper two.

This completes the two-variable case. Figure 4 illustrates that three possible cases could have emerged, corresponding to equations (1)a,

[6] The mathematical symbolism for this function can be written in many equivalent ways: e.g.

$$t_{12}(E_{12}) = T_{12}E_{12} \text{ for } E_{12} \geqq 0$$
$$= T_{21}(-E_{12}) \text{ for } E_{12} \leqq 0$$

and still other equivalent symbolisms (involving absolute values of E_{12}, etc.) can be found.

(1)b, and (1)c. In Figure 4a, region 1 exports to 2 so that the maximum point is smooth; the corner in the curve, due to the discontinuity in the rate of transport cost, is on the vertical axis and does not affect the maximum. Similarly Figure 4c shows a normally smooth maximum

TYPES OF MAXIMA FOR NET SOCIAL PAY-OFF

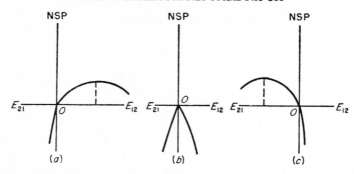

FIGURE 4. Because of transport costs, each curve of net social pay-off has a corner at the origin. In (b) price differentials are too little to surmount transport costs, so trade is zero.

without corners; 2 is then exporting to 1. Figure 4b shows the intermediate case where the maximum point is a cusp with a corner: the transport cost discontinuity is obviously to blame.

* * *

The final point to emphasize is this: Once the separate pay-off functions are set up as areas or integrals of the excess-supply curves and once transport-cost functions are known, a clerk could be given the task of experimentally varying exports so as to achieve a net maximum. He could proceed by trial and error, always moving in a direction that increased the net pay-off, and he would ultimately arrive at the correct equilibrium. The existence of pathological corners would not impair convergence; rather it might accelerate convergence.[7]

[7] Mathematically, calling the excess-supply functions $s_i(E_i)$,

$$NSP = -\int_0^{E_{12}} s_1(x)dx - \int_0^{-E_{11}} s_2(x)dX - t_{12}(E_{12}).$$

By setting $dN/dE_{12}=0$, we arrive at conditions equivalent to equations (1):

(1) $\qquad -T_{21} \leqq s_2(E_{21}) - s_1(E_{12}) \leqq T_{12}, \quad E_{12} + E_{21} = 0$

and with $E_{12} \neq 0$ implying that one of the equality signs holds. A gradient method of making dE_{12}/dt proportional to dN/dE_{12} would always converge for positive sloping s_i functions.

V.—*The General Case of Any Number of Regions*

Instead of two regions suppose we have $i = 1, 2, \cdots, n$ regions. The algebraic amount of exports from i to j we can write as E_{ij} and it will of course be the same thing as the algebraic imports of j from i, $-E_{ji}$. Table I shows the two-way table relating these interregion exports to the total algebraic exports of any region, E_i. (Note that about half the numbers in the table will be negative.) Suppose too that we are given T_{ij}, the transport cost per unit of product moved from region i to region j. These transport costs could also have been arranged in a two-way table. Finally suppose that for each region we have an excess supply function $s_i(E_i) = P_i$, which is calculated by taking the lateral difference between local supply and demand functions.

TABLE I

Region	1	2	$\cdots$	j	$\cdots$	n	Total exports (algebraic)
1	$\cdot$	$E_{12} = -E_{21}$		E_{1j}	$\cdots$	$E_{1n} = -E_{n1}$	$E_1 = \sum_j E_{1j}$
2	E_{21}	$\cdot\,\cdot$		$\cdot$		$\cdot$	$E_2 = \sum_j E_{2j}$
$\vdots$							$\vdots$
i	E_{i1}	$\cdot$		$E_{ij} = -E_{ji}$		E_{in}	$E_i = \sum_j E_{ij}$
$\vdots$							$\vdots$
n	E_{n1}	$\cdot$		E_{nj}		$\cdot$	$E_n = \sum_j E_{nj}$
Total imports (algebraic)	$-E_1 = \sum_i E_{i1}$	$-E_2 = \sum_i E_{i2}$	$\cdots$	$-E_i = \sum_i E_{ij}$	$\cdots$	$-E_n = \sum_i E_{in}$	$0 = \sum \sum_i E_{ij}$ = total net exports

As in the two-variable case, we can define a social pay-off for every region in terms of the area under the excess-demand or excess-supply function. This will depend only upon the total exports of the region and can be written

$$(2) \quad S_i(E_i) = \text{area under the excess-demand curve} = -\int_0^{E_i} s_i(x)\,dx.$$

The transport costs can be written as a function of exports between any two regions; or as $t_{ij}(E_{ij}) = $ a V-shaped curve like that shown in Figure 3.[8]

Now we can form a final net social pay-off for all the regions as the sum of the n separate pay-offs minus the total transport costs of all the shipments:

[8] Mathematically, this function has a corner at the zero export point, and will equal $T_{ij}E_{ij}$ if i exports to j and $T_{ji}E_{ji}$ if j exports to i. Note T_{ij} need not equal T_{ji}, but it can be shown that by definition $t_{ij}(E_{ij}) = t_{ji}(E_{ji})$.

(3)
$$NSP = \sum_{1}^{n} S_i(E_i) - \sum_{i<j} \sum t_{ij}(E_{ij}).$$

Because $E_i = E_{i1} + \cdots + E_{in}$, this is a function of all the E_{ij}'s and when we have found its maximum we have arrived at the final unique equilibrium trade pattern.[9]

Providing that all domestic supply curves cut demand curves from below (as price rises), which is the so-called case of normal or stable intersection, the excess-supply curves will never be falling curves; and it will necessarily follow that the maximum position will exist and be unique. At the maximum point, we will find

(4) $-T_{ij} \leqq s_i(E_i) - s_j(E_j) \leqq T_{ji}$ (for all $i, j = 1, \cdots, n$)

with both inequalities holding only if $E_{ij} = 0 = E_{ji}$; if $E_{ij} > 0$, then the right-hand equality must hold; and if $E_{ji} < 0$, the left-hand equality must hold. Recalling that the s_i's and P's are the same thing, we obviously end up with the proper n-region generalization of equations (1) that were derived for the two-region case.

Our task has now been successfully completed. The problem in descriptive price behavior has been artificially converted into a maximum problem. This maximum problem can be solved by trial and error or by a systematic procedure of varying shipments in the direction of increasing social pay-off.[10]

* * *

Once the exports are determined between any two places, it is obvious that the total exports of any and every place are also determined. Some of the n-regions will end up as positive net exporters; some will end up as net importers (negative net exporters); some may even end up in perfect balance, with zero imports and exports. Reflection will show that we are free to omit all such balanced regions from our further dis-

---

[9] Since we know that the imports of one region are the exports of another, we do not have to specify all the $n^2 E_{ij}$'s in Table I. Instead we can work with all those that are above the hollow diagonals of the Table, inferring those below by using the identity $E_{ij} = -E_{ji}$. Thus, we may adopt the convention of having $i<j$, and may work with $n(n-1)/2$ unknown E_{ij}'s. Incidentally, most of the E_{ij}'s will turn out to be zero: i.e., a typical export region will export to only a few other regions and a typical importer will import from only one or a few regions. More exactly, it is a theorem of linear programming that the number of positive exports need not exceed $n-1$. It will also be true that if T_{ij} and E_i are all integers, the E_{ij}'s will all be integers.

[10] Even if this were not a market problem, we could set up pretended competitive markets whose supply and demand relations might be used to help compute the correct mathematical solutions. Computing clerks could be instructed to act like brokers and arbitragers, etc. Or we could dispense with all markets, and instead watch how NSP is changing as we change each E_{ij}, continuing to move always in the direction of increasing NSP. Doing this long enough will carry us to the top of the hill.

For the case where the excess-supply curves are straight lines Enke has given a simple electric circuit, consisting of resistances, rectifiers, and batteries, which will give the final solution as a measurement of currents and voltages. See Enke, *op. cit.*, Figure 1, p. 45 and the next section below.

cussion, since so long as they remain in balance they need not export or import from any locality.[11]

It follows that we can divide our n-regions up into $i = 1, \cdots, m$ export regions and $i = m+1, \cdots, n$ import regions. Reflection will show that a net import region will never export to any region. (Why send exports out if you have to expensively ship in imports to replace them? Instead ship directly.) Reflection also shows that a net export region will never import from any region. Thus, the only non-zero E_{ij}'s are from an export region i to an import region j.

What does this mean for Table I? It means that we can label our regions so as to give the first m numbers to our export regions and the

TABLE II

Regions	$1 \cdots m$	$m+1,$	$m+2 \cdots n$		Total Exports
exporters 1 2	zeros	$E_{1,m+1}$ $E_{2,m+1}$	$E_{1,m+2}$ $E_{2,m+2}$	$\cdots E_{1,n}$ $E_{2,n}$	(E_1) (E_2)
$\cdot$ $\cdot$ $\cdot$		$\cdot$ $\cdot$ $\cdot$			
m		$E_{m,m+1}$	$E_{m,m+2}$	E_{mn}	(E_m)
importers $m+1$ $\cdot$ $\cdot$ $\cdot$ n	redundant negative numbers		zeros		
Total Imports		$(-E_{m+1})$	$(-E_{m+2})$	$\cdots (-E_n)$	

last $n - m$ numbers to the import regions. Table I will then divide itself up into 4 major blocks: positive numbers will then be in only the upper right-hand block relating the exporting countries to the importing countries; the two blocks relating exporters to exporters and importers to importers will necessarily be full of zeros, and can be neglected. The block relating importers to exporters will consist of negative numbers only and will simply duplicate our positive numbers.

[11] That is $E_i = 0$ implies $E_{ij} = 0 = E_{ji}$ for all j. Note that I am adopting the convention of not treating cargo shipped *through* a port as at all part of its exports or imports. Thus, cargo going from London to San Francisco is not to be treated as both an import and export of Panama. A similar philosophy tells me that T_{ij} data have already been adjusted so that it is no longer cheaper to send cargo from i to j via a third port k: such an "indirect" route would already have been defined to be the cheapest direct route and by our convention the port k would not be explicitly involved. Such preliminary adjustments of the definition of T_{ij} have made it satisfy the "Pythagorean" relations $T_{ij} \leq T_{ik} + T_{kj}$, etc.

Table II shows the relevant configuration. Note that all the numbers shown by symbol are positive: Thus $(-E_n)$ represents positive imports because algebraic exports E_n are negative for an importing country. Note that a table of T_{ij}'s is definable for *all* countries and all blocks; but with the given positive exports and imports shown in the margins of the table within parentheses, we would be interested only in the T_{ij}'s in the upper right-hand corner.

VI.—*Relation to the Koopmans Linear Programming Problem*

In this and the next section, I shall try to relate the results of our international trade problem to the newly developed theory of linear programming (defined austerely by the mathematician as "the maximization of a linear expression subject to linear inequalities"). For the theorist these are important sections, and to an economist who has heard about this new field and would like to get an idea of what it is all about, these will serve to indicate its general flavor. Though I have tried to use only the most elementary tools, these two sections are not summer-hammock reading; and for this reason, the remaining sections, from VIII on, have been arranged so that a reader can go directly on to them, skipping the more technical material.

Imagine now that the positive totals in parentheses $(E_1, \cdots, E_m)$ and $(-E_{m+1}, \cdots, -E_n)$ were given to us by Enke while at the same time he concealed from us the entries $E_{i,m+j}$ giving the detailed breakdowns. Then for us to find the missing numbers so as to minimize total transport cost would be precisely the Koopmans-Hitchcock problem in linear programming.[12]

How do we know that Enke's solution for E_{ij}'s does truly minimize transport cost? Since I have shown that Enke does maximize net social pay-off, and since the expressions $\sum_1^n S_i(E_i)$ in NSP of equation (3) depend only on the regional totals of exports $(E_1 \cdots, E_n)$, it follows that maximizing NSP would be impossible unless the E_{ij}'s were optimal for minimizing transport cost. Thus the Cournot-Enke problem does have inside it the Koopmans problem.[13]

* * *

[12] We minimize

$$\sum_{i=1}^{m} \sum_{j=m+1}^{n} T_{ij}E_{ij}$$

subject to

$$\sum_{j=m+1}^{n} E_{ij} = E_i \qquad (i = 1, \cdots, m)$$

and

$$\sum_{i=1}^{m} E_{ij} = (-E_j) \qquad (j = m+1, \cdots, n) \qquad E_{i,m+j} \geqq 0.$$

[13] A close analogy is the Yntema-Robinson problem of determining best outputs for a monopolist discriminating among independent markets. This includes inside it the problem of best allocating a given total output among markets.

Despite its likeness to the Kirchhoff-Maxwell quadratic maximum property of electric networks, the Koopmans problem cannot be solved by simple Kirchhoff networks unless entirely new laws of resistance can be inserted into such a network.[14] However, we can utilize the Enke network, which uses standard resistances and rectifiers, to solve any Koopmans problem. But we must work backwards: we must experimentally vary Enke's A_i's, which he puts into his network as prescribed voltages, until we achieve the requisite n totals $(E_1, \cdots, E_m, -E_{m+1}, \cdots, -E_n)$.[15] We can read off the required interregional exports as electric currents from the resulting Enke analogue network.

The above method is of interest because it suggests that any linear programming problem may be solvable as an unconstrained extremum problem provided we can imbed it in a suitably generalized problem.[16] Since the Air Forces and Bureau of Standards have set up their electronic calculators so as to solve transportation problems in relatively short time, there is no need to pursue the computational advantage of analogue networks any farther here.

VII.—*Equilibrium Prices and the Dual Problem*

The equilibrium prices as given by equations (4) arise naturally in the Enke problem but are completely absent from the initial formulation of the transport problem. However, as an economist, Koopmans sought to introduce some kind of price mechanism into the calculation

---

[14] See *Activity Analysis*, p. 259.

[15] This can always be done. The theory of the "dual problem" in linear programming assures us that there exists a set of parallel shifts of the excess-supply curves that will bring about any prescribed E_i configuration. The slopes of the excess-supply curves, Enke's b's can be arbitrary positive numbers. The procedure here described has the drawback of involving in effect a need to solve a set of simultaneous equations between the A's and E's. This might be mechanized by servomechanisms. (Query: does the "dual network" to Enke's solve the "dual problem" of linear programming?)

[16] Thus, if we use ordinary matrix notation and are given m arbitrary c's and $m(\geqq n)$ arbitrary x's, suppose we seek to maximize $Z = b'x$ subject to $Ax = c$ and $x \geqq 0$. Then for any $n \times n$ positive definite matrix B, there exists an n-vector v such that

$$Z^* = c'Bc - v'c + b'x = x'A'BAx - v'Ax + b'x$$

will be at a maximum for $x \geqq 0$ only if $Ax = c$. Having somehow found such unknown v's, we can solve Z by solving Z^*, an unconstrained extremum problem. For special A's and B's this can be converted into a simple analogue network problem. In every case we can solve the dual problem by taking proper combinations of the optimal derivatives of Z^*. Actually Z^* need not be quadratic but can be more general. A natural generalization of the Koopmans problem would be to have the flow of shipments vary directly with the marginal costs of transport $T_{ij} + P_i - P_j$. This would differ from the Enke problem in that E_i would then be a function of all P's and not of P_i alone. Dr. Martin Beckmann has written a number of interesting Cowles Commission Memoranda dealing with the case of continuous markets located everywhere in the plane. The partial differential equations of equilibrium correspond very closely to those of the Koopmans problem and a potential function plays a similar rôle. For the continuous case too, we can imbed the problem into a more general situation in which there is an excess-supply function at every point.

and he did succeed in defining a set of prices or potentials that correspond to our s_i's and P_i's. In doing this he was guided by economic and electric analogies and he was able to anticipate the mathematicians' theories of what is called the "dual problem" in linear programming. Mathematical theory assures us that every minimum problem in linear programming can be, so to speak, turned on its side and can be converted into a related maximum problem. The answer to this maximum problem also gives the correct answer for the quantity that was to be minimized.

For sake of brevity I shall simply refer the reader to the theory of linear programming for interpretations and proofs of the following remarks: (1) The P's or s's of equation (4) are the dual variables to the E_{ij}'s of the transport problem;[17] (2) $P_i - P_j$ can be interpreted in the Koopmans problem as an element of indirect marginal cost to be added to direct marginal cost T_{ij},—this term takes into account the money advantages of having an empty ship at j rather than at i; (3) If we change some E_i's, then the resulting increase in total transport cost is related to the P's; (4) Pricing in a competitive market could conceivably keep a system in the proper optimal configuration.[17a]

[17] Defining the profitability of any export from i to j as $\pi_{ij} = P_j - P_i - T_{ij}$, then for all $\pi_{ij} \leqq 0 \leqq P_k$, the maximum of $Z = -\sum P_k E_k$ will equal the minimum achievable transport costs. For any $\pi_{ij} < 0$, $E_{ij} = 0$, and for any $E_{ij} < 0$, $\pi_{ij} = 0$. Z can be rewritten $\sum\sum E_{ij}(P_j - P_i)$ so that we can think of the problem as that of finding the price differentials that will maximize the total *gain* in value of amounts shipped, subject to non-positive profitabilities on each shipment. It may be mentioned that only price differences are determinate and that the "dual variables" corresponding to export regions are related to their prices.

[17a] The present techniques, generalized in the manner indicated by cited work of Beckmann, can be used to throw light on many of the problems arising in connection with the basing point controversy. Oligopolists selling a homogeneous product want some pattern of pricing that will lead to a single *unambiguous price* at any geographical point. Usually, too, the pattern must be such as to lead to a not-too-obviously-wasteful flow of transport, and it must provide for a fairly stable and not-too-lopsided sharing of the market by the different producers. Historically, so long as most production is in fact concentrated in one advantageous place, such as Pittsburgh, a single basing pattern meets these criteria and is not too inefficient. Such a pattern of course encourages consumers to move toward the base; but to the extent that customers do not move, it encourages producers to move out toward them so as to receive in the form of higher net prices the transport costs saved or "phantom freight."

In any case, in a dynamic world any one locality will usually lose its dominant advantages in time and many plants will be operating away from the single basing point. Consequently, the system will lead increasingly to an inefficient pattern of transport and will become increasingly vulnerable to public criticism and to competition. A multiple basing point system may then come into effect and this will represent a compromise between FOB pricing and delivered pricing: within each region, the basing point pattern will prevail but at the shiftable boundaries of the regions there may be price competition between regions.

The requirements for the regional pattern of prices and flow of commodities is so strictly determined by perfect-competition assumptions that it is easy to show how basing point patterns deviate from the spirit and the letter of the competitive pattern: thus when producers all over the country respect a single basing point pattern, the contour lines of equal-delivered-price surround the basing point in a manner superficially similar to a perfect-competition pattern; but the flow of transports is *not* perpendicular to the contour lines of price and so we instantly detect the absence of perfect competition. For any given pattern of producer and con-

VIII.—*Illustrative Case Study*

A numerical example may help to clarify the theoretical relations. Unless there are at least four regions, no problem of optimizing the pattern of exports can arise. So consider regions I, II, III, IV characterized by the following transport costs (in \$ per unit of shipment).

A
$$\left[\begin{array}{cc|cc} \cdot & T_{12} & T_{13} & T_{14} \\ T_{21} & \cdot & T_{23} & T_{24} \\ \hline T_{31} & T_{32} & \cdot & T_{34} \\ T_{41} & T_{42} & T_{43} & \cdot \end{array}\right] = \left[\begin{array}{cc|cc} \cdot & 9 & 8 & 7 \\ 4 & \cdot & 4 & 1 \\ \hline 5 & 1 & \cdot & 5 \\ 6 & 2 & 6 & \cdot \end{array}\right]$$

Let us suppose that initial local conditions of demand and supply are such as to make Regions I and II exporters and III and IV importers. Suppose further that I initially exports only to III while II exports to both III and IV. In that case the data in the upper right-hand block of the transport cost array are alone relevant. The resulting export shipments are perhaps as shown in the following table:

B

Regions	III	IV	Exports	Local Price
I	38	0	(38)	(\$10)
II	2	50	(52)	\$14
Imports	(40)	(50)	90	
Local Price	\$18	\$15		

If only the data in parentheses in Table B were given, we could from the cost data in Table A deduce the remaining numbers in B. To do so

sumer location and observed flow of product, linear programming permits us to calculate the optimal minimum cost of transport and to compare it with the actual.

The optimum pattern never permits of overlapping markets of differently located plants; so it is obvious that an omnipotent combine of oligopolists would never use the arbitrary pattern of price discrimination implied by basing points. Nonetheless, there is nothing at all surprising about the use of this pattern; for after all an omnipotent combine of oligopolists would not engage in competitive advertising and many other things which we expect actual imperfect competitors to engage in. Except in times of formal or informal price control, imperfect competitors customarily administer their prices at more than marginal cost; and since perfect non-discrimination is only one out of an infinity of patterns, we should not be at all surprised by the existence of price discrimination. Moreover, contrary to some views in the literature, the pattern of price discrimination implied by adhering to basing point formulas is *not* particularly a strange or arbitrary one: it can be shown to presuppose that the elasticity of demand of customers for the delivered output of the basing point mills increases slightly with distance from the basing point, an assumption that no one would defend as exact but also an assumption that no assistant vice-president would be motivated to denounce strongly. Under oligopoly the most precious of all devices are those that lead to an informal consensus and the basing point system has the great virtue that within a region it reduces the whole pattern of pricing *to a single unknown*, around which sentiments can form and in terms of which mere price-competing is obviated.

we would have to solve the Koopmans problem and its so-called dual problem; however, in solving the more general Enke problem, all P's would already have been determined by supply and demand conditions, as would have all the unknowns of the problem.

To understand the necessary pattern of price, Figure 5a is useful. It represents what the mathematical topologist calls a "tree," and it shows the flow of exports by means of arrows. Note that all four markets are connected and that competition will freeze all P's as soon as any one P in the tree is known.

FOUR-REGION TRADE EQUILIBRIA

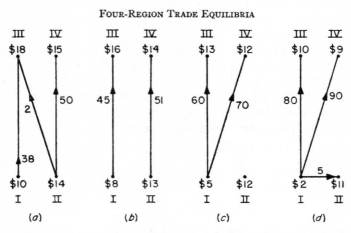

FIGURE 5. The changing network of trade as excess-supply at 1 increases. (Arrows show direction of trade while nearby numbers show its magnitude. Dollar figures refer to regional prices.)

Now let us suppose that there is an increase in domestic supply and a decrease in domestic demand in I, so that I's excess supply function increases. It will be shown in the next section that this must depress P_1. At first, therefore, the *qualitative* pattern of trade will be unchanged; and hence, all P's must decrease by exactly the same amount as P_1 decreases. (Incidentally, algebraic exports of *all* other regions must at first go down if their markets are to be cleared.)

However, if the excess-supply function at I increases enough, region II's export market to III may be completely captured by I. This case is shown in Figure 5b. Our tree has now split off into two trees, or what the mathematician calls a "forest." Now P_2 and P_4 are interconnected but they are independent of P_1 and P_3. This is called the case of "degeneracy" in the theory of linear programming, and its theory is well understood.[18] From this point on further increases in excess-supply at I

[18] This "degeneracy" is not quite the same thing as the following phenomenon: there may for some E's be more than one optimal trade pattern, with choice between the different optima

will depress P_1 and P_3 equally but will leave P_2 and P_4 unchanged, and will not affect exports or consumption in those regions.

But if excess-supply in I increases by still more, it will finally so depress P_1 as to permit I to capture II's remaining export market in IV. II is now isolated as in Figure 4c, which shows a lopsided forest. In this region P_1, P_3, and P_4 all fall equally, and imports of III and IV gradually increase. P_2 and II's consumption remain unchanged, with her export remaining zero.

In the ultimate stage shown by Figure 5d, excess-supply increases so much in I that we again have a tree. I has become an exporter to everybody; all prices are from now on locked together and go down equally.

To clinch his understanding of the principles here shown, the reader should draw the diagrams that would precede Figure 5 as the excess-supply function in I is *reduced*. He can show how all P's rise together until I ceases to export and becomes isolated; how all other P's then remain unchanged, until finally I becomes an importer from II and a tree is formed; still further increases in P_1 will finally cause III and IV to become exporters to I rather than importers, finally putting I in the ultimate importer stage. The reader may also experiment with *ceteris paribus* shifts in excess-supply in some other region. If he rigorously specifies a local excess-supply curve at each point, he can rigorously work out the equilibrium solution at each stage; however, it will be a sufficient test of his understanding if he can correctly infer the qualitative direction in which P's and E's must shift.

IX.—*Comparative Statics*

We can now cash in on our success in converting the spatial equilibrium system into a maximum problem: for such systems it is easy to make rigorous predictions as to the qualitative direction in which the variables of the system will change when some change is made in the data of the problem.

Let me begin with a simple case. Suppose the transport cost rises between i and j. What effect will this alone tend to have on the trade pattern? I think anyone will guess that, however other variables may change, exports from i to j must certainly decrease or at worst remain

---

being a matter of indifference. Thus, Koopmans, *op. cit.* p. 253, has called attention to the following kind of a situation: shipments from London to San Francisco meet shipments from New York to Honolulu in Panama; provided we are dealing with homogeneous shipments of wheat or empty vessels, it is obviously *indifferent* whether we reroute some of the London-Frisco shipments to Honolulu—provided an equal and opposite rerouting of New York cargo is simultaneously made. The cost data of Table A provide such an example when III is exporting say 15, IV exporting 30, I importing 25 and II importing 20. It then becomes a matter of indifference as to how III's exports are divided between I and II, provided that IV's shipments compensate. Professor Robert Solow points out to me that creating a fictitious set of two intermediate ports—V' which receives 45 and V'' which exports 45—will get rid of the indeterminacy.

the same; such exports can certainly not increase.[19] This happens to be a correct conclusion. But how can we be sure that our intuition is correct in a system that may involve hundreds of unknowns? The analytic theory of maximum systems worked out in my *Foundations of Economic Analysis* provides us with just such assurance.

And as a matter of fact, if we try to discover why our intuition suggested the answer it did, we will discover, I believe, that we have consciously or unconsciously been already identifying the system with a maximum and we have been heuristically inputing teleology and wisdom into the system. Again, this happens to be a rigorously correct procedure once the system has been rigorously identified as a maximum one. Indeed, in the physical sciences, the somewhat mystical principle of Le Chatelier, which says that a system tends to react to a stress so as to minimize and counter its effects, is just such a heuristic teleological principle and derives its validity from the maximum conditions underlying thermodynamic equilibrium.

* * *

A more interesting application of the above kind of analysis is provided by the problem of a shift in the excess-supply function at one place alone, say at region 1. Our intuition tells us that an increase in excess-supply at 1 should cause total exports from that region, E_1, to grow.

There is no loss in generality in assuming that the shift in the excess-supply function at 1 is a parallel vertical shift, so that we simply subtract a constant a_1 from the $s_1(E_1)$ expression in order to give the excess-supply curve the desired rightward and downward shift, with more being supplied at every price. Previously our net social pay-off could be written as a function of E_1 and other variables. This is still true, but now in the expression for *NSP* there will be an additional term $+a_1E_1$. The interested reader may be referred to Chapter 3 of *Foundations of Economic Analysis* for a full statement of the reasoning. It is enough to state here that the algebraic sign of the change in E_1 with respect to a change in a_1 must then be positive, or at worst zero. This rigorously confirms the conjecture that an increase in excess-supply at any point tends to increase the algebraic exports of a region and decrease its algebraic imports.

(1) How will such an increase in excess-supply affect price at 1? (2) How will it affect prices everywhere else? (3) How will it affect algebraic exports, E_i, everywhere else? Our intuition does not respond so easily to these further questions. But anyone who has worked through

---

[19] In the Enke formulation of the problem, the total E_i's are not held constant: they are changing as they must to restore the equilibrium. Of course, a similar theorem can be stated in the Koopmans case: an increase in T_{ij}, with all E_i's constant, can never increase E_{ij}.

the numerical example of the previous section will be able to make some fairly shrewd conjectures.

First, we would guess that an increase in excess-supply at 1 will depress P_1. Surprisingly, this turns out to be quite difficult to prove. For the result does not depend upon what happens at 1 alone, and no amount of graphical shifting of the curves in the 1 market can be relied upon for valid inferences. If region 1 were self-contained, an increase in its positively sloping excess-supply curve would certainly have to depress its price in order to get the market cleared. But in the previous paragraph, we have already seen that the net exports out of 1 have gone up, which by itself tends to relieve the redundancy of local supply and to increase rather than depress the local price. Which effect will be larger—the direct depressing effect on P_1 or the indirect upward effect on P_1 of the increased exports?[20]

The correct answer tells us that the final effect on P_1 of enhanced excess-supply at 1 *must* be downward. But how do we know that this is the correct answer? Not, I think, by simple maximum reasoning alone. The following considerations are more rewarding: (1) How does region 1 "force" an increase in its exports on the rest of the world if its price does not actually fall? Surely P_1 must decline or we shall have a contradiction to the rigorously proved result that 1's exports do go up. (2) As to the change of all other P's, how does the rest of the world absorb extra algebraic imports unless prices there have "on the whole" fallen?

Actually, our previous numerical example and the theory of the dual problem in linear programming show us that very stringent conditions must be satisfied by the network of prices in spatial equilibrium. Consequently, a much stronger result can be asserted:

An increase in excess-supply at 1 must have a downward effect on every single price, or at worst leave it unchanged. The downward effect on other prices cannot exceed the downward effect on its own price: for all regions that stay continuously connected by direct or indirect trade with 1, the changes in P_i must exactly equal the drop in P_1; but any regions that at any time remain disconnected from 1 (as in Figure 5b above) the change in P's will be less than the drop in P_1. And so long as we assume "normal" positive sloping excess-supply curves everywhere, we can confidently assert that an increase of excess-supply in region 1 must decrease algebraic exports everywhere else, or at worst leave some of them unchanged.

The proof of these statements can be supplied in a straight-forward fashion by anyone who has mastered the reasoning of the previous

[20] Mathematically, $P_1 = -a_1 + s_1(E_1)$ so that $dP_1/da_1 = -1 + s_1'(dE_1/da_1)$. These last two terms are of opposite sign so the final sign is in doubt.

numerical example relating to spatial price equilibrium. One of the remarkable features of the present model is the fact that economic intuition will lead to correct inferences in a system involving complex interdependence between any number of variables.[21]

X.—Generalized Reciprocity Relations

One last relation concerning reciprocity may be mentioned. Consider the effect on E_j of a unit change in the excess-supply curve at i. And let us compare it with the effect on E_i of a unit change in the excess-supply function at j. Qualitatively, these two effects have been shown to be of the same sign: increased excess-supply at any one point tends to decrease algebraic exports at any other point. We may, however, state a much more astonishing truth: a change in i's excess-supply function has *exactly the same quantitative effect* on E_j that a change in j's excess-supply function would have on E_i.

This reciprocity condition follows immediately from the maximum nature of the problem. Similar relations are known to hold in the field of physics due to the work of Maxwell, Rayleigh, and others. In the economic theory of consumer's behavior similar "integrability conditions" play an important rôle, as has been recognized by Slutsky, Hotelling, H. Schultz, Wold, Houthakker, and others.

I do not imagine that many people would be able to have derived such quantitative relations by intuitive reasoning. Nonetheless, these should not be regarded simply as some rather amusing and paradoxical relations turned up by mathematical reasoning. From a deeper methodological viewpoint, the way that we may test whether a given set of observations has arisen from a maximizing or economizing problem is

---

[21] Perhaps some theoretical economists will feel that the answer to the effect on P's of an increase in 1's excess-supply should have been immediately deducible from the J. R. Hicks stability conditions of *Value and Capital* (Oxford, 1946), Chaps. 5 and 8 and their appendixes. As far as the effect on P_1 itself is concerned, we must beware that we are not simply rewording the problem: "imperfect stability" is a definition and we must answer and not beg the question of whether the concrete specified Enke-Cournot system does or does not enjoy the property of being at least imperfectly stable. The problem is not quite so hopeless as this may sound, in view of the recognition in the 1946 edition of *Value and Capital* of the sufficiency of a maximum position to guarantee perfect and imperfect stability in a wide variety of cases. The present example is *not* directly one such case but it should be possible to make the necessary extensions to the theory so that it would be able to handle cases like the present. Among other things, the present example has the interesting feature of involving functions with corners where no derivatives can be uniquely defined and yet the important logical relations of a maximum position still prevail.

In connection with answering the question of the effect on prices other than P_1, problems of "complementarity" rather than stability are involved. The fact that all P's change in the same direction is related to the Mosak theorem concerning systems in which all goods are substitutes. J. L. Mosak, *General-Equilibrium Theory in International Trade Theory* (Bloomington, 1944) pp. 44, 49–51. Similar matrices have been studied by Leontief, Machlup and Metzler, Frobenius, Minkowski, Hawkins-Simon, Woodbury, Markoff, *et al.*, as discussed in a forthcoming paper by Robert Solow.

in terms of such reciprocity relations.[22] To me, one of the most interesting of the present problems is the fact that the fundamental reciprocity relations implied by a maximum problem turn out to transcend the case where partial derivatives exist.[23]

XI.—*Conclusion*

The problem of interconnected competitive regional markets is one of the rare cases where a reasonably simple and self-contained theoretical treatment is possible. It is a good case to demonstrate the powers of the theory of linear programming since it enables us to give rigorous proofs to plausible conjectures. It so happens that much of the literary discussion of the effects of tariffs and of exchange depreciations is, in the first instance at least, couched in terms of just this model. Thus when a journalist or economist tells you that depreciation of the pound will tend to increase U.K. exports to the United States, to decrease U.K. imports, and to raise pound prices on both categories of goods while depressing dollar prices on them, he is either repeating from memory what someone has worked out from a Cournot-type model or he is himself thinking in terms of such a model.[24] Needless to say, the partial equilibrium assumptions involved in the domestic demand schedules and the neglect of aggregative relations constitute a serious defect of such a model except as a rough first approximation to the answers in especially favorable cases. Good economic theory will recognize these limitations rather than be predisposed to neglect them.

[22] See Henry Schultz, *The Theory and Measurement of Demand*, Chicago, 1938, Chaps. I, XVIII, XVIX.

[23] A more general theory shows that even at corners, where partial derivatives are not uniquely defined, we can extend the definition of a derivative to include all the admissible slopes of "supporting lines or planes" and then generalized reciprocity relations of the following type hold. Plot E_j against a_i and also plot E_i against a_j. The former curve may at some points have a corner so that its generalized partial derivative is anything between, say, $-.33$ and -5.92. It will then turn out that the second curve must also have a corner at the point corresponding to the corner of the first, and its range of indeterminacy of slope must also be between $-.33$ and -5.92. Analogous relations hold in many variables. Thus, within the field of linear programming there exist quite a number of natural generalizations of the relationships that hold for regular differentiable functions.

[24] For elaborations and criticisms see G. Haberler, "The Market for Foreign Exchange and the Stability of the Balance of Payments," *Kyklos*, Vol. III (1949), pp. 193–218; J. Viner, *Studies*, Chicago, 1938, pp. 590–91. Mention should also be made of work by Yntema, Joan Robinson, J. J. Polak, and others.

73

Intertemporal Price Equilibrium:
A Prologue to the Theory of Speculation

By

Professor **Paul A. Samuelson**

Cambridge, Mass.

————

Contents: 1. Introduction. — Part I: Spatial Relations: 2. Established Theory. — Part II: Ideal Intertemporal Spatial Patterns Under Foreseen Stationary Conditions: 3. Case of Instantaneous Harvest; 4. Harvests at Different Times; 5. Steady Production. — Part III: Temporal Equilibrium Under Foreseen Changes in Conditions: 6. Fluctuations in Instantaneous Harvests; 7. Fluctuations in Non-Instantaneous Harvests; 8. Continuous Production and Temporary Fluctuations. — Part IV: Equilibrium Patterns of "Futures" Prices: 9. Multiplicity of Futures Prices; 10. Equilibrium Positive and Negative Price Spreads. — Part V: Elementary Proof of Theoretical Relations: 11. Back-to-Back Intertemporal Diagram; 12. Analysis of Crop Fluctuations. — Part VI: Variable Transport Costs and Interdependence of Temporal Schedules: 13. Supply and Demand for Storage; 14. Vertical Price Relations. — Part VII: Effects of Uncertainty: 15. Basic Issues; 16. Methodological Problems; 17. Penalties for Violating Equilibrium Conditions Under Certainty; 18. Teleology and Competition; 19. A Digression on Dynamic Welfare Economics. — Mathematical Appendix on Speculative Markets.

1. Introduction

Economic relations in *time* have many of the properties of economic relations in *space*. In this paper I apply the tools that analyze spatial competitive relations[1] to the slightly more difficult problems of equilibrium commodity prices over time. The resulting theory shows how prices fall at Harvest time, then rise seasonally until the next Harvest. While the results agree with our intuitive common sense expectations, I

---

[1] See Paul A. Samuelson, "Spatial Price Equilibrium and Linear Programming", *The American Economic Review*, Vol. XLII, Menasha, Wisc., 1952, pp. 283 sqq., for references to writers since Cournot (1838) who have dealt with the space problem.

have not found in the literature a systematic account of the basic theory[1], nor an analysis of how foreseen and unforeseen changes shift the seasonal price patterns.

I call all this a prologue to the theory of speculation because that theory is intimately bound up with *uncertainty*[2]. I am inclined to think that conquering the easier problem, in which future conditions are for simplicity's sake assumed to be forseeable and foreseen, will provide a useful springboard from which to attack the realistic speculative market problems. But future work will have to determine whether beginning with certainty relations is indeed a fruitful method of attacking the harder problems of reality.

While the theory outlined here is overly simple, in that it abstracts from uncertainty, it is hard enough going in its logic. Therefore, I have put in the Mathematical Appendix a symbolic formulation of some of the problems. And at the end of the paper I have sketched some of the questions raised by uncertainty.

Part I: Spatial Relations

2. Established Theory

In two competitive markets separated by space, the prices for the same good may differ, but are subject to the constraint

$$(1) \qquad\qquad -T_{21} \leqq P_2 - P_1 \leqq T_{12}$$

where T_{12} represents the transport costs per unit of the good shipped from Market 1 to Market 2, and T_{21} represents the similar transport cost per

---

[1] See the brilliant early paper, John B. Williams, "Speculation and the Carryover", *The Quarterly Journal of Economics*, Vol. L, Cambridge, Mass., 1935—6, pp. 436 sqq. — Harold Hotelling, "The Economics of Exhaustible Resources", *The Journal of Political Economy*, Vol. XXXIX, Chicago, Ill., 1931, pp. 137 sqq. — Moses Abramovitz, "An Approach to a Price Theory for a Changing Economy", *Studies in History, Economics and Public Law*, No. 453, New York and London, 1939. — Paul A. Samuelson, *Economics, An Introductory Analysis*, New York, Toronto and London, 1948, Chapter 25; 3rd Ed., 1955, Chapter 22.

[2] A few references are Holbrook Working, "The Theory of Price of Storage", *The American Economic Review*, Vol. XXXIX, 1949, pp. 1254 sqq. — *Idem*, "Theory of the Inverse Carrying Charge in Futures Markets", *Journal of Farm Economics*, Vol. XXX, Ithaca, 1948, pp. 1 sqq. — H. S. Houthakker, a forthcoming Cowles Commission Monograph on the grain and cotton markets. — Martin Beckmann, "A Continuous Model of Transportation", *Econometrica*, Vol. XX, Chicago, 1952, pp. 643 sqq., and unpublished Cowles Commission memoranda from 1952 to the present date. — See also the symposium by Kaldor, Dow, and Hawtrey in the *Review of Economic Studies*, Vol. VII, London, 1939—40, pp. 196 sqq., initiated by N. Kaldor, "Speculation and Economic Stability", *ibid.*, pp. 1 sqq. — J. M. Keynes, *A Treatise on Money*, Vol. II: *The Applied Theory of Money*, London, 1930, had discussed the important concept of "backwardation."

unit of the good shipped from 2 to 1. These transport costs consist of
freight, insurance, interest on capital tied up in transit, etc.

With transport costs positive, both equalities in (1) cannot hold
simultaneously; but both inequalities can hold simultaneously, and in this
case no goods will flow in either direction; if one inequality holds and
one equality, then goods will follow the inverse law of gravity and flow
toward the higher price. Thus, with $P_2 = P_1 + T_{12} > P_1$, goods can
flow from 1 to 2 and will do so in whatever amount is needed to satisfy
supplies and demands in the two markets.

Of course, this spatial flow of goods is a subtraction from the net
supply of Market 1 and an addition to the net supply at 2 so that P_1 and
P_2 will be mutually determined along with the spatial flow by the fully
specified demand and supply schedules in both markets and the numerical
transport costs. Figure 1 is a familiar back-to-back diagram used to
describe the simplest spatial model[1].

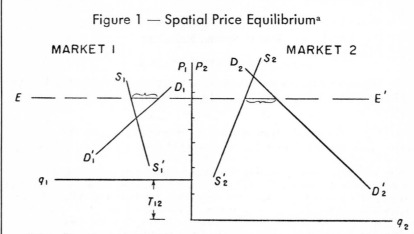

Figure 1 — Spatial Price Equilibrium[a]

a Because Market 2's equilibrium price without trade would exceed Market 1's by
more than the unit transport cost T_{12} between the markets, 1 will export to 2 and
equilibrium will be where the export bracket equals the import bracket and P_2 exceeds
P_1 exactly by the transport cost.

[1] This figure comes from my cited paper but it is standard in the international trade
literature. Note that for short periods of time the relation (1) may be violated if shipping
takes finite time and if shipping is being rationed rather than freely available. Equation (1)
can be formally saved in this case by the artificial device of redefining the relevant T_{12} to
take account of the "emergency" condition; but fortunately the theory is saved from the
charge of emptiness by the fact that solid numerical values can often be given to T_{12} which
almost always hold — note e. g., the stability of the pre-war gold points.

Part II: Ideal Intertemporal Spatial
Patterns Under Foreseen Stationary Conditions

3. Case of Instantaneous Harvest

Now exactly the same analysis applicable to space holds for the simplest model of intertemporal price relations. Thus, Figure 2 shows the ideal seasonal pattern for a crop that is harvested at one definite time in the Autumn and for which there is a uniform demand schedule all year long, dependent on present price but independent of prices at any time other than the present. Everyone is assumed to foresee correctly that there will be no weather variations or shifts in demand and supply.

Note that the price which will prevail in Winter is higher than in the Fall but lower than will prevail in the Spring and Summer. Actually in Figure 2a the price rises from Harvest time until it reaches its maximum just before the next Harvest: the amount of the rise equals the "transport cost for transporting grain from one time to a later future time" — i. e., equals warehouse storage costs, insurance, interest on capital, transport to and from warehouse, etc. For initial simplification, we may assume that these "transport costs" are constants, competitively or administratively determined and independent of the grain market in question; the price increases are made to be more than linear because insurance and interest charges are likely to be constant *percentages* of a growing value. As price rises through the crop year, rate of consumption drops as shown in Figure 2c.

The total stock of grain moves opposite to price: the stock Q is at a maximum just after Harvest; it decreases fairly steadily[1] throughout the year, until just before Harvest in the simplest model it is literally zero. Why zero? Because price drops just at Harvest time, and no one will knowingly incur positive costs in transporting grain from "before Harvest" to "after Harvest" if a price loss is indicated. Such behavior would contradict our economic law of gravity now applied to time as well as space[2].

4. Harvests at Different Times

Of course, all the Harvest does not come in on one Thanksgiving day. Only minor modifications are needed to take account of a regularly

---

[1] Actually, the rising price means that stocks are being eaten into a little more slowly as the year progresses: so Q drops in a slightly concave fashion. If the gradual emptying of warehouses depressed the competitive price of storage, the $P(t)$ curves might reverse their curvatures.

[2] Of course, if transport costs were negative, so that warehouses paid you money to store grain with them, there could be a carry-over into the new crop year.

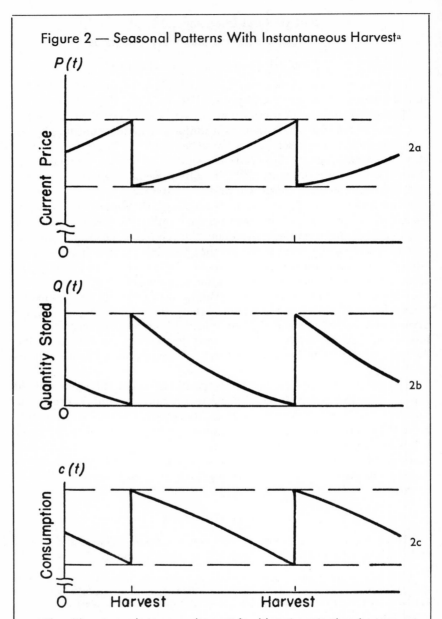

Figure 2 — Seasonal Patterns With Instantaneous Harvest[a]

a If positive storage is to pay, price must be rising at a rate given by transport-through-time storage costs. Anticipating the new Harvest's depressing of price, storage carry-over becomes zero.

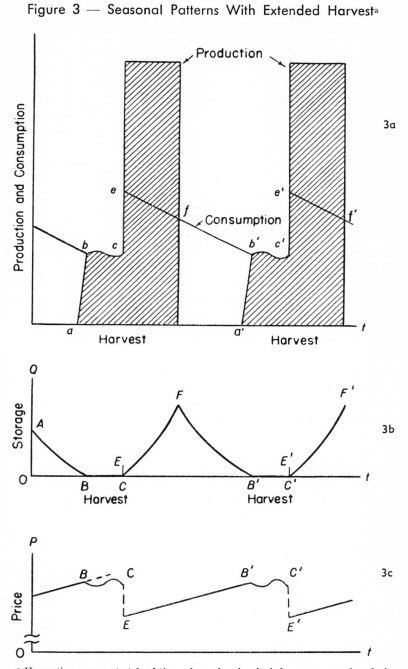

Figure 3 — Seasonal Patterns With Extended Harvest[a]

a Harvesting over a stretch of time, shown by the shaded area, means that during the bc stage (ii) period of zero storage, P may fluctuate with current production — provided only P doesn't ever rise faster than the storage cost gradient of the eb' stage (i).

foreseen pattern of harvesting. Suppose that in Figure 3a the frequency distribution a b c d e f typifies harvesting spread over a month or two in late Summer and Fall. Figure 3c shows what might be the resulting pattern of price. Because in Figure 3b storage is alternately positive and zero, this price pattern now splits up into three phases:

Stage (i): Before any Harvest comes in, price rises as it did in Figure 2. The first driblets of Harvest supply will slow down the rate of using up of the total stocks Q^1. Still price must continue to grow like AB for a while.

Stage (ii): But finally the arrival and impending arrival of great harvestings makes it mandatory for stocks (which are primarily carry-overs from the previous season) to be zero. This second stage of zero carry-over might last but an instant, and new storage of the new crop might begin. However, I have chosen a case where for some weeks the new harvestings are just sufficient to satisfy current demand — no more, no less. But at what current prices? At the wobbly pattern of prices shown in BC, which is just the pattern of P needed to counterbalance the reverse wobbles in currently sold harvestings — shown in bc of Figure 3a.

Note that the only restriction on price movements in this zero-stock Stage (ii) is that price cannot rise by more per unit time than the rate of intertemporal transport cost. Thus, I have drawn in a dotted line at B showing an upper ceiling on price growth. If this ceiling were violated, some of the current harvesting would go into storage, which is to deny our second stage assumption and take us into the next stage.

Stage (iii): Now so much of the harvest is coming in that storage for the new season begins after e. With stocks $Q > 0$, prices must rise in accordance with the intertemporal law of gravity or transport cost. Stage (iii) is of course Stage (i) for the next crop year; and so it goes.

To summarize: harvesting over a period of time differs from the instantaneous Harvest model by introducing a possible intermediate stage in which for a finite time stocks are zero and prices are free to wobble so as to sell current production, subject only to the requirement that price *cannot* grow faster than transport or storage costs[2].

Actually, spatial and temporal patterns were combined in the pre-war grain markets. Harvests in the southern hemisphere come at quite different times than in the northern. The result was several alternations within the year of the ups and downs of Stages (i) and (ii). The extreme case of these

---

[1] Conceivably the new harvestings could even cause Q to grow for a little while.

[2] See footnote 1, p. 184, for a minor qualification which permits price temporarily to grow faster than transport costs.

recurring cycles is seen in markets of perishables where after each ship arrives in an isolated place prices are low, rising until the next ship arrives.

5. Steady Production

What happens if production is not concentrated at certain Harvest times as in the case of grain but instead, like copper, is more or less continuous over the year? Assuming uniform demand over the year and uniform costs, the simplest price pattern of all emerges: under ideal conditions of certainty and stationariness, P is constant over the year with consumption of the good constant. Given perfect synchronization of demands and supplies — admittedly a fantastic oversimplification — inventory stocks of goods that are not in process of being fabricated or consumed will be literally zero.

If we introduce foreseen minor wobbles in production or demand, prices may wobble as in Stage (ii) of the previous discussion. Of course, prices in this stage cannot increase more rapidly than transport costs so long as positive transport of goods from early to later time is stipulated to be absent.

We have now completed a survey of seasonal equilibrium patterns in the simplest model of frictionless foresight and stationary conditions that are known to repeat periodically from year to year. A rigorous demonstration of these intuitive proofs will be given later (Part V) for the simpler cases where the year is divided into but two time periods[1].

Part III: Temporal Equilibrium
Under Foreseen Changes in Conditions

6. Fluctuations in Instantaneous Harvests

Now we can drop the assumption of repetitive stationariness. But I still assume that *future changes are correctly foreseen*. What happens to the equilibrium patterns in the case where the Harvest has proved to be smaller than its future uniform level will be?

In the case of Section 3 where the Harvest always occurs on a single day, the answer is simple. Between now and next Harvest, people must cut down on their consumption. Price will grow according to the usual storage-cost gradient, but now it must start at a higher level and at each time during this crop-year be at a higher level. This suffices to spread the

---

[1] The Mathematical Appendix gives a proof for the continuous-time case involving differential equations of a type analyzed by Dr. Martin Beckmann of the Cowles Commission for Economic Research.

smaller Harvest over the whole year, making it last until just before the next Harvest when Q again will equal zero. Prices and consumption in subsequent years will revert to their previous equilibrium patterns. *So long as carry-over from one distinct crop-year to another remains always zero, Harvest stringency in one year will not affect subsequent years at all*[1]. Robinson Crusoe or a benevolent despot would, on reflection, perceive that this market-induced pattern is indeed optimal.

What happens if we go from the case of crop failure to the case of an especially good crop? So long as the crop is moderately above normal, the above conclusions apply, but of course in reverse: (i) Prices through this crop-year will begin at a lower level than in normal years, rising in accordance with storage costs, but maintaining low enough levels to cause the whole of the abnormal stock Q to be consumed by the eve of the next Harvest; (ii) subsequent years' patterns will be independent of today's moderate abundance.

However, if today's Harvest is *super*abundant, we may have to modify our conclusion about independence of crop-years. Suppose today's crop were big enough to depress this year's price so much as to make its Harvest Eve price *lower* than next-year's post-Harvest price would have been? Then obviously, it would become advisable to carry over some crop from this year to next. The two years then become a single unit with positive storage going on all the time. Hence, price must rise throughout the two years in the familiar Stage (i) pattern. And because grain is being held over from this year to next, price is higher this year than it would have been without carry-over, and consumption is lower. Next year's price and consumption move in opposite directions. Subsequent years are unaffected unless today's superabundance is so colossally great as to make for positive carry-over into the third year or later.

Note that superabundance today must always be gauged relative to the abundance that can be foreseen in subsequent years. This immediately shows us what will be the effects on the *present* of *foreseen future* crop shortages. If next year's shortfall is to be minor, nothing will happen during this crop-year in the instantaneous-crop model. However, if a foreseen shortage is known to be severe enough, it will necessitate positive carry-over from this year into next and will require prices to start higher

---

[1] Actually if the consumer and miller demand for grain at one time depends on future prices, this has to be slightly modified. Families might go without bread before the new Harvest knowing that afterwards they will be able to sate their hunger. Another case of "hidden carry-over" is provided by millers who might wait for the new Harvest to step up their activity, with the community in the meantime depleting its "normal stores" of flour. In a perfect market for flour as well as wheat, a constant time-delay for milling and specified costs of flour storage would recreate a zero carry-over for flour at a slightly later period than the "watershed" for grain between the two seasons.

already during *this* crop-year. An abundant crop, on the other hand, will if foreseen for next year have *no* effect on the present so long as zero carry-over between years was in any case scheduled to take place.

To summarize: Foreseen changes in future supply or demand that will take place within the crop-year or within any period of storage-connected markets (*à la* Stage (i)) must have an *immediate* impact on present and all intervening prices and quantities. But foreseen changes in future supply or demand that will take place beyond an intervening time in which carry-over is zero can have no effects on the present — unless the future change involves an increase in price large enough to shift the period of zero carry-over (so-called Stage (ii) of Figure 3) forward through time. This asymmetrical result — that, in the instantaneous-Harvest model, future price decreases can have no effect on present prices while future price increases if extreme can have an immediate effect — is due to the asymmetrical nature of time itself: I can move goods directly from the present to the future by storage at finite costs T_{12}; but, within this rigid model, for no finite T_{21} can I move goods directly from the future back into the present.

7. Fluctuations in Non-Instantaneous Harvests

The above conclusions concerning the asymmetrical independence of present and far-future prices requires slight modification if we drop the assumption of an instantaneous Harvest at an unchangeable date. With the Harvest coming in over a foreseen span of time, the exact date at which Stage (i) ends (with all of this crop-year's stored grain being zero) will now become a variable of the problem. This variable date must be determined by all the simultaneous equations of supply and demand of this and the next period; and our present problem is to ask how this important date will change when low or high crops occur in the present or in the foreseen future. Generally speaking, we can expect the following:

(1) An extraordinarily large Harvest now will tend, if anything, to lower this year's prices and to lengthen the period for which this year's crop is held: i. e., Stage (i) will tend to be lengthened. For moderate crop increases, any lengthening of Stage (i) is completely at the expense of Stage (ii). I must confess that I had intuitively expected that the terminal date of Stage (ii), which is the beginning date of Stage (iii) when the next year's crop goes into storage, could be delayed by high crops in this present season. This surmise appears to be wrong. What is correct is that the superabundance today may be so great as to cause some of this year's crop to be carried over to next year, thus eliminating Stage (ii) completely

and combining Stages (i) and (iii). This of course will depress next year's prices as well as this year's. But note that the same was true in the instantaneous Harvest case, so that no real modification of the simpler case's conclusion is needed.

(2) A short Harvest today will of course raise this year's price. It may, but need not always, shorten Stage (i), bringing earlier the date at which this year's storage becomes zero. If Stage (i) is shortened, Stage (ii) is lengthened by the same amount: i. e., the initial date of Stage (iii), when next year's crop goes into storage and its price rises along the transport gradient, cannot be brought earlier in time. Hence, we can conclude that, within the framework of this model, next year's prices will be unaffected by this year's shortages.

(3) From the above two results, we can conclude what will happen to this year's normal pattern if for a future year a crop shortage is foreseen. This year's prices can be affected if this year's storage must last longer and be carried over into next year. A moderate shortage foreseen for the next Harvest will lengthen this year's Stage (i) and raise this year's price. A great shortage will wipe out Stage (ii) completely, requiring this year's Stage (i) to stretch out over next year's Stage (iii), and this will raise present prices even more. To have an appreciable effect on present prices, a far distant crop shortage, even if fully foreseen, must be very serious indeed: it must be so drastic as to raise future prices enough to cover transport costs between now and the far future.

(4) A foreseen above-normal Harvest for next year has reverse effects. It can shorten this year's carry-over period, Stage (i), and thereby lower prices this year. For crops whose Harvest is closely bunched, the magnitude of this effect is likely to be minor. Can an abundant Harvest foreseen for more than one year hence have a downward effect on this year's prices? As far as I can tell, within the framework of this model, the asymmetry of temporal transportability — which makes it impossible for the present to borrow directly from the future — makes such a depressing influence of the far-future impossible.

8. Continuous Production and Temporary Fluctuations

Finally let us examine the effects of transient production (or demand) changes on the foreseen equilibrium patterns in the case of non-seasonal uniform supply and demand conditions. An interval of extraordinary production will, if it is moderate in amount, simply depress prices during the period of abundance. The price will not drop enough, relative to later prices, to induce carry-over to the future; and hence, within the framework of our simplest model of independent supplies and demands at different times, future behavior and future economic magnitudes cannot be affected. By the same type of reasoning, we see that a great abundance will depress current prices relative to later prices enough to induce positive carry-over, thereby lowering later prices and increasing later consumption. The interval for which later prices are affected varies, clearly, (a) with the lowness of transport or storage costs, (b) with the degree of superabundance presently current.

Prior to the foreseen abundance, whether major or minor, there will be no depressing effects on prices since no goods can be moved backward in time and there is no normal amount of carry-over that can be reduced.

A temporary production shortage has precisely similar effects. A moderate shortage affects only the period of shortage itself. A more serious shortage will raise contemporaneous prices enough to induce carry-over from earlier periods, thereby lowering their consumption and raising their prices in anticipation of the shortage. Prices and consumption subsequent to the shortage are absolutely unaffected, since no positive carry-over will take place in any case.

For anyone not interested in the details of seasonal patterns, the results of this last section adequately summarize the general effects of foreseen crop fluctuations under asymmetrical intertemporal transport: (a) Minor foreseen changes have only contemporaneous effects (within the "crop-year" if seasonality is present). (b) Important foreseen *shortages* have effects on *earlier* periods similar to their current effects but with attenuating strength. (c) Important foreseen *surpluses* have effects on *later* periods similar to their current effects but with attenuating strength.

Part IV: Equilibrium Patterns of "Futures" Prices

9. Multiplicity of Futures Prices

Up until now, I have been discussing only the "cash" or "spot" price pattern. Such a price is what would currently be quoted for current physical deliveries of the commodity in question (assumed to be perfectly homogeneous and standardized, for expositional simplicity). This current price changes over time, and people know it will change but that does not yet introduce the concept of a "futures" or "forward" market[1].

There is no reason why contracts should not be made that involve delivering at a specified future date. Supply and demand of an auctioneer type can be supposed to settle the prices at which each future delivery is

---

[1] Under my idealized assumption of one homogeneous product, there is no need to distinguish between a forward contract which specifies delivery in terms of a specific quality of grain and a futures contract which permits a delivery of alternative qualities but with an adjusting differential payment to be determined in an agreed-on fashion.

today quoted. For greatest simplicity we may assume that brokerage and margin charges are zero and that there are no indivisible costs of human time and energy in maintaining a broad market for each and every delivery date[1].

The current price with which we have been previously dealing becomes a special limiting case: its time profile, which is designated in Figure 2a by the function $P(t)$, will now have to be written as $P_0(t)$. This denotes the price determined at time t for delivery of the good *zero* periods later. I designate by $P_0(t)$, $P_1(t)$, $\ldots$, $P_\Theta(t)$ the price quoted at time t for delivery $0, 1, \ldots,$ or Θ periods ahead (where our periods are measured in minutes, months, days, weeks, years, or any convenient time unit). Negative Θ's have no meaning.

With the future behavior of prices for current delivery fully foreseen, i. e., with $P_0(t + \Theta)$ known for all values of Θ, there is only one equilibrium pattern that can prevail at time t for all futures of different delivery dates Θ ahead: namely,

$$(2) \qquad P_\Theta(t) = P_0(t + \Theta)$$

Why must the presently quoted futures price for delivery Θ periods ahead be exactly equal to the current price which will then prevail? Because if it did not, arbitragers could make money by buying cheap and selling dear. Thus, if $P_1(t) > P_0(t + 1)$, I could sell a futures contract for $P_1(t)$ and later fulfill it by buying grain at $P_0(t + 1)$, thereby profiting $P_1(t) - P_0(t + 1)$ on each unit. If enough people try to do this, the price $P_1(t)$ will be bid down until the equality $P_1(t) = P_0(t + 1)$ is restored. The reader can show how $P_1(t) < P_0(t + 1)$ will result in arbitragers' purchasing futures at $P_1(t)$, later receiving delivery on them and selling the resulting grain for $P_0(t + 1)$, thereby netting $P_0(t + 1) - P_1(t)$ and of course tending to restore the equality. Unlimited sure-thing excess profit opportunities are incompatible with equilibrium, and if momentarily in existence will set into action powerful forces tending to restore the equilibrium.

Now under conditions of certainty, the equilibrium pattern would result virtually instantaneously. In fact, no futures transactions need ever take place. It is differences of opinion that make horse races and horse markets. And in our model, there are no differences of opinion. Does this mean that the futures prices do not exist? Not at all. These equilibrium prices *do* exist and are posted in the market place. Of course, zero transactions take place at the equilibrium prices, but were the auctioneers to relax their vigilance for a moment and let the futures price patterns differ ever so minutely from the equilibrium pattern, transactions would come

---

[1] Needless to say, this is a gross distortion of reality. Only under very special circumstances will viable futures markets come into existence, as Holbrook Working has observed.

into being and restore the equilibrium. Technically, we have a case of futures' supply and demand intersecting at a unique point, even though that point happens to fall on the vertical price axis where transactions are zero.

Interpreting with strict literalness our absurd assumptions of literally zero transaction costs, we are free, if we want to, to imagine that the number of transactions is indeterminate rather than zero. No one who is going to have grain to sell later *need* under conditions of certainty concern himself to hedge by selling forward at a futures price agreed on now. But, if he wants to, he *can* "short hedge." To whom would he sell? Those who know they will consume grain at the future date have no need to hedge by buying forward. But there is no reason why they should not "long hedge," and an infinitesimal price advantage in the futures' patterns would under our frictionless assumptions permit anyone who wished to hedge to do so, each short hedger transacting with a long hedger and *vice versa*.

Just as we can think of all producers and consumers as being fully hedged in the no-uncertainty model, we are free to introduce speculation on a broad zone of indifference. No long speculator in futures stands to make anything; but in our model he has nothing to lose. Similarly with short speculators in futures (who sell for future delivery). *If all hedging were zero, equilibrium requires a matching of long speculators by short speculators — just as, in the absence of speculation, all long hedging had to be matched by short hedging.* The general rule says: Under conditions of certainty, those who know they have a position to hedge are free to hedge as much or little as they wish; omniscient speculators are free to speculate as much or little as they wish; however, if the known equilibrium pattern is to prevail, the total long position (of hedgers and speculators) must be exactly matched, at the equilibrium pattern, by the total short position (of hedgers and speculators)[1].

Under conditions of perfect foresight, the future literally exists in the present and a perfect futures market gives us a dramatic representation of this fact: the pattern of futures prices $P_\theta(t)$ belongs to the time t and is then being quoted; by scanning the identity $P_0(t + \Theta) = P_\theta(t)$ for all

---

[1] The distinction between speculator and hedger is easy to make in our omniscient model. A hedger is one who knows he is later going to produce or consume physical grain, and anticipates that future transaction by a futures transaction. A speculator in our model has no physical consumption or production counterpart to his transactions. Under conditions of certainty, *arbitrage* cannot be separated from speculation or hedging, but even if we admit a momentary transient state in which equilibrium is "restored," either hedgers or speculators may be the active agents. Perhaps some will choose to say that when hedgers arbitrage they do so not *qua* hedgers but *qua* speculators.

values of Θ, we literally see in present quotations all the prices for physical current deliveries that will develop in the future. (Thus, standing at any point on the curve in Figure 2a, what we see to our right along the diagram can be interpreted as the presently quoted futures prices for all the different values of Θ.)

10. Equilibrium Positive and Negative Price Spreads

Now given any historical pattern of current prices $P_0(t)$ for all t within an interval, you are able to infer what must be the corresponding pattern of futures prices $P_\Theta(t)$. Strictly speaking, we now have three rather than two dimensions: besides P and t we have Θ. If we select any particular value of Θ, say $\Theta = {}^3/_4$ years, so that we are concentrating on contracts for delivery three quarters ahead, we can make a two-dimensional plot of $P_{{}^3/_4}(t)$; of course, this will look exactly like the plot of $P_0(t)$ shown in Figures 2a, 3c, etc., except that the old plot will be shifted leftward by ${}^3/_4$ of a year. In the annually periodic case, the curve for $P_1(t)$ would coincide with that for $P_0(t)$ as would $P_n(t)$ for any *integral* value of Θ. Likewise would $P_{{}^5/_4}(t)$ and $P_{{}^{11}/_4}(t)$ fall on $P_{{}^1/_4}(t)$, and would $P_{{}^7/_4}(t)$ and $P_{n+{}^3/_4}(t)$ fall on $P_{{}^3/_4}(t)$.

It is of interest to examine the seasonal pattern of spreads between current price $P_0(t)$ and various futures prices, such as $P_{{}^1/_4}(t)$, $P_{{}^2/_4}(t)$, $P_{{}^3/_4}(t)$. Note that the price spread is always positive between the current price and the futures price for a period ahead that falls within the same crop-year: the price spread then corresponds exactly to the carrying charges for storage or intertemporal transport.

Note too that a negative or "inverse" price spread always occurs between the high current price at the end of one crop-year and the lower futures price corresponding to delivery early in the next crop-year. Such an inverse price spread[1] I do not designate by the frequently-met expression "inverse *carrying charge*," since in my ideal model no goods are actually carried over such an interval. Actually there are no limits in this model to the extent of the inverse price spread: if the future crop is known to be abundant enough, the numerical value of the inverse spread can be indefinitely large. In contrast, there is a rather inflexible upper ceiling on the positive price spreads, set by actual identifiable carrying charges (interest, storage rates, insurance, and other components of T_{12}).

The interested reader can draw plots of futures price spreads of the form $P_\Theta(t) - P_{\Theta'}(t)$ for all the cases discussed earlier, in which the Harvest period is spread over an interval of time and in which there are abnormal

---

[1] J. M. Keynes has analyzed "backwardation," but the inverse spreads in our pattern are not really of the Keynes' species, which prevails *after* Harvest time and which depends on risk and a positive aversion to risk.

crop fluctuations. He will of course note that the futures price spreads will often reflect past or future-crop conditions: e. g., a foreseen failure in next year's crop will lead to less inversion of the spread between current price and futures' price for delivery in the next crop year; the timing of the positive spreads will be affected, in the manner earlier analyzed, but the size of the positive spread within the same crop-year is so closely geared to storage charges as to be relatively little affected.

Part V: Elementary Proof of Theoretical Relations

11. Back-to-Back Intertemporal Diagram

I have now given a fairly complete description of the properties of the simplest ideal model involving (1) foresight of the future, (2) frictionless and costless intertemporal transport charges, and (3) independence of the supply and demand schedules of different times. The main results will be, I think, intuitively reasonable; and they are, I believe, completely in line with the main stream of the theoretical literature on speculation, allowance being made for the extreme abstractions of my ideal model.

More rigorous proof of these relations is sketched in the Mathematical Appendix. However, many economists will not wish to work through the differential equations that are needed if we assume time to consist of a continuous infinity of points. The full intrinsic content of the theory can be grasped if we make a further useful simplification: suppose that each year is divided up into two intervals (1) post-Harvest (e. g., Fall and Winter) and (2) pre-Harvest (e. g., Spring and Summer). Then we can use Figure 1's back-to-back diagram *to analyze intertemporal relations in exactly the same way that economists have long analyzed interspatial relations.* This is done in Figure 4.

I assume the same demand curve holds in every period of every year, as shown by $D_1D'_1$, $D_2D'_2$, $D_3D'_3$, $D_4D'_4$ in Figure 4, where all periods are numbered consecutively with all post-Harvests being odd numbers and all pre-Harvests even numbers. I assume that there is zero production or supply in the even-numbered pre-Harvest periods; in the first instance, the same positive supply curve or crop in every post-Harvest, as shown by $S_1S'_1$, $S_3S'_3$, etc. Finally, I assume the same intertemporal transport costs $T_{12} = T_{34} > 0$ at which any unit of crop can be carried from post-Harvest to the following pre-Harvest; the transport cost, $T_{23} > 0$, at which grain can be carried from pre-Harvest to the following post-Harvest will be irrelevant until we introduce changes into our model.

Now we can analyze what must happen.

(a) With zero carry-over, price would always be lower in the post-Harvest periods than in the pre-Harvest ones. (Compare prices at points

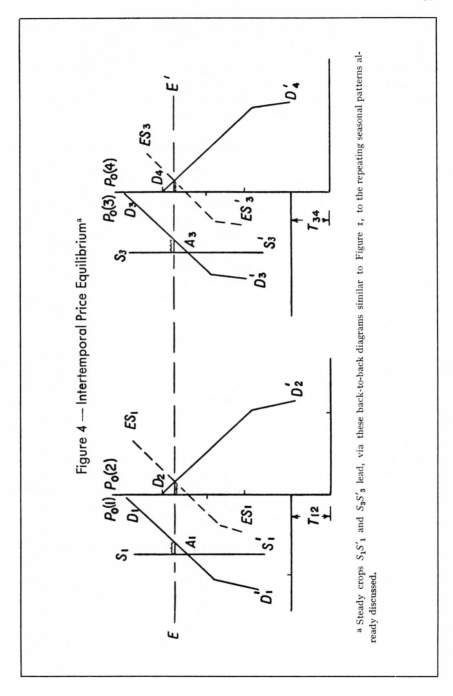

Figure 4 — Intertemporal Price Equilibrium[a]

[a] Steady crops $S_1S'_1$ and $S_3S'_3$ lead, via these back-to-back diagrams similar to Figure 1, to the repeating seasonal patterns already discussed.

A_1 and D_2 or A_3 and D_4.) Therefore, goods will never move from pre-Harvest to post-Harvest, and positive carrying charges for such a move, T_{23}, are irrelevant.

(b) Provided the no-carry-over prices differ by more than storage charges T_{12}, some grain will be carried over from post-Harvest to pre-Harvest, raising $P_0(1)$ and lowering $P_0(2)$ from their "autonomous" values. How much grain will move? And what must be the equilibrium prices?

(c) We raise the post-Harvest diagram by the distance T_{12} and seek the corresponding horizontal level EE' at which the excess of post-Harvest's supply over its demand just matches pre-Harvest's ("excess") demand. Thus, at EE', and no other level, will the two bracketed distances be equal.

The resulting pattern of low price, high price, low price, high price,... can be charted by the reader. Schematically, each post-Harvest market is "connected" with the following pre-Harvest, and under steady crop conditions, each pre-Harvest is "disconnected" from the following post-Harvest. Figure 5a shows the resulting schematic "tree."

Figure 5 — "Tree" Chart of Price Connections[a]

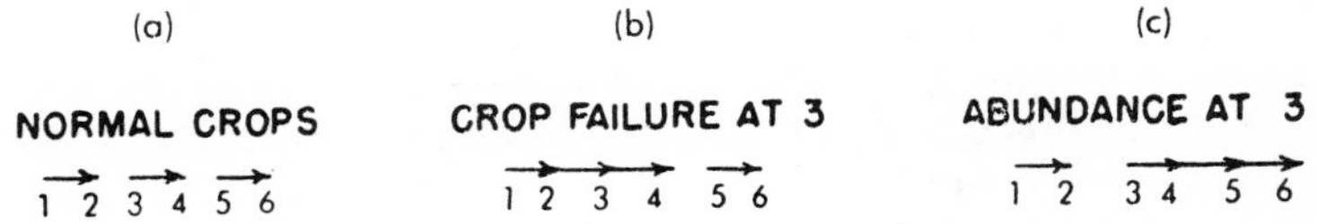

(a)	(b)	(c)
NORMAL CROPS	**CROP FAILURE AT 3**	**ABUNDANCE AT 3**

[a]With steady harvests, each year ends with zero carry-over, and each year's prices are disconnected as first shown. With crop failure anticipated at 3, P_3 and P_4 rise enough to attract carry-over from 2 — so that P_1, P_2, P_3, P_4 show rising price trend determined by storage cost. After crop abundance at 3, P_3 falls so much as to lead to carry-over from 4 to 5, and depression of the connected price pattern P_3, P_4, P_5, P_6.

---

12. Analysis of Crop Fluctuations

Now the reader can shift the supply schedule (or demand schedule) in any one of the periods. The resulting equilibrium pattern can then be rigorously determined[1].

---

[1] A keen reader may wonder whether the infinity of future periods might not create awkward analytic problems. This turns out not to be the case. Dealing with any finite number of periods, we may assume the carry-over at the end of the time in question to be zero, *or any other specified constant*, and solve for a rigorous solution for each value of that constant. But fortunately, with $T_{12} > 0$ and finite, we can be sure that within some sufficiently long (but finite) time after any one-time crop change, there will come a pre-Harvest which carries

What will be the affect of a crop failure at time 3, which shifts $S_3S'_3$ eastward? We find that for a slight shift, P_3 and P_4 are raised but P_1 and P_2 are unaffected. However, a large crop failure raises P_3 so much that it tends to exceed $P_2 + T_{23}$, and then we for the first time have carry-over from one crop year to the next. How much carry-over? We raise the two right-hand diagrams relative to the left-hand ones by the amount T_{23} and seek the unique EE' level which equates total supply and demand for the four periods. This gives us our answer. Figure 5b shows the resulting "tree" connecting 1, 2, 3, 4.

By precisely similar analysis, the reader can show how superabundance in one year may connect it with the following year or years, as shown in Figure 5c.

Part VI: Variable Transport Costs and Interdependence of Temporal Schedules

13. Supply and Demand for Storage

Up until now I have been treating intertemporal transport costs T_{12} and T_{23} as solid single numbers. If warehouses were regulated monopolies with inflexible administered prices and with ever-available capacity, such an approximation might be valid. Or this might be valid if we were dealing with one small crop which used so negligible an amount of available storage space that we could think of it as having no influence on storage prices. Even in this last case where T_{12} is exogenously given to the crop in question, there might be determinate seasonal variations in T_{12} reflecting general Fall stringencies and Spring redundancies of storage and credit; and since such events as crop failures are related to common weather influences, there might result concomitant changes in T_{12} and Harvests of the crop in question, even if the latter is not the cause of the former, both simply being effects of common causes.

To prepare the way for analysis of variable storage costs, Figure 6[1] represents an alternative formulation of the back-to-back diagrams of Figures 1 and 4. Instead of shifting the supply and demand schedules of one period by the amount of transport costs, we plot these schedules *at the same levels*. Clearly only the difference between quantity supplied and

---

over zero to the next post-Harvest; hence the pattern from then on is simply periodic until infinity as seen in Figure 2 and can be ignored. A similar philosophical difficulty threatens from the fact that any future one-time crop fluctuation must be foreseen from the beginning of time. Again, $T_{12} > 0$ leads to the conclusion that there will be substantive effects on the repetitive equilibrium pattern for at most an ascertainable finite number of previous periods.

[1] See Samuelson, "Spatial Price Equilibrium", *op. cit.*, p. 288, Figure 2, for elaboration of this diagram in relation to the back-to-back diagram.

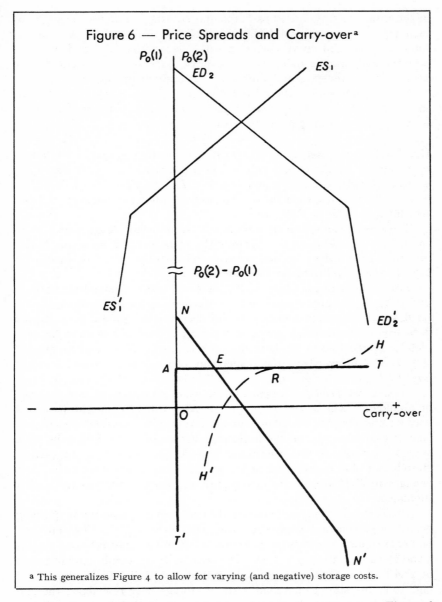

Figure 6 — Price Spreads and Carry-over[a]

a This generalizes Figure 4 to allow for varying (and negative) storage costs.

quantity demanded for each market is relevant: for this reason, Figure 6 contains only the excess-supply curve of period 1, ES_1 to ES'_1 and the excess-demand curve of period 2, ED_2 to ED'_2. These curves are computed in the usual way by *lateral* or horizontal subtraction of respective q's at each price. In our special case where the pre-Harvest has zero supply, the excess-demand curve coincides with the ordinary demand-curve; if post-Harvest crop is independent of price, excess-supply is simply the demand curve reversed and shifted by the amount of supply.

We are interested in the price difference, $P_0(2) - P_0(1)$, or what is the same thing $P_1(1) - P_0(1)$. Our fundamental arbitrage restriction, which is (1) applied to time rather than price, is

$$P_0(2) - P_0(1) \leq T_{12}$$

But $P_0(1)$ we may regard as a determinate function of carry-over from 1 to 2 as given by the excess-supply function ES_1 to ES'_1. Likewise, $P_0(2)$ is given by the excess-demand schedule ED_2 to ED'_2. Their difference $P_0(2) - P_0(1)$ must then be the *net vertical* difference between the two schedules, or NN' in Figure 6.

The crucial point can now be noted: Equilibrium takes place where the *net price* schedule NN' intersects the transport-cost schedule $T'AT$; no other price difference can prevail and no other level of carry-over than at the equilibrium intersection E.

Now what happens (a) if supply increases and/or demand decreases in period 1, (b) if supply decreases and/or demand increases in period 1; (c) if supply increases and/or demand decreases in period 2, (d) if supply decreases and/or demand increases in period 2? Such changes can be completely summarized by shifts in the *net price* curve NN': cases (a) and (d) shift NN' downward, as the reader can verify; cases (b) and (c) shift NN' upward.

We are in a position to demonstrate what the effects of crop shortage or abundance will be on price spreads. We shift NN' in the indicated manner and observe the change in the intersection point. Obviously, any change that leaves us on the horizontal stretch of $T'AT$ keeps the price spread constant. On the other hand, if we begin and end on the vertical stretch of $T'AT$, because the earlier period is disconnected from the later, changes in NN' are free to change price spreads in the manner earlier discussed.

This same diagram can illustrate the effects of dropping the simplifying postulate of constant transport costs. The costs T_{12}, T_{23}, T_{34}, etc. can be made to increase with the amounts being transported between periods 1 and 2, 2 and 3, 3 and 4, ..., etc. The curve $H'H$ represents a modification of $T'AT$ in the manner suggested by Professor Holbrook Working[1]: for high amounts stored, marginal costs of storage may rise above the AT level; for lower amounts stored, marginal costs are below that level.

---

[1] Cf. Working, "The Theory of Price of Storage", *op. cit.*, p. 1259. — *Idem*, "Theory of the Inverse Carrying Charge", *op. cit.*, p. 19.

In accordance with Professor Working's hypothesis, I have permitted costs of storage to actually become negative even when some goods are being carried over to the future. Since I have not yet introduced uncertainty into my model and inasmuch as the desire to hold inventory is critically related to uncertainty about the future, one could cogently criticize the admissibility of negative transport costs in my model. However, without entering into the merits of such criticism, I prefer to introduce a general schedule of the form $H'H$ to show in a formal way how the graph determines equilibrium in any postulated case.

Does dropping the assumption of constant transport cost completely destroy our established qualitative results? I believe not: some modifications are in order, and the reader can judge how serious they are. (i) So long as we remain on the horizontal stretch of $H'H$, the effects are similar to those earlier analyzed for "connected" markets. (ii) Of course, as indicated earlier in qualifying footnotes, when the present crop is *very* abundant relative to the future crop, so much carry-over may take place as to bid up the price of very scarce storage — and therefore we may have an extraordinary price spread as we approach the point H. (iii) A more serious modification is required when the present crop is so short relative to the future that carry-over shrinks and carries us below the horizontal stretch of $H'H$ and on to $H'R$. As in the $T'AT$ case, the price spread will then diminish; indeed it can become negative or inverted. There is just this difference: $H'H$ is *not* perfectly vertical in its lower stretches; hence, there is a slight resistance to the lessened or inverted price spread which a downward shift in NN' tends to cause. Why? Because people act to relieve the present price stringency by cutting down some on their carry-over into the future, as the reader can verify by comparing the effects of a shift of NN' along $H'R$ rather than along $T'A$.

To illustrate: suppose prices are inverted and we are somewhere on $H'R$. Now suppose that a poor crop is newly forecast for the later period, thereby shifting ED_2 and NN' upward. What will happen? (i) Will the future price rise, leaving present price unchanged and widening the spread by the full amount of the change? (ii) Will both prices rise, leaving the absolute or percentage spread largely unchanged? (iii) Will the future price rise, exerting an attenuated pull on present price and widening the spread by a moderated amount?

The classical theory of speculation, which supposes that the $H'R$ curve looks vertical — like $T'A$ — whenever there is price inversion, would answer Yes to (i). Of course, it would answer Yes to (ii), provided we were known to be at the AT level before and after the change, with the markets "connected." The true answer is Yes to (iii), a position intermediate between (i) and (ii). The amount of the widening of the spread depends, naturally, on the quantitative question: How vertical rather than horizontal is $H'R$ in the relevant range[1].

14. Vertical Price Relations

I must briefly qualify the assumption that the demand for each time period depends on the price ruling in that period alone and not on prices of other periods. As mentioned in an earlier footnote, the consumption of nearby periods are probably in some degree "substitutes" for each other. This suggests that foreseen price stringency in any one period will tend to be relieved by resulting increases in demand in adjacent earlier and later periods, thereby tending to raise prices slightly in those periods and to moderate the needed price rise in the period of stringency itself. If correct, this effect confirms and strengthens our main qualitative result that forces producing price changes at any one time are transmitted (in an attenuated way) to the surrounding time periods. (However, no time-*asymmetry* appears to be involved here.)

Again, as mentioned in an earlier footnote, the vertical relations between the price of grain and of, say, flour may also act in the same direction. If flour were auctioned off in a perfect market at current price $R_0(t)$, we might place limits on the spread between it and grain price $P_0(t)$ by introducing transport costs T^* for coverting a unit of grain into an "equivalent" unit of flour. Such transformations take time: the simplest assumption would be that it takes exactly h units of time for the transformation, and that it costs more to store flour than to store wheat, which means — uncertainty aside — that only under unusual price relations will flour be stored in appreciable amounts. Competitive equilibrium requires

$$(3) \qquad\qquad R_0(t + h) - P_0(t) \leq T^*$$

If the inequality holds, millers will not be feeding wheat into the beginning of the milling operation. With T^* and h literal constants, flour storage expensive, and ultimate flour demand steady, we can expect the equality to hold virtually all the time. You might wonder why millers would buy expensive wheat on the Eve of the Harvest rather than wait for wheat to

---

[1] Note that assuming $H'H$ is just like $T'AT$ but with the vertical part falling to the right of zero carry-over has the following effect: it leads to a restoration of all the findings of the simple classical theory earlier outlined; but with the sole difference that there may be positive (albeit "minimal") carry-over in the face of price inversion. Such minimal (or "fiduciary") stocks, which are never drawn on, might just as well be non-existent and by working in deviations from them, we reinstate all the simpler results. To repeat: it is the intermediate slope of the $H'R$ that requires us to alter the simplest conclusions, and to alter them by considering every actual case as intermediate between the asymmetrical polar phases of the classical theory.

fall in price. But when you reflect on the rigidity of our assumptions, you perceive that the price of flour remains high enough — even after the Harvest — to make this just worthwhile. Only h periods after the Harvest will the abundance of grain result in abundance of flour and lower flour prices. Under our conditions of certainty and foresight, the miller is never "squeezed" between falling or low flour prices and rising or high wheat prices. He has no need to hedge, although he may hedge if he wants to. Uncertainty will, of course, introduce hedging needs and other changes in the model. But note that part of the frequently discussed price risks alleged to be experienced by middlemen and processors arise from the, perhaps realistic but not logically inevitable, assumption that they must, or choose to, sell at prices that are not competitively determined in terms of the supplies of flour or finished goods on hand; instead, the argument often proceeds on the assumption (i) they *must* sell at rigidly administered prices or (ii) they must sell at the lower price which present grain abundance will *later* create for finished products[1].

So far vertical price relations have been neutral in affecting our main qualitative conclusion. But now let us recognize that T^* probably, like many marginal cost relations, rises with the quantity of grain being currently milled. As far as I can see, this factor of rising transformation cost simply makes the derived demand for wheat — derived from the steady demand for flour or bread — more inelastic than it would otherwise have been; if anything, this seems to accentuate price fluctuations in wheat.

Probably working in the other direction is the realistic assumption that the time h involved in milling is *not* literally constant. At a cost, it can be speeded up; or if profits come from lengthening h, that can no doubt be done. When grain is especially abundant, its price will tend to fall relative to flour price at times around $t + h$; this will tend to result in quick milling, thereby transmitting the price drop in wheat more rapidly to the price of flour; the extra consumption of flour induced by this earlier price drop serves to reduce the pressure on wheat price during the stringency period and to spread some of that pressure on to wheat prices before and after[2].

---

[1] Perhaps some will argue that h is really very short. But such people can hardly maintain that the price risk on the middleman or processor will then be great. Perhaps storing grain and processing it are highly complementary activities and for many reasons tend to be done by the same people. The storing function does not require "hedging" when uncertainty is absent, but when present, uncertainty makes hedging even more attractive to the storer than to the processor because of the longer time periods involved.

[2] This same variability in the transformation time means that unforeseen price changes in wheat can cause losses to millers and make them want to be hedged against a sudden appearance in the market of rapidly-milled flour following on a sudden grain abundance.

To sum up this section: The facts that (1) ultimate demands of adjacent periods are likely to be *substitutes* for each other and (2) processing and production activities of any era are likely to have *substitutable demands* for inputs of adjacent periods[1] both tend to reinforce the qualitative pattern that stringency or abundance at one time is transmitted (in an attenuated way) to adjacent time periods.

These adjustments can, but need not be, thought of as hidden or indirect forms of "storage of grain" that are going on all the time between present and future; by permitting the amount of such storage to rise as the price gradient $P_0 (t + \Theta) - P_0 (t)$ or $dP_0(t)/dt$ grows, we increase mutual "connectedness" of intertemporal markets and thereby moderate the price gradients.

Part VII: Effects of Uncertainty

15. Basic Issues

A theory of speculative markets under ideal conditions of certainty is Hamlet without the Prince. I hope that such an idealized theory will help to set the stage for fruitful analysis of more realistic markets, but I must honestly admit that this faith has yet to be vindicated. For make no mistake about it, as Frank Knight sensed in his important *Risk, Uncertainty, and Profit*[2], phenomena of uncertainty provide fundamental difficulties to the economic theorist and the descriptive economist. Indeed they raise fundamental metaphysical and epistemological problems that go to the very basis of empirical induction itself.

I must content myself here with some scanty reflections on intertemporal relations under conditions of uncertainty, explicitly recognizing that I leave off where most theoretical discussions begin.

16. Methodological Problems

Realistically no one knows *ex ante* how future prices will move. After time has passed, everyone can know *ex post* how they did behave. Almost everyone, after the fact, has reason to "regret" not having made different earlier decisions. Here regret is defined in the simple sense of recognizing

---

[1] The constant lag h is obviously only one example of a great species. Thus, an animal to be sold some time after Harvest has his weight determined by what he was fed in past days. Naturally he will be fed more intensively *after* the Harvest since at the lower prices then prevailing it will pay to substitute post-Harvest feed for pre-Harvest feed. Such decisions minimize the Harvest drop in grain price. A kind of Le Chatelier Principle, whereby the system reacts almost teleologically so as to relieve stresses put on it, can be seen to be here involved.

[2] Frank H. Knight, *Risk, Uncertainty, and Profit*, Boston and New York, 1921.

that those different decisions would have turned out *ex post* to have been more profitable. On the other hand, depending upon temperament and the nature of developments, an individual may or may not "regret" his past decisions, in the sense of feeling that they were or were not defensible on the basis of *ex ante* knowledge he had when making them.

In what sense can it be said that anyone faced with uncertainty made a "bad decision?" If he followed a system of betting on dice, horses, or wheat prices and subsequently lost his money, naive pragmatists will judge his decisions to have been bad. But if at least one person who followed similar systems made money — and the mathematical laws of probability tell us that within their idealized urn-measure models, at least one out of a sufficiently large number should make money over any finite time — the naive pragmatist is left perplexed.

In case the Observer who passes judgment is able to infer correctly that the phenomena in question constitute (or act as if they do) a "stationary time series" amenable to the mathematical theory of probability with inferable numerical or qualitative properties, he may be able to pass adverse judgment on particular decisions. Even here he must proceed with care, making sure that he knows what it is that the decider is trying to maximize — e. g., expected monetary profit or expected "utility of profit" or something else.

Without passing normative judgments, the Observer — i. e., economist — may hope to state regularities about futures markets, such as: Most small traders lose capital within three years time, futures prices usually show "backwardation" relations to spot prices, futures prices of different dates tend to move together with relatively constant spreads, hedging is costless on the average, etc.

Such macro conclusions are like thermodynamic statements about the air pressure in my room, and may be formulated from observed temperature changes independently of theories about the micro behavior of the individual molecules of air. Such regularities about *groups* can be discussed independently of theorizing about single *individual's* market behavior *and motives*[1]. My own hunch in this field happens to favor an attack on the problem which uses reasoning about individuals to develop hypotheses

---

[1] I strongly repudiate the dogmatic view of Menger and his followers that results based on individuals are necessarily and intrinsically more fruitful than any others. This and its dogmatic equally over-narrow inverse must be appraised pragmatically in each empirical case. Note that our empirical regularities about the past can be extrapolated into the future only on the basis of an uncertain inductive inference about the "stationariness" of some elements of the process. However, in some degree this is true of all economic generalizations and not intrinsically more true of generalizations concerning people's decisions *about the uncertain future*.

which can be stated and tested for groups; but much of our past progress seems to have been derived without going through these stages.

17. Penalties for Violating Equilibrium Conditions Under Certainty

Much of our results under certainty can be summarized briefly as follows:

(A) $P_\theta(t) \equiv P_0(t + \Theta)$:   i. e., today's futures price equals current price for that future date.

(B) $P_\theta(t) \leqq P_0(t) + T_{t,t+\theta}$: i. e., transport costs limit price spreads, and goods are stored only if it pays to do so.

(C) Over any period, current price in each period is determined so as to "clear the market" for sale of what is produced in that period or taken from storage.

The "penalties" for violating these conditions are very great under conditions of certainty. Thus, anyone who knowingly ignores (A) makes a gift to an arbitrager of a substantial sum of money.

Violating (B) does not necessarily result in technological waste corresponding to "cross-haulage" in a spatial Koopmans problem: even if the wrong amount of grain is carried from period 1 to period 3, it may very well be carried in the technologically most optimal way. However, the person who carries an excessive amount loses $T_{t,t+\theta} - [P_\theta(t) - P_0(t)]$ on each unit; and in the rarer case, where he should carry over (indefinitely) more he passes up unit profits of $[P_\theta(t) - P_0(t)] - T_{t,t+\theta}$. These facts would be seen instantly if he hedged his stored grain by sales of futures; but without hedging, the same would show up under conditions of certainty where the futures price $P_\theta(t)$ and the later current price $P_0(t + \Theta)$ are the same thing.

What if the "clearing of the market" conditions of (C) were violated? In a certain sense this is conceptually impossible by definition of an organized auction market. By definition, voluntary transactions record equality of supply and demand. And in still another sense this equality is operationally unrefutable: no one can stop me from putting arbitrary hypothetical supply and demand curves through any recorded price-quantity observation.

But in another sense, we can under ideal conditions make the demand curve operationally meaningful. We are free to imagine hypothetical controlled experiments or interrogations which trace out one and only one true demand schedule; and in terms of this known schedule, we can determine whether people are truly on it.

Now this much can be said: if the demand schedule does reflect each person's relative marginal utility of consumption schedule so that in the simplest case we can measure unambiguously and rigorously his "consumer's surplus," then an arbitrary departure by any individual from his true demand schedule at one time compensated by carrying over the grain to another time can be shown to lower his obtainable "ordinal" utility; and if such behavior is generalized to symmetrical "representative individuals," we can show that everyone would be worse off. For this reason people make sure that they are on their true demand schedules, which is only to say they make sure they are doing what they really want to do.

18. Teleology and Competition

The above considerations lead writers like A. P. Lerner[1] to a normative conclusion about the correct equilibrium pattern: Any deviation from the competitive equilibrium pattern would lower total social utility, provided that the latter quantity can be given content by ethical assumptions about the optimal interpersonal distribution of income.

In our terminology this means that any individual who carries goods through time so as to lead to a deviation from the equilibrium conditions either (1) makes a financial loss on the complete cycle of purchase and sale or (2) incurs a psychic loss by not consuming through time the optimal amounts available to him. His loss tends to create a gain for others; however, if all persons' marginal dollars are equally deserving from the ethical viewpoint so that interpersonal gains and losses are deemed commensurable, the rest of the community gains less than the loser loses. Conversely any action designed to restore the equilibrium pattern leads to an increase in total social (ordinal) utility.

Professor Lerner draws conclusions from these analytic results that I fear will be misinterpreted. Many readers will draw from his discussion the following inferences: (1) A person "deserves" the profits from his successful speculations. (2) The greater the number of voluntary competitive speculators the better. (3) With free entry into competitive speculation, speculative profits will diminish to zero or to the "right" amount.

None of these statements represents a valid deduction or inference from the pure economic theory, and hence an astute reasoner such as Lerner would probably not sanction the above interpretations. All the theory says is that the equilibrium pattern is better than any other. It does not enable us to identify the contribution on this pattern of any individual's single act or collection of acts.

---

[1] A. P. Lerner, *The Economics of Control, Principles of Welfare Economics*, New York, 1946, Chs. 5 and 8.

Suppose my reactions are not better than those of other speculators but rather just one second quicker. (This may be because of the flying pigeons I own or quickness of my neurones.) In a world of uncertainty, I note the consequences of each changing event one second faster than any one else. I make my fortune — not once, but every day that important events happen. Would anyone be foolish enough to argue that in my absence the equilibrium pattern would fail to be reestablished? By hypothesis, my sole contribution is to have it established one second sooner than otherwise. Now even a second counts: and after crops fail, society should even in the first second begin to reduce its consumption of grain. The worth of this one-second's lead time to society is perhaps $ 5, and if we for the sake of the argument accept a Clarkian naive-productivity theory of ethical deservingness, we might say I truly deserve $ 5. Actually, however, I get a fortune. My quickness enables me to reap the income effects of price changes without regard to whether I alone am uniquely capable of producing or signalling the desired substitution effects.

By all means let us remove barriers to entry of other quick reactors so that the $ 5 is spread among many competers. But note that neither the $ 5 nor the much larger revaluation of assets caused by the new development and equal to a "fortune" can be decimated or wiped out by competition among speculators. These algebraic sums are created by the changed conditions: somebody is going to benefit and somebody be hurt by the change and the only question is whether quick speculators can (i) buy up at advantageous terms the positions of those who stand to gain and (ii) sell at advantageous terms any expositions that will shortly be revealed to deteriorate in value. It is true that the sooner everyone realizes the new state of affairs, the sooner will the desired substitutions come into play. But I must repeat: There is no necessary correspondence between the income effects realized by any person's actions and the amount of meritorious substitutions that his actions can alone bring into being. Moreover, increasing entry into speculation until it is perfectly free does not in a world where speculators do not enter the industry with omniscient "crystal balls" lead to the disappearance of speculative profits, i. e., to the disappearance of income effects resulting from changed and unforeseeable conditions.

The pure theory makes us desire a larger supply of omniscience and a smaller supply of uncertainty. It does not tell us what number or manner of recruitment of forecasters is optimal[1]. To gain a pragmatic notion of

---

[1] It will be noted that I have not, in my criticism of inferences from Lerner's discussion invoked elements of (1) monopoly restrictionism by speculators, (2) deliberate rumor spreading or other action by speculators which successfully creates profits by causing *deviations* from the equilibrium pattern, (3) non-deliberate action by speculators which none the less, in a

what are improved policy arrangements in this regard is not in principle impossible or meaningless, but it does itself involve elements of forecasting and inductive inference as to the likely disturbances in society and the likely effects of different communication and social interaction patterns.

19. A Digression on Dynamic Welfare Economics

In an uncertain world "knowledge" is a scarce resource. This is an important fact which has not gone unnoticed. But what has not received any emphasis and yet is vital for dynamic welfare economics, knowledge is a resource loaded with "externality" so that there can be no presumption that pure competition will lead to the optimum. When I give you some of my bread, I have less bread left. When I give you some of my knowledge, I have just as much left. None the less, it is usually to my economic advantage to hoard my knowledge.

Furthermore, as every patent lawyer knows, knowledge can be created by incurring pecuniary costs. So can a loaf of bread. But the loaf I create is mine, and I am motivated to produce more of it up to the point where its benefit to society (as measured by its market price) is equal to its pecuniary *and* social cost. When it comes to making decisions about knowledge, I know in advance that others will be able to imitate my discoveries; so I know that society will benefit by the full amount of the uses of that discovery *everywhere*; but I also know that the pecuniary benefits to me will only under certain special (usually non-competitive) conditions[1] revert fully to me, and therefore in following my self interest, no invisible hand leads me to the social optimum. Pondering over this externality, the reader can resolve the Schumpeter paradox that really perfect competition would stifle dynamic progress, and can discern the *non sequitur* in the *laisser faire* arguments against patents and monopolies. The policy problem becomes completely pragmatic having to weigh the *ex post* harm of monopoly restrictionism against the *ex ante* inducement to creative change.

---

world of uncertainty, turns out to create *deviations* from the equilibrium pattern. Of course, no policy maker can decide on the optimum until he has pragmatically formed empirical judgments concerning the *factual* importance of these elements. However, I have here been content to waive these important qualifications in order to appraise the pure theoretical content of the argument. What we are left with is the statement that equilibrium is a good thing, but cannot pretend by deductive methods to arrive at a definitive program as to how we can get more of this good thing.

[1] After I have made the discovery, *its* marginal costs are zero. So even if I am allowed by monopoly to reap its full pecuniary rewards, the welfare optimum will not be attained, revealing a hole in the Schumpeter doughnut.

Mathematical Appendix on Speculative Markets

1. Assume a single grain market subject to annually periodic fluctuations in price in response to a foreseen constant Harvest H, which becomes available at one instant every Fall. We may let one year equal one unit of time, t, and set the origin at the Harvest instant. The initial stock of grain right after the Harvest is $Q(0+) = H$, and every year $Q(n+) = H$ for all integral n. Just before the Harvest, nothing is left of the crop, or $0 = Q(1-) = Q(n-)$ for all integral n. The amount currently consumed must represent the decrease of stored grain, or $C(t) = -dQ(t)/dt$. At every instant of time we have a uniform demand curve, independent of prices at other times, and relating quantity consumed to ruling current price as follows: $C = f(P)$, with negative slope f'.

The transport or storage costs through time may depend (1) on the season of the year, (2) on the amount of $Q(t)$ still in storage, and (3) because of *ad valorem* interest and insurance charges, on the current price $P(t)$. Call this function $T(t,Q,P)$ and note that with the season being the only cause of change this has the periodic property $T(t+1,Q,P) \equiv T(t,Q,P)$ for all t, Q, and P. So long as $Q > 0$, the rate of increase in price $dP(t)/dt$ must equal this transport gradient.

We may summarize all of our assumptions in the differential equations

(1) $dP/dt = T(t,P,Q) > 0$, $Q(n+) = H, Q(n+1-) = 0$
        $dQ/dt = -f(P)$, $P(n+1-) \geq P(n+1+) = P(n+)$.

Because of the strictly periodic nature of our Harvest, demand, and storage functions, it is sufficient to find the unique solution to these differential equations in the first year where t goes from 0 to 1; thereafter, everything will repeat in annual cycles. Because of the regularity properties of the demand and transport functions, it is easy to show that the two-point boundary conditions on Q alone are sufficient to lead to a unique solution of the differential equations. (One way of showing this is to differentiate the second equation again with respect to t, then substitute from the first equation, and finally invert the original second equation and eliminate all P by substituting the equivalent dQ/dt expression. The result will be a second order differential equation in Q alone, which can satisfy the boundary conditions with but one solution.)

If the transport cost function were a constant, the price profile in Figure 2a would consist of straight-line rises. If T is proportional to P, or $T = kP$, the repeating price profiles will rise in Figure 2a like compound interest curves. If storage costs are higher when there is more Q to be stored, the price profiles will be convex rather than concave, rising most in the Fall and least in late Summer.

2. Now let us assume constant Harvests $H(n) = H$, except in some one year when $H(j) = H_j$. Then when the crop is great with $H_j > H$, we solve the same Equations (1). Provided the abundance is not too great, we find the terminal price inequality of (1) is still fulfilled; this means that the extra crop is absorbed within the one following year, the profile of prices being correspondingly lower.

However, when H_j gets big enough, we find that the solution to (1) will give $P(j+1-) < P(j+1+)$, which would induce storage from before until after the next (normal) Harvest. In this case, the terminal conditions in (1) must be modified to reflect the fact that the two crop years are rigidly connected: now we must write $Q(j+) = H_j$, $Q(j+2-) = 0$, $P(j+2-) \geq P(j+2+)$, and solve the differential equations over the interval of t from j to $j + 2$. Thereafter, everything repeats in the one-year normal cycle.

The reader can easily work out the needed modifications as the crop H_j becomes bigger and bigger, leading to the different "quantum states" where 3, 4, ..., r years become strictly connected in the same crop-era. He can also note the asymmetrical fact that crop abundance never, even when foreseen in previous normal years, affects the earlier periods' price patterns. He can use similar arguments to show how the terminal conditions are changed in earlier periods when there is a foreseen crop failure, leading to carry-over from one or more earlier normal periods and transmitting some of the price increase from crop shortage backward onto earlier prices.

3. We may now use the calculus of variations to show the above differential equations can, at least in the simplest case, be given a maximum interpretation. Define the integral of the demand curve $S(C) = \int_a^C F(c)\, dc$ as kind of a social payoff. Assuming that marginal transport costs depend only on amount Q stored, or $T(Q)$, we define total costs as its integral $R(Q) = \int_b^Q T(q)\, dq$. Recalling $C(t) = -Q'(t)$, set up the following net social payoff integral that is to be maximized

$$NSP = \int_0^1 \left\{ S[-Q'(t)] - R[Q(t)] \right\} dt \text{ with } Q(0) = H, \ Q(1) = 0.$$

The Euler differential equation necessary for a regular maximizing extremal is

(2) $\dfrac{d}{dt}(-S') + R' = 0$

but since by definition $S' = P$, $R' = T$, and $dQ/dt = f(P)$ where f and F are inverse functions, we see that (2) is indeed equivalent to (1). The secondary conditions for a maximum will be assured if the demand curve is always negatively inclined and the transport cost schedule is positively inclined.

4. This periodic maximum property assures us that after a one-time transient disturbance, the resulting equilibrium motions are dynamically "stable" in the sense of approaching asymptotically the equilibrium seasonal pattern. For if $Q(t)$ continued for an indefinitely long time to deviate substantially from the equilibrium pattern, NSP could be bettered by a specifiable motion which does, after a finite transient period, *exactly* *equal* the seasonal pattern forever afterward. But this would be a contradiction to the maximum property of the actual motion. Hence, lim as $t \to \infty$, $Q(t)$ = equilibrium seasonal periodic pattern regardless of the transient disturbance.

5. Suppose the Harvest does not come in all at once, but instead is given by the density function $H'(t)dt$ with $\int_0^1 H'(t)dt = H$, the total annual crop. Now our conditions (1) must be written

(3) $\begin{aligned} dQ/dt &\le H'(t) - C(t) = H'(t) - f[P(t)], \\ dP/dt &\le T[t, Q(t), P(t)] > 0. \end{aligned}$ $Q \ge 0$, $P \ge 0$

The first inequality would hold only if Q were a free good with $P(t) = 0$ at that time; the second inequality can hold only when there is no storage with $Q(t) = 0$. This duality problem reminds us of linear programming. Actually, we have here a new kind of problem: non-linear functional programming, in which the function $Q(t)$ is to be determined for all t so as to maximize a specified integral of a non-linear integrand.

The case where Q is free is of little interest. The case where storage is zero is of more interest and represents Stage (ii) of the text. Where the year separates into two finite stages, we can find the length and terminal dates of Stage (i) by solving (3) with the equality in both relations and seeking the unique values of t_1 and t_2 satisfying the boundary conditions of the problem.

6. The case of continuous production without seasonality can be handled as a special instance of the general formulation in which NSP is written as the same integral as above, but with S now a function of $H'(t) - Q'(t)$ rather than of the latter term alone. This integral is to be maximized over the indefinite future subject only to the condition that $Q(t) \ge 0$. This latter constraint turns the Euler differential equation (2) into an *in*equation, $d/dt(-S') + R' \ge 0$, with the inequality holding only when $Q = 0$.

If production is constant, so $H'(t) = K$ throughout, the obvious solution is zero storage, $C = K = H'$ throughout, and price constant at $P = F(K)$.

Now imagine a transient disturbance in which for a finite time period q we add to $H'(t) = K$ a constant algebraic amount J. Then if J is positive, reflecting temporary abundance, price will have to fall below the equilibrium level. If the time of abundance is long enough, no storage need immediately take place, and the large crop can be auctioned off for what it will currently bring. But sometime before the crop drops back to normal, storage must set in. This is because large enough negative accelerations of the cumulative Harvest *must* cause the inequality in the Euler equation to bump into the equality boundary, and thereafter force price to grow according to the fundamental economic law of gravity. In words: sometime before the abundance ends, the market will foresee the relatively harder times ahead and will ease into them by carrying over in storage some of the abundant crop. The reader can use exactly the same reasoning to prove that in case of foreseen transient crop shortage, the maximal solution given by the Euler differential inequation will involve positive carry-over from the period before the shortage into the shortage period, or at least into the beginning of it. He can also show that a sufficiently gentle foreseen drop in production will be compatible with zero carry-over. Note that the time asymmetry of the text is completely verified. Note too that the Euler differential inequation is, together with our definitions, completely equivalent to (3)'s inequations, which are the generalizations of the special equations of (1).

7. This mathematical analysis points up a fundamental paradox in all problems involving perfect foresight into the future. The future is infinitely long. Infinity is a long time. To avoid infinity, we might be tempted to maximize over a finite time, specifying a final level of inventory, and giving a different maximizing solution for each such level. However, to get a determinate solution, we naturally ask for the "right" final level of inventory. This question can be answered only by extending our time period further. But now we see that we are in an infinite regression. We must always go *beyond* any finite time period.

This dilemma is basic and intrinsic. It cannot be avoided. There are, however, some devices which enable us to avoid some of the extraneous difficulties. First, we can follow the ingenious device of Frank Ramsey[1]. Maximizing NSP over an infinite time interval means that we are maximizing something that is already infinite. Ramsey avoided this infinity by changing the origin of his measure of utility: instead of maximizing utility or NSP he would minimize *deviations* of these from a level of Bliss, defined as that steady state level which is the highest attainable. Since we see we can get to the Bliss level in finite time by paths not

---

[1] F. P. Ramsey, "A Mathematical Theory of Saving", *The Economic Journal*, Vol. XXXVIII, London, 1928, pp. 543 sqq.

necessarily optimal, we are assured that our new integral will be finite even if evaluated over an infinite time interval.

A second device used by Ramsey and many economists to handle the infinite future is to introduce some exponential rate of time discount into our integral. According to many theories of capital interest, such market rates of discount are mandatory, regardless of the mathematician's search for ways of avoiding infinite integrals. As a matter of fact, a positive rate of interest is already implicitly involved in our carrying-cost function T. It is noteworthy that interest enters our formulation only in this way, and not at all in the form of a discount factor applied to future utilities or social payoffs. Thus, the integral which we maximize has purely formal significance: it happens to give us the market equilibrium equations that we deduce from arbitrage and auction conditions; it is most definitely not the integral which Robinson Crusoe or a representative Englishman with Pigouvian time-preference would plan *ex ante* to maximize. These two, quite different, formulations could be reconciled by formal mathematical argument; but here I shall content myself with a warning of their difference. What I want to mention here is the mathematical fact that we can handle the infinite integrals by introducing artificial small discounting factors into the integral, regardless of their economic interpretation, and then watch how the optimal solution changes as the discount factor goes to the limiting case of no discounting.

So much for the avoidable difficulties introduced by infinite time. Now to return to the intrinsic difficulty. I shall call it the "tulip-mania phenomenon." Let the market maximize over any finite time, adding in at the end into the thing to be maximized a value for the terminal amount of grain left. At what level should this terminal grain be valued? We could extend the period in order to find out how much it is really worth in the remaining time left; but this obviously leads us back into our infinite regression, since there is always time left beyond any extended time. We are back into maximizing over infinite time.

But suppose we do what the market itself does in evaluating any stock $Q(t)$ at any given date; suppose we simply evaluate it at the then ruling market price $P_0(t)$. Then we immediately run into the paradox that any speculative bidding up of prices at a rate equal to carrying costs can last *forever*. This is precisely what happens in a tulip mania or new-era bull stock market. The market literally lives on its own dreams, and each individual at every moment of time is perfectly rational to be doing what he is doing.

Of course, history tells us that all tulip manias have ended in finite time. Every "Ponzi scheme" and every chain letter scheme finally runs out[1]. Every bubble is some day pricked. But I have long been struck by the fact, and puzzled by it too, that in all the arsenal of economic theory we have absolutely no way of predicting how long such a "Stage (i)" will last. To say that prices will fall back to earth after they reach ridiculous heights represents safe but empty prediction. Why do some manias end when prices have become ridiculous by 10 per cent, while others persist until they are ridiculous to the tune of hundreds of per cent? Moreover, we do not need the recent Harrod-Domar models to raise in our minds the question whether social progress and secular growth themselves are not self-fulfilling acts of faith which, once interrupted by a serious enough breakdown in the economic and political fabric, may not give way to self-perpetuating trends of disorganization.

The above paradoxes are even more important for general business cycle theory at the macro-level than for a particular grain market, and they play a prominent role in the psychological theories of Bagehot, Pigou, and others. I mention them here because, quite without my suspecting it, the mathematical analysis of perturbations of the equilibrium paths by crop changes revealed some of the same phenomena[2].

8. To avoid extraneous complications introduced into the study of differential equations by "impulsive" changes in crops and initial conditions, I reformulate the problem in terms of discrete time periods, indicated by subscripts such as $Q_1, Q_2, \ldots, P_1, \ldots, Q_t, P_t, \ldots$, where now the unit of time is presumably some small part of a year, such as a month or a day or a season. In order to avoid the extraneous complications introduced by inequalities, I adopt Working's form of the T function, permitting it to assume negative values for values of storage greater than

---

[1] It would be wrong to think that chain letters have to terminate when the geometric progression builds up to more people than exist on the globe. If the game will really send you more money than you put into it, there is no reason why you wouldn't participate any number of times and at any scale. Hence, we are back at the geometric progressions underlying every Ponzi (a famous swindler of the 1920's) scheme or mania. Barnum pointed out there is a sucker born every moment, and some try to construct from this a numerical limit to the process, interpreting Barnum to mean there is *at most one* sucker born every second. But this misses the point that during the Stage (i) process no one is acting irrationally or being a sucker. At the moment Stage (i) collapses, people will realize the losses they incur and that were to be foreseen by an omniscient Observer. But, and this repeats the main point I am trying to make, there is absolutely nothing in the logical, mathematical, and institutional data enabling us to say when the process will end — or for that matter that it *must* ever end.

[2] Concurrent research on growth models by Robert Solow and myself should have alerted me to this phenomenon, as should have an unpublished Cowles Commission Memorandum by Martin Beckmann in which he points out the crucial importance of terminal assumptions in the differential equations of temporal equilibrium.

zero but less than some break-even point. Thus, $\log Q = T$ would be admissible.

Our full equilibrium conditions can now be written

$$C_t = H_t + Q_t - Q_{t+1} \; , \; P_t = F(C_t) \text{ or } C_t = f(P_t) \; , \; P_{t+1} = P_t + T(Q_{t+1})$$

where Q_t represents the amount of crop carried over into period t from the previous period, where C_t represents current consumption, P_t current price, H_t the exogenously specified Harvest, T the positively monotonic storage-cost function and F and f the inverse forms of the demand function for each period, assumed independent of variables of other time periods.

These equilibrium conditions can be rewritten in a number of different ways. Thus,

$$(4) \qquad P_{t+1} = P_t + T(Q_{t+1}), \qquad Q_{t+1} = H_t - f(P_t) + Q_t$$

is one such way. However, this gives the misleading impression that we are dealing with a "causal system" which lives from period to period, determining out of each initial state the subsequent state of the system without any knowledge or consideration of the near or distant future. A world of perfect foresight and certainty should be cast in a more "teleological form." Events have a *rendezvous* with later events, so to speak.

Therefore, a better formulation for our purposes is

$$(5) \quad F(H_{t+1} + Q_{t+1} - Q_{t+2}) - F(H_t + Q_t - Q_{t+1}) - T(Q_{t+1}) = 0.$$

In (5) we are to think of H_t as given for all times, say for $t = 0, 1, \ldots, n$; we are also to think of the initial Q_0 as given and the terminal Q_{n+1} as provisionally given; finally, we are to think of (5) as holding for each time, $t = 0, 1, 2, \ldots, n$. Equations (5) are exactly enough equations to solve for the unknown variables $Q_1, Q_2, \ldots, Q_n$ in terms of the prescribed variables $Q_0, Q_{n+1}, H_0, \ldots, H_n$. Of course prices and consumptions will be determinate also.

Equations (5) represent a second order difference equation in Q_t of non-linear type but free of explicit dependence on historical calendar time. However, if the Harvest goes through regular periodic fluctuations, involving annual or any other cycles, the equilibrium pattern of Q_t will have to be of this same period. Given a periodic function H_t, of period m so that $H_{t+m} \equiv H_t$, we can solve for the periodic equilibrium pattern $Q^0_{t+m} \equiv Q^0_t$ by letting (5) hold for $t = 0, 1, \ldots, m-1$ with $Q_m = Q_0$ and $Q_{m+1} = Q_1$. When these m equations are solved for their m unknowns, we have our equilibrium periodic pattern Q^0_t over its first cycle and we can extend it forward to infinity and backward to minus infinity by means of the relations $Q_{t+m} \equiv Q_{t-m} \equiv Q_t$.

If we now perturb the periodic Harvest in any way, we can calculate the resulting change in Q_t. In particular, the partial derivatives of the form $\delta Q_t / \delta H_i$ can be evaluated by a variety of methods, all related:

continuant determinants, continued fractions, or solutions to a *linear* second order difference equation with coefficients dependent on time. In the neighborhood of the seasonal equilibrium pattern, the coefficients will be periodic functions of time. It may be noted that the partial derivatives of Q_t with respect to specified end conditions Q_0 or Q_{n+1} can be determined as solutions of the same linear second order difference equation, but with special boundary conditions and without any perturbed-Harvest forcing function on the right hand side.

9. Differential equations being more familiar to most mathematicians, I revert to them to indicate the nature of the solution to the latter problem: Perturb a previous equilibrium pattern by prescribing a given algebraic change in $Q(t)$ at either specified point $Q(\Theta)$ or $Q(n)$. What is the resulting change in $Q(t)$ within this interval or outside of it — recalling that under perfect foresight, earlier periods may be as surely affected as later periods?

To avoid inequalities I use the Working form of the transport-cost function, so that $T(Q)$ is negative for Q less than some critical value and always an increasing function of Q. The demand curve is negatively sloped and, as before, independent of prices other than contemporaneous price.

We may suppose, as above, that a periodic Harvest $H'(t) \equiv H'(t+m)$ gives rise to a periodic equilibrium motion $Q(t)^0 \equiv Q(t+m)^0$, and that we are working with variables representing deviations from that pattern — namely, $q(t) = Q(t) - Q(t)^0$. Then from the standard theory of differential equations, we know that for small perturbations the variable $q(t)$ will be small, with its higher powers neglectable to a high order of approximation; hence, the differential equation for $q(t)$ can to a high degree of approximation be written in linear *variational* form with time-dependent coefficients. (Strictly speaking, if we solve for $\delta Q/\delta Q(0)$ or $\delta Q/\delta Q(n)$, this linear approximation is *exact*.)

We rewrite the Euler differential equation summarizing equilibrium

$$(2)' \qquad \frac{d}{dt} F[H'(t) - Q'(t)] = T[Q(t)], \text{ where } F' < 0, \ T' > 0.$$

The variational equations of linear type corresponding to $(2)'$ will be

$$(6) \qquad\qquad A(t) \, q''(t) = B(t) \, q(t) + A(t) \, h''(t)$$

where $A(t) = -F'[H'(t) - Q'(t)] > 0$, $B(t) = T'[Q(t)] > 0$, $h'' = d/dt \, h'(t)$, where $h'(t)$ is any perturbation in the Harvest $H'(t)$ and $q(t)$ the resulting change in amount stored. Note that $A(t)$ and $B(t)$ are periodic functions of period m.

We are most interested in the case where the perturbing conditions can be completely summarized by a change in $Q(0)$ and in $Q(n)$ alone. For both such cases we omit h'', making (6) a homogeneous equation;

to find the effect of $Q(0)$, we add to (6) the initial condition $q(0) = 1$ and the terminal condition $q(n) = 0$; to find the effect of $q(n)$ alone, we specify the alternative boundary conditions $q(0) = 0$, $q(n) = 1$.

Rewriting (6) in the equivalent form $q''(t) = K(t)\,q(t)$ where K is a positive periodic function of period m, we see that q is of the general "catenary type" needed to justify our theory that any disturbance is transmitted forward and backward but *in an attenuated way*.

The simplest periodic function to demonstrate this on is the case of absolutely steady $H'(t) = $ constant, which is to be perturbed by a once- and-for-all change in Harvest. If this algebraic change in Harvest comes at $t = 0$, our equations become

(7) $q''(t) = k^2\, q(t)$, $q(0) = 1$, $q(n) = 0$, $k^2 = K = -(T'/F')^0 > 0$, $K > 0$,

$$q(t) = \frac{e^{k(t-n)} - e^{-k(t-n)}}{e^{-kn} - e^{kn}}$$

This shows that an abundant Harvest at $t = 0$ causes storage thereafter to increase, but the increase is greatest just after $t = 0$ and drops off to zero in subsequent time. The drop in price is greatest right after $t = 0$ and is less, but still finite, by $t = n$ where $Q(n)$ is specified to be unchanged.

Now, if we want to know what the effect of such a Harvest change is by itself, we can let n go to plus infinity and the solution in (7) becomes $q(t) = e^{-kt}$, checking our intuitive expectation that the effect of any Harvest change wears off gradually, depending upon the costliness of storage.

Exactly the same type of reasoning shows us what must be the effect on earlier dates of foreseen changes in crop; thus, for $t < 0$, $q(t) = e^{kt}$, showing that foreseen changes in Harvest have dwindling effects upon the periods far ahead.

*   *   *

74

THE TRANSFER PROBLEM AND TRANSPORT COSTS : THE TERMS OF TRADE WHEN IMPEDIMENTS ARE ABSENT [1]

THE more things change the more they are the same.   After the First World War economists discussed the effects of a unilateral transfer—such as reparations—on the terms of trade.   And in the 1950s, as the end of the Marshall Plan comes into sight, economists must once again consider an identical analytic problem—the possible effects of a cessation of unrequited imports on the terms of trade.[2]

It is perhaps fair to say that most economic theorists subscribe to the so-called " orthodox " doctrine : Any increase in unilateral payments will in probability shift the terms of trade against the paying country; any reduction in its unilateral payments will probably shift the terms of trade in its favor.

In this paper I shall raise a few questions concerning the validity of the reasoning underlying this view; but in the end I shall not seriously impugn its substantive conclusions.   My main purpose here is to treat the rather neglected analytic issues raised for international trade by transport costs, and to show that in their complete absence the orthodox view rests on shaky logical foundations.   Later in a sequel to this paper I hope to analyse in some detail the effects of impediments to trade on international equilibrium, thereby tending to restore some validity to the orthodox position.

BRIEF HISTORY OF DOCTRINE

The debate between Keynes and Ohlin on the effects of transfer will be recalled.   Keynes took the position that if a region like Europe made to a region like America a unilateral transfer (investment, reparations, gifts, etc.), then the terms-of-trade would have to shift against Europe; in addition to the " primary burden " on the paying country of the direct payment,

[1] I am glad to acknowledge helpful comments from Professors R. L. Bishop, G. A. Elliott, C. P. Kindleberger, D. H. Robertson and Jacob Viner; and particularly from Professor G. Haberler, for whose 1936–37 Harvard seminar an earlier mathematical version of this paper was prepared.

[2] A. C. Pigou, " Unrequited Imports," ECONOMIC JOURNAL, Vol. LX (June 1950), pp. 241–54.   See also J. E. Meade, " A Geometrical Representation of Balance of Payments Policy," *Economica*, Vol. XVI (November 1949), pp. 305–20.

there would in addition be a " secondary burden " as her export prices deteriorated relative to her import prices.   Indeed, if the international demand curve of the receiving country were of elasticity of unity or less, there were fears that it would be quite impossible for the paying country to make the transfer—competition would tend to turn the terms of trade indefinitely against her.   This analysis in terms of *price* elasticity was largely concurred in by Taussig, Viner, Pigou and others.

Ohlin and his followers adopted what they called the " modern view."   This took into account income-effects and purchasing power passing between the two countries, and concluded that no change in the terms of trade was necessarily implied by a tribute or transfer.   It was not always clear to the reader just what was meant by this somewhat mysterious flow of real purchasing power; and at times the " modern view " seemed to have about it strong overtones of Say's Law of Markets and conservation of purchasing power.[1]   But abstracting from all dynamic business-cycle effects and from all problems of aggregate demand, we can interpret Ohlin as follows.

The Marshallian international-trade-offer curves of *both* countries are shifted in opposite directions, with this important result : the implied qualitative effect on the terms of trade does not depend upon the *price*-elasticity of one offer curve alone, or on the price-elasticities of the two curves; rather the more crucially important parameters are the *income*-elasticities or propensities in the two countries.[2]

As Viner's masterly survey makes clear, the above analytic formulation was acceptable to the holders of the orthodox view. By the 1930s the holders of this viewpoint had refined their analysis to take account of the mutual shifts of the offer curves. If some had previously thought that a deterioration of the terms of trade was inevitable, they dropped this view in favor of the more careful formulation : A deterioration of the terms of trade of

---

[1] Examination of the historical literature soon suggested that the modern view had its classical precursors : Ricardo, Wheatley, Bastable and others, as against Thornton, Mill and others who favored the orthodox view. See J. Viner, *Studies in International Trade*, Chapter 6, pp. 326–60, for historical discussion.

[2] See D. H. Robertson's essay, " The Transfer Problem," written in 1929, but first published in A. C. Pigou and D. H. Robertson, *Economic Essays and Addresses* (1931).   Robertson pointed out Marshall's error in shifting but one of the curves, and on p. 180 says, " To speak geometrically, both curves must be shifted to a new common starting point . . . [and] it appears that, contrary to common opinion, the degree of change cannot be expressed in terms of the (price) elasticities of the original curves, though it can be expressed in terms of the utility and disutility schedules from which those curves are drawn up." Robertson acknowledges help from Pigou in arriving at this conclusion.

the paying country is not inevitable, but *there is a strong presumption that the income elasticities of the different goods in the different countries will be such as to create some deterioration in the terms of trade.* At the same time holders of the modern view admitted that a change in the terms of trade *might* take place, but argued that it could be in either direction and that there was no presumption as to its direction. Thus, the area of disagreement was narrowed, but not to the vanishing point.

GRAPHICAL ANALYSIS

The definitive analytic treatment of this problem was given by Pigou as far back as 1932.[1] His analysis rests upon a precise set of idealised assumptions, most of which I shall adhere to until contrary notice is given. It would be a great mistake, however, to try to interpret most of the writers as if they had these idealised conditions firmly in mind and as if they made rigorous deductions from them. An intuitionist like Keynes, for example, seems wrongly to have shifted the paying country's curve alone; but he may really have derived his belief about the terms of trade primarily from his notions about monetary effects of international trade on gold, employment and other aggregate magnitudes. In this paper I shall not go into the problems of the foreign-trade-multiplier and other issues of the modern theory of income determination, but will refer the reader to two recent papers.[2] In what follows I shall confine myself to what may be called the pure theory or barter aspects of the problem, and shall ignore all problems concerned with absolute price levels and transitional gold flows. Almost at the beginning of the transfer controversies, Professor Ohlin complained, and I sympathise with the feeling, against mixing "two different and incompatible theories: (1) the

---

[1] A. C. Pigou, "The Effects of Reparations on the Ratio of International Exchange," ECONOMIC JOURNAL, Vol. XLII (1932), pp. 532–42. This is summarised in A. C. Pigou, *A Study in Public Finance*, 3rd edition (1947), Chapter XIX, and duplicates his 1950 article earlier cited. The latter contains a few obvious misprints which can be easily cleared up by referring to the older treatments or to Viner's excellent summary.

[2] Lloyd A. Metzler, "The Transfer Problem Reconsidered," *Journal of Political Economy*, Vol. L (1942), pp. 397–414, and reprinted as Chapter 8 in *Readings in the Theory of International Trade* (1949); Svend Laursen and Lloyd A. Metzler, "Flexible Exchange Rates and the Theory of Employment," *The Review of Economics and Statistics*, Vol. XXXII (1950), pp. 281–99. The former article deals with income-employment effects along the lines of the foreign-trade multiplier analysis of the *General Theory*; the latter considers the interactions of relative price and income-employment effects in terms of a world where effective demand is important. All this is related to work by W. A. Salant, F. Machlup, A. J. Brown, Joan Robinson and others.

barter theory of Mill; (2) a theory of monetary and price mechanism."[1] Since then the confusion of these elements has continued, and, I fear, much to the disadvantage of a clear understanding of either aspect of the problem or of their interaction.

Pigou reduces the transfer problem down to the Jevons–Walras–Edgeworth theory of barter of two goods between two individuals, whom I shall call Europe and America. Call the goods clothing and food, and for simplicity assume that the production of all goods is completely constant throughout our first analysis. If we like, we can think of Europe as producing little (or no) food and much clothing; of America as producing little (or no) clothing and much food. With most of the writers, I shamelessly assume collective indifference curves for Europe and also for America : if this simplification seems too much to swallow, the reader may imagine that he is dealing with the tastes between food and clothing of a representative citizen of each country, all other citizens being identical.[2] It will serve no useful purpose to follow Pigou's assumption that the two goods have independent utilities;[3] any indifference curves of normal concave curvature will do. In the beginning we assume that Europe and America trade under perfectly competitive conditions, with no transport costs or trade barriers. In the beginning there is no unilateral transfer either way.

[1] B. Ohlin, " Transfer Difficulties, Real and Imagined," Economic Journal, Vol. XXXIX (1929), pp. 172–8, and reprinted in *Readings in the Theory of International Trade*, pp. 170–8. This quotation is on p. 174 of the latter. W. W. Rostow, "The Terms of Trade in Theory and Practice," *Economic History Review,* 2nd series, Vol. III (1950), pp. 1–20, gives an excellent survey of the transfer discussion and the Keynes–Beveridge controversy on historical trends, and fairly sums up most of the actual discussion as being " best regarded as an aspect of the short-period monetary theory of prices " (p. 9). It may be remarked that Viner's discussion of Pigou's barter model and of the transfer problem generally is in a chapter entitled " The International Mechanism under a Simple Specie Currency."

[2] Only in one special case can collective indifference curves validly summarise demand conditions for a country : only if all citizens have *identical* taste patterns *regardless* of income level will the ratio of the price of food to the price of clothing be a determinate function of total food and total clothing, *independently of their distribution*. Jacob L. Mosak's definitive study, *General Equilibrium-Theory in International Trade* (1944), pp. 56–63, 75–86, shows how the analysis can be completely freed from the assumption of collective indifference curves, and how the case of any number of people and commodities can be rigorously handled.

[3] I shall later argue that Viner's demonstration, *Studies,* pp. 334–7, that tariff impediments predispose the terms of trade to be affected by transfer in the *unorthodox* way so as to *favor the paying country* is based upon the atypical peculiarity of the Pigou model of strict linearity and independence. The orthodox case is stronger than this model would suggest.

Fig. 1 is the familiar box-diagram that shows the final equilibrium. The base and altitude dimensions of the box are respectively the fixed world totals of clothing and food production. Any point in the box represents four different magnitudes : referred to the lower south-western European corner of the box, a point represents European clothing and food; referred to the upper north-eastern American corner of the box, the same point represents American clothing and food.   Initially, before trade we

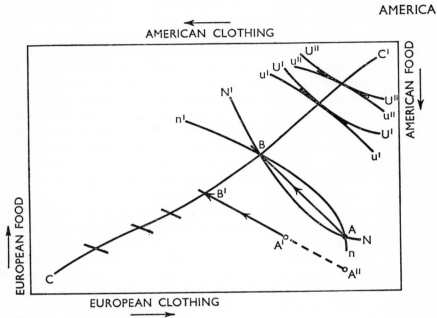

Fig. 1.—CC' is the contract curve where all trade must ultimately end. Reparation payments from A to A' shift the equilibrium from B to B', and the crucial question is how the slope of mutual tangency flattens or steepens as we move down the contract curve.

start off at the point marked A, where Europe is producing little food and America little clothing.   After trade we end up at the equilibrium point B, where Europe is consuming more food than she produces, having exported her clothing surplus for America's food surplus.   The arrow between the production point A and the equilibrium consumption point B represents the amount of clothing traded for food; the arrow's slope represents Europe's terms of trade, the ratio of her clothing-export price to her food-import price.

The exact final equilibrium position is determined by the

intersection at B of the two " offer " or " price-consumption " curves NN' and nn' : at each point on a country's offer curve, the ruling price ratio of clothing to food is just equal (and tangent) to the country's marginal rate of substitution or indifference (as measured by the numerical slope of the indifference curve through that point).

To keep the diagram from becoming cluttered, I have not indicated the indifference curves in the neighborhoods of B and A, but the reader can supply them if he wishes.   I have drawn in the important Edgeworth " contract curve " CC'.   This is the locus with the following defined properties : (1) From any point *on* the contract curve, no mutually advantageous movements are possible; from any point *off* the contract curve, there always exist movements towards the contract curve which do benefit both countries.   (2) Everywhere on the contract curve, the indifference curves of Europe (such as U' or U'') are tangent to the indifference curves of America (such as u' or u'').   The common slopes of mutual tangency are drawn at various typical points along the contract curve.   (3) No matter where we might place our initial starting point A, the final competitive equilibrium *must* be on the contract curve.

Now to introduce a unilateral payment from Europe to America into the picture.   We shall see that it does not matter whether the payment is, in the first instance, expressed in terms of Europe's export good, clothing; or in terms of America's export good, food; or in terms of any combination of them; or, for that matter, in terms of some units of abstract purchasing power.   In any case, the unilateral payment shifts the old initial point A to a new initial point A'.   In Fig. 1, I have adhered to the usual assumption of stating the payment in terms of the paying country's export good, in this case European clothing : so A' is due west of A by the amount of the payment.

From A' the reader can now draw two new offer curves,[1] which will have to intersect at a new equilibrium point on the contract curve, such as B' (which is recognisable by the fact that its slope of mutual tangency " points " directly at A').

[1] This shows the correctness of Robertson's criticism of Marshall for (1) not shifting both curves and (2) for arbitrarily shifting the one curve by the fixed amount of the reparation itself.   See Robertson, *op. cit.*, p. 180, for the correct statement that both curves are probably shifted inward toward each other. This tends to be true so long as the payment is expressed in terms of the payer's export good and does not overshoot the contract curve.   The box-diagram seems superior to Marshall's exchange diagrams for showing up such relations; but it is directly applicable only in the fixed-output case, whereas Marshall's exchange diagram also can handle the case of variable production.

The whole question of the effect of a transfer payment on the terms of trade can now be simply restated : Does a downward movement along the contract curve from B to B' lead to a final slope of mutual tangency that is flatter or steeper ?   If the slope becomes flatter, Europe's unilateral payment causes its terms of trade to deteriorate as in the orthodox view; but if the slope remains the same or becomes steeper, the Ohlin view is vindicated. In this example, I have stacked the cards and drawn in the slopes along the contract curve so that below B there is an orthodox deterioration in Europe's terms of trade.[1]

Our geometrical construction shows us that under truly competitive conditions it does not qualitatively matter whether a reparation is made payable in one good rather than the other. For suppose the payment had been in terms of the receiving country's good and just large enough to take us from A to the point marked A'', which is on the extended line from A' to B'. Obviously such a food payment would end-up both countries in the same point B' as did the postulated clothing payment. In fact, any unilateral payment that involves enough of both goods to shift us from A to *any point on the line A' to A''* will represent an " equivalent payment " and will have exactly the same effects upon the terms of trade.[2]

---

[1] Taussig's concepts of gross barter terms of trade and net barter terms of trade are easily read off the diagram. The former is the slope of a line connecting A and B'; the latter is the slope of the trading line connecting A' and B'. The " secondary burden " on Europe is reflected by the fact that the new net-terms-of-trade arrow from A' to B' is flatter than a hypothetical arrow through A' drawn parallel to AB. See F. W. Taussig, *International Trade*, p. 113.

In the Taussig *Festschrift* volume, *Explorations in Economics* (1936), pp. 84–92, Professor Leontief out-moderned the moderns by presenting a case in which the terms of trade changed so much in favor of the *paying* country as to leave her actually better off after the unilateral payment !   The secondary improvement in net terms of trade more than wiped out the primary transfer burden !   Professor Leontief made sure that his example was consistent with concave indifference curves for both countries.   However, it appears to me from a study of Fig. 1 that, provided we rule out multiple intersections of the offer curves, the Leontief effect becomes impossible.   See my *Foundations of Economic Analysis* (1947), p. 29, for a further comment on this point.   M. Bronfenbrenner, " International Transfers and the Terms of Trades : An Extension of Pigou's Analysis," in *Studies in Mathematical Economics and Econometrics in Memory of Henry Schultz* (1942, Chicago Press, Chicago), ed.   O. Lange *et al.*, pp. 119–31, identifies the Leontief-effect with the " inferior-good " phenomenon; but I should rather relate it to multiple and unstable equlibria, which can certainly be illustrated with superior goods.

[2] One qualification must be made, if the amount of the reparation is specified to be greater than the amount initially possessed (or producible) by the paying country, then the new A' point will be *outside* the box.   In this case it *may* happen that the two new offer curves never meet, making the reparation obligation an impossible one.   See A. C. Pigou, *Public Finance* (1947), p. 176.   It is true that

Why then after the Second World War was there felt to be special virtue in reparations in kind ? Aside from transitional monetary effects, this would have seemed to involve a misapprehension of what it is about tied loans and payments in kind that minimises secondary burdens.[1] If the American Government takes German cameras and dumps them on competitive markets for what they will bring, the effect is no better than if Germany were forced to pay America so much American wheat. This is not to deny that payments in kind and tied loans may go smoothly and minimise transfer problems for a quite different reason from that included in our analysis : namely, when one country lends to another or gives to another, there may be a concomitant *shift* in the desires and needs of the countries (*i.e.*, shifts in their indifference curves or more generally in the demand conditions underlying investment). Nineteenth-century harmonious international lending and borrowing may have been such a case.

But for our problem, the essential question boils down to this : As unilateral payments move the equilibrium along the contract curve, what is happening to the slope of mutual tangency ?

THE CRUCIAL MARGINAL INCOME PROPENSITIES

What is it that determines whether the slopes are getting flatter or steeper as we move down the contract curve below B ? The Pigou analysis, common-sense intuition[2] and Fig. 2's magnification of the neighborhood around B all give the same answer.

---

the qualitative direction of shift in the terms of trade will be independent of the good in which the reparations are expressed. It is also true that any *ex post* burden of reparations and change in the terms of trade resulting from (1) reparations expressed in the payer's exports can be *exactly matched* by (2) some properly large reparation contract involving only *its imports*. But, as Professors Elliott, Viner and Baumol have rightly pointed out to me, before reparations are paid you will know only the *ex ante* price ratios and not the *ex post* price ratios. If *ex ante* 5 food = 1 clothing, it will definitely not be indifferent as to whether reparations are stipulated as 5 billion food, or 1 billion clothing, or as any weighted average in between. Until we know the qualitative and quantitative change in the *ex post* terms of trade, we cannot know which of these combinations would be most onerous.

[1] See Jacob Viner, " German Reparations Once More," *Foreign Affairs*, Vol. 21, July 1943, pp. 666–7 for an excellent statement on this issue.

[2] " If £1 is taken from you and given to me and I choose to increase my consumption of precisely the same goods as those of which you are compelled to diminish yours, there is no Transfer Problem." (J. M. Keynes, " The German Transfer Problem," ECONOMIC JOURNAL, Vol. XXXIX (1929), pp. 1–7, reprinted in *Readings in the Theory of International Trade* (1949), pp. 161–9 ; the quotation is from p. 163 of the *Readings*. See also Viner, *Studies*, p. 329, for a similar 1927 reference of H. K. Salvesen, and p. 354 for triangular expenditure diagrams.

Whether the terms of trade will deteriorate in the orthodox manner or not depends upon *the relative strength of the European and American marginal-propensities-to-consume food and clothing,* and on no terms other than these income propensities.

Call the fraction of each extra dollar spent by Europe on food F_E, and on clothing C_E; call America's similar marginal propensities to consume F_A and C_A. Only the ratios C_E/F_E and C_A/F_A are of importance for the present argument; these ratios are easily compared between the two countries, independently of currency units, etc. Then Fig. 2 will demonstrate the following important results :

If
$$\frac{C_E}{F_E} > \frac{C_A}{F_A}$$

the paying country's terms of trade (*i.e.*, Europe's) will deteriorate. This is because each dollar of income lost went relatively more largely for its own product than did each dollar of extra income received by the foreigner. If $C_E/F_E = C_A/F_A$ or $C_E/F_E < C_A/F_A$, then the terms of trade will remain the same or turn in favor of the paying country.[1]

How can we prove that the above income criterion is a valid criterion to indicate how the terms of trade will change ? Fig. 2 shows a magnification of the contract curve near the original equilibrium point B. It has drawn on it something that was left

---

[1] One should not confuse these marginal *income* propensities with income *elasticities*. Actually, in Fig. 2, the marginal absolute changes in *physical* consumption were the true determinants; it so happens that with equal price ratios in America and Europe, we can convert the latter into marginal propensities expressed as fractions of extra dollars or pounds of income. When tariffs are in the picture, this will not be possible.

Let the European marginal physical propensity to consume $\partial(\text{clothing})/\partial(\text{income}) = C_E/P_C = c_E$, and similarly use small letters c_A, f_E, f_A to denote the other three physical propensities. Analysis like that of Mosak shows that in the " normal " or " stable case," the criterion is $(c_E f_A - c_A f_E)$; if no goods are " inferior," this can be writen as $c_E/f_E - c_A/f_A$, which is P_C/P_F times our previous criterion. In the special case of two goods, no saving and no domestic goods, we can write the same marginal propensities $C_E + F_E = C_A + F_A = 1$. My colleague, Professor Robert L. Bishop, points out that $C_E - C_A$ or $F_A - F_E$ are then equivalent to my above criterion.

Note also, in this two-goods case we can write our criterion in the terms of import propensities alone, $\{(1 - F_E)/F_E\} - \{C_A/(1 - C_A)\}$, which is convertible into $1 - F_E - C_A$. This last form says that the orthodox deterioration of the terms of trade of the paying country will depend upon whether *the sum of the marginal propensities to import of the two countries is less than unity.* Professor Haberler has been using this criterion in his Harvard classes for some years; see also, J. E. Meade, *op. cit.*, pp. 307–8 and Fig. 2. A pitfall in the use of this criterion in the more than two goods case (or in the case with transport costs) is noted in my footnote in the penultimate section.

out of Fig. 1—namely, the *income-consumption* or Engel's curves for each of the two individuals. These are the broken-line curves, which indicate *how people will expand their consumption of food and clothing as income increases but prices remain the same.* Through each point there passes one such income-consumption line for each country. Geometrically we easily draw such a curve by joining together the points on the different indifference curves that have exactly the same slope—*i.e.*, we hold relative prices constant as we vary income. Through the original equilibrium point *B*, *BR* represents Europe's income-consumption line, and *Br* represents America's.

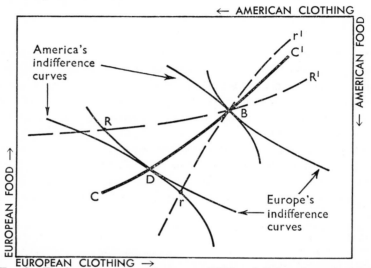

Fig. 2.—The income-consumption curves *RBR'* and *rBr'* are drawn by joining points on adjacent indifference curves that have the same slope as at *B*; they will always contain the contract curve *BD* between them. If *R* is above *r*, it follows that *D*'s slope is flatter than *B*'s.

Let *D* be any nearby point to *B* along the contract curve. Through *D* must pass two tangential indifference curves. It will be noted that as we pass south-east of *D* the slopes along Europe's indifference curves must be getting flatter, while the slopes of America's indifference curves must be getting steeper. This follows from the fact that the box-diagram turns America upside down and makes its indifference curves (which are really also convex to its origin) appear of the opposite curvature to Europe's. Similarly, as we pass north-west of *D*, the slopes of the two indifference curves move in *contrary* directions. It follows from this divergence that the two countries' income-consumption curves through a point like *B* must contain *inside* them the contract curve. For if D were completely above both income curves, its common slopes could not be equal to each other, but would instead have to be both greater and less than the slope at B, which is a contradiction to the tangency condition at D.

Thus in Fig. 2 BD lies inside of BR and Br. It will be noted that by definition of an income-consumption curve, the point R must have the same indifference slope as B; and r, for America, must have the same slope as B. From the fact that R lies above and to the left of r, it then follows that we can infer that D must have a flatter slope than B, representing a deterioration of the terms of trade of clothing against food. Why? Because D lies over r, and hence in terms of the curvature of America's indifference curve it has a flatter slope than at r or B. And with D lying below R, the curvature of Europe's slope tells us that D must have a flatter slope than at R or B.

To sum up: the income-consumption curves through B contain the contract curve inside them; if the paying country's income curve below B lies above the receiving country's, then the slope at the intermediate contract curve point must represent a deterioration of the clothing–food price ratio; the relative slopes of the income curves are our sole criterion of price change.[1]

The common sense of this argument is easily explained. If and only if a movement along one country's income curve causes it to give up the goods in exactly the same proportions as the other country takes them on will there be no change in the terms of trade. It will be noted that crucial slopes of the income curves depend only upon marginal physical income propensities to consume and not directly on the money income propensities expressed in terms of dollars or pounds. However, in the complete absence of impediments to trade, the price ratios will be the same for the two countries, and so we can convert the physical propensity criterion into an expenditure propensity criterion.[2]

[1] The reader can test his understanding of the geometrical argument by working through the details of the case where the two income-consumption curves coincide. The contract curve must then also coincide with them, and must then everywhere show *no* change in the terms of trade. *It will be noted that the present analysis nowhere makes any assumption about linearity or about smallness of the movement.* The only way that the above argument might fail and require qualification would be in the case where two-countries' income-consumption curves were sufficiently twisty to give rise to more than one intersection after some finite movement; even in such a case, the criterion can be made rigorous.

[2] One minor technical point should be noted. Fig. 2 represents normal rather than inferior-good behaviour. No change in the argument is needed to handle the latter possibility; however, a change in algebraic sign of the criterion will result if but one of the countries has food as an inferior good.

PROBABILITY EVALUATIONS: (1) ERRONEOUS SCALE EFFECTS [1]

Our important criterion $C_E/F_E \gtreqless C_A/F_A$ has now been established.[2] It remains to assess the probabilities. Pigou is inclined to argue that there is a definite presumption in favor of the $>$ sign and the orthodox conclusion. The Pigou reasoning on this point is not very clear to me; I have pored over his 1932, 1947 and 1950 treatments, and have not been able to convince myself of the validity of his demonstration. Two separate elements seem to be involved in his argument: first, the assumption that the paying country, Germany in Pigou's example, is smaller in scale than is the receiving country, England, the rest of the non-German world in Pigou's example; second, the assumption that each country spends relatively more on its own products than does the other country spend on those products.

The first of these arguments, hinging as it does on absolute scale, would not necessarily become applicable to the example under consideration—payments between two large and almost equal regions, Europe and America. But aside from this, the argument seems to be logically invalid. Both Bronfenbrenner and Viner [3] have pointed out that mere differences in scale may affect the four terms in Pigou's criterion, but they do so in such a way as to affect the two ratios that must be compared in exactly the same way. We may put the matter most simply as follows: if very small relative to the receiving country, the paying country will " presumably " be spending the same smaller percentage of its income on its own product that the larger country is spending on those same products. Pigou's own mathematical analysis contains the antidote to his view that scale counts. For it shows that the whole problem can be handled by the slopes of the income-consumption curves of the *representative* citizens of the two countries. These are necessarily *independent of scale*, and would be numerically equal to the slope of the aggregate income-consumption curves *whatever the number of identical people in each country*. No amount of converting of these slopes into irrelevant elasticities can obscure this fact, even though after a number of such transformations have been made, one's intuition may have

---

[1] The next five sections are somewhat technical, and can be skipped by the reader satisfied to read the summary that follows.

[2] In Pigou's symbolism, this is $(\psi'/F') \gtreqless (\phi'/f')$. See *A Study in Public Finance*, p. 179, or Viner, *op. cit.*, p. 338. See also G. A. Elliott, " Transfer of Means-of-Payment and the Terms of Trade," *Canadian Journal of Economics and Political Science*, Vol. 2 (1936), pp. 481–92, for a valuable definitive treatment of all these issues.

[3] M. Bronfenbrenner, *op. cit.*, p. 125; J. Viner, *Studies*, p. 341.

become so blunted as to make one prone to wrong assumptions about what is " equally likely."[1]

PROBABILITY EVALUATIONS :   (2) INCONSISTENT APPEAL TO TRANSPORT COSTS

Nonetheless, one does feel that there is something plausible about the fact that Europeans spend relatively more on European goods than do Americans.   This brings us to the second and more interesting strain in the Pigou argument.

To establish a definite presumption in favor of the > sign in the criterion, and therefore to lead to the orthodox conclusion, Pigou leans on the simple econometric fact that Europeans tend to spend more relatively on European products than Americans do ; Americans likewise have a greater average propensity to consume American products than do Europeans.

There seems to be no good reason to question this fact.   And yet it is well to realise that there is no theoretical necessity that this should be so.   What makes it so is the fact that transport costs and tariffs are *not* zero.   This means that European products are relatively cheaper in Europe than they are in America ; and similarly for the relative cheapness of American products in America as compared to European products.   Already in assessing the realistic probabilities, we seem to be departing from the strict assumption of the model—which assumed literally zero

---

[1] Cf. H. G. Johnson and C. F. Carter, " Unrequited Imports and the Terms of Trade : A Note," ECONOMIC JOURNAL (Vol. 60, 1950), pp. 837–9, for the view that Pigou's demonstration is " possibly suspect." They suggest that instead he argue his case in terms of the non-elasticity criterion mentioned above, their implication seeming to be that then a more plausible presumption can be stated for it.

In *Public Finance*, p. 184, Pigou notes, " Contrary to what might perhaps be exacted, it is immaterial to this conclusion [that disparity of scale leads to the orthodox presumption] whether the reparation-paying or the reparation-receiving country is the larger of the two." At first this does seem paradoxical. However, further reflection concerning the symmetry of the situation—where an increased algebraic payment of one country is the same as a decreased algebraic payment of the other and where one country's terms of trade are necessarily inverse to those of the other country—shows that if Pigou's argument were valid (as I argue it is not !) for a small Germany and a large England, it would have to be valid for a small England and a large Germany.

Once this symmetry is grasped, we are instantly alerted to the necessary falseness of a conclusion like that of Bronfenbrenner, *op. cit.*, pp. 130–1, which holds that a duty levied by the receiving country would lead in the " orthodox " direction, while a duty levied by the paying country would lead in the unorthodox direction. Actually, as will be argued later, both duties necessarily lead in the same direction—probably the orthodox direction rather than the reverse as in the Viner model. Where Bronfenbrenner seems momentarily to have erred is in failing to see that duties of either country lead to the same type of discrepancy between the two local price ratios.

transport costs ! Viner has called explicit attention to this inconsistency in the Pigou argument.

But let us for the moment not cavil at this inconsistency in the Pigou argument.   First let us accept the fact of transport costs and impediments to trade.   It still requires some complex argument to deduce from this the orthodox presumption about the relative marginal propensities and the deterioration of the terms of trade.

One great source of complexity in any valid demonstration arises from the desire of many writers to infer from factual data on average-propensities conclusions about marginal propensities. Therefore, it would greatly simplify the argument if an orthodox adherent, as long is he is referring in a casual way to empirical experience, were simply to assume that everyone knows that the European *marginal* propensity to consume tends to be greater for European products than is the American *marginal* propensity. Such a fact would still depend on an implicit recognition of transport costs or tariffs, and we should still have to show by more extensive analysis what is the correct criterion when impediments are present; but nonetheless by directly assuming knowledge about marginal propensities, we shall be able to avoid the tricky analysis based on the " probable " relations between average and marginal propensities.

The cited 1929 essay of Professor Robertson early placed the focus on marginal concepts.   Thus, he says on p. 80—

"... in all probability German goods have more nearly the character of money (which can be surrendered or gained without leading to a change in its marginal utility) to Germans than they have to Englishmen, and English goods have more nearly the character of money to Englishmen than they have to Germans.   Hence, there is a considerable balance of probability . . . that the ratio of exchange will be turned against Germany the paying country."[1]

The use of the word " money " in this connection can be taken to be figurative rather than literal.   Demands for liquidity, transaction balances, media of exchange, store of value and unit of account or speculative hedges against price uncertainties would have little relevance in the static barter model under consideration.[2]   That " money " is used only as a figure of speech is clearly shown by a more recent paper on the " Terms of

---

[1] The expression in parentheses represents a footnote in the original.

[2] Even if we were to introduce dynamic considerations of effective demand into our model, we could not point to any empirical tendency for objects of local manufacture to be used as money proper.   (Actually some anthropologists claim the reverse to be more frequently true : other things equal, African gold and European wampum are preferred as money to local produce.)

Trade " delivered by Professor Robertson at the 1950 Monaco meeting of the International Economics Association.

> " For normally it may be presumed that any country is more easily glutted by receiving a given-sized extra wad of foreign goods than by receiving an equal extra wad of home-made goods, but is less severely inconvenienced by going without a given-sized wad of home-made goods than by going without an equal wad of foreign goods. (Its utility schedule for foreign goods is steeper in both directions than its utility schedule for home-made goods . . .) And if this be true, the appetite of the transferor country for bilateral trade will be less impaired by the fact of unilateral transfer than that of the transferee country, and the terms of trade more apt therefore to move against it." [1]

No explicit reason is given for this econometric fact about the propensities, which appears superficially to be the direct contrary of the commonly met facile assumption that imports have something of the luxury about them and hence tend to have high income elasticities. To a casual observer like myself, the first of these contradictory hypotheses is not implausible. But when I try to analyse the reasons for it, I inevitably find the cause to be rooted in non-zero transport costs—in the most general sense of the term, inclusive of all impediments to trade and imperfections of competition. *If transport costs are literally zero and had never been other than zero, there would be absolutely no localisation of demand : the place of origin of a good would be completely a matter of indifference to the consumer.* Patterns of consumption might differ over the globe, but there would be no reason for these differences to be correlated with the geographical pattern of production. (*E.g.*, I heat my home with oil, while someone near coal-mines heats his with coal; but this is not because he has any inborn love for coal, as becomes abundantly clear when the relative costs of the two fuels permanently change.) [2]

PROBABILITY EVALUATIONS : (3) AMBIGUOUS EFFECTS OF TRANSPORT COSTS ON RELATIVE EXPENDITURE PROPENSITIES

In summing up the implications of the Pigou *transport-free model*, I shall argue that the above considerations completely

---

[1] Taken from privately circulated typescript, pp. 6–7. The expression in parentheses represents a footnote in the original.

[2] Professors Bishop and Viner have reminded me that *past* transport costs may have a lingering effect on tastes and demand even after they have largely disappeared. The role of monopolistic and imperfect competition in actual international trade is crucial and may transcend in importance mere transport cost, narrowly defined. This is hardly touched on in my discussion and needs extensive further examination.

destroy the orthodox presumption in that model.   But before leaving this topic, let me note one further complexity that has not to my knowledge been noted and analysed in the transfer discussions.   Suppose we agree that no systematic predictable differences in expenditure are to be expected when transport costs are zero.   Does it follow that the systematic differences which result from transport costs are in the direction of the alleged facts ? Transport costs of imports do raise their prices relative to those of home goods.   Will people then spend relatively less or relatively more on imports ?   Simple considerations of the price elasticity of demand show that there is no necessity that relatively less will be spent on imports : it all depends on inelasticity or elasticity of demand whether people will tend to spend more or less on imports.

Are we entitled to assume that there is an *a priori* presumption that price elasticity of demand is greater than unity as is usually unconsciously taken for granted in these discussions ?   I should argue that no such general presumption exists.[1]   It all depends upon the facts.   Typically we should expect every commodity price to go through two opposite stages : when it is very cheap, raising its price will encounter inelastic demand; when it becomes sufficiently expensive, its demand will become elastic and eventually nothing will be spent on it.   Sufficiently great transport costs should probably in the end work in the direction of decreasing relative expenditure on import goods, ultimately of course creating so-called domestic goods which do not move at all in interregional trade.

PROBABILITY EVALUATIONS :   (4) WHAT CRITERION WHEN THERE ARE IMPEDIMENTS ?

The above remarks, inconclusive as they are concerning the direction in which transport costs must affect expenditure propensities, are a little misleading in that they refer exclusively to

---

[1] If we take the weighted average of all price elasticities, including cross-elasticities of the ith good with respect to changes in the jth price alone and with each good's elasticities being weighted by the percentage of income spent on it, then it can be shown by intuition or from the mathematical properties of homogenous functions that the average of these elasticities is exactly -1.   To suppose that the average " own-elasticity " of a good is greater than unity (*i.e.* algebraically less than -1), we should have to presume that the average " cross-elasticity " is positive rather than negative.   I cannot demonstrate in terms of any of the customary economic theories why this should be so.   If this is to be assumed an as econometric fact from casual observation, we might as well short-circuit the process and assume from the beginning we know that demands tend to be elastic.   The typical statistical study reports otherwise; but there is good reason to believe from the Haavelmo theories of econometrics that the typical estimates are biased in the direction of inelasticity.

ordinary *ceteris paribus* price elasticities. Impediments to trade change the situation in a much more complex fashion than does a simple price change with fixed money income and fixed other prices. Transport costs and duties create differentials in relative prices of the goods and give rise to familiar " substitution effects." In addition, to the extent that we are talking about real transport costs that use up product in shipping it, there are substantial " income effects " which will be shared between the countries in a complex way, depending upon reciprocal supply and demand. If the impediments consist of artificial tariffs whose revenues represent mere transfers of income, substitution effects are more heavily involved, the only income effects being the transfers between and within countries and the " deadweight loss " resulting from interferences with perfect competition. As will be shown later, those writers who lump together tariffs and real transport costs and treat their effects on the transfer problem as equivalent are being misled into false conclusions and criteria.

Surprisingly enough, it will be shown in the sequel that our task may be lightened by the fact that price elasticity is *not* the dominating consideration. In geometrical terms, it is simplest to think of impediments to trade as shifting the final equilibrium point or points of Fig. 1 from the center part of the diagram containing the contract curve toward the lower right-hand corner from which the original trade began. Our problem then involves the following questions : (1) When each country ends up with relatively more of her own goods, will the income-consumption curves tend to be systematically flattened out or steepened ? (2) Will the income propensities be moved in any systematic direction ?

The second of these questions is very hard to give any conclusive answer to, as we have seen from the ambiguity of price-elasticity and as can be verified if one asks what is happening to the division of expenditure between food and clothing as one moves south-east along an indifference curve. However, while no hard and fast answer can be given to question (1), you can go a long way toward giving it an answer if you are willing to indulge in *a priori* probability argumentation. If you are willing to follow the next section's identification of average and marginal propensities, what is there called the Basic Convention underlying the reasoning of Viner and others, then you can definitely assert the following : raising the price of imports relative to exports causes a country's income-consumption curve to flatten out in slope in the direction of its own good; *i.e.*, the marginal *physical* propensity to consume home goods is raised relative to that of foreign goods.

Doesn't this vindicate the conclusions of Pigou and the orthodox adherents ?   Can't we now apply the same reasoning of Fig. 2 concerning relative slopes to the case where there *are* impediments to trade ?   Can't our answer to question (1) give us a presumption as to what must be the only reasonable presumption as to changes in the terms of trade ?

It would be premature to answer Yes to these questions.   I hope in the sequel to indicate how the transport-free analysis can be broadened in the directions suggested by the above lines of thought.   And I may anticipate the results of further investigation to report that tariff duties can be shown by such reasoning to favor orthodox expectations.   But the same weight of probability cannot be adduced in the case of real transport costs.   For the answer in the latter case will be shown to depend on the answer to ambiguous question (2) rather than question (1).

This warns us that the criterion derived from the Pigou-type transport-free model is directly applicable in that model only. In that model, with relative prices the same in the two countries, it does not matter whether we state our criterion in terms of (marginal) propensities to spend money income or in terms of marginal *physical* propensities to consume more of a good. Without further analysis of a more general model, we do not even know which of these is the proper criterion to use when there are transport costs or tariffs, or whether some third criterion must be found.

PROBABILITY EVALUATIONS : (5) A DIGRESSION ON METHOD

There remains as unfinished business the question of possible inference concerning marginal propensities from presumed knowledge of average propensities.   The fullest treatment of this problem is that of Viner.[1]   He recognises that the marginal and average propensities need not be equal ; that *marginal* will equal (exceed, fall short of) *average* if the average propensity to consume a commodity remains the same (increases, decreases) as income alone increases.   (The exact numerical relation between average and marginal propensity we can state : marginal propensity ÷ average propensity = income elasticity.)   Using a variant of what is known among *a priori* probability philosophers as the

---

[1] *Studies*, pp. 324–5.   In what follows I try to state in statistical jargon what seems to be Viner's intended meaning.

principle of sufficient reason (or of insufficient reason, or of equi-probability of the unknown) Viner argues that if we were given data on average propensity alone, " it was theoretically to be expected " that the average propensity would go neither up nor down with income, so that the unknown marginal propensity could best be estimated as equal to the known average propensity. (In terms of the above stated numerical relations, we may interpret Viner to assume that if we don't know whether the income elasticity is greater or less than one, equi-probability of the unknown considerations suggests that the best estimate is unity. Perhaps the argument will gain in plausibility to some if I add that for all goods, including saving as a good, the average of income elasticities of all goods, each weighted by the percentage spent on it, must exactly equal unity.)

To-day many, perhaps most, statisticians will have little to do with the equi-probability-ignorance arguments that were so beloved by Edgeworth and others. Instead they take the high-and-mighty attitude that out of ignorance can come only ignorance. For the purpose of the present paper, the main conclusion of which is *against* the existence of any presumptions in the zero-impediment case, such an austere attitude is perfectly satisfactory.

But for the sequel, in which the biases introduced for the reparations problem by transport cost are subjected to analysis, some linkage between average and marginal propensities would be useful. In particular, I should like to work out the implications of the Viner view that in the absence of further knowledge, we had better equate marginal propensities to average propensities. If anyone refuses to accept such a use of the principle of sufficient reason, I shall not quarrel with him.

What the Viner convention means in geometrical terms can be simply put. Consider any point in the box-diagram of Fig. 1. Suppose we know nothing of the slope of the income-consumption curve through that point; so that its slope might point in any direction with " equal likelihood." Then what I shall call the Basic Convention requires us to draw in the slope of the income-consumption curve so that it points directly toward the origin of the country in question. The income-consumption curves proceed out from the origin in radial spokes, looking much like the typical casual blackboard drawing of indifference curves.[1]

---

[1] Given more knowledge, such as that food is a necessity and clothing a luxury, we could, of course, do better. Interestingly enough Pigou's assumption of linearity of marginal utility and of independence leads to indifference curves that are concentric ellipses around a center of satiation; all the income-consumption curves point inward toward the satiation point; along any indifference

In statistical jargon, Viner believes the average propensity to consume can be regarded as the *modal* estimate of the unknown marginal propensity to consume. He defends himself against a criticism of Roland Wilson and Harry D. White by stating definitely that he does not think the probability of this mode to be greater than one-half or, for a continuous variable, even necessarily greater than zero; but being the mode, its probability or probability density is greater than that of any other *single* number. This modal value, Viner suggests, will minimise the " probable error " of the estimates.   In terms of any of the usual definitions of probable error and of modes, this is too strong a statement to make—unless, as would probably seem plausible to Viner, we can regard the unknown probability distribution as being a peaked symmetric one with coincidental mean, median and mode.

Among practitioners of the arts of *a priori* probability we more commonly encounter the assumption of a perfectly flat, so-called " rectangular distribution " of probability than that of a peaked unimodal distribution.   Viner quotes as a precedent the argument of John Stuart Mill alleging that the equilibrium in a simple Ricardian foreign-trade example was more likely to be at the mid-point between the limits set by comparative advantage than at any other single point, but with the recognition that the probability at this mid-point mode would itself be small.   Actually many commentators have noted that Mill in his *Logic* showed a great, and uncharacteristic, ignorance of probability matters, a serious weakness in a writer purporting to treat the problem of induction and one which makes him an uncertain guide to follow. However, Mill was in good company among economists, a number of whom (including Carl Menger) have argued that the half-way point between limiting price ratios enjoys some special probability privileges.

The present example is a perfect one for critics of the assumption of equi-likely probabilities, who point out its fatal dependence upon arbitrary specification of original categories and variables so that its conclusions are *not* invariant under reclassifications of categories and transformation of variables.   These critics point out that the method can lead to the presumption of equal males and females on the moon or equal males, female humans and female tigers, depending upon the whim of the practitioner. In the present example it is obvious that transforming from the

---

curve of the special Pigou family of curves, the more expensive a commodity becomes the *greater* becomes its relative marginal-physical-propensity-to-consume, which is just the opposite of what is implied by our Basic Convention.

variable " price of Portuguese wine ÷ price of English cloth "
to its reciprocal causes a substantive change in the mid-point.[1]

Because of its interest in connection with the main stream of
philosophic thought, I have dwelt at some length on this matter.
It will be clear to any careful reader that only the minutest
fraction of Viner's analysis is affected by this issue. And I must
myself confess to a lingering interest in the case covered by the
Basic Convention, not so much for the present paper but for the
analysis of more general problems involving transport costs and
trade impediments.

Summary of Failure of Orthodox Presumption in Absence of Transport Costs

The above sections have arrived at a far-reaching conclusion.
If we rigidly adhere to the assumption of literally zero transport
costs and admit no impediments to trade or imperfections of
competition into our analysis, then the orthodox presumption that
the terms of trade of the paying country will tend to deteriorate
turns out to fall completely to the side. In every case where an
orthodox presumption has been established, it turns out that
somewhere in the chain of reasoning, consciously or unconsciously,
impediments to trade have been brought into the picture.

Once we push the assumption of zero transport costs to its
ultimate limit, there is absolutely no localisation of demand, and
there can be no *a priori* correlation between regional patterns of
production and tastes. This is the crucial point to be understood.
We can number countries $a, b, c, \ldots$ and goods $1, 2, 3, \ldots$ All
permutations of marginal propensities are then equally admissible
a priori, and when we come to compute a criterion of movements
in the terms of trade this turns out to be a symmetric function
with no basis for the presumption that it will be of one sign or
another. In this limiting case of literally zero transport cost,

---

[1] In connection with a different but analogous problem, Viner employs a
quite different assumption that is more nearly in accordance with the usual
assumptions about equi-likelihood. In connection with the relation of mint
parity to foreign exchange he says : " Equilibrium . . . is as likely to be reached
at any one as at any other rate within the limits of the specie points " (*Studies*,
p. 379). Here he is assuming a rectangular distribution without peaks. Unfortunately, if ignorance tells us the above about the dollar price of the pound,
this implies that it tells us something quite different and inconsistent about the
pound price of a dollar : in technical parlance if x has a rectangular distribution
of equal probability between A and B, then $1/x$ will turn out *not* to have a rectangular distribution of equal probability. The arithmetic mean, the geometric
mean and the mode lack invariance under inversion ; and only under special
conventions will the median and geometric mean possess invariance for this
problem. The geometrical argument for our Basic Convention could be closely
linked with the paradoxes of the classic Buffon random-needle problem.

it seems to me logically inescapable that the Ohlin or Modern View is correct in its agnosticism : there is no presumption that the terms of trade will deteriorate rather than favor the paying country.[1]

Figs. 1 and 2 illustrate this.   As drawn, they seem to favor the orthodox view.   But that is simply because, to be agreeable, I stacked the cards.   What if the original A point had been on the other side of the contract curve, as would certainly have been possible before I labelled the axes ?   Then the behaviour of the slopes below B would have negated the orthodox view.   Or suppose I had stipulated that America rather than Europe were the paying country.   Then a careful examination of the diagram *above B* will show that I have stacked the cards against the orthodox view.   The principle of sufficient reason—in its correct formulation, which out of ignorance deduces only ignorance—shows that until transport costs introduce asymmetry into the picture, no *a priori* presumptions are possible.

VARIABLE OUTPUT AND MULTIPLE COMMODITIES

My main task is done.   But to underline this far-reaching conclusion in the zero-transport-cost case, let me briefly show that relaxing the assumptions that production is fixed and that there are only two goods will still not lead to the orthodox result. The box-diagram of Fig. 1 does not tell all the story once production becomes a variable.   Each new pattern of output gives rise to new dimensions for the box.   Nonetheless, students of the

---

[1] One reader has asked me whether this identification of the orthodox presumption with transport costs is analytically related to the Heckscher–Ohlin view that many differentials in regional factor prices would be wiped out if it were not for transport costs of finished commodities, a subject that I have discussed in two earlier articles in the ECONOMIC JOURNAL, 1948 and 1949.   I believe these are not essentially related : the present analysis in terms of fixed production is one in which the Heckscher–Ohlin analysis becomes irrelevant, and yet it is a case where transport costs are relevant for the transfer problem.   To forestall another misunderstanding of the above statement of our ignorance, let me add that in any one case, countries a, b and c will in fact tend to have a definite pattern of production of goods as determined by comparative advantage (factor endowment, etc.).   But without transport costs, the way that each country spends what income it does have will not depend in any causal way on the pattern of its production.   Until we are told more about the two countries—such as the fact that the payer has a marginal propensity to consume good 2 of exactly 0·3333 or that the receiver happens to produce a luxury good, etc.—there seems to be no *a priori* systematic basis for predicting the direction of changes in the terms of trade : the effects of differing production patterns on the distribution of income may be in the direction of increasing or decreasing the relative demand for home versus foreign products; the example of the woodworker who is in that occupation because he is the sort of man who will spend his increments of money and leisure on fine wood carvings is matched by the example of the sadist who will spend his increments on the masochist, etc.

pure theory of international trade know that a determinate equilibrium can still be determined even when production is admitted as a variable.[1]

Graphical or mathematical analysis of the two-country two-good case, where production of the goods is variable along a given technological transformation curve, shows that our *exact same criterion* determines the qualitative direction in which the terms of trade must change as a result of transfer; so again no orthodox presumption is possible. I shall relegate to a footnote a statement of the mathematical system involved for any interested reader to check, and shall very briefly formulate in common-sense terms the reason for this surprisingly simple result.[2]

First suppose the equilibrium configuration of production and consumption has determined itself. Now introduce a unilateral payment of the usual type. Presumably everything will have to change, including of course production. But just suppose we were able to find *a* new equilibrium *without* any change in output; then since the equilibrium is assumed unique, that lucky guess of

---

[1] Ricardian constant costs is one simple case. The next simplest case is one in which costs are variable and in which for each price ratio between the two goods, there is an optimal production pattern for each good, as determined by tangency conditions along a production-possibility or (opportunity-cost) production transformation curve. See G. Haberler, *Theory of International Trade*; W. Leontief, " The Use of Indifference Curves in the Analysis of Foreign Trade," *Quarterly Journal of Economics*, 1933, reprinted in *Readings in the Theory of International Trade* (1949). General equilibrium handles these and more general cases with complete rigor.

[2] Throughout, let capital letters stand for European variables and small letters for American; let X_1 and x_1 represent consumption of clothing and X_2 and x_2 consumption of food; let Y_1, y_1, Y_2, y_2 represent the corresponding production figures, which are related in each country by transformation functions of the usual convex type, $Y_2 = T(Y_1)$ and $y_2 = t(y_1)$; let Ps stand for prices and let primes and double primes stand for differentiation; let the tastes for each country be given by indifference curves that are defined by the following marginal-rate-of-substitution functions for food and clothing $R = R(X_1, X_2)$ and $r = r(x_1 x_2)$; finally, let the algebraic payment or transfer paid by Europe to America in terms of clothing be B. Then the conditions of equilibrium determining all variables are given by

$$X_1 + x_1 = Y_1 + y_1, X_2 + x_2 = Y_2 + y_2, (X_2 - Y_2) = \frac{P_1}{P_2}(Y_1 - X_1) + B,$$

$$- T'(Y_1) = R(X_1, X_2) = \frac{P_1}{P_2} = \frac{p_1}{p_2} = r(x_1, x_2) = - t'(y_1).$$

This Leontief-type system becomes the Pigou–Jevons system if we make the Ys all constant, dropping the outside equations in the last line, and if we specialise R and r to be ratios of independent and linear marginal utilities. The criterion for the algebraic sign of the change in P_2/P_1 with respect to a change in B can be shown to be $(\partial R/\partial X_1)(\partial r/\partial x_2) - (\partial R/\partial X_2)(\partial r/\partial x_1)$, which is equivalent to our earlier criterion. (To introduce tariffs in the picture we must distinguish between the Ps and the ps; to introduce real transport cost, we must in addition modify the relations between the total Xs and Ys.)

ours would correctly portray *the* new equilibrium.   A little reflection tells us when we can hope to find a new equilibrium without any change in production : it is when the criterion worked out in the previous section is exactly zero, and it is only in this case. This can be verified by the box-diagram, which, so long as we are tentatively holding production constant, can be legitimately applied.   This diagram has told us which is the one critical case where no change in price will be necessary.   The case where $C_E/F_E = C_A/F_A$ is the razor's edge; in this case, existing production gets re-allocated between the countries without any relative price change; and without any relative price change, no change in production can take place.[1]

From this reasoning it follows that the criterion of the fixed-production case still provides us with the watershed between the two possible directions of change in the terms of trade.   Variability of production may affect the quantitative intensity of the change in export–import prices, but it cannot affect their qualitative direction.[2]   Income propensities alone are relevant for the qualitative question.

[1] Professor Viner has noted the singular case where the orthodox presumption breaks down regardless of income propensities.   In the Ricardian case of constant cost, where one of the countries incompletely specialises and the price ratio is at its limiting comparative cost ratio, the transfer cannot affect the terms of trade.   In this singular case of infinite elasticity of supply, we may think of our criterion as trying to indicate a change in the terms of trade but as having zero leverage in doing so.   See Viner, *Studies*, p. 349.

We may relax the assumption that output depends on relative prices alone. Thus people in the receiving country may now feel rich enough to work fewer hours, while the payers work more hours.   But when we permute the assumption concerning the labor intensity of the payer's export good, the symmetry of our ignorance seems to permit of no definite presumption.

[2] A similar statement can be made about the role of price elasticities of demand and of supply generally, although the literature abounds with contrary statements.   A more subtle mistake appears in some of the better analyses of the transfer problem; there is believed to be some asymmetry between the roles of supply elasticity and demand elasticity, between the elasticity involving marginal utility and that involving marginal disutility; and this asymmetry is made to work in favor of the orthodox view. Cf. Pigou, *Public Finance*, pp. 183–5; and Bronfenbrenner, *op. cit.*, pp. 125–6, where the following appears : " In general, suppliers (including exporters with a choice between several markets for disposal of their products) are more sensitive to differential profits than are consumers to differential satisfactions.   *Ceteris paribus*, then, elasticity of supply is greater than elasticity of demand, and so, in general, terms of trade may be most likely to shift in favor of receiving countries."   This is inconsistent with my previous analysis, and stems, I suspect, from the non-essential relationship between price and income derivatives introduced by the special features of the Pigou independence and linearity assumptions, and from the transformation of the terms in the criterion into elasticity coefficients.   Earlier in the section dealing with scale effects I have commented on the treacherous nature of such elasticities in probability reasonings.

Thus, we have seen that (1) whether production is constant, (2) whether costs are increasing or (3) whether costs are constant, there is the same absence of presumption concerning the effects of transfer on the terms of trade.

There remains the question of what happens to our results when we go beyond the two-goods case. Of course, when there are more than two goods the concept of the terms of trade becomes ambiguous. We could try to define some index number, but for the present purpose no such approximation is necessary; there is nothing that prevents us from considering the effects of a transfer payment on *all* price ratios of each possible pairings of the goods.

So long as transport costs are literally zero, there is again no localisation of demand and no *a priori* correlation between regional tastes and regional comparative advantages in production. We are again in a position of symmetrical ignorance : with transport costs literally zero, the orthodox presumption becomes completely untenable.

To my knowledge the only logically air-tight successful defense of the orthodox view is that given by Viner, in which he explicitly introduces into the problem transport costs great enough to make international trade prohibitive for some " domestic commodities." [1] Naturally a high percentage of our income is spent on such commodities. And from this fact it is often concluded that the orthodox presumption can be justified. Actually, Professor Viner has shown how all this can be made completely rigorous in a model. His model involves the reasonable assumption that outputs of a country's export and domestic goods are variable and substitutable and will be discussed in the sequel.

Nonetheless, I should like to report an illuminating experiment that definitely failed. Years ago, before Viner's masterpiece had appeared, I attempted to deduce the orthodox presumption by postulating, in addition to the two freely traded international

---

[1] *Studies*, pp. 348–9, seems the best reference for this; note the interesting use in 1937 of Hicks-like composite commodities. Viner and Bronfenbrenner also make frontal attacks on the effects of tariff duties, but Viner's conclusion in this case seems to be against rather than for the orthodox position. As indicated in my earlier footnotes, I believe this result to be due to the peculiar concentric ellipses of the Pigou model and that upon later analysis the orthodox case can be defended if we are willing to use the Basic Convention to identify more closely marginal and average propensities. G. A. Elliott, " Protective Duties, Tributes, and Terms of Trade," *Journal of Political Economy*, Vol. XLV, 1937, 804–7, showed that a prohibitive tariff can convert a traded commodity into a domestic one, and thereby increase the presumption that the terms of trade will move in the orthodox direction.

goods, the existence of domestic goods in one or both countries. But I assumed *production of each good to be absolutely constant and inelastic in supply*. Mathematical and logical analysis then showed that the orthodox presumption could not be maintained.[1]

In terms of graphs, a box-diagram like Fig. 1 was still applicable to this case. But in drawing up each party's indifference curves, I had to hold constant the consumption of the domestic goods. Depending upon taste patterns of complementarity and competitiveness between the domestic and traded goods, the levels at which the domestic goods were held constant could cause shifts in the slope and appearance of the indifference curves, but need not affect their general curvature. Exactly the same reasoning of Fig. 2 could be used to show that the same criterion $(C_E/F_E) - (C_A/F_A)$ would apply, provided these marginal propensities were calculated *ceteris paribus*, *i.e.*, with domestic goods' production and consumption held constant.[2]

This being so, I was in for a surprise. In trying to evaluate this criterion so as to arrive at the orthodox presumption, I soon found that the modern view continued to hold. In the absence of knowledge concerning the pattern of complementarity, and provided the traded goods were absolutely free of transport costs and non-localised in their demand, it was just as easy to imagine a world in which the paying country produced an export that would appreciate rather than depreciate in relative value. So long as our ignorance is thus symmetrical,[3] there is nothing to do but study the econometric facts of each situation and be prepared for a change in the terms of trade in either direction.

---

[1] G. A. Elliott in the 1936 cited article had already arrived at this conclusion.

[2] Suppose Europe spends her extra income on food, clothing and European houses in the proportions (10%, 20%, 70%), and America spends her extra income on food, clothing and American houses in the proportions (6%, 12%, 82%). Many writers would then seem to want to compare Europe's 10% expenditure on America's goods with America's 88% expenditure on her own goods. With production fixed, this is wrong. Assuming that the change in house prices is " neutral " in its effect on income propensities, we must here compare 20/10 with 12/6, which gives *no* change in the terms of trade. Note too that the Haberler–Meade criterion, if uncritically applied, would here yield $0{\cdot}10 + 0{\cdot}12$, which is much less than unity, and might wrongly be interpreted to necessitate a deterioration and a sharp one to boot.

[3] Viner's successful vindication of the orthodox presumption was possible because of his (quite realistic) introduction of an element of asymmetry into the problem : his domestic good is made (infinitely) substitutable for the region's export good production and not at all substitutable for the import good production.

CONCLUSION

This completes what has been a fairly exhaustive analysis of the transfer problem. I have pursued the implication of literally zero transport costs to the bitter end, and have arrived at the conclusion that there is then no presumption in favor of the orthodox view that transfer will tend to deteriorate the terms of trade of the paying country. This serves to clear the way for a later more detailed analysis of transport costs in the international trade mechanism, in the course of which the orthodox view will turn out to be partially vindicated.

PAUL A. SAMUELSON

Massachussetts Institute of Technology,
Cambridge, Mass.

75

THE TRANSFER PROBLEM AND TRANSPORT COSTS, II : ANALYSIS OF EFFECTS OF TRADE IMPEDIMENTS

I. INTRODUCTION

THE first part of this paper [1]

(1) surveyed the theoretical literature;

(2) developed graphically and logically for the transport-free two-country two-good case a fundamental criterion to determine how the terms of trade of the paying country change;

(3) showed that the criterion involves marginal *income* propensities of the different countries and goods in an essentially *symmetric* way, so that *in the complete absence of all trade impediments absolutely no probability presumptions concerning the criterion or the terms-of-trade change were possible ;*

(4) argued that the usual defense of the orthodox view appeals to empirical elements premised on transport costs in order to be able to get a definite answer from a criterion whose validity and applicability had been derived on the explicit banishment of all transport costs.

These results do not—and were not intended to—demolish the orthodox doctrine of a presumption that unilateral transfer payments will tend to deteriorate the terms of trade of the paying country. But they do suggest that the orthodox doctrine is still in need of vindication and further examination.

The present paper : (1) introduces transport costs explicitly into the Jevons–Pigou barter model to analyse the probable effects of transfer, and (2) discusses briefly some other aspects of impediments to trade.

II. EQUILIBRIUM CONDITIONS

As in Part I, Europe and America consume clothing and food. Because Europe is relatively well endowed with clothing (or clothing-producing factors), she exports clothing for American

[1] P. A. Samuelson, " The Transfer Problem and Transport Costs : The Terms of Trade When Impediments are Absent," ECONOMIC JOURNAL, Vol. LXII (June 1952), pp. 278–304, hereafter referred to as Part I. Certain extensions to the many-good case were also made.

food. The price ratio in Europe's markets of clothing to food represents her net terms of trade, and must in equilibrium equal Europe's indifference-ratio or relative marginal utilities of the goods. A similar equilibrium condition will hold for the price ratio in the American market and America's indifference ratio. If there are zero transport costs, these price ratios will be identical even though an ocean intervenes.

With no unilateral payments, trade must balance. For each country, value of imports = value of exports, expressed in common units. These units may be dollars, francs, ergs, food units or clothing units. There is no need to write a separate balance equation for each country, since the exports of Europe are the imports of America and vice versa.

Now we admit a unilateral payment from Europe to America. The common balance equation of the countries becomes

Value of American imports = value of American exports + value
of unilateral payment

or

Value of Europe imports = value of Europe exports — value
of unilateral payment

Part I and Pigou's earlier discussion showed that it matters little for our model in what units the unilateral payment is prescribed. Readers seem to find it most natural to imagine that Europe's unilateral payment to America is initially pre-scribed in terms of Europe's own export good—clothing in my example. Let then the payment be K clothing units per unit of time. So long as clothing and food prices, P_c and P_f, are the same in both countries, we may rewrite the balance of payments

P_f (American Food Exports) = P_c (European Clothing
Exports) — $P_c K$

or using Pigou's notation of X for the receiving country's export and Y for the paying country's export, we get

$$(1) \qquad \frac{P_c}{P_f} = \frac{X}{Y - K}$$

as an expression for Europe's net terms of trade. (Without the K units of clothing payments, we would have Taussig's gross barter terms of trade; and if $K = 0$, the two concepts are identical.)

All this is familiar ground. If we write down our demand or

marginal utility conditions, the full equilibrium conditions are summarised by

$$(2) \quad \left(\frac{\text{M.U. of Clothing}}{\text{M.U. of Food}}\right)_{\text{America}} = \frac{P_c}{P_f} = \frac{X}{Y-K} = \left(\frac{\text{M.U. of Clothing}}{\text{M.U. of food}}\right)_{\text{Europe}}$$

where the marginal utility or indifference ratios depend upon consumption in the respective countries—and hence, with production determined, on the export variables X and Y alone.[1]

The three equations of (2) are sufficient to determine the three unknowns: X, Y, P_c/P_f. If we change K—say from 0 to $+100$—new equilibrium values of the unknowns are determined. How the price ratio changes was shown to depend on the relative slopes of the Engel or income–consumption curves of the two countries (i.e., upon the derivatives of their relative-marginal-utility functions).

III. A Numerical Example of Cost-free Transfer

The following concrete example will pave the way for our further explorations. Suppose Europe produces 0 food and 200 clothing, America produces 0 clothing and 200 food. Suppose with Pigou that for each consumer utilities are measurable and independent. For simplicity, let each good have a strictly linear marginal utility, and for both America and Europe let the same linear formulas apply: M.U. = 8 — 0·04 (consumption), applying to both food and clothing.

Remember that each country consumes of its import good exactly what it imports, and of its export good what is left over from its production after exporting. Thus (2) now becomes the specific equation

Case of no transfer, $K = 0$:

$$\frac{8 - 0\cdot04Y}{8 - 0\cdot04(200 - X)} = \frac{X}{Y - 0} = \frac{8 - 0\cdot04(200 - Y)}{8 - 0\cdot04X} = \frac{P_c}{P_f}$$

---

[1] In *Public Finance*, p. 179, Pigou writes (2) in the form

$$\frac{\phi(Y)}{f(X)} = \frac{X}{Y - K} = \frac{\psi(Y)}{F(X)}$$

Because he usually expresses Europe's payment in terms of the receiving country's good, he usually (see p. 176) writes instead of $X/(Y - K)$ the equivalent expression $(X + R)/Y$, where R is Europe's payment expressed in physical units of America's export product. I have set the number of representative individuals equal to one in each country and have omitted Pigou's m and n.

Case of transfer, $K = +100$:

$$\frac{8 - 0{\cdot}04Y}{8 - 0{\cdot}04(200 - X)} = \frac{X}{Y - 100} = \frac{8 - 0{\cdot}04(200 - Y)}{8 - 0{\cdot}04X} = \frac{P_c}{P_f}$$

By cross multiplication, each of these sets of equations can be combined into quadratic expressions in X and Y. Eliminating one variable, we are left with a 4th-degree equation in the other that can be solved for its relevant root. Actually, as the reader can verify by quick substitution, the solution to the first case is given by :

Before transfer : $\dfrac{P_c}{P_f} = 1$, $X = 100$, $Y = 100$

which is not surprising in view of the assumed symmetry of the relations.

The transfer case can also be solved without setting up 4th-degree equations. The bold-face coefficients in the equations give us the criterion [1] $0{\cdot}04/0{\cdot}04 = 0{\cdot}04/0{\cdot}04$, so we know that the net terms of trade will be unaffected. Knowledge of $P_c/P_f = 1$ gives us three linear relations between X and Y, permitting us to solve by inspection :

After transfer : $\dfrac{P_c}{P_f} = 1$, $X = 50$, $Y = 150$

After transfer—which means with a unilateral payment being currently made and remade !—the receiving country consumes more of both goods, importing more clothing and retaining at home more food. The payer consumes less of both goods, exporting more of her clothing production and importing less food. Although the unilateral payment was prescribed in terms of clothing, the actual transfer has taken place as much in the form of curtailed food imports as in expanded clothing exports. (See Table I for a numerical summary.)

The terms of trade are unchanged because the income–consumption curve of America just happens to coincide with the income–consumption curve of Europe.[2] Before and after transfer, the two countries divide their incomes in the same way between the two goods. This is a highly unrealistic case, but I refer the reader to the earlier discussion as to why there can be

---

[1] This is Pigou's $|\psi'/F'| = |\phi'/f'|$, proportional to my $C_A/F_A = C_E/F_E$. See ECONOMIC JOURNAL 1952, p. 286.

[2] In Part I's graphical terms, here the contract curve coincides with the two income–consumption curves, which for the linear Pigou model are straight lines. See Fig. 1 below for a scale drawing of the case.

TABLE I

Zero Transport Costs and Transfer

	Before transfer $K = 0.$	After transfer $K = +100$ from Europe to America.
Terms of trade of clothing to food .	1·00	1·00
Europe :		
Terms of trade of clothing to food	1·00	1·00
Clothing—		
Production	200	200
Consumption	100	50
Exports (+) or imports (−) .	+100	+150
Food—		
Production	0	0
Consumption	100	50
Exports (+) or imports (−) .	−100	−50
America :		
Terms of trade of clothing to food	1·00	1·00
Clothing—		
Production	0	0
Consumption	100	150
Exports (+) or imports (−) .	−100	−150
Food—		
Production	200	200
Consumption	100	150
Exports (+) or imports (−) .	+100	+50

no systematic presumption about relative expenditure if we adhere pedantically to the strait-jacket of literally zero cost-impediments to trade.

IV. Explicit Introduction of Real Transport Costs

I now propose to come directly to grips with transport costs. The simplest assumption is the following : To carry each good across the ocean you must pay some of the good itself.   Rather than set up elaborate models of a merchant marine, invisible items, etc., we can achieve our purpose by assuming that just as only a fraction of ice exported reaches its destination as un-melted ice, so will a_x and a_y be the fractions of exports X and Y that respectively reach the other country as imports.   Of course, $a_x < 1$ and $a_y < 1$, except in the costless model, where they were each unity.

With transport costs in the picture, we must distinguish between price ratios in the two countries and also between the numerical exports of one country and the numerical imports of the other.   America's clothing imports are now less than Europe's clothing exports Y, being instead $a_y Y$.   Similarly, Europe's food imports are now $a_x X$ rather than X.

The balance of payments for either country can most simply be written using her *domestic* price ratios and her exports and imports. Thus, for America

$$\left(\frac{P_c}{P_f}\right)_A \text{ clothing imports = food exports}$$

all transfers being provisionally assumed away. Or

$$\left(\frac{P_c}{P_f}\right)_A = \frac{X}{a_y Y}$$

For Europe

$$\left(\frac{P_c}{P_f}\right)_E \text{ clothing exports = food imports}$$

Or

$$\left(\frac{P_c}{P_f}\right)_E = \frac{a_x X}{Y}$$

These two relations enable us to deduce the discrepancy between the two price ratios that transport costs must create and maintain. So long as goods are flowing in both directions

$$(3) \quad \left(\frac{P_c}{P_f}\right)_E = a_x \frac{X}{Y} = a_x a_y \frac{X}{a_y Y} = a_x a_y \left(\frac{P_c}{P_f}\right)_A < \left(\frac{P_c}{P_f}\right)_A$$

Interpretation : goods are relatively cheapest in their place of origin for two reasons—there is a transport cost saved on the export good and a transport cost paid on the import good. Thus, if clothing were to cost $\frac{1}{4}$ of itself to transport west and food to cost $\frac{1}{3}$ of itself to transport east, the European price ratios of clothing to food would be $\frac{2}{3}$ of $\frac{3}{4}$ or $\frac{6}{12}$ of the American price ratio. The reader can verify that the American price ratio of food to clothing will be cheaper than the European for the same reason and *by the same numerical factor* of $\frac{6}{12}$; *i.e.*, symmetrically with (3), we have

$$\left(\frac{P_f}{P_c}\right)_A = a_x a_y \left(\frac{P_f}{P_c}\right)_E < \left(\frac{P_f}{P_c}\right)_E$$

These fundamental price relations were derived from comparing balances of payments. A more fundamental derivation would be via arbitrage relations that maintain " purchasing-power parity " relations among transportable goods. One unit of cloth is worth $(P_f/P_c)_E$ units of food in Europe. By sending it abroad we can buy $a_y(P_f/P_c)_A$ units of food in America, of which $a_x a_y(P_f/P_c)_A$ can be brought back to Europe. This last expression must not exceed $(P_f/P_c)_E$, or arbitrage will set in, restoring the equality. Q.E.D. If transport costs are great enough to make all trade unprofitable, then the equality [1] of (3) is to be replaced by $(P_f/P_c)_A > a_x a_y (P_f/P_c)_E$ and $(P_c/P_f)_E > a_x a_y (P_c/P_f)_A$, with similar inequalities holding in terms of opposite directional transport costs.

How shall we measure *the* terms of trade between clothing and food? By Europe's price ratio, $(P_c/P_f)_E$? Or by America's $(P_c/P_f)_A$? So long as the spatial markets remain connected by trade, these measures differ only by an invariant scale factor, $a_x a_y$.[2] Therefore, transfer payments and any other disturbance will affect either measure in the same direction and relative degree. So we can use either as our measure of the terms of trade. Or for that matter, we can define a more symmetrical in-between measure, $(P_c/P_f)_I = a_y (P_c/P_f)_A = (P_c/P_f)_E/a_x$. This intermediate measure, which differs only in scale from the local measures, will be found to be a convenient variable for later use.

Now to combine our elements into a determinate trade equilibrium taking account of transport costs. Assuming no transfer payments, for America

$$\left(\frac{\text{M.U. clothing consumed}}{\text{M.U. food consumed}}\right)_A = \left(\frac{P_c}{P_f}\right)_A = \frac{\text{food exports}}{\text{clothing imports}} = \frac{X}{a_y Y}$$

for Europe

$$\left(\frac{\text{M.U. clothing consumed}}{\text{M.U. food consumed}}\right)_E = \left(\frac{P_c}{P_f}\right)_E = \frac{\text{food imports}}{\text{clothing exports}} = \frac{a_x X}{Y}$$

where in every case, imports are derived by applying the transport-cost a coefficient to our old symbols for exports.

These equations can be conveniently combined

$$a_y \left(\frac{\text{M.U. clothing consumed}}{\text{M.U. food consumed}}\right)_A = \frac{X}{Y} =$$
$$\frac{1}{a_x}\left(\frac{\text{M.U. clothing consumed}}{\text{M.U. food consumed}}\right)_E = \left(\frac{P_c}{P_f}\right)_I = a_y\left(\frac{P_c}{P_f}\right)_A = \frac{1}{a_x}\left(\frac{P_c}{P_f}\right)_E$$

Note that the relative marginal utility expressions for each country are determinate functions of food and clothing consumed; call this function r (clothing, food) for America and R (clothing, food) for Europe, where these functions have the usual curvature properties of marginal rates of substitution. With America producing O clothing and $\overline{F}$ food, and Europe O food and $\overline{C}$

---

[1] See P. A. Samuelson, " Spatial Price Equilibrium and Linear Programming," *A.E.R.*, Vol. XLII (June 1952), pp. 283–303, for a discussion of some of these spatial price relations.

[2] If transport costs varied with volume of trade, the *a*s would not be constants. Realistically, since there are joint costs of a round trip, a_x and a_y will tend to move in opposite directions, depending upon the strengths of demands for east and west transport.

clothing, we can express these demand functions in terms of exports alone : namely, $r(a_y Y, \overline{F} - X)$ and $R(\overline{C} - Y, a_x X)$.

To take account of a transfer payment from Europe to America, recall that this is stipulated in terms of Europe's export good. But is it to be so much clothing *in Europe*, or does the stipulated amount refer to clothing *delivered* in America ? With transport costs, there is a difference. It is of no consequence which convention we adopt : a smaller stipulated amount of delivered clothing will be identical in its effects to a large stipulated amount of clothing paid in Europe itself.

For convenience, I shall let the stipulated unilateral payment K stand for clothing payable in Europe to America. In Europe's balance of payments, K will be seen to be a direct subtraction from its clothing export credit items, Y—exactly as in the transport-free case.

Hence, we can write down our final equilibrium system, including all previous ones as special cases.[1]

$$(4) \quad a_y r(a_y Y, \overline{F} - X) = \frac{X}{Y - K} = \frac{1}{a_x} R(\overline{C} - Y, a_x X) =$$

$$\left(\frac{P_c}{P_f}\right)_I = a_y \left(\frac{P_c}{P_f}\right)_A = \frac{1}{a_x}\left(\frac{P_c}{P_f}\right)_E$$

With the parameters a_x, a_y, $\overline{C}$, $\overline{F}$ specified, we can vary the payment K and determine the resulting shift in the terms of trade.

V. Example of Real Transport Costs and Transfer

Our previous numerical example can provide a good illustration of some properties of our new system. We leave tastes and production as before. To bring out strongly the effect of transport changes, set $a_x = 0.5 = a_y$, so that fully one-half of each good is used up in crossing the ocean. Substituting into the linear marginal utility relations $8 - 0.04$ (consumption), gives

$$\frac{a_y(8 - 0.04 a_y Y)}{8 - 0.04(200 - X)} = \frac{X}{Y - K} = \frac{8 - 0.04(200 - Y)}{a_x(8 - 0.04 a_x X)} = \left(\frac{P_c}{P_f}\right)_I$$

or

---

[1] With $a_x = 1 = a_y$, we have the transport-free case; with $K = 0$, we have no transfer. In the case of independent utilities, this may be written in Pigou's notation as

$$(4)' \qquad \frac{a_y \phi(a_y Y)}{f(X)} = \frac{X}{X - K} = \frac{\psi(X)}{a_x F(a_x X)}$$

which differs from his original equations only because of the a_x and a_y coefficients.

$$(5) \quad \frac{4 - \dfrac{0 \cdot 04}{(2)(2)} Y}{8 - 0 \cdot 04(200 - X)} = \frac{X}{Y - K} = \frac{8 - 0 \cdot 04(200 - Y)}{4 - \dfrac{0 \cdot 04}{(2)(2)} X} =$$

$$\left(\frac{P_c}{P_f}\right)_I = \frac{1}{2}\left(\frac{P_c}{P_f}\right)_A = 2\left(\frac{P_c}{P_f}\right)_E$$

Before transfer, we solve these equations with $K = 0$. From the symmetry of the problem, it is easy to guess $X = Y$, $(P_c/P_f)_I = 1$. It is then easy to deduce that the common value of exports is $X = 80 = Y$, with imports being only half as great because of transport costs. See Table II for a summary of the

TABLE II

Real Transport Costs and Transfer

$(a_x = 0 \cdot 5 = a_y)$

	Before transfer $K = 0$.	After transfer $K = +100$ from Europe to America.
Intermediate terms of trade of clothing to food	1·00	1·48
Europe :		
Terms of trade of clothing to food	0·50	0·74
Clothing—		
Production	200	200
Consumption	120	69·2
Exports (+) or imports (−) .	+80	+130·8
Food—		
Production	0	0
Consumption	40	22·75
Exports (+) or imports (−) .	−40	−22·75
America :		
Terms of trade of clothing to food	2·0	2·96
Clothing—		
Production	0	0
Consumption	40	65·4
Exports (+) or imports (−) .	−40	−65·4
Food—		
Production	200	200
Consumption	120	154·5
Exports (+) or imports (−) .	+80	+45·5

results. In America food consumption is 120 and clothing only 40. In Europe food consumption only 40 and clothing 120. As Pigou, Robertson and others have insisted all along, one's home produce is relatively cheap and one buys relatively more of it in physical terms. Actually $(P_c/P_f)_E = 0 \cdot 5$ and $(P_c/P_f)_A = 2 \cdot 0$, so there is a four-fold difference in price.

What is not inevitable outside this particular model is the fact that each country spends relatively more money on its own good than on the imported good. Before transport costs were introduced, America spent 50% of its income on food and 50% on clothing. With heavy transport costs, clothing imports have become twice as expensive as food; but such is elasticity of demand that physical clothing consumption has dropped off by more than half—from 100 to 40. And more of food production is retained for home consumption because of the transport barrier to exports. So America ends up spending 60% of its income on its own good, food. A similar story holds for Europe's export and import goods.

Now introduce a unilateral payment of $K = +100$ clothing units payable in Europe to America. Table II shows the resulting pattern of trade and the resulting shift of the terms of trade in favor of the paying country.[1] This 48% shift in favor of Europe is a direct and dramatic reversal of the orthodox expectation that the payer's net terms of trade should deteriorate.

Such a perverse result is not coincidental. If we adhere rigidly to the strictest Pigouvion model of (a) identical unchanging tastes, (b) independent marginal utilities and (c) strictly linear marginal utilities, an anti-orthodox result is inevitable.[2] That further analysis of the orthodox view is needed must be apparent from this discussion.

VI. EQUILIBRIUM WITH ARTIFICIAL TARIFF IMPEDIMENTS

So far we have confined attention to " real " trade impediments that literally use up resources in transporting goods. The almost as important case of artificial impediments such as tariffs or quotas has certain analytic similarities. But there are important differences, which must not be glossed over, and which require separate analysis and conclusions.

For simplicity of exposition suppose that all Custom duties are levied in terms of the imported goods themselves : thus an importer who brings a unit of clothing into America from outside finds that the government leaves him with only $a_y < 1$ units of

---

[1] To solve equations (5) for $K = +100$, no short cuts are possible. Rather than solve a quartic equation, I used trial-and-error iterations; the interested reader can substitute Table II values for X and Y into (5) and verify that the resulting ratios do agree to the indicated number of decimal places.

[2] The general mathematical reasons for this are given later. At this stage any reader can examine the bold-faced coefficients, which in the zero transport cost case yield $0.04/0.04 = 0.04/0.04$, a criterion for no change in the terms of trade. He can compare these with the bold-face coefficients, which in the real impediment case where $a_x = 1/2 = a_y$, gives as a criterion for an *improvement* in the payer's terms of trade, $0.04/(0.04/2^2) > (0.04/2^2)/0.04$.

clothing after he has passed through Customs; similarly, a European importer of food is left with but a_x units of food after he has paid the duty on a unit of imports.

Now as far as arbitragers are concerned, they do not care whether the impediments to trade are " natural " or " contrived." Clearly purchasing power parity relations between the spatial prices will be exactly the same as in the case of real transport costs. *I.e.*, so long as duties are not prohibitively high and goods are actually flowing in both directions, equilibrium requires

$$(3)' \quad \left(\frac{P_c}{P_f}\right)_E = a_y a_x \left(\frac{P_c}{P_f}\right)_A < a_y \left(\frac{P_c}{P_f}\right)_A = \left(\frac{P_c}{P_f}\right)_I < \left(\frac{P_c}{P_f}\right)_A$$

This is the exact equivalent of equation (3), which showed the degree to which a country's own export good is relatively cheap at its place of origin.

Tariffs affect our balance-of-payments expressions quite differently from real transport costs. No matter how Custom officials alter the price tags of goods, the physical imports of each country are still fully equal to the physical exports of the other country. Tariffs do not literally *use up* goods as do transport costs. Our convention that governments collect duties in kind brings into prominence the problem that always vexes the theorist dealing with tariffs : What does the government do with the tariff receipts ? The usual convention followed is the one that is most natural for me to adopt here : The government is assumed to distribute the receipts to the (representative) consumer in a *lump-sum* fashion so that each consumer can act as if the true price to him for any expansion of purchase is equal to the price quoted within his country's markets.[1]

The balance of payments of America, or for a typical American consumer, can be written in either of the following ways when transfer payments are zero

Imports valued just outside of America =
                    exports valued just outside of America
Imports valued inside America =
                    exports valued in America + Lump-sum Tariff Rebate

---

[1] The case of quotas does not directly give us a_x and a_y coefficients, but for any degree of import limitation these can be defined implicitly as the ratio of the price the importer must pay to the higher price that competition produces internally. By auctioning the limited quotas, the government can collect the difference and give it to whomever it deems worthy. More often, the difference is pocketed by importers, and for simplicity their tastes and demands are assumed to be like that of the populace at large. The same assumption was implicitly made about the government's disposition of the transfer payment.

Applying similar reasoning to Europe, and using our symbols, we get

(6) $$\left(\frac{P_c}{P_f}\right)_I Y = X$$

and

$$\left(\frac{P_c}{P_f}\right)_A Y = X + \left\{\left(\frac{P_c}{P_f}\right)_A - \left(\frac{P_c}{P_f}\right)_I\right\} Y$$

Similarly, for Europe

$$\left(\frac{P_f}{P_c}\right)_E X = Y + \left\{\left(\frac{P_f}{P_c}\right)_E - \left(\frac{P_f}{P_c}\right)_I\right\} X$$

where the terms involving brackets represent the lump-sum rebates of tariff receipts.

Of these relations, we need only (6). To take account of transfer payments expressed in terms of the export good of the paying country, the specified place of delivery is no longer of substance. In all of our balance-of-payments relations, the transfer of K units of clothing must be regarded as a subtraction from Europe's credit items of exports, and so we simply rewrite (6) in the more general form

(6)′ $$\left(\frac{P_c}{P_f}\right)_I = \frac{X}{Y - K}$$

Recalling that the representative consumer in each country equates his indifference-ratio or relative marginal utility to the domestic price ratio he faces, we can combine this fact with (3)′ and (6)′ to get our final conditions of equilibrium under tariffs :

$$(7)\ a_y r(Y, \bar{F} - X) = \frac{X}{Y - K} = \frac{1}{a_x} R(\bar{C} - Y, X) =$$
$$\left(\frac{P_c}{P_f}\right)_I = a_y\left(\frac{P_c}{P_f}\right)_A = \frac{1}{a_x}\left(\frac{P_c}{P_f}\right)_E$$

This should be compared with (2), the Jevons–Pigou equilibrium condition with no trade impediments and with (4), the equilibrium conditions with real as distinct from artificial trade impediments. Note that the a_y and a_x factors appear in (7) outside the r and R indifference functions exactly as they do in (4). But they do not appear inside the indifference functions because there is no literal using up of goods in transport.

The substantive difference between equilibrium conditions under artificial and real impediments described above is ignored in the following type of arguments. To the view that if the foreigner passes restrictive tariffs we should do the same, the analogy is brought forward : " If Nature silted harbors abroad, would you think it necessary or desirable to ruin your own harbors ? " For polemical purposes and with non-specialists, this is a suitable argument to use. But to a pedantical specialist, there is a difference between the kinds of trade obstructions that needs to be analysed at least once.

VII. Example of Transfer with Artificial Impediments

Using the numerical marginal utility functions of our previous examples, (7) takes the form

$$(7)' \quad \frac{4 - \dfrac{0.04}{2} Y}{8 - 0.04(200 - X)} = \frac{X}{Y - K} = \frac{8 - 0.04(200 - Y)}{4 - \dfrac{0.04}{2} X} = \left(\frac{P_c}{P_f}\right)_I$$

Table III summarises the results where $K = 0$ and no transfer payment is made and where $K = +100$, representing a unilateral payment from Europe to America of clothing. The case of $K = 0$ is easily solved when we note the symmetry of our

Table III

Artificial Impediments and Transfer

$$(a_x = 0.5 = a_y)$$

	Before transfer $K = 0.$	After transfer $K = +100$ from Europe to America.
Intermediate terms of trade of clothing to food	1·00	1·40
Europe :		
Terms of trade of clothing to food	0·50	0·70
Clothing—		
Production	200	200
Consumption	133⅓	79·7
Exports (+) or imports (−)	+66⅔	+120·3
Food—		
Production	0	0
Consumption	66⅔	28·4
Exports (+) or imports (−)	−66⅔	−28·4
America :		
Terms of trade of clothing to food	2·0	2·80
Clothing—		
Production	0	0
Consumption	66⅔	120·3
Exports (+) or imports (−)	−66⅔	−120·3
Food—		
Production	200	200
Consumption	133⅓	171·6
Exports (+) or imports (−)	+66⅔	+28·4

numerical assumptions. This tells us X and Y must be equal. Hence $(P_c/P_f)_I = 1$, and we have merely to solve a linear equation for $X = 66\frac{2}{3} = Y$.

Introducing a transfer payment turns out to shift the terms of trade in favor of the paying country.[1] We expect this unorthodox result from our experience with Tables I and II : the artificial barrier case is intermediate, so to speak, between the zero-cost and real-cost cases. The terms of trade have not shifted so much in Europe's favor as in the previous example, but they have shifted in favor of the payer by 40%.

VIII. Graphic Solution of Tariff Case

Fig. 1 is an exact replica of Fig. 1 of the previous paper, but now the difference curves have been made to be concentric circles in accordance with the special numerical assumption of linear marginal utilities.[2] The dimensions of the box diagram are equal to total world production of the respective goods ; Europe's origin is the lower left-hand corner of the box ; America's origin is the upper right-hand corner. To approximate Jevons more nearly, I have placed the initial endowment point at the southeast corner of the box, marked A : this represents zero food production for Europe and zero clothing production for America, an extreme but inessential assumption.

With no impediments to trade, the offer curves through A will intersect at the equilibrium point B. Both the net and gross barter terms of trade are measured by the numerical slope of a line adjoining A to B. At B both countries' indifference curves are tangential, with their common tangent pointing at A ; of course, B is on the contract curve of points of common tangency, which in this numerical case happens to be the straight-line diagonal joining the two origins.

A transfer payment of 100 clothing paid to America shifts the initial point from A to A'. New offer curves drawn through A' will intersect in a new equilibrium point, marked B'. With zero impediments, this new point must also be on the contract curve, where the nations' indifference curves are mutually tangential and pointing at the new initial point A'.

---

[1] With $K = +100$, I had to solve (7)' by iterative trial and error : the reader can perform the substitutions to verify that the ratios of (7)' are equal, up to the indicated number of decimal places.

[2] By changing commodity units, we could change the circles to ellipses. My choice of numerical coefficients is special in its symmetry between goods ; also, it is an inessential coincidence that the world totals of production would, if given to either country, lead to its exact point of saturation.

For this special numerical case, the income–consumption or Engel's curves through B happen for both countries to have the same slope.[1] It follows from Part I's demonstration that $A'B'$ must then be parallel to AB, so that the unilateral transfer payment causes no orthodox deterioration of the payer's net terms of trade, and no anti-orthodox improvement.

All the above duplicates the reasoning of Part I, and depicts

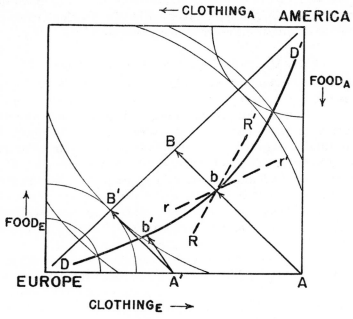

Fig. 1

With zero transport costs, transfer leaves terms of trade AB unchanged at $A'B'$. With tariffs, transfer improves payer's terms, from Ab to $A'b'$: along DD', where domestic prices differ by duties, indifference slopes steepen from b to b' because Pigou model makes Engel's slopes RR' steeper than rr'.

graphically the numerical data already given in Table I. To handle tariffs, we must recognise that the countries must end up—not with indifference-curve slopes equal as on the contract curve—but with Europe's final slope always in a constant ratio to America's. Why? To reflect the relative cheapness of each country's export good in its own market; i.e., the slopes must differ by the constant factor, $a_x a_y < 1$.

---

[1] In the absence of transport costs and special information, Part I argued that we have no reason to presume either country's marginal income propensities will be dominant for either good.

The locus of points with indifference-curve slopes agreeing up to the specified numerical factor is given by DD'. All the final equilibria under tariffs must end up on this locus. Without transfer, the final equilibrium point is shown by Table II to be at b.[1] Graphically, this can be recognised by the fact that the intermediate slope at b, which is between the two countries' indifference slopes in the same degree as $(P_c/P_f)_I$ is intermediate between $(P_c/P_f)_A$ and $(P_c/P_f)_E$, points directly at b.

Just as transfer without tariffs moved us along the contract locus toward the payer's origin, so will transfer with tariffs move us along our new DD' locus from b to b', toward the payer's origin and away from the receiver's. The problem of what happens to the payer's net terms of trade can now be reworded in graphical terms :

> As transfer moves us along this DD' locus of final equilibrium points under tariffs, what is happening to the indifference slopes of either (and both, since the prices are in constant ratio to each other) country ? Are they becoming flatter, as in the orthodox view ? Or steeper ? Or remaining unchanged ?

Readers of Part I will easily see that the reasoning applied there to Fig. 2 can also be applied here. A comparison of the relative steepness of the two countries' income–consumption curves through any point on DD' tells us how the indifference-slopes are changing as we move along DD'.[2]

To summarise :

> The paying country's net terms of trade will, under tariffs, *improve* (*remain the same, deteriorate*), depending on whether its own product expands relative to the other product *more slowly* (*at the same rate, faster*) along its own income–consumption curve than it expands along the receiving country's income–consumption curve.[3]

---

[1] Geometrically, b could be defined by intersecting " offer curves," where the latter are newly defined so as to be generated—not by points on each country's indifference curves that are pointing directly at A—but by points that would be pointing at A after modification by the a_y and $1/a_x$ factors. After transfer shifts us from A to A', a similar argument can determine b'.

[2] See ECONOMIC JOURNAL 1952, p. 287, for the detailed reasoning.

[3] The relevant criterion depends on relative *physical* marginal propensities— *i.e.*, upon the relative slopes of the Engel's curves in the Figures—and can be written as $c_A/f_A \gtrless c_E/f_E$. Since the nations' price ratios differ, this is no longer equivalent to $C_A/F_A \gtrless C_E/F_E$, the criterion previously defined in terms of non-physical marginal income propensities. See ECONOMIC JOURNAL 1952, p. 286. Paradoxically, the latter criterion will turn out to be the correct one when the trade impediments are real rather than artificial, as will be shown in Table IV.

We now see why the anti-orthodox result occurred in this case. The strict Pigou case of independent and linear marginal utilities is seen graphically to imply income–consumption curves that become steeper as the indifference curves become flatter ! *I.e.*, as a good becomes cheap, more of it is bought and its average propensity to consume increases; but its marginal income propensities—both physical and in terms of value—here move in the opposite direction. Thus, through b and b', Europe marginally contracts its purchase of America's product (relative to its own product) faster than America expands its purchase of its own product (relative to Europe's product). Note how Europe's Engel's curve RR' through b is in the Pigou model steeper than America's Engel's curve rr'. This causes the intermediate slope between the two indifference curves to steepen as transfer moves us down DD' from b to b'. (See Fig. 2 of Part I for expansion of this argument.)

IX. Orthodoxy Defended in the Tariff Case

Our analysis has no need for assumptions of independent or linear marginal utilities. And since they lead to bizarre results, the time has come to drop them. In Part I, I discussed at length the alternative convention that Viner and others have put forward. By use of the principle of sufficient reason or other argument, Viner assumes that the single best assumption in the presence of ignorance is the following : Average and marginal income propensities are equal, so that indifference curves should be drawn with income–consumption curves that fan out in straight-line spokes from the origin.

I shall not go through again my previous lengthy evaluation of this Basic Convention.[1] It is enough to show that our assuming it will restore the orthodox presumption in one of our three cases, namely in the present case of artificial tariff barriers. Fig. 2 provides a graphical demonstration. Every American indifference curve is simply a radial blow-up of any other. The same is true of Europe. Assuming tastes to be the same, a fair assumption by our earlier arguments, we would still have no change in net terms of trade until we introduce trade impediments.

But tariffs cause the final equilibrium to shift—not from B to B' along the diagonal contract curve—but from b to b' along the DD' locus of final equilibria with proper spatial price relationships. Obviously, the tariff has made imports dear and shifted

[1] See ECONOMIC JOURNAL, 1952, pp. 295–8.

each country's physical consumption toward its own local goods. Europe's consumption is shifted south-eastward toward more clothing and less food; America's south-eastward toward more food and less clothing. We cannot tell whether a country spends a larger fraction of its income on imports or not. But that does not matter! We do know that in this case as a nation buys

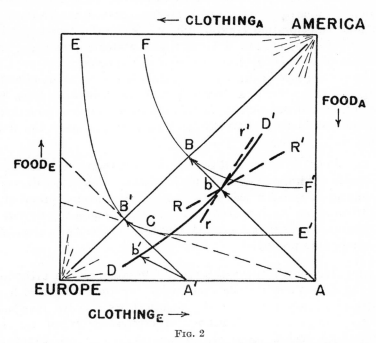

Fig. 2

Basic convention implies Engel's curves are spokes out from origin, so tariffs produce orthodox deterioration. None the less, as Europe moves from B' to C, dearer imports cause relative expenditure on imports to rise; with "elasticity of substitution" less than one for both countries, terms of trade change in anti-orthodox fashion in real impediment cases.

relatively more of its own good its income–consumption curve flattens out in an unambiguous manner. Hence, everywhere on the DD' locus, Europe's income–consumption slope is flatter than that of America: with $c_A/f_A < c_A/f_A$, we know that Europe's terms of trade must deteriorate in the orthodox fashion.[1]

[1] Mathematically $r(Y, \bar{F} - X) = g[Y/(\bar{F} - X)]$, with $g > 0$, $g' < 0$; also $R(\bar{C} - Y, X) = G[(\bar{C} - Y)/X]$, with $G > 0$, $G' < 0$. The criterion $c_A/f_A - c_E/f_E$ turns out to be $(\bar{F} - X)/Y - X/(\bar{C} - Y)$; because DD' lies eastward of the diagonal, this is seen to be algebraically negative.

X. Inconclusive Results in Case of Real Impediments

If we are willing to postulate the Basic Convention of unitary income elasticities (*i.e.*, equal average and marginal propensities to consume), can we also re-establish the orthodox presumptions in the case of real transport costs ?   The answer is, Not necessarily. Our graphical analysis applied only to the tariff and zero-impediments.   It fails to handle the real transport cost case, because then the final consumption equilibrium points for the two countries do *not* coincide, instead differing by a vector representing the amounts of the goods actually used up in transport.

As yet we have deduced no rigorous criterion to handle the real cost case.   Such a criterion will be developed later by straightforward but tedious mathematical argument.   For those uninterested in such derivations, I may briefly state the final result :

> When there are real transport costs, the payer's terms of trade will improve, remain unchanged or deteriorate, depending upon whether the payer's marginal (income) propensity to consume its own product is less than, equal to or greater than the receiver's marginal (income) propensity to consume that same product.[1]

Now even with the assumption favorable to the orthodox view, namely Viner's Basic Convention, we *cannot* be sure how cheapening one's export good will affect its relative marginal (income) propensity to consume.   Its physical output can be expected to decline relatively, but as argued in pp. 292–4 of Part I, no iron-clad presumptions are possible concerning *marginal propensities*.

Actually, our Basic Convention postulates unitary income elasticities, and therefore we can completely identify the marginal propensity to consume with the average propensity to consume. Casual econometricians, a class to which I belong, feel more confident in speculating about the latter than about the former. None the less, as the example of Fig. 2 shows, relative expenditure on clothing may decline for Europe as it becomes cheaper. Europe's indifference curve EE' has been drawn with the usual

---

[1] In symbols $C_A \gtreqless C_E$ is our valid criterion for this case—or what is almost the same thing, $F_E \gtreqless F_A$, or $C_A/F_A \gtreqless C_E/F_E$.   Note that the geometrical slopes of income–consumption curves are no longer relevant : such expressions as c_A/f_A and c_E/f_H must first be multiplied by $(P_c/P_f)_A$ and $(P_c/P_f)_E$ before they can be compared, and these last now differ by the factor $a_x a_y < 1$.

shape and curvature : however, by measuring the relative
lengths of the stretches on the budget line from each consumption
point to the two axes, the reader may verify that for a considerable stretch eastward of the diagonal, the relative clothing price
drops faster than its consumption expands. The crucial determinant of how relative expenditure changes can be shown to be
the so-called " elasticity of substitution," whose magnitude
permits of no uniform predictions.[1]

Unlike the case of tariffs, the case of real transport costs
cannot therefore be definitely brought into the orthodox camp,
even by means of the Basic Convention. As far as a pedantical
economist can go seems to be the following :

> Even with unitary income elasticities, real transport
> costs may cause average and marginal propensities to con-
> sume to decrease as a good becomes cheap, thereby reversing
> the orthodox effect on terms of trade.[2] Perhaps as transport
> costs become very great, thereby raising the costs of imports
> a great deal, there may be a presumption of ultimate ex-
> tinction of consumption of the imported good permitting
> us to infer an ultimate move of marginal and average pro-
> pensities to consume in the direction needed for the orthodox
> result.[3]

XI. FUNDAMENTAL CRITERIA FOR ALL CASES

In this section I present mathematical derivations of terms-
of-trade criteria for all three cases : (i) zero impediments to
trade, (ii) real cost impediments, and (iii) artificial impediments
of tariffs or quotas.

[1] Geometrically, the " elasticity of substitution " of Robinson–Hicks–Pigou
may along an indifference curve be greater than, equal to or less than unity in
magnitude. Nothing prevents Nature from presenting us with indifference
curves that for stretches, and even everywhere, have elasticities of substitution
less than unity. See R. G. D. Allen, *Mathematical Analysis for Economists*,
for discussion of the elasticity of substitution concepts and further references.

[2] Extreme transport costs and tariffs will almost certainly ultimately choke off
imports by raising their prices beyond the point at which competing domestic
supplies can fulfil the total domestic demand : when the markets have become
split up and separated, the transfer will have to take place completely in terms
of whichever good is specified in the payment contract. The result will be to
shift the clothing–food terms of trade in opposite directions in the two countries,
raising its price where one of the goods has become relatively scarce and lowering
it where the good has become abundant. The orthodox view is not particularly
realised in this extreme case of unconnected markets : indeed, with no sale of
exports, the concept of a country's net terms of trade becomes vacuous.

[3] This presumption exists if the indifference curves are postulated to intersect
the axes; if they become horizontal at interior saturation levels, the opposite
presumption exists.

Equations (4) define equilibrium in case (ii). Note that for $a_x = 1 = a_y$, (4) will also cover case (i). By differentiating the relation (4) with respect to the unilateral payment, K, we easily get three linear relations in the derivatives $d(P_c/P_f)_I/dK$, dX/dK, and dY/dK. Solving these, by determinants or otherwise, we can find the criterion that governs the algebraic sign of the derivative of the price ratio with respect to the indemnity.

We differentiate (4) totally with respect to K to yield equations that are linear in the three derivatives dY/dK, dX/dK, and most important for the present purpose, $d(P_c/P_f)_I/dK$:

$$
(8) \quad
\begin{aligned}
a_y(a_y r_1) \frac{dY}{dK} - a_y r_2 \frac{dX}{dK} - 1 \frac{d(P_c/P_f)_I}{dK} &= 0 \\
-\frac{1}{a_x} R_1 \frac{dY}{dK} + \frac{1}{a_x} (a_x R_2) \frac{dX}{dK} - 1 \frac{d(P_c/P_f)_I}{dK} &= 0 \\
+1 \frac{dY}{dK} - \frac{1}{(P_c/P_f)_I} \frac{dX}{dK} - \frac{Y-K}{(P_c/P_f)_I} \frac{d(P_c/P_f)_I}{dX} &= +1
\end{aligned}
$$

where numerical subscripts on the r and R functions indicate partial derivatives with respect to the indicated argument, so that $r_1 = \partial r(c, f)/\partial c$, etc.

By means of determinants, or otherwise, we can solve these linear equations to determine what the change in the terms of trade depends on, namely

$$
(9) \quad \frac{d(P_c/P_f)_I}{dK} = \frac{\begin{vmatrix} a_y(a_y r_1) & -a_y r_2 \\ -R_1/a_x & \frac{1}{a_x}(a_x R_2) \end{vmatrix}}{\Delta} = \frac{\left(-\dfrac{r_2}{r_1}\right) - a_x a_y \left(-\dfrac{R_2}{R_1}\right)}{a_x(-r_1)(-R_1)a_y^{-1}\Delta}
$$

where Δ is the determinant of all the left-hand coefficients of the linear equations (8), which can be shown to be positive as a condition for " stability " of our system. If neither good is an inferior good, every factor in the denominator of the last expression in (9) can be verified to be positive, and hence the numerator alone provides a rigorous criterion for the shift in the terms of trade. Since it is easy to show that the terms in parentheses in the numerator are the slopes of the income–consumption curves of the respective countries, namely c_A/f_A and c_E/f_E, we can rewrite our criterion in the form

$$
\frac{d(P_c/P_f)_I}{dK} \gtreqless 0, \text{ if } \frac{c_A}{f_A} \gtreqless a_x a_y \frac{c_E}{f_E}
$$

or

$$
\left(\frac{P_c}{P_f}\right)_A \frac{c_A}{f_A} = \frac{C_A}{F_A} \gtreqless \frac{C_E}{F_E} = \left(\frac{P_c}{P_f}\right)_E \frac{c_E}{f_E} = \left(\frac{P_c}{P_f}\right)_A a_x a_y \frac{c_E}{f_E}
$$

Of course, if $a_x = 1 = a_y$ because there are zero impediments, then the physical marginal propensities, written in lower-case letters, will be proportional to the dimensionless marginal-income propensities, written in capital letters; and then either may be used as a criterion.

All our criteria are summed up in Table IV. To handle the tariff case rigorously, the reader can supply for himself the differentiation of equations (7) with respect to K to get the linear equations in the derivatives. Because (7) differs from (4) only in the fact that the factor a_y no longer appears within r and a_x no longer within R, the new linear equations will differ from (8) only by the replacement of $(a_y r_1)$ and $(a_x R_2)$ by r_1 and R_2. Hence, for the artificial barrier case, our criterion becomes

$$\frac{d(P_c/P_f)_I}{dK} \gtreqless 0 \text{ if } \frac{c_A}{f_A} \gtreqless \frac{c_E}{f_E} \text{ or } a_x a_y \frac{C_A}{F_A} \gtreqless \frac{C_E}{F_E}$$

Table IV also relates Pigou's form of the criterion, based on independent utilities, to the different types of transport costs. Equation (4)′ of an earlier footnote showed how the Pigou analysis is modified by the appearance *inside* and *outside* of the r and R functions of the factors a_y and a_x. The reader can easily verify how the tariff-case version of these coefficients outside the functions leads to Table IV's version of the Pigou criterion.

It will be noted that whether impediments are real or artificial, the Pigou criteria are modified so as to lead in the direction opposite to the orthodox presumption : *i.e.*, the a_x and a_y terms always appear as depressants on the right-hand side of the criteria. Clearly Professor Pigou intends the assumption of linearity of marginal utility to be only a local approximation. If we permit his coefficients ϕ', f', ψ' and F' to be variables rather than constants, we can muster up some comfort for the orthodox view : Providing the rate of change of the rate of change of marginal utility (*i.e.*, the *third* derivative of the utility function) is assumed to be sufficiently negative for all goods, then the depressing effects of the a_x and a_y coefficients may be more than offset by the change in the ϕ', f', ψ' and F' coefficients, and the orthodox effect can result. Since rightly or wrongly, economists usually draw marginal utility curves that are concave from above, the orthodox case is not necessarily refuted by the assumption of independent utilities.[1]

[1] All this can be understood best in terms of a plotting of the indifference curves and their income–consumption curves. If each good becomes free at a finite level of consumption, the independent utility assumption does near the

TABLE IV

Summary of Criteria for Paying Country's Terms-of-trade Change

	Zero trade impediments.	Real transport costs $(a_x < 1, a_y < 1)$.	Tariff and artificial barriers $(a_x < 1, a_y < 1)$.
Marginal income propensities to consume (dimensionless)	$C_A \gtrless C_E$ or $\dfrac{C_A}{F_A} \gtrless \dfrac{C_E}{F_E}$	$C_A \gtrless C_E$ or $\dfrac{C_A}{F_A} \gtrless \dfrac{C_E}{F_E}$	$a_x a_y \dfrac{C_A}{F_A} \gtrless \dfrac{C_E}{F_E}$
Physical marginal propensities or relative slopes of income–consumption curves	$\dfrac{c_A}{f_A} \gtrless \dfrac{c_E}{f_E}$	$\dfrac{c_A}{f_A} \gtrless a_x a_y \dfrac{c_E}{f_E}$	$\dfrac{c_A}{f_A} \gtrless \dfrac{c_E}{f_E}$
Pigou criterion	$\left\lvert\dfrac{\psi'}{F'}\right\rvert \gtrless \left\lvert\dfrac{\phi'}{f'}\right\rvert$	$\left\lvert\dfrac{\psi'}{F'}\right\rvert \gtrless (a_x a_y)^2 \left\lvert\dfrac{\phi'}{f'}\right\rvert$	$\left\lvert\dfrac{\psi'}{F'}\right\rvert \gtrless a_x a_y \left\lvert\dfrac{\phi'}{f'}\right\rvert$
Strict linear marginal utilities, identical tastes	No change in terms of trade	Anti - orthodox change in favor of payer	Anti - orthodox change in favor of payer
Basic convention of unitary income elasticities, $(MPC = APC)$, identical tastes	No change in terms of trade	Either change depending on whether elasticity of substitution along an indifference curve is numerically greater than one (orthodox) or less than one (anti-orthodox)	Orthodox change against payer
Export and import good with outputs variable	Same as above but with " less leverage."		
" Domestic " goods	Orthodox view favored, provided domestic goods are " more competitive on the production side " with export goods than with import goods.		

XII. VARIABILITY OF OUTPUT

Dropping the assumption of fixed production of the two goods in both countries will not affect qualitatively our above analysis and conclusions, for reasons that were discussed in Part I. Even if food can be substituted for clothing along a familiar production-possibility schedule, no change in production will take place unless our criterion dictates a change in relative prices.[1] The

---

saturation levels lead to income or Engel curves that fan *inward*, thereby negating the orthodox view (see Fig. 1). But in between the zones of saturation, we can easily find examples of independent utilities where the Engel's curves fan out in a more realistic fashion. Note that the independence assumption is incompatible with the Basic Convention of unitary income elasticities. If I were forced to accept one simple assumption, I should perhaps prefer the latter to the former.

[1] To prove this rigorously, see ECONOMIC JOURNAL, 1952, p. 300, n. 2. The factors a_y and a_x must be introduced into the systems shown there in an obvious

only difference is this : If the criterion does dictate a change in relative prices, the elasticity of response of outputs can be expected to moderate the quantitative degree of the resulting change in prices.

The late Frank D. Graham for thirty years insisted that " net elasticities " in international trade were greater than most writers thought. Indeed, in Graham's view, they are infinite or almost so because of his extreme constant-costs assumptions of the classical type.[1] I see no point at this date in re-arguing whether both blades of the Marshallian scissors do the cutting in such extreme cases. But on the substantive point of the effect on elasticities of assuming many countries or many sources of supply, I should put the matter this way : Introducing many alternative supply sources exactly like what one already has seems to increase the scale of all processes, and hence naturally leads to the same-sized disturbances having smaller price effects ; but it is not clear to me why as the world grows in scale, the size of the postulated disturbances should not grow commensurately. Note, too, that introducing new supply sources which produce at *different* constant-cost levels seems, in my view, to work *against* the Graham thesis of almost infinitely elasticity. Similarly, introducing many goods producible at constant costs will lessen the impact of one small micro-economic disturbance ; but

---

way, and then the equation must be differentiated to verify that our same criteria do apply. This involves about ten equations in as many unknowns ; by the following simple analysis, we can fortunately reduce the problem to a single derived equation in one unknown.

Let small letters stand for America, capitals for Europe, let p and $P = a_x a_y p$ be short for $(P_c/P_f)_A$ and $(P_c/P_f)_E$. For each country, output will be determined so as to yield, for each domestic price p or P, a maximum value of national product or income expressed in, say, food-numeraire units ; call these respectively $i(p)$ and $I(P)$, where $i'(p) > 0$, $I'(P) > 0$.

The quantity of clothing supplied in each country will be given by positively inclined functions $s(p)$ and $S(P)$, and the demands for clothing will be given by functions d and D ; these depend upon clothing price (in food-numeraire units) and upon each country's income (expressed in numeraire units) including algebraic transfer payments of $+pa_yK$ for America and $-PK$ for Europe.

The equilibrium is defined by equality of the net demand of America for clothing to the net supply of Europe's clothing that comes through to America after real transport costs : or, recalling $P = a_x a_y p$, we have the single equilibrium equation

$$\{d(p, i(p) + pa_yK) - s(p)\} - a_y\{S(P) - D(P, I(P) - PK)\} = 0 = E(P, K)$$

This defines either unknown price in terms of the transfer K. Differentiating, we get

$$\frac{dP}{dK} = a_x a_y \frac{dp}{dK} = \left(p\frac{\partial d}{\partial i} - P\frac{\partial D}{\partial I}\right)\Big/\Delta_1$$

where $\Delta_1 = -\partial E/\partial P > 0$ for a " stable " system, and where increases in the supply slopes S' and s' cause the denominator to grow.

[1] See *Theory of International Values* (Princeton, 1948).

it is not at all clear to me that the effect of, say, a post-war disturbance of macro-economic type will be quantitatively different in its impact on an economy that concentrates its consumption on a few goods producible at constant costs than on an economy that chooses to spend a very little on a great many such goods. Only if one brings in Chamberlinian phenomena of monopolistic competition do substantive effects arise, and then I suspect analysis of market imperfections due to product differentiation will show that this works against rather than for Graham's thesis of high elasticity.

XIII. Final Qualifications

The Pigou–Jevons two-good model in its slightly generalised form has been squeezed dry of its implications. Yet we are still a long way from the conditions of the real world, involving many goods and various types of market imperfections and trade impediments. With some diffidence, I venture a few tentative speculations as to what the effects of these complications are on the transfer problem.

Many goods with varying transport costs, $a_x, a_y, a_z \ldots$ can be first handled on the assumption of fixed outputs : Any criteria sufficient to hold all relative prices invariant under these conditions can apply to the case of varying outputs—since outputs will not in fact vary without relative prices varying. Expressing the indemnity or payment in terms of specified goods of one or both countries, we can ask the question : In addition to the " primary burden," what is the " secondary burden " on each country as measured by each country's price changes weighed by its *algebraic* imports.

Economic theory does not permit me to give an answer to this question. Even in the case where domestic goods are created in each economy by transport costs (which suggest that elasticity of substitution for the imported goods ultimately becomes elastic in the orthodox manner), it is not clear that the terms of trade, as defined in the previous paragraph or by comparing non-domestic import goods' prices with export prices, can be presumed to change in any one direction.[1]

Yet, as Part I indicated on p. 302, the Viner model of one or more domestic goods in each country which are perfect substitutes on the production side for export goods does provide us with one rigorous and impressive defense of the orthodox view. With

[1] See Part I's discussion, Economic Journal, 1952, pp. 302–3 of the inconclusive case of fixed production with domestic goods.

export and domestic goods always having the same relative costs and prices, we may lump their expenditure together *à la* Hicks; then the Basic Convention will permit us to assume that less is spent marginally and on the average on imput goods, so that our criterion leads to the orthodox presumption.

In a pure Ricardian constant-cost world, a country can usually be assumed to produce none of the goods it imports. Therefore, domestic goods must compete with export goods alone, as in the Viner case. Professor Haberler has asked me whether it would not be possible to find models in which domestic goods were substitutable on the production side for imported goods, thus leading to anti-orthodox criteria. A number of such models are easily constructed.

Thus, suppose the same factors produced bricks in America as produced clothing; suppose, too, that the production-possibility schedule between food and clothing shows strongly increasing relative marginal costs, with the result that in equilibrium some clothing is produced as well as imported. Then for America bricks and clothing may be treated as a composite Hicksian commodity of high expenditure relative to food. Similarly, in Europe there will be low relative expenditure on its export goods relative to remaining goods. Assuming identical average and marginal propensities, we can deduce $C_A > C_E$ and an anti-orthodox improvement in the payer's net terms of trade.

The real world may be somewhere in between : domestic goods or goods whose transport costs are so heavy as to discourage their import relative to their home production may turn out to be substitutable on the production side with both *imports* and *exports*, being infinitely substitutable with neither. It then becomes a case of nice quantitative weighting, beyond the powers of casual econometricians and indeed under present conditions often beyond the powers of the most intensive statistical measurement and inference, to provide us with any final answers. On the whole, I—and I think Haberler—would be inclined to regard the relations between export and domestic goods as outweighing those between import and domestic goods, in accordance with the Viner hypothesis and the orthodox conclusion.

It is well to know just how strong or weak the orthodox view on the effects of transfer are. Findings of the present research on pure barter models are summarised in Table IV.

PAUL A. SAMUELSON

Massachusetts Institute of Technology.

PART X

Welfare Economics

76

Commentary on Welfare Economics

I

I am concerned lest some of the homely truths expressed in the last part of Professor Stigler's recent sermon on welfare economics come under discredit because of loose statements in the earlier parts.[1] More specifically, his Section I does not in my opinion give an adequate summary of the so-called "new welfare economics"; the criticisms embodied in Section II, which are not jejune or obscure, do not seem well taken; and the alternative suggested in Section III is in no sense an alternative.

These points may be developed in reverse order. Speaking as but one of the authors cited,[2] I must emphatically state that the "new welfare economics" is not intended as a *substitute* for the "old,"[3] all pretensions notwithstanding. It is an attempt to derive *necessary* conditions whose validity is independent of value judgments as between individuals, or more accurately, whose validity depends only upon less restrictive, and less well-defined value judgments than had previously been assumed. It involves the implications of the relatively mild assumptions that (1) "more" goods are "better" than "less" goods; (2) individual tastes are to "count" in the sense that it is "better" if all individuals are "better" off.

I am not concerned to discuss here whether the propositions which emerge are or are not "interesting and important." Suffice it to say, (1) that progress is made in economic thought when old confusions are clarified (unfortunately for the subject at hand, the reverse is also the case); (2) that anyone, like Professor Stigler and myself, who wishes to enter into the third realm in which assumptions concerning interindividual comparisons are entertained will find that the earlier work has somewhat simplified his task, rather than served as a hindrance or distraction.[4]

[1] G. J. Stigler, "The New Welfare Economics," *Am. Econ. Rev.*, Vol. XXXIII, No. 2 (June, 1943), pp. 355-59.

[2] The single most important paper in this field was not included in the list of representative writers. I refer to the classic memoir on this subject by Abram Bergson, which appeared in the *Quarterly Journal of Economics,* under the title "A Brief Formulation of Certain Aspects of Welfare Economics," February, 1938. Subsequent writers have not improved upon this statement, and many have fallen short of it. Mention should also be made of the recent contributions of T. Scitovsky, "A Note on Welfare Propositions in Economics," *Rev. of Econ. Stud.,* Vol. IX, No. 1, pp. 77-88.

[3] As Bergson has shown, the more recent developments proceed in an evolutionary fashion out of the contributions of Pareto and Barone, and represent no break in thought.

[4] It would not be possible or fair to appraise Professor Stigler's own welfare program and philosophy from so brief an account. One could wish that he had elaborated on the General Electric example, bringing the same analysis to bear upon the problem of grade-labeling, upon whether or not Canadian gold mines should be enabled to run in time of war, and a host of other social dilemmas much in need of the light which the magic word of consensus can yield.

Thus, it is only through a misapprehension that the Stigler message could be conceived as an alternative to the welfare economics under discussion; nor can the grave charge be sustained that anything in the latter subject is at odds with the precepts of elementary sociology textbooks. However, frankness necessitates the regrettable admission that neither the old nor new welfare economics qualifies as sprightly conversation in the Dale Carnegie, the Oscar Wilde, or even the Oxford Movement sense.

II

The assertions that economic welfare is not the sole or "primary" social end, that a change in policy may alter indifference curves and tastes, etc., are not so novel or so relevant to a criticism of the new part of the "new welfare economics" as to require any notice here. Stigler's relevant objections are confined to a caliginous illustration designed to show that the new welfare economics leads to the absurd conclusion that society should cease wasting resources on the prosecution and prevention of theft. However, his salvo is misdirected since this conclusion, whether absurd or sensible, cannot be deduced as a theorem from the new welfare economics. The latter does not tell us which of *any* two situations is better, and it does not tell us when society really has the choice between two given situations. For a *limited* set of pairs of situations, it does tell us which *would* be better *if* we had the choice between them. Most important of all, it does *not* tell us that a movement about which it can give a determinate answer as to its desirability is better than a movement about which it can give no such answer.

The choice between present institutions relating to theft and an anarchic policy is one which involves the third realm of value judgments; the choice between present institutions and an alternative situation in which thieves are bought off instead of driven off is also of this third variety, unless a new situation is defined in such a manner as not to be a legitimate alternative open to society (*e.g.*, society will pay only those thieves whose supply of services has not been elicited by the professed bribe).[5]

I suspect that Professor Stigler was attempting to express something like the remarks of the last paragraph. If so, he did not succeed very well, and part of the failure may be attributed to the wish to score a point against the new doctrines. On the whole, the best way to ascertain what a theory does not cover is to investigate what it does include. I turn therefore to a brief criticism of Stigler's summary of the doctrines in question.

III

As Professor Stigler has suggested, the recent writings have been rather formidable; his own attempt to state matters very simply suggests that the

---

[5] The new welfare economics does not imply that "exhaustive" expenditure of resources which only serves to redistribute income is a bad thing. It is all right for the Social Security Board to use up punch cards!

difficulties are intrinsic rather than expositional. Although difficult to apprehend for the first time, the subject, once mastered, is easy enough.

In his summary, the author fails to mention what is at the heart of the matter—that the conditions referring to marginal cost and price, and to individuals' rates of substitution are necessary but not sufficient to determine an equilibrium. Speaking technically, the number of equations is less than the number of unknowns, so that we are left with a manifold infinity of values, constituting what I have elsewhere called a "generalized contract locus."

This lack of emphasis explains the occurrence of what can only be a momentary lapse, which leads the author to state that "income (of all countries together) is maximized by free trade." Aside from the meaningless expression in the parentheses, the statement is wrong from almost any point of view, and most particularly from the standpoint of the new welfare economics. Having discussed this briefly in the article cited by Stigler and at length in the other article referred to above, I need not elaborate on this point. The importance of the matter far transcends the field of international trade, since the same problem is raised by those who discuss the senses in which perfect competition is optimal.[6] As far as I know, this was adequately analyzed for the first time by the "new welfare" economists, and I would welcome any earlier citations.

IV

A theory cannot have pretensions, although a theorist may. Much of Professor Stigler's argument is *ad hominem* rather than *ad rem*. Utilizing similar arguments, how can we account for Professor Stigler's depth of feeling which leads him to describe the new welfare economics, as "bizarre," as an "analytical trick," as "pretentious"? Is it possible that he was sold a bill of goods, perhaps by an English economist, and now that he has examined the purchase more carefully has found it not to be quite what he had expected? It is natural to shout "false Messiah" under the circumstances, and highly desirable to purge one's mind of previous misconceptions. However, it would seem more decorous for this catharsis to take place in private, rather than on the printed page.

On the other hand, the above analysis may be over subtle. Perhaps a sufficient explanation is to be found in simple *Weltschmerz*, induced by excessive brooding over the assault by the O.P.A. on the chastity of the economics profession.

PAUL A. SAMUELSON

Massachusetts Institute of Technology

[6] Consider for example, the following quotation from F. H. Knight, *Ethics of Competition*, p. 218, "whether the fundamental tendencies of free contractual relations under competitive control lead to the maximum production of value as measured in price terms."

77

EVALUATION OF REAL NATIONAL INCOME
By PAUL A. SAMUELSON

Introduction

1. Improved measurement of national income has been one of the outstanding features of recent progress in economics. But the theoretical interpretation of such aggregate data has been sadly neglected, so that we hardly know how to define real income even in simple cases where statistical data are perfect and where problems of capital formation and government expenditure do not arise.

In 1940 J. R. Hicks made an important advance over the earlier work of Professor Pigou. This has given rise to recent discussions between Kuznets, Hicks, and Little, but the last word on the subject will not be uttered for a long time. I have tried to treat the problem somewhat exhaustively in this paper, relating it to the modern theories of welfare economics of Pareto–Lerner–Bergson type. The result is not easy reading even to the author—but without such a careful survey I doubt that even the classical writings of Pigou can be adequately gauged.[1]

2. In Fig. 1, the point A represents observed consumption data for a single consumer in equilibrium at the indicated price-slope line through A. All the other points are each to be regarded as alternative to A and have nothing to do with each other. The following statements are immediate consequences of the modern theory of a single consumer's behaviour and are based on $\sum pq$ data such as the national income statistician might be able to measure:

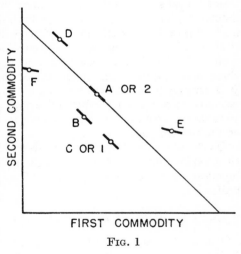

FIG. 1

    (*a*) We can immediately infer that B is on a lower indifference curve than A.

[1] The principal references are to J. R. Hicks, 'The Valuation of the Social Income', *Economica*, 1940, pp. 105–24; Simon Kuznets, 'On the Valuation of Social Income—Reflections on Professor Hicks' Article', *Economica*, Feb. 1948, pp. 1–16, and May 1948, pp. 116–31; J. R. Hicks, 'The Valuation of the Social Income—A Comment on Professor Kuznets' Reflections', *Economica*, Aug. 1948, pp. 163–72; I. M. D. Little, 'The Valuation of the Social Income', *Economica*, Feb. 1949, pp. 11–26; A. C. Pigou, *Economics of Welfare*, 4th ed. (1932), Part I, especially chaps. ii, iii, v, vi; P. A. Samuelson, *Foundations of Economic Analysis* (1948), chap. viii. Since writing this article I have benefited from reading two

  (*b*) Less directly, but with equal certainty, C reveals itself to be inferior to A.

  (*c*) The point D reveals itself to be superior to A.

  (*d*) The points E and A reveal nothing about their order in the consumer's taste-pattern.

  (*e*) The point F is inconsistent with A. The consumer has changed his tastes, or he is not in equilibrium at the indicated points.

Problems of Inference from Group Market Data

3. Let us now regard Fig. 1 as applying to market data for two or more individuals, so that each quantity, q, represents the total of two or more individuals' consumption, $q'+q''+,...,$ &c. The slope through A or any other point represents the market-price ratio of the first and second goods, the only commodities in our simplified world.

What can we now say about our points? Advances in the theory of welfare economics since 1940—many of them growing out of Hicks's own researches—suggest that certain of the definitions and propositions then laid down need to be modified. I resurrect these matters only because most people who have seen the recent discussion between Kuznets, Hicks, and Little must find their heads swimming, and must be in considerable doubt as to what the proper status of this vital matter is.

4. First we may clear up one misunderstanding, in itself unimportant, but giving an initial clue that we cannot make any very sweeping inferences from aggregate price-quantity data. In 1940 it was held that a situation like that of A and F is quite impossible on the assumption that individuals preserve the same well-defined tastes and are in true equilibrium in competitive markets.[1] It was held that, for national totals,

$$\sum p_2 q_2 > \sum p_2 q_1 \quad \text{implies} \quad \sum p_1 q_1 < \sum p_1 q_2.$$

As stated earlier, for a single individual this would be a correct assertion; but it is definitely false for group data involving two or more individuals. Examples to show this can be given *ad lib*. No recourse need be made to the Kuznets case of necessaries and luxuries (understanding by the latter, goods which some individuals do not choose to buy at all)—but, of course, there is no reason why such examples should not also be used. Perhaps the very simplest example to illustrate the possibility of a contradiction would be one in which we keep the exact national totals of the point A, but reallocate goods between the individuals so that they come into final equilibrium with a new and different price ratio. Then already we are on

further papers by Little and from corresponding with him. See I. M. D. Little, 'The Foundations of Welfare Economics', *O.E.P.*, June 1949, and an addendum to his *Economica* article 'A Note on the Significance of Index Numbers'.

[1] See *Economica*, May 1940, pp. 112–13.

the borderline of a contradiction, and by making a slight change in the totals we can obviously get a strong outright contradiction.

Already we are warned that $\sum p_2 q_2 > \sum p_2 q_1$ cannot imply that the second situation represents an 'increase in social real income' over that of the first—since this implication would leave us with the real possibility that each situation is better than the other!

This should also warn us against thinking that we can save such a definition by applying it only where there is no such outright contradiction. For suppose that we consider a case which just escapes *revealing* itself to be contradictory; being so close to a nonsense situation, such a case can in no wise escape being subject to the same *fundamental* (as yet undiagnosed) difficulty, even though it may not be advertising the fact to us.

Inadmissibility of the 1940 Definition of Increased Real Income

5. This tells us already that either there is something inadequate about the 1940 definition of an 'increase in society's real income' or else there is something faulty about the logical proof that the index-number criterion $\sum p_2 q_2 > \sum p_2 q_1$ implies such a defined increase in real income.

The 1940 passage in question is so compact that one must be careful in interpreting it. In my judgement the root of the trouble lies more in the inadequacy of the definition enunciated than in the logic of the demonstration that the stated index-number criterion does imply an increase in defined real income. Although it has already been extensively requoted, the relevant 1940 passage is so brief that it can be given completely here.

'. . . What does it signify if $\sum p_2 q_2 > \sum p_2 q_1$?

'It should first of all be noticed that since this condition refers only to the total quantities acquired, it can tell us nothing about the distribution of wealth among the members of the group. There may be a drastic redistribution of wealth among the members and the aggregates will remain exactly the same. Thus what the condition $\sum p_2 q_2 > \sum p_2 q_1$ tells us is that there is *some* distribution of the q_1's which would make every member of the group less well off than he actually is in the II situation. For if the corresponding inequality were to hold for every individual separately, it would hold for the group as a whole.

'As compared with this particular distribution, every other distribution of the q_1's would make some people better off and some worse off. Consequently, if there is one distribution of the q_1's in which every member of the group is worse off than he actually is in the II situation, there can be no distribution in which everyone is better off, or even as well off. Thus if we start from any actual distribution of wealth in the I situation, what the condition $\sum p_2 q_2 > \sum p_2 q_1$ tells us is that it is impossible to reach, by redistribution, a position in which everyone is as well off as he is in the II situation.

'This would seem to be quite acceptable as a definition of increase in real social income. Let us say that the real income of society is higher in Situation II than in Situation I, if it is impossible to make everyone as well off as he is in Situation II by any redistribution of the actual quantities acquired in Situation I. If this definition is accepted, our criteria can be applied to it without change.'[1]

[1] J. R. Hicks, 'The Valuation of the Social Income', *Economica*, May 1940, p. 111.

6. A diagram that we shall place major reliance on in the later discussion can be used to illustrate exactly what is involved in this definition of an 'increase in social real income'. On the axes in Fig. 2 there is laid out the ordinal utility of each of two individuals: the exact scale of U'' or U' is of no consequence, only the north–south and east–west orderings being important. Corresponding to the point A or 2 in Fig. 1, there will actually be some allocation of the total of goods between our individuals, and hence some determined level of well-being for each. Let the point labelled 2 in Fig. 2 represent that actual level of ordinal well-being. Now consider the other situation that was labelled C or 1 in our earlier figure. Behind the

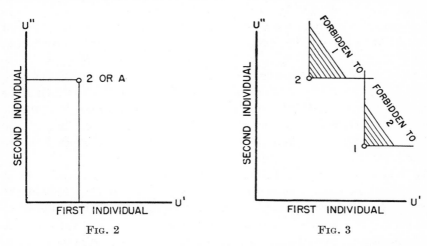

FIG. 2   FIG. 3

scenes, unknown to us from the totals, there is again an actual allocation of the goods to the individuals and again a new point in Fig. 2. If we knew where it was, we could write it in and label it 1. We do not know where this new point will fall: it may be south-west of point 2 so that all individuals are worse off, or south-east so that one individual is better off and the other worse off, and so forth.

Hicks's 1940 definition of an increase in real income from the point 1 to 2 consists of this: if we can be sure that neither point 1 nor any reallocation of its quantities among individuals lies north-east of point 2 (with both individuals better off in 1 than in 2), then point 2 is defined to represent an increase in real income over point 1.

How acceptable is this definition, leaving aside for the moment the question of whether the index-number criteria does permit us to place such a restriction on the admissible position of point 1 ? Upon reflection, we will all agree, I think, that such a definition is not very satisfactory. By means of it a point 1 may be both better and worse than another point 2. This is shown in Fig. 3. Also the definition has small claims on our affections in terms of our common-sense intuitions. Its last disadvantage is a subtle but important one: correctly stated, the new welfare economics is a body of doctrines which attempts to go as far as possible in preparing the way for the final a-scientific step involving ethical judgements; it should never, therefore, prejudice the final step, but only make statements which are uniformly valid for a wide class of ethical systems. Suppose now that we have given to us in Fig. 2 a set of social indifference curves (the contours of a Bergson social welfare function). It is more than possible that a 'point' or 'situation' (they are not quite the same thing) judged by the 1940 criterion to be the superior one may actually be the 'inferior' one in terms of the wider ethical judgements.

7. Instinctively Hicks was reaching out, I believe, for a rather different definition than the one he actually enunciated. The simpler problem of comparing A and B in Fig. 1 will bring this out and at the same time require no intricate index-number reasoning. As before, corresponding to the point A in Fig. 1 there is in Fig. 2 a point 2 representing the ordinal well-being of all individuals. Now with less of *all* goods available to society as shown by B, there will be a new point of individuals' well-being in Fig. 2. Where will the new point lie with respect to the former point 2 ?

We would have to give the unsatisfactory answer 'anywhere' were it not for one important assumption. We have assumed that behind the scenes of A all individuals are in competitive equilibrium facing the same price ratio. This assures us that all marginal rates of substitution are equal and that there exists no reallocation of the goods of A between them which will permit them both to be better off. (In technical parlance the competitive solution lies somewhere on the *Edgeworth contract locus*.) *A fortiori*, for a point like B, which involves smaller totals for *every* commodity, there is *no* reallocation of goods that could possibly make all individuals better off than they were in A. Without introducing price or index numbers, we know therefore that the point B is forbidden to be northeast of the point A—and we know that B corresponds to a decrease in real income over A according to the old 1940 definition.

But that is not really saying much. It is possible that one individual may be worse off even though the other individual is better off. And we must still entertain the darkest suspicions of a possible contradiction. But this simple case turns out to have at least one surprising feature: if we try to reallocate goods in either of the two situations—always letting the individuals come ultimately into competitive equilibrium—it turns out that we shall *never* find a case where on the 1940 definition the situation B turns out to be 'better' (as well as 'worse') than A. I have not yet proved this in my discussion; but, accepting this fact as true, we find

ourselves on the trail of a better way of defining an increase in real income
—or more accurately, an increase in *potential* real income.

The Crucially Important 'Utility-Possibility Function'

8. Let us consider all possible reallocations between individuals of the
consumption totals corresponding to A or 2. For each way of allocating
the goods there will be a given level of well-being for each and every
individual—as can be indicated by a point on the $U'-U''$ diagram. The
totality of all such possible points obviously cannot go indefinitely far in
the north-east direction; equally obviously there is a frontier curve or
envelope giving, for each amount of one person's utility, the maximum
possible amount of the other person's utility. This frontier is the important
'utility-possibility function' corresponding to A.

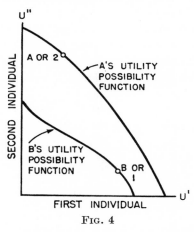

FIG. 4

The point 2 happens to lie on the frontier because at 2 all individuals
are known to be in competitive equilibrium. Corresponding to the smaller
totals of point B, there is also a utility-possibility function. We can now
state the sense in which A or 2 is *potentially* better than B.

The total of all goods being greater in A than in B, the utility-possibility
function of A is uniformly outside and beyond the utility-possibility function of B. (This is shown in Fig. 4.) The reason for this statement is
intuitively obvious and can be expressed in the language of a currently
popular song: A can do everything B can do—(and) better.

9. This, then, is the sense in which we can, without introducing detailed
ethical assumptions, define an 'increase in society's potential real income
in going from point B to point A'. Such an increase means a uniform outward shift in society's utility-possibility function.

Let us now return to the index-number problem. Can we infer that A
is superior to C in terms of our new definition of potential real income?

If we can, then with minor modifications the 1940 analysis can be accepted. But, unfortunately for economic theory, we cannot make any such inference about potential superiority from the index-number analysis of aggregate price-quantity data.[1]

Any single counter-example will prove the falsity of the index-number criteria as applied to more than one individual. Perhaps the simplest such example would be one in which the first individual cares only for so-called necessaries. If less of total necessaries are available in A, then A's utility-possibility curve must cut inside of B's when we get in the region of the U''–U' quadrant favouring the necessary-loving individual; and hence A cannot represent an unequivocal increase in potential real income. Simple as this example is, it is open to the objection that it seems to involve the case where the individuals consume nothing of some commodity. Actually this is an irrelevant feature of the example.

But, in any case, greater insight into the nature of the problem can be had if we examine the steps in the reasoning linking up the index-number criterion and the 1940 definition of an increase in real income.

10. If we have between the points A and C, or 2 and 1,

$$\sum p_2(q_2'+q_2''+\ldots) > \sum p_2(q_1'+q_1''+\ldots),$$

then according to the 1940 argument we can find some redistribution of the quantities in C or 1, so that the new quantities of every good going to each individual, which we may call

$$q_3'+q_3''+\ldots = q_1'+q_1''+\ldots,$$

are such as to make the crucial index-number criteria hold for each and every individual; namely,

$$\sum p_2 q_2' > \sum p_2 q_3', \qquad \sum p_2 q_2'' > \sum p_2 q_3'', \ldots.$$

Hence there exists a new situation resulting from the reallocation of the q_1's which is worse for *every* individual than is situation 2.

A missing step in the 1940 logic must be filled in at this point. The fact that we can reallocate the q_1's to get a new point q_3 which makes both individuals worse off than they are in 2 is taken to mean that the utility-possibility curve of 1 must be south-west of the point 2. But nothing has been said to show that q_3 is a frontier point on the utility-possibility function of point 1. Fortunately, it can be easily proved that there does exist at least one (and actually an infinite number) reallocation of the q_1's that

[1] Simple logic tells us that this negative answer must be forthcoming in a comparison of A and F since each of two curves cannot both lie uniformly outside of each other; and already we have seen reason to believe that the A and F comparison does not differ materially from that of A and C.

(*a*) lies on the utility-possibility function of 1, and (*b*) causes our index-number criteria to hold for each and every individual.[1]

With the above provision, we may accept the 1940 demonstration that when aggregate data satisfy the index-number criterion, the 1940 definition of superiority is definitely realized.[2] But there is nothing in this demonstration that tells us whether the utility-possibility function of 2 lies above (or below) the point 1 ;[3] all we know is that 1's utility-possibility function lies somewhere south-west of the point 2.

---

[1] Fig. 5 shows all this. An Edgeworth–Bowley box has been drawn up with the dimensions of the quantities in the q_1 situation. From the south-west corner of the box we measure off the consumption of the first individual, U'. From the north-east corner we measure downward and to the left the consumption of the U'' individual. Any point in the box represents a possible allocation of the total q_1 quantities, with the point marked q_1 being the one actually observed.

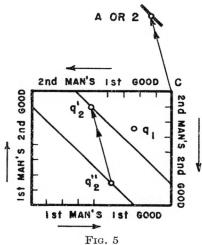

Fɪɢ. 5

On this same diagram we may also show the actual quantities consumed by the individuals in the q_2 situation. But now it takes two points in the box, as far apart from each other as C is from A. They are marked q_2' and q_2'' respectively, and the price-lines through their points are drawn in with the slope of the p_2 situation.

As the picture stands q_1 does not satisfy the index-number criteria for the U' individual since q_1 does *not* lie inside the crucial triangle of the point q_2'. Hicks's statement is that there is some reallocation which will move the point q_1 to a new point q_3 which lies between the two parallel lines. For any such point our index-number criteria are satisfied for both individuals. The missing step is to show that there exist points in this strip which are also on the Edgeworth contract curve. Since the contract curve must go from one corner of the box to the other and pass through all levels of U' and U'', it must obviously somewhere pass through the intervening strip between the parallel lines. This supplies the missing step. Readers of Kuznets should note that it is the totals of q_1, not of q_2, that are reallocated so as to lead to Hicks's conclusion.

[2] This is apparently what Little means when he concludes that the 1940 definition is 'immune from Professor Kuznets conditions' (loc. cit., p. 13).

[3] In any case, no one should think that the condition

$$\Sigma\, p_1\, q_2 > \Sigma\, p_1\, q_1$$

which is satisfied in C (but not in F) helps to rule out a contradiction.

11. Our final conclusions may be summarized briefly. The index-number criterion

$$\sum p_2(q'_2+q''_2+\ldots) > \sum p_2(q'_1+q''_1+\ldots)$$

tells us that the utility-possibility function of 2 does lie outside of that of 1 *in the neighbourhood* of the actual observed point 2—but that is all it tells us. The curve may intersect and cross elsewhere—as shown in the later Fig. 6.

The Hicks–Kaldor–Scitovsky Version of New Welfare Economics

12. Having failed to relate the stronger definition of potential superiority to index-number criteria, we must reconsider whether, after all, the 1940 definition of superiority may not be tolerably acceptable. If we examine this definition, we find that it is in all essentials the same one as that earlier suggested by N. Kaldor and by Hicks in his earlier article on the 'Foundations of Welfare Economics'.[1] It will be recalled that these two writers had ruled that situation X is better than situation Y if there exists a reallocation of the goods in X which makes everybody better off than he was in Y. Except that the 1940 definition applied to a *decrease* in well-being between 2 and 1, this is identical with the earlier 1939 definition.

Dissatisfaction early developed over the 1939 definition. In particular T. Scitovsky[2] came forward with the objection that it seemed to assume that there was something right (ethically) about the distribution of income in the *status quo ante* of the Y situation. To get around this he suggested (in effect) that a *double* test be applied.

To say that 'X is better than Y' we must be sure that (a) there exists a reallocation of the X goods that could make everybody better off than he actually was in Y; and (b) we must make sure there exists a reallocation of the goods in Y that could make everybody worse off than he actually was in X.

Or, in our terminology, the Scitovsky definition of superiority requires the utility-possibility curve of one situation to be beyond that of the other in the neighbourhood of *both* actual observed points.

13. In his criticism of the 1940 definition Kuznets can be generously interpreted to be trying (presumably independently) in effect to reiterate the Scitovsky double criterion. Kuznets says at one point that we must

---

[1] N. Kaldor, 'Welfare Propositions in Economics', *Economic Journal*, xlix, 1939, pp. 549–52; J. R. Hicks, 'Foundations of Welfare Economics', *Economic Journal*, xlix, 1939, pp. 696–712.

[2] T. Scitovsky, 'A Note on Welfare Propositions in Economics', *Review of Economic Studies*, 1941, pp. 77–88, and 'A Reconsideration of the Theory of Tariffs', *Review of Economic Studies*, 1942, pp. 89–110. To be precise Hicks is in 1940 riding the Scitovsky and Kuznets the Kaldor horse.

supplement the Hicks condition [that there must be a reallocation of the q_1's that makes everyone worse off than he actually was in the q_2 situation] by the further condition that '[it must not be] impossible to make *everyone* as well off as he is in situation I by any redistribution of the actual quantities acquired in situation II' (*Economica*, 1948, p. 4).

Kaldor has explicitly accepted the Scitovsky correction, and as far as I know so has Hicks. Therefore they would both presumably have no quarrel with this Kuznets reversibility condition.[1] But both Kuznets and Hicks do not seem to realize that the difficulty is basic and has nothing to do with the question of substitutability of necessaries or luxuries. On the Scitovsky-amended definition, the whole demonstration of superiority of one position over another by aggregate index-number criteria breaks down completely.[2]

14. Our whole theory of arriving at a measure of real income by aggregative price-quantity data has broken down. But the worst is still to come. The Scitovsky conditions are themselves very definitely unsatisfactory. It is not enough to double the 1939 conditions—we must increase them infinitely. Instead of a two-point test we need an infinitely large number of tests—that is to say, we must be sure that one of the utility-possibility functions *everywhere* lies outside the other. Without this test at an infinite number of points, no acceptable definition of an increase in potential real income can be devised at the non-ethical level of the new welfare economics.

Just as Scitovsky has criticized Kaldor and 'compensationists' for assuming the correctness of the *status quo ante*, so we must criticize him for

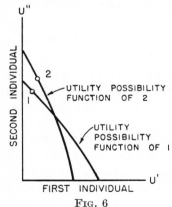

FIRST INDIVIDUAL

Fig. 6

assuming in some sense the correctness of the *status quo ante* and/or the *status quo post*.

Suppose, for example, we have *everybody actually* better off in situation 2 than in 1. Kaldor and Hicks will be satisfied to call 2 better than 1. So will Scitovsky. But the utility-possibility curves might very well cross as in Fig. 6, so that according to many ethical welfare functions both Scitovsky and the others would be rendering false statements.

What Scitovsky should have done was to free all of his comparisons from any depend-

[1] Little has argued (*Economica*, 1949, pp. 12–16) that there is a confusion in Kuznets on the point of reversibility. Perhaps I am setting down what Kuznets should have meant rather than what he meant to say.

[2] The best that we can say is the following. Imagine the change from point 2 to point 1 to be a continuous one. So long as the two points are sufficiently (!) close together, then the condition $\Sigma\, p_2\, q_2 > \Sigma\, p_2\, q_1$ assures us that 2 is better than 1 in the Scitovsky sense. For changes of any size $\Sigma\, p_2\, q_2 > \Sigma\, p_2\, q_1$ tells us that 1 *cannot* be superior to 2 in Scitovsky or in my sense, and that is all it tells.

ence upon either *actually observed* $U''-U'$ situation. He should, instead, have made the comparison depend upon the totality of all *possible* positions in each situation. This would have led to the definition of potential real income earlier proposed, which seems to be the only satisfactory, self-consistent definition within the sphere of the 'new' (relatively *wert-frei*) welfare economics. Aggregate index numbers can tell us little about this except in a negative way. Even this definition is not—by itself—worth very much of anything for policy purposes, as will be shown.

Inadequacies for Policy of the New Welfare Economics

15. We have seen that the new welfare economics is able to define an increase in potential real income which is unambiguous, consistent, and which will not turn out to contradict a wide class of ethical social welfare functions that must later be introduced into any problem. The new welfare economics does not go all the way in settling the problems of normative policy: taken by itself, and without supplementation, it goes virtually none of the way; but taken in conjunction with later ethical assumptions, it attempts to clear the way of all issues that can be disposed of in a noncontroversial (relatively) ethical-free fashion. This is the solid kernel of usefulness in the new approach begun by Pareto, and this should not be lost sight of in the welter of exaggerated claims for the new welfare economics.

The inadequacy for actual policy decisions—even in the most idealized, simplified world—of all of the discussed measures of 'real income' can be illustrated by numerous examples. Consider the very best case where we can establish the fact that situation 2 is *potentially* better than 1 (in the sense of having a uniformly farther-out utility-possibility function). Would a good fairy given the chance to throw a switch from 1 to 2 be able to justify doing so ? Upon reflection we must, I am afraid, answer *no*. Potentialities are not actualities—and unless she can give a justification of her act that will satisfy all reasonably defined social welfare functions, she cannot know whether or not to pull the switch.

A few negative remarks are possible: for any ethical system with the property that an increase in one individual's well-being is, others' being equal, a good thing[1]—for all such systems a final optimum position must necessarily be on 2 and not on 1. That we can certainly say. But without going into the realm of (modern, streamlined) 'old' welfare economics, we cannot say more or get conclusive advice on this problem of policy. The attempt to divide the problem into two parts so that one can say 'a change from 1 to 2 is *economically* desirable in the sense of objectively increasing

---

[1] i.e. for all social welfare propositions W, with the property $W = F(u', u'',...)$ and $\dfrac{\partial W}{\partial u'} > 0 < \dfrac{\partial W}{\partial u''}, \; ....$

production or wealth, whether or not the actual resulting situation will be ethically superior', only gets one into a semantic snarl and glosses over the intrinsic difficulties of the problem.

How much more severe are the policy limitations of some of the modern even weaker 'compensationist' definitions. Following them, the good fairy might do perpetual and irremediable harm. Suppose, for example, that our two *actually observed* points, 1 and 2, both lie above the intersection of the two schedules in Fig. 6, but with the point 1 being south-east of point 2, so as to represent an increase in well-being of one individual and a decrease for the other. The Kaldor condition would be satisfied and so would the Scitovsky condition. Suppose that once the angel has thrown the switch, she can never again reverse it (e.g. capital sunk into a mine may be irrecoverable). Let her now follow the counsel of the compensationists and throw the switch from 1 to 2. According to any ethical view that considers individual U' to be of the elect (or relatively so) and U'' to be relatively undeserving of consideration, the good life lies in a rather easterly direction. For ever and ever 'society' is condemned to 'unhappiness' because of the premature decision based on the Kaldor–Hicks–Scitovsky rules.[1]

Production Possibilities and Group Inferences

16. This completes the problem of making group inferences from simple index-number comparisons. At the non-philosophical level there are still two more grave difficulties to be faced. Up till now I have always spoken of the utility-possibility function of *point A*, not of situation A. But the totals of goods at A or 2 do not fall from heaven in fixed amounts. Obviously other total quantities might instead have been produced. Therefore, the true utility-possibility function corresponding to situation A is really wider and out farther than the one defined for point A. At best, if all markets are perfect and there are no external effects or government distortions, the utility-possibility function for point A may just touch that of situation A at the actual observed point, elsewhere being inside it. The wider schedule is the envelope of a family of schedules corresponding to each *possible* point of total consumption goods. (See Fig. 8.)

Obviously it is the wider possibility function of a 'situation' rather than of a 'point' with which we should be concerned, and before we go throwing

---

[1] If both individuals are better off in the observed 2 point than in the observed 1 point, how reasonable it seems to counsel that the switch be pulled. And if the only alternative were these two situations, almost all old welfare economists might agree. But this need not be our choice of alternatives at all. Realistically, the choice may be between these two points and a third ethically superior point that lies on 1's locus. As a matter of tactics and *realpolitik*, one will sometimes want to follow such simple criteria *and* actually give compensation, or perhaps fail to compensate. But tactics aside, these rules are in principle incomplete.

any switches or making policy decisions we must make sure how alternative production possibilities affect the problem. A few truths continue to remain self-evident, but, generally speaking, this new element makes the problem of definite inference even more difficult—an important but sad fact.

Let us consider an example. Up till now the one unshaken truth that remained was this: If more of every good is observed in point A than in point B, then A represents an increase in potential real national income over B. Even this is no longer necessarily valid! Suppose we draw up production-possibility curves showing how much of each good can be produced in total when the total of the other good is specified. Such a chart might look like Fig. 6 except that now the two outputs rather than utilities are on the axes. In Fig. 7 our observed point A lies north-east of the observed point B, and yet it is obvious that the production-possibility curves can still cross; and it is also obvious, upon reflection, that depend-

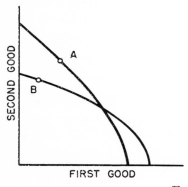 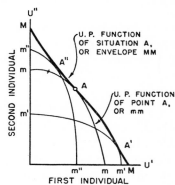

FIGS. 7 and 8

ing upon how much people like one good as compared to another, the *corresponding utility-possibility curve can most definitely cross*—making no unambiguous inference about an increase in potential real income possible.

17. So long as commodities are really economic rather than free goods, this much can be said: *If the production-possibility function of one situation lies uniformly outside that of a second situation, then the utility-possibility function of the one will also be outside that of the other.* In the limiting case where one or both individuals do not care at all for one of the goods, the schedules might just be touching at one or more points. Also it is to be understood that if the total of resources (land, labour, &c.) is not the same in the two situations, these resources are to be treated just like negative commodities, and it is in this sense that one production-possibility function must lie uniformly outside the other.

Hicks attempted in 1940 to explore the relationship between index-number criteria based on price-quantity data and productivity as measured by the position of the production-possibility function of society. His treatment was brief and much of it he had abandoned prior to Kuznets's 1948 criticisms. But even after the recent exchange of views I do not feel the subject is left in its proper state. To analyse the problem in its entirety would be too lengthy a task, but a number of observations are relevant to our discussion. In all that follows I shall assume that there are no excise taxes, so that the irrelevant distinction between income-at-factor-prices and income-at-market-prices can be disregarded.

Under this last assumption, would the same $\sum pq$ tests relevant to indicating a (1940-defined) increase in welfare also serve to indicate a shift in productivity? One is almost tempted to read such a belief into the following passage:

'If competition were perfect, and if state activities were so designed as not to disturb the *optimum* organization of production, marginal utilities and prices and marginal costs would all be proportional, so that the same valuation which would give us the social income as a measure of economic welfare would also give us the social income as a measure of productivity.'[1]

Kuznets objected to all this on the grounds that production-possibility curves, unlike indifference curves, can intersect and can be of variable curvature. His instinct that something is rotten in Denmark may be a sound one, but the precise trouble has not really been isolated, nor a worse difficulty brought to light.

In the first place, there is no need for an individual's indifference curves always to be concave: he need only be assumed to be in equilibrium at the observed points. In the second place, it is untrue that collectively defined indifference curves (*à la* Scitovsky or otherwise) are forbidden to intersect and cross. Our earlier discussion of the points A and F may be referred to in this connexion. Neither of these two reasons can serve to isolate the basic difficulties of making production inferences.[2]

---

[1] *Economica*, 1940, p. 122. Hicks goes on to say, parenthetically: 'It would not be very reliable as a measure of productivity, but it might usually satisfy the productivity tests for small displacements, over which the substitution curves might not differ very much from straight lines.' To make the only comparisons between different situations that are valid, this last linearity assumption can be shown to be unnecessary; but it foreshadows Hicks's later desire for an approximate representation of the production-possibility function in the neighbourhood of an observed optimal point. A straight line gives, under the assumed conditions, an upper (rather than a conservative, lower) bound as to what is producible.

[2] Kuznets has a third objection which has little or nothing to do with the problem here discussed. Working by analogy with the consumption problem, he makes the strange and unnecessary assumption that a perfect price system is in some sense maximizing 'producers' surpluses', and he raises the question whether specificity of some resources may not make it impossible for every producer to be as well off as previously. Both Hicks and I would consider producers and consumers to be the same units, who buy goods and also sell services; all such services can be treated as negative goods and all ordinal disutilities treated along with ordinal utilities. Firms (corporations) provide the place where producers work but themselves have no welfare feelings, although their owners' welfare is important. The problem at hand is what we can or cannot say about the production-possibility functions *of society* in two situations.

In the production or firm field we have an institutional difficulty absent from the household markets: few families act like monopsonists, but many, if not most, firms sell in markets which are less than perfectly competitive. Let us waive this difficulty for the moment and assume that technological and market conditions are most suitable to perfect competition: namely, constant-returns-to-scale prevails and there is 'free entry'. In this case, any observed point of total output—such as A or 2 in Fig. 1—would represent a *maximum* of $\sum p_2\, q$ subject to all the production possibilities of the situation. Geometrically the straight line running through A can never be inside the true production-possibility schedule.

Does this mean that the criterion $\sum p_2\, q_2 > \sum p_2 q_1$ in Fig. 1 assures us of *both* of the following: that 2 is better than 1 *in welfare*, and 2 is better *in a production-possibility sense* than 1 ? It must *not* be so interpreted. The production problem involves a certain *maximum* condition, the consumption case a related *minimum* condition. The same index-number calculation can never serve as a crucial indicator for the two problems: if it is a reliable criterion for welfare, it tells us nothing about production; if it has unambiguous production implications, then welfare inferences are impossible.

There are essentially only four possible cases that have to be considered: a comparison of A and C in Fig. 1, of A and D, of A and F, and the almost trivial case of A and B. In this last case, where the A situation has more of every good than the B, we know immediately that the production-possibility function of A lies outside that of B in the neighbourhood of both observed points, and we also know that A's utility-possibility function (defined narrowly for the points rather than broadly for the situations) lies everywhere outside of that of B. All this is obvious, so we can concentrate our attention on the three other possible comparisons. To keep the notation simple we can always give the point A the number 2 and give all other compared points the number 1. Our cases, then, are as follows:

	Concerning 1940 def. of welfare	*Concerning position of production-possibility function (p.p.f.)*
Case A (or 2) and C (or 1):		
$\sum p_2\, q_2 > \sum p_2\, q_1$ tells us	2 better than 1	nothing
$\sum p_1\, q_2 > \sum p_1\, q_1$ tells us	nothing	p.p.f. of 1 inside of p.p.f. of 2 near point 2
Case A (or 2) and D (or 1):		
$\sum p_2\, q_2 < \sum p_2\, q_1$ tells us	nothing	p.p.f. of 1 outside of p.p.f. of 2 near point 1
$\sum p_1\, q_2 > \sum p_1\, q_1$ tells us	nothing	p.p.f. of 2 outside of p.p.f. of 1 near point 2
Case A (or 2) and F (or 1):		
$\sum p_2\, q_2 > \sum p_2\, q_1$ tells us	2 better than 1	nothing
$\sum p_1\, q_1 > \sum p_1\, q_2$ tells us	1 better than 2	nothing

Under the present assumptions we can make inferences about the shifting of production-possibility functions that are no less strong than those about welfare. We can never hope to infer from index-number tests that one production-possibility curve has shifted *uniformly* with respect to another—but then we have earlier seen that we can never hope to make such welfare inferences either. It will be noted from the table that where light is thrown on productivity it is withheld from welfare, and vice versa. This might almost seem to offer comfort: we seem always to be able to say *something* about any situation. But, alas, this is an illusion.

The Impossibility of Unequivocal Inferences

18. Even that which we have in the field of welfare indicators is to be taken away from us now that we have enlarged our alternatives to all the production possibilities of each situation rather than to the single observed points. *We shall never be able to infer a genuine change in potential real income as I have earlier defined the term*—no, not even in the simplest comparison of A which shows more of every good than the point B. (This was already shown in Fig. 7.) Unsatisfactory as the 1940 definitions of welfare were, we are tempted to beat a hasty retreat back to them. But to no good purpose: even these fragile reeds are blown down by the new winds.

Specifically, the observation $\sum p_2 q_2 > \sum p_2 q_1$ no longer implies that the utility-possibility function of *situation* 1 lies inside that of A even in the neighbourhood of the point 2, or anywhere at all for that matter! The whole 1940 proof by Hicks—as supplemented in my earlier lengthy footnote concerning the box-diagram—breaks down completely. The demonstration fails, the argument no longer leads logically to the desired conclusion. By itself this does not show that there may not be found some different proof. However, the theorem can be proved to be false, so that no valid alternative proof exists.

A single example provides a decisive exception to the theorem (that we can infer a local shift in the utility-possibility function). The point F in Fig. 1 has a utility-possibility curve which may be almost anywhere with respect to that of A, as far as anything we know. There is no reason why it could not always lie outside of A's; there is also no reason why the point F should not lie on C's production-possibility curve; there is also no reason why the utility-possibility function of the general situation C should not be close to or identical with the utility-possibility function of the point F (except possibly at the observed point C itself). It follows that we can easily imagine the utility-possibility function of the situation C to lie *above and beyond* the observed point A—which contradicts the Hicks-like theorem that situation C's curve must lie somewhere south-west of the A point. This example shows that the Hicks's proof remains no longer valid when it ceases to be simply a question of reallocating a given fixed total in the 1 situation.

The Interrelation between Production and Utility-Possibility Functions

19. Production possibilities as such have no normative connotations. We are interested in them for the light they throw on utility possibilities. This is why economists have wanted to include such wasteful output as war goods in their calculations of national product; presumably they serve as some kind of an index of the useful things that might be produced in better times. Our last hope to make welfare statements lies in spelling out the welfare implications of any recognizable shifts in production possibilities.

A uniform outward shift in the production-possibility function—such as can never be revealed by index-number comparisons—must certainly shift the utility-possibility schedule outward. The converse is not true. An outward shift in the utility-possibility function may have occurred as the result of a *twist* of the production-possibility curve. This is because people's tastes for different goods may be such that the points on the new production schedule that lie inward may be points that would never be observed in any optimal competitive market. An 'observable' point is one which, as the result of some allocation of initial resources or so-called 'distribution of income', would lead to one of the points on the utility-possibility frontier.

In the typical case where $\sum p_1 q_1 < \sum p_1 q_2$, so that we know that the production-possibility function of 2 is outside of that of 1 somewhere near the observed point 2, we should like to be able to say that 2's utility-possibility function lies outside that of 1 in the neighbourhood of the observed point 2. But we cannot. The utility-possibility functions of situation 2 and of point 2 both lie outside the utility-possibility function of the points which are known to lie south-west of the observed point 2 on the production-possibilities diagram. But all such points might turn out to be non-observable ones. Only if an observable point 2 is known to give more of all goods than an *observable* point of the situation 1 can we even infer that situation 2 is superior to 1 in the weak 1940 sense. Index-number data are never enough to provide us with knowledge of two such observable points except in the trivial case (like A and B) where one point is better in respect to every good, and where index-number calculations are unnecessary to establish the only fact that can be established: namely, the production-possibility function of A must lie outside that of B near the observed points and the same must be true about the related utility-possibility function.

Under the best conditions of the purest of competition very little indeed of welfare significance can ever be revealed by price-quantity data alone. Needless to say, with the actual statistical problems in a world of imperfect competition and decreasing costs, observed prices have even less significance as indicators of the shape of society's true production-possibility curve.

Political Feasibility as a Crucial Condition in Welfare Economics

20. The last limitation on the applicability to policy of the new welfare economics concepts is in practice one of the most important of all. It hinges around the practical unattainability of the production-possibility and utility-possibility function earlier discussed. It is not simply that imperfections of competitions are so widespread as to keep society from reaching its optimal production frontier; or that government interferences inevitably cause distortions; or that external diseconomies and economies can never be recognized and computed. All these are true enough.[1]

The essential point now to be stressed is that we could move people to different points on the utility-possibility function only *by an ideally perfect and unattainable system of absolutely lump-sum taxes or subsidies*. In point of fact, suppose that, in the simplest case, competitive *laissez-faire* puts us at one point on the utility-possibility function. Then we can only seek to change the distribution of income by a system of *feasible* legislation: e.g. progressive income tax, rationing, &c. All such policies involve a distortion of marginal decisions, some involving great distortions but in every case some distortion. They move us then *inside* the utility-possibility curve. We can pick policies which strive to minimize the harmful effects of redistribution, but in practice we cannot reduce such effects to zero. A 'feasible utility function' can conceptually be drawn up which lies more or less far inside the utility-possibility function, depending upon how Utopian were our assumptions about legislation, public opinion, &c.

All this is shown in Fig. 9. The point L represents the imputation resulting from a situation of relatively *laissez-faire*. It is made to lie on the heavy-line utility-possibility function—which it would only do in a very perfect competitive world.

Let us suppose that the tastes and abilities of the two individuals are identical so that we can use similar indicators of their ordinal preferences. But let them differ in their ownership of resources (say land) so that the

---

[1] They can be thought of as forces keeping us from reaching the true possibility frontier; or if we are in a non-perfectionist mood and willing to compromise with evil, they may be thought of as defining a not-so-far-out but pragmatically obtainable frontier. If the latter interpretation is made, we must be careful to realize that the slopes of the defined frontiers need have little correspondence with market prices, marginal costs of production, &c. As I have earlier pointed out (*Foundations*, p. 221), the constraints under which society is conceived as working are arbitrary and must be given by non-economic assumptions. England's production possibilities would be different if the laws of physics could be disregarded or if we could assume that all workers would do their 'best', or . . . or.

income of U'' is much greater than that of U', as indicated by the position of L relative to the 45°-line of 'equal income'. In a Utopia there might be some way of redistributing wealth or income that would move us along the outside curve from L to the point of complete equality, E, or even beyond. But in practice the only feasible path that Congress or Parliament could follow would be along the light-line utility-feasibility curve.[1]

Space does not permit me to work out the far-reaching implications of this point of view. It is enough to point out here that situation A may have a uniformly better production-possibility function than B, and also a uniformly better utility-possibility function.

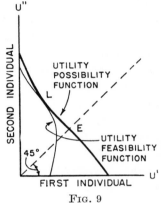

FIG. 9

But a change from B to A might so alter the distribution of market-imputed income away from the 'worthy' and towards the 'unworthy' as to make it an undesirable move from many ethical viewpoints. The *utility-feasibility function* of A may very well cross that of B, so that no statement about potentialities, much less about actualities, can be validly made.

By all means let us pray that feasibilities and possibilities be brought closer and closer. But let us not indulge in the illusion that our prayers have been answered and that we can issue new-welfare-economics prescriptions accordingly.[2]

Final Summary

21. This has been a long and closely reasoned essay. A brief summary may pull the threads together.

1. Certain $\sum pq$ calculations tell us when a single individual has improved himself.

2. The only consistent and ethics-free definition of an increase in potential

---

[1] A strong ethical equalitarian would have to reckon with this fact; and unless his social welfare functions had complete L-shaped corners along the 45° line, or even bent back *à la* Veblen and like the dog-in-the-manger, he would find his feasible optimum at some distance from equality of incomes. All this has a bearing, I believe, on the debate between Meade and Kahn as to whether rationing and food subsidies ought necessarily to be rejected by rational equalitarians in favour of greater reliance on income taxes or other more orthodox devices.

[2] A few comments on the cited Little article on 'Foundations' are perhaps in order. There is much I agree with in this paper, and much I do not yet understand. His semantic jousts with the post-Kaldor school falls under the first heading; his analysis of the meaning of a *social or economic welfare function* under the second. The part of his paper that is most relevant to the present technical discussion is his proposed 'foundations' for a 'system' of welfare economics. In my present understanding of it—still admittedly vague—Little has stated a few theorems of one type. These are understandable in terms of the language of a welfare function, and are more in the nature of one arch or wing of a structure than its foundations. The technical content of the theorems is discussed in the last footnote of the appended Pigou note.

real income of a group is that based upon a uniform shift of the utility-possibility function for the group. $\sum pq$ calculations based on aggregate data never permit us to make such inferences about uniform shifts.

3. The condition $\sum p_2 q_2 > \sum p_2 q_1$ does tell us that the utility-possibility function of the *point* 2 is outside the utility-possibility function of the *point* 1 somewhere near 2. It is not acceptable to define this as an increase in real income for a number of reasons, not the least being that we may end up with 2 defined to be both 'better' and 'worse' than 1.

4. Scitovsky and later Kuznets have suggested a partial strengthening of the earlier definitions of superiority so as to rule out certain revealed inconsistencies. But even these two-sided requirements are not stringent enough; when made infinite-sided, as they must be to avoid inconsistency or implicit ethics, they become equivalent to the definition based upon a uniform shift of the utility-possibility schedule. And even when this rigid definition is realized, we cannot properly prescribe complete policy prescriptions without bringing in ethics.

5. When we come to make inferences about two *situations*, each of which involves a whole *set* of production possibilities rather than about just the observed *points*, even the limited welfare inferences of point 3 break down completely. Under the most perfect conditions suitable for pure competition (where the production-possibility curve can never be concave) a few inferences concerning the local shifts of the production-possibility schedules are possible: e.g. $\sum p_2 q_2 < \sum p_2 q_1$ implies that 1's production-possibility function is outside 2's in the neighbourhood of the observed 2 point.

6. The inferred shifts of production-possibility functions are not enough to permit similar inferences about the utility-possibility functions. This is because that portion of a production-possibility curve which has clearly been revealed to be inside another or 'inferior' may (for all we know) consist entirely of 'unobservable points' that have no correspondence with the truly observable points along the related utility-possibility frontier.

7. The utility-possibility functions defined above are not really possible or available to society; they would be so only in a Utopian world of 'perfect' lump-sum taxes and other ideal conditions. Depending upon how optimistic our assumptions are, we must think of society as being contained within a *utility-feasibility function* which lies inside the *utility-possibility function*. At best these are close together in the neighbourhood of the 'points of relative *laissez-faire*'. Other things being equal, redistribution of income will usually involve 'costs', which have to be weighed against the ethically defined 'advantages' of such policies.

8. All this being true, we come to the paradoxical conclusion that a policy which seems to make possible greater production of all goods and

a uniformly better utility-possibility function for society may result in so great (and ethically undesirable) a change in the imputation of different individuals' incomes, that we may have to judge such a policy 'bad'. Such a judgement sounds as if it necessarily involves ethics, but it may be reworded so as to be relatively free of value judgements by being given the following interpretation: A policy that shifts society's utility-possibility function uniformly outward may not at the same time shift the utility-feasibility function uniformly outward, instead causing it to twist inward in some places. One last warning is in order: to define what is feasible involves many arbitrary assumptions, some of them of an ethical nature.

The above analysis enables us to appraise critically Pigou's important definitions of real income; this has been reserved for a separate appendix, which—except for a few cross-references—is self-contained.

MASSACHUSETTS INSTITUTE
OF TECHNOLOGY.

A NOTE ON PIGOU'S TREATMENT OF INCOME

1. Despite the vast efforts of government agencies and bureaux in the last 20 years, Pigou's *Economics of Welfare* remains the classic discussion of the definition of real national income. Our previous analysis permits us to make a rapid critique of his masterly analysis. Even if I am right that certain of his formulations need minor amendation, his conclusions for welfare economics remain untouched. Pigou's principal theorem—that each resource should have equal marginal (social) productivity in every use, with price everywhere equal to marginal (social) cost—does not depend for its demonstration upon the elaborate discussion of the national dividend in Part I. In these days, when the national income approach is all the rage as a pedagogic device for coating the pill of elementary economics, it is worth noting that Pigou had seized upon this method of exposition more than a quarter of a century ago. Whether it would have been possible for him to have side-stepped completely the introductory discussion of real national income is irrelevant, since by choosing not to do so Pigou was led to make substantial contributions to the modern theory of economic index numbers (of the Könus, Bowley, Haberler, Staehle type).

2. According to Pigou, economic welfare is 'that part of social welfare that can be brought directly or indirectly into relation with the measuring-rod of money'. The national dividend or real national income is 'the objective counterpart of economic welfare'. Pigou would like to adopt the intuitive position that the dividend should be a function of objective quantities of goods alone, and not depend on 'the state of people's tastes'. But since (a) there is not a single commodity, and (b) all commodities do not move in the same proportion, or (c) even all in the same general direction, Pigou reluctantly considers such an objective definition not feasible, and settles for a more subjective definition according to which *the real income of any person is said to be higher for batch of goods II than for I if II is higher up on his indifference or preference map.*

These are not his words but my interpretation of them, expressed so as to be theoretically independent of any relationship with money or market-price behaviour. Pigou's exact statement for the case of a single individual is as follows:

'Considering a single individual whose tastes are taken as fixed, we say that his dividend in period II. is greater than in period I. if the items that are added to it in period II. are items that he wants more than the items that are taken away from it in period II.' (*Economics of Welfare*, 4th ed., p. 51.)

The wording is cast in a comparative form to pave the way for consideration of the more complex case of many individuals where it may be especially difficult to ask people about their wants and desires and theoretically difficult to define what is meant by the *wants* of the *group*. Pigou extends his definition further:

'Passing to a group of persons (of given numbers), whose tastes are taken as fixed and among whom the distribution of purchasing power is also taken as fixed, we say that the dividend in period II. is greater than in period I. if the items that are added to it in period II. are items *to conserve which they would be willing to give more money than they would be willing to give to conserve the items that are taken away from it in period II*.' (Ibid., pp. 51–2.)

For the moment let us accept the assumption of constant tastes and 'distribution of purchasing power' and the assumption that people know their own minds and correctly identify *ex ante* desire with *ex post* satisfaction. Pigou then gives another verbal reformulation of his definition, saying that the dividend is higher in period II than in I if 'the economic satisfaction (as measured in money) due to the items added in period II is greater than the economic satisfaction (as measured in money) due to the items taken away in period II' (p. 54). Under the assumptions stated, Pigou believes this method of definition to be 'the natural and obvious one to adopt' (p. 52).

3. I wonder. One can sympathize with the attempt to introduce into the definition something that a statistician might sink his punch-cards into, but has the introduction of money left the problem unambiguous ? I have repeated the definition to myself aloud again and again ; and yet even in the case of a single consistent individual about whom unlimited data were available, I would still not be sure how to proceed.

Pigou himself, according to my interpretation of his various writings, is also put in an ambivalent mood by his definition. In the next chapter he proceeds to work with index-number expressions of the form $\sum pq$ where the p's and q's are observed market data. To my mind this is a perfectly valid procedure in the case of a single individual (and it can be given a measure of validity for the case of a group along the lines indicated in my present article). But it is not at all clear that Pigou regards his own procedure as really valid. Again and again he states that the proper procedure is to measure the monetary strength of people's desires not by the marginal price data observed but rather by some kind of consumers-surplus type of construction indicating how much they could be made to pay rather than do without the thing altogether.[1]

Pigou's definition has for the moment betrayed him, and I am willing to defend his practice against his precept. I suspect that what happened is something like the following: instead of continuing to look for an ordinal indicator of utility, Pigou suddenly caught a glimpse of the butterfly of cardinal utility and set out in hot

---

[1] Ibid., pp. 57, 59. In his 1945 introductory work, *Income*, p. 13, Pigou still shows a desire to use some measure of consumers' surplus (or total utility) rather than market values. In the 1949 *Veil of Money* he is even more explicit in insisting that the relative weight of goods should in principle depend upon 'how much of their money income people *would have been willing* to spend . . . [rather than on] how much money they *actually do spend*. . . . Weighting by reference to this entails, other things being equal, giving a smaller weight to changes in items of inelastic and a larger weight to changes in items of elastic demand than "ought" to be assigned to them if our object is, as I have suggested it might be, to measure importance by reference to impact on economic satisfaction, given that tastes are constant. Thus at the very basis of any structure we may erect there is an incorrigible flaw. At the best, we shall have to content ourselves with a makeshift measure, what exactly in the last resort it is measuring being ill-defined and blurred' (pp. 60–1). Cf. J. R. Hicks, 'Foundation of Welfare Economics', *Economic Journal*, xlix, 1939, p. 697, for a related criticism of Pigou's treatment of marginal and intra-marginal concepts.

pursuit. But he realized that the difficulties of this approach were more than statistical, necessarily involving all the familiar difficulties of Marshallian consumers' surplus. Whether or not the butterfly is obtainable or of any use once caught, we must take care not to belittle the solid fruits of index-number theory that are in our grasp.

4. What Pigou does establish—on pp. 62–3—is that

$$\sum p_2\, q_2 > \sum p_2\, q_1$$

means that II is better than I for any consistent individual. The reasoning is exactly that of the A and C comparison in my Fig. 1. Likewise

$$\sum p_1\, q_1 > \sum p_1\, q_2$$

would have meant that I was better than II. Pigou prefers to make the comparisons in the more usual Laspeyre and Paasche index-number ratios[1]

$$P = \frac{\sum p_2\, q_2}{\sum p_2\, q_1} \gtrless 1 \quad \text{and} \quad L = \frac{\sum p_1\, q_2}{\sum p_1\, q_1} \gtrless 1.$$

If we treat work and other efforts as negative commodities, our analysis becomes slightly more general.[2] But our $\sum pq$ expressions may then be zero or negative, so that the method of ratios may be inapplicable even though the proper comparisons can be made in non-ratio form. As we shall see, the use of such ratios has the further disadvantage that it tempts people to attach *cardinal* significance, in an exact or probalistic sense, to the numerical value of the $\sum pq$ ratios.

5. If both P and L are greater than unity, II is clearly better than I. If both are less than unity, then I is better than II. If they are numerically almost equal—and Pigou seems to think they often will be—then the measurement of welfare is thought to be fairly definite. When they differ numerically, Pigou would often measure welfare by some kind of intermediate mean between them: because the geometric mean—which is the Irving Fisher so-called 'Ideal-Index'—has certain convenient properties, Pigou accepts it 'as the measure of change most satisfactory for our purpose' (p. 69).

I cannot persuade myself to follow Pigou's use of the numerical value of the P and L ratios. In the first place, he—along with Kuznets and many others—treats the measures much too symmetrically. When $P > 1$, we already know that II is better than I. If we learn in addition that $L > 1$, we cannot regard this as further corroboration that II is superior to I; at best it serves as corroboration of the fact that we are dealing with a consistent individual.

The case is much different when you tell us that $L > 1$, and nothing else. We have no right to presume that II is definitely better than I. If now you volunteer to us the second bit of information that $P > 1$ also, we cannot regard this as corroboration of an earlier presumption or certainty yielded by the first bit of information. *In its own right* the second fact, that $P > 1$, tells us all we want to know.

With respect to the opposite case, of recognizing when I is better than II, we must attach crucial importance to $L < 1$; and once again the behaviour of P is corroboration of nothing, except of the presence of inconsistency and changed tastes.

---

[1] Pigou lets x, y, z,... stand for q's and a, b, c,... for p's and writes these expressions in the form

$$P = \frac{I_2}{I_1} \frac{x_1\, a_1 + y_1\, b_1 + \dots}{x_1\, a_2 + y_1\, b_2 + \dots} \text{ or } \frac{\sum p_2\, q_2}{\sum p_1\, q_1} \frac{\sum p_1\, q_1}{\sum p_2\, q_1} = \frac{\sum p_2\, q_2}{\sum p_2\, q_1},$$

$$L = \frac{I_2}{I_1} \frac{x_2\, a_1 + y_2\, b_1 + \dots}{x_2\, a_2 + y_2\, b_2 + \dots} \text{ or } \frac{\sum p_2\, q_2}{\sum p_1\, q_1} \frac{\sum p_1\, q_2}{\sum p_2\, q_2} = \frac{\sum p_1\, q_2}{\sum p_1\, q_1}.$$

[2] Pigou's difficulty concerning an increase in the dividend at the expense of leisure, p. 87, n. 1, could then have been avoided.

6. Looking into Pigou's probability argument, we will find one difficulty that stems from his treating of P and L as symmetrical indicators of welfare. Suppose $P = 3 > 1$ and $L = 0.99 < 1$, and these measurements are known to be perfectly accurate, statistically speaking. Then the testimony of the two measures is contradictory, one being greater and the other less than unity. But P exceeds unity by a greater ratio than L falls short of unity, so that $\sqrt{PL}$, the ideal-index, is much greater than unity. Pigou would conclude—according to my interpretation of pp. 65–6—that II is *probably* greater than I.

My conclusion would be different. I would say that either the individual's tastes have definitely changed between the periods or that he was not in equilibrium in both situations. This is because $P > 1$ tells me that II is higher on his indifference curves than is I, and $L < 1$ tells me the exact opposite, and that is the end of it. There is no sense that I can see in believing that, because P is much greater than 1, its testimony is in a loud enough voice to shout down the whisper of $L < 1$.

7. Actually all is not lost as far as exact inference from such a case is concerned. We can validly state: $P > 1$ implies that the batch of goods II is higher *on the indifference curves that prevailed in period II* than *is* the batch of goods I; and $L < 1$ implies that the first batch of goods is higher than batch II *on the indifference curves that prevailed in period I*.

It would be tempting to argue that P always measures welfare from the II period's tastes and L always measures welfare from the I period's tastes. This would be quite wrong, as Pigou is clearly aware. If $P = 0.99$ and $L = 3.0$, we most certainly cannot state the reverse of the previous paragraph's conclusions. We cannot even infer anything about inconsistency. By its nature P can only give definite evidence concerning batch II's superiority over I, and L can only give definite evidence concerning batch I's superiority over II.[1]

8. The case where $P < 1$ and $L > 1$ is the only one to which Pigou explicitly applies his probability reasoning. As in Fig. 1's comparison of A and E, no certain inference is possible. The unknown indifference curve through A could pass above or below the point E. Now the closer is E to the budget-line through A, or what is the same thing the closer is P to 1, then, 'other things being equal', we should expect that the chance of A's indifference curve's passing above E would be increased. The same chance would be increased, the more L is reduced towards unity, 'other things being equal'. This is the basis for Pigou's common-sense view that the degree to which $\sqrt{(PL)} \gtrless 1$ determines the likelihood of II's being better or worse than I. Between 1928 and 1932 Pigou felt compelled to abandon an argument based upon 'the principle of sufficient reason' that attempted to establish this common-sense conclusion. His reason for abandoning it was not because of any impregnation with the modern tendency among statisticians and philosophers to question arguments based on ignorance or on the 'equal-probability of the unknown', but because of technical difficulties previously unnoticed. I think that some of these difficulties could be side-stepped, but since Pigou is content to abandon his old view, and since I am not enamoured of the principle of sufficient reason, I shall confine my attention to the exact inferences possible.

Consider a point A on an individual's indifference map. Consider the region of all alternative points in comparison with A, A being regarded as II and each of these

---

[1] In § 5, chap. vi, p. 58, Pigou leans over backward too far on the issue of the inferences possible when tastes have changed. He believes that the best we can hope for is to devise measures giving the correct results *when tastes have not changed*. This is because he thinks that to make the inference that the batch II is better than the batch I on the basis of the indifference curves of II, we must know what the batch I *would have been* if the indifference curves of II (rather than the actual indifference curves of I) had then prevailed. This is incorrect, as can be noted from the above discussion and from the fact that in my earlier Fig. 1 the inference about A and C was independent of the actual indifference-ratio slope *through C*.

points as I. Consider the contour lines of any symmetric mean of P and L, such as $\sqrt{(PL)} = $ constants. Also consider the contour lines of $P = $ constants and $L = $ constants.

Then this much is true: the contour lines $P = 1$, $L = 1$, and $\sqrt{(PL)} = 1$ all go through A and are tangent to the indifference curve through A. Suppose we use any of the three measures $P \gtrless 1, L \gtrless 1$, or $\sqrt{(PL)} \gtrless 1$ to decide whether A is better or worse than the other point tested. Then the 'percentage of points' for which we get wrong answers by these methods goes to zero as we confine ourselves to smaller and smaller regions around A. Also the probability will approach one, as we confine ourselves to ever closer regions around A, that all three methods will give the same testimony. In the limit as the region around A shrinks, the use of the P criterion in those rare cases when it disagrees with the L criterion will lead to a biased estimate —in that all points under such conditions of contradiction will in the limit be declared to be worse than A, including those points which are really better than A. Exclusive reliance on L in case of contradiction will result in an opposite bias towards declaring all doubtful points better than A. In the limit as the second point is constrained to lie in ever closer regions to A, the use of $\sqrt{(PL)} \gtrless 1$ criterion will lead to a percentage of wrong decisions that approaches ever closer to zero.[1] These are exact statements about limits.

9. Besides Pigou, other writers such as Kuznets and Little have seen fit to attach significance to the numerical values of the P and L ratios. (Readers not interested in technicalities can skip this section.) Kuznets argues as follows:

Suppose as we go from I to II, both P and L are greater than they are when we go from I to III. Then II is 'generally' better than III, provided that the shift in prices from II to III has effects on the ratios of certain identical quantity aggregates of an [allegedly] usual sort.[2]

It will be noted that Kuznets is attempting to use certain numerical or cardinal comparisons for the sole purpose of arriving at a purely *ordinal* comparison. There is nothing methodologically objectionable about this; but none the less the Kuznets result is a self-contained truism that does not permit us to make any general inferences of certain validity in any empirical situation.

First an example may illustrate the loopholes in Kuznets's results. Back in my Fig. 1, let us consider the three points A, B, C. Kuznets will find that P and L computed for A and B are *exactly* the same as for A and C. According to his theorem, C and B should be equally satisfactory or approximately so. Actually the indifference curve through C passes above that of B, and if there were any sense in speaking of 'well above' we might use this stronger expression. More than that, by moving C south-west a little or B north-east a little, we could arrive at the even falser presumption that B is better than C.

There is nothing faulty about Kuznets's arithmetic or the truism he derives from his substitution. He would have to say in this connexion: 'My proviso about price-quantity correlation has been violated in the example.' And why should it not be? When Kuznets says that P is 'in general' less than L, he does not mean by the words 'in general' what a mathematician means when he says that the two sides of a triangle are 'generally' greater than the third. Kuznets means, I think it is clear, that *usually* the price-quantity correlation will be such as to make P less than L. (Actually a long line of writers in index-number theory fell into the actual error of thinking that $P \leqslant L$ and between them lies some 'true' value; an almost equally

---

[1] Mathematically, the indifference curve through A is tangential to the $P = 1$ and $L = 1$ contours, lying 'half-way' between them. The contour $\sqrt{(PL)} = 1$ also has their mean curvature and is an osculating tangent to the indifference curve, differing only in its third and higher derivatives. See my *Foundations*, p. 148.

[2] This is my brief transcription of Kuznets's Appendix, *Economica*, 1949, pp. 124–31 and his remarks on p. 5.

long line of writers have pointed out the falsity of this relation.) I venture the conjecture that Kuznets formed his belief concerning the usual or normal numerical dominance of L over P from considering the special case where there are no real income changes and where any increase in the price of a good (or set of goods) is followed by a necessary decrease in its quantity. But it is precisely when we are trying to arrive at an estimate of whether II is better or worse than III that we must not beg the question by assuming that they are on the same indifference locus.

Even in a loose probability sense, it would be dangerous to say that P is usually less than L. If all goods had an income elasticity of exactly one—so that a pure income change resulted in proportionate changes in every item of consumption—then this would be a certainty. But so long as the well-attested Engel's laws and observed budgetary patterns hold, we must *certainly* have a reversal of the P–L relations throughout the area between the income-expenditure curve through A and the straight line joining A to the origin. This shows that my ABC example is not an isolated case, but is typical of what will always be true in some region.[1]

10. So far I have discussed only the single-individual aspects of Pigou's treatment of real income. All these pages of the Appendix were necessary to cover what took scarcely more than a page of my main text. But now I must consider Pigou's analysis of national income in its group-welfare aspects. Because this problem was treated so fully in the main text, my treatment here may be rather brief.

It will be recalled that Pigou regards his inferences as being valid if the members of the group always have 'a fixed distribution of income' (and, of course, unchanging tastes). When we subject his book to microscopic examination, two questions immediately come to mind. (1) Exactly what is meant by 'a fixed distribution of income' between two situations? And (2) even after this by-no-means-simple question has been adequately disposed of, what is it that Pigou thinks is true of the group or of the individuals in the group as we go from one situation to another? Is there a group-mind that registers more utility? Or is it the algebraic sum of utility that has gone up for the group? Or is it that every single member of the group is now better off than before?

11. One must read between the lines to answer these questions—at least, I have not been able to find their explicit answers. I suspect that Pigou does not have any place in his philosophy for any group-mind. But his technical argument seems to come very close to the following Wieser construction:

'The theory of the "simple economy" ... begins with the idealizing assumption that the subject is a single person. However, we do not have in mind here the meagre economy of an isolated Robinson Crusoe ... [but] the activities of an entire nation. At the same time millions of people are regarded as a massed unit.'[2]

We may read elements of this general line of reasoning in Pigou's concern with the question of whether market prices can be considered as given to society in the way that they can be assumed to be prescribed for a single small competitive individual. If Fig. 10 applied to a single individual, he could legitimately regard the straight line NN through A as being open to him. But if the chart holds for society, there could be shown on it the true (but possibly unknown) production-possibility or opportunity-cost curve of type MM or of some other shape.

Pigou is uneasy about applying the argument to the group as a whole. 'But, when it is the whole of a group, or, if we prefer it, a representative man who shifts his consumption in this way, it is no longer certain that prices would be unaffected' (p. 61). For a moment, Pigou seems to lapse into the assumption that the representa-

[1] Little gives a probability interpretation of the significance of the cardinal size of P on pp. 46–7, *Economica*, 1949. He has in mind a closely related, but distinct, group inference from that discussed in this paper. He also relies on our rough empirical knowledge of preference patterns in evaluating his probabilities.

[2] F. v. Wieser, *Social Economics* (1927), pp. 9–10.

tive man knows that he is an image of the group and therefore acts collusively as if a group decision were being made. The group mind knows that the only choice really open to it is along MM; therefore in the initial A situation it does not think that C is obtainable; consequently we cannot infer that A has been revealed to be better than C by a deliberate act of choosing A over C. Something like this Pigou must have believed for the moment, else he would not have felt the need to add a 'certain assumption' of paragraph 8, ruling out the possibility that the production-possibility curve of society is like MM, but instead requiring it to show constant slope like NN. It is fortunate that Pigou's argument can be salvaged without making this extraneous assumption—fortunate because I cannot agree with his appraisal of the *a priori* probabilities: 'In real life, with a large number of commodities, it is reasonable to suppose that the upward price movements caused by shifts of con-

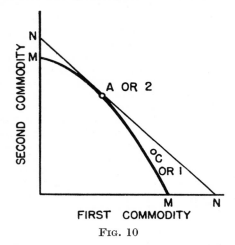

FIG. 10

sumption would roughly balance the downward movements' (p. 62). That is to say, concave or convex curves are equally likely, so we may assume the curve to be a straight line. Rather, I would think that in the conditions most suited to healthy competition—where external economies either balance external diseconomies or both are negligible and where tendencies towards increasing or decreasing returns *to scale* are absent or just balancing—we would still be left with the good old law of diminishing returns in the classical (qualitative and quantitative) senses, so that convex production-possibility schedules are the 'normal' case.

Actually, if Pigou is concerned to make normative statements about points like A and C that hold valid for groups, it does not matter that the true production-possibility curve is something other than NN.[1] We have seen in Hicks's paper and in the text what these valid inferences are. Another way of looking at the problem is by means of the 'collective indifference curves' that Professor Scitovsky has taught us to use in the second of his cited papers.

12. But first we must settle what is meant by Pigou's 'fixed distribution of income'. How tempting to think of money as being concrete and the distribution of income to be fixed if everybody's money income changes proportionately. But money itself means nothing. If two men each have the same money income and if one likes meat and the other cheese and the terms of trade between meat and cheese

---

[1] Pigou does not stand alone. 'Unless the groups considered are small in relation to the whole, market prices cannot be considered as constant, and therefore the condition $\Sigma\, p_2\, q_2 > \Sigma\, p_2\, q_1$ would no longer indicate that goods of situation I were rejected in favour of those of situation II' (Little, *Economica*, 1949, p. 17).

change, then would Pigou consider the distribution of income to have remained fixed ? Probably not. Moreover, if we follow the convenient practice of treating the services of labour and property that people supply as negative commodities, then in the absence of government taxes we might say that everybody has a zero (net) income *always*.

Probably in the beginning Pigou had in mind the simple case of identical individuals, any one of whom is representative, and where they all fare alike. Then when situation II is better than I, it is also true that both individuals are better off. When we leave the case of perfect symmetry, it becomes difficult to say that the extra welfare of one man is always to be some fixed multiple of the increment of welfare of another since this involves ethical inter-personal comparisons that Pigou is trying to avoid in these chapters dealing with the relatively objective aspects of welfare and the national dividend. But for his purposes Pigou needs only to assume that the ordinal well-being of all individuals are required to move always *in the same direction* according to some prescribed relationship. [Some complicated monetary shifts must be assumed to take place to bring this about.]

If I am right in this interpretation, then the comparison of A or 2 and C or 1 in terms of

$$\sum p_2 q_2 > \sum p_2 q_1$$

is immediately obvious and independent of the shape of MM or of any assumptions of group-consciousness. The fortunes of all being linked, any one person reflects the fate of all. Now, obviously, for some one person we must have

$$\sum p_2 q_2 > \sum p_2 q_1,$$

because if the opposite were true for each and every person, how could the totals show this relation ? But if at least one has been made worse off in I than in II, then the 'fixed distribution of income assumption' means that they must all have been made worse off. Q.E.D.

In terms of Scitovsky indifference curves, the story runs as follows: For a prescribed amount of both people's ordinal utility, U' and U'', we can draw up a collective indifference curve. For any prescribed distribution linking U' and U'' in a monotonic fashion we can draw up a family of collective indifference curves. If each person has concave indifference curves, the collective curves will also be concave. But regardless of concavity, the collective curve through A is never permitted to cross below the NN line. This will be obvious to every reader in the case of concave curves ; and the same can be shown to be true in general by simple mathematical argument. It follows that C lies on a lower collective indifference curve than A— *regardless of the true shape of society's production-possibility curve MM.*

13. Pigou's argument has been removed from any dependence on constant (opportunity) cost assumptions. But a worse restriction remains. For him to make any inference, *everybody* in the community must have been made better or worse off. The wind scarcely ever blows that brings good to absolutely everyone. Lucky it is that the remaining fifty-odd chapters of the *Economics of Welfare* do not depend in an essential way upon the results of the early chapters of Part I dealing with the national dividend. Fortunately, too—just as was seen to be true when tastes change —we can make some valid inferences when the distribution of income is known *not* to remain fixed. From our earlier analysis we know that $\sum p_2 q_2 > \sum p_2 q_1$ implies that the II's utility-possibility curve lies outside of I's at least in the neighbourhood of the actual observed situation II.

14. One last case not yet considered by any of the writers. Suppose we have given to us certain well-defined ethical notions concerning inter-personal well-being. In the simplest case they can be summarized in a Bergson social welfare function, $W = W(U', U'',...)$, with the usual property that anything that helps one man without hurting anyone else will mean an increase in W.

As before, let us observe prices, p, and total quantities for all society, q. And finally, suppose that *the distribution of income is ethically optimal both in situation 1 or C and 2 or A*. What can we now infer from the condition $\sum p_2 q_2 > \sum p_2 q_1$? The answer is that situation A lies higher on the ethical social welfare function than does C.[1]

The logical proof of this result is not so easy as I at first thought it would be. This is because our move from C to the better position A need not represent an improvement for all individuals. U' may go down provided U'' goes up relatively more, as measured, of course, by the W function. Hence, when cost conditions change in such a way as to make it optimal to alter the relative 'distribution of income', our earlier argument cannot apply.

To prove that $W(A) > W(C)$, we can use 'social indifference curves'. But they are not the arbitrary ones of the Scitovsky new-welfare-economics type. They are a unique old-welfare-economics set of curves showing the combinations of total goods capable of giving (when all optimal arrangements have been made) equal levels of W. In the 'normal' case, where playing the game of competition can be depended to follow the invisible hand to bliss, these social indifference curves will be concave.* It follows that whenever C lies inside the straight line NN going through A, it must also lie inside the social indifference curve (of equal W) going through A. This proves our result.[2]

[1] This is related to Bergson's interesting interpretation of Pigou in infinitesimal terms. Bergson, 'Reformulation of Certain Aspects of Welfare Economics', *Q.J.E.*, lii (1938), p. 331.

[2] In the last two of his cited papers Little has stated theorems a little bit like the one above. There are two or three different versions, but the typical Little theorem shows that a certain point A is better than another point C because we can imagine going from C to A in two steps: one of these involves an improved distribution of real income (somehow defined) and the other an improvement in each and every person's well-being. I give an abbreviated interpretation of one of the variants discussed in *O.E.P.*, pp. 235–7.

    1. Suppose we have a W function as defined above, with $\partial W/\partial U' > 0$, &c., and start at a point C and end up at a point A.

    2. The point A is assumed to lie out and beyond the utility-possibility locus of the point C; e.g. there is a point C' on the latter locus that is south-west of the point A in the $U'-U''$ plane. Thus the Scitovsky test is satisfied.

    3. Now make the assumption that in terms of W 'the distribution of real income is better' at C' than in C. (Thus, ideally, we should not have been in C in the first place.)

    4. Then it follows that A is higher on the assumed welfare function than is C. (This conclusion does not depend upon whether the Hicks–Kaldor test is satisfied.)

    5. It does not follow that a little angel, given the choice of throwing a switch that moves society from C to A, ought to throw that switch. There may be an infinity of points on C's locus still better than A. Little's policy conclusion is to be qualified, therefore, by the following statement that he has been kind enough to send to me in private correspondence: 'The shift from C to A ought to be made if the shift does not prejudice any other move which might result in a position still more favourable than A.'

The chain of reasoning involved in 1–4 is simple once we pin down what is meant by 'the distribution of real income being better'. This means $W(C') > W(C)$. Since the Scitovsky test implies $W(A) > W(C')$, the Little result $W(A) > W(C)$ immediately follows. Just as Little talks prose, he can be said to be using a *welfare* function whenever he talks welfare economics. But like the new welfare economists, he wants to see what results he can get with an *incompletely* defined welfare function—a commendable effort, perhaps useful for an important class of policy decisions, but necessarily not complete for all policy situations.

* Jan de Graaff of Cambridge University has pointed out to me that I must introduce an extra (and arbitrary) axiom to be sure that the social indifference curves have the stated concavity.

78

SOCIAL INDIFFERENCE CURVES

By Paul A. Samuelson

I. Introduction: widespread use of community indifference curves, 1. — II. Attempts to justify the use of community indifference curves, 3. — III. Proof of the nonexistence of community indifference contours, 4. — IV. Nature of Scitovsky's community indifference contours, 6. — V. Problem of family preference: a parable, 8. — VI. Optimal ways of achieving income redistribution, 12. — VII. Regular properties of social indifference contours, 14. — VIII. Perfect competition and bliss, 19. — IX. Final summary, 21.

I. Introduction: The Widespread Use of Community Indifference Curves

I remember a meeting with Tibor Scitovsky, in Washington just before the war, at which he told me he was writing a paper on "community indifference curves." I risked a new friendship by replying: "That's strange. Long ago I proved that community indifference curves are impossible — they don't exist."

It is fortunate that Scitovsky paid no attention to my remarks, since otherwise he might have been inhibited from writing his properly-celebrated 1942 article, "A Reconsideration of the Theory of Tariffs."[1] His paper did contain what he calls community indifference curves, and it is the essence of its contribution that such defined community curves can — and in many circumstances must — intersect and cross each other.

What was it I thought (and still think) I had proved? Assume two countries each containing more than a single consumer; let each person be rational solely in the sense of having consistent concave indifference curves for two goods. To eliminate nonessential com-

---

1. *Review of Economic Studies*, IX, 89–110 and reprinted in *Readings in the Theory of International Trade* of the American Economic Association, 358–89. See also T. de Scitovsky, "A Note on Welfare Propositions in Economics," *Review of Economic Studies*, IX, 77–88.

plications of production, assume each person's initial endowment of each of the goods given. Then, of course, one can easily define an equilibrium of international trade.

This Jevons, Walras, Edgeworth, Marshall, Wicksell, Bowley, and others long ago proved; and Lerner's (1934) paper on international trade[2] gives a complete graphical account. Note that no use of community indifference curves is involved. Jevons[3] himself had insisted on the lack of need to compare or compound different persons' marginal utilities; and it is simple addition of observable market demand or offer curves that gives us our equilibrium (which by the way most certainly need not be unique, as Walras and Marshall showed in the 1870's).

None the less, by the late 1930's the common way of depicting such an international trade equilibrium was through the use of community indifference curves for each country, which somehow "consolidate" separate individual's tastes. This device Lerner had used (or hinted at) first in his 1932 article;[4] and, indeed, the first pages of his 1934 article reassert by dubious analogy with the single-man's indifference curves the validity of using community indifference curves. Leontief's[5] celebrated international trade article also employs community indifference curves. Much more recent examples from the literature could be given: lest I seem to be throwing stones, let me say that some of my own papers and lectures have employed community indifference curves.[6]

2. A. P. Lerner, "The Diagrammatical Representation of Demand Conditions in International Trade," *Economica*, N.S., I (1934), 319–34, reprinted in A. P. Lerner, *Essays in Economic Analysis* (1953), 101–22.

3. In his *Theory of Political Economy* (1871), chap. 4, Jevons exhibits some confusion over the concept of a collective "trading body," and Walras was perhaps the first to give a rigorous theory of exchange.

4. A. P. Lerner, "The Diagrammatical Representations of Cost Conditions in International Trade," *Economica*, Vol. 12 (1932), 346–56, reprinted in A. P. Lerner, *Essays in Economic Analysis*, 85–100.

5. W. W. Leontief, "The Use of Indifference Curves in the Analysis of Foreign Trade," this *Journal*, XLVII (1933), 493–503 and reprinted in the earlier cited *Readings*, 229–38.

6. Of all the modern writers on international trade theory, only Haberler has, I believe, refrained from using community indifference curves. In "Some Problems in the Pure Theory of International Trade," *Economic Journal*, LX (1950), 223–40, he says, p. 226: " . . . a shift in production will usually be accompanied by a redistribution of income. This precludes the uncritical application of community indifference curves. . . . Scitovsky has made the only serious attempt, as far as I know, at constructing community indifference curves, taking into account changes in the income distribution. His solution is, however, not entirely satisfactory in my opinion."

II. Attempts to Justify the Use of Community Indifference Curves

What defense do we make when challenged on the use of community indifference curves for a country or group of individuals? I suppose one of the following:

(a) We may claim that our country is inhabited by Robinson Crusoe alone and claim only to show how trade between such single-person countries is determined. This is admittedly not very realistic.

(b) In order to give the appearance of being more realistic, we may claim that our country is inhabited by a number of identical individuals with identical tastes; they must also have identical initial endowments of goods if this artifice of examining what happens to the representative individual's indifference curves is to give us a true description of the resulting market equilibrium.[7] This case, too, is not very realistic, though it may seem a slight improvement over Robinson Crusoe.

(c) We may claim to be depicting trade of a totalitarian nation. One dictator determines demand within his country and *his* consistent indifference curves provide us with the community indifference curves for that country. Some might regard this as Robinson Crusoe brought painfully up to date.

(d) None of the previous explanations meets the case of two (or more) dissimilar individuals within each country. We might, therefore, try to argue that (say) two men within a country are to be treated as if *each* were a separate country. Then instead of having trade between two countries, we now speak of trade among $4 = 2 \times 2$ "countries" — or in the general case, of trade among nm countries. Now, with each man a country unto himself, his "community indifference curves" are really individual and not at all collective. So we have ended up with an adequate description of international exchange. But we have abandoned rather than defended the use of community indifference curves. Actually, within the framework of elementary international trade theory, where transport costs are ignored, two men within a country have no more in common than do any two men selected from anywhere in the world. Logically, therefore, it will be as hard or easy to draw up community indifference curves for the whole world as to do it for any subgroup of individuals.[8]

7. J. E. Meade in *A Geometry of International Trade* (1952), p. 9, adopts this postulate.
8. Lerner's 1932 article does in fact draw a world indifference curve, but Leontief and others usually do not.

III. Proof of the Nonexistence of Community Indifference Contours

None of the above four defenses succeeds in providing a justification of the existence and use of community indifference curves. I suspect that a careful search of the literature would turn up still other, equally inconclusive, proposals.[9] It will be most economical to turn at this point to the proof that community indifference curves, defined in the usual sense and with the usual properties, are "impossible."

It will suffice to consider a country composed of two individuals, each with different tastes and with arbitrarily given initial endowments. The "rest of the world" with whom they trade need not be brought explicitly into the argument. Superscripts will identify the men.

What is it that community indifference curves do for us in handling this group of two men? Careful examination of how we use such curves will lead to the following answer: Community indifference curves between the totals of two goods X and Y — where $X = X^1 + X^2$, $Y = Y^1 + Y^2$ — give us a "demand relationship" between prices and quantities of the following form, $p_x/p_y = F(X^1 + X^2, Y^1 + Y^2)$, where the latter can be called the marginal-rate-of-substitution function characteristic of the group.[1] They provide this *and essentially nothing more.*

Now to show the general impossibility of going from the individual's indifference function $p_x/p_y = F^1(X^1, Y^1)$ and $p_x/p_y = F^2(X^2, Y^2)$, which is all that Mother Nature provides us with, to the collective function $F(X^1 + X^2, Y^1 + Y^2)$ or $F(X, Y)$. Mathematically, can we reduce the individual's system on the left to the aggregate one on the right? Is

---

9. Thus Viner, in his *Studies in International Trade Theory*, p. 523, says a country-indifference contour must refer to combinations of goods of "equal market value" with a distribution of income consistent with their production. Even in the one-person country, where no logical problem of defining indifference curves can arise, such a total-value concept would seem to jumble together hopelessly budget lines and indifference curves. And even if we avoid any confusing interminglings by a tautological definition of an iso-utility price deflator, when we come to the group case it is the essence of the problem that values may differ for the same totals of every good, depending upon the detailed distributive breakdown of the totals among individuals; hence, as Viner says, such defined indifference curves can intersect each other. Whatever the many defects of the opportunity cost doctrine, Viner seems wrong in blaming *it* for the community-curve pathologies.

1. If the indifference curves are to be convex to the origin, $(\partial F/\partial X) - (F)(\partial F/\partial Y) < 0$.

$$\frac{Y^1 - \overline{Y^1}}{\overline{X^1} - X^1} = \frac{p_x}{p_y} = \frac{Y^2 - \overline{Y^2}}{\overline{X^2} - X^2} \qquad \frac{(Y^1 + Y^2) - (\overline{Y^1} + \overline{Y^2})}{(\overline{X^1} + \overline{X^2}) - (X^1 + X^2)} = \frac{p_x}{p_y}$$

equivalent

$$F^1(X^1,Y^1) = \frac{p_x}{p_y} = F^2(X^2,Y^2) \qquad \text{to} \qquad F(X^1 + X^2, Y^1 + Y^2) = \frac{p_x}{p_y}$$

The first row on the right follows by direct algebra from the first row on the left. The problem reduces to this: are the two equations in the second row on the left equivalent to the equation on the right? The mathematical answer is: generally no.[2] It was this result that I was referring to in my original comment to Scitovsky.

The common sense of this impossibility theorem is easy to grasp. Allocating the same totals differently among people must generally change the resulting equilibrium price ratio. The only exception is where tastes are identical, not only for all men, but also for all men when they are rich or poor. Gertrude Stein might well have said of this case: "A dollar is a dollar is a dollar." Little wonder that this singular case of "expenditure proportionality" — which is known from casual and detailed econometric investigation to be unrealistic — does admit of community indifference curves.[3]

2. Implicit function theory gives us the sole condition under which $F^1(X^1,Y^1)$ $= p_x/p_y = F^2(X - X^1, Y - Y^1)$ can for preassigned values of p_x/p_y, X, and either X^1 or Y^1 give a solution for Y that is independent of the prescribed value of X^1 or Y^1. E. B. Wilson in *Advanced Calculus*, p. 129, demonstrates that the Jacobian $(\partial F^1/\partial X^1)(\partial F^2/\partial Y^2) - (\partial F^1/\partial Y^1)(\partial F^2/\partial X^2) \equiv 0$ at all values satisfying the equations is a necessary and sufficient condition for there to be the desired relation between $p_x/p_y = F(X,Y)$. This means that each man's income-consumption paths must be straight lines and at a given p_x/p_y their respective income-consumption paths must be parallel straight lines with equal slopes. Readers familiar with the famous transfer problem will recognize that these are the special conditions needed if a redistribution of income among traders is to leave price ratios unchanged. See P. A. Samuelson "The Transfer Problem and Transport Costs, I," reprinted in this volume as Chap. 74, for discussion and references. W. M. Gorman in "Community Preference Fields," *Econometrica*, Vol. 21 (1953) 63–80 and H. Theil in *Linear Aggregation of Economic Relations* (Amsterdam, 1954) have derived similar conditions; and in the field of fiscal policy it has long been realized that lack of great diversity in the *marginal* propensity to consume of rich and poor will reduce the purchasing power leverage of income redistributions.

The above condition of parallel income-consumption curves can be sharpened a little. Once we recognize that no good can be negative, our parallel Engel's lines are really forbidden to *cut* any axis: so they must all be rays through the origin, corresponding to unitary income elasticities for every good, and thus $F^1(A,B) \equiv g(A/B) \equiv F^2(A,B) \equiv F(A,B)$. See Meade, *op. cit.*, p. 9 for a similar remark by Ralph Turvey. Many years ago, Wicksell had noted that similar conditions would be needed to justify Jevons' "trading body" and various constructions of Launhardt. See K. Wicksell's 1893 book, *Value, Capital, and Rent* (1954 English translation), pp. 72–73.

3. This far-fetched but valid fifth defense of community indifference curves can be explained graphically: If the marginal rates of substitution along the

IV. Nature of Scitovsky's Community Indifference Contours

If community indifference curves have been proved impossible, how could Scitovsky have succeeded in defining them? Obviously we must be facing a case where the same name is being applied to two quite different animals. Community indifference curves of the type needed for the derivation of community demand do not exist. But

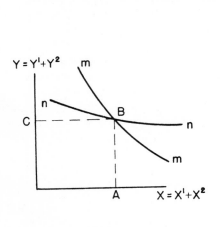

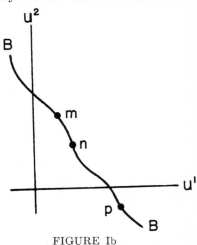

<table>
<tr><td align="center">FIGURE Ia</td><td align="center">FIGURE Ib</td></tr>
</table>

Each point indicates given totals of goods. The locus of points mm or nn give the alternative minimum requirements to achieve the ordinal utility levels m or n. A point in one diagram goes into a curve in the other, dually.

Each specified level of ordinal well-being for all men is depicted by a point like m or n. The utility frontier BB gives the alternative efficient interpersonal allocations of the totals of B in Figure Ib.

these are not what Scitovsky was looking for. He sought what I might call "minimum-total-requirements contours" for society or for a group.[4] They are defined as follows: If each and every man is specified to be on arbitrarily prescribed levels of well-being, what are the minimal combinations of total X, Y, ... that are "needed" to achieve these goals? The Scitovsky community contours are the answer to this question. And generally, as he pointed out, there will be an

contract curve within any Edgeworth box-diagram are to be everywhere equal, the contract curve must always be the diagonal of the box and income elasticity must be unitary.

4. Scitovsky was well within his rights to call them community indifference curves. After all, the name had not been copyrighted; and along any one such curve, every person is left precisely indifferent, by virtue of its definition. Moreover, in pointing out the infinite multiplicity of his contours running through any given point (X,Y), Scitovsky was demonstrating the nonexistence of the type of community indifference contours needed to generate group demand.

infinite number of such contours through any given point in the
(X, Y) plane, one for each of the infinite different preassigned levels
of "relative well-being" among the separate individuals.[5]

Figures Ia and Ib may help to refresh the reader's memory concerning the basic relation. Look at B in Ia. It depicts given totals of
both goods. We could easily construct a separate box-diagram with
dimensions $OABC;$ and we could orient man 1's indifference curves
with respect to its southwest corner 0, and man 2's indifference curves
with respect to its northeast corner. I have not drawn this box, but
I ask the reader to recall that such a diagram would generate a contract curve going from O to B. Every point on that contract curve
would be Pareto-optimal in the sense that from it we cannot reallocate
the given totals so as to make both men better off. The totality of
frontier points of the utility-possibility locus that would be generated
by such a contract curve, I have indicated by the BB locus on the
ordinal utility diagram Ib. (Because any monotonic stretching of
each man's indicator of ordinal utility is admissible, only the degree of
"eastwardness" or "northwardness" in Ib matters; hence, I have not
given BB any one particular convexity or concavity, requiring only
that it never turn northeastward.)

The important fact is this: A single point, like B in Ia, corresponds
to an infinity of points in Ib — like m, or n, or p.[6] (A double-infinity
of loci can be traced in Ib by all the single points in Ia.)

Now essentially, what Scitovsky did was to point out the opposite
or dual relationship between the diagrams. He showed that to any
single point, such as m in Ib, there corresponds a minimum-total-
requirements contour mm in Ia that will have the same convexity-to-
the-origin property as does each man's indifference curve — and,
indeed, at B itself it will have the common slope that each man's
indifference contour has at that point on the contract curve in $OABC$
corresponding to m.

Thus, we have a dual relationship: Each point in one diagram
corresponds to a curve in the other. Just as a point of totals in Ia
like B corresponds to a utility frontier in Ib like BB, so does a specified ordinal utility point like m in Ib correspond in Ia to a Scitovsky
community indifference curve like mm.

Exactly how are these minimum-total-requirements curves

5. The remainder of this Section IV can be skipped without interrupting the
continuity of the present contribution. However, without mastering these
simple geometrical facts, a reader will find it hard to interpret many of the last
two decades' writings.

6. Of course, points inside of the BB frontier are attainable within the $OABC$
box, but such off-the-contract-curve points are clearly nonoptimal.

defined geometrically? By "adding" the indifference curves of each man corresponding to m. Do we add them vertically? No. Horizontally? No. Along a 45° diagonal? No. How then? Obviously, on the different indifference curves we pair points that have equal slopes; then we add, respectively, the co-ordinates of these points to get our Scitovsky curve; only in this way will we, for given levels of each man's satisfaction and prescribed totals of all but one good, be truly succeeding in minimizing the needed total of the remaining good.[7]

All this suggests a different way of characterizing the essential peculiarity of Scitovsky-type social indifference curves. Adding a single indifference curve of one man to the infinity of indifference curves of the other would give us a one-parameter family of resultant curves of the type we need for demand analysis. But that first man in fact has an infinity of curves not a single one. There are just too many ways to add each man's infinity of curves: there results a two-parameter family of Scitovsky curves, with an infinite number going through each and every point in the plane.

We could use these Scitovsky-defined community indifference curves to show the impossibility of a singlefold infinity of consistent community indifference curves capable of giving rise to group demand functions observed on the market.

Start at B in Ia. What slope or price ratio will it determine? We can allocate B's totals to get individuals' well-being corresponding to m in Ib. This takes us back to mm in Ia with its indicated slope at B. But we could just as legitimately have gone from B to n, and back to nn's slope at B. This proves the impossibility of a unique slope at B.[8]

V. THE PROBLEM OF FAMILY PREFERENCE: A PARABLE

Now I have proved the impossibility of group or community preference curves. But haven't I in a sense proved too much? Who after all is the consumer in the theory of consumer's (not consumers') behavior? Is he a bachelor? A spinster? Or is he a "spending unit"

---

7. See Wolfgang F. Stolper, "A Method of Constructing Community Indifference Curves," *Schweizerische Zeitschrift für Volkswirtschaft und Statistik*, Vol. 86, nr. 2, 1950. Lerner in 1952 gave a similar rule for "adding" transportation curves.

8. The singular case of uniform expenditure of all dollars must be an exception. Here mm and nn happen to coincide. Why? Because the movement from m to n merely shifts real income from man 1 to man 2 and both men spend their incomes alike.

as defined by statistical pollsters and recorders of budgetary spending? In most of the cultures actually studied by modern economists the fundamental unit on the demand side is clearly the "family," and this consists of a single individual in but a fraction of the total cases.

This faces us squarely with what has been called the "Dr. Jekyll and Mrs. Jekyll" problem. If community indifference curves are impossible, how can we expect family demand functions observed in the market place to obey the consistency axiom of revealed preference or any other regularity conditions? Why shouldn't the pluralistic decisions of the family group result in price-quantity situations in which the point *A* was at one time selected even though *B* was cheaper, while at another time *B* was selected "in preference to" *A*? Could not this contradiction occur even though nobody had changed his or her preferences?

Of course, we might try to save the conventional theory by claiming that one titular head has sovereign power within the family and all of its demands reflect his (or her) consistent indifference curves. But as casual anthropologists we all know how unlikely it is in modern Western culture for one person "to wear the pants." It is perhaps less unrealistic to adopt the hypothesis of a consistent "family consensus" that represents a meeting of the minds or a compromise between them. (Perhaps Arrow will produce a proof that such a consensus is impossible.)

Still every close student of the family will have noticed that it behaves neither like a dictator nor a unanimous committee. There is discernible a decentralization of decision-making with respect to at least some of its functions. Only rarely do my daughters confer with me as to the ordinal preferability of peppermint over chocolate. We all have our little allowances which within limits we are free to spend as we like. The intrafamily decentralization in Western culture is admittedly not so complete as a thoroughgoing libertarian might desire: just as we may have sacrificed efficiency during World War II by not assigning to each general (or for that matter each noncommissioned officer) his predetermined quota of abstract purchasing power which he could use to bid resources away from his colleagues, so in our internal family life do we fail to decentralize completely decision-making among the clan's separate babies, children, and elders.

Where the family is concerned the phenomenon of altruism inevitably raises its head: if we can speak at all of the indifference curves of any one member, we must admit that his tastes and marginal rates of substitution are contaminated by the goods that other members consume. These Veblen-Duesenberry external consumption effects are the essence of family life. They require us to build up an interpersonal theory that sounds more like welfare economics than like positive demand analysis. Such problems of home economics are, abstractly conceived, exactly of the same logical character as the general problem of government and social welfare.

Elsewhere I have sketched a simplified pure theory of public expenditure,[9] and I have no intention here of tackling this basic problem of all social life. Instead I am content to analyze one extreme polar case of family organization. This family consists of two or more persons: each person consumes his own goods and has indifference curves ordering those goods, and his preferences among his own goods have the special property of being independent of the other members' consumption. But since blood is thicker than water, the preferences of the different members are interrelated by what might be called a "consensus" or "social welfare function" which takes into account the deservingness or ethical worths of the consumption levels of each of the members. The family acts *as if* it were maximizing their joint welfare function.

Concretely, if $u^1 = u^1(X^1, Y^1, \ldots)$, $u^2 = u^2(X^2, Y^2, \ldots)$ are respectively ordinal indicators of the separate indifference curves of members 1 and 2 of the family, then the family ordinal social welfare function can be written as

$$(1) \qquad U = f[u^1(X^1, Y^1, \ldots), u^2(X^2, Y^2, \ldots), \ldots]$$

where f is an ordinal indicator function that grows when any u^i alone increases. Note that f is not necessarily the cardinal sum of separate cardinal utilities. But note that this formulation does conform to the special requirement that each member's separate tastes are to count. (Obviously, this must be a family of adults, or at least of very unusual children.) It is by virtue of this quasi-independence that we can avoid need for family council meetings at which detailed decisions concerning *all* consumptions are jointly arrived at. The only joint consensus decisions that have to be made by the family have to do with the allocation among the different individuals of the total family income I. If this is properly broken down into $I = I^1 + I^2 + \ldots$, then each member confronted with market prices $(P_x, P_y, \ldots)$ can be counted on to maximize his own ordinal $u^i(X^i, Y^i, \ldots)$ — and each will be led, as if by an invisible hand, toward the maximization of $U = f[u^1, u^2, \ldots]$.

9. "The Pure Theory of Public Expenditure," *Review of Economics and Statistics,* XXXVI (Nov. 1954), pp. 387–89; reprinted as Chap. 92.

Our previous analysis of the impossibility of community indifference curves for a country must logically also apply to one family group. It alerts us to some basic difficulties in formulating proper rules for the optimal allocation of I into $I^1 + I^2 + \ldots$

Thus we might at first thought be tempted to stipulate a rule like the following: Papa is always to receive 10 per cent of all income, Mama 51 per cent, and Junior 39 per cent. But such a rule can be shown to be what in *Foundations of Economic Analysis*, Chapter 8, I called a "shibboleth."[1] It is generally incompatible with the maximization of a social welfare function $U = f[u^1, u^2, \ldots]$ that involves real goods. For such an arithmetic rule itself to be given ethical significance, for its own sake and regardless of levels of well-being, is to set up a rather special kind of an end. (Of course, I do not dictate that people must refrain from setting up shibboleth social welfare functions; if, having realized what they were doing, they still want to do so, that is their privilege.)

What is the common-sense explanation of the fact that a stipulated percentage breakdown of income cannot be an optimal rule for a nonshibboleth social welfare function? A little thought will convince us that an admissible optimal rule must have the following familiar property: Income must always be reallocated among the members of our family society so as to keep the "marginal social significance of every dollar" equal, i.e.,

(2)
$$\frac{\dfrac{\partial U}{\partial u^2} \dfrac{\partial u^2}{\partial I^2}}{\dfrac{\partial U}{\partial u^1} \dfrac{\partial u^1}{\partial I^1}} = 1, \text{ etc.,}$$

where $\partial u^i / \partial I^i$ is the marginal utility of income to the ith family member. Now suppose the (10 per cent, 51 per cent, 39 per cent) is truly optimal at the initial price situation $(P_x^0, P_y^0, \ldots)$. When we change one or more of those prices, the different members will be affected differently according to their different tastes; and we cannot, in general, expect the social significance of their last dollars to be any longer equal unless we change the percentage quotas in an optimal way.[2]

1. A better word is needed. Perhaps "fetish," although that has too pejorative a ring. Regardless of names, the phenomenon is unambiguously defined in this last paragraph.

2. Readers of Pigou will be familiar with the meaning of (2), which in fact was widely discussed earlier by Irving Fisher, Launhardt, Wicksell and others. See e.g., I. Fisher, *Mathematical Investigations in the Theory of Value and Price* (1892), p. 99. Bergson in "A Reformulation of Certain Aspects of Welfare Economics," this *Journal*, Feb. 1938, is the first known to me to sense the point about the nonoptimality of fixed percentage allocations in the face of price changes.

To the reader who has pondered over the earlier proofs of the impossibility of community indifference curves, further elaboration of this point should not be necessary. Actually this last line of reasoning can be extended to give an additional proof of the impossibility of community indifference curves. For suppose some hard and fast way of allocating the family's initial total endowment $(\overline{X}, \overline{Y}, \ldots)$ into $(\overline{X}^1 + \overline{X}^2 + \ldots, \overline{Y}^1 + \overline{Y}^2 + \ldots, \ldots)$ were adequate to maximize a function $U = f[u^1, u^2, \ldots]$. Then by straightforward but tedious reasoning we could show that the contours of constant U would provide us with the community indifference curves we were vainly seeking.

VI. Optimal Ways of Achieving Income Redistribution

The demonstration that fixed initial allotments of $(\overline{X}^1, \overline{Y}^1, \ldots)$, $(\overline{X}^2, \overline{Y}^2, \ldots)$ cannot be an optimal rule for family allocation has a vital social implication that we can now explore. What we have been calling a family is after all but a disguised version of society itself — i.e., a collection of more than one person. Some biological families are perhaps less cohesive than the French nation, and even more may lack the cohesion of the Japanese.

By 1890 when Marshall came to write his *Principles* it was a commonplace among technical economists that laissez faire could not be expected — even under favorable market and technological conditions — necessarily to achieve an ethical optimum. The neoclassicists realized something that had escaped both the classicists and the believers in predestined social harmonies such as Bastiat: these marginal utility economists realized that in order for laissez faire to lead to the optimum, there would have to result an equal marginal social utility of each and every person's income. Because Marshall, Edgeworth, Walras, Wicksell, Böhm-Bawerk, and the others thought that men were much alike and subject to interpersonally summable diminishing marginal utility, they all tended to regard existing capitalistic society as too unequal in its income distribution.[3] They felt that only after there takes place a redistribution of the initial wealth could one regard the dollars voted in the market place as being of ethically equal weight; only then would the invisible hand of perfectly competitive markets lead to the social optimum.

Usually followers of this school think that you ought to introduce rules (such as inheritance taxes or even capital taxes) that redetermine the initial endowments $(\overline{X}^1, \overline{Y}^1, \ldots ; \overline{X}^2, \overline{Y}^2, \ldots)$. *After* this

3. Throughout capitalism's rise it was subjected also to the logically admissible countercriticism which held that a free market would give too little to the more-deserving aristocratic class.

has been done properly, competition has, so to speak, been equalized and with each man given a fair start, each is free to elbow his way in the race as best he can. Incentives are thought to be undistorted, and any resulting inequality is of the legitimate variety.

There is something plausible about all this. And undoubtedly it fits in well with one of the diverse strands of Western (and particularly American) social thought. None the less, our previous analysis will show that such an initial redistribution can only under special circumstances be compatible with maximizing a nonshibboleth social welfare function.

First, there is the obvious point that the redistribution cannot (at least in a world of uncertainty) be once-and-for-all. The nineteenth century objection to the redistributing of wealth, which alleged that by the evening of the day of redistribution all the wealth would have gravitated back to its original owners, has some factual validity to it. But, of course, to Marshall's contemporaries its implication for policy was that each day some new judicious redistributive tax would have to be enacted. And since people could learn this *ex post*, it could hardly avoid having some *ex ante* distortions of incentives. Hence, some pragmatic compromise between "equity" and "efficiency" would be in order.

Second, and more relevant to our discussion, is the fact that the original redistribution must be determined with the final equilibrium configuration in mind. Except in the singular symmetric case where all men will *always* be exactly alike,[4] you cannot stipulate an arithmetic rule of initial quotas and then, no matter how crops or other data change, leave it to the competitive market to determine the detailed outcome. To see this, re-examine the argument above (51 per cent, 10 per cent, 39 per cent) in the case of a family.

What does this mean specifically for policy? It means that just before the final equilibrium is struck, you must introduce lump-sum transfers (either of abstract purchasing power or of $\overline{X}$, $\overline{Y}$ endowments) that ensure ending up with equal social marginal utilities.[5] Of course,

4. How could John Stuart Mill, a rather sentimental do-gooder, have believed that once you started men with equal education, each should be free to gain as much inequality of wealth as competition would permit? When you remember that he swallowed the environmentalist view of the nature of man held by his father and by Bentham, according to which all men would *then* be alike, you see that he did not expect there would be any considerable degree of inequality. However, it is precisely this symmetry condition on the nature of man that most inequalitarians deny. So they stress (1) the ethical merits for its own sake of the competitive struggle, (2) the pragmatic incentive and efficiency problem, and (3) the ethical deservingness of the group that gets wealth.

5. You must do this not to please me but to make sense of the statement that you are realizing the ethically specified social optimum possible under the given conditions.

if you have great prophetic vision so you can guess in advance where the final equilibrium will be, the expression "just before" can be interpreted to be compatible with an "initial" redistribution. And if you face steady, repeating conditions, the time distinction disappears: then in each period, you will know from earlier periods, what lump-sum redistribution is needed to realize the optimum. The technical point to be stressed is my earlier proof that no prior allocation of endowments or "rule" for so doing can be counted on to be uniformly optimal whatever the accompanying conditions of technology and tastes.

A third and final point. I prefer to think of the ultimate lump-sum transfers as taking place in terms of abstract purchasing power. This can include as a special case any redistribution in kind of endowments of the form $(\overline{X}, \overline{Y}, \ldots)$. However, if we examine the reasons for undesired income inequalities, we find that they are often associated with personal qualities that literally cannot be transferred among individuals in a lump-sum way. Consider, for example, Bing Crosby's larynx, which makes him a millionaire while I starve. Can you give me his larynx? Of course not. But, you may argue, we can give you a property-right share in the earnings of his larynx. True, in part. However, under our system of jurisprudence, where property rights in men and slaves is severely restricted, you are limited in making such personal-wealth transfers. Still more important is the following fact. Crosby's brain and will are needed to direct his larynx; without regard to legal restrictions, there is literally *no lump-sum way* that you can transfer to me 100 per cent or 50 per cent property ownership in his voice; such a transfer *must* distort his decisions in a way that is incompatible with lump-sum transfers.

There are numerous less fundamental pragmatic objections to transfers in kind. Society taxes an estate in dollars;[6] it does not decide that Henry Ford's gold watch should go to John Doakes for him to use or sell.

For all these reasons, I prefer to write each man's final budget equation in the form

$$P_x X^i + P_y Y^i + \ldots = P_x \overline{X}^i + P_y \overline{Y}^i + \ldots + L^i$$

where L^i is an algebraic lump-sum transfer term that society can theoretically allocate so as to achieve a prescribed ethical optimum.

VII. Regular Properties of Social Indifference Contours

Our digression of the last section can be summarized by reasserting the requirement that incomes are always to be allocated (by

6. In imperfect capital markets there are problems and distortions arising from the need to liquidate assets.

lump-sum devices) among the family or group so as to keep the social welfare function at a maximum through the device of keeping the social (ordinal) utility of every person's last dollar equal as in Equation (2).

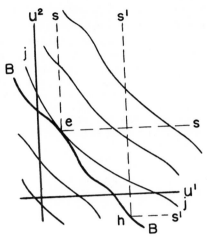

FIGURE II

The tangency point *e* gives the highest level of social welfare attainable along the Pareto utility frontier *BB*. Here the ratio of each man's social marginal utility of income (or any good) equals the marginal rate at which one's utility can be efficiently substituted for the other's.

Figure II redraws Ib to show what this achieves. Plotting $f[u^1,u^2, \ldots]$ = various constants gives us new indifference contours in the ordinal-utilities plane. (Because of the arbitrariness of any cardinal indicator of ordinal utility, these have no particular convexity: by a monotonic renumbering of utility we can stretch Figure II's indifference contours into any convexity we please.) Where is the point on the utility frontier *BB* that maximizes the prescribed social welfare function? Obviously the tangency point *e* where the frontier touches but does not cross the highest attainable contour of welfare. This checks with (2) since the arithmetic slope of the indifference contour is easily seen to be $(\partial U/\partial u^1)/(\partial U/\partial u^2)$, and since with a little greater difficulty we can verify that the slope of the utility frontier must equal the ratio of the two men's marginal utilities of income (or of any other good).[7]

Granting this utopian condition of optimal transfer, what can

7. Note that all these conditions are intrinsically ordinal in content and remain invariant under admissible monotonic stretchings of *U*, of u^1, or of u^2.

we infer about family or group demand? Specifically, let us observe all money going out from the family to the market, and observe the *totals* of all goods demanded at prevailing market prices. We need not be observing how the money and goods are being divided up within the group at any time. Then the following basic theorem of revealed group preference can be stated:

Theorem: (a) If each group member's demand and indifference contours have the conventional "regular" convexity, and (b) if the social welfare function is defined to have similar regular convexity properties,[8] and (c) if within the group optimal lump-sum transfers are always made, then it follows:

(1) there will result observable demand totals that are functions of market prices and total income alone, and (2) that these demand functions will have all the Slutsky-Hicks or revealed preference properties of any single consumer's demand, and (3) there will exist a set of indifference contours relating the totals $X, Y, \ldots$ that has all the regular properties of any individual's contours and which we can pretend a single mind is engaged in maximizing.

Figure III draws the resulting community or social indifference curves. Unlike the Scitovsky curves, these can never intersect, being

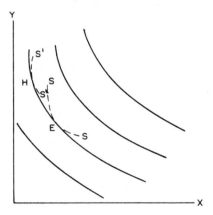

FIGURE III

The regularly convex contours of maximized social welfare provide us with "community indifference contours." These differ from the Scitovsky contours in that they have all the regular nonintersecting properties of individual indifference contours. The social contour through a point like E, corresponding to a point like e in Figure II, necessarily lies inside the Scitovsky contour SS generated by the locus ses in Figure II, being the inner envelope of the family of curves like $S'HS'$ or SES.

8. This is a diminishing marginal rate of substitution and roughly means: as you take away equal amounts of a good from one man, you must give increasing amounts to another if social welfare is to stay constant.

only a one-parameter infinity of curves. To be able to prove that these contours exist with the conventional curvature and non-intersecting properties is equivalent to proving our theorem. Note that as external observers, we can "see" at best what is shown in Figure III; we do not see Figure II or Figure Ib. From external observation alone, we are unable to tell whether our family consists of one or two or n persons. Nor have we any way of knowing that within the family decisions are really made by decentralized decision-making and utopian transfers. What we can infer is this: the observable data behave as if they came from a regular indifference field.

How is the theorem proved? Economists with bold intuition may feel it is obvious and needs no proof. Such confidence can come from ignorance: often we rashly make conjectures and think them theorems, even though they are false. If, therefore, we try in this case to analyze what our intuition seems to be telling us, I think it will amount to something like the following: Adam Smith's invisible hand seems so often to be vindicated by competitive price behavior that we use this doctrine as a heuristic line of reasoning. When we pursue these considerations in enough detail, we are on our way to giving a rigorous proof that is free of all teleology, and we also begin to perceive the necessity of some of the theorem's separate hypotheses.

Rigorous proof can be briefly sketched. First, we write down what is meant by the regular convexity assumptions (a) and (b) of the theorem. Express U in terms of each good separately, so that

$$U = f[u^1(X^1, Y^1, \ldots), u^2(X^2, Y^2, \ldots), \ldots] = F(X^1, Y^1, \ldots, X^2, Y^2 \ldots)$$

and assume it has the following convexity property. If A represents one configuration of *all* goods, and B another, with C being some weighted average of them so that $C = wA + (1 - w)B$, where w is any positive fraction — then $F(A) = F(B)$ implies $F(C) \geqslant f(A)$. This regularity assumption is stronger than realism can justify. (E.g., rational men often have indifference curves that are not convex to the origin.) It also implies a restriction on the admissible class of social ethical norms. However, to save space, I shall not go beyond this popular regularity assumption. Our task is to show that there exists a social welfare function that depends upon the totals of goods alone, $U = W(X, Y, \ldots)$, and whose contours are our new kind of "community or social indifference contours" with all the nice regularity properties of individual's indifference contours.

After devising some straightforward but lengthy proofs of the theorem, I realized that the beautiful Hicks theorem on composite goods will do the trick in a couple of simple steps. First, we note that $U = f[u^1,u^2, \ldots] = F(X^1,Y^1, \ldots ,X^2,Y^2, \ldots)$ is going to be truly maximized in any $(P_x,P_y, \ldots ,I = I^1 + I^2 + \ldots)$ situation. Now think of each $X^1,X^2, \ldots$ as having a separate price $p_x{}^1,p_x{}^2, \ldots$ but with each of these prices held constant and equal to the consumer market price $P_x = P_x{}^1 = P_x{}^2 = \ldots$. Similarly for Y or any good. We note that F regarded as a function of *all separate goods* has the curvature properties of regular indifference contours, and it therefore generates well-behaved separate demand functions of the form

$$X^1 = D_x{}^1(P_x{}^1,P_x{}^2, \ldots ,P_y{}^1,P_y{}^2, \ldots ,I), \text{ etc.}$$

These are definitely not the demand functions of any single family member; they are what his demand might be if family welfare were maximized and if his goods had different prices than the same goods had for other family members.

However, holding $P_x{}^1 = P_x{}^2 = \ldots P_x$ meets the conditions for defining a Hicksian composite good $X = X^1 + X^2 + \ldots$ or $P_x(X^1 + X^2 + \ldots)$. So we know from *Value and Capital*, pages 33–34 and 312–13, that these composite commodities have *all* the usual Slutsky-Hicks demand properties. Then working backwards from the fundaments of revealed preference,[9] we deduce the existence of a well-behaved family of contours defined in terms of the totals $(X,Y, \ldots)$. This essentially completes the proof.[1]

To keep our newly derived community indifference contours distinct from the Scitovsky-type community indifference contours, we might call our new ones the *social welfare contours*.[2]

---

9. P. A. Samuelson, *Foundations of Economic Analysis*, p. 116.
1. My colleague, Robert Solow, has suggested the following simple alternative proof. Consider two situations A and B which have totals that do lie on the same $U = F$ contour. It is feasible (but probably not optimal) to consider a third point which puts each man at C halfway between these points. Then $F(A) = F(B)$ implies $F(C) \geq F(A)$, and since the best point must give a higher U than will the feasible $F(C)$, it follows that U at every intermediate point between A and B must be better than or as good as at A or B. This proves the desired convexity property. Note that this proof fully applies to the more general case where government provides collective goods which enter simultaneously into every man's consumption. Cf. P. A. Samuelson, "The Pure Theory of Public Expenditure," reprinted in this volume as Chap. 92; note that in the notation of that paper, we can define a set of social preference contours $U = W(X_1, \ldots ,X_n,X_{n+1}, \ldots .X_{n+r})$ with all the usual convexity properties.
2. By comparing Figures II and III, the reader can relate these different concepts, proving that the social welfare contours cannot lie outside the Scitovsky minimum-requirements contours. Indeed, if through every point on jj of Figure II you draw a box like ses, then you will find that the welfare contour through E of Figure III is necessarily the inner envelope of the resulting one-parameter family of Scitovsky contours of the type SES.

VIII. Perfect Competition and Bliss

How can one use these new social or community indifference contours? Various applications will be presented in subsequent publications. Let me simply in conclusion point out some important considerations suggested by this analysis.

Does perfect competition lead to bliss even under the technological conditions of constant returns to scale? We know that there is nothing in laissez faire that guarantees the proper ethical weighting of dollar votes in the market place as expressed in condition (2) above. We, therefore, reask the question: Using optimal lump-sum reallocations of initial endowments $(\overline{X}^1, \overline{X}^2, \ldots, \overline{Y}^1, \overline{Y}^2, \ldots)$ or of abstract purchasing power, can we be sure that the device of perfect competition can be counted on to lead to *the optimum?*

Immediately, various objections suggest themselves: decreasing costs (including all the momentous issues of product differentiation and welfare optima which this entails), external economies or diseconomies on the technological or consumption side, knowledge imperfections and uncertainty, irrational or improper consumer tastes (including seller-induced as well as spontaneous changes in taste), contrived scarcities, improper convexity of the individual indifference contours, and improper convexity of the social welfare function $U = f[u^1, u^2, \ldots]$. But let us waive all these. Our analysis suggests still another flaw in the pricing mechanism that seems never to have been mentioned in the literature. It also answers some questions of sixty years ago and of the early 1930's when the late Abraham Wald[3] tried to prove the existence and uniqueness of competitive equilibrium.

Recall Wicksell's[4] well-founded objection to the view that competitive equilibrium must represent the optimum. What about the admitted case in which competitive supply and demand curves intersect more than once? Obviously, both cannot be *the* optimum; Wicksell thought this should alert us to the possibility or virtually certain fact that neither represents an optimum.

Does this possibility of multiple equilibrium still hold when we assume optimal interpersonal distributions of income are always being made so that (2) will always be satisfied. Wald, following Schlesinger and many other writers, writes price ratios as single-valued functions of all market totals. This is simply illegitimate in general, and in point of fact Walras did not rely on such a device. But what has all

3. A Wald, "On Some Systems of Equations of Mathematical Economics," *Econometrica*, Vol. 19 (1951), pp. 368–403, a translation of a German paper of the 1930's.

4. K. Wicksell, *Lectures on Political Economy*, Vol. 1 (1934 English translation), p. 75.

my present analysis been for if not to justify this assumption of Wald in the special case where optimal interpersonal lump-sum allocations are being made! Indeed, in such a case, as we have just seen, the price ratios behave exactly *as if* they obey all the weak and strong axioms of individual preference; therefore, we have for the first time justified Wald's assuming for total market behavior the so-called "weak axiom of revealed preference."

Now Wald proves something very powerful indeed: he not only proves the *existence* of a competitive equilibrium, but with his weak axiom he is even able to deduce its *uniqueness*, which is something much stronger. At first one might think that this rules out the multiple intersection of the offer curves of the different individuals if these offer curves have been generated from optimally redistributed initial endowment points. But this can be shown to be a premature and false inference. All that can be properly inferred is that of all the multiple equilibria that may take place, at most one will correspond to the final equality of marginal social significance of money to all parties.

Is there any reason why the proper optimal intersection, out of the multiplicity of intersections, must be a stable one? It is easy to supply examples in which the answer is shown to be No; i.e., we can construct examples in which the proper ethical intersection is necessarily an *unstable* intersection of the offer curves generated by the rectified initial endowment points. Because of this instability, it would be manifestly impossible in the actual world to keep the slightest disturbances (which are ever present) from sending the market equilibrium away from the ethical optimum point. I conclude that in such a case the mechanisms of competitive markets might not be a useful administrative device for attaining the social optimum.[5]

5. It can be shown that all is not hopeless. There is more than one initial endowment point which will generate offer curves going through the bliss point. Usually it doesn't matter which of the infinity of such initial points we use. But in this pathological instability case it does matter. If we correctly diagnosed the difficulty, we might contrive to select an initial endowment point sufficiently near the final bliss point to assure us of a single stable intersection. Best of all, of course, would be to make our initial point the final bliss point, but it is the essence of the administrative or computing problem that we are unable initially to make such a perfect guess. (An interesting interpretation can be given of this pathological phenomenon of instability: the effect of instantaneously optimal lump-sum redistribution is not only in the direction of "equity," but it is as well a stabilizing force.)

IX. Final Summary

1. It is shown that the various defenses which have been offered for the use of community indifference curves are all open to some serious questioning.

2. The Scitovsky community indifference contours are shown to be "minimum social requirements" contours of total goods needed to achieve a certain prescribed level of ordinal well-being for all. The dual properties of the Figures Ia and Ib, relating points in the commodity and ordinal-utility spaces, are demonstrated.

3. By means of mathematical reasoning or by the demonstration of intersections of Scitovsky contours, a fundamental impossibility theorem is proved: Except where income elasticities are all unity and tastes are absolutely uniform for all, it is proved to be absolutely impossible to solve for unique market price ratios in function of market *totals;* hence, we must lack collective indifference curves capable of generating group demand.

4. All this is shown to entail the nonoptimality of any shibboleth rule which once and for all and independently of changes in technology and taste data predetermines the initial distribution of income or endowments.

5. Since most "individual" demand is really "family" demand, the argument can be made that such family demands have been shown to have none of the nice properties of modern consumption theory. However, if within the family there can be assumed to take place an optimal reallocation of income so as to keep each member's dollar expenditure of equal ethical worth, then there can be derived for the whole family a set of well-behaved indifference contours relating the totals of what it consumes: the family can be said to *act as if* it maximizes such a group preference function.

6. The same argument will apply to all of society if optimal reallocations of income can be assumed to keep the ethical worth of each person's marginal dollar equal. By means of Hicks's composite commodity theorem and by other considerations, a rigorous proof is given that the newly defined social or community indifference contours have the regularity properties of ordinary individual preference contours (nonintersection, convexity to the origin, etc.).

7. This analysis is used to clear up the ancient question of what multiplicity of market equilibria does to our interpretation of the optimality of the competitive mechanism. Our analysis gives a first justification to the Wald hypothesis that market totals satisfy the "weak axiom" of individual preference. The resulting uniqueness of

the equilibrium demonstration of Wald is shown to be subject to the possibility that the resulting equilibrium point is one of multiple supply-demand intersections generated by the contrived initial reallocation point. Only one of these multiple points is ethically optimal, but that one could be an unstable intersection point. If so, the market mechanism will not be a good administrative device for reaching the ethical optimum — unless the difficulty is diagnosed and rectified by selection of some other proper initial endowment point. (This does not rule out still other familiar instances in which the competitive market mechanism is computationally not optimal.)

8. Future publications will show how these social indifference contours can be used to throw light on international trade policy and on the methodological problems of the older and newer welfare economics. The foundation is laid for the "economics of a good society."

PAUL A. SAMUELSON.

MASSACHUSETTS INSTITUTE OF TECHNOLOGY

79

Theories of Welfare Economics. By HLA MYINT. The London School of Economics and Political Science. Longmans, Green & Company, London. 1948. xiv + 240 pp.

This book will challenge the interest of economic theorists everywhere. Dr. Myint has been privileged to study under two great teachers, Hayek and Hicks, and he has brought to his researches an obviously judicious, analytical, and articulate intelligence. The result can be regarded as a fair sample of modern Anglo-Saxon economic thought—that body of written and unwritten analysis, recently infused by Austrian blood and lightly kissed by mathematics. In appraising the book, I shall pay it the compliment of judging it in the unsparing fashion appropriate to an important contribution to modern thought.

Myint attempts to give a survey of welfare economics since the time of Adam Smith and also attempts to find out what types of welfare economics are likely to prove most useful for the purpose of practical policy. The first third of the book deals with the classical writers prior to the so-called marginal revolution of the 1870s. Part II, which is about half the book in length, deals with the neo-classical views on welfare economics, including Pareto and up through Pigou's *Economics of Welfare.* The final brief section brings in the broader philosophical questionings of Knight, J. M. Clark and others as to whether the preferences in terms of which people act in the market-place have ethical validity, and whether formal economic theorising about behaviour is very fruitful.

About Part III's philosophical inquiries, I have little to say. Myint is judicious and he has read widely; the topics covered are ones upon which views differ greatly and at many points a different synthesis of judgment would be possible. In some ways, the most interesting part of ethics is what is left out—all *inter-personal* normative comparisons. At the beginning of the book Myint tells us that this is not part of " economic welfare " but belongs to the field of " *general* social welfare which cannot be analysed in purely scientific and quantitative terms " (p. xi). *Ergo,* the subject is almost never discussed.

Now at the time when Lionel Robbins wrote his *Essay on the Nature and Significance of Economic Science*, it was probably necessary for students steeped in the traditions of Edgeworth, Cannan, Marshall, and Pigou to divest themselves of the quaint notion that there exists a quantity of social utility, made up of a sum of the cardinal satisfactions of different individuals, and of about the same degree of objectivity as the observation that price and quantity are inversely related along a market demand curve. But this does not justify the belief on the part of anyone that policy prescriptions can be made independent of normative judgments concerning different people ; and that there exists no analytical field of welfare economics concerned with the deductions of the implications of various arbitrarily given ethical precepts (i.e., Bergson " social welfare functions "). For a brief period, those who took their Robbins too literally grasped at the straw of a " new welfare economics " which was to be independent of inter-personal ethical elements. But freed from the obscurities of geometry and Paretian French, the new welfare economics stands revealed as being merely a set of *incomplete necessary* conditions whose whole *raison d'être* disappears if the additional ethical conditions are not adjoined.

No reader of Myint is likely to gain from the book many notions as to what the above paragraph is all about, or how to go about relating the " old " to the " new " welfare economics. Nonetheless, Part II, particularly Chapter VII dealing with " The Theory of the General Optimum " along the lines of Pareto and Hicks, will probably prove to be the most valuable part of the book to the student of intermediate and advanced economic theory. I myself most enjoyed the retrieving of Henry Sidgwick from out of Marshall's corona ; Myint brings out the little-known fact that Pigou's welfare economics traces back to Sidgwick almost more than to Marshall.

Aside from giving samples of Marshall's " Victorian morality ", Myint devotes the longest chapter of the book to an approving discussion of the " Marshallian Surplus Analysis ". He seems to regard this as " practical ", or at least more so than the analysis of Pigou and Pareto ; but just why Myint thinks it practical, I cannot find out. This is a realm in which Marshall was not only vague but full of blunders : much of what he says is nonsense and is unsaid at other parts of the book ; and the fact that Marshall avoids some of the errors of his followers is a tribute to him and not to his brain-child, consumer's surplus. And yet this doctrine is usually regarded as Marshall's most important analytical contribution—a damning and cruel verdict, indeed. Only Hicks has given a defensible formulation of consumer's surplus and in his hands it becomes nothing more nor less than a particular reformulation of indifference loci : the single important purpose of the concept is to help make decisions *in the large*—i.e., to decide whether it would be better to take a large finite (rather than small) step away from a particular position ; and to this aspect of the problem Myint devotes almost none of his thirty pages. Instead he reproduces, without apparent disapproval, Figures 30, 31 and 32 from Marshall's *Principles*, designed to show that increasing cost industries should usually be taxed in order to expand decreasing cost industries. Yet Myint is clearly aware that these unwarrantedly neglect producer's surplus in arriving at their conclusion, and he is also aware that in Figure 33 Marshall in effect points out the errors in reasoning of Figure 31.

Part I impressed me as the least satisfactory part of the book. Myint argues that modern economists believe that efficient allocation of resources was the " central problem " of classical economics ; he argues that this was not their central problem ; and if it was not, he asks what was ? After casting about for an answer, he comes up with the thesis that their " central problem " was that of raising the technical productivity of the economy, and that their labour theory of value predisposed them to a man v. nature view of the economic problem rather than to a tightening up of the efficiency of the economy by means of marginal conditions. He warns against the anthropomorphic sin of reading into earlier writers the analysis of present-day economic theory.

He works hard to establish this thesis, desperately hard, and succeeds in giving it a certain superficial plausibility. But upon closer examination of his dialectics and after chasing down his references, I found it increasingly unconvincing. There was no one central problem of classical economics, and to knock one out as pretender does not pave the way for establishing another on the throne. The author is so carried away with his own argument that he even ends up with the conclusion that Smith's afterthought on " productive labour ", one of his few belated quasi-borrowings from the physiocrats, is the most important part of his doctrines.

As I chased down the author's references, again and again I felt his thesis led him to read things *out* of his authors that were there. For example, Smith did realise and state the consumer's surplus arising from exchange ; secondly his analysis of the advantages of the division of labour can be interpreted (and in effect has been by Ohlin) in terms of the later Hicks-Kaldor diagrams (p. 113). Smith did cheerfully acquiesce to Bentham's criticism of his own uncharacteristic leniency toward the laws of usury. And as Myint himself clearly shows, the classical theory of comparative advantage is a perfect example of modern welfare economics ; and the classical rent theory, telling how new units of labour will be added to different plots of land, is another such example, beautifully illuminated by the Hicks-Kaldor construction.

In short one ends up with the feeling that there is a worse sin than the anthropomorphic one of reading modern analysis into older writers' works. There is in addition the sophisticated-anthropormophic sin of not recognising the equivalent content in older writers because they do not use the terminology and symbols of the present.

Space does not permit a more thorough documentation of my skepticism concerning Part I. When a man sets out to prove that England is not an island or that Lytton Strachey wrote the *Economic Consequences of the Peace*, perhaps we should judge him not by how persuasive is his total argument but by whether he gives us a run for our money ; by whether his points are at least *near-* rather than *far-*fetched. But then there is the sterner view that *Dogmengeschichte* is a game only worth playing if it is played very well indeed. From any viewpoint, *Theories of Welfare Economics* is a distinguished contribution to economic theory.

PAUL A. SAMUELSON.

80

Theoretical Welfare Economics. By J. DE V. GRAAFF. (London: Cambridge
University Press, 1957. Pp. x + 178. 22s. 6d.)

OF the many books that are now available on welfare economics, I judge
this to be one of the best. It was written as a thesis by a brilliant South
African, who left his impress on the Cambridge environment but who subsequently revealed a preference to be a non-economist. We are indebted to
those friends of Graaff who rescued the work from the obscurity of a library
vault and got it published in book form. (Although dated 1957, the book
gives internal evidence of having been largely completed around 1951. For
example, only perfunctory notice is taken of Arrow's important book, and all
references to Little are to the articles that preceded the appearance of Little's
book.)

Modern welfare economics has suffered from pretentiousness. So in this
rather advanced discussion, Graaff is careful to lean over backwards—meticu-
lously pointing out the limitations of his findings. His discussion of each
point is brief, almost too brief. Twelve chapters and four mathematical
appendixes are packed into 170 small pages. The variety of subjects can
be judged from a listing: technology (principally external effects); tastes
(utility frontiers of the Pareto type, Bergson inter-personal social-welfare
economics); indivisibility; uncertainty; foreign trade (optimal tariffs);
marginal cost pricing; social income and index numbers.

While Graaff's discussion is not elementary, those just beginning their
study of welfare economics will probably feel they are getting something
from the book. For the most part the sexy symbols of mathematics are confined to Appendix ghettos or to footnotes. Even the theorist without much
interest in welfare economics *per se* will benefit from the book—by seeing how
Graaff grapples with problems of externality, indivisibility, uncertainty and
other pathological phenomena.

Where does Graaff fit into the history of welfare economics? Since the
days of Smith and before, economists have felt that perfect competition—
when conditions for it are right—does accomplish something. By the time
of Marshall and Walras, they had begun to realise that the initial " distribution of income " had to be ethically right if the competitive mechanism were
to get you to the best state of the world. A little later, economists began to
realise that they could not prove, from inside of technical economics and by
the usual tools of science, that one ethical evaluation is " better " than another. Pareto at the turn of the century sensed (but perhaps never rigorously stated) the theorem that by means of lump-sum redistributions the
device of perfect competition could in ideal circumstances be used by
any ethical observer (who respected individual's tastes) to compute *his* best

state of the world.   This is the nub of what it is that is valid in Smith's Invisible Hand doctrine.

An ethical observer who respects people's tastes could not call a situation an optimum if there exists a movement from it which will make everyone feel better off.   So it is a necessary (but not sufficient) condition for his social optimum that it fall at a point on what we might call Edgeworth's " generalised contract locus " (both in a production and consumption sense)—or on the set of " Pareto-optimal utility frontier points."   Pareto, for reasons that I have never found convincing, tried to elevate these *necessary* conditions for an optimum into a *wertfrei* system of " new welfare economics."   By the mid-1930s, Lerner's writings had rediscovered the content of Pareto's necessary conditions.   And around 1938, Bergson (and I following him) had straightened out the interrelations: first, between the old, hedonistic welfare economics and one involving general, interpersonal comparisons, and, second, between partial, necessary conditions for a normative optimum and complete necessary and sufficient conditions.   In 1939 Kaldor and Hicks rediscovered the Pareto urge to elevate into a new welfare economics the subset of necessary optimality conditions which can be written independently of a social-welfare function.   In addition to a technical criticism or correction by Scitovsky, there was considerable criticism in the war and post-war years of this attempt—with Little's book typifying the general disillusionment with the claims of welfare economists.   Arrow's fundamental 1951 book breaks ground into the important realm of political philosophy and mathematical politics.   It proves the non-existence of a reasonable " constitutional function " or " method-of-compromising-and-scoring-all-possible-ballots function."   I believe such a constitutional function ought not to be confused with a Bergson social-welfare function, which makes interpersonal ordinal comparisons among a *given* set of individuals' tastes.

Graaff is in the mainstream of Bergson's kind of welfare analysis—which is no doubt why I found him so sage on point after point.   He takes for granted, in rather a merciless way, the untenability of most *simpliste* versions of welfare economics and proceeds with the business at hand of analysing such realistic difficulties as externalities, indivisibilities, and the like.   It is partly a matter of temperament that his findings are stated in a somewhat nihilistic manner: one who accepts the universe in a cheerful David Hume way might state the same conclusions and yet give a quite different impression.

Among arguments so numerous and detailed, the slips are remarkably scarce.   Whereas a few of Graaff's arguments might have benefited from linear programming developments of recent years, it is astonishing how up to date the discussion reads.   Personally, I should have been willing to sacrifice a few pages of the now overworked optimal tariff for a longer and more constructive attack on the problem of " the feasible optimum " along the lines of Ramsey and Boiteux.   (I do not call this the economics of the " second best," because it is the economics of the feasible first-best.)   But we must all be grateful for this able last testament of Graaff, and lament that economics has lost so able a mind.

PAUL A. SAMUELSON

Massachusetts Institute of Technology,
Cambridge, Massachusetts.

81

COMMENT ON WELFARE ECONOMICS

What is the most useful supplement that I can provide to Professor Boulding's brilliant survey of welfare economics?[1] Upon reflection, it appears to me best to provide some informal notes for the reader. For welfare economics is a rather complicated subject, with, however, the one saving grace that, once understood, it turns out to be a fairly simple theory after all.

1. The "new welfare economics" can have two entirely different meanings: (1) the now-admitted-to-be-misguided claim that welfare economics can be solidly based on objective economic criteria, independently of ethical notions about interpersonal distributions of income; (2) a systematic way of introducing from outside of economics various ethical norms (as embodied technically in what is called a social welfare function) — and so ordering the exposition of the conditions for an optimum that we first state those which require only the weakest postulates, and which therefore hold for the widest possible set of cases, and only later introduce the narrower and more restrictive hypotheses.

I know of no present-day defender of the first and narrower version of welfare economics.[2] One by one, each writer who has not remained

---

[1]Kenneth E. Boulding, "Welfare Economics," in *A Survey of Contemporary Economics*, Vol. II, edited by Bernard F. Haley (Homewood, Ill.: Richard D. Irwin, Inc., 1952).

[2]To understand the 1939 Kaldor and Hicks articles, we must remember that Kaldor is answering Harrod's 1938 assertion that the repeal of the Corn Laws can be justified only "if individuals are treated in some sense as equals." . . . "If the incomparability of utility to different individuals is strictly pressed, not only are the prescriptions of

silent has explained the modified sense in which the doctrines are to be understood.[3]

2. Without norms, normative statements are impossible. At some point welfare economics must introduce ethical welfare functions from outside of economics. Which set of ends is relevant is decidedly *not* a scientific question of economics. This should dispel the notion that by a social welfare function is meant some one, unique, and privileged set of ends. Any prescribed set of ends is grist for the economist's unpretentious deductive mill, and often he can be expected to reveal that the prescribed ends are incomplete and inconsistent. The social welfare function is a concept as broad and empty as language itself — and as necessary. Whether we call it W, or G, or describe it in words is, of course, immaterial.

Note that ethical notions concerning the relative deservingness of different individuals are by their nature completely ordinal. There is no necessary connection with cardinal measurable utility of the individual, or with the addibility of the independent utilities of different individuals into some grand national total. Except for a few utilitarians, drunk on poorly understood post-Newtonian mathematical moonshine, I can find in the ethical writings of recorded cultures scarcely any importance attached to the special social welfare functions of additive cardinal utility.

3. It is agreed then that the Pareto-Lerner necessary conditions for an optimum must be supplemented by distributional considerations if a sufficient set of conditions for an optimum and for policy prescriptions is to be given. But so long as we (1) do later supplement them, (2) assume that social welfare goes up when each and every individual becomes better off, and (3) assume that more goods and less inputs are always desirable, we can formulate these conditions independently of the interpersonal conditions. In summary:

Necessary Marginal Conditions for an Optimum. Between any two variables, the marginal rates of substitution must be (subjectively) equal for all individuals, and (technically) equal for all alternative processes, with the common technical and subjective ratios being equivalent; otherwise there exists a physically attainable position that makes everyone better off.

---

the welfare school ruled out, but all prescriptions whatever." All the discussants suffered from a bad case of the jitters as a result of Lionel Robbins' important 1932 *Essay on the Nature and Significance of Economic Science,* which correctly pointed out that ethical ends were ascientific by their very nature, but which lent itself to the false interpretation that welfare economics was therefore without content.

[3]The only remaining divergence of belief seems to be on pragmatic tactical questions: e.g., shall all changes which *could* make everyone better off but which might in fact hurt some people be made mandatory in the expectation or hope that the cumulative effects of following such a rule will be better (for all or some) than if some other rule is followed? Shall we set up a rule of unanimous consent for any *new* change so that compensating bribes must be in fact paid? To answer such questions we must go beyond economics.

By calling some variables inputs and some outputs, or inputs and outputs of different time periods, etc., this rule can be expanded into many separate rules, including that of price exactly equal to marginal cost, discounted marginal productivity proportionalities, etc. In reasonably efficient societies, these necessary conditions are not very important because they are already near to being realized. But in less fortunate societies, their violation may be very important. Therefore, I dissent from much of the recent skepticism and calumny that those marginal conditions have evoked.[4]

[4]Part of this distrust stems from the correct feeling that it may not be feasible to price all goods at marginal costs with losses financed out of optimal lump-sum taxes; or that with many of the necessary optimum conditions violated, it is not ideal to have any particular subset of them alone satisfied. These considerations suggest that, instead of throwing out the baby with the bathwater, we solve the theoretical problem of the "feasible optimum" and deduce the relevant policy considerations.

PART XI

Dynamics and Statics of Income Determination

82

INTERACTIONS BETWEEN THE MULTIPLIER ANALYSIS AND THE PRINCIPLE OF ACCELERATION

FEW economists would deny that the "multiplier" analysis of the effects of governmental deficit spending has thrown some light upon this important problem. Nevertheless, there would seem to be some ground for the fear that this extremely simplified mechanism is in danger of hardening into a dogma, hindering progress and obscuring important subsidiary relations and processes. It is highly desirable, therefore, that model sequences, which operate under more general assumptions, be investigated, possibly including the conventional analysis as a special case.[1]

In particular, the "multiplier," using this term in its usual sense, does *not* pretend to give the relation between total national income induced by governmental spending and the original amount of money spent. This is clearly seen by a simple example. In an economy (not necessarily our own) where any dollar of governmental deficit spending would result in a hundred dollars less of private investment than would otherwise have been undertaken, the ratio of total induced national income to the initial expenditure is overwhelmingly negative, yet the "multiplier" in the strict sense must be positive. The answer to the puzzle is simple. What the multiplier does give is the ratio of the total increase in the national income to the total amount of investment, governmental and private. In other words, it does *not* tell us how much is to be multiplied. The effects upon private investment are often regarded as tertiary influences and receive little systematic attention.

In order to remedy the situation in some measure, Professor Hansen has developed a new model sequence which ingeniously combines the multiplier analysis with that of the *acceleration* principle or *relation*. This is done by making additions to the national income consist of three components: (1) governmental deficit spending, (2) private consumption expenditure induced by previous public expenditure, and (3) induced

private investment, assumed according to the familiar acceleration principle to be proportional to the time increase of consumption. The introduction of the last component accounts for the novelty of the conclusions reached and also the increased complexity of the analysis.

A numerical example may be cited to illuminate the assumptions made. We assume governmental deficit spending of one dollar per unit period, beginning at some initial time and continuing thereafter. The marginal propensity to consume, a, is taken to be one-half. This is taken to mean that the consumption of any period is equal to one-half the national income of the previous period. Our last assumption is that induced private investment is proportional to the increase in consumption between the previous and the current period. This factor of proportionality or *relation*, β, is provisionally taken to be equal to unity; i.e., a time increase in consumption of one dollar will result in one dollar's worth of induced private investment.

In the initial period when the government spends a dollar for the first time, there will be no consumption induced from previous periods, and hence the addition to the national income will equal the one dollar spent. This will yield fifty cents of consumption expenditure in the second period, an increase of fifty cents over the consumption of the first period, and so according to the *relation* we will have fifty cents worth of induced private investment. Finally, we must add the new dollar of expenditure by the government. The national income of the second period must therefore total two dollars. Similarly, in the third period the national income would be the sum of one dollar of consumption, fifty cents induced private investment, and one dollar current governmental expenditure. It is clear that given the values of the marginal propensity to consume, a, and the *relation*, β, all succeeding national income levels can be easily computed in succession. This is done in detail in Table 1 and illustrated in Chart 1. It will be noted that the introduction of the acceleration principle causes our series to reach a peak at the 3rd year, a trough at the 7th, a peak at the 11th, etc. Such oscil-

[1] The writer, who has made this study in connection with his research as a member of the Society of Fellows at Harvard University, wishes to express his indebtedness to Professor Alvin H. Hansen of Harvard University at whose suggestion the investigation was undertaken.

TABLE I.—THE DEVELOPMENT OF NATIONAL INCOME AS A RESULT OF A CONTINUOUS LEVEL OF GOVERNMENTAL EXPENDITURE WHEN THE MARGINAL PROPENSITY TO CONSUME EQUALS ONE-HALF AND THE RELATION EQUALS UNITY

(Unit: one dollar)

Period	Current governmental expenditure	Current consumption induced by previous expenditure	Current private investment proportional to time increase in consumption	Total national income
1	1.00	0.00	0.00	1.00
2	1.00	0.50	0.50	2.00
3	1.00	1.00	0.50	2.50
4	1.00	1.25	0.25	2.50
5	1.00	1.25	0.00	2.25
6	1.00	1.125	−0.125 *	2.00
7	1.00	1.00	−0.125	1.875
8	1.00	0.9375	−0.0625	1.875
9	1.00	0.9375	0.00	1.9375
10	1.00	0.96875	0.03125	2.00
11	1.00	1.00	0.03125	2.03125
12	1.00	1.015625	0.015625	2.03125
13	1.00	1.015625	0.00	2.015625
14	1.00	1.0078125	−0.0078125	2.00
....	...	....	....	....

* Negative induced private investment is interpreted to mean that for the system as a whole there is *less* investment in this period than there otherwise would have been. Since this is a marginal analysis, superimposed implicitly upon a going state of affairs, this concept causes no difficulty.

latory behavior could not occur in the conventional model sequences, as will soon become evident.

For other chosen values of α and β similar model sequences can be developed. In Table 2 national income totals are given for various selected values of these coefficients. In the first column, for example, the marginal propensity to consume is assumed to be one-half, and the *relation* to be equal to zero. This is of special interest because it shows the conventional multiplier sequences to be special cases of the more general Hansen analysis. For this case no oscillations are possible. In the second column the oscillations in the national income are undamped and regular. In column three things are still worse; the oscillations are explosive, becoming larger and larger but always fluctuating around an "average value." In the fourth column the behavior is no longer oscillatory but is explosive upward approaching a compound interest rate of growth.

By this time the investigator is inclined to feel somewhat disorganized. A variety of quali-

tatively different results emerge in a seemingly capricious manner from minor changes in hypotheses. Worse than this, how can we be sure that for still different selected values of our coefficients new and stronger types of behavior will not emerge? Is it not even possible that if Table 2 were extended to cover more periods, new types of behavior might result for these selected coefficients?

Fortunately, these questions can be given a definite negative answer. Arithmetical methods cannot do so since we cannot try all possible values of the coefficients nor compute the endless terms of each sequence. Nevertheless, comparatively simple algebraic analysis can be applied which will yield all possible qualitative types of behavior and enable us to unify our results.

The national income at time t, Y_t, can be written as the sum of three components: (1) governmental expenditure, g_t, (2) consumption expenditure, C_t, and (3) induced private investment, I_t.

$$Y_t = g_t + C_t + I_t.$$

But according to the Hansen assumptions

$$C_t = \alpha Y_{t-1}$$
$$I_t = \beta [C_t - C_{t-1}] = \alpha\beta Y_{t-1} - \alpha\beta Y_{t-2}$$

and

$$g_t = 1.$$

Therefore, our national income can be rewritten

$$Y_t = 1 + \alpha[1 + \beta] Y_{t-1} - \alpha\beta Y_{t-2}.$$

CHART I.—GRAPHIC REPRESENTATION OF DATA IN TABLE I

(Unit: one dollar)

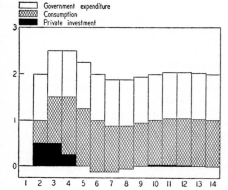

In words, if we know the national income for two periods, the national income for the following period can be simply derived by taking a weighted sum. The weights depend, of course, upon the values chosen for the marginal propensity to consume and for the *relation*.

This is one of the simplest types of difference equations, having constant coefficients and being of the second order. The mathematical details of its solution need not be entered upon here. Suffice it to say that its solution depends upon the roots — which in turn depend upon the coefficients a and β — of a certain equation.[1]

TABLE 2.—MODEL SEQUENCES OF NATIONAL INCOME FOR SELECTED VALUES OF MARGINAL PROPENSITY TO CONSUME AND RELATION

(Unit: one dollar)

Period	$a= .5$ $\beta = 0$	$a= .5$ $\beta = 2$	$a= .6$ $\beta = 2$	$a= .8$ $\beta = 4$
1	1.00	1.00	1.00	1.00
2	1.50	2.50	2.80	5.00
3	1.75	3.75	4.84	17.80
4	1.875	4.125	6.352	56.20
5	1.9375	3.4375	6.6256	169.84
6	1.9688 *	2.0313	5.3037	500.52
7	1.9844	.9141	2.5959	1,459.592
8	1.9922	− .1172	− .6918	4,227.704
9	1.9961	.2148	−3.3603	12,241.1216
.. ..	.....	......	....	....

* Table is correct to four decimal places.

It can be easily shown that the whole field of possible values of a and β can be divided into four regions, each of which gives qualitatively different types of behavior. In Chart 2 these regions are plotted. Each point in this diagram represents a selection of values for the marginal propensity to consume and the *relation*. Corresponding to each point there will be a model sequence of national income through time. The qualitative properties of this sequence depend upon whether the point is in Region A, B, C, or D.[2] The properties of each region can be briefly summarized.

[1] Actually, the solution can be written in the form

$$Y_t = \frac{1}{1-a} + a_1[x_1]^t + a_2[x_2]^t$$

where x_1 and x_2 are roots of the quadratic equation

$$x^2 - a[1+\beta]x + a\beta = 0,$$

and a_1 and a_2 are constants dependent upon the a's and β's chosen.

[2] Mathematically, the regions are demarcated by the conditions that the roots of the equation referred to in the pre-

Region A (relatively small values of the *relation*)

If there is a constant level of governmental expenditure through time, the national income will approach asymptotically a value $\frac{1}{1-a}$ times the constant level of governmental expenditure. A single impulse of expenditure, or any amount of expenditure followed by a complete cessation, will result in a gradual approach to the original zero level of national income. (It will be noted that the asymptote approached is identically that given by the Keynes-Kahn-Clark formula. Their analysis applies to points along the a axis and is subsumed under the more general Hansen analysis.) Perfectly periodic net governmental expenditure will result eventually in perfectly periodic fluctuations in national income.

Region B

A constant continuing level of governmental expenditure will result in damped oscillatory movements of national income, gradually approaching the asymptote $\frac{1}{1-a}$ times the constant level of government expenditure. (Cf. Table 1.) Governmental expenditure in a single or finite number of periods will result eventually in damped oscillations around the level of income zero. Perfectly regular periodic fluctuations in government expenditure will result eventually in fluctuations of income of the same period.

Region C

A constant level of governmental expenditure will result in *explosive*, ever increasing oscillations around an asymptote computed as above. (Cf. column 3 of Table 2.) A single impulse of expenditure or a finite number of expenditure impulses will result eventually in explosive oscillations around the level zero.

Region D (large values of the marginal propensity to consume and the *relation*)

A constant level of governmental expenditure will result in an ever increasing national income, eventually approaching a compound interest rate of growth. (Cf. column 4 of Table 2.) A

vious footnote be real or complex, greater or less than unity in absolute value.

CHART 2.—Diagram Showing Boundaries of Regions Yielding Different
Qualitative Behavior of National Income

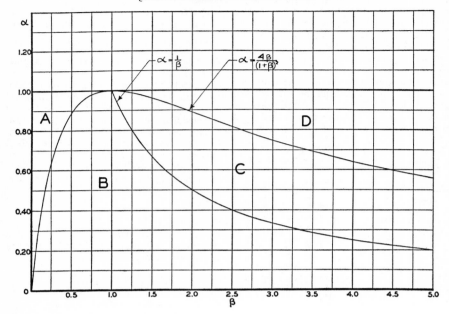

single impulse of net investment will likewise send the system up to infinity at a compound interest rate of growth. On the other hand, a single infinitesimal unit of disinvestment will send the system ever downward at an increasing rate. This is a highly unstable situation, but corresponds most closely to the pure case of pump-priming, where the total increase in national income bears no finite ratio to the original stimulus.

The limitations inherent in so simplified a picture as that presented here should not be overlooked.[1] In particular, it assumes that the marginal propensity to consume and the *relation* are constants; actually these will change with the level of income, so that this representation is strictly a *marginal* analysis to be applied to the study of small oscillations. Nevertheless, it is more general than the usual analysis. Contrary to the impression commonly held, mathematical methods properly employed, far from making economic theory more abstract, actually serve as a powerful liberating device enabling the entertainment and analysis of ever more realistic and complicated hypotheses.

[1] It may be mentioned in passing that the formal structure of our problem is identical with the model sequences of Lundberg, and the dynamic theories of Tinbergen. The present problem is so simple that it provides a useful introduction to the mathematical theory of the latter's work.

PAUL A. SAMUELSON

HARVARD UNIVERSITY

83

A SYNTHESIS OF THE PRINCIPLE OF ACCELERA-
TION AND THE MULTIPLIER

PAUL A. SAMUELSON
Harvard University

THE principle of acceleration is one of the few tools of business-cycle analysis whose importance is universally conceded. Carefully stated, it can be made to yield information concerning the movements of investment from a knowledge of the movements of consumption. In particular, cyclical fluctuations in the latter will yield intensified periodic fluctuations in investment. C. O. Hardy, Ragnar Frisch, and other critics have rightly pointed out that it is a single relation between two series and does not constitute a self-contained, determinate business-cycle theory. Fluctuations in consumption will yield fluctuations in investment, but how do the original fluctuations in consumption arise?

It can hardly be maintained that the original propounders of the principle were unaware of this fact. J. M. Ciark, for example, mentions explicitly that the volume of consumption demand is itself influenced by the level of investment through income payments to the factors producing investment goods. The following quotation will illustrate the point:

> For a full explanation, however, one must take account of factors acting in the reverse direction, namely, the fact that actual movements of consumer demand depend on the movements of purchasing power; and these in turn are governed by the rate of production in general, including that of capital equipment, and also that of durable consumption goods, such as housing and automobiles, to which the same essential principle applies.
>
> Thus, if we take as our initial fact a moderate decrease in the rate of growth of consumer demand (such as needs no particular explanation), this may result—with a lag—in a positive decline in rate of production of durable producers' or consumers' goods. This in turn reduces purchasing power, unless offset by opposite movements elsewhere, and results in a positive decrease in consumers' demand, presumably extended to more commodities than those originally affected. And this in turn further extends and intensifies the shrinkage in production of durable goods, etc. This may serve as

an answer to a criticism of this theory, made by C. O. Hardy before the American Statistical Association last December [1931], to the effect that the theory presupposes a cyclical alternation of expansions and contractions in consumer demand, and leaves these movements to be explained. As stated above, the actual contractions (and the more rapid expansions), if they do arise as original movements produced by "outside causes," can be explained as results of an intensifying mechanism whereby a fluctuation in the rate of growth may be converted into alternations of rapid expansion and absolute contraction, through the interaction of the two sets of forces indicated.[1]

Although the adherents of the principle of acceleration undoubtedly have this second independent relation in mind, its implications are not systematically explored, even to the extent of the construction of arithmetic examples illustrating the mutual interactions of these two principles.

On the other hand, J. M. Keynes in the *General Theory* has concentrated on the manner in which net investment acts upon and generates income and consumption. This is the so-called doctrine of the multiplier, the applicability of which is not confined to the analysis of governmental expenditures. Here, too, Clark has made substantial contributions. We have then two distinct analytical relations growing up side by side, and until recently their mutual interactions have not been exhaustively examined. R. F. Harrod and G. Haberler and A. H. Hansen have to a considerable degree endeavored to remedy matters in this respect.[2]

There remain, nevertheless, as I hope to show, many ambiguities and oversimplifications, to say nothing of incorrect conclusions. Mention may be made of a few such problems. Must the combined action of the acceleration principle and the multiplier lead to a turning-point? Can the increase in replacement demand be regarded as an offset to a decline in the rate of growth of consumption? What is the role of frictions, time lags, and immobili-

[1] "Capital Production and Consumer-taking: A Further Word," *Journal of Political Economy*, October, 1932, pp. 692–93. This is a reply to Frisch's article, "The Interrelation between Capital Production and Consumer-taking," *Journal of Political Economy*, October, 1931, and to a subsequent article in the same journal in April, 1932.

[2] *The Trade Cycle* (Oxford: Clarendon Press, 1936); *Prosperity and Depression* (Geneva: League of Nations, 1937); *Full Recovery or Stagnation* (New York: W. W. Norton & Co., 1938).

ties of the factors of production? About what level will the system fluctuate? Are the results independent of the quantitative strengths of the various factors and the shape of the consumption function?

PRESENT STATUS OF THE THEORY

It may be well to review, if only in a superficial way, the views of preceding writers upon these controversial issues. No attempt is made throughout to appraise the importance of the factors considered as compared to other forces making for modern business cycles; this can be done only after the nature of these processes is clearly understood.

All writers are agreed that an advance in consumption can induce investment which in turn may lead to a further increase in consumption, and the process may continue for some time. Why must it end? Clark, Frisch, Haberler, and Hansen stress the fact that the ceiling of full employment, or at least perverse price-cost movements due to the appearance of bottlenecks, is the cause of the downturn.[3] Harrod appeals to the action of two dynamic determinants, each of which lowers the average propensity to consume for the community.

Are we to believe, then, that in the absence of depressing price-cost and interest movements the expansion would never cease? Must we invoke the action of the dynamic determinants? In the following section model sequences will be developed showing that neither of these views is necessarily correct.

ASSUMPTIONS UNDERLYING THE ANALYSIS

According to the acceleration principle in its simplest form, net investment, or at least some portion of it, is directly proportional to the time increase in consumption, the factor of proportionality or "relation" being the amount of equipment necessary to produce one unit of consumers' goods. Of course, gross investment will

---

[3] There are minor inconsistencies here. Thus, Clark (*Economics of Overhead Costs* [Chicago: University of Chicago Press, 1923], pp. 393–94) attributes the downturn to the fact that capital-goods industries reach full capacity and cannot expand output. Haberler's explanation of the turning-point seems to emphasize the limiting of real demand by the ceiling of full employment leading to a falling-off of investment orders. The losses in this sphere spread cumulatively.

exceed net investment by an amount equal to replacement. Frisch has pointed out some errors which may result if replacement demand is completely ignored.[4] Hansen has quoted with approval this argument in his review of Harrod's *Trade Cycle*, charging that the neglect of replacement leads fallaciously to the conclusion that the downturn is inevitable. Later an attempt will be made to show that for the purpose in hand Harrod's neglect of replacement is not only permissible but almost mandatory.

The national income of any period is equal to the sum of consumption expenditures plus the value of net investment. According to the Keynesian analysis, consumption expenditure is related to income received by a definite psychological law. As income increases the marginal and average propensities to consume fall, and the former is always less than unity.[5] There is some ambiguity as to the time sequence involved in this relationship. As long as one's interest is in equilibrium states, as is most of the Keynesian analysis, the issue does not arise. But for present purposes it must be squarely faced since entirely different results emerge from different assumptions.

At least two alternatives suggest themselves. The first is to assume that consumption bears an invariant relation to income at some previous point in time (or over a previous interval of time). Another is to assume that current consumption bears an invariant relationship to current income. It is certainly true that concomitantly with an existing amount of income there will be an existing amount of consumption. But unless the relationship is an invariant one, this "instantaneous" multiplier is a poor foundation upon which to build a theory. Nevertheless, we shall consider both possibilities.

If we have two relationships holding between two variables, it should be possible merely from a knowledge of the system over some initial periods of time to deduce its movements from then on. Let us first consider the position of the equilibrium state

[4] *Op. cit.*

[5] This holds for a single individual. For society as a whole these tendencies may be made stronger by the fact that at high levels of income profits may be high, affecting the distribution of income in such a way as to diminish the propensity to consume.

which, if established, would maintain itself and around which all oscillations take place. For the moment let us neglect the existence of any spontaneous, anticipatory investment unrelated to the increase in consumption. In the stationary condition the time increase of consumption must be zero, and hence induced investment must be equal to zero. What stationary level is compatible with no net investment? Obviously, in order that businesses as a whole shall not make losses, they must receive back from consumers the whole amount which they pay out to factors as costs

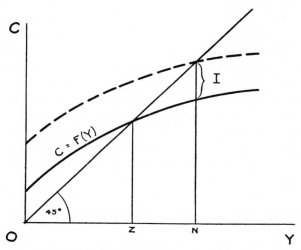

FIG. 1.—Determination of the level of national income

of production. Thus, in the absence of spontaneous net investment the stationary level around which the system will oscillate is that determined by the condition that the average propensity to consume be equal to unity. In Figure 1 a typical consumption function is indicated. The equilibrium is determined at the level of income OZ where a 45° line intersects the consumption function.

In any healthy society, however, there will be some continuous stream of spontaneous net investment. The effect of this is to raise the level at which income can remain stationary. People can save that part of the income paid to them as factors of production which does not represent costs of current production but is net investment, and there will not result losses for enterprises as a whole. The existence of spontaneous net investment can be regarded as raising the consumption function to the level of the dotted curve in Figure 1. The stationary equilibrium level in our healthy society would be at ON.

There is, of course, no reason why the stationary equilibrium level could not be very near the level of full employment. *The acceleration principle can determine the nature of the oscillations but not the average level of the system.* As we shall see, there is less to be feared from the operation of the acceleration principle than from the shrinkage of investment outlets in a stagnant society. Moreover, there is good reason to believe that in an economy whose levels of spontaneous investment and income are high the operation of the acceleration principle will be less strong than in an economy whose level of stationary equilibrium is low.

Let us proceed to show the development of our system from its initial state. Let us suppose that we know the amount of consumption in two successive periods. The national income, Y_2, for the second period will be equal to the amount of spontaneous net investment, assumed throughout to be equal to a constant, A, plus induced private investment, assumed to be proportional to the difference between consumption of that period and the previous period, plus the amount of consumption of that period, C_2, or

$$Y_2 = A + \beta(C_2 - C_1) + C_2,$$

where β is the numerical value of the "relation."

According to our first hypothesis, national income paid out in one period yields consumption in the following period as given by our consumption function. Hence

$$C_3 = F(Y_2)$$
$$= F(A + [1 + \beta]C_2 - \beta C_1),$$

where F is a function having the properties indicated in Figure 1. More generally, if we know consumption at time $t - 1$ and $t - 2$, we can easily compute it for time t by the following formula:

$$C_t = F(A + [1 + \beta]C_{t-1} - \beta C_{t-2}).$$

Given our consumption function, the level of spontaneous invest-ment, the strength of the "relation," and the value of consumption in two initial periods, the behavior of all future consumption and na-tional income is easily determined.

In order to investigate the possible types of behavior to be ex-pected, let us for the moment consider the special type of a linear consumption function with marginal propensity to consume less

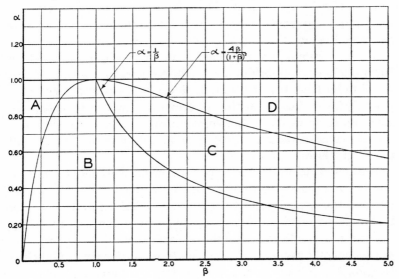

Fig. 2.—Diagram showing boundaries of regions yielding different qualitative behavior of national income   (Reproduced from *Review of Economic Statistics*, May, 1939, p. 78.)

than unity. This case has been discussed by the writer in connec-tion with the analysis of governmental expenditure, and we may draw upon the results there derived.[6]

By simple numerical examples three misconceptions can be re-vealed. First, even without the action of Harrod's two dynamic determinants and without any price or interest-rate changes, an expansion will always come to an end for certain values of the marginal propensity to consume, *a*, and the "relation," *β*. Thus,

[6] P. A. Samuelson, "Interactions between the Acceleration Principle and the Multiplier," *Review of Economic Statistics*, May, 1939, pp. 75–78.

for the marginal propensity equal to one-half and the "relation" equal to one, any expansion must lead to a downturn. (This is true of all values of a and β lying in Regions B and C in Fig. 2, reproduced from p. 78 of the article referred to above.)

Second, the fact that the marginal propensity to consume is always less than unity so that there is always some extra saving out of income is not sufficient to lead to a downturn or to the end of a cumulative movement. Thus, for $a = 0.6$ and $\beta = 5.0$, any cumulative movement would go on indefinitely at an increasing rate (see Region D in Fig. 2).

Third, a cumulative movement can end with an approach to the stationary equilibrium level with no downturn at all. If this equilibrium level is just below the level of full employment, it is possible for the action of the acceleration principle to lead to an asymptotic approach to full employment. For $a = 0.9$ and $\beta = 0.5$, any constructed numerical example will bear this out (see all points in Region A of Fig. 2).

It is desirable, moreover, to pursue the development of the system beyond the first turning-point to examine its possible behavior. For the special linear case the results derived previously can be briefly summarized. With any given value for the propensity to consume, small values of the "relation" yield no cyclical behavior, merely asymptotic approaches to stationary equilibrium (Region A). For the same a, slightly larger values for β lead to cyclical oscillations which become smaller and smaller (Region B). Still larger values of the "relation" result in cyclical oscillations becoming greater and greater but oscillating around the position of stationary equilibrium (Region C). Very large values of β lead to explosive cumulative movements growing at a rate of compound interest (Region D).

EFFECT OF CHANGES IN THE MARGINAL PROPENSITY TO CONSUME

We have seen that large constant values of the marginal propensity to consume yield "explosive" types of behavior. Obviously, these have no empirical counterparts. At worst, this would compel us to the interpretation that cumulative movements would never come to an end in the absence of price-cost and interest-rate changes. In the real world the latter must take place at sufficiently high levels of income, and these anomalous behavior patterns will not be exemplified.

Fortunately, however, it is not necessary to introduce elements extraneous to our model in order to exclude these phenomena. If we drop the assumption of linearity of the consumption function and let the marginal propensity decrease as income increases, approaching zero in the limit, we shall effectively dispose of the possibility of an unending, cumulative upward movement. This destroys the mathematical simplicity of our model, but the broad qualitative behavior patterns can still be traced. Moreover, the elaborate analysis of the linear case is still useful for understanding the behavior of our system in the neighborhood of the stationary equilibrium level.

Of course, the decrease of the marginal propensity to consume with high levels of income cannot help to end a cumulative downward movement but will rather aggravate the difficulty. It is necessary, therefore, to relax the assumption of linearity with respect to the "relation." Strictly speaking, net investment can be negative only to the extent of deferred replacement or consumption. This provides a lower bound to the movements of our system. It must be emphasized that this lower bound will not be reached except possibly for systems with large values of the "relation" and of the marginal propensity to consume, and even here it may depend upon the original conditions.

We may summarize the results of our analysis in the following propositions. (1) The combined action of the acceleration principle and the multiplier can result in cumulative movements. (2) For particular numerical values of the relations assumed there may result an asymptotic approach to the stationary equilibrium level justified by the amount of spontaneous net investment and the marginal propensity to consume. In other words, not all cumulative movements are disequilibrating. (3) There may result cumulative movements which go past the position of equilibrium. Even without the action of Harrod's first two dynamic determinants, for all except large values of the multiplier and "relation" the cumulative movements will come to an end. For large values of the multiplier and "relation" (in the neighborhood of the stationary equilibrium level) the fact that the relationships are not linear (of which Harrod's dynamic determinants are one expression) leads to the reversal of any disequilibrating cumulative movement in every case. (4) Again, depending upon the numerical strength of the different factors, the cyclical patterns which result (if any do!) may or may not be self-perpetuating. They may well be damped, depending upon the initial conditions and numerical values of the system's determinants.[7] Moreover, successive cycles need not be similar in timing or amplitude. (5) Small values of the multiplier and "relation" are conducive to stability. Therefore, systems with a large volume of investment outlets and with small propensities to consume are least likely to be affected seriously by the acceleration principle. (6) From the long-run point of view Keynes was partially justified in ignoring the acceleration principle completely. The average level of the system is independent of its operation, depending rather upon the level of investment outlets.[8]

CRITICISM OF EXISTING VIEWS

A comparison of the foregoing results with Harrod's brilliant chapter ii will reveal many discrepancies. Upon rigorous analysis his exposition will be found to abound with *non sequiturs* and oversimplifications. On the whole, Harrod's intuition surpasses his reasoned conclusions—of what investigator worth his salt is this not true? In addition to differences adumbrated above, it may be well to point out that Harrod does not use the acceleration principle to explain the lower turning-point but introduces an extraneous factor—the accumulation of deferred replacement.

---

[7] There remains one interesting problem still to be explored. Mathematical analysis of the nonlinear case may reveal that for certain equilibrium values of a and β a periodic motion of definite amplitude will always be approached regardless of initial conditions. Such a relation can never result from systems of difference equations with constant coefficients, involving assumptions of linearity. This illustrates the inadequacy of such assumptions except for the analysis of small oscillations.

[8] A. H. Hansen makes this same point in more detail in a forthcoming volume.

This explains why according to his analysis the recession must every time go to "the bottom." Simple arithmetical examples readily show that such need not be the case. The same examples suggest that Harrod is wrong in his belief that the height of the boom has no effect on the depth of the depression. These indicate that the height of the boom determines the rate at which income is falling at the point of stationary equilibrium, and this in turn determines the depths to which the system must fall before the upturn comes.

It may be further noted that at the upper turning-point it is not necessary to have immobilities of the prime factors in producers' and consumers' goods industries. According to the Keynesian analysis, at this point the level of effective demand is such that no additional workers can be absorbed in the consumption trades. Non-Keynesian economists will only require that the general wage rate be not perfectly flexible. Finally, as previously stated, I believe that the possibility of a low secular level of spontaneous investment is more to be regarded with gloom than the action of the acceleration principle as such.

On the other hand, Harrod can be defended against one adverse criticism. Hansen charges him with ignoring the Frisch argument that total capital construction can level out, even if the rate of increase of consumption begins to fall. This is correct but hardly relevant to the present purpose. As Hansen himself has pointed out to the writer, it would involve double-counting to include in the computation of the national income both consumption and the replacement expenditures imputable as costs of that consumption. Only net investment is "multiplied" to give the national income; as a first approximation Harrod was justified in neglecting replacement in the formal relation.[9]

It may be briefly noted that the time lag between income paid out and consumption is necessary if there is to be a cyclical pat-

[9] Actually, there remain problems connected with the age distribution of durable equipment. What is needed is a concept of investment which is "net" for the period in question, even though it is replacement from the standpoint of history. Still better, we need a concept of net income creating expenditure of business enterprise, analogous to the concept of governmental net income creating expenditure employed by some American economists.

tern. Otherwise, there can be only a one-way movement away from equilibrium. Thus, if we start out with consumption above the equilibrium level, in the following period consumption must rise, or else income will not be at the level given by the multiplier analysis—i.e., unless consumption rises an appropriate amount, people will not be saving and spending the amounts necessary to make savings and investment in the Keynesian sense simultaneously equal. The action of Harrod's first two dynamic determinants makes the disequilibrating movement worse. The same argument holds if the instantaneous rate of change of consumption is considered in place of a period analysis.

CONCLUSION

It is a matter of indifference for the present purpose what terminology one employs with respect to savings and investment. These can be defined in the Keynesian manner to be equal, or the Robertsonian terminology may be preferred, in terms of which they can be unequal. Neither offers any advantage. The numerical relations of the acceleration principle and the multiplier generate the behavior of our system. The equality of savings and investment throws no light on the process; the inequality of the Robertsonian magnitudes is equally fruitless, being no more than a reflection of the fact that the level of income is changing. From a strictly logical standpoint controversy over terminology is sterile; the flexible mind will adopt the terminology of his opponent of the moment.

In concluding I should like to point out that, throughout, all relations have been assumed to hold rigidly. Obvious qualifications must be made before the results can be applied to the real world.

84

ALVIN HANSEN AND THE INTERACTIONS BETWEEN THE MULTIPLIER ANALYSIS AND THE PRINCIPLE OF ACCELERATION

Paul A. Samuelson

Scientific theories are like children in that they have a life of their own. But, unlike children, they may have more than one father. It is only fitting, therefore, as the multiplier-acceleration theory [1] celebrates the twentieth birthday of what has been a lusty existence, that credit be given where credit is due. I refer to the all-important role in the formulation of this model that was played back in 1938 by Alvin Hansen. While I have always tried orally to have it designated as the Hansen-Samuelson model — with emphasis on the indicated order of names — Hansen has never received the credit that is rightfully his, and which he is the last man to try to claim.

So it may be of some interest on this twentieth anniversary of the theory to recall its genesis.

I

Just at the time Professor Hansen arrived at Harvard as the first Littauer professor, economists were still absorbing the new Keynesian income analysis. Unlike most Anglo-Saxon writers, Hansen had long been interested in the important role of such exogenous factors as technological and population change in connection with the business cycle. Hence, he was receptive to the new analysis and anxious to formulate its fiscal policy implications.[2]

At the same time he recognized how "undynamic" was the bulk of the *General Theory*, particularly from the standpoint of economists who had long been working with the acceleration principle. For this reason he reviewed favorably Harrod's 1936 *Trade Cycle*, which did try to bring the accelerator into the modern income analysis. (He also expressed his surprise and amusement that anyone should in 1936 rediscover or rename a principle which had already been so much discussed by writers like Aftalion, Hawtrey, Bickerdike, J. M. Clark, and Frisch. This is to say nothing of the mathematical literature of Tinbergen, Frisch, Kalecki, and Theiss, with which I think Hansen was not familiar at that time.)

[1] Paul A. Samuelson, "Interactions Between the Multiplier Analysis and the Principle of Acceleration," this REVIEW, XXI (May 1939), 75–78.

[2] See Alvin H. Hansen, *Full Recovery or Stagnation?* (New York, 1938) for the background of his thinking. Rereading that book has reminded me of its refreshing impact at the time.

Around 1938 though, Hansen's major task was to analyze the 1937–38 recession. It was inevitable, therefore, that he should try to "dynamize" such Keynesian models as, say, that in Lange's 1938 "The Rate of Interest and the Optimum Propensity to Consume." Assuming (1) the multiplier hypothesis that consumption is half of yesterday's income, (2) the acceleration principle that the stock of capital is twice the level of consumption, with capital's change constituting net investment, Hansen worked out a determinate numerical example of developing national income. (Later, under Lundberg's tutelage, such general numerical models ceased to be so novel; but at the time this was still rather a bold step.) To Hansen's surprise, national product's initial rise terminated not in a new plateau of income, but instead went into a *decline*!

This decline naturally reminded him of the post-1937 drop in business. So he enunciated the tentative hypothesis that the upswing of the 1930's was not a full-bodied recovery attributable to basic exogenous factors, but rather a temporary recovery attributable to the temporary investment induced by a transient rate of rise of consumption. Such a consumption recovery, he said somewhat ambiguously, will only go as far as it is pushed.

II

It was only at this point that I entered the scene. It was a case of mathematics not as the Queen of the Sciences but as the Handmaiden of the Sciences. I took *Hansen's* model, recognized its identity to a second-order difference equation with constant coefficients, and proceeded to analyze its algebraic structure.

At once I made the inference that the drop in income which had so struck Hansen was not the end of the story. Quite by chance, he had picked numerical values for the marginal propensity to consume ($a = \frac{1}{2}$) and for the "relation" ($\beta = 2$) which were on the razor's edge that yielded perpetual oscillations, with no damping and no exploding. In other words, if he had continued his numerical example far enough, his downturn too would have come to an end; and he would have been able to generate a succession of never-ending expansions and contractions.

The numerical model was easily generalized to the case of *any* marginal propensity and relation coefficients a and β. Today it would be merely a matter of turning the deductive crank to analyze the stability regions corresponding to the different possible roots of the quadratic equation that constituted the dynamic system's characteristic equation; but even then, once Hansen had handed me the problem on a silver platter, the work went quickly. He himself was delighted to learn that for different values of a and β, one could generate damped or undamped economic cycles, damped one-way movements (of the Kahn-Clark-Robertson dynamic multiplier type), or never-ending one-way movements (of what we now call Harrod-Domar type).

And so this particular theory was born. As theories go, it was born with a silver spoon in its mouth. Dealing with fundamentals easy to grasp, it was apparently just deep enough to pique the interest and curiosity of business cycle students and to serve as a pedagogical introduction to dynamic economic models. While I am proud of my own modest contribution to its development, I think this is a fitting occasion to give credit where credit is due — to Alvin Hansen.

85

THE THEORY OF PUMP-PRIMING REËXAMINED[1]

Prior to a discussion of the basic problems of fiscal policy, explicit attention must be paid to the characteristic features of the private economy. The necessity of sufficient *net* investment must be stressed. The two problems of timing and general level of expenditure must be distinguished. In connection with the latter, reasons are advanced in favor of an early spending plan to combat a downward movement, and against a policy relying upon the remedial, cathartic action of the depression. The doctrine of the Multiplier is described, and its incompleteness as a theory of government expenditure is indicated. The neglected effects upon private investment must be considered, particularly the interactions of the acceleration principle and the Multiplier. Pure pump-priming is to be regarded as an extreme case. Expenditure has reactions on subsequent revenues, but it is not possible to reduce deficits by an increase in outlay, regardless of how progressive the tax system. Other things being equal, however, incomes with low marginal propensities to consume should be taxed most heavily. Finally, the experience of the last decade is considered and qualifications noted.

The Great Depression stimulated an interest in the problems of governmental fiscal policy culminating in the development of the doctrine of the Multiplier by Clark, Kahn, and Keynes. Similarly, the Recession of 1937 has once again brought to the fore the pressing problem of the effects of governmental expenditure upon the level of the national income and business activity. It is the purpose of the present paper to indicate certain difficulties and possible sources of confusion encountered in the analysis of this process.

Nature of the Private Economy

Of course, governmental expenditures do not take place in a vacuum. It is necessary in the beginning to set forth explicitly the basic features of the private economy forming the environment within which governmental action must take place. No attempt is made to justify the characteristics stressed beyond the assertion that in the recent business cycle literature they are regarded as fundamental. These are enumerated briefly as follows:

(1) The economic system is not perfect and frictionless so that there exists the possibility of unemployment and under-utilization of productive resources.

(2) More specifically, as emphasized in the recent economic literature, there exists the possibility of, if not a definite tendency toward, cumulative movements of a disequilibrating kind. That is to say, a substantial movement either upward or downward generates secondary forces which tend to act in the same direction and prolong the initial trend.

(3) There exists a desire of individuals to save on balance out of income; *i.e.,* to accumulate assets, earning or otherwise. This means that the average propensity to consume is less than one, at least at high levels of the national income. As a result, in the absence of substantial amounts

[1] A portion of this paper was delivered before a Round Table Conference of the American Economic Association at Detroit, Michigan, December 30, 1938. I wish to thank, but not implicate, Professors Fritz Machlup and Alvin H. Hansen whose respective unpublished manuscripts relating to this subject were kindly placed at my disposal.

of net investment, there will necessarily be a large degree of unemployment and a low level of business activity. For under the circumstances outlined, business enterprises as a whole cannot possibly recoup in consumption sales their previous disbursements to the factors of production; and a vicious downward spiral must necessarily follow.[2] If there is sufficient net investment, however, the dilemma immediately disappears. In this case the total amount paid out by business enterprises to the factors of production represents more than the costs imputable to the production of current consumers' goods, the excess being attributable to the creation of new productive equipment. It now becomes unnecessary for all of earned income to be spent on consumption. Equilibrium can still be maintained so long as new business assets are being created to an extent sufficient to compensate for factor income not expended on consumption.

(4) Although all business cycle theorists now grant the importance and necessity of proper amounts of net investment, there is perhaps insufficient recognition of the fact that *even in a perfect capital market there is no tendency for the rate of interest to equilibrate the demand and supply of employment.* The interest rate and asset price structure serve to equilibrate the holding of new and old securities of all kinds. This does not imply any tendency for the rate of interest to fall to a level which will call forth an amount of net investment sufficient to absorb all unemployment. In fact, the schedule of the marginal efficiency of capital may be extremely inelastic with respect to the interest rate so that no fall in the rate of interest, even into negative levels, would result in full employment. On the other hand, the outlets for capital investment might conceivably be so favorable that there would result more than "full employment," price increases, forced savings, windfall profits, etc. The amount of net investment must be regarded as dependent on dynamic factors of economic progress such as the amount of as yet undeveloped innovations, trend of population, past net investment, as well as upon the shifting state of confidence and expectations. We should expect, therefore, its behavior to be volatile and capricious, and that shifts in the schedule of the marginal efficiency of investment would dwarf into insignificance changes along the schedule caused by variations in interest rates. If we add to this the overshadowing effect upon savings of variations in the level of income as compared to changes in the interest rate structure, there remains still less basis for a belief in the equilibrating potency of the capital market. This means that in any community there exists a possibility of insufficient net investment, and perhaps in a wealthy community a likelihood of such an insufficiency.[3]

[2] Space does not permit a consideration of the necessity of assumption (1) in this analysis. For the sake of the argument, I neglect price changes in much of what follows.

[3] Mr. Keynes has made a point similar to this based upon the existence of liquidity preference, but the latter is not a necessary condition for this possibility of deficient net investment.

(5) Unless explicit reference to the contrary is made, I shall assume in what follows any fixed schedule of tax rates; it is also supposed that there exist no technical difficulties to prevent the government from financing deficits of the magnitudes discussed. No *a priori* assumptions are made concerning the future level of innovations and investment outlets.

The Timing of Governmental Expenditures

Under these circumstances the government is in a position to determine its own level of expenditure at each instant of time, to influence more or less strongly the subsequent behavior of all parts of the private economy, and to affect its own future tax revenues. The nature of these relations we must investigate. In order to free ourselves from possible preconceptions, it should be pointed out that although there may exist a set of tax rates which will balance the budget over time at a level of expenditure considered necessary or desirable, there need not necessarily be such a set which will do so and at the same time lead to full (or $3/4$, or $1/2$) employment. We must not be committed in advance to a naïve belief that over time surpluses will always balance deficits.

For purposes of the analysis it is convenient to introduce a somewhat artificial distinction between two aspects of fiscal policy. (a) Suppose we are given an arbitrarily preassigned cumulative deficit which we are permitted to run over a period of time (say, two decades), how shall we "spend" this deficit as wisely as possible? This is the problem of timing of expenditures.[4] (b) The other aspect of perhaps even greater interest centers upon the determination of the optimal amount of cumulative deficit that should be incurred over a period of time.[5]

As we shall see, these two aspects must necessarily be mutually interdependent. The better timed a policy of spending is, the smaller need be the long-time level of expenditures. On the other hand, given a low level of governmental expenditures covering only administrative expenses, there will be little room for the discretionary determination of expenditures.[6] As relief and welfare activities become mandatory, another non-discretionary element is introduced, even though deficits now are likely to vary inversely

[4] Of course, to those who determine actual policy, the problem does not present itself in this form. One cannot know in advance what level of deficit will be best, and it would be poor management to act in terms of some preassigned limit. Even more important, correct decisions necessarily involve a detailed diagnosis of the state of the private economy and correct foresight as to its future movements; no amounts of theorizing can guarantee this. But waiving the problem of foresight, over a period of years *some* cumulative deficit will in fact have been incurred. With time stretched in back of us there will necessarily be some time shape of expenditure which will result in the most desirable pattern of national income, and it is this which we seek.

[5] The deficits referred to need not be positive. Sound policy under some circumstances may require debt retirement over time; or in the absence of an outstanding public debt, the sterilization of surplus tax receipts.

[6] Of course, room for discretionary action in the realm of tax policy still exists.

with the state of business activity. If still higher levels of expenditures and deficits are to be permitted, then the problem of timing becomes of interest. However, if an extremely liberal view is taken toward deficits, timing again becomes relatively unimportant; in this case, one merely spends whenever it is needed, and only the boom period offers analytical difficulties. It is the intermediate level, where there is room for the exercise of discretionary powers and yet a need for weighing carefully the comparative advantages of spending each dollar at different times, that is emphasized here.

In order to investigate the optimal time shape of expenditures, it is fruitful to employ a marginal analysis weighing the effects of a dollar's worth of expenditure at different phases of the business cycle. This done, almost anyone will give assent to the proposition that a given level of deficit spending in time of full or high employment is less beneficial at the margin than during depression; in time of price rise, high boom, excess spending may be absolutely as well as relatively harmful. If it is necessary as a condition of the problem to cut expenditures at some time, other things being equal, it is surely best to do so when employment is high and rising.[7]

Really burning differences of opinion concerning proper timing of policy exist only with respect to the period of collapse and depression. There prevail two sharply opposed schools of thought, typified respectively by Professor Slichter and Mr. Harrod. The former holds that expenditures should not be undertaken until the bottom of the depression has been reached, lest by alleviating the situation the government should prevent necessary corrective adjustments in the price-cost structure. From this point of view the depression is a cathartic device by means of which the maladjustments of the boom can be eliminated.

There may perhaps be noted a growing reaction in the literature against this point of view. Increased stress is being placed upon the *disequilibrating,* cumulative aspects of the downward movement with a consequent emphasis upon the need for early strong governmental expenditures in order to check an unnecessary, undesirable, vicious downward spiral which as it proceeds creates more maladjustments than it cures. Even if the deficit spending does not turn the tide, its beneficial indirect effects in slowing down and preventing decreases in the national income are likely to be very high at this time.

Even if it is granted that an increase in wage and other costs is one of the factors responsible for the downturn, it does not necessarily follow that

---

[7] However, strongly discontinuous changes in policy are to be avoided; there should be a gradual tapering off of expenditures rather than a sudden break. Similarly, continuous and smooth operations are desirable at any phase of the cycle. A sustained effort at spending during depression may be much more effective than an equally costly series of abortive spurts which do not attain the "threshhold" at which spending begins to "catch on."

the best policy is to let things get so bad that they will correct themselves. In the first place, as has been seen, the downturn breeds maladjustments of its own which may be far worse than those of the boom. Second, there is good reason to doubt that much downward flexibility exists in an economy such as our own; certainly our experiences of the last decade must raise doubts on this score. Finally, we must not lose sight of ends in our pre-occupation with means. Our aim is a higher national income and employment. It is not a policy of wisdom to let business become *bad* merely in order that it can be improved.[8]

However, each decision must be made in terms of the previous behavior of the economic system. It is necessary to consider each downturn on its own merits in deciding whether or not expenditures should be hastened. Some general types may be considered. First, consider a downturn due simply to the giving out of investment opportunities. Suppose that previously there has been a fairly long period of high business activity during which a considerable volume of investment in durable equipment, housing, utilities, etc., has taken place. As a result several new industries have grown to maturity and henceforth require only replacement in small amounts, and no new outlets appear on the horizon. If, then, business begins to slump, shall the government immediately begin its spending or wait until the process has worked itself out for some time?

In such a case there seems to be no good reason for letting the system go into a vicious downward spiral. The least that governmental policy can do is to attempt to minimize the "secondary depression" which will ensue. The reader will perhaps recognize in this example some of the features characteristic of the Great Depression of 1929. While I do not wish to exaggerate the potency of fiscal policy in combating such a widespread slump, I do feel that it would have been wiser for the government to have spent more heavily in 1930, 1931, 1932, and 1933, even at the expense of the later years.[9] This would probably have proved to be cheaper in the long run, and certainly cheaper to accomplish the degree of recovery actually attained.

Another type of downturn of great interest today is one which follows

[8] To put the matter most crudely, the point of view under consideration represents the large-scale application of the principle of the industrial *lock-out*. The most favorable case for its employ would be when (1) the period of decline and downward revision is very short; (2) prices of cost factors really can be made to fall more than prices of products; (3) the factors of production actually "learn their lesson" so that costs stay down, or rise less rapidly than they otherwise would when business begins to improve. The last point must be emphasized. A little thought will show that it is crucial for the success of this program; otherwise the depression will have been a needless period of destitution, curtailed consumption, and foregone investment.

[9] Of course, federal deficits were run in the closing years of the Hoover administration. On the other hand, there was a precipitous decline in capital investment by the state and local governments in the early thirties.

the accumulation of excessive inventories, premised upon a rate of price increase which cannot be maintained. Once the rate of price increase slackens, even though prices do not fall absolutely, the inventories are seen to be excessive, and new orders drop off sharply. Experience suggests that such a recession is not likely to be as serious and long lasting as the previous type mentioned, provided that the downward movement does not generate strong secondary momentum. Orders being curtailed, inventories can be worked off as long as sales are maintained. Waiving the difficulties of quickly engineering a spending policy, there seems to be every reason in this case for the government to act promptly so as to sustain the national income and aid in the orderly reduction of inventories.

The Multiplier

Before turning to the consideration of the optimal level of long-time deficit financing, it is necessary to examine various mechanical aspects of the impact of governmental expenditures. We have seen from the beginning that in a community where there is a desire to save out of income, consumers' buying will not be large enough to cover their cost of production unless the deficiency is made up by means of private investment, or what comes to the same thing, by governmental expenditures in excess of receipts. That these last two are essentially similar can be shown if we look more closely into the nature of net investment. From the present point of view, the importance of investment consists in the fact that it involves disbursal of income to the factors of production while not at the same time bringing to the market goods which must be currently sold. Because of this, the dilemma of thrift can be averted, provided that the excess of factor income over current costs of production is large enough to offset saving on the part of individuals.

It should be noted, and this is a factor insufficiently stressed by most writers, that all kinds of investment are not equally useful from this point of view.[10] For after all, private investment is motivated by the hope to make profits; sooner or later the currently produced new capital equipment will result in an increased flow of consumers' goods upon the market. The current outlay on investment is a surplus from the point of view of the present, but must be paid out of future consumption revenues. The most favorable kind of investment from the standpoint of bolstering up the national income is that which does not increase the supply of consumers' goods for a long time to come. It is not surprising that the construction of a building which will yield consumers' services over an amortization period of half a century should be regarded as more important in this respect than

---

[10] In the modern literature investment means many things; in this paper I stress its "expansionary demand" aspect.

investment which takes the form of a temporary increase in inventories.[11]

We see, therefore, how an excess of governmental expenditures over revenue is income creating in the same sense as investment. Indeed, it is likely to be the best kind of investment since it need not involve the future sale of extra consumers' goods. When account is taken of the qualitative differences between categories of investment, the strategic importance of fiscal policy becomes apparent, even though the absolute magnitudes of government deficits are a relatively small fraction of total net investment.

This also suggests that the present emphasis upon *self-liquidating* public investment may be misplaced. Aside from the fact that it is poor social economy to saddle overhead charges upon the use of governmental services (as is done in the case of a toll bridge), it may be equally undesirable for government activity to ape the business practices of private enterprise. If the government employs the same calculations with respect to action as private business, it may soon find itself in the same dilemma as confronts a purely individualistic economy.[12]

The doctrine of the Multiplier is nothing more than a recognition of the strategic importance of investment in determining the level of the national income. The crucial assumption upon which it stands or falls is that consumption expenditures and savings are rigidly related to the level of national income. The passive character of consumption cannot be sufficiently stressed. There has been some controversy over the timing of this relationship, Mr. Keynes being of the opinion that it holds necessarily instantaneously. There is no question that at every instant of time there will exist respective amounts of investment, consumption, and national income, but this instantaneous relationship will be anything but stable; an increase in investment will in the extreme short run result in little or no additional consumption.[13] An increase in income can make itself felt in increased consumption only after some period of time; at the risk of oversimplification

[11] The point to be emphasized is that the last kind of investment is likely to be followed by disinvestment in the near future.

[12] As the Swedish experience shows, there may be a tendency for investment activity of governmentally owned industries to follow the same perverse cyclical pattern as that of private concerns. At this point a word of caution is in order concerning the advisability of transplanting other commercial practices into governmental administration, as for example, automatic amortization of any deficit incurred over a given period of time, or the keeping of a capital budget. The latter is usually regarded with favor because it helps to "sell" a spending program. However, the knife may cut both ways. The proposed accumulation of a large Old Age Insurance Reserve Fund was after all a straightforward application of the principles of a capital budget! Correct public policy, like correct entrepreneurial behavior, implies freedom from the conventions and shibboleths of bookkeeping techniques.

[13] Unfortunately, the timing of the consumption-income relationship has become involved in the equality of savings and investment controversy. Space does not permit a discussion of the reasons why I regard this to be a mistake. It should be pointed out, however, that in most contexts the "instantaneous" relations of Mr. Keynes are best regarded as stationary state relationships of the type met with in comparative statics. As such, they are special cases of the dynamic time sequence analysis.

we can assume that consumption of one "period" is related in an invariant way to income of the previous "period."

By means of the Multiplier we can deduce the time behavior of income and consumption from a knowledge of the time shape of investment, provided we know the initial level of consumption. If we know consumption and investment in the first period, the national income is automatically known by addition. From the consumption function the consumption of the second period is immediately determined. This plus investment of the second period provides us with income of the second period. Consumption of the third period is derived by means of the consumption function from the second period's income, and so the process continues indefinitely.[14]

Let us consider now the various shapes of income which will result from certain investment patterns. If investment has always been identically zero in the indefinite past, the national income will be at a level where the average propensity to consume is equal to unity with consumption equal to income. A constant positive level of net investment will result in a constant higher level of the national income. The ratio between the increase in income and the increase in investment will exceed unity, being equal to the reciprocal of the marginal propensity to save averaged over the range of movement. A regular periodic fluctuation in investment will be accompanied by a regular periodic movement in income, the latter lagging behind at the turning points. If the average propensity to consume is sensibly constant, the average level of income over the whole cycle will bear the same relation to the average level of investment as do stationary levels; otherwise the ratio will be somewhat smaller.

Assuming that the time shape of private investment is given, preferably at some constant level, let us now introduce *net income creating expenditures* of the government. For simplicity the marginal propensity to consume will be assumed to be constant, and price and cost changes will be ignored. Each pattern of expenditure will result in a new pattern of additions (or subtractions) to the national income as compared to its level in the absence of governmental action.

The first pattern of expenditure to be considered is fundamental, since by superposition we can construct all other patterns from it. It consists of a single impulse of expenditure. From the work of J. M. Clark and others it is well known that this results in additional income in the first period equal to the original governmental expenditure. Because the marginal propensity to consume is less than unity, and there is no additional investment forthcoming, the national income decreases in geometric progression, in each period being only a fraction of that of the previous period, until

---

[14] It is necessary to emphasize that investment can take any preassigned shape. It must not be thought that investment of one period must be equal to what people *wish* to save out of the previous period's income. To insist on this equality would be to determine investment rigidly and freeze the national income at a constant level.

finally the effect of the initial impulse of expenditure is completely dissi-pated.[15]

A second pattern of interest consists of the sudden introduction of a positive, maintained level of expenditure. This causes the additional na-tional income to increase at a decreasing rate until finally an asymptote is approached equal to the reciprocal of the marginal propensity to save.

A third pattern which is really the reverse of the previous one consists of a sudden reduction of expenditures from a previously maintained level. In this case, symmetry demands that the national income fall at an ever de-creasing rate approaching asymptotically the level of income which would exist in the absence of any expenditure. In fact, any finite amount of expenditure will result ultimately in a return to the previous level of the national income. It may also be mentioned that cyclical movements in the deficit will result in cyclical changes in the national income, lagging behind at the turning points.

The Effect of Expenditure upon the Level of Total Investment

It is sometimes thought that the principle of the Multiplier as outlined above provides a complete analysis of the effects of governmental ex-penditures upon the national income. This is completely without founda-tion. Given the level of total net investment, the Multiplier determines the movements of national income. But, in and of itself, knowledge of the level of government deficits throws no light upon movements of total investment. Our problem may be broken up into two components: (a) What is the effect upon national income of any given change in total net investment brought about by a given fiscal policy? (b) What change in total net investment will result from a given amount of expenditure? The latter question is as important as the former and is left unanswered by the Multiplier analysis.

Thus, it is conceivable that a dollar's worth of government investment might cause a simultaneous disinvestment of ten dollars on the part of private individuals, which with a marginal propensity to consume of two-thirds would result in a total *decrease* in the national income of twenty-seven dollars. The *government Multiplier* would therefore be negative even though the *total investment Multiplier* is positive. The former is equal to the investment Multiplier times the ratio of total additional net investment to the initial governmental expenditure. The latter ratio depends upon the amount of private investment induced throughout all time by the initial governmental net income creating expenditure, and it is to this problem that we must now turn our attention.

We have seen earlier that the amount of private net investment is related

---

[15] If the marginal propensity to consume were equal to, or greater than, unity, the national income would never return to its previous level. A single dollar of expenditure would in sufficient time add any preassigned amount to the national income. This case bears

to dynamic factors of growth and change operating within the economy. Given no fall in interest rates, no technological, institutional change, and no increase in the level of consumption and income, net investment would take place only until the level of capital equipment became optimally adjusted to the existing state of the system. When this has been accomplished, net investment will cease completely and the production of capital equipment will consist entirely of replacement. Obviously, from what has been said before, such investment will provide no stimulus to sales and income, being indistinguishable from outlays to direct factors of production; in the calculation of the national income it would involve double counting to include both consumption sales and the costs of production of the consumption goods.

To facilitate the systematic consideration of the induced effects on private investment of governmental expenditure, Professor Hansen has developed a simplified model sequence which ingeniously combines the familiar *acceleration principle* or Relation with the Multiplier analysis. He assumes that induced private net investment is proportional to the increase in consumption from one period to the next, the numerical factor of proportionality being known as the Relation.

On the basis of this assumption, it is possible to trace out the effects upon income of different patterns of expenditure. I have done this in detail elsewhere[16] and so confine myself to a brief summary of the results obtained from the sudden introduction of a constant level of expenditure. As expenditure is introduced, consumption will grow as determined by the Multiplier. This increase in consumption will induce some amount of private investment, which together with the new stream of government expenditure constitutes the new total of investment. This in turn leads to further consumption, induced private investment, etc. Depending upon the numerical values chosen for the marginal propensity to consume and the Relation, the following different qualitative behavior patterns of income emerge:

(a) For small values of the Relation and marginal propensity to consume, the rate of growth of consumption tapers off so that induced private investment becomes smaller and smaller approaching zero in the limit. Additional national income increases more and more slowly, finally approaching the level which can be maintained by "multiplication" of the continued stream of the deficit alone. The effect of the acceleration principle has been to increase somewhat the governmental Multiplier, but not to change the level of the new stationary equilibrium.

(b) For larger values of the Relation, the induced private investment

a superficial resemblance to the pure case of pump-priming to be discussed later, but is not really what the adherents to that point of view have in mind.

[16] P. A. Samuelson, "Interactions between the Multiplier Analysis and the Principle of Acceleration," *Rev. of Econ. Stat.*, May, 1939, pp. 75-78.

will be of greater magnitude during the first few periods. However, the rate of increase of consumption will taper off so rapidly that the national income will turn down, even though a steady stream of governmental expenditure has been maintained. As the system slumps, there will be some induced private disinvestment; this will decrease as the decline becomes less and less precipitous. Before the additional national income becomes zero, the system will again turn up. But this time the upswing will not go as far as previously, and the subsequent downswing which follows will be of smaller amplitude than its predecessor. Succeeding fluctuations will be damped until finally the national income will approach the asymptote justified by the governmental spending alone. The induced private investment, even though transient, results in a still larger governmental Multiplier.

(c) If we consider a system characterized by still larger values of the marginal propensity to consume and Relation, the successive oscillations of the national income are of ever increasing amplitude, even though the average level of the system is that given by the Multiplier formula.

(d) For very large values of these parameters, the induced private investment will be so great that the time increase of consumption will be unchecked. Consumption grows ever more rapidly, leading to more and more induced private investment, which yields in turn still greater increases in consumption. The system never comes to a turning point, but continues upward at a geometric rate of increase. Throughout all time an infinite amount of private investment is induced, yielding a governmental Multiplier of infinity. The gradual cessation of governmental expenditure will not stop the upward movement.

The Pure Case of Pump-Priming

The last type of behavior exemplifies the situation that may be termed the pure case of pump-priming. It suggests that some minimum initial amount of spending will "break the log jam of private investment," "form the spark to ignite business activity," "act as a catalyst to speed the upward movement," etc. Not attempting to pursue too literally the features of these physical analogies, we find that there is one essential common element. All presuppose that the private economy is in *meta-stable* equilibrium, that a sufficiently strong upward displacement will "set off" forces powerful enough to return the economy to a high level of employment, and keep it there. An infinitesimal upward impetus need not be sufficient; else, why should not a single individual rather than the government bring about the revival?

Not all pump-primers base their case upon the action of the acceleration principle. Some attribute the insufficiency of net investment to the fact that the slump in business has produced a perverse state of pessimistic expectations which inhibits the entrepreneur and prevents him from performing bold acts of investment. They argue that the introduction of known innovations is a function of the current state of activity of the system. Investment waits upon an upturn of business, but business cannot improve except with the aid of substantial investment. The government by breaking through the vicious circle can motivate the business community to do the things which will ultimately prove to be justified.

It is to be emphasized that pure pump-priming is an extreme case. Actually, there is a continuum of possible values for the ratio of induced to initial investment, ranging from zero to infinity.[17] No one should be seriously disappointed if a spending policy over a number of years does not create prosperity in perpetuity. It is to be presumed that any upturn will eventually come to an end, either dying a natural death as investment outlets give out or succumbing to self-created maladjustments. One must be content, therefore, with the "multiplier" effects of spending and any possible induced private investment which may be forthcoming.

The Reaction of Expenditures on Revenue

Throughout it has been implicitly assumed that high expenditure levels and deficits must go hand in hand. This assumption has completely ignored the increasingly important school of thought which argues that a maintenance of government expenditures will so increase the national income that even the same schedule of tax rates will yield revenues sufficient to balance the budget. According to this point of view, it is cheaper in the long run to spend more rather than less.

I shall examine the validity of this belief *under the assumption that our economy may be facing a period of reduced investment outlets so that the induced investment and pump-priming aspects of expenditure can be neglected.* Any tax system can be assumed regardless of how progressive it may be, the only restriction being the obvious one that the total tax bill of any person must not be increased by as much as one dollar as a result of an extra dollar's income. This is not a serious restriction, since any tax formula which is administratively feasible will meet this requirement.

Under the hypotheses made, it can be stated as a theorem of the Multiplier analysis that *the increase of expenditure of an extra dollar cannot result in increased tax revenues of as much as a dollar even though all succeeding time is taken into consideration.* This conclusion holds even though tax rates are almost completely confiscatory, and marginal propensities to consume are very small. It also holds if there are two or more

---

[17] It is, of course, possible that there may be disinvestment induced by a fear of mounting deficits. The empirical record of the behavior of private investment in the thirties suggests, although not conclusively, that whatever the entrepreneur may think or say, he still regards high and rising current revenues as the most powerful motivating factor in making investments. Also, there may be disinvestment due to the reduction of inventories made possible by government spending.

groups in the community, one of which has a very low marginal propensity to consume and is taxed very heavily, and the other has a high marginal propensity to consume and a relatively low tax rate.

The truth of this proposition is not intuitively obvious. It can be expressed in another equivalent form which may gain more ready acquiescence. *A higher maintained level of expenditure will result eventually in a higher national income and higher tax revenues; but the increase in tax revenues will necessarily fall short of the increased expenditure so that there will be a larger deficit per unit time.*

A rigorous numerical proof will not be presented here, but the reasoning involved can be briefly sketched. In the case of a single dollar of expenditure, the subsequent taxes collected out of the additional national income created are essentially of the nature of leakages. The higher the rate of taxation, the less the increase in national income, and the smaller tax revenues at a later date. The sum total must add up to less than one. Looking at the problem from the second point of view, let us suppose for the sake of the argument that higher expenditures do result in higher national income and higher tax revenues sufficient to balance the budget. The result is a contradiction, since at the new high level of the national income there is no longer a deficit to be "multiplied." In the absence of increased private investment, the system must fall back to the level which can be maintained without deficit financing.

The objection may be raised that the cash deficit is not so important as the net income creating expenditures of the government. Cannot a progressive tax system be devised which will balance the budget through taxation of the increases in income contributing little to consumption, and at the same time provide a positive amount of net income creating expenditures? Unfortunately, the answer is incontrovertibly in the negative. The net income creating expenditure under our hypotheses is necessarily directly proportional (but not equal) to the cash deficit. Of course, the more we tax incomes with low propensities to consume, the smaller need be the deficit to accomplish the same purpose. In fact, a new canon of taxation can be enunciated as follows: *private investment being given, any amount of revenue should be raised by taxation of income with the lowest marginal propensity to consume up to the point where marginal propensities to consume are equalized.* This will maximize the national income.

Conclusion

I should now like to turn to a consideration of the experience of our own economy in recent years. Professor Hansen, writing in 1937, put forward the point of view that

The recovery experienced in the United States in 1935-37 can be characterized as a consumption recovery. By that I mean that the expansion in income, employ-

1137

ment and output was based mainly on a rise in consumption. There had occurred, to be sure, a very considerable increase in real investment, but investment for the most part followed consumption; it did not, except in limited degree, lead the way. . . . Two factors were of primary importance. The first was the rise in the demand for durable consumers' goods of which automobiles were the most important single category; the second was the income-stimulating expenditures of the federal government.[18]

This was in contrast with previous recoveries which were mainly initiated and sustained by large bursts of anticipatory private investment. Because of its consumption nature a dilemma must be faced. Such a recovery can proceed no farther than it is pushed. It has no momentum of its own. It has no inner power to complete its own development.[19]

This illuminating and challenging thesis merits careful consideration. It can be subjected to only a brief examination here. First, some question must be raised as to the signficance of the distinction between this "consumption" recovery and other types. As far as investment in durable consumers' goods is concerned, it is well known that they partake of the nature of investment goods in general. There are, of course, differences in the contractual relations incident to purchase, ownership, and financing, but these must not hide the essential similarities. It is hard to find basic differences between the purchase of an automobile, a taxicab, or a truck, between the purchase of many home power units and a central dynamo, between the construction of a house for personal use or for leasing. Moreover, investment in durable consumers' goods follows the same pattern as other investment; *i.e.,* fluctuations in new installations greatly exceed those of the total stock; there is a tendency toward "death by natural causes" of such investment, etc. On the whole, economists and statisticians have wisely emphasized the likenesses of these two types of investment instead of concentrating upon the consumer and producer aspects.

The other feature justifying the characterization of the recovery as a consumption one also rests upon a verbal distinction. It is true that governmental deficit spending stimulated consumption, but by the Multiplier so would have an initiating burst of private investment. Only by not looking upon deficit spending as investment and by skipping to the following time period can the recovery be made to seem a consumption one.

Finally, can a distinction be drawn upon the basis of the operation of the acceleration principle? Analysis suggests that a burst of private investment in one isolated section of the economy should induce private investment elsewhere according to the familiar acceleration principle. This may lead to a temporary peak in income followed by a decline to the level which can be sustained by the net investment stimulus without the aid of induced

[18] Alvin H. Hansen, *Full Recovery or Stagnation?* (New York: W. W. Norton and Company, 1938), pp. 276-277.

[19] *Ibid.,* p. 282.

effects. If the net investment stimulus ceases, the system must still further decline just as it must if a maintained level of deficits is suddenly contracted. There is a point for point correspondence and isomorphism, therefore, between recoveries initiated by private and governmental investment.[20] The long-run implication of Professor Hansen's hypothesis of a possible secular stagnation of industry must, however, be regarded with the greatest interest.

I have not supplied an answer to the question as to the desirable long-time level of expenditure. That must depend upon what the future holds in store for us and upon the weighing of political imponderables. It is my personal conviction, however, that in the uncertain modern world we must heavily discount costs in the far future of present policies. Some doubt may be entertained as to the possibility of maintaining a balanced budget in a democracy under adverse international and institutional conditions. If the real national income can be increased by five or ten per cent over a long period of years only at the cost of incurring a debt of some tens of billions of dollars, I for one should consider the price not exorbitant.

PAUL A. SAMUELSON

Harvard University

[20] Much of the analysis of the downturn which seems to rest upon the operation of the acceleration principle follows equally from the action of the Multiplier alone. An uncompensated decline in deficits must lead to a downturn. From the Multiplier, consumption should lag behind income; this is strengthened by the occurrence of business losses following the downturn, and by the drawing upon savings and cash reserves by individuals at the onset of the depression. The relation between gross business investment and the increase in consumption does not appear to be strong in the yearly data of this period.

86

FISCAL POLICY AND INCOME DETERMINATION

SUMMARY

Scope of the paper, 575. — Negative multipliers, 576. — Level and growth of income in relation to level and growth of investment, 577. — Reaction of expenditure on revenue, 581. — Financial implications of deficits, 587.— Tertiary effects upon private investment, 595. — Public works vs. other expenditures, 599. — The multiplier and velocity approaches, 601. — Conclusion, 605.

Economic analysis advances discontinuously. After a great forward step, time must be taken to consolidate the gains achieved. This is nicely illustrated by the so-called "multiplier" analysis. When first announced in simple terms, its appeal was immediate, because it neatly expressed latent vague and intuitive notions of "purchasing power"; but because of its oversimplification, disappointments were inevitably aroused, and the doctrine received considerable criticism from economists who realized that important elements of truth were omitted. In many cases, however, the true difficulties were not localized, and sometimes false ones were conjured up. The present paper attempts a two-fold constructive task: (1) that of isolating some current misapprehensions, in order to clear the ground for further advance; and (2) that of carrying forward the analysis of important empirical and theoretical factors, usually assumed constant or neglected in the oversimplified versions of the theory.[1] The first sections deal with the *formal* relationships between economic variables which the multiplier analysis implies; the next sections are concerned with the reactions of investment and deficits on financial markets and on interest rates; this leads to a discussion of probable, induced tertiary private investment, including a discussion of the relative merits of public works expenditure and consumption expenditure for relief and social security; in the last section the implications of this discussion for the vitally important comparison of the "multiplier hypothesis" and the "velocity-of-money hypothesis" are developed.

[1]. This paper was written in the summer of 1941. While I have documented the discussion wherever necessary, I should like to make special reference to Professor Villard's recent invaluable review of the whole subject. (H. H. Villard, Deficit Spending and the National Income, New York, 1941.)

Negative Multipliers?

To many economists the doctrine of the multiplier appears as a rationalization of a free spending policy. Actually, they might argue, it is only too easy to conceive of an economy in which government spending is, on balance, harmful to employment and production. If one must use the terminology of the multiplier, under conditions which they consider to be realistic, it must surely be negative. Few, however, would now argue in exactly these terms. It has come to be realized that the multiplier doctrine as such is neutral with respect to public spending. The multiplier only amplifies what is put into it. If public spending is accompanied by negative private investment, the multiplier works in reverse, because the *multiplicand* (public expenditure plus net private disinvestment) is on balance negative.

More sophisticated writers familiar with the fact that the multiplier (M) equals the reciprocal of one minus the marginal propensity to consume (a), or $M = \dfrac{1}{1-a}$, suggest that the multiplier can very easily be negative if the marginal propensity to consume is greater than unity, causing the denominator and the whole of the above expression to be negative. It is certainly possible to imagine a world in which an extra dollar's income would result in more than a dollar's extra consumption expenditure and induced dissaving. On the other hand, untutored common sense suggests that in such a world a dollar of expenditure should be especially potent in raising the national income. It is not hard to dispel this paradox of an apparent negative multiplier in a world of particularly strong positive secondary repercussions to spending. The formula cited above was derived by a now familiar summation of an infinite series as income is spent and respent, namely,

$$1 + a + a^2 + a^3 + \cdots$$

If a exceeds one, the series is not convergent, and the usual summation formula, $\dfrac{1}{1-a}$, becomes untrue and must be replaced by $+\infty$.

Whether or not one adopts the time sequence analysis upon which the above geometric series[2] is based, it remains true that a

---

2. While dynamic time sequence analysis of the above type is often omitted when it should be present, the reverse procedure is also met. Super-sophisticated economists find it necessary to explain instantaneous algebraic

marginal propensity to consume greater than unity means that the system is unstable. It is impossible, then, to appraise the effects of any change in such a system, since finite changes involve infinite and indeterminate changes in all the magnitudes of the system. Although this is not the place to go into the matter, the facts themselves do not lend credence to the hypothesis of an unstable system.

LEVEL AND GROWTH OF INCOME
IN RELATION TO LEVEL AND GROWTH OF INVESTMENT

Perhaps most economists will admit that the marginal propensity to consume is less than unity, in view of the fact that *all* statistical investigations bear this out.[3] But it is difficult for them to account for domestic leakages, since they are accustomed to think of saving[4] as equivalent to investing, the rate of interest performing the equilibration under normal conditions. According to this point of view, the marginal propensity to consume plus the marginal propensity to invest equals unity, and again the system cannot be in stable equilibrium.

It will be instructive, in view of what is to follow, to revise our previous discussion of multiplier and multiplicand. Recent discussion in the field of foreign trade[5] has shown the arbitrariness of any one division of a total effect into *multiplier* and *multiplicand*. By modifying our definition of the multiplicand, we can derive a new multiplier. This may be done as follows: as before, let α equal the marginal propensity to consume; define β as the marginal propensity to invest $\left(= \dfrac{\Delta I}{\Delta Y} \right)$, namely the increase in investment

relations by means of summed infinite series taking place in hypothetical time such that all "rounds" take place contemporaneously. See Joan Robinson, Introduction to the Theory of Employment.

3. On the basis of existing facts it appears to be the reverse of the truth to argue that in the short run when income first increases, the marginal propensity to consume may be very large. Existing evidence suggests rather that there is a delay in becoming adjusted to a given level of income, and so the short run marginal propensity to consume is lower than the long run. This conclusion would be strengthened if durable consumers goods were treated as investment rather than consumption.

4. Not defined in strict Keynesian terms.

5. See especially D. H. Robertson, "Mr. Clark and the Foreign Trade Multiplier," Economic Journal, June, 1939.

induced by a given increase in income. Then our successive rounds of income subsequent to a given dollar expenditure are

$$1, (\alpha+\beta), (\alpha+\beta)^2, (\alpha+\beta)^3, \cdots$$

This series has a finite sum only if the arithmetical sum of the two coefficients is less than unity. In this case we have a multiplier of $\dfrac{1}{1-(\alpha+\beta)}$. If spending is adverse to private investment, β may be negative, so that this multiplier is less than the usual one. However, the whole expression cannot become negative if the system is to be stable. Actually, if the system is not to undergo successively greater oscillations, the adverse secondary effects can wipe out at most one-half of the primary stimulus.[6]

Those whose thinking runs in terms of velocity concepts often fall into the habit of implicitly regarding the sum of these coefficients as equal to unity. The creation of a single new dollar results in a *permanent* increase in income, while the creation of a constant number of new dollars per unit time results in an ever increasing national income.[7] This is pump-priming with a vengeance. Naught stops the dollars on their appointed rounds. If deficits disappear, the system does not decline; it merely ceases to grow.

One version of this view has been so ably exploded[8] that it would seem unnecessary to discuss it here, were it not for the fact that it keeps reappearing. It is not true, in good or bad times, that the rate of interest must fall so as to keep the velocity of circulation constant over time, nor did any "classical" economists hold this to be the case. Moreover, the marginal propensity to invest reflects an essentially short run phenomenon. As the stock of capital grows through cumulation of positive net investment, an increase in income will finally result in zero net investment.[9] Even in the shortest run the marginal propensity to invest appears,

6. When $\alpha+\beta=-1$, the system becomes explosive, i.e. when the multiplier $=\dfrac{1}{1-(-1)}=\frac{1}{2}$. It should be pointed out that the present analysis does not take into account less mechanical "once and for all" adverse effects, not operating via income changes.

7. Nevertheless, in finite time the national income is still finite, although increasing without bound.

8. See Walter S. Salant, "A Note on the Effects of a Changing Deficit," this Journal, February, 1939.

9. A. H. Hansen, Fiscal Policy and Business Cycles (New York, 1941), Chapter XIV.

on the basis of our incomplete statistical data, to be compatible with a stable system. A rise in anticipations which shifts the investment schedule upwards is not to be confused with the slope of an instantaneous schedule.[1] Later I discuss other aspects of velocity and multiplier concepts.

We may dispose briefly of a diametrically opposite point of view which seems to hold that ever increasing deficits are necessary to maintain a given level of income.[2] This belief seems to stem from a simple confusion. If the marginal propensity to consume declines with income, larger and larger deficits are needed to achieve given *increases* in income. But this only implies that larger *constant* deficits are needed to achieve higher *constant* levels of income. The multiplier decreases with income, but is still positive and finite.[3]

Related, but distinct from the above version, is the view that the permanent increase in public debt following a transitory deficit lowers income throughout all time.[4] This would require a *deficit* (and debt) increasing at least in geometric progression to maintain the same level of income. However, the possible harmful effect of debt on income has yet to be definitively treated; and as will be shown later, Clark's own analysis suggests that at least one harmful effect of a growing debt is in fact inoperative.

Rejecting as extreme the views of those who hold that a constant income level requires an ever decreasing deficit and those who believe that a constant income level requires an ever increas-

1. Simple calculations on the above velocity hypothesis lead to the ridiculous suggestion that a deficit of three-quarter billions per month over the next four years would (even if full employment were not reached!) increase the national income to almost 200 billion dollars yearly or to 64 billions per four month period (=present four month income plus addition of three billion dollars for each of twelve such periods). We may well have deficits at least this large, but clearly the facts will reveal a different story when we come to look at the data in retrospect. Cf. J. W. Angell, "Defense Financing and Inflation," Review of Economic Statistics, May, 1941, pp. 79–80; Investment and Business Cycles (New York, 1941).

2. C. J. Friedrich and E. S. Mason, ed., Public Policy, Vol. II, Chapter by R. A. Musgrave and B. H. Higgins.

3. In the case of the above writers, part of the confusion may have arisen from their belief, repeatedly asserted, that saving is increasing secularly. If one turns to the facts, it is obvious that total saving is decreasing, not increasing. However, this is not relevant. But it is relevant to point out that any secular changes in saving *out of a given income* are also downward, not upward. Of course, these writers are not alone in overlooking this fact.

4. See J. M. Clark, "An Appraisal of the Workability of Compensatory Devices," American Economic Review, Supplement, March, 1939.

ing deficit, we must examine the middle position, which holds that a single impulse of expenditure results in dwindling, finitely summable increases in income, and that over time a given constant level of spending will lead to a constant level of income. If the spending then goes back to the previous level, income will fall.

With characteristic originality and penetration Professor Clark has shown clearly that, just as an increase in investment leads to a rapid initial increase in income, finally tapering off to a new level, so a sudden decrease in deficit results in a great initial decrease in income, after which the rate of decrease tapers off. This is an illuminating criticism of any who might think that there is mirror symmetry in the rise and fall of income as plotted against time. Unfortunately, Clark was led too far by his analysis. On the basis of these observations he argues that national income is very sensitive to increases and decreases in investment expenditure. Now his own diagnosis, and algebraic analysis as well, proves just the reverse. Completely discontinuous changes in deficits he has shown to result in only gradual changes in income. It is true that the change is not so gradual as some economists may have believed, but it is nevertheless more gradual than the changes in the deficit.

For any who do not see this intuitively the following considerations are advanced: income by the familiar J. M. Clark-Kahn analysis is a weighted sum of past as well as present investment, the distributed-lagged-weights being $(1, a, a^2, a^3, \ldots, a^n)$. It is a mathematical theorem that the positively weighted sums of a fluctuating variable have a *smaller* (per cent) coefficient of variation than the variable itself.[5] If the reader plots cyclical fluctuations in investment around the average level unity against the resultant fluctuations in (increments of) income, where the latter are divided by $\dfrac{1}{1-a}$ to make the units comparable, he will see which has the smaller amplitude of fluctuation. The lead of investment at the turning points will confirm the reader's guess that in dynamic multiplier analysis income and investment are *formally* related, just as they are according to the acceleration principle.[6]

5. See the Mathematical Appendix in G. Haberler, Installment Credit and Economic Fluctuations. National Bureau of Economic Research, New York, 1942.

6. There is the non-essential difference that, in the acceleration principle, when replacement is neglected, the distributed-lagged-weights are not at all dwindling but constantly equal to one. Thus the contrast with respect to vola-

I conclude that whatever be the merits of a positive fiscal policy to meet cyclical or secular needs, no particular problems of timing arise from an alleged sensitivity of income to changes in deficit spending. The reverse is more likely to be true.

REACTION OF EXPENDITURE ON REVENUE

Some years ago it became fashionable to argue that a courageous *spending* policy, far from resulting in mounting debts, would raise the level of national income to the neighborhood of full employment, and thereby, through increased tax collections, for the first time permit the budget to stay in permanent balance. It is not clear whether, or to what extent, this was devised simply as a persuasive argument to back a policy considered good for other reasons or was intended as a scientific doctrine. In any case, it is perhaps worth discussing, because it permits an examination of expenditure from still another point of view, and because a previous brief discussion of mine on this same topic seems to have given rise to a certain amount of misunderstanding.[7]

While tax collections vary continuously as business activity fluctuates, tax rates are only periodically revised. At any one time there is in existence a *tax system* consisting of the totality of all tax rates. Under a given tax system, each level of national income tends to be associated with a given amount of tax revenue. Strictly speaking this is true only to a first approximation, because any given level of income can have been achieved in a variety of different ways — with much or little risky investment and profits, high or low consumption, rapid rate of increase or decrease, etc. Nevertheless, useful estimates can be made of the tax-income function.

For the Federal Government this is always an increasing function of income, but because of progressive income taxation and the shift to profits as income increases, the rate of increase is at an increasing rate. The following table illustrates the historical behavior of Federal revenues and national income.

tility and sluggishness of the series is not so great in the multiplier as with the acceleration principle. However, if one adopted the rejected Gayer-Angell view mentioned above (p. 579), the *formal* analogy would be exact.

7. "The Theory of Pump-Priming Reëxamined," American Economic Review, September, 1940; reprinted in this volume as Chap. 85.

ESTIMATED TAX YIELDS AT DIFFERENT LEVELS OF NATIONAL INCOME

National Income (Millions of Dollars)	Federal Tax Yield (Millions of Dollars)
42,430 (1933)	2,721
50,347 (1934)	3,765
55,870 (1935)	4,244
65,165 (1936)	5,379
71,172 (1937)	6,149
63,610 (1938)	5,071
69,378 (1939)	5,780
90,000*	11,200
100,000*	13,400

* Estimated at 1940 rates; calendar years throughout.
Source: Report of the Secretary of the Treasury, 1940, p. 5.

Since tax rates were changing upward throughout the period, the increase in revenue with income is greater than would have been true for any given statical curve. It is clear, therefore, that at the rates which prevailed in the middle 'thirties a dollar's increase in national income above existing levels would raise Federal revenues by less than twelve cents; i.e. the marginal propensity to tax was less than .12 at low levels of income. Because of the elements of progression in our Federal system, the tax-income curve would be increasing at an increasing rate. Today we are moving into higher income ranges, and at the same time have levied new taxes which will increase both the average tax and the marginal propensities to tax. It follows that the marginal propensity to tax must surely exceed .22 and probably does not fall short of .4.

While it used to be considered a canon of taxation that a good tax system should produce a steady yield, i.e. the marginal propensity to tax should be almost zero or even perhaps negative, it seems likely that the economist of the future will praise income taxes precisely because they fail to meet this canon, all questions of equity aside. For a high marginal propensity to tax acts as a stabilizer on the system, against both upward and downward movements.

Can we find an invariant relationship between expenditure and income, as we have been able to do in the case of taxes and income? It is true that some governmental activities, such as the post office, do increase with income. It is also the unfortunate truth that in the past legislatures have succumbed to the psychology of the private entrepreneur and have increased expenditure most during booms and curtailed them during depressions, thus *relatively* increasing the fluctuations of business. But if policy is to be discussed, we cannot freeze the action of the government by talking in terms of a fixed expenditure-income schedule. We can always imagine such schedules, but it is precisely the shifts in these, hereafter labelled *autonomous* changes in expenditure, that are of interest.[8]

Let us now make a simple calculation. Suppose that the national income is at ninety billion dollars with a purposely assumed high marginal propensity to consume of about three-quarters, and hence a multiplier of four. The expenditure of two and one-half billion dollars will then raise the national income by ten billions. However, a glance at the table or figure will show that this raises revenues by around four billion dollars. It begins to look as if the Secretary of the Treasury is overlooking an easy way of raising income and paying off the debt at the same time. Of course there is a flaw in this argument, but where it is may not be immediately obvious. As multiplicand we have used the total amount of expenditure, and applied to this the usual multiplier described in earlier sections. Actually, the latter is appropriate only if as multiplicand we use the deficit, i.e. first subtract additional taxes.[9]

Does this mean that we must always use net expenditure (deficits) as multiplicand and never gross expenditures? This is not unlike the problem encountered in the field of international trade to which reference has already been made. Shall exports or exports minus imports be used as multiplicand to appraise the resulting increase in employment? Much of the argumentation on this point has not been very helpful, but we now know that either multiplicand may be used if the multiplier is adjusted appropriately.

8. In strict logic, policy might dictate the analysis of autonomous changes in taxes. I am in sympathy with this point of view, although I suspect that such changes had best be adjusted to the secular outlook. To aid in the cyclical problem, the tax function should be devised so as to have a very high *marginal* propensity to tax. More taxes might be geared *directly* to the national income; e.g. lowered corporate tax *rates*, when national income is low. This will twice lower revenue, once through the decline in corporate incomes and secondly through the change in rates via national income change.

9. The unwary will be tempted at this stage to use 2.5−4.0 billion as the (negative) multiplicand, coming out with the conclusion that income will fall by six billion as a result of the one and one-half billion surplus. Of course, this would be grossly fallacious, for reasons which can be left to the reader.

If exports are used as multiplicand, imports must be treated as leakages which reduce the value of the multiplier. So in the domestic sphere; if we use gross expenditure as the multiplicand, taxes must be treated as leakages. The appropriate multiplier is not $\dfrac{1}{1-a}$, but rather $\dfrac{1}{1-a(1-\tau)}$, where τ is the marginal propensity to tax, and where we reckon as income, income before taxes.

In terms of the previous example where $a=.75$, $\tau=.4$, $2\frac{1}{2}$ billion dollars expenditure will raise income before taxes by about $4\frac{1}{2}$ billion dollars $\left(\text{approximately equal to } \dfrac{1}{1-.75(1-.4)}2.5\right)$. The increased deficit will be only equal to about .7 billion dollars, or the original expenditure minus the new taxes of approximately 1.8 billion dollars. The increase in income after taxation, which is the important thing, if the government expenditure is not devoted to a useful purpose, is equal to about 2.8 billions, or just four times the deficit.[1] While the deficit has increased by not nearly so much as expenditure, it has nevertheless increased somewhat. Not even so powerful an agency as the Treasury can lift itself by its own bootstraps.

1. Simple rigorous proofs are as follows. Throughout induced private investment is neglected, and all symbols refer to increments of income (thus $Y=\Delta Y$). Let

Y = net income after taxes

C = consumption assumed to equal a times net income after taxes

Y^* = gross income before taxes

T = tax collections = τY^*

E = expenditure

Then by definition

$Y^*=C+E$

$Y=Y^*-T=C+(E-T)$

$C=aY=a(1-\tau)Y^*$

By substitution we have

$$Y^*=\frac{1}{1-a(1-\tau)}E$$

$$Y=\frac{1}{1-a}(E-T)$$

$$T=\frac{\tau}{1-a(1-\tau)}E$$

$$E-T=\frac{(1-a)(1-\tau)}{1-a(1-\tau)}E=\frac{(1-a)(1-\tau)}{\tau+(1-a)(1-\tau)}\quad E>0,\text{ if }\begin{array}{l}0<\tau<1\\0<a<1\end{array}$$

1149

We have been generous in selecting a marginal propensity to tax of .4. Even if we were more generous, the qualitative picture would not change. No tax system has ever been devised which is administrable if an increase in gross income before taxation does not result in some increase in retained income. (One might construct a "freak" case in which an individual was taxed less than the total increment of income, but where the rates confronting all individuals increased with national income so as to lead to a final increase of revenue greater than the increment of income.) Hence, the marginal propensity to tax must be less than unity by at least a small fraction. This being the case, if a government spends, without at the same time making autonomous changes in tax *rates*, it cannot raise the national income *in a stable system* without at the same time raising deficits by *some* amount. The induced increase in taxes resulting throughout all time from given expenditure must fall short of that expenditure.[2] Of course, the larger the propensity to tax, the less the Treasury will lose, but there must always be some finite loss.

I should like to emphasize what the above analysis does *not* imply. First, it does not mean that we cannot have full employment and a balanced budget. Even in the face of adverse secular trends, we can hope to revise our tax system to reduce saving so that full employment can be maintained, perhaps with a surplus over time. But this is an effect of autonomous changes in the tax function; with a given function, it remains true that increased expenditure means less additional revenue and somewhat higher deficits. Expenditure and tax policy should be kept analytically distinct for clear thinking, even though we should use both weapons simultaneously.

Secondly, my analysis does not mean that a dollar of expenditure could not *set off* a perpetual boom, and hence yield throughout time taxes many times itself in amount. If the system is in *unstable* underemployment equilibrium, and this is what pump-priming implies,[3] any push, not necessarily that of government expenditure,

2. If the marginal propensity to consume is unity, the only leakages are taxes. Consequently, throughout all time the full expenditure returns to the Treasury. Here we can have our cake and eat it too. But the system must be ruled out as not being stable. In such a world, one would not have to rely on fiscal policy, but rather could depend on the reëmployment of all the idle as a result of one private dollar of continuous investment per unit time.

3. Samuelson, op. cit.

may send it forward. But for such, the whole multiplier analysis, if not all analysis, explodes in our hands.[4]

Finally, although the simple algebraic version given above assumes a single average marginal propensity to consume for all classes, more complicated analysis shows that it is not vitiated by the changes in income distribution which result from expenditure. Of course, the important changes in income distribution and the average propensity to consume resulting from changes in the tax system fall under the heading of autonomous changes in taxes, and were excluded above.

The above case illustrates the point that it is not so important which multiplier is used as that it be matched with the appropriate multiplicand. Much needless controversy has resulted from such confusions. It would be extremely unfortunate if the multiplicity of multipliers were to be regarded as a defect of the analysis, when in fact it is rather a tribute to the flexibility of the concept. The question nevertheless inevitably is asked: which is *the* correct multiplier? Inasmuch as all are algebraically and conceptually consistent, there is not much point in the question.

Still, in a world where none of the relationships hold exactly, we should select that formulation which presents the greatest invariance, not over time in a simple statistical historical sense, but for the purpose at hand. *The different formulations are consistent but not equivalent.* In international trade the use of exports as multiplicand coupled with its appropriate multiplier contains *more* than the use of the trade balance as multiplicand, since the latter does not utilize at all our knowledge concerning a stable propensity-to-import schedule (if this is a fact!). If the latter relationship exists, we are throwing away information by not using it; we leave unsolved part of the problem, that of determining what the trade balance multiplicand will be. On the other hand, if we are interested in the effects of devaluation, a deliberate "autonomous" shift in the propensity-to-import schedule is implied, and so the last mentioned multiplier, because of its incompleteness, is to be preferred. Similarly in the domestic sphere, if the effect of expenditure under

---

4. It may be simpler to consider the matter in the following way. Any initial expenditure is followed throughout all time by exactly an equivalent amount of leakage, *if the system is stable*. The leakages are taxes and saving. Since the latter is positive, the tax collections must fall short of revenue expenditure. This conclusion is unmodified by the assumption of induced investment, provided the system remains a stable one.

given tax rates is desired, the appropriate multiplier is that which includes taxes as a leakage, even if the irregularity of the statistical facts makes this the more difficult one to estimate.[5]

In the last analysis, the choice of the appropriate *multiplier* does not depend upon past statistical invariance. For each question asked, a different answer is required; hence there is a different multiplier for each multiplicand, i.e. for each question asked. The degree of past statistical invariance is of relevance only in assessing the amount of confidence to be placed in the answer.

FINANCIAL IMPLICATIONS OF DEFICITS

The usual multiplier analysis represents a useful over-simplification in stressing the secondary effects of investment on consumption while more or less neglecting other elements of the system. For example, one rarely sees a detailed time sequence analysis of the effect on the rate of interest of a single impulse of government or private expenditure or of a continuing stream of net investment. This is unfortunate, since investigation of kindred problems sheds light on some of the puzzling phenomena of the day.

For the last decade we have seen the maintenance of continuously large and increasing deficits, with a concomitant prodigious increase in the public debt. Repeatedly, respected economists and economic foundations of reputation have seen in these facts the peril of imminent collapse of the government's credit. Each time they have been proved to be wrong by subsequent events, but this has not deterred them from announcing imminent doom at a later date. They have cried "Wolf" so many times that even they themselves do not believe with the same fervor, but have removed the evil day to the next generation.

In terms of the dominant thought and teaching in American universities during the first quarter of this century, their beliefs are not hard to explain.[6] Nor is there any place here for a political discussion as to whether they are right or wrong in attacking a spending policy. The fact worthy of emphasis is simply that they

5. Compare the somewhat similar point of view expressed by Professor Haberler in the third edition of his Prosperity and Depression, pp. 461–473.

6. It is interesting to note that a similar orthodoxy never grew up in England of the same period. Presumably, the intense political agitation over bimetallism in the United States of the 'nineties, resulting as it did in a victory of the "gold bugs," was a significant factor in the crystallization of thought along these lines, just as the post-war continental inflations left indelible prints upon the economists of those countries.

were bad theoretical and applied economists in observing and interpreting events of the 'thirties. A bank, an insurance company, or a
private investor would have done better, *ex post*, to have paid no
heed to their analyses.

Leaving aside any approval or disapproval of governmental
policy, how can we explain the continuance of low interest rates
coupled with a growing debt? In the case of the United States,
there has been at the same time a net increase of gold holdings
amounting to almost twenty billion dollars. This can be accounted
for by our devaluation, which raised the purchasing price of gold
to thirty-five dollars an ounce, and to capital flight from a politically frightened Europe. It is to be stressed that, except for the
recent war period and during the United States recession of 1938,
the gold flowed in on capital account, not in order to pay for an
excess of United States exports; but the latter might have been
smaller were it not for the gold policy. Undoubtedly this contributed to the low interest rates which prevailed in the United States;
but by the same token it cannot explain the low rates prevailing
in large parts of the world at the same time that an armament
race was leading to ever larger deficits. The depressed state of
private investment outlets the world over also is of undoubted
relevance here in explaining the low level of interest rates, but does
not explain why they stayed low as the debt increased.

When analysis fails, there is often an only too familiar recourse
to primitive animism. Many, therefore, have in desperation pointed
to the government — i.e. Treasury and central bank — as the
perpetrator of a "rigged" market. In the absence of coercion
(certainly not as yet pertinent for the United States), economic
analysis tells us that the government can influence market behavior
only along the familiar mechanism of purchase and sale. A nation
is on the gold standard because the Treasury will both buy and
sell gold at the mint ratio; an exchange equalization account
affects exchange rates only by purchase and sale. The Federal
Reserve System can operate only via legal reserve requirements,
rediscount rates, open market purchase and sale. These truths
are elementary, but it seems necessary to emphasize that no secret
weapons exist or are being used. It is a matter of open record that
throughout most of the period under consideration the Federal
Reserve System was *not* acquiring governments in an attempt to
peg their price.

While it has not been operating as an artificial source of demand, it has nevertheless supported the market in time of threatened crisis, such as the spring of 1937 and the fall of 1939. Moreover, it is the opinion of the financial community that it will continue to do so in the future. This indirectly affects demand, since it causes governments to have for the public new properties of liquidity and nearness to money. However, the System would be lax in its duty if it did not so act, and in my opinion we should long since have had even more effective guaranteeing of the market value of long-term securities, so that there would be a great lessening in their differential premia over short-term securities. These premia have been necessary in order to compensate for the risk of capital loss, a risk believed in so greatly by investors who think in terms of previous normal yields.[7]

All of the above facts help to explain why rates should start from a low level, but cast little light on why the growth of debt does not finally increase them. The answer is not hard to find, since it is implicit in the multiplier analysis from Kahn onwards, and is nowhere better stated than in the work of J. M. Clark.[8] A continuous deficit raises the national income until a constant level is reached. It is a condition of this constancy that there is automatically guaranteed out of the new income level an amount of *voluntary* saving per unit time exactly equal to the deficit per unit time. Investment per unit time creates, so to speak, its own sustenance. This crucial fact is often overlooked and is periodically rediscovered. When income has ceased to grow, a *constant* deficit, *which means a continuous linearly increasing debt*, is associated with no upward pressure on interest rates. The rate of interest depends upon the rate of increase in debt, not upon the amount of the debt itself. As far as the multiplier analysis is concerned, we can have a five billion dollar annual deficit for a quarter of a century with no upward pressure on interest rates as the debt exceeds 100 billion dollars, 125 billion, and so forth. While this is an oversimplified picture of reality, it does contain an important grain of truth providing a helpful mechanism to explain the undoubted

7. It is not unusual to find writers who are opposed to spending because of adverse effects upon the public credit expressing disappointment that such adverse effects are not forthcoming in sufficient amounts to curtail spending!

8. Op. cit. and Capital Formation and its Elements (National Industrial Conference Board, 1939), pp. 54–85.

historical, statistical facts of secular rising debt, public and private, with constant and falling interest rates.[9]

It is important to note that a high level of deficit spending does to some extent tend to result in higher interest rates[1] — but not increasingly higher ones. As income is growing, more money is required to finance transactions, leaving less available to satisfy the speculative motive. Consequently, interest rates tend to rise somewhat. By the time income has reached its maximum, rates will rise no further. The government is returning money to the community as fast as it is borrowing it; individuals bring to the capital markets savings out of the increment of income just balancing the government's deficit expenditure and security flotations.

In Figures I and II are portrayed two sets of four charts. In each case chronological time is measured along the horizontal axis. The intersection of the axes marks the time when a given act (such as government spending) is assumed to begin. To the left of this point the system is assumed to be at its previous level with respect to all economic variables, taken as zero, since we work only with deviations from the previous levels. The vertical axes are not labelled, since space will be economized if the same diagram is used to typify the behavior of more than one variable, the vertical scale being modified accordingly. Figure I will refer in every case to a sudden increase in the deficit which is thereafter maintained at a positive constant level (see Figure Ia), while Figure II refers exclusively to a single impulse of expenditure followed by a return to the previous level (see Figure IIa).

We are now in a position to demonstrate geometrically the behavior over time of income, interest, deficit, debt, hoards, etc.

9. I myself do not argue that this would, should, or could happen. Over long periods of time much can take place both economic and political. I reserve for a later discussion the general problem of the equilibrating efficacy of cumulated rates of flow, i.e. stocks (capital, wealth, debt, hoards, etc.). It is not possible to infer from statistical data of the '30's whether interest rates were really independent of the height of the public debt, or whether the influx of new money supply offset such pressure.

1. Among non-academic financial writers one encounters repeatedly the incomprehensible statement that the government's floating of bonds at low interest rates is the cause of the low rates of interest on private securities. To this crude confusion of cause and effect is added the further fallacy that prevailing low yields are discouraging the supply of saving and jeopardizing the community's existing capital stock. How low interest rates, if they really prevail, can be other than conducive to investment and maintenance, and how rates can continue to be low, if savings are deficient, is left unexplained.

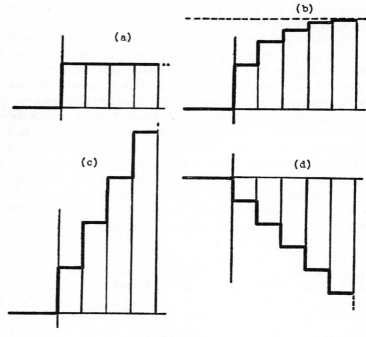

FIGURE I

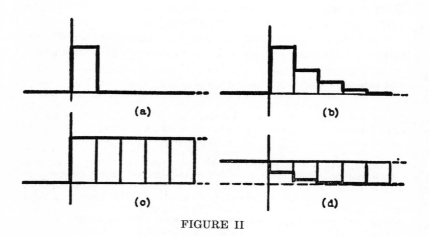

FIGURE II

It is necessary to distinguish carefully, as is too rarely done, three main cases: (1) where the debt is financed by borrowing from individuals, as would have to be the case if the banking system were loaned up; (2) where the excess expenditure is financed by fiat money or through central bank purchase; (3) where the bonds are sold to a banking system with excess reserves. In the past, combinations of (1) and (3) have been of great importance, except in time of war and emergency, when recourse is had to (2).

In case (1) we must refer to Figure I. I assume a new positive deficit held constant through time as in Ia. Then income behaves as in Ib, and the debt grows as in Ic. To a first approximation interest behaves as in Ib, i.e. like income, but of course with a different scale according to its own units. Induced tax collections also behave like income, but greatly reduced in scale. Attention is called to the steady growth of the debt with a constant interest rate. Private money holdings (deposits and cash in circulation) remain constant throughout, the active part growing with income. The repeated government expenditure is necessary to keep so large a fraction circulating. With unemployment in existence before and after expenditure, prices need not change. Later, as a second approximation, I shall discuss the behavior of private investment.

Still adhering to case (1), involving no credit creation, it is important to analyze the effect of a single impulse of expenditure, since we can get from this the effects of any time shape of expenditure by superposition. Deficits behave as in IIa; the debt as in IIc; income, interest, taxes with respectively appropriate scales as in IIb. Total money holdings do not change, the impulse of expenditure leading to a transitory increase in velocity which gradually dwindles away. Again note that a permanent increase in debt is associated with no permanent change in interest.

Let us next consider case (2), in which expenditure continuously in excess of revenue by a constant amount is financed by outright money creation. Figure Ia illustrates the behavoir of the deficit over time. Figure Ic no longer illustrates the growth of debt, but rather the growth of money ("non-interest debt") in the system. To a first approximation income increases as in Ib, just as in case (1). In the first period the new money is all tied up in income transactions, so that interest rate remains the same; on subsequent rounds more and more of the money pumped into the system is released for non-transaction holding, with consequent downward pressure on interest rates. Finally, when income ceases to rise, none of the newly created money is required for transaction purposes, and holding of inactive money increases linearly with time (Ic), and to a first approximation the interest rate drops off linearly (Id). Of course, under conditions such as prevailed in the 'thirties, when there seemed to exist a broad margin of indifference between money and governments, the decline in interest rates may be infinitesimal; in terms of the diagram the scale of the ordinate (Id) must be infinitely enlarged.

I will simply state without explanation the corresponding effects when there is a single impulse of monetary creation (IIa). At first the increase in income absorbs all of the new cash, but as income dwindles (IIb), more and more is released for speculative holding, with the result that the interest rate is depressed until it reaches a level compatible with the inactive holding of the whole increment of new money (IId). An increase in money (m), if brought about by temporary government spending, implies no necessary decrease in v in the very short run, *but subsequently v falls by as much as the increase in m*. Even when we turn to a consideration of induced private investment, we shall see that the neglected factor only puts off the evil day.[2]

Case (3), in which the deficit is financed by sales to banks with excess reserves, is in many ways the most complicated of all. Very often Keynes regards the banking system as peculiarly subject to policy decision via Central Bank controls, so that its behavior is not amenable to analysis, but is taken as an independent datum. This treatment avoids the problems of greatest interest from the present point of view. I shall go to the opposite extreme in regarding the banks simply as specialized financial institutions dealing in particular sectors of the Securities markets, and making decisions in essentially the same manner as other investors. As soon as one abandons the hypothesis of a tendency for the velocity of circulation to be constant or even to have causal significance in its own right, it is possible to strip the process of monetary

---

2. The ultimate collapse in velocity of newly created money is not peculiar to government spending. In a non-Euclidean world involving permanent underemployment, an increase in money purchasing power due to private net investment, gold imports, etc. will not be permanent. Ever new net investment must be forthcoming. On the other hand, in a Euclidean world, where employment is always full, so that monetary creation permanently raises all prices and costs à la Quantity Theory, this effect is not present.

creation via multiple bank expansion of the aura of importance and mysticism which so often surrounds it. At the same time the insoluble problem of the proper definition of money (currency, demand deposits, time deposits, negotiable instruments, etc.) is shown to be artificial and unimportant. The more precisely one defines m, the more shiftable becomes v, and conversely.

Despite the common tendency to regard excess reserves as being an unnecessary surplus, the bank *feels* that it needs them. The legal ratio is only a lower limit, but not necessarily operative. Thus in Great Britain, where no legal ratios exist, the customary ratio felt to be needed is the only relevant one.[3] Additional governments will be purchased only if the yield is somewhat higher (under modern conditions infinitesimally) than it otherwise would have been. As the proceeds of the loan are spent and respent, less and less of the newly created deposits are required to finance the dwindling income (IIb). The newly created deposits do not leave the banks, but gravitate from government ownership to private ownership. It is to be emphasized that the banks keep the deposits, but only as liabilities. The public and not the banks receive the government expenditure and its aftermath as income. But private individuals will not hold idle the new larger amount of cash at precisely the same interest rate, and so they tend to bid up the price of governments and lower their yield. In the process they acquire some of the banks' governments, destroying some of the newly created money. In the new equilibrium the rate of interest would be almost the same as previously, with the money supply

3. This does not imply that the banks feel the reserves to be necessary to cover possible withdrawals. It is more and more being realized that reserves do *not* perform the function of till money. Rather they are felt to be necessary for the maximization of income over time in a world where uncertainty dictates a diversification of portfolios. This the Reserve authorities overlooked when they raised reserve requirements in 1936–1937. They were unprepared for the resulting pressure on the market for governments, since they regarded excess reserves as surpluses. Actually, the banks tried to reëstablish old excess reserve ratios. The fact that they did not succeed in doing so — on balance the public acquired few governments from the banking system — is still compatible with the hypothesis that they attempt to do so. Paradoxically, the break in early 1937 came when the budget was almost balanced for the first time in years, as a result in large part of the new Social Security taxes. In connection with the increase in reserve requirements in the fall of 1941, it may be said that the changed business outlook made it unlikely that an attempt would be made to restore the old amount of excess reserves. However, some pressure was put upon the market; and this was after all the goal of the move. More than this oversimplified picture cannot be attempted here

almost the same as previously. In other words, the amount of new money behaves very much like IIb.

This hypothesis of a "reflux" action whereby the banks create new money to bridge a period of expansion, after which the deposits themselves dwindle away, is as far as I know novel.[4] It could be verified only if we could isolate our impulses. Even then this would be difficult in the recent period for two reasons. First, there has been a gradual downward shift in the banks' liquidity preference schedules in recent years. Over time they would be willing to hold more and more governments and less and less cash at the same rates of interest, in consequence of their fading recollection of past high rates. (Our observations of growing excess reserves are not inconsistent with the above statement, if careful distinction is made between shifts of a schedule and movements along the schedule). Second, the liquidity preference schedules of both banks and the public have been so elastic as to create a broad margin of indifference between the holding of money substitutes and money (deposits for individuals, Federal Reserve deposits for banks). Consequently, induced changes in the interest rate are negligible. Under this condition, it is of almost no importance that the banks instead of individuals acquire new issues. This raises the amount of money, but by depriving individuals of money substitutes for holding, it insures that money will be inactive. The creation of fiat money would have the same effect as cases (1) and (3).

In these considerations lies the key to the failure of monetary policy to promote recovery. Even in the war years ahead, they may lead to deviations from conventional monetary behavior, although presumably to a lessened degree.

TERTIARY EFFECTS UPON PRIVATE INVESTMENT

Because the consumption function is highly stable, we can be relatively certain of the secondary reaction of induced consumption to income. Our first multiplier, the reciprocal of one minus the marginal propensity to consume, is presumably most invariant of all, and will form one part of any explanation of the effect of expansionary investment expenditure. Its usefulness stems from the fact that the stable predictable elements are segregated from

4. For continuous deficits, instead of a single impulse, we should expect from the reflux principle that the process would begin as in case (3), but after the period of expansion merge into case (1).

the volatile, capricious variables, lumped together into the multiplicand.[5]

In appraising the *tertiary* effects of government deficits upon private confidence, I do not believe that I have anything to add to the usual discussion. Any lack of confidence must be related to the whole political and social environment (public regulation, trust busting, business baiting, labor legislation, etc.). I do not think the deficit is quantitatively important in the face of these factors; whatever importance it has had is by now historical. For better or worse, we have departed from the path of strict financial respectability. The human mind cannot comprehend the astronomical figures involved in public finance, and even the alarmists have become accustomed to continuous deficits.[6]

Turning to less psychological factors, changes in the interest rate might be thought to have an influence upon private investment. Deficits of recent years have largely been financed by

5. At one point in the General Theory Keynes seems to base his multiplier analysis upon the logically impeccable equation

$$\Delta Y = \left(\frac{1}{1 - \dfrac{\Delta C}{\Delta Y}}\right) \Delta I$$

which is only a transcription of the identity, $Y = C + I$. He therefore seems to lay himself open to Haberler's charge of having a purely formal, irrefutable theory. But just as we must distinguish between the Quantity Equation and the Quantity Theory (better termed Hypothesis), so we must interpret the multiplier "theory" as hypothecating stability, invariance, and predictability to the term in parenthesis. This multiplier, badly named *psychological*, is of the utmost importance in laying out the complex answer to a change in a given datum (call it A), even though it is *not* the whole answer. The whole answer is given by

$$\Delta Y = \left(\frac{1}{1 - \dfrac{\Delta C}{\Delta Y}}\right) \frac{\Delta I}{\Delta A} \Delta A$$

The real difficulties, now under discussion, are involved in appraising $\Delta I/\Delta A$, but this does not justify us in throwing away that part of the analysis which is known and determinate. Cf. G. Haberler, "Mr. Keynes' Theory of the Multiplier,' " Zeitschrift für Nationalökonomie, 1936.

6. Until the onset of the defense program I should have been inclined to minimize the factor of confidence. The reluctance of business to invest seemed adequately explained by the prospects of profitable investment. Not venture capital but good ventures seemed lacking. When deficits and income were high, private investment was high, whatever the financial community said at the time; when deficits decreased at the same time that income was falling, business disinvested on a vast scale. However, events of the last two years in connection with defense orders make this hypothesis less certain.

methods (1) and (3) of the classification used above, i.e. by security sales to the public, to the banks, and to insurance companies or other non-banking commercial institutions.   We should expect, therefore, continuous deficits to have had some, limited, upward influence on interest rates over what yields otherwise would have been. Depending upon the slope of the marginal efficiency schedule, this might be expected to have a tendency towards inhibiting private investment.[7]   Diametrically opposed to this tendency, however, is that resulting from the expansion, primary and secondary, of sales as a result of deficits.   We are now accustomed to regard the investment marginal efficiency schedule as depending upon income (or consumption) as well as upon the interest rate.[8] Sales financed by deficit spending should bring in their train net private investment.

Which of these tendencies, interest or income, was the stronger? The answer depends, as Professor Lange has shown in dealing with a related problem,[9] upon the relative elasticity of the investment marginal efficiency schedule with respect to interest and income and upon the elasticities of the liquidity preference schedule. In the decade of the 'thirties the harmful effects of interest rate changes must have been negligible for two analytically distinct reasons. (1) The broad margin of indifference between the holding of money and governments meant that the induced increases in the interest rate were at a minimum.   This is further accentuated by the lack of perfect substitutability of government securities for private issues.   (2) The little evidence we have suggests that investment was very inelastic with respect to interest rate changes for technical and psychological reasons, as well as for the reason that corporations were in a relatively favorable position to finance expansions internally.

In the early 'thirties, when the system was at a low level and declining, the existence of excess capacity implied that investment was also inelastic with respect to income (sales).   This became less and less true as output increased and deferred replace-

7. This effect, and those which immediately follow, could take place only in the short run, since after the stock of capital has adjusted itself to a change in the rate of interest, induced private investment (positive or negative) will disappear.

8. See O. Lange, "The Optimum Propensity to Consume," Economica, 1938.

9. Ibid.

ment accumulated. On balance, there seems to be a clear presumption in favor of the view that the tendency towards positive investment induced by income changes outweighed the tendency towards disinvestment induced by interest rate changes.

Again I must emphasize that this gain is only transitory. A single impulse of expenditure, resulting as it does in an ultimate return to the previous income level, implies that the far future will wipe out with disinvestment (induced by income decline) the near future's investment. Nevertheless, if one impulse follows another in a continuing steady stream, we may put off the evil day. In the beginning we shall have transitory induced investment; later, when the capital stock is adjusted to the new level of income and interest rate, there will be neither induced investment nor disinvestment. If the deficit were curtailed, there would follow disinvestment, equal, in a first approximation which disregards windfall losses, to the induced investment.

Thus, from the long-run point of view we may disregard tertiary reactions on private investment, whatever the short run implications. The formulae $\frac{1}{1-a}$, or $\frac{1}{1-a(1-\tau)}$, are not *part* of the answer to the question of the permanent level of income corresponding to a given level of sustained deficit spending; they provide virtually the whole answer to this question.[1]

We have neglected one important aspect of the short-run picture. When recipients of government expenditure make purchases from business concerns, in the shortest run they will receive goods out of inventories. The government expenditure will be offset by involuntary, private disinvestment But in subsequent periods we may expect enterprises to re-order, so as to restore their inventories to their appropriate levels. If the government expenditure persists, the new higher income level should require even more inventories. In the process of building these up, there will be transitory induced tertiary investment, as described above. But if income is falling, or is lower than it had previously been, inven-

---

1. One particular example of the short-run pattern of induced investment was developed in my paper, "Interactions between the Multiplier Analysis and the Principle of Acceleration," reprinted in this volume as Chap. 82. There it was assumed that the capital stock maintained a constant ratio to consumption, thereby invoking the acceleration principle. In the short run there was on balance induced private investment, but for every stable system, income settled down to the usual level given by the multiplier.

tories may already have been excessive before the occurrence of government expenditure. The induced purchases help to work off the inventories, being followed by no re-ordering. From this it is sometimes concluded that governmental expenditure is peculiarly ineffective in depression.[2]

Clearly this conclusion is not validly derived. Expenditure may be particularly effective when income is low and falling. For in any case inventories would have been reduced. There is no induced disinvestment compared with what there would otherwise have been. It is true that deficits permit the disinvestment to take place earlier, but in the same measure they advance the day of eventual restoration of inventories.[3] While the behavior of inventories does not invalidate our broad quantitative results, it does modify considerably the description of the impact over time of investment on the economic system.

Public Works vs. Other Expenditures

At this stage of the analysis I should like to examine the controversial problem of the relative merits of expenditure upon public works and expenditure upon relief, social security, etc. In general, the preponderance of opinion seems to be in favor of the view that a special potency inheres in public work expenditure. With this I cannot agree. It is desirable, therefore, to examine the powerful arguments recently advanced by Professor Hansen.[4]

He admits that, as far as the first round of expenditure is concerned, relief expenditures are spent more certainly, more speedily, and more fully. But on subsequent rounds there is no presumption in favor of one or the other. In this connection I should like to point out that, if the general community's marginal propensity to consume is approximately $\frac{1}{2}$, the first round involves one-half the total effect. Moreover, if expenditure on public works means that on the first round there is a leakage of $\frac{1}{2}$ leading to a series ($\frac{1}{2}$, $\frac{1}{4}$, $\frac{1}{8}$, $\cdots$) as compared with a relief series

2. Cf., for example, National Resources Planning Board, Public Works Expenditure, Appendix.

3. To some extent inventories would otherwise have been sold at prices which involve losses, so that less disinvestment would take place in the absence of expenditure. This is the grain of truth in the belief that there may be net induced disinvestment. Even in this case the deficit could be justified on the basis of its contribution to capital-repair and orderly liquidation.

4. A. H. Hansen, op. cit., pp. 90–92.

$(1, \frac{1}{2}, \frac{1}{4}, \frac{1}{8}, \cdots)$, relief expenditure is twice as potent, as far as consumption is concerned.

Professor Hansen rests his case, however, upon the induced private investment in the durable goods field. As we have seen in the previous paragraphs, these effects can only be transient. In support of this I cited the work of Professor Hansen on the marginal propensity to invest and the acceleration principle. Once the heavy industries become geared to the government expenditure, they will need no further net investment. Moreover, the government itself (at once or over time through amortization) will pay for the new plant built. It would be double counting to include the government's expenditure in the multiplicand and also induced private investment which the government in effect pays for.[5]

Three final points are advanced in connection with public work expenditure. First, it is an undoubted fact that the heavy industries feel depressions exceptionally strongly. Their output declines greatly.[6] This often suggests a doubtful ethical presumption in favor of helping the underdog, the one who suffers most. To me this seems unconvincing, particularly since the long-run outlook may necessitate a reorganization of the economy in the direction of more consumption and less heavy industry. Second, we may dismiss completely the naïve belief that, since booms are characterized by activity in the heavy industries, it is particularly important to stimulate these channels. Third, and this seems to be most important in Hansen's treatment, public works represent concentrated expenditure as compared with diversified expenditure. He writes:

> In the case of relief expenditures, the additional purchases by reliefers is relatively small compared to the large volume of consumption expenditures made by the community as a whole, even in periods of deep depression. The additional purchases are spread very thinly over the vast consumption industries, thus giving very little stimulus to increased output, and are, therefore, likely to induce hardly any increase in employment.[7]

In my opinion this represents a confusion commonly met, a belief that the same mass is necessarily lessened if cut into numer-

5. This is very important in connection with present military plant expansion.
6. This extra excess capacity suggests that a given amount of expenditure should be particularly ineffective in inducing investment. Actually, how much steel capacity was built after years of public work expenditure?
7. Op. cit., p. 91.

ous pieces, each so small as to be negligible. This forgets that there are very many such pieces. Perhaps the economist, in his rôle as an observer, behaves according to the Weber-Fechner law in regarding equal percentage changes as of equal importance. If so, this is a failing and should not blind him to the fact that the sum of the absolute changes may constitute the total. I do not believe that employment would be larger if the government spent all its funds on one product, say golf balls, even though the percentage change would thereby be maximized. In any case, arguments should be brought forward to show why diversified expenditure is relatively unstimulating.

If the previous arguments are correct, an analysis of each dollar spent in the two fields will not be unfavorable to direct consumption expenditure. In this field, probably less rather than more of each dollar goes to profits; probably more labor and less equipment is used per unit of output; in my opinion, during the last decade not less investment was induced per dollar spent. Finally, even if the last assertion is believed to be incorrect, the previous analysis shows that the induced private investment is soon financed by the government via amortization and depreciation, and this is peculiarly likely to be so where the government is the most important purchaser.[8]

I conclude, therefore, that direct consumption expenditure is not only in line with the needs of the times (the war period excluded), but also has no less favorable effects than public works expenditure. The latter must stand or fall on their direct utility and their flexibility in a well-timed, anti-cyclical spending policy.

THE MULTIPLIER AND VELOCITY APPROACHES

It is unfortunate that ancient astronomers selected the period of revolution of the earth around the sun as the conventional unit of time reckoning, because with present financial habits this yields a figure for the income velocity of money of two or three, not dissimilar to the figure usually derived for the multiplier. The likeness is, of course, purely coincidental and only an indication of confusion. If we used the ten-year cycle as our unit of time, income velocity would be somewhere around thirty, while the multiplier would remain two.

8. If directed, concentrated expenditure is considered desirable — and I am not of the opinion that it is — it might well be in the line of consumption needs, public health, etc., rather than public works.

Now numerous writers have attempted a "reconciliation" of the multiplier and velocity approaches, and it would be gratifying to be able to report on their successes. Unfortunately their reconciliations have either been trivial, as one-sided as an agreement between a totalitarian state and one of its puppet creations, or else have been founded upon error. With respect to the trivial reconciliations, it is clear that one may always retain a velocity terminology and a quantity equation (implicitly defining v). Then *ex post* the most elaborately specialized multiplier analysis can be translated into the velocity approach, v playing the rôle of a pawn in the game, always moving so as to make things come out right. As soon as one has arbitrarily defined money and income, one may always define velocity. In the above discussion, I have gone to some pains to make explicit the effects upon v of various changes.

But this is to do an injustice to the older monetary writers. Whatever their shortcomings, they did not concern themselves only with questions of definition and with irrefutable identities. They had a definite hypothesis in mind concerning the effect of change in m and concerning the invariance of v. Just as there is an empty multiplier equation which is to be distinguished from the multiplier hypothesis based upon the alleged (refutable) invariance of the consumption-income function, so with the older writers there was a definite velocity hypothesis.[9]

Under the conditions envisaged in recent fiscal policy discussions, this hypothesis is inconsistent with the multiplier hypothesis; both cannot be correct, one at least must be wrong. I venture the opinion, based upon the above analysis and the whole trend of the best modern writing, that the multiplier hypothesis is more fruitful than that based upon extrapolation of velocities. By the multiplier analysis we understand why public expenditure does not necessarily prime the pump, but rather increases income only transiently. It explains why an easy money policy is ineffective at

9. With less than full employment, this is not equivalent to the "quantity hypothesis" that the price level varies with m. Induced variations in real income are consistent with the "velocity hypothesis," but not with the strict "quantity hypothesis." I cannot attempt here the ambitious task of reappraising the quantity theory in all generality, but rather confine myself to a discussion of conditions of less than full employment, uncertainty, and relatively low interest rates. Lest it be thought that the relationships discussed consist only of "depression economics," I should like to state my belief that they are extremely important in the analysis of full employment and even hyperinflation, although not without some modifications.

the same time that deficit spending may be very effective. It shows why the effects of deficits upon income are not greatly different if financed by money creation, credit creation via bank expansion, or simple sale of securities to the public. These basic facts constitute a challenge to the velocity hypothesis, which admits of them only by devious interpretation.

Various technical attempts have been made to perform a marriage between the two opposing theories. In no case which has come to my attention have there resulted legitimate, viable off-spring. Either the fruit of the attempt has been nebulous and non-existent,[1] or it has consisted of unworthy hybrids, at times partaking of the worst qualities of each — the arrogance and oversimplification of the multiplier approach with the misleading features of the velocity approach.

In his path-breaking Economics of Public Works, J. M. Clark, almost as an afterthought, attempted such a reconciliation. By refusing to push the analysis beyond a year's time, and by taking advantage of the fact that a convexly growing time shape of income can in a finite range be approximated by a straight line, the two hypotheses are given a semblance of compatibility, which will, I fear, please neither camp. If the analysis had been continued in time, Professor Clark would have found it necessary to introduce a sudden, arbitrary, unexplained and unexplainable collapse in velocity, in order to maintain consistence with the multiplier time sequence.

In the case of Professor Angell, the result is a denial of the dwindling secondary effects of spending and a great exaggeration of the induced tertiary, private investment. In his world, except when expectations are falling, the task of the Treasury would be the agreeable one of holding down booms. While modification of the multiplier analysis is needed in boom times to take account of commodity and factor price changes, I do not believe that it should be along the lines suggested by the velocity approach.[2]

1. Thus, in Professor Machlup's useful and interesting article, "Period Analysis and Multiplier Theory," in *QJE*, November, 1939, the velocity discussion of the first ten pages bears little or no relation to the brilliantly formulated subsequent analysis.

2. Professor Gayer seems to have performed the feat of simultaneously riding the divergent horses — but to the pleasure of neither a velocity exponent such as Professor Marget nor a multiplier disciple such as Mr. Salant. Cf. W. S. Salant, "The Demand for Money and the Concept of Income Velocity," Journal of Political Economy, June, 1941, pp. 395–421. It is hard to know

Many people now agree that velocity throws no light on the final level of the system, but nevertheless believe that it is relevant to the process of adjustment to a change in investment. Again I must dissent. Normal velocity figures (of active money) are based upon institutional payment habits in a more or less synchronized system; in the adjustment to new investment entirely different reaction patterns are involved, depending upon anticipation reformulation, production gestation periods, etc. At best the normal speed of turnover of money is one minor limiting factor; at worst, it is irrelevant and misleading.[3]

The conventional geometrically contracting or expanding block diagrams are greatly oversimplified pictures of reality. They neglect the wavelike process of successive investment and disinvestment (particularly in inventories) which actually follows net expenditure. If interpreted literally they imply instantaneous production to order, with no time lost by money in the hands of businesses. The appropriate time unit along the axis would not be the conventional four-month income period, but rather an average heavily weighted with the one-week period of workers, the less important monthly period of salary earners, and the quarterly and yearly period of property income receivers. The result would presumably be much shorter than the average period of a complete income or consumption circuit, because of neglect of business transactions. Even in this simple case, if individuals gear consumption decisions to (say) previous five years' income, that is the relevant period to use, although cash turnover has a time period of four months.

what to say of Professor Villard's preoccupation with velocity. With the general tenor of his thought I am in hearty agreement, and I have profited much from his exposition. But after an examination, as sympathetic as I could manage, I am forced to the conclusion that his valid propositions emerge independently of, and sometimes in spite of, his velocity terminology. Fortunately, he does not push the velocity analysis to its logical conclusion. Thus I am in utter disagreement with his belief that a balanced budget will be expansionary if the government spends its tax revenue faster than the private community spends its income (op. cit., p. 204, passim), or that in a long enough finite time period all of a given increase in income will be spent (p. 184). This last view, if strictly interpreted, is a complete denial of the fundamental principle that the long-term marginal propensity to consume plus the long-term marginal propensity to invest must be less than unity. Otherwise the system is in unstable equilibrium.

3. As an example, Keynes' whole analysis of the "finance" motive for holding money is an emphasis upon the distortion of static patterns resulting from dynamic change.

Nor can we relate normal income velocity to the length of time required for the effect of spending to reach a given fraction of its total impulse. Professors Machlup and Villard have both shown that, even in the simple consumption case, this depends upon the size of the multiplier. When induced inventory and income changes become relevant, this consideration is strengthened by those above.

The multiplier analysis is guilty of oversimplification. It is tragic that velocity considerations have so often deflected writers from the constructive task of refinement and adumbration.

CONCLUSION

This paper has attempted within a few pages to meet some of the pressing difficulties involved in current discussions of income determination. It has avoided glossing over fundamental divergences of opinion and logic. At the same time no effort has been made to indicate the substantial unanimity now achieved by informed writers on many issues. Thus, because of the political implications of fiscal policy, many of the processes described above secure more ready acceptance if applied to bursts of private expenditure, the expansion of instalment credit, etc.

PAUL A. SAMUELSON.

MASSACHUSETTS INSTITUTE OF TECHNOLOGY

87

Statistical Analysis of the Consumption Function

by
Paul A. Samuelson

AMONG the most striking uniformities yet uncovered in economic data are the relationships between various categories of expenditure and family income. Their regularity is substantiated by studies which go back as far as the nineteenth-century investigations of Le Play and Engel.[1] In fact, so strong are these income effects that it is very difficult to find empirically the influence of price, the variable customarily related to demand by the economic theorist.

In recent years business cycle theorists have tended more and more to be of the opinion that *investment* is the strategic moving factor underlying fluctuations and determining the level of the system. This view implies as a corollary that *consumption expenditure should be related passively to income*. This is a fundamental assumption not only of the Keynesian system (e. g., the doctrine of the multiplier), but of most other schools as well.

Recent statistical material provides the opportunity to test this relationship, and numerous attempts have been made. Three general methods have been employed: [2] (a) the analysis of budgetary data, representing a cross section of the different income levels at the same time; [3] (b) the use of time series of national income, consumption, capital formation, etc.; [4] (c) more or less plausible

---

[1] For citations see the voluminous bibliography in *Studies of Family Living in the United States and Other Countries* by Faith M. Williams and C. C. Zimmerman, U.S. Dept. of Agriculture, Publication 223; C. C. Zimmerman, *Consumption and Standards of Living*, Van Nostrand, 1936; R. G. D. Allen and A. L. Bowley, *Family Expenditure*, P. S. King, 1935.

[2] R. and W. M. Stone, *Review of Economic Studies*, October, 1938, gives a good summary of work done up until that time.

[3] Maurice Leven's Brookings Study, *America's Capacity to Consume*; Stones, *op. cit.*; National Resources Committee and W.P.A. study, *Consumer Expenditures in U.S., 1935–36*; H. Mendershausen, *American Economic Review*, September, 1939, *Review of Economic Statistics*, August, 1940; E. W. Gilboy, *Review of Economic Statistics*, August, 1940.

[4] Colin Clark, *Economic Journal*, June, 1937, and September, 1938; Clark and Crawford, *The National Income of Australia*, Angus and Robertson, 1938; Kalecki, *Essays in the Theory of Economic Fluctuations*, Farrar and Rinehart, 1939.

rough estimating of the numerical magnitude of the marginal propensity to consume, such as have been made by Kahn, Keynes, J. M. Clark, and others. It is quite possible that the estimates under this last heading are the most useful of all for policy decisions. Nevertheless, it is impossible to appraise their validity by unambiguous statistical methods; consequently, no discussion of them will be attempted here.

However, recent data on national income provided by Kuznets [5] suggest the possibility of utilizing the second method for a new statistical appraisal of the consumption function. A rudimentary discussion of the comparability of the results of methods (a) and (b) will be attempted, but this will not be treated in the exhaustive fashion it deserves.[6]

ADJUSTMENTS OF OBSERVATIONS

Kuznets presents *national income produced* and *consumption outlay,* each in current prices, for the years 1919–35. The first two years may be presumed to contain the anomalous effects of the first World War period and are, therefore, excluded from this discussion. It would be very desirable to secure data for the five years which have elapsed since 1935, and Kuznets has presented elsewhere data for the first two of these years. However, the National Resources Planning Board has made provisional estimates of these magnitudes for the four years through 1939. While admittedly tentative, and despite their lack of strict comparability, these were considered sufficiently informative to be included in the analysis.

If dollar consumption figures are plotted against dollar national income figures for the nineteen years (see page 236), no simple relationship is apparent. Perhaps if the period were subdivided into the twenties and into the thirties, a linear relationship might be found for each half of the data. But these would differ, and the data for the whole period could be represented only by an irregular curve with a definite twist between the two levels.

A correction would seem to be in order if a reversible analytical

[5] S. Kuznets, *National Income and Capital Formation,* National Bureau of Economic Research, 1937.

[6] Cf. J. Marschak, *Canadian Journal of Economics and Political Science,* August, 1939; Hans Staehle, *Review of Economic Statistics,* August, 1937, and August, 1938.

relationship is sought rather than simply a historical description of past happenings. Because of changes in prices, changes in money income and consumption are not the same thing as changes in real income and consumption. From economic theory and from observation, we should not expect to find an invariant relationship between money consumption and money income, regardless of the real levels which these represent. A doubling of *all* prices simultaneously would presumably leave each individual in the same position as previously; we should expect, therefore, no change in real quantities, abstracting from the dynamical effects of *changing* prices. Unless a correction were made for price changes, it would appear that two different observations on the consumption function were available, and that the marginal propensity to consume were equal to the average propensity to consume. Thus, if previously money consumption equaled national income (investment being zero), and suddenly all prices doubled evenly, presumably money consumption would double as income doubled. This might be erroneously interpreted to indicate a marginal propensity to consume of unity, when in fact only one observation of the true *real* consumption function had been made, and no basis exists for inferring the magnitude of the marginal propensity to consume.

For the years before 1936, Kuznets presents a deflated series of income and consumption in terms of 1929 prices. The precise method of adjustment employed by him is a complicated one and could not be applied to the last four observations. Experimentation with the data for the 1921–35 period showed, however, that simply deflating both income and consumption by the Bureau of Labor Statistics Wage Earner's Cost of Living Index led to almost precisely the same relationship as that derived from the more complicated adjustment. Therefore, this technique was used on the whole series, homogeneity for the whole period being preferable to greater exactness in the earlier years.

A second correction readily suggests itself. The same real income divided up among more people cannot be expected to yield the same real consumption expenditure. Perfectly balanced extensive population growth, in which each individual is exactly as well off as previously (derived, for example, by combining statistics of many homogeneous countries), would, as in the case of price changes discussed above, introduce only spuriously new ranges of observation of the consumption function. A need arises, therefore, to place the data upon a standardized or per capita basis. By the use of midyear census estimates the observations were adjusted to the 1929 population level.

These two corrections yielded a series of observations of United States 1921–39 consumption outlay and national income produced, each in terms of 1929 prices and 1929 population.[7]

CONSUMPTION AND INCOME PRODUCED

In Chart 12 is plotted the scatter of real per capita consumption against real per capita income. The corrected observations present a much more unified picture, the data being no longer divisible into two heterogeneous parts. Moreover, the scatter gives at least the appearance of linearity. Determining by conventional least squares technique the regression of consumption on income, we found a constant marginal propensity to consume of .54 (i. e., a multiplier of about 2.2) and a level of income at which savings would be zero of about 59 billion dollars. The closeness of fit as indicated by the Pearsonian coefficient of correlation exceeds + .97.

This is a high correlation, even for the field of economic time series, where sizable correlations are the rule. However, detailed examination of the data suggests that the deviations from the line of best fit are not randomly distributed.

Therefore, we tested the hypothesis that a secular trend may have been operating throughout the period. We resorted to multiple correlation in which *time* was included as a linear factor. Utilizing only the pre-1936 data, a significant improvement in fit resulted, the consumption schedule being shifted upward by about .2 billion dollars per year. The point of zero saving was still around 60 billion dollars in 1929, but shifting upward at a rate of some-

---

[7] Without these adjustments the results would be not at all comparable with budgetary studies. These were made as of *constant prices,* and relate to individual and family decisions. Moreover, from the standpoint of a reversible relationship of relevance to the problem of (say) the effect of new investment expenditure upon income, clearly population will not increase *pari passu* with such investments. However, the case for eliminating price changes is, from this latter point of view, not so strong. If the price changes recorded in the data were rigidly related to changes in income (hence, investment), then the "pure" *ceteris paribus* relationship with prices removed may be an irrelevant one; we may seek rather the resultant of its shifts. It is precisely considerations of this latter type which we should use to justify our *not* taking into account the effects of changing distribution of income.

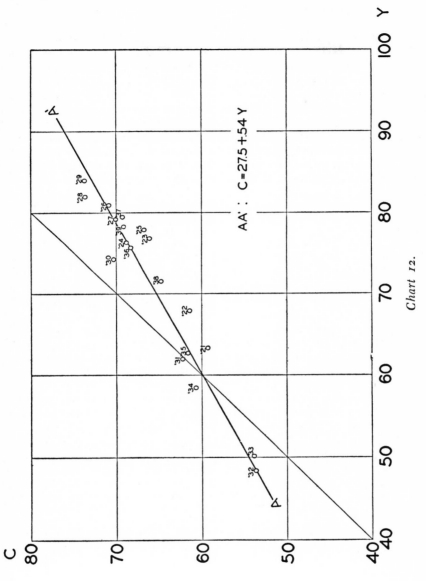

Chart 12.

The Consumption Function in Terms of 1929 Prices and Population

thing less than .1 billion dollars per year. The marginal propensity to consume was found to be only slightly higher, namely, .56; i. e., a multiplier of 2.23.

But, two considerations argued against the validity of the previous multiple correlation analysis. When the last four observations became available and were included in the analysis, there no longer appeared to be a sizable trend factor. The multiple regression coefficient of consumption on time was not found to differ significantly in a sampling sense from zero; and the slight increase in the goodness of fit of the multiple regression over the simple regression was insufficient to justify the introduction of a new parameter with a subsequent loss of one degree of freedom.

Besides, analysis of other components of Kuznets' study suggested an alternative explanation of the upward drift of consumption prior to 1936. This is explored in the next section.

CONSUMPTION, AGGREGATE INCOME PAYMENTS, AND ENTERPRISE SAVING

May not the secular trend discussed above simply be the reflection of a variable whose influence can be explicitly appraised? More specifically, in the early thirties income actually received by consumers, i. e., *aggregate income payments*, exceeded *national income produced* by billions of dollars because of calculated business dissaving and government dissaving (deficits).[8] The reverse was true in the twenties. This provides a possible explanation of the upward drift in *consumption* as compared to *income produced*. It is also in line with experience and theory which suggest that individuals' consumption outlay should depend primarily upon income received.

To check this hypothesis we plotted in Chart 13 *consumption* (1929 prices and population) against *aggregate income payments* (deflated as above for price and population changes), using the data available through 1935. The points lies almost upon a straight

[8] There has been some controversy over the problem of whether the volume of real dissavings may not be overstated because of changes in values of inventories and other business losses, and whether the volume of dissavings represents an equivalent splashing of the community with purchasing power. This is not the place to enter into this confused discussion. It will suffice to point out that *aggregate income payments* is the primary observable series, and that errors in reckoning enterprise savings will distort only the value of *income produced*.

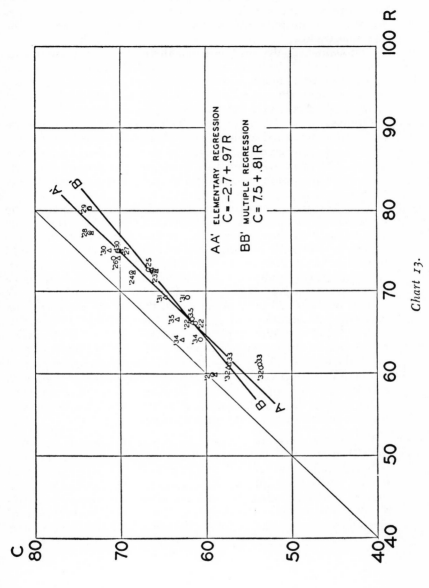

Chart 13.

The Consumption Function in Terms of Aggregate Income Payments

line, the coefficient of correlation being almost $+ .96$. There is no noticeable drift toward increasing consumption. This was confirmed by multiple correlation analysis; the influence of time was found to be insignificant and in the opposite direction to the previous trends.

Thus, closer analysis suggests that there was no increase in consumption out of the same income received. The thirties' increase in consumption compared to income produced seems explicable on the grounds that corporations were saving less (dissaving), not that less was being saved out of income received.

Quite surprisingly, *aggregate income payments* ($=$ national income paid out) varied *less* in this period than did consumption outlay. Savings appeared at all levels of the *aggregate income* payments. The marginal propensity to consume computed from the elementary regression of consumption on income payments has the high value of .97.

If we compute the marginal propensity to consume from the regression of income payments on consumption, we arrive at the anomalous coefficient of 1.06. This seems to indicate an unstable system in which the secondary effects of new expenditure would be unlimited and cumulative. Actually, the leakages incident upon enterprise saving induced by extra income would serve to make the system stable and all secondary effects finite.

This is illustrated in Chart 14 which shows *total enterprise savings* (1929 population and prices) against *national income produced* (1929 base). The simple correlation is $+ .91$. A least squares calculation of the marginal propensity of total enterprise to save yields the very high figure of $+ .49$. An increase of income produced of one dollar results in 49 cents of saving (or less dissaving). This accounts for most of the leakages incident upon net investment; as far as these data go, the leakages incident upon household savings are much smaller and possibly negative.

While income received should be expected to be the dominating determinant of consumption, income produced but not distributed might be expected to have some effect. In a perfect capital market where book and market values coincide, corporate earnings plowed back into the business would thereby increase individuals' equities and make them less anxious to save out of given income received. (Alternatively, individuals may reckon their

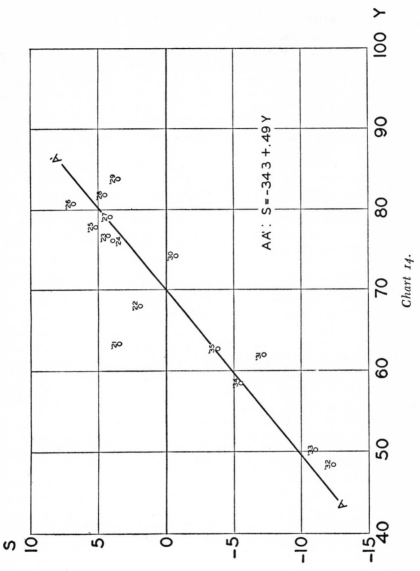

Chart 14.

Total Enterprise Savings in Relation to Income

AA': S = -34.3 + .49 Y

true income as that produced, not that actually received, and would, therefore, consume more.) Similarly, when dividends exceed earnings (as in amortization of "wasting" mining properties), not all income received may be regarded as true income out of which to determine consumption.

In the real world we should expect the relationship between consumption and enterprise savings to be tenuous. By multiple correlation analysis an attempt was made to evaluate the effect of such savings upon consumption for given levels of income received.

The small triangles in Chart 13 show the net regression between consumption and income received for the level of enterprise saving in 1929. The "net" marginal propensity to consume is reduced to $+.81$. An increase in enterprise savings of one dollar increases consumption by approximately 23 cents; i. e., shifts the schedule up by that amount. This seems plausible; while unreceived produced income has some effect upon consumption, such "dollars" are only about one quarter as effective as dollars actually received.

The following statistical magnitudes are included for possible further exploration by others:

TABLE XXIII

A. Means and Standard Deviations

	Means of Series †	Standard Deviations
X_1 Consumption (corrected) (millions of $)	64,857.6 (65,490.3) *	6,286.23
X_2 Income Produced (corrected) (millions of $)	69,540.0 (70,934.5) *	11,153.69
X_3 Aggregate Income Payments (corrected) (millions of $)	69,733.3	6,207.84
X_4 Total Enterprise Savings (corrected) (millions of $)	— 189.73	6,019.13
X_5 "Time" (years; 1920 = o)	8.0 (10.0) *	4.32 (5.48) *

† Unless otherwise indicated, all magnitudes are for the period 1921–35.
* 1921–39.

TABLE XXIV

B. Correlation Coefficients (1921–35, unless otherwise indicated)

	X_1	X_2	X_3	X_4
X_1				
X_2	+ .96			
	(+ .97) *			
X_3	+ .96	+ .92		
X_4	+ .79	+ .91	+ .71	
X_5	— .29	— .50	+ .92	+ .91
	(— .05) *	(— .15) *		

* 1921–39.

The square of the multiple correlation coefficient of consumption on *aggregate income payments* and *enterprise savings* equals .95, and the square of the partial coefficient of correlation between consumption and aggregate income payments equals .85. The analysis must be taken with a grain of salt because of the high intercorrelation between the independent variables, *income payments* and *enterprise savings* $(= + .7)$. This renders a precise determination of the respective weights of income and savings impossible. An even higher intercorrelation between savings and income produced $(= .9)$ rendered meaningless multiple correlation analysis of these variables and consumption.

In conclusion, the opinion may be ventured that the statistical observations bear out the expectations of theory except with respect to the very sensitive relation of *consumption* to *aggregate income payments*.

88

CONCERNING SAY'S LAW*

Professor Samuelson said that a belief in the validity of the law of markets was a necessary badge of membership in the Classical school of political economy, and comprehension of its logical derivation formed the *pons asinorum* for the budding theorist. Nevertheless, rather than one organic principle, at least three aspects of this law can be discerned. First, and most zealously held, there is a metaphysical formulation which is irrefutable under all conceivable circumstances and hence empirically meaningless. According to this view, supply *is* demand since goods exchange against goods. Overproduction in one sphere necessarily implies underproduction elsewhere, all values being relative. Second, there is the view that purchasing power is indestructible. What is not spent on consumption is automatically invested; indeed, from Smith on it was held that what the saver did not consume was passed on as consumption to someone else since capital was regarded in part at least as an advance of subsistence to workers. This second point of view has empirical content and is admittedly false. Effective purchasing power, MV, changes constantly in an upward and downward direction. Finally, and most deserving of attention, is the view that general involuntary unemployment is impossible in a world of perfectly flexible prices. Under this heading is discussed (1) Keynes' somewhat unfortunate concept of *involuntary unemployment* resting upon an alleged monetary illusion on the part of the working classes; (2) the validity of the classical inverse relationship between employment and the real wage; (3) the misleading Pigouvian capitulation to the Kaldor argument that wage changes increase employment only via effects of the rate of interest; (4) the contrast between this argument and the more fundamental Keynes-Lerner thesis that the influence is only through the rate of interest. In conclusion a "classical" model was sketched in which unemployment could be eliminated by falling wage rates not necessarily through stimulation of *real investment*, but through a process of bidding up existing asset values until individuals are motivated to spend out of their capital gains sufficient amounts on consumption to keep employment full. In this connection two problems must be kept distinct: Will any level of prices, however low, lead to full employment? Will prices changing at some rate keep employment full? The reply to the latter question may be in the affirmative, while the first may conceivably admit only a negative answer.

* Abstract of a paper presented before the Econometric Society, at New Orleans, Dec. 1940. Reprinted from *Econometrica,* Vol. 9, No. 2 (April 1941), pp. 177–178.

89

PROFESSOR PIGOU'S *EMPLOYMENT AND EQUILIBRIUM*[1]

I

When Professor Hicks wished to discover what a "classical" economist believed to be the determinants of the level of employment, he was very much in the position of the man who, having lost his donkey, had no recourse but to ask himself what he would do if he were a jackass, and then do the same thing. But now the animal has come forward to speak for himself, and all economists will welcome Professor Pigou's new and stimulating book.

Just as Marshall[2] in his review of Jevons' *Theory of Political Economy* did Jevons, and himself, less than justice, so Pigou[3] reacted to Keynes in a remarkably parallel fashion. Apart from Marshall's vexation at prior publication in less perfect form of doctrines which he was himself developing, and only here does the parallel begin, his annoyance was generated by Jevons' treatment of earlier writers. "[Jevons] seemed perversely to twist his own doctrines so as to make them appear more inconsistent with Mill's and Ricardo's than they really were . . . [Marshall's] youthful [!] loyalty to [Ricardo] boiled over."[4]

That Pigou was justified in his reaction to Keynes's treatment of the "classical" economists, particularly of their beloved mutual master, there can be no doubt. Whether Keynes was deliberately Machiavellian in this, only he can tell, and whether or not such tactics helped the spread of his doctrines, only his biographer will be able to tell us.

In any case, it is clear that the time has come for the calm reconsideration which the present work attempts. In his preface, Professor Pigou makes generous acknowledgment to the stimulus of Keynes's thought, and this is borne out by a comparison of this book with his own previous review and with the *Theory of Unemployment*. *Employment and Equilibrium* is for the most part not such difficult reading as the former book, and in my opinion more important.

With respect to methodology, it is almost ideal. Following introductory discussions of definitions, Part II treats the conditions of equilibrium determining employment, income, savings-investment, interest, etc. This section will probably be of major interest to most readers. It is less technical in character than Part III, which is concerned, along rigid lines of comparative statics, with the effect after equilibrium is re-attained of changes in various parameters such as banking policy, productivity, thriftiness, etc. The

---

[1] *Employment and Equilibrium—A Theoretical Discussion.* By A. C. PIGOU. (London: Macmillan. 1941. Pp. xi, 283. $3.00.)
[2] A. C. Pigou, ed., *Memorials of Alfred Marshall,* pp. 93-100.
[3] A. C. Pigou, "Mr. J. M. Keynes' General Theory of Employment, Interest, and Money," *Economica,* May, 1936, vol. iii, pp. 115-32.
[4] *Memorials of Alfred Marshall,* pp. 99-100. Brackets mine.

problem of the dynamic approach to equilibrium is left to Part IV, but even here the treatment is sketchy rather than complete. In particular, the dependence upon dynamics of the stability conditions, which are of such great importance for the preceding parts, is not brought out. Some consequences of this will be touched upon later.

II

Because of the disproportionate attention paid in the literature to the equality of saving and investment, notice is taken here of Pigou's complete acceptance of the Keynesian definitions, despite the "plain" man's wish to regard these magnitudes as not necessarily equal. For the system as a whole, saving and investment, as observables, are defined as the same thing: the difference between income and consumption *when appropriate allowances are made for capital revaluations in the reckoning of income;* or as the value of the increment of capital equipment. For a single individual who can hoard and not consume, and thereby induce dishoarding and income decreases on others, they need not be the same. From the discussion on page 24, one might get the impression that he attributes the final equality to the fact that individuals cannot on balance increase their holdings of a given total amount of cash. If this is his meaning, it reflects a momentary lapse, since as he himself shows elsewhere (pp. 21-22), the equality of the above definitions holds even if new money is being created per unit time.

In the above senses, saving and investment may be called for clarity saving-investment. It is not true, however, even in the Keynesian system that for *virtual* displacements, which by their nature cannot be simultaneously observed, the saving (saving-investment) which households *would* perform out of a given income need equal the investment (saving-investment) which entrepreneurs *would* make at that same income. It is precisely because of their being unequal except at one point that income is uniquely determined. The idea of saving and investment being equilibrated, in the sense of schedule intersections, by income and by the other variables of the system, is implicit in the minds of most Keynesians (*e.g.,* Harrod), but is often badly expressed. The concepts *ex ante* and *ex post* attempt to convey the idea, but seem less suitable than the terminology *virtual* and *observable*.

Equality in the above sense may take time to be established. Until the intersection of schedules defining equilibrium is reached, saving-investment may be inappropriate for both households and enterprises. It is precisely this "inappropriateness" which acts as the moving force leading a stable system to equilibrium. The problem of time, so carefully worked out by Marshall for partial equilibrium markets, is only beginning to receive the attention it deserves in connection with aggregative equilibrium.

Professor Robertson has provided definitions which permit the inequality of saving and investment. Today it is fashionable for most writers when they speak of inequality hastily to add that they are using the Robertsonian rather than the Keynesian terminology. But not one out of five who make this disclaimer seem actually to have in mind these extremely specialized definitions. More often they seem to have in mind their virtual inequality at full employment (which is thereby unattainable!), or their inequality for the individual, or the treatment by individuals of capital gains and losses as income. While Pigou's criticism (p. 26) of Robertson's system on the basis of the difficulty of slicing time into discrete units does not seem well taken and seems confused on the question of synchronization, he very rightly points out that the Robertsonian inequality is not what the plain man has in mind, nor is it anything but a reflection of the change in income level of the system. However, it would be like throwing the baby out with the bath water to let the sterility of the Robertsonian definitions deflect attention from the fruitful detailed time-sequence analysis of the path to equilibrium characteristic of Robertson, Kahn, J. M. Clark, Lundberg, Keynes at an earlier stage, *et al.*

But Professor Pigou wishes to concentrate on the intermediate short run "flow" equilibrium reached over a time period long enough to insure constant, appropriate values of saving, investment, income, employment, etc.[5] This implies that unintended changes in investment have been rectified. However, the time period is not so long as to lead to any appreciable change in capital through the cumulation of positive net investment. Previously, Pigou criticized Keynes for using this same device, but he has now come to realize its value in separating short-run from long-run effects. Moreover, if investment is regarded as the instantaneous rate of increase of capital ($=$ d capital/d time), there is no inconsistency in taking capital as constant at the same time that it is changing, Zeno and the ancient philosophers notwithstanding. As a special, singular case of "flow" equilibrium, we have long-run equilibrium in which net saving-investment per unit time equals zero, and the stock of capital is strictly constant.

III

In the second part when he states the conditions which determine flow equilibrium, Professor Pigou selects almost exactly the same equations as those suggested by Professor Hicks[6] as being in the minds of the "classical" economists, although he may have been unaware of the close similarity. In two respects there are differences. The first is the minor one of allowing

[5] The term "flow" is used in contrast to the momentary market equilibrium discussed by Marshall. Because "stocks" as distinct from "flows" are equilibrated in even longer runs as well as in shorter runs, it is possible that some such term as intermediate short-run equilibrium is preferable to flow equilibrium.

[6] J. R. Hicks, "Mr. Keynes and the 'Classics'; A Suggested Interpretation," *Econometrica*, vol. v (1937), pp. 147-59.

for monopolistic competition by equating price times a correction for the elasticity of demand (= marginal revenue) to marginal cost. Secondly, as will be seen, more specific assumptions are made with respect to bank policy.

A classical system even simpler than that of Hicks and Pigou, implicit in many discussions of Say's Law, is simply as follows:[7] The velocity of circulation of money is taken as constant, and the amount of money is fixed. Curtailing of consumption results then automatically in investment. The attempt to save leaves employment just where it was before, but not necesarily full. However, if money has "legs" as described, unemployment can be prevented by lowering wages and costs. This lowers prices and, with total value of sales constant, necessarily means greater output and employment. In the simplest case prices may be made proportional to costs (wage rates), as would be the case if there were not increasing or diminishing returns. Thus, the quantity equation is not used to determine the price level directly, for wages determine prices. With fixed wage rates the quantity equation determines output and employment. But if the wage always falls to guarantee full employment, both it and prices are simultaneously determined by the quantity equation.

The above model is instructive because it shows clearly how misleading it is to phrase the problem of guaranteeing full employment as one of lowering the *real wage of labor* in order to increase employment along a given real productivity curve. Keynes himself has accepted uncritically the classical law of diminishing marginal productivity, permitting his critics to interpret an increase in effective demand as simply a round-about way of lowering the real wage. Actually, in the above example, a decrease in money wages by lowering prices with fixed money income directly increases effective demand and employment. To the limited extent that one can speak of cause and effect in a closed interdependent system, it is more nearly correct to regard effective demand as increasing employment, and the increased employment as raising, lowering, or leaving marginal productivity the same, depending upon the laws of returns.

In Keynesian terminology full employment is guaranteed in this model, not because the propensity to consume is always unity, but because the marginal propensity to consume plus the marginal propensity to invest are always unity. As of a fixed money wage level, the system is in neutral equilibrium. If the money wage is flexible, the system is in stable full employment equilibrium. Any decreases in consumption are automatically made up by investment. An act of saving does inevitably become an act of investing.

Professor Pigou's model is not so simple. He follows Keynes in assuming a consumption schedule varying positively with income, but also depend-

---

[7] *Cf.* Ricardo, *Principles of Political Economy and Taxation* (Everyman's Library), chap. xxi, especially pp. 192-93.

ing on the rate of interest. The nature of this dependence cannot be definitely determined; some forces make for a positive supply curve of saving, others for a negative, while institutional factors argue in favor of independence. In a long chapter (Part II, chapter VI) an attempt is made to squeeze out an answer to the problem by the utility calculus, but the assumptions made are highly restrictive. He holds that within some range saving must increase with the interest rate, "for otherwise, in a state of full employment, there will be no machinery through which an enhanced demand for labour for investment could evoke a correspondingly enlarged supply" (p. 57). To many this will carry no weight, for aside from the mechanism of forced saving via price increases, there is no evidence that an increased demand does evoke an increased supply. If the supply curve is backward rising, but stable in the Walras, Hicks, Marshall-of-international-trade sense, an increase in demand will only raise the interest rate.

This is a matter of considerable moment, because Pigou's whole rosy theory of long-run equilibrium in contradistinction to Keynes's gloomy "Day of Judgment" rests upon Pigou's rather diffident assertion that reductions in the rate of interest can wipe out net saving completely. I fear that few economists will follow him in believing that under modern conditions there exists a positive rate of interest at which saving out of full employment income would be zero. This means that in the absence of dynamic, new investment outlets, the rate of interest will approach a lower limit—be it zero or two per cent—and investment will be zero after the capital stock has adjusted itself. But at this rate of interest people are still attempting to save with the inevitable consequence that income remains at a sufficiently low level to make actual saving abortive. (It is a common fallacy to believe in this connection that any hoarding either in the sense of money accumulation or lowered velocity will take place in the new equilibrium.) To avert the Day of Judgment, most of us will continue to hope for the appearance of dynamic new investment outlets and broad institutional changes in saving habits brought about by changes in the age distribution, changes in public and private finance, etc., rather than rely upon the slender reed of the interest rate's effects on motivation.

To return to flow equilibrium, Professor Pigou assumes a marginal efficiency schedule inversely relating investment to the rate of interest. He does not go on to point out that, as of a given stock of equipment, investment will certainly depend upon the level of consumption and/or income. Thus, he is unable to duplicate the Malthus-Lange argument which shows that an increased *desire* to save, even if it lowers the rate of interest, may result in less actual saving-investment, although he recognizes that it will involve less real income in the absence of perfect wage flexibility.

To the two Keynesian pillars of the propensity to consume and the marginal efficiency of capital must be added a third. Rather than deal directly with a liquidity preference schedule, the author prefers to take the level of money income (MV) as a function of the rate of interest, the form of which varies with the particular Central Bank policy followed. Since the velocity of circulation is itself a function of the rate of interest and the level of income, it is by no means clear that the Central Bank can in fact make MV what it likes. It can hope to influence M, but under moderately realistic conditions this may be completely compensated by changes in V. By a slight change of emphasis, Pigou is able to short-circuit the determination of income by saving and investment decisions to a quasi-quantity theory determination, in which the combined action of the Central Bank in determining the amount of money income (MV) and the working class in determining the money wage and prices, directly determine the level of real output. So to speak, only after total output is determined can the propensity to consume and the marginal efficiency schedule together parcel out income between saving and consumption in the appropriate proportions. More precisely, of course, in so doing the interest rate is affected, and this affects Central Bank action reciprocally.

Thus, in the system of Pigou, as in the system of Keynes, a cut in the money wage increases employment only by making money so redundant as to lower interest rates and thereby increase investment and consumption. It cannot be more effective than cheap money. But as Professor Hansen has pointed out, a decade of gold inflows from abroad has given us a laboratory experiment in cheap money beyond the wildest dreams of earlier writers, and the result has been extremely disappointing. Perhaps a 75 per cent cut in wages and prices would not have released so much money from the transaction sphere as to affect interest rates comparably.[8]

Analytically the error in Pigou's formulation consists of the failure to recognize the compensating adjustment of V when one of two conditions is filled: (a) the liquidity preference schedule is almost perfectly elastic so that absorption of money takes place with little change in the interest rate; (b) the schedule of the marginal efficiency of investment is extremely inelastic. It is the primary virtue of recent business cycle theory to have recognized the strategic significance of both of these hypotheses for the period of the thirties, rather than to have formulated aesthetically elegant models of aggregative equilibrium.

To defend the "classical" notion that the money wage was sufficiently flexible in the pre-World-War era, Pigou cites the lack of a secular trend in the degree of unemployment. Our knowledge of unemployment for this period is notoriously incomplete, but even if the facts were better established, from the nature of Pigou's system one could not tell whether

---

[8] Because of a preoccupation with flow equilibrium, the author does not discuss the possible effects on employment of continued changes, upward or downward, in money wages. But this is not the place to discuss the economics of hyper-deflation and inflation.

it was not bank policy rather than wage policy which kept employment full; or extensive growth coupled with foreign investment; or fortunate dynamic changes in investment outlets. In the interpretation of history we must insist upon as rigid standards of isolation and control as in the statistical analysis of the recent past.

In this connection it is necessary to discuss the chapter on stability conditions (Part II, chapter III). For as Professor Pigou's sound methodological instincts have suggested, almost all meaningful hypotheses emerge from them. It is unfortunate, therefore, that he simply generalizes mechanically the Marshallian market conditions. These are not necessarily correct even for a simple market, as countless writers have shown. He further identifies them with the maximum conditions for a single firm (*i.e.*, that marginal cost must cut marginal revenue from below). This leads to the identification of a minimum as a position of unstable equilibrium when it is in fact no equilibrium at all. Actually the stability of a market is only indirectly and distantly related to the stability of a single unit facing prices or given demand and supply curves. It is interesting to note that his stability condition that a change in interest rate must not change saving more than investment, while correct, is so only because he slips in applying the Marshallian conditions and instead derives the Walrasian conditions relevant to a backward-rising (as distinct from forward-falling) supply curve of saving.

Most important is the failure to distinguish the changing elasticity of demand *as it appears to a single seller in the neighborhood of a given level of output* from the change in his elasticity if effective demand increases all employment by (say) fifty per cent and shifts the demand curve for one small producer. While it probably can be shown on the basis of dynamical considerations that in the systems of Keynes and Pigou a change in money wage *cannot* change employment in the same direction, Professor Pigou shamelessly deduced this from the properties of the *ceteris paribus* demand curve confronting a single firm. Probably the analytic device borrowed from Mr. Harrod of assuming extreme symmetry between goods and then concentrating upon one as typical of all blinded him to the fact that changes for all mean shifts, albeit equal ones, in the demand of each. Actually he should have relied upon the changes in interest rate, real investment, real income, and finally employment; and then it would be clear, as mentioned earlier, that the increase in employment might come about even though prices fall more than wages so that real wages rise.

IV

Part III and the tables in the mathematical appendix present a somewhat formidable and technical appearance. Nevertheless, they contain the empirically meaningful content toward which all the previous material was aimed. Pigou, as much as any economist, has grasped the fundamental principle that the statement of equilibrium conditions is empty without specification of their structural properties, on the basis of which refutable hypotheses concerning empirical magnitudes can be formulated.

Moreover, the complexity results in part from the rich variety of assumptions which are examined. Permutations and combinations of the four alternative banking policies—(a) that in which money income increases with the interest rate, (b) that aimed at keeping money income constant, (c) that aimed at constant prices of consumers' goods, (d) that aimed at a constant interest rate—are combined with varying assumptions of monopoly and competition, and distribution of income. In particular, the discussion (chapters IX and X) on various multipliers represents a long overdue contribution.

Part IV on the dynamic transitions between positions of flow equilibrium seems almost an afterthought. For simplicity only transitions resulting from shifts in investment demand are considered. Most readers will grant these to be the most important factors in the trade cycle, but the cited positive correlations between employment and short term interest rates will not add much to this conviction. The conjecture (pp. 230-231) that any factor which displaces equilibrium states in a given definite direction will also displace a moving system in the same direction should be rigorously demonstrable on the basis of truly dynamic mathematical analysis.

The last chapter on cumulative movements rather refreshingly controverts the notion that the economic system is so unstable that a change in behavior in any small sector may spread cumulatively. While a glance through any review of business cycle theories, such as Haberler's, confirms the need for this emphasis, Pigou's method of proof is not conclusive. As he himself points out, the question is begged as to whether a given change is followed by a "once-for-all" adjustment, or a never-ending one. On the other hand, it is not inevitable, as he believes, that the psychological factor of expectations, generated by price changes and generating changes in the same direction, should lead to an unstable system. The key to all these difficulties must be found in the failure to supplement the detailed algebraic analysis of previous sections by a detailed differential or difference equation analysis (or its literary equivalent) of the approach to equilibrium.

While most of my discussion has been concerned with questioning details of Professor Pigou's book, this is so only because of the richness and fertility of his analysis and conclusions. Judged in shotgun fashion only by hits, or riflelike by hits compared to misses, this is one of the most important books of recent years. Moreover, it reveals with remarkable force the extent to which the Keynesians all along have been speaking classical prose, at the same time that "classicists" have thought in Keynesian poetry.

PAUL A. SAMUELSON

Massachusetts Institute of Technology

90

A FUNDAMENTAL MULTIPLIER IDENTITY

By PAUL A. SAMUELSON

I

TWO ALTERNATIVE DEFINITIONS of the multiplier are met with in dynamic sequence analysis. The first measures the multiplier by the increased level of income finally reached as the result of a *continual* stream of a unit expenditure, repeated in every period. The second, which may be called the cumulated multiplier, is measured by summing throughout all time the increments in income resulting from a unit, nonrepeated, impulse of expenditure.

For the familiar Kahn-Clark model sequences in which induced investment is neglected, the two measures are quantitatively equal for all stable cases, being respectively $1/(1-k)$ and the limit of the sum $(1+k+k^2+\cdots)$, where k is the marginal propensity to consume. It is a condition for stability in such a process that k be less than one in absolute value, and it is precisely in this case that the latter sum can be shown to be equal to the former expression by means of well-known formulae on geometric progressions.

In private correspondence in connection with more complicated sequences, I encountered a numerical discrepancy between two such measures. Although I suspected a numerical computational error, it occurred to me that no one had ever proved the identity of the two measures in the general case of more complicated sequences.[1] It is the purpose of this note to call attention to this identity and briefly indicate its proof.

II

Consider a process obeying a general difference equation of any order m with constant coefficients, which may be written in the form

$$(1) \quad L[Y(t)] = Y(t) + a_1 Y(t-1) + a_2 Y(t-2) + \cdots + a_m Y(t-m) = I(t),$$

where Y represents national income measured in deviations from some level, and I represents autonomous investment. To derive the first measure of the multiplier we set $I = I_1(t)$ with the properties

$$(2) \quad \begin{aligned} I_1(t) &= 0 & (t < 0), \\ I_1(t) &= 1 & (t \geq 0). \end{aligned}$$

[1] See for example the sequences in Lundberg's *Studies in the Theory of Economic Expansion;* P. A. Samuelson, "Interactions of the Multiplier and Acceleration Principle," *Review of Economic Statistics*, Vol. 21, May, 1939, pp. 75–78; Lloyd A. Metzler, "The Nature and Stability of Inventory Cycles," *Review of Economic Statistics*, Vol. 23, August, 1941, pp. 113–129.

Let $f_1(t)$ be the resulting solution in Y, and consider the limiting value of $Y(t)$ as t goes to infinity. Then

(3) $$\lim_{n \to \infty} f_1(t) = \text{the first multiplier.}$$

To arrive at the second measure we set $I = I_2(t)$ with the properties

(4)
$$I_2(0) = 1,$$
$$I_2(t) = 0 \text{ everywhere else.}$$

If the resulting solution for income is $Y = f_2(t)$, then its algebraically summed value

(5) $$f_2(0) + f_2(1) + \cdots = \sum_0^\infty f_2(t)$$

is the cumulated multiplier.

It is to be shown that these two different expressions are identical for all possible sequences regardless of order. Actually I shall prove a more general theorem which holds even for unstable systems and includes the above identity as a special case.

First, the concept of a "truncated" multiplier must be defined. As in the case already discussed, two cases must be distinguished: that corresponding to a steady stream of expenditure, and that representing the cumulation of the effects of a single impulse. By a truncated multiplier of the first kind I mean simply the level of income reached in some specified number of periods as a result of a continuous stream of expenditure. There is such a multiplier for every time period, and from its definition it is clearly equal to $f_1(t)$ as defined above.

The truncated multiplier of the second kind, or the cumulated truncated multiplier, is simply the sum of effects realized up to some given time period. Its value is given by a summation of $f_2(t)$ from zero to a finite time and differs from the ordinary cumulated multiplier in that the summation is not over infinite time.

THEOREM: *The two truncated multipliers are necessarily equal.*

COROLLARY: *The two ordinary ("untruncated") multipliers are necessarily equal.*

It is only necessary to prove the general theorem since the second follows from the first by evaluating the truncated multiplier at $t = $ infinity.

Since

(6) $$L[Y(n)] = I_1(n)$$

has for its solution $f_1(n)$, and since the solution is unique, the demonstration that

(7)
$$L\left[\sum_0^n f_2(t)\right] = I_1(n)$$

will imply

(8)
$$f_1(n) \equiv \sum_0^n f_2(t)$$

or that the two truncated multipliers are identical.
 By definition

(9)
$$L\left[f_2(t)\right] = I_2(t).$$

We may sum this expression from $t=0$ to $t=n$, and we get

(10)
$$\sum_0^n L\left[f_2(t)\right] = \sum_0^n I_2(t).$$

Because of the linearity of the system, the summation sign may be transferred to within the brackets; and recalling that from their definitions

(11)
$$I_1(n) = \sum_0^n I_2(t),$$

we come out with the relationship

(7)
$$L\left[\sum_0^n f_2(t)\right] = I_1(n)$$

which was to be proved.[2]

III

One further generalization may be briefly indicated. If we are given a system involving many countries, as in the analysis of the foreign-trade multiplier, it still remains true that the two possible definitions of the multiplier effect of a unit of one country's expenditure upon the income of a second country turn out to be identical, both in the ordinary form and in the more general truncated form. By treating $y(t)$ and

---

[2] Grateful acknowledgment is made to one of my students, Joseph L. Ullman, whose algebraic analysis of the second-order case persuaded me to believe the stronger truncated theorem to be true in the most general case.

$I(t)$ as column matrices representing s countries' national incomes and investments, the system may be written in the normal form

$$(12) \qquad\qquad y(t) = ay(t-1) + I(t)$$

where a is an s-by-s matrix representing the marginal propensities to consume of country i from country j.

The theorem stated just above could be proved by substitution as in the previous section. Or the weaker theorem dealing with the completed multiplier can be derived from the formal matrix identity

$$(13) \qquad\qquad (E - a)^{-1} = E + a + a^2 + \cdots$$

where E is the identity matrix. In the stable case, where all the roots of the characteristic equation of a are less than one in absolute value, the left-hand side will represent the first multiplier, and the right-hand side the cumulated multiplier. The stable case is precisely the one in which the formal expansion is valid.

To establish the stronger truncated theorem, we note that the matrix initial conditions corresponding to the continuous-stream-of-expenditure case and the single-impulse case are given by equations exactly like (2) and (4) except that matrices rather than scalars are implied, and unity is to be replaced by the identity matrix, E.

With the insertion of these initial conditions, the corresponding solutions are respectively $(E-a^t)(E-a)^{-1}$ and a^t, as can be verified by substitution in (12). Our strong theorem is then a consequence of the rearranged matrix identity.[3]

$$(E - a)^{-1} = E + a + a^2 + \cdots + a^{t-1} + a^t(E - a)^{-1}.$$

This holds regardless of stability. It may be noted that the set-up of this section includes that of previous sections as a special case.[4]

IV

There is a third concept of the multiplier which is essentially non-dynamic in nature. It is represented by the solution of the statical algebraic equation derived from substituting in the difference equation an unknown constant solution, z,

$$L(z) = 1.$$

[3] Harold Hotelling, "Some New Methods in Matrix Calculation," *Annals of Mathematical Statistics*, Vol. 14, March, 1943, p. 13.

[4] Still further generalizations are possible if we replace our discrete sums by Stieltjes integrals, leading to linear integro-functional equations, for which the principle of superposition is still valid. In the important case of a Volterra integral equation of the second kind, the analogue of $f_2(t)$ is given by the so-called resolvent kernel.

Clearly, z is given explicitly by the formula

$$z = 1/\sum a_i,$$

or in the matrix case by

$$z = (E - a)^{-1}.$$

In all stable cases, this is precisely equal to the other two (untruncated) dynamic multipliers. But in unstable cases, this is no longer true, the first two multipliers being explosive. Failure to recognize this adequately has given rise to some confusion in the literature. Thus, it has sometimes been considered remarkable that a marginal propensity to consume greater than unity should result in a negative multiplier, because $1/(1-k)$ is negative. Actually, the "multiplier," instead of being less than in normal cases, is much greater, being equal in the limit to infinity because of the explosive upward movement of the system.

What meaning then can be given to the coefficient $1/(1-k)$ or the third statical multiplier when it does not agree with the previous two?[5] Clearly, it no longer has the interpretation of the new stationary level of income which the system will approach under continuous spending, there being no such level. *What it does give is the only possible stationary level of income which is maintainable with continued expenditure.* Being unstable, this level is never approached, and even if artificially established by outside forces, it would hold only transitorily since slight shocks would cause the system to recede in either direction.

Perhaps, this helps to explain some of the paradoxical results encountered in some cases by Marschak[6] in his interpretation of the Wicksellian system. The anomalous cases met are precisely those which correspond to instability, in which case comparative statics is largely irrelevant and academic. This is merely one more example of what I have called the correspondence principle: systems which are well-behaved dynamically tend to be well-behaved from a purely comparative statical viewpoint; likewise those which are unstable give rise to anomalous comparative statical conclusions.

---

[5] It is suggestive but perhaps not quite accurate to characterize such cases as involving a "faster than infinite" rate of growth of the system. See J. J. Polak, "European Exchange Depreciation in the Early Twenties," ECONOMETRICA, Vol. 11, April, 1943, p. 162.

[6] Jakob Marschak, "Wicksell's Two Interest Rates," *Social Research*, Vol. 8, November, 1941, p. 475 *passim*. Comparative statics seem to suggest that cumulative inflation or deflation take place only if Marschak's m and n (propensities to save and invest) are equal. If true, this would be infinitely rare in occurrence. But dynamic analysis shows that there is cumulative inflation or deflation whenever n equals or exceeds m.

V

It is to be noted that the functions $f_1(t)$ and $f_2(t)$, particularly the latter, are *basic* special solutions of a linear difference equation system, out of which all solutions for an arbitrary $I(t)$ can be constructed by superposition according to theorems analogous to the Duhamel relations in a physical differential equation system.[7] However, such extensions lie outside the scope of the present note.

Massachusetts Institute of Technology

[7] Karman and Biot, *Mathematical Methods in Engineering*, pp. 403–405.

91

The Simple Mathematics of
Income Determination

⇛ BY ⇚

PAUL A. SAMUELSON

I. INTRODUCTION

THANKS in large measure to Professor Hansen and his associates, advanced students in business cycle theory have become proficient in calculating a large variety of different "income multipliers." In fact the subject has become something of a black art. Black because, to the uninitiated, the jargon must necessarily appear mysterious if not vicious; and an art because even the most adept are hard put to it to remember all the complex terms required for any particular multiplier formula.

Once we drop the most simplifying assumptions concerning income determination, and once we begin to seek the answer to a number of different policy or factual questions, most of this complexity is intrinsic. But by no means all. A large part of the difficulty of the subject—looked at from the standpoint of teacher or pupil—results from the practice of working with "multipliers," rather than concentrating on the equilibrium conditions which give rise to these expressions. The relations determining income are logically prior to those describing the way the equilibrium income changes. They are also easier to remember, easier to handle without making over-narrow straight-line assumptions, and they easily yield the appropriate multiplier formula for any particular problem.

Paul A. Samuelson

The present discussion is purely expositional, dealing as it does with problems that have been thoroughly thrashed out in the advanced literature. It attempts to show, with the use of the simplest mathematical language, (1) the simplest Keynesian model by which "saving and investment" determine income; (2) how government expenditure and taxes enter into this picture; (3) the role of international trade; and (4) how the corporation and its savings are to be handled.

II. THE HEART OF INCOME ANALYSIS

By definition, *national income* (at market prices), Y, can initially be set equal to the sum of consumption expenditure, C, and *net investment*, I:

$$Y = C + I$$

If Keynes had stopped with this identity, we should be left with an indeterminate system. In his simplest model of income determination, he added the following two hypotheses: (a) consumption is a function of income, and (b) investment may provisionally be taken, at any one time, as a constant. Mathematically, these relations may be written

$$C = C(Y) \text{ and } I = \bar{I}$$

When we substitute these into our first identity, we come up with the simplest Keynesian income system:

$$(1) \qquad\qquad Y = C(Y) + \bar{I}$$

This is a determinate system, being one equation to determine one unknown variable. While much of the anti-Keynesian and Keynesian world was still arguing over the tautological character of the Keynesian concepts, Professor Hansen had quickly cut through the non-essentials to isolate the critically important role of the propensity-to-consume schedule, as embodied in this fundamental equation.

Equation (1) is crucially important for the history of economic thought. It is the nucleus of the Keynesian reasoning. If it *in no way* gives insight into the analysis of employment, then the Keynesian system is sterile and misleading. In its oversimplification, this relation must be compared with two other seminal single equations which contain by implication much of the remainder of economic theory: namely the equating of supply and demand to determine market price,

$$D(p) - S(p) = O;$$

and the determination of a firm's best output, q, (or anything else) by the condition that its profits, π, be at a maximum through the balancing of the effect of any decision on *total revenue*, R, and *total cost*, C,

$$\frac{d\pi}{dq} = \frac{dR(q)}{dq} - \frac{dC(q)}{dq} = O$$

Geometrical Representation

Graphically, the simplest Keynesian equilibrium can be shown on a by now familiar 45° line diagram.[1] On the vertical axis the consumption function, C(Y), is plotted against income. Investment is then superimposed onto consumption. The two together constitute the right-hand side of equation (1). The left-hand side, Y, is simply income itself plotted against income, or in short a 45° line. The intersection of $C(Y) + \bar{I}$ with the 45° line gives us our simplest "Keynesian-cross," which logically is exactly like a "Marshallian-cross" of supply and demand.

As an alternative to this geometrical presentation, we may let the intersection of a saving schedule with investment depict the determination of income. This amounts simply to transposing the consumption term in equation (1) over to the left-hand side, which now gives us the difference between income and consumption, or what may be called the *propensity-to-save* schedule, S(Y). In its new version (1) reads,

[1] See, for example, the contribution of Robert L. Bishop, in L. Metzler *et al.*, *Income, Employment and Public Policy* (New York: Norton, 1948), p. 319.

(2) $$Y - C(Y) = \bar{I} \text{ or } S(Y) = \bar{I}$$

As before, income is plotted on the horizontal axis; but now on the vertical axis we must allow for both positive and negative amounts of saving or investment. The amount of investment is plotted as a horizontal schedule. The saving schedule will intersect it from below to yield the same equilibrium income as is shown in the 45° line diagram.

How does the fundamental income equation yield us the usual multiplier? Very simply, when we ask for the change in income which results from a change in the parameter investment, $\bar{I}$.[2] From (1) it follows that $\frac{d\bar{I}}{dY} = 1 - C'(Y)$; or the multiplier formula becomes

(3) $$\left[\frac{dY}{d\bar{I}}\right] = \frac{1}{1 - C'(Y)}$$

where C' is the familiar margin propensity to consume at each different income level. Of the two equations, (1) and (3), the former is the more fundamental. By it we can appraise the effect of a large as well as a small change in investment, and without making the usual linear approximation to the consumption function.[3]

[2] The only mathematical technique used in this paper is the simple one of determining the derivative of one variable, Y, with respect to another variable or parameter, a, to which Y is related by an implicit equation. Thus, if Y depends on a as determined by

$$F(Y,a) = 0$$

so that $dF = \dfrac{\partial F(Y,a)}{\partial Y} \, dY + \dfrac{\partial F(Y,a)}{\partial a} \, da = 0$, then necessarily

$$\frac{dY}{da} = - \frac{\dfrac{\partial F}{\partial a}}{\dfrac{\partial F}{\partial Y}}$$

where the symbol ∂ refers always to partial differentiation with "all other variables being held constant." An expression like $C'(Y)$ or C' always means $\dfrac{dC(Y)}{dY}$.

[3] If $C = a + bY$, a linear function on income, then the reader can show that

$$Y = \frac{1}{1-b} (a + \bar{I}) \text{ and } \Delta Y = \frac{1}{1-b} \Delta \bar{I}$$

Simple Mathematics of Income Determination

Autonomous Consumption Shifts and Induced Investment

Before leaving the simplest Keynesian system, we may briefly mention that an autonomous upward shift of the consumption schedule will have exactly the same multiplier effects upon income as will an increase in investment. Thus, we may rewrite the consumption schedule to include a new element, a, of autonomous consumption—or $C = a + C(Y)$. The reader may easily verify that in the new Equation (1), the a term can be grouped with $\bar{I}$ with exactly the same quantitative effects upon income. "Investment dollars are high-powered dollars." Consumption dollars are, too.

The problem of "induced" investment introduces no formal difficulties. From a long-run economic viewpoint, it is doubtful that net investment can be related to a stationary income level in the way that consumption can. But in the short run, when the stock of capital is more or less constant, and when each different level of income can be thought of as a *change* in income as compared to previous periods, then it may be legitimate to write investment as a rising function of income, $I(Y)$. This *propensity-to-invest schedule* will intersect (from above) the *propensity-to-save schedule* of (2) to give the equilibrium level of income.

If we now wish to calculate a "multiplier" coefficient, the problem is more complicated. Exactly what question do we really wish to ask? What "multiplicand" are we changing in order to appraise its effect on income? The reader should verify for himself that once induced investment enters the picture, the appropriate multiplier to show the effect on Y of an *autonomous* shift, a, in either the investment or consumption schedule is given by [4]

If C is curvilinear, then

$$\Delta Y = \frac{1}{1 - \bar{C}'} \Delta \bar{I}$$

where now the $\bar{C}'$ will be some marginal propensity to consume intermediate between the old and new income situations, and which can only be evaluated with perfect exactitude by Equation (1).

[4] More generally, a may be an autonomous factor which shifts the I or C

$$(4) \qquad \left[\frac{dY}{da}\right] = \frac{1}{1 - C'(Y) - I'(Y)} = \frac{1}{S'(Y) - I'(Y)}$$

III. TREATMENT OF GOVERNMENT IN INCOME ANALYSIS

So far we have been ignoring the presence of government expenditure on goods and services, G, and of net algebraic tax collections or withdrawals, W (positive when people pay taxes, negative when they receive transfer payments such as old-age pensions, veterans' allowances, etc.). Actually, Net National Product at market prices consists of three components

$$Y = C + I + G$$

To make our four-variable system determinate we must be willing to commit ourselves to some additional hypotheses. As before, we may provisionally make investment a constant. Since government expenditure is primarily a matter of policy (particularly, since we are excluding from G, relief and other transfer items which vary with income), we may provisionally set it equal to a constant. But now the dependence of consumption upon national income becomes more complicated. If we abstract from changes in the distribution of income—and empirical studies suggest that the *marginal* propensities to consume of different income classes do not differ enough to make this a disastrous oversimplification—then as a first approximation we can make consumption a function of "disposable income *after* net algebraic taxes or withdrawals," $Y - W$. By adding W as a variable, we must now demand that an additional hypothesis be made about its behavior. The simplest assumption is that net taxes or withdrawals are equal to some constant, set by policy. (We shall see in the next section that this is a rather misleading assumption.)

---

schedules (either or both) in a *non-parallel* fashion. Our multiplier then becomes

$$\left[\frac{dY}{da}\right] = \frac{1}{\left(1 - \dfrac{\partial C}{\partial Y} - \dfrac{\partial I}{\partial Y}\right)} \frac{\partial(C + I)}{\partial a}.$$

Simple Mathematics of Income Determination

In symbols, our hypotheses are as follows

$$I = \bar{I}, G = \bar{G}, W = \bar{W}$$
$$C = C(Y - \bar{W})$$

which when substituted in the first definitional equation of this section, gives us a determinate equation for income

(5) $$Y = C(Y - \bar{W}) + \bar{I} + \bar{G}$$

The 45°-line diagram is well designed to illustrate this equilibrium; our only change is to add government expenditure (whether on capital or current goods) to private investment, and to shift the consumption function rightward (and downward) in a parallel fashion by a distance equal to net tax withdrawals, $\bar{W}$.

The saving-investment diagram is now not quite so convenient to interpret, and a number of alternative re-groupings of terms can be imagined. The method which is most closely akin to the definition of saving of the Department of Commerce would be as follows

(6) $$Y - C(Y - \bar{W}) - \bar{W} = \bar{I} + (\bar{G} - \bar{W}).$$

Consumption has been transposed to the left-hand side and $\bar{W}$ has been subtracted from both sides. The left-hand side, saving, is equated to private investment plus the deficit (whether financed by borrowing or printing of money).

An alternative possibility, which is perhaps nearer in formulation to the National Bureau definitions, would be to treat the deficit as negative government saving, and transpose it to the left-hand side, so that investment is equated to private and public saving. The only advantage to this second formulation is that it makes more plausible to beginning students such a statement as, "A reduction of taxes will raise income by reducing the community's saving." Intuitively, the student feels that a reduction of taxes will increase consumption, (private) saving, and income. Of course, either formulation is identical to Equation (5).

Now that income is a determinate function of $\bar{I}, \bar{G}$, and $\bar{W}$, it is simple to determine the appropriate multipliers for a unit change in each of these quantities. Using the technique described in the second footnote to this paper, it is easy to show that

$$
(7) \quad
\begin{aligned}
\left[\frac{dY}{d\bar{G}}\right] &= \left[\frac{dY}{d\bar{I}}\right] = \frac{1}{1 - C'(Y - \bar{W})} \\
\left[\frac{dY}{d(-\bar{W})}\right] &= \frac{C'(Y - \bar{W})}{1 - C'(Y - \bar{W})} = \left[\frac{dY}{d\bar{G}}\right] - 1
\end{aligned}
$$

In words, government expenditure has the same favorable effect on income as does private investment, both effects being equal to the reciprocal of the marginal propensity to save out of disposable income. Tax reduction will also increase income, but dollar for dollar its effects are always less than those of increasing expenditure. *In fact a dollar of expenditure always increases income by exactly one dollar more than does a dollar reduction of taxes.*

The "Balanced-Budget Theorem"

This is the basis for the significant "balanced-budget theorem." [5] According to this theorem, a deficit is not at all necessary for an expansionary fiscal policy. A balanced increase in expenditure and taxes—assuming no shift in the functional relationship of consumption to disposable income and no change in private invest-

---

[5] This theorem has been developed by several writers; see A. H. Hansen and H. S. Perloff, *State and Local Finance in the National Economy* (New York, 1944), pp. 245–246; T. Haavelmo, "Multiplier Effects of a Balanced Budget," *Econometrica*, Vol. XIII (1945), pp. 311–318; and the further comments by G. Haberler, R. M. Goodwin, E. E. Hagen, and T. Haavelmo, *Econometrica* Vol. XIV (1946), pp. 148–158; H. C. Wallich, "Income-generating Effects of a Balanced Budget," *Quarterly Journal of Economics*, Vol. LIX (1944), pp. 78–91; N. Kaldor's Appendix C to W. H. Beveridge, *Full Employment in a Free Society* (New York, 1945), pp. 346–347; P. A. Samuelson, "Full Employment after the War," in *Postwar Economic Problems*, edited by S. E. Harris (New York, 1943), p. 44. W. A. Salant's privately circulated memorandum was held up in publication by his war service. See also the early paper with similar notions developed from a different point of view by H. Somers, "The Impact of Fiscal Policy on National Income," *Canadian Journal of Economics and Political Science*, Vol. VIII (1942), pp. 364–385.

ment—will result in an exactly equivalent increase in net national product.[6]

The explanations given for this paradoxical result are numerous:

(1) Mr. Salant pointed out that taxes do not enter directly into the net national product on the very first round, so that the two multiplier chains resulting from G and $- W$ are respectively

$$1 + C' + (C')^2 + (C')^3 + \ldots\ldots,$$
$$- C' - (C')^2 - (C')^3 - \ldots\ldots$$

with the difference being 1 regardless of the magnitude of C'.

(2) Another mode of explanation is to say that to some degree taxes must "come out of saving as well as consumption." Haavelmo has, with some justification, objected to this explanation on the ground that it erroneously suggests that the expansionary effect of a balanced budget is proportional to the quantitative size of the marginal propensity-to-save coefficient—which it is not.[7]

(3) A similar explanation follows the line that when the government's tax-financed expenditure is expanded, this amounts to adding an element in the system with a propensity to consume of unity. Increasing the weight of such an element must pull up the weighted-average propensity to consume of the community as a whole.

(4) The last explanation, which Hansen himself emphasized, stresses that tax-financed government expenditure constitutes a

[6] If private investment is a rising function of total NNP, then the resulting increase in income and employment will be even larger; if, on the other hand, the net effects upon private investment are adverse, the increase in income will be smaller. Also it is quite possible that some changes in the distribution of disposable income might result, so that the saving and consumption schedules would shift in relationship to total disposable income. Consequently, the total income effects may differ, depending upon the type of taxes and the type of expenditures in question. For a development of this point, see R. A. Musgrave, "Alternative Budget Policies for Full Employment," *American Economic Review*, Vol. XXXV, No. 3, June, 1945, pp. 387–400.

[7] But he perhaps stretches his case too far when he argues that the same result is achieved when the marginal propensity to consume is exactly unity. For in that limiting case, our system becomes indeterminate and its multiplier o/o so long as $G \equiv W$. If $W \neq G$, the system is inconsistent.

part of the "circular flow" of society's self-sustaining income. If the concept of net national product at market price had been adhered to from the beginning in our national income statistics, we should have more quickly emancipated ourselves from the Grover Cleveland notion of government expenditure as a *subtraction* from private national product.

To realize that government expenditure on goods and services is itself part of national product is almost, but not quite, enough to demonstrate the validity of the balanced-budget theorem. Just one further step of reasoning is necessary for a logically rigorous proof: It must be shown that private disposable income will actually remain constant when tax-financed government expenditure is superimposed upon it.

That private disposable income will remain constant is easily seen from Equation (5) or (6). Rearranging terms and designating *disposable income* as y and the deficit as D, $(= G - W)$, we now have

(8) $$Y - \bar{W} = C(Y - \bar{W}) + \bar{I} + (\bar{G} - \bar{W}) \text{ or}$$
$$y = C(y) + \bar{I} + \bar{D}$$

Obviously, with $\bar{G}$ and $\bar{W}$ increased equally, with $\bar{D}$ and $\bar{I}$ unchanged, this equation determines y as a constant, $\bar{y}$. Hence, total Y must increase one for one with the superimposed amount of $\bar{G}$ or $\bar{W}$ added onto the fixed base of private disposable income, $\bar{y}$. Thus, the balanced-budget expenditure has a multiplier of exactly one; without recognizing this quantitative fact, we miss the kernel of the theorem.

A few concluding observations may be made: (1) The above analysis shows that there is, strictly speaking, no true unique multiplier to be associated with a deficit; i.e., $dY/d(G - W)$ is undefined until we know how the deficit is brought about in terms of the relative weights going to G and W. Such a "pseudo-multiplier" can be made to vary between minus and plus infinity. (2) Government transfer expenditure, as distinct from "exhaustive" expenditure on goods and services, tends to have a relatively weak

multiplier exactly like that of taxes. In fact, raising taxes and transfer expenditure simultaneously will (apart from redistribution between income classes and indirect tax-distortion effects) have no
effect on $\overline{W}$ or income. (3) The old Currie-Villard concept of
"net income creating expenditure" of the government is seen to be
slightly misleading. With no deficit, income may be created. It
would be a little more appropriate to call this concept the "net dis-
posable-income creating expenditure" of the government. This is
because a unit increase in deficit has the same effect on disposable
income as a unit increase in investment (or government expenditure) has on total net national product, as the reader may verify.

Collections from a Given Tax Structure vs. Changing Rates

Realistically, it is misleading to treat net tax withdrawals, W, as a
direct policy parameter. Congress legislates government expenditure, $\overline{G}$; but it can never legislate tax receipts. All it can do is
legislate tax *rates* which determine the government's net take at
each different level (and composition) of national income. Any
change in rates will necessarily change income, so that the legislators can never quite know what tax collections will be—without
estimating the solution to the simultaneous equations of income
determination.

Instead of assuming W constant, therefore, we shall assume that
it is a given function of income for each set of Congressional decisions concerning different tax rates and transfer expenditures For
simplicity, we may assume that the complex of rates can be summarized in a single parameter, $\bar{r}$, which shifts the whole tax schedule up or down at each income level. Hence [8]

[8] It would be more general to permit $\bar{r}$ also to "twist" the tax schedule as well
as raise or lower it. This will produce only higher-order curvature effects on income which will be negligible for small changes in tax rates. In the general case,
$W = W(Y,\bar{r})$ and $\dfrac{\partial W}{\partial r}$ depends upon the level of income.

Nevertheless, $\dfrac{dY}{dr} \Big/ \dfrac{\partial W}{\partial r}$ will be independent of any twist effect imparted
by the term $\dfrac{\partial^2 W}{\partial Y \partial r}$.

$$W = \bar{r} + W(Y)$$

where $W'(Y) = \dfrac{\partial W}{\partial Y}$ is the marginal propensity to tax, a quantity which increases progressively with income. Our equation of income determination now gives us Y in terms of $\bar{G}$, $\bar{I}$, and $\bar{r}$:

(9) $$Y = C[Y - \bar{r} - W(Y)] + \bar{I} + \bar{G}$$

If we wish to illustrate the equilibrium graphically, we can easily do so as long as net tax rates, $\bar{r}$, are constant. This being so, disposable income, $y = Y - \bar{r} - W(Y)$, becomes a determinate function of net national product, Y. Therefore, consumption itself becomes indirectly a function of Y, but now with a slope which is less than the marginal propensity to consume out of disposable income—perhaps by about a quarter. For fixed $\bar{r}$, we plot

$$C = C[Y - \bar{r} - W(Y)] = C(Y,\bar{r})$$

where

$$\frac{\partial C(Y,\bar{r})}{\partial Y} = C'(y)[1 - W'(Y)]$$

As we decrease $\bar{r}$, the consumption schedule is shifted leftward (and upward), but now by an amount greater than the reduction of taxes, and to an increasing degree as income increases.

Equation (9) will yield us an income multiplier with respect to $\bar{G}$ or $\bar{I}$, and also one with respect to $\bar{r}$. These three are the only basic multipliers possible. But when any given combination of these three parameters has been changed, it is always possible to relate the resulting change in income to the resulting change in any other variable of the system. Such a ratio can be called a multiplier if one pleases, but really it is a *mutatis mutandis* concept and had better be recognized as a chameleon creature whose numerical value can be changed at will by specifying different combinations of variation in the basic parameters, $\bar{r}$, $\bar{G}$, and $\bar{I}$. Examples of such a pseudo-multiplier will be provided later.

Simple Mathematics of Income Determination

From Equation (9), we get the following two identical multipliers when we change only $\bar{G}$ or $\bar{I}$:

$$(10) \qquad \left[\frac{dY}{d\bar{I}}\right] = \left[\frac{dY}{d\bar{G}}\right] = \frac{1}{1 - \dfrac{\partial C(Y,\bar{r})}{\partial Y}}.$$

$$= \frac{1}{1 - C'(y)[1 - W'(Y)]}$$

Because the marginal propensity to tax, W', is about one-fourth, the marginal propensity to consume out of national income will be only three-fourths as large as that out of disposable income. Consequently, our new multiplier will be much smaller, its weakness being due to the superimposition of "tax leakages" on top of "savings leakages." Even if people consume all their disposable income, the tax leakages would be a heavy drag—in either direction—on the system's movement.

For a change in $\bar{G}$, we could easily calculate a pseudo deficit multiplier:

$$(11) \qquad \left[\frac{dY}{dD}\right] = \frac{\dfrac{dY}{d\bar{G}}}{\dfrac{d(\bar{G} - W)}{d\bar{G}}} = \frac{1}{1 - \dfrac{\partial C}{\partial Y} - W'}$$

$$= \frac{1}{(1 - C')(1 - W')}$$

This may be very large indeed, because an increase in expenditure —after it has had a multiplied effect upon income—may be accompanied by a substantial increase in taxes, with the result that a sizable change in income is associated with a small change in deficit. For a change in $\bar{I}$ only, the deficit goes down and income goes up, yielding a negative pseudo deficit multiplier, whose exact value the reader can easily verify to be the reciprocal of the marginal propensity to tax.

Our last basic multiplier will be that giving the change in income resulting from a unit autonomous downward shift of the tax schedule:

$$(12) \qquad \left[\frac{dY}{d(-\bar{r})}\right] = \frac{C'(y)}{1 - C'(y)[1 - W'(Y)]}$$

This results from differentiating Equation (9) with respect to $\bar{r}$ according to the stated rule of implicit functions. Note again, that (given the assumption of constant investment) tax reduction is less powerful than expenditure. Beardsley Ruml does not have quite the leverage of Harry Hopkins.

Three Paths to Full Employment

Professor Bishop, in *Income, Employment and Public Policy*, has elaborated upon the three fiscal paths to full employment: (1) deficit spending (a change in $\bar{G}$ only, in our notation); (2) spending without deficit (an equal change in $\bar{G}$ and $\bar{W}$); (3) a deficit without spending (a reduction in net taxes, W, brought about by reducing rates, $\bar{r}$, in $W[Y,\bar{r}]$). Any two of the three cases can be combined to produce the third. Bishop prefers to regard (2) and (3) as "pure" cases, the former involving only expansion of the government component of net national product, and the latter involving only a change in the private sector. His first case is then simply a blending of these two.

From the standpoint of policy manipulation, it might be preferable to regard (1) and (3) as pure cases, the former involving a simple change in $\bar{G}$, and the latter a simple change in $\bar{r}$ or $\bar{W}$. The balanced-budget case (2) would then represent an equal blending of the two pure cases. Either viewpoint is equally admissible.

However, one thing is clear: Financial orthodoxy aimed at minimizing deficits turns out to be really most radical from the standpoint of maximizing free, private enterprise and minimizing the role of government. To a *laissez-faire* economist, route (3), which is the least orthodox, is the best path to follow when income is to be expanded.

Simple Mathematics of Income Determination

IV. INTERNATIONAL TRADE AND INCOME DETERMINATION

Very briefly, the treatment of international trade, neglecting the government and corporations, may be indicated. Net national product is now the sum of home-produced consumption goods, c, home-produced investment goods, I, and home-produced goods for export, X. In exports are included such invisible service items as shipping and (net) interest and dividends from abroad. Then

$$Y = c + I + X$$

If for simplicity we assume that imports, M, are all consumption goods, we may subtract and add M and rewrite this equation as

$$Y = (c + M) + I + (X - M)$$
= total consumption goods + investment + foreign balance on current account

The Department of Commerce includes the foreign balance in private net capital formation.

As far as a single country is concerned, *exports* may often be taken as an autonomous factor, independent of income, without too great error. However, this is not strictly true with respect to some components of dividends payable to foreigners; also there will be some small reflex influence of our income on our own exports via the effect of our imports on income and imports of foreigners. These effects I disregard. Our demand for domestic consumption goods may be taken as a function of our national income, $c(Y)$, exchange rates and relative prices being given. With domestic investment, $\bar{I}$, being given, our income equation becomes

$$(13) \qquad Y = c(Y) + \bar{I} + \bar{X}$$

and our multipliers become

$$(14) \qquad \left[\frac{dY}{d\bar{I}}\right] = \left[\frac{dY}{d\bar{X}}\right] = \frac{1}{1 - c'(Y)} = \frac{1}{S'(Y) + M'(Y)}$$

where the marginal propensity to consume, $c'(Y)$, falls short of unity by the marginal propensity to import, M', plus the marginal propensity to save, S'. The increase in imports and the pseudo balance of trade multiplier can be shown to be given respectively by

$$(15) \qquad \frac{dM}{d\bar{X}} = \frac{M'}{M' + S'}$$

and

$$(16) \qquad \frac{dY}{d(\bar{X} - M)} = \frac{1}{1 - c' - M'}$$

These formulae, and indeed the whole analytical problem of exports versus balance of trade as multiplicand, are formally analogous to the problem of government expenditure versus deficit.[9]

An autonomous shift in imports would, other things being equal, have no effect on domestic income, except possibly through indirect effects which are excluded in this discussion. But most things which affect the propensity to import, such as tariffs, exchange rates, and relative prices, would also affect the domestic propensity to consume in the opposite direction. Therefore, I shall not present a formal multiplier for a shift in imports.

Are there not circumstances under which the balance of payments, $(X - M)$, rather than X is the appropriate autonomous variable or multiplicand? If so, and if $C = c + M$ is a determinate function of income, $C(Y) = c(Y) + M(Y)$, then the appropriate income equation becomes

$$(17) \qquad Y = C(Y) + \bar{I} + \overline{(X - M)}$$

and

$$(18) \qquad \frac{dY}{d(\overline{X - M})} = \frac{1}{1 - C'(Y)} = \frac{1}{1 - c'(Y) - M'(Y)}$$

the same result as given just above. But now the pseudo-multiplier

[9] See D. H. Robertson, "Mr. Clark and the Foreign Trade Multiplier," *Economic Journal*, Vol. XLIX (1939), pp. 354–356, for the classical treatment of this problem.

has become the genuine article; and through our change of hypothesis, the basic multiplier has become a chameleon.

A few concluding observations may be made concerning international trade: (1) It is true that price changes, such as result from gold flows or exchange rates, find themselves supplemented by income effects. Nevertheless, when a country's exports increase, the resulting induced change in imports brought about by the income multiplier will always fall short of restoring equilibrium by an amount which depends on the relative strength of the marginal propensity to save and the marginal propensity to import. See Equation (15).

(2) When relative price changes are introduced into the picture, it becomes even more possible that domestic employment may be improved by a change in conditions which simultaneously expands exports and contracts the trade balance. This cannot be elaborated upon here.

(3) The cases in which the trade balance can be treated as an autonomous element are necessarily those in which—through the action of exchange control, exchange depreciation, or lender-borrower psychology—capital movements prove to be the bottleneck to which trade movements adjust themselves. The post-World War II world, where the availability of dollars calls the tune, may be such an example. In many if not most of such cases, imports are adjusted to exports so as to realize the preassigned balance of trade (for the foreign country at any rate) and the assumed relations between home-consumption goods, imports, and income cannot be assumed to hold, so that Equation (17) must be used with caution.

(4) Throughout part of this discussion, I have been following the customary loose practice of treating the foreign trade multiplier as if it were concerned only with the balance of trade and not with the more inclusive balance on current account. Usually, this does not matter since everyone realizes that shipping is just like exports, and tourist expenditure just like imports.

But confusion almost always arises in connection with interest and dividend payments. Very often one encounters the following type of statement: "Foreign lending for a while creates domestic employment. But finally, when interest payments become larger than new lending, the balance of trade will become unfavorable—*with necessary adverse effects upon domestic employment*." The italicized passage is absolutely wrong.

Interest received from abroad, *per se*, increases domestic employment through its favorable secondary effects on consumption spending. To some (small) degree it increases our imports and thus tends to solve its own "transfer problem." But, alas, this effect is necessarily an incomplete one, so that exchange depreciation may be necessary for the paying country; the unfavorable employment effect of this must be compared with the favorable effect previously mentioned. Strangely enough, from the standpoint of modern income analysis, the Ohlin position of "conservation of purchasing power" becomes something of an archaic throwback to the classical Say's Law; and the orthodox economists (including Keynes), through bumbling reasoning, seem to have approached the correct position.

(5) A simultaneous increase in exports via reciprocal lowering of trade barriers will improve the efficiency of the international division of labor. But ordinarily its favorable effects upon employment are likely to be unimportant—except to the quite limited degree that the release of exchange controls can be expected to diminish thriftiness. This follows from Equation (17) and the earlier remarks concerning an autonomous shift in the import schedule.

Throughout the remainder of this paper, I shall follow the convention of including the foreign balance in *private net capital formation*, I, and shall not attempt to isolate that part of each component of net national product which can be imputed to home-owned factors. Therefore, international trade will be implicitly, rather than explicitly, in the income system.

Simple Mathematics of Income Determination

V. THE BUSINESS CORPORATION AND INCOME
DETERMINATION

The public's disposable income, y, falls short of net national product, Y, by more than taxes or net withdrawals once we admit the corporation into the picture. Taxes may now be split into business and personal, although the dividing line becomes rather arbitrary. But more important, corporate earnings (after corporate income taxes) may not all be paid out in dividends; undistributed profits may be ploughed back into the business, or in very bad times dividends may be maintained in excess of stated earnings. In short, algebraic net business saving, B, must be subtracted from net national product, along with taxes, before we get the disposable income of consumers.

If initially we ignore the role of government, our simplest income equation now becomes

$$(19) \qquad Y = C(Y - \bar{B}) + \bar{I}.$$

An increase in investment will increase income; an increase in net business saving will, by itself, reduce disposable income, consumption, and income. The reader should be able to compute the appropriate multipliers $[dY/d\bar{I}]$ and $[dY/d\bar{B}]$. But first compare this last equation with our earlier treatment of government in Equation (5). It is easy to see that $\bar{I}$ and $\bar{B}$ are—in their relation to income and each other—playing exactly the same roles as did $\bar{G}$ and $\bar{W}$ respectively. This tells us immediately that a reduction in corporate saving is not quite so stimulating as an increase in investment.

The Income Stimulus of Corporations

It also casts light on the way to measure the stimulating influence of business enterprise. Among income analysts, the notion is thoroughly discredited that corporations are flooding the community with purchasing power whenever they pay out more in dividends than they receive in earnings. Fortunately, this is so because in most years, net business savings are positive rather than negative, and a logical application of the discredited viewpoint would have led to the anomalous conclusion that business enterprise is normally *deflating* the community. At the other extreme are those who seem to argue that any real corporate investments made out of ploughed back profits, are fully income creating so that when corporate taxes take away funds that would be added to surplus, employment is being greatly reduced.[10]

Probably most income analysts will prefer a third magnitude to measure the income stimulus emanating from corporations— namely, the difference between net business investment and net business saving (or what is the same thing, the difference between these gross magnitudes). Even this third measure, however, turns out to be not quite correct. Just as a balanced budget increases income with a multiplier of one, so will a balanced increase in business investment and business saving increase employment and income. But, and this the reader can verify by treating Equation (19) the way (5) was treated, there will be no secondary multiplier effects.

The Corporate Propensity to Save

It would be more realistic to modify (19) by making net business saving some function of net national product or $B = B(Y)$. This would give us

$$(20) \qquad Y = C[Y - B(Y)] + \bar{I} = C(Y) + \bar{I}$$

and

$$(21) \qquad \left[\frac{dY}{d\bar{I}}\right] = \frac{1}{1 - C'(Y)} = \frac{1}{1 - C'(Y - B)[1 - B'(Y)]}$$

[10] This would be nearly true if stockholders treated undistributed profits as part of their disposable income for consumption purposes. This is not realistic because capital gains are not actually, or believed to be, equal to additions to book surplus.

Simple Mathematics of Income Determination

Between the wars, the marginal propensity of corporations to save appeared much more important than that of families. This may, however, be a short-run cyclical phenomenon which would not be true of the secular growth of high and stable levels of income. Much more statistical study of corporate behavior is needed, especially since there is no reason to expect the invariance of any unique simple hypothesis.[11]

VI. SYNTHESIS

One of the great advantages of quantitative econometric model building is the fact that the writer is pinned down by the concreteness of the arithmetical figures to making specific hypotheses about all the relevant magnitudes. We may summarize, therefore, all the special cases considered up until now by considering the simplest complete income model which takes account of all components of national product.

As always, net national product is the sum of consumption, C, investment, I (including the net foreign balance), and government expenditure on goods and services, G:

$$Y = C + I + G$$

For simplicity, G and I may perhaps still be taken as autonomous factors, although the reader may easily modify this assumption. But if consumption is to depend upon disposable income, a long list of assumptions must be made concerning the numerous subtractions which first have to be made from net national product before we get disposable income. These subtractions are:

(a) *Business taxes*, BT, which we may assume are a function of income.

(b) *Net corporate saving*, B, which is the difference between corporate earnings (after taxes), E, and dividends, D, not to be confused with the deficit referred to earlier. Earnings may, for

[11] For example, in (19) B may be made a function of I rather than Y giving a multiplier of $(1 - C' \frac{\partial B}{\partial I}) \div (1 - C')$.

simplicity, be assumed equal to a function of income; although a good argument could be made for the alternative assumption that earnings before taxes are an invariant function of Y regardless of tax policy. Dividends may most simply be made a function of earnings, although their simple correlation coefficient has not been very high in the past.

(c) *Net personal taxes or withdrawals*, PW, where transfer payments have been treated as negative items. (Obviously, PW + BT = W.) This term PW might be made a function of "income paid out," but for simplicity in grouping it with business taxes, we shall make it a function of total net national product, or PW(Y).

Mathematically our hypotheses are

$$C = C(Y - BT - B - PW) = C(Y - W - B) = C(Y)$$
$$W = BT(Y) + PW(Y) = W(Y)$$
$$B = E - D = E(Y) - D[E(Y)] = B(Y)$$
$$I = \bar{I}, G = \bar{G}$$

Our simple income equation finally becomes

(22) $$Y = C[Y - W(Y) - B(Y)] + \bar{G} + \bar{I}$$

The interested reader may depict this equilibrium graphically, and introduce policy parameters—such as tax rates, $\bar{r}$, or corporate "thriftiness"—into various places in this equation and work out the appropriate responses.[12] He may also introduce induced investment if he pleases, or otherwise vary the hypotheses.

In all essentials, our final equation epitomizes the important previous equations, which are respectively (1), (5) or (9), (13) or (17), and (19) or (20).

---

[12] The response to a change in $\bar{G}$ or $\bar{I}$ can be verified to be given by

$$\left[\frac{dY}{d\bar{G}}\right] = \left[\frac{dY}{d\bar{I}}\right] = \frac{1}{1 - C'(Y)\,[1 - W'(Y) - B'(Y)]}$$

where $B'(Y) = E'(Y)\,[1 - D'(E)]$. This is placed in a footnote to emphasize that the parent income equations are more important than their multiplier offspring.

In conclusion, I would not be doing justice to the pragmatic realism of Professor Hansen, if I did not emphasize the violence done to complex reality by the simplified statical abstractions of this paper.

BOOK FOUR

Economics and Public Policy

PART XII

Pure Theory of Public Expenditure

92

THE PURE THEORY OF PUBLIC EXPENDITURE

Paul A. Samuelson

1. *Assumptions.* Except for Sax, Wicksell, Lindahl, Musgrave, and Bowen, economists have rather neglected the theory of optimal public expenditure, spending most of their energy on the theory of taxation. Therefore, I explicitly assume two categories of goods: ordinary *private consumption goods* $(X_1, \cdots, X_n)$ which can be parcelled out among different individuals $(1, 2, \cdots, i, \cdots, s)$ according to the relations $X_j = \overset{s}{\underset{1}{\Sigma}} X^i_j$; and *collective consumption goods* $(X_{n+1}, \cdots, X_{n+m})$ which all enjoy in common in the sense that each individual's consumption of such a good leads to no subtraction from any other individual's consumption of that good, so that $X_{n+j} = X^i_{n+j}$ simultaneously for each and every ith individual and each collective consumptive good. I assume no mystical collective mind that enjoys collective consumption goods; instead I assume each individual has a consistent set of *ordinal preferences* with respect to his consumption of all goods (collective as well as private) which can be summarized by a regularly smooth and convex utility index $u^i = u^i(X^i_1, \cdots, X^i_{n+m})$ (any monotonic stretching of the utility index is of course also an admissible cardinal index of preference). I shall throughout follow the convention of writing the partial derivative of any function with respect to its jth argument by a j subscript, so that $u^i_j = \partial u^i / \partial X^i_j$, etc. Provided economic quantities can be divided into two groups, (1) *outputs* or goods which everyone always wants to maximize and (2) *inputs* or factors which everyone always wants to minimize, we are free to change the algebraic signs of the latter category and from then on to work only with "goods," knowing that the case of factor inputs is covered as well. Hence by this convention we are sure that $u^i_j > 0$ always.

To keep production assumptions at the minimum level of simplicity, I assume a regularly convex and smooth production-possibility schedule relating totals of all outputs, private and collective; or $F(X_1, \cdots, X_{n+m}) = 0$, with $F_j > 0$ and ratios F_j/F_n determinate and subject to the generalized laws of diminishing returns.

Feasibility considerations disregarded, there is a *maximal* (ordinal) *utility frontier* representing the Pareto-optimal points — of which there are an $(s-1)$fold infinity — with the property that from such a frontier point you can make one person better off only by making some other person worse off. If we wish to make normative judgments concerning the relative ethical desirability of different configurations involving some individuals being on a higher level of indifference and some on a lower, we must be presented with a set of ordinal interpersonal norms or with a *social welfare function* representing a consistent set of ethical preferences among all the possible states of the system. It is not a "scientific" task of the economist to "deduce" the form of this function; this can have as many forms as there are possible ethical views; for the present purpose, the only restriction placed on the social welfare function is that it shall always increase or decrease when any one person's ordinal preference increases or decreases, all others staying on their same indifference levels: mathematically, we narrow it to the class that any one of its indexes can be written $U = U(u^1, \cdots, u^s)$ with $U_j > 0$.

2. *Optimal Conditions.* In terms of these norms, there is a "best state of the world" which is defined mathematically in simple regular cases by the marginal conditions

$$\frac{u^i_j}{u^i_r} = \frac{F_j}{F_r} \qquad \begin{matrix} (i = 1, 2, \cdots, s; \; r, j = 1, \cdots, n) \text{ or} \\ (i = 1, 2, \cdots, s; \; r = 1; \; j = 2, \cdots, n) \end{matrix} \qquad (1)$$

$$\sum_{i=1}^{s} \frac{u^i_{n+j}}{u^i_r} = \frac{F_{n+j}}{F_r} \qquad \begin{matrix} (j = 1, \cdots, m; \; r = 1, \cdots, n) \text{ or} \\ (j = 1, \cdots, m; \; r = 1) \end{matrix} \qquad (2)$$

$$\frac{U_i u^i_k}{U_q u^q_k} = 1 \qquad \begin{matrix} (i, q = 1, \cdots, s; \; k = 1, \cdots, n) \text{ or} \\ (q = 1; \; i = 2, \cdots, s; \; k = 1). \end{matrix} \qquad (3)$$

Equations (1) and (3) are essentially those given in the chapter on welfare economics in my *Foundations of Economic Analysis*. They constitute my version of the "new welfare economics." Alone (1) represents that subset of relations which defines the Pareto-optimal utility frontier and which by itself represents what I regard as the unnecessarily narrow version of what once was called the "new welfare economics."

The new element added here is the set (2), which constitutes a pure theory of government expenditure on collective consumption goods. By themselves (1) and (2) define the $(s-1)$-fold infinity of utility frontier points; only when a set of interpersonal normative conditions equivalent to (3) is supplied are we able to define an unambiguously "best" state.

Since formulating the conditions (2) some years ago, I have learned from the published and unpublished writings of Richard Musgrave that their essential logic is contained in the "voluntary-exchange" theories of public finance of the Sax-Wicksell-Lindahl-Musgrave type, and I have also noted Howard Bowen's independent discovery of them in Bowen's writings of a decade ago. A graphical interpretation of these conditions in terms of *vertical* rather than *horizontal* addition of different individuals' marginal-rate-of-substitution schedules can be given; but what I must emphasize is that there is a different such schedule for each individual at each of the $(s-1)$fold infinity of different distributions of relative welfare along the utility frontier.

3. *Impossibility of decentralized spontaneous solution.* So much for the involved optimizing equations that an omniscient calculating machine could theoretically solve if fed the postulated functions. No such machine now exists. But it is well known that an "analogue calculating machine" can be provided by competitive market pricing, (a) so long as the production functions satisfy the neoclassical assumptions of constant returns to scale and generalized diminishing returns and (b) so long as the individuals' indifference contours have regular convexity and, we may add, (c) so long as all goods are private. We can then insert between the right- and left-

hand sides of (1) the equality with uniform market prices p_j/p_r and adjoin the budget equations for each individual

$$p_1 X^i_1 + p_2 X^i_2 + \cdots + p_n X^i_n = L^i$$
$$(i = 1, 2, \cdots, s), \qquad (1)'$$

where L^i is a lump-sum tax for each individual so selected in algebraic value as to lead to the "best" state of the world. Now note, if there were no collective consumption goods, then (1) and (1)' can have their solution enormously simplified. Why? Because on the one hand perfect competition among productive enterprises would ensure that goods are produced at minimum costs and are sold at proper marginal costs, with all factors receiving their proper marginal productivities; and on the other hand, each individual, in seeking as a competitive buyer to get to the highest level of indifference subject to given prices and tax, would be led as if by an Invisible Hand to the grand solution of the social maximum position. Of course the institutional framework of competition would have to be maintained, and political decision-making would still be necessary, but of a computationally minimum type: namely, algebraic taxes and transfers $(L^1, \ldots L^s)$ would have to be varied until society is swung to the ethical observer's optimum. The servant of the ethical observer would not have to make explicit decisions about each person's detailed consumption and work; he need only decide about generalized purchasing power, knowing that each person can be counted on to allocate it optimally. In terms of communication theory and game terminology, each person is motivated to do the signalling of his tastes needed to define and reach the attainable-bliss point.

Now all of the above remains valid even if collective consumption is not zero but is instead *explicitly set* at its optimum values as determined by (1), (2), and (3). *However no decentralized pricing system can serve to determine optimally these levels of collective consumption.* Other kinds of "voting" or "signalling" would have to be tried. But, and this is the point sensed by Wicksell but perhaps not fully appreciated by Lindahl, now it is in the selfish interest of each person to give *false* signals, to pretend to have less interest in a given collective consumption activity than he really has, etc. I must emphasize this: taxing according to a benefit theory of taxation can not at all solve the computational problem in the decentralized manner possible for the first category of "private" goods to which the ordinary market pricing applies and which do not have the "external effects" basic to the very notion of collective consumption goods. Of course, utopian voting and signalling schemes can be imagined. ("Scandinavian consensus," Kant's "categorical imperative," and other devices meaningful only under conditions of "symmetry," etc.) The failure of market catallactics in no way denies the following truth: given sufficient knowledge the optimal decisions can always be found by scanning over all the attainable states of the world and selecting the one which according to the postulated ethical welfare function is best. The solution "exists"; the problem is how to "find" it.

One could imagine every person in the community being indoctrinated to behave like a "parametric decentralized bureaucrat" who *reveals* his preferences by signalling in response to price parameters or Lagrangean multipliers, to questionnaires, or to other devices. But there is still this fundamental technical difference going to the heart of the whole problem of *social* economy: by departing from his indoctrinated rules, any one person can hope to snatch some selfish benefit in a way not possible under the self-policing competitive pricing of private goods; and the "external economies" or "jointness of demand" intrinsic to the very concept of collective goods and governmental activities makes it impossible for the grand ensemble of optimizing equations to have that special pattern of zeros which makes *laissez-faire* competition even *theoretically* possible as an analogue computer.

4. *Conclusion.* To explore further the problem raised by public expenditure would take us into the mathematical domain of "sociology" or "welfare politics," which Arrow, Duncan Black, and others have just begun to investigate. Political economy can be regarded as one special sector of this general domain, and it may turn out to be pure luck that within the general domain there happened to be a subsector with the "simple" properties of traditional economics.

93

DIAGRAMMATIC EXPOSITION OF A THEORY OF PUBLIC EXPENDITURE

Paul A. Samuelson

IN the November 1954 issue of this REVIEW my paper on "The Pure Theory of Public Expenditure" presented a mathematical exposition of a public expenditure theory that goes back to Italian, Austrian, and Scandinavian writers of the last 75 years. After providing that theory with its needed logically-complete optimal conditions, I went on to demonstrate the fatal inability of any decentralized market or voting mechanism to attain or compute this optimum. The present note presents in terms of two-dimensional diagrams an essentially equivalent formulation of the theory's optimum conditions and briefly discusses some criticisms.

A polar-case model of government

Doctrinal history shows that theoretical insight often comes from considering strong or extreme cases. The grand Walrasian model of competitive general equilibrium is one such extreme polar case. We can formulate it so stringently as to leave no economic role for government. What strong polar case shall the student of public expenditure set alongside this pure private economy?

One possibility is the model of a group-mind. Such a model, which has been extensively used by nationalists and by Romantic critics of classical economics, can justify any, and every, configuration of government. So there is perhaps little that an economic theorist can usefully say about it.

My alternative is a slightly more sophisticated one, but still — intentionally — an extreme polar case. It is consistent with individualism, yet at the same time it explicitly introduces the vital external interdependencies that no theory of government can do without. Its basic assumption is an oversharp distinction between the following two kinds of goods:

(i) A *private* consumption good, like bread, whose total can be parcelled out among two or more persons, with one man having a loaf less if another gets a loaf more. Thus if X_1 is total bread, and X^1_1 and X^2_1 are the respective private consumptions of Man 1 and Man 2, we can say that the total equals the sum of the separate consumptions — or $X_1 = X^1_1 + X^2_1$.

(ii) A *public* consumption good, like an outdoor circus or national defense, which is provided for each person to enjoy or not, according to his tastes. I assume the public good can be varied in total quantity, and write X_2 for its magnitude. It differs from a private consumption good in that each man's consumption of it, X^1_2 and X^2_2 respectively, is related to the total X_2 by a condition of *equality* rather than of summation. Thus, by definition, $X^1_2 = X_2$, and $X^2_2 = X_2$.

Obviously, I am introducing a strong polar case. We could easily lighten the stringency of our assumptions. But on reflection, I think most economists will see that this is a natural antipodal case to the admittedly extreme polar case of traditional individualistic general equilibrium. The careful empiricist will recognize that many — though not all — of the realistic cases of government activity can be fruitfully analyzed as some kind of a blend of these two extreme polar cases.

Graphical depiction of tastes and technology

The first three charts summarize our assumptions about tastes and technology. Each diagram has a private good, such as bread, on its vertical axis; each has a public good on its horizontal axis. The heavy indifference curves of Chart 1 summarize Man 1's preferences between public and private goods. Chart 2's indifference curves do the same for Man 2; and the relative flatness of the contour shows that, in a sense, he has less liking for the public good.

The heavy production-possibility or opportunity-cost curve AB in Chart 3 relates the total productions of public and private goods in the usual familiar manner: the curve is convex from above to reflect the usual assumption of increasing relative marginal costs (or generalized diminishing returns).[1]

[1] Even though a public good is being compared with a

Because of our special definition of a public good, the three diagrams are not independent. Each must be lined up with *exactly the same horizontal scale.* Because increasing a public good for society simultaneously increases it for each and every man, we must always be simultaneously at exactly the same longitude in all three figures. Moving an inch east in one diagram moves us the same amount east in all.

CHART 1. — INDIFFERENCE CONTOURS RELATING MAN 1'S CONSUMPTION OF PUBLIC AND PRIVATE GOODS

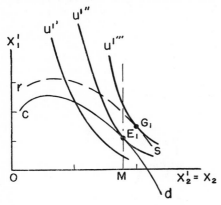

The private good on the vertical axis is subject to no new and unusual restrictions. Each man can be moved north or south on his indifference diagram independently. But, of course, the third diagram does list the total of bread summed over the private individuals; so it must have a larger vertical axis, and our momentary northward position on it must correspond to the sum of the independent northward positions of the separate individuals.

Tangency conditions for Pareto optima

What is the best or ideal state of the world for such a simple system? That is, what three

vertically-aligned points corresponding to a determination of a given total of both goods and a determinate parcelling out of them among all separate individuals will be the ethically preferred final configuration?

To answer this ethical, normative question we must be given a set of norms in the form of a *social welfare function* that renders interpersonal judgments. For expository convenience, let us suppose that this will be supplied later and that we know in advance it will have the follow-

CHART 2. — INDIFFERENCE CONTOURS RELATING MAN 2'S CONSUMPTION OF PUBLIC AND PRIVATE GOODS

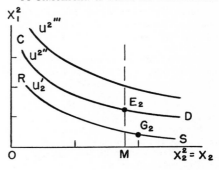

CHART 3. — TRANSFORMATION SCHEDULE RELATING TOTALS OF PUBLIC AND PRIVATE GOODS

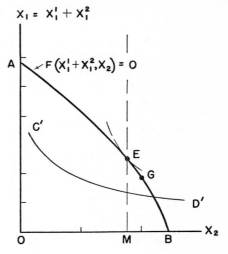

---

private good, the indifference curves are drawn with the usual convexity to the origin. This assumption, as well as the one about diminishing returns, could be relaxed without hurting the theory. Indeed, we could recognize the possible case where one man's circus is another man's poison, by permitting indifference curves to bend forward. This would not affect the analysis but would answer a critic's minor objection. Mathematically, we could without loss of generality set X^1_2 = any function of X_2, relaxing strict equality.

ing special individualistic property: leaving each person on his same indifference level will leave social welfare unchanged; at any point, a move of each man to a higher indifference curve can be found that will increase social welfare.

Given this rather weak assurance about the forthcoming social welfare function, we can proceed to determine tangency conditions of an "efficiency" type that are at least necessary, though definitely not sufficient. We do this by setting up a preliminary maximum problem which will eventually necessarily have to be satisfied.

Holding all but one man at specified levels of indifference, how can we be sure that the remaining man reaches his highest indifference level?

Concretely, this is how we define such a tangency optimum: Set Man 2 on a specified indifference curve, say his middle one CD. Paying attention to Mother Nature's scarcity, as summarized in Chart 3's AB curve, and following Man 1's tastes as given by Chart 1's indifference curves, how high on those indifference curves can we move Man 1?

The answer is given by the tangency point E_1, and the corresponding aligned points E_2 and E.

How is this derived? Copy CD on Chart 3 and call it $C'D'$. The distance between $C'D'$ and AB represents the amounts of the two goods that are physically available to Man 1. So subtract $C'D'$ vertically from AB and plot the algebraic result as cd in Chart 1. Now where on cd would Man 1 be best off? Obviously at the tangency point E_1 where cd touches (but does not cross) his highest attainable indifference contour.[2]

How many such Pareto-optimal points are

---

[2] The reader can easily derive rs and the tangency point G_1 corresponding to an original specification of Man 2's indifference level at the lower level RS rather than at AB. He can also interchange the roles of the two men, thereby deriving the point E_2 by a tangency condition. As a third approach, he can *vertically add* Man 2's specified indifference curve to each and every indifference curve of Man 1; the resulting family of contours can be conveniently plotted on Chart 3, and the final optimum can be read off from the tangency of AB to that family at the point E — as shown by the short broken-line indifference curve at E. It is easy to show that any of these tangencies are, in the two-good case, equivalent to Equation (2) of my cited paper; with a single private good my Equation (1) becomes redundant.

there? Obviously, for each of the infinite possible initial indifference curves to put Man 2 on, we can derive a new highest attainable tangency level for Man 1. So there are an infinity of such optimal points — as many in number as there are points on the usual contract curve. All of these Pareto-optimal points have the property that from them there exists no physically-feasible movement that will make every man better off. Of course we cannot compare two different Pareto points until we are given a social welfare function. For a move from one Pareto point to another must always hurt one man while it is helping another, and an interpersonal way of comparing these changes must be supplied.

Chart 4 indicates these utility possibilities on an ordinal diagram. Each axis provides an

CHART 4. — UTILITY FRONTIER OF PARETO-OPTIMAL EFFICIENCY POINTS AND ITS TANGENCY TO HIGHEST ATTAINABLE SOCIAL WELFARE CONTOUR

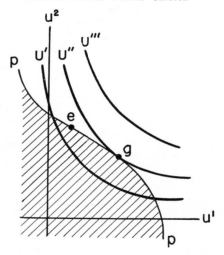

indicator of the two men's respective indifference curve levels. The utility frontier of Pareto-optimal points is given by pp: the double fold infinity of "inefficient," non-Pareto-optimal points is given by the shaded area; the pp frontier passes from northwest to southeast to reflect the inevitable conflict of interests characterizing any contract locus; the curvature of the pp locus is of no particular type since we have no need to put unique cardinal numbers along the indifference contours and can content ourselves with east-west and north-south relationships in Chart 4 without regard to numerical degree and to uneven stretchings of either utility axis.

The optimum of all the Pareto optima

Now we can answer the fundamental question: what is the best configuration for this society?

Use of the word "best" indicates we are in the ascientific area of "welfare economics" and must be provided with a set of norms. Economic science cannot deduce a social welfare function; what it can do is neutrally interpret any arbitrarily specified welfare function.

The heavy contours labelled U', U'', and U''' summarize all that is relevant in the provided social welfare function (they provide the needed ordinal scoring of every state of the world, involving different levels of indifference for the separate individuals).[3]

Obviously society cannot be best off inside the utility frontier. Where then on the utility frontier would the "best obtainable bliss point" be? We will move along the utility frontier pp until we touch the highest social indifference curve: this will be at g where pp tangentially touches, without crossing, the highest obtainable social welfare level U''. In words, we can interpret this final tangency condition [4] in the following terms:

(i) The social welfare significance of a unit of any private good allocated to private indi-

viduals must at the margin be the same for each and every person.

(ii) The Pareto-optimal condition, which makes relative marginal social cost equal to the sum of all persons' marginal rates of substitution, is already assured by virtue of the fact that bliss lies on the utility frontier.[5]

Relations with earlier theories

This completes the graphical interpretation of my mathematical model. There remains the pleasant task of relating this graphical treatment to earlier work of Bowen [6] and others.

To do this, look at Chart 5, which gives an alternative depiction of the optimal tangency condition at a point like E. I use the private good X_1 as numeraire, measuring all values in terms of it. The MC curve is derived from the AB curve of Chart 3: it is nothing but the absolute slope of that production-possibility schedule plotted against varying amounts of the public good; it is therefore a marginal cost curve, with MC measured in terms of the numeraire good.

The marginal rate of substitution curves MRS^1 and MRS^2 are derived in a similar fashion from the respective indifference curves of Man 1 and Man 2: thus, MRS^1 is the absolute slope of the u''' indifference curve plotted against varying amounts of the public good; MRS^2 is the similar slope function derived from Man 2's indifference curve CD. (All three are "marginal" curves, bearing the usual relationship to their respective "total" curves.)

These schedules look like demand curves. We are accustomed to adding horizontally or laterally the separate demand curves of individ-

---

[3] These social welfare or social indifference contours are given no particular curvature. Why? Again because we are permitting any arbitrary ordinal indicator of utility to be used on the axes of Chart 4.

An ethical postulate ruling out all "dog-in-the-manger phenomena" will make all partial derivatives of the social welfare function $U(u^1, u^2, ...)$ always positive. This will assure the usual negative slopes to the U contours of Chart 4. However, without hurting the Pareto part of the new welfare economics, we can relax this assumption a little and let the contours bend forward. If, at every point there can be found at least one positive partial derivative, this will be sufficient to rule out satiation points and will imply the necessity of the Pareto-optimal tangency condition of the earlier diagrams.

[4] This tangency condition would have to be expressed mathematically in terms of numerical indicators of utility that are not invariant under a monotonic renumbering.

However, it is easy to combine this tangency with the earlier Pareto-type tangency to get the formulation (3) of my cited paper, which is independent of the choice of numerical indicators of U, u^1, or u^2.

[5] A remarkable duality property of private and public goods should be noted. Private goods whose totals add — such as $X_1 = X^1_1 + X^2_1$ — lead ultimately to marginal conditions of simultaneous equality — such as $MC = MRS^1 = MRS^2$. Public goods whose totals satisfy a relation of simultaneous equality—such as $X_2 = X^1_2 = X^2_2$—lead ultimately to marginal conditions that add—such as $MC = MRS^1 + MRS^2$.

[6] Howard R. Bowen, "The Interpretation of Voting in the Allocation of Economic Resources," *Quarterly Journal of Economics*, LVIII (November 1943), 27–49. Much of this is also in Bowen's *Toward Social Economy* (New York, 1948), ch. 18.

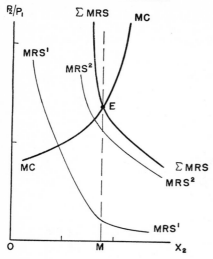

uals to arrive at total market demand. But this is valid only for private goods. As Bowen rightly says, *we must in the case of public goods add different individuals' curves vertically.*

This gives us the heavy ΣMRS curve for the whole community. Where is equilibrium? It is at E, where the community MC curve intersects the community ΣMRS curve. Upon reflection the reader will realize that the equality $MC = \Sigma MRS = MRS^1 + MRS^2$ is the precise equivalent of my mathematical equation (2) and of our Pareto-type tangency condition at E_1, E_2, or E. Why? Because of the stipulated requirement that Chart 5's curves are to depict the absolute slopes of the curves of Charts 1–3.

Except for minor details of notation and assumption, Chart 5 is identical with the figure shown on page 31 of the first Bowen reference, and duplicated on page 177 of the second reference. I am happy to acknowledge this priority. Indeed anyone familiar with Musgrave's valuable summary of the literature bearing on this area [7] will be struck with the similarity between

[7] Richard A. Musgrave, "The Voluntary Exchange Theory of Public Economy," *Quarterly Journal of Economics,*

this Bowen type of diagram and the Lindahl 100-per-cent diagram reproduced by Musgrave.[8]

Once the economic theorist has related my graphical and mathematical analysis to the Lindahl and Bowen diagrams, he is in a position, I believe, to discern the logical advantage of the present formulation. For there is something circular and unsatisfactory about both the Bowen and Lindahl constructions: they show what the final equilibrium looks like, but by themselves they are not generally able to find the desired equilibrium. To see this, note that whereas we might know MC in Chart 5, we would not know the appropriate MRS schedules for *all* men until we already were familiar with the final E intersection point. (We might know MRS^2 from the specification that Man 2 is to be on the AB level; but then we wouldn't know MRS^1 until Chart 1's tangency had given us Man 1's highest attainable level, $u^{1''}$.) Under conditions of general equilibrium, Charts 1–3 logically contain Chart 5 inside them, but not vice versa. Moreover, Charts 1–3 explicitly call attention to the fact that there is an infinite number of different diagrams of the Lindahl-Bowen type, one for each specified level of relative interpersonal well-being.[9]

Concluding reflections

I hope that the analytic model outlined here may help make a small and modest step toward understanding the complicated realities of polit-

LIII (February 1939), 213–17. This gives citations to the relevant works of Sax, De Viti de Marco, Wicksell, and Lindahl. I have greatly benefited from preliminary study of Professor Musgrave's forthcoming treatise on public finance, which I am sure will constitute a landmark in this area.

[8] Musgrave, *op. cit.*, 216, which is an acknowledged adaption from Erik Lindahl, *Die Gerechtigkeit in der Besteuerung* (Lund, 1919), 89. I have not had access to this important work. This diagram plots instead of the functions of Chart 5 the exact same functions after each has been divided by the MC function. The equilibrium intersection corresponding to E now shows up as the point at which all persons will together voluntarily provide 100 per cent of the full (unit? marginal?) cost of the public service. (If MC is not constant, some modifications in the Musgrave diagram may be required.)

[9] The earlier writers from Wicksell on were well aware of this. They explicitly introduce the assumption that there is to have been a *prior* optimal interpersonal distribution of income, so what I have labelled G. But the general equilibrium analyst asks: how can the appropriate distribution of income be decided on

ical economy. Much remains to be done. This is not the place to discuss the wider implications and difficulties of the presented economic theory.[10] However, I should like to comment briefly on some of the questions about this theory that have been raised in this REVIEW.[11]

(i) On the deductive side, the theory presented here is, I believe, a logically coherent one. This is true whether expressed in my original mathematical notation or in the present diagrammatic form. Admittedly, the latter widens the circle of economists who can understand and follow what is being said. The present version, with its tangencies of methodologically the same type as characterize Cournot-Marshall marginal theory and Bergson-Pigou welfare theory, should from its easily recognized equivalence with the mathematical version make clear my refusal to agree with Dr. Enke's view that my use of mathematics was limited "to notation."

(ii) In terms of the history of similar theories, I hope the present paper will make clear relationships to earlier writers. (In particular, see the above discussion relating my early diagrams and equations to the Bowen-Lindahl formulation.) I shall not bore the reader with irrelevant details of independent rediscoveries of doctrine that my ignorance of the available literature may have made necessary. Yet is it presumptuous to suggest that there does not exist in the present economic literature very much in the way of "conclusions and reasoning" that are, in Dr. Margolis' words, "familiar"? Except for the writers I have cited, and

a prior basis *before* the significant problems of public consumptions have been determined? A satisfactory general analysis can resist the temptation to assume (i) the level of government expenditure must be so small as not to affect appreciably the marginal social significance of money to the different individuals; (ii) each man's indifference curves run parallel to each other in a vertical direction so that every and all indifference curves in Chart 1 (or in Chart 2) give rise to the same MRS^1 (or MRS^2) curve in Chart 5. The modern theorist is anxious to free his analysis from the incubus of unnecessarily restrictive partial equilibrium assumptions.

[10] At the 1955 Christmas Meetings of the American Economic Association and Econometric Society, I hope to present some further developments and qualifications of this approach.

[11] Stephen Enke, "More on the Misuse of Mathematics in Economics: A Rejoinder," this REVIEW, XXXVII (May 1955), 131–33; Julius Margolis, "On Samuelson on the Pure Theory of Public Expenditure," this issue, p. 347.

the important unpublished thoughts of Dr. Musgrave, there is much opaqueness in the literature. Much of what goes by the name of the "voluntary exchange theory of public finance" seems pure obfuscation.[12]

(iii) Far from my formulation's being, as some correspondents have thought, a revival of the voluntary exchange theory — it is in fact an attempt to demonstrate how right Wicksell was to worry about the inherent political difficulty of ever getting men to reveal their tastes so as to attain the definable optimum. This intrinsic "game theory" problem has been sufficiently stressed in my early paper so that it has not been emphasized here. I may put the point most clearly in terms of the familiar tools of modern literary economics as follows:

Government supplies products jointly to many people. In ordinary market economics as you increase the number of sellers of a homogeneous product indefinitely, you pass from monopoly through indeterminate oligopoly and can hope to reach a determinate competitive equilibrium in the limit. It is sometimes thought that increasing the number of citizens who are jointly supplied public goods leads to a similar determinate result. This is reasoning from an incorrect analogy. A truer analogy in private economics would be the case of a bilateral-monopoly supplier of joint products whose number of joint products — meat, horn, hide, and so on — is allowed to increase without number: such a process does not lead to a determinate equilibrium of the harmonistic type praised in the literature. My simple model is able to demonstrate this point — which does have "policy implications."

(iv) I regret using "the" in the title of my earlier paper and have accordingly changed the present title. Admittedly, public expenditure and regulation proceed from considerations other than those emphasized in my models. Here are a few:

a. Taxes and expenditure aim at redistrib-

[12] See Gerhard Colm, "The Theory of Public Expenditure," *Annals of the American Academy of Political and Social Sciences*, CLXXXIII (January 1936), 1–11, reprinted in his *Essays in Public Finance and Fiscal Policy* (New York, 1955), 27–43 for an admirable criticism of the Graziani statement, "We know that the tax tends to take away from each and all that quantity of wealth which they would each have voluntarily yielded to the state for the satisfaction of their purely collective wants" (page 32).

uting incomes. I am anxious to clear myself from Dr. Margolis' understandable suspicion that I am the type of liberal who would insist that all redistributions take place through tax policies and transfer expenditures: much public expenditure on education, hospitals, and so on, can be justified by the feasibility consideration that, even if these are not 100 per cent efficient in avoiding avoidable dead-weight loss, they may be better than the attainable imperfect tax alternatives.[13]

b. Paternalistic policies are voted upon themselves by a democratic people because they do not regard the results from spontaneous market action as optimal. Education and forced paces of economic development are good examples of this.

c. Governments provide or regulate services that are incapable of being produced under the strict conditions of constant returns that go to characterize optimal self-regulating atomistic competition.

d. Myriad "generalized external economy and diseconomy" situations, where private pecuniary interest can be expected to deviate from social interests, provide obvious needs for government activity.

I am sure this list of basic considerations underlying government expenditure could be extended farther, including even areas where government probably ought not to operate from almost anyone's viewpoint.

(v) This brief list can end with the most important criticism that the various commentators on my paper have put forth. They all ask: "Is it factually true that most — or any! — of the functions of government can be properly fitted into your extreme category of a public good? Can education, the courts, public defense, highway programs, police and fire protection be put into this rigid category of a 'public good available to all'? In practically every one

of these cases isn't there an element of variability in the benefit that can go to one citizen *at the expense* of some other citizens?"

To this criticism, I fully agree. And that is why in the present formulation I have insisted upon the polar nature of my category. However, to say that a thing is not located at the South Pole does not logically place it at the North Pole. To deny that most public functions fit into my extreme definition of a public good is not to grant that they satisfy the logically equally-extreme category of a private good. To say that your absence at a concert may contribute to my enjoyment is not to say that the elements of public services can be put into homogeneous additive packages capable of being optimally handled by the ordinary market calculus.

Indeed, I am rash enough to think that in almost every one of the legitimate functions of government that critics put forward there is to be found a blending of the extreme antipodal models. One might even venture the tentative suspicion that any function of government not possessing any trace of the defined public good (and no one of the related earlier described characteristics) ought to be carefully scrutinized to see whether it is truly a legitimate function of government.

(vi) Whether or not I have overstated the applicability of this one theoretical model to actual governmental functions, I believe I did not go far enough in claiming for it relevance to the vast area of decreasing costs that constitutes an important part of economic reality and of the welfare economics of monopolistic competition. I must leave to future research discussions of these vital issues.

Economic theory should add what it can to our understanding of governmental activity. I join with critics in hoping that its pretentious claims will not discourage other economic approaches, other contributions from neighboring disciplines, and concrete empirical investigations.

---

[13] See my "Evaluation of Real National Income," *Oxford Economic Papers*, N.S. II (January 1950), 18 ff. for analytic discussion of this important truth.

94

ASPECTS OF PUBLIC EXPENDITURE THEORIES *

Paul A. Samuelson

ECONOMIC theorists have done work of high quality and great quantity in the field of taxation. Public expenditure seems to have been relatively neglected. To illustrate this, let me turn to Professor Pigou. I do so with some diffidence, remembering what Ralph Waldo Emerson said to Oliver Wendell Holmes when Holmes showed him a youthful criticism of Plato. "When you strike at a King," Emerson said, "be sure you kill him."

I have no wish to assassinate Professor Pigou. Nor even to criticize him. But immortality does have its price: if one writes an outstanding treatise such as Pigou's *A Study in Public Finance*, one must expect other men to swarm about it, picking a nugget here and probing for a weakness there.

Of a book of some 285 pages, Pigou devotes most attention to taxes. At least 200 pages to taxes; of the rest, most are concerned with fiscal policy and its impact on the business cycle. What about the pure theory of public expenditure? I can find barely half a dozen pages devoted to the heart of this matter — specifically, pages 30–34. And even if we widen the category — to include Pigou's definitions of transfer and exhaustive expenditure and his discussion of pricing of state-operated public utilities — we still cannot bring the total of pages much beyond twenty.

Now it may be that this ratio of 200 on taxes to 20 on expenditure is the proper one. Perhaps there is really nothing much to say about expenditure, and so heavily overbalanced a page budget may be truly optimal. On the other hand, we must admit that fashion has a great influence in economics, which suggests that we ought periodically to survey the neglected areas of theory to make sure that they do deserve to be left in their underdeveloped and backward states.

I have previously published (this REVIEW, XXXVI, November 1954, 387–89) some thoughts on public expenditure theory; and in order to

* This is a slight revision of a paper delivered at the December 1955 meetings of the Econometric Society and the American Economic Association. Acknowledgment to the Ford Foundation for research aid is gratefully made.

widen the discussion among economic theorists, I later gave a non-mathematical exposition (*ibid.*, XXXVII, November 1955, 350–56). I do not propose here to give a detailed review of these theories. Rather, I'd like to think aloud about some of the difficulties with expenditure theory and with political decision-making. On these subjects, Richard Musgrave and Julius Margolis have done outstanding research and I must confess my obligation to them for much friendly counsel.

I

Let me first take a fresh look at the nature of government and of public finance from a purely analytical viewpoint. I must give warning: the result will be rather like a New Yorker's map of the United States, in which vast areas of the country are compressed into almost nothing and certain places — like Hollywood, Cape Cod, and Times Square — are blown up far beyond their true proportions.

Similarly, I shall commit all the sins of those bad historians and anthropologists who recreate the history of the human race according to their *a priori* conceptions of the moment. To keep from getting caught, I'll imagine a planet rather like the earth.

Once upon a time men on this planet were all alike and very scarce. Each family hunted and fished its symmetrical acres; and each ended with the same production and real income.

Then men turned to cultivating the soil and domesticating animals. This left even more of the globe vacant, but did not disturb the symmetry of family incomes.

But finally population grew so big that the best free land was all occupied. Now there was a struggle for elbow room. According to the scenario as I choose to write it, the struggle was a gentlemanly one. But men did have to face the fact that recognizing squatter's rights and respecting *laissez-faire* did result in differences of real incomes among families.

Optimal transfer expenditure. Here then for the first time, government was introduced on this planet. A comprehensive program of redistributing income so as to achieve a maximum of the community's social welfare function was introduced. The budget was balanced at a non-zero level: taxes were raised in a non-distorting lump-sum fashion, and transfer expenditure was allocated among families so as to achieve the marginal conditions necessary to maximize the defined social welfare function.

Now here on earth, things don't seem to have worked out exactly according to such a time-table. In fact, look at Adam Smith's 1776 discussion of the three duties of government — protection against external aggressors, maintenance of order at home, and erecting those public institutions and works "which though they may be in the highest degree advantageous to a great society, could never repay the expense to any individual." We could interpret the last of these in so broad and tautological a way as to be compatible with anything. But if we stick to a narrower non-empty interpretation, it would appear that our planet began with redistributional governmental functions that Smith had not even dreamed of and which would most surprise him if he were to come to life and revisit any modern nation.

Now why do I describe so bizarre a model? It is to underline this theoretical point: Given a social welfare function, and given the absence of all technological and taste externalities, and given universal constant returns to scale, there would be needed only one type of public policy — redistributive transfers. (Under some ethical assumptions, these might be from poor to rich rather than rich to poor; but only by chance alone would zero redistributions maximize a specified social welfare function that depends solely on real incomes.)

Minimal collective expenditure. But what about the neglected exhaustive elements of public expenditure that even the most thoroughgoing *laissez-faire* economy will want to make — e.g., courts of justice to enforce contracts or any of the other items under Smith's first two duties? Later I shall review a possible theory of such expenditure. But first let me mention why the problem of financing such expenditures is, so long as they remain small, secondary to that of transfers.

Even on other planets, perfectionist lump-sum taxes are rarely feasible. We tax the objects that we can feasibly tax. And this must introduce deadweight-theoretically-avoidable tax burdens in addition to the unavoidable real burden involved in having to use resources for public purposes. (This doesn't mean the public services aren't worth their costs; on well-run planets, they are.)

Years ago, when studying this problem, I encountered what was to me a surprising fact. It turns out that, so long as exhaustive expenditure is "small," the deadweight burden is "negligible" no matter what system of taxation is used. Only in the second approximation, so to speak, does it matter what tax structure we use to "cover" the needed program. At least this would be the case if incomes were already distributed optimally. *If*, as is more likely, *incomes are distributed prior to taxation in a non-optimal manner* (not as determined by me but as determined by the relevant social welfare function), *then the manner of taxing is very important even at the first level of approximation; and it is the interpersonal distributive elements that are all important in defining an optimal tax structure.*

It is because of this conclusion that my planet had to start out with transfer taxation. As I have said, this result seemed odd to me at first; but having been led there by the invisible hand of mathematical logic, I was forced to draw my map in this way.

Sizable exhaustive public expenditure. Once we admit the possibility of public collective services on our planet, we have to face the possibility that they will be large rather than small; and in any case they will be finite rather than zero or infinitesimal. So we do need an analysis of their logical nature.

We can approach this indirectly. What is our theory of *non*-public expenditure? So long as goods are producible at constant returns to scale and so long as each person's consumption of a good is measurably distinct from any other person's, the perfect-competition model of markets can be used as *an* optimal social computing device. If we deny constant returns to scale — and technology on this or any other planet may make this denial mandatory in many areas — an opening wedge for an alternative kind of social allocation arises. And if we deny that every good's consumption is purely individualistic, instead insisting on strong "external effects," we will have still another reason why the ordinary private marketing calculus must be non-optimal.[1]

To handle one difficulty at a time, let's keep to a strict assumption of constant returns to scale in all production. But let's introduce important externalities ("neighborhood" effects, etc.) into the consumption sphere. Thus, the battleship that protects your rights and investments also protects mine.

I don't suppose that anyone, upon reflection, would try to build up a theory of public expenditure without bringing in some kind of externality. Yet it is surprising that Pigou, who above all welfare economists has reminded us of external diseconomies of the smoke nuisance type, should in his brief discussion of expenditure theory have left this externality element almost completely implicit.

Now remembering that we theorists like to work with extreme polar cases, what is the natural model to formulate so as to give strongest emphasis to external effects? I have long thought that this is best brought out by the following model.

Assume that some goods, like bread, are privately consumed: this means that the total of bread can be written as the sum of the bread consumptions of each separate individual. But along with such purely private goods, assume public goods — like national defense — which *simultaneously* enter into many persons' indifference curves. Then assuming no transcendental group mind, but only a set of individual tastes and an ethical social welfare function dependent upon these tastes and ranking them in order of deservingness, we can prove that the perfect-competition market model will not work optimally. We can prove that there exists an inefficient configuration from which all men can be made better off, and a frontier of efficient points from which no universally advantageous movements are possible; of all the infinity of

such efficient points, a socially best one is definable in terms of a specified normative welfare function.

It is this model that I explored in the two cited papers. And it is also this model that Sax, Wicksell, Lindahl, Musgrave, Bowen, and other economists of the last 75 years had considered under the "voluntary exchange theory of public finance" name or some other. The principle conclusions of this analysis seem to be the following:

1. Efficient, inefficient, and socially optimal configurations can be theoretically defined: a point on the efficiency frontier requires equality between the vertically-added marginal rates of substitution of all men for the public and private goods; and the best of such points requires lump-sum redistributions of the transferable private goods until they have equal marginal social significance.

2. Although the optimum is definable, rational people will not, if left to themselves, be led by an invisible hand to the bliss point. On the contrary, it will pay for each rational man to dissemble, trying to mask his preference for the public goods and to engage in other game-strategy maneuvers which, when all do them, will necessarily involve deadweight loss to society.

Having called attention to the nature of the difficulty, I do not wish to be too pessimistic. After all, the world's work does somehow get done. And to say that market mechanisms are non-optimal, and that there are difficulties with most political decision processes, does not imply that we can never find new mechanisms of a better sort. (Example: skillful use of the symmetry that prevails between individuals may enable us to find optimal computing algorithms. Example: Interrogate people for their tastes with respect to public goods in such large homogeneous groups as to give each respondent the feeling that his answer can be a "true" one without costing him anything extra.)

Decreasing-cost phenomena. Once people have understood the above model, they are likely to object to its unrealism. Thus, Drs. Stephen Enke and Julius Margolis have both pointed out that many, if not all, government expenditures can be qualitatively varied so as to confer more

[1] There are still other basic reasons for governmental action or interferences: e.g., "paternalistic" dissatisfaction by the electorate with the effective tastes that they will all display in their day-to-day market preference acts — leading to public policies in the field of education, capital formation, etc.; exercise of economic entrepreneurship and decision-making by public officials; and many more.

benefit on one man at the expense of another man. This raises the question whether we cannot bring back the market pricing mechanism, charging fees for public services and letting their quantity and quality be determined by money voting of the supply and demand type.

Certainly, it should be possible for the theorist to go beyond the polar cases of (1) pure private goods and (2) pure public goods to (3) some kind of a mixed model which takes account of all external, indirect, joint-consumption effects. I shall not write down such a mathematical model. But if I did do so, would we not find — as Pigou and Sidgwick so long ago warned us is true of all external economies and diseconomies — that the social optimum could not be achieved without somebody's taking into account all direct and indirect utilities and costs in all social decisions?

Now in connection with running a particular railroad, highway, or concert, we might find just the right conditions of scarcity of space and of independence of consumptions so that ordinary market pricing could lead to the optimum. In such a case, we can really reduce matters to our first category of purely private goods, and self-policing perfect competition might be an optimal social signalling and computing device.

However, generally, a mixed model that refuses to fall in my polar case of a pure public good will not thereby obligingly go into the other polar case of a pure private good. The mixed case has elements of both in it. And while we cannot by pure logic alone deduce that the intermediate case must qualitatively be a blend of the properties of the two poles, we can by logic know that ordinary pricing will be nonoptimal unless it happens to be able to pick up each indirect external marginal utility.

Here is a contemporary instance. The Federal Communications Commission is now trying to make up its mind about permitting subscription television. You might think that the case where a program comes over the air and is available for any set owner to tune in on is a perfect example of my public good. And in a way it is. But you would be wrong to think that the essence of the phenomenon is inherent in the fact that the broadcaster is not able to refuse the service to whatever individuals he pleases. For in this case, by use of unscramblers, it is technically possible to limit the consumptions of a particular broadcast to any specified group of individuals. You might, therefore, be tempted to say: A descrambler enables us to convert a public good into a private good; and by permitting its use, we can sidestep the vexing problems of collective expenditure, instead relying on the free pricing mechanism.

Such an argument would be wrong. Being able to limit a public good's consumption does not make it a true-blue private good. For what, after all, are the true marginal costs of having one extra family tune in on the program? They are literally zero. Why then prevent any family which would receive positive pleasure from tuning in on the program from doing so?

Upon reflection, you will realize that our well-known optimum principle that goods should be priced at their marginal costs would not be realized in the case of subscription broadcasting. Why not? In the deepest sense because this is, by its nature, not a case of constant returns to scale. It is a case of general decreasing costs. So long as increasing returns prevail in the actual range of consumption, we know that perfect competition will not be self-preserving and market behavior is unlikely to be optimal.

The case of decreasing costs may be empirically very important. Certainly, when you try to analyze why public utilities are public utilities and why certain activities (like railroads, water supply, electricity, and postoffices) may fall into either the category of public or private enterprise, you will usually find that some significant deviation from strict constant returns to scale is involved. I cannot then be completely satisfied with Pigou's statement:

> These are not problems of Public Finance, as I understand that term. I do not propose, therefore, to discuss at all the question over what classes of enterprise it is desirable that public operation should be extended, but to proceed on the assumption that this is already determined. (Page 24.)

Considerations concerning waste thus enable us to say, with regard to several classes of goods and services [primarily those which do not have an inelastic demand], that, if the government decides to provide them, it should finance their provision by fees. (Pages 27–28.)

It is precisely in such cases that uniform average cost pricing will sin against the rule that prices should equal marginal costs. As Hotelling has insisted, there is here a *prima facie* case for government subsidy. To argue, as some economists have done, that the government budget is already so loaded with necessary expenditure as to make it undesirable for it to have to take on such subsidy expenditures, is to miss the point I am trying to make. This *is* one of the needed functions of government, and in making compromises because of fiscal necessities, there is no *a priori* reason why this function should be particularly neglected.

There is a related significant point that needs stressing. It is not enough in the decreasing cost case to come closer to marginal cost pricing in the Lerner-Lange manner, making up the deficits by general taxation. As soon as decreasing cost and diversity of product appear, we have the difficult non-local "total conditions" to determine what finite mix of product is optimal. This involves a terrible social computation problem: we must scan the almost infinite number of possible products and select the best configuration; we cannot feel our way to the optimum but must make judgment at a distance to determine the *optimum optimorum*.

All this is familiar. But what I have to point out are the complications that arise when there are two or more people on the planet. I like my cider sour; you like it sweet. With constant returns we could both get what we want, or at least what we deserve. But with initial indivisibilities or other forms of increasing returns, what I get will depend on what you get. (This is true even if we pay in the form of fees the marginal costs of our separate consumption.)

Now, how can society decide on the product mix which will maximize a specified social welfare function? It must weigh in all the different individuals' utilities from each decision. And *this is a problem that is analytically almost exactly like my model of public expenditure.*

Given the individual indifference curves and the social welfare function compromising them, one could define the theoretical optimum. (In practice, finding the solution might be very tedious.) But now try to devise a system of "benefit taxation" that will in some sense make people pay for what they get — either because justice or equity requires this, or, more subtly, because the necessity of having to make such payments is thought to be a way of helping to determine the proper place for society to arrive in the end. Instantly, you will discover that the same game-theory reasons that compel rational men to hide their desires for public goods will be motivating them to hide their consumers' surpluses from different product configurations.

II

Once again, in contemplating the dilemmas that most forms of political voting involve, we are reminded of the beautiful and special simplicities of the *laissez-faire* model. But, alas, the difficulties are those of the real world. And it would be quite illogical to conclude from all this that men and technology should be different, should be such as to make the competitive game all-sufficient. That would be as silly as to say that we should all love sawdust because its production is so beautiful.

Conclusion. Unfortunately, I have only gotten my planet started. Time hasn't permitted me to do more than describe its transfer expenditures, to relate them to the financing of small public services, and to formulate some of the analytic difficulties with a theory of public services. Though my model of pure public goods has turned out to be an unrealistic polar case, it turns out that almost all deviations from constant returns to scale and almost all externalities must inevitably involve some of the same analytic properties and dilemmas of my polar case.

We must leave to other times and other stars the exploration of those momentous coalitions of decision-making that are part of the essence of the political process. To the theorist, the theory of public finance is but part of the general theory of government. And at this frontier, the easy formulas of classical economics no longer light our way.

Appendix: *Strotz and Tiebout Discussions*

1. *Distributional aspects of public goods.* I should like to comment briefly on two papers that have grown out of the earlier discussion. In the present issue Professor Robert H. Strotz has pointed out a formal implication of my original equations (1) and (2): they define a Pareto optimality frontier [2]

$$u^1 = f(u^2, u^3, ..., u^s);\qquad\text{(A)}$$

and each point on that frontier will generally determine a set of all public goods

$$X_{n+j} = g^j(u^2, u^3, ..., u^s) \quad (j = 1, 2, ..., m). \quad\text{(B)}$$

Now under what conditions can the left-hand variables in (B) be regarded as independent variables? If $s - 1 = m$ and the Jacobian matrix $[g^i{}_j]$ is well-behaved, (B) can be inverted. Or if $s - 1 > m$ and the Jacobian $[g^i{}_j]$ is of rank m, m of (B)'s right-hand u's can be solved for in terms of the public goods $(X_{n+1}, ..., X_{n+m})$ and the remaining right-hand u's. So the Strotz conclusion follows: Any public good configuration is optimal if only the "distribution of income" is such as to get us to a point on the Pareto-frontier compatible with that public good configuration.[3]

In view of the modern trend to regard mere Pareto-optimality or efficiency as incomplete necessary conditions, what follows from the above conclusion? To me, this.

It is wrong to make, as some have made, a sharp separation between correct public-good decisions and correct redistributional-taxation decisions. Changing public goods *does* materially affect the distribution of income and all decisions have to be made *simultaneously*.

As Professor Strotz says, there is no disagreement between our analyses.

2. *Local finance and the mathematics of marriage.* A second paper of interest in the present connection is that of Professor Charles M. Tiebout.[4] He argues that the public expenditure theory simplifies itself at the local level — as people spontaneously join in forming homogeneous communities which will legislate what each (and all) want in the way of collective goods.

This attempted solution fits in under one or another of the "symmetry" principles that I had referred to. That it goes some way toward solving the problem, few would doubt. As a solution, though, it raises a number of serious questions.

Thus, when you study in detail a supposedly homogeneous suburb, you find it riddled with conflicting desires. The old, with grown-up children, oppose the desire of the young for more school expenditure. And so it goes. It avails little for one group to say to another: "If you don't like it here, go back where you came from." Ours is a fluid society, with little respect paid to hard-to-identify charter members. People want to "improve" their community, not abdicate from it.

Secondly, people often like heterogeneity even though it involves conflict. The old don't want to live in homogeneous ghettos with their own kind, and the same goes for many other groups. In an interdependent world, one man's privacy is another man's condemnation to loneliness.

Thirdly, there is the political and ethical question whether groups of like-minded individuals shall be "free" to "run out" on their social responsibilities and go off by themselves. At the national level, society respects no such freedom: e.g., migration control, compulsory taxation, etc.

A simple mathematical model will illustrate a few of the intricacies of the problem. If a group of men and women have each a preference rating for members of the opposite sex, who will end up marrying whom? This assignment problem — which is stated in biological terms only for concreteness — is also faced by colleges and students choosing each other, by clubs and fraternities, etc. In real life, it is solved by dynamic reconnoiter, contact, proposal, refusal or acceptance — in short, by general trial and error, which is not guaranteed to represent any optimum.

Consider the trivial case of 2 boys A and B and two girls 1 and 2. Each boy has an ordinal preference rating of the girls, which in this simple case must be either the permutations (1, 2) or (2, 1). Each girl's rating of the boys must be (A, B) or (B, A).

Now what are the possible preference configurations? In this simple case, they are essentially only the following (where the first row lists people, with their choices shown in the columns below them):

1	2		A	B
A	B		1	2
B	A		2	1
		or		

[2] I use my original notation, which is related to Strotz's by $X_{n+j} = S_j$, $s = I$, $m = K$, $L^i = s_i$, etc.

[3] When you reflect that the degrees of freedom to *completely specify* a single post office exceed the number of people in the United States, the case where $s - 1 < m$ may seem most realistic. In such a case, or in case people's preferences for public goods are so alike as to lead to ill-behaved Jacobians, an arbitrary choice of (X_{n+j}) will be compatible with no Pareto-optimal point.

[4] Charles M. Tiebout, "A Pure Theory of Local Expenditures," *Journal of Political Economy*, LXIV (October 1956), 416–24.

I	2		A	B
A	A		I	2
B	B		2	I

or

I	2		A	B
A	B		2	I
B	A		I	2

or

I	2		A	B
A	A		I	I
B	B		2	2

Of these four cases, the first fits Tiebout's attempt best. All the guinea pigs are in agreement: 1 and A want to marry; so do 2 and B; all get their first choices. The solution (1,A; 2,B) is Pareto-optimal; being the only Pareto-optimal solution, it is also Bergson-optimal, maximizing *any* social welfare function that respects individual's tastes.

But now turn to the last case. A and 1 are preferred by all of the other sex. If we give persons the "property right" to form bilateral compacts, the favored ones will presumably marry each other with (1,A; 2,B) the resulting equilibrium.

However, given a social welfare function which respects tastes, this outcome is not necessarily optimal. The other possible outcome (2,A; 1,B) might be "ethically better" (e.g., where 2 has a "great"

preference in favor of A but 1 is "almost" indifferent, and 2 is "ethically deserving" of great social respect). Or we can put the matter a little differently: (2,A; 1,B) is just as Pareto-optimal as is (1,A; 2,B). When you leave the former and go to the latter, you make two people happier and two people unhappier.

In the second case, there is likewise no unique Pareto-optimal point. Left to themselves with certain "freedoms" and "property rights" to make bilateral collusions, probably 1 and A will marry, ignoring 2 and B. And B will be glad. But 2 will not be glad, showing that the configuration (2,A; 1,B) is also Pareto-optimal. Of course, if you used a crude majority vote rule, (1, A; 2, B) would be the winning position. But — as Arrow, Black, and others have shown — majority-rule devices are subject to many intransitivities and drawbacks.

Finally, the third case is like the last in that both outcomes are Pareto-optimal and in going from one to the other you sadden two people and gladden two. Whether the girls or boys are to be made glad cannot be decided except in terms of a given determinate social welfare function.

I conclude from all this that there remain many important analytical problems of public-good determination that still need investigation at every level of government.

PART XIII

Principles of Fiscal and Monetary Policy

95

THE EFFECT OF INTEREST RATE INCREASES ON THE BANKING SYSTEM

By Paul A. Samuelson*

Simple truths need constant repetition. Current American discussions suggest that it may be advisable to assert the following propositions:

1. *The banking system as a whole is not really hurt by an increase in the whole complex of interest rates. It is left tremendously better off by such a change.*

2. *A typical single bank, taken by itself, is not really hurt by an increase in the whole complex of interest rates. It is left better off by such a change.*

The author wishes to emphasize that he does not believe interest rate increases to be probable or desirable.

I

If a bank were a university, nobody would doubt that it would be made better off by an increase in the interest rate. At worst, it could continue to hold all existing gilt-edge securities to maturity and be no worse off. As these matured, the proceeds could be invested at higher rates with a resulting increase in income. It would be better off in the sense that *ceteris paribus* it could hire more teachers per year, spend more money on buildings and stadia, engage in more research.

The only exception would be in the limiting and unrealistic case where all its money was invested in perpetuities. But even here it would be no worse off. In every other case it would be better off.

If the treasurer of the college has had a college course in financial mathematics, or if his secretary owns a book of compound interest tables, he should be able at each instant of time to calculate the *present value* of his assets: *i.e.*, the discounted value of all future income streams. In any case, in a reasonably perfect capital market this will be done for him and will be reflected in the quoted prices of the securities he holds.

Obviously, when the rate of interest goes up and is expected to remain up, the present value of his assets goes down. Now there are many purposes for which the reckoning of present value is indispensable.

* Mr. Samuelson is now on leave from his position as associate professor of economics at Massachusetts Institute of Technology while he is engaged in technical warwork.

But it will be readily seen that the problem of forming a judgment of the good or bad effects of an interest change is not one of them. We have seen that the university is better off in the only reasonable sense of the term (disposable real income over time), and yet *present value* seems to give an opposite indication.

Does this mean that a university should buy bonds without taking account of probable future long-term rates of interest? Of course not. Suppose the treasurer of Siwash buys a bond today, and the treasurer of Sweet Briar does not. Let interest rates rise tomorrow. The price of bonds will drop. Obviously, the woman treasurer has done better than the man. She can buy the same income stream for less money, or can get a larger income stream for the same money.

If, on the morrow, an angel came to Siwash and asked the treasurer whether he wished rates of interest to rise, what would he answer? Unless he were a fool, or an ingrate who valued his own reputation for sagacity more than the welfare of his Alma Mater, he would of course answer, "Yes." It would be but human for him to add wistfully, "If you had only come around yesterday. . . ."

Clearly then, an interest rate increase which you have not anticipated is a good thing, even though an increase you have anticipated and gambled on is a better thing. If interest rates rise without your having speculated on their doing so, you should not feel any worse than at not having picked the winner in yesterday's horse race, or at not having sold short stocks which events later proved would fall. And certainly any unavoidable feelings of recrimination should not cause one to forego very great gains just because only partial advantage of them can be taken. It is better to "place" or "show" than not to be in the money at all. *Ex ante* decisions should be directed to *ex post* advantage; *ex post* advantage should never be sacrificed to *ex ante* decisions.

Conclusion: *A university is not really hurt by an increase in the whole complex of interest rates, declines in its capital values notwithstanding. It is really left better off by such a change.*

II

So much for the case of a university, where no one can fail to draw correct conclusions. Let us turn now to the intermediate case of an insurance company. How does it differ from a university? Each receives inpayments, owns earning assets, and must make outpayments. The contractual nature of these outpayments differs, and therein lies a partial distinction. But not too much should be made of this difference. Many of the expenses of a university are relatively fixed and even subject to legal commitment, while the insurance companies, by the prevailing practice of setting rates higher than cost (as revealed by subsequent experience), are able by variable dividend policy to control an important part of their outpayments.

As far as the policies already in force are concerned, an insurance company can pretty well tell in advance the whole future pattern of its net outpayments. The contingencies which occasion outpayments are specified in the policy, and the actuarial large-scale frequency of these contingencies is relatively predictable. Indeed knowledge of future outpayments on insurance now in force would be almost perfect were it not for the options (changeover, lapse, waiver, borrowing, etc.) included in insurance policies. But even these factors can be estimated, in terms of various probabilities, with a considerable degree of accuracy.

Of course, insurance companies are not loath to sell new policies. With perfect knowledge of the future course of interest rates, the application of sound actuarial principles makes this a factor of no great importance because each group of like policies can "stand on its own feet." This, after all, is the important purpose of reserves in private insurance. In any case it should be pointed out that the general course of future sales is in large measure predictable as to trend. Except for national income, which is subject to cyclical fluctuations, the relevant factors such as age distribution change slowly. And, in fact, every insurance company tacitly proceeds in its administration upon a "going concern" basis and indeed upon a "growing concern" basis. This is only proper.

If charges in the past have not been set too low, and if dividend policy has not been overly generous, it would be possible for an insurance company to arrange its portfolio in relationship to the future time pattern of commitments so that the company would be perfectly hedged against all future interest rate changes. Bond coupons and retirements would be staggered so as to produce exactly the right amount of cash even if no new business were taken on, and regardless of what happened to the market value of securities held. This is not the current policy of insurance managements. Although no criticism is implied by the statement, they usually take an implicit speculative position.

Can we say then that under these conditions of perfect hedging on old business, insurance operations are not affected by interest rates? No. An increase in rates would still benefit the insurance business and policyholders. But its benefits would go completely to *new* policyholders, who would pay less for the same coverage, or get more coverage for their money.

Realistically, we encounter a combination of these extremes. The benefit is divided between new and old policyholders. Guaranteed interest rates on new policies are (quite properly) relatively slow to change over time. Increased earnings are distributed in dividends to all policyholders, old and new. In addition, because insurance companies take an implicit speculative position, there is a further effect as a result of interest rates increase.

The following theorem will indicate the exact conditions under which interest rates help or hurt a given person or institution: *Increased interest rates will help any organization whose (weighted) average time period of disbursements is greater than the average time period of its receipts.*[1]

In our previous discussion we implicitly assumed that the disbursements of a university were spread evenly over an indefinite time in the future, and so an interest rate increase was good for it. *Present discounted value* proved to be a false indicator, not so much because the concept is at fault as because it was applied to only one part of present values, *i.e.*, to the income stream. If we had considered the steady stream of outpayments of the university as negative inpayments, had discounted them and added them *algebraically* to present value, then we should have found the whole expression to be algebraically increased rather than decreased by an increase in interest rates.

The only figures relating to the maturity dates of life insurance portfolios at hand refer to holdings of government bonds. These figures suggest that up to 1943 the average maturity date was less than 10 years. On existing policies in force the average date of outpayment could not conceivably be less than ten years, because of the fact that there is a growing population of insured individuals who buy level premium policies in the productive age years. Therefore, insurance companies were speculating explicitly or implicitly that interest rates would rise. If we consider insurance as a growing business, which

---

[1] Let N_t = inpayment t years after the present, C_t = corresponding outpayments, V = present value, i = interest rate per annum averaged over time.

$$\text{Then } V = \sum \frac{N_t}{(1+i)^t} - \sum \frac{C_t}{(1+i)^t}$$

$$\text{and } \frac{dV}{di} = -\frac{\log_e (1+i)}{(1+i)^2} \left\{ \sum \frac{tN_t}{(1+i)^{t-1}} - \sum \frac{tC_t}{(1+i)^{t-1}} \right\}.$$

By rearranging terms, we find that $\frac{dV}{di} \gtrless 0$ depending upon whether $\bar{N} \gtrless \bar{C}$ where $\bar{N}$, $\bar{C}$ are respectively weighted average periods of inpayments and outpayments, whose weights are proportional to discounted dollar amounts.

means that net outpayments in excess of inpayments will *not* occur, except temporarily, for a long period of time in the future, this conclusion is strengthened. (It should be pointed out in the last connection that the companies can partially protect themselves from a *fall* in interest rates by revising the terms upon which new business is written.)

TABLE I.—OWNERSHIP OF MARKETABLE SECURITIES ISSUED OR GUARANTEED BY THE UNITED STATES

Securities Due or Callable:	(In billions of dollars) Amounts Held February 29, 1944						
	Com-mercial Banks	Savings Banks	Insur-ance Com-panies	Other In-vestors	All except Govern-ment	Federal Reserve, etc.[a]	All In-vestors
Within 1 Year	22.3	0.3	0.7	13.0	36.2	9.8	46.0
1 to 5 Years	16.0	0.6	1.6	4.4	22.5	1.7	24.2
5 to 10 Years	17.2	2.3	3.3	5.7	28.6	1.4	30.0
10 to 20 Years	3.4	2.2	5.1	4.8	15.5	1.3	16.8
After 20 Years	0.9	1.3	4.7	4.1	11.1	1.5	11.6
Total	59.8	6.7	15.4	32.0	113.9	15.7	129.6
Securities Due or Callable:	Amounts Held November 30, 1942						
	Com-mercial Banks	Savings Banks	Insur-ance Com-panies	Other In-vestors	All Except Govern-ment	Federal Reserve, etc.[a]	All In-vestors
Within 1 Year	10.2	0.3	0.5	3.7	11.6	2.1	16.7
1 to 5 Years	10.5	0.7	1.8	4.5	17.4	2.5	19.9
5 to 10 Years	10.5	2.0	2.6	3.1	18.2	2.2	20.4
10 to 20 Years	2.6	0.8	3.8	2.6	9.8	1.2	11.0
After 20 Years	0.7	0.3	0.6	0.7	2.5	0.3	2.8
Total	34.5	4.1	9.3	14.5	62.5	8.3	70.7

[a] Federal Reserve Banks, government agencies and trust funds.

In the last eighteen months, there has been an interesting shift of insurance companies into bonds of long maturity. (See Table I.) With 60 per cent of their bonds having a duration of more than 10 years, insurance companies will be in a fairly neutral position with respect to interest rates as far as their old business is concerned and they would stand to gain on their new if interest rates were to rise. This must be modified by the realization that their non-governmental assets are probably of shorter duration.

Final conclusion: *each insurance company, all companies together, and the families who hold or buy insurance would not be hurt by an increase in interest rates. On the contrary, they would be made really better off, regardless of misleading comparisons of present or market values.* If properly computed along the lines indicated above, present value could be shown to bear out this conclusion.

III

I turn now to the case of the banks, particularly the system as a whole. Let us assume the following specific permanent change in the interest rate structure on government bonds:

Duration to maturity	Assumed average duration	Old rates per annum	New rates per annum
1 year or less	.33 years	0.5%	1.5%
1 to 5 years	2 years	1.0%	2.0%
5 to 10 years	7 years	2.0%	3.0%
10 to 20 years	14 years	2.0%	3.0%
over 20 years	22 years	2.0%	3.0%

This is intended only as an hypothetical example and not as a prediction. The old rates are chosen to be approximately equal to present rates. The new rates represent a flat one per cent increase at all levels. If the present differential between short and long rates can be attributed to a fear that rates will harden, and if after that hardening has taken place there is no further expectation of increase, then it would not be unnatural for the short rates to firm relative to the long rates. Witness the reverse movements from the twenties to the thirties.

Would the banking system be worse off for such a change? Let me ask another question: if the government were to bestow upon the banking system some 60 billion dollars, or what is the same thing under existing rates, grant a perpetual annual subsidy of .6 billion dollars, would the banking system be better or worse off? Would bank stocks—which for some city banks are already beginning to sell for more than the book value of capital plus surplus—go up or down in price? Would public confidence in banks rise or fall? Over a period of years would the capital structure of banking be more or less sound?

Or let me pose the question in another way. What if all banks were to subscribe 2 billions to a perfectly safe but non-negotiable term loan, to be paid back in equal installments over three years' time and to yield a rate of compound interest of some 15 *thousand* per cent per annum! Would any sane bank examiner rule that the non-negotiability of such

a loan, which amounts to less than 2 per cent of all bank assets, over-
weighs the fabulous return on a safe investment?

To ask such questions is to answer them. Any one of these alternatives would involve the greatest boon in history to the commercial
banks, with the possible exception of the stimulus to bank earnings
provided by World War II, a stimulus which will not be confined to the
war years as in the case of most war producers.

Yet the relatively moderate, permanent increase in rates considered
above is essentially equivalent to either of the above alternatives! Only
the intricacies of bookkeeping prevent this from being seen.

But what about the collapse of capital values when rates harden?
Will not an average doubling of interest rates wipe out 50 per cent of

TABLE II

Securities Due or Callable:	Ratio of New Capital Value to Old	New Yield on New Base	New Yield on Old Base
Within 1 year	.997	1.5%	1.50%
1 to 5 years	.981	2.0%	1.96%
5 to 10 years	.938	3.0%	2.81%
10 to 20 years	.887	3.0%	2.67%
after 20 years	.841	3.0%	2.52%

the value of securities held? Even if it did, we have seen in the previous
cases the irrelevance of *present value* as traditionally computed, and
I shall show it to be equally so for the banking system. But we need
not fall back on this theoretical argument.

*Applying the usual bond tables and formulas to a portfolio of the
composition given in Table I, we find that its capital value will fall
only 3 per cent in going from the old to the new rates.* Maintainable
net income from governments, however, will almost double even if
shorts and longs are held in the same proportions in the new situation.
Table II shows the *new* capital value of each dollar previously invested
in each maturity. By weighting these factors according to the required
proportions, we can make a similar calculation for any portfolio. The
results for each of the groups listed in Table I are indicated below in
Table III.

On a capital value reduced only by 3.29 per cent, a bank portfolio
will earn a yield of 2.15 per cent, which is 2.08 per cent on its old
capital value. This is almost double its previous yield of 1.17 per cent.
The corresponding old and new yields are shown in Table III, for all
groups.

It is occasionally recognized that higher rates will increase earnings *after* old bonds mature and their proceeds are reinvested. This is a relatively slow process. It is rarely realized that immediately after interest rates have risen and capital values have been scaled down, *all parts of the portfolio,* old as well as new, begin to earn higher rates. We must not forget that the earning of a bond is *not* its coupon, but rather its coupon corrected for amortization of bond premium or dis-

TABLE III

Ownership of Securities	Percentage Decline in Capital Value	Dollar Decline in Capital Value (in billions)	Old Average Yield	New Average Yield on Old Base
Commercial banks	3.29%	1.96	1.17%	2.08%
Savings banks	9.11%	0.61	1.84%	2.57%
Insurance companies	10.13%	1.56	1.83%	2.53%
Other investors	5.22%	1.67	1.25%	2.10%
All except government	5.11%	5.83	1.33%	2.18%
Federal Reserve	3.40%	0.53	0.96%	1.86%
All investors	4.91%	6.36	1.28%	2.14%

count. In this case bonds which were previously at par will be at a discount, and true earnings or yield will exceed coupon rates by amortization of bond discount.

If the banking system maintains the same operating expenses and dividend policy, it will be able by ploughing back the new higher earnings to replace the 3 per cent decrease in values *in less than three years' time*—without changing its proportions between longs and shorts expressed in value terms. This does not mean that in three years' time the bank will have got over the damage done them by interest rate increases. There is no such damage; from the very beginning banks are "really" better off; and at the end of three years, they are much better off because the old capital value can be invested to give twice the old yield.

One technical point should be mentioned. In the new situation, banks may not choose to keep the same proportions between longs and shorts. Indeed, with the new capitalizations, *all* investors will not be able to do so in value terms even should they wish to. But if a bank or the banking system should wish to do so, and if the new rates remain as stated, there may have to be some reshuffling of portfolios in which other than new issues are bought.

In the above calculations, we have treated the bank portfolio like any other portfolio. But what is the basis for the widespread opinion that what is true for a university or insurance company is not true for the banking system? Our fundamental theorem provides a rationalization of the answer: *a rise in interest rates hurts the banking system if the average time period of its inpayments exceeds that of its outpayments.*

But what are the future outpayments of the banking system? If it is assumed each night that tomorrow is the day of judgment, that all depositors may wish to withdraw all their money, then the average period of outpayments is one day, and of course the banking system would be hurt by interest rate increases. In such an absurd world, it would be criminal for banks to have anything but 100 per cent reserves. It is equally absurd to assume that savings banks have an average period of outpayments of 30 days.

It should not be necessary to argue before economists that the banking system is a going concern, and is to be treated as such. But some practical bankers, noting that their own business has gone up during the war, share the common opinion that—along with the business of the butcher, the baker, the candlestick maker—after the war their business will go down. When the war is over, it is not impossible that business activity should decline. But as far as volume of deposits is concerned, banking is one business which cannot go back to its previous level.

Deposits are unmade in much the same way that they are made. Deposits were created in banks by the process of expanding earning assets, largely war bonds. Deposits can only be destroyed if banks lose assets. There are only three conceivable ways in which banks could be expected to lose deposits.

1. After the war, the federal government might run surpluses and retire debt. Even high annual surpluses would require a very long time to make a dent in the huge volume of bank deposits. The most confirmed optimist knows that the quantitative rates of surpluses cannot be a fraction of the rate of wartime deficits, although he may hope for a long period of such surpluses. Realistically, there is as yet little reason to believe that economic and political conditions will be such as to permit rapid debt reduction.

In any case, it will be obvious that reduction via this process will create no problems for bank portfolios. Withdrawals and debt retirement will be linked, with equal average periods.

2. The second way in which deposits might decrease is as the result of a changed preference of the public for cash and security. If individuals should come to prefer government bonds to non-earning bank balances, we could witness in the post-war world a gradual purchase of government bonds by the public from bank portfolios, with a resulting destruction of deposits. This second process is the only one of

the three which seems at all probable, and it must be considered as only a doubtful possibility.

But should it materialize, it would obviously not create difficulties for the banks. They would be losing deposits precisely because of an increased demand for government bonds. Interest rates would then be falling, and banks would be making capital gains rather than losses.

3. If the public should distrust banks and wish to hoard cash, deposits would of course decrease. It may be stated pointblank that such a contingency will not materialize, and cannot materialize. Not only does deposit insurance greatly decrease the chance of its happening, but also any sensible conception of public responsibility would envisage drastic use of Federal Reserve and governmental powers to prevent such a situation from developing, and to meet it should it develop. Realistically, banking experts anticipate that peace will cause a reverse flow of currency back to the banks.

The reader may work out for himself the details of the case where the public develops a desire for securities other than governmentals and attempts to use up its deposits in such purchases. Government bond yields could harden but bank outpayments would not increase.

Legalists and bank examiners nevertheless will still worry about the instantaneous effects of higher interest rates on capital values. Balm may be found for them in the following considerations: government securities may be carried at cost rather than market; capital surpluses may be large enough to absorb a 3 per cent drop in portfolio book value; bank stockholders, confronted with the possibility of doubled earnings, will be in a receptive mood to subscribe to new stock issues to meet any deficiencies in *apparent* capital;[2] in special cases, the government may aid where it is in the public interest to do so. *Conclusion: the banking system as a whole is immeasurably helped rather than hindered by an increase in interest rates. Indeed, it receives much greater benefit than either universities or insurance companies, and commercial banks would profit more than savings banks.*

IV

Since the line of thought and conclusion are fairly obvious, the reader may work out the details of the argument as applied to individual banks. Let him consider the case of a boom-town bank in (say) Bath, Maine or Portland, Oregon; the case of New York banks; the case of rural banks; etc.

---

[2] Some city bank stocks are already selling for more than book and market value of the capital account.

It will be seen that problems of bank examination with respect to government securities do not disappear completely. But it will be equally clear that they are to be determined within the framework of a *realistic* appraisal of benefit and harm.

V

Sometimes right policies are followed for the wrong reasons. Not long ago I was privileged to hear a public address by a distinguished American economist, in which he argued in favor of the use of a tight money policy to control a post-war boom. He was immediately pounced upon by *all* his colleagues, and his argument was completely damned by the assertion that such a policy would create great difficulties for the banking system because of its holding of governments. Perhaps the critics argued with tongue in cheek, hoping to gain support for the perfectly sound and eminently desirable policy (of preventing high interest rates) by a faulty but effective argument. And perhaps silence is maintained on the obvious true analytic relationship between interest rates and bank positions by tacit agreement not to debunk a shibboleth which happens to be conducive to correct policy.

Why, then, do I now give away the secret which all wise men know but which no wise man will tell? First, I plead the usual excuse of all scoundrels: if I don't tell, somebody else will, and I at least can make certain that the antidote is given at the same time. Second, if rightly interpreted, it will be seen that mine is an argument against interest rate increases, not one in favor of them. They imply *enormous,* unneeded, unnecessary, undesirable, and arbitrary gifts to certain investors at the expense of the Treasury. In addition, their long-run harmful effects greatly outweigh, in my opinion, the doubtful minor benefits in controlling a hypothetical situation, which can in any case be better handled in other ways, even within the framework of banking policy. I shall not dwell here on the considerations which make it seem likely that the post-war epoch will witness even lower rates than the present.

Finally, and most important, the fancied difficulties arising from a hardening of rates is now being used as an argument against the lowering of rates, on the grounds that there will be great harm if they have to be raised later. I hope to have demonstrated the weakness of this argument.

In truth, the United States Treasury and Federal Reserve have missed a great opportunity. This war is a 2-per-cent war. *It should have been a one-per-cent war*. Literally, nobody has argued that the interest rates offered have had any substantial effect upon private consumption or investment in a war world of direct controls and inflationary gaps. They may have had some minor effects upon the form in which wealth is held, but to explore the fancied advantages and disadvantages of these would require another, equally long paper.

I hope I am giving away no secret when I say that the American authorities have in this (fortunately relatively unimportant) sphere pursued an uninspired policy whose full implications will be felt for a long time to come. May we hear from the wise men on this subject?

96

The Turn of the Screw

I

It would be churlish of a writer who has issued a trumpet call for wisdom not to accept it gratefully from all sources. Professor Harris's comments are most welcome, particularly since I am in agreement with many of them. Also, I must admit that there is some interest in Mr. Coleman's suggestions in connection with my previous paper that maturity dates as well as call dates be used in reckoning bond yields. In better days of peace ahead, if time hangs heavy, this additional arithmetic can be computed.

But I should by no means accept the relevance or validity of the rest of Mr. Coleman's comments. The differences between us are important and many, but most have little to do with anything discussed in my article, where I explicitly abstained from analysis of the desirability of low and lower interest rates. For what they are worth, my views on this subject are expressed in popular form in a debate with a formidable opponent, H. Christian Sonne; the interested reader may be referred to the January issue of *Modern Industry*. Although owning up to the fact that a sample of 50,000 top management executives proclaimed me the loser by a 3 to 1 landslide, I remain unrepentant.

But rather than enter upon this controversial subject, in a titanic battle between Mr. Coleman's bank clerk and my economic sophomore, it would be more useful, I think, to survey in a cursory fashion the dramatic changes that have taken place in the government bond market, especially since the summer of 1944 when my article was written. In doing so, I hope that I may be forgiven for the Reinhardt-like procedure of answering to my own horn.

II

When the war broke out, the financial community, aware of the movement of interest rates in previous wars and of the great financial needs of the government, anticipated higher interest rates. Instead the Treasury in effect guaranteed in the fall of 1942 a definite pattern of interest rates about as follows: 3/8 per cent on 90-day bills; 7/8 per cent on 1-year certificates; 1½ per cent on 4-4½ year notes; 2 per cent on 8-10 year bonds; 2½ per cent on long-term bonds. And at the same time, the Federal Reserve banks, in effect, took upon themselves the task of seeing that there would be adequate bank reserves to meet the needs of government finance and to support the bond market.[1]

Such a guaranteed structure in itself represented something of an anomaly since the pre-war structure of short-term rates persistently far below long-terms was a reflection of the fact that the existing structure could *not* be guaranteed to persist. In the new state of affairs it became practically a

---

[1] On these matters see the excellent treatment, C. R. Whittlesey, "Bank Liquidity and the War" (New York, Nat. Bur. of Econ. Research, 1945, Occasional paper 22); also, the March, June, and July, 1945, issues of the National City Bank of New York's Newsletter.

sure thing to buy the higher yielding securities; indeed by purchasing 2 per cent with eight years to run, one could confidently count on a capital gain of ½ per cent per year as they approached the 1½ per cent yield of four-year maturities.[2]

As Mr. Coleman remarks, every lowly bank clerk knows that banks have been speculating on or hedging against, a rise in interest rates. But not even bank presidents have been able to explain why they persisted in so odd a belief when in every year of the past decade (except for three transitory flurries) it proved to be wrong. In fact, those few banks which broke away from this obsession, repeatedly scored higher yields and capital gains by concentrating upon longer durations. A spinster who sees a man under her bed once can be forgiven. But what are we to think of the judgment of anyone who cries wolf for eleven years?

After the Treasury guarantee of the rate structure, it is to be wondered that there was not a greater shift to higher yielding bonds. Apparently, the government's guarantee was not understood or not taken seriously. In addition, banks were forbidden to participate directly in the later Victory Loan drives, and the new longer issues were barred to commercial banks (except for small amounts related to saving deposits) for considerable periods of time.

Gradually, however, the suspicion began to infiltrate the market that the longer maturities were better buys, and the Federal Reserve actually had to sell some few long-terms in 1943 to help maintain the structure, at the same time that it kept the buying and selling peg on ⅜ per cent bills.

When in November, 1944, the British gave the easy money screw another twist by replacing the 2½ per cent 52-50 with 1¾ per cent 50, the American money market belatedly realized that the U. S. Treasury had a firm grip on the money market and was in a position to push for lower rates. This realization, by causing purchase of intermediate and longer issues and sending their yields down, created its own fulfillment. Since then, banks and other investors have been reaching out for the longest maturities available to them.

Thus, the yield curve has shifted and twisted downward. The market is split now into three parts with ascending yields: partially tax exempts eligible for bank investment; fully taxables eligible for bank investment; fully taxables not now eligible for bank investments. The latter category is essentially a new phenomenon, inviting careful study by economists.

III

So much for the factual survey of the reasons why the Treasury has a firm grip on the bond market. What future policies are implied?

First, bond drive oversubscription should cease to be a dominating goal of policy. It is to be hoped that the new Secretary of the Treasury, Mr. Vinson, will stop regarding bond selling drives as glorified community chest campaigns and morale builders, except with respect to Series E, F, and G sales.

Second, if the Treasury's victory is not to be an empty (and wanton!) one, it is time for another turn of the "cheap money" screw. The 2½ per cent

[2] Everett Smith, "Securities for the Bond Portfolio," *Federal Home Loan Review*, May, 1945, p. 220.

market issues should be replaced in future Victory Loan drives by not more than 2¼ per cent issues, with further downward pressure all along the line. As the July, 1945, monthly news letter of the National City Bank of New York puts it so well: "Undoubtedly a helpful factor in *preventing* a further decline in long-term interest rates generally would be for the Treasury to make clearer its intention to continue issuance of 2½ per cent bonds in subsequent war loans" (p. 75; my italics).

In a sense, it would be more correct to say that the screw has already turned itself, with little credit due to the Treasury. But at least the screw's thrust should be used to lower the carrying charge of the public debt, rather than simply create profits for existing holders, free-riders, and margin purchasers. Cheap money arrived at by drying up the supply of securities to banks is nugatory, representing little more than a punitive drive on bank earnings.

The semblance of logic for such a move is provided by the unsubstantiated belief that bank purchases of government bonds are essentially more inflationary than sales to ordinary buyers of market issues. In view of the pledge of both political parties to maintain bond prices—*i.e.*, their ready convertability into cash—and in view of the fact that market issue purchases rarely come out of income and rarely represent a permanent renunciation of consumption, there is little in this notion.

The announced policy of Secretary Morgenthau that there will be no refunding of all short-term debt after the war is an eminently sound one and should be strongly reaffirmed. The great premium placed upon liquidity by our financial institutions and the gullibility of investors concerning a rise in yields should be harnessed for the benefit of the taxpayer. The notion that short-term debt "hangs over the market" is no more tenable than a similar notion applied to bank deposits payable on demand. The constant turning over of the debt is not essentially different from the turning over of bank deposits, and should give the Treasury no cause for alarm—unless, indeed, it too is a victim of the obsession of rising rates!

Mr. Vinson enters upon office with all the wartime powers of the Treasury at full tide. In many respects, his peacetime powers will be even greater. It is a propitious moment, I believe, to initiate, while in admitted strength, determined policies in the nation's long-run interest.

PAUL A. SAMUELSON*

* The author is associate professor of economics at Massachusetts Institute of Technology.

97

The Business Cycle and Urban Development

Mr. Paul Samuelson, *of Massachusetts Institute of Technology, read a paper on this subject. Since it constitutes a study of primary importance to the matters under examination, it is here reproduced in full:*

Almost everybody would agree that it is unwise to predict the far future from the happenings of one particular moment. If, during the present war period, there is reversion to horse-and-buggy days, that does not mean that the automobile will cease to play an increasingly important part in the future development of our economy. And if, during the Great Depression, there was a temporary reversion of the centuries-old trends towards increased urbanization, neither does this mean that the long-run outlook is for more and more decentralization. For in the post-war period we shall and must succeed in maintaining a high level of effective demand and employment.

The present discussion will raise the question as to whether some town planners may not have misinterpreted events of the last decade in giving too much credence to the belief that unemployment is caused by cities as such; with the corollary that in making plans for a better world we must turn our back on the city and build a new kind of town. The present writer is an economist with no special competence in the field of city planning. It is with some trepidation, therefore, that he ventures to enter upon a discussion of those problems. His excuse for doing so lies in the fact that implicit in many treatments there is economic theorizing involving detailed diagnosis of the causes of unemployment together with prescriptions for its cure.

It may be convenient, therefore, to summarize some of these implicit economic theories in rather gross and exaggerated terms, not in order to criticize specific writers but rather to bring out certain points of view more sharply. The following beliefs are sometimes encountered in the literature on Housing:

(1) Unemployment is of greater quantitative importance in urban centers than in rural areas.

(2) Furthermore, it is of greater numerical importance in the larger cities than in the smaller ones.

(3) In the recent past the rate of growth of the larger cities has been less than that in smaller towns.

(4) Unemployment in large cities results from "industrial blight" which is in its origins not unlike the blight which attacks neighborhoods and produces slums. In the words of one extremely intelligent and moderate discussion this is stated as follows: "It is safe to say—with many reasons in the background— that all of these factories became obsolete and lost their competitive strength in the battle with other factories in this country and abroad."

It may well be that the American people would prefer to desert large cities of the present pattern in order to create a new way of life. In doing so, there would no doubt be important economic costs, balanced somewhat by economic savings. But the community might in fact be willing to incur these costs, regarding the expenditure of productive resources upon town building as preferable to expenditure upon other items of consumption or upon capital formation. In ascertaining and making clear the comparative economic costs of urban rehabilitation or the construction of a new and different basic urban unit, the economist can be of assistance; but he could hardly presume to advise the community as to the intensity of its preference for one way of life as compared to another.

On the basis of the statements of alleged economic fact cited above, it is held that the greater unemployment in the cities can hardly be a coincidence. Remove the cities and you will remove unemployment. If obsolete factories give rise to obsolete homes and obsolete men, build a new type of factory and you will help to cure our depression problems. If the craving of modern man for space and air is not great enough by itself to justify a costly rebuilding of our urban structure, this craving plus substantial gains in employment together may offer rewards greater than their cost.

I shall attempt in the discussion that follows to appraise the validity of these notions in terms of the best tested findings of economic specialists in the fields of statistics and business cycles.

Rural v. Urban Centers in Depression: Cursory observation by the man on the street would suggest in the first instance that unemployment is of truly greater quantitative importance in the urban centers than in rural areas. It is not easy to find bread lines in the countryside. Nevertheless, a detailed factual investigation shows the opposite to be the case. There is more unemployment in rural areas, but as will be seen it tends to take the form of *disguised unemployment.*

For more than a century towns have been growing at the expense of rural areas. The differential rate of growth takes place despite a comparatively unfavorable balance of births and deaths and is the result of migration. While this movement has continued steadily over many years it has not proceeded smoothly and without interruption. The older economists ventured the prediction, since borne out by the facts, that the flow of people from country to city would be greatest in times of prosperity and would languish in periods of depression and unemployment.

The "push" from the country actually operates continuously because of the relatively unfavorable standards of living, which seem to characterize rural areas in all countries and in all times. While this "push" is a necessary force in the process it is still not sufficient. It is the "pull" of the city which forms the proximate causal force in leading to migration, and it is this "pull" which oscillates with the business cycles. When jobs are not to be had in the city, it is pointless for individuals to move from the country to the city. In fact, we now know that during a period of great depression such as prevailed in the early thirties there is not only a cessation of the normal country-to-city movement, but there is even a reverse flow back to the farm of those previous migrants who have not succeeded in remaining in employment.

These speculations of the older economists have been verified by all of the statistical material which has since become available. Similarly, an examination of the statistics of immigration from foreign countries into the United States shows the influence of the business cycle, even in the days before any restrictions were placed upon entrance.

It has long been recognized that the Swedish Vital Statistics are among the best in the world with regard to accuracy and detail. Recent works of Dorothy S. Thomas, Gunnar Myrdal and others on these Swedish data have produced findings completely in accord with the above hypotheses.

For the United States no records are kept of the changes in domicile of our residents; so we are thrown back upon cruder observations and estimates. At first glance, one would think that an examination of unemployment statistics could prove conclusively whether unemployment is greater on the farms than in the cities. Unfortunately this is not the case. Except in census years or as a result of partial or total specific census, we have no direct measures of unemployment in this country. Various agencies, such as the National Industrial Conference Board, the A. F. of L. and others have, nevertheless, prepared estimates of unemployment. The disagreements between them are not too great and are attributable in part to differences of definition rather than to disagreement with respect to quantity. In all of these estimates as well as in the census the assumption is made that any person who returns to rural areas because of failure to achieve steady employment in the city is nevertheless to be counted as employed regardless of whether he is doing no more than living with his parents or relatives on a farm. Actually he contributes little or nothing to the already redundant production of agricultural products, and so we are confronted with a clear case of *disguised unemployment*.

It is common knowledge that with rationalization our present farm production could be maintained with little more than half of our existing acreage under cultivation and with a considerable reduction in the rural working force. Therefore, we should probably count as *disguisedly unemployed* not only the migrants who return from the city to the country but also that number who normally move to the city but were prevented from doing so by the absence of employment opportunities there.

As we have moved into the period of acceleration of our Victory effort, we have found that our largest labor reserve among the gainfully occupied consisted of the three million odd persons who were *disguisedly unemployed* in agriculture.

Not only is it true that unemployment in rural areas tends to exceed even that of our urban centers, but in addition the per capita income falls more markedly in these sectors. This is borne out by the fact that in years of depression there tends to be greater inequality of income between the highest and lowest income states; that is, between the predominantly urban and the predominantly rural states. Poverty in the cities is noticeable because of its concentration and its contrast with the more prosperous neighborhoods; poverty in the country is in many regions all-pervading and hence escapes almost unnoticed. It is outdoor life. Nutritional studies of the South and elsewhere reveal some of its less glamorous aspects. Vitamin deficiencies prevail; meat, vegetables, and milk are scarce; sanitation is bad rather than the reverse, etc., etc. For misery in its most concentrated form one must look at a half-dozen odd rural problem areas, such as the northern and southern Dust Bowls, the Appalachian Plateau, the Deep South, the Michigan cut-over area, and so on.

Having examined the differential behavior of unemployment and income between rural and urban areas in the Great Depression, we now turn to the prospects for each in a period of revival such as the present or in a period of high income such as we are determined to maintain in the post-war era. It is to be emphasized that both urban and rural communities will benefit greatly from an increase in employment and national income, but the manner of their benefiting will be somewhat different. An upswing of business will open up vast employment opportunities in our cities and towns, because with a high level of income people choose to buy the kinds of things that are produced in cities and towns. Countless budgetary studies have shown that with increased income, expenditure is not divided in a uniform way among different commodities. Other things being equal, expenditure upon food does not keep pace with increases in income; rather is there a shift in favor of luxuries, services, durable consumers goods, etc. These are the products of our cities and towns.

This is not to say that agricultural and extractive industries will not benefit markedly from the attainment of high levels of national income. On the contrary, as the economists of the Agriculture Department are the most insistent in pointing out, the prosperity of agriculture is crucially dependent upon the prosperity of industry. The most important single step in solving the agricultural problem lies therefore in the provision of more and better jobs in the cities.

Other things, to be sure, will not remain equal. Agricultural products tend to be inelastic in supply even though the income elasticity of demand for them at constant prices tends to be small. Nevertheless, even a small increase in a demand schedule which is itself already inelastic and which faces an inelastic supply schedule can result in a great increase in price. High prosperity, by raising agricultural prices more than others, may actually lower the income inequalities between agriculture and industry and thereby weaken the "push" from rural to urban areas. But this effect upon migration will be as nothing compared to the greatly enhanced "pull" which will be set up by the existence for the first time in many years of freely available employment opportunities in the cities. Already reports are heard of roads in the Ohio Valley crowded with migrants from the Appalachian "Hillbilly" region of the South to the industrial regions of the North. One need only remember the experience of the last war and the prosperity thereafter, when the largest fraction of our present metropolitan negro populations was attracted for the first time to northern cities by the exceptional employment opportunities then prevailing.

The results of our factual survey of the incidence of depression and prosperity upon rural and urban areas may be summarized as follows: destitution and unemployment are present no less in rural areas than in urban centers but their effect tends in many ways to be disguised. The present defense prosperity reveals the favorable upturn of employment opportunities in the cities. The long-range outlook, based upon what we know to be the changes in demand for different types of goods as income increases, is also favorable to urban centers.

Unemployment in Large and Small Cities: Let us turn to the second implicitly assumed hypothesis, that unemployment is of greater numerical importance in the larger cities than in the smaller ones. Even within the limits of our inadequate statistics it should be possible to corroborate or refute this point of view. We have at least three censuses of unemployment available to us, that of the regular 1930 census, the special postcard census of unemployment in 1937, and the recent regular 1940 census. Tabulation of the complete returns for 1940 has not yet been made, and so the figures which I present will be confined to the returns from the 1930 and 1937 census.

Scatter diagrams have been made which attempt to throw some light upon the variation of the intensity of unemployment with variation in city size. The first fifty cities in the United States are ranked according to size in 1930—New York being one, Chicago two, etc. At the same time each city is ranked according to the intensity of its unemployment in that year as measured by the percentage which the partially and totally unemployed bear to the total population of the city. In the first chart is plotted a scatter diagram showing the correspondence between these ranks. If the correspondence were perfect, that is, if the largest city had the largest percentage of unemployment and the fiftieth city the smallest, then all of the points would fall upon the indicated 45 degree line. Actually this is far from being the case. The points are distributed haphazardly over the diagram with only the faintest drift from the lower left hand corner to the upper right hand corner, a drift so small as to be capable of being attributed simply to chance. Statistical computation of the rank correlation coefficient does not yield a significant positive correlation.

The second chart is drawn up just as before except that an attempt has been made to take account of possible differences in the age distribution of different cities. This has been done by relating the unemployed to the total number in theory gainfully occupied, that is, the total labor force seeking employment in 1930. Instead of leading to a more significant positive relationship, the result is an even more dispersed scatter with a completely negligible coefficient of correlation.

In a third chart a similar scatter is presented, utilizing the 1937 unemployment data and the 1940 rank of cities by size. If anything, the correlation is less significantly positive than in 1930. We may conclude from the three charts referred to that workers in larger cities are not appreciably exposed to greater risks of unemployment than workers in medium-sized urban centers, and

SCATTER DIAGRAMS SHOWING RELATIONSHIPS BETWEEN
SIZE OF CITIES, UNEMPLOYMENT, AND SPECIALIZATION

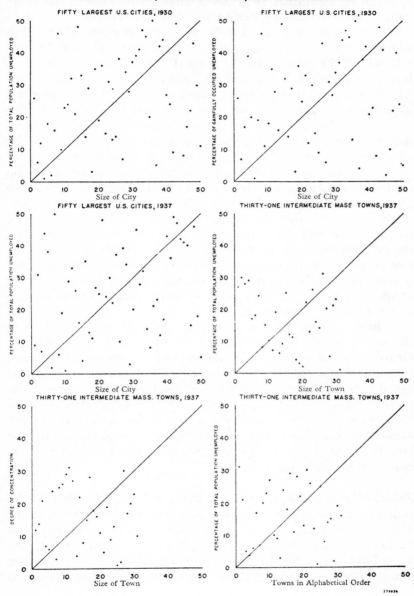

FIFTY LARGEST U.S. CITIES, 1930

FIFTY LARGEST U.S. CITIES, 1930

FIFTY LARGEST U.S. CITIES, 1937

THIRTY-ONE INTERMEDIATE MASS TOWNS, 1937

THIRTY-ONE INTERMEDIATE MASS. TOWNS, 1937

THIRTY-ONE INTERMEDIATE MASS. TOWNS, 1937

that during the Great Depression what inequalities of risk there were tended to be mitigated rather than the reverse.

These facts tell the story only for the larger cities. Three additional charts were made for medium-sized towns, no one of which falls within the class of the fifty largest cities. They are thirty-one intermediate-sized Massachusetts towns, from which the largest Massachusetts cities have been excluded. Within this intermediate classification there again appears to be no significant positive relationship between town size and intensity of unemployment. An examination of the fourth chart in the series shows it to be very similar in general character to the previous three.

It was thought that differences in the degree of specialization or diversification among the various towns might have tended to obscure a significant relationship between size and unemployment. To see whether this could be the case, a chart was made of the degree of industrial concentration of each town as measured by the percentage importance of the five industries against the size of the town. Again there is no significant relationship either positive or negative. In other words, for intermediate-sized towns of Massachusetts, it is just as likely for a small town to be specialized as for a large town.

There remains for discussion only the sixth and last chart of the series, which is something of an anticlimax. To bring out clearly what is meant by a scatter such as might have arisen through chance alone, percentage unemployment was plotted against the alphabetical order of the town. As might be expected, there is no significant relationship, although such relationship as there is turns out to be slightly positive. As far as the statistics are concerned, one might just as well blame unemployment on the fact that a town received its name from the first half of the alphabet as on the fact that it is large.

Relative Trends of Large and Small Cities: It is conceivable that the centuries-old persistent trend towards urban concentration might have gone too far, so that in this century indications might be forthcoming of a reversal of this trend. I have attempted to throw some light upon this question by an examination of data to be found in our decennial census. Cities are classified according to whether they fall in the group of over 1,000,000 population, 500,000 to 1,000,000, 250,000 to 500,000, 100,000 to 250,000, 50,000 to 100,000, 25,000 to 50,000, 10,000 to 25,000, 5,000 to 10,000, 2,500 to 5,000 and below. Not only is the number of places in these categories given but also the percentage of the total population which reside in those cities respectively. I have listed below the relative figures for 1940 in terms of numbers of cities in each classification and percentage of total population. In columns 3, 4, 5, and 6 I have listed the net change between the given decade and the previous decade of the percentage of population in each class.

PERCENTAGE URBAN POPULATION OF THE UNITED STATES
CLASSIFIED BY SIZE OF PLACE

Area and class of place	No. of places 1940	% of total pop. 1940	1930–40	Changes in % of total pop. 1920–30	1910–20	1900–10
Greater than						
1,000,000	5	12.3	−0.2	+2.7	+0.4	+0.7
500,000–1,000,000	9	4.7	+0.2	−1.2	+2.6	+1.1
250,000– 500,000	23	5.9	−0.6	+2.2	0.0	+0.5
100,000– 250,000	55	5.9	−0.2	−0.1	+0.9	+1.0
50,000– 100,000	107	5.6	+0.3	+0.3	+0.5	+0.9
25,000– 50,000	213	5.6	+0.4	+0.4	+0.4	+0.7
10,000– 25,000	665	7.6	+0.2	+0.8	+0.6	+0.3
5,000– 10,000	965	5.1	+0.3	+0.1	+0.1	+0.2
2,500– 5,000	1,422	3.8	0.0	−0.5	+0.1	+0.2
Total (above 2,500)	3,464	56.5	+0.3	+4.7	+5.6	+5.6

Total population of U. S. in: 1900 was   75,994,575
                                             1910 was   91,972,266
                                             1920 was 105,710,620
                                             1930 was 122,775,046
                                             1940 was 131,669,275

The result is rather illuminating. We find a steady increase in the proportion of the total population living in towns with population of 2,500 or over from only 40 per cent in 1900 to 56.5 per cent in 1940. However, the increase in this percentage is much less between 1930 and 1940 than was typical of the preceding three decades. What is true for all the urban centers is true for urban communities of every class. Throughout the twentieth century large, medium-sized and small cities have in every case increased not only absolutely but in percentage importance. Again, however, there is a break in the rapidity of this trend between 1930 and 1940 with some of the larger groups losing in percentage importance although not absolutely.

If we consider the decade of the twenties as one of relative prosperity and perhaps more like the decade to be experienced in the immediate future, it becomes clear that the large city, far from being outmoded, shows the most rapid rate of increase. If the ten years ahead are by and large more like the depressed period of the thirties, we may expect this trend to slow down or even to be reversed. It is not true, however, that the very largest cities have shown in the last decade the greatest loss in percentage importance. This is true rather of the quarter million to half million sized towns.

One must be cautious in interpreting these statistics, since there is good reason to believe that they are biased in the direction of minimizing the true rate of growth of urban areas. If in the last decade Philadelphia and Boston showed no positive rate of growth but rather a decline, it would be misleading to infer a significant trend from this fact. A city does not end at its legal boundaries. One must consider the Greater Philadelphia and Greater Boston regions. As is to be expected from the outward movement within all growing cities, the regions around these metropolises would grow much more than enough to compensate the loss of the center. Today practically nobody lives in the City of London, but it would be absurd to suggest that the Greater London area has been declining in relative or absolute importance. It would be illuminating if a tabulation were made of the rate of growth of the population of greater metropolitan areas, and I have no doubt that the pattern presented above would, for the thirties at least, be substantially modified.

It would perhaps be a fair summary of the statistical findings of this section to say that the twentieth century has revealed no reversal of the trend towards urban centralization, although there has been marked decentralization to the suburbs of the urban communities themselves and the depressed conditions of the last decade have slowed down and in some cases reversed the growth of the towns and cities.

Urbanism as a Cause of Unemployment: It is, of course, neither possible nor desirable to enter here upon a detailed discussion of what the best informed opinion believes to be the major forces responsible for unemployment, but still it may be useful to mention a few of these findings. Our economic system is subject to periodical ups-and-downs in employment, income, production, profits, prices, etc. This movement is all-pervading, affecting all regions of the country and communities of all sizes. The magnitude of the effect is of course not equal, but as a first approximation the differences can be disregarded. It is important to emphasize the general character of the phenomenon, for if this be borne in mind, remedies which carry a superficial appeal because of their likeness to the procedures by which a single individual can ameliorate his condition, are seen to be no remedies at all. Thus, a single individual, if he studies Dale Carnegie, takes correspondence courses, works over-time, and does the thousand and one things which from time immemorial have been thought of as leading to success, can without doubt succeed in finding employment. But all cannot do so. If everybody became a go-getter, none would be much better off than before. One man can see the parade better by standing upon a chair, but what works for one will not work for all simultaneously, and the single individual who secures a job by self-improvement tends to do so by displacing another worker. There has been a growing realization of the fact that unemployment is not an individual problem, and this is reflected in our legislation and our attitudes towards Social Security, Relief, etc.

Very much the same considerations apply to cities. The country as a whole will not be pulled out of a slump by vigorous advertising of different cities' Chambers of Commerce, although any one city may benefit by these tactics. Nor is it necessarily true that a given city benefits from a growth in employment elsewhere. If this growth resulted simply in migration of the unemployed to the new center, the old might be benefited; but the products of the new center may compete with the products of the old. And for every man who leaves, there will tend to be an equivalent loss in employment in the old city, its relative status probably being unbalanced worse because of fixed charges.

The picture I have painted of a relative fixity of the number of jobs at any one time should not be thought of as a gloomy one. Something can be done about this situation and I suspect in the years to come something will be done about it, but piece meal methods will not serve. Beggar-my-neighbor methods on balance show zero net results. Only a comprehensive program which tackles directly the problem of effective demand can hold out hope of a solution.

In closing, I should like to express the hope that urban and housing specialists will premise their long-range plans upon the assumption that we will effectively overcome the specter of unemployment and the most flagrant cases of poverty. Proceeding upon this assumption, the economists can say with some confidence that the findings of their subject are neutral with respect to the long-range desirability of furthering the development of urban communities of different sizes. It is up to the planners to give us the kinds of cities we want in as perfect a form as we are able and willing to afford.

98

Principles and Rules In Modern Fiscal Policy: A Neo-Classical Reformulation

PAUL A. SAMUELSON

I. Introduction

In this essay I should like to give an appraisal of certain trends in modern fiscal theories. My viewpoint is that of a general neo-classical theory that incorporates into the classical tradition whatever parts of the Keynesian and neo-Keynesian analysis that seem to possess descriptive validity for the present-day economy. In its general outlines, I think this is the viewpoint that Marshall, Walras, and Wicksell would subscribe to if they were alive today; and I am inclined to think that Adam Smith himself would claim an important share in its formulation.

To the extent that these general principles are true, I am sure that they will seem to involve a semblance of belaboring the obvious: such is the fate of truth; it is only error that is spicy. For this and other reasons, I shall let the general tenor of this neo-classical position reveal itself through a running commentary on certain aspects of recent fiscal theorizing.

II. A Modern Fallacy Concerning Government Expenditure

During the last half dozen years there has grown to some popularity in this country a new and special doctrine of fiscal policy. In reaction against the earlier emphasis on variation of public expenditure as a countercyclical device and to the earlier underemphasis on tax policy, the new view holds that it is optimal to rely on changes in tax revenues alone to contribute to over-all business stability, and that both strategic necessity and basic economic principle decree that *government expenditure on goods and services not be varied in the light of variations in business-cycle demands but be held at fixed levels as determined by a calculation of the intrinsic merits of the desirable level of public services.*[1]

I believe that there is much that is valuable in this emphasis. The built-in flexibility of taxes and the possibility of changing tax rates so as to contribute toward stability was too long neglected by economists. Similarly there was in the 1930's too great a belief in the efficacy of public works programs and too naive a neglect of the forecasting and administrative-legislative difficulties in bringing about a desired time-profile of government expenditures.

The Neo-Classical View of Policy

These last strategic considerations have by now received a thorough airing in the economic journals so that there is no need to add to what may already be excessively pessimistic appraisals of their difficulties. I should like to address myself to the following question of basic principle.

In an economy where the tastes of individuals are to count, is it an optimal condition of welfare economics that the level of public services be determined independently of the state of private investment demands and of the business-cycle situation and of the other use-alternatives open to resources that may be devoted to public services?

From the way I have asked the question, it must be obvious in which direction I conceive the answer to lie. All decisions must be made in terms of alternatives: when these change, the optimal decision must change. Public services at all times must be regarded as competing with each other for the use of our limited resources and they must be thought of as competing with all other uses as well—with current desires for private consumption goods, with current private capital-formation programs for resource use, etc.

It follows, I believe, as a matter of basic logic that when the need for, let us say, a heavy war program is great, then private consumption, private capital formation, and civilian government programs should all have to retrench. On the other hand, if for any reason private

---

[1] In some degree or other this view is to be found in the economic journals, in publications of the Committee for Economic Development (CED), and the National Planning Association, and occasionally even in government utterances. In Part III specific forms are further discussed.

capital formation should have gotten into an extremely depressed condition so as to have resisted all the feasible methods of stimulating it, what then follows? Clearly a wastage of resources in unemployment is not optimal according to modern neo-classical welfare economics. If some other useful activities *can* be made to expand, they *should* certainly be encouraged to do so. But in any case the residue of resources released in any one direction should be used in other directions. Sound economic bookkeeping tells us that in real terms people can now (1) afford to have more private consumption goods, including leisure; and *exactly the same considerations* tell us that they can now (2) also afford to have more public or governmental goods and services. How they will choose to apportion the extra released resources between the private and public categories must rationally depend on the shapes of their preference patterns ("indifference contours") between public and private goods.

All the indicated optimal expansions in the public and private sphere will not necessarily take place spontaneously. To the extent that they do not, and always assuming that appropriate policies in the monetary and pricing spheres are being pursued, there remains a problem for fiscal policy. To bring about the desired expansion in private goods, tax reduction—or its (algebraic) counterpart, increased transfer expenditure—is called for. To bring about the desired expansion of government goods and services, an increase in government expenditure is called for, since public services are by definition not purchased by the consumer directly but are provided for him by the government.

This same point may be expressed in an equivalent way. Just as there are budgetary regularities (the so-called Engel's laws) summarizing how families wish to parcel out their extra incomes on food, clothing, shelter, saving, recreation, etc., so there are similar income patterns between public and private services. A rich country will feel it can afford a network of roads and public parks that a poor country cannot. The effective quantitative pattern of these income-relations will depend upon peoples' tastes, upon the distribution of incomes and democratic voting power, and a host of such institutional factors. The curious fiscal policy that I am criticizing makes the special and completely arbitrary and gratuitous assumption that the income elasticity of public services must be 0.00. No reason, except the political one regarding "rules," to be treated later in this essay, has been advanced so far as my reading of the relevant literature is concerned to show why this should be the case. And, of course, it is not the case, as several proponents of the view will concede.[2]

Some Important Implications

Let me stress that accepting the general neo-classical view here enunciated, as against the narrower one criticized, need involve (1) no relaxation of vigilance over inefficiency in government, (2) no relaxation of vigilance against invasion by government of private consumption and personal liberty, (3) no acceptance of boon-doggling as a necessary evil at any time, and (4) no minimization of the strategic problems in programming either public expenditure or tax legislation. Let me enlarge on each of these points.

(1) The view that we resolve every activity into its true costs in terms of real resources is inimical to inefficiency in government for two reasons: it stresses that to get any given range of public services we should take away as few resources from the private sphere as possible; and that for any given amount of resources made available to the public sphere at the expense of the private, we should get the most possible government services of the type that people most want. Both of these considerations are opposed to inefficiency in government.

(2) The neo-classical viewpoint formulated here is a powerful

[2] Because the above common-sense discussion may be thought to be inconsistent with more intricate economic reasoning, I shall redundantly add a mathematical proof of the error in the special fiscal policy under discussion. If we call private consumption goods C_p, public consumption goods C_g, private capital formation I_p, and public capital formation I_g, then we may over-simplify the political consensus and write down a national taste pattern or "welfare" function $W = W(C_p, C_g, I_p, I_g; i, E, \alpha, \ldots)$ where i represents the structure of interest rates, E the state of expectations, α a general catch-all parameter of business cycle disturbance (innovation, etc.). W is to be maximized subject to the fact that over-all resources are scarce. In the simplest case we could imagine, that with full employment and given productivity, the menu or production-possibility schedule for the system is defined by $C_p + C_g + I_p + I_g =$ constant minus "tax-collection-deadweight-loss." Without writing down the details of the conditions of equilibrium, it is obvious that there is complete formal symmetry between C_p and C_g and unless it can be shown that their income elasticities are of different sign, then they can be expected to have qualitatively similar adaptive patterns to changes in investment, in α, or anything else; and hence the doctrine of active tax *rather* than expenditure policy is shown to be false. An extension of this line of reasoning shows that there is an optimal division-of-labor between fiscal and monetary policy that has little recognizable relation to the more precisely formulated programs put forward by private economists and advisory groups. I myself have given my approval to compromise recommendations, some of the *details* of which seemed lacking in logical rigor.

It should be noted that the above analysis does not assume that the "real needs" of the economy for capital formation fluctuate as wildly as the motivated private investment demand does; or that private investment demand would fluctuate so greatly if an appropriate stabilization environment were established; or that fiscal policy must accept the variability of investment demand as a fact, unalterable by non-fiscal measures or by fiscal policy itself. All that is insisted upon is the formal qualitative symmetry of tax and expenditure policy, of private and public consumption goods.

argument against any undue expansion of the government sector. Each proposed program, old and new, is to be subjected to the test of whether its desirability outweighs its true costs. At the same time the present doctrine does not stand in the way of any expansions that do meet this test.

(3) This same viewpoint represents a rejection of such counsel of despair as is embodied in deep-depression defenses made for useless public projects on the ground that they do succeed in getting the money out and do have favorable secondary effects on consumption respending and production. Tax reductions, worthy transfer expenditures, and useful projects can be expected to have the same favorable effects—and in addition, to lead to a more optimal distribution of resources. But to rule out boon-doggling is not to vitiate the fundamental argument of the present paper: appraisals of how worth while it is for private and public goods to expand must be made in terms of the alternatives open. Thus if one knew that a certain population was *temporarily* immobilized near a Maine shipyard, or that in five years time one would want to expand shipbuilding for reasons of defense, then a project that would not pay in the absence of these considerations might become optimal in light of them.[3]

(4) Instead of blinding one to the strategic difficulties involved in forecasting and in the timing of tax and expenditure programs, the present approach helps to make clear their nature and the direction in which optimal decisions may lie. Take for example the case of a depression that is sure to be temporary. A public works program that would be slow in getting under way and that would be sure to result in heavy use of resources and money outlay after the labor market had become tight would be roundly condemned—and precisely for the reason that it would utilize resources that it is felt could be better utilized elsewhere.[4] The same might be said of a tax-cut, designed to meet a temporary situation, but which could not be reversed politically even after inflationary pressures required such a reversal. The present approach is neutral and lets the strategic facts decide whether

[3] In weighing benefits against costs one should of course not omit any slowing down of mobility that might result from the government program. Also as a matter of strategy it might be a very dangerous precedent for the government to appraise each project by correcting its pecuniary cost by some estimate of corrected non-pecuniary cost. But in principle, as distinct from strategy, this is not objectionable.

[4] If, over the business cycle, the irreducible residue of fluctuations in private investment should release special categories of resources, which are more or less suitable for use in the private consumption sector rather than the public, then a rational policy will take this into account.

certain of these difficulties of timing weigh more heavily against one kind of fiscal policy than another. There is no implication in the present approach that some ascertainable simple income-elasticity ratio can be calculated to settle these complex problems.[5]

One important strategic element should be fully taken account of in applying the present neo-classical view. In the past it has often been argued that an expansion of government expenditure during a depression is likely to have adverse effects upon business confidence and to have depressing effects on private investment. The reverse has also been argued. But let us suppose that it were established that in a future depression the adverse effects will be predominant. Would the present neo-classical doctrine wish to take this adverse incentive effect into account? The answer is *definitely yes:* in appraising any policy *all* its consequences are to be taken account of and weighed in the balance.

III. The False Dichotomy between Discretionary and Other Policies

All that I have said is merely an elaboration of the obvious. So much so that economists who begin by upholding the one-sided view that I have criticized quickly abandon it, but then go on to argue: does the neo-classical view say more than that one should be against sin and for virtue? Does it provide rules of thumb and standards that legislatures and advisers on public policy can use to arrive at optimum decisions?

There is certainly some force in these questions. The analysis outlined here is in itself neutral as to the specific policies that should be followed. It is a language and not a particular poem or story in that language. Still, I cannot think it unimportant to be against sin and for virtue; and especially to set forth the general considerations that help one to recognize arbitrary identifications of sin as compared to justifiable ones.

But the search for rules of thumb persists and this raises some perplexing questions in political economy. We can meet the request for standards by enunciating certain formal crypto-rules that are not

---

[5] My colleague, Max Millikan, has pointed out a needed qualification. Suppose that a slump in private investment has reduced income and has induced multiplier reductions in private consumption. If government expenditure has been held constant, there is then some presumption that private consumption has greatest utility at the margin. After tax-reductions or other consumption stimulants have eliminated the secondary-multiplier reductions in private consumption, from that point on public and private consumption can be treated symmetrically.

untrue but are almost completely empty of specific content. Thus if a family comes for advice on how to spend its income, we can answer: "Equalize the marginal utility of the last dollar in every use, or, what is the same thing, make the marginal-rate-of-substitution between any two goods equal to their price ratios." Likewise, I could have reworded the neo-classical fiscal doctrines in terms of equalizing the social marginal utilities all around, etc. I cannot believe that it is this kind of a reformulation of the basic problem of choice that those who seek standards have in mind; if it is, then they are easily bamboozled.

Instead of simply telling the family to think carefully in making its decisions, advice which if helpful is so only in a limited sense, some would offer more definite suggestions: "Take your paycheck right home from the factory, detouring around the corner saloon; and when you get home, put so much in a red envelope for the rent, so much in a green envelope for the insurance man, etc., etc." Similarly, the student of public administration may be able to say that a certain committee structure and accounting set-up is better than another. Such considerations as this are by no means unimportant; but if anything is clear, it is certain that the student of economics has no particular professional competence in this sphere.

Still a different kind of rule is the following: "A family should spend about one week's salary on its monthly shelter." I do not doubt that countless families have had grounds for self-congratulation that they have observed such a rule and that innumerable people have come to regret that they have not done so. But, of course, this ratio has no intrinsic economic validity, and a judicious person with indifference curves between housing and other things that were quite inconsistent with this rule would be foolish to disregard his true tastes. Likewise in the sphere of fiscal policy, there is no intrinsically valid quantitative pattern that should be followed independently of (1) people's tastes as democratically resolved and of (2) all the alternatives present when decisions have to be made. Once again we are thrown back onto fundamentals rather than rules of thumb.

I could go on and enumerate still other kinds of rules that people might seek or give. But it seems to me that the minute such rules have real content, they become arbitrary and only accidentally compatible with the true optimum position. And when they are without content, it is hard to see that they are of economic significance.

Yet arbitrary though particular rules, habits, and procedures may be from the standpoint of an ideal optimum, I am sure that, in fact, such behavior patterns and slogans are very important. I feel that most sophisticated people who put forward a particular package of rules to be followed do so because they regard this as *the lesser of evils*. They are resigned to not being at the optimum anyway; they believe they detect in actual reality a deviation from the optimum in a particular direction; and they propose a new slogan, automatic mechanism, or budgetary procedure in the belief or hope that the adoption of this package will reduce the distortion and bias away from the optimum.

Let me illustrate. One may favor a gold-coin standard because the expected variability of gold production and stocks will be less than the variability and inflation that the Prince or the mob may bring about in the absence of such a standard. A similar case can be made out for playing the rules of the gold standard rather than going in for inept monetary management. Or one may favor balancing the budget in every year, not because that will necessarily lead to efficiency in government or a proper division of resources between private and public uses and unemployment, but simply because legislators who abandon that rule may engage in worse follies. Or one may argue that expanding government expenditure on goods and services as a supplement to a tax-reduction depression program may be a bad thing—not in principle, but because under present voting conditions the secular trend of government expenditure will then grow faster than you desire, or faster than you think "the people as a whole" really desire.

Or one may set up an arbitrarily designed automatic mechanism consisting of specified reserve ratios, marginal-propensities-to-tax according to frozen tax legislation or according to "formula-flexibility," parity-price programs of expenditure, commodity-money, wage-price flexibility, and so forth in greater or lesser detail. Such an automatic mechanism is often contrasted with a so-called "discretionary" system. Now over the years I have struggled with this distinction and for the life of me I am unable to isolate any real logical difference, either at the philosophical or pragmatic level. It is not simply that such a mechanism is set up by discretion, is abandoned by discretion, and is interfered with by discretion—although this consideration is itself enough to destroy the notion of a genuine difference of kind. But even my efforts to establish a logically rigorous difference of degree has not met with success.

Imagine the detailed response of the economic system under some particular uninterfered-with automatic mechanism that is specified in detail. Its description could be written down in words or in mathematical equations in much the same way that the behavior of an automatic-pilot on an airplane can be so described. Now generally we can write down a set of words or equations that will describe an exactly *equivalent* discretionary program—not just exactly equivalent under a specific historical pattern of the system, but equivalent in its response to *any* virtual pattern. Neither system is better or worse than the other: they are simply logical equivalents. Now it may be inconvenient for Congress or the Executive to be standing in a perpetual state of preparedness to take precisely the action that would duplicate the result of the automatic mechanism; or we may not be able to trust Congress to follow such action, or for that matter to keep hands off the mechanism. There may therefore be a strong *pragmatic* case to be made for instituting that kind of discretionary action which a mechanism provides: we all recognize the merits of an automatic-pilot in commercial aviation; and if we can, we do install thermostats in our homes so that we do not have to get up in the cold or keep our eyes glued on off-and-on switches located all over the house. But in all logic it still seems to be a case of pragmatic choice between two discretionary policies.

At the practical level there is much to be said for various quasi-automatic devices provided they are carefully watched and judiciously interfered with. Administrative convenience, quickness of action, minimization of manpower and other advantages can be pointed to. Also, private individuals can predict what the government will do. But, of course, this predictability would also be true under even the most perverse discretionary programs provided only they were consistently perverse; and it should be remembered, too, that our experience with stabilization funds and other policies indicates that it is not *always* desirable for such private prediction to be possible.

As I write in 1950 it appears that such automatic devices are rather academic and must wait upon the $81 + n^{\text{th}}$ Congress for enactment. In part this is because Congressmen look upon such policies as an enhancement of the omnipotent powers of the modern State. This is a little ironical, inasmuch as eloquent opponents of State power like my late teacher, Henry Simons, thought of "rules" as opposed to "authorities" and of the ancient distinction between a "government of law rather than of men."[6] In terms of precise logic this appears to be really

[6] H. C. Simons, "Rules *vs.* Authorities in Monetary Policy," *Journal of Political Economy*, February 1936, XLIV, No. 1, pp. 1–30, reprinted in H. C. Simons, *Economic Policy for a Free Society* (Chicago, University of Chicago Press, 1948), pp. 180–183.

a plea for democracy to pursue certain discretionary policies which preserve certain "rights" of an individual and of any minority group against encroachment by other minority groups or by the majority itself. My own ethical belief attaches tremendous importance to these considerations. But they have little to do with the logical distinction between "discretion" and "non-discretion." The personal tyranny of a Genghis Khan might be even less horrible than automatically-meted out mass-death in a gas chamber.

IV. A Sample of False Rules

A few examples may be chosen from the modern literature at random to illustrate how arbitrary become the rules of conduct deduced from anything but the most general of principles. First may be cited the excellent and straightforward fiscal policy programs of the CED.[7] Its requirement that government expenditure be scheduled for years ahead as a constant with respect to the business situation may or may not involve good strategy and lucky postwar forecasting, but it certainly is at variance with the general neo-classical principles here enunciated.

Or consider the following clear fiscal proposal:

A policy of determining the volume of government expenditures on goods and services—defined to exclude transfer expenditures of all kinds—entirely on the basis of the community's desire, need, and willingness to pay for public services. Changes in the level of expenditure should be made solely in response to alterations in the relative value attached by the community to public services and private consumption. No attempt should be made to vary expenditures, either directly or inversely, in response to cyclical fluctuations in business activity. Since the community's basic objectives would presumably change only slowly—except in time of war or immediate threat of war—this policy would, with the same exception, lead to a relatively stable volume of expenditures on goods and services.[8]

Now if there is any validity at all to the previous discussion of neo-classical doctrines, then it must be clear that the third of these four sentences does not follow from, and indeed is inconsistent with, a correct interpretation of the first two. If this contention be granted, the fourth of these sentences must also be very carefully qualified.

[7] See, for example, Committee for Economic Development (CED), *Taxes and the Budget; a Program for Prosperity in a Free Economy* (New York, CED, 1947).

[8] Milton Friedman, "A Monetary and Fiscal Framework for Economic Stability," *American Economic Review*, June 1948, XXXVIII, No. 3, p. 248. A qualifying footnote on the need to distinguish, when prices change, between constant real government expenditure and constant money expenditure has not been quoted.

No one can predict with certainty whether fluctuations in autonomous private investment will be sharp or mild in the years ahead or whether non-fiscal programs can be counted on to reduce their residual fluctuation down to a broad or narrow range; thus the neo-classical doctrine does not tell us whether the indicated optimal pattern of cyclical fluctuation of government expenditure will be sharp or mild. But that (1) there should be such a cyclical pattern is the contention of the neo-classical doctrine here outlined; and also that (2) its qualitative pattern should differ from the indicated cyclical pattern of transfer expenditures, tax collections, and fiscal-induced consumption expenditures *only* as income-elasticities and pragmatic administrative-political strategies decree, and not as a matter of basic economic principle— this, too, is implied by the neo-classical view.

The Rule of Marginal-Balance

The cited CED report has given a careful criticism of the rule of the annually-balanced budget, both in terms of principle and in terms of strategy designed to lower the secular level of government expenditure and of public inefficiency. Consequently, only a more sophisticated version of annual balancing need be discussed here. A group of American economists were called to Princeton in September 1949 by the Douglas-Flanders Congressional sub-committee on Monetary, Credit, and Fiscal Policies, and by the National Planning Association. The present author was one of the signers of an unanimous report dealing with certain general principles. One recommendation, I then felt and continue to feel, will not stand up under a too-literal interpretation. It may be called the principle of the "marginally-balanced budget" and may be quoted as follows:

... in conditions of continued prosperity, a modified version of the balanced budget rule could be used as a guide: taxes should grow or shrink corresponding to desired changes in expenditures. Thus proposed increases in expenditures would be exposed to the traditional test of whether they are worth their cost in terms of taxes.[9]

As a check against government extravagance, this appears to me to be if anything too weak. The electorate and their representatives should apply more stringent tests to proposed expenditure than that

[9] "University Economists' Statements on Fiscal Policy," Princeton, September 16–18, 1949, reproduced in *A Collection of Statements submitted to the Subcommittee on Monetary, Credit and Fiscal Policies of the Joint Committee by Government Officials, Bankers, Economists and Others*, 81st Congress, 1st Session, November 7, 1949 (Washington, U. S. Government Printing Office, 1949), p. 437.

new money tax revenues can be found to match them: they must ask themselves whether the particular expenditure-tax pattern implied represents the way the nation wants to divide up its resources between private consumption and public services. Such an obvious point few would question. Less obvious is the fact that matching extra expenditure by equal dollars of tax revenues is almost certain to leave an inflationary bias in the combined program. [Briefly the reasons for this are as follows: suppose the government takes an extra $10 billion of resources for cold war or European recovery purposes. If employment is already full and if we are to avoid inflation, private expenditure on resources must contract by the full $10 billion. But so long as the private marginal-propensity-to-*spend* (MPS), is less than one, we must obviously reduce private disposable income by taxes of *more than* $10 billion—in fact by approximately $10 billion/MPS.]

To fiscal specialists, this is an obvious modification. Nonetheless, I am not fond of a "marginally-balanced budget" principle even when reworded to take account of its inflationary bias. It is bad public housekeeping to keep on old and no longer wanted public projects just because the tax revenues are conveniently forthcoming to pay for them. A policy of bracketing expenditure programs with specific tax proposals is both unsound in principle and has worked badly in practice. I am left, therefore, with the following statement of principle, which to some may sound simply as if I am against sin, but which to me seems to be the only theoretically defensible one:

Avoid "taxation by inflation" until you have exhausted all better taxes, which probably means almost indefinitely; remember that the primary function of taxes is to bring about a release of command over resources in what is regarded as an optimal and equitable pattern, and that in practice no perfect tax is likely to be found completely without "dead-weight-loss" distorting effects on incentives, production, and consumption. Hence, there is all the more reason to scrutinize carefully *all* government expenditure programs—old, new, and newly proposed—to see whether they are worth their real costs and are being obtained in the cheapest and most efficient manner.

Still further examples of the dangers that lurk as soon as one leaves the realm of fundamental principle can be culled from the very stimulating essay on fiscal policy contributed to the American Economic Association sponsored *A Survey of Contemporary Economics*.[10]   While

[10] See H. S. Ellis, ed., *A Survey of Contemporary Economics* (Philadelphia, The Blakiston Company, 1948), Arthur Smithies, "Federal Budgeting and Fiscal Policy," Ch. 5, pp. 174–209.

the tax canons of A. Smithies include notable improvements over those of A. Smith, even so fine a theorist and judicious a public servant seems to me to have laid down rules for action that clash with what I understand to be sound neo-classical doctrine. After giving a brief but able discussion of that doctrine on pp. 192–193, on the very next page Smithies goes on to argue that the level of long-run government expenditure should be determined in formal correspondence with the CED's "stabilizing budget."[11] By this Smithies means the following:

The long-run policy would determine tax yields and expenditures at high levels of employment and income when no compensating action is required to offset deflationary and inflationary influences in the private sector of the economy.

This policy would be subject only to gradual change . . . (p. 194).

I should like to avoid discussing here the administrative device of distinguishing between the long and short run by means of an "extraordinary budget." Except for the purpose of propaganda and window-dressing, I suspect that such a device will either be meaningless or, even worse, will serve to create a situation like that prevailing in the 1930's: at the same time that important regular agencies of the government, like the Bureau of Standards, were being ruthlessly and foolishly squeezed in an attempt to present an economy normal budget, Hopkins was vying with Ickes to see who could first spend a billion dollars. Two pools of money with widely differing net utilities at the margin violates all rational principles of allocation.[12]

But let me avoid this whole problem by considering the ideal situation where employment could be considered not to undergo short-run variations around a long-term high level. I would consider it most unwise to try to forecast for years ahead just what the composition of such a full-employment income might be. There are no stable investment propensities, nor consumption propensities either for that matter,

[11] But with a difference, not relevant to the present criticism, in that Smithies does not try to decide in advance, as the CED does, on a target budgetary surplus for years of high employment.

[12] But this is not to suggest that in every depression I would expand such agencies as the Bureau of Standards to whatever level would be suggested by an attempt to equalize the *short-run* marginal utilities of different kinds of expenditure. Rather would I advocate departing from a double budget in the direction of triple-, quadruple-, and thousand-fold set of criteria, in which each of the thousands of government projects would have to be considered in terms of the resource commitments *of every time-period* that might be involved and in terms of implicit and explicit estimates of future alternatives. Naturally, such calculations or deliberations are not properly to be summarized in any accounting statement such as the budget. Still they cannot be avoided; if not made explicitly, they will be made implicitly.

that, together with any general notions about the electorate's preferences between private goods and public services, tell us much about
what the proper level of government expenditure should be. Our
problem has been rephrased and not answered. As rapidly as private
investment demand fluctuates in its total, as rapidly as the electorate
changes its mind as to its rate of indifference between ordinary consumption and ordinary public services, as rapidly as the polls show
reversals in sentiment with respect to economy-mindedness among
the voters, as rapidly as the exigencies of the cold war and the foreign
situation change, then so too must government expenditure change—
and all this regardless of any stabilization motivation in government
programs.

Capital Operations of Government

While upon close examination, any apparent similarity between
Smithies and the CED-Friedman view concerning government expenditure programs is seen to be non-existent,[13] let me in passing use
two other dicta in the Smithies essay as an introduction to the vital
problem of determining how the stabilization function shall be divided
between fiscal policy and such other policies as monetary policy.

The first dictum says: The conventional view that public investment
projects should be financed by loans rather than taxes is incorrect, as
is the view that loans made to private business by the government are
to be financed by loans rather than taxes.

This is a somewhat startling break with tradition, much more so
than the second related dictum which fits in well with prevailing
fashions of opinion. This second dictum may be quoted as follows:

Should reserves be accumulated now to avoid raising taxes in the future
when old-age payments increase as the population grows older? . . .

To this question our analysis gives an unqualified negative. The accumulation of a cash reserve is itself deflationary. To offset it, either government
expenditures must be increased or other taxes must be lowered. The disburse-
ment of the reserve would in itself be inflationary. To avoid the inflation,
taxes would then have to be increased or expenditures reduced. In fact, the
budgetary situation would be the same as it would have been if the reserve
had never been accumulated. Thus, there is no justification for distorting the
budget in order to make possible the accumulation of the reserve in the first
place. (p. 198)

[13] Cf. *National and International Measures for Full Employment* (Lake Success, New
York, United Nations, 1949), drafted by Smithies and four other experts for a more positive
statement on the proper role of expenditure.

I personally am inclined to think that it was a good move to abandon the original social security program of an actuarially-determined reserve fund in favor of a pay-as-you-go system; but in all fairness let me summarize the argument in favor of the former and compare it with the Smithies position.

Let us assume that in forty years or so the proportion of retired older workers will be greater than it is today and that between now and then these workers are willing to sacrifice some current consumption in favor of future consumption when retired. They, of course, cannot set up a fund of consumable goods and store it away in a deep-freeze chest; nor will a mere storing of money or securities in itself provide extra subsistence goods for the later period. But if current resources are shifted away from producing current consumption goods and are devoted to extra capital formation over and above what would otherwise have taken place, then forty years from now we shall end up with a larger stock of real capital goods. The net productivity of this capital stock will under the capitalistic system take the form of interest payments; within limits, even further consumption may be secured during the worker's period of retirement if the capital stock is deliberately allowed to run down, the resources for its replacement being channeled into consumption products.

In a well-running neo-classical system, something like this is supposed to happen in the realm of purely-private actuarially financed life insurance. The savings of young policyholders are channeled into bonds and equities. The counterpart of this is supposed to be an enhanced flow of real investment. In the future, the accumulated stock of real capital provides the real counterpart of the monetary interest earned by the reserve fund. And when the policyholders have become old, the fund is gradually depleted, either by sale of securities and passing on of going-concern investment projects to other age-groups or, if the total population is going downhill, by some degree of physical amortization of capital (within the limits made possible by technology).

If for the moment we assume a reasonably functioning system in which attempts to save are not allowed to become abortive through unemployment and limitation of investment, exactly the same thing could be expected to follow from a government reserve fund. The increased social security tax collections in the early years are in excess of the benefit outpayments, and it is assumed that this is not *made* the excuse to reduce other taxes or to expand beyond what would otherwise have been the level of other government expenditure. What will then have to be done with the surplus collected on account of social security? It matters not an iota whether Congress does or does not set up a reserve fund with bits of paper in it. But what does matter is that the proceeds are used to accomplish either of the following: a reduction of the actual public debt in the hands of the public (including commercial banks, etc.); or if not an absolute reduction of the debt, a reduction as compared to what would otherwise have been the case if the surplus tax collections had not taken place. Note that a substantive change has taken place, despite the confusions of those non-economists who are surprised to find government bonds and not cans of soup in the reserve fund, and who are surprised to learn that the taxes collected have already been "spent" by the government; and despite the primitive arithmetic of those who argue that the interest earned by the reserve fund in the distant future must really be paid by the Treasury out of then current taxes so that the fund has made no substantive difference.

Where Smithies differs from the orthodox analysis is very clear. He believes that the surplus of tax collections on social security account must induce unemployment if previously employment was just full; hence, this surplus will either be wiped out directly by changing old-age benefits or tax rates, or will have to be offset by tax reductions or expenditure increases elsewhere. Hence, no real fund of capital formation will be created, and no genuine financial fund will be created over and above what would otherwise have been the net creditor-debtor position of the government.

For the moment Smithies is making a strong non-classical assumption that all capital formation is perfectly fixed and will not be affected by the social security financing.[14]

I am quite prepared to agree with Smithies that there are numerous institutional reasons for denying an extreme classical view in which all savings get automatically translated into real investment with no effects on unemployment. But I shall argue in favor of a neo-classical synthesis of classical Keynesian, and neo-Keynesian theories; in

---

[14] Except in deep-depression when the investment schedule is completely interest-inelastic and/or the Keynesian liquidity preference schedule is infinitely interest-elastic, Smithies' unqualified negative is a little too strong even in terms of Keynesian economics. The surplus on social security account with its financial counterpart of absolute or relative debt reduction and its real counterpart of a reduced level of private consumption can be expected to result in lower interest rates and some inducement of investment; as Lange has shown in his discussion of the optimum propensity to consume, we must set against this favorable effect on investment any unfavorable effects that result from a reduction in total consumption and employment.

terms of this synthesis, private investment demand cannot be taken as a constant, subject to negligible influence by monetary and other non-fiscal policies. I do not doubt that over the next forty years central bank policy and public debt-management—in short the financial-capital rather than current-fiscal operations of the government—can have very substantial effects on the availability of finance for investment and upon the total level of capital formation. A financial surplus on account of social security can thus be offset by measures which will increase private capital format on and thus provide the real capital counterpart of the financial reserve financing. Moreover, a substantial amount of capital formation is in the public rather than private sphere, so that we can in effect prepay part of the far future's expenses of government by advancing the date of construction of public projects, and we can also count on the increased net productivity of such projects to help provide or to release the resources needed to provide consumption goods for the retired aged. I would, nonetheless, agree with Smithies that all this can be done, if desired, without invoking the mechanism or paraphernalia of an actuarial social security reserve.

But now let me return to the first Smithies dictum that government capital formation ought always to be financed in the same way as current services consumed by the government. This too follows from his assumption that private investment is a constant, and that both private investment and consumption cannot be substantially influenced by monetary and debt operations of the government; consequently there is no way for resources currently being used in the private sector to be attracted into the public sector to be used on investment projects yielding future public services—there is no way via the structure of interest rates, public borrowing, central bank operations, but only the one way of using tax increases to release the needed resources.

I imagine that most economists today, including Smithies, would no longer be so pessimistic as he was in the immediate postwar period concerning the impotence or unfeasibility of monetary policy to reinforce or counteract short-run fiscal policy.[15] But in any case we are

---

[15] Smithies (*Survey of Contemporary* . . . , *op. cit.*, p. 208) then said: "In the field of compensatory action I believe fiscal policy must shoulder most of the load. Its chief rival, monetary policy, seems to be disqualified on institutional grounds. This country appears to be committed to something like the present low level of interest rates on a long-term basis. There is not much room for reductions to alleviate depressions and it seems generally agreed that with the national debt at its present size, any appreciable increase in rates would cause serious financial disorders." It is clear that this is intended to apply only to the short-run cyclical stabilization aspect of the problem and not to the long-run aspects of fiscal policy.

almost all agreed that over the long run, monetary policy has considerable leverage in helping to determine the mix of high-employment
national product between consumption and investment goods of
different categories, and that fiscal policy need not take as ultimate
data quantitatively predetermined deflationary or inflationary gaps.
We must not forget that both the problems of social security finance
and of government capital formation have most important *long-run*
aspects. According to the neo-classical doctrines here enunciated, it is
not assumed that under any-old spontaneous banking arrangements
the classical assumptions underlying the Say's Law of Markets will be
valid. But it is assumed that central banking policy and debt management can be relied on to have substantial effects on private investment
decisions, and in the direction of substantially vitiating the novel
dicta under review.

Optimal Reliance on Monetary v. Fiscal Policy

This opens up an important question. What are the principles by
which a neo-classical economist is to determine the optimal mix
between fiscal and monetary policies? I shall not enter upon this
problem here in any detail, but it is obvious that some general considerations can be laid down. It depends in part upon the degree to
which we think that the cyclical fluctuations in effective demand are
irrationally aggravated by moods of pessimism and optimism and fail
to reflect the true "worthwhileness" (somehow defined) of capital
formation to the community; in part upon the nature of the preferences between time-periods that individuals do express in their
consumption-savings habits; and in part according to the weight that
the people as a whole democratically care to give to the claims of the
present generation and the future.

In any case an explicit or implicit decision will have to be made. To
let a secular trend of inflation do the deciding is not to avoid a decision;
to let the cumulative "wealth effects" of past changes in the volume of
currency and government bonds bring about the desired level of average saving is not to avoid a decision. One of the features which I like
least about the various rules of thumb and automatic mechanisms that
have been put forward is their arbitrary and implicit resolution of this
problem, which according to my neo-classical views should be resolved
in terms of ultimate ends and not at the level of means and devices.[16]

[16] Thus to gear monetary policy rigidly to fiscal policy according to a one-to-one gear
ratio has no *a priori* merits in principle: I should prefer to see the gear-ratio be 1.99 or 3.33,

In short, what the Bureau of the Budget needs is an Arthur Smithies and not his will and testament of rules of thumb. Unless based on general principles, these will go out of date very rapidly and not lead to optimal behavior or even be conducive toward tolerably adequate strategic compromises. And when stated in general terms, all principles turn out to be a set of procedures for asking the right questions and concentrating on the right considerations rather than slide-rule formulas for pre-fabricated optimal decisions.

V. Conclusion

In my judgment the most devastating case that can be made against the search for convenient rules-of-thumb of fiscal policy lies in the various rules that have been currently proposed. As soon as one leaves the realm of general principle and attempts to write down cook-book prescriptions, the result seems to be dicta that will not stand up under careful examination: either they turn out to be empty or they turn out to be arbitrary.[17]

not only to call attention to the arbitrariness, but also to show that under certain implicit forecasts of the years ahead this will lead to a more efficient and sensible stabilization program. Better still, I would not attempt to prejudge the nature of the tasks ahead by fixing upon any one gear-ratio, nor would I outlaw a determination of monetary policy in part on considerations other than fiscal policy. Even if I were to accept the unwise assignment of designing a servomechanism which automatically created surpluses in inflation and deficits in depression and which depended upon cumulations in these algebraic magnitudes to result in changes in the community's total financial wealth so as to have, via the "Pigou effect," a stabilizing influence on total employment and prices, I would have to determine and defend its constants in terms of a specific forecast as to the future load that the servomechanism is likely to bear. As compared to a mechanism that held tax collections constant as income changes, a servomechanism that causes a $\frac{1}{4}$ change in taxes for every unit change in income, might be defended as preventing about one half of the unemployment created in the short run by an unoffset new reduced plateau of investment. If slow changes of the sort described could be expected in the future, it would be hard to justify the 50 per cent of residual unemployment that remains in the short run. True one might argue that over the long run, the Pigou effect of the cumulated deficit might in $n = 10$, 1 or 100 years wipe out half the residual unemployment and in another n years wipe out half of what remained, etc., but that is cold comfort. One would be strongly tempted in the case considered to step up the "gain" of the servomechanism. But this would be done at the peril of getting too fast an over-response in a situation where investment is varying rapidly. Precisely because of the uncertainties of our forecasting abilities we cannot rely upon automatic mechanisms with constant coefficients! This is the reverse of the usual view, and I base it on the fact that the optimum "constant coefficients" of the mechanism (the marginal propensity to tax, the marginal propensity to extinguish currency when the budget runs a $1 surplus, etc.) cannot rationally be decided in advance of what the future may bring.

[17] Regarded as discretionary programs, most of the automatic mechanisms put forward turn out to have a detailed arbitrary quantitative structure which would be optimal in only one out of an infinity of conditions; instead of obviating any need for forecasting, such mechanisms are premised on certain *implicit* forecasting and knowledge assumptions. They are to be appraised in terms of whether or not they are truly the lesser evil as compared with alternatives.

Their real appeal to economists does not reside in their economic validity so much as in the success they may have in countering the great modern myth of our time that voters can afford to expand government activities without considering their costs. I am prepared to believe that those people may be correct who hold that rational principles will not succeed in countering the myth of costless government expenditure as successfully as will some newly-created myth. But I am inclined to doubt that the professional economist has much of a comparative advantage in myth countering. And so he may, with better conscience, resign himself to the prosaic pastimes of empirical and logical inference.

99

Full Employment versus Progress and Other Economic Goals

BY PAUL A. SAMUELSON

I. INTRODUCTION

Full employment is an important goal; but it is not the only goal of modern economic society. We all wish for men to be employed rather than idle; but we also wish for them to be employed at useful tasks and under conditions of personal freedom. We wish for our parents to enjoy old-age security beyond that enjoyed by our grandparents; but we also profess to desire for our children a standard of living beyond any we have known. Attacks on the rights of property and on gross inequality in the distribution of wealth and income seem to elicit resonant responses in modern democracies; at the same time, our mixed system of private and public enterprise does require incentives to elicit human efforts and it does still depend upon pecuniary profits and losses to organize the bulk of economic activity.

Suppose economic science were more exact than it is, so that all experts could agree in prescribing a legislative package to abolish unemployment; and even suppose that good will among men were to overcome partisan and class differences, so that the American people, through Congress, were willing to buy this legislative package. Would a new Utopia on earth then follow? The answer is, obviously, no.

If anyone doubts this, he need only look at many countries of western Europe, such as Britain. In the postwar period such countries have had to worry about almost every conceivable economic problem except that of job shortages. They have been concerned with the low volume of imports that can be bought for their exports and with the virtual disappearance of their prewar investment income from abroad. They have been concerned with the problem of increasing the efficiency of manufacturing industry and with the need to increase their defensive strength. And this is only the beginning of a long list of basic economic difficulties other than those raised by depression unemployment.

I think it no exaggeration to say that for a dozen or more years following 1930 economists were obsessed with the problem of full employment. Probably this was only as it should have been. In time of plague one does not worry about sunburn nor even about senescence. But any single one note—whatever its quality and timbre—if held a long time becomes a little offensive to the ear. It was only to be expected, therefore, that many people should have begun to be a little bored with the continuous discussion of employment policy, particularly during the war and postwar years when the demand for labor seemed almost insatiable. And there is still another understandable reason for suspicion of full employment policies. For many years reform legislation of all kinds—social security, farm aid, etc.—has been advanced not only for its own sake but also in the name of full employment and as a device to bolster purchasing power. It is ironical that the argument used against the early New Deal—which asserted the opposition between reform and recovery—should in the end have been displaced by the opposite political allegation which tried to claim that reform was necessary for full employment.

The present chapter is concerned with one central theme: What are the relationships between employment stabilization policies and other goals of economic life? Does job security go hand in hand with technical progress, the one reinforcing the other? Or is the price of full employment some sacrifice in our rate of material progress? Does the twentieth-century democratic demand for so-called "greater equity" as between rich and poor subtract from, or contribute to, the growth of productivity? Will continued full employment strengthen us in case of war, or will it provide an extra obstacle to be overcome in some future political emergency? These are all complex issues that will become increasingly pressing as we succeed in maintaining high employment. To the extent that we fail in this goal, to the extent that mass unemployment prevails, these questions will be treated as academic and will be shelved in the face of an insistent political demand for governmental action.

II. Full Employment and Other Short-Run Goals

1. *Full employment, in itself, bad?*

The arguments against a full employment stabilization program are numerous and of varying quality. There are enough sound objections and enough real dilemmas of national policy to permit us to dismiss summarily a number of the more extreme and foolish viewpoints that have received expression in past years. Only in this way can we hope to clear the air for a consideration of the more thoughtful and rational doubts that have been expressed.

First we may dismiss the ascetic view that unemployment causing adversity and suffering is a good thing in itself. Such arguments carried considerable weight in nineteenth-century discussions of the poor laws, but they only injure the cause of those who advance them today. Congressional oratory, newspaper editorials, sermons and encyclicals, and the expressed votes of the electorate at poll after poll all clearly indicate that the American people are against unemployment. They apparently do not take seriously the argument that with plentiful job opportunities the family will be weakened, as women (and youths) are called out of the home. Just as the public is "agin sin" it is against unemployment.

2. *Effects on productivity*

There is a second, less crude, argument that deserves more consideration. Suppose that public policies do succeed in maintaining high employment levels so that any qualified person looking for a job can hope to find a reasonably good opening in not too long a time. What will happen to labor turnover and to factory discipline and productivity when workers no longer need fear being thrown into long-term unemployment and onto relief or worse?

In advancing the argument that unemployment is needed to police workers' willingness to do an honest day's work, extreme conservatives are often unknowingly repeating the thesis of communist critics of the capitalistic system. One of the central tenets of Marxism has always been the belief that a "reserve army of the unemployed" is absolutely necessary to the functioning of a profit system. As observers we may chuckle, but as analysts we cannot reject a view simply because of its bipolar sponsorship. The contention that unemployment may be good for productivity merits careful examination.

At the beginning we must be clear on one thing. This is not particularly an attack on government-created full employment. If valid it is an attack on full employment itself, and it scores a point against the desirability of a "new era" of spontaneous prosperity sustained by private enterprise just as much as it does against an era of publicly created prosperity. Again, this is not to deny the possible validity of the view under examination.

a. LABOR MOBILITY

On the face of it, I think it reasonable to expect higher voluntary labor turnover on the part of workers when they know the penalty of quitting a job is not likely to be long-time unemployment. And to some extent this is certainly an evil, an economic cost whose value must be measured

in terms of lower realized national output. But labor mobility and turnover is not an unmixed evil. One of the attributes of the good life is
variety and change; when a worker changes jobs his pay is interrupted,
but who is to say that (in moderation) this is not an acceptable way
for him to spend his available income? More than that, we know from
studies of geographical labor markets that much of labor turnover is
among the very young; and it is by means of shopping around and by
trial and error that the youthful entrants to the labor force finally settle
down into their suitable niches.

Full employment is blamed for causing too high labor mobility. It is
also blamed for causing too little! Thus an inventor who wishes to set
up a factory to produce a new product is supposed to be unable in
prosperous times to recruit a labor force for this worth-while purpose.
Likewise the flexibility of the system in adjusting to changing tastes and
conditions is believed to be impaired by full employment.

Implicit in all this is the hidden premise that high or full employment
necessarily means a "seller's market" for labor. Must this always be so?
When there is a high demand and supply for wheat, we do not regard
it as impossible for a new baker to buy extra wheat for some new
purpose. Of course his need (and his pecuniary ability) must be great
enough to enable him to bid away wheat from other uses. Likewise,
under conditions of full employment, any one enterprise should be able
to draw labor from other uses, provided it can offer sufficiently attractive working conditions and wages. It would be an uneconomic use of
limited national resources to keep pools of manpower or equipment
idle on the off-chance that some worthy innovator might like to use them
in his experimental promotions. This would clearly involve a hidden
subsidy to such activities, perhaps an excessive one in terms of economic cost and efficiency. If we do want to adopt a national policy of
providing subsidies to pioneering activities, let us do so with our eyes
wide open, knowing what costs we are incurring and not throwing the
burden on the groups least able to afford them, namely, the families of
the unemployed.[1] Policies designed to aid retraining and mobility of
labor come to mind at once in this connection.

My preceding paragraphs do not meet squarely the contention that,
while full employment policies do not *necessarily* mean a seller's market
for labor (in which it becomes almost impossible for any one employer
to expand his working force even if he has the money to meet an ex-

---

1. This raises the whole problem of our patent system, antitrust policies, regulation of capital flotations, Reconstruction Finance Corporation programs, and general credit and tax policies.

panded payroll), nonetheless full employment policies as pursued in many countries are in fact likely to lead to conditions of "repressed inflation." Indeed one leading exponent of such policies, Lord Beveridge, the author of *Full Employment in a Free Society*, has declared it as a goal of action that there be reached so high a level of monetary demand as to require direct price and output controls; and critics of European labor governments have sometimes alleged that there have been cases where factories have been completed only to find that no labor could be recruited for them.

I conclude that there is considerable force in the argument that we are here faced with something of a dilemma in our choice between 1) full employment and 2) price-wage stabilization. But this problem has been explored by other writers in this symposium and I shall for the most part neglect it in my discussion, interpreting my task to be that of appraising the costs of a successful two-sided stabilization program that guards against inflation as well as deflation.[2]

b. WORKER MORALE AND PRODUCTIVITY

Let me return to the problem of factory discipline and productivity. All of us are familiar with the more extreme examples of union featherbedding and make-work rules: limited-size paint brushes, stand-by musicians, etc. But it appears that even the experts in the field of labor economics cannot make up their minds on the *net* effects of unionization on productivity.[3] It is still harder to form an estimate of the relationship of full employment to productivity. Pretty clearly, some forms of work slowdowns grow out of a fear on the part of the workers that if they are "eager-beavers" they will quickly work themselves and their fellows out of a job. Good, plentiful employment opportunities can be expected, over time, to lessen this motive for such harmful practices; the growth of mass unemployment, on the other hand, can be expected to intensify such practices.

In the past workers were stimulated to put forth effort and skill by holding out wage incentives and by prodding them with the threat of discharge. From a hard-boiled production standpoint, no one has been able to work out the optimal combination of rewards and penalties, of carrots and kicks. Relaxed men may fall asleep; tense, frightened men may be equally poor producers. Psychologists and sociologists who have studied the modern factory place great emphasis—under present-

2. See Chapter 11 for discussion of the wage-price spiral problem.
3. See S. H. Slichter, *The Challenge of Industrial Relations* (Ithaca, Cornell University Press, 1947).

day conditions—upon factors of morale and teamwork and upon non-pecuniary aspects of the workers' environment.[4]

One further relationship between full employment and productivity deserves investigation. Unionization has grown in importance over the past years but it is still far short of covering all of American industry. Does full employment contribute to or work against the growth of this important but controversial institution? No pat answer can be given. Generally the historical record seems to show that expanding business conditions are good for the growth of unionization and depressions are bad. The two world wars, with their accompanying "overfull employment," represent high-water marks of organized labor; and in our more distant past depressions were associated with recessions in unions' strength and influence. Still, the prosperity era of the 1920's represents a major (and perhaps unrepeatable) exception; organized labor lost ground in those years. It is significant that in the years of expansion following 1932 organized labor, with the aid of new government attitudes, made its greatest peacetime advance; perhaps it is no less significant that the period 1933–36 was also one in which, although there was strong recovery from the depression trough, there still remained a sizable amount of unemployment.[5]

C. STABILIZATION AND GOOD MANAGEMENT

Labor productivity is in many ways a misleading concept. It tends to distract our attention from the important factors, other than personal attitudes and skills of workers, that are responsible for more or less efficient production. To the extent that continued high employment results in sellers' markets and protects business from the pinch of adversity, there may be a gradual relaxation of effort on the part of management and a slackening or slowing down of productivity improvements. Needless to say, such an outcome is not inevitable since, even with general demand being continuously maintained, there may still be such vigorous competition from rivals that productivity is kept up to par. Moreover, to the extent that costs rise and prices are held down by direct controls or other rigidities, there is a great incentive for management to introduce cost-saving methods. From the historical evidence we cannot be sure that there have been *any* significant differences in productivity growth during good and bad times.

Stabilization of business activity should carry with it some improve-

---

4. The pioneering work of Elton Mayo, Fritz J. Roethlisberger, and other Harvard Business School workers may be cited.

5. See Horace B. Davis, "The Theory of Union Growth," *Quarterly Journal of Economics*, 55 (August, 1941), 611–637.

ments in productivity even if management and worker attitudes are not particularly favorable. Stop and go production is expensive production. The fear of a decline in markets often prevents firms from using methods which would be extremely productive in turning out steady streams of output. This explains why many firms on their own initiative engaged in internal stabilization programs which guaranteed a certain continuity of employment and wages to their workers.[6] A quite similar favorable effect on productivity results from the fact that if borrowers and lenders did not have to fear sudden precipitous declines in business activity, the risks of capital formation would be greatly reduced, thereby making it possible for firms to use a more efficient amount of capital.

It should be noted that many of the points discussed in the last few paragraphs are more crucially affected by the stabilization of business activity than by the quantitative level of employment and output at which stabilization takes place. Thus, if we were to forego the target of full employment, replacing it instead by the goal of holding steadily to some 5 or 10% level of unemployment, many of the favorable effects on productivity would still take place. Too often stabilization of activity and maintenance of full employment are treated as if they were synonymous.

No final evaluation of the relationships between full employment and productivity can be attempted here. On balance I am inclined to the view that there are some net losses of potential productivity that must be charged against such a program and that perhaps these costs increase at an accelerated rate as we try to squeeze out the last little drop of extra employment from our system. Much research remains to be done in this area and other observers may, quite properly, read the record in the opposite way. Furthermore, the costs I have mentioned can perhaps be expected to become less important in the future and possibly even to reverse their net direction. Collective bargaining seems here to stay; when full employment has helped to unionize an industry it cannot unionize it again, and further full employment may help to make the unions "mature" and "responsible." In the future, gentle prods rather than the whiplash of chronic unemployment may be the better part of wisdom in handling the human animal.

Nor should we forget that man does not live by bread alone. High scores in productivity are not the sole ends of the good life. We do not

6. There is a voluminous literature on guaranteed annual wage plans of the Procter & Gamble or Hormel type. See *Guaranteed Wages*, Report to the President by the Advisory Board of the Office of War Mobilization and Reconversion, January 31, 1947, for references and discussion.

tell the American people they are wrong in taking out part of the historical increases in productivity in the form of shorter working weeks and more leisure. Similarly, we cannot say nay to the American worker if he wishes to give up something of material goods in exchange for working at a slower pace and enjoying greater independence and personal dignity on the job. The difficulty is to make sure that the worker is in fact getting something commensurate with his sacrificed output, and is not simply frustrating his instincts of craftsmanship in return for senseless bravado. Moreover, there may be dangers to traditional middle-class values in a worker-dominated society.

3. *Effects on total output*

Whatever the net effects are of a tight labor market on productivity of people on the job, they should not be confused with the changes in total output that will result from full employment. More people on the job should, other things being equal, result in larger total output available for current consumption or capital formation. Longer hours per week should have the same effect. In addition, there is the more subtle effect of upgrading of people into better jobs, this being the reverse effect of "disguised unemployment" that results from depressed levels of total effective demand. In prosperity marginal farm laborers leave the country for higher-productive city jobs. Door-to-door salesmen can give up the attempt to make a bare living at what is too often not very productive work by any criterion. And similarly with other examples of disguised unemployment.

Since increased employment may itself affect productivity, the percentage changes in output may be greater or less than the changes in employment. To the extent that the people brought into employment are qualitatively inferior, the resulting change in output may be expected to be less than proportional to the change in people or total man-hours. To the extent that short-run bottlenecks of full plant capacity are encountered short of the point of full employment, the law of diminishing returns may also be operative; and to the extent that natural resources are limited, this short-run effect may be carried over even into the indefinitely long run.

On the other hand, there is a possible countertendency in the form of increasing returns to scale: by "spreading overhead factors" and overcoming "indivisibilities" of productive organization, increased employment may actually result in increases rather than decreases in productivity. Again the statistical record is not clear. We cannot isolate the effects of employment changes from other concomitant variations. The statistical data, such as they are, do not seem to indicate any clear-cut tendency toward diminishing returns during upswings in the business cycle; if the recent wartime indexes of production could be taken seriously, the possibilities of the countertendency toward increasing returns would have to be taken seriously. Particularly must we recognize the "upgrading" that comes with expansions so that, even if productivity in each occupation were constant, average productivity for the community would rise because of shifts from low productivity jobs to high.

The existence of increasing returns can create some difficulties for the theoretical economists' vision of perfect competition—since it is often under these conditions that competition becomes "ruinous" and monopoly firms tend to drive out competitors. On the whole, depressions make this worse and full employment may help keep competition viable by so increasing the level of total demand as to permit a larger number of effective competitors to remain in the industry.

Our findings with respect to the problem of this section can be briefly summarized: *higher employment probably means higher output,* but not necessarily in the same degree. There is no conclusive evidence as to whether long-run returns of output would be in greater than or less than proportion to the increase in total man-hours worked. As to effects on progress, this will be discussed in the latter half of this chapter.

4. *Full employment and our national security strength*

We live in troubled times. Great interest attaches to the economic sinews of war. Would full employment increase or decrease our defensive and offensive strength in the next war years? The question of our *long-run* military strength—or economic war potential—is closely related to the question of our long-run rate of economic progress and may be deferred to a later section; but discussion of the short-run aspects belongs here.

An economist cannot pretend to give an expert opinion on some of the intangible political aspects of the question. Would mass unemployment help the growth of communism in America and lessen the fighting morale of our armed services and civilian labor force? Would it contribute to radical legislation having no immediate relation to recovery and that would be weakening to our productive system?

To some extent the answer to the first of these questions, I should suppose, must be yes. But it is probably *sudden* deterioration in people's economic position that causes them to be disappointed and to seek desperate solutions. If failure to achieve full employment were to mean that in the next few years we were to slip undramatically behind our true economic potential with the situation being glossed over by shorter hours and unemployment compensation of one form or another, the dangers to our democracy may perhaps have been exaggerated in the discussions of recent years. I question whether our democratic system is quite so fair-weather a flower as some have come to regard it. But undoubtedly failure to maintain high employment will involve important noneconomic costs of this character. Moreover, the rest of the world's opinion of us and of our way of life would be seriously blackened if we were to succumb to a great depression.

There is an opposing argument, according to which unemployment actually adds to the military potential of a nation. It used to be said that Hitler was fortunate to have come into power at the bottom of the depression, because this enabled him to syphon off the subsequent increase in German output almost entirely into war preparations. (Recent data made available by surveys of the German war effort show that consumption in Germany grew more after 1933 than it was fashionable for us then to believe, but this does not refute the point.) By the same token the war effort of the United States was considered to be helped after 1940 by the fact that we then still had eight million unemployed who could be moved into the war effort. This enabled us to have extra guns *and* extra butter; had employment been full, we should, according to this argument, have been forced to give up civilian goods for war products. A popular present-day extension of this type of reasoning leads to the conclusion that if war should break out in an atmosphere of full employment, such as prevailed in the early 1950's, consumption would have to be cut instantly and sharply.

On the factual side this last conclusion overlooks important hidden buffers of manpower in the American economy. These result from the fact that, as compared with other nations and with war conditions, we Americans work, even under full employment conditions, a small number of hours per week or year; and only a relatively small number of Americans of working age are normally in the working force. Simply by working longer hours and by having women, youths, and the aged return to the labor force, according to the pattern of World War II, we could substantially expand our military use of resources without cutting down on consumption. The further fact that consumers' and producers' durable goods are such an important part of the American economy makes possible an additional expansion in our war effort without any great reduction in *current* consumption of the *services* of those durable goods by final consumers or by producers.

Aside from being factually misleading, the view that unemployment actually improves our military potential is theoretically weak in the following respect. It is probably not easier or quicker to transfer an unemployed worker (say, in Detroit) from the relief rolls to war work than it is to transfer him from a peacetime job making automobiles to a wartime job making tanks. When employed, he has not evaporated away and been made unavailable for war purposes. Under modern conditions we must convert *whole enterprises* to military production; and it is perhaps easier to do this when people are attached to productive employment than when their skills are rotting in idleness. When total demand is depressed, it is employment in the durable goods trades that suffers most; and it is peculiarly these trades which, when they are in operation, can be regarded as stand-by military resources. The present argument is only strengthened when we add to these manpower considerations the fact that our plant capacities and inventories of goods and skills are likely to be more favorable for war purposes after a period of high rather than low employment. Undoubtedly our high levels of civilian production of steel and durables in the 1945–50 postwar period added to our strength to meet the post-Korean challenge.[7]

Starting out from full employment rather than depression, we are able to reach as high or higher a level of military strength (compatible with the same level of minimum civilian consumption). But in moving to this wartime position from a full employment starting point, it is indisputable that we appear to be giving up more of civilian consumption, investment, and governmental goods than if we were to move to that same position from a starting point of mass unemployment. In the latter cases we give up, so to speak, the goods we have been wasting in idleness.

People probably strive harder to maintain the consumption levels that they have already been enjoying than they do to reach levels they have never known. Here lies the essential truth in the view that unemployment makes it easier to run a war. Depression does not really add to our war potential, but it may put us in the frame of mind where we are more willing to make the civilian sacrifices necessary to reach that full potential.

For example, suppose that America and her allies need very heavy defensive military expenditures. If there should be heavy unemployment in the next few years, Congress and the people might be more willing to approve these necessary expenditures than they would if the civilian demand for goods is extremely brisk. Moreover, since need is a relative thing, this would be a rational decision, because the alternative needs

7. It should be admitted that high production does create problems in connection with the more rapid depletion of exhaustible resources such as copper, nickel, oil, etc.

for capital formation would be exercising a correspondingly smaller pull. Undoubtedly, high employment in western Europe complicates the problem of quickly building up effective defense programs.

Related to the problem of getting people to give up resources to a postulated war need, there is the problem of getting them to do so in a manner that will minimize inflation and the need for stringent price or fiscal controls. The problem of maintaining financial stability and preventing inflation will probably be more difficult if we start out our war program from a position of full employment. Having experienced rising prices recently, people are less likely to save voluntarily so large a fraction of their expanded money incomes; they probably will not respond so fully to patriotic drives to increase thrift and bond purchases; possibly the excess income which they cannot spend because of rationing and direct controls will not pile up so peacefully and harmlessly in the form of savings but instead will exert greater pressures on black markets and the enforceability of direct controls.

We may conclude that *full employment makes more difficult the problem of financing a war without inflation and undue controls,* and may increase the resistance of people within a democracy to endure austerity in the interests of the war effort. But these effects should not be confused, as they are in current discussions, with the view that depression unemployment actually boosts real war potential. The reverse is probably true, as we have seen.

5. *Full employment and proper use of all economic resources*

In my discussion up to this point, I have been able to take up the effects of stabilization policies in the abstract without having to go into the specific character of the public or private policies adopted to achieve full employment. To do justice to the question of whether such policies result in an inefficient pattern of labor and material resource use, our inquiry must become more specific: we must analyze the different effects of different possible employment programs on the wise allocation of economic resources.[8]

It is only too easy to imagine antidepression government program that do lead to a wasteful use of resources. Hiring people to dig holes and fill them up is a well-known example. During the worst years of depression and general despair, some people became so pessimistic as

8. There are of course many problems with which stabilization programs are not primarily concerned (e.g., monopoly, distressed areas, tariffs, quotas, etc.). It is remarkable how even these may be favorably affected by successful full employment programs (viz., our success during boom times in lowering tariffs, the almost miraculous impact of the war on distressed areas, etc.).

to think that governments had no other choice than to adopt such measures. They even defended such measures, arguing:

> Old-fashioned economists of the extreme "classical" persuasion have been talking palpable and patent nonsense for years. During the past century, when the world has gone through two score well-documented periods of boom and bust, these old fossils have been stubbornly denying that general overproduction is possible—that you can no more create or destroy purchasing power than you can create or destroy energy. This perverted form of the classical doctrine is not only logically erroneous but it is historically utter nonsense. Mass unemployment is a fact. The only cure is to "get purchasing power out" somehow; and for this purpose the government must find *by hook or crook* public work projects that will put people to work, and it must look for foreign markets upon which we can dump our exports and from whom we must stop buying goods. [So goes the argument.]

Of course this is a caricature of what may be called the *neomercantilist* doctrine—so named because it represents a return to the prenineteenth century views of the mercantilist writers who thought it important for people to work rather than to consume and to export goods rather than to import them. The neomercantilist view is as extreme and fallacious as the classical dogmas against which it is reacting. Careful students of economics are increasingly in agreement that our system is such as to permit us—by appropriate fiscal and monetary policies—to keep our resources from being wasted in mass unemployment, *and to do this in a great variety of alternative ways so as to yield almost any desired pattern of want fulfillment.*[9]

Specifically, we can make work by digging holes and filling them up, but why should we want to? We can pursue beggar-my-neighbor policies of foreign exchange depreciation and import controls. These may add to our total of domestic purchasing power; they may offer what appears to the worker to be useful work for his eager hands to do; they may even, from a narrow national viewpoint, seem preferable to a policy of do-nothing-at-all. But such policies—that get us nothing useful for our efforts and dollars—are demonstrably worse than alternatives that do have all the same favorable repercussions on total purchasing power and *also* give us useful public or private consumption and capital goods. There is nothing such despairing neomercantilist policies can do for us that an earthquake or a war catastrophe cannot do as well. If the people as a whole prefer private consumption goods to government public

9. See Chapters 5–9 for detailed discussion of alternative programs.

works, then we can fight mass unemployment by cutting taxes rather than by increasing public construction; we can improve the environment for venture capital; or we can expand welfare expenditure (such as social security, etc.), which will enlarge private consumption rather than government use of goods and services, if that is what is desired.

It took technical economists a decade to grasp this principle: *through a variety of such different actions, large-scale wastage of economic resources can be avoided, and the only sensible policy to be followed is that which yields the final pattern of production that a democratic people want.*

This may be called the neoclassical doctrine.[10] It, too, has been oversimplified in this exposition and should be qualified in a number of ways (e.g., there are problems of timing, of prediction, of wage-price spirals, of pressure groups, etc.). Within a framework of maintained high employment, the old and important classical problems of scarcity and economic cost and divergent group interests come into their own.

What does this rather optimistic viewpoint imply concerning the pattern of appropriate policies? The answer depends in part upon what the American people, as individuals and as interdependent citizens, really want. (To be sure none of us really knows his own mind completely, and we are all tempted to vote public projects whose true costs [11] to ourselves are not very apparent, since at the time we make our decision no down-payment may be exacted. On the other hand, we often neglect to carry out some public collective activities, which if we had them might seem worth while to most of us. A community can afford the governmental activities that it wants provided it is prepared to make the requisite sacrifices.)

The optimal policies also depend upon the choices open to us. For example, the desirable amount of public spending is a variable thing. If private investment opportunities happen to be very strong, so that many highly useful capital projects are crying to be done, most of us would consider it only prudent to contract the resources engaged in useful public activities. Correspondingly, when the pull of private capi-

10. By analogy with neomercantilism and not to be confused with the narrower neoclassical doctrine of pure theory. See my chapter in *Money, Trade, and Economic Growth: In Honor of John Henry Williams* (New York, Macmillan, 1951), entitled "Principles and Rules in Modern Fiscal Policy: A Neo-Classical Reformulation," for an elaboration of this neoclassical view. See also Chapter 8 of this book.

11. The exact nature of these costs cannot be expressed simply in terms of the tax dollars that one should raise in order to finance all or part of any given expenditure. We must also remember that no "neutral" tax system can ever be devised which will not "distort" production and consumption decisions; tax burdens of this kind must be considered as part of the cost of government outlay. See Chapter 6.

tal or consumption needs is relatively relaxed, the margin of desirable governmental use of resources should expand.[12] All this follows from the simple logic of rational choice and setting of priorities among alternatives.

The reader has missed the point of what I have called the neoclassical doctrine if he thinks that this boils down to the familiar notion that public works should be contracted in time of boom simply *in order to curb inflation* and expanded in depression simply *in order to stimulate purchasing power.* These are *not* the reasons for a countercyclical policy of government expenditure according to the neoclassical doctrine, since this already accepts it as axiomatic that deflation and inflation can be moderated by a variety of other devices. Except under highly special value standards, public works have no prior claim over other stabilization devices (such as variable tax collections and tax legislation). The only sound reason for justifying public works, or any other policies, is in terms of society's preference for the resulting pattern of output and resource use.

If this whole line of reasoning is acceptable—and I think it follows from traditional economic analysis—then we must raise our eyebrows at certain special prescriptions that have been popularized in recent years. I refer to the notion that while the total of the tax collections should vary anticyclically, the total of government expenditure should not be varied in this manner; and to the even more narrow dictum that *tax rates* should be kept constant over a long period of years, sole reliance for stabilization being placed on automatic variations in the taxes that will be collected out of varying national income. In principle, these are false guides to national policy—although occasionally there is something to be said for them on pragmatic grounds under special circumstances.[13]

12. If the reduction of private investment is due to "irrational" psychological expectations, there is a strong case for measures that expand private activity. Even if private investment is "genuinely" low, the gap it leaves should usually *not* be completely filled up by expansion of government expenditure, but rather by a mixture of extra private consumption and extra public expenditure.

13. The view that I am criticizing has been widely advocated in recent years. E.g., in the 1947 *Economic Report of the President* there is the statement (p. 40): ". . . we should attempt to stabilize public-works construction according to our long-term needs." Later this is qualified. See also Beardsley Ruml and H. C. Sonne, *Fiscal and Monetary Policy*, National Planning Association, Pamphlet No. 35 (1944) and *Taxes and the Budget: A Program for Prosperity in a Free Economy*, Committee on Economic Development (New York, 1948). In the following four-sentence quotation, the first two sentences are reasonably satisfactory, but the final two represent an illegitimate inference from the first two. ". . . government expenditures on goods and services . . . [should be determined] entirely on the basis of

6. *Some qualifications*

My optimistic account of the broad variety of paths to full employment must be realistically qualified. In a world subject to rapid unpredictable dynamic change, it would not be possible to act quickly enough to offset all upward and downward movements in output and prices, even if we should want to do so. Moreover, the repercussions of any governmental program are themselves distributed over time in a not completely predictable fashion, so that in trying to make a transient situation better we may actually make it worse. It is more realistic, therefore, to admit that short-run fluctuations of some amplitude are to be expected even in the face of a successful stabilization program. But mass unemployment and long-time deviations in one direction should be capable of being largely avoided if we are agreed to do so.

A second warning may be needed lest my exposition be misunderstood. Although our arsenal of antidepression measures is a broad one, it is not necessarily the case that in it are any weapons that achieve their purpose *without costs*. Even when we have picked those which, in terms of our set of ethical ends are least costly, there may still be an irreducible minimum of costs. Therefore, full employment itself must be regarded as one of many goals, and we must be prepared to pursue it only to the extent that the gains outweigh the costs. This means that the last ounce of high employment may be deemed not worth the sacrifices it would entail; and where high employment programs entail losses in other directions—such as private autonomy, incentives, growth, etc. —a calculation of alternative benefits is in order.

As a corollary of the above reminder, we must not reject any one antidepression measure solely because it entails some disadvantages: such a rejection would be rational only if there were a perfect alternative, and there is not. We must choose among the lesser of evils or among the greater of goods. When we reject a measure like boondoggling on the ground that a better measure is possible, we must be sure

the community's desire, need, and willingness to pay for public services. Changes in the level of expenditure should be made solely in response to alterations in the relative value attached by the community to public services and private consumption. No attempt should be made to vary expenditure, either directly or inversely, in response to cyclical fluctuations in business activity. Since the community's basic objectives would presumably change only slowly—except in time of war or immediate threat of war—this policy would, with the same exception, lead to a relatively stable volume of expenditure on goods and services." M. Friedman, "A Monetary and Fiscal Framework for Economic Stability," *American Economic Review*, 38 (June, 1948), 246. See my previously cited essay for further elaborations and also Chapter 8 of this volume.

that this better method is in fact being used and that the relevant political choice is not between a half-good measure and no action at all.

Most of the above qualifications refer to the problem of avoiding mass depression. Unfortunately the problem of inflation and the problem of deflation are not simple opposites: there is no simple algebraic 'flation problem. Inflation usually can be taken to mean generally rising prices; but deflation, in its most objectionable sense, is not simply a falling of prices but rather a general decline in output and employment.

Provided we can forestall a great slump from getting under way and cumulatively sending the system downward—and in my view this should be within our powers—the nature of the policies needed to fight general unemployment is fairly well understood. But our experiences in the last fifteen years suggest that the problem of maintaining reasonably steady prices is much more difficult than that of preventing mass unemployment. It is possible that whenever we attain enough steam in the purchasing power boiler to lead to high employment and to get rid of much disguised unemployment, we will encounter upward wage pushes on prices. Hence, under modern labor market conditions, perhaps we must choose between high employment and steady prices; perhaps we cannot have both.

This is the heart of the so-called wage-price problem and it presents us with a dilemma. If every upward thrust in wages, beyond improvements in real productivity, is accompanied by fiscal and monetary policies that enable full employment output to be sold at the new higher prices, then we may be able to keep full employment but with rising prices. Moreover, single unions and employers will then have every reason to continue the process. On the other hand, if we try to buck the upward pressure on prices from the supply side by fiscal and monetary policies that reduce demand or do not permit it to rise enough to absorb the full employment output at higher prices, then production and employment must fall. If we stubbornly insist on having average prices remain constant, and if trade unions stubbornly prescribe too high money wages, then the drop in employment may have to be very considerable.

Now it is possible that a very small degree of unemployment in the labor market might serve to persuade or to force unions from asking and getting increases in their money wages greater than productivity changes. If so, we are lucky and the wage-price dilemma does not exist. Unfortunately, our knowledge of the true empirical relations is necessarily scanty since nature has not performed the requisite controlled experiments for us. The price rise and course of events since 1935 is not inconsistent with the optimistic or pessimistic interpretation.

Much further investigation and observation are needed in this important realm.[14]

7. *Stabilization efforts and income distribution*

The first half of the present essay—that part dealing with current short-run effects of full employment policies as distinct from the effects on long-run trends—can be brought to a close after we have discussed one final issue. Do such stabilization programs fall in with the modern tendency—so dear to demagogues but also apparently so deeply rooted in our culture [15]—toward favoring a less unequal distribution of income? Do they tend to lead to soaking the rich and favoring the poor? If so, is this an inevitable consequence of such policies?

Among many early Keynesian writers there was, I think, the belief that America's problem in future years is more likely to be that of fighting deflation than inflation. There was also a belief that the rich have a much lower (marginal) propensity to spend their incomes than do the poor; so that aside from any intrinsic merits in heavily progressive income taxation, there was supposed to be an additional purchasing power argument in favor of such measures. More recent statistical studies of family spending habits have cast some doubts as to the quantitative leverage of redistribution of income on the total of American saving: the income of the very rich does not bulk large, and the spending habits of the rest of the income classes do not differ greatly in respect to *changes* in income. Also, it follows from the neoclassical viewpoint outlined above that if it were desirable on general ethical or other grounds to leave higher income in the hands of the wealthy, then means (other than income redistribution) can certainly be found to prevent unemployment. Hence, a move toward greater equality of income is never mandatory for stabilization purposes.

Nonetheless, any judicious person will have to admit that the existence of heavy unemployment has the effect, politically and economically, to reinforce any latent ethical and political tendencies favoring the adoption of policies designed to redistribute income in favor of the poor, especially since relief and other welfare programs are usually designed for the poor rather than the wealthy.

But by the same logic an honest person should admit that the reverse policies are indicated to the degree that our problem is one of inflation

14. See Chapter 11. Also see the essay by E. S. Mason cited in the Williams volume (n. 10, above) and the views expressed by John H. Clark, G. Haberler, Edward H. Chamberlin, and Milton Friedman in *The Impact of the Union* (New York, Harcourt, Brace, 1951), David McCord Wright, ed.

15. See Chapter 1.

rather than deflation, of too much rather than too little monetary demand. What is sauce for the goose is sauce for the gander, and many economists must feel a little uneasy advocating, during the inflationary cold-war period, tax increases that impinge most heavily on the more well-to-do.[16] Unfortunately, if one is really to fight inflation, some pressure has to be put upon consumption spending, unpalatable as such action may be.

On the whole, every large group stands to gain in the long run from stable prosperity, but it is the poor whose position deteriorates most in depression and improves relatively most in revival. The inequality of income (as measured by a so-called Lorenz curve or other statistical device) shows that inequality declines in prosperous times. Minority groups and those who stand at the bottom of the income pyramid— Negroes, marginal farmers, domestic servants—have the largest stake in a militant stabilization program. In short, the usual modern notions of so-called equity reinforce and are reinforced by full employment programs. And to the extent that you wish to give great weight to the well-being of the economically less fortunate groups, you should be all the more willing to push such programs, at the same time frankly recognizing the harm done to those with fixed money incomes.

III. STABILITY AND PROGRESS

The second half of this chapter is concerned with the problem of economic progress. For more than a century the American economic system has increased its productivity in each decade. Statistical measurements of real income show that—after corrections and adjustments have been made for changes in the purchasing power of the dollar—output per capita has increased, at the same time that the average hours each person works per week or year have gone down. Comparative statistics also

16. At least three valid loopholes to this criticism can be found. The past rise in prices had in effect raised the effective tax of the poorest classes beyond what was apparently considered "equitable," so that they were entitled to some relief. Also, the economists were almost alone in fighting for more taxes and they may have felt that it would not be possible politically to salvage a half-loaf of remedial action if one advocated more regressive taxation. In addition, perhaps one can make out a case that during boom periods the middle and wealthy classes are most likely to invest what they do not consume so that taxing them does reduce current total effective demand appreciably; this serves to damn the rich whether the winds are inflationary or deflationary and neglects favorable effects of capital on subsequent output. Finally, some government economists may have felt that there are worse things than mild inflation. It should be added that once we admit that investment incentives are affected by tax rates, we must admit the possibility that more unemployment could require lower taxes on the rich relative to the poor in order to stimulate private investment.

show that real wages are higher in the United States than anywhere else in the world. This increase in our standard of living is not something that can be taken simply for granted. There is nothing inevitable about material progress. There is no divine governor or thermostat that guarantees an increase in productivity of 2 or 3% per year. Historians and anthropologists record numerous examples of economic societies that have regressed from high to low standards of living. In our own annals the record of progress has not always been smooth or uniform.

Public policy must be concerned with dynamic economic development, and programs of stabilization must be scrutinized for their possible unfavorable or favorable effects upon the trend of productivity. Perhaps the booms and the busts of the last century were the inevitable costs of progress, the necessary price we must pay for vital growth. If such is the fact, let us face it unflinchingly and, facing it, decide whether the gains of progress are worth their social costs, or whether there is some golden mean involving neither a maximum of progress-*cum*-instability nor complete security-*cum*-decadence. On the other hand, it may turn out that certain types of stabilization programs are not so drastically opposed to economic growth but may even contribute toward healthy economic development. The problem is a thorny one to which no slick answer can be given. We must review and weigh the economic issues involved.

1. *The meaning of stabilization*

Of course, by stabilization we do not mean a state of suspended growth. Nor do we simply have in mind a dampening down of the roller coaster of business activity until the curve of total output is flattened into the shape of just any old trend. By stabilization we do mean 1) an absence of large fluctuations upward and downward in total employment, 2) absence of mass unemployment, overemployment, or "disguised unemployment," 3) the absence of excessive price inflation resulting from too-high effective demand and "overfull-employment" conditions. In short, the economic system is to hug relatively closely the line of its full *potential* (or producible) national output. The *task of progress is to further the growth of this "potential national product."*

The kind of over-all stabilization being discussed here has nothing to do with—and indeed is quite opposed to—stabilization of price or output in any particular market or industrial sector or geographical region. The needs and wants of consumers are constantly changing and so are the resources and technology of production. All this makes the numerical measurement of *potential output* difficult and approximate. It also implies that relative prices and outputs must be constantly varying and readjusting themselves; otherwise the optimal goal of full potential output cannot be achieved. It is only too clear, therefore, that some kinds of policies that have occasionally been associated with the name of stabilization—control agreements to stabilize output or price, legislation to protect the interests of particular workers or farmers—may be diametrically opposed to progress. They have, and should have, nothing to do with the full employment programs discussed in this volume.

Progress is an obstreperous and often cruel disturber of the *status quo*. It flings windfall gains to some and inflicts heavy economic penalties on others, often on groups and persons least able to afford them. Fear of change may breed more insecurity than its actual impact. People and institutions very naturally and understandably react to prevent or forestall adverse changes. And governments, feeling that there is a conflict or clash between progress and equity, take various actions designed to alleviate the losses of the afflicted. Some of these government actions can slow up economic progress, just as the steps taken by private trade unions or corporations to resist change may delay improvements in technology.

I cannot deal here with all such aspects of the problem. What I am concerned with is the effects of the successful maintenance of a high level of monetary demand upon such resistance to change. Surely the essence of the problem of, say, technological unemployment is not how to keep a man from losing his old job so much as to make sure that alternative jobs become available, at as high a wage as his revalued skill can command. The problem is similar in the case of displaced demand for the output of any particular plant or item of capital equipment. To the extent that people can be dissuaded from vetoing needed technological changes, a successful over-all stabilization program can be said to be favorable rather than opposed to a healthy rate of progress.

2. *Inevitability of business cycles and growth trends*

But are not most modern economists increasingly in agreement that technological change, innovation, and dynamic economic growth are the important causes of business cycles? [17] Are progress and the business cycle not inseparable? If governments had been successful in moderating the business cycle over the last century, would world productivity be as high as it now is? Could even a collectivized society succeed in

17. Continental writers such as Joseph A. Schumpeter or Arthur Spiethoff were most strongly associated with this view, but D. H. Robertson and (in more recent years) John M. Keynes, Alvin H. Hansen, and other Anglo-Saxon writers have increased their emphasis on such factors. See any work on business cycles, such as G. Haberler, *Prosperity and Depression*.

banishing the business cycle without at the same time killing off all progress? These questions have been widely discussed by economists.

Though progress may often have been the cause of the business cycle in the past, it does not follow that progress is the effect of the business cycle in the sense that when you abolish or moderate the cycle you will necessarily banish or lessen progress. A relatively small fluctuation in innovations may, unless something is done about it, set up a violently amplified oscillation in total business activity, since cumulative economic forces pile onto any upward or downward movement carrying it far beyond the initial push. In the train of genuinely important innovators are a host of imitators who, caught up with the boom fever, may carry the expansion to excess; when the crash comes the most inefficient firms may be eliminated, but there may follow a cumulative downward spiral which causes even the soundest firms and banks to become bankrupt or to curtail activity. Public policy designed to moderate the "secondary" excesses set up by primary fluctuations in investment opportunities can prevent much economic waste, while at the same time having little or no adverse influence on innovation and technological progress.

Granting that cycles of historically observed amplitude are not inevitable, we must critically examine a more recent notion that the rate of growth of an economy is foreordained by its rate of population growth and by the ratio of its capital stock to income. This secular aspect of the acceleration principle has been studied by Roy F. Harrod, Evsey D. Domar, and others. Moreover, it seems to lend weight to more intuitive notions of "balance," according to which there is during any period, such as the 1920's, some appropriate rate of capital formation which cannot be long exceeded without giving rise to depression. Now if we recognize all the rigidities in our system and if we set up a model of a laissez-faire system in which each investor's fears of future depression may be only too fully realized, then I have no doubt that high rates of capital formation for one period may be regarded as being at the expense of low rates later. Perhaps the great depression of the 1930's is to be explained partially in precisely these terms.

But if we revert to the optimistic neoclassical doctrines outlined above, and if we recognize that the amount of capital needed for any level of income is a variable depending upon the rate of interest and other factors, then I do not see why a well-run economy cannot have almost any rate of capital formation it wanted to. To show that there is nothing intrinsically in the technological nature of a system that limits its rate of growth, imagine a fully centralized and planned economy. It might be subject to many evils of arbitrary power and authority and of errors in judgments about particular investment projects, but I do not see why it could not make its capital grow at any desired yearly increase—at least up to the point where the net productivity of capital had been brought down practically to zero. This is because the parameters in the accelerator models must be regarded as variables rather than as constants.[18]

3. *Stabilization and investment incentive*

Stabilization policies may serve to further progress in two ways. First, the memory of a great speculative orgy such as 1929 may last so long as to discourage more investment in subsequent years than can be credited to the boom period itself. Hence in checking the excesses of the boom we may be advancing the average rate of economic growth. Second, and perhaps even more important, in offsetting slumps and preventing great declines in employment and incomes we are lessening their adverse influence on investment and risk-taking.

No more favorable environment could be imagined for venture capital and innovation than one in which businessmen could look forward to a steadily growing market not prone to sudden epidemics of general bankruptcy and insecurity. They could then scrutinize each bold new project on its merits without at the same time having to look into a crystal ball to foretell the course of general business conditions. While it is not yet within our power to provide such assurances, the favorable effects upon the trend of productivity of even partially successful stabilization programs seem hardly open to doubt. This of course assumes that the stabilization policies are not of the type which will give rise to grave ideological concern on the part of entrepreneurs.

There will not be smooth monotonous growth as a result of even the luckiest and most successful full employment policies. The true line of potential output can be expected to be subject to some ripples and accelerations. Inventions will not appear with perfect regularity and their promotion and economic introduction will show even greater clustering; but there need no longer be such great swings of investment once the

18. For a discussion of the nature of the business cycle in a planned economy, see the views of G. Haberler, Abram Bergson, and David McCord Wright in *Conference on Business Cycles,* held under the auspices of Universities–National Bureau Committee for Economic Research (New York, National Bureau of Economic Research, 1951). Note that the same jerkiness of progress, replacement waves, and backlogs might arise in a collectivist society as in our own: to the extent that these were not foreseen, we can make adverse ex post evaluations of the mistakes in planning; to the extent that they were foreseen and nonetheless rationally accepted as optimal programs, the shifting of resources occasioned by such jerkiness need not be regarded as wastes.

feedback effects of boom-bust pessimism, optimism, and money-market convulsions have been moderated. When change is proceeding at an especially rapid rate, layoffs and frictional unemployment will be at their peak; this is in part unavoidable if the advantages of progress are not to be indefinitely thwarted. But the measure of success of high employment programs will be the degree to which new productive job opportunities are found for those displaced and the degree to which cumulative slumps in jobs and sales can be avoided.

Some costs in terms of progress may have to be charged against stabilization programs. Historically, booms have often resulted from the creation of money and credit by the banking system at the behest of speculative investors. The result has often been inflation, with individuals being forced into lower consumption by shrinkage in the buying power of their wages and property income. This process of "forced savings" (forced doing without would be the better term, since the abstainers have no assets to show for their sacrificing) has been reinforced by the increase during inflationary boom periods in profits accruing to the more active speculators and risk-takers, who are just the people most ready to experiment with new products and processes. Especially for young developing countries, where investment opportunities always seem (at conventional interest rates) to be running beyond the full employment voluntary saving of the community, control over inflationary banking policies may slow down the rate of progress; and this possibility should be admitted.

On the other hand, if over the years the public authorities find themselves pursuing expansionary monetary and fiscal policies in order to offset incipient stagnation, then savings which would have been abortive may be brought into effective being. Under these circumstances full employment policy may be materially contributing to the rate of growth of industrial productivity. The degree to which this is true will depend upon the qualitative and quantitative composition of the program adopted.

4. Factors underlying progress

Before examining the different effects of various alternative government programs on the growth of productivity, we must catalogue some of the conditions necessary to improved levels of output. There is first the availability of resources, material and human. America has been singularly blessed in respect to land and mineral resources, and a significant fraction of our superiority can be attributed to this factor beyond our control. But the presence of resources in this land as of 1492 cannot explain our rising standard of living; and over the world as a whole the association between degrees of productivity and natural endowment of resources is by no means a close one.

From the standpoint of welfare rather than national power, we are probably more interested in per capita output than in total output. Therefore the type of growth to be explained is not that associated with mere increase in numbers of our population. A century ago population growth was a more significant cause of the total growth in our production than it will be in future years when our natural rate of increase will be smaller and when the flow of immigration into this country will be narrowly limited by law. Above and beyond the mere expansion in numbers, there has been a historical increase in output per capita, which requires all the more explanation since more workers means a dilution of the amount of God-given resources per worker.

The explanation may lie partially in the quality of our workers, the word "quality" having to be carefully limited in its meaning. Certainly few experts would attach great weight to any biological difference in our citizenry, since we are notoriously a nation of mixed ethnic, language, and anthropometric strains. Even if the difference cannot be traced to the germ cell, it is still true that the American worker by training and experience is often a more efficient agent of production than his counterpart abroad. He is not exerting greater physical efforts —usually much less; and even the mental and nervous strain of a week's work in an American factory is probably less instead of greater than prevails elsewhere. From birth the American grows up in a highly efficient, industrialized environment so that he unconsciously and easily acquires the skills and attitudes conducive to efficient production. He is no superman and, in any case, most of the credit is not his; nonetheless, no one who has tried to help less advanced nations improve their productivity is likely to underestimate the importance of the effective human skills available in the American labor force.

This is simply one reflection of the single most important reason for our productivity—namely, the advanced state of our technological know-how. The steady world-wide growth of fundamental scientific knowledge has been drawn upon by American engineers to further industrial productivity. The result has been dramatic new products and industries—electrical, chemical, etc. But equally important have been the almost unnoticed, undramatic steady improvements in machinery and methods. Not only has the level of technology been high within each plant, but in addition we have succeeded in building up a relatively large free-trade area in which an elaborate division of labor enables any one firm to purchase the precision instruments, raw materials, and parts it needs—a great advantage for which foreign producers greatly envy us.

All this has been built up largely through individual initiative and without active government direction. In fact some of our largest concerns, frowned on by the antitrust branch of the government, have often been focal points of most rapid technological progress. Perhaps as applied science becomes even more complex and costly, the advantages of size enjoyed by such large corporations in the research field may increase still more and their share in the growth of technology may swell. This may raise certain conflicts of social goals and certain dilemmas for government policy. Thus there may be a clash between our antipathy toward monopolistic concentrations of power and our desire for progress. On the one hand we are tempted to dangle before would-be innovators the promise of patent protection; on the other hand we deplore the influence of the dead hand of old patents upon competition, price, and output.[19]

All this takes us beyond stabilization policy. The important thing for our purposes is the emphasis on *effective technological knowledge* as the single, most important factor in economic progress. Closely related to technology is the role of *capital formation* in advancing productivity. The two cannot be entirely separated, but in earlier years economists put undue emphasis, I believe, on the mere accumulation of capital. Historically, it is true, as capital grew so did productivity. Any comparative cross-sectional view of different countries today will also show that those countries with the highest productivity also tend to have the most real capital per head. Abstract economic theory tells us, too, that as the interest rate is lowered, even without any new technical knowledge, processes which were previously unprofitable will now be adopted and the result will be greater output and labor productivity.

While the role of capital formation in progress is obviously an important one which no developing nation can afford to minimize, still it must be remembered that the historical association between capital abundance and high standards of life [20] is partly that of the latter making possible the former rather than vice versa. Also very much of capital formation consists of duplicative "widening" of existing, known facilities; a century later it will not matter whether there are one dozen or

19. See Chapter 10.

20. It may in part result from the way we measure capital. If labor's noncapitalizable share of the national income is somewhere around two-thirds of the total, and if property income is capitalized into wealth at an annual interest rate of between 5 and 10%, then the stock of capital will always appear to be about 4 to 7 years' national income *whatever* the *technological* relationship may be.

one thousand generators built in 1952, whereas the discovery of one fundamental principle today—which may be "free" capital—may change the face of the world forever. Thus I believe it is quite possible that, if the United States economy throughout its history had saved only one-twentieth of its income instead of roughly one-eighth and if a larger share of what was saved had gone into scientific research, pure and applied, into pilot-plant operations, and experimentation, we should today enjoy even larger levels of output than we now do. The significance of this for the future lies in the fact that less-advanced nations, simply by imitating the best known technological methods, can hope to improve their standards of living even with a minimum of available capital. Our Point Four program is based on this recognition. In some ways knowledge is the most important form of capital, and here as elsewhere in life it is often the best things that are free.

I must not underestimate the importance of capital formation. Even if a firm or nation could contrive to make progress just by replacing its old capital with better-designed new capital and without doing any "net" saving, its upward progress would presumably be even greater if new capital formation were also available. Resources used to produce such new capital processes must be taken away from the production of current consumption goods, once full employment is assured. Depending upon the people's habits of thrift and their expectations concerning the present and the future, people may voluntarily abstain from present consumption and channel their savings into investment assets. Historians such as Max Weber, Werner Sombart, and R. H. Tawney consider it no accident that the industrial revolution has been associated with the "Protestant ethic" and its emphasis on effort and thrift. Sometimes a country's capital needs are met by imports from outside; during the nineteenth century Britain made private development loans to Canada, Argentina, and the United States. Other countries such as Japan and Russia have, through choice or otherwise, been relatively self-reliant in their development. Japan is perhaps an example where a very unequal distribution of income between rich and poor has served the purpose of augmenting the savings available for capital development. In Russia the government through its successive five-year plans deliberately planned to hold down current consumption of the people in favor of industrialization and military expenditure.

5. To save or not save?

Let us turn to the policy aspects of the problem. It is doubtful that the government can by orthodox measures influence greatly the amount that people choose to consume out of their available disposable income.[21] Only by affecting the general environment of expected future prices can public policy do much about saving-consumption patterns. But questions may be asked—what *ought* we to wish for with respect to saving, and what problems will face the government as a result of different saving decisions?

The orthodox position with respect to saving used to be: the more the better; "a penny saved is a penny earned." While it is possible to be too miserly and to die too rich because one has not lived richly enough, the followers of Poor Richard would maintain that most people save too little and are insufficiently prudent and parsimonious. Moreover, in saving, the individual is thought to be not so much helping himself as aiding the laboring classes and society at large by providing new capital that will increase future real income. From the time of Adam Smith's bumbling definitions of "productive" and "unproductive" labor down through Pigou's emphasis on people's defective "telescopic faculty" that causes them to discount the future unduly, there has been a feeling that people if left alone tend to save too little. This feeling carries over into communistic and socialistic economies. Even those writers who think that people should be able under socialism to buy the goods they like better—apples rather than oranges if that is their choice—usually balk at letting people decide individually for themselves how much capital the present generation will pass on to the future generations; this, the state is to decide. The conservation movement reveals most clearly the latent notion that the present generation does not have the right to decide in terms of its own individual preferences how fast it shall use up exhaustible natural resources; instead the people set up their government as kind of a trustee to protect the interests of the as yet unborn.[22] Even within capitalistic countries a good deal of capital formation is governmentally and institutionally determined.

Against the orthodox glorification of saving there early grew up a whole school of critics who argued that excessive thrift might *reduce* rather than increase the rate of real capital formation. This was well expressed more than a century ago by the English economist, Malthus,

21. Corporate saving and investment is more amenable to the influence of changes in the tax structure. Also the government by its tax policy can affect the levels of disposable income that will prevail at full employment.

22. Since J. M. Keynes has in recent years been associated with the view that oversaving may be a problem, it is interesting to note his earlier statement in the *Economic Consequences of the Peace* (1919) that the middle classes have their *raison d'être* in the fact that they do save and not consume, and that post-World War I Europe might not quietly permit them to dis-save should they want to.

who far from being a radical agitator was an Anglican clergyman with the interests of the country gentry at heart. He said:

> No considerable and continued increase in wealth could possibly take place without that degree of frugality which occasions capital formation . . . and creates a balance of produce over consumption; but it is quite obvious . . . that the principle of saving, pushed to excess, would destroy the motive to production. . . . If consumption exceeds production, the capital of the country must be diminished, and its wealth must be gradually destroyed from its want of power to produce; if production be in great excess above consumption, the motive to accumulate and consume must cease from the want of will to consume. The two extremes are obvious; and it follows that there must be some intermediate point, though the resources of political economy may not be able to ascertain it, where taking into consideration both the power to produce and the will to consume, the encouragement to the increase of wealth is greatest.[23]

In England the followers of David Ricardo (particularly James Mill and J. R. McCulloch) made it a condition of membership in the economic profession to abjure such underconsumption heresy and to subscribe to the tenets of the so-called Say's law of markets which held that supply created its own demand and that overproduction or underconsumption were logically (and empirically?) impossible, so that excessive thrift could never be a problem. Nonetheless, the underconsumptionist view smoldered on both in England and on the Continent, until in our own day it burst forth in the new form of the modern theory of income determination.[24]

This analysis distinguishes sharply between the attempt to save and the amount of real saving and investment that society succeeds in making. The attempt by individuals to consume less of their income, if it is not translated into equivalent investment, will prove abortive: people will only succeed in reducing their own incomes to the point where they finally give up the attempt; or some people may succeed in adding to

23. T. R. Malthus, *Principles of Political Economy* (1820), pp. 6–7 of the London School of Economics reprint of the 1836 edition.

24. Associated in its beginning with Keynes, *General Theory of Employment, Interest, and Money* (London, Macmillan, 1936). But even prior to 1936 Harold G. Moulton and his associates at the Brookings Institute had insisted that an increase in the desire to consume might sometimes help rather than hinder capital formation.

their financial savings by forcing others to dissave. The situation may be even worse from the standpoint of increasing society's real capital formation and productivity: the fall in incomes resulting from attempts to save will make existing plants redundant and undermine confidence and the volume of capital formation.

This "paradox of thrift" needs a number of qualifications. If there is an "inflationary gap" with total spending tending to outrun the value of full employment output, then an increase in thriftiness may reduce the rate of inflation and lead to a stable full employment condition characterized by a high rate of capital formation. Even when there is some unemployment, an increase in thriftiness can be expected to lower interest rates via its downward impact on money incomes; this favorable lower-interest rate effect will oppose the unfavorable lower-income effect upon investment and, if thriftiness is not too great, the result may be increased capital formation.[25]

The neomercantilists were inclined to make much of this paradox of thrift. Claiming to desire more capital formation, they were able to advocate progressive taxes and other fiscal measures designed to redistribute income from rich to poor. Earlier I have mentioned that evidence from budget studies of different income groups' saving habits suggests that such redistribution has limited quantitative effects on total consumption and savings. (See p. 564 above.) Also we must not neglect any adverse effects upon investment resulting from the impact of high marginal rates of taxation (and inadequate loss offsets). There is the additional fact that the qualitative character of the saving done by the lower income groups—saving, accounts, insurance policies, etc.—may for institutional reasons be available primarily for gilt-edged bond investment rather than for equity capital.

If the proponents of the paradox of thrift overlooked its limitations, the critics of the doctrine were blind to its grain of truth. Thus when Alvin Hansen spoke in the 1930's of the need to make America a "high consumption economy," many interpreted this to mean a low investment economy, a deduction which would be tenable only if resources were always fully employed and if unemployment were not a variable in the problem. In my interpretation, by a high consumption economy Hansen

---

25. See O. Lange, "The Rate of Interest and the Optimum Propensity to Consume," in *Readings in Business Cycle Theory* (Philadelphia, Blakiston, 1944), ch. 8, and reprinted from *Economica*, New Series, 5 (1938). If prices and costs are flexible downward, the reduction in money income may not imply an equivalent loss of real income; also, the lower prices may increase the propensity to consume so that a smaller amount of *net* thriftiness finally ensues. This last so-called Pigou effect reinforces rather than negates the paradox of thrift.

meant one in which net capital formation would be absolutely high and even higher relative to income than in a depressed system.

6. *The optimal rate of saving*

How does our neoclassical doctrine stand on these matters? It will be recalled that earlier this was defined to mean that *high employment can be achieved by a wide variety of alternative programs so as to yield almost any pattern of resource use between the public and private sector* and—it now may be added—*between capital formation and present consumption goods.* If the policies described elsewhere in this volume are successful, then we need no longer fear thrift's possible damage to real income and capital formation. An effective stabilization program being assured, we can ask the purely classical question: How much of current national income ought to be saved, and how fast a rate of progress should be our goal?

The answer that we should save as large a percentage of income as possible and aim for the most rapid rate of progress makes little sense. Obviously it would be absurd to try to invest 100% of national income or to try to put everyone in the land into a scientific laboratory. Each increment of capital formation must be at the expense of current consumption; and while one can conceptually imagine a nation that uses *all* its machines and labor to produce more machines which will in turn make still more machines, no one would seriously set this up as a goal. To the extent that each new unit of capital will yield a net return (in terms of real output) over and above the depreciation costs for its ultimate replacement, we can think of each present sacrifice of consumption goods as making possible a perpetually higher flow of (real) income. But the more we invest, the more precious becomes each unit of the consumption that is left to us. The problem is how to strike the right balance.

Under certain heroic assumptions—such as the absence of any "time-preference" and the addition of independent utilities spread over all future time, etc.—some rather fine-spun theories as to the optimal rate of capital growth have been put forward.[26]

Moreover, the problem of saving is peculiarly one in which the actions

26. The Ramsey mathematical analysis of saving, made in 1928 by a brilliant short-lived philosopher-protégé of Keynes, is summarized in less technical terminology in J. E. Meade and C. J. Hitch, *An Introduction to Economic Analysis and Policy* (New York, Oxford University Press, 1938), Pt. IV, ch. 3. This theory assumes that society tries to maximize over all time the sum of "utilities," the latter being the same concave function of current consumption of each time period. Society should then do positive saving until either the "net productivity of capital" is zero or "bliss" has been attained with all goods free. The rate at which this

of people when left to themselves are widely regarded as not necessarily optimal. This view and its negation both involve ascientific ethical value judgments, and it is only in the role of a reporter and not as a special pleader that I call attention to this fact. An illustration of what I have in mind can be cited.

It is not at all impossible that the citizens of many countries of western Europe, living in the mid-century shadow of the atomic bomb, would if left to themselves dis-save on balance. Their "governments" will not let "them" do so. Is this good or bad? It all depends upon the philosophical viewpoint. The individuals who spend their patrimony may later regret it; to which some will reply that everyone is entitled to his own mistakes and having made one's bed. . . . On the other hand, even in the most individualistic society people are limited in the harm they can do themselves—especially if it is serious harm such as suicide. Also some will argue that there are military needs of society and a "right" for society to avoid its own economic suicide which should take precedence over the right of the individual to dissipate "his" property. Just as Louis XV is criticized for having said "après moi, le déluge," so a citizenry that has a net reproduction rate far below that necessary for group survival is often criticized, collectively and individually. To add to the paradox, the whole of the populace may give a vote of confidence to government's performing such "trustee" powers over capital formation, even though taken separately as individuals they distrust their own powers to resist excessive consumption. It is like the case where few will enlist in the army but all will vote to subject themselves to (risk of) the draft. However, the problem of insuring that government is responsive to our democratic collective wills is a more difficult one because of the quantitative nature of the investment process.

Leaving out the clash between present and future generations and between individuals and society, we must recognize a philosophical ambiguity in all decisions taking place over time that makes normative statements especially difficult. Our tastes change over time; the man who makes a decision today for tomorrow is different from tomorrow's man and also from the man who will reminisce the day after tomorrow.

---

happy state should be reached is determined by balancing the loss of present satisfaction from one more increment of present saving against the gain in future satisfaction involved in advancing the date that we reach bliss. This means that society should ultimately save a percentage of the national income almost equal to the percentage-income by which we fall short of bliss: e.g., if society now enjoys only three-fourths of the maximum producible income, it should save almost one-fourth of its current income. This is a rather fanciful prescription based on fanciful assumptions.

I may hate myself in the morning for what I do tonight; paradoxically, I may now know that I will be hating myself in the morning; and tomorrow, while hating myself, I may know perfectly well that given the same situation I would again behave in the same way. In technical parlance there are no invariant indifference curves over time, and where tastes are changing there is no frame of reference for normative decisions. This point has been strongly made by Professor M. Allais of Paris, who is otherwise a staunch advocate for free pricing.

It all adds up to this: there are no rules as to the optimum rate of progress. Richer societies are better able to save, but also they may have less reason to do so. Public policy, democratically arrived at, may be directed toward accelerating or holding down the rate of capital formation, or it may attempt to be neutral, letting people in some sense decide for themselves how much they will save. But since every decision about taxes, expenditures, and other economic matters impinges on the environment within which individuals make up their minds, the concept of neutrality would have to be given a very special meaning.

Fortunately, the sweeping neoclassical doctrine outlined in this chapter can sidestep the question of how much shall be saved. This is not the business of a stabilization program to decide. High employment can be achieved, theoretically, with almost any pattern of investment and consumption. If individuals are trying to save so much that their efforts threaten to become abortive through a fall in employment, this can be offset by policy and high employment can be maintained. If the resulting pattern of employment involves too little capital formation according to some prescribed standards, there exist other combinations of policy measures that will result in a more rapidly growing stock of capital. As an example, we could have full employment with money so cheap and plentiful as to be conducive to private capital formation, but with a federal budget strongly overbalanced to curb inflation; or, if we wish it, present consumption standards may be higher, with private investment expenditure being limited by a tight money market that rations out capital funds sparingly. Or we might have anything in between.

I do not wish to convey the impression that monetary policy, within the range of usually discussed changes in interest rates and credit availability, has the same potency as fiscal policy does within its usual range. Nor do I wish to imply that, by taking various mixtures of monetary and fiscal policy, you can bring about exactly the same kind of restriction of total demand: the effects of fiscal and monetary policy may be qualitatively and quantitatively different, and it is for this reason that we must choose the mixture best suited to prescribed ends.

In recent years it has become fashionable among technical economists to stress the possible effects on consumption and thriftiness of the real level of people's money and public debt holding. Price deflation is regarded as one way of bringing full employment saving into alignment with investment outlets. Such a view carries with it the empirical corollary that people do not possess deep invariant patterns of time preference and that they will be content to save much or little depending upon how we manipulate their financial wealth. This presents us with a three-way choice of a full employment program: 1) heavy reliance on fiscal policy; 2) heavy reliance on interest-rate monetary policy; 3) heavy reliance on price flexibility and so-called Pigou effects. But what mixture is optimal? Should every child be endowed with a nest egg of negotiable government bonds so as to overcome his feeling of insecurity? If the saving pattern changes greatly with the size of the nest eggs of these fictitious claims on wealth, which is the proper *natural* or *neutral* pattern of interest rates and asset structure? If we are willing to make heroic assumptions about the invariance of individuals' time preferences, and if we were given the ethical criteria by which we determine the proper "share" and deservingness of the born and unborn, a formal answer could be given.

In closing I must make one general qualification. Throughout this chapter I have been concerned with conflicts of ultimate goals at the high strategy level. I have not attempted to do anything like full justice to the tactical difficulties of achieving stabilization goals. I have been concerned with the problems we would face even after our stabilization policies were most successfully realized. This should not be interpreted as a belief that stabilization can be fully or easily attained; as the other chapters of this book show, the problems are many and difficult and go beyond the narrow confine of economics.

100

THE NEW LOOK IN TAX AND FISCAL POLICY

PAUL A. SAMUELSON, Massachusetts Institute of Technology

I

There is much talk about taxes. When I flick on the dial of my radio in the morning, I hear a Congressman quoted on how our high level of taxes is ruining the Nation or a Senator's tape-recorded alarm over the unfair burden the poor man has to carry because the administration has been favoring big business. My morning paper at breakfast brings me the view of its editor that the United States has been pursuing unsound fiscal policy for the last 25 years. Scratch the barber who cuts my hair and you find a philosopher ready to prescribe for the Nation's monetary ills.

This is as it should be. We expect sweeping statements in a democracy. We hope that out of the conflict of extreme views there will somehow emerge a desirable compromise. Yet such sweeping statements have almost no validity from a scientific, or even from a leisurely commonsense point of view: spend as little as a year going over the factual experience of American history and of other economies, devote as little as a month to calm analysis of probable cause and effect, or even spend a weekend in a good economics library—and what will you find? Will you find that there breathes anywhere in the world an expert so wise that he can tell you which of a dozen major directions of policy is unquestionably the best? You will not. Campaign oratory aside, the more assuredly a man asserts the direction along which salvation is alone to be found, the more patently he advertises himself as an incompetent or a charlatan.

The plain truth is this, and it is known to anyone who has looked into the matter: The science of economics does not provide simple answers to complex social problems. It does not validate the view of the man who thinks the world is going to hell, nor the view of his fellow idiot that ours is the best of all possible tax systems.

I do not wish to be misunderstood. When I assert that economic science cannot give unequivocal answers to the big questions of policy, I do not for a moment imply that economists are useless citizens. Quite the contrary. They would indeed be useless if any sensible man could quickly infer for himself simple answers to the big policy questions of fiscal policy. No need then to feed economists while they make learned studies of the obvious. It is precisely because public policy in the tax and expenditure area is so complex that we find it absolutely indispensable to invest thousands of man-years of scholarly time in scholarly economic research in these areas.

Make no mistake about it. The arguments that we all hear every day of our lives on the burning partisan issues have in every case been shaped by economists—by economists in universities, in business, in Government, and by that rarest of all birds, the shrewd self-made economist. What economists do not know about fiscal policy turns out, on simple examination, not to be known by anyone.

II

With this necessary preamble out of the way, let me record the general views that studies have led me to, about the current state of our fiscal system. This will clear the way for a more detailed analysis of taxes and growth, taxes and stable full employment, taxes and equity, taxes and the level of public expenditure programs.

Here then are the major facts about our system as I see them.

(1) The postwar American economy is in good shape. There is nothing artificial or unsound about its underpinnings. For more than a decade we have had generally high employment opportunities. Our production efficiency has been growing at a steady rate that compares well with anything in our history or in the history of countries abroad. For all this we must, in our present-day mixed economy, be grateful to both public and private institutions.

(2) The existing structure of Federal, State, and local taxes is in its broad features highly satisfactory. Repeatedly at the polls and through all the legitimate processes of government, the citizens of this Republic have indicated that they want our present type of fiscal structure—its substantial dependence at the Federal level on personal and corporate income taxes, its eclectic dependence on selective excises, on payroll levies for social security, on property and sales taxes at the local levels. If the consensus of citizens in our democracy were to be other than it is—toward less or more equalitarianism, toward less or more local autonomy—there is no reason that the careful analytic economist can see why our fiscal system is not capable of being altered in the desired direction. In other words, there is nothing in the mechanics of a modern economy which makes it impossible or difficult for the citizenry to get the kind of a tax system that they want; our tax system has plenty of give, plenty of room for adaptation and change.

All the above does not imply that we are living in a new era of perfection. The American economy now faces, and will continue to face, many tough problems, many hard decisions. And, to be sure, there are numerous imperfections, inconsistencies, and loopholes in the present tax structure; these do need improving.

What the optimistic diagnosis of the modern-day economist does contradict is the following:

(1) The view that America has long since departed from an orthodox fiscal policy and that it is only a matter of time until a grim Mother Nature exacts retribution from us for our folly in departing from the narrow line of fiscal rectitude. (This is a philosophical position that any dissenter from current trends is free to assume; but it is not a factually verifiable view about reality that dispassionate study of statistics and facts can substantiate.)

(2) The view, shared in by the extremes of both left and right wings, that our economy generally is moving in unsound directions so that we must ultimately end up in some unnamed disaster or convulsion. (In terms of business-cycle stability and efficient growth, the

United States has in the last dozen years dramatically refuted the sour expectations both of those who look back on a fictitious past golden age and of collectivists who look forward to a golden age that only a revolution can usher in.)

III

Turning now to the goals of any tax system, we can ask: What tax structure will give us the most rapid rate of growth? What tax system will give us the highest current standard of living? What tax structure will make our system most immune to the ups and downs in employment and prices that make American families insecure? What tax structure will realize most closely the community's sense of fairness and equity? What tax structure will have the least distorting effects on our use of economic resources, instead of maximizing the efficiency with which we produce what our citizens most want?

Upon careful thought it will be obvious that there cannot exist a tax system which will simultaneously maximize these five quite different goals of social life.

It is easy to see that high current living standards and rapid growth of our ability to produce are conflicting ends: you have only to look at a collectivized society like the Soviet Union, which decides to sacrifice consumption levels of the current generation in favor of a crash program of industrialization; you have only to reflect that historically in the slums of Manchester working families might have lived longer in the 19th century if England and the other nations had during the industrial revolution slowed down their rates of material progress; you have only to consider the problem of conserving scarce exhaustible natural resources to realize that every society must all the time be giving up higher future resource potentials in favor of keeping current generation consumption as high as it is.

You can imagine a society that decides to devote its income in excess of the bare physiological existence level 100 percent to capital formation. You can imagine it—but there never has been such a society. Nor would any of us want to live in such a one. It should be obvious, therefore, that no sane person would ever seek a tax program which literally maximized our rate of economic growth. (Yet how many times over the chicken a la king have we all heard speakers reiterate this nonsensical goal.) It is just as obvious that no sane person would want to maximize present living levels if this meant eating up all our capital on a consumption bender that would leave us an impoverished Nation.

There is no need to go through all the other pairs of the five listed goals to show their partial incompatibility. If we are willing to frame a tax system that strongly favors thrifty men of wealth, we may thereby be able to add to our rate of current growth; if we encourage a gentle rate of inflation, we may be able to increase the profits in the hands of the quick-reacting businessman, perhaps thereby stepping up our rate of growth. So it goes, and one could easily work through the other permutations and combinations.

But not all of our five goals are necessarily competing. Some when you realize them, help you to realize the others. If we succeed in doing away with the great depressions that have dogged the economic record, we may thereby add to our rate of growth. If we shape a graduated-tax system that enables lower income groups to maintain minimum standards of life, we may ease the task of stabilizing business activity. If we replace distorting taxes by less distorting alternatives, the fruits of the resulting more efficient production can add to our current consumption and to our rate of progress in capital formation.

I shall not prolong the discussion of the degree to which the diverse goals of tax policy are competing or complementary. For it will turn out that we can formulate proper policies without having to measure these important, but complicated, relationships.

IV

Upon being told by the economist that it is absurd for Congress to aim at the most rapid rate of growth possible and that it is equally absurd for Congress to aim at the highest possible current level of consumption, the policymaker may be tempted to say: "I understand that. Won't you therefore as an economist advise us as to just what is the best possible compromise between these extremes?"

A good question but, unfortunately, not one that the expert economist can pretend to give a unique answer to. If he is honest, he must reply: "The American people must look into their own hearts and decide on what they consider to be the best compromise rate of growth."

Just because I have advanced degrees in economics and have written numerous esoteric works in the field, I am not thereby empowered to let my personal feelings, as to how much the present generation ought to sacrifice in favor of generations to come, become a prescription for society. It would be as presumptuous for me to offer such specific advice as to let my family's notions about dental care determine how much the typical American family ought to spend on toothpaste. But it is legitimate for me as an economist to say this: "Whatever rate of capital formation the American people want to have, the American system can, by proper choice of fiscal and monetary programs, contrive to do." This can be shown by an example.

Suppose the vast majority of the American people look into the future or across the Iron Curtain at the rate of progress of others. Suppose they decide that we ought to have a more rapid rate of capital formation and technological development than we have been having recently. Then the economist knows this can be brought into being (*a*) by means of an expansionary monetary policy that makes investment funds cheaper and easier to get. Admittedly, such an expanded investment program will tend, if it impinges on an employment situation that is already full and on a price level that is already stationary, to create inflationary price pressures and overfull employment—unless something is done about it. What would have to be done about this inflationary pressure? Clearly (*b*) a tight fiscal policy would be needed to offset the expansionary monetary policy: By raising taxes relative to expenditure, we would reduce the share of consumption out of our full employment income, releasing in this way the real resources needed for investment. (It should be unnecessary to go through the reverse programs which would be called for if the national decision were to slow down the rate of capital formation as compared to that of recent years.[1])

From these remarks it will be clear that economic science is not only neutral as to the question of the desired rate of capital accumulation— it is also neutral as to the abilty of the economy to realize any decided-on rate of capital formation.

I repeat: With proper fiscal and monetary policies, our economy can have full employment and whatever rate of capital formation and growth it wants.[2]

V

The optimistic doctrine that our economy can have stability and the rate of growth it wants may seem rather novel. Perhaps even a little shocking. But there are worse surprises yet to come.

The reader may think that my argument rests on something like the following reasoning:

Suppose that political party R is more concerned with progress than political party D, which shows a greater concern for the little man, with security, and with current consumption. Then if the Nation gives its approval to the general policy goals of R, the Government will have to change its emphasis away from reducing taxes on individuals—particularly rapid-spending lower-income people; and it will have to change its emphasis toward reducing taxes on business, in an attempt to bolster the incentives toward investment. In short, it is by changing the qualitative pattern of taxation, by sacrificing equity to incentive, that the community succeeds in getting higher levels of capital formation when it desires such higher levels.

I predict that much of the testimony before this subcommittee will proceed along these lines. Certainly much of the political discussion of the last 3 years, when it has had the courage to be frank, has been along these lines.

---

[1] The fact that variations in the overall deficit or surplus of the Government can, if properly reinforced by monetary policy, determine the rate of society's capital formation puts a sobering responsibility on democratic governments. Ordinarily, we assume that each individual is to be the best judge of whether he will spend the income society leaves him after taxes on more butter or on more margarine. We do not ordinarily assume that I, as an individual, am free to determine the amount of smoke my chimney can eject into the public air; I am willing to enter into a compact with my neighbors whereby we all decide democratically how our liberty or license is to be curbed in order to further the good of each one of us. A nation's saving seems to be treated by most 20th century nations as something in between these 2 polar cases: to some degree we all act as if we consider ourselves trustees for future generations, and we desist from using up all the irreplaceable resources of nature. In both the advanced and the underdeveloped parts of the globe, citizens act at the polls as if they do not completely approve of the saving-investment decisions that they would make in private life; they reinforce and alter these decisions by voting public fiscal and monetary policies which increase (or decrease) the capital formation which private thrift would by itself dictate. Why do they do this? Often they do so implicitly. But often explicitly because, technically speaking, they attach qualified weight to their own changeable ex ante indifference curves between present and future. If full ethical primacy were to be given to these indifference curves and if short-run irregularities were ignored, the proper goal of social policy might be a constantly balanced budget accompanied by an active monetary policy that maintains full employment.

[2] Space does not permit me to give the needed qualifications to this simplified exposition. I have elsewhere explained at some length what might be called the important neoclassical synthesis, which combines the essentials of traditional economics pricing theory with the essentials of the modern theory of income determination and which underlies the asserted proposition. See my chapter entitled "Full Employment Versus Progress and Other Economic Goals," appearing in (Max F. Millikan, editor) Income Stabilization for a Developing Democracy, Yale University Press. 1953, pp. 547–580. Also see my related discussion entitled "Principles and Rules in Modern Fiscal Policy: A Neo-Classical Reformulation," in Essays in Honor of John Williams. the Macmillan Co., New York, 1951, pp. 157–176. The third edition of my Economics, McGraw-Hill, 1955. ch. 29 (Interest and Capital), contains an elementary exposition to show how fiscal and monetary policy interact in the determination of alternative mixes of consumption and investment at full employment.

But this is not at all the train of thought that I wish to emphasize in my testimony. I want to cap the daring doctrine that an economy can have the rate of capital information it wants with a doctrine that may seem even more shocking. Naturally, I cannot here develop all of the underlying reasoning, nor give all the needed qualifications. But I do in advance want to stress the earnestness with which I put it forward, and to underline that it does spring from careful use of the best modern analyses of economics that scholars here and abroad have over the years been able to attain. The doctrine goes as follows:

A community can have full employment, can at the same time have the rate of capital formation it wants, and can accomplish all this compatibly with the degree of income-redistributing taxation it ethically desires.

This is not the place to give a detailed proof of the correctness of this general proposition. It will suffice to illustrate it with two extreme examples.[3]

In the first, suppose that we desire a much higher rate of capital formation but stipulate that it is to be achieved by a tax structure that favors low-income families rather than high-income. How can this be accomplished? It requires us to have an active expansionary policy (open-market operations, lowering of reserve requirements, lowered rediscount rates, governmental credit agencies of the FHA and RFC type if desired) which will stimulate investment spending. However, with our taxes bearing relatively lightly on the ready-spending poor, consumption will tend to be high at the same time that investment is high. To obviate the resulting inflationary pressure, an increase in the overall tax take with an overly balanced budget would be needed.

Alternatively, suppose the community wants a higher level of current consumption and has no wish to make significant redistributions away from the relatively well-to-do and toward the lower income groups. Then a tighter money policy that holds down investment would have to be combined with a fiscal policy of light taxation relative to expenditure. But note that in this case, as in the one just above, any qualitative mix of the tax structure can be offset in its effects by appropriate changes in the overall budget level and in the accompanying monetary policy.

VI

My discussion has covered a great deal of ground and has necessarily been brief. But I shall be glad to enlarge on the subject if that should be desired.

---

[3] I do not recall ever seeing mathematical economics in congressional committee hearings. This drought can be ended by the following brief proof of the reasoning underlying my basic proposition. To the initiated the symbols will be almost self-explanatory; to the uninitiated no harm is meant.

Let Y = real national product, y = disposable income in real terms = Y − taxes. Let I and C stand for investment and consumption, G for Government expenditure on goods and services. Let i stand for the cost (and the availability) of borrowing for investment purposes. Let m be a parameter indicating the degree to which the tax structure is income distributing toward the poor and, possibly harmful to investment incentives: the tax structure can be summarized by $T = T(Y,m)$. Our whole system can be defined by the conditions:

$$Y = C(y,m,.....) + I(Y,i,m,.....) + G, \text{ where } y = Y - T(Y,m)$$

For prescribed levels of G and m, there will always be a level of i and a level of the tax function T that simultaneously leads to full employment and to any desired ratio I/Y. (The dots in the functions will permit one to add stocks of wealth or money as further variables and also to make various wage and price level assumptions.)

101

PAUL A. SAMUELSON
Massachusetts Institute of Technology

Economic Forecasting and National Policy

Introduction

AT OUR party to commemorate the tenth anniversary of the Employment Act of 1946, we must invite the Bad Fairies as well as the Good. For in 1956 we also commemorate another memorable anniversary—that of the famous Wrong Postwar Forecast.

At the war's end, we relearned the hard way that economics is not an exact science: a vast number of our best economists, using the most advanced models and statistics that a great government can afford, predicted the drop in war expenditure would create considerable unemployment—but the facts of the postwar boom proved otherwise. And disillusionment with forecasting naturally followed so dramatic a failure.

We should not minimize this bad omen under which the Employment Act was born.[1] It is important to know and to avow explicitly our scientific limitations. Yet pessimism can be carried too far; and in the last years of the 1940's, some economists let their disillusionment with our ability to forecast drive them into nihilistic positions which, paradoxically, represented bad forecasting both of our ability to forecast and of the required accuracy of forecasting needed by stabilization policy.

For make no mistake about it. We are here to celebrate a happy birthday, not a wake. In the last decade the American economy has performed wonderfully well: unemployment has been kept lower than even the most optimistic of the Act's godfathers dared hope.[2] To be

---

[1] I can think of no other occasion in the history of economics or of any other discipline, when the aspirations of a budding science were dealt so sudden and sharp a blow. Perhaps the nearest parallel case is the failure of prewar demography, with its confident extrapolation of falling net reproduction rates, to anticipate or even acknowledge the war and postwar population upsurge. Still there is no comfort for the economist in the fact that other social sciences make poor forecasts; and only cold comfort in the fact that economic forecasters were much quicker than the demographers to cut their losses and to make *post mortem* studies which tried to find out why their forecasts went wrong and what could be learned from the episode for the future.

[2] Our record in achieving stable prices has, of course, been less good; but I venture to think this has not been so much because of any failure to read the future as because of the nation's apparent unwillingness to compromise the goals that conflicted with price stability.

sure, this was not all due to fine government policies. Luck and extraneous events were with us. But why didn't we thwart our luck by bad policies—as we could have done, but didn't? And will not a careful rereading of the general direction of policies followed by our government over the past ten years suggest that there was no six-month period in which we pursued wrong-directional policies that better forecasting ability could have prevented?

I conclude that our experience of the last ten years imparts an optimistic view concerning the ability of policymakers to diagnose the general trends and needs of our modern economy. Still we must guard against complacency. I propose, therefore, in the brief space given me, to review the scientific problems of forecasting in their relationship to policy.

What Official Forecasts Should be Published?

During the war itself economists constantly made forecasts and extrapolations. Many were routine. Not a few were provocative and unpopular. The general wartime batting averages of economists, allowing for cancelling errors and luck, were in my view remarkably high. This led some of the partisans of the Employment Act to envisage the following postwar procedure of a responsible Economic Council:

1. Economists and statisticians would at the beginning of each year make and publish careful quantitative estimates of the feasible goals of high-employment production and income. These targets were thought to be rather objectively specifiable.

2. They would next make up and publish careful quantitative models of the probable level and composition of national income and production under various policy assumptions. It was thought by some that such predictions, if based upon elaborate econometric model-building and modern income analysis, would also have a high degree of precision.

3. Finally, the expected or predicted values would be compared with the target projections. In the unlikely event that they closely agreed, well and good—no change in policy was thought called for. In the more likely event that they significantly differed, showing either general deflationary or general inflationary "gaps," the Council would then be in a position to recommend generally expansionary federal policies or generally contractionary policies.

4. Congress, being told the findings of science, would proceed to take the needed action and there would follow full employment at all times, or a close approximation to it.

To put matters so simply is of course to caricature.[3] Yet the above was undoubtedly a strand in the thinking of many.

Needless to say, no such proposal as this has been followed over the last ten years by our government.[4] Under Nourse and Keyserling, the Council of Economic Advisers did occasionally set out semi-quantitative goals or targets much like point 1 of my outline. But primarily in a qualitative way did the Council make its predictions under point 2: thus at the beginning of any year, the reader could usually infer whether the Council thought that the outlook was significantly inflationary, deflationary, or roughly in balance. Under Eisenhower the Council has refused to venture quantitative published "predictions" concerning the desired targets. For this it has been criticized by members of Congress.[5]

From the scientific view we must distinguish between (i) the prediction of feasible targets and (ii) the prediction of the economy's likely performance under existing or specified policy measures. These are different in nature. Some might even wonder whether targets involve predictions at all. Predictions of actual performance can be proved right or wrong by subsequent events: but can predictions of goals be validated?

Admittedly, if I predict in 1960 that the economy could be producing in 1961 $500 billion GNP, and if we produce only $450 billion, I may never be able to know whether my feasible goal was wrong or whether our policies were inadequate to realize that goal. So simple validation is not always possible. However, if my friend argues that $450 billion was the feasible goal, and if in 1961 expansionary fiscal policies send the real GNP to $515 billion, then I think that most economic

---

[3] I have not mentioned a distinction between (i) the school which thought that an elaborate mathematical-statistical model of the Tinbergen-Clark-Klein type would provide the accurate forecasts and (ii) the more general group who would add much broad judgment to any statistical equations in making projections. Let me only say that I welcome the elaborate models for their scientific interest; but based upon our experience with them to date, they do not yet seem capable of as reliable forecasts as we can hope for from more informal, eclectic techniques which place much reliance on the elusive factor of "judgment." Recall Colin Clark's disastrous U. S. prediction for 1954, more important, see the thoughtful researches and discussion of Carl Christ, Lawrence R. Klein, and Milton Friedman in the *Conference on Business Cycles* of the Universities-National Bureau Committee for Economic Research (New York, 1951), pp. 35-130. The demonstrated fact that "naive models" which predict no change do so well will be later shown to be a powerful aid to the policy maker rather than a cause for pessimism.

[4] The National Budgets of Norway, Sweden, Denmark, the Netherlands, and the United Kingdom have in some postwar years come a little closer toward the described procedure. For an account of the partly good, partly bad success of such budgets see *Economic Bulletin for Europe*, Vol. V (July, 1953), pp. 63-82.

[5] I do not care to go into the question, argued in the Joint Committee, whether this failure is contrary to the letter or spirit of the Employment Act. For it is obvious that sponsors of the Act differed among themselves and that many of those who finally voted for the revised Act did so disbelieving in it and its purposes, and as a political choice among evils.

historians will conclude that my guess of a $500 billion 1960 target was much nearer the mark than his guess of $450 billion. And further validation of one view or the other can often come from examination of concomitant economic time series, such as the percentage of the labor force unemployed and the movements of prices.[6]

For the President to make published quantitative estimates of goals does put his Administration somewhat on the spot. However, as I review our general experience with projections *of this type,* in the government and outside of it, I think our ability to foresee the short-run trends in population, labor force, productivity, etc. has been fairly free of truly embarrassing errors. Reluctance to make such forecasts I would realistically attribute to scientific temperament of the members of the Council who happen to be serving and to the natural reluctance of the more conservative of our two political parties to be forced into what might be regarded as an over-activistic full employment policy.

When I turn to the advisability of publishing detailed quantitative estimates of next year's actual magnitudes and of inflationary or deflationary gaps, I must admit that forecasting experience of the last two decades does not give one high confidence in the accuracy of such estimates. In the first place, sophisticated forecasters realize that they envisage a range of probable future values for any economic magnitude rather than a single figure. But the clients of forecasters, in Congress and out, tend to be confused by anything but a single figure, and few have learned how to use such probability spreads in private or political decision-making.

I conclude therefore that whereas within the government itself such detailed quantitative estimates are necessary, there is a good case at this time against requiring the President or any important government agency to put single-valued official predictions into the record.[7]

---

[6] I write "can *often* come" because one must admit that in many years there may arise a sharp conflict between high employment and price stability. Prices may rise even when unemployment is an intolerable percentage. A subjective or political judgment as to a compromise goal must be made. Such a judgment is nonfactual and cannot be later tested in the way that ordinary forecasts or predictions can be tested. Of course, this makes the setting of goals more rather than less important.

[7] This is a pragmatic view based on our experienced accuracy. I have not been led to this view by the frequently heard argument that the government's influence is so important as to make it undesirable for it to make pronouncements that will adversely affect private expectations. If the government were to predict unemployment ahead, it is truly possible that some might say: "Aha, even the President admits things are bad; if that is so, think how bad they must really be!" We should recognize, but not exaggerate, a tendency for official predictions to become self-fulfilling. Nonetheless, a strong pragmatic case can be made for brutal frankness on the part of the government: after this has been followed for some time, it will gain on the swings what it loses on the round-abouts. People will be less prone to the opposite pattern in which they say, "Things are worse than we're being told about."

John Jewkes in *Economics and Public Policy* (Brookings, 1954) and in *Lloyd's*

Conclusion

Space does not permit a full appraisal of the demands on the forecaster required by successful employment stabilization policy. So I must simply state that they are not as onerous as many have thought.

All our facts show that the economic system is very sluggish. It moves, but it moves slowly. Predict for six months ahead that it will not be far from its present level or present trend, and you will rarely be wrong. This is a great help to the policymaker. For if, in every six-month period, he zealously seeks policies that will not lead to grossly excessive or grossly deficient over-all demand, and if he at all well succeeds in these policies, then the great depressions which plagued the history of capitalism cannot come to pass.

And as we continue to succeed to avoid serious slumps, there will emerge this paradox: Reasonably successful stabilization policy will tend to leave the economic system in such a position that the forecaster will find it difficult to know whether it will be likely to rise or fall significantly. It is precisely because our economic system was historically so deficient in its stabilization programming that successful (but irrelevant) forecasting of the major swings was relatively easy.

Bank Review (April, 1953) has forcefully stated the case against economists' ability to forecast. He reminds us of the view that even if unpublished forecasting were possible, the public announcement of the forecast would change reality and falsify the forecast. That this theoretical point is not, itself, sufficient to prove the impossibility of correct forecasting is shown by proof that—provided accurate unpublished forecasting is postulated to be possible—there will, under a wide set of conditions, exist a published forecast which, taking account of its own influence, will still be correct. For this see E. J. Greenberg and F. Modigliani, "The Predictability of Social Events," *Journal of Political Economy*, V. LXII (1954), pp. 465-478.

102

ANALYTICAL ASPECTS OF ANTI-INFLATION POLICY

By Paul A. Samuelson *and* Robert M. Solow
Massachusetts Institute of Technology

I

Just as generals are said to be always fighting the wrong war, economists have been accused of fighting the wrong inflation. Thus, at the time of the 1946-48 rise in American prices, much attention was focused on the successive rounds of wage increases resulting from collective bargaining. Yet probably most economists are now agreed that this first postwar rise in prices was primarily attributable to the pull of demand that resulted from wartime accumulations of liquid assets and deferred needs.

This emphasis on demand-pull was somewhat reinforced by the Korean war run-up of prices after mid-1950. But just by the time that cost-push was becoming discredited as a theory of inflation, we ran into the rather puzzling phenomenon of the 1955-58 upward creep of prices, which seemed to take place in the last part of the period despite growing overcapacity, slack labor markets, slow real growth, and no apparent great buoyancy in over-all demand.

It is no wonder then that economists have been debating the possible causations involved in inflation: demand-pull versus cost-push; wage-push versus more general Lerner "seller's inflation"; and the new Charles Schultze theory of "demand-shift" inflation. We propose to give a brief survey of the issues. Rather than pronounce on the terribly difficult question as to exactly which is the best model to use in explaining the recent past and predicting the likely future, we shall try to emphasize the types of evidence which can help decide between the conflicting theories. And we shall be concerned with some policy implications that arise from the different analytical hypotheses.

History of the Debate: The Quantity Theory and Demand-Pull. The preclassical economists grew up in an environment of secularly rising prices. And even prior to Adam Smith there had grown up the belief in at least a simplified quantity theory. But it was in the neoclassical thought of Walras, Marshall, Fisher, and others that this special version of demand determination of the absolute level of money prices and costs reached its most developed form.

We can oversimplify the doctrine as follows. The real outputs, inputs, and relative prices of goods and factors can be thought of as determined by a set of competitive equations which are independent of the absolute level of prices. As in a barter system, the absolute level of all prices is indeterminate and inessential because of the "relative homogeneity" properties of these market relations. To fix the absolute scale factor, we can if we like bring in a neutral money. Such money, unlike coffee or soap, being valued only for what it will buy and not for its intrinsic utility, will be exactly doubled in demand if there is an exact doubling of all prices. Because of this important "scale homogeneity," fixing the total of such money will, when applied to our already determined real system of outputs, factors, and relative prices, fix the absolute level of all prices; and changes in the total of such money must necessarily correspond to new equilibria of absolute prices that have moved in exact proportion, with relative prices and all real magnitudes being quite unaffected.[1]

As Patinkin and others have shown, the above doctrines are rather oversimplified, for they do not fully analyze the intricacies involved in the demand for money; instead they ignore important (and predictable) changes in such proportionality coefficients as velocity of circulation. But by World War I, this particular, narrow version of demand-pull inflation had more or less triumphed. The wartime rise in prices was usually analyzed in terms of rises in the over-all money supply. And the postwar German inflation was understood by non-German economists in similar terms.

But not all economists ever agree on anything. Just as Tooke had eclectically explained the Napoleonic rise in prices partially in terms of the war-induced increase in tax, shipping, and other costs, so did Harold G. Moulton and others choose to attribute the World War I price rises to prior rises in cost of production. And it is not without significance that the great neoclassical Wicksell expressed in the last years of his life some misgivings over the usual version of wartime price movements, placing great emphasis on movements in money's velocity induced by wartime shortages of goods.

Of course, the neoclassical writers would not have denied the necessary equality of competitive costs and prices. But they would have regarded it as superficial to take the level of money costs as a predetermined variable. Instead, they would argue, prices and factor costs are

[1] But as Hume had early recognized, the periods of rising prices seemed to give rise to at least transient stimulus to the economy as active profit seekers gained an advantage at the expense of the more inert fixed-income, creditor, and wage sectors. The other side of this Hume thesis is perhaps exemplified by the fact that the post-Civil War decades of deflation were also periods of strong social unrest and of relatively weak booms and long periods of heavier-than-average depressions—as earlier National Bureau studies have suggested.

simultaneously determinable in interdependent competitive markets; and if the level of over-all money supply were kept sufficiently in check, then the price level could be stabilized, with any increases in real costs or any decreases in output being offset by enough backward pressure on factor prices so as to leave final money costs and prices on the average unchanged.

Many writers have gone erroneously beyond the above argument to untenable conclusions such as the following: A rise in defense expenditure matched by, say, excise taxes cannot raise the price level if the quantity of money is held constant; instead it must result in enough decrease in wage and other factor costs to offset exactly the rise in tax costs. Actually, however, such a fiscal policy change could be interpreted as a reduction in the combined public and private thriftiness; with M constant, it would tend to swell the volume of total spending, putting upward pressure on interest rates and inducing a rise in money velocity, and presumably resulting in a higher equilibrium level of prices. To roll back prices to their previous level would take, even within the framework of a strictly competitive neoclassical model, a determined reduction in previous money supply. (This illustrates the danger of going from the innocent hypothesis, that a balanced change in all prices might in the long run be consistent with no substantive changes in real relations, to an overly simple interpretation of a complicated change that is actually taking place in historical reality.)

While the above example of a tax-induced price rise that takes place within a strict neoclassical model might be termed a case of cost-push rather than demand-pull, it does not really represent quite the same phenomena that we shall meet in our later discussion of cost-push. This can perhaps be most easily seen from the remark that, if one insisted on holding prices steady, conventional demand reduction methods would work very well, within the neoclassical model, to offset such cost-push.

Demand-Pull à la Keynes. Aside from the neoclassical quantity theory, there is a second version of demand-pull associated with the theories of Keynes. Before and during the Great Depression, economists had become impressd with the institutional frictions and rigidities that made for downward inflexibilities in wages and prices and which made any such deflationary movements socially painful. Keynes's *General Theory* can, if we are willing to oversimplify, be thought of as a systematic model which uses downward inflexibility of wages and prices to convert any reduction in money spending into a real reduction in output and employment rather than a balanced reduction in all prices and factor costs. (This is overly simple for at least the following reasons: in the pessimistic, depression version of some Keynesians, a hyperdeflation of wages and prices would not have had substantive effects in restoring employment and output, because of infinite elasticity of liquidity preference and/or zero elasticity of investment demand; in the general form of the *General Theory,* and particularly after Pigou effects of the real value of money had been built in, if you could engineer a massive reduction in wages and costs, there would have been some stimulating effects on consumption, investment, and on real output; finally, a careful neoclassical theory, which took proper account of rigidities and which analyzed induced shifts of velocity in a sophisticated way, might also have emerged with similar valid conclusions.)

While the Keynesian theories can be said to differ from the neoclassical theories with respect to analysis of deflation, Keynes himself was willing to assume that attainment of full employment would make prices and wages flexible upward. In *How to Pay for the War* (1939), he developed a theory of inflation which was quite like the neoclassical theory in its emphasis upon the demand-pull of aggregate spending even though it differed from that theory in its emphasis on total spending flow rather than on the stock of money. His theory of "demanders' inflation" stemmed primarily from the fact that government plus investors plus consumers want, in real terms among them, more than 100 per cent of the wartime or boomtime available produceable output. So prices have to rise to cheat the slow-to-spend of their desired shares. But the price rise closes the inflationary gap only temporarily, as the higher price level breeds higher incomes all around and the real gap reopens itself continually. And so the inflation goes on, at a rate determined by the degree of shifts to profit, the rapidity and extent of wage adjustments to the rising cost of living, and ultimately by the extent to which progressive tax receipts rise enough to close the gap. And, we may add, that firmness by the central bank in limiting the money supply might ultimately so increase credit tightness and so lower real balances as to bring consumption and investment spending into equilibrium with available civilian resources at some higher plateau of prices.

Cost-Push and Demand-Shift Theories of Inflation. In its most rigid form, the neoclassical model would require that wages fall whenever there is unemployment of labor and that prices fall whenever excess capacity exists in the sense that marginal cost of the output that firms sell is less than the prices they receive. A more eclectic model of imperfect competition in the factor and commodity markets is needed to explain the fact of price and wage rises before full employment and full capacity have been reached.

Similarly, the Keynes model, which assumes stickiness of wages even in the face of underemployment equilibrium, rests on various assumptions of imperfect competition. And when we recognize that, considerably before full employment of labor and plants has been reached, modern prices and wages seem to show a tendency to drift upward irreversibly, we see that the simple Keynesian system must be modified even further in the direction of an imperfect competition model.

Now the fact that an economic model in some degree involves imperfect competition does not necessarily imply that the concepts of competitive markets give little insight into the behavior of relative prices, resources allocations, and profitabilities. To some degree of approximation, the competitive model may cast light on these important real magnitudes, and for this purpose we might be content to use the competitive model. But to explain possible cost-push inflation, it would seem more economical from the very beginning to recognize that imperfect competition is the essence of the problem and to drop the perfect competition assumptions.

Once this is done, we recognize the qualitative possibility of cost-push inflation. Just as wages and prices may be sticky in the face of unemployment and overcapacity, so may they be pushing upward beyond what can be explained in terms of levels and shifts in demand. But to what degree these elements are important in explaining price behavior of any period becomes an important quantitative question. It is by no means always to be expected that by observing an economy's behavior over a given period will we be able to make a very good separation of its price rise into demand and cost elements. We simply cannot perform the controlled experiments necessary to make such a separation; and Mother Nature may not have economically given us the scatter and variation needed as a substitute for controlled experiments if we are to make approximate identification of the causal forces at work.

Many economists have argued that cost-push was important in the prosperous 1951-53 period, but that its effects on average prices were masked by the drop in flexible raw material prices. But again in 1955-58, it showed itself despite the fact that in a good deal of this period there seemed little evidence of over-all high employment and excess demand. Some holders of this view attribute the push to wage boosts engineered unilaterally by strong unions. But others give as much or more weight to the co-operative action of all sellers—organized and unorganized labor, semimonopsonistic managements, oligopolistic sellers in imperfect commodity markets—who raise prices and costs in an attempt by each to maintain or raise his share of national income, and who, among themselves, by trying to get more than 100 per cent of the available output, create "seller's inflation."

A variant of cost-push is provided by Charles Schultze's "demand-shift" theory of inflation. Strength of demand in certain sectors of the economy—e.g., capital goods industries in 1955-57—raises prices and wages there. But elsewhere, even though demand is not particularly strong, downward inflexibility keeps prices from falling, and market power may even engineer a price-wage movement imitative in a degree of the sectors with strong demand. The result is an upward drift in average prices—with the suggestion that monetary and fiscal policies restrictive enough to prevent an average price rise would have to be so very restrictive as to produce a considerable level of unemployment and a significant drop in production.

II

Truths and Consequences: The Problem of Identification. The competing (although imperfectly competing) theories of inflation appear to be genuinely different hypotheses about observable facts. In that case one ought to be able to distinguish empirically between cost and demand inflation. What are the earmarks? If I believe in cost-push, what should I expect to find in the facts that I would not expect to find were I a believer in demand-pull? The last clause is important. It will not do to point to circumstances which will accompany any inflation, however caused. A test must have what statisticians call power against the main alternative hypotheses.

Trite as these remarks may seem, they need to be made. The clichés of popular discussion fall into the trap again and again. Although they have been trampled often enough by experts, the errors revive. We will take the time to point the finger once more. We do this because we want to go one step further and argue that this problem of identification is exceedingly difficult. What appear at first to be subtle and reliable ways of distinguishing cost-induced from demand-induced inflation turn out to be far from airtight. In fact we are driven to the belief that aggregate data, recording the *ex post* details of completed transactions, may in most circumstances be quite insufficient. It may be necessary first to disaggregate.

Common Fallacies. The simplest mistake—to be found in almost any newspaper discussion of the subject—is the belief that if money wages rise faster than productivity, we have a sure sign of cost-inflation. Of course the truth is that in the purest of excess-demand inflation wages will rise faster than productivity; the only alternative is for the full increase in the value of a fixed output to be siphoned off into profits, without this spilling over into the labor market to drive wages up still further. This error is sometimes mixed with the belief that it is possible over long periods for industries with rapid productivity increase to pay higher and increasingly higher wages than those where output per man-hour grows slowly. Such a persistent and growing differential is likely eventually to alter the skill- or quality-mix of the labor force in the different industries, which casts doubt on the original productivity comparison.

One sometimes sees statements to the effect that increases in expenditure more rapid than increases in real output necessarily spell demand inflation. It is simple arithmetic that expenditure outrunning output by itself spells only price increases and provides no evidence at all about the source or cause of the inflation. Much of the talk about "too much money chasing too few goods" is of this kind.

A more solemn version of the fallacy goes: An increase in expenditure can come about only through an increase in the stock of money or an increase in the velocity of circulation. Therefore the only possible causes of inflation are M and V and we need look no further.

Further Difficulties. It is more disconcerting to realize that even some of the empirical tests suggested in the professional literature may have little or no cutting power in distinguishing cost from demand inflation.

One thinks automatically of looking at the timing relationships. Do wage increases seem to precede price increases? Then the general rise in prices is caused by the wage-push. Do price increases seem to precede wage increases? Then more likely the inflation is of the excess-demand variety, and wages are being pulled up by a brisk demand for labor or they are responding to prior increases in the cost of living. There are at least three difficulties with this argument. The first is suggested by replacing "wage increase" by "chicken" and "price increase" by "egg." The trouble is that we have no normal initial standard from which to measure, no price level which has always existed and to which everyone has adjusted; so that a wage increase, if one occurs, must be autonomous and not a response to some prior change in the demand for labor. As an illustration of the difficulty of inference, consider average hourly earnings in the basic steel industry. They rose, relative to all manufacturing from 1950 on, including some periods when labor markets were not tight. Did this represent an autonomous wage-push? Or was it rather a delayed adjustment to the decline in steel wages relative to all manufacturing, which took place during the war, presumably as a consequence of the differential efficiency of wage control? And why should we take 1939 or 1941 as a standard for relative wages? And so on.

A related problem is that in a closely interdependent economy, effects can precede causes. Prices may begin to ease up because wage rates are expected to. And more important, as wage and price increases ripple through the economy, aggregation may easily distort the apparent timing relations.

But even if we could find the appearance of a controlled experiment, if after a period of stability in both we were to notice a wage increase to a new plateau followed by a price increase, what could we safely conclude? It would be immensely tempting to make the obvious diagnosis of wage-push. But consider the following hypothetical chain of events: Prices in imperfect commodity markets respond only to changes in costs. Labor markets are perfectly competitive in effect, and the money wage moves rapidly in response to shifts in the demand for labor. So any burst of excess demand, government expenditure, say, would cause an increased demand for labor; wages would be pulled up; and only then would prices of commodities rise in response to the cost increase. So the obvious diagnosis might be wrong. In between, if we were clever, we might notice a temporary narrowing of margins, and with this information we might piece together the story.

Consider another sophisticated inference. In a single market, price may rise either because the demand curve shifts to the right or because the supply curve shifts to the left in consequence of cost increases. But in the first case, output should increase; in the second case, decline. Could we not reason, then, that if prices rise, sector by sector, with outputs, demand-pull must be at work? Very likely we can, but not with certainty. In the first place, as Schultze has argued, it is possible that certain sectors face excess demand, without there being aggregate pressure; those sectors will indeed show strong price increases and increases in output (or pressure on capacity). But in a real sense, the source of inflation is the failure of other sectors, in which excess capacity develops, to decrease their prices sufficiently. And this may be a consequence of "administered pricing," rigid markups, rigid wages and all the paraphernalia of the "new" inflation.

To go deeper, the reasoning we are scrutinizing may fail because it is illegitimate, even in this industry-by-industry way, to use partial equilibrium reasoning. Suppose wages rise. We are led to expect a decrease in output. But in the modern world, all or most wages are increasing. Nor is this the first time they have done so. And in the past, general wage and price increases have not resulted in any decrease in aggregate real demand—perhaps the contrary. So that even in a single industry supply and demand curves may not be independent. The shift in costs is accompanied by, indeed may bring about, a compensating shift in the subjectively-viewed demand curve facing the industry. And so prices may rise with no decline and possibly an increase in output. If there is anything in this line of thought, it may be that one of the important causes of inflation is—inflation.

The Need for Detail. In these last few paragraphs we have been arguing against the attempt to diagnose the source of inflation from aggregates. We have also suggested that sometimes the tell-tale symptoms can be discovered if we look not at the totals but at the parts. This suggestion gains force when we recognize, as we must, that the same general price increase can easily be the consequence of different causes in different sectors. A monolithic theory may have its simplicity and style riddled by exceptions. Is there any reason, other than a desire for symmetry, for us to believe that the same reasoning must account for the above-average increase in the price of services and the above-average increase in the price of machinery since 1951 or since 1949? Public utility prices undoubtedly were held down during the war, by the regulatory process; and services ride along on income-elastic demand accompanied by a slower-than-average recorded productivity increase. A faster-than-average price increase amounts to the corrective relative-price change one would expect. The main factor in the machinery case, according to a recent Joint Economic Committee study, appears to have been a burst of excess demand occasioned by the investment boom of the mid-fifties. And to give still a third variant, Eckstein and Fromm in another Joint Economic Committee study suggest that the above-average rise in the wages of steelworkers and the prices of steel products took place in the face of a somewhat less tight labor and product market than in machinery. They attribute it to a joint exercise of market power by the union and the industry. Right or wrong, it is mistaken theoretical tactics to deny this possibility on the grounds that it cannot account for the price history in other sectors.

Some Things It Would Be Good to Know. There are at least two classical questions which are relevant to our problem and on which surprisingly little work has been done: One is the behavior of real demand under inflationary conditions and the other is the behavior of money wages with respect to the level of employment. We comment briefly on these two questions because there seems to us to be some doubt that ordinary reversible behavior equations can be found, and this very difficulty points up an important question we have mentioned earlier: that a period of high demand and rising prices molds attitudes, expectations, even institutions in such a way as to bias the future in favor of further inflation. Unlike some other economists, we do not draw the firm conclusion that unless a firm stop is put, the rate of price increase must accelerate. We leave it as an open question: It may be that creeping inflation leads only to creeping inflation.

The standard way for an inflationary gap to burn itself out short of hyperinflation is for the very process of inflation to reduce real demands. The mechanisms, some dubious, some not, are well known: the shift to profit, real-balance effects, tax progression, squeeze on fixed incomes. If price and wage increases have this effect, then a cost-push inflation in the absence of excess demand inflicts unemployment and excess capacity on the system. The willingness to bear the reduced real demand is a measure of the imperfectness of markets permitting the cost-push. But suppose real demands do not behave in this way? Suppose a wage-price rise has no effect on real demand, or a negligible one, or even a slight positive one? Then not only will the infliction not materialize, but the whole distinction between cost-push and demand-pull begins to evaporate. But is this possible? The older quantity theorists would certainly have denied it; but the increase in velocity between 1955 and 1957 would have surprised an older quantity theorist.

We do not know whether real demand behaves this way or not. But we think it important to realize that the more the recent past is dominated by inflation, by high employment, and by the belief that both will continue, the more likely is it that the process of inflation will preserve or even increase real demand, or the more heavily the monetary and fiscal authorities may have to bear down on demand in the interests of price stabilization. Real-income consciousness is a powerful force. The pressure on real balances from high prices will be partly relieved by the expectation of rising prices, as long as interest rates in an imperfect capital market fail to keep pace. The same expectations will induce schoolteachers, pensioners, and others to try to devise institutions to protect their real incomes from erosion by higher prices. To the extent that they succeed, their real demands will be unimpaired. As the fear of prolonged unemployment disappears and the experience of past full employment builds up accumulated savings, wage earners may also maintain their real expenditures; and the same forces may substantially increase the marginal propensity to spend out of profits, including retained earnings. If there is anything to this line of thought, the empirical problem of verification may be very difficult, because much of the experience of the past is irrelevant to the hypothesis. But it would be good to know.

The Fundamental Phillips Schedule Relating Unemployment and Wage Changes. Consider also the question of the relation between money wage changes and the degree of unemployment. We have A. W. Phillips' interesting paper on the U. K. history since the Civil War (our Civil War, that is!). His findings are remarkable, even if one disagrees with his interpretations.

In the first place, the period 1861-1913, during which the trade-union movement was rather weak, shows a fairly close relationship between the per cent change in wage rates and the fraction of the labor force unemployed. Due allowance must be made for sharp import-price-induced changes in the cost of living, and for the normal expectation that wages will be rising faster when an unemployment rate of 5 per cent is reached on the upswing than when it is reached on the downswing. In the second place, with minor exceptions, the same relationship that fits for 1861-1913 also seems to fit about as well for 1913-48 and 1948-57. And finally Phillips concludes that the money wage level would stabilize with 5 per cent unemployment; and the rate of increase of money wages would be held down to the 2-3 per cent rate of productivity increase with about $2\frac{1}{2}$ per cent of the labor force unemployed.

Strangely enough, no comparably careful study has been made for the U.S. Garbarino's 1950 note is hardly a full-scale analysis, and Schultze's treatment in his first-class Joint Committee monograph is much too casual. There is some evidence that the U.S. differs from the U.K. on at least two counts. If there is any such relationship characterizing the American labor market, it may have shifted somewhat in the last fifty to sixty years. Secondly, there is a suggestion that in this country it might take 8 to 10 per cent unemployment to stabilize money wages.

But would it take 8 to 10 per cent unemployment forever to stabilize the money wage? Is not this kind of relationship also one which depends heavily on remembered experience? We suspect that this is another way in which a past characterized by rising prices, high employment, and mild, short recessions is likely to breed an inflationary bias—by making the money wage more rigid downward, maybe even perversely inclined to rise during recessions on the grounds that things will soon be different.

There may be no such relation for this country. If there is, why does it not seem to have the same degree of long-run invariance as Phillips' curve for the U.K.? What geographical, economic, sociological facts account for the difference between the two countries? Is there a difference in labor mobility in the two countries? Do the different tolerances for unemployment reflect differences in income level, union organization, or what? What policy decisions might conceivably lead to a decrease in the critical unemployment rate at which wages begin to rise or to rise too fast? Clearly a careful study of this problem might pay handsome dividends.

III

A Closer Look at the American Data. In spite of all its deficiencies, we think the accompanying scatter diagram in Figure 1 is useful. Where it does not provide answers, it at least asks interesting questions. We have plotted the yearly percentage changes of average hourly earnings in manufacturing, including supplements (Rees's data) against the annual average percentage of the labor force unemployed.

The first defect to note is the different coverages represented in the two axes. Duesenberry has argued that postwar wage increases in manufacturing on the one hand and in trade, services, etc., on the other, may have quite different explanations: union power in manufacturing and

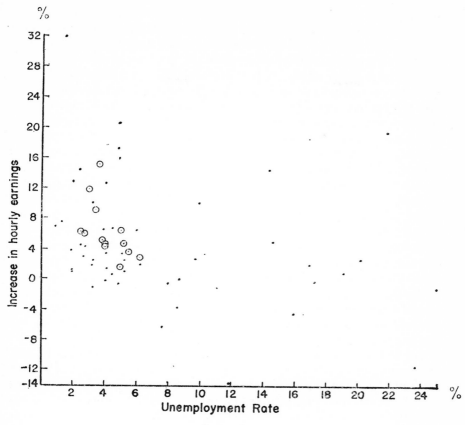

PHILLIPS SCATTER DIAGRAM FOR U.S.
(The circled points are for recent years.)

simple excess demand in the other sectors. It is probably true that if we had an unemployment rate for manufacturing alone, it would be somewhat higher during the postwar years than the aggregate figure shown. Even if a qualitative statement like this held true over the whole period, the increasing weight of services in the total might still create a bias. Another defect is our use of annual increments and averages, when a full-scale study would have to look carefully into the nuances of timing.

A first look at the scatter is discouraging; there are points all over the place. But perhaps one can notice some systematic effects. In the first place, the years from 1933 to 1941 appear to be *sui generis:* money wages rose or failed to fall in the face of massive unemployment. One may attribute this to the workings of the New Deal (the 20 per cent wage increase of 1934 must represent the NRA codes); or alternatively one could argue that by 1933 much of the unemployment had become structural, insulated from the functioning labor market, so that in effect the vertical axis ought to be moved over to the right. This would leave something more like the normal pattern.

The early years of the first World War also behave atypically although not so much so as 1933-39. This may reflect cost-of-living increases, the rapidity of the increase in demand, a special tightness in manufacturing, or all three.

But the bulk of the observations—the period between the turn of the century and the first war, the decade between the end of that war and the Great Depression, and the most recent ten or twelve years—all show a rather consistent pattern. Wage rates do tend to rise when the labor market is tight, and the tighter the faster. What is most interesting is the strong suggestion that the relation, such as it is, has shifted upward slightly but noticeably in the forties and fifties. On the one hand, the first decade of the century and the twenties seem to fit the same pattern. Manufacturing wages seem to stabilize absolutely when 4 or 5 per cent of the labor force is unemployed; and wage increases equal to the productivity increase of 2 to 3 per cent per year is the normal pattern at about 3 per cent unemployment. This is not so terribly different from Phillips' results for the U.K., although the relation holds there with a greater consistency. We comment on this below.

On the other hand, from 1946 to the present, the pattern is fairly consistent and consistently different from the earlier period. The annual unemployment rate ranged only narrowly, from 2.5 per cent in 1953 to 6.2 per cent in 1958. Within that range, as might be expected, wages rose faster the lower the unemployment rate. But one would judge now that it would take more like 8 per cent unemployment to keep money wages from rising. And they would rise at 2 to 3 per cent per year with 5 or 6 per cent of the labor force unemployed.

It would be overhasty to conclude that the relation we have been discussing represents a reversible supply curve for labor along which an aggregate demand curve slides. If that were so, then movements along the curve might be dubbed standard demand-pull, and shifts of the curve might represent the institutional changes on which cost-push theories rest. The apparent shift in our Phillips' curve might be attributed by some economists to the new market power of trade-unions. Others might be more inclined to believe that the expectation of continued full employment, or at least high employment, is enough to explain both the shift in the supply curve, if it is that, and the willingness of employers (conscious that what they get from a work force is partly dependent on its morale and its turnover) to pay wage increases in periods of temporarily slack demand.

This latter consideration, however, casts real doubt on the facile identification of the relationship as merely a supply-of-labor phenomenon. There are two parties to a wage bargain.

U.S. and U.K. Compared. A comparison of the American position with Phillips' findings for the U.K. is interesting for itself and also as a possible guide to policy. Anything which will shift the relationship downward decreases the price in unemployment that must be paid when a policy is followed of holding down the rate of wage and price increase by pressure on aggregate demand.

One possibility is that the trade-union leadership is more "responsible" in the U.K.; indeed the postwar policy of wage restraint seems visible in Phillips' data. But there are other interpretations. It is clear that the more fractionated and imperfect a labor market is, the higher the over-all excess supply of labor may have to be before the average wage rate becomes stable and the less tight the relation will be in any case. Even a touch of downward inflexibility (and trade-unionism and administered wages surely means at least this) will make this immobility effect more pronounced. It would seem plausible that the sheer geographical compactness of the English economy makes its labor market more perfect than ours in this sense. Moreover, the British have pursued a more deliberate policy of relocation of industry to mop up pockets of structural unemployment.

This suggests that any governmental policy which increases the mobility of labor (geographical and industrial) or improves the flow of information in the labor market will have anti-inflationary effects as well as being desirable for other reasons. A quicker but in the long run probably less efficient approach might be for the government to direct the regional distribution of its expenditures more deliberately in terms of the existence of local unemployment and excess capacity.

The English data show a quite clearly nonlinear (hyperbolic) relation between wage changes and unemployment, reflecting the much discussed downward inflexibility. Our American figures do not contradict this, although they do not tell as plain a story as the English. To the extent that this nonlinearity exists, as Duesenberry has remarked, a given average level of unemployment over the cycle will be compatible with a slower rate of wage increase (and presumably price increase) the less wide the cyclical swings from top to bottom.

A less obvious implication of this point of view is that a deliberate low-pressure policy to stabilize the price level may have a certain self-defeating aspect. It is clear from experience that interregional and interindustrial mobility of labor depends heavily on the pull of job opportunities elsewhere, more so than on the push of local unemployment. In effect the imperfection of the labor market is increased, with the consequences we have sketched.

IV

We have concluded that it is not possible on the basis of a priori reasoning to reject either the demand-pull or cost-push hypothesis, or the variants of the latter such as demand-shift. We have also argued that the empirical identifications needed to distinguish between these hypotheses may be quite impossible from the experience of macrodata that is available to us; and that, while use of microdata might throw additional light on the problem, even here identification is fraught with difficulties and ambiguities.

Nevertheless, there is one area where policy interest and the desire for scientific understanding for its own sake come together. If by deliberate policy one engineered a sizable reduction of demand or refused to permit the increase in demand that would be needed to preserve high employment, one would have an experiment that could hope to distinguish between the validity of the demand-pull and the cost-push theory as we would operationally reformulate those theories. If a small relaxation of demand were followed by great moderations in the march of wages and other costs so that the social cost of a stable price index turned out to be very small in terms of sacrificed high-level employment and output, then the demand-pull hypothesis would have received its most important confirmation. On the other hand, if mild demand repression checked cost and price increases not at all or only mildly, so that considerable unemployment would have to be engineered before the price level updrift could be prevented, then the cost-push hypothesis would have received its most important confirmation. If the outcome of this experience turned out to be in between these extreme cases—as we ourselves would rather expect—then an element of validity would have to be conceded to both views; and dull as it is to have to embrace eclectic theories, scholars who wished to be realistic would have to steel themselves to doing so.

Of course, we have been talking glibly of a vast experiment. Actually such an operation would be fraught with implications for social welfare. Naturally, since they are confident that it would be a success, the believers in demand-pull ought to welcome such an experiment. But, equally naturally, the believers in cost-push would be dead set against such an engineered low-pressure economy, since they are equally convinced that it will be a dismal failure involving much needless social pain. (A third school, who believes in cost-push but think it can be cured or minimized by orthodox depressing of demand, think that our failure to make this experiment would be fraught with social evil by virtue of the fact that they expect a creep in prices to snowball into a trot and then a gallop.)

Our own view will by now have become evident. When we translate the Phillips' diagram showing the American pattern of wage increase against degree of unemployment into a related diagram showing the different levels of unemployment that would be "needed" for each degree of price level change, we come out with guesses like the following:

1. In order to have wages increase at no more than the 2½ per cent per annum characteristic of our productivity growth, the American economy would seem on the basis of twentieth-century and postwar experience to have to undergo something like 5 to 6 per cent of the civilian labor force's being unemployed. That much unemployment would appear to be the cost of price stability in the years immediately ahead.

2. In order to achieve the nonperfectionist's goal of high enough output to give us no more than 3 per cent unemployment, the price index might have to rise by as much as 4 to 5 per cent per year. That much price rise would seem to be the necessary cost of high employment and production in the years immediately ahead.

All this is shown in our price-level modification of the Phillips curve, Figure 2. The point A, corresponding to price stability, is seen to involve about 5½ per cent unemployment; whereas the point B, corre-

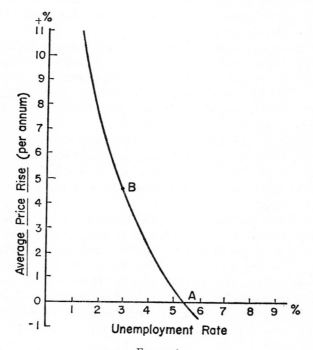

FIGURE 2

MODIFIED PHILLIPS CURVE FOR U.S.

This shows the menu of choice between different degrees of unemployment and price stability, as roughly estimated from last twenty-five years of American data.

sponding to 3 per cent unemployment, is seen to involve a price rise of about 4½ per cent per annum. We rather expect that the tug of war of politics will end us up in the next few years somewhere in between these selected points. We shall probably have some price rise and some excess unemployment.

Aside from the usual warning that these are simply our best guesses we must give another caution. All of our discussion has been phrased in short-run terms, dealing with what might happen in the next few years. It would be wrong, though, to think that our Figure 2 menu that relates obtainable price and unemployment behavior will maintain its same shape in the longer run. What we do in a policy way during the next few years might cause it to shift in a definite way.

Thus, it is conceivable that after they had produced a low-pressure economy, the believers in demand-pull might be disappointed in the short run; i.e., prices might continue to rise even though unemployment was considerable. Nevertheless, it might be that the low-pressure demand would so act upon wage and other expectations as to shift the curve downward in the longer run—so that over a decade, the economy might enjoy higher employment with price stability than our present-day estimate would indicate.

But also the opposite is conceivable. A low-pressure economy might build up within itself over the years larger and larger amounts of structural unemployment (the reverse of what happened from 1941 to 1953 as a result of strong war and postwar demands). The result would be an upward shift of our menu of choice, with more and more unemployment being needed just to keep prices stable.

Since we have no conclusive or suggestive evidence on these conflicting issues, we shall not attempt to give judgment on them. Instead we venture the reminder that, in the years just ahead, the level of attained growth will be highly correlated with the degree of full employment and high-capacity output.

But what about the longer run? If the per annum rate of technical progress were about the same in a low- and high-pressure economy, then the initial loss in output in going to the low-pressure state would never be made up; however, in relative terms, the initial gap would not grow but would remain constant as time goes by. If a low-pressure economy could succeed in improving the efficiency of our productive factors, some of the loss of growth might be gradually made up and could in long enough time even be more than wiped out. On the other hand, if such an economy produced class warfare and social conflict and depressed the level of research and technical progress, the loss in growth would be compounded in the long run.

A final disclaimer is in order. We have not here entered upon the important question of what feasible institutional reforms might be introduced to lessen the degree of disharmony between full employment and price stability. These could of course involve such wide-ranging issues as direct price and wage controls, antiunion and antitrust legislation, and a host of other measures hopefully designed to move the American Phillips' curves downward and to the left.

103

REFLECTIONS ON MONETARY POLICY
Paul A. Samuelson

So great is the compulsion for a professor to convert all evaluations into grades that I find myself making out the following report card: the performance of the Federal Reserve over the last few years, its laboratory work so to speak, would rate only a B; the Fed's rationalization of what it is doing, its essay questions, earn for it, I fear, a bare gentleman's C.

Lest these grades seem harsh, we must remember that modern problems are difficult. Were one to fill out a similar report card for the eloquent opposition to the Fed, while it would certainly earn an A for effort, one could not conscientiously award it high marks for the subtlety of its economic analysis. Perhaps the best that can be said for it is this: ours is a pluralistic society involving the competing pressures of diverse interests and bodies, and had not the opposition been snapping at the Fed's heels, there are reasons to fear its monetary policies might have been even less good than they were.

In all seriousness, I must append some disclaimers to the above remarks. These are of course my subjective valuations, not objective ratings that all informed experts would be expected to agree to. Life is not a classroom. We are dealing here with open questions that only a fool could think were capable of True or False answers. Throughout the Federal Reserve System there are intelligent, well-trained, zealous men, whose goal is the furthering of the national interest. Maybe they are right and I am wrong. Nor is the System a monolithic structure: there is more academic freedom within the Federal Reserve than in any central bank in the world, and for all I know than in any central bank throughout all history. We economists generally have a wholesome Freudian love for the Fed; its problems are our problems; and quite naturally therefore we henpeck the System and try to improve it according to our own lights.

I

Let me stress that what some would regard as shortcomings in the recent performance of the System have been due more to the indifference curves of its highest authorities than to any technical economic weaknesses. For example, many have criticized the Fed, rightly I think, for continuing to pursue tight money into October and November of 1957. Was this because the cycle analysts within the Fed were slower than the bulk of the experts in recognizing the mid-summer turning point? Not at all. If you had fraternized with research economists within the System whose business it is to follow current business conditions, I believe you would have found that most of them were beginning to have anxieties as early as May at the latest. But if you gave the weight that the Board does to (1) price stability in comparison with (2) the difference between 5 and 4 per cent near-term unemployment and (3) the desirability of purchasing further short-term physical growth by credit ease, then I suspect you too would have been led by the slow price creep of 1955–57 to overstay your market somewhat as they did, even if not by so long a period.

Note that I am not expressing the cocksure view that the authorities should have been wise enough to see that from mid-1956 on the boom was largely spent and was hanging on by its teeth. These things are much easier seen in retrospect. On the other hand, I do wish the Board would embrace more warmly the Viner view that it should be prepared at any time to reverse its policy, experimentally and tentatively, and should feel there is no cause for self-reproach when it soon finds itself forced back to a previous policy. One of the virtues of monetary policy is that it can move by small steps and change its mind. One wishes that the Board would more frequently avail itself of this womanly privilege.

Wouldn't it be nice if the National Bureau of Economic Research did not have to register

money behavior and interest rates so often among its *lagging* rather than leading or coinciding time series? Leaning against the wind is indeed a good stabilizing philosophy. Since it takes some time to guess how the wind has been blowing, some lag there will tend to be. And because the effects of present-day monetary policy, like those of fiscal policy, will be distributed over some future times, the lags are in a sense intensified and can weaken or reverse the stabilizing effects of a lean-against-the-wind policy.

But, taking into account the view that the Federal Reserve should expect often to have to reverse any new credit trend it is now putting into effect, and taking into account the actual *ex post* batting averages of short-run forecasts rather than merely tea room talk of how badly the experts did in 1929 and 1945, I would say that the problem of lags should predispose us even more toward the following view: instead of adapting policy passively to the recent past, the authorities should try to form a judgment of what a prudent informed man thinks the rough probabilities are for the couple of quarters ahead and should take action accordingly, being perfectly prepared to change their tack as new evidence becomes available to modify these prudent probabilities.

II

Specifically, I should like to see in some future cycle the following pattern: the Fed's easy money has helped to create an upturn; perhaps early in that upturn the Fed has begun to put more restraint on the market than was done in 1955, though on this point I am not so sure as are the critics of the Board or the authorities themselves after reviewing that experience; as the expansion progresses and as more and more price and wage rises begin to accompany the rise in physical output, the Board continues to apply credit restraint more or less as was done in 1956; but later, and here I come to my point, I would at least once like to see the Fed ease off on the structure of interest as soon as output begins to level off or grow less rapidly than its trend value, even though, as can be expected, price and wage rises concomitantly show no particular abatement; so that there might then ensue a period of falling interest rates as the Fed deliberately strives to prolong a prosperity period by encouraging every possible deepening of capital.

It is possible that 1960 might present the opportunity for such policy.[1] But my proposal has nothing to do with that. I simply want to raise the question whether we might get, within the same pattern of average longtime price rises, a better degree of attainment of high production and growth if we tried varying the present cyclical pattern of generally leaning against the wind until *after* a turn was pretty clearly recognizable.

Admittedly certain limited risks with respect to forecasting are here involved. But there is no escaping the problem of forecasting: he who refuses to do it is thereby simply binding himself to a special kind of implicit forecasting. And he who thinks he can replace judgment by freezing action in advance into certain formulas or rules is exercising the most extreme kind of discretion possible when setting up those rules and must be implicitly or explicitly claiming that he knows how to predict for the distant future the kinds of instabilities and problems that are likely to arise. In matters of this sort rather than turn to the philosopher for generalities, consult with an electrical engineer whose task it is to set up automatic servomechanisms and learn from him how the design of optimal characteristics must depend critically upon the postulated statistical properties of the loads that are to be put on the system. The notion that man has now the wisdom to set up machines that will be endowed with, or can be expected to learn from, experience, the wisdom needed to cope with the uncertain future, is only less naive than the expectation that men will in real political life stand by and passively abide by the decisions of some past Frankensteins.

III

A careful reading of the Federal Reserve positions suggests the authorities are willing to entertain the hypothesis that there are important cost-push mechanisms operating in the present

[1] This was written some months before the June 1960 lowering of the discount rate.

system. As Solow and I indicated at the 1959 meeting of the American Economic Association, in our paper [Ch. 102] on the apparent "Phillips curve" that roughly relates American wage increases to the degree of unemployment in our system, I agree that tendencies toward sellers' inflation and related inflexibilities in the face of demand changes do seem to throw up something of a dilemma for fiscal and monetary policy. Chairman Martin seems to conclude from this that it is *all the more necessary* for the Fed to hold a tight rein on credit. In the sense that unlimited credit at pegged interest rates would contribute toward a secular inflation under the postulated conditions, one can agree. But that is very different from accepting the implication that in the presence of important cost-push pressures, one should act all the harder to *insure price stability*.

With important cost-push forces assumed to be operating, there are many models in which it can be shown that some sacrifice in the requirement for price stability is needed if short- and long-term growth are to be maximized, if average long-run unemployment is to be minimized, if optimal allocation of resources as between different occupations is to be facilitated. I confess I have not found in writings of the Board a careful and judicious appraisal of these *possibilities* — I will not call them certainties.

Perhaps all we can expect of a public body, charged with grave responsibilities, is that it should in its public utterances make out cases stronger than it really believes in. Or perhaps, because its opposition deals in overly strong criticisms, it may for political reasons and for understandable psychological reasons provide overly strong rebuttals. Or perhaps it is the case that the authorities believe that there are no sensible reasons to doubt the following view: *The way to maximize growth, to maximize the long-run degree of achieved employment, to maximize equity among the various social groups that could be affected by price level changes is, in the absence of important cost pressures and even more in their presence, for the Federal Reserve to insist upon the attainment of essentially stable long-run price levels.*

If they feel *confident* in the correctness of so definite a view, which involves relationships that are universally thought to be of exceptional complexity and which is itself at one extremity of the spectrum with respect to the viewpoints that have been soberly discussed by academic economists, then I simply have to report that the Reserve authorities are not to be regarded as skilled economists in the academic sense of the term. Thoughtful students of these problems generally feel that *no one* has the evidence to be confident with respect to any single view in this difficult area, and that the above position imputed, I hope not wrongly, to the Fed is but one of a number of possible hypotheses and perhaps not the most plausible single one at that. It is not out of spite, partisan commitment, or mere ignorance that have come the many academic criticisms which the Reserve authorities seem to find so unconstructive.

IV

Here are some tentative observations on the potency of monetary action and an evaluation of different mechanisms. I agree that *open-market operations* are the important weapon of control. Changes in *required reserve rates* can have powerful effects but should probably be used primarily to attain long-run objectives or is reserved for an emergency when strong results are needed in a short time.

I think that criticisms of the *discount function* are overdone. While it is true that discounting often acts counter to open-market operations, there is no evidence that a unit change in open-market operations induces an opposing change in discounting large enough to reverse or substantially wipe out the original effect. So it is not really difficult for the planners of open-market operations to take all this into account; and precisely because they know that the discount window provides an escape valve, they can be more courageous in the use of open-market operations. To repeat a phrase that I previously borrowed from Schumpeter for use in this connection: giving a car brakes may seem to slow it down, but actually cars go faster because they have brakes. So it may well be that the discount window strengthens the efficacy of open-market operations despite superficial appearances to

the contrary, particularly since it most definitely can strengthen the potency of moral suasion. Let me finally say that these considerations do not argue against the view that the discount rate might be moved more often to keep in closer relation to market conditions. Nor am I particularly opposed to the Canadian practice of setting the discount rate in fixed relations to competitively determined market rates for bills; it is just that I think the degree of improvement will be much less than the adherents of this view hope. And the same goes for the policy of abolishing all discounting.

I must be brief here on the problem of "bills only" or "bills usually." Economists have long thought that short- and long-term interest rates are related, but by no means *perfectly* related.[2] Experience here and abroad has led also to the view that many components of investment expenditure, some of which one certainly might want to influence in the concern for stabilization, are more potently affected by variations in long-term interest rates and their associated capital value changes than by variations in short-term interest rates alone. If the Reserve authorities really think they have evidence to refute these findings of experience, it is incomprehensible why they insist on the importance of having Treasury debt management conducive to stability. In justice I must add that the Joint Economic Committee show the same inconsistency in their writings: if you agree with them that contracyclical management of debt maturities is unimportant, then how can you go along with their vehement criticism of the "bills only" doctrine?

My own position departs from both these views. Legislative and administrative ceilings on FHA and VA interest rates have, fortuitously, given strong leverage for cyclical credit

---

[2] The quantitative *degree of substitutability* among different parts of the money market is an extremely important question for investigation. Thanks, however, to unpublished theoretical analysis by Tobin (Cowles Foundation Discussion Paper No. 63), we can know that under certain plausible assumptions each and every imperfectly substituting sub-market (e.g., that involving longs rather than shorts, that involving intimately such *financial intermediaries* as insurance companies rather than commercial banks, etc.) will be affected *qualitatively* in the same direction by an open-market bill purchase as will the rates in the bill market itself. Needless to say, this valuable finding does not imply that all sub-markets are affected in equal *quantitative* degree.

management and have produced in the postwar period an important stabilizing contribution from the field of residential housing. Even if there were no objections to such a mechanism, one suspects that such a situation is unlikely to last. And should there arise cycle movements somewhat more serious than our three mild postwar recessions, there might come a time when the "bills only" doctrine could involve significant social costs.

Taking the Treasury and Reserve System together, and this we should do since all of the latter's extra earnings are turned over to the Treasury, we must face the fact that minimizing interest costs to the government is incompatible with a policy of enhancing stabilization by pushing long terms on the public in times of overexpansion and pulling out long terms in times of underexpansion. For this involves selling bonds when they are cheap and buying them back when they are dear. While no one favors spending money unnecessarily, we must never forget that it is the business of the government to spend money in good causes — a principle that Senator Douglas ought to appreciate more than most.

V

Economists of my generation have had to unlearn a lot in the sphere of monetary policy. First we had to discover that the velocity of circulation of money is not a constant, independent of interest rates or of business optimism and investment opportunities generally. Then we learned from questionnaire investigations by Hall, Harrod, Hitch and others at Oxford that investment spending could be expected to react very inelastically to changes in interest rates; from case studies by Ebersole of the Harvard Business School pretty much the same thing; from statistical studies by Tinbergen and others that the interest rate did not figure importantly in multiple correlation equations to explain investment.

Subsequent experience with respect to verbal replies in interviews and questionnaires and with correlation studies would, I suppose, cause us today to give less weight to that kind of evidence. But in the years after 1933 we did have experience with an extensive gold flow into the United States that resulted in short-term interest rates which were practically zero and in sizeable excess reserves by banks. Although there has since become available much fuller information about the behavior of the money supply and velocity in the last century, nothing in that experience suggests that a person in, say 1935, should have expected a hundred million dollars of open-market purchases by the Fed to have had expansionary effects on output and prices as sizeable as a similar purchase might have had in the decade of the 1920's. When you have forced down the bill rate to one quarter of one per cent at a time of pessimistic risk aversion, forcing it down a little more seems unlikely to affect real expenditure very much.

Still, the 1950's and the 1960's are not the late 1930's. Although even now I hear some bankers say that they have never met a business that couldn't get, even in tight money days, the credit it "really needs," the evidence does seem inescapable that increases in the cost and tightening of the availability of credit do have substantial effects on investment spending: as mentioned, they have sharp effects on housing expenditure under present institutions; they affect the timing of state and local spending; in my opinion they affect the timing of many components of business investment, and also possibly their average level over a period of time.

We used to think interest was too unimportant a cost to have much influence on short-lived projects; that with respect to long-lived projects it would be swamped by the larger factor of subjective uncertainty about the distant future. I am not sure now that this is even a half truth. Swings in inventory accumulation are so great as to be a predominant factor in short cyclical swings; it is by no means certain that credit policy can have only negligible effects on inventory policy. But more important is the problem of long-lived investment projects. Decisions about them do involve uncertainty; but if you watch the pencil work that goes into planning a toll road, a hotel, or even a piece of durable equipment, you will find that the decision whether to go ahead or not *is*, in a given state of expectation, crucially affected by the postulated interest charges. A change of interest rate from 5 to 6 per cent may seem small; but to the entrepreneur who is taking on himself the residual risk, it may make the difference between his ending up with an expectation of 40 per cent on *his* commitment rather than the inadequate 10 per cent which he may feel is not adequate compensation for the risks involved. And for reasons not entirely clear to me, when money is tight enough to produce 6 per cent rather than 5 per cent on high-grade bonds, the optimistic entrepreneurs often find they simply cannot get the supplementary finance they need for their investment programs. (The history of Webb & Knapp and similar investment promoters would be interesting in this connection.)

Monetary policy used to be sometimes criticized on two seemingly inconsistent grounds: on the one hand it was argued that conventional monetary contraction had little potency to affect spending; on the other, that it was in danger of causing a collapse of business. This at first glance appeared to be illogical, and defenders of monetary management argued that this simply raised the problem of proper intermediate dosage. While I think, as a matter of mere logic, one can construct a servomechanism that will be so unstable as to produce little effect at first and then hard-to-predict avalanche-like effects almost impossible to control, it would seem better to consider actual experience since 1950. Careful observation suggests that the effects of monetary policy on the real economy are likely to be continuous rather than discontinuous, even though it will be true of the bond market, as of all supply and demand markets, that with changes in expectations there can result quick swings in prices. But there has been nothing in the experience here, or the more extensive experience in postwar Britain, to suggest that a nation will be ruined if its bonds stand 15, 20, or even 40 per cent below par.

I do not wish to exaggerate the potency of monetary measures. In particular I must record the judgment that the interesting "new theory of money" promulgated by Williams, Roosa, and others around 1950 has been valuable in its emphasis upon the attitude of lenders, but it has expected more potency from small changes in interest rates than the subsequent experience has actually recorded; and its mystique of uncertainty as a powerful weapon of the central bank still needs to be spelled out.[3]

I suppose nobody believes today, as did some of the generation of economists just before my day, that the relative way that the expansionary impacts of changes in M affect the Q and P of the equation of exchange is any different than could be expected from an equivalent expansion in fiscal policy. Economists of my day may be entitled to regard velocity as an unfruitful variable for the understanding of how monetary policies work; they may feel that expansions in M resulting from a unit addition to open-market purchases will be weaker at some times than at others, and that such changes in M that do take place will at times tend to be largely offset by induced drops in V; but they have no right to conclude, either from experience or from theorizing about an elaborated Keynesian system, that contrived changes in M are likely ever to be *reversed* in effect by induced drops in V larger than the original M increase. So they have no right to deny that changes in M can lead to the right *qualitative* responses in the system (i.e., $\partial(MV)/\partial M$ is not negative, in a *ceteris paribus* sense). And in conditions like those of the last decade, it seems unwise to expect that induced changes in V will largely undo the effects of central bank operations; at times they could be reinforcing. The Radcliffe Report seems to me to give misleading impressions in this regard, whatever its other merits.

But having said all this, I must make clear that a careful study of the concomitant *mutatis mutandis* changes in M and V over past short cycles does not seem to me to give an adequate

---

[3] The much talked-about "locked in" effect makes insiders smile: the important portfolio managers in this country, far from being reluctant to sell bonds that will show a realized loss, carefully pick the years in which money has tightened as loss years and *other things equal* decide to sell the certificates showing the *greatest* loss, knowing that there is a loophole in our tax laws permitting banks to charge off all such losses against ordinary (highly taxed) income and permitting them to pay light long-term capital gains taxes on realized profits when in periods of easy money they sell bonds that have appreciated in value. However, once an interesting myth gets into the economics literature it is hard to get it out again.

basis for estimating *ceteris paribus* effects; i.e., it is a false identification to try to infer $\partial V/\partial M$ from observations on past $(dV/dt)/(dM/dt)$.

And while I am on the subject of "identification," what about the following argument, taught me as an undergraduate: business cycles since the Federal Reserve Act have been greater in amplitude than in the period before 1913; ergo discretionary muddling by the Reserve authorities has made things worse, and the System should be abolished in favor of an inflexible system of rules. Although I was a docile child, I was at the same time being taught how terribly difficult it is to estimate the demand elasticity for a single crop of corn from masses of statistical data; so I was not tempted, even though this proposition received massive support from W. Randolph Burgess, to adopt this line of reasoning, which, inci-dentally, could also hold the Fed responsible for two world wars. What I want to report on is how bad the prophecies generated by this view have been: friends of mine who had adhered to these views could have wrung from them in 1945 or 1951 the prediction that post-war business cycles should prove worse than those in the good old days of 1870 to 1912. How wrong such prophecies have been! And how high must be their grades for the Federal Reserve in producing in the last decade a stability in the growth of M according to the fondest wishes of my earliest teachers.

Now that I have come to the end of my story, what grades ought to be given to my-self and more particularly my generation? I do not think it is modesty that makes us prefer to leave this for posterity to decide.

104

REFLECTIONS ON CENTRAL BANKING[1]

Contrary to the opinions of many contemporary economists (and to some of my own earlier views), I believe that monetary and credit policies have great potency to stimulate, stabilize, or depress a modern economy. This belief is based on my evaluation of the tremendous amount of empirical data given by (1) history, (2) current statistics, and (3) case studies of business behavior. These data are diverse, conflicting, and often inconclusive, and therefore have to be interpreted with the help of all the tools of economic analysis inherited from the past and developed by the present generation of scholars.

In thus differing from the pessimists, I want to make clear that I am *not* agreeing with that much smaller group of older economists who think that monetary policy by itself is the sole or principal mechanism for controlling the aggregative behavior of a modern economy. I believe such a view to be factually wrong or irrelevant; and would add that, even if monetary policies truly had this exaggerated degree of potency, I would not deem it optimal social policy to rely exclusively or primarily upon that weapon alone.

Today all experts dismiss the ancient view that *laissez-faire* can properly hold in the field of money and banking. "Money will not manage itself." Banking institutions are not perfectly competitive self-regulating enterprises that can be free from strict governmental regulations and

[1]This article is based upon the author's testimony before the Canadian Royal Commission on Banking and Finance in October 1962. Pages 1361–1377 were originally published in *The National Banking Review*.

controls. They are "public utilities vested with public interest" and the same is true in equal or lesser degree of various financial intermediaries, such as savings institutions, finance companies, and insurance concerns. Let me make clear that all this is stated from the standpoint of one who philosophically values individual freedoms. A person who cheerfully accepts the idea of direct price, wage, and production controls can afford to give a relatively large measure of freedom to credit institutions; but one who wishes to minimize (except in emergency periods) the use of such direct controls will realize that we maximize total freedom in a society by limiting it in the areas which crucially determine the aggregate of effective demand.

I must firmly disassociate myself from the small but important group of writers who, agreeing that money will not run itself, go on to argue that it ought to be determined permanently by certain automatic formulas. Sometimes this is put in the fancy language of "rules versus authorities," or "laws versus men," or "automaticity versus discretionary action." Of course, no one, myself included, will admit to favoring arbitrary caprice of bungling rulers over the even-handed justice of well-formulated rules. If every form of explicit cooperative action set up by men is bound to be completely nearsighted, venal, and blundering, then recourse to astrological rules might pragmatically be defended — although no wise man could have any secure belief that such bungling human beings would ever bind themselves and stay bound to such arbitrary mechanisms. The vicissitudes of ancient coin standards — which were at the mercy of the accidental discovery of precious metals in Latin America, Australia, California, Alaska, South Africa, and now Soviet Russia — would certainly be preferable to some forms of "managed money."

In practice, however, there have always been — for both good and evil — substantial departures from any automatic coin, bullion, or other kind of gold standard. In principle, the choice has never been between discretionary and nondiscretionary action: for when men set up a definitive mechanism which is to run forever afterward by itself, that involves a single act of discretion which transcends, in both its arrogance and its capacity for potential harm, any repeated acts of foolish discretion that can be imagined. Since I have argued elsewhere the philosophical principles involved in this choice and have never seen any written refutation of these arguments by adherents of the "automaticity" school, I shall merely state here that the relevant choices have to be made pragmatically in terms of the goodness or badness of behavior patterns that result from various kinds of discretionary action.

Specifically, consider the suggestion of a money supply which is to grow at exactly 3 per cent per year, a policy advocated by some who think no other actions would then be required. Suppose this had been enacted in the United States in a random recent year, without knowledge of the balance-of-payments problems just ahead, and without knowledge of the massive shift to time deposits such as we have been experiencing as a result of both raised interest-rate ceilings on such deposits and the natural shift to such deposits as interest rates generally rise. The results could have been quite bad in comparison with what actually happened; and if the balance-of-payments situation had, for unpredictable reasons, been a great deal worse, the results could have been disastrous. I realize the adherents of such proposals will argue that such dire results might have been avoided if there had been floating exchange rates, perfectly flexible wage rates, and never, never any interest-rate or other ceilings. But since we do not and shall not live in such a never-never land, legislating part of the package would surely do more harm than good.

I. The Quantity Theory and Monetary Policy

There are many reasons why any automatic gadget can be improved upon by decision makers, even by fallible decision makers. This statement will be denied by those who are firm believers in the ancient Quantity Theory of Money. If it were true *in a causal sense* that there is an invariant relationship between, on the one hand, total dollar income and spending, and, on the other, the supply of money defined in such a way as to be capable of predetermination by the central bank, then an autogyro which kept total money supply growing smoothly would, by hypothesis, keep total money income growing smoothly. While I know that some modern scholars have tried by historical studies to establish an empirical concomitance between money supply and aggregate income, let me simply state here that I find the implied proof of a simple, controllable, causal proportionality relationship unconvincing.

It is the easiest sport in the world to shoot down any crude formulation of the Quantity Theory. But I think it quite illegitimate to conclude from this what the Radcliffe Committee and many modern scholars have stated: namely, if total money supply, M, does not invariably create an exactly proportional total income and product because the income velocity of circulation of money, V, is not a constant, then it follows that we should turn our attention away from conventional central bank controls and rely instead upon some global concept of "liquidity." As will become evident, I attach considerable importance to various concepts of liquidity.

But I think it wrong to believe that recognizing such concepts should undermine the belief that conventional central bank operations of open-market purchase and sale of securities, discount lending, and reserve-ratio changing are likely to have important effects upon the total of investment and consumption spending. Emphasizing "liquidity" quite properly serves to debunk a crude quantity theory, and it thereby scores a fatal point against advocates of simple automaticity gadgets. But it leaves the position I am here expounding unscathed, and it is for this reason that a number of reviewers have criticized the Radcliffe Report.[2]

Because of the human temptation to deify any concept that has been defined and to tend to regard, as approximately constant, the last variable that one has defined, I do not find the velocity variable, V, a very useful one. But older economists did, and some younger ones are beginning to again. So I shall restate the heart of the matter in such terms.

If the requisite V were a strict constant, $P \times Q$ would, by hypothesis, be exactly proportional to the requisite definition of money, M. Experience shows that V is not a constant: it shows certain historical trends in the long run; in the course of the business cycle, it has generally shown fluctuations that are sympathetic with the cycle itself, rising in good times and falling in bad. After more studies have been made, I believe V will also show certain fluctuations with interest rate and other conditions, tending, other things equal, to rise when interest rates are high and the opportunity cost of cash balances is great, and tending to fall when short-term investment opportunities all have a very low yield.

The behavior of V will also be quite sensitively affected by the particular concept of the money supply that is adopted, being quite different if currency alone is considered (as with the nineteenth-century Currency School and Edwin Cannan in the 1920's) than if demand deposits are included and various categories of time deposits and close money substitutes are, or are not, included in the definition of money. Some of the movements of V will be erratic and relatively unpredictable; others will be in some measure predictable. In particular, although they are operationally hard to identify in the empirical record, certain changes can always be expected in V that are themselves induced by the change in M itself and, certain other things being held constant, are part and parcel of such a change in M. Some sensible probability statements can be made about these induced changes in V at various phases of the business cycle and at various time points in history.

Now, if it were the case that recognition of the importance of money substitutes and various concepts of liquidity were to imply that changes of M in one direction could be expected to be followed systematically by opposite changes in V just large enough to offset any resulting induced changes in $MV = PQ$, then the casual reader of the Radcliffe Report would be right in thinking that central banks are unable to affect significantly aggregate spending by conventional open-market and lending operations. But none of the testimony or arguments in connection with the Radcliffe Committee succeed, in my judgment, in establishing a pre-

[2]See John Gurley, "The Radcliffe Report and Evidence," *American Economic Review* (September 1960).

sumption in favor of this doctrine of induced-velocity-changes-that-just-offset-money changes.

Not only is this not demonstrated in the historical record, but, in addition, such a finding is not in accordance with that type of analysis which is thought to have displaced the old Quantity Theory. For, in the various Keynesian models, there is generally a presumption that an increase in M engineered by the central bank will cause such a reduction in interest rates and such increases in credit availability as to generate an increase in investment and total spending just large enough to create an extra level of income which would absorb in transaction balances the new increment of money created. While the mechanism just described holds for the most primitive Keynesian model, the same conclusion is found to be valid for more sophisticated models, which pay explicit attention to wealth and other stock effects and which distinguish a long chain of assets that range from being very near to money (like short-term government bonds) to being very illiquid and difficult to sell or evaluate (like built-in machinery that is highly specific to a particular location and owner). And the qualitative nature of the conclusion — that the central bank can expand spending by expansive open-market, lending, and reserve-ratio fixing operations — will still hold, even after we have admitted the existence of relatively-less-controlled financial intermediaries such as savings banks, finance companies, insurance companies, mutual or unit-trust funds, and various forms of equity and loan participants.

With his permission, I will refer briefly to an interesting demonstration by Professor James Tobin of Yale in an unpublished manuscript[3] privately circulated several years ago. Suppose that we have a chain of substitutes, which instead of being called tea, coffee, and cocoa are called bank money, short-term bonds, long-term bonds, insurance assets, and so forth; call them M_1, M_2 — and suppose that their respective prices are N_1, N_2, $\cdots$. If the central bank could decrease all of the M totals together by operations and fiats that apply to insurance companies as well as to banks and to all financial intermediaries, then no one doubts that the total of "liquidity," however measured, would go down and that this would, other things equal, tend to have a depressing effect on aggregate spending and general inflationary pressures. Specifically, with every M_i decreasing because of direct central bank action, the unweighted or weighted sum of the M's and every other recommended measure of "liquidity" would also go down. But now suppose that the central bank can only decrease directly M_i, having no direct controls on the reserve-ratios or totals of any other sectoral M_j. A reader of the whole of the Radcliffe Report and Hearings might be forgiven for infer-

[3]Cowles Commission Study Paper #63.

ring that in this case nothing positive could be said about the ability of the central bank to affect total liquidity, as measured by some kind of total of the M's or weighted-sum of the M's or other measure of liquidity; and hence that we should abandon the simple notion that a modern central bank can by its conventional operations push aggregate spending in a desired direction. Tobin, however, in his unpublished memo, has shown that, provided the M's are all *substitutes* (in the sense that the excess demand for each M_i *de*creases when its own N_i price rises but *in*creases when some other M_j's N_j goes up — as, for example, that an isolated increase in the price of short-term bonds should cause less of them to be demanded and more of long-term bonds to be substituted for them), then the central bank can cause *every* M_j to go down by simply depressing M_i! (The theorem is like the Leontief one which says that raising the consumption requirements for hats must raise gross output of every good in a well-behaved input-output system, and like the Metzler-Keynes theorem that an increase in domestic investment in one country must to some degree raise outputs everywhere in a well-behaved many-sector multiplier model.) This important Tobin result accords well with intuition. One should not push it beyond its actual statement: each indirect effect is, generally speaking, weaker than each direct effect, *and* the central bank may have to push undesirably harder on M_i to get the same change in over-all M's than it would have to do if it were given direct powers to affect financial intermediaries.[4] Later I shall have to point out some important limiting cases where the potency of central bank action becomes quantitatively zero or almost zero.

It has often been said that monetary policy is more effective in contracting an economy than in getting it to expand. There is an important grain of truth in this observation. Thus, when the bank rate or the discount rate is 6 or 7 per cent, and the commercial banks' excess reserves are at a minimum and the business community is heavily dependent upon bank borrowings for its current investments in inventories and other items, then further restrictive action by the central bank can, by a variety of channels, cut deeply into the aggregate of investment and total spending.

On the other hand, in a period like the 1930's, when the market yield on short-term government securities has already been driven down to a fraction of one per cent, and when banks have copious excess reserves and business firms are regretting their past investing and regarding the marginal profitability rate on all further investments as negative, there

---

[4]This corresponds to a theorem that, in appropriate units, $\partial N_i/\partial M_i > \partial N_j/\partial M_i > 0$ for certain systems of Leontief, Metzler, and Mosak-Hicks type, as has been recognized by diverse writers, such as Hicks, H. Johnson, Morishima, and others. It does not deny that in certain limiting cases of perfect substitution these effects will be equal, or that in certain limiting cases one or both may be zero.

would be little potency indeed in conventional central bank operations. (Buying short-term bonds in the open market would then merely take from the community a very close money substitute and replace it by money itself.) This would not have much further depressing influence on the interest rate structure and would not make credit more readily available to borrowers (who are in any case virtually nonexistent and automatically regarded as suspiciously risky chaps, if they should come forward with a loan application).

From the technical fact that monetary policy works more effectively at high than at low interest rates, no one should make the mistake of concluding that the goal of policy should be to avoid low rates. Forks must be made to fit fingers, not fingers, forks: when an economy will suffer from tight markets and the technician will benefit, it is of course the technician who must properly give way.

This last case then is one where an induced change in velocity can be expected to wipe out almost completely any contrived change in money narrowly defined. It is the case often referred to as the Depression-Keynes model, where (1) there is a liquidity trap near to a zero rate of pure interest, at which the Keynesian liquidity preference schedule is practically infinite in elasticity so that the system will absorb great amounts of M at practically the same interest rate and credit-availability; and/or where (2) the rate of investment spending is almost completely inelastic with respect to changes in the interest cost and availability of credit.

I believe, in the face of some doubters, that such a depression model has occasional empirical validity — certainly in the short run and possibly for a vexingly long time. Moreover, bitter experience in the United States of the last few years leads one to suspect that it is not always so easy to engineer a deepening of capital by conventional central bank operations, even when one is not in a deep-depression liquidity trap: for, even when gilt-edge rates are lowered farther and farther, the effective profit rates that businessmen must anticipate to get them to make somewhat risky investments may remain quite high — say 15 per cent before corporate taxes or 8 per cent after taxes. Thus, even massive open-market purchase of government bonds may not be able to push the system down through a high-profit floor that acts rather like the older Keynes liquidity trap interest floor in keeping investment resistant to expansion.

I know it can be argued that the central bank, provided it is ready to abandon notions of feasibility and force the market rates of interest up to 40 per cent in boom times and down to zero or, for that matter, down to negative rates of interest, can control the amount of total money and spending activity at any desired levels, regardless of adverse fiscal policies and adverse behavior propensities on the part of business and the public. Personally, I consider it irrelevant to talk about 40 per cent bank rates, and in any case undesirable to put the burden of such extreme adjustments on the narrow sectors most affected by monetary actions. And as far as forcing extremely low interest rates is concerned, it is simply not true that lending money to people at negative interest rates is guaranteed to result in any desired expansion in spending: making gifts might, but if these are loans that have to be paid back, it would be rational for people to borrow at negative interest rates and just hold the proceeds in safety lock boxes, thereby earning a handsome yield. The total of something called M might rise, but that does not mean that the requisite MV can be achieved in any short period by *conventional* central bank operations.

My purpose here is not to score a point against some extreme Quantity Theory formulation, but to call attention to the fact that in many social situations a well-running democracy will want its central bank to engage in *unconventional* activities. (Examples: in the 1930's Federal Reserve Banks made loans directly to certain small businesses; in a future balance-of-payments crisis, the central bank might want to provide certain guarantees and investment insurance to desired domestic investments, while keeping up the yields on short-term government bills; and the day could come when the central bank would want to make loans at negative interest rates to applicants who satisfied certain requirements, such as a guaranteeing that the proceeds would go into resource-using investment; if *laissez-faire* conditions should prove to choke off deepening of capital when profits rates are still as high as 10 per cent and conventional credit operations proved not able to overcome this, the intrinsic logic of central banking requires recourse to new, unconventional programs.)

Finally, I once felt it necessary to point out a minor flaw in certain descriptions of the asymmetry of monetary policy's potency. It is not correct to say that monetary policy can contract an economy more easily than it can expand it. In buoyant times when interest rates are already high and credit already tight, monetary policy is quite potent enough to *both* expand and contract the system from its previous situation; in slack times when interest rates are near the floor and the system is swimming in liquidity, monetary policy is quite impotent with respect to contraction and expansion of the system from its previous level. Thus, the true asymmetry is not that depicted by a corner in the schedule relating general activity and central bank activity, with the slope for an up movement being greatly different from the slope for a down movement; the asymmetry merely refers to the putative difference in slope at any given point in a slack as against a tight credit market.

Central bankers abhor a situation which they feel is not closely responsive to their control. So they naturally dislike being so expansive as to create a "sloppy market." As shown above, the consequences of this abhorrence may not be too costly in the short run; yet they should often brave the displeasure of commercial bankers (who abhor sloppy markets for the good commercial reasons that such markets are hard on bank earnings) and flood the market with a view to the longer-run stimulus in investment that may come from gradual penetration of alleged liquidity-trap floors. One has no right to assume away such longer-run benefits from a policy of "over-ease." The central banker will tend to feel that the cost of such a policy will be the danger that in the subsequent recovery period the redundant credit, which had previously done no harm and precious little good, will come to life and create the possibility of an over-fast expansion and of undue inflationary pressures. This is just another aspect of his reluctance to let the money market get out of his immediate control.

While recognizing some merit in this view, I would point out that the goal of policy is not to minimize the unease of central bankers; they are supposed to suffer psychic pain when that is in a good cause. Moreover, some quickening in their contractionary actions early in the recovery may serve to undo much of the harm to be expected from an earlier policy of over-ease, and such a quickening would in many cases be a worthwhile price to pay for improving the slump situation. What I am saying here would not be so important if the only thing to fear were a regular cycle involving a recession known to be short-lived. But when an economy moves into an epoch when profit rates are sluggish (having been competed down by the plentifulness of capital stock relative to labor, and the nature and speed of contemporaneous technical change) and investment is hard to coax out at still lower profit rates, the best policy for conventional central banking operations is to keep the money market flooded with reserves, with a view to eroding gradually resistant long-term interest rates and the profit-rate floors that businessmen insist upon getting, if they are to make resources-employing investments. Specifically, in the U.S. environment of the 1930's, it was right to have great excess reserves and minimal short-term rates: the slow, too-slow, drop in long-term interest rates was thereby encouraged. With due regard to future international payments considerations, the same strategy will be needed in certain future times; and American central bankers are wrong to reproach themselves for over-ease in the 1953–1954 and 1957–1958 recessions.

Zealots for monetary policy are, somewhat pardonably, infuriated by a related asymmetry that used to be argued by critics. These critics would say in one breath, "Monetary action is practically impotent," and in the next breath they would add, "But using monetary policy determinedly will plunge the system into a crisis and major depression." This argument is thought to involve almost a self-contradiction. How can a thing be simultaneously both weak and strong? Formally, this can be saved from being utter nonsense by modifying it to say, "For a small exercise of monetary policy, the results will be not only small but disappointingly small; for a really large exercise, the results will be disastrously large." To this, defenders of the view that M can take care of everything will naturally reply, "Aha, then, it is really only a matter of using the right (intermediate) dosage."

On the whole, I have to agree with this defense of monetary policy, particularly in the historical context of the postwar U.S. debates as to whether letting War Bonds fall below par would entail uncontrollable disaster. But in terms of the logic of all the situations that could possibly arise, two qualifications ought to be made: (1) If the response to a control lever satisfies a function that changes suddenly from a low slope to a high one, and at an unknown spot, then a correct dosage is extremely hard to reckon or to work out experimentally; so in some, perhaps rare and unrealistic, situations the asymmetry arguments of the pessimists might have a measure of validity. (2) There is a second complication that may have been envisaged by users of this asymmetry argument: namely, the possibility that in certain situations market expectations are important, with investment demand depending on the bond prices that the central bank engineers and also on the *rate of change of prices*; given differential equation relationships of the form $F(I,P,dp/dt, M, \cdots) = 0$, there could result discontinuities in the solution. An example would be the case where shoveling a little snow up hill may, at an unknown and quite unpredictable point, set off an avalanche of snow. To say in such a situation, "It is only a question of the right intermediate dosage," is to miss the point.

II. Effects of Monetary Policy on Price and Output

It was once widely believed, and some central bank authorities still believe it, that the central bank operates to control money, or M, and that M operates directly to control the price level, P. In the old days the quantity of output, Q, was not thought to need determining by any particular agency, since something like full employment was more or less taken for granted. In more recent decades, holders of the present view have been prone to think of government *fiscal* policy as somehow having the ability to control Q, with monetary policy controlling P. The point I want to make is a purely mechanical one and has nothing to do with subjective value judgments. It is simply untrue that money and credit programs have any way of peculiarly affecting the P or price factor: successful monetary expansion will, as I have shown earlier, have some favorable effect on the dollar value of total output $P \times Q$, and so will expansionary fiscal policy. The resulting change in $P \times Q$ will get distributed between expansion in Q as against expansion in P, depending upon how much or how little labor and capital remains unused to be drawn on, and upon how strong or weak are the cost-push upward pressures that come from the institutional supply conditions of organized and unorganized labor, of oligopolistic price administrators and more perfectly competitive enterprises.

No one has been able to establish any presumption that either monetary policy or fiscal policy has some special impact upon the price as against the output factor. Indeed, one cannot too often correct the view widespread among noneconomists, that a "natural" upswing in consumption or investment spending is less inflationary than an equivalent upswing in aggregate spending, $P \times Q$, brought about by deliberate public policies. (It is true that one expects a somewhat different mix of expenditures to result from new investment spending induced by credit policy than from new consumption spending induced by tax rate reduction. Likewise, a private inventory boom will encounter price rises from bottleneck pressures different from those of a private equipment boom or those of a defense boom. But there is no differential price-level presumption associated in general with deficit, credit, or private stimulation.)

I have been careful to state the Quantity Theory of Money in terms of proportionality between M and $P \times Q$, rather than in the older terms of proportionality between M and P. The first of these formulations has the advantage that it allows real output to increase considerably from an underemployment situation without there having to be much price rise up to the time that bottlenecks and resource scarcities appear. It allows also for the occurrence of "sellers' inflation," in which there may be an upward push on prices from the wage, profit, and raw material cost side. Since V and Q both tend to rise with the business cycle, Irving Fisher and older writers thought that the ratio of P to M might be approximately constant; however, the facts of the last 40 years do not accord well with such a hypothesis.

Facts aside, there is one model or case in which the older Quantity Theory would indeed be true. Imagine a new situation in which *every* price and every value magnitude has exactly doubled or halved, so that *all* price ratios and real quantities are absolutely unchanged. The essence of money — be it shells, or gold, or bits of paper (and in contrast to drinkable coffee or any good where consumption gives psychic satisfaction) — is that we want it only for its ultimate indirect utility in getting goods that can give direct utility. Basically, we want to hold money only in order to be able to spend it some day in exchange for something directly useful. Therefore, when all prices have exactly doubled or halved while all real magnitudes and exchange ratios and interest rates have stayed exactly constant, the desired amount of money holding can be thought of as exactly doubling or halving.

In this sense and situation, there is an underlying truth in a strict Quantity Theory that makes P and M exactly proportional. (Technically, economists describe this by saying that all real quantity relations are homogeneous of degree zero in *all* absolute prices and all value magnitudes like $p_i \times q_i$ are homogeneous of degree one in terms of all p's; hence the needed amount of money — the number of wampum beads or ounces of gold or items of paper currency — is a homogeneous function of degree one in all the prices when expressed in terms of that unit. Note that whenever a substance used as money also has a direct utility — as in the case of gold for teeth or of beaver skins for coats — this strict Quantity Theory no longer applies: double the amount of beaver skins by central bank or other activity, and the price of wool will not double even if the price of mousetraps should. From this formulation it will be evident that, along with the total of any useless M stuff, be it shells or metal or fiat paper money that represent non-interest-bearing I.O.U.'s of the government, we should also take account of any interest-bearing I.O.U.'s of the government (which people think of as an asset but fail to think of as involving a personal liability for future taxes).

The strict Quantity Theory now says: double fiat M and fiat government bonds, and you will exactly double all prices and value in a classical model that has all its real magnitudes and relative prices unchanged. These fiat bonds are important without regard to the fact that they are usable directly for exchanges or are close money substitutes. As will be seen shortly, some conventional credit operations that involve the same change in M will differ markedly in their "Pigou effects" and potency, a fact ignored by simple-minded theorists. Note too that this version of a quantity theory would hold even if the real part of the model were different from the classical one involving full employment, as in the case of some of the deep-depression Keynesian models of underemployment where so-called Pigou effects were deemed not to operate. If the economist stipulates a real model that lacks unique equilibrium, then a change in absolute price levels might jar the system from one admissible equilibrium to another, thereby jeopardizing the "neutrality" of money.

III. Price Changes and Distribution Effects

Simple models do great good in clarifying issues. They can also do great harm if carelessly applied to real life in all its complexity. History does not record nicely balanced changes in all prices that are as neutral with respect to real effects as would be a dimensional transformation in which one chooses to reckon in terms of cents rather than dollars, or in terms of dozens of eggs rather than single ones. And what is more relevant, when the central bank increases one or another measure of the money supply by 10 per cent, this will not, and cannot, result in a nicely balanced change in all prices and values. It literally cannot do so because all past contracts and past prices are already determined: as a debtor your real position is altered by this new change in M, just as my position as a creditor is altered. Nor is there the slightest guarantee that what I gain you will lose, since there is no law of conservation of total well-being under such a change. Indeed, since the time of David Hume, it has been generally thought that mild *unexpected* price rises tend to expand the degree of utilization of resources and to channel resources into the hands of the more active entrepreneurial elements at the expense of more inert classes. During periods of mild or severe inflations, certain *changes in relative prices* have been considered to be characteristic.

While the conditions for a strict Quantity Theory to be valid are unrealistic, they probably become somewhat less so in the long run. I suspect that after more research has been done we shall learn that many of the systematic changes in *relative* prices induced by transitional inflations are not so great as has been believed; for it seems odd that continuing price rises should keep coming as a surprise to people. Moreover, the longer the run, the less important will be the effects of past contracts and remembrance of lower levels of past prices. The past is, one supposes, as long as the future. But well-behaved and stable price systems tend to have the property of gradually "forgetting" the past. If that were not so, the way that the War of the Roses was financed would be as important for 1962 behavior as the sliding-scale wage contracts of 1961. So a once-and-for-all doubling of money will eventually imply that the distortion inherent in the fact that past prices certainly have not doubled will become less and less relevant. The simpler-minded Quantity Theory is thus seen to have its greatest measure of empirical validity in the longest run.

Having emphasized this kernel of truth, I must quickly add the warning that it is precisely in the long run that other things will not have remained equal: exogenous and endogenous shifts in the relations determining equilibrium will certainly have taken place, thereby vitiating any simple price-scale change as an interpretation of the empirical facts. Even if one could rule out purely exogenous disturbances, real economic life does not consist of a return to the same predetermined real equilibrium after a transient change in money supply. I live but once, and if an inflation wipes out my real net worth, that is an irreversible fact. The distribution of income and corporate power was never (including the position of Hugo Stinnes) quite the same after the 1920–1923 German inflation: even if a Lorenz curve depicting the inequality of distribution of income or wealth begins to revert toward its earlier form, the class ownership of wealth could be permanently different. Even the same Lorenz curve will not imply the same people in the background and the same behavior propensities. Capitalism, as we know it today, probably would have been systematically different if Columbus had never discovered the New World with its vast areas of gold and silver. All that I have just been saying is rather hypothetical. But there can be no doubt that if Canada and the United States had followed policies which prevented the Great Depression of the 1930's, today we would have an entirely different stock of capital goods. And it is wrong to argue that this means merely that we arrive today at the state we would have otherwise reached in 1953 or 1945: to have arrived at our present "capital abundance" prior to knowing the discoveries of *recent* science would imply a qualitatively and quantitatively different pattern of economic history. (Technically, the theorist describes all this by saying that every economic equilibrium displays important *hysteresis* effects; where the very location of the equilibrium position depends upon the actual historical path of the system, and thus, there can never be truly neutral changes in the absolute price level. As a craftsman, I could wish that reality corresponded to the mechanics of a system without hysteresis, because this would make my task of analyzing economic reality so much more pleasant and simple. But just as the purpose of evolution has not been to give central bankers an easy life, neither has it been to give theorists restful nights and plenty of time to play golf or chess.

While my examples have been primarily taken from price rises, the hysteresis effects from price declines are greater still because of price and wage rigidities which persist even in the long run. The attempt after World War I to roll back the price rises by reverting to 1913 gold parities has aptly been compared to the act of running over a man and then backing up over him a second time to undo the first effects. The corpse would recognize hysteresis effects even if many of the best economists of that day did not.

All this may seem abstract, and admittedly it is expressed in technical language. Yet it does have fundamental economic implications. Simple believers in M as the determinant of total effective demand do not feel the need to distinguish between, say, an increase in M that comes from the Treasury's (or central bank's) printing new dollar bills and (1) sending them to all family heads, or (2) lending them at interest to investors, or (3) spending them on subsidies to investors, or (4) buying back Treasury bills with them. The same increase in M leads, they allege, to the same change in $P \times Q$ (and by strict "homogeneity" reasoning to the same real magnitudes). This is, of course, patent nonsense in the short run, as they concede when challenged. Under (1) consumption is presumably stimulated and interest rates, if anything, raised; under (2) interest rate falls, and presumably V too, depending upon how much investment rises. Only in the longest run, if then, can one assume that the new M gets distributed "ergodically" (i.e., independently of its original point of entry): I say *if then* because at best the stock of capital is permanently different. Note that (4) is without direct Pigou effects and hence is presumably permanently different.

Gustav Cassel's famous purchasing-power-parity theory of war-dislocated foreign exchange rates was, prior to its reformulation by Keynes and others as a mere condition of spatial price equilibrium, based originally upon precisely the homogeneity assumption I have just described. It could be precisely applied only to balanced inflation — a situation which did not exist around the time of World War I. As a matter of fact, in such a hypothetical balanced inflation resulting from a mere change in the absolute amount of an essentially neutral money, we would not get any predictive power from the purchasing-power-parity formulation, since in such a world of perfect flexibility the exchange rates would already be at their equilibrium; but to this Cassel would no doubt reply that his theory would have predictive powers in cases where there are only short-term transient departures from balanced inflation and deflation, and during such times his theory would point to the longer-run equilibrium. Eclectic defenders of the usefulness of the reasoning that underlies the strict Quantity Theory and purchasing-power-parity doctrines will gladly jettison the notion that a trillion-fold increase in 1920 German marks will result in an exactly trillion-fold change in domestic prices and foreign exchange rates: it is enough for their purpose, and mine, to stress that such massive changes in M and related magnitudes will inevitably be associated with massive changes in price levels; and that such massive changes in price levels cannot take place if the total of currency, bank deposits, and related magnitudes are kept fairly constant.

IV. The Timing of Monetary Policy

The effects of monetary policy are not instantaneous. This is not surprising, since there are no effects in nature that are secured instantaneously. Even when I turn my key in the lock, the fact that there are no perfectly rigid metals means that a slight twisting and delay is inevitably involved. But the intrinsic delays involved in effectuating monetary policy are much longer than this. It is widely believed that monetary policy delays are considerably less than those involved in fiscal policy actions — such as public works. And this is considered to be one of the great advantages of monetary policy. Actually, however, not a great deal is known in this area, and the empirical researches performed so far are only a beginning. (I find it interesting that Lord Cobbold of the Bank of England in his testimony to The Royal Commission on Banking and Finance of Canada referred to his experience of a six-month lag in monetary policy.) I merely want to point out that the inevitable lags both underscore the lack of perfection to be expected from monetary control and condition the procedures to be followed in making optimal decisions.

If monetary policy acted almost instantaneously and were subject to easy cancellations,[5] the central bank would find its task a much easier one: thus it might not have to take *anticipatory* action prior to a turn down of business activity from a full-employment level; for many purposes it would be sufficient to recognize a turn after it had already happened, which would be a procedure relatively immune from the false forecasts of turns which always plague practical forecasters. But once we recognize that lags of some considerable number of months are involved in securing the effect of new actions, there may be grave harm in a policy which tries to offset a new movement only after enough months have passed to make the direction of that movement terribly obvious. "Don't try to look over hills or beyond valleys" is the sage advice often given by those leery of our ability to forecast. This can be very bad advice, and, in fact, one has to be very arrogant concerning his understanding of the exact degree of a government's ability to forecast, in order to be able to set down this rule or any other specific rule concerning the sluggishness with which an adapting mechanism is to adjust and react to the information input available. If an airplane follows a relatively smooth path with moderate random errors superimposed on it, the electrical engineer knows he should set up a target computer which is based on considerable extrapolation of previous trajectory. If the statistical properties to be expected of the airplane are quite different — for example, involving almost completely random and unpredictable movements — the optimal servomechanism should be a much more sluggish one.

Thus few *a priori* rules can be stipulated in advance and certainly none by those who profess to be nihilistic about man's ability to forecast at all. We must get the best guidance possible from experience itself. I'm quite sure that economic historians will feel that the Federal Reserve system was not premature in taking anticipatory action to ease the money market in the spring of 1960, which was prior to the May turning point and which definitely involved looking over hills and not waiting to find out exactly which way the wind was blowing in order to lean against it. It is precisely the consideration that optimal stabilization policy must vary with the probability pattern of the system to be stabilized, which makes it rather ridiculous to specify in advance and for all times that some particular gadget like 3-per-cent-money-increase-per-year should be adhered to, in season and out of season. Were the

---

[5]This inability to cancel out previous action without delay is the one valid argument, which I referred to in an earlier section, for not relying upon the flooding of the money market in time of presumably short recession; note, however, the need to be able to forecast correctly the shortness of the recession.

cold war suddenly to end, imagine the avoidable evil consequences that would follow from such a predetermined policy.

V. Goals and Functions of Central Banking and Monetary Policy

Anyone who has studied carefully the evolution of central banking will have noted the steady broadening of its functions and goals. In the beginning, most central banks, being first among equals and merely endowed with certain special privileges and duties, were hardly distinguishable from a commercial bank. Long-run profit maximization was their proper criterion of action. Gradually the profit motive became subordinate, and today it should be of no consequence at all. (The various money creation privileges given by the government to the central bank usually have implied more than enough profits anyway; and in a modern economy the accumulated earnings beyond a nominal minimum must be thought of as reverting, eventually or continuously, to the government — and note that I did not write the Treasury, since that is merely an administrative subdivision.) Profit maximizing is at least a definite task, and its disappearance makes the job of decision-making all the more ambiguous and difficult.

After central banks had been recognized as quasi-public institutions, there continued to be an evolutionary broadening of their functions and goals. And I ought to say that these purely factual trends are regarded by most economic experts as desirable developments. The same cannot always be said about the attitude of bankers. And even central bankers are not to be regarded as reliable authorities on the proper role of the modern central bank. Governor Strong of the New York Federal Reserve Bank and Montagu Norman of the Bank of England agreed on many things; from beyond the grave they undoubtedly would disapprove of most changes in central banking which are not even matters of controversy today. If Canada appoints another Royal Commission to look into this matter 25 years from now, the witnesses before it will take for granted many changes that would shock the present generation of central bankers. I suspect that the direction of many such changes can be fairly confidently predicted today. I should add that these developments impress me as being, for the most part, salutary moves in the battle to improve the performance of nontotalitarian mixed-enterprise systems.

Nor are they unique to central banking and monetary policy. If it was once true — and the evidence for this is remarkably skimpy — that taxation was never properly to be used for any purpose other than the raising of revenue, one has only to look around at the modern world to realize how untrue this is now and how much would be sacrificed in an attempt to return to some hypothetical earlier regime. I should also emphasize that many of the paths of future development are not easily foreseen now, and that the evolutionary process does not move smoothly toward any inevitable goal of perfection. We proceed by trial and error, and many entrenched developments can be looked upon as grave mistakes from the standpoint of social efficiency.

Monetary policy, both as handled by the central bank itself and by the government, does not have different ultimate goals from fiscal or any other social policy involving economic aggregates. Thus fiscal policy should aim at the proper degree of price stability in comparison with other major goals just as much as should monetary policy. And debt management, if it happens to be in the hands of the Treasury, should no more aim at unduly low interest rates, in order to cater to the vanity of the ruling Chancellor or in order to keep down unduly the tax burden of servicing the debt, than should central bank policies. It is amazing how such a simple truth should be lost sight of in the usual discussions of these matters, including, I make bold to say, some of the testimony offered you by eminent witnesses. I consider myself the simple child of the Hans Christian Andersen fairy tale who blurted out the secret that the King was wearing no garments at all, fine or otherwise. In a properly running democracy of the modern mixed-enterprise kind, the ultimate goals of macroeconomics are simply the following:

1. There must be best utilization of resources, in the sense of no chronic pools of human and property resources that are involuntarily out of work for reasons connected with the level of total dollar spending.

2. These resources must be efficiently combined at producing the kinds of goods that the various citizens really want and need (which rules out as optimal various make-work activities like building unattractive pyramids or digging holes to be later refilled, etc.).

3. There must be what society, within the framework of its agreed-upon system of property rights, deems to be an appropriate division of command over resources among different age and social classes (which means that society is to have the minimum standards of life provided for various people in accordance with its constitutionally expressed decisions).

4. There must be the appropriate allocations of current resources between production of goods for present consumption as against goods that involve capital formation and widen the opportunities for future consumption.

All these decisions are made by the people of the democracy both in their individual capacities as spenders of their personal incomes on consumption goods and saving instruments and as spenders of various business funds as owners or agents of owners of property, and in their civic capacities as electors of responsible representative government to take care of the cooperative and coordinating functions of economic life and any welfare activities of responsible representative government. It is of course not the function of the Governor of the central bank to impose his own or anyone else's opinions on society, any more than it is the function of the Undersecretary of the Treasury or the Secretary or the Budget Bureau Director or the Chief Executive or particular Members of Parliament to do so. But since it is a fact of life, quite unavoidable, that the way central banking and fiscal policy interact has substantive effects on unemployment and the distribution of income among persons and among present and future time periods, it follows inescapably that such considerations as these must have an appropriate role in the decision making of monetary policy as well as fiscal policy.

What about the important goal of "price stability"? What about "exchange rate stability"? What about economic growth? Of course, such problems are not overlooked. But it is useful to point out that we want price stability because that may be necessary to keep the aged from being cheated by inflation, or may be necessary to permit efficient business planning and long-term contract formation, or may be necessary to avoid unsettling exchange rate depreciations, and so forth. Put this way, we do not prejudge the question of just what sacrifices have to be made in order to achieve this or that degree of price stability, or even this or that degree of secular price decline or rise. I shall say a great deal more about the problem of price stability, and a little about the merits for a country like Canada of various foreign exchange rate policies. Here I need mention only that the problem of growth has already been included in my statement of primary goals or objectives, since the previous formulation included the problem of achieving the desired allocation of goods between present and future. Since money and credit policies, almost by definition, involve decisions about interest rates and capital availability, which are the key terms of trade between present and future goods, one would have thought that out of any ten witnesses before a Royal Commission on Money and Finance, almost all would have given a pivotal role to the central bank in helping a democratic society achieve its best feasible growth rate. Yet it is an empirical fact that many central bankers would, at first inquiry, be inclined to deny that growth was at all within their province of preoccupation. It will be clear that I, along with a great number of modern economists, am unable to concur in this view.

"Surely everybody cannot worry about everything, and there must be some division of labor in a pluralistic society between various public agencies. If the central and monetary policy tries to do everything, it may end up accomplishing nothing. Whereas if it sticks to a narrow category of objectives, it will eventually contribute, along with other agencies in the division of labor that characterizes modern society, its maximum to the broad objectives of society." Something like this will be argued against my previous remarks, and more still. "What, after all, is the distinction between monetary policy and any other kind of policy? The answer to this must be given, and after it has been, it will be recognized that it is outside the field of central banking and monetary policy that most of these broad social objectives must be realized." These are all legitimate questions, and I now propose to give a tentative answer to the last one. Monetary policy differs from fiscal policy in that it is primarily concentrated with *stocks* of assets — like cash, or short-term bonds, or long-term bonds, or borrowings, or various near-moneys and less-liquid net worth items; whereas fiscal policy is more involved with current *flows* of income — like tax receipts levied against current income and sales or like current resource-using government expenditures or current welfare-transfer government expenditures. This contrast between stocks and flows as the key element in defining the realm of monetary policy will help to make clear why President Holtrop of the Netherlands Bank insisted in his testimony before the Royal Commission that whenever debt management is being conducted by the Treasury rather than the central bank, one must recognize that an essential part of *monetary* (or, just as accurately, *asset*) policy is being controlled outside the central bank. Thus, monetary policy is not that which central banks do and ought to do; nor is what central banks do, and ought to do, monetary policy. Monetary policy is asset policy wherever it takes place, and in various times and institutional setups it will be divided in various ways by organization. One can even imagine and observe, if not recommend, institutional cases where more than one agency in a country has been exercising central banking functions. And I fear that adherence by those individuals who have been historically identified as central bankers to a narrow definition of their function will simply cause the growth elsewhere in society of just those activities which they deplore. Before giving an opinion about the useful relationship between central bank and government, I want first to give a caricature of certain views about what constitutes central banking. While this is avowedly a caricature, it cuts too close to the bone for comfort.

Against the preceding viewpoints, here is another: The job of a central bank is to guard the stability of the price level. It controls money, and every schoolboy knows that money is what determines price levels. It never interferes with or affects relative prices or the sectors in which activity takes place. It leaves all those functions to the free market place because a belief in freedom requires this, and because this is a more efficient way for society to organize itself. Democracy, as well as government generally, is always biased in the direction of producing inflation. This is the great evil against which the central bank must always guard. Because democracy can never be trusted, the central bank must be set up as an insulated nonpolitical bastion of price stability, responsible to no one in the community but only to its function. It must therefore issue public statements of warning against public excesses. It must refuse to finance government deficits, and particularly must never finance them by issue of notes or by purchase of short-term floating debt. It should rarely even take on the long-term debt of the government. When a particular gang in office is behaving particularly badly from the standpoint of fiscal soundness, it is the duty of the central bank to contrive or help a flight away from the currency, calling upon central bank cousins abroad who act according to the motto approved by Professor T. Gregory, "Who hurts one, hurts all." It is a lonely and unpopular life, redeemed only by a good cuisine and a sense of righteousness at a distasteful task performed well. Secrecy is all-important. The wisdom of private bankers, who understand these issues and are less inflationary minded than the community generally, should constantly be sought. Balance-of-payments problems, which domestic wastrels look upon as a necessary evil, the central banker regards as a blessing not in disguise: it enforces the discipline so shockingly absent in these parlous times. Career men, who begin life not overly burdened with academic knowledge, make the best successors to similar chiefs; but a few sound academics are useful too, not for helping to run day-to-day affairs — since outside help for that is to be found in men who know and make their money from the money market — so much as for providing general ideological defenses for the beneficent institution. Central bank employees are like ballerinas who must practice each day; you must never let them go off on tours of duty in other branches — scratch out the word "other" — of the government, for that will blunt their abilities. Moreover, they are pure-bred ballerinas, and you must not introduce into the central bank barnyard outside government officials, even on temporary tours of duty, since their contact with the ballerinas may involve a certain contamination that will be detrimental to proper performance. There is no point in prolonging such a cruel caricature. Like most caricatures, it does serve the purpose of portraying in an exaggerated way some not uncommon attitudes. Moreover, although I have called it cruel, there are some writers, fewer today than in the past, who would claim literally that a central bank ought to be secretive and lean over backward as the only watchdog of the stability of prices in a world where all other interests seem biased toward inflation. A more moderate and defensible position would frankly assert that the monetary authorities should overstate their case so that in an adversary procedure a better balance between inflation and deflation would be achieved. I think it is interesting, for example, that President Holtrop in his testimony attached prime importance to the stability of the internal and external value of the currency. And Lord Cobbold, in his image of the automobile, instinctively thought of the central banker as the one who kept his foot on the brake while others pumped against the accelerator. On an *a priori* basis a lack of coordination between the government and the bank could involve an interchange of positions half the time; but that is not the way things seem to modern central bankers. (Later, in discussing growth, I shall have to make the point that this kind of lack of coordination between central bank and government is a powerful drag on growth because it uses a lessening of capital formation as the offset to over-spending on private and collective consumption.)

There are three interesting possibilities for the trend of average prices: steadily and slowly downward; steadily and slowly upward; essentially level.[6] Which of these three patterns is best? This is a difficult and perhaps even meaningless question to ask if nothing is specified about the uncertainties and errors of foresight that are supposed to accompany each pattern. However, certain normative evaluations can be made if we are willing to consider the rigorously abstract model where un-certainties and errors of foresight are absent. I fear that an unwary reader of the testimony presented to the Royal Commission by my long-time friend Sir Dennis Robertson may form an incorrect opinion on this subject. If I understand Sir Dennis, he argues that, feasibility aside, it is a more proper pattern to have prices slowly falling with the increase in technological productivity so that the fruits of technological progress are distributed even-handedly among workers, property owners, re-tired persons, and so forth. Feasibility aside, is this a correct finding of economic theory, as was argued by many economists in the 1930's? I think not. A world in which there is and has been and will always be a positive exponential rate of rise in absolute prices would have *exactly the same real allocations* among labor and nonlabor factors of production and among young and old as would a world with a foreseeable expo-nential fall in prices, or a world with stable prices. Indeed as Thornton, Marshall, Wicksell, Fisher, and others have argued, there tends to be built into the money rate of interest a full allowance for the foreseeable change in price levels; and my study of the interest rates that insurance companies and others pay on fixed-money contracts suggests to me that something like this has already happened to some degree in America and abroad. I conclude from this that there is no presumption in the purest theoretical model in favor of the view that a slowly declining price level is optimal.

The criterion that the ideal situation is that which would correspond best to an idealized state of barter, where money has no so-called distorting effects and is allegedly "neutral," strikes me as a rather

[6]On this subject, see also my article, "D. H. Robertson (1890–1963)," *Quarterly Journal of Economics*, Vol. LXXVII, No. 4 (November 1963), pp. 518–535, and reprinted in the present volume as Chapter 119.

gratuitous criterion. It completely ignores the fact that one has to have an agreed-upon social welfare function that adjudicates the worthiness of those who gain from price change before any real normative statements can be made. But adhering to that criterion, I hope I have shown that within the abstract model involving no rigidities and uncertainties, the Robertson presumption in favor of declining prices has no particular validity, since a golden age with price stability or steady price rise leads to no worse results.

But I must not put words in Professor Robertson's mouth. He, no doubt, had in mind a world with a reasonable degree of uncertainty. Once any appreciable elements of uncertainty appear, it is remarkably hard to make normative statements at all: we pass this way only once, the Bible says, and even a lunatic can say, "If you believed what I believed was going to happen, and feared what I feared was going to happen, you would have to admit that it was not irrational of me to wear knight's armor to the factory." But let us be pragmatic in good English fashion and try to form normative judgments. Professor Robertson, as I understand it, has not said that in principle falling prices are good because that happens to splash *his* cautious friends with extra real goods; because to that you could answer that rising prices are good because that splashes your deserving risk-taking friends with real goods. His attempt to set up as in some sense approximately good the condition that would tend to prevail if money were "neutral" and did not distort natural barter arrangements would at bottom, I suppose, reflect the rough notion that, interpersonal equity aside, a situation free from price-level distortions is more likely to be efficient in the technical sense of "Pareto-optimality." Now it has come to be conceded pretty much everywhere that there is no guidance to choosing generally between feasible situations to be found in concentrating only on Pareto-optimality properties of alternative situations. But is it true that balanced falling prices with the dollar buying more as technology improves bring a greater degree of Pareto-optimality than would stable prices or slowly balanced price rises? To the extent that foresight prevails, the answer is obviously no. To the extent that there are errors of foresight, no one that I can recall has demonstrated a presumption of greater Pareto-optimality in gentle secular deflation as compared to steady price levels or, for that matter, gently rising price levels. Unless I have overlooked something, some new types of argumentation would have to be supplied before one could draw any such conclusion.

Abstract models having established no presumptions, we must turn to feasibility conditions. Here, fortunately, there can be general agreement. Given the institutional rigidities of a modern economic system, most experts agree that the attempt to shape fiscal and monetary policy to produce a trend of declining prices will have grave consequences for total unemployment and production growth. At best (or worst), it is argued that society should want to aim for steady prices. As the American Commission on Money and Credit has concluded, this involves the difficult choice of which index to stabilize: wholesale prices, consumer prices (or the so-called cost of living), or the Gross National Product deflator? Stabilizing wholesale prices would entail in the modern world a rise in the consumer price index of more than one per cent per year in the long run, because there is slower productivity gain (as the statistician measures it) in the services sectors of the economy than in the goods sectors. A still greater rise in the GNP deflator would seem probable. The Commission on Money and Credit also pointed out that recent researches have suggested that official index numbers are almost necessarily biased upward in that they fail to make appropriate allowances for quality improvements: if the official consumer price index is reported to rise at one per cent per year, the error here involved suggests that a dollar is probably just about holding its own in terms of true purchasing power as measured by the utility of goods it will buy. A small economy that is open to the rest of the world must have a price trend to a large extent set for it from abroad if it insists on fixed foreign exchange rates. If world price indexes could be held to a long-term rate of increase that averaged out over buoyant and dull epochs to not much more than one per cent, there would still be the problem that certain elements in the community — particularly in the lower income classes — will find that the savings they set aside for retirement in the future are likely to show a diminution of real yield. With higher rates of price increase this problem becomes still worse. Since statistical researches suggest that the principal victims of mild inflations are the old rather than the young, there is a strong case for helping these groups adjust to the problem. This might involve: (i) purchasing-power bonds, annuities, savings accounts, and equity funds being made available to people on favorable terms by government aid, but in limited amounts; (ii) more pay-as-you-go private pensions; and (iii) what is already a universal fact of modern life, social security benefits that keep up with the taxable capacity of the nation and with the price level. Such measures need not weaken the fight against undesirable inflation. Nor is it true that the "purpose" of the inflations to be feared is precisely the cheating of the old, so that sliding-scale adjustments in their favor will only speed up the rate of demand inflation to accomplish again this purpose. The inflation dangers ahead are more likely to be of the "cost-push" or "sellers" type, or of the cataclysmic type that come in the wake of war and social disorganization.

It would be nice if modern mixed societies had the frictionless price flexibility to permit us always to have price stability without jeopardy to sustainable growth and efficient employment at high levels. It would also be nice if motors turned with less friction and if television sets could grow like weeds. The facts of life, alas, are not all ideal; and while they are mutable, it is one of the facts of life that they cannot be changed in the easy way men might wish. As evidence accumulates, suspicion mounts that there will arise many occasions when society will find a clash between approximate price stability and tolerable sustained high employment and growth. I know that some experts deny this: in my files I have a number of such denials by eminent bankers and scholars. I wish that they were more convincing, because life would be better if there were no "trade-offs" between objectives and no need to compromise between evils. The Commission on Money and Credit was worried by this problem; and it is my guess that even its report is too optimistic. This is not an issue that can be decided by reason or be decided on the basis of past experience. Nor is there a need to come to a firm decision before the fact. Yet it is essential to have one's thinking altered to the problem and to prepare tentative strategies for handling events as they materialize. Now precisely because it is economically false that monetary policy has some special potency to affect the P in $P \times Q$, I must assert boldly: *The problem of determining how much price rise will be tolerated in the interest of a longer and growing output and employment is just as much a problem for fiscal policy as for monetary policy.* There is no reason in logic or ethics why the central bank should be the agency for pulling the compromise in one direction — say, the disinflationary direction — rather than the government (be it Parliament, the Executive, or the Treasury). Indeed, nonelected officials who hold long-term office and who are permitted wide freedom in their actions are not at all the ones in a responsible democracy to resolve these problems. This does not deny that the people through their legislature may choose to set up a quasi-independent agency to represent them in this regard. Except by the Darwinian test of survival of certain older central bank attitudes, there seems to be little evidence that the people have chosen to make such a social compact It is in this sense that every central bank is responsible to government and not really independent.

VI. Conclusion

This testimony is already long. Yet I have barely scratched the surface of many relevant issues. Since time will not permit discussion of them in the depth they deserve, I shall simply list a number of opinions that could be elaborated on at some later date.

1. A country like Canada might gain a good deal from a system of *flexible exchange rates*, in contrast to the stable exchange rates of some large powers like the United States.

2. While open-market operations and required reserve requirements are the important tools of conventional central banking, the earlier Canadian experiment with a *discount rate that changed rather flexibly* with respect to market bill rates has much to recommend it. The limited advantages of having something dramatic to announce when a change in market conditions is desired might still be preserved by having certain special differentials decreed at such times.

3. The goal of faster *growth* can be achieved in a mixed-enterprise economy, if at all, primarily by one mechanism — namely, by conventional and unconventional monetary policies designed to stimulate a long-term deepening of capital, with the corresponding reduction of the proportion of consumption as a fraction of full-employment product being achieved by a compensatingly tight fiscal policy that prevents demand-pull inflation. This means that money cannot by its nature be "neutral"; hence, the notion that central banking can be above and beyond responsible political decision making is quite untenable.

4. Every modern central bank should be made clearly responsible to the democratic government in power. This does not mean that it should be a mere branch of the Treasury. Nor does it require short terms of office for central bankers. Nor does it deprive the governor of the central bank of his freedom in day-to-day operations. Nor does it rob him of his power to nag publicly and privately. Nor does it take away from him his ultimate weapon — dramatic resignation in public protest against what he deems to be bad policy. But it does mean that, after due process and agreed-upon delay periods, he must either yield to governmental policy or be subject to removal from office. There is no room in a modern democracy for a Fifth Estate, which serves as an insulated pocket of power set up to accomplish its own purposes, be they good or be they bad. Freedom of a democracy to make its own mistakes is not merely a *desideratum*: it is an inevitability.

105

PAUL A. SAMUELSON
FISCAL AND FINANCIAL POLICIES FOR GROWTH

Mr. Samuelson: Gabe Hauge, David Rockefeller, distinguished guests on this panel, Miss Porter and gentlemen.

Economists find bankers fascinating. After all, you are the white mice we study; that is what we get paid for. It is no wonder then that I should have accepted eagerly your invitation to speak here today on fiscal policy and growth. What does perhaps require explanation is why the guinea pigs should want to fraternize with the "nosey Parkers" who spy on them, and should go so far as to invite their tormentors to this Centennial birthday party.

However, a guest must not question his welcome. What I can do in return for your hospitality is to speak my mind frankly. Not because it is my mind or because I have any official status—I definitely do not, and speak for myself as professor—but because of all the economists on today's program, I perhaps represent most typically the modern generation of academic economists whose unorthodox views bankers must reckon, even if not agree, with.

Indeed picture if you can the 50th birthday party at the halfway point to this Centennial. What would the elder J. P. Morgan, that forceful mind, make of our discussions here today? If I am the devil's advocate, he shall serve as the angel's.

WHERE WE STAND

Time is brief: Morgan and I will agree to the following stipulations.

1. The earlier numbers game, as to whether America's growth rate has been decelerating in the latter part of the postwar period, has now been resolved by the facts. Our achieved rate of progress has, since 1956 (or even since the cessation of the Korean War in 1953), fallen below the earlier trend rate. It is below that of the Soviet Union, even after their official claims have been deflated by our most antagonistic experts. The miracle nations of Japan, Western Germany, France, Italy and the Common Market have been growing most rapidly of all, narrowing in a decade their technical gap behind us.

2. For the whole of the postwar period, our annual growth rate compares well with the 3 per cent average rate that has characterized historic capitalism here and abroad. One important reason for this has been success in taming the business cycle's worst excesses. Our four postwar recessions have been mild, averaging less than a year in length. Much of the big change I, if not Morgan, would attribute to active Federal fiscal policy.

It is a fact that people's disposable income is no longer permitted to fall appreciably, thereby banishing the vicious spiral whereby drops in production undermine income, which in turn undermines production further, in a self-aggravating cumulative secondary depression. Why, and how?

There is the new built-in automatic stabilization stemming from our welfare expenditure, tax and corporate structure. These are coupled with various anti-recession expenditure and monetary policies of a discretionary type. Consequently *Final* Gross National Product—which is defined as ordinary GNP with inventory investment and disinvestment removed—is well maintained, with the important result that inventory recessions sooner or later burn themselves out.

Furthermore, the shortness of recessions interacts with the downward stickiness of modern wage rates and administered prices to obviate the dramatic collapse in price levels which used to plague bankers and other creditors. When I declaim against creeping inflation, I must in the interest of scientific objectivity call attention to the following fact: for a quarter of a century we have not had to have real estate, stock markets and manufacturing all go through the wringer of bankruptcy together, culminating in the debt-deflation spirals of prewar American history. Who would have predicted that or is rash enough to predict it for the next quarter-century?

3. To explain the disappointing vigor of recent expansion periods, one has primarily to focus on sluggish private investment. Defense needs have led to a rising trend of Federal expenditure; the population boom has led to a rising trend of state and local expenditures on schools and roads. The consumer has not run wild in spending his money, but he has not shirked his duty and year in and year out has spent on goods and services about 93 per cent of his disposable income. Except for the 1956-57 boom in plant and equipment, private investment—particularly when we leave out residential construction and other assets not acquired with profits as a goal—has been a disappointing percentage of total GNP.

Concomitant with disappointing investment performance and a serious balance-of-international-payments deficit have been (1) a growth in the percentage of the labor force unemployed throughout most of the business cycle, (2) a growth in percentage of excess capacity in industry, and (3) a decline in profits expressed as a percentage return on capital invested or as a percentage of the wage bill.

4. While the elder Morgan had never heard the name of Kuznets' cycles, he knew that our history was characterized by long cycles of 15 to 25 years in duration which were characterized by fluctuation in total resource availability (work force, native and immigrant); in degree of resource underutilization (unemployment and

underemployment of men and machines) ; and, possibly, in productivity improvements. He might have welcomed the suggestion that we may now be moving in the less buoyant phase of a postwar Kuznets' cycle and feel there is nothing specially new in that.

Here my generation of economists might take sharp issue. We do not today regard the various waves and afflictions that nature throws up as burdens that man can do nothing about and should cheerfully bear. Whatever may be true of earthquakes, modern man does do something about floods, hurricanes and even the weather. And it is not the case of puny man, standing defiant and waving his fist childishly at forces he cannot touch. Modern man does not accept a cycle of locusts or influenza as an immutable force : he uses insecticides and counterparasites ; he relies on sulpha and penicillin, on isolation and immunization.

So it is with Kuznets' cycles : most economists today would agree that countercyclical monetary and fiscal policies, if we had had them in the last century, would have possessed the potency to moderate Kuznets' and shorter cycles. That is water over the dam. Today we know about the potency of these weapons, and the nation is determined to use them. Of course, just as there are risks in building bridges, using DDT, and prescribing antibiotics, so there will be risks and mistakes and political misuse of the weapons of economic policy. But such arguments will not prove such policies should be eschewed, nor will they carry weight in the political arena of any modern democracy. We have eaten of the fruit of the Tree of Knowledge, and there is no going back.

How High the Sky?

Let us return to certain stipulations and depositions that all parties can agree to provisionally. Mere wishing and willing cannot give America any growth rate it wants. What is a realistic possibility?

The modern discussion may perhaps be traced back to the justly famous 1957 Rockefeller Brothers Study. Its Panel IV Report mentioned the magic figure of a 5 per cent growth target for the United States. Although this number was mentioned merely in passing and along with more detailed alternative projections, it did capture the public's fancy. Dr. Leon Keyserling, who had been Truman's economic adviser, has published a number of "Conference for Economic Progress" statements calling for a full-employment growth target of 5 per cent. Governor Nelson Rockefeller and the 1960 Democratic party platform have each formally espoused the 5 per cent target; however, it is of some interest that Candidate Kennedy never once in his 1960 campaign speeches interpreted "getting the country moving again" to mean "getting it moving at a sustained growth rate of 5 per cent per year."

I suspect this caution on the part of the New Frontiersman was well-advised, for in the last couple of years we have had a new wave of scholarly revisionism. As economists have studied in detail long-run trends in population and work force, technical productivity trends here and abroad and the effect of a once-and-for-all solution to the problem of excessive unemployment, they have generally been unable to hold out genuine hope of our achieving an annual growth rate of 5 per cent over a sustained period of time. According to this revisionist view, America can do much better than we have been doing this last decade, but sober study of the various components which can contribute to annual growth suggests that anything much above sustained $3\frac{1}{2}$ per cent will require a great intensification of social and private efforts.

THIS HIGH: A FEASIBLE GOAL

If one wants to set a goal high enough to call forth greater energy but not so high as to be discouragingly beyond reach, I think the long-term target of 4 per cent per annum is a good round number to aim for.*

---

* Dr. Gerhard Colm at the National Planning Association has been making projections in this general realm, some of which for earlier dates turned out to be amazingly accurate. President Kennedy and his Economic Adviser Walter Heller have frequently referred to the desirability of attaining at least a $3\frac{1}{2}$ per cent annual increase, being made up of a $1\frac{1}{2}$ per cent increase in labor and a 2 per cent annual increase in productivity. Perhaps the most detailed quantitative study on this subject is that by Edward Denison, done for the C.E.D. last year (Edward F. Denison, "The Sources of Economic Growth in the United States and Alternatives before Us," Supplementary Paper No. 13, New York; Committee for Economic Development, 1962). Denison tries to quantify the contribution that various measures might make to force up America's average growth rate 1960-1980 above a $3\frac{1}{3}$ per cent per annum rate. Such a base rate is manifestly below the approximate 4 per cent target to 1970 recently agreed upon for the United States (and Britain) as part of a concerted O.E.C.D. projection. Already we are slipping behind this projected path.

Starting from current levels of underemployment, we could reasonably hope for about three years of 6 per cent real growth. But after a high-employment ceiling of about 4 per cent unemployment has been achieved, the subsequent rate of progress must be limited by the rate at which we can make our *Potential* (or high-employment) National Product grow, which in turn depends on the following factors:

1. *Population* and labor force trends, taking into account desired changes in the length of the workweek and of vacations.

2. *Technical progress*, related to science, innovation, development, competition, management, effort and morale.

3. *Capital formation and resource development*, to give each unit of labor more productive equipment to work with and to add to the stock of private and public assets that provide useful economic services.

4. *Investment in humans*, in the form of education (basic and higher); training, retraining and moving; health research and care, for its own sake as an end in life worth as much as anything in the GNP, but also as a way of increasing the quantity and quality of labor inputs.

While the fourth item in this list might seem surprising to the elder Morgan, there is nothing in the first three to occasion much of a lift in eyebrows—and biographers tell us that the lifting of those eyebrows could be a formidable thing to observe. Victorians would have taken it for granted that capital formation will add to future national product but would be surprised to learn that Government had aught to do with the matter. So let me now turn to the specific subject of my assignment, fiscal policy and growth.

Before presenting the following list, I want to make clear its essential nature. It is a list of programs that can have important bearings on economic growth. It is a fairly comprehensive list. But it most definitely is not the list of measures that I personally would favor for the United States. It is not even a list of measures that I personally would favor if there were no political feasibility constraints upon American policy.

GOVERNMENT EXPENDITURE POLICY FOR GROWTH

1. Expenditure on useful public assets that are *durable* is more conducive to growth than expenditure on current public items.

2. Government expenditure, directly or by subsidy, to basic and applied *science* and to *research and development* is an important growth policy. (Why shouldn't private enterprise carry this ball? It does in part; but since no private firm can hope to keep to itself the social fruits of its innovational work, there is a prima-facie case for public expenditure and subsidy. While improvements in knowledge are an unmixed blessing, the effect of rapid innovation *can* be to lower profits and to intensify the problem of sluggish investment; or it *can* stimulate profits and investment, depending upon its qualitative character.)

3. Public expenditure on *education* and *training* programs can contribute much to growth. Human capital has a profit yield like that material capital, but our market system does not carry human investment to an optimal point. (I personally believe that much of education ought to be defended on other grounds than growth, and suspect that many current economists have gone overboard in reckoning the social yield on educational investment in humans. But, like all professors, I am for more and better education on its own current merits.)

4. Public expenditure on *health research and care,* by the Federal Government or by its subsidies to states and localities, can contribute to growth. (I personally think this effect may be overrated and that these should stand and fall largely on their great human welfare merits in the here and now.)

5. Public expenditure on various forms of *social overhead capital,* including conservation and perhaps some cautious experiments with "indicative planning" of the French type, are policies conducive to growth.

6. Public expenditure to *reduce risk of private investments,* by insurance, subsidy or bail-out devices, or by joint participation or direct Government ownership and operation represents contributions to growth that are not quite the same thing as the ordinary notion of Government capital formation. Provided the good effects are not offset by harmful effects (psychological and/or real), these could be further devices for accelerating growth. Also, many public expenditure programs have directly favorable effects on private production and should be expanded in a balanced program for growth.

All the above public expenditure programs were designed to increase the rate at which America's full-employment potential national product can be made to grow. The next point has relevance to the problem of helping achieve growth by contriving to reduce underemployment and cut into the gap between actual and potential production.

7. *Any public expenditure on goods and services,* if not offset by more-than-equivalent new taxes and if it impinges on an under-employed economy which, for balance-of-payments or other reasons, cannot be brought to full employment by expansionary monetary policy, will cause real GNP to grow; aside from the first-round creation of useful public product, there will be the induced further rounds of private product (consumption and investment). In all candor, if one takes very seriously the international constraint and the ideological constraint against large deficits, then the Administration's avoidance of expanding civilian Government expenditures cannot be defended as economically mandatory.

8. Expansion of *welfare transfer expenditure,* not offset by taxation, would also have the above effects. But there is no presumption that this can be done with less need to create a sizable deficit.

TAX POLICIES FOR GROWTH

9. Obviously, tax policies designed to spur *research* are desirable. We have already legislated loopholes in our tax law to encourage patents, and the 1963 tax bill will further liberalize the right to expand research expenditures. There is really not much more that taxation can do in this important field.

10. Allowing *faster depreciation* for tax purposes can stimulate capital formation and growth. The 1954 legislative change and the 1963 guidelines are important here. Policies, like those in Germany, Sweden and other nations, in which a large fraction of the value of an asset can be written off in the first and second year, *cannot* be justified as a return to fair recognition of true economic depreciation (inclusive of obsolescence) needed to measure true *money income;* let us face it, they are deliberate bribes to coax out faster growth. (Note that faster depreciation of an item merely puts off the day of taxes: it is an interest-free equity-type loan from government to business, and if business is already liquid, its effect can be weak.)

11. *The tax investment credit,* proposed by Kennedy and Dillon and so spurned by business, is a genuine give-away designed to coax out investment. The ante on this could be raised.

12. *Permitting assets to be depreciated on a base that is inflated along with the price level* would represent a change from the present system that taxes money income toward a new system that taxes *real* income. This ought to shift the balance away from hoarding money toward investing in things—just as our present LIFO methods for treatment of inventory represent a give-away from the standpoint of correct taxation of *money* income.

13. *Lenient treatment and definition of what is called "capital gain"* rather than ordinary income ought to encourage "venturesome" investment. Indeed, raising ordinary tax rates and lowering "capital-gains rates" should be very stimulating to investment and capital formation as well as to wheeler-dealer speculation. Loopholes can be bribes to coax out investment, albeit they can also distort resource use.

14. Improving devices for *"tax averaging,"* through generous carrybacks and carryforwards and other income-spreading devices, should remove the most important penalties against risk taking in our tax system. This gets the least attention in popular discussions of the present day, but it is economically about the most important policy for growth and equity. If the 1963 Kennedy-Dillon spreading reforms are enacted, our tax structure will be fairly optimal in this vital respect.

15. Changing from a graduated system of income taxation to a *graduated system of consumption and wealth taxation,* if it were politically and administratively feasible, would perhaps be the single most important policy to achieve growth without sacrifice of "equity." The penalty on investing for the future would then be removed and the fruits of windfall gains would get taxed when spent or held.

16. It is popularly believed that our *high marginal rates of taxation on upper incomes* are the most important obstacle to dynamic investment and growth and reducing them is crucial. Careful study of the effects upon personal effort and on risk taking show this popular notion to be much exaggerated, and even to be possibly the reverse of the truth. The present system practically drives a rich man into venturesome investment, so as to convert ordinary income into what are treated as capital gains. I favor the Kennedy-

Dillon 1963 tax package in which high marginal rates are brought down from a 91 to a 65 per cent top. But I do so primarily because the present system, in which people are subject to high rates which they can avoid by taking advantage of loopholes, is both unaesthetic and distorting. It is not because I expect it immediately to give our system a strong fillip toward growth and capital formation.

17. *A reduction in the corporate tax rate* might be stimulating to investment and growth.* Corporations early in 1963 look to be rather unusually liquid, so the actual increase in the funds left with them perhaps cannot be expected to be as stimulating to investment as in more normal times. There are some economists who think that excess capacity implies a marginal profitability to further investment of practically zero, so that it would be much more potent to engineer an increase in output toward capacity than to try to induce an increase in the ratio of capital to existing output. I am not of this school, but I must admit that events of the last few years have not strengthened my case. This group believes that stimulating current investment, so that you engineer a spurt like that of 1956-57, will merely mean excess capacity in subsequent years and you will pay in sluggishness then for anything you contrive now. (A shrewd Wall Street analyst told me he disliked the fast depreciation of the 1954 tax code because he thought it had led to the 1956-57 over-investment which was eroding profits; he favored a cut in corporate taxes instead, precisely because he thought it would accrue to the stockholders and not be used to stimulate capital formation and undermine profits.)

Whether a cut in the corporate tax rate will stimulate investment much depends on the perplexing problem of the incidence of that tax. Gaylord Freeman, Vice Chairman of The First National Bank of Chicago, told a recent LIFE forum on tax cutting that such a tax may well get passed on to consumers; so removing it would not swell profits and thereby coax out investment. Professor Richard Musgrave, at the same conference, reported on a statistical investigation in which he found that the corporate tax was shifted on to consumers. Even if it were true that the tax was shifted completely on to consumers but that the mechanism by which this came about was through the creation of less capital formation, this

---

* Wiping out the corporate layer of taxation is an extreme case of this. Back in 1945 when many economists favored such a move, I regarded the corporate tax as a lesser evil than any feasible alternatives, precisely because corporations are good poolers of risks.

Mustgrave-Freeman point would not invalidate the hope that cutting rates from 52 per cent to 47 per cent or lower would stimulate investment and growth. (This has been pointed out by the C.E.D. report, "Reducing Tax Rates for Production and Growth," December 1962, pp. 15-26.) Musgrave, however, suspects that the incidence takes place primarily through the fact that businessmen will administer their prices at lower levels if they have to pay less corporate tax: I must confess that this notion that businessmen are successful in pricing to a certain after-tax profit and no more seems unlikely to me. And I must report that Professor Arnold Harberger of Chicago has done research that casts doubt on the shifting of the corporate tax away from capital.

It would seem plausible that certain modernization and other investment projects that yield only a 16 per cent before-tax profit and a bare 8 per cent after-tax profit might be refused by business this year; however, a sizable reduction in the corporate or individual tax rate could convert the after-tax yield into a return high enough to motivate this investment. To be sure, lowering the cost of debt and equity capital by massive Federal Reserve expansionary credit policies could achieve this same result and more; but a country—like Canada—with an overvalued currency might not be able to afford such policies, whereas the tax-cut route could extend to domestic investors, a privilege not bestowed on investment abroad. If this be discrimination, lay the blame on the overvaluation of the currency.

Fifteen years ago Musgrave, together with Professor Evsey Domar (now of M.I.T.), made an important point that is overlooked in most modern discussions. When the Government taxes so as to become your senior partner, it shares in your losses as well as gains; so *reducing* the tax rate does to some degree have the offsetting result of *increasing* the riskiness of private investment. It is not necessary that businessmen master this argument for it to be valid; it is enough that their profits be subject to the effect, and that habits and decisions adjust to the facts of the situation. This is not the place for me to become technical; but you can see that depressing points like this are what undermine to some extent the rosy hopes for strong results from business tax reduction. Later a similar point will come out.

18. *Shifting from a system that depends heavily on graduated income taxes to one that depends on ungraduated consumption tax-*

ation would be conducive to thriftiness out of a full-employment income. If such thriftiness tended to become abortive and led to unemployment, growth would be hurt not helped. The result could be a mix of demand at full employment more conducive to capital formation rather than current consumption. Historically, capitalism has, teleologically speaking, used income inequality as a source of growth. If profits are the reward to people with a knack for picking good investment and if such people are thrifty, then leaving profits in their hands ought to lead to a good qualitative mix of venturesome investment as well as to a good over-all total of investment. Whether modern democracies wish to purchase growth of this type at this cost is not a matter that I pronounce on here.

It is important to note that the mere fact that a man is in a high tax bracket does not discourage his investment. If I can expense my investment by ultrafast depreciation or by any means, or if my 90 per cent tax is one based upon my consumption, then wiping out all taxation would seem to convert a project with a before-tax return of 20 per cent and an after-tax return of 2 per cent into a project with after- and before-tax return of 20 per cent. What could be more stimulating to investment than that after-tax rise from 2 to 20 per cent, a tenfold change? Alas, the calculation is wrong and misleading. While subject to a 90 per cent tax, a dollar of investment does not cost me $1 but rather only 10¢ since the Government pays the other 90 per cent. If I relate my 2¢ gain to *my* 10¢ investment, I come out with the same 20 per cent after-tax return that 20¢ on a dollar gives me when there is no tax at all.* New businesses, it is true, do not have this advantage.

While countries like Germany and Sweden and Britain tax relatively more than we do, they get a smaller fraction of their revenues from graduated income taxes. In the case of Sweden and Britain, this is not because our marginal rates are so much higher than theirs: at comparable levels of income they are not even so high. But it is because we are more prosperous, so that many more of our people are in high enough income brackets to pay appreciable direct taxes. Fostering inequality to stimulate capital formation, as we have seen, does have cause-and-effect validity. There is an alternative way of producing the same increase in capital formation but leaving its fruits more evenly divided among the populace; but this

---

* The day after writing these lines I met the head of a large corporation who mentioned that they were test marketing a profitable new product "half at government expense."

will appear later in the "expansionary credit policy *cum* fiscal austerity package" discussion.

If I were hired as an economist for the whole group of people who have incomes above $15,000 per year and asked to develop a program best designed in terms of their self-interest, I could not come up with any proposal better than that our present reliance on graduated income taxes be altered by drastically reducing the degree of graduation, exchanging for much of the revenue lost a sales or value-added tax at the Federal level. Professional ethics would require me to state to my clients that the evidence does not suggest to me that, in the present decade, such a change would contribute much to economic growth or to over-all efficiency; but it would have significant effects (what we economists call "income" rather than "substitution" effects) in moving us back toward the greater inequality of incomes that prevailed in 1929. If hired by the rest of the community, it would of course be my duty to make this last point clear to the public.

19. *Using ad hoc tax baits to promote worthy causes could be part of a growth program.* I may illustrate this point by quoting a German economist who appeared as a guest at a C.E.D. meeting. "I realize that the American and German practices are quite different. We in Germany are supposed to be a free enterprise economy, but we freely use the tax system to accomplish what we think needs to be accomplished. Thus, if we want more construction, Dr. Erhard shapes tax programs that subsidize building. If we wish to push exports, we use the tax system to do so. Then when times change and we don't want these activities emphasized, we remove the tax bait and push something else. On the other hand, you economists in America seem to try to set up fairly what is to be defined as true income and then you try to tax the different kinds of incomes at uniform rates: while there is much to be said for this as a matter of equity, it ties your hand as far as achieving special purposes." I think this quotation speaks for itself and needs no comment from me.

MONETARY POLICY AND FISCAL POLICY

Here at the end I come to the most important part of my subject. While it is right that fiscal policy should receive much emphasis these days, it is in the realm of monetary policy that a mixed enterprise system like ours can do the most to slow down or step up its rate of growth. Classical economists have always emphasized that channeling resources away from current consumption and toward capital formation is an important way of increasing the ability of an economic system to produce more in the future. Indeed the classical economists were hipped on this subject and tended to place all their emphasis on capital formation as the sole source of progress. Today we have redressed the balance: we also emphasize the crucial role of the technical innovations that can take place even when a nation is doing no net saving according to the usual way of measuring saving and capital formation. Perhaps we have gone too far in redressing the balance: numerous studies by Solow, Fabricant, Kendrick and others abroad have led to the tentative conclusion that the largest fraction of progress comes from changes in the production function rather than from increases in the stock of capital. Nonetheless, for each extra dollar of resources that the nation can channel into capital formation, there is made possible more than a dollar of additional future consumption: depending upon whether you believe the estimates of Denison or other writers, you will find that society earns 10 to 20 per cent per annum on its effective investments. These rates are not riskless, to be sure; but they are far greater than the 4 per cent gilt-edge rates which prevail for long-term bonds of the highest quality.

20. *Central bank credit policies that reduce the cost of borrowing and increase the availability of credit to formers of real capital are the single most important programs for causing the "deepening of capital" which steps up the growth potential of a nation.* It is odd that the expressions "easy money" or "cheap money" have such a risqué connotation to them: actually they are the puritanical way of shifting a well-run nation away from consumption and toward more rapid growth. If Max Weber, Tawney and Sombart wanted to preach the Protestant Ethic for a Twentieth Century economy, their emphasis would have to shift away from the Calvinist emphasis upon nonconsumption toward programs which ensure the channeling of resources into capital formation. For me to give up wanting to buy today's bread is not enough to guarantee that bridges and plants will get built: only if the interest rate and capital market mechanisms which create an effective demand for capital are brought into play does my Calvinistic abstention result in anything but unemployment and unused capacity. How wrong,

therefore, on cause-and-effect grounds are arguments like the following, which I collect in my files from utterances by distinguished
men of affairs: "Higher interest rates will encourage more saving
and less consumption; since we need more investment, the best thing
the Federal Reserve can do to promote capital formation is make
money tight enough to cause interest rates to firm up." Economists
regard this as a fine example of incorrect reasoning; and if this
day's sun sets after having had someone here make sense of it, I
shall consider today's visit the most valuable one of the year, for it
will have taught me something very important.

I realize, of course, that our present international balance of payments makes it difficult to use this most important growth policy
and will comment on that matter in a moment. I realize, too, that
when easy money brings a nation too much demand-pull, this can
contribute to inflation and have bad social effects and bad repercussions for growth; my next point will deal with that matter.
But right here I ought to comment on whether an easy money policy
which is good for the country is also good for the banking industry
and for property owners generally. On the whole, since there is
considerable evidence that the relative shares of property and of
labor do not change much, one would expect that the owners of
property as a whole are benefited by an easy money growth policy.
I do not see that banks are any exception to this rule, and indeed
policies which expand their reserves and earning assets might be
expected to help them even when other property owners are being
hurt by a decline in yields. The whole point of such a growth policy
is to cause investment to take place that will bring down yields;
so particular *rentiers,* particularly retired persons, might find
themselves worse off even when the total return to property has
gone up. And I must admit that there is the possibility that inducing a "deepening" of capital could cause its yield to decline at such
a rate as to reduce the total return to property. Even a euthanasia
of the *rentier* class is an eventual possibility, though unlikely: this
points up the fact that there need not always be a harmony of
interest between the part and the whole; what is good for the
United States need not be good for some special part of it.

A number of recent econometric studies suggest that lower
interest rates do have a stimulating effect on capital formation
spending, which is in contrast to the more pessimistic findings of
economists one or two decades ago. I do not wish to make too much
of such fragmentary studies. And one has to admit that much of

capital formation is financed by large corporations out of internal funds generated from undistributed profits and from depreciation accruals. Short-run variations in Federal Reserve policy are not likely to affect much the decision of the Aluminum Company or of du Pont to build a factory that is clearly needed. Yet even their decisions can, in the longer run, be influenced by the general environment of credit tightness or ease. This general environment can influence stock prices and corporate payout ratios. It can encourage or discourage firms from using their internal funds to buy up other firms or to go into new lines. While internal funds can be thought of as a separate pool from external funds, these two are loosely interconnected. Just as the Pacific and Atlantic oceans do not have the same level, as the locks in the Panama Canal show, so the effective yields externally may differ from those internally. But there is enough indirect connection between the two oceans to keep their levels from deviating by too much; and in the same way, lowering the levels of yields in the external market can help bring down gradually the yields within even the largest firms.

21. *A strong growth-inducing policy of monetary ease, if it succeeds in producing over-all employment, can be combined with an austere fiscal policy, in which tax rates are kept high enough and/or expenditure rates low enough, so as to remove inflationary pressures of the demand-pull type and succeed in increasing the net capital formation share of our full-employment income at the expense of the current consumption share.* Such a package has been advocated for many years by such liberal economists as James Tobin, E. C. Brown, R. A. Musgrave, and me; and it has been greeted with some skepticism by the labor movement and by such economists as Alvin Hansen, Gerhard Colm, Robert Eisner and Leon Keyserling. The Kennedy Administration, because of the international deficit problem, has not been able to make progress with such a program. So long as monetary policy is limited by international constraints, this "new look" program cannot get off the ground. If such a program cannot be tried, or if it actually lacks technical potency because of the impossibility of engineering an increase in the capital-output ratio by increasing the availability of capital, then a nontotalitarian economy like ours cannot do a great deal to speed up its growth.

22. *To the extent that a currency is temporarily or permanently overvalued, the case is strengthened for various unorthodox mone-*

tary policies designed to reduce long-term interest rates and increase the availability of risk-capital to domestic users, while not at the same time letting short-term interest rates fall to levels that will cause cool money to migrate to foreign markets and thereby worsen our international balance of payments. Thus, the costs in terms of growth of an adherence to a "bills only" (or "—preferably") doctrine would be intensified in an era of international deficits. Conventional monetary policy has not usually been interpreted to include policies designed to bring the rates of risky investment down toward the gilt-edge rates; if such measures could be devised, they would do much to energize private capital and promote growth.

The wage inflation that is now going on in Europe is doing as much to correct our international balance of payments as anything we have yet contrived. Still there are some academic economists who claim that this is too slow a process and that the American dollar may be overvalued. If that should some day prove to be so, some of them would favor direct import and capital controls. Some would favor suspending gold payments and letting the dollar be a floating currency. To the criticism that other countries can be expected to devalue as much as the United States, this reply is given: "If other countries are willing to hold our obligations at the same value in terms of their own currencies, well and good; the important thing is not to hamstring employment and growth domestically." Because some members of the press construed my remarks as favoring or contemplating a change in the external value of the dollar, I want to repeat that the above remarks report on academic attitudes and refer to vague future contingencies rather than to present actualities. What I do personally want to stress is this: When a currency is overvalued, adjusting to that situation by running a sluggish slow-growth economy is a remedy worse than the disease. The correct things should be done and if that should reveal the untenability of existing parities, it will have been time to learn about the hard facts of life.

One final apology: I wish I could have come here and promised that balancing the budget, preserving monetary discipline, reducing Government expenditures and busting the monopoly powers of labor unions would usher in an era of prosperity and growth without inflation or tears. It was not my heart that kept me from doing so; it was my head, and my fear of being in violation of the laws of fraud, that compelled me to say less agreeable words.

PART XIV

The Individual and the State

106

PAUL A. SAMUELSON : *Modern Economic Realities and Individualism**

T O AN ECONOMIST THE WORD "INDIVIDUALISM" IS TIED UP WITH *laissez-faire.* Or with liberalism in the nineteenth-century Manchester-School sense as distinct from the modern American connotation of a liberal as a kind of New Dealer who is just to the left of the moving center but not quite over the brink into radicalism. Perhaps John Stuart Mill is the archetype of an individualist. And perhaps the apotheosis of individualism is that social order which Thomas Carlyle contemptuously dismissed as "anarchy plus the constable." In this last century the world has obviously moved away from rugged individualism. Presumably in the century before that the Western world had been moving toward a greater degree of individualism. Yet it would be a mistake to think that there was ever a golden age of unadulterated individualism.

Eden in Equilibrium

Physicists have a model of a dilute gas. The air in this hypothetical balloon I hold in my hand is supposed to consist of a number of hard little atoms in continuous motion. So small is each atom as to make the distances between them very large indeed. It is a lonely life, and the encounters between atoms are very few and far between—which is indeed fortunate since the encounters are envisaged by the physicist as involving collisions with elastic rebounds. Something like this is pictured by the extreme individualist. Daniel Boone, who moved farther west when he could begin to hear the bark of his neighbor's dog, would regard this model of a dilute gas as very heaven. Those who cherish family life, or at the least have an interest in biological survival, will gladly extend the notion of an individual to include the family group. Nor will this daunt the physicist, who is happy to think of the air in this balloon as consisting of molecules, which in their turn consist of clusters of parent-and-children atoms rather than detached bachelors.

* Acknowledgment is made to Felicity Skidmore for research assistance. Part of this discussion was adapted from my contribution to a Swarthmore symposium and research for a workshop sponsored by the Industrial Relations Division of the University of California at Berkeley.

I will tell you a secret. Economists are supposed to be dry as dust, dismal fellows. This is quite wrong, the reverse of the truth. Scratch a hard-boiled economist of the libertarian persuasion and you find a Don Quixote underneath. No lovesick maiden ever pined for the days of medieval chivalry with such sentimental impracticality as some economists long for the return to a Victorian marketplace that is completely free. Completely free? Well, almost so. There must, of course, be the constable to ensure that voluntary contracts are enforced and to protect the property rights of each molecule which is an island unto itself.

Where Carlyle envisaged an anarchy that was veritable chaos, a jungle red in tooth and claw, the antiquarian economist sees Newtonian order—an impersonal system of competitive checks and balances.

Life in this other Eden is neither nasty, brutish, nor short. Law, labor, and capital end up getting combined in an optimal way, so that the best menu of apples, automobiles, Picasso paintings, comic books, gin, applesauce, xylophones, and zebras is offered to the consumer. He chooses from the lot what pleases him best. As Bentham said, all pleasures are one: Push-pin is as good as poetry provided individuals deem it so. Applejack gives a less pure pleasure than apple juice, but not for the reason that alcohol is morally bad. Rather only for the reason that its positive pleasure tonight must be carefully adjusted for the negative pleasure of tomorrow's hangover: if the net balance yields more utils than apple juice, then bottoms up! If at some midpoint between tonight's revelry and tomorrow's hangover, you decide to walk over Niagara Falls on a tightrope, that is just your way of maximizing utility. Should that turn out in some altitudinal way to have been a mistake, well each man who is free and twenty-one is entitled to make his own mistakes without the nosy interference of his neighbor or of artificial government.

Special allowance might have to be made for lunatics and minors. While most Benthamites would certify women as "competents"—i.e., free-wills whose tastes should be respected—few of them would go as far as Albert Schweitzer and extend the felicific calculus to animals, insects, and plants. The formula, each to count for one and only one, was not expected to include chimpanzees or amoebae: the total utility which the Universe was to minimize apparently did not include an algebraic contribution from the likes of them.

On the other hand Bentham would not have recognized an inferior caste of slaves whose pleasures were not to count. What would he think of a person who sold himself into perpetual slavery, in order to give a weekend *potlatch*? I am not sure, but if it had been a sober arms-length transaction at the *going competitive market price*, I dare say Bentham would have wanted such contracts to be legally enforceable.

What Smith Hath Wrought

The first human was Adam. The first economist (if one can make the distinction) was Adam Smith. The year 1776 was a vintage one: it gave us the Declaration of Independence, the work of Thomas Jefferson and a committee; and it gave us *The*

Wealth of Nations, the work of an individual. Smith was an urbane and skeptical Scot nurtured on the same branch water as his friend David Hume. No zealot he, Smith gave two resounding cheers for individualism; but for state interference of the pre-nineteenth-century type, he could muster up only a Bronx cheer.

And make no mistake about it: Smith was right. Most of the interventions into economic life by the State were then harmful both to prosperity and freedom. What Smith said needed to be said. In fact, much of what Smith said still needs to be said: good intentions by government are not enough; acts do have consequences that had better be taken into account if good is to follow. Thus, the idea of a decent real wage is an attractive one. So is the idea of a low interest rate at which the needy can borrow. None the less the attempt *by law* to set a minimum real wage at a level much above the going market rates, or to set a maximum interest rate for small loans at what seem like reasonable levels, inevitably does much harm to precisely the persons whom the legislation is intended to help. Domestic and foreign experience—today, yesterday, and tomorrow—bears out the Smithian truth. Note that this is not an argument against *moderate* wage and interest fiats, which may improve the perfection of competition and make businessmen and workers more efficient.

Smith himself was what we today would call a pragmatist. He realized that monopoly elements ran through *laissez-faire:* when he said that Masters never gather together even for social merriment without plotting to raise prices against the public interest he anticipated the famous Judge Gary dinners at which the big steel companies used to be taught what every oligopolist should know. Knowing the caliber of George III's civil service, Smith believed the government would simply do more harm than good if it tried to cope with the evil of monopoly. Pragmatically, Smith might, if he were alive today, favor the Sherman Act and stronger antitrust legislation, or even public utility regulation generally. He might even, in our time, be a Fabian. Certainly Jeremy Bentham, with his everlasting concern for maximizing utility, would in our nonindividualistic age have been a social activist—at the very least a planner of the present French type.

The Invisible Hand

One hundred per cent individualists skip these pragmatic lapses into good sense and concentrate on the purple passage in Adam Smith where he discerns an Invisible Hand that leads each selfish individual to contribute to the best public good. Smith had a point; but he could not have earned a passing mark in a Ph.D. oral examination in explaining just what that point was. Until this century, his followers—such as Bastiat—thought that the doctrine of the Invisible Hand meant one of two things: (a) that it produced maximum feasible total satisfaction, somehow defined; or (b) that it showed that anything which results from the voluntary agreements of uncoerced individuals must make them better (or best) off in some important sense.

Both of these interpretations, which are still held by many modern libertarians, are wrong. This is not the place for a technical discussion of economic principles, so I shall be very brief and cryptic in showing this. First, suppose some ethical observer —such as Jesus, Buddha, or for that matter John Dewey or Aldous Huxley—were to examine whether the total of social utility (as that ethical observer scores the deservingness of the poor and rich, saintly and sinning individuals) was actually maximized by 1860 or 1962 *laissez-faire.* He might decide that a tax placed upon yachts whose proceeds go to cheapen the price of insulin to the needy might increase the total of utility. Could Adam Smith prove him wrong? Could Bastiat? I think not. Of course, they might say that there is no point in trying to compare different individuals' utilities because they are incommensurable and can no more be added together than can apples and oranges. But if recourse is made to this argument then the doctrine that the Invisible Hand maximizes total utility of the universe has already been thrown out the window. If they admit that the Invisible Hand will truly maximize total social utility *provided the state intervenes so as to make the initial distribution of dollar votes ethically proper,* then they have abandoned the libertarian's position that individuals are not to be coerced, even by taxation.

In connection with the second interpretation that anything which results from voluntary agreements is in some sense, *ipso facto,* optimal, we can reply by pointing out that when I make a purchase from a monopolistic octopus, that is a voluntary act: I can always go without alka-seltzer or aluminum or nylon or whatever product you think is produced by a monopolist. Mere voluntarism, therefore, is not the root merit of the doctrine of the Invisible Hand: what is important about it is the system of checks and balances that comes under perfect competition, and its measure of validity is at the technocratic level of efficiency not at the ethical level of freedom and individualism.* That this is so can be seen from the fact that such socialists as Oscar Lange and A. P. Lerner have advocated channeling the Invisible Hand to the task of organizing a socialistic society efficiently.

---

* What perfectly competitive equilibrium, the Invisible Hand, achieves is this: if production functions satisfy appropriate returns conditions, if all externalities of production and tastes are appropriately absent (which includes the absence of public goods and of neighborhood effects), then competitive equilibrium is such that not *everyone* can be made better off by any intervention. This is not a theorem about ideal *laissez-faire* for it holds just as validly after good or bad (lump-sum) interferences have determined the initial distribution of wealth and earning powers. There are literally an infinite number of equilibrium states just as "efficient" as that of laissez-faire individualism. Such an efficiency state is a necessary but not sufficient (repeat, not) condition for maximization of a social-welfare function that respects individuals' tastes. It is a tribute to competitive pricing that under the severe returns and externality conditions specified, and then only, it can maximize an ethically prescribed social-welfare function provided the initial "distributon of resources" has been rectified so as to make each consumer dollar voting in the market of equal social deservingness. All this is complex and was not understood until this century at the earliest. A. Bergson, P. Samuelson, and O. Lange can, I think fairly, be cited for the present formulation; but parts of it had been understood, and sometimes misunderstood, by such distinguished economists as V. Pareto, E. Barone, A. P. Lerner, N. Kaldor, J. R. Hicks, and T. Scitovsky. Mention should be made of the useful intuitions of the neoclassi-

In summary: these individualistic atoms of the rare gas in my balloon are not isolated from the other atoms. Adam Smith, who is almost as well known for his discussion of the division of labor and the resulting efficiency purchased at the price of interdependence, was well aware of that. What he would have stressed was that the contacts between the atoms were *organized* by the use of markets and prices.

The Impersonality of Market Relations

Just as there is a sociology of family life and of politics, there is a sociology of individualistic competition. It is not a rich one. Ask not your neighbor's name; enquire only for his numerical schedules of supply and demand. Under perfect competition, no buyer need face a seller. Haggling in a Levantine bazaar is a sign of less-than-perfect competition. The telephone is the perfect go-between to link buyers and sellers through the medium of an auction market, such as the New York Stock Exchange or the Chicago Board of Trade for grain transactions. Two men may talk hourly all their working lives and never meet. It is alleged that many women have developed affection for the local milkman, but few romances have blossomed over a Merrill Lynch teletype.

These economic contacts between atomistic individuals may seem a little chilly or, to use the language of wine-tasting, "dry." They remind one of those nunneries which receive sustenance from the outside world only through a contrivance like a dumbwaiter which bars all human confrontation. Or they are like the anthropological custom in which certain tribes trade with their neighbors by laying out gifts at dead of night, which the others pick up and reciprocate. Presumably custom keeps the balance of trade about even, which is more than custom has been doing for the weak American balance of international payments in recent years.

---

cal economists L. Walras, K. Wicksell, A. Marshall, F. von Wieser, A. C. Pigou, A. Young, J. B. Clark, P. Wicksteed, F. Edgeworth, F. Taylor, F. Knight, J. Viner, and still others. For a partial review of doctrine, see P. Samuelson, *Foundations of Economic Analysis* (Cambridge, Mass., 1947), Chapter Eight.

An economist might wonder whether the later work of K. Arrow does not cast doubt on the concept of a social-welfare function. Valuable as it is in its own right as a contribution to mathematical politics, Arrow's demonstration, that it is impossible to have a "constitutional function" that compromises differing tastes of individuals and at the same time satisfies certain plausible requirements, does not rob the Bergson formulation of its validity. A constitutional function is not a social-welfare function, even if it is given the same name as one. I should mention that Harsanyi, in the last decade, has made the notable contribution that the Bergson Social Welfare Function can be written as additive in individuals' utilities provided certain plausible postulates about social choice in the presence of probabilities are accepted. The view that R. Coase has shown that externalities—like smoke nuisances—are not a logical blow to the Invisible Hand and do not call for coercive interference with *laissez-faire* is not mine. I do not know that it is Coase's. But if it had not been expressed by someone, I would not be mentioning it here. Unconstrained self-interest will in such cases lead to the insoluble bilateral monopoly problem with all its indeterminacies and non-optimalities.

This impersonality has its good side. If money talks, you and I do not have to fabricate conversation. That is one reason my wife buys our toothpaste at the self-service supermarket rather than at the corner drug store—which as a matter of fact is no longer there, for reasons that are obvious. The prices have been equalized by Massachusetts law, and she is liberated from talking about the New England weather, being able to save her energies for our dialogues about Plato and Freud. On the other hand that Southern editor, Harry Golden of North Carolina, claims he has never bought an entire box of cigars in his life, since that would deprive him of pleasurable daily contacts. Under perfect *laissez-faire,* those who want to talk about the weather have only to put their money in the telephone slot and dulcet tones will present the latest betting odds. I understand you already can call for a spiritual message each day; and if the demand warrants it, you will be able to dial for a set of random digits whenever your statistical work has soiled the old ones and calls for a fresh set.

Believe me, I do not wish to jest. Negroes in the South learned long ago that their money was welcome in local department stores. Money can be liberating. It corrodes the cake of custom. Money does talk. Sociologists know that replacing the rule of status by the rule of contract loses something in warmth; it also gets rid of some of the bad fire of olden times.

Impersonality of market relations has another advantage, as was brought home to many "liberals" in the McCarthy era of American political life. Suppose it were efficient for the government to be the one big employer. Then if, for good or bad, a person becomes in bad odor with government, he is dropped from employment and is put on a black list. He really then has no place to go. The thought of such a dire fate must in the course of time discourage that freedom of expression of opinion which individualists most favor. Many of the people who were unjustly dropped by the federal government in that era were able to land jobs in small-scale private industry. I say small-scale industry because large corporations are likely to be chary of hiring names that appear on anybody's black list. What about people who were justly dropped as security risks or as members of political organizations now deemed to be criminally subversive? Many of them also found jobs in the anonymity of private industry. Many conservative persons, who think that such men should not remain in sensitive government work or in public employ at all, will still feel that they should not be hounded into starvation. Few want for this country the equivalent of Czarist Russia's Siberia, or Stalin Russia's Siberia either. It is hard to tell on the Chicago Board of Trade the difference between the wheat produced by Republican or Democratic farmers, by teetotalers or drunkards, Theosophists or Logical Positivists. I must confess that this is a feature of a competitive system that I find attractive.

Moreover, there is no law preventing people from falling in love over the broker-age telephone. And the warm personal relationships that are lacking in the economic sphere can be pursued in after hours. Medieval guild crafts are not the only human associations that are worthwhile, and the price to retain them may be too high in terms of their inefficiency.

I have now finished describing the ideal equilibrium of the gas, which has individual atoms in dilute form. We have seen how a perfect model of competitive equilibrium might behave if conditions for it were perfect. The modern world is not identical with that model. As mentioned before, there never was a time, even in good Queen Victoria's long reign, when such conditions prevailed.

To elucidate this, let us ask what happens when we squeeze the balloon. Or what is the same thing if we permit a Malthusian proliferation of molecules within the same space. The gas is no longer dilute, the atoms no longer lonely.* The system heats up. Now the collisions are frequent and uncomfortable. It is no longer a question of hearing our neighbor's dog: we toss with insomnia while his TV blares. In revenge, our electric shaver distorts his morning symphony. For better or worse the human race has been joined.

Whatever may have been true on Turner's frontier, the modern city is crowded. Individualism and anarchy will lead to friction. We now have to coordinate and cooperate. Where cooperation is not fully forthcoming, we must introduce upon ourselves coercion. Now that man must obey the stop lights he has lost his freedom. But has he really? Has he lost something that he had? Was he free to race his car at the speed he wished and in the direction he wished? Of course not. He had only the negative freedom of sitting in a traffic jam. We have, by cooperation and coercion, although the arch individualist may not like the new order, created for ourselves greater freedom.

The principle of unbridled freedom has been abandoned: it is now just a question of haggling about the terms. On the one hand, few will deny that it is a bad thing for one man, or a few men, to impose their wills on the vast majority of mankind, particularly when that will involves terrible cruelty and terrible inefficiency. Yet where does one draw the line? At a fifty-one per cent majority vote? Or, should there be no actions taken that cannot command unanimous agreement—a position which such modern exponents of libertarian liberalism as Professor Milton Friedman are slowly evolving toward. Unanimous agreement? Well, virtually unanimous agreement, whatever that will come to mean.

The principle of unanimity is, of course, completely impractical. My old friend Milton Friedman is extremely persuasive, but not even he can keep his own students

---

* Density of population produces what economists recognize as external economies and diseconomies. These "neighborhood effects" are often dramatized by smoke and other nuisances that involve a discrepancy between private pecuniary costs and social costs. They call for intervention: zoning, fiats, planning, regulation, taxing, and so forth.

But too much diluteness of the gas also calls for social interfering with laissez-faire individualism. Thus, the frontier has always involved sparse populations in need of "social overhead capital." In terms of technical economics jargon this has the following meaning: when scale is so small as to lead to unexhausted increasing returns, free pricing cannot be optimal and there is a *prima facie* case for cooperative intervention.

in unanimous agreement all the time. Aside from its practical inapplicability, the principle of unanimity is theoretically faulty. It leads to contradictory and intransitive decisions. By itself, it argues that just as society should not move from *laissez-faire* to planning because there will always be at least one objector—Friedman if necessary—so society should never move from planning to freedom because there will always be at least one objector. Like standing friction, it sticks you where you are. It favors the status quo. And the status quo is certainly not to the liking of arch individualists. When you have painted yourself into a corner, what can you do? You can redefine the situation, and I predicted some years ago that there would come to be defined a privileged status quo, a set of natural rights involving individual freedoms, which alone requires unanimity before it can be departed from.

At this point the logical game is up. The case for "complete freedom" has been begged not deduced. So long as full disclosure is made, it is no crime to assume your ethical case. But will your product sell? Can you persuade others to accept your axiom when it is in conflict with certain other desirable axioms?

Not By Reasoning Alone

The notion is repellant that a man should be able to tyrannize over others. Shall he be permitted to indoctrinate his children into any way of life whatsoever? Shall he be able to tyrannize over himself? Here, or elsewhere, the prudent-man doctrine of the good trustee must be invoked, and in the last analysis his peers must judge— *i.e.*, a committee of prudent peers. And may they be peers tolerant as well as wise!

Complete freedom is not definable once two wills exist in the same interdependent universe. We can sometimes find two situations in which choice A is more free than choice B in apparently every respect and at least as good as B in every other relevant sense. In such singular cases I will certainly throw in my lot with the exponents of individualism. But few situations are really of this simple type; and these few are hardly worth talking about, because they will already have been disposed of so easily. In most actual situations we come to a point at which choices between goals must be made: do you want this kind of freedom and this kind of hunger, or that kind of freedom and that kind of hunger? I use these terms in a quasi-algebraic sense, but actually what is called "freedom" is really a vector of almost infinite components rather than a one-dimensional thing that can be given a simple ordering.

Where more than one person is concerned the problem is thornier still. My privacy is your loneliness, my freedom to have privacy is your lack of freedom to have company. Your freedom to "discriminate' is the denial of my freedom to "participate." There is no possibility of unanimity to resolve such conflicts.

The notion, so nicely expounded in a book I earnestly recommend to you, Milton Friedman, *Capitalism and Freedom* (Chicago, 1962), that it is better for one who deplores racial discrimination to try to persuade people against it than to do nothing at all—but, failing to persuade, it is better to use no democratic coercion in these matters—such a notion as a general precept is arbitrary and gratuitous. Its absurdity is perhaps concealed when it is put abstractly in the following form: If free men follow Practice X that you and some others regard as bad, it is wrong in principle to coerce them out of that Practice X; in principle, all you ought to do is try to persuade them out of their ways by "free discussion." One counter-example suffices to invalidate a general principle. An exception does not prove the rule, it disproves it. As a counter-example I suggest we substitute for "Practice X" the "killing by gas of five million suitably specified humans." Who will agree with the precept now?

Only two types would possibly agree to it: (1) those so naive as to think that persuasion can keep Hitlers from cremating millions; or (2) those who think the status quo achievable by what can be persuaded is a pretty comfortable one after all, even if not perfect.

I exclude a third type who simply accept an axiom without regard to its consequences or who do not understand what its consequences are. The notion that any form of coercion whatever is in itself so evil a thing as to outweigh all other evils is to set up freedom as a monstrous shibboleth. In the first place, absolute or even maximum freedom cannot even be defined unambiguously except in certain special models. Hence one is being burned at the stake for a cause that is only a slogan or name. In the second place, as I have shown, coercion can be defined only in terms of an infinite variety of arbitrary alternative stati quo.

The precept "persuade-if-you-can-but-in-no-case-coerce" can be sold only to those who do not understand what it is they are buying. This doctrine sounds a little like the "Resist-Not-Evil" precepts of Jesus or Gandhi. But there is absolutely no true similarity between the two doctrines, and one should not gain in palatability by being confused with the other.

Marketplace Coercion, or The Hegelian Freedom of Necessity

Libertarians fail to realize that the price system is, and ought to be, a method of coercion. Nature is not so bountiful as to give each of us all the goods he desires. We have to be coerced out of such a situation, by the nature of things. That is why we have policemen and courts. That is why we charge prices, which are high enough relative to limited money, to limit consumption. The very term "rationing by the purse" illustrates the point. Economists defend such forms of rationing, but they have to do so primarily in terms of its efficiency and its fairness. Where it is not efficient—as in the case of monopoly, externality, and avoidable uncertainty—it comes under attack. Where it is deemed unfair by ethical observers, its evil is weighed pragmatically against its advantages, and modifications of its structure are introduced.

Classical economists, like Malthus, always understood this coercion. They recognized that fate dealt a hand of cards to the worker's child that was a cruel one, and a favorable one to the "well-born." John Stuart Mill in a later decade realized that mankind, not Fate with a capital F, was involved. Private property is a concept created by and enforced by public law. Its attributes change in time and are man-made, not Mother Nature-made.

Nor is the coercion a minor one. Future generations are condemned to starvation if certain supply-and-demand patterns rule in today's market. Under the freedom that is called *laissez-faire,* some worthy men are exalted; and so are some unworthy ones.* Some unworthy men are cast down; and so are some worthy ones. The Good Man gives the system its due, but reckons in his balance its liabilities that are overdue.

Anatole France said epigrammatically all that needs to be said about the coercion implicit in the libertarian economics of *laissez-faire.* "How majestic is the equality of the Law, which permits both rich and poor alike to sleep under the bridges at night." I believe no satisfactory answer has yet been given to this. It is certainly not enough to say, "We made our own beds and let us each lie in them."* For, once Democracy rears its pretty head, the voter will think: "There, but for the Grace of God and the Dow-Jones averages, go I."

How Unequal Is Equal? Is Unequal?

The game is up for abnegation of all social decision making. To "do nothing" is not really to do nothing but to continue to do what has been done. Since coercion is willy-nilly involved, and there is no algebraic magnitude of it that can be minimized in the interests of maximizing algebraic freedom of n men, what can abstract reasoning deduce concerning the "equitable" exercise of coercion, or, what may be the same thing, concerning the setting up of optimal arrangements for cooperation? Very little, as experience has shown and as Reason itself confirms.

"Equals are to be treated equally." Who could disagree with this sage precept. But what does it mean? And how far does it carry us? No two anythings are *exactly* equal. In what respect are they to be treated as essentially equal? What differences are to be ignored? Here are two organisms, each with a nose. Should they be treated equally, and what does it mean to do so? If the state taxes a brunette a dollar, then few will argue it should tax a redhead two. That seems discriminatory. But what if the redhead has a million dollars of income or wealth and the brunette has a thousand? Many would consider it indiscriminate to treat them as equals, to tax them each the same number of dollars or the same percentage of dollars.

A true story points up the problem of defining equality as a guide to "equity." In the Second War, Professor Ragnar Frisch, a world-famous economist and a brave Norwegian patriot, was put into a concentration camp by the Nazis. Food was scarce there and rationed. Frisch, according to legend, raised the question: Is equal rations

---

* "I am kept from attending college because my family is ——." To discern the coercion implicit in a competitive pricing system, note that any of the following can be substituted into the blank space: Negro, bourgeois, Jewish—or, poor.

* If one disagrees with Malthus and France and thinks that we all had equal opportunities and *have* made the beds we are to lie in, our judgment of *laissez-faire* improves—as it should. But note it is because of its fine welfare results, and *not because the kind of freedom embodied in it is the end-all of ethics.*

per man equitable? or, since nutritional need depends on metabolism which depends on body area and size, should not bigger men get larger allotments—their fair share, but no more? (If the result seems circular, a case of giving to him who hath, Frisch would no doubt be able to devise a measure of "inherent bigness." In any case no important vicious circle would be involved since the infinite series would be a rapidly converging one, as in the case where Gracie Allen found that the heavier a package the more stamps she had to put on it, and the heavier still it became.) This is not a trifling matter. Colin Clark has pointed out that 1800 daily calories for a small-boned man in the Tropics is not quite so bad as it sounds.

"Do unto others as you would have them do unto you." Shaw has not so much improved on this Golden Rule as given its antidote. "Do not do unto your neighbor as you would have him do unto you: his tastes may be different." This is, of course, the Anatole France point about asymmetry made general. It illustrates how little guidance can be derived from Kant's Categorical Imperative: Act (or create institutions that will lead to acting) in such a way that if your action were generalized to all, the total welfare and welfare of each would be maximized. Such a precept has meaning only in a perfect symmetry situation; in real life even approximate axes of symmetry cannot be found and agreed upon.

The whole matter of proper tax policy involves issues of ethics, coercion, administration, incidence, and incentives that cannot begin to be resolved by semantic analysis of such terms as "freedom," "coercion," or "individualism."

Mine, Thine, and Our'n

Life consists of minimizing multiple evils, of maximizing multiple goals by compromise. What is inevitably involved is a "rule of reason." But this kind of rule is misnamed, for it cannot be generated by abstract reason. It depends on ethics and experience. I shall not labor the point but merely give some examples of the inability of deductive reasoning to infer what is the optimal pattern of freedom and coercion, of individualism and cooperation.

Mill, and anyone, will agree: You are to be as free as possible so long as you do not interfere with the freedom of others. Or as Mrs. Pat Campbell, Bernard Shaw's pen pal, put it: Anyone can do whatever he likes so long as he does not scare the horses in the street. In an interdependent world the horses scare easily.

In practise, as recent Reports in Britain illustrate, the gist of these modes of reasoning lead to the view that the law should not interfere with, say, the relationships between homosexuals so long as these are carried on in private. But, as these Reports say, there are certain special issues connected with the problem of enticement of the young or simply enticement in general. Quite similar problems exist in connection with heterosexuality but almost escape notice in our post-Victorian world.

Let me leave this whole issue by reminding you of a well-told anecdote. A gay young blade is blithely swinging his umbrella and is told off by an irate oldster.

GAY YOUNG BLADE: What's the matter, this is a free country, isn't it?

IRATE OLDSTER: Yes, young man, but your freedom ends where my nose begins.

Actually, this is an understatement. Just as we have the rule of a three-mile limit, so there is intrinsically involved here a six-inch rule of nasal *Lebensraum*. And really life is much more complicated even than this: for, just as we live by taking in each other's washing, we live by breathing in each other's breath. Abstract reasoning cannot *find* a line between individuals, nor *draw* a line.

Finale

My time is almost up. I shall conclude by asserting that we live in an interdependent world. Just as God knows about every sparrow that falls, Einstein's theory of general relativity shows that everything does depend on everything else: when that sparrow falls, it creates a wrinkle in space-time which changes space everywhere. The doughnut which is an individual man is a collection of cells, each of which is a collection of smaller individuals. The skin that surrounds us is thin skin.

My body is remaking itself every moment: the I who is talking is the heir to the I's that were and the sire to those that will be. Radioactive isotopes show that even our teeth are tenants on a short lease; they are remaking themselves every day, and the half life of the charter-member calcium is measured in weeks not years. Only our serial number has soullike persistence.

Before Rousseau, people made the mistake of treating children as merely adults shrunk small. The Bible and Freud go farther and tell us that an adult is merely a child grown large. Man is imperfect, and so is woman. And so is We, Incorporated, who paternalistically put restraints upon ourselves. Not even an individual's perfections are his alone; like his imperfections, they are group made. We entered a world we never made, and leave one we did not unmake.

Carry the notion of the individual to its limit and you get a monstrosity, just as you do if you carry the notion of a group to its limit. You get not Nietzsche's superman, nor even Mill's imperfect-perfect Victorian entitled to his own mistakes. You get Wolf-Boy.

The Edward Everett Hale story of *The Man Without A Country* made a lasting impression on the boy that was I. You recall that Lieutenant Philip Nolan said in a fit of temper that he wanted never to hear the name of his country again. Fate gave him his wish, and how cruel his fate was. Likewise, I have thought, should an extreme individualist be given the wish of every child—to be able to travel anywhere with the gift of being invisible, inaudible, untouchable, and for that matter, inedible. To be condemned to dwell with mankind and never experience the interaction of others—I almost said other individuals—would be misery enow. It is not human to be such a human, and he would soon beg to join some committee—any committee.

Like a Beethoven symphony, my lecture does not end abruptly but it does come to an end. Perhaps what I have been saying comes to this. Wherever the true home of man is, it certainly is not in Coventry.

107

THE ECONOMIC ROLE OF PRIVATE ACTIVITY[1]

Introduction: Matter and Antimatter

Thoreau, disapproving of the Mexican War, would not pay his taxes and was put in jail for civil disobedience. His Concord neighbor, Emerson, went to visit him down at the hoosegow and called out: "Henry, what are you doing in there?" Thoreau replied, "Waldo, what are you doing out there?"

Illustrative of the same point was a conversation I had once with an economist for one of the great international oil companies. I was astonished to learn from him that their crews and engineers did not drill for oil in the Middle East. He explained the paradox as follows: "The Sheiks there are always anxious to make us sell immediately more oil than the market will bear; and they would take a dim view if we slackened on the job of exploration. So we drill in the hope of getting dry holes, but follow a research procedure that will mark off for us where oil really is to be found."

By now you will have perceived my point. One way of approaching the question "What is the proper role of government?" is to ask, "What is the proper role of nongovernment?" While you cannot be confident that the man who is most proficient in playing regular checkers (or tic-tac-toe) will also be best at playing "give-away" (or cot-cat-cit,

[1]Presented as part of a dialogue on "The Proper Economic Role of the State," at Swarthmore College. George J. Stigler was the other principal participant. The full version was originally published by the University of Chicago, Graduate School of Business (Selected Papers, No. 7).

in which the loser is made to have three of his symbols in a linear array), conventional wisdom or logic does ensure that by finding the optimal role for non-government, you can thereby define the proper role for government. Not taking the bull by the horns should at least give us a fresh perspective on the animal.

Lincoln's Formula

Some people begin the discussion of a concept by telling you how it is defined in Webster's dictionary. I follow the other fork and quote Abraham Lincoln. You may remember that the fellow who ran against Kennedy in 1960 quoted Lincoln on the proper role of government. It went something like the following:

> I believe the government should do only that which private citizens cannot do for themselves, or which they cannot do so well for themselves.

One would think this is supposed to be saying something. Let us try it in its converse form:

> I believe the private economy should be left alone to do those activities which, on balance after netting out all advantages and disadvantages, it can best do.

Obviously, what I have stated is an empty tautology. It is no more helpful than the usual answer from Dorothy Dix to a perplexed suitor that merely says, "Look into your own heart to see whether you truly love the girl. And then, after you have made up your mind, I am sure it will be the right decision."

But are these mere tautologies? Do the two Lincolnesque statements say exactly the same thing? There is a certain literal sense in which they can be interpreted to be saying the same thing. But we all bring to the words we hear certain preconceptions and attitudes.

I think Lincoln meant to imply in his formulation that there is needed a certain burden of proof that has to be established by anyone who proposes that the government do something. The balance of advantage in favor of the government must be something a little more than epsilon, or you should stand with the *status quo* of private enterprise.[2]

---

[2]Most people will, in fact, tend to give the benefit of the doubt to the *status quo* — any *status quo*. In our day the government does many things it did not do in Lincoln's time. When one of these activities is brought open to question, its being the *status quo* could shift the burden of proof onto the man who wants to bring the activity back into the private domain. I doubt that Lincoln would have agreed with this interpretation; in good nineteenth-century fashion, he thought of private activity as *natural* unless the contrary was demonstrated.

Why? Lincoln does not say. But he takes it for granted that his listeners will understand that "personal liberty" is a value for its own sake and that some sacrifice of "efficiency" is worth making at the optimal point where activity is divided so as to maximize the total net advantage of "efficiency *cum* liberty" and vice versa.

The second statement that I have formulated also carries certain connotations. At a first hasty reading, it might suggest to some that the burden of proof is put on or against any proposal for *laissez faire* and individualism. And so it would be naturally construed in 1963 Soviet Russia.

After a second or more careful reading, it is seen to contain certain weasel words of qualification — such as "on balance," "netting," and "advantages" and "disadvantages." So interpreted, it can be made consistent with any desired emphasis on liberty as well as efficiency. So interpreted it could suffice for Stalin or Rousseau, for Keyserling or Friedman. And yet, even when almost completely emptied of its meaningful content, my formulation is left with a subtle connotation. It says: there are no absolutes here. The subject is an open one — open for debate and open to compromise. At some terms of trade, efficiency can be traded off against liberty. (Of course, Lincoln has already implied *this*, but not quite so strongly.)

Overture to the Program

So much for introduction. My Act I has prepared the way for what is to follow. In Act II, I want to examine the conditions under which efficiency is realizable by free enterprise or *laissez faire*. This is familiar ground, but too familiar and needs re-examination.

Then in Act III, I want to raise some questions about the notion that absence of government means increase in "freedom." Is "freedom" a simply quantifiable magnitude as much libertarian discussion seems to presume? In case the time clock catches me somewhere in Act II, let me give you a hint of the kind of thing I have in mind: Traffic lights coerce me and limit my freedom, don't they? Yet in the midst of a traffic jam on the unopen road, was I really "free" before there were lights? And has the algebraic total of freedom, for me or the representative motorist or the group as a whole, been increased or decreased by the introduction of well-engineered stop lights? Stop lights, you know, are also go lights.

Then I shall conclude on what may seem a *nihilistic* note, but which I hope is actually a *liberating* one.

Technical Requirements for Competitive Optimality

Consider a society with limited resources. Let certain facts about technology be "known" (in varying degrees). Let there be more than one person, so that we can speak of society. Let people have their tastes and values. And if you like, let there be one or more sets of ethical beliefs in terms of whose norms various situations can be evaluated and ordered.

What I have now specified is so terribly general. Yet already I have been guilty of tremendous idealization and abstraction in comparison with any real-life situation.

To some observers, none of the preceding admits of quantification. It is all quality, quality, quality. There is a possible utopia; there are a variety of actualities; one contemplates these as a whole and reacts to them. And that's it. Such observers, patently, have little use for economics or economists.

Many observers, however, will note that one grain of sugar is much like another and rather different from grains of salt or Norwegian sweaters. Quantification is, so to speak, rearing its idealized head. Then one notes that five fingers and one nose tend to go together, and by a long chain of not-too-cogent arguments there emerges *Cogito, ergo sum* rather than *Cogitamus, ergo sumus*. Now individualism has reared its single head. And if I — or should it be said "we"? — can coin an Irish Bull, there is almost an anthropomorphic fallacy in considering that individuals exist in the sense that atoms exist.

Now, to save time, we plunge into heroic assumptions.

1. Each person's tastes (and values) depend only upon his separable consumptions of goods. That is, there must be no "consumption externalities."

2. Strict constant-returns-to-scale prevails.

3. Perfect competition, in senses too numerous to list here, prevails.

4. The interpersonal distribution of property (inclusive of personal attributes) is ethically correct initially or is to be made so by ideal lump-sum transfers of a perfectly nondistorting type.

Then, and only then, has it been rigorously proved that perfect competitive equilibrium is indeed optimal. So strict are these conditions that one would have thought that the elementary consideration that a line is infinitely thinner than a plane would make it a miracle for these conditions to be met. Real-life optimality, or an approach to it, would seem to cry out, not merely for departure from *laissez faire*, but for never having been remotely near to *laissez faire*. Yet, you might almost say by accident, our world is not galaxies away from this thin line.

Lawrence J. Henderson, a distinguished physiologist and philosopher at Harvard in my day, saw far beyond Darwinian evolution in which selection led to individuals that possessed fitness for the environment. He wrote a charming book on *The Fitness of the Environment*. For example, life as we know it depends critically on the peculiar properties that water happens to have (with, I believe, only ammonia as a substitute). How remarkable that one planet should have the temperature in that special range where water is liquid! This planet got selected for its suitability to sustain life.

I say how miraculous that Victorian England came anywhere near the homogeneity-of-the-first-degree production conditions that perfect competition truly needs. If all production functions were homogeneous of degree 2 or $3.14159\cdots$ — and why shouldn't they be? — George Stigler would be out of work; he would be a brewer or a Nobel Prizeman in physics.

And note this. We each belong to many circles: the United States, the Elks, the Samuelson family, the office pool, etc. In almost none of these relationships is the organizing principle that of decentralized competitive pricing. Let Abraham Lincoln ponder over that one.[3]

A Final Law

At the end I must lay down one basic proposition. If you remember only one thing of what I say, let it be this. If you don't remember anything of what I say, let this be the last thing you forget:

There are no rules concerning the proper role of government that can be established by *a priori* reasoning.

This may seem odd to you, for to state the rule that there are no rules may sound like a self-contradiction, reminiscent of the breakfast-cereal box that contains an exact picture of itself . . . of itself . . . of itself. . . . However, no Bertrand Russell theory of types is involved here. For, my proposition — call it Samuelson's Law if you like — does not claim to be established by Reason, but merely to be a uniformity of experience. Whose experience? My experience, and that of every (I mean, almost every) man of experience.

If I am wrong, it will be easy to prove me wrong: namely, by stating one valid nontrivial proposition about the proper role of government derived by cogent *a priori* reasoning alone. After I have digested it, I shall have no trouble in eating my own words.

Let me illustrate by a few rules that have been proposed and that will pass neither the test of experience nor the test of logic.

[3]P. A. Samuelson, "Modern Economic Realities and Individualism," in *The Texas Quarterly*, November 30, 1962. See pp 130–136. This is an adapted excerpt.

> JEFFERSON'S LEMMA: That government is best which governs least.

I waive the formal objection that there exists no least positive real number. Just as the only good Injun is alleged to be a dead one, this says that the best government would be one which committed suicide. By a social compact and constitution, anarchy would be proclaimed. Not even being sure just what is meant by the chaos the Bible tells us existed before Genesis (white-noise chaos? of Gaussian or Pareto-Lévy type?), I am certainly not sure just what anarchy is, although I have an idea what it is not. Taken *literally*, no one — certainly not Jefferson — will buy this dictum of zero government. Such sweeping rules are like soap bubbles: Literally take them and you find nothing in your hands to take. In this they differ from the Pythagorean or other theorem about Euclidean space derived by logic: Imagine saying "I believe the three angles of a plane triangle add up to 180° — but of course, not to the degree of taking the belief literally."

Here is another proposed law:

> ACTON'S CONJECTURE: All power corrupts, and absolute power corrupts absolutely.

Of course, Lord Acton didn't say quite this in his letter to Bishop Creighton; nor did he profess to deduce it *a priori*. Yet, since Lord Acton was unfamiliar with the anthropology of the Samoan islands, neither he nor anyone else, with the possible exception of Margaret Mead, can testify to its universal correctness. Even within the experience of the history known to nineteenth-century Cambridge dons, this cannot be established unless the words "corrupt" and "power" are defined tautologically. The Spearman rank correlation coefficient between the power of rulers and their abusive rulings is certainly not $+1$; to say the correlation is positive in a wide sampling of history is to say something interesting, but this is the kind of nonsweeping *empirical* uniformity that I am pleading for here as against dogmatic arguments from the nature of things.

Here is another branch whose graft never took on the tree of wisdom.

> COLIN CLARK'S LAW: The role of government must be held below a ceiling of 25 per cent of the national income.

This is not a two-halves truth or even, I fear, a 25 per cent truth. A number of nations whom we all point to as having accomplished miracles in the last decade never had the erudition to know of Clark's law or the instinctive good sense to desist from violating it. That Western Germany, the showplace of free enterprise, should collect 34 per cent of her national income for taxes is as shocking and thoughtless a violation of Clark's natural law as that a column of mercury should, after 30 vertical inches, neglect to remember that Nature abhors a vacuum.

I could go on. But why do so? My point is made: No *a priori* reasoning has yet been found to demarcate the role of nongovernment and of government. However, I must not be dogmatic. Having found cause to reject laws of Jefferson, Acton, and Clark, I must out of courtesy and caution reserve judgment on any laws that Professor Stigler may unveil. For, as I learned when our friendship began long ago, George Stigler can do anything — anything but be boring.

PART XV

Comments on Economic Programs

108

FULL EMPLOYMENT AFTER THE WAR

Paul A. Samuelson

As this essay is written, America's most important task is that of winning the present conflict.   Therefore, the difficult problems which our economy must again face when peace is at last reattained have very properly been pushed into the background.   The most important of these problems is that of providing for *continuing full employment.*   Before the war we had not solved it, and nothing that has happened since assures that it will not rise again.   And yet it is vitally important that we win victory on this economic front. Not alone for the tremendous material advantages which full employment will bring, but also because politically a democracy cannot flourish under conditions like those of the great depression.

It is necessary to emphasize these simple fundamental facts because in the years just prior to 1939 there were noticeable signs of dwindling interest in the problem of unemployment, which took the form of ostrich-like attempts to "think" away the very fact of unemployment by recourse to bad arithmetic and doubtful statistical techniques.   And even among professional economists there was increased emphasis on the recovery of production and income to 1929 levels.

At the present time, there are clear indications of increasing optimism among our better informed observers concerning the likelihood of a postwar boom of some duration.   In this respect, the experts are far ahead of the business community and the man on the street; but those who take the pulse of public opinion profess to detect some signs of increased optimism even among these groups.

No doubt this is a healthy corrective against the undue pessimism concerning the postwar period which characterized public opinion in the recent past.   But it would be unfortunate if we were to build up an attitude of complacency which might inhibit constructive policy formation designed to promote effective demand and combat unemployment should it develop; unless, of course, facts have become available which show conclusively that a lasting postwar boom is indeed inevitable.   This essay will be concerned with weighing the strategic factors and considerations upon which the validity of this point of view depends.   However, it may be said in the beginning that whether optimism may or may not be justified, complacency certainly cannot.   Precision in forecasting is simply out of the question.   There exists no new facts, secret or otherwise, which can justify the relaxation of our vigilance or of our conviction to combat a downward spiral of income and employment.

SIZE OF THE PROBLEM

By this I do not mean to imply that there is a serious prospect that we shall return to national income levels such as characterized the deep depression of 1932–1933.   Regardless of plans and intentions, any party in power would be forced by the mere sweep of catastrophic political events to provide sufficient demand to prevent this from happening.   The real danger lies in the possibility that we shall lag ever farther behind our true productive potential—that we shall be content with a half loaf instead of insisting upon the whole loaf which can be ours.   The thing to fear is an ever-widening gap between our attained levels of output and employment and our true productive potential.

It has taken the heavy wartime expenditure to show us how big the gap already is.   Throughout the thirties productivity increased tremendously so that we were able to reach the 1929 levels of real income with considerably reduced employment.   Until the defense program, all these gains plus the whole of our population increase were dissipated in unemployment or shared underemployment.   Any doubts as to the magnitude of this dissipation are removed by the fact that we are currently producing real national incomes 50 per cent greater than those of 1929.[1]   Given time in

[1] It is not certain but what our current peacetime potential would be greater than that now attained.   For war products must be produced hurriedly and in the face of bottlenecks, with shortages of strategic metals and with equipment not completely adapted to the changed character of production.   In addition, some millions of able men are taken by the military forces

which to make adaptations of equipment and manpower, it is only conservative to estimate that by the middle of this decade we shall be able to produce real national incomes 50 per cent greater than *prewar* levels; and by the closing years of the decade, real national incomes more than 70 per cent greater than *prewar* levels. In terms of *1935–1939 dollars* this means net national incomes of around $110 billion and $120 billion respectively.[1]

However, there is no special reason to believe that we shall necessarily return to prewar price levels. Indeed, despite our best efforts to control the price level by fiscal and direct measures, he would be an optimist who did not allow for at least a 25 per cent increase over the price levels prevailing in the summer of 1942. Consequently, within little more than the next half-dozen years, we may witness money national incomes of not much less than $170 billion.[2] Such a figure may seem fantastic, but so have all the estimates of one or two years ago—estimates which have already proved to be too cautious. Furthermore, our figure is premised upon the successful maintenance of full employment. And if events prove the estimate to be excessive, no harm will have been done since it will simply bring home by exaggeration the qualitative nature of our problem.

In drawing up fiscal plans for the future we must begin to think in larger numbers. Out of $170 billion income we shall have more money to spend on food, clothing, housing, recreation, leisure, education, saving, and personal security. We shall also be able to afford more in the way of public works, urban reconstruction, social

---

at fractions of their previous incomes. Against these factors must be mentioned the increased intensity of work under multiple-shift operations and the fact that national income figures are swelled by the less prudent expenditure of funds which the emergency necessitates. The incommensurability of war output makes it impossible for statistical deflation of money income to remove the latter source of bias.

[1] These figures are offered with due allowance for apparent productivity trends and population changes. Needless to say, they imply no forecast and are introduced only for purposes of exemplification. If anything, they are probably too low.

[2] Most of the rudimentary caculations that are presented in this essay are independent of the price level in terms of which real magnitudes are expressed. Should the increases in productivity upon which all the above estimates are based *lower* prices below the hypothesized levels, only a scale change in the value of various magnitudes will be required. An exception is provided by the case of such fixed-money magnitudes as the national debt. Changes in the price level will then mean real changes in its "burden."

security, welfare expenditures, etc. And by hypothesis only a small part of the increase in our total disposable money income will be offset by the higher prices for which everything will sell.

This is the promise which the future holds for us, provided that we are lucky or provided that we manage our affairs well. But bitter experience of the last dozen years, if not of the last century and a half, shows that there is no invisible hand guaranteeing that we shall always be lucky. Whether or not we should prefer it that way, the only alternative is deliberate, purposive, intelligent social action on whatever scale is necessary to ensure continuing full employment.

PROBLEM OF EFFECTIVE DEMAND

Anyone with the slightest knowledge of the existing standard of living of the various economic groups in our economy, and of the want patterns characteristic of modern society, cannot doubt that our *needs* will not begin to be filled by a 70 per cent increase in output, nor even by a doubling and quadrupling of output. We may take it as axiomatic that within the visible range human wants are insatiable, so that we shall not lack for employment for the reason that there is nothing useful left to be done.[1]

Why then can there be any problem of unemployment? A few of the older economists might even have denied its possibility on the basis of a discussion of human needs. But these would be in the minority. Bitter experience has taught us that it is not enough to be able to produce and to be able to consume. Demand must become effective if those who are willing to work are to find employment. At the bottom of the great depression our wants were if anything greater than before, our abilities to produce no less, and yet there was no mechanism by which these could be brought together.

It is not possible to reach full agreement among economists on any subject, much less on the fundamental reason why the above paradox should prevail. But increasingly there is a trend toward a theory of income determination, such as is about to be described.[2]

---

[1] In that dim distant (and probably ever-receding) day when human wants are satiated, the alternative to work will not be enforced unemployment, but rather play and leisure, *i.e.*, activity undertaken for its own sake.

[2] To a first approximation, with given technology and capital, the level of employment is determined as soon as the level of income is given, increasing as the latter does. This is not exact because the same level of income can be

It is associated largely with the name of John Maynard Keynes, although others have aided in its development. While its crystallization can be dated from the appearance of the *General Theory*[1] in 1936, it can be shown to have its roots in the earlier thinking of Keynes and other economists, and also to represent an amusing "throwback" to discredited doctrines of earlier days. Although the appellation "Keynesian" is usually applied to individuals of a certain viewpoint with respect to monetary and fiscal policy, this should not be confused with the use of the term as applied to those economists who use the technique of analysis which is about to be described. In itself the technique of analysis is neutral on policy questions, and that is why a majority of modern economists can continue to employ it while still dissenting vigorously from the views of the small but growing minority who constitute the inner circle.

THE SAVING-CONSUMPTION-INCOME PATTERN

We may approach our problem by way of an investigation of the manner in which an individual family expends an increase in its income of, say, 10 per cent.[2] Its expenditure on each item purchased does not ordinarily go up in the same proportion. Despite some shifts to better grades of food, its total expenditure on food will in all probability increase by less than 10 per cent. On the other hand, its expenditure upon recreation may increase by more than 10 per cent. But if all consumption items are added

---

weighted more or less heavily with products requiring much or little labor per unit. But for the present purpose it will be satisfactory to regard employment as being determined as soon as income is determined.

[1] J. M. Keynes, *The General Theory of Employment, Interest, and Money* (London, 1936).

[2] Literally thousands of "budget" studies have been made of income patterns in different countries and cities. *Cf.* Faith M. Williams and C. C. Zimmerman, *Studies of Family Living in the United States and Other Countries*, (U. S. Department of Agriculture, Publication 223). The consistency of results is impressive, suggesting that here we have a fairly stable and fundamental relationship. One of the most complete studies ever made for a country as a whole is outlined in *Consumers Expenditure in the United States*, 1935–36 by the National Resources Committee. This one undertaking represented the joint work of the above committee, the Bureau of Labor Statistics of the Labor Department, the Bureau of Home Economics of the Agriculture Department, and the Works Progress Administration. Despite inevitable inadequacies, it has rightly come to be regarded as a basic social document.

together, it is almost invariably found that they increase in smaller percentage than income; that those families with higher incomes devote an increasing percentage of their income to saving, *i.e.*, to the purchase of securities, life insurance, or to the accumulation of saving accounts. Even more certain is the generalization that *with higher incomes, some fraction of the increase goes into saving so that the total of saving increases absolutely with income whether or not it does so in less or greater proportion.*

In view of the relationship between family savings and family income, it is to be expected that there should be a fairly stable relationship between the total of all family savings and total national income; or what is only the other side of the picture, between total consumption and national income. Examination of the data provided by the painstaking efforts of Prof. Simon Kuznets of the National Bureau of Economic Research shows this to be the case.[1] For when national income rises, the incomes of most groups do also, and if not in the same proportions, nevertheless in a pattern sufficiently regular as to lead to the same result.

To individual and family savings we must add the savings of business and corporate enterprise. Indeed, it would appear from statistical examination that although these sources provide only a fraction of total saving, nevertheless they provide almost the whole of *extra* savings made out of additions of national income. Their so-called *marginal propensity to save* exceeds that of individuals.

Statistically, theoretically, and institutionally, everything points toward a consumption-savings-income pattern which is relatively stable, which is qualitatively predictable, and which changes only slowly over time. At low levels of national income net savings are negative; at some intermediate break-even point considerably below the full-employment level, they are zero; as we approach full employment, they mount rapidly, increasing more than proportionately with income.

[1] S. Kuznets, *National Income and Its Composition*, 1919–1938, Vols. 1 and 2 (New York, 1941). The interested reader may also refer to the following statistical investigations: A. H. Hansen, *Fiscal Policy and Business Cycles* (New York, 1941), Ch. XI and Appendix; M. Ezekiel, "Saving, Consumption, and Investment," I and II, *American Economic Review*, March and June, 1942; O. L. Altman, *Saving, Investment, and National Income*, T.N.E.C. Monograph 37; M. Abramovitz, "Savings and Investment; Profits vs. Prosperity?" *American Economic Review*, Supplement, June, 1942, pp. 53–89. R. Bangs, "The Changing Relation of Consumer Income and Expenditure," *Survey of Current Business*, April, 1942, pp. 8–12. For other countries, the reader may consult C. G. Clark, *The Conditions of Economic Progress* (London, 1940).

As a second approximation to bring the picture into greater conformity with reality, we must modify the above notion of a stable consumption-savings-income pattern to allow for *secular* and *cyclical* alterations.   The first is most easily understood.   As real income increases over time, commodities that were once luxuries become necessities.   Today, modest incomes can buy more than a king's fortune could command in former times.   And yet such incomes are often not large enough to finance "absolutely necessary" purchases, so that their possessors cannot break even, much less save on balance.

What is true for the individual is true for the community. Whatever the concept of oversaving is supposed to mean, it certainly does not imply that at the same levels of real income modern communities consume less than they used to.   Rather is the reverse true.   Not only does consumption at the same income levels increase secularly, but our rudimentary statistical data indicate that in each decade for the half century prior to 1929 about the same percentage of national income was saved.[1]   Since national income was increasing rapidly throughout this period, the most plausible explanation of this is to be found in the hypothesis that our enlarged scale of wants was causing an upward shift in the consumption function at about the same rate as improvements in our production potential, yielding a stable relation between percentage consumed out of national incomes corresponding to a given fraction of *full-employment* income.

Indeed, were it not for this upward shift of consumption, it would have become increasingly difficult to approximate as closely to full employment as we have in the past.   And in the future, the outlook for employment would be very black if we could not count upon expanded standards of life.   But this is not to imply that there is any guaranty that the upward shifts of the consumption schedule will be at a rate rapid enough to keep up with our productive potential; especially if the war and a prolonged period of depression keep us from knowing what we are missing in the way of new good things of life, so that our consumption "requirements" increase more slowly than our productive potentialities.

---

[1] S. Kuznets, "Capital Formation, 1879–1938," *Studies in Economics and Industrial Relations* (Philadelphia, 1941), pp. 53–78.

The customary relation is not to be found in 1941 and 1942 when restrictions on flows of consumers' goods and patriotically induced subscriptions to war bonds stimulated savings.—EDITOR

It is all very well to deal with the amount which would be consumed out of a given income level if that income were maintained *constant* for some time; but, in fact, income oscillates with business activity.   What are the *cyclical* distortions of the consumption and savings picture?   While income is rising (falling), does consumption change by more or less than its increase (decrease) from one stable level to another maintained stable level?   This question cannot be given a definitive answer on a priori grounds, since there are considerations supporting either an affirmative or a negative answer. On the one hand, it would seem plausible to argue that some time is required to become adjusted to increased levels of income so that in the short run consumption increases less with increased income than it does in the long run, saving taking up the slack. Moreover, when income drops, consumption is maintained at the expense of savings.   According to this first point of view, the short-run marginal propensity to consume is less than the long-run marginal propensity to consume.[1]

Diametrically opposed to this is the hypothesis that an increase in income will immediately cause families to make durable-goods purchases in excess of the increase in income, either through use of installment credit or out of previously accumulated wealth.   This would imply a "reverse acceleration effect" whereby a positive rate of change of income would induce consumption expenditure over and above what would be forthcoming at the same level of income steadily maintained.

Only the facts can decide between these opposing theories.   On the whole, the statistical data seem most in accord with the first hypothesis.[2]   In the short run when income is rising (falling), consumption does not increase (decrease) as much as its change from one stable level to another.   This would be even more true if we included in consumption expenditure only the value of consumers'

---

[1] By the marginal propensity to consume we mean the slope of the consumption-income schedule, or the fraction of an additional dollar of income which is spent upon consumption.   Since every dollar of income is either spent upon consumption or goes into saving, the marginal propensity to consume is one minus the marginal propensity to save.   The marginal propensity to consume should not be confused with the propensity to consume which refers to the whole consumption-income schedule or to some point on it; nor should it be confused with the average propensity to consume which gives the percentage of total income which is consumed.   Despite the fact that savings and investment are equal as observables, the reader is warned against identifying the marginal propensity to save with the marginal propensity to invest.

[2] Ezekiel, *op. cit.*, p. 33.

durables actually used up in the given period.   There is ample precedent for such a procedure, but the fact that it involves a difficult reckoning of the imputed use value of consumers' durables militates against its adoption.

The accompanying chart summarizes what has been said.   The dark line, AA, represents what the static consumption function would be at any instant of time if income were to be maintained

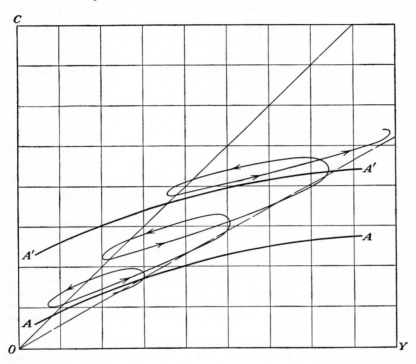

stable at each given level.   As time passes, the consumption schedule shifts upward to the higher dark line, $A'A'$.   Strictly speaking, under modern conditions these schedules are not observable since income rarely holds to a plateau of income, but moves cyclically. This point is indicated in the lighter curve which takes the shape of ascending spirals; these are counterclockwise in direction because of the delayed adjustment of consumption to new levels of income. In this diagram, both the cyclical and secular distortions of the static pattern have been exaggerated for emphasis.   However, in accord with the statistical findings of the last half century, the spiral has been drawn so that at each peak of the cycle, assumed for simplicity to correspond to full employment, about the same percentage of total income is consumed. This can be seen from the fact that the upper right-hand "corner" of each spiral falls almost on the dotted straight line through the origin.[1]

I have dwelt at some length on the behavior of consumption and savings in relation to income because this relationship is crucial for all business-cycle theories and provides the setting within which all analysis must take place.[2] At high levels of income corresponding to full employment, billions of dollars will be saved every year.[3] These sums are saved each year because people have incomes in excess of their consumption needs, because of a desire for personal security, because of power considerations or greed, because of automatic institutional arrangements, and for a thousand other reasons. It is irrelevant whether the process is deliberate or unconscious, whether prudence and thrift are involved or greed and lust, whether or not there is pain and abstinence. The desire to accumulate is a social *fact*, to be taken as such. And whatever might or might not be true of a Robinson Crusoe economy, it is clear that in modern societies individuals save regardless of the magnitude of investment outlets. Even if no new securities were floated, attempts to save would continue; and if old securities were not avail-

---

[1] Some might choose to interpret the dotted line as a very long-run consumption function, although I myself would not. Even if regarded as such, the fact that it does not show an increased percentage of saving as income rises does not in any way vitiate the application of the usual saving-investment analysis. It is necessary to emphasize this because in some quarters Prof. Kuznets' historical findings are taken as disproving the Hansen-Keynes long-run analysis.

[2] My omission of a discussion of the effects of interest rates and of stocks of wealth upon savings is a reflection of my belief, which cannot be justified here, that these are relatively minor in importance.

[3] If the 1935–1936 expenditure patterns and the 1935–1936 *relative* distribution of income were maintained, *real net savings* expressed in prewar dollars might be as large as $22 billion. In then current dollars this might be $28 billion. To this must be added some billions of net corporate saving, giving total net saving of around $32 billions. If a gross figure is desired, some further billions of depreciation must be added. Furthermore, in recent months it has become customary to distinguish between net national product and the total value of national expenditure valued at final prices. The latter magnitude exceeds the former by the amount of indirect business taxation. *Cf.* Milton Gilbert, "War Expenditures and National Product," *Survey of Current Business*, March, 1942, pp. 9–16. A comparable figure for saving could be derived by blowing up ours by some percentage.

able, it would still be possible to accumulate noninterest-bearing assets such as cash.

It is important to emphasize the stability of the savings-income pattern because of the insight it yields into historical income determination. Yet it is also important to remember that this pattern can be modified by *deliberate social action*. This does not mean that "Buy now" campaigns will end a depression, nor that exhortations to acquire government bonds will end a wartime inflation. However, by appropriate changes in our personal and corporate income taxes, we can affect the distribution of final disposable income in terms of which saving decisions are made. But such action must dig deep, for the institutions and habits relating to saving lie deep in our economic and political organism.

NECESSITY TO OFFSET SAVINGS

Aside from deliberate social action modifying the distribution of income, there does exist one process which is an effective regulator of the supply of saving. Precisely because of the stable income-saving pattern, declines in national income will make the community so poor that it will not save at all, or will dissave. For upon one thing all modern economists, of whatever school of thought, are agreed: *the amount which the community wishes to save at full-employment income levels must somehow be offset, or income will fall until the community is so poor and wretched as to be willing to save no more than can be offset.* In terms of time-period analysis, the community must return to the income stream in each period as much as it received in previous periods, or else there will ensue a cumulative downward spiral of income and employment.

We are confronted with the paradox that while no one attempts to save with any thought of investment outlets or of offsets, yet the amount which all together succeed in saving is brought into alignment by the movements of income and employment. But the alignment is performed on a cruel Procrustean bed, with employment and income being lopped off if the desire to save is excessive in comparison with available offsets, and with an inflationary straining of demand if investment is excessive.

It is important to understand this process because it throws light on countless other paradoxes. It is not that effective demand is independent of economic law. On the contrary, no view could be more fallacious than that which regards a depression as simply the result of a vicious spiral of unfortunate circumstances which, if once set right, would usher in permanent full employment.   Many times during the thirties we had incipient boomlets; if only optimism and an upward start were needed, they would never have come to an end.   But today we have come to understand that a system may be in *stable* underemployment equilibrium.   Economic law is operative but in a non-Euclidean, or rather a non-Ricardian, world in which the "topsy-turvy" may be right and the plumb line may be crooked.   It is characteristic of such a world that things may not be what they seem; a country may be in need of capital, its citizens may be imbued with prudence and thrift, and yet the *attempt* to save will not only be abortive but through its adverse effects upon income may lessen the amount actually saved and invested.[1]

If full employment is to be maintained, all savings that are made must be offset.   Two extreme schools of thought have drawn opposite conclusions from this.   On the one hand, the classical economists in their formulation of the celebrated *Say's Law of Markets* simply denied that there ever could arise a problem of offsetting savings.   For them, what was not consumed was automatically invested.   The exact elucidation of this doctrine is always obscure, and it takes on suspiciously many unrelated forms—from the innocuous assertion that goods exchange against goods and that all values are relative, to vague notions of conservation of purchasing power and absence of leakages.   In other formulations, a lowered real wage is believed to be effective in expanding demand along a "general demand curve for labor" drawn up in analogy with the negative sloping partial equilibrium demand curve for a single commodity.   Or still again, it used to be argued that the interest rate, if flexible, would somehow equilibrate the demand and supply of savings and investment, and at the same time in some manner equilibrate the supply and demand for labor.   Finally, in its most sophisticated form, reference was made to the fact that a general equilibrium system with flexible prices had for its mathematical and economic solution the equating of supply and demand in all markets. In the last analysis, then, only *inflexibility* in prices or costs could give rise to unemployment.

[1] Much of this had been intuitively realized for a long time.   But only in the last half-dozen years has an unambiguous analytical formulation been possible.   And even today the same facts can be given a favorable interpretation by the judicious use of the word *investment* or, if the opposite case is to be made out, by the use of the word *saving*.   More careful analysis shows that the intrinsic empirical phenomenon cannot be changed simply by revising our descriptive vocabulary.

This is not the place to attempt to deal adequately with so complex a doctrine. It can be said, however, that just as those economists who were free traders have developed the best arguments for protection, so it is those economists who use the Keynesian analysis who have been able for the first time to patch together a reasoned defense of the proposition that price flexibility may have salutary effects upon employment.[1] The process can only be briefly indicated.

Broadly speaking, downwardly flexible wages are supposed to cause prices to fall, thereby to produce redundant money supply and low interest rates, and hence stimulate investment. Other favorable effects are supposed to flow from the stimulus to consumption that the increased real value of money stocks will allegedly bring.

All in all this is not an impressive case, involving as it does the inadequacies of a cheap money policy, plus a dependence upon favorable expectations. Furthermore, closer investigation shows that its effects are transient since it depends not on *low* wages and prices, but on *ever-falling* ones. In view of the adverse psychological and real effects upon the marginal efficiency of capital and the propensity to invest which an ever-falling price and cost level would entail, it is by no means certain but that even moderate rates of deflation would be disequilibrating and self-aggravating rather than favorable to employment and income.

Therefore, I shall not discuss further the now extreme view that price-wage inflexibility is a necessary condition underlying the existence of unemployment, and that its removal is a sufficient or important remedial measure. At the same time the equally doctrinaire viewpoint that the existence of saving must necessarily cause unemployment in all circumstances can be treated only briefly. Whatever the excesses of some older underconsumption writers, it is today recognized that there is nothing in the structure of production itself (value added, depreciation payments, Major Douglas' *A* and *B* payments, etc.) which makes impossible the realization of full employment over any finite time period. Provided that sufficient new capital outlets exist, any amounts which

[1] *Cf.* Prof. Lange's forthcoming monograph on flexible prices; J. R. Hicks, *Value and Capital* (Oxford, 1939), Ch. 20; A. C. Pigou, *Employment and Equilibrium* (London, 1941); G. Haberler, *Prosperity and Depression* (3d ed., League of Nations, 1942), Ch. 13; Gardiner C. Means, *Structure of the American Economy*, Vol. II (National Resources Planning Board, Washington, D. C.), pp. 9–17.

people wish to save can be offset.[1] It may be bad theology, but it is sound economics that a *sufficiently lucky* community can cheat the devil of ineffective demand indefinitely. Thus, the significant contributions of these earlier writers must be found in their realization that unemployment would arise unless very special conditions were met, and perhaps in their belief in the unlikelihood that these conditions will prevail.[2]

OFFSETS TO SAVINGS

It is the upshot of our discussion that the prospects for unemployment and depression cannot be determined on a priori or deductive grounds. An analysis of income determination can help in isolating the strategic factors involved and in suggesting the appropriate questions to ask of our available empirical statistical data. Specifically, we must answer the question, what are the processes by which savings can be offset. Broadly speaking, these can be divided into at least the following categories: (1) private net capital formation, (2) private losses, (3) foreign investment, (4) governmental expenditure in excess of tax receipts, (5) governmental fiscal policy aimed at changing the primary distribution of imputed income into a secondary distribution of net income after taxes, which is conducive to greater consumption out of the same total income, (6) increased governmental expenditures matched by equivalent taxes, (7) an upward shift in the propensity to consume at each level of income.[3]

Let us examine briefly each of these in turn. The most widely recognized is the first, private net capital formation. Historically this has taken the form of new heavy capital goods, primarily of

---

[1] This holds even after the output of the newly created capital goods comes upon the market provided that sufficient further investment outlets are forthcoming. *Cf.* the doctrines of Foster and Catchings, *Money* (Boston, 1923).

[2] It may be appropriate to record the belief that the future historians of economic doctrines will dispense with the false distinction between underconsumption and underinvestment or undersavings, and that the under consumptionist writers will attain to a level of respectability hitherto denied them, if only because their instincts led them to see obscurely the elements upon which the modern income analysis is based.

[3] This mode of classification is arbitrary, but useful. Several of these items could be consolidated, and the careful reader will note that some of the offsets to savings are ways of preventing savings from arising rather than neutralizers of performed savings. The sum of these components will not equal total savings.

durable types.   It is to be noted that public utilities, railroads, and residential construction have throughout our history over-shadowed manufacturing industry in importance as a source of investment outlets.   Since we exclude replacement expenditures, it is clear that this offset depends upon discovery of new ways of doing things, new products, dynamic growth and expansion.   In behavior it is sporadic, volatile, and capricious.   Its effective determinants are almost completely independent of current statical factors (level of income, etc.).

It is tempting to construct a theory of income determination analogous to the "Marshallian cross" of supply and demand by which price in a single market is determined; *i.e.*, to erect schedules of both saving and investment, at whose intersection income is determined.   However valid this may be formally, it is necessary to insist that investment in anything but the shortest run cannot be related to income in the way that savings can.   Even in the shortest run it is not the statical level of income, but its time pattern of change taken in conjunction with the existing stock of capital equip-ment, which determines investment.   In the present writer's opinion, this cannot be emphasized too much, particularly in view of recent statistical attempts to estimate what the level of invest-ment would be at high levels of national income.[1]   At worst, such attempts simply indicate what levels of investment are *necessary* if income is to be at a high level, since the past coexistence of high investment and high income may represent causation from the former to the latter rather than vice versa.   At best, they might hope to give the cyclical pattern of investment peaks which can be touched for a moment at the top of a boom; but even this is extremely doubtful since there is no necessary repetition from cycle to cycle of the sectors which lead in investment outlay.

While it is customary to think of capital formation as taking the form of heavy durable capital goods, there is no necessity for this to

[1] Ezekiel, *op. cit.;* R. Bissell, in this volume and in *Fortune,* May and June, 1942.   Both of these authors attempt, by dealing with split-up components, to avoid the gross statistical error of deriving two independent schedules from essentially the same data.   I do not believe that they succeed in this attempt.   In any case, the data which both use are consistent with the alternative hypothesis that the scatter of investment outlay is traced out by shifts in the investment schedule.

It may be noted that one of these studies comes out with a pessimistic quantitative estimate of the ability of private investment outlay to lead to full employment, while the other paints a rosier picture.

be the case.   Outlay to the public by private business enterprise in excess of its consumption sales constitutes income and employment creating expenditure.   It may be for the purpose of building up (via advertising expenditure) such intangible assets as good will; it may take the form of a price reduction which only after a considerable period of time will pay for itself.   Most important, such expenditure provides an offset to saving even if no asset, tangible or intangible, is created for the business enterprise.   *Business losses* arising from imprudent or unfortunate expenditure are dollar for dollar as employment-creating as other private investment and provide equally potent offsets to savings.   Historically such losses have been extremely important as an offset to savings.   Recent trends, however, suggest that a considerable sector of business enterprise, particularly large corporations, are learning to adapt themselves to an unfavorable environment so as to avoid losses.   It is quite possible that many of these could make adjustments so as to stay out of the red even at levels of national income corresponding to 50 per cent of full employment.   On the whole, this is not necessarily an undesirable trend, since imprudent and wasteful expenditures are not the most desirable ways to provide employment.   Nevertheless, this trend must be taken account of in reckoning the prospects for the maintenance of full employment on the basis of private demand alone.

It is too early to speak with any assurance concerning the future of foreign lending.   On the whole, it seems to be the consensus of informed opinion that the prospects are not good for any substantial revival of private flotations in the form that we have known them in the past.   No doubt we shall forge new quasi-public instrumentalities for the purpose of aiding in international reconstruction. These are best included under a discussion of governmental offsets to savings.   Aside from these it may well turn out to be the case that the new international responsibilities which are forced upon the United States by her leading position in world affairs will require a renunciation of beggar-my-neighbor attempts to export without importing, so that in the postwar world the foreign balance may be an unfavorable rather than a favorable offset to savings.[1]

During the last decade we have had to rely heavily upon the fourth offset to saving, *viz.*, deficits.   A realistic appraisal of the future would suggest that these can only be wiped out by a sub-

---

[1] *Cf.* essays in this volume on "International Economic Relations."

stantial strengthening of our tax system. It seems extremely unlikely that postwar Federal expenditures can shrink to prewar levels. Nor is it certain that the retention of many parts of our wartime tax structure will yield enough revenue to balance the budget. There is the further paradox that the heavy yields of our tax structure may depend upon high levels of national income, which levels are premised upon large sustaining deficits. This inevitably raises the question as to the perils involved in a growing public debt.[1] If orthodox central banking operations are not adequate to prevent large increases in debt service charges and interest rates, careful thought should be given to the alternative of the controlled issuance of noninterest-bearing debt. It is becoming increasingly apparent that this would have little or no effect upon the magnitude of public expenditure and would differ in no significant degree from bond sales as a contributing factor to inflation. Whether or not we embark upon such a policy, it is highly desirable that the Treasury follow a militant policy of interest rate reduction except where subsidies are to be granted on the basis of broad social desirability.

Because the same fraction is not saved out of the *last* dollar of a man's income, the amount which will be saved out of a given volume of total income depends upon its distribution among individuals. This distribution is not to be regarded as a fundamental datum, but can be altered by means of tax collections which have a differential effect upon the different income classes, and by government expenditure which does not go to all classes in the same proportion. Progressive income taxes are one way of achieving this result, as are estate and capital taxation. In view of the administrative limits to steep income taxes,[2] the corporate tax may be useful in giving us a tax system with less sag in the middle. On the expenditure side an expanded welfare program involving public health, old-age pensions and assistance, unemployment compensation, family allowances, educational aids, as well as relief for the underprivileged, all contribute toward a distribution of income more favorable to consumption. As yet we do not fully realize how large a fraction of our welfare expenditures are *not* associated with depression and unemployment, but rather with the higher social standards which our democracy has adopted. Consequently, even continuing full

---

[1] See S. E. Harris, on *"Public Debt,"* in this volume.
[2] H. C. Simons in his *Personal Income Taxation* (Chicago, 1939) indicates how we may strengthen our progressive tax system.

employment will not cause a shrinkage of welfare expenditure to predepression levels.[1]

While substantial gains in consumption can be made by these distributional methods, it would be well not to expect too much of them. For the difference between the *marginal* propensity to consume of poor and wealthy is by no means so great as between their *average* propensities to consume. Consequently really large changes in the inequality of income distribution are necessary to reduce savings by even 10 per cent. And at the same time that savings are being reduced, there is some adverse effect upon the offset to saving provided by new investment. I cannot do justice to these aspects here. But it may be said that the modern corporation provides a mechanism for the pooling of risks so that the government does share in the risk takers' losses.[2] Undoubtedly democratic communities will continue to attach primary importance to the equity considerations in favor of a more equal distribution of income, letting the favorable effects upon consumption form a secondary argument for them.[3]

Only recently have I become convinced that item 6 does provide a genuine offset to saving—that a budget balanced at a high level, with "nonprogressive" taxes and expenditure, is nevertheless employment- and income-creating. A proof cannot be attempted here. However, if valid, this form may provide an important method by which our economy can hope to maintain the level of effective demand.

[1] The government by nonfiscal policies such as wage regulation, price regulation, trust busting, etc., can hope to offset the primary distribution of income in a more favorable direction.

[2] Furthermore, it is the curvature of the tax structure rather than the steepness of the tax gradient which introduces the unwillingness to invest because the government pockets winnings without sharing in losses. A careful study of the economic history of the United States and England would probably show that "venture capital" in the usual sense has not provided an important fraction of total offsets to savings. Its real importance lies in their productivity-increasing aspects rather than in their stimulating effects upon employment. Even here the reluctance to assume risk because of modern tax systems results in a delay between the discovery of new processes and their introduction rather than in their total loss. Instead of accumulating an ever greater pool of unused inventions, we become synchronized some few years behind our maximum potentialities.

[3] Space does not permit a discussion of the influence of wartime fiscal policy upon the distribution of wealth holdings at the end of the war and upon interest income in the postwar period.

The seventh process by which one generation develops new consumption wants and needs so as to offset the amount which would be saved under earlier patterns has been of the greatest historical importance in sustaining effective demand.   In a sense, the others are only makeshifts.   Private investment only puts off the evil day.   It must be followed by more investment in all succeeding time.   Increased consumption standards, on the other hand, are more or less irreversible.   They provide in each period sustaining demand.

Nor is it to be thought that a high consumption economy means a low investment-savings economy.   On the contrary, only where consumption demand is high are large savings and investment possible.[1]   A high consumption economy may mean low investment in percentage terms; but it means higher absolute levels of investment.

As we have seen in earlier sections, the United States seems historically to have increased its consumption standards at about the same rate as its productive potentialities.   Even if this should continue to be the case in the future, it is quite possible that the problem of offsetting savings would become more acute as we grow more wealthy.   For with increasing real income, constant percentages saved means that we must find ever-increasing absolute volumes of offsets.

Besides, there is no mechanism, no natural law, which guarantees that these processes will develop in balance during the years ahead. In the past the country-to-city movement has resulted in higher propensities to consume, but now this process has decreased in importance.   The war itself has meant a reversion to lower consumption standards and may leave us a generation behind where we would otherwise have been.   Despite our backlog of deferred consumers' durable goods purchase, considerable time may be required to thaw out frozen consumption habits.   Most important of all, since 1929 we have had a distinct break in trend.   The great depression meant an intensification of the desire to save because of personal insecurity.   Throughout this decade our income ceased to grow but our productive potential increased steadily.   The con-

---

[1] For completeness it should be pointed out that under exceptional circumstances low consumption can lead to a fall in income and interest rates sufficient to stimulate investment more than unfavorable consumption sales discourage it. See O. Lange, "The Optimum Propensity to Consume," *Economica*, February, 1938.

sumer did not know what he was missing in the way of new good things of life and so was not able to develop new tastes at the same old rate.   As in other branches of economic analysis, there is something of a vicious circle here.   Provided we succeed in maintaining high levels of income, habits are developed which make it easier to continue to hold to these levels.   If once a slump is permitted to develop, the situation may be stabilized at a low level.

BALANCE SHEET OF THE FUTURE

With the theory of income determination outlined in the previous section we are now in a position to evaluate the factors favorable and unfavorable to high levels of employment in the postwar years. Those who are optimistic concerning the prospects for a spontaneous postwar boom of some duration based upon private demand alone entertain this belief for one or more of the following three reasons:

1. They point to the impressive ease with which demobilization took place after the First World War.

2. Others attach importance to the fact that as a result of the current struggle we will necessarily use up our stock of producers' and consumers' capital equipment in excess of replacement.   The unavailability of goods during the war, taken in conjunction with high monetary incomes, means that family savings will necessarily increase, taking the form of government bonds, savings accounts, and life insurance.   Installment debt has already declined greatly, and by the end of the war the same will be true of mortgage indebtedness.

Once the war program has ceased to accelerate, the same process of increased liquidity will become true of business enterprise as well, particularly large business.   Depreciation allowances in excess of gross investment will eventually go into cash, government bonds, and reduction of liabilities.   These gross savings will be swelled by earnings on war contracts, rapid amortization of war equipment, and eventually by war end indemnity payments from the government to armament-producing firms.   Already the tendency toward greater liquidity is getting under way, as yet unnoticed by observers who fear that the war will strip corporations of liquidity.

If we add to this the forced saving plans which the future will certainly bring, as well as postwar tax refunds to corporations, it will be seen that the *real backlog of deferred demand* as a result of wartime depletion of capital will be accompanied by the financial means to make it effective.

3. The third group of optimists are those who all along, regardless of the war, have thought that prosperity was just around the corner—or would be if sound governmental policies were adopted. This group looked forward throughout the great depression to the imminent appearance of a large block of deferred demand, which until the war had not yet developed. If the war were to end early, they would still expect prosperity even though no backlog of wartime deferred demand had as yet arisen. This is the most difficult view to substantiate or refute, resting as it does in part upon faith and in part upon the fulfillment of political conditions other than those we are likely to face for a considerable time in the future. Needless to say, the validity of this viewpoint is unaffected by the war. It is worth as much or as little as before 1939.

Because it rests upon historical facts, the first viewpoint may be discussed at greatest length. This is done in the next section. After a few words on point 2, some sources for pessimism will be indicated.

AFTERMATH OF NOV. 11, 1918

An examination of the popular and learned periodicals issued during the last war shows almost no preoccupation with problems of postwar planning. As victory finally loomed ahead, a number of programs for "Reconstruction" did emerge, but these were almost exclusively international. A few cautious souls warned that temporary problems of glut in the labor market might arise if soldiers were demobilized too rapidly, and that consequently the speed of discharges should be regulated with reference to unemployment. But on the whole, in the radical and in the conservative press, there was little concern over the problem of achieving or maintaining full employment.

As soon as the Armistice was signed, a feverish anxiety swept over the country to return to prewar "normalcy," to "get the boys out of the trenches by Christmas." Those soldiers who had not gotten overseas were discharged largely in December, while the A.E.F. was disbanded rapidly all through the first half of 1919. By one year after the Armistice, about 4 million soldiers, sailors, and marines had been disbanded, or all but a skeleton force.

On Nov. 12, the long-distance wires were kept busy canceling war contracts wherever possible. Within a year, 2 billion of these were settled, with cash payments by the Treasury averaging about one-eighth of the face values of the contracts.[1]   Price and production controls were also removed as soon as possible, many by the end of 1918.   The administrators of the emergency agencies, largely recruited from private industry for the "duration," were eager to return to private business.

The picture is clearly that of a planless rush to wind up the war activities as quickly as possible, without thought of possible adverse consequences.   And all this was done without appreciable dismissal pay for soldiers, in a system not yet possessing unemployment insurance, with primitive labor exchanges and placement services, and with little or no provision for direct or work relief.

The upshot of all this is well known.   There was no market crash or crisis, no great increase in unemployment, no deep cumulative downward deflationary spiral.   Instead, we witnessed the very mild recession of the winter of 1918–1919.   This was followed in the spring of 1919 by an upturn in prices and activity rising to a crescendo in the first half of 1920.   The 1919–1920 boomlet came to an end with the collapse of farm prices in the summer of 1920 and was succeeded by the very sharp, but fairly brief, recession of 1921.

These events are a matter of record.   They are interpreted by many to mean that private industry at the end of the last war was able by itself to solve the problem of demobilization and postwar transition.   Some will take a further step and ask whether similar tactics are not feasible when the Second World War comes to an end. Unfortunately, the argument fails at the first step.

Closer examination of the facts reveals that the picture painted above of the 1919–1920 boomlet is superficial and seriously distorted. *It was not a privately maintained boom.   It did not rest upon backlogs of deferred demand.   It did not bring with it the material prosperity usually associated with a boom.   It was not based upon stable, enduring foundations.   Many of its characteristic features are precisely those which can be expected not to be present at the end of the present war.*

The single most important fact to be emphasized is that, however anxious we were to end the war immediately after Nov. 11, 1918, this was nevertheless not possible.   Economically speaking, the First World War did not end with the Armistice, but continued until well into 1920.   In the first months after November 11, our war expenditures were larger than at any previous time.   It was these unprecedentedly high "net income-creating expenditures" of the Federal government which eased the demobilization of that period.

[1] *Annual Report of the Secretary of War*, 1919, p. 43.

Nobody wished to spend this money; it was not part of a plan, but simply proceeded from the necessities of the moment.   Projects almost completed could not simply be terminated in mid-air.   After the Armistice we lent $2 billion to the Allies, and spent hundreds of millions of dollars to feed the continent of Europe.   Because of this, our favorable balance of trade was greater in 1919 than at any time during the war or during the decade of the twenties.   The shipping shortage operated more to reduce imports than exports, again contributing artificially to offsets to savings.   While not all the favorable balance of trade was financed by the government, some substantial fraction being financed by extraordinary short-term capital lending, there is no indication that the latter phenomenon will be present when the Second World War comes to an end.

Not knowing the troublesome times ahead, the private business community greeted peace with optimism.   As the spring of 1919 wore on, sales increased in retail lines such as clothing for returning soldiers, household goods, etc.   With the removal of price controls, the wholesale price index began to rise, in the end soaring from the final war level of around 200, on a prewar base, to almost 250.   This set off a wave of inventory accumulation, or attempted accumulation, which formed a substantial fraction of total offsets to savings; and the paper increase in inventory values was considerably greater.

From its nature this was an unhealthy base upon which to erect a boom.   Price increases led to attempted inventory accumulation, further accentuating the price increases.   But it was not enough for prices to stay at these abnormal levels; once they ceased to rise, or leveled off, the whole structure had to collapse.   It is worth contrasting this 1919–1920 boomlet with the longer sustained prosperity plateau of the twenties.   The latter was not at all based upon the stimulus provided by a temporary upward price and inventory spiral.   In this respect 1919–1920 was more like the incipient boomlet of 1936–1937.   In both cases an unstable price situation was aggravated by the rather drastic reductions in net Federal spending, giving rise in one case to the recession of 1938 and in the other to the 1921 recession.

In one important respect the picture of the 1919–1920 boomlet as simply a paper upswing must be qualified.   From mid-1919 to the end of 1920 American industry spent unprecedentedly large sums upon gross plant and equipment.[1]   The rate of expenditure exceeded

[1] Lowell J. Chawner, "Capital Expenditures for Manufacturing Plant and Equipment, 1919–1940," *Survey of Current Business*, March, 1941.

that of the late twenties or of any other period until the present war effort.   In view of the definitely secondary importance of manufacturing as a source of investment outlets, and in view of the *unprecedentedly high rate of saving immediately after the First World War I*,[1] these outlays are not to be given too much importance as offsets to saving and as income maintainers in this period.   Nor did they contribute much to the output of that period, which available indices of production show to have been lower than 1916 levels despite the alleged boom conditions.[2]   But they were undoubtedly of importance as a tooling up for the mass-production levels of the golden twenties and for the later economies in the use of labor which increased productivity per man-hour made possible.

Despite this qualification it remains broadly true that the 1919–1920 boomlet is nothing to look back upon with pride.   It was a boom without prosperity initiated by the inevitable large government expenditures necessary to wind up the war.   It continued on the momentum of these expenditures plus transient speculative elements of inventory accumulation induced by booming farm and industrial prices.   The bubble necessarily had to burst sometime, and the fact that the resulting depression was short-lived and was followed by a period of sustained prosperity must be explained in terms of a concatenation of fortunate circumstances, of which only a fraction can be related to private investment outlets or to the war itself.

Furthermore, careful study of the First World War leads to the conviction that it was utterly different from the present conflict and that analogies with it are more dangerous than otherwise.   It was not total war as this one is.   There was relatively little conversion of peacetime activity.   Most important, our military production, aside from operations begun in response to Allied orders, literally never got under way on an appreciable scale.[3]   No more illuminating contrast could be found than in a comparison of the roles of both the automobile and aircraft industries in this and the last war.

[1] S. Kuznets, *National Income and Its Composition*, 1919–1938, Table 1, p. 137, and Table 58, p. 322.

[2] S. Fabricant, *The Output of Manufacturing Industries*, 1899–1937 (New York, 1940).

[3] Apparently the year 1918 was planned to be a year in which we were to build up our military productive capacity for an all-out struggle in 1919, and thereafter.   The speedy end to the war seems to have come as a surprise to expert and layman alike.

When this war comes to an end, more than one out of every two workers will depend directly or indirectly upon military orders. We shall have some 10 million service men to throw on the labor market. We shall have to face a difficult reconversion period during which current goods cannot be produced and layoffs may be great. Nor will the technical necessity for reconversion necessarily generate much investment outlay in the critical period under discussion, whatever its later potentialities. The final conclusion to be drawn from our experience at the end of the last war is inescapable—*were the war to end suddenly within the next 6 months, were we again planlessly to wind up our war effort in the greatest haste, to demobilize our armed forces, to liquidate price controls, to shift from astronomical deficits to even the large deficits of the thirties—then there would be ushered in the greatest period of unemployment and industrial dislocation which any economy has ever faced.*

This does not deny that there may be a boom after the war. In this the experts may still be correct. For the release of controls upon demand coupled with plentiful amounts of monetary demand might well give rise to price increase, inventory buying, feverish speculation and all the superficial earmarks of a boom. But it would be the antithesis of a prosperity period, constituting instead a nightmarish combination of the worst features of inflation and deflation. Nor, having spent itself, could it be expected to evolve into healthier channels. Instead, the final outcome would undoubtedly be a cumulative hyperdeflation from which, at best, we should lose a decade of progress and which, at worst, our democracy would not survive.

Of course, this is not intended as a picture of what will in fact happen. For there is every reason to believe that we shall not be lulled into a feeling of false security by the last war's experience or by the half-truth that the end of the war will witness a boom. No doubt, we shall retain direct controls for a period after the conflict ends. We shall taper off war production gradually. We shall undertake income maintenance in the form of dismissal pay for soldiers, unemployment compensation, direct and work relief expenditure. It is probable, although less certain, that, in addition, the Federal government will initiate employment maintenance measures such as large scale public works, etc. But even these will not necessarily be adequate to maintain full employment or any approach to it. In the next section, I shall discuss factors favorable to employment in the period after the immediate demobilization and reconversion crisis. It may be said in advance that, however favorable these are, they can be completely nonoperative if we do not take very far-reaching measures to bridge the immediate transition period—measures much stronger than those envisaged in current discussions.

THE BACKLOG OF DEFERRED DEMAND

Undoubtedly this factor will be of the greatest importance in the postwar period. What is needed most of all is a series of detailed quantitative studies, sector by sector, of the extent to which the war is depleting consumers' and producers' stocks of capital equipment, in order that more precise estimates can be made. While such studies would confirm the importance of this source of demand, they would also, I believe, provide a healthy corrective to many currently held inflated expectations.

Until the summer of 1942, no deferred demand on balance had accumulated. On the contrary, inventories of producers' and consumers' durable and nondurable goods were at an all-time high. In the two years following 1939 we had added almost one-half as much manufacturing plant and equipment as we had been able to accumulate in all our previous history. Much of this will be convertible after the war, resulting in some fields in tremendous reverse backlogs —surpluses and not deficiencies. No conceivable increase in peacetime demand could possibly absorb the capacities for aircraft production and machine-tool production which the war will leave us. The same is true of many of the metal trades.

Furthermore, implicit in the usual reckoning of deferred demand is the assumption that there is a fixed total over time which must necessarily be spent. Given the technological change which the war will inevitably bring, this is by no means necessarily the case. We must take care also to avoid double counting. If a man goes without an automobile for 6 years, he does not then have a demand for six automobiles, nor will he necessarily spend in all subsequent time upon automobiles an extra amount equal to the 6 years' expenditure forgone. This means that the backlog will increase with the length of the war, but not in direct proportion. For nondurable goods there need be no backlog at all. Consumption forgone today is gone forever.

Upon even the most optimistic reckoning the magnitude of the backlog is necessarily finite. If bunched into a short enough period, one can produce as large a boom as is desired, but it will not last. If spread over a long enough period of time, its contribution to the rate of employment may be quite small.   A last point to be mentioned is the fact that deferred demand is a fair-weather friend.   What has been postponed can be postponed longer.   Even if individuals and corporations have adequate funds to finance expenditure, they are unlikely to do so if the bottom is falling out of the market for goods, and if unemployment is mounting.

All this suggests that deferred demand represents a favorable reinforcing factor, but not one which in and of itself can be relied upon to initiate and sustain a lasting prosperity.   There is no justification to envisage a "generation" or decade of prosperity from this factor.   On a fairly liberal estimate of the amount of war bonds which individuals will accumulate, the stock of unused automobile miles at the end of the war, the level and potentialities of installment selling, etc., it is certain that under no circumstances could automobile production after the war require the employment for as long as 2 years of the $1\frac{1}{2}$ million laborers who will be in the automobile and aircraft industries.   In fact, without striving to be pessimistic, it is possible to derive the estimate that the total backlog of deferred demand could be made good by our productive capacity at the end of the war in a period from 18 months to 2 years, and this on the favorable assumption that we successfully meet the immediate demobilization crisis.   Compared with a deficit of $40 billion per year, this is not of primary importance.

CONCLUSION

All our findings lead to the conclusion that there is serious danger of underestimating the magnitude of the problem of maintaining continuing full employment in the postwar period.   Those who complacently predict a boom are likely to find their expectations fulfilled, but not with respect to the employment and real-income aspects usually associated with a prosperity period.

Even if correct, the realistic appraisal presented here does not provide grounds for pessimism.   We can, and I am confident that we will, pursue policy measures appropriate to the challenging situation.   The penalties for failing to do so will be serious, but the rewards for courageous action will be commensurately great.

109

RECENT AMERICAN MONETARY CONTROVERSY

BY PAUL A. SAMUELSON

Professor of Economics, Massachusetts Institute of Technology

VOLTAIRE DEFINED HISTORY as a fable agreed upon. In this sense of the word I can briefly sketch the history of American central banking as a background for discussion of current monetary issues.

1. Institutional Developments

In the first years of this century we had periodic crises and panics in the money market. These pathologies were diagnosed as being due to the *inelasticity* of our National Banking system. So, after a decade of hot debate, in 1913 the Federal Reserve System was established.

Characteristic of our American distrust in centralisation was the decision to create twelve regional Federal Reserve Banks. This agreeable fiction of decentralisation and regionalism has many small advantages in terms of communication with the hinterland: it provides listening posts for grassroots public opinion; it improves the architecture of some of our great cities; and it provides honorific posts for representatives of industry, agriculture, banking and the public. But very soon it became clear to all that we had indeed created a central bank, inevitably and not improperly dominated by New York and Washington. And this trend toward centralisation continues even into the present day. To illustrate: If I find myself in violent disagreement with current monetary policy, my friends at the local Boston Federal Reserve Bank would think me mad to subject *them* to bitter criticism. The privilege to be criticised bitterly is recognisably located in Washington and New York, and in that order.

It is more than forty years since the Federal Reserve was founded. Most of the giants who then walked the earth are now gone. Only their children, principally daughters, remain. And most of these, it would seem, make great claims on behalf of their sires for *the* basic idea underlying the Federal Reserve. This gives rise to an adding-up problem in which the imputed claims add up to more than 100 per cent of the whole – surely an harmonious and harmless social solution. But what is perhaps more notable is the fact that people seem most anxious to claim credit for that basic feature of the Federal Reserve System which has come in time to be almost completely repudiated. I refer to the notion that the Federal Reserve exists for the purpose of providing automatic *elasticity* of our currency and credit through its mechanism of providing new reserves to the commercial banks whenever they bring to its 'rediscount window' the endorsed promissory notes of their customers as collateral for a loan or rediscount. I do not know whether Glass, or Warburg, or Willis, or President Wilson himself is primarily responsible for this clever gadget by which the monetary supply can be made infinitely elastic in response to the 'legitimate needs of industry and trade'. In any case, by the 1920's President (or 'Governor') Benjamin Strong of the New York Federal Reserve Bank, who was the first of our three great American central bankers, had come to realise that the essential function of the Federal Reserve Authorities is to thwart both automatic inelasticity and automatic elasticity of the credit system, replacing these by discretionary actions hoping to moderate unemployment and inflation.

After the First World War the Federal Reserve stumbled on to a second and more powerful weapon of monetary control: open-market operations in government securities to expand or contract member bank reserves and deposits. And fortunate this was, since in the years following the 1929 Stock Market crash the supply of promissory notes to be rediscounted and the desire of the member banks to rediscount them almost completely dried up. The basic reforms of the Federal Reserve Act in 1933 and 1935 made government securities eligible as collateral for advances, with the result that rediscounts ever since have been on the basis of government securities as collateral. But even this fundamental reform could not keep the rediscount mechanism from withering away to nothing in the twenty years after 1933. The rediscount rate itself became a dead letter; use of the rediscount privilege was negligible from 1934 until the end of the war, and it came again to be of some significance only since 1950.

It is easy to see why this was the case. During most of the 1930's and early 1940's the commercial banks had excess reserves. If you were a sensible banker, the last thing in the world you would have thought of doing would be to pay interest in order to get more of such idle reserves. Then during the Second World War, when the structure of yields on government securities of different maturities was assured by Secretary of the Treasury Henry Morgenthau, our central bank always bought enough of the newly issued war debt to keep the commercial banks adequately supplied with enough reserves to purchase that part of the new war debt which the insurance companies and general public were unwilling to buy.

It is true that in recent years the Reserve officials have had to sweep the dust off the rediscount window and scurry around for old clerks who remember its mechanisms and procedure. Specifically, the Accord of 1951 recognised the independence of the Federal Reserve from the Treasury and its freedom to stop pegging government securities' prices; during much of the time since then, the Federal Reserve Open Market Committee has deliberately kept the reserves of the banks so low as to force them into the rediscount window, with late 1952 being a strong case in point and this last year being another.

The British boast of having an unwritten constitution. American institutions too grow like Topsy and in wonderful and mysterious ways undreamed of by their legislative founders. Thus, in private a present-day Federal Reserve official may speak of the banker who 'flagrantly abuses' the rediscount privilege in almost the same indignant tones that I might use in referring to a scoundrel who steals from the church or to a traitor who tramps on the flag and damns Motherhood. And to whom is he thus referring? To one who brings forged or stolen collateral to the window for rediscount? Not at all: simply to a commercial banker naïve enough or brassy enough to think he can augment his investible funds by continual or continuous use of the ancient rediscounting 'privilege'. I daresay that whoever it was who really originated the built-in elasticity of the Federal Reserve rediscount mechanism must be turning over in his grave when he hears of this fundamental – and from the economist's viewpoint, salutary – change in Federal Reserve philosophy and practice.

Nor did the founding fathers of the Federal Reserve System envisage the frequent use of what, after open-market operations, has become the principal monetary weapon of American central banking – namely, changes in the legal reserve requirements that member banks are required to hold at the Federal Reserve Banks in proportion to their demand deposits. Prior to the great depression the legal reserve ratio of all city and country member banks averaged about 10 per cent of demand deposits and was fixed by statute. In 1936, a year after Congress gave the Federal Reserve Board power to double the required reserve ratios, the Board became apprehensive over inflationary pressures and over its inability to exercise tight control of the member banks when they were possessive of so much excess reserves. It therefore ordered drastic increases in legal reserve ratios in order to mop up excess reserves. Anyone having more exaggeratedly romantic notions about the potency of monetary policy than I do would have to put much of the blame for the 1937 recession on the hardening of interest rates that came about early in that year as a result of the increased reserve requirements. (The authorities themselves were not fully prepared for what followed from their actions because they had a shallow theory of liquidity preference; according to this theory, excess reserves were truly 'excessive' in the eyes of the commercial banker, so that one could expect that he would indifferently give up these excess reserves and refrain from attempting to replenish any part of them by security sales.) As an objective historian I must mention without comment that all this was going on while (i) there was some noticeable tendency for the cost of living to be rising at a rate of about 5 per cent per year, and at the same time that (ii) the economy was enjoying sizable unemployment at the rate of perhaps 15 per cent of the labour force, with the index of physical production being some 25 per cent below what in retrospect appears to be the long-run trend of our producible potential.

Throughout the war and most of the post-war years the legal reserve ratios bumped against the ceiling levels that the Reserve Board was legally able to prescribe. At one time in the post-war period when inflation seemed particularly virulent, many members of the Board wanted Congress to increase this discretionary ceiling, thereby restoring to the Board two-way freedom, to contract or expand reserve requirements. (The regional Reserve Banks and the banking community generally took a dim view of this way of strengthening the Reserve Authorities' powers to fight inflation, for the prudent reason that use of this weapon would lower bank earnings.)

In the last few years, the Board has so frequently changed

reserve requirements as to make it necessary for us to begin to wonder whether we were right in thinking that this weapon of monetary control is one to be used only at infrequent intervals. For, after all, the purpose of the monetary authorities is to put different amounts of predictable and unpredictable pressure upon the member banks' availability of credit, and is there any logical reason why this should not be done by frequent changes in legal reserve ratios?

In mid-1953, when the Board rightly feared that the hard-money crusade of the early Eisenhower Administration had gotten out of hand and might be held responsible for any ensuing recession, it dramatically lowered reserve requirements. Less understandable in terms of the older doctrine of sparing and once-and-for-all use of changing reserve ratios was the further lowering of requirements in 1954 when the economy had long been in a mild recession and when the Federal Reserve wanted to intensify the easiness of money.

Congressional critics of the 'Fed' hasten to attribute the lowering of reserve requirements to its desire to increase bank earnings or, as the critics prefer to put it, bank profits. Such critics are right in pointing out that the same degree of monetary tightness or ease can often be achieved either by open-market operations or by reserve requirement changes; in a real sense, therefore, the 'Fed' is like a public utility commission which passes on the desirable or fair level of earnings that it will allow the companies under its jurisdiction; and in appraising the degree to which the banks and other interests in the economy are to be given representation in the Federal Reserve structures, this element of self-interest must be given its proper weight. None the less, until Congress legislates an increase in the reserve requirements that the Board is empowered to prescribe – and you'd lose your money if you bet that this was likely to happen in the foreseeable future – a case can be made for the Board's gradually working down the required reserve ratios toward the middle of its discretionary range, so that it again has two-sided freedom in the use of this powerful weapon of monetary control.[1]

2. The Primacy of Open-Market Operations

For the present purpose there is no need to go into the other less-important credit weapons of the Reserve Authorities. They do have the power to set margin requirements for loans on listed stocks: e.g. this last year the government became fearful of a speculative bull market, and the Board raised margin requirements from 50 per cent to 60 per cent and again to 70 per cent, the present figure. (This means that I can borrow from my broker or banker only 30 per cent of the value of listed stocks; if I certify to my banker that my loan is not made for the purpose of 'carrying listed securities', I might be able to avoid this restriction.)

Also, in the past the Board has had the power to regulate down-payment terms and length-of-contract terms of instalment purchases (so-called Regulation W) and of house mortgages (Regulation X). There is a good deal of evidence that these selective credit controls had great potency, but they have now lapsed.[2] The Federal Reserve Board has never appeared to be very comfortable exercising these selective controls, which are philosophically at variance with its general belief in over-all non-discriminatory credit control; and there is no

---

[1] Politics aside, an economic case can be made for abolishing our obsolete distinctions between country banks, city banks and reserve city banks, instead bringing them gradually to a uniform basis. While there are powerful economic reasons why the thousands of banks outside the Federal Reserve System should be subject to the over-all monetary controls deemed appropriate for the nation's well-being, the issue will not become crucial except in the remote contingency that the non-member banks should become a significantly larger fraction of our total banking system.

[2] President Allan Sproul of the New York Federal Reserve Bank, our third great Central Banker (after Strong and Eccles), asked at the end of 1955 that the power to regulate instalment credit be restored; and President Eisenhower in his Economic Message (January 1956) has asked Congress to consider stand-by powers to regulate instalment credit.

fundamental reason why these regulatory powers should have to be given to the Central Bank rather than to an administrative agency of the Executive Branch of the government.

Concerning 'moral suasion', the last of the traditional weapons of central banking, I don't know quite what to say. When it is recalled that the American banking system consists of some 14,000 separate banks, with no few banking chains having a dominant position, a case can be made for the traditional American view that this weapon has no potency. I must confess that mine is a minority view in having doubts on this matter: I suspect that there is some considerable potency in the short run in verbal statements made by the Authorities to the banks; for bankers after all operate in a less-than-perfectly-competitive industry and are notoriously sensitive to public opinion. Since Central Bankers live from day to day and week to week in a series of short runs, even limited potency of moral suasion can be of social importance.

What does our review of the changing institutional structure of the Federal Reserve System leave us with? Primarily with the recognition of *open-market operations as the important weapon of monetary policy*. Whether or not frequently changing reserve requirements could play an important role, we have not yet arrived at a time when they are likely to do so. And the recently revived rediscount mechanism owes its effectiveness to prior contractionary Federal Reserve open-market sales, which cut down on commercial bank reserves and force them to the rediscount window, where they come under the whip-hand of the 'Fed' and become subject to real moral suasion.[1] In a literal sense, rediscounting operates as an offset to open-market operations rather than as a rein-

---

[1] Some writers, here and abroad, have alleged that a change in the rediscount rate will itself have great announcement effects conducive to stability: men will interpret a rise to mean that the end of the boom is in sight, and will thus be led to cut down on their spending and to confirm their expectation. Careful observation of our money market sug-

forcing weapon: when open-market sales tighten bank reserves, bank borrowing from the rediscount window tends to relieve the stringency and hence to serve as an offset; similarly, when the banks are in debt to the 'Fed', open-market purchases aimed at expanding bank loans and real investment may be partially thwarted by the natural tendency of the banks to use at least part of their new reserves to repay their borrowings.

Recognising this 'perversity', some critics have criticised the 'Fed' for leaving rediscount rates so low as to cause the rediscount mechanism to come back into effectiveness. Without denying their offsetting tendency, I think a defence can be made for use of rediscounts. They do provide an important safety valve, and without this safety valve the authorities might not dare to apply as much contractionary or expansionary pressure. My old teacher, Joseph Schumpeter, was fond of pointing out that good brakes make cars go faster, an analogy which applies perfectly to the present point.

---

gests that this announcement effect would not, by itself, be of the desired potency. For when money is becoming tight in a boom, the market is getting new signals of this fact every day and the rediscount rate is only one of the following many signals: weekly changes in bill rates, commercial paper rates, bond yields, banks' prime lending rate, finance company borrowing rates, the call rate, banks' published reserve position and Reserve Banks' open-market reports, etc. The rediscount rate moves as a result of these, though admittedly its movement does serve to confirm the suspected movement and to initiate some further moves. Only gullible textbook writers attach full weight to the rediscount rate and to the postulate that the Central Bank is certainly going to achieve what it sets out to do; the men in the market-place are too eclectic to believe in one simple theory or one key indicator.

Moreover, with each passing year of flexible monetary policy there is a developing tendency for announcements of monetary tightness to be given an interpretation just opposite to that relied on by the older writers. Today, financial men know that the Federal Reserve 'leans against the breeze', tightening money when it thinks the forces of expansion are strong and easing money when deflation seems a threat. Therefore it is rational for an investor to say, 'Aha! the "Fed" is raising interest rates; they must know that the current outlook is very bullish, and if that is going to be so, I'd better expand my operations'. Conclusion: announcement effects are often ambiguous.

I think it important to have inferred from our review of developments the primacy of open-market operations. Indeed, speaking teleologically, one might say that the whole evolution of the Federal Reserve System has been towards a perfecting of the open-market operations weapon of credit control. Yet, since 1952, a fundamental debate has been raging over the proper use of this weapon. A new doctrine has been formulated and been given a measure of official acceptance. This new doctrine would alter seriously the traditional use of the open-market weapon. Many economists think it would weaken seriously the potency of monetary policy; and to these critics the hamstringing of the open-market weapon, which had been developed after a long evolution, is rather like the case of a higher ape who, having come down from the trees, and having learned over the aeons to use his thumb and brain, then appoints an *ad hoc* committee, which negates the evolutionary development by a decision to limit the use of thumb and brain.

3. The New Doctrine of Operating only in Short-Term Issues
Economists and the general public first learned of the new Federal Reserve Doctrine from the *Fortieth Report* (1953) *of the Board of Governors of the Federal Reserve System.* There had been no previous full-scale discussion and debate over the issues. Even the brief statement in that Report might have escaped appropriate notice if there had not been an almost unprecedented eruption into print of the controversy that had been taking place within the system, as a result of the forthright dissent registered by President Sproul of the New York Federal Reserve Bank.

It was then remembered that there had been earlier set up an *Ad Hoc* Sub-committee on the Government Securities Market, which after much labour and investigation had prepared a Report in November 1952. The new doctrine embodied in this Report, to cease open-market purchase and sales of intermediate- and long-term government securities, has been badly in need of a name. It has been referred to as the Craft Doctrine, after Robert H. Craft, the New York banker who took leave of absence to serve as its full-time technical consultant. It has been called the *Ad Hoc* Doctrine. I have even heard it referred to in academic circles as the 'Riefler Doctrine', in honour of the distinguished monetary economist Winfield W. Riefler, who as an adviser to Chairman Martin is held, perhaps unfairly, to be the good or evil genius behind the doctrine. I think it would be more appropriate to attribute the doctrine to Chairman of the Federal Reserve Board William McChesney Martin, Jr., formerly the president of the New York Stock Exchange and holder of many high offices under the Democratic Administrations. Therefore, I christen it the 'Martin Doctrine' and shall so refer to it.

Once economists heard about the new doctrine, its split vote, and the New York Federal Reserve Bank criticism of it, we were of course anxious to get hold of a copy of the *Ad Hoc* Report; but it was tantalisingly unavailable, and we had to conduct our investigations of the doctrine in the dark as to the exact arguments advanced in its favour. (It was subsequently learned that the questions about the government securities market had been addressed solely to financial specialists; only about one and one-half of the names in the interrogated list would be regarded as economists by members of our exclusive guild.)

Finally, in December 1954, the two-year veil of secrecy was pierced when the so-called Flanders Hearings on monetary policy[1] forced the Federal Reserve System to make public the

---

[1] 'U.S. Monetary Policy: Recent Thinking and Experience.' Hearings before the Sub-committee on Economic Stabilization of the Joint Committee on the Economic Report. Congress of the United States. Eighty-third Congress, Second Session. See also articles by Alvin H. Hansen and Sidney Weintraub in the 1955 *Review of Economics and Statistics*, and by Deane Carson in the 1955 *Quarterly Journal of Economics*.

Ad Hoc Committee Report. Since that time there has sprung up in our academic journals a lively discussion over the merits of the Martin Doctrine and the Sproul objections to it. Undoubtedly, this is only the beginning and the score cannot yet be given; but up until now almost all the academic discussants have been critical of the new doctrine. Specialists in the money market, who might be expected to favour a doctrine explicitly designed to foster growth of their function, have been divided: particularly in the hard-money debacle of Spring 1953 was there much criticism of the new policy, and this at the same time that the Reserve Board was congratulating itself on the smoothness of the new régime. Since then, though, I think I can discern a move in the New York money market towards more favourable acceptance of the Martin Doctrine, and I confidently predict that the specialists will come to favour it unanimously if it is allowed to remain in effect for a number of years.

What about the United States Treasury? The Democratic Secretaries, Morgenthau, Vinson and Snyder, had all wanted the Reserve System to help keep government security prices orderly and to support the government bond market directly or indirectly. Their reasons for wanting this were various, ranging from a childishly vain desire to have government bonds over-subscribed, to the desire to keep interest costs on the public debt down, to a concern for the capital values in bank and insurance company portfolios and to fear of disorderly market avalanches. I do not wish to go into the merits of the struggle between the Treasury and Federal Reserve. Let me simply state dogmatically that the Secretary of Treasury should be just as concerned for the nation's stability as the Central Banker. He is not appointed to have a pleasant life, either as a taxer or a borrower. This being the case, there is no legitimate clash between Treasury and Central Bank policy: they must be unified or co-ordinated on the basis of the over-all stabilisation needs of the economy, and it is unthinkable that these two great agencies could ever be divorced in function or permitted to work at cross purposes. (In particular it is nonsense to believe, as many proponents of monetary policy used to argue, that fiscal policy has for its goal the stabilisation of employment and reduction of unemployment, while monetary policy has for its goal the stabilisation of prices. In comparison with fiscal policy, monetary policy has no differential effectiveness on prices rather than output.)

Fortunately for analytic clarity – I hesitate to say, for the country – there has been no clash between the Treasury and the Central Bank during the Eisenhower Administration. W. Randolph Burgess, the Deputy Secretary of Treasury who went twenty years ago from the Federal Reserve System to become a leading New York banker, was in 1953 even more disposed toward tight money than the Reserve Authorities.

The Martin Doctrine has many facets: (i) the decision to confine operations to the short end of the market; (ii) the negation of any target of desired yield patterns, with 'intervention in the Government securities market . . . solely to effectuate the objectives of monetary and credit policy (including corrections of disorderly markets)'; (iii) the tentative decision not to aid new Treasury financing directly.

I wish to concentrate on the important core of the doctrine – that it is legitimate for a Central Bank to affect credit by open-market operations in short-term governments – principally bills – and that all other intervention is illegitimate. I have already asserted that the Treasury and Central Bank have to be co-ordinated in the interests of national stability, so I am little interested in the division of labour between them. Hence the December 1955 support of a new government issue, which represented an apparent departure from the Martin Doctrine or a use of its escape clause relative to 'disorderly markets', I do not find as exciting an incident as have the Board's

Congressional critics. I prefer to stick to fundamentals.

What are the arguments for the Martin Doctrine? Really it stands or falls on the basis of one major premise. Deny that premise, and all the subsidiary arguments concerning the desirability of developing a more 'self-reliant' money market having the oft-repeated properties of 'depth, breadth and resiliency' cease to be relevant to the issue. The major premise is this:

> By confining operations to short terms, the monetary authorities can realise all the desired effects on credit and spending and can do this in the manner that is philosophically most compatible with the ethical goals of a free society.

It will be seen that this premise has in it an assertion about the facts of the modern money market – namely an alleged close relationship between induced changes in (i) short-term interest rates and in bank reserves and the resulting changes in (ii) long-term interest rates, credit availability, and investment spending.[1] It also has in it an ethical assertion that is neither open to scientific proof nor disproof, but whose feasibility and costs in terms of other ethical ends will depend very much on questions of fact and logic.

I do not think we need spend much time on the question of tradition and legitimacy. As far as precedent goes, there are Central Banks of the present and past which could provide a precedent for anything that someone might suggest doing, however fantastic or collectivistic. Even if we look to the Great Tradition of Central Banking, whether it be in the England of Queen Victoria or in the United States of Governor Strong, we are merely re-posing our problem. My account of the organic evolution of Federal Reserve could be used by

---

[1] Some defendants of the Doctrine ride a horse in two directions on this technical issue. After asserting that intervention in the long-term market is bad because it will affect capital values and open the way for espionage and venality as investors try to learn in advance the course of policy, in the next breath they assure us that the effects of short-term purchases on long-term yields are immediate and strong!

one unsympathetic to the Martin Doctrine to brand it as a departure from tradition; and an Edmund Burke, if he were alive today, might in eloquent terms damn the new doctrine on this account alone. Moreover, in its deduction of broad policy principles by logical syllogisms from fixed axioms, the Martin Doctrine is at odds with the pragmatic and even fuzzy development that has characterised Anglo-Saxon institutions, here and abroad. If the Doctrine is right, no appeal to legitimacy is needed; and if it is wrong, such an appeal cannot save it.

Another red herring should be cleared away from the argument. The issue is not between pegging or aiming at some definite structure of interest yields as against adopting the Martin Doctrine of dealing in shorts only. Few of the critics of the Washington view propose any pegging. The genuine issue is between feeling free when the occasion seems to call for it to put pressure *directly* on the whole spectrum of interest rates rather than to abdicate this freedom by a self-imposed restriction requiring you to operate in shorts alone, in the belief that your pressure will be indirectly applied to longs with the desired speed and potency.

Nor is anyone against the development of the money market. Without the Martin Doctrine, the pursuit over a period of time of flexible monetary policy was bound eventually to strengthen the dealer mechanism, for the simple reason that there would be an increasing function for such dealers and therefore an opportunity for entry and competitive profit making. The notion that such a development could not come into existence so long as the 'Fed' operates in long-terms is, in my judgment, incorrect inference and forecasting: if there is money to be made in the long run from taking risks, dealers in a free market will increasingly take these risks.[1] If the

---

[1] Lessening the 'Fed''s power to create uncertainty in the minds of the men in the market is to rob the New York Federal Reserve writers of one of their choicest weapons. While I am not sure that Allan Sproul,

Martin Doctrine were deemed wrong on the basis of the stability needs of the nation and our philosophical ethical goals, it would be wicked to adhere to it for the purpose of creating the vacuum into which bond specialists increasingly are pulled.

4. Conclusion

I have now laid out what seem to be the important background considerations to the debate. What is my own evaluation of the issue? Any reader by now must have guessed that my studies have led me to favour the New York view and to regard the Washington Martin Doctrine as a backward, and unnecessary, step. My reasons are simple and can be briefly stated.

First, there is the ethical issue. I do not wish to force my own philosophical beliefs on anyone, but will simply posit that the greatest feasible amount of freedom is our goal. Yet experience tells us: Freedom is a scarce commodity, not a free good; it is to be conserved; to maximise over-all freedom, you do not try to maximise it in every direction, instead you must 'spend' a little of it wherever that will add to the sum-total.

This is the *rationale* for Central Banking (and for that matter, for stabilising fiscal policy). For its own sake, no one wants a Board of men to decide on over-all quantitative monetary measures – any more than we desire price-fixing boards or utility-regulation boards for their own sake. Conservative political philosophers have become resigned to Central Banking itself as one of the necessary costs of a stable economy. The Washington philosophers – and in this area the opinions of money-market philosophers have no expert

Robert V. Roosa and John H. Williams themselves always knew quite what they meant when they preached the virtues of creating uncertainty, this device may have its place in the Central Banker's arsenal and should not be thrown away or limited without careful consideration.

standing[1] – take the curious view of 'this far and no farther'. It is legitimate to infringe liberty and freedom by selling short-term securities and affecting reserves, so long as you stay within some semantically meaningless definition of 'neutrality' with respect to your affects on the structure of interest yields; debt management operations that directly affect the structure of interest rates are all right, but only as long as they are carried on by the Treasury and only so long as they are operations in connection with new offerings and refundings; the momentary and ever-changing liquidity preferences of the market-place are to be taken as sacred, and if you affect them more than indirectly, you are being paternalistic and are heading down the road to serfdom. So go the arguments. One slip of the pen and the Federal Reserve philosophers are in danger of slitting their own throats, since Professors Ludwig von Mises and Milton Friedman, who claim to know what freedom really requires, use as impeccable logic to prove that all Central Bankers should be abolished.

The enemies of monetary policy, who may or may not be opponents of freedom, are of course delighted with the Martin Doctrine. They know that the more the Federal Reserve circumscribes its own powers, the greater the probability that selective credit agencies will spring up elsewhere in the government – in the fields of housing, small business finance, farm credit and elsewhere.

And this leads finally to the technical non-ethical question. Can the Central Bank achieve all it ever wants to achieve, or ought to achieve, by operating in short-terms alone? I am inclined to think that since the beginning of the 1953–54 Reces-

---

[1] I can now quote someone more respectable than Voltaire, namely Kipling: 'And what should they know of banking, who only banking know?' In doing so I open myself to the *riposte* I once heard Alfred North Whitehead give when Kipling's quotation was used against him. Whitehead replied, 'What do they know of England, who don't know England?'

sion, adherence to the Martin Doctrine has done no particular harm or good. True, the policy of active ease had to push short-term rates down farther than would have been needed to achieve the same expansion of long-term credit, but that is no great social evil. None the less, the fact that long and short markets have been rather intimately connected in these prosperous times should not blind us to the lessons of experience. We may devoutly hope that private investment demands and stabilising fiscal policies will always be so fortunate as to leave to monetary policy only the minor problem of contributing modestly to over-all stability. (That, wishful thinking aside, is the considered claim that can be made for monetary policy in the last few years.) We may hope that a great depression like that of the 1930's will never have to be faced; and we can even be optimistic that our new powers of fiscal and monetary control will handle such a situation if it were to arise. But we forget at our peril how during the great depression our short-term interest rate was forced down essentially to zero, how banks were flooded with excess reserves by the inflow of gold from abroad, and yet how slow long-term interest rates were to fall and how unavailable credit was to risky capital formation.[1] What then was the interconnection of long and short markets? In any such future depression, how much of the life-blood of capitalism will have to be lost before the Martin Doctrine is repudiated?

I end, as I began, with a quotation. A couple of years ago I received a communication from a scholar, who said that he

---

[1] Had not the New York Bank quoted, tongue in cheek, an earlier finding of Riefler on the interconnection of markets, I should not have dared cite the National Bureau study which he headed, and which showed the perverse and recalcitrant depression pattern of low short rates and high long. See *Occasional Papers*, Nos. 3 and 6, of the National Bureau of Economic Research. Aside from these, there is a vast literature on the general subject.

had been looking for the source of the quotation: 'Those who ignore history are condemned to repeat it'. He finally traced it down to my *Economics*. Though flattered, I had to disclaim priority. Was it from Acton? Buckle? From whom? To my surprise I could not find it in any of the standard reference works. (Actually, it was later discovered to be due to the philosopher Santayana.) So I asked Professor Crane Brinton of Harvard, thinking that if any historian would recognise it, surely he would. He answered: 'I don't know the source of your quotation, but I'll improve on it for you'. And this is what he said. 'Those who are ignorant of history are condemned to repeat it. And those who know history are condemned to repeat it too.'

I hope in the field of monetary policy Professor Brinton is wrong.

February 1956

110

THE ECONOMICS OF EISENHOWER:

P. A. Samuelson

Contemporary notes on business cycle development during the Eisenhower Administration may be of some interest to the economic historian of the future. By and large this has been a period of great regularity — I might almost say predictability. For once in our history, most economists found themselves in fairly close agreement as to what was happening, and the facts were nice enough to be in substantial agreement with their theories. The simple textbook models and formulations seemed almost to work, so that we economists kept pinching ourselves to ask "What went right?"

The Honeymoon Period. The New Team came enthusiastically into office, raring to go after 20 years of involuntary unemployment. To understand the hard money episode of the first five months of 1953, we must turn our eyes from the prosaic facts of the contemporaneous sluggishness of wholesale, staple, and futures prices and instead concentrate upon the preconceived theories brought into office by the new men in the Treasury, Budget Bureau, and Executive Departments generally. Thus, one who had read the pre-1953 writings of the able and forceful banker-economist, W. Randolph Burgess, who came in to direct debt management policy in the Treasury, could understand better what was happening from day to day in that period than could one who merely measured current price changes and observed income flows.

The verdict of history will be that hard money was overdone in this period. Still it would be unfair to fasten all the blame on the Treasury. The Federal Reserve System *did* have its independence; and anyone who indulges in the amiable pastime of allocating praise and blame must include its authorities as accessories before and after the fact. Thus, utterances by the Chairman of the Reserve Board during this period contributed as much to the uncertainty and rumors that swept through the free market place as did the speeches of any other single individual.

But the economic historian must not be too harsh in his judgments. It was a new team and new relationships had to be worked out with the Central Bank. In addition, we now know what men in Wall Street and university economics departments did not then realize — namely, that early 1953 just happened to be the occasion when the long-run structural reform embodied in the Martin "Bills Only" Doctrine was being introduced. It is mere chance that this new doctrine did not become actual policy during a period of business cycle relaxation, and as a consequence of this coincidence the market place in 1953 went wrong in interpreting some of the Federal Reserve statements as indicating more tightness than the Reserve authorities may have intended.

At the end of this period a happier note can be sounded. Whatever one thinks of the hard money crusade, all are agreed that nothing became the Reserve Board so well in its tight money policy as the speed and finality with which it dropped that policy. Why this quick turn-around? We shall never know exactly, but some pretty good guesses can be hazarded.

First, it was not because the Reserve authorities were so clairvoyant by late May 1953 as to foresee the 1954 recession. Events were predictable, but not *that* predictable! Rather I think can the turn-around be explained by the feeling of many within the Federal Reserve

System that the tightness of credit was getting out of hand, that they were being subjected to heavy criticism both from the Left and the Right, and that if the tightness had not already led to a recession if persisted in it might very well do so. Therefore, the path of prudence was to shift gears into reverse. And mind you, the Board always had the ability later to change its decision and return to tightness if the much talked about inflation should actually materialize. This is one of the beauties of monetary policy: you don't have to guess correctly the far future; you only have to live from week to week.

The Gathering Storm. Business started to go down in the middle of 1953. Each month the Federal Reserve Board Index of Production slipped one or two points downward from the July peak of 137. The Democratic opposition early, perhaps too early, sensed the recession and called it to the attention of the American people. While I have tried objectively to appraise the role of "confidence," a variable that has been much talked about by Eisenhower administration spokesmen, this is a difficult subject to clothe with operational meaning. So I shall simply record my tentative conclusion that the mere act of calling attention to the developing recession did not play an important role in accentuating it. Nor did the Administration's refusal to admit the existence of the developing recession contribute substantially during the last months of 1953 to its worsening.

The recession seems best diagnosed as an inventory turn-around of the type familiar in American economic history, but particularly sparked off in mid-1953 by the increasingly-certain prospect of government expenditure reduction at year's end, and accentuated by the strong expansion in business for the full year prior to mid-1953 as an aftermath of the 1952 steel strike.

The Inventory Inflection Point. The first Economic Report of the President, appearing at the end of January 1954, must be deemed to have been overly optimistic. This is easy to say in retrospect, but if we examine the testimony of Winfield W. Riefler a fortnight later before the Joint Committee on the Economic

Report, we see how even at the time the Report contrasted with the prevailing consensus of professional opinion.

The Council of Economic Advisers, which must be absolved from all blame in the early 1953 period since at that time it was scarcely operative, was through no fault of its own unacquainted at the time its Report was being prepared with the actual testimony of the new unemployment census and with the current rate of government expenditures. Moreover, because of the well-known doctrine that "admissions against interest" are held to be especially damning, it may be argued that any report signed by the President must inevitably be biased on the optimistic side lest the public at large think "If he has admitted so much, things must surely be even worse than he says."

We now know from the published revelations of the Eisenhower Administration that behind the scene there was actually much concern over the recession within the Administration. Its claim to have decided in September 1953 to let tax reductions go into effect has been treated with considerable derision, since such a decision in the political context of that period was a little like deciding to let the sun set at eventide. But we must emphasize in the strongest terms that the lessons of the New Deal had been learned, and that no responsible persons in either political party came forward — as they had during the 1930 Hoover days — to suggest that the built-in stabilizers of our system be vitiated by the perverse discretionary action of raising tax rates in order to avoid budget unbalance.

As a result of our built-in stabilizers and reinforcing discretionary actions, a more than 10 per cent drop in production was not permitted to have any net reducing effects upon disposable incomes. Most outside economists, and I think many within the Administration, believed that with final incomes maintained it would be only a matter of time before inventory reduction brought stocks to levels at which the desire to decumulate inventory at so rapid a rate would weaken. At this fundamental *inflection point*, a lessening of the rate of inventory accumulation could be expected to provide some expansion to the production index. I myself at the time thought that, with construction so strong and equipment expenditure down so little, the inflection point would probably be reached by May or June, but this seems to have been too early an estimate. The turn actually came somewhat later, perhaps too late for the ensuing expansion to have gone far enough to keep the Democrats from regaining control of Congress in November 1954.

The Post-Keynesian Thinking of Our Times. All in all it has been an experience of which we can all be proud. The opposition performed the extremely important role of needling the Eisenhower administration into taking action. Intelligent counsel within the Administration kept the situation under fairly accurate diagnosis, and President Eisenhower made the type of utterance that contributed much more to basic confidence than all the slogans of his cabinet officers.

One may agree with the 1954 utterances of Professor Slichter that unnecessary risks were being taken by the Administration in its policy of patient waiting. Nevertheless, a protagonist of Arthur Burns could forcibly offer rebuttals to this argument, pointing to subsequent events as testimony to the wisdom of that policy.

Here we are at the limits of economic science and no definitive conclusion can yet be reached, nor will the economic historian of the future necessarily be able to resolve so close an issue.

Return of the Dilemma? Finally, I should like to put forward the hypothesis that the relatively minor economic differences between the Republicans and Democrats during 1953–56 has been in the nature of a lucky accident. For reasons that will not necessarily be relevant in the future, *we have been able since early 1951 to have a very high degree of prosperity and also to have stable prices.* The drop in farm and other staple prices made this possible.

In the future the dilemma between very high employment and stable prices is likely to reassert itself with increasing force. Then it will be found that the Republicans do differ from the Democrats in the greater weight that they will give to the goal of maintaining an honest dollar in comparison with the clashing goal of keeping unemployment extremely low.

In this clash of ideologies, social welfare functions and not scientific economic principles must play the decisive role.

111

ECONOMIC FRONTIERS

I. THE ECONOMIC OUTLOOK

1. *Recession.* Economic experts are generally agreed that the nation's economy is now in a "recession." The slide since mid-1960 cannot be termed a "depression" like that after 1929, but so widespread a decline in production deserves more than the euphemism of a "rolling readjustment."

Prudent economic policy must face the fact that we go into 1961 with business still moving downward. This means that unemployment, now above 6 per cent of the labor force, may this winter rise more than seasonally. It means still lower profits ahead.

The fact of recession also has significant implications for the prospective Budget. It means a falling off of tax receipts from earlier estimated levels. This recession is wiping out the previously estimated Budget Surplus for the fiscal year ending June 30. Many experts now believe that as of today it is reasonable to forecast a deficit for this fiscal year, assuming only expenditures already authorized and in the absence of desirable new expenditures from an accelerated effort. Recalling the experience of the 1957-58 recession may be useful: due largely to the impact of a recession that everyone but the authorities admitted was then taking place, the announcement in early 1958 of a small fiscal 1959 Budget Surplus was actually followed by a final fiscal 1959 Budget deficit of more than 12 billion dollars! Not even the ostrich can avert the economic facts of life. He misreads the role of confidence in economic life who thinks that denying the obvious will cure the ailments of a modern economy.

No one can know exactly when this fourth postwar recession will come to an end. A careful canvass of expert opinion and analysis of the economic forces making for further contraction suggest this probability:

With proper actions by the government, the contraction in business can be brought to a halt within 1961 itself and converted into an upturn. Recognizing that many analysts hope the upturn may come

---

Credited solely to Dr. Paul A. Samuelson, Professor of Economics at M.I.T., who headed a task force on "economic conditions in the United States."

by the middle of the year but recalling how subject to error were their rosy forecasts for 1960, policy makers realize the necessity for *preparing* to take actions that might be needed *if* this fourth recession turns out to be a more serious one than its predecessors.

2. *Chronic slackness.* In economics, the striking event drives our attention from the less dramatic but truly more fundamental processes. *More fraught with significance for public policy than the recession itself is the vital fact that it has been superimposed upon an economy which, in the last few years, has been sluggish and tired.* Thus, anyone who thought in 1958 that all was well with the American economy just because the recession of that year bottomed out early was proved to be wrong by the sad fact that our last recovery was an anemic one: 1959 and 1960 have been grievously disappointing years, as the period of expansion proved both to be shorter than earlier postwar recoveries and to have been abortive in the sense of never carrying us back anywhere near to high employment and high capacity levels of operation. This is illustrated by the striking fact that unemployment has remained above 5 per cent of the labor force, a most disappointing performance in comparison with earlier postwar recoveries and desirable social goals.

If what we now faced were only the case of a short recession that was imposed on an economy showing healthy growth and desirable high employment patterns, then governmental policies would have to be vastly different from those called for by the present outlook. But this is not 1949, nor 1954.

Prudent policy now requires that we also combat the basic sluggishness which underlies the more dramatic recession. In some ways a recession imposed on top of a disappointingly slack economy simplifies prudent decision making. Thus, certain expensive programs that are worthwhile for their own sake, but that inevitably involve a lag of some months before they can get going, can be pushed more vigorously in the current situation because of the knowledge that the extra stimulus they later bring is unlikely to impinge upon a recovery that has already led us back to full employment.

The following recommendations try to take careful account of the fact that the recession slide is only the most dramatic manifestation of the grave economic challenge confronting our economic system.

II. Feasible Economic Goals

3. *Our economic potential.* Had our economy progressed since

1956—not at the dramatic sprint of the Western European and Japanese economies or at the rush of the controlled totalitarian systems but simply at the modest pace made possible by our labor force and productivity trends—we could have expected 1961 to bring a Gross National Product some 10 per cent above the $500 billion level we are now experiencing. With unemployment below 4 per cent, with overcapacity put to work, and with productivity unleashed by economic opportunity, such a level of activity would mean higher private consumption, higher corporate profits, higher capital formation for the future, and higher resources for much-needed public programs. Instead of our having now to debate about the size of the Budget Deficit to be associated with a recession, such an outcome would have produced tax revenues under our present tax structure sufficient to lead to a Surplus of around ten billion dollars; and the authorities might be facing the not unpleasant task of deciding how to deal with such a surplus.

4. *The targets ahead.* Looking forward, one cannot realistically expect to undo in 1961 the inadequacies of several years. It is not realistic to aim for the restoration of high employment within a single calendar year. The goal for 1961 must be (1) to bring the recession to an end, (2) to reinstate a condition of expansion and recovery, and (3) to adopt measures likely to make that expansion one that will not after a year or two peter out at levels of activity far below our true potential.

Indeed policy for 1961 should be directed against the background of the whole decade ahead. Specifically, if the American economy is to show healthy growth during this period and to average out at satisfactory levels of employment, we must learn not to be misled by statements that this or that is now at an all-time peak; in an economy like ours, with more than a million people coming into the labor force each year and with continuing technological change, the most shocking frittering away of our economic opportunities is fully compatible with statistical reports that employment and national product are "setting new records every year."

5. *Prudent Budget goals.* A healthy decade of the 1960's will not call for a Budget that is exactly balanced in every fiscal year. For the period as a whole, if the forces making for expansion are strong and vigorous, there should be many years of budgetary surpluses and these may well have to exceed the deficits of other years. Economic forecasting of the far future is too difficult to make possible any positive statements concerning the desirable decade average of such surpluses

and deficits. But careful students of sound economic fiscal policy will perhaps agree on the following:

(i) The first years of such a decade, characterized as they are by stubborn unemployment and excess capacity and following on a period of disappointing slackness, are the more appropriate periods for programs of economic stimulation by well-thought-out fiscal policy.

(ii) The unplanned deficits that result from recession-induced declines in tax receipts levied on corporate profits and individual incomes and also those that come from a carefully designed anti-recession program must be sharply distinguished from *deficits that take place in times of zooming demand inflation.* This last kind of deficit would represent government spending out of control and be indeed deserving of grave concern. The deficits that come automatically from recession or which are a necessary part of a determined effort to restore the economic system to health are quite different phenomena: they are signs that our automatic built-in stabilizers are working, and that we no longer will run the risk of going into one of the great depressions that characterized our economic history before the war.

III. THE CONSTRAINTS WITHIN WHICH POLICY MUST WORK

6. *Gold and the international payments.* Granted that the New Administration is preparing a whole series of measures to correct our balance of payments position, the days are gone when America could shape her domestic stabilization policies taking no thought for their international repercussions. The fact that we have been losing gold for many years will, without question, have to affect our choice among activist policies to restore production and employment. The art of statecraft for the New Administration will be to innovate, within this recognized constraint, new programs that promote healthy recovery.

It would be unthinkable for a present-day American government to deliberately countenance high unemployment as a mechanism for adjusting to the balance of payments deficit. Such a policy would be largely ineffective anyway; but even were it highly effective, only a cynic would counsel its acceptance. It is equally unthinkable that a responsible Administration can give up its militant efforts toward domestic recovery because of the limitations imposed on it by the international situation. What is needed is realistic taking into account of the international aspects of vigorous domestic policy.

7. *The problem of inflation.* Various experts, here and abroad, believe that the immediate postwar inflationary climate has now been

converted into an epoch of price stability. One hopes this cheerful diagnosis is correct. However, a careful survey of the behavior of prices and costs shows that our recent stability in the wholesale price index has come in a period of admittedly high unemployment and slackness in our economy. For this reason it is premature to believe that the restoration of high employment will no longer involve problems concerning the stability of prices.

Postwar experience, here and abroad, suggests that a mixed economy like ours may tend to generate an upward creep of prices *before* it arrives at high employment. Such a price creep, which has to be distinguished from the ancient inflations brought about by the upward pull on prices and wages that comes from excessive dollars of demand spending, has been given many names: "cost-push" inflation, "sellers" (rather than demanders) inflation, "market-power" inflation,—these are all variants of the same stubborn phenomenon.

Economists are not yet agreed how serious this new malady of inflation really is. Many feel that new institutional programs, other than conventional fiscal and monetary policies, must be devised to meet this new challenge. But whatever be the merits of the varying views on this subject, it should be manifest that *the goal of high employment and effective real growth cannot be abandoned because of the problematical fear that reattaining of prosperity in America may bring with it some difficulties; if recovery means a reopening of the cost-push problem, then we have no choice but to move closer to the day when that problem has to be successfully grappled with.* Economic statesmanship does involve difficult compromises, but not capitulation to any one of the pluralistic goals of modern society.

Running a deliberately slack economy in order to put off the day when such doubts about inflation can be tested is not a policy open to a responsible democratic government in this decade of perilous world crisis. A policy of inaction can be as truly a policy of living dangerously as one of overaction. Far from averting deterioration of our international position, a program that tolerates stagnation in the American economy can prevent us from making those improvements in our industrial productivity that are so desperately needed if we are to remain competitive in the international markets of the world.

History reminds us that even in the worst days of the Great Depression there was never a shortage of experts to warn against all curative public actions, on the ground that they were likely to create a problem of inflation. Had this counsel prevailed here, as it did in pre-Hitler

Germany, the very existence of our form of government could be at stake. No modern government will make that mistake again.

IV. GENERAL POLICY RECOMMENDATIONS

8. *Introduction.* The two principal governmental weapons to combat recession and slackness are *fiscal* (i.e., tax and expenditure) policy and *monetary or credit* policy. In ordinary times both should be pushed hard, so that they are reinforcing rather than conflicting. These are not ordinary times. Until our new programs have taken effect, America does not have the freedom from balance of payments constraints that she enjoyed for the 25 years after 1933.

The usual balance between fiscal and monetary policies will have to be shifted in the period just ahead toward a more vigorous use of fiscal policy because of the international constraint. Some of the conventional mechanisms of credit policy may have to be altered to meet the new situation we face. While credit was made very easy in the 1954 and 1958 recessions in order to induce housing and other investment spending, a similar reduction of the short-term interest rate on government bills down to the one per cent level might lead in 1961 to a further movement of international funds to foreign money markets, thereby intensifying our gold drains. Because our monetary institutions are slowly evolving ones, the following recommendations deal less fully with monetary policy than the subject deserves in a full-scale study of stabilization.

9. *The need for flexibility.* Since experience shows that no one can forecast the economic future with pinpoint accuracy, the policy maker cannot plan for a single course of action; he must be prepared with a list of programs, reserving some on the list for the contingency that events in the early months of 1961 may turn out somewhat worse than what today seems to be the most likely outcome. The following recommendations of this report, therefore, fall into two parts.

First come those minimal measures that need to be pushed hard even if the current recession turns out to be one that can be reversed by next summer at the latest. Expansions and accelerations in expenditure programs that are desirable for their own sake, improvements in unemployment compensation, new devices that permit use of flexible credit policy within the international constraints and stimulus to residential housing are examples of measures that belong in our first line of defense and which are already seen to be justified by what we know about the recent behavior of the American economy. Now in January the wisdom of such policies can already be verified.

Second comes a list of other measures of expansion which represent sound programs to combat a sagging economy, but which are more controversial at this time. If we could read the future better, they might be just what is now needed. But given our limitations, it may be safer to hold such measures in reserve. As the months pass, and the February and March facts become available, we shall be in a position to know whether more vigorous actions are called for. Flexibility in decision making deserves emphasis: there is nothing inconsistent about asking for measures in March that one does not ask for in January, if events have provided us with new information in the meantime. The annual Budget should itself be a "living document." Just as Congress should begin to explore measures that will enhance the flexibility of tax rates by giving certain discretionary powers to the Executive, so should Congress itself be quite prepared to flexibly reverse its field in tax legislation when new economic conditions are recognized to call for new measures.

10. *Important warnings.* It is just as important to know what *not* to do as to know what to do. What definitely is not called for in the present situation is a massive program of hastily devised public works whose primary purpose is merely that of making jobs and getting money pumped into the economy. The Roosevelt New Deal inherited a bankrupt economy that was in desperate straits. Whatever the wisdom of anti-depression "make work" projects in such an environment, they are definitely not called for at the present time. There is so much that America needs in the way of worthwhile governmental programs and modern stabilization has so many alternative weapons to fight depression as to make it quite unnecessary to push the panic button and resort to inefficient spending devices.

Similarly, as was mentioned earlier, massive spending programs designed to undo in a year the inadequacies of several years do not represent desirable fiscal policy. Planned deficits, like penicillin and other antibiotics, have their appropriate place in our cabinet of economic health measures; but just as the doctor carries things too far when he prescribes antibiotics freely and without thought of proper dosage, so too does the modern government err in the direction of activism when it goes all out and calls for every conceivable kind of anti-recession policy. The golden mean between inaction and overaction is hard to define, and yet it must be resolutely sought.

Finally, it is worth repeating the warning against concentrating exclusively on ending a downward slide of activity and ignoring the suboptimal level at which the economy may then be operating. Even if this recession ended early in 1961, and even if its initial stages seemed to show a tolerable rate of improvement, that would not alone be enough to render unnecessary policies aimed to get us back to, and keep us at, high employment levels. Satisfactory growth is not something one procures by a once-and-for-all act; eternal vigilance, as with so many other good things, is the price that must be paid for good economic performance.

V. "First Line of Defense" Policies

11. *Expenditure programs.* Pledged expenditure programs that are desired for their own sake should be pushed hard. If 1961-62 had threatened to be years of over-full-employment and excessive inflationary demand, caution might require going a little easy on some of them. The opposite is in prospect. The following measures are not being advocated in the faith that they will help business from declining in the first months of the new year. Some of them will, at best, pay out money only after a considerable delay. They are advocated for their own sakes as builders of a better, fairer, and faster-growing economy. And even should their expenditures come into play after we have reversed the recession tide, they should be helpful in making the next recovery a truly satisfactory and lasting one.

(i) *Defense expenditures* ought to be determined on their own merits. They are not to be the football of economic stabilization. Nor, as was so often done in the past, ought they to be kept below the optimal level needed for security because of the mistaken notion that the economy is unable to bear any extra burdens. Certainly a recession drop in tax receipts should not inhibit vital expenditures any more than should the operation of artificial limits on the public debt. And they should certainly not be maintained at high levels merely for the purpose of substitution for other measures designed to keep employment high. On the other hand, any stepping up of these programs that is deemed desirable for its own sake can only help rather than hinder the health of our economy in the period immediately ahead.

(ii) *Foreign aid* is likewise to be determined by the need for development abroad. An increase in this program, skillfully tailored to take account of the international payment position, deserves high national priority in a period like this one.

(iii) *Education programs* including funds for school construction, teachers' salaries, increased loans for college dormitories should be vigorously pushed. Some of these could have an impact even within the calendar year 1961 itself.

(iv) *Urban renewal programs*, including slum clearance and improvement of transportation facilities, represent desirable projects that should come high on the policy agenda.

(v) *Health and welfare programs*, including medical care of the aged, increased grants for hospital construction, and continued large grants for medical research, are desirable even though some of them—such as health for the aged financed by social security—will not add at all to dollar demand in the near future.

(vi) *Improved unemployment compensation* is one of the most important of all the measures on this list from the standpoint of anti-recession action. The fairest and most effective step the Federal government can take to help fight the recession would be to expand unemployment compensation benefits. Such expenditures go to those who need them and who will spend the money promptly; they also go up at the right time and in the right place and will come down at the right time and in the right place. It is a sad fact, however, that the Nation's unemployment compensation system cannot possibly do the job it is expected to do. Under present arrangements, it was shown to be inadequate in the 1957-58 recession and it will be inadequate in the present recession as well.

For the immediate future, emergency legislation is needed to permit all states to continue paying unemployment benefits (perhaps at a stepped-up rate) for at least 39 weeks, regardless of the condition of their insurance reserves and even if they have not yet repaid the loans received to tide them over in 1958.

For the long pull, we need a system with basic Federal standards that will (a) cover employees in all firms regardless of size; (b) provide unemployment benefits of at least one half of the employee's earnings; and (c) extend the term of benefits to a minimum of 26 weeks in all states, supplemented by an additional 13 weeks during periods of high national unemployment. Federal standards are also needed to provide for adequate financing and solvency of the system. Consideration should also be given to the possibility of equalizing the burden of financing unemployment benefits among the states, and to varying the benefits in such a way that they will go up when unemployment in the nation as a whole is high and go down when unemployment is low. These measures would reinforce the stabilizing effectiveness of the system in all stages of the business cycle and would eliminate the need for hasty action during periods of emergency.

(vii) *Useful public works programs* should be accelerated to the extent feasible without disrupting their orderly execution. This applies to Federal and federally-supported programs, such as (a) water resources, (b) highways, (c) post office construction, (d) public building construction by the General Services Administration, and (e) military construction. Prompt additional appropriations and authorizations by the Congress are needed in most cases. Opportunities for speeding up authorized public works exist also at the State and local levels. Cooperation of all levels of government strengthens an antirecession program.

(viii) *Highway construction programs* can be accelerated. Cement capacity and labor availability is such as to make this a potent nearterm stimulant. An aggressive Federal highway program might involve any of the following measures: (a) relaxing contract controls over State obligations, and assuring States their obligations will be met; (b) authorizing repayable advance to the States to meet their 10 per cent matching requirements under the Interstate program; (c) waiving the pay-as-you-go amendment if required to permit full apportionment of future Interstate authorizations and, if deemed necessary, increase these authorizations.

(ix) *Depressed area programs* are desirable both in the short run and the long. The Douglas Report spells out needs in this matter and makes comment unnecessary here.

(x) *Natural resource development projects*, including conservation and recreation facilities, provide further examples of useful programs.

The above list does not pretend to be exhaustive. Certain other expenditure measures could be added to a first line of defense program, but enough has been said to indicate the nature of the needed actions. The order of magnitude contemplated here might be in the neighborhood of $3-5 billion above already planned programs in Fiscal 1962 and does not involve the inflationary risks of an all-out anti-recession Blitzkrieg. This does not purport to make up for the accumulative deficiencies in those vital areas.

12. *Residential housing stimulus.* The last two recessions were helped immensely by a successful program to make credit more available to residential housing. No experts could have predicted the anticyclical potency that housing has shown in the postwar period. Already we have seen some easing of credit in this area, but such steps do not seem this time to have been so successful in coaxing out a new

demand for home construction. There is perhaps some reason to fear that less can be expected from the housing area in the year ahead. Down payments are already quite low, as are monthly payments. Vacancy rates, particularly in certain areas and for certain types of housing have been rising. The age brackets that provide the greatest demand for new housing are hollow ones because of the dearth of births during the depression of the 1930's.

None the less, so great is the need for housing a few years from now when the wartime babies move into the house-buying brackets and so useful is the stimulation that a resurgence of housing could bring that it would seem folly not to make a determined effort in this area. In particular, loans for modernization of homes, which now bear so high an interest rate, might provide a promising source for expansion.

Many specific actions will be required. Mortgage rates might be brought down to, say, $4\frac{1}{2}$ per cent interest, with discounts on mortgages correspondingly reduced; consideration might be given to further extended maximum amortization periods. The insurance fee for single dwellings under FHA programs might well be reduced from $\frac{1}{2}$ per cent to $\frac{1}{4}$ per cent. The Federal National Mortgage Association (FNMA or "Fannie May") could step up its mortgage purchasing program, especially for high-risk mortgages lacking private markets. Housing for the elderly is another program, desirable for its own sake. Measures that tie in with urban renewal and college dormitories, as covered above, also hold out promise.

Particularly because our international balance of payments inhibits certain types of activistic monetary policy will it be necessary to push hard on specific credit programs in the housing field. Innovation ingenuity, and experimentation with new instrumentalities will be needed in this matter; it is not reasonable to believe that the patterns earlier arrived at are the last word in feasible programming.

13. *The role of monetary policy.* Were it not for the international constraint, an economy that faced recession in the short run and which had been falling below its potential for several years would naturally call for a considerable easing of credit. Indeed a growth oriented program would entail a combination of low interest rates and widely available credit with an austere fiscal program designed to create Budget Surpluses large enough to offset any resulting overstimulation of demand. But such a program must await a solution of our international economic difficulties that will free our hands in domestic monetary policy.

The first order of business is to get nearer to high employment. Expansion by the Federal Reserve of bank reserves, in order to increase the supply of money and to stimulate investment spending, will naturally tend to lower short-term interest rates. But in view of the volatility of funds as between our money markets and those abroad which pay higher interest, we can plan only limited use of this conventional mechanism. New exploration is needed.

(i) In the days after the 1951 Accord when the lesson had to be learned that government bonds were not in peacetime to be arbitrarily pegged at artificial price levels, it was perhaps defensible for the monetary authorities to concentrate almost wholly on open market operations in the shortest-term government securities. Without entering into the merits of this position—and the problem is indeed anything but a simple one to be decided by emotional slogans—responsible economists realize that the new international situation requires some change in emphasis. Indeed it is encouraging to note that the Federal Reserve authorities have themselves already been experimenting with actions designed to adjust to the new situation. Still further actions may be desirable in order to help bring long-term interest rates down relative to short-term. It is long-term rates which are most decisive for investment spending; and it is short-term interest rates that are most decisive for foreign balances. This is not an area for hasty improvisation or doctrinaire reversal of policies; but it is one for pragmatic evolution of procedures and policies.

Nor is this merely a task for the Federal Reserve. The Treasury too must consider the wisdom of relying primarily on short-term issues in the period just ahead. Those in Congress who have thought that recession times are the best period in which to issue long-term debt at low interest rates will have to go through the same agonizing reappraisal of their view as a result of the new international situation.

The whole problem of debt management by the Treasury, as coordinated with the Federal Reserve in the interest of over-all stability, will require rethinking in these new times. No conflict of desires between the Executive and the Federal Reserve is to be involved, since both have the same interest in economic recovery and defense of the dollar.

(ii) Decisive actions to improve our international balance of payments position are desired for their own sake as well as to liberate domestic stabilization policies. This is not the place to describe the numerous programs that are needed in the international area. Fortunately there are some reasons to think that our net export position is an improving one and that the task is not an impossibly difficult one.

The primary need is to make sure that our productivity is improved so that our costs will remain competitive in international markets. But there are also certain psychological measures that can alleviate the drain on gold.

VI. "Second Line of Defense" Policies

14. *Two alternatives.* All the above has been premised upon a specific, and perhaps optimistic, forecast of how the economy is likely to behave in 1961. This first alternative could be called the "optimistic model" were it not for the fact that it turns out to involve unemployment that does not shrink much or any in 1961 below present levels of some 6 per cent. It seems nevertheless to agree most closely with the likeliest expectations revealed by a careful canvass of economic forecasters in business firms, universities, and public agencies.

Concretely, the optimistic model assumes that the Gross National Product will decline for at most one or two quarters. It assumes that the calendar year GNP will average out to between $510 and $515 billion, which represents an improvement in real GNP of about 2 per cent in real terms (after correction for price changes has been made). It assumes that by the end of the year the economy will be running some 3 per cent above the present rate. It assumes that even in the absence of any needed programs by the New Administration the current Budget will have lost its surplus and more likely will show some deficit. It assumes that our new jobs will be barely enough to provide work for the 1.2 million workers who are added to the labor force in 1961 and that unemployment remains a grave social problem.

Evidently such an outlook cannot be regarded as an optimistic one; and it is to improve upon this situation that the above programs were prescribed.

It is only wise, though, to be prepared for an even worse outlook. Suppose inventory decumulation continues longer than expected above; that consumers continue to save as large a percentage of their disposable incomes as they have recently been doing; that plant and equipment expenditures by business accelerate their downward slide; and that construction generally proves to be disappointing. What then?

In that case unemployment will rise toward and perhaps beyond the critical 7½ per cent level that marks the peak of the postwar era. In that case corporate profits will sink far below their present depressed levels, and a sagging stock market may add to the public's feeling of pessimism. In that case we shall certainly automatically incur a large deficit. While many hope and expect this more pessimistic model will not happen, it cannot be ruled out by careful students of economic history and present indications.

15. *A temporary tax cut.* If economic reports on business during the early months of the year begin to suggest that the second, more pessimistic, outlook is the more relevant one, then it will be the duty of public policy to take a more active, expansionary role. This is not the place to spell out the details of such a program. But certainly the following tax-cut measure will then deserve consideration.

A temporary reduction in tax rates on individual incomes can be a powerful weapon against recession. Congress should legislate, for example, a cut of 3 or 4 percentage points in the tax rate applicable to every income class, to take effect immediately under our withholding system in March or April and to continue until the end of the year.

In view of the great desirability of introducing greater flexibility into tax rates, it would be highly desirable for Congress to grant to the Executive the right to continue such a reduction for one or two six-month (or three-month) periods beyond that time (subject to the actions being set aside by Joint Resolution of Congress) with the clear understanding that the reduction will definitely expire by the end of 1962.

At this time it would be urgently important to make sure that any tax cut was clearly a temporary one. With the continued international uncertainty and with new public programs coming up in the years ahead, sound finance may require a maintenance of our present tax structure and any weakening of it in order to fight a recession might be tragic. Even if it should prove to be the case that growth makes reduction of tax rates possible in the long run, that should be a decision taken on its own merits and adopted along with a comprehensive reforming of our present tax structure. (Various tax devices to stimulate investment might also be part of a comprehensive program designed to eliminate loopholes, promote equity, and enhance incentives.)

VII. A FINAL CAUTION

16. *Direct attack on the wage-price spiral.* The above programs have been primarily concerned with fiscal and monetary policy. This is as it should be.

It is important, though, to realize that there are some problems that fiscal and monetary policy cannot themselves come to grips with.

Thus, if there is indeed a tendency for prices and wages to rise long before w reach high employment, neither monetary nor fiscal policy can be ι ,ed to the degree necessary to promote desired growth.

What may then be needed are new approaches to the problem of productivity, wages and price formation. Will it not be possible to bring government influence to bear on this vital matter without invoking direct controls on wages and prices? Neither labor, nor management, nor the consumer can gain from an increase in price tags. Just as we pioneered in the 1920's in creating potent monetary mechanisms and in the 1930's in forging the tools of effective fiscal policy, so may it be necessary in the 1960's to meet head on the problem of a price creep. This is a challenge to mixed economies all over the free world, and is not to be met by government alone.

112

ECONOMIC POLICY FOR 1962
Paul A. Samuelson

TO look ahead one must first look back. 1961 was a year of recovery from a mild recession that followed on the short and weak 1958–60 boom. The general pattern for 1961 envisaged in my task force Report to President-Elect Kennedy on the American Economy (January 4, 1961) turned out, by some sad miracle, to have been right:

(i) the thing to fear was not the persistence of the recession itself, but rather the danger that the next recovery would be a disappointing one like that of 1959–60;

(ii) unemployment looked to remain a problem well into the new recovery;

(iii) the American economy appeared to need nothing so much as a *stimulus in its over-all demand spending*, such as a vigorously expansionary monetary policy and *a planned* ("prudent") *deficit* could alone give it.

Ideology as a Debit

In pointedly opposing the Eisenhower philosophy of contained government expenditures and "sound" budget balance (like that appropriate to any civilian or army family), I was merely reflecting the considered opinions of the bulk of economists who have been analyzing the facts about national income determination and American growth. While these are the views that scholars all over the free world are almost unanimous in holding, they have never been the views of the man in the street. And in Congress itself, the Eisenhower philosophy, as interpreted by Secretary George Humphrey (in opposition to Arthur F. Burns) and by Secretary Anderson (in opposition to no heard voice in the last Eisenhower Administration), had led to a *reversion* of economic understanding even among the moderate leadership of the Democrats — as exemplified by such men as Vice-President Johnson and Congressman Rayburn. Needless to say, the Byrds and Goldwaters in Congress required no Eisenhower influence to make them revert to a position they had never left.

I linger on this irrational question of ideology because it must have made the job of the new Administration a hard one. Had President Kennedy come out boldly for the sizeable deficit which objective economic analysis called for, he would have run into severe opposition in the divided Congress; and, by becoming tarred with the asinine label name of an "irresponsible spender," the President might have put all his new programs in jeopardy. Here then, was one of those reminders that politics is the art of the feasible: while it is always easy for expert advisers to urge that the Head of State exercise his "leadership," he must ever deliberate on how best to spend and conserve his limited bank-balance of leadership.

Though the outgoing Administration bequeathed a budget document purporting to show a budget in balance, it was readily apparent to any intelligent observer that it was bequeathing an economy which was already running a deficit and which could not possibly end up the fiscal year without a still bigger one. The fact that the deficit could be blamed on the previous Administration eased the ideological task; and in the early messages, President Kennedy described his own program as one of "balancing the Eisenhower Budget," in the sense of recommending programs that would not of themselves unbalance the budget if it had been true that the Eisenhower Budget has been itself in balance — which, because of the decline in tax revenues due to the recession, it clearly was not. (If the above sentence is an involved one, no blame attaches to me as a writer but must instead be attributed to the subtlety of its content.)

Bluntly, the straight economics of the 1961 situation required a sizeable deficit. How might this best come about? There were a number of new Kennedy programs that could be justified on their intrinsic merits, independently of any anti-recession need. A temporary tax cut, with or without some relinquishing by Congress of discretionary authority, was a possibility. Structural improvements in our unemployment compensation system and in other transfer programs naturally recommended themselves. On the other hand, the outlook for defense expenditures at the beginning of 1961 was cloudy and expert opinion could be found suggesting that these would not have to rise in any appreciable amount.

Whatever the economic merits of a tax cut, it seemed politically out of the question. The President had run on a platform that asked sacrifices of the American people. How then could he begin by giving them what many would regard as a "handout?" Also, how could one be sure that the new civilian and defense programs might not require maintenance of the tax base? And what about the possibility of raising our growth rate by changing our full-employment composition of demand away from comsumption and toward net capital formation by means of maintaining tax rates and offsetting the ultimate implied budget surplus by a militant policy of credit expansion?

Muddling Through To The Needed Stimulus

In brief, the first Kennedy program was a modest one: designed to help bring the recession to a speedy end, it was not large enough to lead to so rapid a recovery as would be wanted by those anxious to bring unemployment substantially down from its 7 per cent rate and anxious to speed up America's real growth rate. If, for fiscal 1962, the economy needed a $5–10 billion deficit, it did not look at that time as if it could be got.

But all that did not reckon with Mr. Khrushchev and the tendency for our agricultural programs to become more expensive. As a result of two or three new upward revisions of our defense budget, and not as a result of a cool decision on the part of the New Team to disregard ideology and prescribe for the nation what its sound economic health required, fiscal 1962 looks to end up with the sizeable deficit designed to promote a healthy rate of recovery and expansion.

The Craft of Statesmanship[1]

President Kennedy, one gathers from his intimates, has an intuitive grasp of economics that is the envy of the lawyers in the White House and Cabinet. He also has something that his economic experts naturally lack, namely, an appreciation of the degree to which Congressmen have to be educated and re-educated in these economic matters. ("It takes a Senator to know a Senator," so goes an old Potomac proverb.) Also according to usually accurate

---

[1] This section is adapted from a recent article in the *Nihon Keizai Shimbun.*

gossip, the President combines with his social concern a cool head and prefers to proceed in a pragmatic and gradual way.

The resulting program of expansion has been something less than all that could be desired by academic perfectionists (the caste to which I happen to belong). But it has been something more than could have been hoped for by political realists, who knew how closely divided this Congress is and how much the middle-of-the-roaders need in the way of of persuasion. Guile will not get one very far with a sophisticated Congress; but adroitness, plus notable courage at several junctures in 1961, have helped to give us the programs designed to promote economic growth and recovery. To be sure, the decisions of Mr. Khrushchev to bring about a Berlin crisis and to resume nuclear testing must be given some of the responsibility for the quantitative expansion in federal spending.

The Moral: A Governmental Recovery

This backward look is important. For somewhat similar problems face the policymaker at the beginning of 1962, and he must recognize the most important lesson from our recent past: the 1961 expansion was largely a governmental one. It was helped in the expected way by a transient shift from inventory accumulation to decumulation. Net foreign investment could hardly have been expected to continue as a stimulus at the early-1961 rate; and as our imports rose, this did lose strength. Some slight rise in plant and equipment was induced after the turn was clearly behind us; but nothing like the 1956–7 boom in fixed investment is indicated in the factual surveys yet available. Residential housing received some stimulus from a determined easier credit policy (private and public); but the pattern of previous post-war recoveries, in which we could induce a tremendous stimulus from housing to reinforce the rise, can apparently no longer be repeated.

At best, then, private investment rose slightly to reinforce the government expansion. As yet it has not shown signs of running away with the ball, as in some of our historical revivals.

What about the consumer? Until the last months of the year he did not seem to be the hero of the scenario. But with auto and retail sales picking up in the last quarter, analysts have come to the opinion that he will probably continue to pass along in spending about 93 per cent of his disposable income, which means he will be doing his duty even if not performing remarkably beyond the call of duty.

The Treacherous Concept of Balance

If it be the case that the 1961 recovery will go down in the history books as primarily a governmental recovery, the implications for fiscal policy are enormous. I have in mind particularly the following:

The resolution to balance the budget after the recovery has got underway has always been used as a powerful argument to meet the ideological block against a needed deficit. If temporary government stimulus is followed by a massive release of private stimulus — as in the case of the pump-priming image — the desire to balance the budget can be honored without jeopardizing the economic wisdom of fiscal policy. Indeed, if the private revival is an especially vigorous one, a budgetary surplus is economically called for and the best policy may even require a reduction of the public debt over the complete business cycle.

But the above is only half the story. And in rereading my Report to President-Elect Kennedy, I am grateful for the caution expressed there concerning the certainty that the budget can be expected to be in balance over the cycle or over the decade. Good policy will, in some eras, require overbalance most of the time; in some other eras, good policy will want the public debt to grow over a decade at some optimal rate; by rare chance, a perfect balance might be called for in some singular eras.

Unfortunately, our powers of economic prediction are not so perfect as to enable us to know *in advance* what target to aim for over an extended period. This is the mortal weakness in the view that one should aim for a balance over the cycle; and it indicates the theoretical flaw basic to the more sophisticated *Committee For Economic Development* concept that the budget should be made to balance at a full-employment level of income. Good policy may require a full-employment surplus at one time; and at another time, it may require a full-employment deficit. It would be the height of arrogance, or a stroke of good luck, if one could specify in advance the proper goal.

Avoiding a Premature Balance

I must, alas, call attention to the peculiar ideological problem that is again paramount in deciding fiscal policy for the next 18 months. Shall the fiscal 1963 programs be restricted to the constraint of a balanced budget?

Ideology can never be met on its own terms by reason. It has to be matched by ideology.[2] But unfortunately, as time passes, ideological *ripostes* remain to plague one. The notion that

[2] Of course, all this can lead to upside-down economics. Thus, I must bear some of the credit for the following gambit: if ideology prevents us from having the needed deficit in recession times, let us channel that ideology so as to negate the built-in dampening stabilizer in our system. This involves upside-down arguments of the type, "Now that recovery is rising enough to give us more tax receipts, we can afford (sic) to *increase* our expenditures or *cut* tax rates." The economics illogic is apparent: yet in political economy, two wrongs *may* come nearer to a right *than one alone*.

the fiscal 1963 budget could be balanced was a powerful one in quieting the irrational opposition to needed fiscal expansion. If private spending had boomed, that notion would today do us no harm. But facts are facts.

It was harmful to let a large budget surplus develop in the weak 1959–60 revival and thereby help to choke off that recovery. Similarly, it would be tragic if a premature budget balance were to weaken the momentum of the present recovery long before we have come close to healthy employment and growth levels.

That I believe is the basic policy question of 1962.[3] My own views on how to answer the question must be obvious from the above remarks. *Fiscal and monteary policy should tighten only when substantial misbehavior on the price, wage, and international fronts has developed and cannot be well met by more specific remedies.* They should *not* be tightened as a sop to outmoded ideology.

[3] An experienced observer would have to admit that the odds favor the view that the fiscal year will end up with a larger deficit than is forecast in the original budget estimates — a significant factor to keep in mind.

BOOK FIVE

Economics — Past and Present

PART XVI

Essays in the History of Economics

113

ECONOMISTS AND THE HISTORY OF IDEAS*

By PAUL A. SAMUELSON

"For there are, in the present times, two opinions: not, as in former ages the true and the false; but the outside and the inside."

J. M. Keynes (1921)

"The proper study of Mankind is man." So said the infallible poet. And past experience at these annual gatherings of the sons and daughters of Adam Smith suggests that the popular subject of discussion among economists is not so much economics as economists. Usually the annual presidential address is an exception—an exception that does not always improve upon the rule.

According to our annals, an expiring president of this occult body begins with two choices. He may, on the one hand, give an address that summarizes his lifework or his basic contribution to some important field of scholarship. Thus, my old teacher, Paul H. Douglas, just as he was about to come out of his academic cocoon and emerge as a senatorial butterfly, gave his 1947 address on the Laws of Production, summarizing his decades of work measuring statistical production functions.

I am afraid this choice is not open to me. My own scholarship has covered a great variety of fields. And many of them involve questions like welfare economics and factor-price equalization; turnpike theorems and osculating envelopes; nonsubstitutability relations in Minkowski-Ricardo-Leontief-Metzler matrices of Mosak-Hicks type; or balanced-budget multipliers under conditions of balanced uncertainty in locally impacted topological spaces and molar equivalences. My friends warn me that such topics are suitable merely for captive audiences in search of a degree—and even then not after dark.

This leaves me still with several possible choices. For one thing, I can always talk about methodology. But although my children think of me as a remnant of "the olden days," to myself I seem just re-

* Presidential address delivered at the Seventy-Fourth Annual Meeting of the American Economic Association, New York, December 27, 1961.

cently to have become emeritus from the category of *enfant terrible;* and the only thing more terrible than the sight of an immature youth is the sight of a half-baked elder statesman. So, that part of methodology which consists of passing on good advice concerning the scholarly pitfalls to avoid and the proper paths to climb, I had better avoid.

But there is another possibility: I could give a sermon tonight on the use and misuse of mathematics in economics. This subject is the only commodity in the world that seems not subject to Gossen's law of diminishing marginal utility. It was only yesterday that three successive presidential addresses touched upon this delicious topic; and the strongest of those attacks on mathematics led to so resonant a response with this annual audience as to give rise to a standing ovation for the speaker.

Thomas Hardy remarked, "If the Archbishop of Canterbury says that God exists, that is all in the day's business; but if he says God does not exist, there you have something really significant." What a Daniel-come-to-Judgment I would be, if I, the lamb that strayed fustus' and mustus' from the fold, were to testify before God and this company that mathematics had all been a horrible mistake; that right along, it has all been there in Marshall, Books III and V; and that the most one needs for life as an economist is a strong voice, and a compass and ruler.

I wish I could be obliging. Yet even if my lips could be brought to utter the comforting words, like Galileo I would hear myself whispering inside, "But mathematics does indeed help."

I am left then finally with one choice. This evening I shall talk less about technical economics than about economists. Where do we members "of the most agreeable of the moral sciences" fit in the great stream of ideas and ideologies? On this solemn occasion I shall eschew gossip, leaving that to the corridors and lobbies. But I shall unavoidably have to deal with personalities and names if I am to explore the interrelations between professional economic thought and the general history of ideas.

I. *Within the Looking Glass*

As my old teacher Schumpeter used to say, "We are all girls here together." Hence, mine can be the view of an insider looking in, and an insider looking out.

I begin with two books. One is a work of scholarship; the other is, and you will excuse the distinction, merely a textbook. Compare *The History of Economic Analysis* by Joseph Schumpeter with *The History of Economic Doctrines* of Gide and Rist, which students used to study in my day when preparing for general examinations. I dare say that all the names mentioned by the latter authors can be found in Schumpeter's index. But how different is the emphasis: reading Gide and Rist you would be forgiven for thinking that Robert Owen was almost as important as Robert Malthus; that Fourier and Saint-Simon were much more important than Walras and Pareto. The A. Young in their index is, of course, Arthur Young, not Allyn Young.

Now turn to Schumpeter. Everything is there; no name left out. But now it is Marshall, Walras, Wicksell and such people who steal the stage. Of course Adam Smith is given his due. But what a due! He is rather patronizingly dismissed as a synthesizer who happened to write the right book at the right time: his analytic contributions are certainly minimized.

How can we account for these differences? By the fact that Schumpeter is writing some 40 years after Gide and Rist? Only in the smallest part, I think. By 1913 Wicksell, Wicksteed, and Wieser had done their great work, but only Wieser gets a mention from Gide and Rist —one mention. The treatment of Walras is even more indicative. Walras is indeed mentioned by them; but yet not primarily for his work as a theorist so much as for his views on nationalization of land, free trade, and the State—views which Pareto and Schumpeter thought of as simply silly, like Irving Fisher's food fads and teetotalism. To verify that I am not having sport by picking on a particular set of authors, turn from Gide and Rist to Alexander Gray's brief book, the busy student's friend, to see how Walras fares there. In Gray, Leon Walras is "crowded out" by his father Auguste and is referred to as the "younger Walras," which is a little like referring to Maynard Keynes as the "younger Keynes."

No one can really deny that we have two different sets of standards here. When I began graduate study at Harvard in 1935, Schumpeter rather shocked me by saying in a lecture that of the four greatest economists in the world, three were French. (I had thought the non-Frenchman was English, probably Adam Smith; but after looking into Schumpeter's later book for the purpose of checking, I think my inference must have been incorrect and that he then meant Alfred Marshall rather than Smith.) And who were the Frenchmen?

Of course, one was Leon Walras, whom Schumpeter had no hesitation in calling the greatest economist of all time, by virtue of his first formulation of general equilibrium. Today there can be little doubt that most of the literary and mathematical economic theory appearing in our professional journals is more an offspring of Walras than of anyone else (and I stress the adjective *literary*). The comparison that Lagrange made of Newton is worth repeating in this connection: Assuredly Newton was the greatest man of science, but also the luckiest.

For there is but one system of the world and Newton was the one who found it. Similarly, there is but one grand concept of general equilibrium and it was Walras who had the insight (and luck) to find it.

I ought to add that this rating by Schumpeter deserves more credit, coming in 1935, than it would coming today. For it had predictive value as to what was to happen to our professional writings. Back in 1935, Marshall was still propped up on his throne and in large parts of the world even the zealots of the mathematical method tended to look upon Walras merely as the predecessor of the great Pareto. The bourse for professional reputations shows changing price fluctuations: if at one time Alfred Marshall was overpraised and quoted at an inflated price which left little of consumer's surplus to the buyer, he had to pay for this by later being sold at an overdiscount—as will become evident.

Since I ought not to leave you waiting for the other shoes to drop, I hasten to name the other Frenchmen. One is Cournot, a choice that will not seem too surprising. Certainly there is a professional competence about the 1838 Cournot, in the field of partial equilibrium, monopoly and oligopoly, that the modern literature only reattained by 1930. (Think only of the *re*discovery in *this* century of the concept of marginal revenue!) I do not know that the name of Schumpeter's final giant will seem so obvious a choice. It is Francois Quesnay, who is deemed to be great on account of his cryptic *Tableau* and anticipation of the circular flow of economic life. Back in the days before Leontief and the resurrection of Karl Marx's Volume 2 model of circular reproduction, I thought this last choice even more far-fetched than I do today.

II. *The Pecking-Order of Analysts*

I need not labor the point farther. Within economics, we economists rate writers of the past in a quite different order than does the outside world. And, as far as economic analysis itself is concerned, the present generation of economists gives a quite different ranking than did earlier generations of economists.[1]

Now I am not really concerned here with the history of pure theory and the changing fortunes of different writers. A critic can rightly argue that Gide and Rist were writing a history of economic *doctrines*, while Schumpeter was writing a history of economic *analysis*; and hence I ought not to be surprised if there turns out to be a considerable difference in emphasis. Who would want to deny that Cournot,

---

[1] There is a great deal of evidence that this is more than the view of the *avant garde* and more than a passing fad. One straw in the wind would be to examine the successive revisions since 1939 of a book that did not begin with any prejudice in favor of economic analytics, Eric Roll, *A History of Economic Thought*, 3d ed., Englewood Cliffs, N.J., 1956.

writing in 1838, had an analytical power and freshness that is breathtaking? But who in his right mind could argue that Cournot had been a great force on the history of ideas: what Paris *salon* preoccupied itself with sellers of mineral water? Except through possible indirect influences of his teachings, Cournot's impact on ideology must surely have been negligible.

I quite agree. In many ways the history of a subject's technical analysis is easier to write precisely because it need not involve the determination of social influencings.[2] Tonight we do not want to linger on analytics, except perhaps to draw the obvious moral that, if economists spend more and more of their time on highly technical mathematics and statistics, they must not be surprised if the intelligent man of affairs comes to ignore this part of their activities. It is true that Voltaire and Madame du Châtelet, his great and good friend, wrote profusely on Newton's universal law of gravitation; but this really amounted to vulgarization of that subject, gross vulgarization on the part of Voltaire and neat vulgarization on the part of that gifted lady. While we should not minimize the importance of vulgarization—I mean communication—we must not blink the fact that this is an area where Gresham's Law operates in its most remorseless fashion: vulgar vulgarization drives out subtle, just as strong ideology outsells weak.

The split, between "the inside look" of a subject in terms of the logic and experience of its professional development and its implications for the man-in-the-street or the academician down the campus, is well recognized. No one gets a Nobel Prize for an essay on the relationship of quantum mechanics to free will and God; but one who has already received such a prize will get a better hearing for his random or systematic thoughts on the topic. Nor, these days, do you get appointed to chairs of economics by virtue of your social elo-

---

[2] If the history of science is still generally in a crude form, that is primarily because scholars have just recently begun to take it seriously. In the case of mathematics, there is a most ludicrous ignorance of the true sequence of contributions: if a formula, such as Lagrange's interpolation formula, is attributed by name to a person, the betting is good that small research will show it appeared in earlier writings. What I have in mind here is not the statement that there is nothing new under the sun and all knowledge is a repetition of previously known knowledge: on the contrary, such a statement is the reverse of the truth; mathematical knowledge has been cumulative and, with enough research and luck. we might hope to clean up the false history of the subject. The situation in mathematics is especially simple if one takes the view that the objects of mathematical research are theorems and that most importance attaches to the date of their first rigorous *proof*. Thus, it is meaningful to say that the "strong ergodic theorem" goes back to G. D. Birkhoff in 1931, and that J. v. Neumann deserves the credit for two-person zero-sum game theory. (But if one is also interested in conjecture, heuristics and partial insight, the matter is not so simple. Some modern mathematicians, one feels, will rename Fermat's Last Theorem to Schwartz's Theorem if the first man to prove it happens to be named Schwartz.) In economics, datings are harder: thus I cannot tell you who first disproved "the labor theory of value," much less who originated it.

quence; indeed, until academic tenure has come, you are best advised not to write for *Harpers* or the *Manchester Guardian* (to say nothing of the *National Review* or the *New Republic*) lest you be indicted for superficiality.

Good writing itself can be suspect. (I interject that if good literary style is indeed a sin, it is not a sin that is very widespread among our economics brotherhood.) John Stuart Mill tells us in his remarkable autobiography that his father, James Mill, thought poetry was overrated; but that since poetry *was* overrated, young John ought to try his hand at it. I believe it was Yale's Tjalling Koopmans, himself a creative economist blessed with clarity of style, who advanced the austere argument that exceptionally fine writing is a biasing factor which might bring to an argument more attention and credence than it really deserved. There is something to this: but no one should be taken in by the false corollary that the *intrinsic* worth of an argument is enhanced by virtue of its being phrased obscurely. Having said this, one must add grudgingly that, while obscurity may not add to the intrinsic worth of an argument, it has often been a contributory ingredient to fame. How many Marxians have read *Das Kapital*—I mean read it through? Bernard Shaw once claimed that he was the only man in England, including H. M. Hyndman and contemporary Marxian leaders, who had read the book. Shaw himself was observed at the British Museum by Harcourt[3] in the act of reading Marx (in the French translation, of course); so at least part of Shaw's claim may be true. But Shaw was sitting in the British Museum with a copy of *Capital* stretched before him and beside it a copy of the score of *Lohengrin*; one can guess on which he could have earned the higher exam grade.

This brings me to mention one of our members who is far away tonight toiling on a distant shore. I refer of course to J. Kenneth Galbraith and have in mind *The Affluent Society*. To compare this book with *The Theory of the Leisure Class* would be in some of our common rooms, to damn it; in some, to praise it. Gibbon tells us how he found his *Decline and Fall* on every boudoir table soon after its publication. When we economists think how often in recent years people have been asking us, " What do you think of *The Affluent Society*?"—and how embarrassing the question has been to so many of us busy beavers— we can appreciate that this work stands as good a chance as any of being read and remembered twenty years from now.

Yet always members of a guild have their defenses against the man who ventures away from home. "It was all in Keynes's 1930 *Saturday*

---

[3] This gives Sir William Harcourt a second claim to fame, beyond that of his famous one-tenth truth: "We are all socialists now."

Evening Post article, 'Economic Possibilities for Our Grandchildren.' "
"Two-thirds of the title came from Tawney's *The Acquisitive Society.*"
"The point about the need to spend more these days on public rather
than private wants was already made eloquently by Alvin Hansen and
others; in any case it involves a value judgment not a scientific finding." "Harvard professors may have incomes high enough to satiate
them, but most people do not." "So what's the matter with big auto
fins? Didn't you ever hear of Freud? And how about Jeremy Bentham's dictum concerning the equality of pleasures, 'Pushpin is as
good as poetry?' " "Are commercially created wants different, or less
satisfying, or less worthy than natural wants, whatever those may be?"
"The book's style is superficially attractive but its message is not
profound."

I am afraid people in the boudoir, today or twenty years from now,
will not seek the benefit of our professional reactions. Within the body
of economics itself, *The Affluent Society* will find a place that is proportionate to the new predictions about economic regularities it may
suggest. But whatever the later verdict about the operational meaning
of its propositions, we can no more recall it or wipe out half a line of
it than we can—by professional exegesis—expunge Henry George's
Progress and Poverty from the historical record.

III. *Political Economists: Ourselves to Know*

Leaving aside how our own profession rates and ranks the craftsmen
of its trade, I now want to close in on the differences between our
view of ideologies and *Weltanschauungen* and that of the intelligent
man of affairs. Who do *we* think were the great *political* economists
as against just great economists?

Adam Smith. Going back no earlier than Adam Smith, we can let
Smith stand for the classical tradition. And, in my telescope, he stands
on a pinnacle. While I think Smith is underrated as an economic
theorist, it must be admitted that his impact as a political economist
does not rest upon his having improved upon theories of his friend
David Hume; nor upon his having anticipated the various refinements
of Malthus, West, Ricardo, Torrens, and John Stuart Mill.

Here is a case where the inside view and the outside view are one.
The intelligent man of affairs, and even Macaulay's schoolboy, were
profoundly influenced by Smith's attacks on mercantilism and state
interference and by his spirited championing of *laissez faire*. To be
sure, the amateur never appreciates the nuances of Smith's position:
e.g., his skepticism about the businessman's passion for tough competition; his definite role for limited government; his general pragmatism rather than dogmatism.

Still, it is significant that the great critics of the classical tradition generally chose to controvert the *Wealth of Nations* rather than the writings of later members of his school.

David Ricardo. In time Ricardo came to be the whipping boy for continental romantics and historicists. Yet there is not much evidence that they had to read him closely in order to find fault with his abstract methodology. I must confess that I find Ricardo hard to give semester-type grades to. He is par excellence an economist's economist. A sweet man, Ricardo is certainly one of the luckiest that ever lived. And here I have not so much in mind his success in speculating; although he was no slouch in that department, as some facts from his biography illustrate.[4]

Ricardo was lucky in being on the spot when the Napoleonic Wars were causing the value of money to misbehave in the most interesting fashion. He was lucky to have James Mill as taskmaster and press agent. He was lucky in having been deprived of higher education, so that his resulting written expositions had the clumsiness necessary to give that ingredient of obscurity so conducive to a reputation for great profundity. Finally, and I hope it comes as no anticlimax, Ricardo was lucky in being profound.

[4] Cut off for marrying outside his faith with a few thousand dollars, within twenty years Ricardo had become a millionaire a few times over, the equivalent in this present day of taxes, higher prices and higher general real incomes, to tens of millions of dollars. The Duke of Wellington may have regarded the battle of Waterloo as "a damned near close-run thing," but David Ricardo urged before the battle that his friend Robert Malthus go the limit in holding British government bonds; and Malthus, a parson with small means and a convex-from-above utility function, lived to reproach himself for not having followed that advice. Retiring young from business to devote himself to leisure, study, politics, and being a gentleman, Ricardo astutely realized that his numerous children were not chips off the old block in financial acumen; so, and this is purely my conjecture, being convinced by his studies that land rent tends to rise as capital and labor progressively grow, Ricardo arranged to buy self-sufficient gentry estates for his offspring, succeeding so well in his purpose as to keep his descendants out of shirtsleeves until the end of the century and, at the same time, conferring upon them the bonus of being absorbed into county society. At the urging of his friends, Ricardo indulged in conspicuous consumption by buying his way into Parliament. (He did this by invoking the later doctrine of "opportunity cost": *i.e.*, he lent £20,000 interest-free to an Irish holder of a rotten borough, one which Ricardo never bothered to visit.)

Ricardo's parliamentary career was something of an anticlimax. He was not a gripping speaker, and the build-up of his reputation was a grave handicap. It is interesting that Ricardo was a genuinely disinterested man and generally favored measures that were against the interest of landlords. When once accused of having a special interest in some proposal, he candidly replied that his interests were so diverse that he himself could not tell on which side the balance of his Hicksian income effects would fall, thus showing himself to be a master of *quadratic* programming of the type needed for optimal Markowitz portfolio balancing; and little wonder, since in 1817 Ricardo's comparative cost theory had involved him in linear programming. One feels he was a natural at trading in, and arbitraging, Lagrangean multipliers and other dual-price variables. See Volume 10 of the Sraffa edition of Ricardo's work for most of the facts from which this account has been fabricated.

Still, when I once heard George J. Stigler say that Malthus was the most overrated of economists, I heard myself replying: "That's funny. I think David Ricardo is the most overrated of economists." Probably this conversation tells more about Stigler and me than about Ricardo and Malthus. What I had in mind was this: Ricardo was a keen reasoner and almost always comes out to be logical in the end, if you accept his implicit and explicit definitions and assumptions. But he makes unnecessarily rough weather of the matters he deals with, and the reader is inclined to think him miraculous for being able to get out of the holes he has dug for himself by his mode of attack and exposition. Analytically, his theory of rent is excellent but not clearly better than or earlier than the contemporaneous theories of rent of Sir Edward West and Malthus. Ricardo did have a rigorously handled general equilibrium model of primitive type; but its dynamics merely elaborate on what is already in the population theory of Malthus and Smith, and ought not today to be regarded as very "magnificent."

His greatest tour de force was the theory of comparative advantage; and though it would be simply irrelevant to point out that Isaac Gervaise had developed similar notions in the preceding century, one has to take into account that Colonel Torrens, a mere mortal, had also developed pretty much the same analysis at pretty much the same time. Moreover, in most of the debates that Ricardo's work gave rise to, the points of his critics were well taken, not so much in proving that Ricardo's reasoning was wrong in terms of its assumptions, as in pointing out that his conclusions were apt to be misunderstood and were of limited significance. Instead of regarding it as a scandal that so much ink has had to be split over Ricardo's flirtations and retreats from a labor theory of value, his admirers think this makes him a seminal thinker.[5] In short, the notion of Keynes that "Ricardo's mind was the greatest that ever addressed itself to economics" does not agree with my assessment of his high I.Q. or creativeness in relation to that of other economists.

Ricardo's name was certainly used as a rallying cry for the school that favored freer trade in England. But Smith had already made the needed points; if exaggeration is what was needed, Herbert Spencers and Bastiats can usually be found who are unencumbered by the subtleties of refined economic analysis. Moreover, detailed researchers will more and more reveal that the Ricardian School provided the background for early Victorian thinking but did not, in a detailed fashion

---

[5] See my two papers on Ricardian systems, which elaborate on my views and give a physiocratic interpretation, "A Modern Treatment of the Ricardian Economy," *Quart. Jour. Econ.*, I, Feb. 1959, 73, 1-35; II, May 1959, 73, 217-31; also my paper on related Marxian models, "Wages and Interest: A Modern Dissection of Marxian Economic Models," *Am. Econ. Rev.*, Dec. 1957, 47, 884-912.

satisfactory to the historian of direct political development, have important influences upon such legislative events as the repeal of the Corn Laws. Indeed, Ricardo was subtle enough to muck up the simple-minded case for harmonious free trade.

Jeremy Bentham, a friend of James Mill and Ricardo, was a character who would have been unbelievable if he had appeared in a book. (He once seriously asked James Mill for his eldest son. James thought that an excessive demand on friendship, but did lease him John to help clean out the Augean stables of Bentham manuscripts; this was but one of the feats of Hercules that John accomplished with distinction and at incredibly early ages.)

Bentham's influence on modern law and institutions has always been recognized by historians as having been great: the nineteenth century where legislation is concerned is truly Bentham's shadow writ large, as Dicey has said. Crane Brinton once quipped: "The New Deal had a good deal of old Bentham in it."[6] And I have dared to suggest that the logic of Bentham's position would in later times have gone beyond his fortuitous individualism, so that his thought is really congenial to that of Fabians like Sidney Webb. Bentham, though not an economist's economist nor even primarily an economist, had I am sure an influence far greater than that of Ricardo.

Have I now not proved too much? Why then has Ricardo had the good press with posterity if my strictures are at all near the mark? I think the answer depends upon a different kind of luck. David Ricardo happens to be the darling both of the liberal economists who followed in his direct line and of the Marxian critics of capitalism. Like me, you may not agree with Ricardo's famous letter to Trower which says, "Political economy . . . should rather be called an enquiry into the laws which determine the division of the produce of industry amongst the classes who concur in its formation." But you can perceive how Ricardo's laconic and unsparing remarks about distribution would stimulate the so-called Ricardian socialists who regarded property incomes as exploitation of labor. And once Karl Marx took him up as an object of worthy study, Ricardo was, so to speak, in on both sides of the street. Having Piero Sraffa as an editor merely capped Ricardo's good luck.

John Stuart Mill. I pass by Nassau Senior and the other classical writers to mention Mill briefly. Mill was modest; Marshall was not. The world takes people too much at their word. The result is that Marshall's claims to analytical originality are received too seriously;

[6] C. C. Brinton, *Ideas of Men: The Story of Western Thought,* London 1951, p. 392. Incidentally, Brinton's index has between Rhodes, Cecil and Richards, I. A. no Ricardo, David.

and Mill's forging of the general-equilibrium concept of demand and supply schedules, even before the 1838 date of Cournot's definitive partial-equilibrium formulation, is ignored by all but the true gourmets of economic theory, who recognize it as an analytical contribution of the first magnitude.

John Stuart Mill, son of a dogmatic father, was himself eclectic and had an engaging ability to change his mind when new facts or arguments became available or merely from rethinking old attitudes.[7] It is almost fatal to be flexible, eclectic, and prolific if you want your name to go down in the history books: get known for one idea, however farfetched it may be—such as that the rate of interest has to be zero in the stationary state or that land is the source of all value—and you are sure to get at least a paragraph in the history books for it. Also, Mill had what Nietzsche once referred to as an offensively clear style.

Yet so great was Mill as a thinker and reflector that he was able to overcome these handicaps. His views on liberty will, even in the post-Freud world, never go out of date and can perhaps be summarized in the words of Mrs. Pat Campbell, Bernard Shaw's pen-mistress: People should be allowed to do anything they like—provided only they don't scare the horses in the street.

Mill is truly a transitional figure. Shaw shows this in one of his wittiest plays, *You Never Can Tell.* A typical Shavian New Woman returns from the West Indies after an absence of some 20 years to find that all her revolutionary Millian notions have become old-hat, superseded by new Fabian notions. The same conflict between the eighteenth and twentieth century went on in Mill's own mind: it was fa-

[7] Sweden's Gustav Cassel, whom the public regarded as about the world's leading economist in the 1920's and who might have become a truly outstanding scholar if his temperament had been different, is shown by the following story to be a good opposite to Mill. H. C. Sonne, the distinguished merchant banker and chairman of the National Planning Association, has told how Cassel visited at Sonne's family home in Denmark in the days around the First World War. A guest happened to mention that some scholar had just made a fresh study of the relationship between the price level and gold supply and had come up with conclusions strongly at variance with the famous Cassel thesis. When asked what he intended to do about it, Cassel replied as follows. "I have a son-in-law whom I have put through Divinity School at some considerable expense. Now that he has graduated and qualified for his diploma, he comes to me and says that he has lost his faith and asks what to do. My advice to him was simple: 'Just carry on as if nothing had happened'."

Relevant too is a conversation I had last month in London after I had given the Stamp Memorial Lecture in the University of London for 1961. In that lecture I discussed, among other things, some of the problems of economic forecasting and stressed the need for scientific validation and the desirability of each forecaster's going back ruthlessly to review *ex post* his *ex ante* predictions. "A great mistake," I was told by one of the best forecasters in English academic life. "It is fatal ever to read what you have earlier written. It breaks your nerve as a forecaster." His lips were smiling but his eyes looked serious.

ther James against friend Harriet with John advancing two steps and going back one. It is ironical that evolutionary socialism in England and elsewhere finds itself today backing up from its post-Benthamite insistence on nationalization of the means of production to something like the society dimly envisaged by Mill. No wonder Karl Marx hated Mill and denounced him as a vulgar bourgeois economist. Marx could recognize the enemy when he saw him. (Curiously, the well-read Mill either never heard of Marx or never thought him worth mentioning—this despite Mill's interest in the Revolution of 1848, the *Communist Manifesto* by Marx and Engels of that date, and Mill's survival beyond the 1867 date of *Capital* Vol. 1.)[8]

Karl Marx. From the viewpoint of pure economic theory, Karl Marx can be regarded as a minor post-Ricardian. Unknowingly I once delighted a southern university audience: my description of Marx as a not uninteresting precursor (in Volume 2 of *Capital*) of Leontief's input-output analysis of circular interdependence apparently had infuriated the local village Marxist. Also, a case can be made out that Marx independently developed certain vague apprehensions of underconsumptionist arguments like those of the *General Theory*; but on my report card no one earns too high a grade for such a performance, since almost everyone who is born into this world alive experiences at some time vague intimations that there is a hole somewhere in the circular flow of purchasing power and production. This seems to come on the same chromosome as the gene that makes people believe in Say's Law; and Marx's bitter criticisms of Rodbertus for being an underconsumptionist shows us that he is no exception.

As long as I am being big about admitting small merits in Marx, I might mention a couple of technical suggestions he made about business cycles that are not without some interest: Marx did formulate a vague notion of 10-year replacement cycles in textile equipment as the determinant of cyclical periodicity—which is an anticipation of various modern "echo" theories. He also somewhere mentioned the possibility of some kind of harmonic analysis of economic cycles by mathematics, which with much charity can be construed as pointing toward modern periodogram analysis and Yule-Frisch stochastic dynamics. A much more important insight involved the tying up of technological change and capital accumulation with business cycles, which pointed ahead to the work of Tugan-Baranowsky (himself a Marxian), Spiethoff, Schumpeter, Robertson, Cassel, Wicksell, and Hansen.

What can be gold in the field of fluctuations can be dirt in the context of pure economic theory. Marx claimed in Volume 1 that there was some interesting economics involved in a labor theory of value,

[8] *Cf.* A. L. Harris, *Economics and Social Reforms,* New York 1958.

and some believe his greatest fame in pure economics lies in his attempted analysis of "surplus value." Although he promised to clear up the contradiction between "price" and "value" in later volumes, neither he nor Engels ever made good this claim. On this topic the good-humored and fair criticisms of Wicksteed and Böhm-Bawerk have never been successfully rebutted: the contradictions and muddles in Marx's mind must not be confused with the contradictions and muddles in the real world.

Marx, like any man of keen intellect, liked a good problem; but he did not labor over a labor theory of value in order to give us moderns scope to use matrix theory on the "transformation" problem. He wanted to have a theory of exploitation, and a basis for his prediction that capitalism would in some sense impoverish the workers and pave the way for revolution into a new stage of society. As the optimism of the American economist Henry Carey shows, a labor theory of value when combined with technological change is, on all but the most extreme assumptions, going to lead to a great increase in real wages and standards of living. So the element of exploitation had to be worked hard. Here Marx might have emphasized the monopoly elements of distribution: how wicked capitalists, possessed of the nonlabor tools *that are essential* to high production, allegedly gang up on the workers and make them work for a minimum. Or, were it not for his amazing hatred toward Malthus and his theory of population, Marx might have kept wages dismal by virtue of biological conditions of labor supply. The monopoly explanation he did not use, perhaps because he wanted to let capitalism choose its own weapons and assume ruthless competition, and still be able to show it up. Marx tried to demonstrate the same dramatic minimum character of real wages by means of his concept of the "reserve army of the unemployed."

Here is the real Achilles' heel of the Marxian theory of distribution and its implied prophecies of immiserization of the working classes. Under perfect competition, technical change will raise real wages unless the changes are so labor-saving as to raise the rate of maintainable profit immensely; Joan Robinson and others have pointed out how contradictory is Marx's notion that both profit rates and real wages can fall once Marx jettisons Ricardo's emphasis on the scarcity of land and the law of diminishing returns. Marx simply has no *statical* theory of the reserve army. If an appeal is made to a vague dynamic theory of technological displacement or recruitment from the country, close analysis will suggest that Marx (like Mill) was a very bad econometrician of his times, not realizing how much real wages in Western Europe had been raised by new techniques and equipment; and he was a bad theorist because his kind of model would almost certainly lead to shifts in schedules that would raise labor's wages tremendously, in a way more consistent with the 1848 *Communist Manifesto's* paeans of praise for the capitalistic system than with his elaborated writings.[9]

In brief, technical change was gold in giving Marx cyclical insights, and dirt in giving him secular insights or an understanding of evolving equilibrium states. I should warn you that this is my opinion. and that I have always been surprised that I should be a virtual monopolist with respect to this vital analysis.

So far I have been talking about Marx as an economist. And I have been doing my best, subject to truth, to find some merit in him. (You may recall Emerson's neighbor in Concord: when he died the minister tried to find something to say at the funeral eulogy and ended up with, "Well, he was good at laying fires.") Even this represents a resurrection of Marx's reputation. Keynes, for example, was much more typical of our professional attitudes toward Marxism when he dismissed it all as "turbid" nonsense. (In view of the tendency of the radical right—for whom all Chinese look alike—to equate Keynesianism with Marxism, this ironical fact is worth noting; and also its converse, since there is nothing communists deplore more than the notion that capitalism can be kept breathing healthily by the Keynesian palliatives of fiscal and monetary policy.)

Technical economics has little to do with Karl Marx's important role in the history of human thought. It is true that he and his followers felt that their brand of socialism differed from the sentimental brands of the past in that Marxist socialism was scientifically based and, therefore, had about it an inevitability and a special correctness. I need not labor the point before this group that the "science" involved was not that body of information about commercial and productive activity and those methods of analyzing the behavior relations which *we* would call economics. Political economy in our sense of the word was the mere cap of Karl Marx's iceberg. *Marx's bold economic or materialistic theory of history, his political theories of the class struggle, his transmutations of Hegelian philosophy* have an importance for the historian of "ideas" that far transcends his façade of economics.

Finally, one must never make the fatal mistake in the history of ideas of requiring of a notion that it be "true." For that discipline, the slogan must be, "The customer is always right." Its objects are what men have *believed;* and if truth has been left out, so much the

---

[9] If migration from the country kept wages down to a city minimum, then the average wage and living standard of country-*cum*-city would be raised in accordance with the optimization desired by a technocrat—unless, again, Malthusianism is admitted back into the rural hovel.

worse for truth, except for the curiously-undifficult task of explaining why truth does not sell more successfully than anything else. Marx has certainly had more customers than any other one aspiring economist. A billion people think his ideas are important; and for the historian of thought that fact makes them important, in the same way that he would have to regard as diminished in importance the subject of Christianity, were it conceivable that it had been the religion merely of a transitory small group who once occupied the present country of Jordan or the state of New Mexico.

Alfred Marshall. What killed Mill for economists was not the socialism that killed it for Shaw's no-longer-New Woman. The marginalist school of Jevons-Walras-Menger perpetrated the murder. The roster of neoclassical economists would include the names of Böhm-Bawerk from Austria, J. B. Clark from the United States, Pareto from Italy, Wicksteed from England, and Wicksell from Sweden. But, for all that I have said earlier about his overvaluation in the market for reputations, few will doubt that Alfred Marshall of Cambridge is the prototype as *political economist* for this group. Marshall may now be old hat, but in his day he was some headpiece.

Marshall had strong social sympathies. At the same time he realized the harms that precipitate reform may bring. He was the prophet of moderation. If you graft Keynesian models of income determination on his thought and update his Victorianisms, you come close to the median member of this Association. His pupils filled, Foxwell could say by 1888, half the chairs of political economy in the United Kingdom; his influence permeated the other half and, methodologically speaking, today we are all Marshallians in the same sense that we are all higher primates.

But what has been Marshall's role in the history of ideas, the panorama of human thought? Never has he had one-hundredth the notice of, say, Henry George. I remember talking to the aged Frank Taussig at a Harvard Society of Fellows dinner before the war. Taussig quoted in despair a recent remark of John Dewey that Henry George was the greatest economist America had ever produced. George was the whipping boy for the economists just before my time; but within my time as a high school student in the Middle West, you could still find vestigial single-taxers, the old principal of my high school being one and my civics teacher another. George was not original in attacking incomes that come from land; as Foxwell said long ago, nationalizers of land we have always with us. This is understandable from the Hume-Ricardo recognition of rent as a price-determined (rather than price-determining) surplus to a factor in inelastic supply; but, as I have recorded elsewhere, my implicit belief that George gave a good statement of Ricardian rent theory will not stand up after a search through *Progress and Poverty* for suitable quotations to put in an anthology. While the single-tax movement is recognizable today as being adverse to socialism, Henry George's attack on the inequality of property ownership in land was influential in turning many people toward socialism: thus Shaw tells us he became a socialist after hearing Henry George speak in London.[10]

Let us leave aside impact on the *hoi polloi*. What was Marshall's influence over his long life on the educated man of affairs? For years I looked for every trace I could find in books to show that someone other than a professional economist or student had read Marshall. I realize Marshall himself thought he was writing for the businessman; but anyone who looks at the *Principles* will realize that no businessmen in good Queen Victoria's time or since would be likely to find it attractive. (Actually Marshall's literary style is excellent, his graphs are in footnotes, and his rather awkward mathematics is buried in special notes at the end; but all this was to no avail.) I was able to come up essentially with only two bits of evidence, one negative and one positive. Pollock in his letters to Justice Holmes urged him to read Marshall; Holmes, who was a man of the most catholic interests, replied that he had tried it and it was not the dish for him. On the positive side, C.C.N.Y.'s great philosopher, Morris Cohen, reported somewhere that his inclination to be an eclectic in philosophy had received inspiration from Alfred Marshall's eclecticism in economics.

To be sure, Marshall taught at a leading world institution where half the English upper classes received their instruction. But actually he taught at Cambridge little more than 20 years, not very much longer say, than, I have taught at M.I.T. Sixty was a generous number for those who attended his popular lectures, and that was the beginning attendance not the final. As I know from personal conversations with Alfred North Whitehead, Marshall's contemporaries at Cambridge did not like him as a man ("He was a popish man who treated Mary Marshall very badly." "A second class mind?"); and one gets

---

[10] Later Shaw went successively from Marxism to Jevonsism with a Fabian twist. Philip Wicksteed's conversion of Shaw away from Marxism is one of the most amusing and incredible incidents in the history of thought: for once a rational argument changed, or seemed to change, someone's mind.

It must have been on that same trip to England that Henry George debated Alfred Marshall in Oxford: little David beat Goliath, if we can believe the record; in part perhaps because Marshall was a home-boy, and the well-to-do undergraduates of those days started out hostile to George; there is also the fact gleaned from Henry George's biography that he slept miserably on that trip and the night before the debate. Playing the parlor game of Charles Lamb and William Hazlitt as to which characters in history one would like to meet, I would plunk for being present when Alfred Marshall debated Henry George.

the impression from autobiographies of such contemporaries as J. J. Thomson, the discoverer of the electron and Nobel Prize winner, that they had no great opinion of the economics being offered at that time in Cambridge.

IV. *We Happy Few*

If then Marshall and neoclassical writers have had influence upon the affairs of men, and I think they have had pronounced influence, we must regard these influencings as being indirect rather than direct.

For a long time John Maynard Keynes was known for one famous quotation, the casual remark: "In the long run we are all dead." Now that Keynes himself is dead, he is best known for a different quotation:

> . . . the ideas of economists and political philosophers, both when they are right and when they are wrong, are more powerful than is commonly understood. Indeed the world is ruled by little else. Practical men, who believe themselves to be quite exempt from any intellectual influences, are usually the slaves of some defunct economist. Madmen in authority, who hear voices in the air, are distilling their frenzy from some academic scribbler of a few years back. I am sure that the power of vested interests is vastly exaggerated compared with the gradual encroachment of ideas. Not, indeed, immediately, but after a certain interval; for in the field of economic and political philosophy there are not many who are influenced by new theories after they are twenty-five or thirty years of age, so that the ideas which civil servants and politicians and even agitators apply to current events are not likely to be the newest. But, soon or late, it is ideas, not vested interests, which are dangerous for good or evil.

This is fine writing. And no doubt it is flattering to our egos. But is it really true? Keynes did not specify what academic scribblers he had in mind, and I am not sure how easy it would have been for him to do so. (Thus, when we see a politician favoring protective tariffs or a balanced budget, do we have to look for any profound analysis from some earlier thinker or can we not simply reflect that most people generate such notions almost unthinkingly? Yet, even if that is so, what are we to conclude in the case where we observe a politician favoring free trade or deficit-financing? The issue is certainly not a simple one.)

The leaders of this world may seem to be led around through the nose by their economist advisers. But who is pulling and who is pushing? And note this: he who picks his doctor from an array of competing doctors is in a real sense his own doctor. The Prince often gets to hear what he wants to hear.

Where does that leave us then as economists? It leaves us where we ought to be. Our map of the world differs from that of the layman. Perhaps our map will never be a best seller. But a discipline like economics has a logic and validity of its own. We believe in our map because we cannot help doing so. In Frank Ramsey's beautiful quotation from William Blake:

"Truth can never be told so as to be understood and not be believed."

Ours is an uncertain truth and economic scholars are humble about its precision—but our humbleness is built out of knowledge, not out of ignorance.

Not for us is the limelight and the applause. But that doesn't mean the game is not worth the candle or that we do not in the end win the game. In the long run, the economic scholar works for the only coin worth having—our own applause.[11]

[11] Lest I be misunderstood, I elaborate. This is not a plea for "Art for its own sake," "Logical elegance for the sake of elegance." It is not a plea for leaving the real-world problems of political economy to noneconomists. It is not a plea for short-run popularity with members of a narrow in-group. Rather it is a plea for calling shots as they really appear to be (on reflection and after weighing all evidences), even when this means losing popularity with the great audience of men and running against "the spirit of the times."

114

PAUL A. SAMUELSON

The General Theory

[1946]

THE DEATH of Lord Keynes will undoubtedly afford the occasion for numerous attempts to appraise the character of the man and his contribution to economic thought. The personal details of his life and antecedents very properly receive notice elsewhere in this volume.

It is perhaps not too soon to venture upon a brief and tentative appraisal of Keynes' lasting impact upon the development of modern economic analysis. And it is all the more fitting to do so now that his major work has just completed the first decade of its very long life.

THE IMPACT OF THE GENERAL THEORY

I have always considered it a priceless advantage to have been born as an economist prior to 1936 and to have received a thorough grounding in classical economics. It is quite impossible for modern students to realize the full effect of what has been advisably called "The Keynesian Revolution"[1] upon those of us brought up in the orthodox tradition. What beginners today often regard as trite and obvious was to us puzzling, novel, and heretical.

To have been born as an economist before 1936 was a boon— yes. But not to have been born too long before!

> Bliss was it in that dawn to be alive,
> But to be young was very heaven!

The *General Theory* caught most economists under the age of thirty-five with the unexpected virulence of a disease first attacking and decimating an isolated tribe of south sea islanders. Economists

---

[1] I owe much in what follows to discussions with my former student, Dr. Lawrence R. Klein, whose rewarding study published by Macmillan Company bears the above title.

beyond fifty turned out to be quite immune to the ailment. With time, most economists in-between began to run the fever, often without knowing or admitting their condition.

I must confess that my own first reaction to the *General Theory* was not at all like that of Keats on first looking into Chapman's Homer. No silent watcher, I, upon a peak in Darien. My rebellion against its pretensions would have been complete, except for an uneasy realization that I did not at all understand what it was about. And I think I am giving away no secrets when I solemnly aver—upon the basis of vivid personal recollection—that no one else in Cambridge, Massachusetts, really knew what it was about for some twelve to eighteen months after its publication. Indeed, until the appearance of the mathematical models of Meade, Lange, Hicks, and Harrod, there is reason to believe that Keynes himself did not truly understand his own analysis.

Fashion always plays an important role in economic science; new concepts become the mode and then are passé. A cynic might even be tempted to speculate as to whether academic discussion is itself equilibrating: whether assertion, reply, and rejoinder do not represent an oscillating divergent series, in which—to quote Frank Knight's characterization of sociology—"bad talk drives out good."

In this case, gradually and against heavy resistance, the realization grew that the new analysis of *effective demand* associated with the *General Theory* was not to prove such a passing fad, that here indeed was part of "the wave of the future." This impression was confirmed by the rapidity with which English economists, other than those at Cambridge, took up the new gospel: e.g., Harrod, Meade, and others, at Oxford; and, still more surprisingly, the young blades at the London School, like Kaldor, Lerner, and Hicks, who threw off their Hayekian garments and joined in the swim.

In this country it was pretty much the same story. Obviously, exactly the same words cannot be used to describe the analysis of income determination of, say, Lange, Hart, Harris, Ellis, Hansen, Bissell, Haberler, Slichter, J. M. Clark, or myself. And yet the Keynesian taint is unmistakably there upon every one of us.

Instead of burning out like a fad, today, ten years after its birth, the *General Theory* is still gaining adherents and appears to be in business to stay. Many economists who are most vehement in criticism of the specific Keynesian policies—which must always be carefully distinguished from the scientific analysis associated with his name—will never again be the same after passing through his hands.[2]

It has been wisely said that only in terms of a modern theory of effective demand can one understand and defend the so-called classical theory of unemployment. It is perhaps not without additional significance, in appraising the long-run prospects of the Keynesian theories, that no individual, having once embraced the modern analysis, has—as far as I am aware—later returned to the older theories. And in universities, where graduate students are exposed to the old and new income analyses, I am told that it is often only too clear which way the wind blows.

Finally, and perhaps most important from the long-run standpoint, the Keynesian analysis has begun to filter down into the elementary textbooks; and, as everybody knows, once an idea gets into these, however bad it may be, it becomes practically immortal.

THE GENERAL THEORY

Thus far, I have been discussing the new doctrines without regard to their content or merits, as if they were a religion and nothing else. True, we find a gospel, a scriptures, a prophet, disciples, apostles, epigoni, and even a duality; and if there is no apostolic succession, there is at least an apostolic benediction. But by now the joke has worn thin, and it is in any case irrelevant.

The modern saving-investment theory of income determination did not directly displace the old latent belief in Say's Law of Markets (according to which only "frictions" could give rise to unemployment and overproduction). Events of the years following 1929 destroyed the previous economic synthesis. The economists' belief in the orthodox synthesis was not overthrown, but had simply atrophied: it was not as though one's soul had faced a showdown as to the existence of the deity and that faith was unthroned, or even that one had awakened in the morning to find that belief had flown away in the night; rather it was realized with a sense of belated recognition that one no longer had faith, that one had been living without faith for a long time, and that what, after all, was the difference?

The nature of the world did not suddenly change on a black

---

[2] For a striking example of the effect of the Keynesian analysis upon a great classical thinker, compare the fructiferous recent writings of Professor Pigou with his earlier *Theory of Unemployment*.

October day in 1929 so that a new theory became mandatory. Even in their day, the older theories were incomplete and inadequate: in 1815, in 1844, 1893, and 1920. I venture to believe that the eighteenth and nineteenth centuries take on a new aspect when looked back upon from the modern perspective, that a new dimension has been added to the rereading of the mercantilists, Thornton, Malthus, Ricardo, Tooke, David Wells, Marshall, and Wicksell.

Of course, the Great Depression of the thirties was not the first to reveal the untenability of the classical synthesis. The classical philosophy always had its ups and downs along with the great swings of business activity. Each time it had come back. But now for the first time, it was confronted by a competing system—a well-reasoned body of thought containing among other things as many equations as unknowns; in short, like itself, a synthesis; and one which could swallow the classical system as a special case.

A new *system*, that is what requires emphasis. Classical economics could withstand isolated criticism. Theorists can always resist facts; for facts are hard to establish and are always changing anyway, and *ceteris paribus* can be made to absorb a good deal of punishment. Inevitably, at the earliest opportunity, the mind slips back into the old grooves of thought, since analysis is utterly impossible without a frame of reference, a way of thinking about things, or, in short, a theory.[3]

Herein lies the secret of the *General Theory*. It is a badly written book, poorly organized; any layman who, beguiled by the author's previous reputation, bought the book was cheated of his five shillings. It is not well suited for classroom use.[3a] It is arrogant, bad-tempered, polemical, and not overly generous in its acknowledgments. It abounds in mares' nests or confusions: involuntary unemployment, wage units, the equality of savings and investment, the timing of the multiplier, interactions of marginal efficiency upon

---

[3] This tendency holds true of everybody, including the businessman and the politician, the only difference being that practical men think in terms of highly simplified (and often contradictory) theories. It even holds true of a literary economist who would tremble at the sight of a mathematical symbol.

[3a] The dual and confused theory of Keynes and his followers concerning the "equality of savings and investment" unfortunately ruled out the possibility of a pedagogically clear exposition of the theory in terms of schedules of savings and investment determining income.

the rate of interest, forced savings, own rates of interest, and many others. In it the Keynesian system stands out indistinctly, as if the author were hardly aware of its existence or cognizant of its properties; and certainly he is at his worst when expounding its relations to its predecessors. Flashes of insight and intuition intersperse tedious algebra. An awkward definition suddenly gives way to an unforgettable cadenza. When finally mastered, its analysis is found to be obvious and at the same time new. In short, it is a work of genius.

It is not unlikely that future historians of economic thought will conclude that the very obscurity and polemical character of the *General Theory* ultimately served to maximize its long-run influence. Possibly such an analyst will place it in the first rank of theoretical classics, along with the work of Smith, Cournot, and Walras. Certainly, these four books together encompass most of what is vital in the field of economic theory; and only the first is by any standards easy reading or even accessible to the intelligent layman.

In any case, it bears repeating that the *General Theory* is an obscure book, so that would-be anti-Keynesians must assume their position largely on credit unless they are willing to put in a great deal of work and run the risk of seduction in the process. The *General Theory* seems the random notes over a period of years of a gifted man who in his youth gained the whip hand over his publishers by virtue of the acclaim and fortune resulting from the success of his *Economic Consequences of the Peace*.

Like Joyce's *Finnegan's Wake,* the *General Theory* is much in need of a companion volume providing a "skeleton key" and guide to its contents: warning the young and innocent away from Book I (especially the difficult Chapter 3) and on to Books III, IV, and VI. Certainly in its present state, the book does not get itself read from one year to another even by the sympathetic teacher and scholar.

Too much regret should not be attached to the fact that all hope must now be abandoned of an improved second edition, since it is the first edition which would in any case have assumed the stature of a classic. We may still paste into our copies of the *General Theory* certain subsequent Keynesian additions, most particularly the famous chapter in *How to Pay for the War* which first outlined the modern theory of the inflationary process.

This last item helps to dispose of the fallacious belief that Keynesian economics is good "depression economics" and only that. Actually, the Keynesian system is indispensable to an understanding of conditions of over-effective demand and secular exhilaration; so much so that one anti-Keynesian has argued in print that *only* in times of a great war boom do such concepts as the marginal propensity to consume have validity. Perhaps, therefore, it would be more nearly correct to aver the reverse: that certain economists are Keynesian fellow travelers only in boom times, falling off the band wagon in depression.

If time permitted, it would be instructive to contrast the analysis of inflation during the Napoleonic and first World War periods with that of the recent War and correlate this with Keynes' influence. Thus, the "inflationary gap" concept, recently so popular, seems to have been first used around the spring of 1941 in a speech by the British Chancellor of the Exchequer, a speech thought to have been the product of Keynes himself.[4]

No author can complete a survey of Keynesian economics without indulging in that favorite indoor guessing game: wherein lies the essential contribution of the *General Theory* and its distinguishing characteristic from the classical writings? Some consider its novelty to lie in the treatment of the *demand for money,* in its liquidity preference emphasis. Others single out the treatment of *expectations.*

I cannot agree. According to recent trends of thought, the interest rate is less important than Keynes himself believed; therefore, *liquidity preference* (which itself explains part of the lack of importance of the interest rate, but only part) cannot be of such crucial significance. As for expectations, the *General Theory* is brilliant in calling attention to their importance and in suggesting many of the central features of uncertainty and speculation. It paves the way for a theory of expectations, but it hardly provides one.[5]

---

[4] In the present writer's opinion this "neo-Austrian" demand analysis of inflation has, if anything, been overdone; there is reason to suspect that the relaxations of price controls during a period of *insufficient* general demand might still be followed by a considerable, self-sustaining rise in prices.

[5] See Chapter XXXI, [of Seymour Harris, ed., *The New Economics.* Knopf, New York, 1947].

I myself believe the broad significance of the *General Theory* to be in the fact that it provides a relatively realistic, complete system for analyzing the level of effective demand and its fluctuations. More narrowly, I conceive the heart of its contribution to be in that subset of its equations which relate to the propensity to consume and to saving in relation to offsets-to-saving. In addition to linking saving explicitly to income, there is an equally important denial of the implicit "classical" axiom that motivated investment is *indefinitely expansible or contractable,* so that whatever people *try* to save will always be fully invested. It is not important whether we deny this by reason of expectations, interest rate rigidity, investment inelasticity with respect to overall price changes and the interest rate, capital or investment satiation, secular factors of a technological and political nature, or what have you. But it is vital for business-cycle analysis that we do assume definite amounts of investment which are highly variable over time in response to a myriad of exogenous and endogenous factors, *and which are not automatically equilibrated to full-employment saving levels by any internal efficacious economic process.*

With respect to the level of total purchasing power and employment, Keynes denies that there is an *invisible hand* channeling the self-centered action of each individual to the social optimum. This is the sum and substance of his heresy. Again and again through his writings there is to be found the figure of speech that what is needed are certain "rules of the road" and governmental actions, which will benefit everybody, but which nobody by himself is motivated to establish or follow. Left to themselves during depression, people will try to save and only end up lowering society's level of capital formation and saving; during an inflation, apparent self-interest leads everyone to action which only aggravates the malignant upward spiral.

Such a philosophy is profoundly capitalistic in its nature. Its policies are offered "as the only practicable means of avoiding the destruction of existing economic forms in their entirety and as the condition of the successful functioning of individual initiative."[6]

From a perusal of Keynes' writing, I can find no evidence that

---

[6] *General Theory,* p. 380.

words like these resemble the opportunistic lip service paid in much recent social legislation to individual freedom and private enterprise. The following quotations show how far from a radical was this urbane and cosmopolitan provincial English liberal:

> How can I accept [the communistic] doctrine which sets up as its bible, above and beyond criticism, an obsolete economic textbook which I know to be not only scientifically erroneous but without interest or application for the modern world? How can I adopt a creed which, preferring the mud to the fish, exalts the boorish proletariat above the bourgeois and intelligentsia who, with all their faults, are the quality of life and surely carry the seeds of all human advancement. Even if we need a religion, how can we find it in the turbid rubbish of the Red bookshops? It is hard for an educated, decent, intelligent son of Western Europe to find his ideals here, unless he has first suffered some strange and horrid process of conversion which has changed all his values. . . .
>
> So, now that the deeds are done and there is no going back, I should like to give Russia her chance; to help and not to hinder. For how much rather, even after allowing for everything, if I were a Russian, would I contribute my quota of activity to Soviet Russia than to Tsarist Russia.[7]

Nothing that I can find in Keynes' later writings shows any significant changes in his underlying philosophy. As a result of the Great Depression, he becomes increasingly impatient with what he regards as the stupidity of businessmen who do not realize how much their views toward reform harm their own true long-run interests. But that is all.

With respect to international cooperation and autonomy of national policies, Keynes did undergo some changes in belief. The depression accentuated his post-World War I pessimism concerning the advisability of England or any other country's leaving itself to the mercy of the international gold standard. But in the last half dozen years, he began to pin his hopes on intelligent, concerted, multilateral cooperation, with, however, the important proviso that each nation should rarely be forced to adjust her economy by *deflationary* means.

---

[7] J. M. Keynes, *Essays in Persuasion* (1932), pp. 300 and 311.

PORTRAIT OF THE SCIENTIST

There is no danger that historians of thought will fail to devote attention to all the matters already discussed. Science, like capital, grows by accretion, and each scientist's offering at the altar blooms forever. The personal characteristics of the scientist can only be captured while memories are still fresh; and only then, in all honesty, are they of maximum interest and relevance.

In my opinion, nothing in Keynes' previous life or work really quite prepares us for the *General Theory*. In many ways his career may serve as a model and prescription for a youth who aspires to be an economist. First, he was born into an able academic family which breathed in an atmosphere of economics; his father was a distinguished scholar, but not so brilliant as to overshadow and stunt his son's growth.

He early became interested in the philosophical basis of probability theory, thus establishing his reputation young in the technical fields of mathematics and logic. The *Indian Currency and Finance* book and assiduous service as assistant editor and editor of the *Economic Journal* certified to his "solidity" and scholarly craftsmanship. His early reviews, in the *Economic Journal,* of Fisher, Hobson, Mises, and of Bagehot's collected works, gave hints of the brilliance of his later literary style. The hiatus of the next few years in his scientific output is adequately explained by his service in the Treasury during the first World War.

The first extreme departure from an academic career comes, of course, with the Byronic success of the *Economic Consequences of the Peace,* which made him a world celebrity whose very visits to the Continent did not go unnoticed on the foreign exchange markets. As successful head of an insurance company and bursar of King's College, he met the practical men of affairs on their own ground and won the reputation of being an economist who knew how to make money. All this was capped by a solid two-volume *Treatise on Money,* replete with historical accounts of the Mycenean monetary system and the rest. Being a patron of the ballet and theater, a member of the "Bloomsbury set" of Virginia Woolf and Lytton Strachey, a governor of the Bank of England, and peer of the realm simply put the finishing gilt on his portrait.

Why then do I say that the *General Theory* still comes as a surprise? Because in all of these there is a sequence and pattern, and no one step occasions real astonishment. The *General Theory*, however, is a mutant, notwithstanding Keynes' own expressed belief that it represents a "natural evolution" in his own line of thought. Let me turn, therefore, to his intellectual development.

As far back as his 1911 review of Irving Fisher's *Purchasing Power of Money*,[8] Keynes expressed dissatisfaction with a mechanical quantity theory of money, but we have no evidence that he would have replaced it with anything more novel than a Cambridge cash balance approach, amplified by a more detailed treatment of the discount rate. All this, as he would be the first to insist, was very much in the Marshallian oral tradition, and represents a view not very different from that of, say, Hawtrey.

Early in life he keenly realized the obstacles to deflation in a modern capitalistic country and the grief which this process entailed. In consequence of this intuition, he came out roundly against going back to the prewar gold parity. Others held the same view: Rist in France, Cassel in Sweden, *et al.* He was not alone in his insistence, from the present fashionable point of view vastly exaggerated, that central bank discount policy might stabilize business activity; again, compare the position of Gustav Cassel. Despite the auspicious sentence concerning savings and investment in its preface, the *Tract on Monetary Reform* on its analytical side goes little beyond a quantity theory explanation of inflation; while its policy proposals for a nationally managed currency and fluctuating exchange are only distinguished for their political novelty and persuasiveness.

In all of these, there is a consistency of pattern. And in retrospect it is only fair to say that he was on the whole right. Yet this brief account does not present the whole story. In many places, he was wrong. Perhaps a pamphleteer should be judged shotgun rather than rifle fashion, by his absolute hits regardless of misses; still one

---

[8] This is a characteristically "unfair" and unfavorable review, to be compared with Marshall's review of Jevons, which Keynes' biography of Marshall tries weakly to justify. That Keynes' first publication of a few years earlier was a criticism does not astonish us in view of his later writings.

must note that, even when most wrong, he is often most confident and sure of himself.

The *Economic Consequences of the Peace* proceeds from beginning to end on a single premise which history has proved to be false or debatable. Again, he unleashed with a flourish the Malthusian bogey of overpopulation at a time when England and the Western European world were undergoing a population revolution in the opposite direction. In his controversy with Sir William Beveridge on the terms-of-trade between industry and agriculture, besides being wrong in principle and interpretation, he revealed his characteristic weakness for presenting a few hasty, but suggestive, statistics. If it can be said that he was right in his reparations transfer controversy with Ohlin, it is in part for the wrong reasons—reasons which in terms of his later system are seen to be classical as compared to the arguments of Ohlin. Again, at different times he has presented arguments to demonstrate that foreign investment is (1) deflationary, and (2) stimulating to the home economy, without appearing on either occasion to be aware of the opposing arguments.

None of these are of vital importance, but they help to give the flavor of the man. He has been at once soundboard, amplifier, and initiator of contemporary viewpoints, whose strength and weakness lay in his intuition, audaciousness, and changeability. Current quips concerning the latter trait are rather exaggerated, but they are not without provocation. It is quite in keeping with this portrait to be reminded that in the early twenties, before he had an inkling of the *General Theory*, or even the *Treatise*, he scolded Edwin Cannan in no uncertain terms for not recognizing the importance and novelty of modern beliefs as compared to old-fashioned—I might almost have said "classical"—theories.

Where a scientist is concerned, it is not inappropriate, even in a eulogy, to replace the ordinary dictum *nihil nisi bonum* by the criterion *nihil nisi verum*. In all candor, therefore, it is necessary to point out certain limitations—one might almost say weaknesses, were they not so intrinsically linked with his genius—in Keynes' thought.

Perhaps because he was exposed to economics too young, or perhaps because he arrived at maturity in the stultifying backwash of Marshall's influence upon economic theory—for whatever reason,

Keynes seems never to have had any genuine interest in the theory of value and distribution. It is remarkable that so active a brain would have failed to make any contribution to economic theory; and yet except for his discussion of index numbers in Volume I of the *Treatise* and for a few remarks concerning "user cost," which are novel at best only in terminology and emphasis, he seems to have left no mark on pure theory.[9]

Just as there is internal evidence in the *Treatise on Probability* that he early tired of somewhat frustrating basic philosophic speculation, so he seems to have early tired of theory. He gladly "exchanged the tormenting exercises of the foundations of thought and of psychology, where the mind tries to catch its own tail, for the delightful paths of our own most agreeable branch of the moral sciences, in which theory and fact, intuitive imagination and practical judgment, are blended in a manner comfortable to the human intellect" (*Essays in Biography,* pp. 249–50).

In view of his basic antipathy to economic theory, it is all the more wonder, therefore, that he was able to write a biography of Alfred Marshall which Professor Schumpeter has termed one of the best treatments of a master by a pupil.[10] Never were two temperaments more different than those of the two men, and we can be sure that the repressed Victorianism and "popish" personal mannerisms which Keynes found so worthy of reverence in a master and father would have been hardly tolerable in a contemporary.

From Marshall's early influence, no doubt, stems Keynes' antipathy toward the use of mathematical symbols, an antipathy which already appears, surprisingly considering its technical subject, in the early pages of the *Treatise on Probability*. In view of the fact that

---

[9] Indeed, only in connection with Frank Ramsey's article on "A Mathematical Theory of Saving" (EJ, 1928) does he show interest in an esoteric theoretical problem; there he gave a rather intricate interpretation in words of a calculus-of-variations differential equation condition of equilibrium. His reasoning is all the more brilliant—and I say this seriously!—because it is mathematically unrigorous, if not wrong. The importance which Keynes attached to this article is actually exaggerated and can be accounted for only in terms of his paternal feeling toward Ramsey and his own participation in the solution of the problem.

[10] Keynes' discussion of Marshall's monetary theory is much better than his treatment of Marshall's contribution to theory.

mathematical economists were later to make some of the most important contributions to Keynesian economics, his comments on them in the *General Theory* and in the Marshall and Edgeworth biographies merit rereading.[11]

Moreover, there is reason to believe that Keynes' thinking remained fuzzy on one important analytical matter throughout all his days: the relationship between "identity" and functional (or equilibrium-schedule) equality; between "virtual" and observable movements; between causality and concomitance; between tautology and hypothesis. Somewhere, I believe in his early writings, he already falls into the same analytic confusion with respect to the identity of supply and demand for foreign exchange which was later to be his stumbling block with respect to the identity of saving and investment.

Perhaps he was always too busy with the affairs of the world to be able to devote sufficient time for repeated thinking through of certain basic problems. Certainly he was too busy to verify references ("a vain pursuit"). His famous remark that he never learned anything from reading German which he didn't already know would be greeted with incredulity in almost any other science than economics.[12] What he really meant was that his was one of those original minds which never accepts a thing as true and important unless he has already thought it through for himself. Despite his very considerable erudition in certain aspects of the history of thought, there was probably never a more ahistorical scholar than Keynes.

Finally, to fill in the last little touch in this incomplete portrait of an engaging spirit, I should like to present a characteristic quotation from Keynes:

---

[11] Keynes' critical review of Tinbergen's econometric business cycle study for the League of Nations reveals that Keynes did not really have the necessary technical knowledge to understand what he was criticizing. How else are we to interpret such remarks as his assertion that a linear system can never develop oscillations?

[12] Around 1911–15, he was the principal reviewer of German books for EJ; also he must have read—at least he claimed to have—innumerable German works on probability. That he could not speak German with any fluency is well attested by those who heard him once open an English lecture to a German audience with a brief apology in German.

In writing a book of this kind, the author must, if he is to put his point of view clearly, pretend sometimes to a little more conviction than he feels. He must give his own argument a chance, so to speak, nor be too ready to depress its vitality with a wet cloud of doubt.

Is this from the *General Theory*? No. From the *Treatise on Money* or the *Tract*? No and no. Even when writing on so technical a subject as probability, the essential make-up of the man comes through, so that no literary detective can fail to spot his spoor.

THE ROAD TO THE GENERAL THEORY

It was not unnatural for such a man as I have described to wish as he approached fifty to bring together, perhaps as a crowning life work, his intuitions concerning money. Thus the *Treatise* was born. Much of the first volume is substantial and creditable, though hardly exciting. But the fundamental equations which he and the world considered the really novel contribution of the *Treatise* are nothing but a detour and blind alley.

The second volume is the more valuable, but it is so because of the intuitions there expressed concerning bullishness, bearishness, etc. And even these might have been prevented from coming into being by too literal an attempt to squeeze them into the mold of the fundamental equations. Fortunately, Keynes was not sufficiently systematic to carry out such a program.

Before the *Treatise* was completed, its author had already tired of it. Sir Isaac Newton is alleged to have held up publication of his theory for twenty years because of a small discrepancy in numerical calculation. Darwin hoarded his theories for decades in order to collect ever more facts. Not so with our hero: let the presses roll and throw off the grievous weight of a book unborn! Especially since a world falling to pieces is ripe to drop Pollyanna and take up with Cassandra on the rebound.

Perhaps not being systematic proved his salvation. A long line of heretics testifies that he is not the first to have tried to weld intuition into a satisfactory unified theory; not the first to have shot his bolt and failed. But few have escaped from the attempt with their intuition intact and unmarred. In an inexact subject like economics, concepts are not (psychologically) neutral. Decisions based upon ignorance or the equi-probability of the unknown are not invariant under transformation of coordinates or translation of concepts. Simply to define a concept is to reify it, to breathe life in it, to create a predisposition in favor of its constancy; viz., the falling rate of profit and the organic composition of capital, the velocity of circulation of money, the propensity to consume, and the discrepancy between saving and investment.

The danger may be illustrated by a particular instance. Shrewd Edwin Cannan, in characteristic salty prose, throughout the first World War "protested."[13] At first his insights were sharp and incisive, his judgments on the whole correct. But in the summer of 1917, to "escape from an almost unbearable personal sorrow," he undertook to set forth a *systematic* exposition of the theory of money. The transformation of Cinderella's coach at the stroke of twelve is not more sudden than the change in the quality of his thought. Here, I am not so much interested in the fact that his voice becomes shrill, his policies on the whole in retrospect bad—as in the fact that his intuitions were perverted and blunted by his analysis, almost in an irrecoverable way! Not so with Keynes. His constitution was able to throw off the *Treatise* and its fundamental equations.

While Keynes did much for the Great Depression, it is no less true that the Great Depression did much for him. It provided challenge, drama, experimental confirmation. He entered it the sort of man who might be expected to embrace the *General Theory* if it were explained to him. From the previous record, one cannot say more. Before it was over, he had emerged with the prize in hand, the system of thought for which he will be remembered.

Right now I do not intend to speculate in detail on the thought process leading up to this work, but only to throw out a few hints. In the 1929 pamphlet, *Can Lloyd George do it?* written with H. D. Henderson, Keynes set up important hypotheses concerning the effects of public works and investment. It remained for R. F. Kahn, that elusive figure who hides in the prefaces of Cambridge books, to provide the substantiation in his justly famous 1931 *Economic Journal* article, "The Relation of Home Investment to Unemploy-

[13] E. Cannan, *An Economist's Protest* (1927).

ment." Quite naturally the "multiplier" comes in for most attention, which is in a way too bad, since the concept often seems like nothing but a cheap-jack way of getting something for nothing and appears to carry with it a spurious numerical accuracy.

But behind lies the vitally important consumption function: giving the propensity to consume in terms of income; or looked at from the opposite side, specifying the propensity to save. With investment given, as a constant or in the schedule sense, we are in a position to set up the simplest determinate system of underemployment equilibrium—by a "Keynesian savings-investment-income cross" not formally different from the "Marshallian supply-demand-price cross."

Immediately everything falls into place: the recognition that the *attempt* to save may lower income and actually *realized* saving; the fact that a net autonomous increase in investment, foreign balance, government expenditure, consumption will result in increased income *greater* than itself, etc., etc.

Other milestones on the road to Damascus, in addition to the Lloyd George pamphlet and the Kahn article, were Keynes' contributions to a report of the Macmillan Committee[14] and his University of Chicago Harris Foundation lectures on unemployment in the summer of 1931. In these lectures, Keynes has not quite liberated himself from the terminology of the *Treatise* (*vide* his emphasis on "profits"); but the notion of the level of income as being in equilibrium at a low level because of the necessity for savings to be equated to a depressed level of investment is worked out in detail.

From here to the *Means to Prosperity* (1933) is but a step; and from the latter to the *General Theory* but another step. From hindsight and from the standpoint of policy recommendations, each such step is small and in a sense inevitable; but from the standpoint of

---

[14] Young economists who disbelieve in the novelty of the Keynesian analysis, on the ground that no sensible person could ever have thought differently, might with profit read Hawtrey's testimony before the Macmillan Committee, contrasting it with the Kahn article and comparing it with Tooke's famous demonstration in his *History of Prices,* Volume I, that government war expenditures as such cannot possibly cause inflation—*because what the government spends would have been spent anyway, except to the extent of "new money" created.*

having stumbled upon and formulated a new system of analysis, each represents a tremendous stride.

But now I shall have to desist. My panegyric must come to an end with two conflicting quotations from the protean Lord Keynes between which the jury must decide:

> In the long run we are all dead.

> . . . The ideas of economists and political philosophers, both when they are right and when they are wrong, are more powerful than is commonly understood. Indeed, the world is ruled by little else. Practical men, who believe themselves to be quite exempt from any intellectual influences, are usually the slaves of some defunct economist. Madmen in authority, who hear voices in the air, are distilling their frenzy from some academic scribbler of a few years back. I am sure that the power of vested interests is vastly exaggerated compared with the gradual encroachment of ideas . . . Soon or late, it is ideas, not vested interests, which are dangerous for good or evil.[15]

---

[15] *General Theory,* pp. 383–4.

115

A Brief Survey of Post-Keynesian Developments

[1963]

Muᴄʜ ʜᴀs ʜᴀᴘᴘᴇɴᴇᴅ in the quarter century since Keynes published his *General Theory*. What are some of the changes that a second edition might call for? Had he lived Keynes would be eighty today, hard as that is to imagine. And having worked all his life (overworked, according to his friend Bertrand Russell), Keynes might be excused from the chore of preparing a revision—particularly since, for better or worse, the *General Theory* is a classic and even its creator must not tamper with a classic. The pyramids may not be perfect, but they are the most perfect pyramids we shall ever know.

Still Keynes at eighty would be younger than most of us at thirty. Toward the end of his life he declared that, if he had it to do all over again, he would drink more champagne. Heaven protect us from that! As William James said, there are some men who are born with a bottle of champagne to their credit; in the case of Keynes, it must have been a jeroboam. Believing in creative obsolesence, Keynes would not be content to change a few commas and improve a few derivatives. Instead he would write a sequel, which might be entirely new—as different from the *General Theory* as that was from the *Treatise on Money*. The body of economics could not take another such shock in the same century.

In the long run we are *each* dead. And now posterity must take care of itself without the promptings from J. M. Keynes. Very briefly, therefore, I shall give a personal interpretation of some major trends in macroeconomic analysis that have grown out of the *General Theory*.

THE PIGOU EFFECT

The most shocking view in the *General Theory* was the allegation that economic equilibrium need not produce full employment. Economists like Schumpeter found this to be simply incredible. Smith's Invisible Hand was brought under direct attack. This was revolution, not evolution.

What is most shocking in a book is not necessarily most important and lasting. Had Keynes begun his first few chapters with the simple statement that he found it realistic to assume that modern capitalistic societies had money wage rates that were sticky and resistant to downward movements, most of his insights would have remained just as valid—particularly in view of his later discussions that showed how money wage cuts were, apart from interest rate changes, by no means followed by commensurate real wage cuts.

We usually associate with the wartime writings of A. C. Pigou the demonstration that within a Keynesian system full employment can in all probability be fully restored by the following mechanism:

> Let unemployment drive down money wage rates and price levels to, say, one-hundredth of their previous levels; the real

wealth of people embodied in their hard coin, their fiat currency, and [part of] their holdings of government securities would then be one hundred times as great as previously; at the same level of real current income, a man possessed of much real wealth can be expected to want to save less and consume more; hence, this Pigou effect can shift downward the community's real saving schedule enough to make it intersect even a low investment schedule at full employment.

While Pigou, rightly in my opinion, did not consider this mechanism a useful one for policy, it did serve to save face and honor for the believers in the harmony of equilibrium. This was a worthy achievement, purchased at little cost. And now the air was cleared to tackle matters of substance and not of ideology.

Later writers, such as Oskar Lange, Don Patinkin, and Franco Modigliani pursued these issues further.[1] Writers before Pigou, such as Gottfried Haberler, in his *Prosperity and Depression,* had of course anticipated the Pigou effect. Indeed from 1932 to 1936 at Chicago and Harvard I was generally taught that at low enough wages all could get employed, although just exactly what was the general demand curve for labor along which we were to travel was never made clear to me. Here are two instances: I can remember Wassily Leontief saying: "If wages are low enough, this dime in my hand will employ everyone in the nation; and my only requirement on them is that they not show up at my office for work." That was around 1935-6, and, although the term had not yet been invented, I was left with the feeling that some kind of "disguised unemployment" was involved in the Leontief operation. Any student of the quantity theory who had been assigned the works of such a writer as Sir Dennis Robertson had before 1936 the feeling that prices would fall enough so that an irreducible MV could form a full-employment output ratio $Q = MV \div P$. It is noteworthy that Pigou's *Theory of*

---

[1] Space does not permit discussion of the revival of the sophisticated quantity theory of money in recent years by Friedman, Modigliani, and others. Let me only note that in the most abstract model, instead of having the absolute price level be proportional to M narrowly defined, it should be made a homogeneous function of the first degree in the variables (M, GB), where GB is the total of interest-bearing public debt unbacked by public capital assets. If n is the finite average expectancy of human life, the form of the homogeneous function varies with n and many other variables.

Unemployment, written just before the *General Theory* and to which Keynes was partially reacting, did *not* anticipate the Pigou effect. I have long argued that the *General Theory* provided the tools of analysis for classical writers to understand and defend their own views. If only Say, James Mill, and Ricardo had lived after 1936, think of what sense they might have made of Say's Law!

STOCKS AND FLOWS

Much of the *General Theory* is concerned with *flows* of income, with *stock* effects being implicit rather than explicit. (Liquidity preference and money provide an obvious exception.) An important development subsequent to 1936 was to make explicit the role of stocks and to give them increased emphasis. Indeed, the Pigou effect just discussed could be placed under this heading.

Sir Roy Harrod, in his 1936 *Trade Cycle,* had already made explicit the accelerator relationship between capital stock and output flow, foreshadowing his famous 1939 *Economic Journal* article and 1948 book on *Dynamic Economics;* Evsey Domar was led to similar analysis, as were Alvin H. Hansen and myself. Even prior to the *General Theory,* Gustav Cassel had worked with what would today be called Harrod-Domar growth paths, and in the 1935 *Econometrica,* the Hungarian economist Edward Theiss had published a similar model.[2]

Nicholas Kaldor, in a justly famous 1940 *Economic Journal* article, proposed a model of the trade cycle which made investment explicitly a function directly of the level of income and inversely of the stock of capital. This may be considered either as an alternative to the acceleration models; or, as Hollis B. Chenery, Richard M. Goodwin, and others have shown, as a generalization which includes the "tight accelerator" as the special case when investment succeeds in adjusting so rapidly to the discrepancy between actual and desired capital as to lead to a reasonably stable capital-output ratio. From the standpoint of business cycle analysis, the Kaldor model placed

---

[2] Since the *General Theory,* there has grown up a fascination with exponential rates of growth of the Harrod-Domar and J. Robinson type, and which Sir Dennis Robertson had experimented with in the 1920's. Some later remarks touch on these matters but I shall not here attempt a survey of this area.

emphasis on nonlinearity of structure, thereby making possible a theory of determinate *amplitude* of fluctuations. (Harrod had elements of this in the *Trade Cycle;* and my 1939 *Journal of Political Economy* synthesis of accelerator and multiplier had shown how nonlinearity could accomplish this.) Richard M. Goodwin, in numerous articles, lectures, and in a long-awaited book, had explored such nonlinear models in the war and postwar years. The *Trade Cycle* (1950) of J. R. Hicks built on nonlinearity, combining it with exogenous exponential trends.

THEORIES OF THE CONSUMPTION FUNCTION

Most of the stock effects above put emphasis on real capital relationships. At the same time, writers like Franco Modigliani and James Tobin[3] were emphasizing the role of financial wealth effects on the propensity to consume. In particular, Modigliani and Brumberg worked out in detail the implications of a model involving lifetime patterns of saving and consuming. And in recent years American economists have been much interested in Milton Friedman's hypothesis that permanent income (as against transitory income) gets spent in about the same percentage whether its average level is $5,000 or $15,000 per year.

A little background to this discussion may be usefully sketched. Around 1940, Simon Kuznets estimated American consumption and income for the decades going back to 1900. His finding that the ratio of consumption to income did not fall with long-run higher income levels was thought by some to be a deathblow to Keynesianism. However, writers like Hansen had already been insisting on the shift of living standards and consumption propensities through time, having been led to this position by common-sense observation and by comparative budget studies—as for example the 1919 and 1935 evidence on Washington civil servants' saving habits. As Keynes had earlier insisted in controversy with H. Staehle and E. W.

---

[3] I am omitting in this brief survey an important post-1936 development: the analysis of liquidity and general asset preference in terms of attitudes toward uncertainty and probability distributions, associated with the writings of J. Marschak, J. R. Hicks, J. Robinson, H. Markowitz, J. Tobin, F. Modigliani, Musgrave-Domar, A. G. Hart, L. J. Savage, M. Richter, H. Houthakker, P. Cootner, and others.

Gilboy, a straight-line propensity-to-consume schedule was grist for his mill, the only important requirement being that but a fraction of extra income go into consumption spending.

Being a skeptic by nature, I was not willing to go so far as Hansen in postulating a long-run consumption function showing about the same percentage of saving at full employment levels. In Seymour Harris' *Postwar Economic Problems* (1943), I preferred to state: the consumption function shifts upward through time as tastes and habits change and as new consumption items are developed to tempt us; at the same time our full employment potential shifts upward as technical invention and capital formation improve productivity; the fact that these counter trends have about canceled each other out for half a century can be regarded as in the nature of a coincidence, and provides no guarantee of repetition in the future. Despite twenty more years of experience, I incline to pretty much the same opinion, having learned how treacherous are economic "laws" in economic life: e.g., Bowley's Law of constant relative wage share; Long's Law of constant population participation in the labor force; Pareto's Law of unchangeable inequality of incomes; Denison's Law of constant private saving ratio; Colin Clark's Law of a 25 per cent ceiling on government expenditure and taxation; Modigliani's Law of constant wealth-income ratio; Marx's Law of the falling rate of real wage and/ or the falling rate of profit; Everybody's Law of a constant capital-output ratio. If these be laws, Mother Nature is a criminal by nature. Experience has also taught me not to be necessarily suspicious of coincidences; in many cases, even if they do not explain the facts, they do describe the facts, up until they cease to describe the facts.

In the Harris book I pictured the hysteresis loops characteristic of cyclical moves in the production function. In principle, a quick transitory increase in incomes during an upswing might get spent more fully on durable and other goods than might a slow and steady rise to a new level; in principle, the opposite could happen. Turning to the facts, we learn that the latter view is the realistic one: when incomes fluctuate in a cycle, consumption is maintained above the steady-state curve during a downturn and loops back below the curve as recovery takes place. Actually, as pointed out in my diagram, the cyclical loops are shifted upward by the mentioned long-term trend, with all the data averaging out around a quasi-uniform long-run linear consumption path function whose general position depends on a race between improvers of productivity and inventors of new human wants.

James Duesenberry, and at the same time Modigliani, introduced at the war's end the specific mechanism of a "ratchet" to produce these cyclical loops: they hypothesized that the amount consumed out of current income would be affected by the last highest peak of income. This approximation helped explain the facts very well; but neither author would insist that a peak like 1929 would be remembered indefinitely, nor that some kind of a distributed lag with fading memory would be inferior to a simple ratchet.

In connection with the longer-run trends, the Duesenberry insistence on the role that convention and emulation play in determining consumption standards was an important one. He introduced the Veblen-like hypothesis that the fraction of income a man saved depended much upon his percentile rank in the income pyramid of his peer group (whether he be a Negro in Columbus, Ohio, at the top of the income pyramid with $3,000 income in 1935-6, or an executive in Scarsdale, New York with a $12,000 income). W. Fellner and budget analysts had already been led to similar theories.

All these developments are of interest for national policy as well as for history of doctrine. One of the important reasons why so many economists went wrong in the notorious prediction of substantial postwar unemployment was their failure to adjust their consumption functions for (a) the upward shift from the passage of time itself; (b) the war accumulation of liquid wealth; (c) the accumulated backlog of needs and desire; and (d) the lower propensity to save out of permanently higher incomes.

Within the last decade, thanks to the work of Friedman—and also of Margaret Reid and Modigliani—the bolder hypothesis has been promulgated that the average propensity to consume is a constant at all income levels once adjustment for transitory income has been made. Much evidence has been forthcoming consistent with this Permanent Income Hypothesis, as for example abundant demonstrations that transitory income gets saved more than permanent. Since there is nothing in pure theory to make the Permanent Income Hypothesis mandatory or particularly probable, since ordinary experience suggests to me that it is truly harder for a $5,000 year man to save as great a percentage as his brother who (partially through being conditioned to more thrift) enjoys a permanent income of $50,000 a year, and since much of the evidence provides not so much a crucial test of how high and low permanent incomes get spent as a test between transitory and permanent income propensities—for these reasons, I would expect in the end that the verdict will probably be this: there is a slight tendency for the permanent-income consumption relationship for the affluent to involve relatively less saving and savings at comparable years of active adult life; but this difference is much less than differences relating to short-term income fluctuations and to other factors such as family size and those arising from intra-group variation. The fact that so many would like to make a reputation as the refuter of Friedman's permanent-income hypothesis, and yet have made so little progress in denting it, is both a tribute to Friedman and to the empirical usefulness of his approximate hypothesis.

I conclude this discussion of asset effects by the observation that so far surprisingly few behavioral equations have been found from the valuable flow-of-funds data that Professor Morris Copeland and the Federal Reserve System have made available to economists. And when clients ask me to forecast next year's GNP, I go through the motions of computing the asset-effects of stockmarket declines on the propensity to consume, but I find myself in the end estimating C as .93 $\pm$ per cent of expected disposable income with a few adjustments relating to probable auto and durable demand and recent saving trends. An anticlimax?

THE COST-PUSH PROBLEM

As indicated earlier, much of the *General Theory* can be regarded as pretty much independent of the money wage rate. It is not surprising then that the book lacks a developed theory of the wage and price level, even though some sage things are said about their fluctuations. It is a caricature of Keynes to say that wages and prices stay constant until we move the system to full employment; after that point, there is an inflationary gap and we must turn to his *How To Pay For The War* (1939) to describe the resulting demand-pull inflationary process. Yet this caricature is a useful classroom expository model.

Actually, in Professor Richard Kahn's original multiplier article of 1931, he had noted that some of any income expansion will be dissipated in wage increases. And in the book itself, Keynes had followed the Marshallian tradition of assuming statical diminishing returns and rising marginal cost curves; so higher levels of employment could be expected to be associated with higher price levels relative to unchanged wage units. Shortly after the *General Theory* was published, Joan Robinson pointed out that unions and market conditions would cause money wages to rise long before any point of full employment. And associated with the wartime overfull-employment, which so obviously was having its prices restrained by rationing and other fiats, there came the realization—as for example in Lord Beveridge's 1945 *Full Employment in a Free Society*—that high *levels* of employment would be associated not merely with high *levels* of wages and prices but with *rising* wages and prices. How then can a society enjoy simultaneously full employment, price stability, and free markets? This question was asked by Beveridge, by Hansen, and by many others.

We still don't know the answer to it. Although in many years of the immediate postwar period the influence of cost-push or "sellers" inflation had been overstressed relative to conventional demand-pull inflation, there is good reason to fear that America may, along with other lands, suffer from an institutional problem of cost-push. I mean by this that at levels below those corresponding to reasonably full employment, our institutions of wage bargaining and price setting may be such as to lead to a price and wage creep, a creep which can be lessened by conventional depressing of demand by monetary and fiscal policy measures but only at the cost of creating greater unemployment and excess capacity.

Professor Robert M. Solow and I have dramatized this notion by use of the convenient Phillips Curve, named after Professor A. W. Phillips, who correlated English unemployment levels with the percentage rates of wage and price changes. The neoclassical demand models I was brought up on, and also certain simple Keynesian models, will work rather badly if—as Solow and I fear—America has a bad Phillips curve, meaning by "bad" a curve that crosses the axis of price stability only at a high level of unemployment, such as 5 per cent or more. I should add that the Phillips Curve, which involves both supply and demand and all kinds of institutional elements, is itself a slippery concept and we do not explain much by using it. But the first duty of an economist is to describe correctly what is out there: a valid description without a deeper explanation is worth a thousand times more than a clever explanation of nonexistent facts.

How can one get a better Phillips Curve? Conservatives say, "Treat labor rough. Legislate and prosecute. Bargain hard. And run a low-pressure economy in the hope that keeping unemployment high will reduce price pressure and perhaps shift the Phillips Curve itself gradually downward. And if that doesn't materialize, forego high employment." Radicals say, "Use direct price and wage controls. Don't believe that these are inefficient or will soon become inefficient. Don't believe that these involve undue interferences with natural freedom. Or, if they do involve some of these various evils, still this is the cost we must pay for reasonable prosperity and stability." Optimists in between say, "Be clever. Think up new devices which preserve freedom, prosperity, and price stability." The late Sumner Slichter said: "If some price creep is the price we must pay for growth and prosperity, and perhaps it often is, then it is the lesser evil to pay this price; nor is it true that every price creep must turn into a trot."

After looking at Dutch, Swedish, British, Italian, German, Canadian, and American experience, I leave all this as an open question.[4]

THE NEOCLASSICAL SYNTHESIS

The postwar preoccupation with economic development and growth represents no particular departure from the thinking of Keynes. In his 1937 *Eugenics Review* article "The Economic Consequences of a Declining Population," Keynes was already aware of the effects associated with different exponential rates of natural growth. Hansen's prewar hypothesis of secular stagnation was based upon similar elements.

In the 1950's there grew up a new emphasis on models of capital

---

[4] Bent Hansen, *A Study in the Theory of Inflation*, (1951) put valuable emphasis on the interactions between demands in factor and commodity markets. When E. S. Phelps pointed out to me the omission of continental names in this survey, I had no answer to give him. Had I been reviewing econometric investigations since Keynes, names like that of Jan Tinbergen would have received attention.

accumulation and technical change. Some of this involved as much microanalysis as macroanalysis. Particularly in the writings of such American economists as Solow, Tobin, and myself, attention was focused on a managed economy which through skillful use of fiscal and monetary policy channeled the Keynesian forces of effective demand into behaving like a neoclassical model. All this can be found in all but the first two editions of my elementary textbook, in Tobin's *Journal of Political Economy* article of 1955, in T. Swan's *Economic Review* article of 1956, and in Solow's *Quarterly Journal of Economics* article of 1956. Whether couched in terms of an oversimplified Frank Ramsey model of capital or more elaborately, these involved departures from the special "depression version" of the Keynesian system in which making credit cheaper and more easily available could have no substantial effect on investment spending because of either a liquidity trap floor on interest due to liquidity preference or a virtually inelastic schedule of the marginal efficiency of investment. I cannot honestly say that Keynes would have disapproved of such a model: there is considerable evidence, even up to his last years, that he had some confidence in coaxing out new investment by a genuine decrease in *long-term* interest rates. Certainly some members of the Keynesian camp would disapprove of these doctrines. Still, I do not want to make anything of the distinction between the views of Keynes and some of his followers, because it is not a very operational distinction and it reminds one rather unpleasantly of the easy tendency to say, "Franco is not so bad, it is just the men around him," or "President Kennedy is a sound fellow, but you had better watch out for Dr. Heller."

One of the consequences of the neoclassical synthesis was the sanguine hope that a modern society could increase its rate of growth at full employment by coaxing out a deepening of capital through expansionary monetary policy, while using an austere enough fiscal policy to prevent demand-pull inflation. These combined devices could, in effect, lower the share of full employment income going to consumption and yet not jeopardize full employment itself.

Of course this mechanism presupposes that there is no fixity of the capital output ratio. Many American economists, like Hansen, Gerhard Colm, and Robert Eisner, have questioned the practical validity of this hypothesis. They would perhaps point to the sluggishness of capital formation following the 1956-7 equipment boom as evidence that any deepening of capital contrived in the short run is unlikely to be sustainable and will tend to be followed by such investment sluggishness. A final judgment is not yet possible. Chronic deficits in America's international balance of payments have inhibited the use of expansionary monetary policy and so a test case has not been possible.

Even greater hostility toward the neoclassical synthesis would be encountered among English economists. The Radcliffe Report, despite its emphasis upon something called liquidity, shows that the academic Establishment is skeptical about the efficacy of monetary policy to bring about a deepening of capital or a significant stabilization of activity.

Often in our field controversial issues that are conceptually independent get linked together in professional debates. Thus, the neoclassical synthesis that I have described above has nothing intrinsically to do with the approximate validity of econometric investigations that, like those of Solow, employ the concept of an aggregate of real capital. Yet it is a good bet that a Cambridge economist who distrusts Solow's use of aggregates will also happen to be dubious about the possibility of inducing a deepening of capital. Similarly, those who think that marginal productivity notions have little bearing on trends in the distribution of income are likely to be skeptical of an elaborate neoclassical model involving thousands of heterogeneous physical capital processes.

Disagreements like these among economists do not arise solely out of the internal logic of professional discussion. Events in the real world have an unmistakable influence. As an example of this, consider a remark made by Harry Johnson in his Invited Lecture before the American Economic Association at the St. Louis convention in December 1960. His oral statement that nobody takes seriously any more the problem of stagnation or underconsumption was received with some lifting of eyebrows, not so much because people disbelieved in elaborate models that could provide full employment no matter what level was prescribed for the propensity to consume, as that many economists shared with the public a concern over the apparent sluggishness of the American economy since the mid-fifties; and, of course, events in the last two years have accentuated the concern over sluggish labor markets and lagging growth.

KALDORISM VERSUS KEYNESIANISM

As an American I find it a little ironic that just in the decade when our problems of unemployment have seemingly become chronic, Nicholas Kaldor has been reverting to a theory of full employment. Had an obscure economist in Tennessee put forth such a notion, worshippers at Keynes' shrine might have been expected to greet it with indifference or laughter; and, if for some reason the world had begun to take such notions seriously, I should have expected them to be regarded as anti-Keynesian. Kaldor, however, has as much a right to interpret Keynes as any single person—and I understand it to be his claim that the full-employment notions of the *Treatise* are, after all, superior to the retrogressive notions of the *General Theory*. But far from being branded in Cambridge as a renegade, Kalor is apparently orthodox in having an equilibrating theory of income distribution. Kahn, Robinson, and Pasinetti would apparently adhere to somewhat similar notions and regard them as generalizations of the *General Theory,* as can be gleaned from various passages in Robinson's *The Accumulation of Capital* (1956) and various journal articles.

Earlier than these Cambridge publications, Kenneth Boulding's *A Reconstruction of Economics* (1950) and Frank Hahn's macroeconomic theory of "Share of Wages in the National Income" in the 1951 *Oxford Economic Papers,* had looked for the key to income distribution outside neoclassical formulations; pretty much as a lone wolf, Sidney Weintraub has also been formulating macroeconomic theories of income distribution. Since there is ample evidence that all of these thinkers have been pursuing their investigations for a considerable period of time, the dates of these various contributions are of no particular interest. My reason for concentrating on Kaldor's particular formulation is that he very clearly adheres to a theory of full employment brought about by equilibrating shifts in the distribution of income; and on this occasion I am not concerned with the merits or demerits of a macroeconomic versus neoclassical theory of distribution, but rather with developments in employment analysis since the *General Theory*.

The usual Kaldor formulation involves the setting out of certain identities. Then there is set up a factual hypothesis concerning the propensity of profit receivers to save a larger fraction of their incremental incomes than do poor wage receivers. Finally, the Keynesian schedule of the marginal efficiency of investment is assumed to be vertical and subject to purely autonomous shiftings. There is nothing in this that a typical Keynesian would want to quarrel with, although many Keynesians would consider it more realistic to suppose that a point on the marginal efficiency schedule is a function of such variables as capital stock, credit availability, income levels and growth, *and* of profit and interest rates, and internal cash flows.

The new element in Kaldor is the implicit or explicit behavior equation which says that the aggregate of profit or the ratio of profit to income can be expected to fall so long as actual employment is less than full employment. For brevity, I write down the Kaldor system in two symbolic equations, involving autonomous investment, $\bar{I}(t)$; desired saving S; the actual level of income and employment, Y, and the full-employment level Y^*; the ratio of profits to income, $\pi =$ profit/income, which is of course $1-($wage bill/income$)$.

(1) $\quad S(Y,\pi) = \bar{I}(t)$, where $\partial S/\partial Y > 0$ and $\partial S/\partial \pi > 0$

(2) $\quad \dfrac{d\pi}{dt} = K(Y - Y^*)$, where $K(0) = 0$ and $K' > 0$

This last behavior equation involving the function identified by the honorific symbol K is a Kaldor innovation and is quite necessary if this system is to lead to full-employment equilibrium. Conversely, provided $\partial S/\partial \pi$ is empirically sufficiently large,[5] the system can be shown to be unique and stable.

I have had eight years now to study the empirical validity of Kaldor's basic equation (2) and I cannot find telling evidence in its

---

[5] An important post-Keynesian development I have not mentioned is the apparent tendency of some part of corporate earnings and cash flow to go into investment spending endogenously. E. Kuh and J. Meyer in *The Investment Decision: An Empirical Study* (1957) have found American evidence for this. If there is a positive marginal propensity to invest out of profits, this will serve to attenuate and even possibly to reverse the sign of $\partial S/\partial \pi$, where S in (1) is now given the interpretation of a general leakage, with negative endogenous investment being contained in it. In the case where all profits are automatically reinvested endogenously—admittedly an extreme, unrealistic case—we have something like the balanced-budget multiplier theorem of J. Gelting, Hansen, William Salant, Kaldor, myself, and wartime budget speeches prepared for the Chancellor by

favor. Indeed our unemployment rates at persistent 6 per cent levels over half a dozen years suggest that to whatever economic system it may apply, it does not apply to American capitalism. The mechanism of Jean Baptiste Kaldor seems to involve an extremely invisible Invisible Hand. In particular one should not mistake the common-sense tendency of corporate profits to fall sharply when businessmen experience a drop in sales that they had not counted upon when contracting their overhead expenses, for the strong Kaldor equation (2). The empirical validity of the one does not testify to the validity of the other.

If only the Kaldor syllogisms were empirically valid, how nice the world would be. Raising labor's share in the national income would be child's play. By following an austere budget policy of surplus financing, which even the late Montagu Norman would consider orthodox, you could introduce an additive constant on the left-hand side of equation (1) which would be sufficient to squeeze profits down to a much reduced level. Who believes that possible? Anyone who subscribes to the above Kaldorian system should.

Having rejected Kaldor's central doctrine of employment-equilibrating relative income shares, I hope it will not seem patronizing to express approval of his attempt, considerably prior to Kenneth J. Arrow's *Review of Economic Studies* (1962) paper, to relate technical change to the history of the investment process itself; and of his attempt to build a theory of a liquidity trap not at a gilt-edge floor of, say, 1 per cent interest, but at a minimum profit level of, say, 8 or 10 per cent, below which risky investment may have to be coaxed out by new policy measures. While neither of these insights seems to me to be crucially dependent on non-neoclassical lines of analysis, that may be merely a matter of taste and interpretation or may reflect my personal blindness.

Keynes. In this extreme case, (1) determines nonprofit income uniquely as a function of exogenous investment alone, being quite independent of (2). Here, $\partial S / \partial \pi$ is definitely negative; the system will not return to full employment but will diverge endlessly in either direction away from it. It is easy to find the less extreme critical value for the Kuh-Meyer coefficient which will cause the Kaldor system to break down. This footnote is not to be regarded as a criticism of his system.

Time does not permit me to go farther into all these matters. I trust that any reader will agree with the statement of Keynes that scribblers do continue to have an influence after they are dead—sane ones as well as mad.

SUPPLEMENTAL REFERENCES

J. S. Duesenberry, *Income, Savings, and the Theory of Consumer Behavior* (1949).

R. Eisner, "On Growth Models and the Neoclassical Resurgence" *Economic Journal* (1958); James Tobin, "Reply to Professor Eisner" *Economic Journal* (1959); Robert Solow "Is Factor Substitution a Crime, and if so, How Bad? Reply to Professor Eisner" *Economic Journal* (1959).

M. Friedman, *A Theory of the Consumption Function* (1957).

R. M. Goodwin "The Business Cycle as a Self-Sustaining Oscillation" *Econometrica* (1949); and "The Nonlinear Accelerator and the Persistence of Business Cycles" *Econometrica* (1951); see also Chapter 22 of A. H. Hansen, *Business Cycles and National Income* (1951).

R. F. Kahn, "Exercises in the Analysis of Growth," *Oxford Economic Papers* (1959).

N. Kaldor, "Alternative Theories of Distribution," *Review of Economic Studies* (1955-56); *Essays on Economic Stability and Growth* (1960); *Essays on Value and Distribution* (1960); *Essays on Economic Policy* (1962).

S. Kuznets, *National Income: A Summary of Findings* (1946).

Franco Modigliani (and Albert Ando), "The 'Life Cycle' Hypothesis of Saving," *American Economic Review* (March 1963) discusses and gives references to earlier work by R. Brumberg and Modigliani, and by Modigliani.

L. Pasinetti, "Rate of Profit and Income Distribution in Relation to the Rate of Economic Growth" *Review of Economic Studies* (1962).

Don Patinkin, *Money, Interest, and Prices* (1956) gives references to earlier work by himself, Lange, and Pigou.

A. W. Phillips, "The Relations Between Unemployment and the Rate of Change of Money Wage Rates in the United Kingdom 1861-1957," *Economica* (1958).

A. C. Pigou, *Employment and Equilibrium* (1941). This has hidden in it the Pigou effect, prior to Pigou's wartime papers' explicit application of it to short-term equilibrium. See also Pigou, *Keynes' General Theory* (1951), an admission of error and of admiration almost without precedent in the history of any science.

P. A. Samuelson, "The New Look in Tax and Fiscal Policy" *Joint Economic Committee Compendium* (1956); also reproduced in E. S. Phelps, ed., *The Goal of Economic Growth* (1962); P. A. Samuelson and R. M. Solow, "Analytic Aspects of Anti-Inflation Policy" *American Economic Review* (1960).

R. M. Solow, "Technical Change and the Aggregate Production Function" *Review of Economics and Statistics* (1957); and "Investment and Technical Progress" K. Arrow, Karlin, and Suppes (ed.), *Mathematical Methods in the Social Sciences, 1959* (1960).

116

SCHUMPETER AS A TEACHER AND ECONOMIC THEORIST

Paul A. Samuelson

THERE were many Schumpeters: the brilliant *enfant terrible* of the Austrian School who before the age of thirty had written two great books; the young Cairo lawyer with a stable of horses; the Austrian Finance-Minister; the social philosopher and prophet of capitalist development; the historian of economic doctrine; the economic theorist espousing use of more exact methods and tools of reasoning; the teacher of economics.

From the long-term viewpoint the first of these roles is the most important. Schumpeter will unquestionably be labeled by future historians of thought as a business-cycle theorist who placed primary stress on the role of the innovator. Of this he was well aware. He always remained faithful to his youthful vision, not only because of its intrinsic merits, but also — I venture to think — because he was too self-conscious an artist to let old age clutter up the aesthetic life line laid down by the genius of youth.

But enough will be written of this long-term contribution of Schumpeter. Here I should like to concentrate on Schumpeter as a teacher, and on Schumpeter as a patron of economic theory. It was in these two capacities that I knew him best. But aside from that, you might say of Schumpeter that, although he had an absolute advantage both as a scholar and a personality, his comparative advantage was if anything almost greater as a personality. His books speak for themselves but only his pupils can recapture the impact of his colorful personality.

II

I saw Schumpeter for the first time at the 1934 Christmas meetings of economists in Chicago when, as an undergraduate, I accidentally walked in on a meeting where he was speaking. I saw him for the last time at the 1949 New York meetings, where in marvelous form he was expounding good sense about the Walrasian theory of money and bringing life back to an audience wilted by two hours of confusing technical discourse. The intervening fifteen years constituted almost half my lifetime — the important years according to Schumpeter's strong view on the biology of scholars. For Schumpeter these same fifteen years constituted less than a quarter of his life-span; and it is remarkable in view of his own theories on the aging of the creative impulse that they did not represent an anticlimax to his career.

This was the period of his two-volume *Business Cycles*, of his *Capitalism, Socialism, and Democracy*, and of his yet-to-be-published *History of Economic Analysis*. A grand work on economic theory was part of his plan: a work on Money, and a separate volume on Banking; a book on mathematical logic for his old age, his seventies. And as relaxation for really old age, he spoke of writing a sociological novel in his eighties. He even once did field work on the latter: after a long and rather tiring walk, Mrs. Schumpeter with some difficulty persuaded him to ride on the subway back to Harvard Square. This, he reported, had been a very interesting experience; and what was more, when he came to write his sociological novel, he was going to do it again.

Professor Smithies, who knew him much more intimately than I ever did, has indicated in his obituary essay the importance in Schumpeter's life of having been born in the closing era of the Austro-Hungarian empire. With the disappearance of that world, he became completely qualified to play the important sociological role of the alienated stranger. The America of Mickey Rooney and coca-cola he knew almost nothing about; in 1913, while at Columbia, he first saw a football game, and that was enough to last him the rest of his life; if anything, he went out of his way to exaggerate his naïveté with respect to all such matters.

As a judge of short-term events, this could not help but prove a serious handicap; in compensation, his long-term view may have gained.

On the psychological side, Schumpeter's was a temperament not uncommon among gifted minds, and perhaps peculiarly characteristic of those who have been precocious in their youth. Obviously, he was ambitious to make his mark and it was no accident that the figure of the innovator should have intrinsically appealed to him. There was in him a consciousnes of great powers, and this served as an irritant urging him toward creative activity. Moreover, this was not an irritant that ceased to operate on weekends and holidays; I don't suppose that he ever crossed the Atlantic without spoiling the trip by taking along a book on tensor calculus or partial differential equations, which inevitably he succeeded neither in reading nor ignoring.

This feeling of great personal powers was of course of tremendous importance in connection with his professional work. It also showed itself in every aspect of his life: he was quite prepared to talk expertly on anything from Etruscan Art to medieval law; to read, or feel that he could read, Italian, Dutch, and Scandinavian; to outline a theory of metaphysics. This lack of inhibition was extremely important in giving him the freedom to make daring and interesting sociological hypotheses concerning phenomena on the fringes of politics and economics.

The one field in which he did show real humility was in connection with mathematics — a statement that may seem surprising to some. It is true that he never tired of pointing out to the non-mathematical the virtues for economics of mathematics. It is also true that he would often refer with a wave of his hand to quite difficult problems as if they were elementary and easy. But nonetheless he was quite aware of his own lack of facility with mathematics and cheerfully admitted the difficulties he had in mastering and retaining mathematical techniques.

I think to the end he regarded it as a slightly mystical fact that a mixed-difference-differential equation of the Frisch-Tinbergen type involves complex exponentials which in a miraculous manner give rise to sinusoidal periodicities. He waited eagerly (the uncharitable might almost say credulously) for some new mathematical method to turn up that would solve the mysteries of the ages: the tensor calculus, linear operators, symbolic logic, etc.

Moreover, it was his conviction that mathematics itself had grown up as a servant of physics and was not adapted to economics; so that real progress in economic theory would require new methods tailor-made to economics. In this expectation he foreshadowed in a sense what actually came to pass in the von Neumann-Morgenstern *Theory of Games*, which dispenses completely with the tools of modern mathematical physics and falls back upon the more fundamental notions of point-set theory and topology. Schumpeter held this expectation all the more confidently because of his conviction that the processes of logical thought had themselves been biologically developed in the human species as the result of a Darwinian process in which man had to learn to solve successfully the *economic* problems of living: Schumpeter expected therefore that logic and economics would turn out to be closely interrelated. Such an inference may have a slightly far-fetched flavor but it illustrates the character of his speculations. It is not unrelated to Schumpeter's views concerning the naturalness of econometrics: in an early issue of *Econometrica*, he argued that the economic marketplace is by its nature concerned with monetary magnitudes of a measurable sort so that while other disciplines may gradually feel their way toward exact quantitative analysis, economics has this problem thrust upon it from the very beginning.

Call this faith of Schumpeter's naïve if you will. Still it was a beautiful thing to see. And it kept him young. Every scholar, as he grows in years, experience, and judiciousness, faces two insidious enemies which in the end usually take over: disillusioned skepticism and loss of enthusiasm. Schumpeter held these at bay. Only in the last year of his life did Schumpeter express before the National Bureau of Economic Research Conference on Business Cycles the view that mathematical models in business-cycle research had been relatively sterile: that as between the alternative methods of cycle research, (1) theoretical, (2) statistical, and (3) historical, the last was by far the most important. It is not necessary here to ask whether there is any antithesis between these alternative methods, whether there is not one single problem of empirical induction which is necessarily to be attacked by means of hypothesis formation and abstraction so that (2) and (3) are methodologically indistinguishable in principle and both inseparably intertwined with (1), with the only real issue being the pragmatic one of degree. The only point of the incident is that it represents one of those rare occasions when Schumpeter gave what was from his viewpoint "comfort to the enemy." For the real enemy to him was first and foremost those who opposed — and I now employ the words uttered a thousand times by him in the classroom — "the use of exact methods in economic analysis." [1]

Patron of mathematical economists is perhaps the best way of describing his rôle. He was quite the opposite of those celebrated scholars who rarely make an error and who instill in their best students an inferiority complex. Schumpeter's very imperfections gave hope and drive to his students.

Conscious of his scholarly achievements outside of mathematical economics, he very wisely refused to make small contributions to this field. Subconsciously he may have realized that the last part of the 19th century was a bad time for a theorist to be born. It was either too late or too soon — too late to lead the pack in the 1870 "revolution," and too soon to participate fully in the post-1925 era. In Austria, England, and America the first quarter of the 20th century proved fairly arid for economic theory.

However, if a bad time for theory, the first years of this century were tremendously fertile for trade-cycle analysis, culminating around the beginning of World War I in a series of brilliant studies by Spiethoff, Schumpeter, Aftalion, Mitchell, Hawtrey, and Robertson. Primarily as a pioneer in this development will Schumpeter be remembered.

[1] Aside from the merits of Schumpeter's view, I do not think we have to invoke old age as an explanation for this uncharacteristic performance. He loved to oppose the popular side; and in the Cowles Commission, I respectfully suggest, he met a faith not less fervent than his own, thereby reversing completely his usual motivation.

III

Let me turn to Schumpeter as a teacher. Schumpeter was a great showman. In all probability he spoke before more economists the world over than any other scholar in history, so I do not have to try to describe his manner. But good as was his average performance, he was really at his best in his own classroom. I don't suppose that ever in his life he *read* a paper in the literal sense. He spoke from notes only very rarely. On really serious occasions, such as his Presidential Address at the 1948 Meetings, he was in a sense caught between stools and his best spontaneous speaking was inhibited.

What his German speech was like I cannot judge. His English was, of course, easy, grammatical, and flowery; but with an accent that was *sui generis*. On that occasion at the 1934 meetings referred to above, he was quite incomprehensible to one who had never been out of the Middle West. On every subsequent occasion my ear seemed to have acquired the proper key so that I never again had the slightest difficulty. This experience, however, seems to have been quite typical.

Schumpeter liked to talk too well to be at his best in leading a small seminar. He loved to lecture! And to large audiences. If left to himself, he would probably have swallowed up imperialistically all fields of economics and lectured on all subjects. At Harvard, I dare to think, he was not left to himself in this respect; but, nonetheless, for the semester after his death he had been scheduled to give a course on Economic Theory, one on History of Economic Thought, and one on Socialism — and all this when he was past the age of retirement!

In 1935 when he first took over Taussig's famous Ec-11, the basic Harvard graduate course in economic theory, the class met at 2 o'clock in Emerson Hall. After, and not before, the students had assembled for the class hour, in would walk Schumpeter, remove hat, gloves, and topcoat with sweeping gestures, and begin the day's business. Clothes were important to him: he wore a variety of well-tailored tweeds with carefully matched shirt, tie, hose, and handkerchief. My wife used to keep track in that period of the cyclic reappearance of the seemingly infinite number of combinations in his wardrobe: the cycle was not simple and it was far from random.

The hour after lunch is the most dangerous of all to the lecturer, but no one ever felt tempted to enjoy a siesta in his class. Humor always eludes description and defies analysis. In Schumpeter's case it is clear that he never told jokes and had no prepared-in-advance booby traps; he was never dead-pan and ingenuous, but somehow made the class itself seem witty, so that even earnest Radcliffe students felt themselves to be engaging in brilliant sortie and repartée. He was free of the congenital vice of the veteran college professor: he never repeated his stories, as I know from careful count kept over a span of years. Only after some years of teaching have I learned to appreciate the real significance of this.

I do not know what the effect has been of the postwar flood of graduate students, but back in the 1930's his typical class was about 50 in number. He did not lecture in the strict European sense of a unilateral monologue. He called on people in the class, and he was constantly interrupted by his audience. If anything, he tolerated too many interruptions from grade-chasers, fools, and exhibitionists. In the beginning years when he was carrying on Taussig's famous course, he aimed particularly at carrying on the Socratic method of Taussig.

This requires some explanation, which I offer with some diffidence since I was the very first of the post-Taussig generation. The year 1935–36, my first at Harvard, was also the first year of the age of Schumpeter: Taussig had given one half of Ec-11 the previous year; Bullock too had just finished his last course; Gay had still one more year to go; and Carver was long-since emeritus. The Socratic method of teaching, which Taussig had perfected to its highest art, had tremendous prestige and was universally imitated — even down to the rawest instructor in elementary economics.

What did it consist of? For one thing, the teacher never presented the answers to questions to the student. The student was supposed to work out all answers by himself, but he was never to be told whether he had or had not arrived at the correct answer. Furthermore, different members of the class were called upon to discuss the question at issue, and it was part of Taussig's greatness that he would plan out his campaign in advance, knowing exactly who could be counted on to give the appropriate stupid reply and who must be avoided lest he give the show away. Taussig, himself, was a rather austere gentleman of the old school so that most of the class sat in fear and trembling until he had announced his immediate victim, whereupon all the rest relaxed to enjoy the fun.

All this is of course grossly over-simplified and not a balanced view of the method, but it will suffice for the present purpose. What shall we conclude about the Socratic method? That it represented a performance of consummate skill and artistry on the part of Taussig, none can deny; and, apparently, those who went through it had an unforgettable experience. It is equally clear that in the hands of most teachers — and not just beginners — it was a disastrous method: disastrous both to students and teacher. Moreover, even at its best it was not — and here I am expressing my own opinion — a very good method for teaching graduate economic theory of the modern type. If you believed as Taussig did that economics consisted of a few great thorny problems — such as "the" index-number problem, "the" problem of value, etc. — that no one had ever solved and that no one ever would solve, but concerning which there were a number of aspects to be explored along the lines laid out by Ricardo and others — then it was a good method. You never got anywhere very fast, but since there was nowhere to get to anyway it didn't really matter very much, just so long as you had a good ride through the traditional back-country.

All this that I am saying is, I realize, heresy. I have never said it before, but I have thought it; and so too did many of the people of my generation, who had constantly thrown at them the almost-mystic accounts of the Taussigian method, which none could describe but to the excellence of which all testified.[2]

[2] I am the more emboldened to say it because once when Taussig was a dinner guest at the Society of Fellows, a year or two before his death, he told me that in his own opinion his economic theory course had not, since the time of the First World War, been very good. Caught up in war-time duties, he felt himself getting out of touch with developments in economic theory; and being about 60 years old at the war's end, he preferred to throw himself into International Trade rather than pick up the modern theoretical developments.

Schumpeter was perhaps not at his best in conducting a first course in graduate economic theory, and after two or three years he confined himself to more advanced courses. For one thing, he was considered too difficult for an important fraction of the class, many of whom had scarcely heard of Marshall and J. B. Clark before coming to Harvard, to say nothing of Pigou or Frisch. Aside from the intrinsic difficulties of economic theory, there was the added fact that Schumpeter darted about, "opening doors" on new theories and topics. Furthermore, he was addicted to the cardinal vice of introducing mathematical symbols into the economic classroom; and it must be confessed that his blackboard equations were not a model of neatness. Sometimes we spent half an hour looking for a lost Walrasian equation or getting rid of a redundant one.

I have said that he was consistently amusing and in a way that counted against him. Whereas he never gave a lecture that a one-day visitor would have found dull, the regular class attendant became a little numbed and jaded and began to wish for a little more systematic instruction. At the time I was a fairly conscientious note taker, but I find not infrequently in my class notes the following type of entry for a full hour's lecture:

A. Particular Expenses curve: Array (cumulative) of average cost curves of different firms. It is not a supply curve.

And that is all.

But now that I have stated the case against him, let me restore the balance. His 1935 theory course more nearly resembled the courses now being given in every graduate school than did any course then being given in America, excellent as were many of the contemporaneous courses. He took you out of the flat dull textbook world and into the three dimensional world of living economics and economists; his enthusiasm over the latest article to appear in the *Review of Economic Studies* on the elasticity of substitution was real and catching. In the last analysis, the poor students were the ones who were critical. The good ones — and in the long perspective isn't it they who primarily matter? — found his course the most valuable of all. I believe it was David McCord Wright who once summed up the general re-

action: a year or two after taking Schumpeter's course, you began to appreciate what you had got.

The subject matter of his 1935–36 Ec-11 course was excellent. It involved readings in Marshall, Wicksell, Pigou, Böhm-Bawerk, Knight, and Wicksteed. In addition, much was made of Chamberlin, Robinson, and current journal articles by Hicks, Harrod, Sraffa, and others. Such advanced authors as Cournot, Edgeworth, and Hotelling were at least sampled. The "Cost Controversy" was, understandably for the time, given great weight — probably too much weight we would now say. Monopolistic competition received a great deal of attention, as one could expect from the time. The order of topics was: The Individual Firm, Industry, Monopolistic Competition, General Equilibrium, Marginal Productivity (including capital theory), Welfare Economics (which he never got to by the year's end). In awarding final grades, he completely depreciated the currency by his liberality, as has become legendary.

Curiously enough, he rarely mentioned his own theories. The nature of entrepreneurship and profits was discussed; but only once did I hear him discuss the reasons why the interest rate would be zero in a stationary state, and then only in an advanced seminar and under heavy pressure from Paul Sweezy and others.

Although he departed from the practice of his teacher Böhm-Bawerk, in that he rarely bothered to answer criticisms alleging the impossibility of a zero rate of interest, he never abandoned his early views.[3] On the occasion of his sixtieth *Festschrift*, I had occasion to review the various logical contradictions allegedly involved in his notion of a zero rate of interest. None of the following stood up under careful logical analysis: (1) the bizarre notion that a zero interest rate has the logical implication that all goods must be free; (2) the incorrect belief that at a zero rate of interest capital will necessarily not be maintained or replaced; (3) the quaint belief that someone who has *no* intention of ever repaying his debts will at a zero rate of interest borrow an infinite amount and squander it on riotous living, but will at a positive rate of interest borrow none

[3] See Haberler's essay, "Schumpeter's Theory of Interest," *Review of Economic Statistics*, May 1951, pp. 122–128.

or only a finite amount; (4) the terror that an asset, such as land, which over perpetual time will yield a perpetual yield, should, in the absence of a discount factor, fail to have a finite value in relation to current flows — as if this were something horrendous or absurd, and as if this same mathematical infinity were necessarily avoided by the usual assumption of an ever falling rate of interest; [4] (5) the dogmatic extrapolation of the laws of technology and of tastes so that the question (of non-vanishing net productivity) is begged by revealed hypothesis. One may consider attainment of a zero rate unlikely or even (under likely empirical assumptions) impossible, but this is no warrant for the still-frequently-met indictment of deductive error and logical contradiction.

In his general views on economic theory, he seemed surprisingly un-Austrian. On the whole, he was much more Walrasian. He always referred to Léon Walras as by far the greatest economist of all time.[5] He usually spoke of Marshall as "Papa Marshall," and although he was always respectful toward Marshall's worth, he obviously regarded him as overrated. Edgeworth he thought underrated, partly because he had written articles rather than books.[6] As a man, he found Irving Fisher a

little comical; as a scientist, he revered his achievement. This was typical of Schumpeter: although himself a genius, he paid exuberant tribute to talent and promise; rather fastidious in his personal likes and dislikes, he never let these stand in the way of giving real encouragement to able economists, whatever the color of their haberdashery.

Though Schumpeter left behind him no band of zealots bent on differentiating his views from those of traditional economic theory, he did leave behind him the only kind of school appropriate to a scientific discipline — a generation of economic theorists who caught fire from his teachings.

---

[4] A concrete case will illustrate the point. Suppose total labor and land are fixed and inventions cease so that the interest rate is determined by the "net productivity of capital" as given by the marginal-productivity partial derivative of a Cobb-Douglas production function with exponents .75 for labor, .13 for land, and .12 for capital. If such a society always accumulates 15 per cent of its income, the interest rate will fall toward zero but never reach it. Nonetheless, if we evaluate the requisite integrals, we find that under conditions of certainty any dollar of perpetual income (such as a consol or land) will in this case have *infinite* present discounted value. Shall we hurriedly shoot the mathematician lest the world come to an end? Or infer that the rate of possible accumulation must be limited relative to technology so as to avoid the infinity?

[5] By virtue of Walras' vision of general equilibrium. In the next rank, Schumpeter placed Smith, Cournot, and (strangely) Quesnay. As a scholarly personality, Kurt Wicksell was his ideal.

[6] He used to tell of visiting Edgeworth in the *ante bellum* Edwardian days and having rock pheasant and champagne at breakfast in All Souls, which was adequate recompense for the dullness of Edgeworth's lectures. At about the same time, Schumpeter, in the full flower of his brilliant youth, visited Marshall, only to be advised not to continue work in economic theory! On another pilgrimage, he asked Mrs. Foxwell whether her "father" was at home. Later when he asked to see the famous library, Foxwell, grieving over his recent necessitous sale of it, merely pointed sadly to his two young children and the shoes on their feet.

117

Economic Theory and Wages

BY PAUL A. SAMUELSON

Note: The following was presented at a symposium of the Institute on the Structure of the Labor Market held at the American University (Washington, D.C.), May 12-13, 1950. [ed.]

WHEN an economic theorist comes to write an *apologia pro vita sua,* he writes certain chapters at great speed and in considerable length, knowing full well the worth of his contributions. The theory of comparative advantage in its applications to practical problems of international economics may perhaps be cited as an example. But I fear that when the economic theorist turns to the general problem of wage determination and labor economics, his voice becomes muted and his speech halting. If he is honest with himself, he must confess to a tremendous amount of uncertainty and self-doubt concerning even the most basic and elementary parts of the subject.

It is not that there is a shortage of wage theories. Indeed there are many: too many and too mutually contradictory, so that they obscure rather than point up important truths. And for all his self-doubts and humility, the economic theorist knows as he surveys the bouquet of wage theories that, thorns, blossoms, and all, they are the creation of economic theorists living or dead. The practical man of labor affairs has always acted by instinct, and to justify his behavior he has shopped around to choose the most suitable economic rationalizations; but their fullest articulation has almost all been the product of fairly academic writers.

In the present paper I propose to sample unsystematically

some of the theories bearing on wages and labor economics. My task is not to explain their content, since fairly widespread acquaintance with their general features can be taken for granted. Rather my efforts can go toward evaluation of the elements of validity and error involved in the various theories and toward identifying those areas in which our existing knowledge seems inadequate.

Over-All Wage Theories

The language and concepts of economics have evolved over centuries, with much of the development being accidental rather than inevitable. Since language is not neutral in its influence on thought processes, we can guess that the classification of productive agents into land, labor, and capital prepared the way for separate theories of rent, wages, and interest. But so long as no member of the triology was treated very differently from the others, the problem was not much more than reformulated.

To writers of earlier centuries it was apparently too dull to treat all productive agents alike, and so we were provided with ingenious figures of speech and analogies to demonstrate that work or something else is the true source of value or of something-or-other. "Labour is the Father and creative principle of Wealth, as Lands are the Mother," or alternatively, land is the source of all *produit net*. Today such romantic distinctions leave us a little cold and we are inclined to wonder how their lack of real content could, for good or evil, have had much effect upon the understanding of economic happenings. But this is to overlook the persuasive role of language in forming people's perception and interpretation of what it is that they see in the world around them. Even at the present time it is a provocative statement to affirm that labor is merely a commodity.

By the time of Smith's *Wealth of Nations* (1776) economic analysis had not yet emancipated itself from the influence of its historical terminology—indeed it has not been able to do so since. Still the terminology had become so varied and ambiguous in meaning that the classical writers could both pay lip service to a labor-theory-of-value (whatever that is) and disregard it whenever it became convenient for them to do so in the course of trying to explain some part of economic reality.

In the last century and a half at least the following general wage theories are commonly distinguished by economists: (1) the *subsistence* theory of wages; (2) the *wage fund* doctrine; (3) the *indeterminacy* or *bargaining power and exploitation* theory of wages; (4) the *marginal productivity* theory of wages; (5) the *purchasing power* theory of wages.

Such a list is of course a logical monstrosity. The various categories are overlapping. They cut across each other logically and their number could easily be expanded or contracted. Nonetheless each involves a catch phrase around which arguments have been marshaled and concerning which writers have felt strongly, both pro and con. For the purpose of the present unsystematic sampling of views, the classification will do.

Subsistence Theory

The world must have been ripe in 1798 for Malthus's population theory because its impact was immediate, substantial, and lasting, while at the same time its facts were inconclusive and its simple reasoning by no means completely new. The dismal iron law of wages deduced from it can be sufficiently epitomized in modern terminology.

Human fertility is such as to cause the long-run supply curve of labor to be horizontal at the minimum level of biological subsistence; because fixity of natural resources brings the law of diminishing returns into play, the general demand curve for labor is a downward-sloping schedule. Although technological change tends to shift the demand schedule upward, fertility can override all; so that equilibrium will (or can) only take place at the very low intersection of supply and demand where the wage is low enough to choke off lives and births so that the population is just replacing itself.

Despite the fact that the next half century was one of rapid increase in life expectancy, in total population, and probably in real wages, this subsistence theory nevertheless remained an important influence on political thought. As a statement of tendency about what would happen, or would have to happen, in a limiting state of equilibrium, the theory was practically immune to any factual attack: indeed, a critic wishing to attack it would have had trouble deciding which facts to play up and which to soft-pedal, and a defender might have faced the same dilemma.

The highly specific content of the doctrine—its exact quantitative character, rooted in the physiological level of subsistence—would have delighted the heart of an ancient Pythagorean or a modern econometrician. But by the time of Ricardo and the late classical writers the horizontal long-run supply curve of labor had been permitted to rise to whatever *conventional* level of wages workers were taught to insist upon prior to their reproducing themselves. Labor then differed not at all from capital, which too had its conventional level of "subsistence interest rate"—or "effective rate of accumulation"—below which all capital growth was thought to cease.

For America and Western Europe the crude subsistence theory of wages possessed no empirical validity, even though it continued to be appealed to in controversies over unionization and governmental aid to the poor.[1] It is an irony of history

[1] Yet as late as the mid-nineteenth century so judicious a writer as John Stuart Mill was led by his preoccupation with the birth control movement to make a famous utterance stating how doubtful it was that the technological improvements of all history had "lightened the toil" of suffering humanity. And he seriously argued that unions should disregard the depressing effects on the wages of others that would follow from raising their own, on the ground that in any event the general class of

that so unrealistic a theory should have given economics so bad a name for so long a time. And as is so often the case with intrinsically weak arguments, every victory it brought to those who used it was ultimately dearly purchased: critics of classical economics and of the existing social order were enabled to make a completely unjustified identification of competition with minimum subsistence wages.[2]

The Wage Fund Doctrines

Discussion of the so-called wage fund doctrine constitutes one of the most sterile chapters in that dreary gap between the classical age and the revolutionary neoclassical discoveries of the last third of the nineteenth century. If the subsistence theory had been true, it would have been important. Even if the wage fund theories were correct—it really would have made no great

---

unskilled labor could always be expected so to change their numbers as to keep their wage level constant.

One grain of truth in Malthus remained truly applicable to Europe in the last century: the great reduction in death rates was not accompanied by an immediate and contemporaneous decline in birth rates, so that population grew tremendously; and to the extent that statical diminishing returns was then operating to counter dynamic technological innovation and cheapening of American food, Europe can be said to have been "spending" some indeterminable fraction of her gains from progress on mere increase in numbers.

[2] Karl Marx replaced the devil of biological fertility by the "reserve army of the unemployed." Their downward pressure on wages was supposed to lead to the same iron law of subsistence wages. Except for the overlaps between this notion and the later-discussed bargaining or exploitation theory, there is no validity in this Marxian notion: in simple competitive models, unemployment causes the real wage to fall to the equilibrium intersection of supply and demand, which for modern nations would presumably have no connection with physiological minima of subsistence. With the same logic Marx could have promulgated the golden law of wages: Unfilled job vacancies will cause wages to reach the level of bliss.

difference, since the controversy was largely over empty words.

It is one of the characteristics of the history of economic doctrines that whenever Adam Smith let fall a casual remark—perhaps defining a desirable canon of taxation, or extolling the superiority of short-term credit, or pointing out the dependence of wages on capital—then throughout subsequent history these casual thoughts have gone reverberating down the corridors of time, ending up in the strangest places and in the strangest forms.

Even before Smith,[3] Turgot had noted a dependence of employment and wages on capital. Smith, Ricardo, and the earlier classical writers gave a prominent place to such considerations. But only in the time of Senior and Stuart Mill, when the subsistence theory was fairly played out, did the doctrine of the wage fund begin to have attention focused on it. Around the middle of the century it ruled triumphant, but in the late 1860's it came under attack by Leslie, Thornton, Longe, Walker, Jenkin, and others. And when Mill made his famous recanta-

---

[3] Smith's view that "industry is limited by capital" is well expressed in Book IV: "As the number of workmen that can be kept in employment by any particular person must bear a certain proportion to his capital, so the number of those that can be continually employed by all the members of a great society, must bear a certain proportion to the whole capital of that society, and can never exceed that proportion." If such an extreme degree of technical complementarity between capital and labor were to hold in each small line of production, and this seems doubtful, still it would not have to hold for society as a whole. Yet this notion dies hard: in a recent U. N. Full Employment Report by able economists, deviation from full employment in backward countries—and not simply low wages and productivity—seems to be attributed to capital scarcity. Few will deny that a disturbance of the supply of raw materials in a country like Italy could cause temporary unemployment; but who can agree that this condition is remediable in the long run only by a restoration of that same flow of materials? I will concede that backward countries do have special disguised unemployment problems, and that the process of their awakening is interrelated with capital formation, but all this needs careful and critical spelling out.

tion in a review of Thornton, there followed for thirty years an era in which the economic theorist was thought to have withdrawn his former objections to the attempts by unions to raise wages. The whole episode represents much ado about practically nothing, and so I may be very brief in my summary.

Just as the subsistence theory was a special theory of the supply curve of labor, the wage fund doctrine was a special theory of the demand curve for labor. In its strictest (meaningful and nontautological) form, it held that the total wage bill is approximately a constant, being predetermined by the money funds of the capitalists set aside for wages, or at the deeper level, by the predetermined total real-wage bill of goods and services to be advanced by the capitalists to the workers. Dividing this constant numerator by the volume of employment would yield by simple arithmetic the average money or real wage. Of course, the issue was rarely stated so clearly and simply as this.

Now if this strange notion had been empirically valid, it is not at all clear that this would have constituted an argument against unionism. On the contrary, the short-run case for workers limiting their numbers would be an especially strong one in this rigid case of *unitary elasticity* in the general demand for labor. And, as a matter of fact, Mill with his weakness for good causes actually used the doctrine as a justification for birth control and as a reason to implore the capitalists to increase their saving and investment.

Union wage increases could be expected in the longer run to lower the profit incomes of the wealthier and thriftier classes, and therefore, to result in less saving and in what Mill and the other classical believers in Say's law of markets regarded as exactly the same thing—less investment. A slower growth of capital would result in lower wages in the future than would otherwise have been the case. Hence for workers to accept lower wages was regarded as equivalent to their putting money in the bank, which would return to *them* with interest in the form of higher wages in the future. Thus Senior's defense of capital and interest by appeal to the saver's real cost in the form of *abstinence* could now be reinforced by the view that investing by the rich involved an act of altruism as well as of self-interest.

Today we would agree that there is an important element of truth in the view that a rapid growth of real capital can be expected to increase labor productivity and real wages. But just as the wage fund theory came into the limelight because of its absurdities, it met its doom for the same reasons. To explain wage rates by the wage bill is to put off an answer and to raise the problem of what it is that determines the wage bill. If we regard wages as a flow per unit time, what factors shape and limit the total of this flow? Today we may provisionally answer that labor's total consumption is limited by the total flow of national product; but even this is not strictly true in the short run, since for a time a nation can enlarge its consumption at the expense of capital.[4] If we grant that 100 per cent of the national product is an upper limit for wages,[5] then we are

[4] In the 1890's Taussig and the Austrians came to the defense of the wage fund using arguments more subtle than those of Mill, Fawcett, and Cairnes. Taussig's *Wages and Capital* (1895) describes the time dimension of the capital process; but as he pointed out in the 1932 reissue, it would have been better to have omitted the name of the wage fund altogether. In this modified form the wage fund has almost nothing to do with any of the issues involving unionization; if anything, a realistic view of the capital process increases the *short-term* gains that a labor monopoly might capture. It might be added that the Taussig view of the capital process is divorced from any dependence upon a numerical average period of production and gives a desirable counteremphasis to the J. B. Clark abstractions of an almost automatically self-renewing capital stock.

[5] The nebulous doctrine of noncompeting groups in consumption, if ever relevant, is so no longer. In this country, workers consume the same articles as anyone else. But even if this were less the case, as in Europe in an earlier century, we could still rely on a free pricing mechanism to put each and every consumption good (including paintings and stickpins) into the hands of those who have the highest monetary demand—and all

granting all that the most avaricious trade unionist could desire; and if we look for exact quantitative principles to determine some more limited fraction, we look in vain in economic books, modern or ancient.

Indeterminacy, Bargaining, and Exploitation Theories

The wage fund doctrine was a weak argument to use against labor unions and it inevitably boomeranged against its users. For once it had been cast in doubt and discredited, the supposition grew up that there was nothing in economic theory that was at odds with the attempts to raise wages by collective bargaining. The sole importance of the wage fund doctrine, if true, would have been to establish a general demand for labor with *negative elasticity*, so that higher real wages would mean lower total employment. We can believe in the fact of negative elasticity without the wage fund doctrine. Consequently the falseness and emptiness of the wage fund doctrine impresses a modern observer as irrelevant.[6] Yet the floodgates had been opened to economists' views more sympathetic toward collective bargaining; and not until the later, scarcely more relevant, marginal productivity theory became known were theorists shunted back to their earlier opposition.

In the last third of the nineteenth century the apparatus of geometrical supply and demand curves was coming into use. This had been implicit in older writers; explicit in Cournot but inaccessible to the unmathematical, which is to say to practically everybody; and all but explicit in Mill's *Principles*, particu-

---

this regardless of the distribution of income. The short-run changes in consumer surplus, it is true, might be smaller than the long-run changes.

[6] W. H. Hutt, one of the modern theorists most uncompromisingly opposed to all collective bargaining, makes this point very strongly (*Theory of Collective Bargaining* [P. S. King, 1930], pp. 2-10). As compared to later quantitative estimates of elasticity of labor demand, − 1.0 is a gross understatement.

larly in the numerical tables relating to international trade. In conjunction with the rediscovery of marginal utility Jevons and Walras were motivated to perfect the analysis of supply and demand. Marshall too—probably from his study of Mill's international values—developed his geometrical cross of supply and demand. Probably a little earlier than Marshall, Fleeming Jenkin, an Edinburgh engineering professor, was led *by his studies of the labor market* to a formulation of supply and demand which appears to me to have *all* the *essential* features of the Marshallian analysis, including an independent rediscovery by Jenkin of Dupuit's consumer surplus and tax incidence analysis.

I mention this history because of the following paradox: During this same thirty years of perfecting of the tools of supply and demand, the labor market was by special dispensation considered to be an exception to supply and demand. The special features of the labor market and the peculiarities of labor as a commodity were dwelt upon at great length, perhaps even at excessive length, with the result that some of the most enlightening comments on the labor market go back to this period.[7]

Loopholes in the laws of supply and demand were eagerly sought out. Thus, Thornton pointed out that if there was a

[7] Fleeming Jenkin, *Papers*, Vol. II (reprinted as a London School of Economics Scarce Tract, 1932) contains the interesting essay, "Trade Unions: How Far Legitimate" (pp. 5-75), written in 1868, a year or two before his paper on supply and demand. This has a most modern air about it and would be worth quoting at length, since it deals with many of the issues debated in connection with the Taft-Hartley Act. The 1870 paper on "Graphic Representation of the Laws of Supply and Demand, and their Application to Labour" (pp. 76-93, 93-106) is a little disappointing in its applications to labor: instead of stating simply that a monopoly can travel up the demand schedule for labor by restricting employment, Jenkin couches the process in the language of cost of production, reserve price, standards of comfort, etc. A. Marshall, *Economics of Industry* (Macmillan, 1899), has an interesting chapter on trade unions (Book VI, chap. xiv. See also Book VI, chaps. iii, iv, v).

coincidental complete inelasticity of both the supply and demand schedule, then competitive price would be indeterminate within that range. To the extent that economic goods or services are discrete and lumpy rather than perfectly continuously divisible, something like this is bound to be true on a small scale at least. Later Böhm-Bawerk, with his tedious horse market, was to exhaust the patience of subsequent theorists by his inordinate dwelling on this point. Consequently modern theorists tend to regard these early discussions as rather piddling.

But in doing so, we must not forget something infinitely more important than the coarseness of the units in which labor comes: namely, the tremendous differentiation of abilities and attitudes as between workers, so that no two are alike—and so that no person can accurately ascertain their differences. This, plus the fact that the performance you get from a man is not something that exists independently of his wage, the wages of others, his past employment experience, and the performance of others, pulverizes the labor market into separate but highly interrelated segments. If each morning people could be hired in an organized auction market, the world would be a very different one—not a slightly different one, but a substantially different one, in my judgment.

Whatever its merits, there came to the fore in this period the endemic notion that the wage bargain was indeterminate, depending much on relative bargaining power, and that the individual workingman would by himself be inferior in bargaining power to the more wealthy employer who was possessed of greater financial resources to outlast a strike and who in any case could almost always be regarded as being in an overt or tacit combination to keep wages down.[8] In its crudest form this view

---

[8] Most of these doctrines go back at least to Adam Smith, that alleged apologist of the bourgeois class. Labor was supposed to be at an additional disadvantage in that its services were perishable, in the sense that the work you don't do today, you can never do; also the cost of maintaining the workers' families was regarded as a recurring overhead cost that went on

pictured each helpless worker as being picked off by a powerful employer and having his wage forced down to a minimum necessary for existence.

Either in defense or for offense, a subgroup of workers by banding together and bargaining collectively could hope to raise their wages. That any reasonable economist should have denied that a monopoly of labor in one given market can affect supply and raise the price above the competitive level, today appears strange. Scarcely less explicable was the factual assertion that trade unions would not be able to make their monopoly power stick and would find their attempts to raise particular wages as unavailing as attempts to stop the ocean's tide by oral exhortation. Those who argued in this way were bad political and market analysts.[9]

In economics it takes a theory to kill a theory; facts can only dent the theorist's hide. Edgeworth in his *Mathematical Psychics* (1881) came forward with an elaborate analysis of two-sided monopoly, thereby giving geometrical content to the old examples of dickering between buyer and seller of unique objects such as musical snuffboxes. One of the most important applications of this theory of bilateral monopoly was felt to be

---

independently of employment. It has been truly pointed out that some— but not all—of the services of capital equipment are also forever lost if not used today; and in many industries today it is simply not true that the days lost on strikes represent a full net subtraction from the days that will ever be worked. (Cf. the Chamberlin paper and discussion, chaps. viii and ix.)

[9] If unions do not raise certain wages relative to what they would otherwise be, it is hard to understand much of the criticism of organized labor. Nonetheless, it is not possible to document the view that unions have substantially raised their wages relative to others. Such is the character of economics! Contrast the views of union power (for good or evil) set down in the Chamberlin and Clark papers and the Friedman paper (chaps. i, viii, x); of course more than the effects of unions on money and real wages must be taken into account. ·

the labor market. The general conclusion of Edgeworth was that the amount of employment and the wage would under imperfect competition be indeterminate rather than uniquely determinable as under perfect competition. By agreement both contending parties might be expected to leave certain mutually disadvantageous settlements; but this would only narrow down the field of battle to (the so-called Edgeworth "contract curve") a point where the interests of workers and of employers were diametrically opposed. An infinite continuum of final settlements could thus eventuate from collective bargaining, depending upon some kind of vaguely defined bargaining power exerted by each side.[10]

Doctrines of inevitability oust issues of morality; doctrines of free will raise questions of norms. When economic theory began to give its blessing to the notion that organized labor might be master of its fate and wages, interest was rekindled in the old question of what is the fair or normal share of labor. Where does exploitation begin? Where are workers organizing defensively to recapture what is rightly theirs, and where are they beginning to go too far?

The term "exploitation of labor" has, of course, myriad meanings. In recent years some economists have tried to give this

[10] Marshall and his pupil Berry tried to define a determinate price even in the case of bilateral monopoly. If the income that employers are bartering against workers' labor has "constant marginal utility" to both parties, then every point on the contract curve will represent the *same* amount of employment, and the final marginal rate of substitution of work for income will be everywhere the *same*. But even under the bizarre conditions assumed, note that the settlement is still highly indeterminate, and that the well-being of workers and employers depends completely on the outcome of the bargaining. See A. Marshall, *Principles of Economics* (8th ed.; *Macmillan*, 1920), Appendix F and Note XII. Recent theorists, such as Leontief and Fellner, have attempted to apply the tools of bilateral monopoly to exposition of some problems of collective bargaining; and in 1932 Hicks set forth a theory of strikes. In my view disappointingly little has yet come from theorists in this field.

concept certain precise and technical meanings representing well-defined deviations from optimum welfare conditions. Thus, Joan Robinson, *Economics of Imperfect Competition* (Macmillan, 1933), follows Pigou and defines two kinds of exploitation of labor. The first kind exists when the employer is an impure competitor or monopolist who equates marginal revenue rather than price to marginal cost—or what is the same thing, who hires inputs until their extra cost to him is balanced by their "marginal value or revenue product" rather than by the "value of their marginal product"; the second kind of exploitation occurs when the employer is a *monopsonist* in the labor market and equates to marginal revenue product the extra cost of a worker, calculated as his wage *minus* the additional amount previous workers must thereby be paid. These definitions are somewhat misleading since the workers in question are not the ones being exploited: a worker employed by a large corporation in a company town will *probably* be getting higher rather than lower than the average wages paid by small nonmonopsonistic firms; and impurely competitive firms probably pay higher wages than purely competitive ones do. As Mrs. Robinson indicates, it is the community that is being exploited, in the sense that there are two kinds of deviations from optimum welfare economic conditions.[11]

[11] In the oral symposium Professor Chamberlin and I discussed at some length whether the first kind of "impure competition exploitation"—i.e., the equality of wages with marginal revenue product rather than with value of the marginal product—did truly represent a deviation from the optimum. I affirmed that it did, and this he questioned. The discussion was continued in correspondence and the area of disagreement was, I think, narrowed. The following summary represents my own personal view and is not at all binding on Professor Chamberlin.

If outputs and inputs have not reached the position compatible with prices everywhere equal to 1.00 times marginal cost, then there is a deviation from the optimum in the following sense: *everybody* can be made better off by some theoretical rearrangement of resources. The equality of P and MC, which is the same thing as the equality of factor prices with

It is not clear that these new meanings are at all what earlier observers had in mind in using the word "exploitation." In fact, I doubt that any one thing very definite lay in the back of the minds of users of the term. "Exploitation" is a general word of opprobrium, and anything that strikes the onlooker as a bad thing seems to deserve this label—whether it be wages low enough to keep a worker thinking about his stomach, or quite high wages paid by a man of great wealth to a poorer man. There is always a latent feeling that it would be nice for us all to live at the level of, say, the upper eighty-fifth percentile of the income distribution; and since most of us must necessarily fall short of such a level, it is clear that wages generally can always be regarded as too low. And this will remain the prevailing attitude even if it can be pointed out that median wages in this country are a multiple of general wages elsewhere; so long as median wages are less than average national income, wages tend by many to be regarded as too low—and among those not well versed in arithmetic this may persist even after the median has been brought up to the mean.

---

the value of their marginal products, may be inconsistent with $p =$ average cost and may require ideal "lump-sum taxes and subsidies" if a perfectionist's optimum is to be reached. These marginal relations are *necessary* conditions for an optimum that must hold *whatever* the ethical norms prescribed. But they are definitely *not* sufficient conditions. To determine which commodities are to be produced at all requires "total conditions" in addition to the marginal ones—as Dupuit, Hicks, Lerner, Meade, Henderson, Chamberlin, and others have shown. See my *Foundations of Economic Analysis* (Harvard Press, 1947), chapter 8.

At the level of workability or feasibility, the above paragraph needs careful qualification. Lowering prices to marginal costs in some subsector of the economy alone may *worsen* rather than improve the situation. And since ideal lump-sum taxes and subsidies are not feasible, the actually feasible optimum is consistent with some degree of both kinds of "exploitation."

Marginal Productivity Theory

A historian of industrial life and of economics books cannot neglect people's attitudes toward the rightness and wrongness of wages. But he must also not forget that the importance of a proposition in this sphere is often independent of its intrinsic logical merits or its empirical validity as a description of what goes on in real markets.

After 1900 the marginal productivity theory of wages became increasingly popular among economists. Its recognition and assertion of substitutability among inputs within the firm does provide one extra reason for elasticity in the sloping demand curve for labor. But except for this I cannot see that this theory is particularly relevant to the question of whether competition will result in low or high wages, or of whether collective bargaining can hope to raise wages. Within the realm of economic theory itself, marginal productivity relations are one subset of the conditions of general equilibrium; and if the existence of the partial derivative postulated by this theory contradicted technological fact, the status of labor economics would be in no significant sense altered.[12]

[12] George J. Stigler, *Production and Distribution Theory* (Macmillan, 1941), is the indispensable reference to the genesis of this theory. Anyone who thinks that marginal productivity analysis adds to the ethical merits of competitive wages should recall that v. Wieser's *Natural Value*, which antedates the theory, gives a full teleological defense of competitive pricing. Cf. also F. M. Taylor, *Principles of Economics* (8th ed.; Ronald Press, 1921), or the modern "nonmarginal" theory of "linear programming." Pareto, it will be recalled, disbelieved in marginal productivity but nevertheless was one of the first to set down the optimizing character of competitive pricing under capitalism or socialism. Between the first and third editions of his *Éléments*, Walras adopted a marginal productivity theory of production: nonetheless, even back in the 1870's he held firm views about the optimum character of general equilibrium pricing. In 1925 in the *Journal of Political Economy*, Professor Knight showed that even in the case where there was no substitutability because of "fixed coefficients,"

A subsistence theory of wages is quite consistent with marginal productivity, and for that matter so is a meaningfully stated wage fund theory. Under appropriate conditions of demand and technology, a marginal productivity theory might impute 99 per cent of the national income away from labor, which would be exploitation enough in the eyes of radical agitators; or it might impute 99 per cent to spendthrift workers, which would be bad indeed in the eyes of those who strain for progress.

Perhaps the importance of the theory is to be found in the use made by it to rationalize the *correctness* of wages as determined in relatively competitive markets.[13] True the theory is too complex ever to have percolated down to the noneconomist public; but then it was never needed at that level, since the earlier mentioned general discontent over low wages has always been matched by an elaborate set of doctrines to explain why this condition must prevail.

J. B. Clark, one of the many developers and expanders of the marginal productivity theory, clearly thought that its importance lay in its demonstration of the ethical merits of competitive wage determination. In his *Distribution of Wealth* he speaks again and again of having identified the "natural law" of wage determination, whereby labor received *its* "normal," "ideal," "specifically produced," "traceable" fair share of the

---

the competitively determined wage would equal the addition to the value of total product resulting from the addition of a single worker (the evaluation of product being at the previous set of prices).

It is in view of these facts that I make the statement that there is nothing in the marginal productivity doctrine as such that adds to the normative significance of competitive pricing.

[13] Even to this day one reads in important economic writings such statements as: If workers get less than their marginal product there may be underconsumption and a crash; or, Workers can be expected to be given their marginal product in good times but not in bad times when profits are under pressure. Not only does some moral connotation still cling to the concept of marginal product, but also there is fuzziness on how this condition of equilibrium comes about or is departed from.

product. Indeed Clark seems to have felt that his most important contribution beyond the earlier work of von Thünen lay, not alone in a different or better description of the facts of the market place, but in the demonstration that the marginal productivity theory is a theory of *justice* and not, as von Thünen believed, of *exploitation*.[14]

[14] *Distribution of Wealth* (Macmillan, 1902), preface; pp. 321-324.

Comment by Clark: I feel I should not let this question go entirely by default. As to the terms in which J. B. Clark's marginal productivity theory was formulated, it was first publicly presented in 1889, by a non-mathematical economist, in the light of prevailing issues far different from those raised by 1950-brand mathematical-welfare theory. On the general horizon, von Thünen bulked less large than Marx, under whose theory any share capital gets is outright robbery. As against this, the marginal productivity theory asserts that the rewards of both labor and capital are in exchange for productive contributions. They embody the (limited) ethics of mutual exchange, as against the nonethics of robbery, just as any sale of a commodity does.

I do not know anyone who has seriously claimed that either settles all ethical questions: certainly not the question whether the unequal distribution of inherited property or innate ability is just, or the more practical question whether one whose innate abilities enable him to produce five times as much as another, should justly receive five times as much (before or after taxes). But the idea that of two who have equal abilities or command of property, the one who uses his to render twice the useful service has a claim to twice the reward (less taxes)—this accords with a widespread feeling that this is *one* important element of fairness, in addition to the obvious elements of expediency and incentive which it involves. I hope that such criteria are not going to be discredited on the ground that they are partial and limited, because I am sure that perfect and all-embracing ethical formulae for concrete actions are impossible, and that limited and partial ones are the only kind we shall ever have.

As to "specific" productivity versus "partial derivatives," the idea J. B. Clark wished to convey was that of the amount of added product dependent on the presence or absence of *any one* of a number of interchangeable productive units, in the setting represented by the presence of the other interchangeable units, and the other factors. If it is wrong to attach the idea of specifically traceable causality to such a relation, I am

J. B. Clark stated his position clearly and strongly, but it is now commonly regarded as such an ethically arbitrary one that he has become somewhat discredited in the eyes of modern economists.[15] Still, this all took a good deal of time and was aided by reinforcement from later social developments. We must not deny, therefore, that the marginal productivity theory did—rightly or wrongly—serve the purpose of refuting the notion that wages are simply a matter of workers' aspirations backed up by organized collective bargaining.

In concluding this section, I should like to add some reflections occasioned by the oral discussion of the significance of marginal productivity. Assuming the absence of uncertainty and of market imperfection, and assuming the existence of continuous partial derivatives of all the production functions in the eco-

---

puzzled as to what causal relations may generally involve which is different from this.

By all means, let us modify the formulation of this principle, for present use, in the light of current methodological attitudes. And let us distinguish more systematically between positive analysis and terms of ethical appraisal.

[15] It is not clear to me that J. B. Clark ever meant what he seems to have meant. Why should a man of his general sentiments have cared to identify the functional distribution of income with the personal distribution of income? Once he agrees to their separation, marginal productivity ceases to be an ethical doctrine and becomes a theory of production (and possibly of incentive). T. N. Carver, among others, pointed this out a half century ago; but I do not know whether Clark ever changed his public position.

Comment by Clark: As to the relation between functional and personal distribution, I had construed the principle as stating that the personal owner of a factor receives the share functionally attributable to the factor he owns. This seems to describe a pretty close relation, compounding the ethical problem of ownership with that involved in marginal imputation. Accordingly, I would not "agree to the separation" of functional and personal distribution in any sense that would completely destroy whatever (limited and partial) ethical implications there may be in the theory, and I doubt if my father would have done so.

nomic system, the Walrasian conditions of general equilibrium (which include a subset of marginal product conditions) *do* determine a configuration of relative prices. In the absence of detailed quantitative knowledge of the production functions, and of consumer supply and demand functions, we cannot state what the quantitative pattern of resulting prices will be, nor how it will quantitatively change when certain changes impinge on the system. We can perhaps formulate a few qualitative laws of behavior simply from our knowledge of the conditions of returns and maximization, yet admittedly we would be happier if the "empty boxes" could be filled with detailed quantitative knowledge. Yet no one should expect to make bricks without straw, and the theory in question should not be blamed for the complexity of the facts and our ignorance of them. Under the above simplified conditions, the general equilibrium theory is the *only* valid description and any competing valid theory must turn out to be identical with it and hence no less complicated.

A more serious accusation against the marginal productivity theory resides in the failure of its assumptions to be realized. Here the problem becomes one of deciding how far the facts depart from the theory's implications, and how good a first approximation is provided by the simplified version of the theory. I personally think it does provide us with some insight but that—especially where imperfections and impurities of competition are concerned—where uncertainties and feed-back influences of wages on management and worker productivity are concerned, and where the uncertainties associated with cyclical investment and technological changes are concerned, the simplified version of the theory needs to be amplified by successively more realistic theories.

But suppose we were to waive the fact of our empirical ignorance, and suppose we were to grant that reality faithfully matches all the premises underlying marginal productivity and general equilibrium theory. There still would remain the question of its normative significance. Does it then simply tell us what will happen if nothing is done? Or does it go further and tell us that what will happen *ought* in some sense to happen? This is the welfare economics aspect of the problem, and to my astonishment I find that the arbitrariness of J. B. Clark's views on the deservingness of competitively determined rewards is not universally recognized, as I had earlier declared. I must refer the reader to the oral discussion and to my own concluding remarks on welfare economics.

Purchasing Power Theory of Wages

For a long time Henry Ford shared with the A.F. of L. the conviction that high money wages helped to create and preserve prosperity all around. While economic outlaws such as John A. Hobson had long preached a doctrine of underconsumption due to inequality of income distribution as lying at the root of depression and the trade cycle,[16] until recently respectable economists regarded such doctrines with some amusement and threw them to their fledgling pupils as exercises in avoiding sloppy thinking.

Then suddenly J. M. Keynes's *General Theory* (1936) reopened the question of the efficacy of money-wage cutting in curbing a depression. In the first years after 1936, the bulk of the discussion emphasized the lack of connection between autonomous changes in general money-wage rates and the resulting real-wage rates. It was often believed that to a first approximation a general change in all wages would be accompanied by an

[16] Wm. T. Foster and Waddill Catchings in *Profits* (Houghton Mifflin, 1925) and in numerous other books published during the 1920's proclaimed an underconsumption doctrine, but pinned their hopes for a remedy on unorthodox government monetary and fiscal policies. The Brookings Institute also placed early stress on the consumption effects of the skewness of our income distribution, but advocated lowering of prices by industrial statesmanship.

equivalent all-around change in the price level, with no appreciable change in real wages.

Keynes himself in one of his early chapters enunciated a peculiar definition of "involuntary unemployment" that hinged on an alleged myopia on the part of workers and unions toward a decrease in money wages as against an equivalent increase in the price level. The author and his readers were misled into thinking this an important concept; actually it later became clear that the concept of involuntary unemployment was only used by Keynes to explain rigidity of money wages in the face of unemployment—a rigidity which can be amply explained by a great number of other factors, such as legislation, trade union activity, imperfect competition in labor markets, general attitudes, etc.

Also, as Keynes came later to realize, he at first put too much emphasis on changes in the level of employment as being finally determined by somehow brought-about changes in real wages *along a fixed real demand schedule for labor, downward sloping by virtue of the classical law of diminishing returns*. Actually the essence of his theory was that fluctuations in total investment demand would, in a regime of fairly invariant propensity to consume, represent *shifts* in the total demand schedule so that even at the same real wage employment might change. When it was pointed out to him that the most careful examination of all known facts could not rule out the possibility of increasing rather than decreasing returns, he was delighted and gladly dropped forever the notion that saving and investment could influence income *only through* their differential effects on money and real wages.[17]

This also opened the way—although in truth that way had never been closed—for considering whether a completely bal-

[17] Even with diminishing returns, if real saving and investment propensities are not changed by extreme changes in money wages and prices, attempts by collective bargaining to accept lower real wages would not

anced hyperdeflation brought about by a fall in all wages accompanied by a proportionate fall in all prices might not have substantive effects on employment. Early it was agreed that so long as the monetary system was not infinitely elastic, the hard-money and fiduciary issues of currency would form a "nonhomogeneous" element which would not necessarily shrink proportionally with the price and wage level. Thus, a policy of hyperdeflation brought about generally by wage-cutting would be one way of making the volume of money redundant, and one roundabout way of engineering low interest rates and easy money. *Unless* the liquidity preference schedule of people is so completely elastic as to make lower interest rates impossible—or unless the general demand schedule for investment is so completely inelastic as to make lowering of interest rates of little potency in promoting recovery—a policy of hyperdeflation was early conceded to be capable of having favorable *statical* effects on employment.

But in the 1930's when the potency of an easy money policy was so widely discounted, to say that an all-around deflationary policy might contribute to easy money was to damn such a policy with faint praise—especially since the authorities had ample powers to ease money far beyond those they were using. Therefore, it was a matter of some interest when Pigou [18] and other neo-Keynesians began late in the 1930's to emphasize a new avenue whereby hyperdeflation could add to the level of real effective demand: namely through *the stimulating effect upon the propensity-to-consume schedule of the increased amount of* (*real*) *money wèalth created by the process of wage-price cuts.* [19]

---

necessarily lead to full employment but perhaps instead to an endless hyperdeflation. I am not here arguing that such a model is realistic, but rather that such a model can be rigorously defined—a logical fact which has been repeatedly denied in the recent literature.

[18] Haberler's 1937 *Prosperity and Depression* (United Nations, 1946) has already emphasized this aspect of the matter.

[19] Since the numerical importance of hard money and fiduciary currency is limited, the asymmetrical character of the public debt was brought

In the absence of much factual or theoretical knowledge about the potency of this "wealth effect," it was seized upon by those who favored wage-price flexibility and minimized by those who did not; and no doubt over the next decades the numerical importance of this effect will continue to be argued in the journals. According to many, including Pigou himself as he tells us in the preface to *Lapses from Full Employment*,[20] deflation is not necessarily to be recommended as a cure for unemployment: real wealth can be put in people's hands more easily and equitably by other measures; other expansionary policies are also preferable. Nonetheless there are undoubtedly some modern economists who believe the wealth effect to be substantial so that deflation need not become hyperdeflation; and who believe that expansionary central bank policy can simultaneously mitigate the money-income-depressing effects of wage cuts; and who believe that the necessary adjustments of relative wages and

---

in as a substantially equivalent factor. As a people, we both owe and own the public debt; but we recognize the debt we own and tend, so it is persuasively argued, to forget about what we owe. Therefore, all-around hyperdeflation will not have canceling-out effects on public debt as it is supposed to have on private debt. Instead the government bonds, in people's hands or in their financial institutions, will be a nonhomogeneous item just like hard money.

Be it noted that open-market operations of the conventional sort *are not by themselves* capable of bringing about the same real expansion in the community's total of *government bonds + cash*. Only to the extent that open-market operations are capable of inducing secondary expansions or contractions of commercial loans—a smaller category relative to total bank assets than it used to be—can they have effects similar to those brought about by hyperdeflation, hyperinflation, or cumulative treasury surpluses and deficits. When a low interest policy has reached an impasse due to interest-elastic excess reserves by commercial banks, interest-elastic cash holding by individuals, or interest-inelastic investment demand schedules, then central bank operations do not have the wealth effects of the other policies named. These latter may be potent even when the central bank is not.

[20] (Macmillan, 1945.)

relative prices that a dynamic economy always requires are more desirably brought about by permitting some wages to fall, whenever unemployment develops in a given sector of the market, rather than by giving the system an inflationary bias through requiring that all relative-wage changes take place as a result of differential increases alone.

In a sense a compromise doctrine has emerged from the combination of classical, neoclassical, Keynesian, and neo-Keynesian analysis. A legitimate and convenient name for this common core is, I suggest, "neoclassical." Neoclassical analysis permits of fully stable *under*employment equilibrium only on the assumption of either frictions or a peculiar concatenation of wealth-liquidity-interest elasticities; and this is in a sense a negation of the more dramatic claims of the Keynesian revolution. On the other hand, this neoclassical doctrine is a far cry from the old notion that unemployment is simply the consequence of imposing too high real wages along a sloping aggregate marginal productivity demand schedule for labor: it goes far beyond the primitive notions that by definition of a Walrasian system, equilibrium must be at full employment; and beyond the view that the same analysis which demonstrates a drop in price will equate supply and demand in any small partial equilibrium market will also suffice to prove that a drop in general wages must clear the labor market. It rejects the question-begging gobbledygook of Say's law of markets, whereby supply creates demand and the flow of purchasing power automatically conserves itself —regardless of saving and investment decisions. Perhaps the cream of the jest is the final vindication of the classical belief in full employment *by means of a mechanism which leans heavily on indirectly destroying thriftiness and on the matching of full-employment saving and investment* so ardently desired by the underconsumption denizens of the academic underworld.[21]

[21] *Comment by Wright:* Regarding the doctrinal history implied in this passage compare chap. xiii, especially pages 289, 290.

All the above is a fairly far cry from the older mechanism by which wage cuts were supposed to lead to increased employment, for it will be noted that if the above process results in extra employment, it does so without necessarily diminishing real-wage rates and almost certainly by increasing rather than decreasing real consumption. Professor Wright has very properly asked whether there is not also *a more direct effect* of wage cuts on employment through directly favorable effects upon investment incentives, the marginal efficiency of capital, or autonomous investment.[22]

That wage cuts may directly stimulate investment is an important possibility; and we must also consider possible unfavorable effects upon net investment. In which direction the final balance is to be struck will depend upon many quantitative crosscurrents. While I do not feel competent to evaluate the empirical magnitudes of the conflicting tendencies, I am prepared to listen with interest to those who do have definite hypotheses on this point.

The problem would of course be a much simpler one to analyze if we were talking about cuts in particular relative wages. No one can doubt that such a cut might, other things being equal, result in some increase in the particular line of employment involved. But when it is a question of a change in all wages—or even more generally of a change in *all* cost items—then the argument must be a quite different one. To take only one example: We often read that increased money-wage rates will favor mechanization and *increase* the propensity to invest. This cannot be uncritically accepted—though, to be sure, there are theoretical models in which exactly this does happen. But there are also models, Leontief's elaborate one, for example, in which a universal increase in wages will raise the price of machinery by exactly the same proportion, with no substitution taking place.

---

[22] The next few pages addressed to this problem were added to my original paper as a result of the oral discussion.

Economic Theory and Wages

Similarly, except in terms of the earlier described "indirect influences," we cannot decide whether a decrease in wages will involve any change in the interest rates relevant to investment decisions.

Moreover, it becomes important to distinguish between changes in real wages and changes in general money wages. To the extent that general wage changes result in proportional, more-than-proportional, or less-than-proportional changes in prices, the leverage of the direct influence may be zero, unfavorable, or favorable to aggregate employment. If we try to avoid this difficulty by working with sliding-scale real-wage formulas of the 1950 General Motors type, the result—in many relevant monetary models—may simply be cumulative deflation or inflation. (Denmark, Finland, and other nations have had not altogether favorable postwar experiences with such devices.) If on the other hand one makes certain other monetary assumptions, so that changes in real wages do result in changes in employment, the mechanism by which this is brought about—whether it is expressed in terms of the consumption-investment propensities of modern income analysis or in terms of the conventional quantity theory of money—is of the "indirect" rather than "direct" type, as I have classified these terms.

In all of the above I have made no mention of "expectations" generated by transitionally *changing* prices and wages, but have concentrated on *levels* of wages and prices. Realistically, these dynamic transition stages with their expectation patterns are very important; but, as Professor Haberler points out, almost anything can be proved by some appropriate assumptions about expectations. Thus, a once-and-for-all wage cut followed by expectations that wages will be higher in the future might be favorable to current employment, whereas the same wage cut regarded as part of a continuing deflationary trend might have opposite effects.

As far as the moving trend of wages and prices is concerned, and assuming that prices and wages do move together with no change in any real relations, we would typically suppose that a rising trend favors investment and employment; and that a falling trend inhibits real investment and encourages attempts to hoard. More realistically, all the quantity theorists since Hume's time have recognized the transitional expansionary effects on investment and employment of rising price and wage levels: A shift toward profit and an increased propensity to invest could be expected, along with "forced saving" resulting from the price rise and the delay in spending income. However, if the question is one of a price rise induced by prior autonomous wage increases, some of the above conclusions need to be modified: businessmen may still not be slow to spend their cash, but there may be a shift *away from* profits in this case of wage-price rather than price-wage inflation.

In all of the above, I have shown what scientific caution suggests must be said on some of the pros and cons of wage increases and employment. But now suppose we take a bolder view and set up the hypothesis—which I understand Professor Friedman to doubt and Professor Wright to affirm—(1) that unions do stand by vigilantly to capture increased real wages from a firm's *ex post* profitable operations, and (2) that this fact or fear operates as one of the important elements in the firm's *ex ante* deliberations. Then the following result seems reasonable: the motivation and ability of firms would be adversely affected and the propensity-to-invest schedule would be shifted downward. The above real-wage change can be expected also to shift the propensity-to-save schedule downward; hence the final effects on employment and inflationary gaps will be in either direction and will be qualitatively different at different times. But whatever the final effect on income, there will probably be a lower rate of real capital formation [23] and hence a lower rate of growth of the future productivity and real wages in the system.

[23] This is a probability, not a certainty: if (1) the shift in income distribution has very adverse effects on thriftiness so that (2) income greatly

The preceding paragraph gives my version of the important issue raised by Professor Wright. The point's importance goes beyond any issues of unionism or nonunionism; it directly involves the possible clash between the present and the future. As the verbatim discussion concerning competition and innovation brought out, the wage-price configuration that would result under vigorously competitive or under union monopoly conditions might very well result in a slower rate of progress than under some other system where wages were, so to speak, "taxed" in order to subsidize entrepreneurial profits.[24]

From the above discussion it will be clear that the analysis of purchasing power aspects of wages remains in a fairly primitive state. Certain dogmatic conceptions have been found to be complex and uncertain, even under simplified assumptions. But the reality of these simplifying assumptions is still very much an open question: Will militant raising of money-wage rates all around succeed—for good or evil—in raising real hourly wage rates? Will the relative share of real income going to labor improve? Will higher wages decrease thriftiness more or less than it will decrease the desire to invest? Will strategic changes in relative prices brought about by wage changes increase or decrease over-all employment, welfare, and effective demand? [25]

---

expands, and (3) if the induced marginal propensity to invest is very substantial, then, paradoxically, real-wage increases are a way of increasing capital formation.

[24] *Comment by Wright:* The semantic connotations of this sentence seem a bit unfortunate. *De facto* I suggest it should rather be put that the *new* wealth created *by* entrepreneurial saltations should not too soon be seized by other groups. Cf. my *Capitalism*, chap. iv.

[25] Bergson and Bissell have shown that increasing the costs of investment projects—such as housing—may in some circumstances add to the total value of investment and consumption spending, and in other cases have opposite results.

I think one must entertain the hypothesis that for a large sector of American industries the relationship between prices and labor costs elsewhere is determined by the institutions and mores of modern business. Competition is real; but for the group as a whole the predictable limits

Our ignorance on all these questions, even at the deductive level, is almost as great as the intensity of our convictions.

Conclusion

The final impression of my historical survey of wage theories must, to a careful reader, be a feeling of their emptiness and irrelevance. But they should not be lightly dismissed: if one were to make an equally careful survey of the pieces of theory that modern economists draw upon to answer these same questions at the present time, one would find that every one of the considerations involved in these historical theories still has relevance.

At the bottom of all of them is an ethical defense of and attack on the inequalities in the distribution of income. This is not confined to labor versus capital; it equally involves the $3500-a-year union man versus the over-$10,000 salaried official, union or corporate. At the bottom of all of these disputes is an aspiration for a standard of living for people generally beyond what the system can provide and beyond what is consistent with other aspirations. The economist can point out some of these basic incompatibilities of desire. But he weakens his case and he loses the audience he ought to persuade if he dogmatically states that the wage and income structure that would eventuate in a relatively competitive order is an optimal one (for society as a whole, for particular workers, or for workers as a whole), and if he blindly regards the existing institutional structure—with or without strong unions—as a good approximation to the competitive regime envisaged in Walrasian general equilibrium.[26]

---

competition sets on behavior are not narrow. I have seen this hypothesis denied (and defended) by assertion, but I know of no careful documentation and appraisal of its degree of validity.

[26] In my judgment the present symposium revealed how important it is to carry out—within professional circles—a meticulous restatement, in

Yet it will be an empty victory for him if he keeps his audience only by telling them what they wish to hear. And hence
the honest economist must stress the limits and uncertainties
that surround any extensive programs for bettering the position
of labor by collective bargaining. This is in any case what, in its
heart of hearts, the labor movement itself increasingly has
learned—as may be witnessed by its increasing resort to politics.
And that the state itself can—for worse or better—greatly alter
economic reality, no one in this century will deny.[27]

terms of the modern logical syntax of welfare economics, of the implicit
ethical value judgments that lie behind much present-day economic
writing on this and other problems. Every economist has the right as a
citizen to propagandize; but as a scientist—as a social scientist—he has
a duty, according to my old-fashioned creed, to give disciplined attention
to the facts of empirical life and logical argumentation.

[27] [*Editor's note:* Professor Clark epitomizes the above argument as follows (with apologies to Hilaire Belloc):

> If workers, low-paid, seek to better their lot
> By grabbing some dough from the rich,
> It makes jobs for more workers—or else it does not;
> I cannot be positive which.]

118

HAROLD HOTELLING AS MATHEMATICAL ECONOMIST

by *Paul A. Samuelson*

Until quite recently the number of mathematical economists was not large. It might have been a relaxing hobby to collect all the first editions of the major works of Cournot, Jevons, Walras, Edgeworth, Wicksell, Irving Fisher, and Pareto—to say nothing of a dozen other minor writers in this vein such as Marshall, Auspitz and Lieben, Launhardt, and many others. Perhaps a careful observer might have been forgiven if in 1920 he had concluded that mathematical economics was a dead-end, and indeed dead, subject. For the original late nineteenth century spurt had largely spent itself before the first war.

The New Dawn

It was in 1925, when Harold Hotelling was almost thirty, that he burst on the scene of economics. Although he took his Bachelor's degree in journalism, Hotelling belongs to that small group of scholars who came into economics from formal training in mathematics; and to the subset of that group whom economists recognize as having made significant contributions to economics proper.

Besides Hotelling's many contributions to the valuable economics tool of mathematical statistics, he wrote more than twenty contributions to economics itself. No one of these is lacking in interest and insights, but it is for his six major papers, published between 1925 and 1938, that he will be most remembered by the historian of economic analysis. As economists of my generation can testify, late comers find it much easier to ride the crest of a renaissance after it has clearly gotten under way than to be one of the pioneers initiating that renaissance. Men like Hotelling, Frisch, and Tinbergen—to say nothing of Griffith C. Evans, Henry Schultz, and Charles F. Roos—were the leaders in the pre-1930 revival of mathematical economics.

Great Days on Morningside Heights

It was at Columbia, in the decade before World War II, that Hotelling became the Mecca toward whom the best young students of economics and mathematical statistics turned. Many of today's leading scholars went through an apprenticeship with him. Even less able students were accorded his legendary attentiveness to their problems, to the degree that some of their work appeared to outsiders to be more a tribute to Hotelling's originality than their own. And so kindly a Master was Hotelling as to make it hard to evaluate his glowing letters of recommendation and his liberal awarding of A grades. (This resemblance to Schumpeter was striking.)

All in all, the combination of Wesley Mitchell, J. M. Clark, and Harold Hotelling made Columbia an exciting place in the 1930's, carrying forward the great tradition of John Bates Clark and H. L. Moore. Alas, Hotelling's increasing preoccupation with mathematical statistics was that discipline's gain but a loss to the literature of economics. All the more worthwhile, therefore, for me to recall his six major papers in economics (1).

Depreciation and the New "Entropy" Economics

It is remarkable that Hotelling's first economic paper, dealing in 1925 with the thorny problem of depreciation, already shows, in addition to a firm mathematical technique, a keen understanding of the subtle economic aspects involved in the problem. From the very beginning, in good Irving Fisher fashion, he sets up the present discounted value of future net receipts and insists that every decision be taken so as to maximize this integral. Simple as this idea is, it puts a whole new light on the purpose of computing depreciation, and enables him quickly to set down the derivative conditions for the determination of the optimal length of life for an asset that will not be replaced. Later writers, such as Gabriel Preinrich, Armen Alchian, and George Terborgh, generalized this problem to an infinite stream of succeeding machines.

We have here then a nice example of what has come to be known as managerial economics, and a particular example of the kind of dynamic programming Richard Bellman and others have studied in our own day. And it must be a gratification to Hotelling to know that all over the land business management is today using methods, developed by George Terborgh of the Machine and Allied Products Institute, to replace machines so as to maximize the firm's present discounted values.

The following quotations from this first paper (pp. 351-2) will show that from the beginning Hotelling realized the importance of maximizing principles to economics:

> . . . the guiding principle is that . . . discounted future profits, is to be made a maximum. Even if the capitalist system is to give way to one in which service and not profit shall be the object, there will still be an integral of anticipated utilities to be made a maximum. Since we must find a function which maximizes an integral we must in many cases use the Calculus of Variations. But the problem here transcends the questions of depreciation and useful life, and belongs to the dawning economic theory based on considerations of maximum and minimum which bears to the older theories the relations which the Hamiltonian dynamics and the thermodynamics of entropy bear to their predecessors . . .
>
> . . . A thorough working knowledge of the Calculus of Variations is a prerequisite to the development of this type of economic theory [the new "entropy" economics]—which doubtless explains why it has not developed further.
>
> All hedonistic and eudaemonistic ethical theories, which declare that the total of pleasure or happiness should be made a maximum, really reduce the question of right conduct to a set of problems in the Calculus of Variations and in the more general theory of maxima of functionals.

There is perhaps an overemphasis upon the calculus of variations and maximizing continuous functionals here, due no doubt to the coeval work of Evans and Roos and the many students of G. A. Bliss; and also to Hotelling's own developing interest in the problem of mining that was to be the subject of his third major paper, that of 1931 dealing with exhaustible resources and giving extremal conditions for various maxima. For the most part economists have found it just as convenient to work with a finite number of variables defined at many discrete periods of time as to deal directly with functionals. And except in connection with capital theory there have been rather few important applications of the calculus of variations in the thirty years that have since elapsed. (2) For all of that, there is a prophetic insight in these early words.

Location and Duopoly

The 1929 paper on "Stability of Equilibrium," which has been reprinted in the American Economic Association's *Readings in Price Theory*, is perhaps Hotelling's most widely known piece. Its happy example of sellers strung like beads along a road is not only of economic import but is interestingly used by Hotelling to show why our two major political parties tend to be so much alike and why cider tends to be too homogeneous. In the realm of location theory, it is a worthy successor to the special models of Thünen, Weber, and Fetter and a worthy forerunner of the Lösch-Christaller hexagonal patterns of two-dimensional location. Like most original investigations, it has been extensively commented on by later writers: e.g. E. H. Chamberlin in his revolutionary *Theory of Monopolistic Competition* (1st edition 1933; 7th edition 1957) and many others.

If quantity demanded of a good is the same at every point on a line-segment and independent of delivered price and if transporting a unit of the good costs a constant amount per unit distance, then social costs are minimized if a single seller locates in the middle of the line. The rational monopolist will in fact go to the central point. But suppose there are two sellers, each regarding the other's price as fixed and setting his own F.O.B. price to maximize his net profits. Then a seller will set his price so as to sell some output at home, and he can be sure of the market "behind him" (i.e., between him and the end of the line segment). As he lowers his F.O.B. price to all, even though the two goods are identical and the demand at each point on the line totally inelastic, he widens his own share of the line between him and his rival because the boundary of his market, the point of equal delivered price from the two sources, necessarily moves towards his rival. Thus, at prices which leave some market to the other fellow, each man's profit becomes a smooth function of his and his opponent's administered prices. The Hotelling-Bertrand point of duopoly equilibrium is then given by the two equations

$$\frac{\partial \pi_1(p_1,p_2)}{\partial p_1}=0, \qquad \frac{\partial \pi_2(p_1,p_2)}{\partial p_2}=0$$

Moreover, empirically one man would find his maximized profits increasing if he moved *toward* his stationary rival. So instead of locating at the social optimum point of $(\frac{1}{4}, \frac{3}{4})$ on a unit line, sellers may tend toward the middle point $(\frac{1}{2}-\epsilon, \frac{1}{2}+\epsilon)$. For $n>2$ sellers, the socially optimal locations $(\frac{1}{2^n}, \frac{3}{2^n}, ..., \frac{2n-1}{2^n})$ will

not be reached; nevertheless whenever too great an empty space appears, it will pay one of the men to move into it. Interestingly enough, if we wind the line around a circle, we get rid of the certain market "behind" the outside men and may find an equally-spaced equilibrium.

Hotelling has built upon the earlier duopoly theories of Cournot, the French mathematician Bertrand, and Edgeworth. It will be recalled that Bertrand repudiated Cournot's market specification that each seller can only name his output and that total output is auctioned off to bring the price given by the demand curve $p_1 \equiv p_2 \equiv ... \equiv p = D(q_1+q_2+...)$. Instead Bertrand assumed a market structure in which each seller independently *names* his own administered price, p_i. With homogeneous goods, the demand relations for each Bertrand seller have infinite cross-elasticity and own-elasticity at $p_1 = p_2$; so naturally this discontinuity can lead to continuous price undercutting down to zeroless cost, or to the common marginal cost of identical sellers. Because of transport cost, Hotelling's $\pi_i(p_1,p_2)$ functions were designed to avoid discontinuities and corners at $p_1 = p_2$ and this gave him his "stability" of equilibrium.

However, as Bowley, Frisch, Edgeworth (in neglected passages), Stackelberg, and Neumann and Morgenstern have shown, the duopoly problem is the same in principle whether you write the demand functions as prices in terms of quantities or as quantities in terms of prices. Indeed, since a seller need not sell all that consumers want to buy at the named price, the strategy space for each one of the sellers may have to involve *both* his p_i and q_i. So generally the profits for each have to be written as the general payoff function $\pi_i(x_i,x_j)$, where the space of the strategy vectors x_i of man i have to be specified *institutionally*.

From this viewpoint, the Hotelling equilibrium point is the same in principle as the Cournot point, the Bertrand point, or the modern-day Nash equilibrium point for a non-constant sum game; namely, each of two or more rivals is supposed to pick his x_i strategy so as to end up with the system's achieving the following simultaneous maximum relationships

$$\text{Max } \pi_1(x_1,\bar{x}_2) \text{ and Max } \pi_2(\bar{x}_1,x_2),$$
$$\{x_1\} \qquad\qquad \{x_2\}$$

where the barred magnitudes are subjectively taken as unalterably given.

Unless we have the special Neumann case where π_1 and π_2 add up to a constant (or can be made to do so by scale changes) there need not be a nice saddlepoint solution and all such proposed Nash solutions are open to numerous economic objections. Edgeworth, Bowley, and Stackelberg pointed out that if one seller picks x_1 to maximize π_1 taking x_2 as given, then the other can usually benefit from *not* pursuing a similar behavior pattern. Nor is it certain, except in a tautological sense, that collusively $\pi_1 + \pi_2$ will be maximized—for the reason that there is no way a rational colluder can know in advance how the maximized total will end up being divided. Nor will economists wish to commit themselves to a different kind of Nash symmetry solution based on various appealing but arbitrary axioms.

Of course none of this commentary thirty years after the fact detracts from Hotelling's 1929 achievement.

Integrability and All That

Hotelling's 1932 article dealing with producer supply and demand conditions and taxation, his 1935 article dealing with demand by a consumer subject to a budget or income constraint, and his 1938 article on welfare marginal cost pricing are all part of a developing pattern. The 1932 preoccupation with the taxation paradox

of Edgeworth well reveals the superiority of mathematics to commonsense reasoning where deductive intricacies are concerned. How can placing a unit tax on one or on two goods actually cause *both* prices to fall? Commonsense tells us, if we tame it, that after two such taxes a monopolist will definitely cut down on his output of at least one good (and he *may* cut down on the other one too). If demands were independent, then with at least one q certainly down at least one p would have to rise. (Giffen effects have been ruled out of order here.) But with interrelated demands, the reduction of one (or more) q_i cannot rule out the possibility that all p's might have to fall.

More important than this curiosity is the detailed analysis of interrelated supply and demand functions of profit maximizers. Hotelling for the first time rigorously derives correct integrability conditions and secondary definiteness conditions that each firm's functions must satisfy and that the *aggregate market* functions must satisfy. In connection with tax and optimality problems, Hotelling beautifully generalizes to related demands the Dupuit-Jenkin-Marshall concepts of consumer surplus and deduces important relations that are approximately true for small taxes. Later writers, such as Hicks, Allais of Paris and his students Boiteux and Debreu, and many others have built on this work of Hotelling. Without apparently knowing the Ramsey-Pigou taxation analysis of 1927, Hotelling poses and gives at least a formal solution to the problem of the optimal pattern of *excise* taxes to achieve a given amount of real revenue with least loss.

Here is a further point to illustrate the penetration of Hotelling's analytical power. The fact that prices as a function of quantities possess a symmetric and definite Jacobian matrix is shown to imply that the inverse functions of quantities in terms of prices must possess the same property. It follows that the integrability conditions have insured the existence of a new function, called by Hotelling a "price potential," whose second derivative symmetric Hessian matrix is identical to the relevant Jacobian matrix. Many later writers, such as Court, Roy, Hicks, Houthakker, and I have had occasion to make extensive use of such inverse or indirect utilities or potentials that were related to Legendre transformations and Gibbsian thermodynamic potentials.

To complete his 1932 program of taking into account demand generated by utility maximized *subject to an income restraint*, Hotelling in 1935 tackled the mathematics of this problem. He began unaware of Slutsky's brilliant 1915 Italian solution. Hicks and Allen and Henry Schultz too did not in the beginning know Slutsky's work, and Hotelling carried on his researches unaware of the Hicks and Allen 1934 conquest of this summit. Because of the simple fact that Harris Hancock had published a detailed account of Weierstrasse's little-known resolution of the secondary condition for a constrained maximum, Hotelling was able to do quickly what Pareto never in all his life succeeded in doing—namely to give the correct bordered-matrix conditions sufficient for a true constrained maximum. This shows the importance of pure mathematical technique in an applied field. Pareto's instincts were perfect; his equipment just not up to his needs. (3)

Marginal Cost Pricing

I come now to the *piece de resistance*. The title of Hotelling's 1938 paper, "The General Welfare in Relation to Problems of Taxation and of Railway and Utility Rates," gives a good idea of its importance. Once the George Washington Bridge has been built and before it has become overcrowded, the social extra or marginal cost of having one more person cross on it is virtually nil. Why then charge a toll, causing some users to go by circuitous routes? It is not the transfer of money from citizen to the state that bothers Hotelling: after all there may be bond interest on the bridge that has to be paid; and it is possible that the user is rich and not especially to be spared unpleasant income effects. It is the citizens who needlessly avoid use of the bridge, and to that degree never pay any money, who are involved in the social problem of inefficiency in the use of resources—or what economists call "deadweight loss" from less than optimal taxation and pricing.

The conclusions of his analysis are sweeping: all industries which are subject to increasing returns (railroads, public utilities, etc.) ought to be charging the lower figure of marginal costs rather than average costs which will permit them to break even; all taxes, to subsidize the deficits of such industries and to provide revenues for desired real public services and for desired redistribution of income involved in various welfare transfer programs, ought to be levied in "lump sum" form so as to leave each person and firm facing market prices that truly reflect correct social costing and are not distorted by various tax excises so as to leave the system with deadweight loss. If this Hotelling-Lerner pattern is not followed, there always exists a rearrangement of society that can make every man better off—the rich, the poor, the worthy, and the unworthy; and if it is followed, there exist redistributions of income that will guarantee that a specified social welfare function for all of society has been truly made a maximum in terms of the technological alternatives open to society.

All this of course is grandly ideal. Hotelling shows in subsequent discussions that he realizes the feasibility compromises that would have to be met. None the less it is his strong empirical inference that if the glaring cases of divergences of price from marginal cost are dealt with that this will with great probability lead to a "better" configuration than if customary practices are followed; and he points up the presumption that, other things equal, small excises on many goods do less harm than a large excise on a few.

Hotelling points out that his general result is not new and can be traced back at least to the French engineer Dupuit and to a number of neoclassical economists (including, I may add, Wicksell who influenced Swedish economists early in this century to favor marginal cost pricing for railroads). But Hotelling, independently of Lerner, Bergson and other contemporaries, was the first to generalize the argument from a Marshallian partial equilibrium analysis of a single market to the rigorous analysis of n interrelated goods.

Because his analysis gave rise to some criticism and misunderstanding, I shall restate it briefly in slightly modified terms. For simplicity suppose society's production of n goods $(q_1,...,q_n)$ involve constant-returns-to-scale production functions in terms of a single primary factor L (standing for "labor" or "land"); hence, production possibilities are summarized by

$$(1) \qquad \pi_1 q_1 + \pi_2 q_2 + ... + \pi_n q_n = L,$$

where the π's represent true social and private marginal costs (expressed in terms of the *numeraire L*).

Now suppose that a single individual wishes to maximize an ordinal utility indicator $\Phi(q_1,...,q_n;L)$. Alternatively Φ could be postulated to hold for each of a large number of identical persons, or could even represent a social welfare function derived after an ethical observer had arranged for optimal transfers that would keep the social marginal utilities of every man optimally equal.

In the absence of governmental services and taxes and changes in L, a technocrat would succeed in maximizing Φ by picking $(q_1^*,...,q_n^*)$ such that

$$(2) \qquad \frac{\partial \Phi}{\partial q_i} = \lambda p_i;$$

together with (1), (2) determines the pre-tax optimum.

A competitive market system which set prices (relative to the wage) equal to marginal cost, $p_i = \pi_i$, and gave the man an income $m = \bar{L}$, would achieve the same optimum if the man used free choice in the market to maximize Φ subject to the income budget constraint $\sum p_i q_i = m$.

Now suppose the government requires goods for public purposes in amounts $(g_1,...,g_n)$, with $r = \sum \pi_i g_i$ the irreducible real tax burden. Then the technocrat would find a new optimum $(q_1^{**},...,q_n^{**})$ satisfying exactly the same equations as (2) but with the right hand expression in (1) now involving L minus the needed government expenditure or revenue r. Unless the public g's affected preferences among the private q's, presumably less would now be consumed of all "superior" goods; etc. To determine the optimal g's, equations of the form $\partial \Phi / \partial g_i = \lambda \pi_i$ would be necessary along the lines of my modernized Wicksell-Lindahl theory of public goods; but that was no concern of Hotelling in 1938.

What pricing system would be optimal? Hotelling shows that the new (q_i^{**}) can be reached by setting $p_i - \pi_i = t_i$, the size of each excise tax, in every case equal to zero; at the same time we must reduce income $m = L$ to $L - r$. Thus, an "income" tax is an optimal tax. Hotelling agrees with Lerner that if $\partial \Phi / \partial L \neq 0$, so that factor supply is variable, then a so-called income tax is really an excise on effort and should really be required to be a "lump sum" tax independent of pre-tax income L. He agrees with R. F. Kahn and Frisch that p_i proportional to π_i in every case, rather than equal, may also be optimal provided L is strictly constant; with any possible variability in L, he has to insist upon full equality to marginal costs rather than mere proportionality. (4)

The Scientist as Man

Enough has been said to point up Hotelling's tremendous originality in dealing with deductive matters, and what is rarer among theorists his fruitful insights into important social and economic problems of modern society. In concluding I trust it will not be impertinent to draw attention to two of his important personality traits.

A mathematical economist need not be of any particular political persuasion. Despite Mussolini's decorating of Pareto, the old canard that "a reactionary is a man who believes in equilibrium" is not sustained by the history of mathematical economists. The dispersion of their views has pretty much matched that of their contemporaneous literary comrades, and if any statistically significant difference could be found it would probably be to the effect that the median mathematical economist has been slightly more in favor of reform than the total universe of economists.

Certainly Hotelling always indicated a strong concern for improving the workings of our economic system and decreasing its inequalities: thus, while showing his usual kindliness toward a sloppy book on economic time series, he could not pass over without protest its claim that the goodness of fit of a Pareto distribution to segments of data on wealth, billiard scores, and executive salaries implied society could not alter the distribution of wealth or could do so only at the cost of ensuing catastrophes like the French and Russian Revolutions or the collapse of the Maginot Line. And it is worthy of note that what is perhaps Hotelling's most important single paper, his 1938 Presidential Address to the Econometric Society which was commented on above, chose to deal with the welfare economics inefficiencies resulting from social pricing different from marginal costs.

Finally, one should mention Hotelling's sense of the importance of his kind of work. From the very beginning he had an optimistic faith in the urgency of applying mathematics to social problems and fostered in others the desire to cultivate this vineyard. In the dark days of World War II, at M.I.T. I heard him express in all seriousness the conviction that the Allies would surely win the conflict, because they had (in Britain,

the United States, and India) the leading masters of modern statistical theory in contrast to Germany and Italy which had none. And I believe it was Hotelling who during that War suggested *Econometrica* be discontinued lest its contents lend aid to the Enemy's war effort! Such faith has to some appear to border on the naive. But the history of ideas shows that strong faith is the pioneer's greatest asset. And it is society's gain that Harold Hotelling is in this regard so generously endowed.

REFERENCES

(1) In chronological order they are: "A General Mathematical Theory of Depreciation." *Journal of the American Statistical Association*, xx (1925) 340-353; "Stability in Competition." *Economic Journal*, xli (1929) 41-57—also appears in K. E. Boulding and G. J. Stigler, ed., AEA *Readings in Price Theory* (1952) 467-484; "The Economics of Exhaustible Resources." *Journal of Political Economy*, xxxix (1931) 137-175; "Edgeworth's Taxation Paradox and the Nature of Demand and Supply Functions." Journal of Political Economy, xl (1932) 577-616; "Demand Functions with Limited Budgets." *Econometrica*, iii (1935) 66-78; "The General Welfare in Relation to Problems of Taxation and of Railway and Utility Rates." Presidential address to the Econometric Society. *Econometrica*, vi (1938) 242-269—also appears in R. A. Musgrave and C. S. Shoup, ed., AEA *Readings in the Economics of Taxation* (1959) 139-167.

(2) The work of Fred Westfield and of Tjalling Koopmans on optimal use of water in hydroelectric scheduling provides significant exceptions.

(3) The 1935 treatment is perhaps not completely satisfactory in its goal of deriving useful inequalities for *market* demand functions arising from aggregating many consumers. Instead of writing market demand as a homogeneous function of degree 0 in all p's and all specified individual incomes, m_a, Hotelling seems to replace implicitly $q_i = \Sigma_a q_{ia} = \Sigma_a h^{ia}(p_1,...,p_n,m_a) = q^i(p_1,...,P_n; m_1,...,m_a,...)$ by $q_i = f^i(p_1,...,p_n)$ or by their (existent?) inverse $p_i = F^i(q_1,...,q_n)$. I may say that my own attempt to do better in *Econometrica* 1938, I no longer like. Perhaps the root of Hotelling's difficulty is that his writings are never fully Walrasian; he improved on Marshall and Edgeworth by generalizing their partial equilibrium to many interrelated goods, but it was no part of his interest to spell out in print the full Walrasian general equilibrium and some of the minor misunderstanding of his 1938 paper may be due to this. As he was aware, a rigorous interpretation of his results was possible in the special case where for everyone the marginal utility of income, λ_a, was strictly constant—not a realistic case but one that does give partial equilibrium analysis a firm deductive base. Certainly Hotelling as much as any of his generation gave the stimulus, by his generalizing partial equilibrium, to the modern revival of full general equilibrium analysis.

(4) This is not the place to consider (1) how the effects of marginal social utilities of income of different men can be handled. Or (2) how Hotelling's use of differentials can be justified by a rigorous analysis of point derivatives. Or (3) how, as Margaret Joseph and others have shown, it is really the Slutsky elasticities and not the *ceteris paribus* $\partial q_i / \partial p_i$ expressions which are crucial in computing minimum deadweight loss. Years ago in a Treasury memo, I showed how the Ramsey analysis can be improved on, and Boiteux has published numerous important contributions to this problem. Suffice it to say that Hotelling's theorems can be defended from all criticisms, and form the springboard for an attack on the more difficult problem of what is the best compromise when all price and marginal costs cannot be equated for feasibility reasons.

119

D. H. ROBERTSON (1890–1963)

Paul A. Samuelson

"Everyone deserves justice — even Cambridge mathematicians." So wrote that eccentric genius of electricity and mathematical operators, Oliver Heaviside, with the evident implication that it would have to be meted out to them in eye-droppers. Cambridge economists, God bless them, also deserve justice; and since they cannot always be counted on to pour it on each other in buckets, it is up to us barbarians to join in the rituals.

Dennis Robertson dead? It is like having one of the fixed stars disappear. To those of my generation, Robertson was always there. In a scholarly field, age is measured not from birth but from the time of first notable publication, which explains I suppose the astonishing fact that Robertson was actually younger than, say Alvin Hansen, and others who came to economics after transitional detours. Robertson's notable book, *A Study of Industrial Fluctuation* (1915),[1] was written before the first war and is very nearly contemporaneous with the classic *Business Cycles* (1913) [2] of Wesley Mitchell. The book was written in good part when Robertson was but twenty-two years of age and in the third year of his economic study! Such precocity is hard to match. It reminds one again of the incredible ability of talented youth to master in a season all that the past has established, and then to push the flag forward another furlong. Galois in mathematics, Ramsey in philosophy, and Abba Lerner (who after months of part-time study at the London School was writing articles of classical stature), all belong in this same remarkable category of precociousness.

1. London, P. S. King.
2. Berkeley, University of California Press.

The Style That Is The Man

Dennis Robertson is well remembered for his quotations from *Alice in Wonderland*. Robertson not only gathered harvest, he produced it. He had the rare vice of being a charming writer. He would sneak up on the unwary reader and gain his acquiescence by a siren song. The man could almost make you believe in such absurd things as cardinal utility. What others had to steal by the bludgeon of matrix calculus, he deftly purloined by the stiletto of wit.

There was, of course, one exception. (There *always* is an exception — save for special cases, such as Alfred Marshall's uncanny ability to avoid lapsing into humor.) *Banking Policy and The Price Level* (1926),[3] which many would regard as Robertson's greatest work, is almost unreadable. Professor John Williams used to be able to say without shame that he had never finished reading it, because every few years, when conscience drove him to the effort, he always got to the same page 40 at which the frailty of the flesh took over. Hoping to benefit by his example, I tried as a student to read it backward but not with greater success: at page 103 minus 40, I too conked out. If we should ever meet in the Pullman club-car an explorer who began his climb at page 40, the three of us might be able to gauge the book's greatness. Fortunately, in several books and articles, Robertson splashed us with the essence of his 1926 contribution to the subject of forced saving and banking (long and short; direct and indirect; spontaneous and induced; applied and abortive). The book's elementary mathematics is not presented gracefully, which is a pity since Robertson can justly claim to have been an originator of the period analysis (i.e., dynamic difference equations and the qualitative analysis of market "days"), which became in the 1930's so useful a tool in the hands of Lundberg, Hicks, J. M. Clark, Metzler, and others. He also made claim — with more than an epsilon of justification — to having been an originator of the geometric progressions that Harrod, Domar, and others have made so famous in the golden age we live in.

If being English were a quantity instead of a quality, Robertson would merit a high cardinal score. First, he was the son of a clergyman headmaster. (Pigou's father was an army officer, Keynes's a don, Marshall's a cashier in the Bank of England.) Robertson proceeded to Eton and apparently belonged to that happy few of public school men who were both (1) literate enough to record memories and (2) possessed of pleasant memories to record. He

3. London, P. S. King.

went up to Trinity and remained in Cambridge virtually all his life. The time he might have spent in learning how to read Spiethoff's German writings on business cycles was better spent on the classics, at which he excelled; and his inability to understand what $e = 2.718$ . . . meant, he wore throughout his life as a badge of honor. From Robertson's writings I had always thought that he must have been among the last of Marshall's protegés, and was surprised to learn from him how few and casual his personal contacts were with the retired Marshall. Pigou, Marshall's emissary on earth, was his teacher, along with Keynes and Walter Layton. Needless to say Robertson mopped up every honor in sight, including those in amateur dramatics.

Although an ardent pacifist, when the war came Robertson signed up at once. He was awarded the Military Cross, and according to rumor, came close to receiving the Victoria Cross. The man who in his bath first said, "Eureka: there does exist something I shall call the Establishment," might well have been thinking of Dennis Robertson when inspiration struck. The only deviation from the Edwardian pattern is the fact that he was mercifully spared in battle.

Before the Break

And so he returned to Cambridge to live happily ever after and pick up his economic studies. There followed in the 1920's what I fancy was the happiest decade of his scholarly life: working closely with Keynes in a mutually productive relationship, Robertson formulated most of his lasting contributions to monetary theory; he also found time to make a number of worthwhile points about economic theory and international finance. Besides his 1926 monograph, he wrote the first two editions (1922, 1928) of the justly famous handbook on *Money* [4] in the Cambridge series of Keynes, and also *The Control of Industry* handbook.[5] (My own earliest introduction to economic theory came from Sir Hubert Henderson's handbook, *Supply and Demand*; [6] my earliest introduction to money from the 1928 Robertson *Money*. I often think I should have quit while I was ahead. Certainly I was well-qualified to run the Bank of England or solve minor Treasury crises.) *Economic Fragments*

4. London, Nisbet.
5. London: Nisbet, 1923.
6. London: Nisbet, 1922.

(1931),[7] the first of his self-selected anthologies, records the theoretical work of that period.

Biography refuses to stay on the nonfiction shelf. At about the end of the decade came Robertson's break with Keynes (or vice versa). The timing is curious. One would not have been too surprised if the revolutionary accomplishments and pretensions of the 1936 *General Theory* [8] had precipitated a rift between them: but it is hard today to imagine anyone's getting aroused over the anticlimactic 1930 *Treatise on Money* [9] — except perhaps for its digs at $MV = PQ$. Perhaps the friction between the two men was quite independent of scholarship: one really does not want to know, except as personal information illuminates scholarly issues. In any case a new note enters into Robertson's writing which was to remain until the end — a querulous note of protest over the pretensions and correctness of so-called new ideas and a somewhat repetitious defense of earlier wisdom. I do not mention this for the reason that full candor is mandatory in an obituary notice. I mention it because it is there, recognized by foe, friend and Robertson himself, and it may put readers off unduly. This Robertsonian querulousness was not, I conclude on reflection, sterile. Many of Robertson's points, had they come from within the Keynesian camp, would have been recognized as valuable contributions. One of the attributes that make the *General Theory* a great book is this uncanny ability to convert its critics (many of them, anyway) into fruitful reformulations — Pigou being a prime example.

LIFE AT THE TOP

Dennis Robertson reached the height of his fame in the mid-1930's, when he was in his mid-forties. Thus, in Haberler's first edition of *Prosperity and Depression* [1], Keynes, Pigou, Hayek and Robertson receive by far the most index references. This fame was also symbolized by Harvard's picking him out of all the world's economists to receive an honorary degree at the time of its 1936 Tercentenary Celebration. Except in one respect, the choice was an excellent one. Robertson was urbane and cultured. He gave a nice speech, in which he pointed out the difference between cycles and secular stagnation; he warned against doing too little, and warned even more against doing too much. One suspects his hosts appre-

7. London, P. S. King.
8. New York, Harcourt Brace.
9. New York, Harcourt Brace.
1. Geneva: League of Nations, 1937.

ciated the latter message, for those who live in Newcastle invariably love to import people whom they expect will bring them coals. As a student at Harvard in the days before Hansen, I can testify that the coals of caution concerning doing too much about unemployment were not scarce goods in 1936 Cambridge. In those days of 15 per cent unemployment, there was coal doled out in each class, every hour on the hour; there were coals piled up in Holyoke House, where wisdom reigned before Littauer was built.

The scandal was not with the man who was there, who had after all been invited to the party. What constituted the scandal in Cambridge, Massachusetts in the fall of 1936 was the man who was not there. The fact that every reader will know his name confirms the justness of my diagnosis, which I may add did not have to be formulated with the wisdom of hindsight.

Robertson's one departure from Cambridge took place in the late 1930's. The pull of a professorship at the London School of Economics must have been a powerful one indeed to draw so attached a Trinity don away from his familiar rooms and walks, from his beloved music and contacts with young people. Probably the push from an environment grown hostile was more powerful still.

The Ever After

The war broke out. Robertson served his government well. And after the war he returned to the Marshall chair of political economy in Cambridge.

To understand Robertson's polemical writings in this final period, one would have to understand Cambridge. And no outsider can do that. Suffice it to say that the reader of his works is merely eavesdropping on an ancient argument that only Cambridge students could witness in full. The whole spectacle does not, an outsider fears, reflect great credit on anyone. It has been acted out a hundred times in continental universities. Yet who is to say that an adversary procedure does not have a constructive role in the long-run history of a science?

Finally, in the years of his retirement, Sir Dennis again became a controversial figure in connection with the Cohen Council on Prices, Productivity and Incomes. Now the issue of personality and doctrine becomes submerged by deeper ideological and political divergences. Will a slow-growing, somewhat open, economy like the United Kingdom benefit from contractionary restraint on aggregate demand so as to engineer (at least temporarily) enough labor

and capacity slack to moderate the upward trend of wage and entrepreneurial costs?   While it is hard to judge wherein lies the proper
balance between expansionary and restrictionist policies, it is easy
to guess how an economist with Robertson's background and lifetime writings would react to such an issue.   Had he not been one
who insisted from the beginning that much of the business cycle was
an inevitable and even a good thing?   Had he not through thick and
thin favored a policy of having the price level decline as technical
productivity rises?   Had he not always warned against "forced
saving?"   Against doing too much?   Against a belief in the complete
impotence of orthodox monetary policy (and also against a belief
in its omnipotence)?   It was inevitable that he should have come out
strongly for restrictionism.   And inevitable that he should have been
criticized bitterly for doing so.   I say this while eschewing all judgment on the merits or demerits of his case.   Suffice it to say that
there are many, in his country and mine, who argue that the only
cure for a bad Phillips Curve (implying upward price drift before
near-to-full employment) is a deliberate investment by the community in temporary deflation.   Once again, for good or ill, Dennis
Robertson had been a leader in formulating a key economic issue.

Some Robertsonian Contributions

Turning away from matters of personality, I should like to
mention a few of Dennis Robertson's lasting contributions to
economics.

1. *Exogenous investment as an important source of fluctuations.*
In *A Study of Industrial Fluctuation* Robertson cultivated a field
too much neglected in the Anglo-Saxon literature.   At a time when
monetary theories of the Hawtrey type were challenged only by
Pigou's emphasis on cumulative psychological factors, Robertson
did well to emphasize real factors in the business cycle, such as innovation and capital intensity.   On the continent, where Spiethoff,
Schumpeter, and Cassel were stressing such factors, his contribution
would perhaps not have had so much *Grenznutzen.*   Time permits us
to filter out Robertson's overemphasis on factors such as agriculture, which experience shows has no simple relationship to business
cycles.

All his life Robertson was predisposed to regard fluctuations in
activity as in some important degree desirable, a view which I
cannot think subsequent experience has fully endorsed.   On the
other hand, this same stubborn insistence kept Robertson from being

the darling of the libertarians: they never liked his skepticism, as expressed to the Macmillan Committee and elsewhere, that monetary policy could succeed in curing a slump; nor would most of them approve of his early emphasis, long before the *General Theory*, on fiscal policy as a partial substitute for the inadequacies of Hawtreyan monetary policy.

2. *Overinvestment aspects of a turn-down.* While never stooping to Hayekian extremes, Robertson always cherished the belief that there is in some sense "a shortage of saving" associated with the underinvestment that leads to a cycle down turn. I am not the one to do this notion justice, having lived in a generation taught every nonsensical variant of what remains a fairly incoherent and mystical doctrine. Certainly it is true that in many expansion periods, prices rise and the labor market gets tight; capital formation takes place under the influence of animal spirits and the profits associated with boom; interest rates tighten naturally and central banks can be counted on to countenance and encourage this tightening. Such a boom may have to run ever faster to stand still. Profits begin to erode as capital accumulates and mistakes become apparent. Like a tulip mania or a stock market bubble, the process lives on its own acceleration: the bubble, for reasons no one has ever been able to codify, will eventually prick itself. Or we can prick it. Or we can feed it some of the things it needs to keep going a little longer. But not all the angels in heaven know how to stretch out this kind of expansion indefinitely. Now let the financial and real bubble burst. If quick compensatory action is taken that is strong enough to resuscitate the mania, we are still on the tiger-ride that cannot last. How long then should we wait before preventing the recession that follows from snowballing into a secondary depression? These are real problems in a subset of upswings, but in what degree do they vindicate an overinvestment-undersaving theory of the peak? An increase in consumption expenditure would seem the least controversial policy in such an early recession; this Robertson perceived in his gentle renunciation of Hayekian deflationism, which Lionel Robbins had marshalled all his talents of persuasion to advocate in *The Great Depression* (1934).[2]

3. *The synthesizer and critic.* Although Robertson once referred to his "natural indolence" as the cause for not having written large tomes, he was in fact a hard and meticulous worker all his life.[3] Here is but one example. At sixty he read through one of

2. New York, Macmillan.
3. Aside from the books already mentioned, the following collections of

my less appetizing articles, and wrote, "Do you not, on page 10, want to add 'not' in the sentence on line 3?" Like Oscar Wilde, who spent all morning putting in a comma and all afternoon taking it out, I passed a morning deciding that Robertson was right and an afternoon in wondering whether he had been.

He embodied the results of his reading in periodic surveys of monetary theory, the interest rate, price theory of the firm, utility and all such. These served a purpose and met a need, one must admit even while disagreeing with some of his formulations. In re-reading Robertson's many collections of essays, I felt anew what a shame it was that his many criticisms of Keynesian writings from 1936 to the mid-1950's had not come from *within* that tradition.

Thus, he rightly pointed out that the equality of saving and investment was by many early Keynesians treated simultaneously as (i) an identity and (ii) as an equality achieved by movement of income to an equilibrium level. And he was also right in asserting that neither (a) $S \equiv I$, nor (b) the fact that investment-induced income increments will "generate" extra saving, can ensure against price inflation. He was right in questioning Keynes's insistence that the multiplier held instantaneously, and (with Haberler) in pointing out the tautological nature of the identity $\triangle Y/\triangle I \equiv 1/(1 - \triangle C/\triangle Y)$, derived from $\triangle Y \equiv \triangle C + \triangle I$ or $Y \equiv C + I$. (But I fear he was wrong in suggesting that the world could be the same after Richard Kahn's 1931 multiplier article, that no useful empirical hypothesis could be made about $\partial C/\partial Y$ and the shifts in schedules of C as a function of Y, and that the doctrine of forced saving was not in need of careful qualification in a world of con-siderable unemployment. When Robertson later referred to Hicks's *Trade Cycle*[4] as a brilliant book, he was thereby conceding that the *General Theory* was a classic.)

Particular credit should be given to Robertson for his fruitful contributions to the post-1936 discussion of interest rates. He often made better Keynesian sense — and good sense — than did some of the writings by those labeled with the epithet Keynesian.

4. *Inequality of investment and lagged Robertsonian saving.* The resistance to Keynes's 1936 definitions of saving and investment

essays and lectures testify to his industry: *Economic Essays and Addresses* (with A. C. Pigou) (London: P. S. King, 1931); *Essays in Monetary Theory* (London, P. S. King, 1940); *Utility and All That* (New York: Macmillan, 1952); *Britain in the World Economy* (London: Allen and Unwin, 1954); *Economic Commentaries* (London: Staples Press, 1956); *Lectures on Econom-ic Principles* (London: Staples Press, 1957–59); *Growth, Wages, Money; The Marshall Lectures for 1960* (London: Cambridge University Press, 1961).

4. Oxford: Clarendon Press, 1950.

as equivalent was given temporary appeasement by Robertson's supplying more dynamic definitions. This led to schizophrenia of the type reported by my colleague, Professor Ralph E. Freeman. "From ten to eleven I teach the equality of saving and investment from an elementary text, and have barely ten minutes between classes to adjust myself to teach their Robertsonian inequality from a money-and-banking text." (Actually, most desires for a neo-Wicksellian inequality of saving and investment were not correctly met by the special Robertsonian period definitions.) Robertson himself never conceded to Hawtrey and Keynes that he was merely uttering a tautology in asserting that income will rise (or fall) when observed investment exceeds (or runs short of) Robertsonian saving, which is defined as the difference between last period's income and this period's consumption. Yet $S_t \equiv Y_{t-1} - C_t$, $I_t \equiv Y_t - C_t$, does *tautologically* imply $Y_t - Y_{t-1} \equiv I_t - S_t$, with no refutable causation being necessarily implied. Robertson never seems to have realized the difference between such a tautology and the dynamic causal sequence involving an hypothesized consumption function $c(Y_{t-1})$, $Y_t \equiv C_t + I_t = c(Y_{t-1}) + I_t$. This last has the testable hypothesis $C_t = c(Y_{t-1})$; it also displays the test criterion for income change $Y_t - Y_{t-1} = I_t - [Y_{t-1} - c(Y_{t-1})] = I_t - [s(Y_{t-1})]$, where the expression in brackets is now Robertsonian saving, $s(Y_{t-1})$, a specific hypothesized *behavior equation* — e.g., with the refutable property $0 < ds(Y_{t-1})/dY_{t-1} < 1$. The above is a particular dynamic model, one actually given earlier by J. M. Clark in *The Economics of Planning Public Works* (1935); [5] Erik Lundberg, Lloyd Metzler, Richard Goodwin and many others showed it to be but one model; the criticism of so simple a model, made by Arthur F. Burns, in his well-read piece, "The Keynesian Thinking of Our Times," could itself be rewritten, without change in substance, so as to appear from within the Keynesian schools as a constructive criticism of the inadequacy of ultra simple models and the need for even more post-1936 elaboration.

5. *Eclectic insights.* When Robertson argued in effect, that a speculative demand for money would (i) arise merely from a willingness to pay a premium to hold safe cash in preference to risk-containing assets, and (ii) all this independently of any one-sided expectation that interest rates would soon harden and produce capital losses, he may have thought he was being anti-Keynesian. And so may some Keynesians of the late 1930's. History knows

5. Washington, Government Printing Office.

better. This is actually a superior statement of Keynesian liquidity preference.

A different case is provided in his disagreement with the view of someone like Joan Robinson, that an increase in thriftiness will lower interest, r, through its reducing income, Y. He argued that it could, even with unchanged total money M, lower interest directly. Now it is easy to imagine a man on his way to buy bread stopping at the broker's office and bidding down the yield on bonds. Hurrah for Marshall. But what happens to the bread piled up on bakers' shelves? To the former bondholder now with cash to invest? It was characteristic of Robertson that he resisted setting up a definite and *determinate macroeconomic system* either of dynamic or static type. The simplest Keynes system $Y - c(Y) \equiv s(Y) = I(r)$, $r = L(M, Y)$ may not be realistic in transitional states (nor better than a crude approximation to stationary equilibrium). But you can look at it, examine its deficiencies, even bomb it. What hostages has Robertson given to fortune — i.e., to testable science? Actually, in the absence of the Pigou effect — which, to my surprise, I have not been able to isolate in all the Robertson pre-1940 literature — Robertson too will come in the end to the conclusion that a lowering of the $c(Y)$ relationship will reduce income. When people save more, income will fall unless there is an easing of interest rate and credit great enough to expand investment in full compensation. Does Robertson really want $r = L(M, Y)$ to be replaced by $r = L(M, Y, s(Y))$ in the steady state, which can certainly be done easily if the facts call for such an alteration of the Keynesian building blocks? Again, when we are reminded that Marshall pointed out how an easing of interest rates *now* may sometimes trigger off a boom that will raise it *later*, are we to conclude that this is an exception to the proposition that creation of more M tends to depress r? If so, a drink now could tend to send me to church tomorrow.

6. *The transfer problem.* To illustrate Robertson's versatility, he and Pigou seem to have been the first to realize that when Germany pays reparation to England, the Marshallian offer curves of *both* countries shift. In simplified modern terms, he is suggesting that the endowment point in an Edgeworth-Meade box diagram be moved northeast to the benefit of the receiver and the detriment of the payer. In 1932 Pigou gave his all-but-definitive treatment of the transfer problem under barter conditions and in 1952–54 I brought to completion the Robertson-Pigou resolution of the issues

debated by Keynes, Ohlin, Taussig, Viner, and earlier writers.[6] Robertson supported the orthodox view that the payer's terms-of-trade would deteriorate by claiming that a country has a greater income elasticity for its own-produced goods than for its imported goods. I showed subsequently that, in the absence of all transport costs and tariff impediments, this is an inadmissible hypothesis and no presumption about terms-of-trade are possible; and that, in the presence of such "frictions," all presumptions become very complicated indeed.

7. *Those four crucial fractions.* Once discussing the waves of fashion in economics — such things as the period of production, elasticity of substitution, the twenty-six ways of measuring consumer's surplus, the Ricardo effect, and other 365–day wonders that sweep and resweep our science — I jokingly said to Robertson: "I don't suppose that even *you* remember your four crucial fractions." I was wrong. He took them very seriously up until the end, as I have been reminded in rereading his lifework: Robertson thought that the great depression and other basic trends might be related to a nonequilibrium development of *the desire of the public to hold in bank money exactly as much as would be consistent with the fraction of circulating capital that the banks would need and be willing to finance in business loans!*

This analysis has two claims to historical interest. First, Robertson was able to point out in his 1953 Harvard-Princeton paper, "Thoughts on Meeting Some Important Persons," [7] that this 1926 strain of analysis has some valid claims to have foreshadowed the Harrod-Domar type of equilibria.

Second, Robertson used his model to refute the ancient, but endemic, "real-bills" doctrine, which alleges that so long as money elastically expands and contracts in response to the desires of manufacturers and merchants for "sound, productive loans," money will manage itself in an optimal manner. This old notion underlay one of the important quarrels between the Banking School and Currency School more than a century ago, between the Qualitative and Quantitative theories of credit debated at Columbia thirty years ago, and it represented a faulty premise underlying our original Federal Reserve System of 1913.[8]

---

6. Essentially this last paper was submitted by name for publication in early 1937 but rejected.

7. This *Journal*, LXVIII (May 1954); reprinted in *Economic Commentaries, op. cit.*

8. See Lloyd Mints, *A History of Banking Theory in Great Britain and the United States* (Chicago: University of Chicago Press, 1945).

Robertson believed that his was a sufficient (and necessary) vindication of orthodox economic tradition, going back at least to Henry Thornton (1803), against its Banking School and practical-man critics. According to Robertson's exposition, it would be practically a miracle if *the velocity of turnover of money* were to be geared just properly with what might be called the (velocity of) *turnover of the average item of circulating capital*, so as to lead to price stability under laissez-faire banking. A summary, and appraisal, of his view seems long overdue. I use his notation for the most part.

First, simplify Robertson and assume all capital goods are circulating capital or goods-in-process, C. Let annual income be R. Then the now-familiar capital output is a crucial fraction C/R. (These variables can be measured in real or deflated terms; or, on the admissible simplifying assumption that the same price level, P, applies to all goods, we find PC/PR gives exactly the same ratio. Usually the capital output ratio is measured in calendar years and exceeds unity rather than being a fraction; but Robertson was thinking only of circulating capital, and in any case we can call 2.5 an honorary fraction.)

Second, simplify Robertson and assume *all* capital assets are financed by bank intermediaries and not by firms or families directly. Bank loans finance all capital assets. (Firm's assets of goods-in-process are matched by their loan liabilities. Banks' assets of loans receivable are matched by their deposit liabilities. Families have as assets their checkable bank deposits, which are matched by their net worth.)

Third, all money is bank-deposit money, M. By good Marshall-Fisher reasoning the average stock of money people will (want to) hold is a crucial fraction K, which is, of course, the reciprocal of the velocity of circulation of money and is measured in fractions of a year.

In this trivial system, since balance sheets must balance and by hypothesis all capital assets are bank financed, the total of money, M, equals the total value of capital, PC (or just C if Robertson assumes the price level is at its base of unity). By school algebra, we can write the equations

$$M \equiv PC$$

$$M \equiv \{K\}\,(PR) \qquad PC \equiv \left\{ \frac{PC}{PR} \right\} PR$$

$$\therefore \{K\} \equiv \left\{ \frac{PC}{PR} \right\} \, .$$

These are Robertson's *two* crucial fractions — two and not four because I have assumed that banks lend *only* on circulating capital and that circulating capital is financed *only* by the banks.

If I understand Robertson (a simplifying supposition), he believes the left side and the right side are quite independent of each other in causation and motivation: K is determined by institutional spending habits — how often we get paid, how near we are to a bank, and all the Fisher-Marshall considerations that determine the income velocity of circulation of M. On the other hand, the capital output ratio is a quasi-technical constant changing only if innovation or something else raises or lowers the average period of production. We have two quasi-constants which must (i) "instantaneously" always be equal or (ii) must "end up in equilibrium" equal. Will they? Won't they? Must they? If they don't — or if they try not to — what will follow from this "contradiction?"

All this is very non-neoclassical. It is very non-Robertsonish. Politics aside, it is like the 1936 Keynes and unlike the 1820 Say or James Mill. It is even like Marx with his everlasting contradictions. It is like Balogh or others who think that a dollar shortage (or glut) is not, of itself, an absurd notion. Since Robertson has commented on Lerner, Kalecki, Robinson, Kahn and others concerning Keynesian identities and behavior equations, their comments on his exposition would seem in season.

As I have written his system, it cannot even be used to controvert the "real bills" doctrine. For suppose producers became optimistic and asked for more loans, and thereby expanded M, say doubling it. Then if prices were to double, the identity of bank loans and firm's capital goods will persist; hence we seem to have no protection against over-issue of M even when the two crucial fractions are always equal. And, cannot the same equality hold in transitions when we have positive dM/dt and not necessarily matching changes in R, or in PR, or for that matter in P itself?

One suspects that Robertson sometimes wants to regard the left- and right-hand sides of the identity as "intended" or "*ex ante*" or "sustainable" or "scheduled" magnitudes, and to let their difference $\left[\{K\} - \left\{ \dfrac{PC}{PR} \right\} \right]$ act as some kind of an "error-signal" in making *something* change. If so, and if that "something" is the price level P, do we have a Wicksell-like theory of secular price change? Or is the adjustment taking place in real output R, so that we have a theory of the great depression? Suppose we do adopt this general kind of interpretation, say for P, and write out

$$-\frac{dP}{dt} \text{ is proportional to } \left[\{K\} - \left\{ \frac{PC}{PR} \right\} \right]$$

does our "inflationary gap" finally "close itself" by virtue of the fact that the right-hand quasi-constants are to be regarded as gradually melting into adjusting functions of the price level? (I must interject the query: "Why in the world should a *balanced* higher-level of prices change spending habits or technical periods of production?")

But one must not brow-beat Robertson for my simplified version of his model. Let's see whether his two other crucial fractions clarify the difficulties.

In real life a fraction of all firms' capital may be financed and owned directly by families: let $1-b$ be that fraction, with $b(PC)$ being the amount of circulating capital actually financed by bank loans.

In real life, some of bank assets will go for other purposes than circulating capital (e.g., government securities, durable-goods financed by term-loans or even by renewable 90-day promissory notes, it being understood that such capital goods are to be designated by a letter different from C). So, to bring in the last of the four crucial fractions, let $aM = a(KPR)$ be the fraction of total bank assets or liabilities that are used for circulating capital financing.

Now our simple algebra turns what was a two-fraction equivalence into a four-fraction equivalence

$$aM \equiv b(PC)$$

$$aK(PR) \quad \equiv \quad b\frac{PC}{PR}PR$$

$$\boxed{\{a\}\ \{K\} \equiv \{b\} \left\{ \frac{PC}{PR} \right\}}$$

Here then are Robertson's four crucial fractions of *Money*.[9]

Is the Robertson Equivalence a balance sheet identity? A definitional identity by virtue of definitions of a and b? Are the two sides quasi-constants, determined by quite different motivational and institutional forces? Are all four fractions such independent quasi-constants? Is some kind of an *ex ante* discrepancy $\left| aK - b\frac{PC}{PR} \right|$ conceivable; and is its intended-sustainable magni-

9. 1928 and 1948 editions, pp. 105–7, 182. There is the trivial difference that I have written the last one as the now familiar capital/output ratio rather than in his symbolism ½D, D being the Jevons-Wicksell range of the period of production.

tude a function of some economic variables like P or R or short-term interest rate or differential 'twixt short- and long-term interest rate? Is the mere fact that a/b is not unity Robertson's principal weapon in refuting the erroneous real-bill doctrine; and, if so, did he on reflection, stand by such an argument? I wish someone had asked Robertson these and other questions.

How a man uses a concept often throws light on what he thinks he means by it. Robertson at times seems to have had in mind something like the following application. In the 1920's the capital output ratio was perhaps shrinking for technical reasons as firms seemed to require less inventories for the same sales. So banks, the principal source of finance for inventories, might begin to have trouble in finding enough loan outlets to keep the community's supply of (checkable) M growing at, say, the 1 per cent rate needed to balance population growth and the resulting output growth. This might put undue downward pressure on the price level and lead to deflationary conditions of a slump.

Coming from a commentator writing in 1928 or 1930, this train of thought makes some logical sense and would appear to have some measure of empirical importance. But can one honestly say much more for it? If a and b and K do not spontaneously match the change in the capital output ratio, why wouldn't banks threatened with excess reserves underbid direct financers of circulating capital and increase b by changing their interest and availability requirements? Why wouldn't banks lower their a by making term-loans? (Robertson could claim to have foreseen this trend by his theory, and to have warned against the institutional and legal lags.) Why not help banks lower their a by providing them with government securities to hold? For a capitalistic system to let itself suffer from a fatal Robertsonian contradiction because it is unwilling to use such traditional methods of public debt management would seem laughable in 1963, and paradoxical even in 1928.

I owe it to Robertson's memory to try to interpret his crucial fractions. But I am not sure I have succeeded in doing so correctly.

8. *Should prices fall with progress?* It was long a matter of debate whether the growth in real output due to technical progress and population should result in (i) stable prices, (ii) falling prices, or (iii) rising prices. Implied in each of these patterns is a corresponding trend in money wage rates.

It is not always clear just what the terms of the debate are. Is the issue purely a *normative* one, with all the widows and *rentiers* naturally favoring a falling price level in opposition to the interests of equity speculators and active entrepreneurs or workers? Indeed if only self-interest is involved why shouldn't an advocate for pensioners advocate a fall in prices much *greater* than the technical cheapening of production? Usually as the issue has been debated, something more than *self-interest* is involved: According to reasonable ethical welfare functions, which price trend is fairer, *more equitable*? Finally, to bring the issue still more within the area of nonsubjective analysis, there is near the surface a feeling that one or another of these patterns is more "natural," in the quasi-objective sense of giving rise to less difficulties, distortions, and dead-weight loss. These are all very slippery notions and it does not help a great deal to repose the problem in terms of which pattern is "more neutral," in the sense of duplicating more closely the putative (optimal?) pattern that would be achieved in a hypothetical world of perfect barter where money could not "distort" things.

From an early date, Dennis Robertson favored a pattern of steady money wages, with the fruits of progress going "even-handedly" to all consumers through a steady fall in the price level. He considered such writers as Haberler, Hayek, and Lord Robbins as his allies, in opposition to the plain man who thought stable prices natural and such pre-Keynesians as Hume and Harrod; and Robertson certainly disagreed with more recent writers, like the late Sumner Slichter, who believed gently-rising prices to be the optimal feasible. In what was probably Robertson's last economic writing, his excellent *Memorandum Submitted to the Canadian Royal Commission on Banking and Finance* on July 28, 1962 [1], he reiterated his scientific view of the matter. While agreeing that political expediency might make stable prices a necessary compromise, he stated that the "more scientific view" called for falling prices, quoting with approval a letter to the *Times* of January 11, 1962 by the Archbishop of Wales:

> To a simple fellow like myself it seems that the lower prices which increased productivity makes possible would benefit everybody, but I recognize that there must be a flaw in my thinking, for increased productivity has not brought — and does not seem likely to bring — lower prices. Presumably there is good reason for this. Will someone explain?

"Nobody did," Robertson added dryly.

In my own *Memorandum Submitted to the Canadian Royal Commission on Banking and Finance* of October 19, 1962, I took mild issue with Robertson's statement on scientific grounds and I

---

1. Now available in the Princeton series *Essays in International Finance*, No. 42, May 1963.

refer the specialist to my rebuttal. The problem is important enough to merit discussion here.

To sum up my Canadian testimony on this point, I argued that a steady foreseeable trend of productivity accompanied by any one of the three patterns of price trend would, as long as the price trend was itself steady, foreseeable and foreseen, result in essentially the same real division of product between labor wages and interest returns to property. Employing good classical Thornton-Marshall-Wicksell-Fisher-Sraffa-Keynes reasoning, the equilibrium money rate of interest r_m would equal the real-natural-own rates of interest r_q plus an algebraic built-in factor $(dP/P)/dt$. E.g.,

$$.06 = r_q = r_m - \frac{dP/P}{dt} = .06 - 0 = .09 - .03 = .02 - (-.04),$$

giving essentially the same 6 per cent interest on profit returns in real terms, under steady, rising and falling price trends. In my idealized model, only once-and-for-all unforeseen inflation achieves appreciable real effects. Reason tells us this. Hume realized it. When Professor Earl Hamilton and others produced contrary evidence for the price revolution of post-Columbus centuries, this seemed odd; but reason cannot quarrel with bullets and facts. Yet cross-sectional experience with chronic inflations in underdeveloped and other lands gives much corroboration to my theory. And now, I believe, further historical research is at least somewhat negating Professor Hamilton's provisional hypotheses. I have before me the report of a large insurance company which earns more than 5 per cent on its new investments: I have no doubt that, if Robertsonian policy pushed the consumer's price index steadily downward by 2 per cent per annum, that company's annuitants would not be earning their current 5 per cent. Actually, if we now agree to bring in practical nonidealized considerations, my strong thesis will have to be qualified: but most economists will think these new elements of expediency will tell more against Robertson's "scientific" claim for falling prices than against his antagonists' claim.

To be specific consider [2] a Model T Solow system (where technical change does not have to be "embodied" in qualitatively new capital equipment). In this miracle country, equidistant from Germany, Japan and France but alas farther away from the United States and United Kingdom, labor grows at 1 per cent per year; versatile physical capital grows at 5 per cent; technical progress proceeds at 3 per cent per annum. The time-dependent production

2. The remainder of this section may be skipped.

function was measured by Solow to be of the following Cobb-Douglas form

$$Q = e^{.03t}\ L^{\frac{3}{4}}\ C^{\frac{1}{4}},\ L(t) = e^{.01t},\ C(t) = e^{.05t}$$
$$= e^{.03t}\ e^{.01t\frac{3}{4}}\ e^{.05t\frac{1}{4}} = e^{.05t}.$$

Thus, total output grows at 5 per cent in all; and because of the constant-relative-shares property of the Cobb-Douglas function, so must total wages and total interest (or profit). Since labor numbers grow at 1 per cent, the per capita real wage grows at 4 per cent; since total capital grows at 5 per cent, the interest rate (or the net rent per unit of capital good) remains constant. Although Kaldor would consider this country unrealistic, it would portray his stylized features of capitalism: constant capital output ratio, constant relative shares, constant profit rate, and even a constant saving income ratio. If we wickedly gave one of his students the data of the country without giving him its name, he could be forgiven for thinking that Kaldorism would "explain" its properties, although we sadists know better.

Now Robertson, if I understand him, would not insist on the price level's dropping by 5 per cent. In his Quantity Equation, $M = KPQ$, he would want M to grow at least as fast as the population increase, or by 1 per cent per year. Prices should then fall by $5-1 = 4$ per cent per year; as a check, note that this would indeed correspond to a constant money wage rate and a rising real wage rate of 4 per cent per annum attained through lower prices of goods. Also, the money price of machines is falling at 4 per cent per annum, and the money rate of interest is 4 per cent less than the real rate of interest, since capitalists can also buy all goods 4 per cent more cheaply each year. While people, or at least Archbishops, take it for granted that the 3 per cent fruits of technical progress — which are sent, so to speak, freely from heaven — should be splashed indiscriminately on all consumers (including workers, capitalists and consumers of capital formation), Robertson does not tell us why the fruits of deepening of capital, from a rising C/L ratio, should be splashed in this indiscriminate way.

Actually in such a crude or refined neoclassical model, any growth pattern for prices — such as $P(t) = e^{.03t}$ à la Slichter, or $e^{.0t}$ à la the plain man, or $e^{-.04t}$ à la Robertson [3] — is optimal provided only that the wage rate and other pecuniary parameters are

3. If money is storable, it is hard to see how the money rate of interest can be made negative: so a price decline exceeding in absolute value the real rate of interest would be impossible to achieve, meaning that in all cases where $r_q < |-.04|$, as is quite possible, Robertson's scientific pattern will be simply unachievable. Pathology illuminates normalcy!

at the appropriate levels — $w(t) = e^{.03t} e^{.04t}$ or $e^{.0t} e^{.04t}$ or $e^{-.04t} e^{.04t}$, respectively.

After returning from Ottawa, I noted one flaw in my own argument of price-trend neutrality If the M used as a medium of exchange bears no interest — a monstrous assumption in an idealized model and, as our banks now are learning in an era when Treasury bills give yields of more than 2½ per cent — the cash-to-income ratio K will be greatest (least) if prices are falling (rising). This is because the opportunity cost of holding sterile money for transaction purposes is greatest when prices are rising and the *money* rate of interest, r_m, is highest. Why impose this (minor) deadweight loss on mankind? [4] This does seem a small point in Robertson's favor; but it does also raise a nice question concerning Pareto-optimality of laissez-faire. Do we have here a case of the fallacy of composition, where each man cuts down on his cash balance because of the extra interest income he can get by so economizing? But when all persons act in this self-serving way, does society really economize on anything real or does it simply end up with a higher nominal price level? To appreciate the point about Pareto-optimality, suppose by collusive agreement we all hold *on the average* twice the cash balance dictated by *ceteris paribus* selfish maximizing. Then we save shoe leather on trips to the broker or savings banker. Doesn't *everybody* end up better off, with less deadweight loss?

*   *   *   *

In leaving this problem of the optimal trend of the price level, I have to warn that I have been discussing it in abstract terms. Realistically, there is much to be said for pay-as-you-go social security, constant-purchasing-power bonds to be made available to the public in limited amounts for various long-term saving purposes, and other devices to compensate the aged who have been irreversibly hurt by wartime or other inflation. Such escalation need not be of a magnitude to make inflation appreciably greater or more explosive.

CONCLUSION

Among the Iroquois it was the custom to do the newly dead more than justice, indicting them so to speak for the offense of virtue and leaving for a later tribunal judgment on the charge. I

4. I have benefited from talk on this point with Professor Edmund Phelps, who was at M.I.T. in exile from Yale last year. See also Harry G. Johnson, "Equilibrium under Fixed Exchanges," *American Economic Review*, LII (May 1963), 113; Robert Mundell, "Inflation And Real Interest," *Journal of Political Economy*, LXXI (June 1963), 280–83.

fear I have done Dennis Robertson less than justice. And perhaps it could not be otherwise, coming from one near to incorporating in himself all that Robertson deplored in modern economics: an addict of mathematics and neat models, a debunker of Alfred Marshall (not in the manner of economists like Joan Robinson who regard him as the best of a bad neoclassical lot, but as one of the new barbarians who deem him third to Walras and Wicksell), a zealot for full employment and critic of inequality, Robertson's friend and yet even more the friend of his antagonists — in short a silly-clever economist at an age when one should know better.

Let my tribute to him stand, then, as an underestimate.

MASSACHUSETTS INSTITUTE OF TECHNOLOGY

120

The Life of Knut Wicksell, by Torsten Gårdlund. Stockholm: Almqvist & Wiksell. 1958. Pp. 355, including an Appendix containing some Wicksell correspondence with Marshall and Walras. 30 kr.

If economists ran a popularity contest among themselves, the chances are Knut Wicksell would be the easy winner. After long neglect his writings on money and on pure theory were rediscovered in in the early 1930's. And what is more remarkable they have survived the challenge of translation into English — which is more than can be said of many other highly-touted rediscoveries.

Aside from the modern quality of his scientific writings, Wicksell's appeal to us is personal. He was generous to his predecessors and contemporaries and utterly candid in admitting difficulties in his own line of thought. How different he is in all this from Gustav Cassel, Sweden's other towering economist of the first quarter of this century. Cassel never ceased blowing his own horn and used the writers who went before him only as objects to be exploited, abused, or ignored. (In most popularity contests, he would end up at the bottom of the list; and history has taken its revenge by valuing Cassel below his true deserts.)

Most of us have probably accepted Schumpeter's view of Wicksell as a jovial Papa Brahms, who except for a passionate interest in neo-Malthusianism led the quiet and retiring life of a scholar. Had that been the case, there could not have been an excellent book-length biography like the present one, which is an English translation of a somewhat longer Swedish version. It turns out that Wicksell was an unusual psychological type, with a built-in need to rebel and to turn the authorities against himself regardless of the cost to his family's welfare. It is these strangenesses — I dare not call them imperfections! — in Wicksell's character that impart interest and even romance to what would otherwise be the conventional *curriculum vitae* of the successful academic.

How can we explain the fact that Wicksell had no professorial appointment until the age of 50? That he did not begin his serious studies of economics until the age of 38, but that most of his best ideas had already been formulated by 10 years later? (None the less up until his death at 74 he was still making contributions to the literature, some of them in the purest of pure theory — for example, his work on Akerman's problem and his review of Bowley's *Mathematical Outline of Economics*.) Why was the second edition of his *Lectures* prefaced from jail, where he had been committed in his late fifties for the blasphemous crime of ridiculing the conception of Christ?

Sex and religion seem to provide the clues. Like so many others of his time, Wicksell at adolescence became strongly religious. Guilt-ridden and an orphan, he feared Hell. To resist the torment of "sensual desires" he gave up all literature and the theatre and did not even dare to set foot in cafés with their "attractive waitresses." It is easy enough to see why he should have been a religious fanatic

from age 15 to 23. What may be harder to explain is why at that stage, he was beset and then convinced by doubt and became for the rest of his life an anti-religious fanatic. Yet we must remember that Scandinavian society of those days was very stuffy indeed, and that Ibsen, Strindberg, and Björnson were all fiercely attacking existing attitudes toward freedom of thought and the emancipation of women. Still Wicksell seems to have had an especially strong case of sexual repression: while he published poems of kissing soft bosoms, he in fact led a life of shy moral abstinence that even Malthus would have applauded.

We are used to long years of graduate study, but Wicksell wins the prize. He spent the years until 34 in somewhat aimless study of mathematics, where he had talent but apparently no signs of genius. Then partially financed by the Lorén Foundation, which had been set up by a dead philanthropic friend, he spent another dozen years studying economics. In the meantime, beyond the age of 45 or 46 he found it necessary in order to get a job as an assistant professor of economics in the Uppsala law faculty to cram into a couple of years the usual four year course of law. And he was not yet out of the woods. When neither Stockholm nor Uppsala would give him a professorship, he finally got a temporary post at Uppsala and then an Associate Professorship there; but he did not receive his full professorship until he was within a dozen years of the retirement age.

The opposition to Wicksell was primarily political and personal, not professional. At the age of 28 he became converted to neo-Malthusianism and made a famous address before a temperance society — in a Lutheran mission hall of all places — advocating contraception and arguing that current society suffered from sex-starvation with the only choice being one between celibacy and prostitution. This received nation-wide attention and for years Wicksell was a controversial name and a lecturer much in demand. (During those same years he, not uncharacteristically, fell in love with someone he had never met and with his best friend's wife!)

I think nothing in this tale should surprise us — except that along with these protest activities, Wicksell should have been able to turn out first-rate scientific work in the field of economics. Here his mathematical aptitudes and training must have been important; he found it a challenge to combine Böhm-Bawerk's capital theory with the equations of Walras. And yet we must admit that there is nothing very mathematical about his theory of interest rates and the behavior of price levels.

In the drama of Wicksell's life, things begin to

get better once he meets and marries the Norwegian Anna Bugge. True, he decides against a marriage ceremony even at the cost of estranging his wife's family. And later when his children have barely enough food to keep alive, he finds it necessary to preach the unpopular cause that Sweden should join the Russian empire in the interests of saving on defense and civilizing the Russians. Finally, when the great goal of a professorship at Lund is at last in sight, Wicksell cannot bring himself to sign his application to the King "Your Majesty's most obedient servant," instead ending up in the face of all his friends' advice with the simple form "Yours respectfully."

The last part of Wicksell's life was a little sad. He seems never to have had at Lund more than a smattering of uninterested law students or a circle of friends. While Wicksell did exercise some important influence during the Stockholm years of retirement, Gårdlund quotes a letter written at seventy:

Nothing in the world gives me pleasure any more — except good food and wine when I have the chance of it — a few weeks ago I went to concerts three days in succession and heard Beethoven's last eight quartets (played by the "London Quartet"). There was no doubt that they were extraordinarily beautiful, but my soul was not ravished as it should have been. All I could say was that it would have been very pleasant — if I had been thirty years younger.

The final irony is that after Wicksell's death his wife, as always not fully sympathetic with her husband's quixotic notions, arranged a funeral complete with hymn ("Am I Ready for Salvation?"), handfuls of earth thrown on the coffin, readings from St. John, and the Lord's Prayer.

PAUL A. SAMUELSON

PART XVII

Lectures and Essays on Modern Economics

121

WHAT ECONOMISTS KNOW
Paul A. Samuelson

Economics is fortunate among the social sciences in that many of its findings are directly applicable to public policy. Within the last twenty-five years great advances have been made in our factual knowledge about the financial system and in our understanding of how that system works and can be made to work. So only recently, you might say, has economics earned the right to its ancient name of political economy.

Thus, as I write in early 1958 the American economy is in the midst of a recession. So well charted these days is the pulse of the nation that this is open knowledge. The casual reader of the newspaper has today an awareness of contemporaneous economics events that was just a few decades ago unavailable even to the most energetic scholar. And beyond this knowledge of the facts of the case there is a calculated confidence• in our ability to battle this scourge

• Since this was written events have confirmed the implicit prediction made in early 1958 that the recession would soon come to an end: the upturn came after April.

of depression. A prediction made two decades ago that our mixed capitalistic system would no longer face the same frequency of chronic slumps as in its checkered past would have been borne out by the subsequent record: today's college undergraduate has scarcely known a full year of business contraction! The previous pattern, that each war must be followed by a slump with the same predictability that night follows day, has not thus far reasserted itself. While it would be rash to say that the business cycle has been banished from American life, it would be foolish to overlook the changed betting odds with respect to the likelihood of the *sustained* deflations that occurred in the 1830s, the 1870s, the 1890s, and 1930s.

If one had to associate this changed knowledge and control over national output and employment with but one name, it would certainly be that of Cambridge's Lord Keynes. If one were permitted a second, it would probably be that of Harvard's Alvin Hansen, the so-called "American Keynes" and himself a prolific developer of the tools of fiscal analysis. But the body of knowledge that I am interested in describing is quite independent of its controversial origin: an expert in business cycles as Arthur F. Burns, formerly Economic Adviser to President Eisenhower and now re-associated with the National Bureau of Economic Research, would without doubt reject the notion that he had received inspiration from Keynesian Theory. And so would Sumner Slichter and many other gifted observers of the passing economic scene. Yet, in the mode of analysis used—the emphasis upon the interrelations of consumption and investment spending, upon the past sequences of statistical time series—economists of varied political persuasions can largely agree. Craftsmanship rises above personalities: this is the fact that makes the dream of a science of economics possible.

A prosaic example can often illustrate, better than can thousands of words about abstract methodology, how a science actually proceeds. Therefore, I propose to illustrate, later in this essay, just what things the practicing economist watches and reasons about if he is approaching the important job of understanding the contemporaneous business cycle—understanding it for its own sake, understanding it in order to make predictions about the future, understanding it in order to give policy advice to statesmen or businessmen.

But a brief digression about the nature of economics and its reasoning would be useful at this point.

Uncommon Common Sense

Economists use terribly complicated jargon: long words, fine definitions, cabalistic mathematical symbols and graphs, complicated statistical techniques. Yet, if they have done their job well, they end up with what is simple common sense.

The noneconomist must naturally ask: Was that trip really necessary? The answer is: Apparently yes. Nothing is so rare as common sense—*i.e.,* the *relevant* common sense. Anything and everything can be phrased so as to be plausible. Black is plausible; so is white; and so is grey. Until you have excluded some possibilities, or reduced their probability, you have accomplished nothing as a scientist. So the content of pure common sense—like that of the self-canceling folk aphorisms of a people—tends to be nil.

Economics of War

A subject that is all too important these days provides an excellent illustration—the economics of war. Let any intelligent layman reflect upon what he conceives to be its principles. Then let him consider the relevant sections of any elementary textbook.[1] How much of the subject did he anticipate? And—what is even more interesting—what additions to these doctrines was he able to make?

Lest any one think all this too obvious, let me hasten to point out that until World War I nothing of war economics was at all well understood. Here are a few examples. (1) At the beginning of that war, in both Britain and America, the slogans "business as usual" were not words of reproach; they were being flashed in full-page advertisments urging the consumer to spend his money on civilian goods. (2) In 1914 the young Keynes told his Bloomsbury friends the war was too costly to be able to last long. (3) It was only after 1914 that economists were able to clarify the problem of whether the current wartime generation could, by financing the conflict through loans rather than taxes, succeed thereby in throwing a sizable burden onto the future, rather than on the present, generation. It took the best economists of that day to show that the enemy must be fought with current real resources; and that only to the degree that less of economy's capital (machinery, plants, roads, etc.) is bequeathed to the post-war generations can those generations be made to bear the burden of the war. (4) In 1917 patriotic Americans were urged to borrow from the banks in order to buy government bonds—as if that would release any real resources to the war effort or differ in effect from merely selling bonds to the banks directly.

Examples of similar folly could be found in World War II—but not among responsible economists.

Economists in Action

War provided another kind of a test case. Economists in some numbers joined the government to help solve military and civilian policy problems. So did numerous businessmen, not all of whom served for a dollar a year. What were the relative achievements of the two groups? If one who was not himself directly involved can be permitted to hazard a guess, I would suggest that the decisions followed tended usually to be those framed by people primarily from university life and that these were on the whole the better decisions.

What were the reasons for this? Certainly not differences in intrinsic intelligence or articulateness. Aside from the fact that it is the economists' business to be thinking about social decision-making, I think there was also the factor that a considerable advantage attends the exercise of ordinary precautions of "loose" scientific method—a wish to dig up relevant evidence, and a respect for such factual data once it had been collected and analysed.

In the realm of decision-making itself, there seemed to be a military role which persons trained in the discipline of economics could fulfill. In one agency, units of historians and economists worked side by side: and I think disinterested third parties would agree that the economists seemed quickest to make the important policy decisions. It is as if the repeated study of the imponderables of economic life—where the data are never complete and where calculated guesses have to be made—were a valuable preparation for the wartime problems. I daresay the same type of considerations are relevant to explain why, in the war-created realm of *operations research,*[2] which involved the use of scientists to aid in decision-making, statisticians and economists often proved less paralyzed by the need to reach conclusions on the basis of incomplete evidence than were those who came from some of the "harder" laboratory sciences.

It is considerations such as those preceding that fortify

the teacher of graduate economics. As he puts each generation through the paces of advanced economics, he is a rare man if he does not sometimes ask himself what the connection is between these rarified concepts and the concrete realities of economic life. But it seems to be a brute fact of experience that, somehow, going through such a training does alert the trained economist to an important way of looking at things—to a concentration on relevant alternatives and a predisposition to question their relative costs and advantages. Perhaps there ought to be some cheaper way of producing this degree of economic sophistication, but no one seems yet to have found it.

A Demurral

Still I must not give the impression that an economist is to be judged by how much money he can make or by how quick and accurate his decisions are. Economics, after all, is not *home economics,* even though its name derives from the Greek word which means that. The economists I know are, by and large, not demonstrably better at spending or saving their money than other people; nor at outguessing the stockmarket. Some of our most gifted economists would be useless in the tent of the Prince either in war or peace—even though as a result of their researches and theories, political economy is in a better position to render needed advice.

Whether a man makes quick decisions, whether he is good at piercing the veil of uncertainty, is after all a matter of temperament. One would not require the same qualifications in appointing someone to fill a chair in economics as one would in deciding on who is to advise a bank or to invest his widow's money.

There is a sense, however, in which all science does involve decision-making. Some years ago, at a Harvard Law

School Symposium on the role of law in a liberal education, Judge Charles E. Wyzanski, Jr. quoted from Lord Beveridge's biography to the effect that the laboratory scientist is lucky because he never has to make decisions. I bristled at this, for it has long been my conviction that the problems of all sciences can be formulated as the making of intelligent decisions with respect to actual or hypothetical courses of action. Of course, these will often be in the nature of "thought experiments"—hypothetical bets or decisions. They need not be actual decisions, with important financial or human consequences.

After all, why does a scientist make one experiment rather than another? And why do scientists consider the results of certain experiments as so much more interesting and important than those of others? To say that the quantum theory is a better theory than the classical theory of mechanics can be construed to mean: If my life was wagered on the probable outcome of as-yet-unperformed experiments, would I—or would I not—base my forecast upon the quantum theory? And my degree of confidence in that theory might be revealed, or at least illuminated, by the odds that I could be forced to give if necessary.

An Interpretation of History: A Digression

With respect to the natural sciences the above reformulation, even if admissible, is not needed. A physicist or chemist need not be much of a methodologist: his disciplines have a logic of their own which often will unobtrusively point the way. It is otherwise with the "softer" social sciences. So little spontaneous guidance is provided by the subject matter, that in some of these disciplines substantive research is displaced by repetitious and inconclusive discussion of methodology.

History is a discipline now passing through some kind of a crisis, as historians are themselves the first to testify. Few still regard it as an exact science. Yet not all historians are willing to have it become mere antiquarianism, sequestered behind the walls of the Humanities and separated from the Social Sciences. Because history borders on economics, the views of the latter may throw some light on the interpretation of history as a discipline.

"We pass this way only once," is the essence of the problem for the historian. If Nature were to provide its own controlled experiments; or if, in the absence of controlled experiments, she were to supply us with repeated experience from which we could infer regularities—in either event the peculiar differences between history and any science would disappear.[3] But things happen as they happen. To say that things might just as well have gone another way than the way they did go cannot be judged.

Yet we do distinguish between good and bad historians. Two writers may both tell the truth, but neither can tell the whole truth. Nevertheless, we find one profound and interesting, the other trivial. For example, if we are interested in the view of a man who has weighed all the available evidence bearing on the historical question of whether the *Odyssey* was written by a woman, it is not because we can ever perform an experiment that will answer the question. Either Homer was or was not a woman, and the concept of probability and forecasting cannot directly apply to that dead fact. But we can ask ourselves the hypothetical question: Suppose new documentary finds should become available in the future. What would a jury of responsible historians or scientists be willing to guess would be the bearing of such documents[4] upon the question?

Some such scientific method as that just described is used

by the historian all the time, and it is by exercise of such methods that we decide that one writer produces foolish and far-fetched history whereas another's is cogent and interesting.

Within the discipline of economics itself, consider the scientist who studies the business cycle. As the 1957-58 recession developed, he pored over the facts that emerged concerning it and tried to discern a pattern from these facts, in order to narrow down the field of open possibilities that were relevant to the immediate future. He was aware that the present recession is exactly like no previous one, but he knew also that, by careful marshaling of the relevant analogous events of past experience, he could gain insight into this unique event.

Let any one who thinks the world was born anew this morning—possessing no tendency to favor certain uniformities with yester-morning—beware of making bets about the future. Such an agnostic will lose his money—I assert this as a fact of experience!

But this is not to say that it is fruitful to regard the whole of past economic history as a homogeneous sample from what the statistician calls a "stationary time series." On the contrary, one feels that new data about 1836 will contribute something—but relatively little—to the dynamics of contemporary capitalism. The system has evolved; and to have a feeling for the rate of its evolution one must apply the canons of ordinary scientific method to study its "stationary part."

The depression of 1893 would certainly be called "history"—if only because the statute of limitations has run out. But you would, in principle and with due respect to gaps in the data, study it by the same methods to be applied to such recent history as the depression of 1932—or, for that matter, the recession of 1958.

We shall return now from the digression on history to the peculiar problems of economics itself.

A Babel of Voices?

According to legend, economists are supposed never to agree among themselves. If Parliament were to ask six economists for an opinion, seven answers would come back—two, no doubt, from the volatile Mr. Keynes! If economists cannot agree among themselves, how can the rest of the world be expected to agree with them and to respect their recommendations?

This is a fair question. It is a matter of record that, on any broad issue requiring decision, you often find economists giving quite different recommendations. The reasons for this are at least twofold:

First, most decisions involve questions of future fact. No one has yet found a crystal ball that will make the future transparent.

Second, most decisions involve *ethical ends* that transcend positive science. Thus, one economist may seem to favor repeal of the oil industry's privilege to go untaxed on its 27½ percentage depletion; another may argue for retention of this tax privilege. Both may, nevertheless, be in agreement that such a change will (1) slow down the search for oil and (2) speed up the equalization of incomes that has been going on for some decades. Their differences may lie in the ethical weights each gives to égalitarianism and to material progress. And such differences of opinion can never be finally arbitrated within the halls of economic science itself, but must be decided in the political arena.

Some other reasons for disagreement among economists can be expected to disappear as our knowledge of the facts and our analytical abilities increase. What needs emphasis to the layman, perhaps, is this truth: when two good economists are arguing with each other, they can quickly narrow down their differences and identify them—in a way that a good economist cannot always do when carrying on economic arguments with noneconomists.

The New Uniformity

It is possible to argue that American economists—and Western economists generally—far from being too divided among a number of competing schools, today present a united front that reflects *too little* basic disagreement on fundamentals.

It was not always so. In the past, particularly in nineteenth-century Germany, there was great methodological conflict between the Historical School and the Classical School. In the first quarter of the twentieth century this same quarrel came to a head in America. The so-called Institutionalist School—associated with such names as Thorstein Veblen, John R. Commons, Wesley Mitchell— rose to challenge traditional economics. But, with the passing of the years, the Institutionalists have not perpetuated themselves. Today, surveying leading graduate schools, one finds them competing for the same men, teaching the same basic economic doctrines and methods. Although there are one, two, or three exceptions to this, even they are moving toward the common pattern—and one might have expected, in a great nation, countless exceptions to any one pattern.

It is impossible to discuss here the detailed reasons for the decline of historicism and the ascendancy of neo-classical economics. Briefly, one reason lies in the fact that the former became stale and sterile and did not produce the results it had promised. A second factor lies in the roots of the Keynesian Revolution, which was developed by economists working within the older Anglo-

Saxon tradition; it provided an outlet and a program for those with strong reform aspirations who had previously provided the best recruits for the anticlassical movements. Finally, the existence in America of numerous business schools and of flourishing areas of applied economics— such as labor economics and industrial relations, market organization and price policy, public finance, etc.—meant that economists with an empirical bent could follow their inclination without necessarily cutting themselves off from the body of economic theory.

Marxian Economics

Obviously, there has been so far no mention of the economic doctrines that are considered official for half the people in the world—for the hundreds of millions in Soviet Russia and China. But there is in fact little contact between the tenets of the economics studied in the Western World and that of the Iron Curtain nations.

For a dramatic indication of the differences between these two traditions, one might consider the elementary textbooks on economics that have been published in both societies (for it may indeed be more important to write a people's songs and textbooks than to write her laws). One of the most widely used American introductory textbooks—one that has been translated into many languages— has outsold in number such past books as those of John Stuart Mill, Adam Smith, and Alfred Marshall. One might assume, from sheer number of sales alone, that it might be taken as representative of Western economics. However, any illusion that it represents the best-seller in the field of economics would be decisively shattered by the information—and reliable information—that the official economics textbook of the Soviet Union, *Political Economy,* sold four or five million copies in its first printing.

It is instructive to compare the two texts. The Soviet book was written by a committee, and within a year after 1954 it had to be revised for deviations from official Soviet ideology. It is required reading for all college students; and units of the Communist Party—be it a cell of engineers or scientists, or a philosophical discussion group—must master its catechism. Of its 800 pages, scarcely 200 are devoted to the economics of the Soviet Union or of a socialist society. (The absence of consecutive statistics and detailed facts is noteworthy.) The rest is devoted to the shortcomings of capitalism. The quotations from economists and other writers are few and extremely selective: Marx and Engels, Lenin, and (to a diminishing degree) Stalin[5] are predominant.

Is it a good book? If it provided a good framework of analysis for the development of capitalistic society, then—however distasteful its dogmatism, however uneven its contents—we of the Western World would mine it for its insights and shamelessly plagiarize it for its conclusions. But, alas, for reasons that would have to be substantiated elsewhere this Marxist economics is not well adapted to predicting the next five months of capitalistic society much less the next fifty years! When the Soviet economists, in actuality, find themselves having to adapt the price analysis of traditional economics to the problems of collectivist planning, and to explain the 1958 decline in American business activity, they will have to go through the same routines of national income calculation as do their Western counterparts.

How To Be Your Own Economic Forecaster

For the remainder of this discussion, I should like then to turn to the area of business cycle control. Here, after all, is the area which signifies to most people the progress made by economic analysis.

There is no easy way to become a sophisticated economic forecaster. But no better introduction to the problems faced by the modern student of business cycles can be had than to go through the prosaic steps followed by the actual forecaster in his day-to-day activities as he advises the government or his business firm. Obviously, the judgment that he brings at each stage to the analysis cannot be learned overnight, and can scarcely be learned at all without a prolonged apprenticeship of economic study.

Can Forecasters Forecast at All?

Anyone who reads the daily paper will have some impression of what is happening to business. But, unless he disciplines his observations, his impression will be a rather chaotic one, and he will not be very prompt in recognizing the turning points in the economic climate.

On the one hand, trained economists are not impressively accurate in forecasting the near-term future, as is attested by the fact that in 1945 most members of the profession wrongly predicted a sizable postwar depression. On the other hand, the month-to-month forecasting that takes place in the financial and industrial community, in government, and in universities will provide a general estimate of the "batting averages" of the different groups. And significantly, in forecasting the economy, economists, poor as they are, do better than noneconomists. A personal impression, drawn from filed records of past behavior, is that the forecasting departments of large corporations do slightly better than their more impressionistic, less systematic, brethren. On the whole, the forecasting done within the government, although far from perfect, is among the best there is; and it is impressive how well informed federal departments are on the changing state of the economy.

Weekly Statistics

Which statistics will the prudent forecaster watch most closely? The layman, probably because he remembers the great stock market crash of 1929, is prone to think that the daily reports of common stock prices is the primary index for the forecaster. True, the day-to-day and minute-to-minute speculator is concerned most with these reports. However, a speculator in onions, studying nothing but onion statistics, is not likely to imagine that such information is pivotal for the economy as a whole.

The stock market, too, is more effect than cause of what is developing in the economy. Its testimony, although of some interest, is hardly of prime importance. The forecaster interested in economic policy will dismiss the daily Wall Street returns in favor of the indexes of stock prices, released later by the Securities Exchange Commission on a weekly or a monthly basis.

The significant weekly reports for the analyst are the Federal Reserve Board figures on department store sales. These are already several days out of date, but any significant changes in them may herald an important change in the consumption spending of the nation. Since consumption is the greatest single component of national income spending, any change in its trend would be of highest interest to the analyst; he would like to know about it early.

There are obvious pitfalls in interpreting the movements of this current series. Have store sales gone up simply because the arrival of Easter has stimulated sales? The experienced economist will invariably make some kind of correction for the season. Thus, he will want to study how this week's sales compares with the similar week one year ago. For seasonal events such as Christmas, which always falls on the same date, such a simple year-to-year comparison may be enough. But he knows that the complicated nineteen-year cycle of Easter makes it harder to judge whether the current sales are ahead of, or behind, the previous year's. Even when he has allowed for the month and day of the year, he knows that a fortuitous event, such as a heavy snow storm on the Eastern seaboard, may contaminate his comparisons. An unusually warm and late winter may reduce apparel spending in a way that is never made up in later months. The analyst must take all these factors into account. If he is experienced, he realizes that, whenever retail spending is weak, a host of apologists will arise who will attribute this weakness to some vagary of the weather. The analyst must be able to give the weather no more than its due—not an easy task.

There are other important weekly indicators, such as railroad freight-car loadings or electric-power production. As the railroads lose ground to the trucking industry, railroad carloadings are subject to a long-term declining trend. The analyst must allow for this—and, likewise, for the strong growth trend characterizing electric-power production. Thus, as the nation goes into a recession, he must not be taken in by reassuring utterances that this week's power production is 1 or 2 per cent above last year's. Such a report is far from cheerful. Ordinarily, in our growing economy, in which electricity becomes ever more important, we expect each year to use 5, 7, or 10 per cent more electricity than did the previous year. It is a severe recession indeed that makes electric-power production go down absolutely. Thus, the ups and downs of business activity in the electric-power production figures are not merely ups and downs in the rate of growth of that series. And this the experienced observer will have learned.

A number of financial services average together several of these weekly indicators of business activity into what they call a comprehensive index, or barometer, of business activity. Thus, there is the New York Times index of business activity, which takes into account electric-power production, carloadings, steel production, paper, and still other indicators of current activity. When corrected for long-term trend, seasonal factors, and fortuitous events such as strikes, these barometers can serve a useful purpose.

Another important weekly source of information is the Federal Reserve report on its balance sheet and the changes in position of its member banks. Ordinarily, the day-to-day operations of the Federal Reserve open market committee, as it buys and sells government bonds, are shrouded in secrecy. Those very close to the money market may suspect on Monday that the Federal Reserve is buying government bills in order to make credit a little easier, but even they cannot be sure. Only at the end of the week, when the new balance sheet of the Federal Reserve Banks is published, do we get a concrete clue as to what has been happening.

Seasonal and irregular factors will becloud the testimony of any one week's report. Certainly a neophyte can be thrown off by changes in such mysterious entities as the "float" and be led into thinking that the Federal Reserve has reversed its policy when in fact nothing significant has been happening. However, one learns to allow for such factors, and in the fall of 1957 careful analysts could anticipate a change in Federal Reserve policy some weeks before the Federal Reserve Board, on November 14, dramatically lowered its discount rate to 3 per cent from 3½ per cent.

The information provided by the reporting member banks may be even more significant than that of the

Federal Reserve itself. For example, 1957 bank loans were languishing for months before the Federal Reserve decided to abandon its policy of credit restriction in favor of a policy of credit ease. Because the movement of business inventories is one of the most important bellwethers of the current situation, and because of the unfortunate fact that estimates of inventory changes are always late in coming out each month and that the corrected rate of inventory change needed for national income information is available only quarterly, it is all the more important for us to watch the behavior of bank loans as a possible quick indicator of what the more complete inventory figures will later show.

Monthly Statistics

Additional important economic statistics become available on a monthly basis. Not long after the end of each month department store and mail order sales data, and also sales data of grocery, variety, apparel, and drug chains are published. These significantly re-inforce the testimony of the weekly department store sales. Indeed, since department stores in many urban areas are losing ground to the suburbs and also to so-called discount houses, they are an imperfect reflector of retail trends. The great department and mail order houses, such as Sears Roebuck and Montgomery Ward, give a surprisingly accurate portrayal of what is happening in the economy at large. They, with the sales data of other chain stores, enable us to guess what the Department of Commerce will later report for retail sales. Early in each month there is a census of unemployment, employment, and size of labor force. Taken together with the reports on employment provided by a sample of business firms, this is a valuable indicator of what is going on in the economy. It can be supplemented by information on hours worked per week and on how many workers are making new claims for unemployment compensation. Moreover, by breaking down the unemployment figures into those relevant to partially and fully unemployed and into those unemployed for a long or short time adds to our ability to guess whether a given upswing or contraction is likely to be especially significant.

Perhaps the most important of all indicators of current business activity is the monthly Federal Reserve Board index of production. This is available some weeks after the month's end and provides a comprehensive measure of physical production in manufacturing and mining. Because it does not include the less volatile item of services, it tends to exaggerate the amplitude of short-term fluctuations—which is really an advantage to the forecaster interested in picking up on his seismograph the slightest rumblings of trouble ahead.

It is interesting that the Federal Reserve Board production index reached its (seasonally corrected) peak in December 1956, some seven months before the majority of the various economic time series turned downward and a good ten months before the Federal Reserve authorities recognized that we were indeed in a recession. Similarly, its turn down in the middle of 1953 served to announce the 1953-1954 recession. A producer of steel, copper, or oil could find it enormously useful to know, in advance, the Federal Reserve Board index of production for twelve months, in order to gauge his output accordingly.

Another important monthly bit of information is given by personal income. This is a seasonally corrected estimate of how much people have received in the form of wages, interest, dividends, government relief and transfer payments, and earnings from unincorporated enterprise. After they pay their direct taxes out of this total, people are left with disposable income, to be spent on consumption goods or saved. If at any period the reports on personal income were down for three or four months in a row—as in the period following August 1957—one would be forced to conclude nervously that some kind of recession was taking place. For it is the usual case that personal income rises from decade to decade, from year to year, and from month to month. The short-term changes in reported personal income give the economist the basis for guessing what the not-yet-reported quarterly figures for national income will later show.

There are a number of other miscellaneous statistical reports that the careful forecaster will take careful note of. If he reads *The New York Times* or *Herald Tribune*—or his *Wall Street Journal* or *Journal of Commerce*—he will watch for the latest reports of sales, new orders, and inventories in the retail, wholesale, and manufacturing sectors, and for data on housing starts and construction awards.

Most of these important magnitudes will be summarized for him in the convenient Congressional publication *Economic Indicators,* which is published late in each month by the Joint Economic Committee for the Council of Economic Advisers. This merely presents the figures without analysis. For a deeper understanding of what is going on, the forecaster will be sure to read the Department of Commerce's *Survey of Current Business* and the monthly *Federal Reserve Bulletin.*

Most monthly newsletters put out by banks are dispensable, although an exception should perhaps be made for the influential First National City Bank monthly letter and for the monthly review of the New York Federal Reserve Bank. These various letters will comment on, and attempt to interpret, the striking events of the passing parade.

Quarterly and General Statistics

Soon after each quarter of the year the economic analyst will receive the first reports on national income statistics. Strictly speaking, the gross national product, the GNP, attracts the most publicity and attention; the particular magnitude that the U. S. Department of Commerce chooses to call "national income" does not become available for some time and does not in any case represent so inclusive and important a magnitude as GNP.

The significant points in these reports are changes in consumption or government spending and changes in the various components of domestic or foreign investment. Among the investment components, the net change in inventories is the one most likely to fluctuate in the short run. And any change in the percentage of disposable income that people save will be examined with great interest.

The quarterly statistics of GNP will be averaged for the year in the new January Economic Report of the President. Still further revised estimates will become available in the February *Survey of Current Business;* but not until the July national income number of that *Survey* will reasonably definitive annual estimates be available ("reasonably definitive" because the time will never come when all such estimates become final: the Department of Commerce is constantly revising its historical estimates as new ways of improving them become available).

Surveys of Future Intentions and Hopes

The statistical observations described so far refer to past facts. Today we have a new and exciting supplement to such timely observation on past facts—the periodic surveys that bear on intentions of businessmen to invest and of families to consume.

Thus, the McGraw-Hill Publishing Company puts out periodically a valuable poll of businessmen's intentions to invest, broken down by industry. The National Industrial Conference Board and *Newsweek* give estimates of the "capital appropriations" of business. The official SEC-Commerce surveys of business investment give estimates for two quarters ahead on such spending, broken down by industrial classification.

The credit rating organization, Dun & Bradstreet, takes periodic polls of businessmen's expectations with respect to their own sales and those of the over-all economy. Purchasing agents of industry draw up reports monthly concerning their own expectations and current experience. There are even continuous observations available upon the opinions of a fixed panel of academic and business economists.

Especially around New Year, there is no shortage of utterances about what can be expected in the coming year. To be sure, the number of independent bits of information in these communications is not great: typically, the year-end forecaster predicts no change in the economic winds for the next six months—followed thereafter by a reversal. However, you will probably be wrong to agree with the old aphorism: "When all the experts agree, watch out, for that's when they are most likely to be wrong." Historical observation does not suggest that such a hypothesis can be validated.

Historical observation suggests that, indeed, "One peek is worth a thousand finesses." It is better to have a man tell you of his plans than to have to guess at them. Consider, as a concrete example, the fall-off in fixed investment spending by business that began in the last quarter of 1957. As early as the summer of 1957, the Conference Board survey of capital appropriations alerted the analyst to this possibility. And by fall both the McGraw-Hill and SEC-Commerce Surveys confirmed the prognosis. Then, in the Spring of 1958, we learned how terribly accurate these surveys had been.

To get a notion of the mood and intention of consumers, the Group Survey Center of the University of Michigan conducts a scientifically random poll of consumers all over the nation. The results of this are published and analyzed in the Federal Reserve Bulletin and give a clue as to whether the typical consumer is feeling more optimistic than before, more thrift-minded, or more disposed to buy durable goods such as homes, cars, and appliances.

It is too soon to make sweeping claims for the validity of usefulness of such information, but experience of the last decade has suggested that this is a promising source of information about the current economic situation. Certainly, in early 1958, the reported pessimism of consumers was worth worrying about.

Three Methods of Forecasting

Economists differ in methodology—specifically, in their techniques of analyzing accumulated data—but the following three categories are roughly representative. First, there are the crude empiricists, who simply form an impression from the variety of pertinent data as to whether things are going to remain the same, go up, or go down. Second, there are the refined empiricists, who look for certain early indicators to alert them to what is later going to happen to the economy at large, or who take careful numerical count of the number of economic time series that are going up in comparison with those that are going down and compute a "diffusion index" in which every statistical time series is given the same weight, although one may be GNP and another pig-iron production. Third, there are the national-income model builders, who try to make estimates of the different components of GNP and who, in order to do this, find it necessary to make consistent estimates of the inter-relations among the different magnitudes.

How do followers of these three different general methods fare? No final answer can be given with confidence, but it would be a personal guess that the crude empiricist does worst of all. Indeed, the human mind being what it is, the crude empiricist rarely remains a nonselective averager of the information fed him but becomes instead the prey of each passing theory and fad.

The refined empiricist who searches for early indicators puts great weight on the following series: stock market prices, sensitive commodity prices, residential and other building contracts, new orders, average hours worked per week, number of new incorporations, and absence of business failures. When any or all of these turn up, he considers this an indication that within a few months general business activity may turn up. And a turn down in any or all of these would indicate to him that business is the more likely to turn down in a few months.

More eclectic economists of this persuasion keep track of the relative number of different economic time series that are currently going up. If the diffusion index shows that only 25 per cent of all series are going up, they reserve judgment as to when the upturn will come. As the diffusion index rises toward 50 per cent, they become more confident that the upturn is imminent. The really cautious ones will not actually call a turn until the 50 per cent level has been passed.

A careful person who follows these methods can hardly fail to detect any sizable movement in the modern economy. Unfortunately, his seismograph is also likely to record many small fluctuations, some of which have to be regarded as false alarms. Watching the more sensitive of the early indicators is calculated to keep the analyst in a constant state of agitation and alarm. Thus, in 1952 the method called for a recession which never came. And in August 1957 a temporary firming of many of the early indicators gave the false signal to some analysts that there was not to be the impending recession. The next month's information decisively corrected this misinformation.

This is not the place to attempt a definitive appraisal of such methods. But a few cautionary remarks are in order. Take the case of a typical early indicator—the behavior of stock market prices. Although business turned down in the middle of 1929, the stock market was some months late in taking account of this fact. So this particular omen did not work well at the outset of the biggest depression in our recent history. Or take the case of the 1937-38 recession, where in hindsight it is given a better score. Here the market did fall in the first part of 1937, but unaccountably then proceeded to recover. Its subsequent decline did agree with the decline in general business activity. But think of the nervous agitation of the analyst who was contemporaneously following this barometer and who didn't have the benefit of our generous hindsight. Still another case is that of 1946 when the market fell in anticipation of a recession that never came. Nor can the behavior of the market in 1953 be considered a triumph for the method. In the first part of 1953 when business was strong the market was weak. Then in September, just as the Eisenhower administration, along with everyone else, began to recognize that we were in for a recession the stock market proceeded to take off on a rise that was to persist throughout and beyond the 1954 recession, ending only at the peak levels reached in the middle of 1956 and again in the middle of 1957.

There seems to be an inherent bias in the way that economists use hindsight to claim validation for the prophetic powers of a volatile series like the stockmarket. The truth is that such economic time series fluctuate a good deal. If every time they go down and the economy does not subsequently go down, you ignore such a movement and only record those cases where you know by hindsight the economy did validate the move, you will get an exaggerated notion of the prophetic powers of the volatile series. (In some experiments at the Massachusetts Institute of Technology we found that experimental subjects, who didn't know the future and who were shown the chart of stockmarket prices with successively larger sections exposed to view, tended to call three times as many turns in the stockmarket as are recognized to have taken place in general business activity!)

It appears that most serious minded forecasters take account of the mehod of economic indicators and diffusion indexes but combine them with some kind of a rough gross national product model. Few such forecasters go to the extremes represented by Lawrence R. Klein of America, Colin Clark of Australia and Britain, and Jan Tinbergen of Holland. These latter have complicated sets of mathematical equations, fitted to the past facts to determine their best numerical parameters; certain recent information is then incorporated into the equations and, with the aid of modern calculating machines, the results state definite forecasts of the future values of gross national product components, employment, production, and prices.

Although few analysts use such elaborate and inflexible models, most of them, in using a process of successive approximation—*e.g.*, in making first rough estimates of an interconnected table of all the variables and then adjusting them for apparent inconsistencies—are trying to accomplish much the same thing.

The process can be only vaguely sketched here. Typically, a relation based on past experience is used to connect consumption spending and disposable income. (If there is reason to think that the past relationship will in this period be a little high or low, this can be built into the model.) Past relations connecting dividends and corporate earnings, taxes and income, welfare expenditure and income, etc., are also utilized. Then, estimates from surveys or recent history are used to introduce investment figures into the model. Finally, the trends in government expenditure and foreign trade are introduced. When all these different figures are made to confront each other systematically, various corrections take place; you will emerge with either a single set of predictions of the various economic magnitudes or a range of predicted values within high and low limits. Depending upon temperament, the analyst may never structure this into a systematic model but may, nonetheless in effect, be solving simultaneous equations in an approximate way by intuition. Some analysts, although they have learned that they speak prose all their lives, have yet to learn that they may be solving complicated simultaneous equations when they exercise judgment about economic compatibility of various estimates.

Hitting the Target

As a result of watching carefully all past and present events and scanning the portents of future events, the analyst usually finds it easy enough to decide whether total dollar spending is too little or too much. If total spending is too much, employment tends to be overfull—the number of job vacancies tends to outstrip the number of unemployed workers, and there is an upward pressure both on money wages and on prices generally. If total spending is too little, there is a residue of unemployed workers and an inadequate level of production and consumption.

When the economy is diagnosed as clearly needing less or more total dollar spending, the government knows what fiscal and monetary programs ought to be followed. Thus, to help increase total spending, the Federal Reserve Authorities will buy government securities in the open money market: this will raise bond prices and lower interest rates; at the same time, it will tend to increase the reserve balances of the commercial banks, which they, in turn, will hasten to offer for loans or investment. The net effect is to make credit more available and also cheaper to investment spenders. In addition to these day-to-day open market operations, the Central Bank can also lower the discount rate at which it lends to banks and can periodically lower the legal reserve ratios that it requires the commercial banks to keep uninvested and on deposit with itself. These measures will also ease credit and tend to add to total investment spending.

What must Congress and the President do to help add to the total of spending and job opportunities? The fiscal authorities must reduce tax collections and/or increase government expenditure in order to add to the total of spending. Because of well-known "built-in stabilizers" the modern economy automatically drops its tax collections and steps up its spending when income falls *even without* any authorities being aware of it or taking any explicit, discretionary acts; but over and beyond these first-line-of-defense automatic attenuators of instability, there are explicit fiscal programs of expansion to be followed.

If economists' diagnosis declares the economy to be suffering from an excess of demand, the needed therapy calls for a reduction in total spending. Then all the above monetary and fiscal programs have to be operated in reverse. For example, taxes must be raised and expenditures cut; credit must be made tight and expensive, by openmarket sales of bonds, by discount rate hikes, and legal reserve ratio increases.

Nor is any of the above academic. In the late 1950's we are getting samples of all these fiscal and credit measures. It is wrong to think that all these decisions must be made with a surgeon's precision, that there must be split-second timing without any delays, and that there must be instantaneous reversal of policy when conditions change. The modern economy is a great sluggish thing. It changes but it changes slowly. Remember that our goal is not the abolition of all business cycles—even if that were feasible, it might not be desirable. Instead we aim to wipe out persistent slump or unsought inflation. If only capitalism had succeeded in the past in this more modest goal, how different would have been the course of human history!

A Final Dilemma

Lest this end on too complacent a note, it must be pointed out that, although economics has solved many problems, the solutions have given rise to new problems. Not the least of these is the fact that many economists feel technologically unemployed: having helped banish the worst economic diseases of capitalism, they feel like the ear surgeons whose function modern antibiotics has reduced to a low level of priority.

From the standpoint of society at large, perhaps the greatest problem still facing the student of political economy is the threat of long-term inflation. In the past, the periodic bouts of economic depression tended to bring prices down. History witnessed the averaging of price drops against price rises, with the long drift being one of caprice and accident. But the contemporary social conscience is very sensitive to what would have been regarded years ago as quite modest levels of temporary unemployment. We seem no longer willing to tolerate distress that is persistent enough to have a downward influence on prices and wages. All our adjustments tend then to be made in the upward direction. This not only shifts the betting odds toward long-term rising prices but also breeds an understandable concern over inflation. The problem of continuous inflation tends to weaken society's motivations to seek perfectionist standards of full employment. And a candid appraisal of some recent attitudes would indicate that, in its effects upon future policy formation, the fear of inflation should awaken some other fears.

But this danger need not strike too dismal a note. As old problems are conquered, we expect to turn up new problems. A discipline lives on its unsolved problems; and so, for better or worse, economics is likely to be a lively subject for as many years ahead as man can see.

NOTES

[1] A typical textbook treatment would be P. A. Samuelson, *Economics* (4th ed.; New York: McGraw-Hill, 1958), Chap. 36.

[2] See Philip M. Morse and George E. Kimball, Cambridge, Technology Press of M.I.T. and Wiley, New York, 1951, for

a first discussion of what has since blossomed out into a vast discipline.

[3] As John Dewey said, "We never step in the same river twice." The river is different and so are we.

[4] Only occasionally are new documents found that enable us to test alternative views or forecasts—which make the problem of validation all the more difficult for the historian.

[5] This book replaced Stalin's *Short Course* as the official textbook of Marxian economics.

122

AMERICAN ECONOMICS*

Graduate School and Other Trends

Since the graduate schools are all-important as the producers of economists and as the places where much research takes place, the trends in their development are worth reviewing. Such early graduate centers as Johns Hopkins and Clark University lost out, for reasons that are not too clear but that probably involved a shortage of financial sustenance. Harvard, Chicago, Columbia, and Wisconsin would probably be recognized as our strong graduate institutions around the time of the First World War but with many other universities not far below in size and prestige.

By the time of the Second World War the degree of concentration of American graduate study, if one could measure it, would probably have shown a centripetal growth. In the early 1930's Chicago — like the London School of Economics — enjoyed, under Frank H. Knight, Henry Schultz, and Jacob Viner, a position of great prestige. Toward the end of the decade Harvard, covering the field of microeconomics with J. A. Schumpeter, E. H. Chamberlin, and W. W. Leontief, and macroeconomics with Alvin Hansen and J. H. Williams, had reached a degree of ascendancy that gave rise to much comment and talk about "the old school tie" and mutual back scratching.

Economists played an important role in World War II. Washington

---

* This is an abbreviation of an extended paper on American economics. The first part of the paper appears in this volume as Chapter 125.

became in a real sense *the* center of economic science. In some numbers economists joined the government to help solve military and civilian policy problems. So did numerous businessmen.

As an outsider, I can testify to the high quality of the technical wartime economics in Washington. Committee meetings were then carried on at a level that would do credit to advanced university seminars. This is in interesting contrast to what our postwar bombing surveys learned from the German records about the caliber of wartime planning in that country. Apparently all calculations had been made for a short war, and the national income and other information needed to coordinate an intense and prolonged war effort were simply not to be had in the Third Reich. In Washington, on the other hand, the general predictions of wartime economic magnitudes were vindicated by the subsequent facts — so much so, in fact, that the economics profession as a whole was becoming a little cocky. Whom the gods would destroy they first raise up. It is an ironical fact worth pondering that the best brains from our best universities using the best economic tools known to our discipline and having at their command the statistical resources of a great nation went significantly haywire in making the famous 1945 prediction that the immediate aftermath of the war would involve mass unemployment. When the facts proved otherwise, this constituted a chastening experience — one which has rightfully increased the humility of a generation of economists.*

After the war there was a great exodus of economists out of Washington back to the universities. One of the interesting postwar trends seems to have been a decrease in the concentration ratio of American economic graduate study: I mean by this that in addition to the few traditionally strong graduate schools, which continued strong and indeed were engulfed by a torrent of returning servicemen, there emerged a number of vigorously competing centers for graduate study in economics. It would be invidious to attempt a comprehensive list, but the names of Stanford, M.I.T., Yale, Michigan, Johns Hopkins, and California will be recognized by anyone familiar with the American scene as providing keen competition to the established centers. (I have named half a dozen schools, but I could easily name others of equal or superior quality.)

The reasons for this postwar decentralization seem to be obscure. On the one hand, by this time America had more topnotch economists than could be hired by only a few graduate schools; and thus there was a willing and eager supply of teachers to man the new pro-

* Careful study of forecasting throughout the postwar years suggests to me that professional economists generally do do better at this chancy game than nonprofessionals. But this is not to deny that there still remains a great deal of unreliability in the predictions of the best of forecasters.

grams. On the demand side, there remained the fact that a venerable institution of learning has the tremendous advantage of inertia working in its favor. It is well known in subjects other than economics that long after a particular department has receded from its peak, it continues to have applicants sent to it by its former students and to attract applicants from the public at large. Working against this centralizing factor of inertia, there was perhaps an accumulated realization that the slightly smaller institutions might have certain advantages on the research side and in connection with the important problem of being placed in a good job after graduation.

Where We Stand

The early American economists would be astonished to look at a present-day learned journal. The professionalization of the subject has been carried to the point where much of it might seem incomprehensible. The most visible manifestation of this is, of course, the use of mathematical symbolism. But even if all mathematical expressions were replaced by their verbal equivalents, there would still remain the increased technical character of modern economics. An economist who recently retired was heard to say: "I'm glad I'm not thirty-five years old, for I'd then feel I had to learn a lot of mathematics." In a way he was right, yet in two ways wrong. First, there are notable examples to prove that a man can do first-class creative work in the field of modern American economic analysis even if he has but a primitive training in mathematics. Second, the intricacies of current discussions are such that mere knowledge of mathematics will not suffice to carry one very far. It cannot be restated too often that mastery of mathematics textbooks is neither a necessary nor sufficient condition for mastery of economics. This is not to deny that it may be a highly useful tool in meeting the miscellaneous statistical and theoretical problems that turn up in the course of a modern economist's year — as students of Harold Hotelling and Henry Schultz learned just a generation ago.

There are many things that a modern economist feels he must know: statistics, economic history, sociology and interdisciplinary subjects, mathematics, foreign languages — and I have seen lists which even included public speaking and the ability to write clear English. In recent years we have been turning out graduates who could pass comprehensive examinations — particularly those of the objective-type format — in a vast range of subjects. (When an international civil service gives such examinations to students from the various countries of the world, there is some evidence which suggests that American students score high grades on the average.) It has sometimes been suggested that our most advanced students know everything except common sense. To this I have heard the reply that that is something which will come with age, whereas if you do not learn the other things in youth, you never will.

One of the notable features of modern American economics is the sheer number of economists. Back in the days of Alfred Marshall one could count on two hands the economists who mattered in England. They were a small group, writing for each other. The time is now here when the members of the American Economic Association will have to be reckoned in five digits. With the individual propensity to write articles the same at all times, it is little wonder that it is harder today to get a marginal article published than it was even a generation ago. With the individual propensity to read articles no greater, mere multiplication of journals cannot restore the old proportion without at the same time creating a feeling of frustration on the part of those who feel guilty when they are not keeping up with the literature. The only solution would seem to be a specialization of function: a journal for econometricians, one for operations researchers, one for linear-programing operations researchers, and so on. And something like this has actually come to pass as new subdisciplines have formed new associations and new official organs.

The number of American economists can itself have an overwhelming impact on the foreigner. Imagine his feeling when he attends for the first time the Christmas meetings of the *AEA!* I remember Lionel Robbins once commenting on the great number of American economists, telling how he had been brought by Harry D. White during the war to meet some American economists in the Treasury — only to learn that they were merely the economists in White's division of the Treasury!

This problem of magnitude leads to an optical illusion, which we must guard against. When a country goes from a few economists to many, there will almost certainly have to be a lowering of *average* quality. Such a move is therefore sometimes deemed a bad thing — as if average quality were what is to be maximized (a goal which would entail there being only one best economist left). Actually, if we are interested in the general advance of a scholarly subject, it is the *total* contribution that counts. So long as we do not lose any of the best men at the top, their work will be supplemented by the contributions made all up and down the line.*

* It has occasionally been suggested that all contributions come from a few great men, but I do not think this Carlylean thesis will stand up under a careful examination of the evolution of a science. To be sure, there is a social cost of maintaining more men in a science, which has to be measured against their scholarly and teaching contributions; and there is even a cost, involved in the drain on other people's attention, whenever someone issues a paper of little scholarly merit. One solution to the problem of the plethora of publication, but

I would not dare to attempt a catalogue of names of topnotch economists today working in America, but they obviously constitute a great number. Within the realm of analytical economics itself, notable progress has been made in such diverse topics as the following: linear programing, welfare economics, game theory, operations research, national income and fiscal policy, subjective probability and decision making under uncertainty, and many others. The National Bureau of Economic Research, the Cowles Foundation for Economic Research, and other research groups continue to add to our knowledge of business cycles and how to moderate them. The study of economic growth and development is today all the rage, and its voluminous literature testifies that the world's demand for treatment of the subject is met by a copious supply.

Throughout all this, as has been true characteristically of American economics, the applied areas flourish. These applied fields provide an outlet for sublimating what in earlier times and other places would have been an antipathy for pure theory and a liking for historicity. The ancient battle between prosaic Baconian description and brilliant Newtonian synthesis still goes on, but it now takes place within the framework of an understanding and respect for economic analysis.

Some Problems

I must not, however, end on a complacent note. There is always plenty to worry about in connection with the development of a live discipline. We certainly have our share of problems. Let me briefly mention a few.

First, we have seen that the present generation of American economists was greatly improved by the importing of able scholars from abroad. Are we now self-perpetuating? Or, in the absence of political uneasiness abroad of sufficient magnitude to keep up the flow of migrants to our shores, will we revert to a lower level of quality?*

---

not one that I would personally favor, has been approached in some countries: a lottery that involves talent, articulateness, and luck manages to pick a few leading scholars who occupy the best posts at the few best universities; they then publish for each other's edification and for the edification of a larger group of scholars who follow their work closely. This makes for more interesting personalities and makes the reading problem more manageable; but it also makes for flurries of fashion and raises questions of fairness and efficiency.

* This raises the economic problem of the mobility of highly skilled factors of production. Being the richest country in the world, America has some pull on artists, musicians, and scholars. Even in the absence of political disorder, we may find that our living conditions and conditions of research assistance will be such as to attract many of the best users of such resources. Certainly many have expressed some concern in the last decade that international agencies such as the United Nations and the International Fund and Bank should have drawn off to our shores some of the better-trained foreign economists who might have been put to very good use at home.

Nobody can yet know the answer to this question, which obviously involves questions about the whole American educational system at the collegiate and precollegiate level.

A second major concern also has to do with the question of quality. During the depression decade of the thirties a great many able minds were attracted to the study of economics. There is some evidence that the economist, in helping to cure the business-cycle ills of the world, has to some degree worked himself out of an exciting job. He may be a little like the children's undertaker or the mastoid surgeon, who have become technologically obsolete in consequence of the discovery of antibiotics. There has been noted in recent years some tendency away from economics as a field of concentration on American campuses. More of the best minds these days go into the fields of physics, law, and medicine. There is even some competition felt now from business management as a career.

Finally, it may be argued that modern society is becoming so affluent as to cause a euthanasia of the economic problem — and with it the euthanasia of challenging problems for the economist. This brings us back to an argument often used a century ago to explain the backwardness of American economics. America, it was said, had no economic problems and therefore could not generate a vital science of economics. Like the rumor of Mark Twain's death, any declaration of the end of economic problems is somewhat premature. But, since political economy is not an end in and of itself, its devoted practitioners can be counted on to help hasten that happy day.

123

PROBLEMS OF
THE AMERICAN ECONOMY:
AN ECONOMIST'S VIEW

I OUGHT at the very beginning to make a confession—lest I be found in violation of the full-disclosure provisions of the U.S. Securities and Exchange Commission. What I am going to talk about is not exactly what would seem to be indicated by the abridged title announced for my Lecture. This is not because we in America have so few economic problems as to make it impossible to stretch out the discussion for all this hour. Nor merely that America has *so many* problems as would require us to stay here until well past midnight before we could find the solution to all of them.

The real reason why my sermon is departing slightly from its text is that you all know so much already about the American economy and its problems. I was tempted to use the hackneyed phrase 'bringing coals to Newcastle', but lately I learned in Washington that Pennsylvania would indeed be sending coal to that and other English ports were complete free trade to prevail.

You all know so much about my country because you are such clever people. America is a peculiar object of interest to all the world and London is well-served by an accurate press. (As an aside, I must confess that some of what you know from your papers about America is news even to us: I was tickled to learn years ago from the *New Statesman* that we Americans are so fearful of a bomb attack that each summer night in Chicago thousands and thousands of cars stream out from the city and into the countryside; the anxiety apparently hits young people even more than old; it wanes with the breeze and waxes with the humidity; and on those weekends that you would call Bank Holidays, it reaches a veritable climax of panic.)

But there is still another reason why you know so much about America's economic problems. They are, alas, so very much like your own. This was brought home to me last Spring when Lady Hall of Somerville College was a visiting professor at M.I.T. The first public seminar she attended was on America's problems and was conducted by an able *New York Times* reporter. The next day I asked her how the meeting went. Remembering our custom, Once a governor always a governor; and remembering the lines

> Not all the water in the rough rude sea
> Can wash the balm from an annointed King:

remembering all this, I should specify it was *Professor* Hall who answered my query, saying: 'I could have cried: he wasn't talking about the once-proud America I used to know. The problems were so drearily familiar, I felt I had never left home.'

How true it is. Thus, for the twenty-five years after 1933 we never had the least bit of concern about gold and our balance of payments. I have recorded elsewhere how after a long day's session in Washington I would often look back over my notes and discover that not once had anybody mentioned international trade. Well, the honeymoon was great while it lasted. But, as our friends are kind enough to remind us, now the United States has rejoined the human race: we too have a balance of payments problem; we too have a wage-price spiral; we too have a languishing growth rate.

Of arms and the gap and all those problems we have in common[1] I shall speak. Yet a balanced description and reasoned analysis of these matters, I could not hope to squeeze into an hour's talk. And I must remember the doctrine of *comparative* advantage: even were it true—as it, of course, is not—that I were America's greatest authority on all these matters, I must not forget that I am an economics professor. A teacher of graduate students and beginners. A thing of roots and vectors. In short an incurable theorist, who would rather be sprayed with chalk dust than with star dust.

---

[1] It will be evident that some of our problems are quite different. Thus, we have a special problem that is no real economics problem but is none the less crucial: I refer to our ideological battle over the question of whether our Budget must be 'in balance'. I can find no one in the U.K. who even knows how your deficit, as *we* measure it and worry over it, is to be calculated. Sweet innocence!

The true subject of my talk, then, is to be: What are some of the analytical problems that the American economy throws up to the economic theorist to puzzle over and try to solve? What is his role as compared to that of the lawyers (who are so important in our setup) and as compared to other policy makers? The honest title of my paper ought really to be something like the following: Problems of the American Economy as Grist and Challenge for the Economist.

In preparation for this occasion, I did some homework and brushed up a little on the life of Lord Stamp, whom we honour today. Stamp felt that there was definitely a place for the economics scholar in public affairs. And I think he would have approved my resolve to know my own place and to stay within it.

*   *   *

But what is the place of the professionally-trained economist in public affairs? I gather that this has been considerably debated in England during the last decade. Much did I learn from two lectures on the subject by Sir Robert Hall, who enjoys practically a monopoly over here in having lived in both the world of government and the world of professional economics. From Professor Devons and Dr Little I was given much to think about, but the views of the one did not quite seem to reinforce those of the other.[1] So perhaps I had better stick to the inductions garnered from my own observation of Washington and the Groves of Academe.

I am led to enunciate three trite theorems.

¶ First, political economy is much too important to leave to the non-economists.

¶ Second, while Denis Brogan may be right in reminding us repeatedly that Calvin Coolidge said 'The business of America is business', I have to insist that much of what is involved in business, far from being nobody's business, definitely is the economist's business.

[1] Sir Robert Hall, 'The Place of the Economist in Government', The Sidney Ball Lecture, 1954, *Oxford Economic Papers*, 1955; 'Reflections on the Practical Application of Economics', Presidential Address to the Royal Economic Society, July 1955, *Economic Journal*, December 1959; Ely Devons, 'The Role of the Economist in Public Affairs', *Lloyds Bank Review*, July 1959; I. M. D. Little, 'The Economist in Whitehall', *Lloyds Bank Review*, April 1957.

❡ Finally, I have an answer to give to the Kipling-like gibe sometimes heard from men of affairs who say: 'What do they know of econ who only econ know?' Whitehead suggested the proper reply: 'And what do they know of economics who *don't know* economics?'

Economists and Business Policy

I intend to develop some corollaries of these theorems. But today is not the time to say very much about the role of the economist in a business firm. Years ago A. C. Pigou claimed that no one would ever think of asking an economist to help run a brewery. If true then, it is not true now. Linear programmers tell firms how each week to mix their chicken feed and dog food (the Stigler least-cost diet problem); how each month to ship most cheaply from plants to customers (the Hitchcock-Kantorowich-Koopmans transportation or assignment problem); how each minute to distribute the power load among alternative generating stations in a network; and how each season to vary stocks (Whitin-Arrow-Bellman dynamic and stochastic programming). The most esoteric discounting methods of Irving Fisher have, through the work of George Terborgh and others, revolutionized the *practice* of capital budgeting in large and middle-sized firms.

I do not want to concentrate on the economist as operational researcher—even though David Ricardo's comparative cost theory seems to be the first historic use of linear programming. But I ought to mention the more traditional role of the economist in business and banks. Very often the man who used to be called the company's economist was merely an ideologue: when he was not editing the corporation house organ and writing about the virtues of free private enterprise, he spent his time as a kind of hatchet man criticizing the critics of business enterprise. Such functionaries 'could never meet a payroll'—the acid test *they* like to apply. I would as soon depend upon the newest accountant or nearest gypsy for a forecast of future gross national product or company sales as on such as these; and to tell the truth, the businessman himself never thinks very highly of such kept men. I find it amusing that the same pattern is apparently to be found in the Soviet Union. Those ideologues who teach what is called political economy—which consists of the apologetics and homiletics of Marxism—are looked down upon as lower-caste by the important economists in the Soviet Union who, working largely outside the universities, concern themselves with the *substantive* business of running the economy and keeping up with developments abroad.

To be candid, even in the large firm which cannot afford to be without economists, economics is not so valuable as it is in government. I do not wish to sound patronizing but to make the following analytical point. Money is so clear-cut a thing to deal with, that unsophisticated men can develop a flair for handling it. (I once heard an old Southerner say: 'You don't have to be smart in order to make money. But you *do* have to be able to make money.' Molière would have approved of this formulation, and so would Wittgenstein.) If money-making is the test, Ricardo and Keynes were successful speculators. And so perhaps are some brilliant economists today. But a number of the best in our profession are terrible at this game.[1] For example, one of the leading scholars in the world told me that he had bought but a single equity share in the postwar years. 'What is it?' I asked with an avaricious gleam in my eye.

'Angostura bitters. I figured it met a real need. And yet, if you can believe it, the price hasn't risen a bit in all the time I've held it.' I found I could believe it.

I shall say no more about business, and turn to the problem of economics and contemporary public policy.

The Few and the Many

I gather from a recent investigation—by P. D. Henderson in the *Oxford Economic Papers*—that your high civil service has scarcely more than a dozen full-fledged economists, or perhaps a score if some concealed economists are counted in. To us this does seem shocking. But I am reminded of the vice-president of a billion

---

[1] To the age-old query, 'If you're so smart, why ain't you rich?' the reply, 'If you're so rich, why aren't you smart?' will serve nine out of ten times. The man who first thought up the expression, 'He who is his own lawyer has a fool for a client' has much gratitude due him from the legal guild. But Shaw will have to answer in Heaven to the academic world for his dictum: 'Those who can, do; those who cannot, teach.'

dollar West Coast firm who sought my aid in his campaign to get the first economist appointed to their staff. His greatest barrier, he told me, was how to answer the question of the company's president who kept saying: 'If it is true that economists are so good, how come we've been getting along so well without one.'

Perhaps the affairs of this sceptr'd isle, this other Eden, have been running so well as to make it inadvisable to rock the boat by adding economists or making any other change. I do not mean to criticize. And, I must confess that, while there is no numerical shortage of economists in Washington, yet we do still have our troubles. Evidently, trained economists are neither a necessary nor a sufficient condition for the solution of an economy's problems. The question is, How helpful are they?

Let me linger a little on the question of numbers. My teacher and friend, Professor Seymour Harris, estimates that America has ten to fifteen thousand professional economists. Even counting Harris himself as but one, the United States supports as many economists as it does veterinarians or chiropractors. In our government itself, we do have numerous economists—even though cutting all their paychecks would not make a perceptible dent in the over-all budget. If you have scarce fifteen economists in all of Whitehall, I must mention that when I was a youth of barely 25—'in the wane of my wits and infancy of my discretion' —I supervised at least that number in the spare time between teaching and antiaircraft war work management. And that was as nothing, a mere epsilon. Lord Robbins years ago made the same point in telling about an occasion when the late Harry White led him into an auditorium to meet economists, and how great was his surprise to learn that not only were these not all the economists in Washington, they were not even all those in the Treasury, being just those in White's division of the Treasury.

Perhaps this will conjure up to you the last stage of the law of diminishing returns and the vision of all those slide rules getting each in the other's way. Nor will I deny that, if some Maxwell's Demon found a way of cutting out the fat without hurting the muscle, he could trim the number of our economists without doing much harm. None the less I insist that the nation could greatly benefit from having many *more* able economists than we have succeeded in enticing into government service. To pick but one example: our regulatory agencies—the Federal Communications Commission, the Federal Power Commission, the Securities Exchange Commission, Department of Justice—all of these are virgin territory waiting to be homesteaded by able economics students.

Turnover Among the Élite

Moreover, until recently our government has been living on its capital. Economists in government have been important ever since Franklin Roosevelt's first New Deal days. During the last war, some of our ablest academics spent a tour of duty in Washington, afterwards returning to the universities. Yet many able people remained. And, fifteen years ago, our best graduate students went into teaching or government service.

All that changed in the days of Senator McCarthy: students began to prefer the lucre from international oil companies to work in Washington. And, quite aside from McCarthyism, I have to relate a sorry fact: after twenty years of sympathetic Democratic rule, most American economists became committed to views that one of our major Parties did not like. I can illustrate this by an actual incident.

Back in 1946 the Republicans captured Congress while Harry Truman was still President. The late Senator Taft at that time asked a friend of mine—a Yale graduate whom Taft could trust— to help in finding a new Director of Research for the important Joint Economic Committee, someone who would understand 'sound' economics. How *I* got involved is one of those irrelevant mysteries. In any case, we drew up lists of all the able scholars we could think of, bearing down heavily on those universities thought to be conservative if not reactionary. Not one acceptable name could we turn up. So-and-so was against social security and minimum wages; but he held the awkward view that the steel companies should be broken up into a dozen smaller units. So it went.

And so it went—with a few notable exceptions—after Eisenhower became President in 1952. When civil servants in Scandinavia and Britain asked what would happen to our civil service when the Republicans got in, they could not believe it when I expressed the guess that many distinguished long-time civil servants in Washington would either quit their jobs or be forced out of them. 'What about Civil Service tenure?' they asked, and were mystified to be told that Civil Service tenure is with us some protection against being fired for *in*competence, but means nothing if a man's job is abolished or if he is deprived of all functions. I, in my turn, found it remarkable that no one seemed to have been deprived of his job or powers when your Conservative Government came into power in 1950.

You must not think that America has reverted to the Jacksonian Era, when it was taken for granted that 'To the victors belong the spoils', and victory provided the chance to throw the old rascals out and put in the new. Far from it. I have had something to do with recruiting economists for public service in the last twenty-five years, and I have been amazed how negligible is the old-fashioned kind of patronage appointment: no ward heeler becomes the Commissioner of Labor Statistics; party contributions may help to get you an Ambassadorship or even a Sub-Cabinet post, but they will not get you on the Staff of the President's Council of Economic Advisers.

The root of the turnover problem lies elsewhere. Our economist civil servants, and here I exclude those concerned with statistics and technical matters or those of junior rank, did not act between 1932 and 1952 as mere servants of the politically-appointed Department Heads.[1] They often fancied themselves as policy formulators, and some of our most important legislation has in fact stemmed from vigorous civil service promotion. How often one heard back in New-Deal and war-time cocktail parties complaints by high civil servants that their bosses of Congress were slow to grasp the merits of their proposals!

Now I suppose one cannot have it both ways. One cannot shape policy, actively and patently, and expect to be immune to shifts in electorate opinion. Most particularly must this be the case if the general policies being pushed—however excellent they may be—

[1] The Bureau of the Budget, having able professional people who survive from Administration to Administration, is an exception; and so are the permanent cadre of non-policy experts in the Commerce, Labor, and Agriculture Departments. On the other hand, the Treasury was almost denuded of economists after 1952.

are in many respects far ahead of public and Congressional opinion in sophistication.[1]

No doubt here and in Scandinavia you handle these matters better. I take it that high civil servants here accept cheerfully the 'indifference curves' of their political chiefs and then calculate for them positions of 'Pareto optimality'. Today they nationalize steel with efficiency. Tomorrow with equal efficiency they de-nationalize it. If, as the wisest believe, Permanent Under-secretaries sometimes manage their superiors, it is all done in oh-so-subtle-and-pleasant a way as to make the Minister feel that throughout he is enjoying Hegelian freedom—that delicious freedom which represents the cheerful recognition of necessity.

There is this advantage to your system. It provides a lifetime career for the able civil servant. One joins up young and stays until retirement. Just as New York is said to be 'a great city to spend a weekend in but I'd certainly hate to live there', Washington is a fine place to spend eight years in; but one must have reservations in recommending it as a lifetime career for an ambitious and able young economist. This deprives our Executive of long experience, and the improved judgment experience can bring with it. But perhaps this is not all loss. Freshness and enthusiasm are also assets. We have all met fine civil servants who have become just a little jaded on the job, a little stale and sceptical. They can tell you a thousand reasons for not doing something, and often they are right; but mere caution is not the greatest talent a modern nation needs in its employees. Moreover, there is practical merit to a system that can still recruit people in their thirties and forties for highest careers—if for no other reason than the difficulty in recognizing which 22-year-olds will turn out to be the best economic decision makers at 45 or 50. Why force oneself to prejudge the matter?

---

[1] It would be wrong to think that government economists were foisting their personal value judgments in a paternalistic way on the public and on elected officials. End conflicts were minor in comparison with differences of opinions on means: would deficits increase unemployment? cause prewar inflation? and so forth. Two further points may be important. We do not have the Ministerial system in which the Government largely controls its majority in the Parliament. Also, while opinions *on ends* may be more widely split in Britain, opinions on means are probably more widely split in the States. *E.g.*, Keynes has always been a fighting word with us, being coupled with Marxism and juvenile delinquency among the *Privatdozenten*.

I shall not pretend to know the best answer. Each system has its merits, and its demerits. To say that a golden mean of them would be better still, might be merely like saying: 'Herring is good. And chocolate is good. How good then must be herring-and-chocolate.'

Perhaps in concluding this international comparison an economist will be forgiven for saying a few words about the economics of public service. If our government is to rely on periodic infusion of blood from the universities, how does its salary scale compare?

In the first New Deal, economists generally bettered themselves by going to Washington: many a young instructor I knew left an $1,800 a year job involving a teaching load of 12-plus hours to take Uncle Sam's four or five thousand dollar salary, with typing thrown in for free. Times have changed. The highest Washington job an economist could get and be an economist would, I believe, pay little over $20,000 per year; and most high positions would fall well short of this figure. Truly it has been said that we now live in the age of the affluent Professor. Many academic chairs (though not so many as one would think listening to academic gossip) would pay more than this now; and since the opportunities for outside income from consulting, writing, and foundation grants is considerable, the man who goes to the New Frontier today probably does so at some considerable financial sacrifice. Before last January I would not have realized how much the terms-of-trade had changed.

Let me compare them with your situation. As far as I know a top professor in one of your Ancient or Red-brick Universities gets about £3,000—only $8,400 at the official exchange rate but undoubtedly much more at the purchasing-power-parity appropriate to dons. I do not know how high is your scale for top civil servants or run-of-the-mill Bank of England economists, but I doubt that it can fail to reach £5,000. On a before-tax basis, your government-university index would be 167 while ours would scarcely be 100. To be sure, the marginal tax rate is heavier here on the differential income; but I think the comparison still has point. The moral is not that your top Civil Servants are overpaid; nor do I pronounce on the question as to whether our lucky professors enjoy unwarranted producer's-surplus. Rather the point is this. It is high time our Supreme Court Justices, Congressmen, and Cabinet Officers had their pay raised from $25,000 per year—even if they do not merit or want it, though of course they do—in order that our government can move up salaries of scientists and other specialists to the levels needed to attract able people. Otherwise, we shall stop getting people responsive to good, clean money and will have to settle for those responsive to bad, dirty power.[1]

Rare Sense and Common Sense

Permit me to put aside all questions of organization and recruitment. What is it that the trained economist can do which is useful and better in government than can be done by persons with some other kinds of training?

If I were to reply, 'Economists know advanced economic theory better than anyone else possibly can', that would be stating a tautology which begs the question. Certainly if you were to read official state papers and overhear the meetings at which final policy decisions are made, you would find they usually involve not much more than so-called common-sense economics. If Macaulay's schoolboy can easily learn elementary economics by reading a certain fat textbook, why is not the same true of a crack classical scholar who has been recruited into government service; or even true, at least to a degree, of an elected official?

There is a ready answer to this. Common-sense economics may indeed be all that anyone must use in the end. But it takes the most uncommon sense and wisdom to know just which part of the

---

[1] Adam Smith pointed out that equalizing differentials in wages are needed to get men into unpleasant occupations like butchering; and in comparison with the pleasant life of the University some differentials may be needed for government. In this connection recall the remark the great physicist J. J. Thomson made when someone pointed out to him that a broker in the City earned three times what he did in Cambridge. 'Yes, but think of the work he has to do.' In pursuit of these sociological investigations, I may anticipate some of the later discussion comparing lawyers and economists in government. While the Kennedy Administration had some difficulties in attracting able economists from their university positions, it seemed to have much less of a problem when it came to lawyers. Apparently the typical New York attorney earning more than a hundred thousand dollars a year has been pining since 1952 to get back from the sticks to the gay, bright capital. It will be a bad day for democracy when only the very poor or the very rich can afford to work for the government.

filing case of muddled notions that men call common sense[1] is relevant to a particular problem.

While it is true that few with advanced training in economics can be trusted to use common-sense economics, fewer still, and maybe no one, *without* advanced training in economics, can be trusted to use common-sense economics. Don't ask me why this is so. I have puzzled over the phenomenon for years and years and never been able to satisfy myself as to the reason. When Margaret Fuller said: 'I accept the Universe!', Thomas Carlyle's reaction was, 'By gad, she had better'. The same goes for me. Though I can't explain why, experience does show that the best economic policy-makers have spent years studying economics and doing scientific research. The alleged exceptions almost invariably turn out to be flukes.

Was not Schacht the genius who stabilized the mark in 1923? Yes, and it was that same genius whose orthodox advice to Hitler contributed mightily to *our* victory. Is not Bernard Baruch the elder statesman who, with no more than his mature shrewdness and practical experience in Wall Street, has been the adviser of Presidents from Wilson to Eisenhower? Yes, but this only tells us something about his supply curve of effort and nothing about the uneven merit of his enthusiasm for direct price and wage controls[2].

Common sense, and folklore generally, lack empirical content. Some particular aphorism, taken by itself, may seem to contain information and contradict my last statement. Thus, 'Absence makes the heart grow fonder' would seem to offer advice to a Ulysses debating whether to leave his Penelope behind. But not really. Common sense is too cagey to commit itself to a refutable hypothesis. It protects itself by coupling with the above aphorism its antidote: 'Out of sight, out of mind.' The two together contain what the electrical engineer would call zero bits of information and constitute what the old-fangled logical positivist would

---

[1] Cf. A. N. Whitehead, *Introduction to Mathematics* (1911), p. 157: 'Now in creative thought common sense is a bad master. Its sole criterion for judgment is that the new ideas shall look like the old ones, in other words it can only act by suppressing originality.'

[2] Some will hold the same things can be said about the Rueffs and Cassels of this world, who, whatever else they may be accused of, have not lacked training in economics.

call a 'meaningless' proposition. I would liken common sense to the hands of a watch, hands so short that they lie in every direction; lying in *every* direction, the hands cannot *point* in any direction and such a watch can tell us the correct time only *after* we have already learned it elsewhere.

On Being Practical

What about the need for policy advisers who are 'practical', as against learned fools who are 'theoretical' or 'idealistic'? Disraeli declared, 'A practical man is a man who practises the errors of his forefathers', an especially interesting definition to have come from a self-proclaimed conservative. If we accept this definition, we are right back in the section on common sense and can proceed to new matters with only a backward reference. But there is something more involved in the notion of being practical that is different from merely exercising common sense. Most sciences make a legitimate distinction between their *applied* and *pure* aspects, even though the borders are fuzzy. In economics the distinction is peculiarly bound up with the problem of *feasibility*. Temperaments differ among scholars as well as chorus girls. It is quite legitimate to write a book analyzing the consequences of abolishing present-day Central Banking, and substituting for it certain automatic money mechanisms; yet it would be quite useless to sign on at the Federal Reserve Board for the sole purpose of advising it, every hour on the hour, to commit suicide.[1]

We laugh at students who, instead of answering the examination question as set, try to brazen it out by answering some quite different question. Some scholars are like that: when you ask them what would be the effects of a cut in personal income tax rates, they say you should be making a study of the effects on the balance of payments of an appreciation of the currency. Or they reply: 'On the assumption of an n-person economy, with indifference curves that are homothetic and production functions that are homogeneous, and assuming workers save nothing and

---

[1] The same point is made by the story of an eminent economist, who arrived in Israel to advise on policy, and came off the plane saying: 'The first thing you must do is devalue your currency by 70 per cent; then I will prescribe the next steps.'

non-workers save all, tax rates enter merely as . . . blank, blank, blank . . .'—leaving you to decide how relevant is the answer and how it must be modified to give a tolerable approximation. Less useless is a third answer: 'It all depends.' 'On what does it all depend?' 'It all depends on everything.' This does say something more than, 'I don't know the answer.' It adds the innuendo, 'And I don't believe anyone else can know the answer, until further data are supplied.'

Now I must not be misleading. As Sir Robert Hall rightly pointed out, every adviser and consultant—whether he be an attorney, statistician, priest, or economist will learn that, just as the facts never tell their own story, 'clients' do not know their own mind and do need a midwife to help deliver them of the questions they ought to be asking. So we should not reproach the practitioner for reformulating the questions to be answered. Nor is it wrong to study idealized models for the purpose of throwing light on particular concrete problems, if we or some others determine that the models do have some describable relevance. Nor is it without use to assert ignorance, where ignorance in fact prevails, and provided one's inability to give an *exact* answer is not used as an excuse to avoid giving the *best possible approximate* answer.

As I said, temperament is all important. To be a research scholar, not particularly informed on current facts and policy matters, is an honourable estate worthy of inclusion in the gross national product and value-added; not only can it be pleasurable, it may even bring fame and the gratitude of later generations. What is unforgivable is for those in this niche to rise to the bait when a journalist calls up to learn what the professor thinks next year's unemployment will be. Instead of telling the reporter to ask someone who has studied the matter, we academics too often will hazard a guess—more often than not, as experience shows hazarding too gloomy a guess. And why not? We are alerted to the sin of unemployment, and as men of good-will are agin' it. Even those who think on the problem never know in advance just where the new stimuli for spending will come from; so naturally those who have not thought on the matter cannot perceive where the requisite spending will emerge from, and may unthinkingly equate to zero what *they* cannot specify.

By temperament some scientists are simply not good decision-makers, are simply not shrewd estimators of subjective probabilities and consequences. I may illustrate by the case of an illustrious mathematician, my M.I.T. colleague Norbert Wiener. He is a good example because no one doubts the originality of his contributions to Banach-Weiner space; the Wiener-Brownian motion; Fourier analysis and ergodic theory; generalized harmonic analysis and Komolgoroff-Wiener-Shannon information theory; Cybernetics; and Wienerism generally. I stay well within the truth when I report that Wiener is not a good chess player: if a colleague's ego needs bolstering or if he has a bright 10-year old son, I always prescribe a victory over Wiener in chess to build up morale.

Once someone asked Wiener: 'How come you are so great a mathematician and—if you will pardon the expression—so lousy a chess player?' Wiener's reply was instantaneous: 'That is because a mathematician is judged by his *best* performances; whereas, alas, a chess player is only as good as his *worst*.'

Businessmen, generals, physicians, speculators or men-of-affairs know that good decision-making is neither like chess nor like creative mathematics. The Great Scorekeeper will judge you by your accuracy averaged over a considerable period of time (accuracy being gauged in terms of the 'utility significance' of error, not its mere numerical magnitude).[1] If this viewpoint can be identified with 'responsibility', then it is simply a fact that many of our best economists are irresponsible. They would as lief be wrong in an interesting way as be right along with the mob.

Some I know get stuck with an investment in a strong position.

---

[1] Playing for blood and money is not the same as playing on paper. Suppose I allocate each member of my class $100,000 on paper at the beginning of the term; and each competes to invest this so as to have the most gains at the end of the term. Inevitably students will take flyers in the most fantastic equities. And they are right to do so in this sociological situation. For either you end up the sole winner or you do not: you might as well be hung for a sheep as a lamb. Real life is not at all like that. There is all the difference in the world between winning second rather than thirtieth place. If only a speculator can repeatedly 'show', he can let a changing group of rivals 'win' and 'place'. One of the dangers of heroes in history—men like Napoleon and Hitler—is that they disregard this distinction between outcomes that are less-than-glorious. When Sombart in World War I complained that England was a nation of shopkeepers rather than heroes, he unwittingly paid you a great compliment.

Thus they may have predicted a great collapse every year since the wars. Knowing they are linked with this view, they will not cut their losses,[1] preferring to wait for that inevitable day when reality will wander into their stationary gunsights. If their eating money were at stake, they would not continue to throw good funds after bad. They remind me of a stubborn brother who refused to change his watch for daylight saving time, knowing that reality would catch up with him the next autumn; but he at least knew how to allow for his own stubborness and such people do not.

There is still another pattern of irresponsibility that often succeeds in impressing the casual onlooker and posterity, but does not impress the Great Scorekeeper and me. Big-picture men like Henry Adams, or Toynbee, or Marx, or Nostrodamus will sometimes produce patches of words that seem to hit the nail on the head.[2] Thus, in the nineties, Adams wrote that Russia would ultimately be the great world protagonist along with the United States. How prescient! Yet, was it really? Henry Adams had a propensity to write numerous letters, and they are a delight to read. But there is every kind of prophecy in them, many woefully off the mark. Like monkeys in the British Museum or Tippetts' random numbers, a man who spread his buckshot so widely could scarcely help but hit some targets.

As Justice Holmes said, we ask of someone like Spengler not that he be right but that the rascal give us a run for our money. Not so the Prince in selecting his advisers: the Prince can stretch

[1] Most economic forecasters have a low cunning that demographic forecasters could emulate. When the forecast by economists of a postwar slump did not materialize, we generally modified our view. Not so with the demographers. The fertility upsurge in France, the United States, and Australia caught them unaware. For this I throw no pebble: there was nothing in our pre-1939 experience to foreshadow the reversion by the middle classes to a sizeable family pattern. But after years of demonstration that such families were having more third and fourth children, it was rather stupid of demographers to keep muttering about the depression backlog of marriages, the draft, the postwar resumption of family life, and to deny the persistence of the new trends. The fact that no convincing explanation for the phenomenon has yet been offered is not a legitimate reason for denying the phenomenon or for predicting its early reversal.

[2] Veblen, Keynes and Schumpeter were interesting *nominators* of patterns that might happen in the long run, but I do not think they provide genuine exceptions to my formulation. Alexis de Tocqueville does, I must admit, shake my confidence; however, if, like Houdini, I were given time to contrive my escape, I might even succeed in explaining this exception away. I hope not.

his mind and get his exercise in some more harmless way. What he requires from an adviser is what we all require of a broker or weatherman—not that he be right, but that he makes the best judgment on the basis of weighing the evidence available *ex ante*, inferring from 7,000 years of recorded history that such use of loose scientific method in the end beats any witchcraft or dialectic yet discovered. E. B. White's diffident definition of democracy as 'the recurrent suspicion that more than half the people are right more than half the time' might appropriately apply to a defence of what I can here call loose scientific method. Paradoxically, the soft sciences that are still akin to an art benefit more from an explicit awareness of the canons of scientific method—the search for relevant data and the need to interpret and analyze the data— than do the hard sciences, where doing what comes naturally will protect even a fool from gross methodological error.

A Bouquet of Problems

Let me enumerate a few American problems, some of which are also your problems.

1. *Our balance of payments deficit.* This surely brings in all the complications of advanced economic analysis. Congressmen and editors could never work out for themselves the distinction between our 'basic balance'—which compares our current surplus of goods and services on private account with our government current deficit and our long-term private investment—and the 'liquidity deficit' which involves the decisions of people to hold more or less of their assets in American obligations rather than gold or foreign securities. While our basic deficit was improving in 1960, our liquidity deficit was worsening.

The superficial view of busy politicians is to identify our deficit with some particular item in the balance of payments, not realizing that it is an organic whole and that if we cut down on a dollar of foreign aid, that is unlikely to relieve our balance by a dollar—since so many of our private exports are geared to our provision of foreign aid. Without comparative cost theory, the government would not realize how an increased productivity abroad in the kinds of goods we specialize in could, if not offset, make ours an overvalued currency. Even when this lesson is taught, there is the much more subtle question of the deterioration of our terms of trade that would be implied in a successful campaign to bring our money costs into line with those abroad. Were this hour not so short, I would lapse into my academic manner and plot on the board a before-and-after comparison between the transformation curves of America and Europe, and American workers' lost monopoly access to management technology.

2. *The effect of defence spending on long- and short-term prosperity.* One need only read the changing economic analysis that comes out of the Soviet Union on this point to realize that common sense is hopeless in isolating the problems here involved.

3. *The alleged effects of alleged automation on unemployment and real wages.* Never did so many write so much that is nonsense and inconclusive as on this topic. The special American problems, that you seem not yet to have met, of whether there is a secular increase in 'structural unemployment', provided a marvellous example of what the new and brilliant team of Economic Advisers (Heller, Tobin, Gordon, Solow and others) could contribute in their first months of office to a murky issue.

4. *Ideological upside-down fiscal doctrine as against cause and effect.* This should be no problem but it is for us: Thus, Congress likes to vote more expenditures when tax collections grow. The U.K. seems to have been spared this nonsense problem.

5. *The problem of price creep at less-than-full employment.* Why Western Germany should have a more favourable 'Phillips Curve' (a concept many of us used in lectures for a long time and which Professor A. W. Phillips has formulated and measured) is almost the major economic enigma of this decade as far as rational fiscal and monetary policy is concerned.

6. *The degree to which a mixed economy can increase its own growth rate by a conscious programme of increasing over-all capital formation through an austere fiscal policy coupled with an expansionary credit policy.* No First in Sanskrit will help much in appraising this most difficult problem of the role of 'deepening of capital' in an environment of rapid technological change

7. *How to test operationally the hypothesis that ours is an 'affluent society'.* What should satiation imply for the personal saving rate, tax consciousness, multiple jobs and moonlighting, and so forth.

One could easily multiply the items on this list, and do so without even broaching the fashionable topic of economic development.

Since time does not permit more than naming these matters, I
had better go on to discuss the conventional problem of how
economists or anyone else can succeed in forecasting the future of
economic events.

Forecasting: A Typical Problem

To illuminate the question of how well economists can forecast
the future, permit me to tell an almost-true story. One of my teen-
age daughters asked me recently: 'Dad, are you a good business
cycle forecaster?'

Believing in the old-fashioned doctrine that truth is the best
policy, even within the family, I replied, 'No, of course not.
Economics is not an exact science like astronomy and physics. I
am often wrong in my predictions about the future.'

'Then, if you're not a good economic forecaster, who is a
better one?' she asked.

Well, I thought and thought. And I thought and I thought.
Finally I said, 'Margaret, go wash your hands for dinner; we
can't stand here all day wasting our time in idle chatter.'

This is not meant to be frivolous. Like Shaw who believed
children should never be spanked except in anger, I hold scholarly
wit should never be tried except to illuminate deadly-serious
problems. When I admit that *economists cannot forecast well*, that
sounds like a humble statement. Yet really it is not. I must add to
it the qualifying clause: *but experience shows they forecast the
economy better than any other group thus far discovered.* Empirical
statisticians, clairvoyants, down-to-earth businessmen, hunch-
players—all these turn out to have a worse 'batting average' than
government, academic, and business economists.

Batting average, by which I mean average performance over an
extended period of trials, must be the relevant criterion here; for,
on any single trial, you are either right or you are wrong. It will
help to use the language of baseball, which I understand is a
reasonably *U* topic. A ball player who has a batting average of
0·380 (that is, 380 successful hits out of a thousand trials at bat)

would be considered a veritable genius these days. While no economist can bat 1·000, the best do score around 0·775, which looks twice as good as the performance of Babe Ruth or anyone in baseball history.[1]

But let us not be deceived: merely by tossing a coin, any forecaster ought to be able to average 0·500 in predicting the direction of economic change; merely by parroting the word 'up', he can hope to score 0·600; and merely by calling out for tomorrow what he has observed to be the direction of change today, he can probably raise his score to 0·650. Adding zealous analysis of the facts as they become available, he may bring up his average to say 0·700. The difference between 0·800 and 0·700 may seem slight. Yet it is precisely the difference, at this stage of economic science, between high-talent and mediocrity.

In the years from, say, 1935 to 1955, Harvard's late Sumner Slichter was perhaps our best economic forecaster. I do not say this because he was a fine gentleman and my friend; or because I admired his methods of analysis. I say it because Dr Robert W. Adams, now head of the economics department of Standard Oil of New Jersey, wrote a doctoral dissertation under my direction on different methods of forecasting. One such method was 'being Sumner Slichter'. Adams studied Slichter's complete writings: sometimes Slichter was saying nothing about the future; not infrequently, he seemed to be stating something but, upon careful reading, Adams perceived that he was saying no more than that 'Business will go up if it doesn't go down or stay still'; often, though, Slichter was making a definite forecast, which Adams could record to compare with the later facts; in some rare cases where Adams could not be sure of what was being stated, he called on independent outside readers for their consensus.

What was the upshot when event was compared with prediction? Sumner Slichter did turn out to have an unusually good batting average—but, of course, a less-than-perfect one. (I might add for the benefit of over-crude pragmatists that the investment trust and other groups who relied on him for advice did very well financially in the postwar period.) On the evidence, I would have

[1] Since the criterion of good forecasting is not solely relative frequency of correctly predicted direction of change, my use of these batting-average numbers is of course to be regarded as figurative.

bet my money on Slichter in preference to any other single person. I daresay there were better analysts of income determination and macroeconomics than Slichter; but they were few indeed and I would not expect their forecasts to turn out as well.

Specifically, I think Slichter was more reliable than any of the elaborate econometric equation-models associated with Jan Tinbergen, L. R. Klein, Colin Clark, Daniel Suits, and other famed experts. To be sure, since that time the models have improved. And Slichter is dead. But if I were Secretary Dillon and Economic Adviser Heller, I would give precedence to forecasts prepared by a jury consisting of, say, James Tobin, Arthur Okun, Geoffrey Moore, Robert Solow, David Lusher and George Jaszi over the forecasts emerging from a giant electronic computer.

Hearing this statement, you may be tempted to conclude: 'Samuelson is trying to sell the notion that advanced economics is helpful in government, yet he is himself admitting that the fancy methods of higher mathematics are inferior to those of judgment.' If so tempted, please resist the temptation. My point is very different.

It takes the most advanced training and skill to render and understand the judgment being made about equation models. The jury I mentioned would want to know the structure and results of a Klein or Suits model and by sophisticated analysis decide what parts of it to reject or keep.

But even this is not the most important point I am making. Although today's 'artists' of forecasting are much better than today's 'scientific' models, the Ford Foundation is well advised to give money for attempts to improve the equation-models. Why? Because Slichter is dead. It took America forty years to grow a head like his; yet, after his passing, *none* of his wisdom could be transferred to pupils or co-workers. I used to study Slichter like a Boswell, but no design in the carpet could I discern. One year he talked about credit; another year it was expectations; a third year, technology. It is my guess that Slichter was, miraculously, greater than the sum of his parts. It is my conviction that he was greater than his explanations and rationalizations. To think that Slichter was merely an *idiot-savant* with luck would be plainly ridiculous; to think he was a cracker-barrel philosopher with no need to rely on the tools of modern economics would be less-plainly ridiculous, but still ridiculous. An Arthur Burns or an Arthur Okun do as well as they do because they have spent years in studying the economics of business cycles.

By now the clever members in the audience will have noted that it is a favourite gambit of mine to give a statement proclaiming great humility over the prowess of economic science, and then gradually to convert it into a statement of arrogance. I am led to this not by immodesty but by the invisible hand of objective truth. And I warn you that here I go once again.

Charles Darwin has told us how he found it necessary to write down any objections he encountered to the theory of evolution; for invariably he found himself tending to forget them. In the same way I steel myself to review my forecasts of the previous year that have appeared periodically in the *Financial Times* or other publications I write for regularly. It is not for me to appraise my own batting average but I usually nurse the feeling that it has been not at all bad. I must confess, though, that upon unsparing re-examination, there usually arises the feeling that last year I had not pin-pointed the ensuing pattern of events quite so precisely as fond memory had suggested.

I mention this to stress the need for the rough scientific procedure of validating forecasting performances—something which is never done in the bathtub full of investment letters that reach my desk in the course of each season. Chartists point to their successes; they ignore their failures; their second sight is nothing but hindsight; no programmer can reduce to automaticity their methods so as to test them comprehensively on a giant calculator.

The fact that I was not so smart *ex ante* as *ex post* I remembered myself to have been, dashes my spirits only for a moment. Then I begin to work the other side of the street saying: 'There is always an irreducible degree of uncertainty in forecasting the future, something like the Heisenberg principle of indeterminacy in quantum mechanics. I would have been cheating the readers of the *Financial Times* had I given precise point-estimates, even had they turned out often to be correct; how generous I was with those readers to have indicated along with my best point-estimate a proper caution as to the approximate width of the confidence interval appropriate to the degree of our possible knowledge.'[1] You will realize that I am slightly pulling your legs —so slightly as almost to constitute pushing them. Through my hollow laughter, though, you will hear the faint echo of truth. A good forecaster uses the numerical language of probability, not as amateurs and some savants think, to give a false impression of precision in estimating, but rather to give a humble indication of degree of ignorance. This ignorance that grows out of knowledge distinguishes itself over a long period of time from the ignorance that grows out of ignorance.

Sometimes writers have thought that there is a kind of danger in unanimity among the experts. 'When they are most agreed, watch out, for they are sure to be wrong. Do not likewise, but do the opposite.' An attractive theory but I am sorry to report one with no substantiation. Just before the stock market crash of 1929 the experts were *not* most in agreement; read the literature and you will find that division of opinion had been growing in the previous years. And if you carefully go over the detailed record of GNP forecasts, you will find that the experts have been least in error when they were least in disagreement.

How nice it would be to find somewhere in the world a person so gifted with ignorance as to make it possible for you to reverse his actions and make precise forecasts. There is no such person or group. Like Tolstoy's unhappy families, each fool is wrong in a different way and wrong in a different direction from time to time.

This brings me finally to the common charge: 'Economists cannot be very helpful because they do not agree even among themselves. Take any point of view however bizarre and you can find an economist to espouse it. It is notorious that among N economists you will always find N different views *at a minimum.* Recalling the definition of a Unitarian as a man who believes that there is at most one God, you can write down the inequality $V \geqq N$.'

I wish I could go more fully into the merits of this charge. Let me merely report that as far as American experience goes, it is not borne out factually. At any time I can tell you just what point

---

[1] In fine, I am the contrary of the New England judge who reprimanded counsel with: 'Sir, this Court is often in error but never in doubt.' While I sometimes escape error, I always profess doubt—as every decision-maker should.

the majority of bank and government forecasters are clustered about; like cider, forecasters are if anything too homogeneous, too much in touch with one another, too sheep-like in their shifts of optimism. We have an apt saying: 'Economic forecasters are like many eskimos crowded into the same bed. You can be sure of one thing, they will all turn over together.' The reasons are not hard to find; what one fool can do, so can another; opinions mingle; finally, it is safer to be wrong with the crowd than take the chance that you may not be right, all by yourself.

Some Final Conclusions

Years ago I wrote that it was commonly found that economists made better decisions than the businessmen who signed up in Washington for the war years. I attributed this merely to adherence to the rules of rough scientific method and evaluation of evidence. And I cited the experience of the Office of Strategic Services as revealing the superior wartime usefulness of trained economists over trained historians. When I wrote this, I expected an outcry from both camps; but it has not yet come. This silence may serve to validate my thesis, but there is always an alternative hypothesis to be kept in mind: it may simply be that businessmen do not read at all, and that historians do not read the kind of book people like me write.[1]

Since then, more experience has accumulated. Anyone who knows anything about our defence planning will realize how great has been the contribution of RAND, despite the unpopularity it has been awarded for its fearless excellence. It is no secret that

[1] P. A. Samuelson, 'What Economists Know' in *The Human Meaning of the Social Sciences*, ed. Daniel Lerner, Meridian Books, Inc. (1959), pp. 186–8. Had I gone on to say that trained economists did better than physicists, I might have brought down on my head the thunderbolts of 'operations researchers'. Yet, the record as a whole is not clear. Without doubt the principal asset will always be generalized *I.Q.*, whatever that may be. Economists, historians, and physicists come in stupid and bright varieties: it is *partial* correlation coefficients we seek not raw ones that do not allow for differences in ability and temperament. The wartime folklore, being folklore, was ambiguous: according to some accounts, philosophers proved the best decision makers; according to others, biologists and scholars in 'soft' rather than 'hard' sciences proved most creative and versatile. In my observation of wartime computer and antiaircraft design, pure mathematicians did well. Less surprisingly, eminent statisticians like Abraham Wald did well at statistics.

the role of economists has been an outstanding one, as I can candidly state because I merit none of the praise. Charles Hitch, the Rhodes Scholar who stayed on, could not have played his important role in RAND (and now in Washington) had not Oxford added to what the Ozarks had begun.

To watch a superb economist at work—a Robert Roosa as Undersecretary of the Treasury; a Heller, Tobin and Gordon at the Council of Economic Advisers—is like watching Jack Dempsey, Blondin, Frank Ramsey or Roger Bannister do what only they can do and do so elegantly. The balm from an annointed Doctor of Philosophy has a half-life that is all too short; I fear the sprint that such versatile people set themselves could never be maintained over the long-pull, without periodic rustication to recharge the batteries of economic insight. Just as Virginia Woolf argued that a woman needs a room of her own and as earthier advisers tell a girl to take 'mad money' along on a date, such people need a place outside of Washington to fall back on—I mean the Frost-kind of home, . . . which is 'where, when you go there, they have to take you in'. Economists in government need this to keep from being too 'practical' in the sense I have so far avoided: of interpreting too narrowly the realm of the feasible. I swear the heavens look down upon no sight o'er this mean globe more tragi-comic than that of an Assistant Secretary who spends his time trying to guess what his Cabinet Secretary will guess the President is going to want next to hear.

Q called political economy an unnatural science, and I shall pay the price of the adjective to get the noun. Pigou and Keynes said our science lacks the beauty of physics and higher mathematics. I tell you they were wrong. Anyone with the aesthetic sense to recognize the beauty of the proof that the diagonal of a unit square is not the ratio of two integers—the acid test of G. H. Hardy—will sense the same harmony that resides in Ricardian comparative cost or Walrasian general equilibrium. Economic theory is a mistress of even too tempting grace.

But having said this, let me call attention to a higher goal that surpasseth even the love of form. When man sets himself the challenge to theorize *and yet stay within the constraint of explaining reality*, the task is much the harder—but how much more satisfying the hunt. At night by the fireside let them who will display their easy tiger skins; for man the greatest quarry of all is the study of man. For what do they know of economics, who political economy do not know?

124

STABILITY AND GROWTH

IN THE AMERICAN ECONOMY

Wicksell, The Economist

It is always an honor to be invited to give a series of lectures abroad. For me as an economist it is an especial honor to receive a call from Sweden, so noted for its eminent economists. Indeed, if I may borrow a theory from two great scholars, namely the late Eli Heckscher and the early Bertil Ohlin, I have to report that Nature has endowed Sweden so fully with the rare natural resource, economics brainpower, that she could not help but specialize in the production and export of brilliant ideas, importing in return and at the generous terms-of-trade heartfelt appreciation and admiration from economists all over the world.

Having been doubly honored, I find that my cup runneth over to be asked to give lectures that go under the name of the great Knut Wicksell. He of course is a Saint of political economy. But just as a child may have, out of all the calendar of Saints, a particular one who speaks especially to him, so I have felt these last twenty-five years an especial affinity for Wicksell. He is *par excellence* "an economist's economist", and Wicksell is to me an intellectual pin-up-boy worthy of the giddiest hero-worship.

Prophet of The Welfare State

Before I tackle those crucial problems of economic policy that face the American and world economy, I hope it will be quite appropriate to linger over the achievements of Knut Wicksell.[1] For, of all that noble tribe who blossomed in the last part of the Nineteenth Century—Marshall in England, Böhm-Bawerk in Austria, Walras in France and Switzerland, and the other great neoclassical writers—Wicksell was in many ways the most truly prophetic figure. A stormy rebel against the traditional religion and prudery

---

[1] It will be evident that I have benefited from: Torsten Gårdlund, *The Life of Knut Wicksell* (Stockholm, 1958); Carl G. Uhr, *Economic Doctrines of Knut Wicksell* (Los Angeles, 1960); Erik Lindahl, "Wicksell's Life and Work", introduction to *Selected Papers on Economic Theory by Knut Wicksell* (London 1958), translated from an article in *Ekonomisk Tidskrift,* 1951, and Bertil Ohlin, "Obituary", *Economic Journal,* 1926, p. 503–511.

of his day, Wicksell had the warm heart of a socialist along with the cool head of a classical economist. As a result he came as near as anyone could, before World War I, to being an exponent of the Welfare State. He could certainly—were he a modern American—be down in Washington with President Kennedy's New Frontier. And Heaven knows we could use his advice in connection with our international balance of payments problem, lagging growth rate, and threat of cost-push inflation.

But life did not rise from the primordial mud nor did man evolve from ape merely to achieve a 1960-type New Deal. Or did it? Back in the 1880's when George Bernard Shaw and Sidney Webb were writing *Fabian Essays,* radicals confidently looked forward to a world of socialism, where government ownership of the means of production would be the key to enhanced happiness. Sixty years later it was not so easy to write *New Fabian Essays.* The Democratic Left had in Europe and elsewhere realized many of the dreams of their ardent end-of-the century founders. But mere nationalization of industries and militant collective bargaining by trade unions had not ushered in utopia; nor did it appear probable, looking forward, that a much higher real wage and general living standard could be secured by an intensification of such traditional programs. On the other hand, redistributive taxation at graduated rates; welfare transfer expenditures to the unemployed, the old, the handicapped, and the unlucky; and public regulation against monopoly and excessive monopoly profits—all these appear to have done more for the workers and low-income classes in the Western World than the more traditional programs of socialism. In this sense Wicksell was prophetic, and could be excused for crowing: "I told you so."

The radical left has not looked too kindly on economists. And perhaps rightly so. For time and again the serious study of economics has captured idealistic reformers and turned them into dull pedants who, once youth is past, lost their idealistic sympathies along with their illusions. There are a few exceptions. Wicksell was one. In my own country, H. J. Davenport was another. Himself an accomplished economic theorist of the World War I generation, Davenport complained that there was no reason why reactionaries should have a monopoly on economic analysis. And he practiced what he preached, being the best friend in academic life that the iconoclast Thorstein Veblen ever had. Indeed on one of the innumerable occasions when that Norwegian descendent lost his academic post for mingled reasons of alleged sexual philandering and radical teaching—he apparently excelled in both—Davenport made room in the coal cellar of his house for Veblen to occupy, and greater love hath no man than this. This reminds me that Wicksell spent part of his time as professor at Lund in jail. Whatever we may think of the state of society then, which could jail a man for the offence of blasphemy, one's admiration goes out to the tradition of academic freedom in Swedish Universities which keeps a professor's livelihood and scholarly privileges immune from his non-scholarly misdemeanors. I wish I were sure that the same could be said of all American colleges.

"Warts and All"

I know from ancient experience that there is nothing that makes Swedes more uncomfortable than unqualified and nondiscriminating praise, as for example from tourists who gush about the wonders of the Middle Way and attribute even an exceptional spell of fine weather to the cleverness of Swedish planning. So let me make clear that I have hero-worship for Wicksell, the economist. But I have no giddy worship for anyone's ideas— not even my own—and I must point out that many of Wicksell's economic judgments have been revealed by history to have been quite wrong.

First and foremost, Wicksell had an absolute fixation on the population question. The Malthusian problem of diminishing returns obsessed him and colored all his thought, leading him to take an uncompromising and unpopular stand in favor of birth control. Whatever we may think today of the perils of overpopulation in underdeveloped countries, hindsight has taught us that scientific invention could be counted on in Europe and the advanced countries to keep the amount of food production growing faster after 1880 than the number of empty stomachs. Moreover, as we now know looking backward, a definite drop in the rate of such advanced countries was already taking place by the turn of the century. It is one of those hollow jokes of fate that Gunnar Myrdal, Wicksell's nephew so to speak, should within a dozen years of Wicksell's death be warning against the perils of Swedish depopulation.

Now, hindsight is certainly not foresight. Wicksell did not have the statistics available to tell him about the downward trend developing for the net reproductive rate (even though Cannan in England and Bortkiewicz in Germany had already sized up the changed outlook). Besides Wicksell was in good company in his concern, since Keynes and other economists were impressed with the slight trend toward higher terms of trade for food relative to European manufactures in the decade before 1914. Finally Wicksell's ghost might argue that it was precisely the agitation by martyrs like himself which helped create the more favorable trend in the birth rate.

Still ... and still, I cannot escape the feeling that he was not using the best economic judgment even *ex ante*. Malthusian problems were at best of secondary importance for his time. If I did not fear your displeasure by departing from my role as economist and donning the mantle of amateur psychoanalyst, I would venture the hypothesis that Wicksell early in life went through an emotional crisis mixed with religion and sex; and that his intellectual concern with diminishing returns proceeded from his early emotional concerns rather than that his concern with marriage and population questions proceeded logically from his economic theories.

Professor Gårdlund's charming biography of Wicksell was an eye-opener to me and to most foreign economists. Quite candidly, I had always respected Wicksell for what I thought to be his placid and sweet nature— as shown for example in his courtesy to other writers and in his non-aggressive modesty. To me he seemed rather like an amiable Papa Brahms, whereas his eminent contemporary Gustav Cassel had always impressed me as more of a Richard Wagner or Richard Strauss. How wrong, apparently, I was about Wicksell.

By all accounts he had an almost neurotic need to stand up and be counted on the side of unpopular causes. Whatever Anna Wicksell may have thought about this trait, in our age when martyrs are scarce and sensible men plentiful, I find this all rather admirable. One man's neurosis is another man's principle. Wicksell's own view of the matter is quoted in Erik Lindahl's penetrating memoir:

"... my fault in the political field is rather that I participate too *little,* not too much. I have espoused the principle never to push myself forward when the things that I think ought to be said on any particular subject have already been said by others; and, conversely, never to remain *silent,* no matter how small and insignificant my contribution may be, when *no one* speaks on a subject that is close to my heart."[1]

However admirable this may be, my earlier assertion that Wicksell would be found today in Kennedy's Washington ought, perhaps, to be modified by the distinct possibility that he might be classified as an unacceptable "security risk". And maybe I ought to reconsider whether Brahms was really the placid spirit of legend.

---

[1] Erik Lindahl, *op. cit.* p. 46.

Indeed, when I tried to identify the person of whom Wicksell so strongly reminded me, the answer kept eluding me. Finally, I realized it was the great early nineteenth century essayist William Hazlitt, another personal idol. Hazlitt was a man of the strongest liberal convictions, which, like Wicksell's, were formed early in life and never abandoned even in the face of the post-French-Revolution period of reaction. Neither would have much liked the term, but both represented the quintessence of Protestantism— the conviction that a man must be true to his own thought, though the whole world think him crazy or despicable and no matter how hot the fire or great his loved ones' suffering. Hail to such men (but pray they be not mistaken)!

A Study in Contrasts

If wrong about Wicksell's character, I was apparently only too right about his great contemporary and foil, Gustav Cassel. No one could call him modest—not even, I think Cassel himself! Lord Melbourne said, "I wish I was as sure about *any*thing as Macaulay is about *every*thing". Wicksell and Davidson must have felt much this way about Cassel. He chose not to be an economist's economist; and as Wicksell's stock rises with posterity, Cassel's quotation falls away to nothing. Like Faust, he made a compact with the Devil and bought immediate popularity at the price of profundity. Schumpeter's epitaph for him as "Leon Walras plus water— much water" is just. Yet shares can go to too great a discount in volatile markets. Cassel was a remarkable mind, who could master languages, mathematics, statistics, and political economy in unbelievably short time. The only thing he could not master was himself. The doctrine of *nihil nisi bonum* must not prevail.

Of the long dead we must say nothing but what is true: we owe that as a threat to the living. (This reminds me of a story I once heard about Gunnar Myrdal and which I preach to my classes. According to the story, the youthful Myrdal was brilliant but outspoken. When one of his teachers, Bagge, took him aside and warned him to beware of hurting the feelings of his elders since his promotion might depend on their good will, Myrdal is supposed to have replied: "Ah, but you forget. It is we youngsters who will have the last word; for it is we who will write your obituaries.") I don't know that the story is true but in any case it is well told.

My function is not to start legends but to preserve good ones known to be true. In this connection last Christmas, in my Presidential Address before the American Economic Association, I had occasion to mention an earwitness account that tells much about Cassel as a scholar. Hans Christian Sonne, our distinguished merchant banker, Chairman of the important National Planning Association, recent Vice-Chairman of our *Commission on Money and Credit,* public benefactor, and *bon vivant* told me of a visit that Cassel made to Sonne's father's home in Denmark. At the dinner table someone interrupted the discussion to mention that a scholar had recently examined Cassel's thesis that accumulation of gold stocks from mining could exactly explain the course of prices in the century before World War I, and found it wrong. When Cassel was asked what he was going to do about it, he (perhaps facetiously) replied: "I have a son-in-law whom I have been helping to finance through Divinity School. Just as he was hoving in sight of graduation he came to me and said he had lost his faith. My advice to him was, 'Just go on as if nothing had happened'. And that suggests my answer to you."

Forgive, but do not forget. This is the stern motto the historian of thought must wear on his crest. I must not pass over in silence, even on these native grounds, an example of Cassel at his worst. In the course of proving that Ricardo was a fool, Cassel goes out of his way to call attention to Bertil Ohlin's work on international and interregional trade. This is a work bursting with original ideas and practical insights. And what does Cassel see in it? Merely, a copying of his important equations—not Walras's mind you, *his.* And he cannot refrain from chiding Ohlin for having paid attention to Eli Heckscher's immortal paper on factor-price equalisation, which Cassel dismisses as complete nonsense. In the course of five short pages,[1] Cassel manages to damn four great economists. I say four, because in addition to Ricardo, Heckscher, and Ohlin, he most damns Gustav Cassel—a great economist in spite of himself. If anyone doubts this let him reflect that Cassel, long before the vogue of the properly famous Harrod–Domar equations, had already discovered their content, and one could extend the list.

The Scientific Accomplishment

Because Wicksell read the works of his predecessors and contemporaries, and acknowledged the fact; because he was eclectic; because he regarded all his own ideas as merely tentative hypotheses; because he happened to

---

[1] Gustav Cassel, *On Quantitative Thinking in Economics* (Oxford, 1936) pp. 168–173.

come to economics after Jevons, Menger, Walras, Böhm–Bawerk, Marshall and J. B. Clark—for all these reasons Wicksell is sometimes regarded as not having been a truly original and creative economist. I am convinced this appraisal is quite wrong.

While Wicksell may have lacked the broad judgment of Marshall and the one-track concentration of Clark, to savor his genius you have merely to read his works on capital and general equilibrium (*vide* Joan Robinson); on marginal productivity (*vide* Solow); on the impact of technological change (*vide* Hicks); on marginal cost pricing and imperfect competition (*vide* Hotelling and Chamberlin); on business cycle rhythms generated by uneven exogenous trends and random shocks of innovation, which impinge on an endogenous system geared to produce quasi-regular rhythms whose periods depend on its internal structure (*vide* Frisch and Tinbergen); on the proper role of government expenditure in an affluent and less-than-affluent society (*vide* Lindahl and Musgrave); on the relationship between interest rates set by the central bank and cumulative trends of inflation or deflation.

It was primarily for his view that a divergence between the market and the natural rate of interest caused cumulative price change that one knew Wicksell in the early 1930's when I was an undergraduate at the University of Chicago. So often when a foreign writer is praised to the sky, the translation of his book comes as a disillusioning anti-climax: the Italian work in public finance of Vito de Marco is a good example. But when Wicksell's German and Swedish works were translated in the mid-Thirties, they exceeded their advanced billing. While passing time has killed off interest in the neo-Wicksellian versions of the business cycle—such as those by Hayek, by Keynes in the *Treatise,* and by various Swedish writers belatedly translated—these notions seem to have served as valuable stepping stones to modern theories of income determination. The elder Marx once said in wry reproof of successors that he himself was not a Marxian. So Wicksell up in Valhalla—perhaps I ought to withdraw the metaphor in view of his repugnance toward all religions—would be the first to go beyond his own tentative hypotheses.

Hope Deferred

I have not thought it necessary to say much about the long trials and tribulations Wicksell had to go through before, at the age of 50 he finally was granted a university post and a living wage. That is a story that has often been told. And when I look back on my own career—receiving scholarship and fellowship aid from the beginning, having great teachers in economics at two world centers, being given research facilities and travel grants at an early age, having stimulating colleagues and more advanced students in a year than Wicksell had in a lifetime, and finally being paid reasonably well to do the teaching that I would pay money to be able to do—I confess to some embarrassment at the contrast. Indeed the thought that at my present age I would have to do what Wicksell had to do to become an assistant professor, namely study up for a law degree, is like a nightmare and my forehead breaks out in cold sweat at the prospect.

Still we must redress the balance a little and take Wicksell's own view of the matter. While food was scarce and his livelihood insecure, he did snatch the leisure from journalism and popular lecturing to consult libraries and do his thinking about economics. Genius handicapped is not nearly so bad as genius suppressed or genius aborted. His books got published, the really important thing to every autodidact. Nor need a Swede blush too much for the universities of that time: Wicksell was not repeatedly passed over in favor of lesser men; economics jobs were scarce and unconventional genius is never easily recognized by Deans and Faculty Boards. In that same age the great American philosopher, Charles S. Peirce, was without an academic chair, for reasons not wholly creditable to Harvard University. And besides, as I sometimes tell our students in flashes of personal immodesty, good teachers can themselves become something of a handicap to the emerging creative mind: Smith, Ricardo, Jevons, Walras and Marshall somehow managed to do all right. (On the other hand John Maynard Keynes is an example to show that it is not mandatory to be brought up in the wilderness for original thinking.)

What I do begrudge is the slowness of our Anglo-Saxon world to recognize the help Wicksell had to offer. His mathematical garb was one factor in this. And part of the blame must of course go to the incredible provincialism of the Edwardian Age, with Edgeworth as editor of the *Economic Journal* doing Marshall's bidding (conscious and unconscious) in suppressing serious interest in foreign theorists' writing. But for the most part it is a sad fact that American and English economists remain incredibly deficient in ability and willingness to read (*really* read) other languages: by this I do not mean Tibetan, but merely German or Italian.

Had Wicksell the good luck of Böhm–Bawerk in having a translator, or Cassel's remarkable facility with English and other tongues, how much farther along we might all hope to be today.

Although I am not regarded as much of a sentimentalist, all my emotions are aroused by one little story told in Gårdlund's biography. The 65-year old Wicksell, really at the top of his powers as an economist, visited London in 1916 and got a chance to see John Maynard Keynes. Keynes was then half his age, a recognized comer and tremendously enjoying his important position in the wartime Treasury. Keynes was able to spare time to have a brief lunch with Wicksell, and even went so far as to let Wicksell extend the discussion by accompanying him on his way to the barber!

Now what gets me in this story is not so much what Keynes did. He was a busy man and a war was on. Wicksell was little more than a name to him and Keynes never was known for overappreciating elders and strangers. Moreover, let us face it: a man must after all shave. What I find so poignant in the tale is the fact that Wicksell was so patently grateful for each little crumb of attention. The image of that plump little man nipping along in the wake of unconscious youth is to me a haunting one that makes me whisper "There, but for the grace . . ." and yet not know to which I am pointing.

Age and Scholarship

Talk of age raises one of the most interesting questions about Knut Wicksell. It is usually believed that scientists and mathematicians bloom young, and someone like Schumpeter carried this belief to the limit. Galois, Newton, Abel, Hamilton, all are examples of men who got their great ideas before the age of 30. Gauss and Euler are examples of men who did *great* work decade after decade. Weierstrass and numerous scholars in such fields as history where knowledge must accumulate and youthful impetuosity evaporate provide examples where a scholar's first notable work is done after youth is some distance behind.

Wicksell would seem to belong to this latter pattern. His great decade was that of the Nineties, which means that his three great classics were both thought up and written in the fifth decade of his life. But his case makes me wonder. In years he was not young. But in terms of the study of economics, he was indeed young and had no more time behind him than would a person fifteen years younger. Perhaps the brain is to be thought of as a Tabula Rasa, it being more important for creative thought that one be in the first ten years of study of a subject than in the first ten years of adulthood.

Wicksell is interesting in another respect. I do not subscribe to the view that after the turn of the century when he had passed 50, he ceased to be a truly creative economist. On the contrary, even his last paper and recorded discussion, when he was already in his midseventies, are among the most interesting he ever wrote. Perhaps this phenomenon is more typical of a questioning mind than of an assertive one. The accumulation of judgment saps the will to believe in one's own grand ideas and inhibits their birth. Perhaps the possession of the technique of mathematics—which, so to speak, does so much of our own thinking for us—stands by one as the years roll on. The old Wicksell may have lost something of the joy of life—there is pathos in his letter about the failure of music to ravish his soul as of yore—but his theoretical powers remained high.

The Ultimate Victory

But enough of sentiment. A scientist wants attention to his ideas not sympathy. With compound interest Wicksell has reaped the harvest of his long waiting. Ragnar Frisch, in his memoir on Wicksell, has quoted an English translation of an introduction written by the late Joseph Schumpeter to a German publication of Wicksell's last paper. I can hear my old teacher talking in the following lines:

... [Wicksell's] significance in wider circles of colleagues is not yet sufficiently valued, his message not yet exhausted. This is owing to the fact that his character excluded every kind of advertisement, that his amiable modesty left no room for any emphasis on his own contributions, and that he never stressed his powerful originality and never neglected to give the researchers to whom he was attached what was their due ... Scarcely any other of the architects who have laid the foundations of modern analysis, have so much to give us today—to give everyone of us who are growing, developing and struggling for new ways and views—as he. This is not only due to his wealth of thought, but also to the traits of his character. As he always thought of the subject only and never of himself and what could serve his own best, he had a style which, indeed, is neither smooth nor simple, but which for that very reason gives us a look into his workshop. We trace the vivid flash of constructive imagination, we see the original formulations, the difficulties and doubts such as they presented themselves to the author. Therefore, he gives us more than the actual result, he teaches research itself and points in every line beyond himself. This is very rare.[1]

Sometimes Schumpeter indulged in fulsome praise to be ironical, but this time he meant it. I can recall him contrasting with Wicksell's openness the dead geometric style in which Newton came to write up in the *Principia* his principles of universal gravitation, couching the argument in the cold form farthest removed from the steps by which he had actually made his discovery, a tactic Schumpeter deplored.

In calling Wicksell "the Swedish Marshall", Schumpeter paid a pretty compliment to *both* men. You will recall that when Laplace was asked who was the greatest mathematician in Germany, he replied with an eminent name. "What, not Gauss?" was the response. "Oh, Gauss, why he is merely the greatest mathematician in Europe." If asked to name the greatest economist in the twenty years before the great war, I would not find the choice easy. But I suspect posterity will award the palm to Knut Wicksell.

At Wicksell's death in 1926, a brilliant young man said that Wicksell had committed the unforgivable crime of being two decades ahead of his time. I think Professor Ohlin will agree with me that political economy has added 37 more years to the accusation against him but has forgiven him the crime.

----

[1] Quoted by R. Frisch from Joseph Schumpeter's introduction to the 1927 German translation of Wicksell's last paper. See H. W. Spiegel (ed.) *The Development of Economic Thought* (New York, 1952) pp. 653–654.

May 8, 1962

[Revised November 2, 1962]

Stability, Growth and Stagnation

Introduction

My over-all title "Stability and Growth in the American Economy" was chosen with some cunning, for under its rubric almost any economic topic could be touched on. The stability part of the topic would have come as no surprise to the economists of thirty years ago, since there was then a great preoccupation with what is called *the* business or trade cycle. Growth, however, was not a usual topic for discussion among economists of that time. Indeed, even after the 1936 publication of Keynes' *General Theory*, an English or American economist would be more likely to have used the title "Stability and Full Employment" than the one I have chosen.

Does this mean that the problem of unemployment has ceased to exist? Or that people have ceased to worry about it? While there has been little unemployment since the war in many European countries and actually a good deal of over-full employment in some of them, there definitely has been a deficiency of job opportunities in America during the last decade. And certainly people in Europe are much more sensitive than they were ever before to even small increases in the rate of unemployment. The American people, too, have shown in the postwar period greater preoccupation with the problem of unemployment than used to be the case before the Great Depression. But, whether or not it maketh the heart sick, hope long deferred does lead to some spirit of resignation and even complacency: Europeans are often puzzled that Congress and the American public tolerate with such apparent equanimity unemployment rates that exceed two per cent of the labor force—to say nothing of the fact that our unemployment has rarely fallen below the five per cent level in recent years and has at times reached the 7 per cent level.[1]

---

[1] It is widely realized that the American way of measuring unemployment—by a monthly interrogation of a scientifically determined sample—tends to give a higher index than the usual European method which relies on a register of unemployed. And there has been considerable research into the comparability of foreign and American measurements, research which has been much helped by pioneering Swedish experiments in applying our methods and concepts to your markets. The final upshot of this research has corrected the first impressions, according to which it appeared that our reports at least doubled the unemployment percentage which would be measured abroad: it now appears that 5 per cent here would correspond to something like 4 per cent if we could use the British or Swedish methods of reporting.

Such amounts of unemployment are perhaps not the same social scourge in our rather affluent society, both because these rates are much less than those typical of former depression times and because various methods are available to alleviate the worst of human misery they might otherwise occasion. Still the problem of unemployment is definitely a social evil that we American economists give a great deal of attention to. And it will be clear from my later remarks, that my use of the word growth does permit the economist to pay a great deal of attention to the problem of high employment. At the same time, the word growth permits him to concentrate in addition on quite other problems and processes, which understandably were pushed to the back of his attention during the tragic decade of the Great Depression.

When I first planned to give these Lectures, I had not expected to add the word "Stagnation" to the present section, thinking with most American economists that this word had lost relevance to the postwar years. However, events since 1957, or 1953, suggest that attention must be given to this possibility.

The Swing of Fashion in Economists

Let me first deal with stability, for this can be handled somewhat independently of the wider topic of growth. If you looked into the course catalogues of American universities a generation ago, you would find that stabilization was largely conceived to be the problem of ironing out *the* business cycle. Prior to 1930, it is fair to say that American economics was colonially dependent on neoclassical English economics. Aside from certain applied fields, like labor and market organization, perhaps the area in which we made our greatest contributions was that of business cycles. I have in mind the important 1913 work of Wesley C. Mitchell and quite a number of other inductive studies. Such writers on the continent as Tugan–Baronowsky, Spiethoff, Aftalion, Schumpeter, and Cassel were also going beyond the neoclassical neglect of these problems and preoccupation with price levels and money. (In this connection the early Dennis Robertson should probably be blanketed in as an "honorary continental".) I think if you look at the 1937 edition of Gottfried Haberler's classical study for the League of Nations, *Prosperity and Depression,* you will get an eclectic summary of what had been learned about the subject of business cycles.

All this went into eclipse in the middle of the 1930's. As a result of writings by Keynes and the Stockholm School, the emphasis shifted from fluctuations in the level of national income to models concerned with the determination of the level of income. People no longer believed in a nebulous "normal" around which oscillations took place: full employment was thought to be an upper-bound, rarely achieved except in war time, rather than as a mean norm; deflation was a greater concern than inflation just before the war. Merely to stabilize economic activity around an under-employment equilibrium was no longer considered to be the goal of policy. Because the college curriculum is slow to change, the courses labeled business cycles actually devoted their time to national income analysis, as did the courses labeled "Money and Banking" at the bigger universities. The cyclical models of Frisch, Tinbergen, Kalecki, Harrod, and Hansen fitted in well with the new income models; and attention shifted away from the preoccupation with price levels and neutral money of such neo-Wicksellians as Hayek and Mises and even away from the Persons–Mitchell statistics of lags and leads in timing.

Twilight of the Business Cycle?

This shift in attention away from traditional business cycles turned out, perhaps somewhat fortuitously, to have been prophetic. In most countries of the world, the old-fashioned business cycle has been less of a problem during the postwar period. Japan and Europe have experienced occasional balance-of-payments crises and they have had bouts of inflation. But they have not experienced depression; even mild recessions have been rare, having been replaced by more innocuous "pauses". To recreate a cyclical pattern for them one would have to revert to the practice of measuring deviations from a smooth trend, so that the years when production increases less than some average growth figure (perhaps 5 per cent in the 1950's) could be called recessions.

The postwar pattern of business cycles has been somewhat more conventional in the United States. For a century prior to 1940 there was a remarkably consistent international pattern of cycles shared by the chief industrial nations. If the U.S. had a recession, it was a good bet that the U.K., France, Germany, and (in the later period) Japan did too. At the end of the war I wondered why, in the face of government management of an economy's macroeconomics, there should continue to persist this common pattern. Even if the U.S. mismanaged its economy, why should Europe have to regard us as the sick old man of Europe who would inevitably spread his plague to them? I was therefore disappointed when America's 1949 sneeze, in the form of our first mild postwar recession, seemed to make Europe's international balance quite ill—culminating in the widespread devaluations of 1949. Fortunately, subsequent fact has subordinated itself to *a priori* reasoning. The old international pattern of business cycles has broken itself up, which is a happy development for all of us. Thus, when we were strong in early 1953, the U.K. economy was languishing. Just as we moved into the 1953–4 recession, our second postwar one, the U.K. picked up strength; so a mutually self-aggravating downward spiral, in which each nation saps the strength of the other, was completely avoided. In Thoreau's words we now act as if we march to a different drum beat and I say, *"Vive la difference!"*

So-called Inventory Cycles

I must now summarize the salient facts about postwar business cycles in America. They have been relatively mild. Not counting the 1945–6 period of reconversion from war to peace, we have had thus far four recessions in 16 years: 1948–9, 1953–4, 1957–8, and 1960–1. Despite my use of two years to designate each recession, they have been short, averaging less than a year apiece in length. The periods of expansion have been correspondingly long: until recently, there were grounds for the optimistic assertion that we can hope to enjoy about three years of advance, punctuated by a year of very modest pause and retreat.

The old "major" business cycle, like the 1920's and 1930's or like 1837, 1872, and 1893, cannot be observed in our postwar annals and may well be extinct. If so, they will not be mourned. These older cycles were associated historically by writers like Schumpeter and Hansen with great undulations in fixed capital investment. The so-called shorter minor cycles used, *faute de mieux,* to be called "inventory" cycles. And so it is common to hear experts say that America today is subject only to the inevitable inventory cycles. I think this may be misleading.[1]

---

[1] I must acknowledge help from an unpublished study by Professor Alice Bourneuf of Boston College and Sonia Mejia; see also Gary Fromm, "Inventories, Business Cycles, and Economic Stabilization", Joint Economic Committee, Congress of the U.S., Part IV, Supplementary Study Papers (1960), pp. 37–133, for evidence on this question. See also other writings in the Joint Economic Committee inventory investigation for affirmations rather than denials of the current importance of inventory behavior.

It is true that our fluctuations are short and mild. And it has been true that, if you take out all inventory changes from Gross National Product to get a new magnitude called *Final* Gross National Product, the resulting series shows practically no declines at all in the postwar period—thereby validating in a formal sense the assertion that our declines today depend on inventory decumulation. Finally, if the variation in inventory investment is divided by the total variation in all private investment, the resulting ratio in the postwar works out to be as large as or larger than in the period between the Wars. This much can be adduced in favor of the characterization of postwar American cycles as inventory cycles. But that is only part of the story.

Actually there seems to be something of a declining trend in the amount of inventories our economy needs. This is not entirely new, as witnessed by the widespread complaints during the Twenties against "hand-to-mouth buying"; but the decline is continuing, as modern computers enable businessmen to know quickly what their sales and inventories are, and as new managerial mathematics permit tighter control over stocks.[1] Helped by the secular rise in the importance of services as against tangible goods, the ratio of inventory (particularly private) to Gross National Product is less rather than more than it used to be. The ratio of inventory variation to total private investment variation is as high as it is not so much because the numerator has increased relative to other factors but because the denominator has decreased, in reflection of the fact that plant and equipment expenditure by business has been overshadowed in the postwar period by the greater importance of government expenditures.

It is notoriously difficult to single out one factor in an interdependent system as being the primary initiating factor of the undulations in aggregate output. But if forced to plunk for one, I should certainly not designate private investment as the most disturbing component in postwar America. Nor, despite the utterance of those who dislike the Keynesian analysis and who think its validity stands or falls on the constancy or inconstancy of the

---

[1] Excess capacity, whose recent persistence will be commented on later, may be thought of as a technical substitute for stocks since the ability to order an item quickly makes storing it less necessary. I have thought the postwar preoccupation with inventory control somewhat ironical: for, inasmuch as the probability of depression has greatly fallen and the likelihood of severe price decline in recession has diminished, there may have been operating here some kind of Parkinson's Law—just as the need to control inventories has become less pressing, business has learned how to control them.

propensity-to-consume function, can I find much fault with the consumer: he has not been a hero but he has been pretty much doing his duty in recent years, spending on consumption a fairly steady 93 per cent of his disposable income quarter-in and quarter-out, and saving the remaining 7 per cent.

Instability From the Government Sector

This brings us, by exhaustion, to government expenditure as the prime villain in the postwar scenario of instability. This is indeed paradoxical: for, according to the textbooks, a modern country is supposed to use government expenditure and fiscal policy as a conscious stabilizing device to moderate fluctuation. But instead of being a counter-cyclical stabilizer, federal government expenditure has acted like an exogenously disturbing factor. Aside from the obvious 1945–6 reconversion dip that resulted from a drop in war expenditure, most of our postwar recessions can be associated with cuts in government expenditure. As Fromm has argued in the paper cited earlier, even such variations as have occurred in inventory behavior may well be considerably derivative from fluctuations in government expenditure rather than initiating factors themselves.[1]

Is some Law, even grimmer than Parkinson's, at work here? Just when economists have taught governments how to *use* stabilizing fiscal policy, is it inevitable that governments will *misuse* it, thereby creating new instability? Or is it the case, as critics of government intervention based in Chicago have long proclaimed, that the forecasting ability of government economists is so irretrievably poor relative to the lags involved in the effects of fiscal decisions being felt by the economy, that the attempt to use fiscal policy for stabilization will inevitably do more harm than good.

My colleague, E. C. Brown, has shown that federal expenditure and tax policy have indeed not been optimally stabilizing factors in the postwar. But primarily this is not because their *effects* are opposite to what modern economic analysis predicts nor even because these mechanical effects are

---

[1] "... fluctuations in Government orders and expenditures coupled with their resulting impact on, and the independent variation of, private business investment appear to bear the principal responsibility for recent stability difficulties in the U.S. economy.

This is not to say that inventory declines have been unimportant, but only that it is unlikely that such reversals, alone, without the impetus and reinforcement of Government expenditure or investment cutbacks, would have produced cyclical reversals of the magnitude that have been experienced in the last decade." *Ibid.,* p. 37.

weaker than theoretical expectation or vitiated by dynamical lags. On the contrary Professor Brown's earlier researches on the facts of the 1930's rather confirms the empirical correctness of our modern theories and quite controverts the single biggest myth dogging American lay discussion, the myth that "We tried deficit spending in the 1930's and it just didn't work out".[1]

A careful review of public debates and private debates within the Truman, Eisenhower, and Kennedy Administrations will not bear out the thesis that postwar fiscal policy has been perverse because of failure to forecast correctly the pattern of developing events. Although far from perfect, forecasting has been pretty good. The only clear case that I can find where the wrong fiscal policy was advocated as a result of faulty diagnosis of the basic economic trend was in the few months after Truman's surprise 1948 electoral victory: though the economy had turned down before the end of that year, Truman and his Council of Economic Advisers remained obsessed by the fear of inflation and for a couple of months into 1949 continued to press for a tax rate increase—which they, fortunately, did not get.

State and local expenditure has shown one of the steadiest trends in the chartbook, appearing to be drawn with the use of a straight edge. With the exception of farm subsidies, whose outlays are not set by Congress so much as by the weather and the vicissitudes of market supply and demand conditions as they interact with parity price supports, the principal fluctuation in federal expenditures has been associated with war and defense: *viz.,* the end-of-war decline, the Korean-war rise and subsequent fall, the post-Sputnik rise in spending for missiles and space research. From the standpoint of cyclical stabilization, these have indeed been exogeneous factors of disturbance, being determined more by Stalin, Berlin, and Castro than by the leading and lagging indicators of business activity.

It is proper that the bulk of government expenditures should fluctuate when the social need for them fluctuates. To make them do otherwise would involve great social waste, since resources should be released for other uses when they are not needed for defense. This aspect of the post-

---

[1] E. Cary Brown, "Federal Fiscal Policy in the Postwar Period", in Ralph E. Freeman (ed.) *Postwar Economic Trends in The United States* (New York, 1960), and also his "Fiscal Policy in the Thirties: A Reappraisal", *American Economic Review,* Vol. 46, 1956.

war serves as a partial refutation of the view that America's cold-war expenditure is merely a transparent prop to support effete capitalism.

It is, however, an interesting fact that other fiscal programs have not been shaped to offset most of the instability originating from government. The dollars not needed for uniforms have not been fully reallocated to public works or welfare transfer expenditures. (Although I have expressed in recent years my belief that monetary policy can have considerable potency, it is significant that the Federal Reserve was not able to create anything like equivalent offsets to the massive savings in defense expenditure. Part, but probably only part, of the reason for this will be traced later to the bias of our central bank authorities toward avoiding price rises rather than unemployment rises.) The question arises: Why has discretionary tax policy not been more effective in offsetting the exogenous fluctuations in government expenditure? Certainly no one will question the wisdom of cutting down on Korean outlays after that shooting-war had come to an end, but why were there not changes on the tax side sufficient to compensate?

There were belated tax reductions in 1954, but their magnitude was not sufficient to offset the reduction in government expenditure and the shortfall of private investment.[1] Indeed one must go beyond the purely cyclical stabilization problems of the postwar to realize that tax rates have probably been too high ever since the end of the Korean war. This was not generally realized then. And if it had been, the Republican Party could not have stomached the implicit massive deficits. In any case tax reductions were then always debated in a cyclical context.

Early in the 1957 recession, many urged that there should be a cut in tax rates. President Eisenhower chose to disregard this advice, which had become almost a public clamor by Easter of 1958. Quite to the astonishment of many experts, that recession proceeded to hit bottom and turn up by April. Those who advocated the tax rate cut purely for short-term cyclical reasons had to admit that it would have been a rather bad thing

---

[1] It might be argued that the tax reductions just after the war were excessive in view of the need to fight a 1946–8 demand-pull inflation generated by the liquidity and backlogs of need inherited from the war itself. I would point out that it is asking a lot of tax policy to have it be applied so vigorously as to prevent any once-and-for-all increase in the price level after a great war and after rationing and direct controls have been holding down the stated quotations on prices so firmly that they no longer register the true scarcities of the situation. A brief once-and-for-all rise in prices might be the lesser of evils in such a case.

if Eisenhower had followed their advice in March. But those who were thinking in longer-run terms, being concerned with sustainable growth and with the possible setting in of a stagnant period characterized by cyclical fluctuations around an inadequate level of average demand and employment, believe that Eisenhower made the wrong decision. And they feel that the weakness of the short-lived expansion of 1958–60 vindicated their position.

It is cold-comfort to this group of economists—I am one of them and can speak with feeling—that the current Kennedy recovery has been such a weak one. For generally, if such a policy had been politically feasible, they would have favored a tax cut when Kennedy came to office in January 1961.

Potency of Automatic Fiscal Stabilizers

One aspect of fiscal policy has been operating just as economic theory had predicted. I refer to the automatic stabilization inherent in our tax system, particularly in the part of the system which relies on personal and corporate incomes. Modern economists have set Adam Smith upside down. You will recall that one of his requirements for a good tax was that its revenue collections be steady through good times and bad. We recognize today that this is a requirement for a very *bad* tax.

It is, therefore, an extra boon to the American economy that we gain in stability from the fact that we rely much more upon income taxes for our federal revenues than does any other nation in the world—including the semi-socialist nations. As incomes fall, tax receipts automatically decline. Because of our pay-as-you-go withholding system, the time lag for personal incomes is no longer important. Although we have lessened the corporate tax lag, this still remains a problem, albeit a minor problem because of the fortunate fact that corporate accounting is quite rational and decisions are made in terms of accruals rather than cash items.

This automatic tax flexibility is augmented by other built-in mechanisms: countercyclical fluctuations in unemployment compensation and other welfare expenditures, in farm support expenditures, and in retained corporate earnings after dividends have been rather steadily paid out.

These structural changes have served well to cushion the declines in people's disposable income associated with fluctuations in production and employment. By themselves, *automatic stabilizers can of course not reverse a movement but only attenuate it.* However, in the postwar years we have

3 – 633032 Wicksell Lectures

supplemented automaticity with various discretionary countercyclical measures: defense expenditures have been pushed forward in time, and civilian public expenditures have been deliberately increased during recession periods. The result has been something remarkable.

Since 1950 governmental action has been such as to prevent any decline in business activity from causing an actual drop in disposable income. With total family disposable income maintained, aggregate consumption is kept from falling. The *primary* contraction remains, but there is banished the old *secondary* contraction, in which a decline in consumption followed a decline in income and production and then caused further declines in those magnitudes in the too familiar pattern of a vicious circle. Mild recessions, therefore, do not snowball into serious ones or into depressions and chronic slumps.

The importance of this structural change cannot be exaggerated. It does not mean that a great depression is impossible—because nothing in economics can be ruled out as literally impossible. But the probability of a great depression, as reckoned by a prudent man or well-informed committee, must today be deemed very small indeed. This is one of the most important facts about modern capitalism in the mixed-enterprise economies of the twentieth century.

Government, The Ultimate Bulwark

Let ut make no mistake about what has caused this basic change. It comes from new governmental attitudes. Democratic governments today have the tools powerful enough to prevent depression collapse, and they are certain to use them. Were government to revert back to its former role, the prognosis for future fluctuations would be little different from that of earlier times. Technology still proceeds in fits and starts. Investor opinion is still capable of cumulative gyrations. Corrective flexibility in prices and wages is, for a variety of institutional reasons, even weaker in a modern economy than it was in the past.

Obviously the system can be improved still further. It is doubtful that much more is required in the direction of automatic mechanisms; they seem already powerful enough, and indeed may be almost too powerful. For do not forget that automatic mechanisms are two-edged swords. They cut for you in attenuating a decline. They cut against you in attenuating a recovery to full employment. It is precisely because we have to worry about a long-run problem, which is quite distinct from a cyclical one, that we would not want a heavier drag on expansion and growth to come from enhanced marginal taxation.

Apart from enhancing built-in automaticity, there is the real possibility of using an intermediate device to promote cyclical stability. To reduce the time lag required for Congress to meet, to deliberate and legislate a discretionary change in tax rates, many experts have advocated that there be granted to the President authority to change tax rates by Executive discretion within certain limits and subject to certain safeguards of legislative review. It is not remarkable that such an idea should occur to academic economists; actually some professors have gone even farther and recommended that tax rates should be changed automatically when certain index numbers of prices or unemployment set off certain agreed upon signals. But such proposals could not be expected to meet with ready legislative acceptance, and they have not as yet.[1]

The National Planning Association and the Committee for Economic Development have lifted out of the realm of academic speculation the proposals for executive authority to change tax rates. The conservative government in the United Kingdom received from Parliament the right to vary at its discretion the rate of purchase tax; and this power has been used recently. Although fiscal policy was not the prime concern of our private Commission on Money and Credit, one of its most newsworthy conclusions was the recommendation that the President be given the power to change tax rates by executive action. My Task Force *Report on the State of the American Economy*, prepared in January 1961 for President-

---

[1] The debate in 1961 over the difficult statistical question of how to adjust unemployment seasonally warned that there could be serious difficulties in finding an *objective index* of genuine changes in the unemployment situation. Several recent investigations into the inadequacy of quality adjustments and coverage of new commodities in the Consumers Price Index show that problems may arise in defining a proper index of price. I do not believe such problems are of major importance; after all, we have long had numerous sliding-scale wage contracts which are geared to the official price index and which perform satisfactorily even if that index is not perfect, so long as there is no question of arbitrariness or fraud in its compilation. Despite the lack of precision of real income measurements by states, the system legislated long ago, in which welfare grants to states are geared to measures of per capita real income, have performed tolerably well. My own primary lack of enthusiasm for automatic formulas, geared to economic indexes that register and set off gongs and whistles, comes from experience on how badly such systems may begin to behave as the years go by—in comparison, of course, with systems that require the exercise of human judgment. Men are fallible but no mechanism has the learning ability of the human brain, or perhaps I should say of a jury of human brains.

Elect Kennedy, made such a recommendation. President Kennedy in 1961 actually asked Congress for such power. Congress has given all such requests a cool reception, which is perhaps not too surprising in light of the thousand-year struggle of legislatures to achieve the power of the purse as a device to ensure democracy and control monarchs.

I am optimistic enough to think that, after the novelty of the proposal has worn off and there is time to weigh its merits, Congress will eventually give the President limited powers to change tax rates, subject to reversal by congressional resolution and to specific time limitations. But that day is not yet near. And, as Professor Brown has cogently pointed out, there is no evidence yet that Congress has failed to act promptly when it has been given strong leadership by the Executive and when Congress is not in disagreement with the President's appraisal of the desirability of a tax change. Pending the day of enlightenment and as a step to hasten that day, our first business is to urge upon Congress prompt action in its own discretionary deliberations.

Deficit Folklore Versus Economics

The real barrier to optimal fiscal policy is not procedural or administrative. It is ideological. If the American people, Congress, and the President all had a desire for the requisite pattern of expenditure and taxing—and the implied budget deficits (and surpluses!)—then without any structural reforms our present system could be more nearly optimally stabilizing. It is simply a matter of fact, though, that Americans attach great ideological importance to that particular arbitrary magnitude which is called the Administrative Budget. The American public simply cannot stomach budgetary deficits of the size sometimes needed for stability, high employment and growth. Or, what is really an indistinguishable variant, the American public cannot be persuaded or persuade itself that such sizeable deficits are truly needed and feasible.

Foreigners may find this surprising. Economists may find it shocking. They may point out that a year is an arbitrary unit and that since the Budget cannot be balanced in every day or every month, there is no particular merit in trying to balance it in the arbitrary astronomical cycle involved in one swing of the earth around the sun. Why not balance it over some other cycle, say the business cycle? Or over the nineteen year cycle of Easter? Or over a decade?

And why balance the so-called Administrative Budget? It differs from, and is inferior to, the Cash Budget, which nets out purely bookkeeping items that involve no flow of funds between government and the public. But why jettison one shibboleth only to take on another? The Cash Budget itself is inferior as a measure of the government's current impact on the economy to the Budget on National Income Account, which takes into consideration the accruals of corporate tax liability as they occur and become a crucial factor in corporate spending decisions. While the Administrative Budget is probably the least meaningful and useful of these three budget concepts, none of them takes into account public capital formation and the increase in assets that is taking place in the governmental sector. It has long been argued that America should adopt some form of a Capital Budget which will distinguish between current and capital items and will bring to attention the public assets that offset the public debt.

An informed economist knows that no single concept of the budget can do justice to the qualitative and quantitative aspects of fiscal policy. No single one can be set up in advance as the desirable goal to be "balanced" in any year, month, business cycle, or decade. Changing the focus of attention from one concept to another one may minimize the economic harm resulting from ideological attitudes. Or changing from focussing upon one concept to spreading attention over several may serve to blunt and confuse ideological preoccupations. In principle though, there is only one correct rule about budget balance—Smith's Law (not from Adam Smith but Professor Warren Smith of the University of Michigan). It goes as follows:

Smith's Law. There is only one rule about Budget balancing, and it is that the Budget should never be balanced.

Never? Well, hardly ever. Economic conditions will generally call for either a surplus or a deficit. Only in the transition as the budget is passing from the black to the red (or from the red to the black) should the budget be fleetingly in balance.

Scope and Efficiency of Government Activity

What about the need for "discipline" in restraining excessive public expenditures? Is not history the history of excesses by the greedy Prince? Will not the future reveal a tendency for democracies to vote higher public expenditures than people want or need—particularly if the curb of the balanced-budget concept is removed and new expenditures do not have to be matched by newly-voted taxes?

Brevity requires me to sound dogmatic. There are indeed three problems of government that have to be faced. None of the three, save by accident, are properly solved by any variant of budget balancing.

1. *Efficiency of public expenditure.* For any total of dollars, or rather of economic resources, put at the disposal of government, it is desirable that we should receive a maximum of useful public services. What is the same thing, each package of useful public services should be produced so as to use a minimum of scarce national resources. This is what efficiency means. A demand for efficiency should not be thought to imply a reduced scope of government. We can have limited government scope with low efficiency or with high; we can have broad government scope with high efficiency or with low. An increased efficiency *may* make it rational to widen rather than narrow the scope of government; or a reduced efficiency might make it optimal to devote more rather than less resources to the public sector. Efficiency is hard to define, even harder to measure, and still harder to improve. It is easy to talk idly about efficiency.

2. *Proper scope of government.* This necessarily involves a group, democratic decision. Since unanimity is unusual, it also involves an overriding of some persons' preferences. But note that narrowing government's scope involves the same lack of unanimity and overriding of some person's preferences. The mechanics of all voting systems[1] known to man or beast are in principle less than perfect: the outcome can be biassed toward too little government or too much. To say that resources should be divided twixt the public and private sector until their marginal social utilities (net) are equal is not to say very much, but it is to say almost all that can be usefully said. The evaluations of social utilities will be subjective and involve group value judgments: if foreign affairs are peaceful, if thieves are scarce, if people care not much for public fireworks, if there are no great indivisible costs of irrigation or transport, if population is sparse and with

---

[1] Wicksell and Lindahl, and in recent times R. A. Musgrave and I, have tried to develop a pure theory of public expenditure. In my view this is interesting, but valuable as much for the problems it calls attention to as for its constructive solutions. K. Arrow has done fundamental work in mathematical politics, which illuminates the basic problems of democracy. See R. A. Musgrave, *The Theory of Public Finance* (N.Y., 1959); K. J. Arrow, *Social Choice and Individual Values* (N.Y., 1951).

much elbow room—then the group decision may be for very narrow scope of public services. But if not, then not.

No simple balancing of a budget has yet been devised that will correctly police the community's decisions on these fundamentals. The analogy with private enterprise—that chewing gum be not produced if a tax in the form of its price to the consumer be not forthcoming large enough to pay for the resources used in its production—is faulty at root. Indeed the only valid reason for having a public sector is that it performs needed functions which cannot be optimally priced by *laissez-faire*. The public business is that which is no man's proper business.

3. *Avoiding inflation or deflation.* My nine-year-old boy asked me recently "Why should there be taxes? Why not just print money to pay for the goods government needs?" He is a dangerous character. The next thing I know he will be questioning capital punishment, the law of gravity, and my own infallibility. But in nine more years he will have learned the facts of life and come to regard his question as a foolish one. Imagine questioning the inevitability of taxes, or death!

It will take another nine years of advanced study in economics before he comes to appreciate the wisdom of his question and the proper answer to it. As given by A. P. Lerner, that answer would go roughly as follows.

Never tax just for the sake of taxing. Tax primarily to reduce the pressure of excessive dollar demand for society's current limited resources, which are limited because of their scarcity in relationship to government and private bids for them. If the sum of private and public dollar demand is sufficiently great, you should legislate taxes great enough to produce a large and persistent budget surplus. If the total of dollar demand is chronically low relative to the value of total resources available at current prices, economic prudence requires you to legislate tax rates low enough to result in a budget deficit. Such a deficit, which results from the indicated pattern of public expenditure and taxes, can be counted on to produce expansionary stimulus needed to offset the deflationary pressures in the economic system. This government stimulus is not more expansionary nor more inflationary than would be an equivalent billions of dollar increase in spontaneous family expenditure on consumption or spontaneous pickup in investment spending.

Budget balance is itself irrelevant. Such a point of balance could be much too inflationary at certain times and deflationary at others. The effects of a budget balance with public expenditure and taxes both high cannot be expected to be the same as an equivalent balance achieved when low taxes match low expenditures. While a nine-year-old might be forgiven for not realizing it, we should know that financing substantial public expenditures by the printing of new money would probably be swelling the total value of dollar spending beyond the likely surplus of private saving over private investment. So we tax just enough to avoid such an inflationary gap, financing the algebraic difference by nothing so crude as the printing of Treasury currency, instead relying upon optimal debt management and central banking credit creation.[1]

I had a teacher who was seven times nine years old but the doctrine of *de mortuis nihil nisi bonum* forbids me to reveal his name, which is just as well since he was always something of an unknown soldier. He used to say pithily: "A dollar of expenditure is a dollar of taxes." A glance at public accounts will show there to be billions of exceptions to that theorem. His doctrine is wrong today; and it was obsolete before it had been enunciated, which is something of a *tour de force*. The history of capitalism, and perhaps of the Darwinian ascent of man, is a history of deficits outweighing surpluses. This is not a matter of mankind living beyond its means but rather up to them.

The Recent American Economy

While these remarks of mine have been brief and perfectionistic, they do have direct relevance to the current American scene. Since 1957, or perhaps even since the end of the Korean War in 1953, private investment spending has not been strong. Private consumption spending by families has fluctuated gently around an average level of about 93 per cent of total disposable income. Government expenditure has been the most dynamic upward force in recent years. As noted above, state and local expenditures have expanded steadily, primarily because our population explosion has created the need for the building of schools and roads. Cold-war rivalry in the area of missiles and space has resulted in a steady increase in defense expenditures. Welfare transfers and agricultural subsidies have continued to grow, as have the interest charges on the war-created public debt; but civilian expenditures of the federal government, contrary to the impression gleaned from reading our newspapers, have not been increasing in proportion to the growth of GNP.

Why has private investment seemingly been so undynamic? Is this due

---

[1] Economists realize that a cumulative deficit or surplus in Budget over a generation can effect the resources available to future generations and their thriftiness. Only under special factual and ethical assumptions is it correct to say that a balanced budget over a generation achieves the "proper" distribution of consumption between generations, that pattern which truly reflects voluntary individualistic desires to save. My colleague Franco Modigliani has treated these issues in the *Economic Journal* (December, 1961).

to a lack of investor "confidence", induced by distrust of the expanding role of government? Or would a more vigorous expansion of government expenditure and lowering of taxes stimulate the growth of real output, resulting in a greater effective demand for private capital formation through the action of the familiar principle of acceleration? Had there been less preoccupation with price stability in the last half decade, would expansionary monetary and fiscal policies have lowered the amount of excess capacity and unemployment, thereby improving corporate profits, the internal funds available to business for investment purposes, and the profitability of new investment?

These are hard questions. Men of affairs disagree with economic experts in providing answers; and indeed American economists are in some disagreement among themselves on diagnosis and prescription. I presume, however, that you invited me to Stockholm to give my opinions in the matter and some indication of the evidence on which they are based. I ought also to report that in this regard my opinions are probably rather typical of the majority of American economists in universities and the government civil service. They would be regarded with some suspicion, I should guess, by a random bank president or trade-union official, but each would agree less with the other than perhaps with me and their own staff economists would differ less with me than they would.

The Role of Confidence

I think it is true that American businessmen are ideologically alienated from the Federal government. After a honeymoon period, President Kennedy began to appear to them "unfriendly toward business". Hatred of him reached a crescendo following his April 1962 intervention with the price raising by the large steel companies. Dislike of him has never equalled that which the business community felt toward Franklin Roosevelt; and probably in various downtown clubs Kennedy would be deemed preferable to Harry Truman. It is in any case harder for a camel to pass through the eye of a needle than for a Democratic President to win popularity contests among business leaders. Even President Eisenhower, a moderate Republican, could not in eight years create a political environment to the taste of entrepreneurs.

Yet we must, I think, distinguish between the ideological statements that businessmen make at night in public conferences and the way they make money decisions during the day down at the office. In 1936–7, when hatred of Franklin Roosevelt was at its worst, the American economy enjoyed a plant and equipment boom. The years 1933–5, a time of Wallstreet disillusionment with the New Deal, involved the most rapid advance in physical production America has ever experienced in peacetime. To be sure we started from a woeful depression base and never recovered during the 1930's to a full employment level; but this does not blunt my point that American entrepreneurs will invest their funds whenever they can envision a good marginal rate of profit, regardless of their alienation from politics.

Herbert Hoover's popularity with business did not prevent the post-1929 slump. Eisenhower's conservative cabinet did not prevent fixed investment from languishing after 1957. This year's weakness in private investment was already clearly discernible before Kennedy's steel intervention and the Spring stock market crash.

Low Investment, Profit Experience, and Credit Policy

With our growth rate having been so slow in recent years and our excess capacity so large, we need not seek for explanations in terms of "confidence" for the weakness of investment performance. I believe that the spurt of capital formation in the first postwar decade could be expected by normal competitive processes to bring down the rate of profit on new investments. It is not so much the predatory wage demands of labor unions as the competition of each capitalist and each unit of capital, one against the other both here and abroad, which has eroded the percentage rate of profit on invested capital. To have superimposed upon this diminishing-returns phenomenon a slack rate of growth in output was merely to have compounded the difficulty.

In all solemnity I must state the belief that our Federal Reserve authorities have erred these last half dozen years in the direction of overtightness of credit. In the beginning they did so because they considered the evil of creeping inflation—whether of a cost-push or demand-pull type—a greater national danger than the evil of unemployment and stagnation. Later when wholesale and many other prices ceased rising, our monetary authorities became impressed with the growing deficit in the American balance of payments. Eisenhower's two Secretaries of the Treasury for the most part encouraged this bias toward over-tight money.

You must realize that this is my personal interpretation. William Mc-Chesney Martin Jr., the experienced chairman of the Board of Governors of the Federal Reserve System, has asserted his belief repeatedly that there is no true conflict between price level stability and sustainable prosperity. He and his colleagues seem to have acted in the belief that there is no demonstrable shift in the American economy toward the mechanism of cost-push inflation; but that if such a mechanism should prove to be present in the American economy, this would call for even tighter rather than looser money.

Since President Kennedy came into office, the Federal Reserve has abandoned its self-imposed 1953–60 doctrine of conducting its open-market operations in short-term bills only, save in special and extraordinary circumstances. The Fed and the Treasury have, mildly, been pursuing "Operation Twist", in which short-term bill rates have been kept high in order to keep cool money from leaving our shores for financial centers abroad, while at the same time the demand for long-term securities has been kept high relative to their supply, in order to keep credit available at low cost to construction and other investment activities.

Treasury and Federal Reserve officials have proclaimed before Congress and the world that our international balance-of-payments problem has not been permitted to be a drag on desirable domestic monetary and fiscal programs. I, and most academic economists, cannot agree. To us it is like the case of a hunchback confidently asserting that there is no hump on his back. Indeed to us it is a self-incriminating statement. If it were true that the international-payments situation were not a real constraint, then they should be reproaching themselves for not having pursued, in this year of high unemployment and decelerating growth, a more militant policy of credit easing to induce that deepening of capital which every orthodox economist knows is an important stimulus to growth. But I must not be harsh. Perhaps they mean to say merely that they have been handling the balance-of-payments constraint as successfully as it can be handled. And certainly our monetary managers have been acting better than they talk, like stern school teachers who surreptitiously perform the good deeds they are ashamed to own up to; and they are much better in their intentions, actions, and analysis than many members of the private banking fraternity, who feel that if there were not a genuine international problem sufficient to impose "discipline" on money and fiscal managers, a fictitious crisis would have to be invented to perform the same function.

I believe our monetary authorities have been behaving better than experience with central banks and debt managers has led cynics to expect. They have even surpassed their own expectations! But, when history judges all the risks involved, one guesses some responsibility for our sluggish economy will be attributed to Federal Reserve policy.

America's Gold Drain

I do not want to belittle the genuineness of America's balance-of-payments problem. During the 1950's there was an insidious changeover from embarrassing surpluses in our export position to embarrassing deficits. The Suez crisis of 1957 temporarily masked this trend, but in the years 1958–1960 it became obvious to all. America continued to have a surplus of exports over imports in our current private account. This current surplus, however, was no longer great enough to offset our military and aid programs abroad as well as the upsurge in American long-term investment abroad. The discrepancy between these items constitutes what President Kennedy defined as our "basic international deficit". This basic deficit could be financed by export of our gold and by foreigners accepting our short-term dollar obligations. (Foreign citizens or central banks could hold deposits in American banks, or our short-term government and private securities.) After 1959 our basic balance began slowly to improve; but just at that time, because of psychological concern over the future of the dollar, of relatively higher interest rates abroad and reconstituted money markets there, and of a desire by many governments to restore historic ratios of gold reserves—for all these reasons there took place massive short-term capital movements out of the United States and hence a substantial gold drain.

Fifteen years ago the United States held 70 per cent of total world gold, a disproportionately large share. Since then we have exported about ten billion dollars worth of gold and are now left with something more than fifteen billion dollars worth of monetary gold, only 40 per cent of the world total. The rest of the world has enjoyed this drain of gold from America. It has helped to replenish international liquidity abroad.

Most American economists think that by and large such a relocation of gold reserves is a good thing—for the world as a whole and even in terms of our own long-run interests. If it were merely a matter of now being at a new equilibrium plateau, all would be well. But the issue is a more difficult one. The end is not really yet in sight for the American gold drain. Because of the economically obsolete 25 per cent gold cover requirement for our central bank, so that its holding of gold certificates by law must not fall below 25 per cent of its note and deposit liabilities, about three-quarters of our current gold stock is technically not available for export. Many bankers, economists, and government officials have expressed the view that this reserve requirement should be abandoned by Congress, or at least lowered substantially. Because gold has always held an irrational fascination for laymen and would-be economists, such legislation would probably face vocal opposition and be delayed in passing. The only rational argument for retention of the gold requirement is that it provides "discipline" in a democracy. Brevity requires me to say that it is of limited efficacy in doing so, that other methods for providing discipline can be had in a democracy that wants discipline, and that the Commission on Money Credit was right in finding the net advantage to be greater on the side of abolishing the gold cover.

I think the issue is primarily legalistic, being more psychological than real. Legal precedents suggest that when the chips are down, with or without congressional action, all of our gold supply can be made available for international purposes if that is the wish of the authorities then in power.

Possible Causes and Cures of The International Deficit

It would bore you if I were to review all the reasons that have been given for America's balance-of-payments deficit. So I desist. I do this with a better conscience because it is simply not true that, in order to make the best prescription for improving a situation, you must first have diagnosed its cause. A fever may have been caused by exposure to streptococcus but be curable by rest; another ailment may result from overwork but be curable by an antibiotic. If it were true that our international deficit was the result of excessive government spending on aid and defense, it might still be curable by devaluation rather than by cutting down on such spending; or be curable by removal of trade restrictions abroad; or by combining an austere monetary policy with a loose fiscal policy.

The mere arithmetic of the problem cannot get you very far. It is very well to say that a cut of a dollar of government aid spending would help our international deficit; but it is well to remember that our private ex-

4 – 633032 Wicksell Lectures

ports might not be what they are if it were not for such aid financing. The trade balance is an organic whole: when you act to change one part of it, you cannot safely make the assumption that other things will remain constant; in double entry bookkeeping not everything can remain constant, and it is a task of most difficult judgment to guess what is the probable pattern of incidence upon all the items in the balance of payments of any one particular policy measure.

Let me be dogmatically brief. The United States *has* not had a greater degree of inflation of wages and general prices in the last few years than most other countries. Yet it is true that the costs in some of our machinery exports have risen much compared to our domestic price levels and compared to money costs in many rival countries. And whether or not our costs have gone up at all, so long as the demands for our exports are fairly elastic, a cut in our costs—through increases in productivity, declines in the trend of money wages, reduction in profit margin, or whatever—might help improve our balance of payments and our unemployment situation.

A Fundamental Hypothesis Concerning Foreign Productivity

For some years it has been my hypothesis that the productivity miracles in Japan, Western Germany, and Europe generally have been among the most important phenomena in connection with the swing away from dollar shortage. This has permitted money wages to rise abroad much faster than our own. It has permitted real wages to rise much faster than our own, even if not so fast as the rise in money wages there. It has permitted relatively lower foreign prices and costs—and here I have in mind not merely stated prices but also the fact that availability of quality goods has improved because delivery lags have been reduced and credit terms have become more liberal. American management has found that it can use with advantage foreign labor and plants to supply foreign markets; it can use with advantage those plants to provide third markets with goods; and, were it not for public relations and union problems, American firms have increasingly discovered that they could supply the domestic market with goods produced abroad.

If two countries start out in trade equilibrium and one has its production functions improved more than the other, an economist expects from the inherent lags in economic adjustments that the less progressive economy will encounter transitional balance-of-payments deficits. Were all this a once-and-for-all thing, we would expect a gradual restoration of equilibrium as price and wage levels became adjusted to the new *status quo*. However, if this is a repeated process in which one country continues to improve its productivity faster than the other, one would expect the disequilibrium to be a more chronic one—even though, given enough time and predictability of the trend, there might ultimately come an approach to dynamic equilibrium.

Once equilibrium has reasserted itself, the technological trends will not show up in the form of payments deficits. But they may still have substantive effects upon the real incomes of each country. Naturally, unless the regions with rapid productivity growth are so large as to face a quite inelastic and limited demand for their exports, we expect *their* well-being to improve rapidly. And this is certainly what has been happening in Japan, Germany, France, Italy, the Netherlands, and other countries enjoying the postwar miracle.

What about the countries enjoying less rapid, or even no, productivity improvements? How their prosperity is affected by technical innovations abroad, after payments equilibrium has been restored, must depend upon what those improvements do to the terms of trade of the countries involved. Were all costs abroad—for domestic goods, export goods, and all—to change in exactly the same proportion, the simplest theories of comparative advantage tell us that our welfare ought *not to be affected at all,* the principal effect being an increase in real incomes there.[1]

However, suppose the improvements abroad come largely in the production of modern goods which the United States has in the past been exporting and producing for her domestic uses. Then, even aside from any transient burden of unemployment and payments deficit, *the country with the less-dynamic technology, can expect to be hurt rather than helped by the technological spurt abroad.*

I suspect, but cannot prove, that something like this has been happening in the last decade. Since America is so affluent, we can afford and applaud the technical revolutions going on abroad even if they narrow the gap of superiority we enjoy, and even if they somewhat slow up the rate of growth

---

[1] As Mill and Ohlin have taught, we must study the effects of demand patterns on these cost situations. If the goods of the sprinting countries are of the type that people everywhere are as anxious to have when poor as when rich, no modifications in the above simple argument is called for.

of our own real incomes. (The U.K., Sweden, and other countries not showing in this miracle sprint might be affected adversely just like America.)

Also, the process I have described could affect the distribution of income within the United States. American corporations have in the past been closely associated with scientific management. To the degree that this is true, *American labor has enjoyed a kind of a monopoly access to such scientific methods and part of our high wages has been the economic rent to such access.* But suppose that now our corporations learn how to utilize their capital and methods in cooperation with *foreign* labor. Labor abroad finds its real wages greatly enhanced. As United States corporations receive high profits or royalties from such arrangements, part of the benefit may be said to accrue to the U.S. national income in the form of repatriated or repatriable earnings and royalties. To this degree, U.S. real income *taken as a whole* need not suffer and might even be enhanced.

But look at the matter from the standpoint of domestic American labor. To the degree that the foreign technical opportunities raise the general profit rates which American capital can command, *there is an actual lowering of American real wages over what they could otherwise be!* Note that this is quite independent of the export of jobs abroad as transitional unemployment is made to grow here. Even if we restored full employment by various means, such as devaluation or fiscal policy or flexible wage rate cuts, the real wage that would clear the market would be a lower one.

Many will regard this as a slightly gloomy finding. I fear they are right, but cannot as a scientist be expected to stick my head in the sand and refuse to describe and interpret a phenomenon that truly exists and which will not disappear merely by ignoring it and indulging in wishful thinking. Of course, an experienced economist will realise on reflection that one cannot counter this effect detrimental to real wages by repeating the popular saying: "Experience shows that when our neighbors' living standards increase, they become better customers for our exports since trade between developed countries is well-known to be greater in volume than between a developed and an underdeveloped country."

A full employment economy is benefited only by being able to sell its exports *at an improved terms of trade* and not merely by being able to sell more goods abroad. The total *volume* of trade does not measure the *consumer satisfaction* (or surplus) gained from trade. It is quite possible that trading with a banana republic at *half* the volume as trading with a country like ourself might be bringing us more material benefit—and be bringing them more too!

Throughout this lecture I have followed the principle that I would rather be right than original. Perhaps in this section I have departed from that principle. I have stressed the possibility that the productivity miracle abroad, in addition to being an important cause of our gold problem, may also have real effects on our equilibrium income levels of a slightly harmful type and may have even stronger harmful effects upon the real wages imputed to American labor. I have stressed this possibility not so much because the effect can be presumed to be large as that this type of analysis seems never or rarely to have been presented in our literature. People like to be cheerful and stress the harmony of interests among classes and nations; they tend to overlook the genuine conflicts of interest that can occur. In addition the analysis I have given is by its nature rather intricate (which is not a synonym for unreliable and unimportant) and comparative advantage considerations themselves suggest that it is more likely to come from an academic economist than from a man of affairs or journalist.

Is the American Dollar Overvalued?

I must now return to the all-important problem of transitional states. I am inclined to agree with the international experts who discern a gradual trend of improvement in what was defined earlier as our basic international balance, but I am perhaps less optimistic than they in appraising the quantitative strength of this trend and the distance left to go before equilibrium is approached. It is true that Detroit auto manufacturers have risen to the Toynbeean challenge of compact cars imported from Europe. It is also true that the lash of competition has caused some reduction of waste in American manufacturing. The fact that our annual money wage increases have been dropping from the 5 per cent rates of a few years ago to rates only half as large, may have at first seemed reassuring; yet this change must surely be associated with the high levels of unemployment we have been tolerating in recent years, and any over-valued currency can disguise its condition if unemployment is made to be high enough.

The most favorable factor working toward solution of our basic deficit has, I think, to be found in conditions abroad rather than at home. I refer to the wage inflation that has at long last burst out in Western Germany and other miracle nations. With productivity reverting there to annual increases of no more than 5 per cent, a continued rise of money wage rates at 10 per cent per annum must eventually lessen the competitive advantage of the surplus countries in comparison to America. Perhaps profits have been so high that they can for some time be squeezed, but eventually increases in cost of such magnitude must begin to show itself in export pricing.

Even though that half of the classical Hume equilibrating mechanism—whereby America, the deficit country, should have its cost and prices come down as a result of the gold drain—does not work well in modern times, the other half—whereby costs and prices are supposed to rise in the surplus countries abroad—does seem to work out slowly in the long run.

This I find to be the most optimistic element in the current situation. For I discount domestic policy acts such as bringing army dependents home, purchasing army supplies here so long as their price does not exceed foreign prices by more than 20 per cent, and tying foreign aid grants. All these measures are necessary, and in the present context even desirable. It is better to give tied aid than none at all. But all such measures primarily represent an adaptation to an exchange stringency rather than a sign that there is no such stringency. International equilibrium should be defined in terms of people and governments being free to do what it is that their tastes and values make them want to do.

When I speak of a possible overvaluation of the dollar, I do not have in mind the question of whether the dollar ought to be devalued now or in the more distant future. American official policy, publicly and privately, is firmly against any such a policy decision. And even if it were not, the feasibility of such a move—unilaterally or multilaterally—would involve many complications not worth mentioning here.

In the present context overvaluation or undervaluation involves the following considerations: (i) If there were a free market with floating exchange rates, would the price of the dollar, relative to the yen and EEC countries but *not* relative to the U.K. and Canada, have fallen or risen in the last few years? (ii) would a deterioration of the quoted dollar rate be avoidable, without hampering a militantly expansionary monetary and debt policy aimed at restoring full employment and more rapid growth, without putting constraints on the size of a prudent budget deficit, without requiring cheese-paring economies in offshore military purchases and tying of various aids, and without involving explicit or implicit discouragements or penalties for private investments abroad?

In terms of such a definition, I suspect that most economists would regard the American dollar as at least temporarily overvalued. Indeed, this is reduced almost to the tautology that any payments deficit involves at least temporary overvaluation. But a little more than that is involved, since most economists would find themselves giving a negative answer to the following hypothetical question. "Suppose at some past date the dollar had somehow been given a lower parity relative to other currencies and this had involved no transitional difficulties? Would you truly be sorry rather than glad that such an event had taken place?"[1]

I mention this whole issue to introduce some of the difficulties involved in a full-employment and growth policy for America. I dot not mention it for the explicit or covert purpose of recommending a change in the dollar price of gold or dollar parities of other currencies. Nor am I entering into the problem of whether international liquidity under the present gold standard and gold exchange standards is now a problem or is likely to become so much of a problem in the future as to require recourse to some kind of Triffin, Bernstein, Jacobsson, or Posthuma plan. Let me say here, tangentially and merely for the record, that I think it is superficial to accept the following argument.

Even if it should prove at some future date that the dollar is overvalued relative to other key currencies, it is fruitless to contemplate any devaluation. For, if the U.S. raised the price of gold other countries would be *sure* to follow suit [and in the same degree].

Of course it is unthinkable that we could raise the price of gold from $35 an ounce to $55 and have the mark, guilder, and franc stay at their old gold parities. But never forget that one country's international deficit problem is somebody else's international surplus problem. We are not yet back in the 1930's, when each country wanted to export its unemployment by depreciating its own currency relative to its neighbors'. When the U.S. rationally needs a depreciation of the dollar to improve its deflationary gap and unemployment, that same act should rationally be pleasing to a country with over-full employment and an inflationary gap. An era of rationally managed money and public finance should, for the first time in the history of capitalism, become immune to mercantilistic policies. (Let me add, quietly, that if it ever came to a competitive race for successive rounds of currency depreciation, technically the deficit country can win out in the end.)

---

[1] Of course there are still some economists—usually older than I—who go on regretting that Roosevelt raised the price of gold by more than 50 per cent back in 1933!

Direct Growth Policies

I return now to the problem of promoting U.S. growth. Before 1961 it was a matter for partisan debate as to whether our growth rate was slowing up in the second half of the postwar period, and whether this was necessarily a bad thing. Now public opinion seems generally to believe that our growth rate has been languishing, and that something ought to be done about it.

There is a fair amount of agreement that government has certain special responsibilities and opportunities in this regard.

Research. Resources devoted to research and development should increase the productivity and growth potential of our land, equipment, and labor force. Since research and development expenditures by a firm lead to benefits for other firms, the marginal social utility of such activities can be presumed to exceed their private marginal utility (expressed in pecuniary terms). Hence, economists have long recognized that such "external economies" create a *prima facie* case for public subsidy. American research and development expenditures have been very high in recent years, and a large fraction of the total is financed directly or indirectly by governments. (Much of this is traceable indirectly to our defense budgets, and one hopes that a reduction in international tension would not lessen federal support for basic research.)

Education. Increasing the skills of the working population will raise our potential GNP and increase its rate of growth. American economists, notably Theodore W. Schultz of the University of Chicago and coworkers, have rediscovered the importance of investing in people by education, training and retraining. Most economists agree that voluntarism is unlikely to lead to sufficient human capital and that government has a crucial role to play here. All this is to the good—especially from the viewpoint of one in the educating business.[1]

---

[1] I must, however, quietly mention that the present fad tends to exaggerate the percentage yield on education as such: as my colleague R. Eckaus's researches suggest, much of education has to be defended on its consumption-utility worth not on its contribution to real product. A man with higher IQ and temperamental effectiveness is likely to be more educated than one with lower; but it is misleading to attribute all the difference to the difference in education and there is, as yet, little scientific evidence suggesting how large should be the fraction of imputation—and the yield on social aid to education depends crucially on this fraction that must be guessed. (Example: a 21-year-old Irishman who has less than 8 years of formal education could, if he displayed ability to pass intelligence and dexterity tests a year or two

Health. Almost any good cause can be sold as making some contribution to growth. To the degree that absenteeism, incapacity to work, strength and vigor are improved, there should be some increase in physical productivity. To the degree that vigorous life is lengthened and the final period of incapacity is shortened, per capita production is improved. The vital role of government in this general area, however, transcends mere growth considerations and should be defended primarily on other grounds. Indeed preoccupation with growth rationalizations could pervert and distort the pattern of activity in this field.

Governmental planning. To the degree that the coordination of economic activities achieved by private-enterprise markets can be improved upon by governmental planning activities, growth could be increased. Underdeveloped countries like India, to say nothing of the Soviet Bloc countries, place considerable reliance on public planning. More recently, much has been heard about the efficacy of French "indicative planning"; and particularly in the U.K., there is a great deal of interest in similar activities. Even under the New Frontier, I detect little such activity in Washington. The matter is a controversial one in the American political scene.

My own guess would be that, since we do so very little of this, pragmatic experimentation on a small scale would be informative. With due regard to experience as to efficacy, and taking into account any conflicts with personal and business freedoms, future decisions to retreat or advance could then be made. Thus far, this has not been an important area and it is unlikely to become one in the next few years.

Growth of Potential and Actual Product

All the above programs can be described as attempts to increase the rate of growth of our potential full-employment GNP or our potential real income per capita.[1] We are not now living up to our potential. So America

after immigration to the States be capable of holding down a high-paying job in most of our manufacturing industries. Six more years of schooling might help but little, or even spoil him for some work. That is my opinion but you would never guess it to be right after perusing many current writings on this subject.)

[1] Since a policy to speed up or slow down population growth is not a matter for American debate, and since I am not concerned here with the absolute levels of GNP that might be relevant in appraising our military strength in comparison with some rival nation, for the most part when I use the word "potential", one can intepret this as "per capita potential". However, with population growth predictable for the next decade, per capita and absolute magnitudes will be affected in the same direction by most policy measures.

could achieve very rapid short-term growth just by getting unemployment down from $5\,{}^1/_2$ per cent to 4 per cent, and excess capacity down from say 20 per cent to 10 per cent.

Thus, in the first year of the Kennedy Administration, our real GNP rose by 8 per cent. This was better than the record in the same period of Japan, Western Germany, or the Soviet Union. But of course such an annual rate could not be maintained for very long. If it were to have been maintained for another couple of years, we should have exceeded in restoring full employment and wiping out completely the *gap* between our potential and actual real GNP.[1]

Once we cease to narrow this fundamental gap between potential and actual GNP, the economy cannot grow any faster than the growth in its potential. Iudeed, in the very long run any economy's average rate of growth cannot be greater than its potential's rate; inasmuch as modern economies never have gaps exceeding some fraction of income, in the longest run the oscillations of the economy cannot make its average actual growth performance deviate significantly from its potential's annual growth rate (albeit cyclical oscillations could depress the potential's long-term growth rate, or in some models even increase it).

Narrowing the Gap

Popular discussion, particularly in liberal circles, has quite naturally put the greatest emphasis on achieving rapid (near-term) growth through restoring full employment.[2] To move nearer to full employment, an increase in consumption, investment, or government spendings is needed.

Expanding government expenditure. So liberals often propose that more be spent on urban renewal, conservation, health and other programs, both because such programs are desired for their own sake and also because (like digging ditches and filling them up again) such government expenditure programs result in increased money and real income, with multiplier effects on consumption and perhaps investment spending, and regardless of whether such programs have any direct bearing on our growth potential.

Expanding consumption. The same people urge that tax rates be reduced

---

[1] As of May 1961 it is already obvious that the second year of the Kennedy recovery is slowing down, and the gap is ceasing to be cut into. [Later in 1961, this impression was validated and strengthened.]

[2] To go from 7 per cent unemployment to $3\,{}^1/_2$ per cent sounds almost like a doubling of something, which seems more impressive than having something go from 93 per cent to $96\,{}^1/_2$ per cent. Yet, where product is concerned, the latter way of looking at the matter is perhaps the more relevant one.

so that consumption spending, particularly of the lower-income ready-spenders, be increased. Such consumption itself adds to the increase in GNP, and in addition can be expected to have secondary effects of a multiplier kind on further consumption and perhaps investment. Ever since the beginning of the Kennedy Administration, and indeed back to 1957, liberal economists like Leon Keyserling have urged tax reductions. Had that been more politically feasible, I daresay that members of my own Task Force would have reported to President Kennedy a similar recommendation before his inaugural.

Expanding investment. Fiscal policy could also be directed toward direct stimulus to investment. President Kennedy early proposed an *investment tax credit* to induce greater net capital formation. This concession to business met a cold reception from businessmen for reasons that lie outside economics: after a long legislative struggle, such an investment tax credit was passed, involving reduced rates and no longer involving extra credit for firms which expanded their investments from earlier levels.

More *rapid depreciation,* which had made some headway in Eisenhower's 1954 Tax Act, was scheduled to go into effect in 1962. Such measures, to the degree that they permit depreciation more rapid than actual decline in economic value as a result of obsolescence and physical wear, represent an interest-free loan to business with the favourable feature that the loan has to be paid back only if business subsequently has taxable income. Like the investment credit, it should provide some extra funds available for investment and increase the incentive to use other funds for investment. Since I am adding quiet remarks, I ought to say softly that the competitive race between the various developed countries of the world to give the fastest depreciation rates has gone beyond the point where true economic depreciation is recognized by the tax authorities; it is now at the point where loopholes have been deliberately created in tax systems alleging to tax (money and not real) earnings, with the design of giving a bribe and bait to expand investment and employment. It is like the case of our municipalities, which vie with each other to give greater tax concessions in order to lure firms away from other areas.

In America we have a double layer of income taxation. Ford Motors is taxed in its earning at a marginal rate of 52 per cent, regardless of how much it pays out in dividends; then whatever is paid out in dividends is taxed to the person who receives the dividends at essentially his regular marginal rate of personal income tax. A *reduction in the corporate tax rate* to below 52 per cent might be expected to have some favorable effect upon capital formation. Thus, if managers insists on a 10 per cent yield after taxes before they will build a plant and if the pre-tax yield is now only 20 per cent, they will not build that plant. However, if the corporate tax rate were cut from 52 per cent down to below 50 per cent, that investment project would now become worthwhile. Moreover, as firms accumulate more money because of the rate reduction, they may bid down the postulated 10 per cent after-tax yield needed to induce certain kinds of risky investment.

Liberals argue that it is inequitable to help owners of property too much. They also argue that, with investment so sluggish in the American economy of recent years, there will be an inelastic stimulus to investment from such tax reductions. On the other hand, more conservative people argue that since it is investment that has been so disappointing in recent years, tax reduction should be specially directed toward it—either as a matter of equity, or because its marginal social worth is so great, or because of a presumed elasticity of its response.

Leaving ethical judgments to the side, my observation of the behavior of decision makers and of their cash positions and opportunities suggests to me that in the short run there is not a great deal of potency in corporation tax reduction. In the longer run, combined with a vigorous full-employment problem and taking into account the international balance constraint on credit ease, there may be merits in such programs in accelerating the "deepening of capital" so helpful for a growth program.

Finally, there is the widespread belief that our investment has been lagging because our *high-income bracket tax rates* are so high and our structure is so complicated by loopholes and exemptions. It is true that we collect a larger fraction of federal revenues from graduated income taxes than does any other nation; but this is primarily because our average incomes are so high and not because we tax more heavily at most levels of real income than do the welfare states abroad.

For aesthetic reasons, I would trade our highest marginal rates which go up to 91 per cent for an elimination of our many loopholes and exemptions that narrow the tax base (although I doubt that this will turn out to be politically feasible). But I do think that the depressing effect upon investment of our present rate structure is romantically exaggerated. For one thing, our capital-gain loophole when combined with high marginal rates makes for much venturesome investment, rather than killing it off.

For another thing, empirical evidence confirms theoretical expectation that many of the features of our tax law can increase rather than decrease the incentive to save and invest, to work rather than enjoy leisure, so that the final factual balance is in doubt.[1] Much time and energy of accountants, lawyers, and entrepreneurs is wasted in taxmanship, no doubt; but the actual magnitude of this in comparison with other drains on resources can easily be exaggerated, and Congressmen who really take this seriously as a problem could enact simplifications in structure without necessarily reducing graduation drastically.

Basic reform of our tax system must be determined essentially on grounds of ethics and morality, not—as recent discussions would lead one to believe—as a vital contribution to economic growth. Historically, many developing economies have relied on *inequality of income distribution* to provide thrift and capital formation: factual studies show the differences in the *marginal* propensities to consume between rich and poor to be moderate, to be much less than the difference in their average propensities; in any case modern nations have alternative choices, as will now be seen.

Public Thrift

For half a dozen years I have been preaching the doctrine that a mixed-enterprise economy can raise its rate of capital formation, and hence the growth rate of potential GNP, by supplementing private thrift by public thrift. Just as people decide their day-to-day decisions about consuming and non-consuming in the marketplace for goods, for bonds and saving accounts and for equities, so they may voluntarily come together at the political polls and vote for an additional rate of capital formation to be brought about through government action. I do not have in mind here merely that people may vote for durable dams, school buildings and other forms of social capital, even though such programs may well be desirable for their own sakes and for growth. What I mean is that we may all democratically vote that our full-employment mix of output should be shifted toward more capital formation and less consumption by a package of the following devices:

(i) *Expansionary monetary policies* by the central bank and other credit agencies is to make credit more available and cheaper to potential in-

---

[1] This is not to deny the finding of advanced welfare economics that "dead-weight" loss is in any case introduced by distortion of substitution effects.

vestors. With effective interest rates low, investment projects which previously didn't pay unless they yielded (say) a 10 per cent equity yield, now will be profitable to carry through. Then 9 per cent projects can be made to be profitable by further credit expansion programs, thereby causing the stimulus to growth coming from technical change to be supplemented by greater "induced capital deepening" than would otherwise have been the case.

(ii) *Austere fiscal policies* will also be necessary whenever (i)'s monetary ease induces so much private investment as to open up an inflationary gap of excessive dollar spending. By raising or maintaining tax rates enough relative to needed government expenditure on current and capital goods and on welfare transfers, we can lower the share of total income accruing to private persons and firms, thereby causing the reduction in consumption needed to release the scarce resources in our postulated full-employment economy that are needed for the induced investment programs.

This "new look" in fiscal policy has also been advocated by such progressive economists as James Tobin (of Yale and Kennedy's first Council of Economic Advisers), Richard A. Musgrave (of Princeton and various economic advisory groups), E. C. Brown and R. M. Solow (of M.I.T.). I call it a "new look" but I am told that Gunnar Myrdal had proposed something like this for Sweden almost 20 years ago, and that there has been much political debate here on the matter.

Many liberal economists—such as my Harvard teacher Alvin Hansen, Gerhard Colm (of the National Planning Association) and Robert Eisner (of Northwestern University)—have all along had doubts about this proposal. Aside from the ethical question as to how much sacrifice of current consumption the present generation of workers ought to make in the interest of growth and enhanced future potential, they are inclined to doubt that much deepening of capital is maintainable. "Does not the capital-output ratio of the accelerator pretty much determine investment needs? Hence, at full employment the rate of capital formation is not much subject to social (or private) decision; and an attempt to force the pace will merely result in capital glut a little later and be self-defeating. Hence, our goal should be to *encourage consumption* enough to get us back on our maximal growth trend, thereby aiding rather than subtracting from investment."

So go the arguments of the critics of the view that a mixed-system like ours can increase its rate of growth by an effective social thrift policy. I must confess that it is to me one of the sadnesses of the Kennedy era that events have been working out in a way that these critics might have expected. I don't mean that this is sad because it proves me in error and others right; these others are my friends and personal vanity is really unimportant. I merely mean that it will be a sad thing if the American mixed-system has no effective control over its own growth rate and must acquiesce in a $3\,^1/_2$ per cent rate rather than aspire to a $4\,^1/_4$ per cent long-run rate.

A deeper look at recent events makes me less sad. After all, we have been laboring under a serious balance-of-payments constraint. The two-step program for growth has not even been tested yet because it was never able to get off the ground: step (i), involving militant monetary expansion, has never taken place because our international deficit would not permit us to have really low short-term and long-term interest rates. Hence, we have no real evidence as to the potency or impotence of easy money to induce capital formation of a deepening kind.[1]

While the factual issue is still open, from the viewpoint of policy in the early 1960's the verdict is clear. So long as we cannot introduce Step (i) of the new-look program, Step (ii) is clearly undesirable and the whole program must be for some time soft-pedalled. It would be too dramatic to say that we are in an era of stagnation. Perhaps it will sound better if we say that we *may* be in one of the slack periods of the so-called Kuznets Long Waves, which at 15 to 25-year intervals seem to appear in American annals of the last 75 years (in construction data, population and immigration data, in various measures involving the scale of economic resources *and their degree of intensity* of utilization).

We no longer regard such swings as immutable facts of nature, like the inevitable plagues that man could do nothing about before the age of penicillin, sulpha, medical care and public health. Fiscal and monetary policies can ameliorate, moderate, and perhaps even compensate fully for such tendencies toward sluggish investment opportunities. But until we regain freedom of domestic monetary policy or experiment further with unconventional credit policies—such as helpful guarantees that reduce riskiness of domestic investment without sending funds abroad to get higher yields in London and other money markets—we must welcome anything which increases public or private consumption.

---

[1] This consideration is of course relevant to my earlier discussion of possible overvaluation of the dollar.

Conclusion

I have raised many problems. Some will be familiar to Europeans; some are characteristically American. Because I have discussed them unflinchingly, I may be in danger of leaving the impression that our problems are terribly difficult, even hopeless. Let me correct any such misapprehension. Ours, for the most part, are the happy problems that come with affluence. We have made strides toward solving many of them; and shall be making further strides these next few years. And the same goes for some economic problems I have not had time to mention. But we do not make progress by being complacent or by sticking to ancient orthodoxies. That reasoning suggested long ago and events of the last few years have amply confirmed.

Moreover, we still have one non-economic obstacle to overcome. I refer to Americans' ideological repugnance for continuing budgetary deficits. It must be evident to any attentive listener that my diagnosis of recent economic history has the implication that the United States *may* be in prudent need of sizeable deficits in the Administrative Budget for at least the next few years of the 1960's and perhaps even longer. As the lungs need air, the heart needs blood and the stomach needs food—and not as a drunkard needs drink, an addict needs dope and a diabetic needs insulin—a modern economy may in some epochs need chronic deficits and a growing public debt (and in other epochs need a chronic surplus, i.e., a chronic over taxation to release resources to investment needs and to curtail inflation and to reduce the public debt). I say this in all seriousness even though scarcely one in a hundred of our opinion makers can yet comprehend my meaning. But here too I am optimistic that rationality will win out over habit.

I shall end with the simple observation that Knut Wicksell in Valhalla, as he listens to this lengthy lecture, must be struck—as I have been struck in recent years—by the realization that each one of the problems of current economic life cries out for analysis by the tools of the professional economist. When by chance I wandered years ago into the study of economics, I hoped my chosen subject would prove useful in real life as well as pleasurable in the university. Reality has—perhaps alas?—more than fulfilled my youthful hopes.

Paul A. Samuelson

December, 1962

125

❧ Economic Thought and the New Industrialism

Paul A. Samuelson

That the history of ideas can be written without paying *serious* attention to changing theories about economics is itself a preposterous idea. Yet, like Samuel Johnson's kicking of the table to disprove skeptics of reality, any doubter can convince himself of this remarkable truth by training his magnifying glass on a random page of a random book from the library shelf labeled "intellectual history."[1] It is not really that historians think economics is unintellectual, but rather that it strikes them as being too intellectual — that the esoteric ideas with which it abounds are too much for the ordinary man.

Evidently there are two fallacies here. First, as will not be evident to those who hold it, there is the mistaken belief that economics is really all that hard. When Carlyle called economics the Dismal Science, he was of course not referring to the mathematical complexity of modern economics or even to the Ricardian syllogisms and supply-demand diagrams of the nineteenth century; but for many learned men he might just as well have been. Here of course we have merely another problem of the two (or n) cultures: the real difference is not between science and the humanities, for both Saint Peter in heaven and Maxwell's Demon recognize that the savant who toils over vocabulary shifts in Tibetan is blood brother to the tireless collector of atomic spectra, while the big-picture man who can trace the rise and fall of civilizations is as incapable of mastering a nice point in literary philosophy as he is in quantum mechanics or growth economics.

The second fallacy renders the first gratuitous. For suppose it really did take a superman to understand basic economic principles. It would not then follow that the bulk of men carry around in their heads no economic ideas at all. Nature does abhor vacuums — a law of Sir T. Gresham, not Sir I. Newton. And simple economic notions, like weeds, homestead wherever they are not forced out by the cultivated flowers of the intellect. Moreover, many a flower is but a weed grown tame: unprune it and you discover its original sins. Just as every chairman of the board is a walking encyclopedia of economic theories, every barefoot econometrician has hidden inside him the full-blown prejudices of his high school civics teacher mingled among the Keynesian theories of deflation and the Paretian theorems on optimal competitive pricing.

All this can be illustrated by the present essay. I am concerned with the development of economists' thought in America, particularly in the period from the Civil to the First World War. While this is of interest for its own sake, I must confess that I began with the following vague hypothesis:

> Businessmen today — and for that matter congressmen, editors, and the American middle classes generally — have economic beliefs which keep the country from doing things that would improve profits, real wages, job opportunities, and living standards generally. The source of these archaic notions is perhaps to be found in the "conventional wisdom" laid down by academic economists in the half-century after the Civil War.

But the more deeply I study the evolution of thought, the less confidence I have in the attractive theory that today's popular beliefs are primarily vestiges of yesterday's science. For one thing, the best economic scholars of the past, even though deprived of access to a good M.I.T. training in economics and ignorant of the experiences of nations in the twentieth century, turn out upon examination to have had a much better understanding of economic principles *for our times* than does a present-day man of affairs. If the rock-and-roll music of popular fashion is not the same as Schoenberg, that does not mean it has to be the Bach or even the Chopin of some past epoch.

Too much, however, should not be read into my assertion that popular notions about economics are somewhat different from those of past and present economists. It does not follow that the history of popular economic notions has to be much like the histories of water closets or of sexual superstitions, which are perhaps best recorded by busy anthropologists working across time and space. Were that so, I suppose we would push the subject out of the category of intellectual history and into the category of "social" or some other kind of history. But to do this would, I think, be a mistake.

How a man feels about a balanced budget turns out to be closely linked with how he feels about the gold standard or minimum-wage legislation. This is merely to say that his various ideas in economics have *analytical and intellectual connections,* even if they do not form an integrated self-consistent system. "I rationalize; therefore I am" might well be the credo of everyman as economist. To be articulate it is well to have something articulated to talk about — which is more than a play on words. All this applies to the radical as well as to the conservative: it is not enough to express hate for a system and implore others to do likewise; one inevitably tries to explain why the hateful is hateful.

At this point of generalization an element of science does enter in at least crudely. If I manufacture dolls, and Japanese imports threaten my income, I do not have to convince my wife that free trade is a bad thing. But in asking Congress and the voters to do something about it, I require arguments that go beyond my own need or greed: so I find myself shopping among economic theories for new points of persuasion, thereby implicitly entering the realm of primitive economic science. Nor should rationalization be thought of as simple reflections of views already arrived at without the need for reasoning: rationalizations do take on a life of their own and do in some degree affect subsequent opinions and actions. Thus, if my wish to be left alone to run my own business convinces me of the virtues of laissez-faire and limited government, I may end up voting against governmental tariff protection for some other industry even though I do not overdo consistency by refraining from asking government to protect my own. One does after all owe something to one's wife!

In summary, while reviewing the developing economic thought among economists is not quite the same as giving a definitive history of American economic opinions, I believe such a review provides an indispensable aspect of the problem. Besides, as any survey of the history of ideas must show, there is more interest for its own sake in the story of connected thought than in a chronological listing of an inventory of notions. The portrait of a baby or a lobster is more memorable than the photocopy of a yeast colony in a washtub.

EARLY AMERICAN ECONOMICS IN BROAD VIEW [*]

Every textbook on the history of economic doctrines includes a separate section on American thought. Invariably the same names appear: Benjamin Franklin, Alexander Hamilton, Henry C. Carey, Henry George, Francis Walker, and John Bates Clark. Certain clichés and stereotypes about the character of American economics are repeated in every discussion. What are some of these?

American economics is first and foremost supposed to be "optimistic." Men living on a bounteous and yet unsettled continent during a time of rapid progress in population and real national product per capita could hardly be expected to take much stock in a gloomy Malthusian vision of diminishing returns and subsistence wages. And they did not. Henry C. Carey, writing just before the middle of the nineteenth century, rebelled against the dismal aspects of classical economics. His logic was often bad and his prolix style atrocious. But his fundamental empirical inferences seem correct for his time and place.

By virtue of technological developments in transportation the ef-

[*] The next three sections are adapted from my essay "American Economics," Chapter 2, pages 33–44 in *Postwar Economic Trends in the United States*, edited by Ralph E. Freeman; copyright © 1960 by Massachusetts Institute of Technology; reprinted by permission of Harper & Row, Publishers.

fective supply of land and natural resources, far from declining relative to labor and capital, was actually increasing.[2] Most important,
real wages were rising as a result of technological change and capital
formation, and in addition could confidently be expected to continue
to rise. No wonder Henry C. Carey saw social harmony everywhere — and before Bastiat, as he himself bitterly pointed out. It is
instructive that the economic theories which Carey used to deduce
those glowing trends were not unlike the labor-theory-of-value models. Yet they were used to deduce predictions about real wages quite
opposite from those of Karl Marx — predictions which we now
know are more nearly in accordance with the historical record than
Marx's expectation of an absolute or relative impoverishment of
labor.

A second characteristic of nineteenth-century economics is its
"theological" character. The typical textbook writer seems to have
been an ordained clergyman teaching as an amateur economist in a
college. As Cliffe Leslie pointed out in his essay, *Political Economy
in the United States* (1881), anyone looking over the leaves of
American treatises would be tempted to classify them as "Sunday"
rather than "weekday" books: they take for granted that God designed the competitive economic system in a harmonious way, regarding this as an axiom rather than as a theorem proved by Adam
Smith.[3]

A third characteristic commented on by most writers is the "protectionist" leanings of American economists. Since this seems hardly
consistent with a belief in the harmonious nature of free private enterprise, most chroniclers have tried to explain protectionism in
terms of aberrations of logic.

A better explanation of protectionist leanings will be found, I
suspect, in a fourth characteristic of American economics, its "nationalistic" nature. Thus to the array of important American economists I would add the name of Friedrich List. Of course List would
usually be considered the arch exponent of German nationalism; but
Joseph Dorfman, in his monumental study, *The Economic Mind in
American Civilization*, has convincingly argued that List's theories
had already jelled prior to his returning to Germany from the
United States, and that it was in the nature of an accident that he
wrote his *National System of Political Economy* in German.[4] Native writers, such as Harvard's Francis Bowen, produced textbooks

with such titles as *American Political Economy;* and as late as the First World War, Thomas Nixon Carver was writing elementary textbooks of an unashamedly nationalistic character.

As an ethical end, Carey and his followers wanted a diversified America. I suspect they were willing to pay an economic price for this,[5] but they were poor enough reasoners to be able to convince themselves that no price would be exacted. Instead of presenting their many specious arguments in favor of a tariff, they would have done better to concentrate on the "infant industry" argument. In retrospect, knowing as we do that America has developed a comparative advantage in many lines of manufacture, it seems to me a legitimate hypothesis that tariffs which speeded up their introduction and *initiated early experimentation* may have had some helpful role in accelerating the pace of American development.

Undoubtedly, however, the most powerful forces pushing economists toward arguments for protection were not the interests of industries yet unborn but the established coal and iron interests. Little wonder that Pennsylvania was a hotbed of protectionism and that no free trader could teach at the University of Pennsylvania.[6]

This brings me to a fifth characteristic of nineteenth-century American economics — its "pro-business, conservative" character. The harmonies of the economic system were the harmonies of ruthless competition. Whereas at the beginning of the century many writers thought that the result would be an equalitarian society, by the end of the century economists observed that the outcome did involve great disparities of wealth. Many followed Herbert Spencer in embracing a crude form of "Social Darwinism," in which the poor were blamed for their misfortune and the rich praised for their success. One such "forgotten man," who enthralled several generations of Yale men with this stern philosophy, was William Graham Sumner.

The final characteristic of earlier American economics that most writers have agreed on is its "untheoretical," even "antitheoretical," nature. This is summed up in the much-quoted view of Harvard's C. F. Dunbar, who said in his essay "Economic Science in America, 1776–1876": ". . . The United States has done nothing towards developing the theory of political economy. . . ." There is much to this, but two reservations must be made.

First, there is the fact that Dunbar was pretty much satisfied with theoretical economics as laid down by the classical economists. (He was the person Eliot picked to teach sound free-trade economics in place of Bowen.) So he could hardly be regarded as an unbiased judge of the newer doctrines of Carey and other Americans.

Second, there is the neglected American theorist John Rae. Rae developed a sophisticated theory of capital and interest and put forth many interesting notions concerning invention and progress. Not only was Rae a theorist of international caliber, but in addition it can be argued that most of what is valid in Carey he might have found in his reading of Rae.

But, all in all, we must accept the charge that early American economics was on the primitive side where economic theory was concerned. Perhaps nothing more could have been expected of amateurs writing in a provincial backwater. The tendency of American thought to be derivative and doctrinaire — as seen by the popularity and repeated imitation of the textbooks of Jean Baptiste Say and John Ramsay McCulloch — fits in with such a pattern too. There may be something also in the notion that Americans are peculiarly pragmatic, content to stay close to the facts and untempted toward long chains of deductive reasoning.

A more flattering interpretation of this untheoretical trait may be found in the nature of the subjects in which American economics excelled. Around the turn of the century Americans did a great deal of work on business cycles, which culminated in Wesley C. Mitchell's magnificent book published in 1913. The fact that American fluctuations were always so much bigger than those abroad led naturally to an interest in this subject. Even those of us who are fondest of economic theory will not argue that cultivating the economic theories of the classical and neoclassical writers would have been an optimal way of then advancing knowledge of business fluctuations.

The second subject that American economists can be said to have been studying with special vigor comprises what would today be called "growth and development economics." Thus the early writers were interested in promoting thrift and capital formation, were stressing progress and technological change, and were emphasizing the economies of large-scale production. It is true that they did not succeed in formulating a simple and comprehensive theory to cover growth and development. But modern economists of the 1960's are least likely to blame them — since in our own day the philosopher's stone that would unify and illuminate this area has long been sought, but the search has as yet produced only a catalogue of important but not unobvious tendencies and countertendencies.

THE TRANSITION TO MODERN ECONOMICS

Does this survey of American economics throw much light on the present position of the subject? I am not sure.

From it one would hardly be prepared for the fact that abstract mathematical economics and statistics are being avidly studied today here in the United States. (That economists should be busily engaged in operations research and programing for large corporations and the armed services fits in a little better with the earlier pattern.)

Nor would reading a survey of the nature of early American economics lead one to guess that today large parts of the business community look on economists with suspicion — as impractical "eggheads" bent on criticizing private enterprise and putting it in fetters. The intervening years of trust formation at the turn of the century and of mass depression in the 1930's substantially changed characteristic patterns of the earlier economics.

The evolution of American economic thought would, however, have prepared one for the emergence in the first part of this century of the *institutionalist* school of economics. This was associated with the names of Thorstein Veblen, John R. Commons, and Wesley C. Mitchell. For the most part this school has not succeeded in reproducing itself and today it seems to be almost extinct. But at the University of Wisconsin and the New School for Social Research in New York in the years after the First World War, this school, with its rejection of abstract "equilibrium" economics in favor of a concentration on economic institutions, did appear to be the wave of the future.

It is hard today to see what such diverse men really had in common, that is, aside from their all being critical of the deductive economics promulgated by complacent classical and neoclassical theorists. Veblen — the American Karl Marx — was primarily an iconoclast and social critic, debunking in murky but brilliant prose the cherished beliefs and institutions of his time. The lasting achievements of Commons and Mitchell would not seem to reside in anything that they had particularly in common with Veblen or with each other but rather with the important work in applied economics that each was motivated to do — Commons in the field of labor economics and Mitchell in the field of business cycles.

Prior to the institutionalists, America was not without its critics of the existing order. About Henry George and his single-tax movement I shall say little, since so forceful a speaker and stylist was able to command for himself an amount of attention disproportionate to his intrinsic importance. The imputation of land income is unlikely to be considered by the economic historian of the future as a problem of the first magnitude, and the expectation by George's followers that the single tax would cure most of the ills of society seems merely crankish.[7]

One would have expected the deflationary decades at the end of the nineteenth century to have created a group of radical economists. In the political field itself we had the era of Populist agitation, and this did have its counterpart in the realm of thought. The young John Bates Clark was a kind of Christian socialist; and Francis Walker at the threshold of his career as an economist felt himself to be a militant critic of the harmonies of laissez-faire. The American Economic Association was founded in the 1880's by the younger economists — many of whom had studied in Germany under so-called "socialists of the chair" and exponents of the historical method — as a protest movement against the older conservative economists. It may not seem remarkable today but it was then a use of strong language for them to propose in their platform the assertion: "We regard the State as an educational and ethical agency whose positive aid is an indispensable condition of human progress." How different this was from the Jeffersonian notion that the best government was that which governed least!

In time the American Economic Association lost its radical tinge and embraced almost all the leading American economists. And it is interesting to observe how many of the men associated with its founding became less radical with advancing age and prestige. In the nineties Richard T. Ely, one of the leading spirits in the founding of the Association, was formally accused at the University of Wisconsin of being a socialist. Not only did he clear himself of this charge, but, what is more remarkable, he agreed that if the charge had been true, it would have been good grounds for disqualifying him from teaching. And Clark ended by formulating in his classic *Distribution of Wealth* the doctrine that the imputation of functional wages and interests by the specific productivity laws that prevail under free competition is *ethically* optimal.

Perhaps the pressures of what was on the whole an intolerant society can explain the increasing conservatism of the transitional generation of economists. Certainly some explanation for the relative unimportance of socialism in modern American thought is called for. As far as the changing ideas of economists themselves are concerned, I have this hypothesis to put forward. By the turn of the century economists were ceasing to be amateurs and were making their livelihoods as college professors. This professionalization of economics may have had as one of its by-products a toning down of radical feelings, for the university environment and the full-time study of economics may make for a reduction of Utopian ardor. (It is interesting to note that Alfred Marshall in England and Léon Walras in France and Switzerland went through similar developments, each starting and ending with warm social sympathies but in the course of time becoming more and more skeptical about proposals for the radical remaking of society.)

The professionalization of American economics greatly improved its analytical quality. Now articles and books were being written by men who had been taught by other economists, not by themselves. What was lost in originality was more than made up for in cogency. The two great figures from the standpoint of analytic contribution undoubtedly were John Bates Clark and Irving Fisher.[8] After the First World War this transitional period culminated in such world-famous economists as Frank H. Knight, John Maurice Clark, and Jacob Viner. These men, the sons of our grandfathers, belonged to the first generation of topnotch economists to have been completely reared by American graduate schools. They provide a fitting bridge to the modern generation of American economists.

THE MODERN SCENE

In giving a survey of American economics and American economists, I must not make the mistake of the patriotic Greek who insisted that the moon of Athens was different from the moon of Sparta. American economics is plainly in the tradition of Western economics generally. Indeed, to a Russian it would be indistinguishable from French or German economics. To a Latin American it would not seem different from English economics. (And even we American economists have our private little joke concerning our great advantage over the English. They read only their own writings, whereas we can get the benefit from reading their papers and our own too!)

Furthermore, by American economics one cannot mean economics as taught and discussed by persons *born* in this country. Scarcely one French professor in twenty was born outside of France. But of twenty outstanding American economists at the time of the Second World War, perhaps two came here from England and six to eight from Europe. (I do not even distinguish Canadian from American economists. Another of our jokes is that we are all Canadians!) An American university that tried to recruit its economics department from *Mayflower* descendants would, I fear, have a tough time of it.

These and other characteristics of the American economic profession would also be quite typical of other disciplines: mathematics, physics, chemistry, classics, sociology, medicine — and in some degree law and history. Many of my remarks then, though couched in terms of the concrete detail of economics, will be applicable to American academic life generally; and this essay can be considered a contribution to the general subject of *comparative academics*.

For about a quarter of a century now, American economics has been first-rate. What does this mean? It means what any competent observer means when he says that a particular university or person is in the forefront in creative research in the field of mathematics, physics, or medicine. Naturally there is an inevitable subjective element in any such appraisal. And there is an inevitable bias that predisposes any observer to magnify the accomplishments of his own town, province, and country. When I state that the *quantity* of economic thought in Cambridge, Massachusetts, is second to none anywhere in the world, I might be able to back this up by a count of the pages of articles published in learned journals, by measurement of the total inches of our theoretical and statistical curves, by the decibel count of the seminars at Harvard and further down the river. But when I go on to state that the *quality* of this thought is second to none, you must make allowance for the fact that Cambridge is where I sip my morning coffee.

In saying that American economics has been first-rate for a quarter of a century, I seem to be implying that prior to that time it was not. One can never be sure about such judgments, but I am inclined to risk the hypothesis that the scholarly research done by Americans in economics prior to, say, 1932 was generally not quite of the first rank. And I suspect this is a judgment that could be risked about mathematics, physics, and chemistry, too.

Let me illustrate by the case of mathematics and physics. Toward the end of the Second World War, when President Roosevelt set up the Bush Committee to survey science, I recall hearing I. I. Rabi, himself an American Nobel prize winner in physics, point out that in our history we had produced only one truly outstanding theoretical physicist (presumably Willard Gibbs). And the story is told that when the young G. D. Birkhoff proved in 1910 a famous conjecture of the dying J. H. Poincaré, the French mathematician C. E. Picard refused to believe that an American could have done it.[9]

It was not purely for reasons of fashion that at the turn of the century Americans went to Germany to do their graduate work. In the natural sciences the best work was being done there, and many Americans who studied abroad were frank to report that they found themselves less well prepared and creative than many of the fellow students they met in Europe.

Returning to economics, can we explain the earlier trek to Germany purely in terms of the world superiority of German *economic* scholarship? I think not. If American economics was years ago clearly inferior to some other economics, one would have to point to English economics as the clearly front-rank effort. So, I suppose, we must invoke the institutional factor that German universities were set up to give graduate instruction whereas Cambridge (and Oxford) were not. If an economist like J. B. Clark could have gained anything from his teachers — and there is little evidence that so self-oriented and original a man could — one would have thought that a W. S. Jevons might have given him more than could a Karl Knies or any other less theoretically oriented German scholar. But Jevons taught undergraduates in a university that was not yet even red brick. And even after the nineties, when Alfred Marshall was widely regarded as the world-leading economist, there was really no way for anyone to do graduate study in his Cambridge classroom — much less at his knee.[10] Had a young American been venturesome enough to break away from the German pattern, how could he get into an English college? And outside the college common room, whom would he have found to talk to? Worst of all, to cap his folly he would have had to return to our shores unanointed by the all-important Ph.D. degree, which was the necessary passport for a successful teaching career.

Demand creates its supply. We have seen that American universities increasingly began to process their own graduate students and to award domestic Ph.D. degrees. And yet, as we have seen, it was perhaps still not true that American economics was first-rate. This led many observers by the familiar *post-hoc-ergo-propter-hoc* reasoning to the inference that our second-rateness must be due to our horrible propensity to insist on doctor's degrees. Even today this view will take one a long way in many a common room of the British Isles, and there are *Gelehrten* here at home who think that the mere *absence* of a degree will convert a mediocre son of the Middle Border into a sparkling and omniscient don.

I must confess my own original predilections were against our Ph.D. until, under the impact of direct empirical observation, I was forced to the view that the absence of a comprehensive Ph.D. program may be the curse of economics abroad. This is not at all because our average doctoral dissertation is a substantial contribution to scholarship, a work of art, or even a literate document. To look at the thesis is to miss the point; it is only the exposed peak of a submerged iceberg. If the Ph.D. program had never existed, we should now have to invent it — for the simple reason that *it gives us the excuse to carry on advanced instruction in economics.*

For, make no mistake about it, modern economics has become a complicated subject — one which takes a long time to learn. Gone are the days when one could give a bright undergraduate a copy of Alfred Marshall's *Principles* to take along with him on his vacation trip to the mountains and expect him to end his undergraduate days as an accomplished economist. True, such a system may generate clever essays about Marshall's use of the representative firm or his concept of quasi rent. But that is not the sort of thing that economists today regard as important work — nor would similar clever essays by Marshall on Mill's use of "derived demand" have earned him *his* world reputation.

AMATEURS AND PROFESSIONALS

My survey has given primary emphasis to the economic ideas of economists rather than of noneconomists. Increasingly as the years went by, being an economist meant being a professor. But the two terms are by no means identical: neither David Ricardo nor John Stuart Mill was an academic teacher or even a college undergraduate; in America people like Rae and Carey were more important *as economists* than academic figures like Bowen and Dunbar, and for this reason I have paid more attention to them. On the other hand, someone like Edward Bellamy, through his novel *Looking Backward* (1888), had a far greater political impact on socialist sentiments in America than did Karl Marx or even Thorstein Veblen. Yet though Bellamy deserves a full treatment in the history of Utopias, I do not think he rates a major place in the history of economic ideas as developed by economists.

Elsewhere I have written at some length on the different rating we in the economics profession give to economic ideas of the past as compared to the rating used by professional historians of ideas and cultivated men of affairs generally.[11] The present essay further illustrates this divergence. Consider Henry Ford. The man in the street attached some importance to the ideas of Henry Ford, and perhaps the eclectic historian of social thought will give him a few paragraphs. Yet in the catalogue of economic ideas and principles, professional economists will spare him scarcely a footnote. His ideas about mass purchasing power are not new or particularly well phrased: his pronouncements about production and about tapping a mass market through price reduction seem not of the importance of an Eli Whitney or even a Frederick Taylor. While Shaw may be right in saying that "Those who can, do; those who can't, teach," it is the latter who survive in books of intellectual history. For history is written, after all, by writers.

The point about Ford is a trite one. More subtle are the examples provided by Henry George and William Graham Sumner. Henry George was long a force to reckon with in the political world and in the marketplace for general ideas. Yet, as I have indicated, he really was not much of an economics scholar. The example I use to illustrate this is a conversation at the Harvard Society of Fellows that I once had before the war with Frank W. Taussig, then the dean of venerable American economists. He told me that a recent remark by John Dewey praising George as the greatest economist America had ever produced simply filled him with despair: in terms of economic analysis — and I am not here referring to any conservative doubts Taussig might have had about the land-tax movement — George appeared to Taussig to be like a confused child. This same Taussig has somewhere written that William Graham Sumner, however important his polemical eloquence might have been, added nothing essential to economic knowledge, not even to the principles a conservative might want to appeal to. Lest I give the impression that Taussig was by temperament a stuffed-shirt and an overcritical judge, let me add that as editor of the austere *Quarterly Journal of Economics* Taussig had encouraged publication of papers by Thorstein Veblen, whom he regarded as a genius, albeit not necessarily a faultless economic reasoner.

One is not surprised that an unoriginal vulgarizer should carry more political weight than a subtle creator of important economic ideas. Part of the hard-sell involves repetition and oversimplification. To be persuasive one should often ignore objections to a thesis: and one way to ignore an objection is to be unaware of it. Yet it can be argued that the advocate of a special view is best armed with the most complete knowledge about the strengths and weaknesses of his own arguments. If this be the case, I think it definitely true that by shopping around among contemporary and past economic scholars, a Machiavellian advocate can construct his most powerful brief. Economic scholars come in all opinions; and since, by definition, they are the ones who have devoted the most time to the pursuit, they are the ones in the best position to enunciate the intrinsic merits (and demerits) of a particular view. As an illustration of all this, consider the dictum of my old teacher and friend, Professor Jacob Viner of Chicago and Princeton. Like most economists, he would regard himself as pretty much of a free trader; and yet he would claim, "The best arguments for tariff protection have been thought up and described by free traders."

Yet, I must confess to lingering doubts. Viner would no doubt have in mind arguments like J. S. Mill's that a temporary protective tariff may enable an "infant industry" to get started and develop into a competitively viable national asset. That is one of the best arguments for a tariff. But in what sense "best"? Best in the sense that free traders, or rather economists generally, will be most likely to deem it best. Evidently there is a danger here of circularity: economic scholars provide the best analysis of important matters, if you use their criteria as the test. Now, the best arguments in this sense are not necessarily the most persuasive ones politically. Thus, the argument for a so-called "scientific tariff" — one that *merely* serves to equalize costs of production at home and abroad! — perhaps had as much political sex-appeal a third of a century ago as any argument. Yet it is widely regarded by economists as a tissue of nonsense, which if taken seriously would wipe out *all* trade and all the benefits of trade. Was it developed by a free trader, or for that matter by a professional economist? I do not know, but if it was, it was probably developed in a fit of absentmindedness. Unless a political protagonist is very Machiavellian indeed, is he not better off *not* realizing how illogical is his use of the scientific tariff argument? I realize it may be argued that in the long run logic will win out over illogic and correct description of reality will win out over incorrect. But as we survey the history of popular ideas, just how confident are we of that?

CONCLUDING REMARKS

Does the history of economic ideas in America fit into any simple patterns? To a first approximation, it seems to me the data can be usefully described in terms of the familiar interpretations.

American economics has, on the whole, been on the conservative and laissez-faire side prior to 1933. The fact that America has always enjoyed about the highest standard of living in the world, and has tended to enjoy a rising standard, does seem important in explaining this. The fact that America started with a clean slate and abundant natural resources does make it seem likely that ours would be a relatively classless society, and hence not too favorably disposed toward interventionist or socialistic ideologies.

This is, of course, a banality. But better a correct banality than an ingenious sophistry. As soon as one proceeds to a closer examination of the record, the shortcomings of a first-approximation description become evident, along with doubts about further theories purporting to "explain" America's thought. Here are a few doubts.

First, why this American prosperity? Climate and abundant resources? No doubt a part of the explanation. Good racial stock? Mm. The perfection of our Constitution and mores? Luck? What kind of an explanation is that? Yankee ingenuity? An answer that raises a new question, albeit possibly a fact as solid as a table and not to be ignored merely on the ground that it is simply a description.

Second, why should Australia and New Zealand, also sparsely settled regions of considerable prosperity, have developed a kind of Fabian socialism that America shunned? At this point one may argue, as Paul Sweezy and others have argued, that radicals were rooted out of American colleges and converted by pressure to conformity. The troubles of Scott Nearing, Thorstein Veblen, Richard T. Ely, and more recent scholars are indeed facts that cannot be ignored. But to the degree that we accept this thesis, we undercut another: thus, the clear-slate freedom from feudalism is widely used to explain our lack of class consciousness; yet it is that same absence of feudal traditions which left American universities at the mercy of their businessman trustees — all this showing the subtlety needed in appraising simple interpretations.

Third, how good is the Max Weber view that the Protestant Ethic and Capitalist Spirit are significantly related? Certainly many religious sermons have a Chamber of Commerce ring about them. But, as Kurt Samuelsson has been the most recent to point out, capitalism has flourished with and without Protestantism and vice versa — so that the historian must turn quantitative in a way he has been reluctant to do. If Weber can use Benjamin Franklin as a prototype of a religious man, then his thesis has been widened into emptiness. (If Adam Smith and David Hume are Protestants, then I am the Pope.) And how does the American observer treat the radicalism inherent in the "social gospel" movement that grew up in the pre-1914 Protestant ministry? Is Herbert Spencer to be given honorary baptism, and W. G. Sumner to be equated with John Wesley? Thus, there is truth and untruth in the Weber thesis; and if a Talcott Parsons should charge that it is a vulgarization of the subtle Weber position which is being attacked, one must reply that the vulgarization of an idea sometimes contains its cash-value in the Bridgman-Carnap sense of operational meaningfulness, while its subtle qualifications may be the antidote that emasculates its empirical dote.

While Charles Darwin lent false respectability to Herbert Spencer, the causal direction between the notions of evolution and economic progress are far from simple. Progress in the sense of size and real-income growth was a solid fact to every Wisconsin schoolboy, and it may be as correct to say that belief in progress led to belief in evolution as vice versa. Certainly it is ironical that both Darwin and Wallace were led by Malthus to natural selection, and yet the America that was so hospitable to Social Darwinism was the same America that thought Malthus just plain wrong. It is partly because Social Darwinism is such a jolly good story, aside from its merits, that it has had its vogue with historians. Sumner spoke to his age, not for it. To ignore what he felt a need to rebut is like reporting one side of a telephone conversation. Also we must not forget that economists as diverse as Mill and Schumpeter and Milton Friedman do attach the greatest importance to "competition" — not the rivalry of Dan'l Drew and Cornelius Vanderbilt so much as the erosion of profits for those who put their noses to the wrong grindstone. The man who builds a better mousetrap makes grass grow in his neighbor's road.

Hardly more satisfying are the attempts to link up American philosophies with economics. The transcendentalists founded collective colonies of good chaps, it is true. But is there not also much of the Horatio Alger, Jr., and Dale Carnegie kind of individualism in Ralph Waldo Emerson? And was not America a natural place for experimental colonies for the same prosaic reason that one does not plant a nudist colony in the high-rent district? To link Veblen with pragmatism because he overlapped with John Dewey at the University of Chicago is as superficial as identifying the know-nothing attitudes of practical businessmen with the ideas of William James and Charles S. Peirce. The facile explanation of Dewey's radicalism in terms of his father's being a rural Vermont merchant of limited means must seem a fine joke to those who knew Davis R. Dewey, the conservative economist who was John's brother: perhaps Freudian historians can explain this by Davis's sibling envy!

I desist from continuing this list of points and counterpoints. If history is not to be an impressionistic arrangement of descriptions that happen to please the historian and his friends, I think one has to be critical of a book like J. F. Normano, *The Spirit of American Economics* (1943), which, along with a review of the troops, includes the usual interpretations of American economic thought together with a few new ones. My point is not that I happen to like a different emphasis, since why cater to my tastes rather than Normano's? My point is that such a book, written within the last twenty years, would lead its readers to expect in the postwar era an entirely different kind of American economics from the mathematical and New Dealish economics that Professor Harris correctly describes elsewhere in this volume. But the latter came as no surprise to competent observers of the 1930's. Good history does not pretend to create accurate predictions, but it should not serve to make its readers' batting average worse than that of a pair of dice.

PART XVIII

Comments on Methodology

126

ECONOMIC THEORY AND MATHEMATICS— AN APPRAISAL

By Paul A. Samuelson
Massachusetts Institute of Technology

It has been correctly said that mathematical economics is flying high these days. So I come, not to praise mathematics, but rather to slightly debunk its use in economics. I do so out of tenderness for the subject, since I firmly believe in the virtues of understatement and lack of pretension.

I realize that this is a session on methodology. Hence, I must face some basic questions as to the nature of mathematics and of its application. What I have to say on this subject is really very simple—perhaps too brief and simple. The time that I save by brief disposal of the weighty philosophical and epistemological issues of methodology I can put to good use in discussing the tactical and pedagogical issues—or what you might even call the Freudian problems that the mathematical and nonmathematical student of economics must face.

The Strict Equivalence of Mathematical Symbols and Literary Words. On the title page of my *Foundations of Economic Analysis,* I quoted the only speech that the great Willard Gibbs was supposed ever to have made before the Yale Faculty. As professors do at such meetings, they were hotly arguing the question of required subjects: Should certain students be required to take languages or mathematics? Each man had his opinion of the relative worth of these disparate subjects. Finally Gibbs, who was not a loquacious man, got up and made a four-word speech: "Mathematics is a language."

I have only one objection to that statement. I wish he had made it 25 per cent shorter—so as to read as follows: "Mathematics *is* language." Now I mean this entirely literally. In principle, mathematics cannot be worse than prose in economic theory; in principle, it certainly cannot be better than prose. For in deepest logic—and leaving out all tactical and pedagogical questions—the two media are strictly identical.

Irving Fisher put this very well in his great doctoral thesis, written exactly sixty years ago. As slightly improved by my late teacher, Joseph Schumpeter, Fisher's statement was: "There is no place you can go by railroad that you cannot go afoot." And I might add, "Vice versa!"

I do not think we should make too much of the fact that in recent years a number of universities have permitted their graduate students to substitute a reading knowledge of mathematics for a reading knowledge of one foreign language. For after all we run our universities on the principle that Satan will find work for idle hands to do; and the fact that we may permit a student to choose between ROTC and elementary badminton does not mean that these two subjects are methodologically identical. And besides, we all know just what a euphemism the expression "a graduate student's reading knowledge" really is.

Induction and Deduction. Every science is based squarely on induction—on observation of empirical facts. This is true even of the very imperfect sciences, which have none of the good luck of astronomy and classical physics. This is true of meteorology, of medicine, of economics, of biology, and of a number of other fields that have achieved only modest success in their study of reality. It used to be thought that running parallel with induction there runs an equally important process called "Deduction"—spelled with a capital *D*. Indeed, certain misguided methodologists carried their enthusiasm for the latter to such extremes that they regarded Deduction as in some sense overshadowing mere pedestrian induction.

Now science is only one small part of man's activity—a part that is today given great honorific status, but which I should like to strip of all honorific status for purposes of this discussion. However, to the extent that we do agree to talk about what is ordinarily called science—and not about poetry or theology or something else—it is clear that deduction has the modest linguistic role of translating certain empirical hypotheses into their "logical equivalents." To a really good man, whose IQ is 300 standard deviations above the average, all syllogistic problems of deduction are so obvious and take place so quickly that he is scarcely aware of their existence. Now I believe that I am uttering a correct statement—in fact, it is the only irrefutable and empty truth that I shall waste your time in uttering—when I say that not everybody, nor even half of everybody, can have an IQ 300 standard deviations above the mean. So there is for all of us a psychological problem of making correct deductions. That is why pencils have erasers and electronic calculators have bells and gongs.

I suppose this is what Alfred Marshall must have had in mind when he followed John Stuart Mill in speaking of the dangers involved in *long* chains of logical reasoning. Marshall treated such chains as if their truth content was subject to radioactive decay and leakage—at the end of n propositions only half the truth was left, at the end of a chain of $2n$ propositions, only half of half the truth remained, and so forth in a geometric multiplier series converging to zero truth. Obviously, in making such a statement, Marshall was describing a property of that biological biped or computing machine called *homo sapiens;* for he certainly could not be describing a property of logical implication. Actually, if proposition A correctly implies proposition B, and B correctly implies proposition C, and so forth all the way to Z, then it is necessarily true that A implies Z in every sense that it implies B. There can be no leakage of truth at any stage of a valid deductive syllogism. All such syllogisms are mere translations of the type, "A rose is a rose is a rose."

All this is pretty well understood when it comes to logical processes of the form: Socrates is a man. All men are mortal. Therefore, Socrates is mortal. What is not always so clearly understood is that a literary statement of this type has its complete equivalent in the symbolism of mathematical logic. If we write it out in such symbolism, we may save paper and ink; we may even make it easier for a seventeen-year-old freshman to arrive at the answer to complex questions of the type: "Is Robinson, who smokes cigarettes and is a non-self shaver, a fascist or is it Jones?" But nonetheless, the mathematical symbolism can be replaced by words. I should hate to put six monkeys in the British Museum and wait until they had typed out in words the equivalent of the mathematical formulas involved in Whitehead and Russell's *Mathematical Principia.* But if we were to wait lcng enough, it could be done.

The Case of Neoclassical Distribution. Similarly, in economics. The cornerstone of the simplest and most fundamental theory of production and distribution—that of Walras and J. B. Clark—is Euler's theorem on homogeneous functions. Now it is doubtful that Clark—who rather boasted of his mathematical innocence—had ever heard of Euler. Certainly, he cannot have known what is meant by a homogeneous function. But nonetheless, in Clark's theory, there is the implicit assumption that scale does not count; that what does count is the proportions in which the factors combine; and that it does not matter which of the factors of production is the hiring factor and which the hired. If we correctly interpret the implication of all this, we see that Clark—just as he was talking prose and knowing it—was talking the mathematics of homogeneous functions and not knowing it.

I have often heard Clark criticized for not worrying more about the exhaustion-of-the-product problem. He seems never to have worried whether rent, computed as a triangular residual, would be numerically equal—down to the very last decimal place—to rent calculated as a rectangle of marginal product. Like King Canute, he seems simply to have instructed his draftsman to draw the areas so as to be equal.

As I say, Clark has often been criticized for not going into this problem of exhaustion of the product. I myself have joined in such criticism. But I now think differently—at least from the present standpoint of the nature of true logical deductive implication as distinct from the human psychological problem of perceiving truth and cramming it into the heads of one's students or readers. Even if Euler had never lived to perceive his theorem, even if Wicksell, Walras, and Wicksteed had not applied it to economic theory, Clark's doctrine is in the clear. His assumptions of constant-returns-to-scale and viable free-entry ensure for him that total revenue of each competitive firm will be exactly equal to total cost. And with this settled in the realm of cost and demand curves, there is no need for a textbook writer in some later chapter of his book dealing with production to suddenly become assailed by doubts about the "adding-up problem of exhaustion-of-the-product."

Now let me linger on this case for a moment. Economists have carefully compared Wicksteed's and Clark's treatment of this problem in order to show that mathematics is certainly not inferior to words in handling such an important element of distribution theory.

What is not so clear is the answer to the reverse question: Is not literary economics, by its very nature, inferior to mathematics in handling such a complex quantitative issue. As one eminent mathematical economist put it to me: "Euler's theorem is absolutely basic to the simplest neoclassical theory of imputation. Yet without mathematics, you simply cannot give a rigorous proof of Euler's theorem."

Now I must concede that the economics literature does abound with false proofs of Euler's theorem on homogeneous functions. But what I cannot admit—unless I am willing to recant on all that I have been saying about the logical identity of words and symbols—I simply cannot admit that a rigorous literary proof of Euler's theorem is in principle impossible.

In fact, I tried a literary proof on my mathematical friend. He quite properly pointed out that it was not rigorous in the way it treated infinitesimals. I fully agree. My argument was heuristic. But I do claim that if my friend and I could spend a week or so talking together, so that I could describe in words the fundamental limit processes involved in the Newton-Leibniz calculus and derivatives, then this problem of lack of rigor could be met. In fact, much more subtle properties of Pfaffian partial differential equations are in principle capable of being stated in basic English. As Professor Leontief has pointed out, the final proof of the identity of mathematics and words is the fact that we teach people mathematics by the use of words, defining each symbol as we go along. It is no accident that the printer of mathematical equations is forced to put commas, periods, and other punctuation in them, for equations are sentences, pure and simple.

Geometry in Relation to Words and Mathematical Analysis. Today when an economic theorist deplores the use of mathematics, he usually speaks up for the virtues of geometrical diagrams as the alternatives. It was not always thus. Seventy years ago, when a man like Cairnes criticized the use of mathematics in economics, probably he meant by the term "mathematics" primarily geometrical diagrams. From the point of view of this lecture, the ancients were more nearly right than the modern critics. Geometry is a branch of mathematics, in exactly the same sense that mathematics is a branch of language. It is easy to understand why a man might have no use at all for economic theory, invoking, instead, a plague on mathematical economics, on diagrammatic textbooks, and on all fine-spun literary theories. It is also easy to understand why some men should want to swallow economic theory in all of its manifestations. But what is not at all clear—except in terms of human frailty—is why a man like Cairnes should be so enamored of literary theory and should then stop short of diagrams and symbols. Or why any modern methodologist should find some virtue in two-dimensional graphs but should draw the line at third or higher dimensions.

I suggest that the reason for such inconsistent methodological views must be found in the psychological and tactical problems which constitute the remaining part of my remarks.

But before leaving the discussion of the logical identity of mathematical symbols and words, I must examine its bearing on a famous utterance of Cairnes. He lived at a time when, as we now know, mathematics was helping bring into birth a great new neoclassical synthesis. Yet Cairnes went so far as to say: "So far as I can see, economic truths are not discoverable through the instrumentality of mathematics. If this view be unsound, there is at hand an easy means of refutation—the production of an economic truth, not before known, which has been thus arrived at." Now this view is the direct opposite of that of Marshall. Marshall in his own way also rather pooh-poohed the use of mathematics. But he regarded it as a way of arriving at truths, but not as a good way of communicating such truths—which is just the opposite of Cairnes's further remarks on the subject.

Well, what are we to think of the crucial experiment proposed by Cairnes? In the first place, he himself was both unable and unwilling to use the mathematical technique; so it might have been possible for us to produce a new truth which Cairnes could never have been capable of recognizing. Indeed, many have cogently argued that Jevons had in fact done so. However, from the methodological viewpoint that I have been expounding, it will be clear that any truth arrived at by way of mathematical manipulation must be translatable into words; and hence, as a matter of logic, could quite possibly have been arrived at by words alone. Reading Cairnes literally, we are not required to produce a truth by mathematics that could not have been proved by words; we are only required to produce one that has not, as a matter of historical fact, been previously produced by words. I suggest that a careful review of the literature since the 1870's will show that a signicant part of all truths since arrived at have in fact been the product of theorists who use symbolic techniques. In particular, Walrasian general equilibrium, which is the peak of neoclassical economics, was already enunciated in Walras' first edition of the *Elements* at the time Cairnes was writing.

Jevons, Walras, and Menger each independently arrived at the so-called "theory of subjective value." And I consider it a lucky bonus for my present thesis that Menger did arrive at his formulation without the use of mathematics. But, in all fairness, I should point out that a recent rereading of the excellent English translation of Menger's 1871 work convinces me that it is the least important of the three works cited; and that its relative neglect by modern writers was not simply the result of bad luck or scholarly negligence. I should also add that the important revolution of the 1870's had little really to do with either subjective value and utility or with marginalism; rather it consisted of the perfecting of the general relations of supply and demand. It culminated in Walrasian general equilibrium. And we are forced to agree with Schumpeter's appraisal of Walras as the greatest of theorists—not because he used mathematics, since the methods used are really quite elementary—but because of the key importance of the concept of general equilibrium itself. We may say of Walras what Lagrange ironically said in praise of Newton: "Newton was assuredly the man of genius *par excellence,* but we must agree that he was also the luckiest: one finds only once the system of the world to be established!" And how lucky he was that "in his time the system of the world still remained to be discovered." Substitute "system of equilibrium" for "system of the world" and Walras for Newton and the equation remains valid.

Summary of Basic Methodology. In leaving my discussion of Methodology with a capital M, let me sum up with a few dogmatic statements. All sciences have the common task of describing and summarizing empirical reality. Economics is no exception. There are no separate methodological problems that face the social scientist different in kind from those that face any other scientist. It is true that the social scientist is part of the reality he describes. The same is true of the physical scientist. It is true that the social scientist in observing a phenomenon may change it. The theory of quantum mechanics, with its Heisenberg uncertainty principle, shows that the same is true of the physical scientist making small-scale observations. Similarly, if we enumerate one by one the alleged differences between the social sciences and other sciences, we find no differences in kind.

Finally, it is clear that no a priori empirical truths can exist in any field. If a thing has a priori irrefutable truth, it must be empty of empirical content. It must be regarded as a meaningless proposition in the technical sense of modern philosophy. At the epistemological frontier, there are certain refined difficulties concerning these matters. But at the rough and ready level that concerns the scientist in his everyday work, the above facts are widely recognized by scientists in every discipline. The only exceptions are to be found in certain backwaters of economics, and I shall not here do more than point the finger of scorn at those who carry into the twentieth century ideas that were not very good even in their earlier heyday.

Differences in Convenience of Languages. I now turn to the really interesting part of the subject. What are the conditions under which one choice of language is more convenient than another? If you are a stenographer required to take rapid dictation, there is no doubt that you will prefer shorthand to old-English lettering. No disinterested third party will ever be in doubt as to whether Roman numerals are less convenient than arabic numerals for the solution of problems in commercial arithmetic; and the same goes for a comparison between a decimal system of coinage and that used by the English.

A comparison between a language like French and one like German or English or Chinese is a little more difficult. We might concede that any proposition in one language is translatable into another. But that is not relevant to the psychological question as to whether one language is intrinsically more convenient for a certain purpose than another. We often hear it said that French is a very clear language, and that German is a very opaque one. This is illustrated by the story that Hegel did not really understand his philosophy until he had read the French translation!

I do not know whether there is anything in this or not. It seems to me that Böhm-Bawerk or Wicksell written in German is quite as straightforward as in English; whereas I find Max Weber or Talcott Parsons difficult to understand in any tongue. I suspect that certain cultures develop certain ways of tackling problems. In nineteenth century German economics it was popular and customary to ask about a problem like interest or value: What is the essence of interest or value? After this qualitative question is answered, then the quantitative level of the rate of interest or price-ratio can be settled. Now I happen to think that this is sterile methodology. But I cannot blame it on the German language.

It is interesting, however, that Menger wrote a letter to Walras on this very subject. As reported by Professor Jaffe's interesting article (*Journal of Political Economy*, 1936), Menger said that mathematics was all very well for certain descriptive purposes, but that it did not enable you to get at the essence of a phenomenon. I wish I thought it were true that the language of mathematics had some special faculty of drawing attention away from pseudo problems of qualitative essence. For, unlike Menger, I should consider that a great advantage.

Baconian and Newtonian Methods. There are many empirical fields where translation into mathematical symbols would seem to have no advantage. Perhaps immunology is one, since I am told not a single cure for disease—vaccination against smallpox, inoculation for diphtheria, use of penicillin and sulpha, and so forth—has been discovered by anything but the crudest empiricism and with sheer accident playing a great role. Here the pedestrian methods of Francis Bacon show up to much greater advantage than do the exalted methods of a Newton. If true, we must simply accept this as a fact. I am sure that many areas of the social sciences and economics are at present in this stage. It is quite possible that many such areas will always continue to be in this stage.

Pareto regarded sociology as being of this type. But curiously enough, he goes on to argue that the chief virtue of mathematics is in its ability to represent complexly interacting and interdependent phenomena. I think we must accept this with a grain of salt. Analogies with complicated interdependent physical systems are valuable if they alert us to the dangers of theories of unilateral causation. But after mathematical notions have performed the function of reminding us that everything depends upon everything else, they may not add very much more—unless some special hypotheses can be made about the facts.

On the other hand, there are areas which over the years have fallen into the hands of the mathematically annointed. Earlier I mentioned the case of symbolic logic. There are still some girls' seminaries where literary logic rules the roost; but no sensible man expects that in the centuries ahead the field of logic will be deloused of mathematics.

Another field is that of physics. Its capture by mathematics is a fact as solid and irreversible as the second law of thermodynamics itself.

It is dangerous to prophesy. But I suspect that in some small degree the same will hold of the field of economic theory. For a century mathematics knocked at the door. Even today it has no more than a foot in the doorway. But the problems of economic theory—such as the incidence of taxation, the effects of devaluation—are by their nature quantitative questions whose answer depends upon a superposition of many different pieces of quantitative and qualitative information. When we tackle them by words, we are solving the same equations as when we write out those equations.

Now I hold no brief for economic theory. I think the pendulum will always swing between interest in concrete description and attempts to construct abstract summaries of experience, with one decade and tradition giving more emphasis to the one process and another time and place giving emphasis to the other. But I do think that when the pendulum is swinging in favor of theory, there will be kind of a Gresham's law operating whereby the more convenient deductive method will displace the less convenient.

Convenience of Symbols for Deduction. And make no mistake about it. To get to some destinations it matters a great deal whether you go afoot or ride by a train. No wise man studying the motion of a top would voluntarily confine himself to words, forswearing all symbols. Similarly, no sensible person who had at his command both the techniques of literary argumentation and mathematical manipulation would tackle by words alone a problem like the following: Given that you must confine all taxes to excises on goods or factors, what pattern of excises is optimal for a Robinson Crusoe or for a community subject to prescribed norms?

I could go on and enumerate other problems. But that is not necessary. All you have to do is pick up a copy of any economic journal and turn to the articles on literary economic theory, and you will prove the point a hundred times over.

The convenience of mathematical symbolism for handling certain deductive inferences is, I think, indisputable. It is going too far to say that mathematicians never make mistakes. Like everybody else, they can pull some awful boners. But it is surprising how rare pure mistakes in logic are. Where the really big mistakes are made is in the formulation of premises. Logic is no protection against false hypotheses; or against misinterpretation of reality; or against the formulation of irrelevant hypotheses. I think it is one of the advantages of the mathematical medium—or, strictly speaking, of the mathematician's customary canons of exposition of proof, whether in words or symbols—that we are forced to lay our cards on the table so that all can see our premises. But I must confess that I have heard of card games—in fact I have participated in them myself—where knowingly or unknowingly, we have dealt cards from the bottom of the deck. So there are no absolute checks against human error.

The Human Dilemma. In conclusion, ask yourself what advice you would have to give to a young man who steps into your office with the following surprisingly common story: "I am interested in economic theory. I know little mathematics. And when I look at the journals, I am greatly troubled. Must I give up hopes of being a theorist? Must I learn mathematics? If so, how much? I am already past twenty-one; am I past redemption?"

Now you could answer him the way Marshall more or less advised Schumpeter: forget economic theory. Diminishing returns has set in there. The world is waiting for a thousand important applications.

This of course is no answer at all. Either the young man disregards your advice, as Schumpeter did. Or he accepts it, and psychologically you have dealt him the cruelest blow of all.

I think a better answer might go somewhat as follows: Some of the most distinguished economic theorists, past and present, have been innocent of mathematics. Some of the most distinguished theorists have known some degree of mathematics. Obviously, you can become a great theorist without knowing mathematics. Yet it is fair to say that you will have to be that much more clever and brilliant.

It happens to be empirically true that if you examine the training and background of all the past great economic theorists, a surprisingly high percentage had, or acquired, at least an intermediate mathematical training. Marshall, Wicksell, Wicksteed, Cassel, and even such literary economists as Nicholson or Malthus provide examples. This is omitting economists like Edgeworth, Cournot, Walras, Pareto, and others who were avowedly mathematical economists.

Moreover, without mathematics you run grave psychological risks. As you grow older, you are sure to resent the method increasingly. Either you will get an inferiority complex and retire from the field of theory or you will get an inferiority complex and become aggressive about your dislike of it. Of course, those are the betting odds and not perfect certainties. The danger is almost greater that you will overrate the method's power for good or evil. You may even become the prey of charlatans who say to you what Euler said to Diderot to get him to leave Catherine the Great's court: "Sir, $(a + b^n)/n = x$, hence God exists; reply!" And, like Diderot, you may slink away in shame. Or reacting against the episode, you may disbelieve the next mathematician who later comes along and gives you a true proof of the existence of the Deity.

In short—your advice will continue—mathematics is neither a necessary nor a sufficient condition for a fruitful career in economic theory. It can be a help. It can certainly be a hindrance, since it is only too easy to convert a good literary economist into a mediocre mathematical economist.

Despite the above advice, it is doubtful that when you check back five years later on that young man he will be very different. Indeed, as I look back over recent years, I am struck by the fact that the species of mathematical economist pure and simple seems to be dying out and becoming extinct. Instead, as one of my older friends complained to me: "These days you can hardly tell a mathematical economist from an ordinary economist." I know the sense in which he meant the remark, but let me reverse its emphasis by concluding with the question: Is that bad?

127

SOME PSYCHOLOGICAL ASPECTS OF MATHEMATICS AND ECONOMICS[1]

When Boswell once asked Johnson's opinion about the previous evening's engagement, the great man replied: "It was a good enough dinner, but not one to ask a man to." Mr. Novick's reflections on mathematics in economics seem to be regarded in pretty much the same critical vein by the eminent practitioners of that art who have leaped to the defense of mathematics. I wonder though whether Novick's piece, unpolished as it is, does not gain all the more in interest from its very casualness. It seems to come right from the stomach. And as Pascal almost said, The stomach has reasons that Reason will never know.

For make no mistake about it: to every economist of the present generation, mathematics presents a psychological problem. Each meets this problem in his own way. Some sublimate their feelings and transfer from economic theory into the area of history of doctrines or . . . labor economics. Others wrestle with the devil and pass sleepy weekends browsing and rebrowsing through the early chapters of R. G. D. Allen's invaluable handbook. Still others ultimately reach a kind of equilibrium without ever having made up their minds whether the hills far off are truly green or whether instead the grapes therein are truly sour.

Of course, none of this talk about psychology has anything to do with the deeper substantive problems of scientific methodology. My own

[1] *Ed. note:* The following is one of a series of replies to David Novick's attack on mathematical economics in *The Review of Economics and Statistics*, Vol. XXXVI, No. 4.

views on the deeper substantive methodological questions and on the pragmatic fruits of mathematics have been expressed elsewhere.[2] Rather than discuss the problem further in general terms, I submit in concrete evidence the paper "The Pure Theory of Public Expenditure" which is published elsewhere in the present issue. In length it takes about the space of Novick's note. I think it fair to say that it contains most of the imperfections of communication so often charged against mathematical economics.

Yet I should not be honest if I didn't state my conviction that it represents a substantial, if modest, contribution to an important problem. Before and after Adam Smith, *benefit theories* of taxation of a most muddled sort have cluttered up the literature; and one who does not understand — in words or symbols or both — the logic involved in this mathematical note cannot, in my view, hope to have a proper grasp of these theoretical issues. This is not to say that a practical budgeter like Mr. Novick need disturb his busy brain over this abstract matter; but there always have been, and there always will be, some who will address themselves to it; and they might as well get the matter straight, appreciating some of its more subtle nuances.

Reverting now to the spicier psychological aspects of mathematics in economics, I should like to throw off a few casual observations — these do not pretend to be connected points of the sort you would invite people to hear, but they may still be of some interest.

1. Mathematics is thought to be a young man's game. Certainly mathematics is easier to learn in one's youth than in one's older years. And it is historically true that the really great achievements in pure mathematics have usually been made by men when they were in the first brilliance of their youth. Nevertheless, I have noted as a glad fact of experience that the *applied* mathematician seems to age gracefully. Pigou, E. B. Wilson, and numerous others provide examples of men who have kept their zest for creative work over the decades.

[2]See T. C. Koopmans' comments in *ibid*, p. 377, note 14. I accept his correction to my earlier empirical conjecture that the race of *pure* mathematical economists is perhaps becoming extinct. I ought also to state that the apparent disagreement between myself and Dorfman as to the sense in which mathematics is a language will evaporate once it is realized that I regard logic as a language in exactly the same sense. I have no substantive disagreement with Tinbergen's admirable list of elements in any contribution to economics; but, semantically, I might prefer to replace his contrast between use of mathematics and non-use by a related but different contrast between use of induction and deduction. In my view mathematical reasoning is formally of the same essence as all logical reasoning, whether the logic is expressed in words, Euler diagrams, or symbols. This raises another issue dealt with by Tinbergen. Not knowing Dutch I cannot properly appraise his cited methodological paper; but from his account, I think I might question whether the usual syllogisms of logic cannot be given a "simultaneous-equation" formulation making them formally identical with the conventional mathematical formulations.

2. There is a viewpoint, which I used to share, that the mathematics of pure mathematics and of physics is intrinsically beautiful, but the mathematics of economics is of an inferior aesthetic order. I think this view is wrong. The simple Ricardian theory of comparative advantage is beautiful, and let no mathematical snob persuade you otherwise.

But let me not be misunderstoood. Part of the extra beauty of any applied mathematics lies in its applicability to some reality. Extra zest comes from following the rules of the game; and it is part of the rules of the game of economic theory that your deductive creations be of *empirical relevance*. Who wants easy victories?

3. That some mathematical researches constitute rather trivial economics no sensible person would deny. I think we can find at least one psychological reason for this: the classical notion that past costs or pains produce value applies in the creative sphere; so if we have worked hard over something, it often gains a value in our own eyes for that reason alone, and independently of its pragmatic merits. I have noted a number of cases where an economist has gone through precisely this pattern of long and difficult creative turmoil, and at the end has been as fascinated as Jack Horner at what he has accomplished.[3]

Granting the validity of this point, you will infer that it chiefly applies to poor and imperfect mathematicians. The cure, you will say, lies primarily in having economists become better mathematicians so that they will quickly and efficiently derive their results and not be bewitched by their own imperfections. I agree with this counsel. But I don't think it entirely solves the problem.

For, no matter how much mathematics you study, there is a frontier at which things become hard: by working with ever more general premises — in which for example you replace the strong assumption of continuity and smoothness by weaker assumptions of bounded variation or upper-semi-continuity — you can succeed in making almost any problem hard. In fact, as puzzle-solving animals, that's part of where our fun comes from. A final optimal solution to this problem can come only from the theorist using his judgment on how refined a treatment the problem merits and his readers will stand for.

[3]Here is a personal instance. As a young student who knew no calculus, I happened to learn about Joan Robinson's rules for relating marginal revenue to average revenue. At the time I was learning a little analytical geometry and I had somewhere picked up the rule for differentiating a simple power x^n: so I wrote out a general polynomial, painfully differentiated it to get the slope of its tangent line at a given point, wrote out the equation for its tangent line, and applied Robinson's geometrical rule about straight-line curves; at the end, after miraculously making no algebraic errors in the long chain of reasoning, I came up with the simple result $d(xp(x))/dx = p(x) + xdp(x)/dx$, which has an obvious literary interpretation. Of course had I known the simplest rule for taking the derivative of a product of two functions, I'd have arrived at this result immediately and for all functions and not just polynomials. But I am sure that I'd never have been so impressed with the result if it had not come as a sudden and beautiful simplification after a long process of sweating.

Moreover, it is counsel of perfection to tell economists to learn more mathematics. Many will remain clumsy. You may therefore jump to the conclusion that they should stay out of mathematical economics completely. And of course ordinary considerations of comparative advantage tell us that many should. None the less I must strongly dissent from the Carlylean notion, held by Colin Clark and others: according to this, only the few great minds of any generation should be economic theorists; the rest of the ordinary folk should fly about busily gathering facts, bringing them back to the hive for the genius queens to turn into grand principles. I believe that knowledge is additive and that the history of economic doctrines suggests that progress comes from unpredictable and varied sources.

4. My final psychological point will at first appear to be opposite to the previous point that the scientist's work input imparts an illusory value of his output. I shall now argue something different.

At the end of every deductive reasoning, after we have finally gained understanding of the implications of our premises and exactly how they lead to various conclusions and theorems — at the end, I say, there almost inevitably enters in a certain disillusionment. "Is that all there is to it?" our mind then feels. "How obvious!"

Consider Newton's famous statement: "I do not know what I may appear to the world, but to myself I seem to have been only like a boy playing on the seashore and diverting myself in now and then finding a smoother pebble or a prettier shell than ordinary whilst the great ocean of truth lay all undiscovered before me."

Most commentators have taken this for excessive modesty — false or genuine. I cannot agree. I think it is a completely honest and characteristic reaction. It can be matched by similar feelings on the part of other great thinkers, such as Lagrange and many others. This same sentiment is expressed in a perceptive statement by Ernst Mach, the physicist: ". . . every general principle brings with it, by the insight which it furnishes, *disillusionment* as well as elucidation. It brings with it disillusionment to the extent that we recognize in it facts which were long before known and even instinctively perceived, our present recognition being simply more distinct and more definite; and elucidation, in that it enables us to see everywhere throughout the most complicated relations the same simple facts."

Why do I dwell on this psychological point? Because often poor mathematicians, such as Novick claims to be, do find it necessary to work through the logical conclusions of some branch of technical economics. This with work they can always do: for there is absolute truth in the saying "What one fool can learn so can another." Now what happens when finally they do grasp the contents of the theory? Quite usually, they genuinely say, "Is that all there is to it? Why poor little me with my infinite ignorance can easily understand that — in fact I probably knew it all along. What was all the fuss about?"

This disillusionment, which is a legitimate phenomenon for the reasons I have just discussed, leads in a natural but illegitimate way to the feeling that some charlatan has been caught perpetrating a swindle. Actually, to those adept at symbols, *there has been no fuss*! On the contrary, the matter has been dispatched in the simplest fashion toward its common-sense — for all logico-mathematic derivations simply depict common-sense implications — conclusions.

Charlatans and self-impressed scholars exist in every field. But no one who seriously studied empirically the very real psychological stresses and tensions between literary and non-literary economists will find that serious problems are created by swindling second-raters who dabble in symbols. It was Cournot, and Walras, and Edgeworth, and Pareto — yes, and Marshall, too — who gave ulcers to the older generation of economists. And today it is Pigou, and Hicks, and Hotelling, and Koopmans, and Frisch, and — but why prolong the list? — who pose grave issues for the student. Only if you swallow Novick's deep-down view — that all their work has been trivial — can you regard the problem of charlatanism as one of any importance. The real problem goes much deeper and will, I think, long persist.

128

COMMENT ON "PROFESSOR SAMUELSON ON OPERATIONALISM IN ECONOMIC THEORY"

Professor Donald F. Gordon* has listed five criticisms of the methodology of my *Foundations of Economic Analysis*. To the extent that I understand his arguments, it is primarily his fourth criticism concerned with the Correspondence Principle relating dynamic stability and comparative statics that seems to me to be in need of amplification and

---

*"Professor Samuelson on Operationalism in Economic Theory," *Quarterly Journal of Economics*, May 1955, pp. 305–310. His criticisms were briefly as follows:

1. The principles of maximization and dynamic stability of the foundations are insufficient. To them must be added the hypothesis that the functions do not shift unpredictably, a "foundation" which can only be established by hard empirical work.

2. "There is no point to Samuelson's analysis of the effects of a shift in a function due to a change in 'tastes,' or a shift which is presumably an autonomous change in behavior patterns since it is left unexplained."

3. ". . . the two hypotheses may be, from a methodological point of view, not even necessary."

4. "Recent theories of the business cycle, as well as various forms of the cobweb theorem, suggest that actual economic variables may possess *no* stable equilibrium values over the observable range, yet the values observed may all be points on stable functions." The points observed are neither of dynamically stable nor of nonstable-equilibrium.

5. Samuelson asserts that what "little success" economists have had in arriving at propositions in comparative statics is due to the use of the correspondence principle. Older economists, such as Smith, did not use the principle in arriving at comparative statics conclusions, such as that when the supply of a commodity falls short of the demand, the price will rise, but rather based such statements on empirical observations.

qualification. Here are my reactions to the specific points Gordon makes. I hope that these hasty interpretations will be regarded as tentative.

Criticism 1. The hypothesis that a competitive firm with an unchanging cost curve will never reduce its quantity supplied when market price rises is according to my use of terms a meaningful proposition: i.e., it is conceptually an empirically refutable proposition. I continue to aver that the hypothesis of profit maximization is sufficient to deduce this hypothesis.

Gordon's criticism seems to me to be concerned not so much with the sufficiency of my reasoning but rather with the quite different problem of how we go about deciding that a conceptually meaningful proposition is or is not a fruitful hypothesis and whether as a result of any particular observations we are to decide that it has or has not been refuted.[1] This is an important question: indeed much of the whole theory of statistical inference is concerned with little else, and in the last decades due to the work of Haavelmo, Koopmans, Frisch, Elmer Working, and other writers on the problem of "identification" a small start on a satisfactory theory has been made. I do not think that I discussed this issue anywhere in *Foundations*, and in retrospect I feel little urge to have done so. To test, refute, or "verify" a meaningful proposition is a tough empirical job and no amount of flossy deduction can obviate this. Realizing this should not be disillusioning; and it certainly should not tempt one to belittle meaningful propositions in favor of empty ones.

Criticism 2. This does overlap with the first point. Again Gordon seems to me to be saying: "In real life, observed changes are often the result of simultaneous changes in numerous parameters; but just which parameters have changed or how great are the relative quantitative magnitudes of the changes is a most difficult question to answer. Therefore, it is wrong (or misleading? or useless?) to try to set up meaningful hypotheses about the *ceteris paribus* effects of changes in each datum taken separately." I do not think the second sentence follows from the truth of the first.

There is one special point in this second criticism that may require special comment. I do indeed think there is point in analyzing changes in "tastes." How will thriftiness affect capital formation? How will a shift from beer to tea affect markets? How will knowledge on the part of the consumer that liver is good for anemia affect the relative prices of kidneys and liver? These are perfectly legitimate questions to ask, whether or not we have an "explanation" for the change in tastes. Indeed, in a fundamental methodological sense, it is precisely the

---

[1]E.g., a fall in quantity supplied by a maximizing competitor may have been due to a simultaneous factor price increase.

changes in the parameters or data of a system that are, within the framework of *that* system, unexplainable. I do not see that I, or Schelling, or Hicks (some of whose *Value and Capital* theorems refer to defined changes in tastes) have any reason to avoid trying to answer such questions. I only wish that we had better success in doing so.

Criticism 3. To me this says that there may be ways of forming meaningful hypotheses other than by postulating maximization or dynamic stability. Of course, there are. No one has ever doubted it.

Observe market behavior over time; make statistical scatter diagrams; and if the result suggests to you the hypothesis that the marginal propensity to consume is exactly .925, or that the elasticity of demand for rye is $-.70$, or that the propensity to save schedule is concave from above — then well and good, for these are all meaningful, refutable hypotheses.

Criticism 4. The point made here seems to me to be a very fruitful one. The Correspondence Principle is a vague line of deductive reasoning by which we can under certain circumstances deduce, from the hypothesis that a stipulated system is dynamically stable, various implied hypotheses about its comparative statical properties appropriate to a permanent shift in a parameter to which corresponds a new stationary equilibrium position. There is much that is unsatisfactory about the exposition of this heuristic principle and about our knowledge of its deductive properties. But the point that Gordon is here concerned with is a different one. In *Foundations* I did not content myself with deriving these formal properties: in addition, I stepped forward as a man of the world and casual empiricist and stated my opinion that the hypothesis of dynamical stability was a "realistic" one to make. I am no longer so sure of this.

True, there is something vaguely persuasive about the doctrine of "the nonpersistence of unstable states" that Gordon quotes from my book: indeed, as my reference to L. J. Henderson will show, this is not a new thought originated by Keynes to refute criticisms made in this *Journal* concerning the properties of the marginal propensity to consume; instead it can be traced back to Hippocrates, to Maxwell, to Gibbs, to Darwin, and to a host of philosophers; and when the Smyth Report told us that a certain sized arrangement of Uranium 235 would explode, most of us amateurs used this heuristic reasoning to predict that such concentrations of Uranium 235 were not likely to be found in nature by geologists.

None the less, you never get something for nothing and never empirical hypotheses from empty deductive definitions. At best your observation can tell you only that the real world (or some subset of it) is not exploding; your theoretical model or system will always be an idealized representation of the real world with many variables ignored; it may be precisely the ignored variables that keep the real world stable, and it takes a significant act of inductive inference to rule this out and permit the Correspondence Principle to deduce properties of the idealized model.

Here is an example. Some critics of Keynes alleged that he did believe, and needed to believe, that the consumption function is convex. Closer reading of his book shows this not to be so. Keynes replied arguing that all that he required was a marginal propensity to consume of less than one. And even if this were not granted, he felt that this would simply throw on the doubter the need to explain why the capitalistic system is not hopelessly unstable.[2]

Well, maybe the system *is* unstable. That is one possibility, and as Gordon is cogently pointing out, many of the cobweb cycles and auto-relaxation trade cycle theories of such moderns as Kaldor, Goodwin, Hicks, and others are squarely based on the notion of a system that is locally unstable at its stationary levels so that it oscillates — but because of such nonlinear elements as full-employment ceilings, capacity limitations, impossibility of disinvesting faster than at certain limiting rates, the system oscillates with a preferred finite amplitude.

A priori reasoning will not settle this empirical question. During the late 1930's I felt, and so perhaps did writers like Professor Lloyd Metzler, that the observed behavior of the macroaggregates of the American economy was most compatible with the hypothesis of dynamic stability: in those days it seemed hard rather than easy for the system to generate self-aggravating cumulative movements of explosive type. This view may have been wrong, and we may have been too confident in expressing it.[3] Or it may have been a fruitful hypothesis for that period but not one for the present decade. Or it may still be fruitful. These are important empirical questions that cannot be answered by dividing dichotomously the world's possibilities into categories of stable and unstable and inferring that our observed world by its not having exploded away is necessarily in the stable category. So I concur in Gordon's misgiving.

---

[2]My discussion of the Correspondence Principle should have made clearer the possibility that the world is stable but that our model — in this case a simple income model — is too simple to portray the world correctly. Thus, the marginal propensity to consume might exceed unity, but tightness of the money supply and movements of interest rates might be what prevents explosion. This raises questions of empirical judgment.

[3]Readers of the modern cycle literature may receive the misleading impression that economists started with linear models and then arrived at nonlinear ones. The historical patterns are the reverse: most of the literary models that antedate the work of Frisch, Tinbergen, Metzler, and myself were very definitely nonlinear. One of the things we thought worth showing was the fact that no separate theory of the turning points or of the four phases of the cycle was needed: the same linear model could be shown to be theoretically capable of producing all phases of the cycle. This does not deny that there may be some truth to Haberler's gibe that with their nonlinear models the econometricians are almost catching up to the literary economists.

Criticism 5. Here the question is whether older economists used the so-called Correspondence Principle in arriving at comparative statical results. And did they know they were using it? To the latter question the answer is surely, No. They could not have known the name, obviously; and they were not so self-conscious as to analyze the logical structure of many of their intuitions. But were they, so to speak, talking prose all their lives without knowing it?

I have never seriously examined the writings of Adam Smith and other economists to see just how much of the logic involved in the Correspondence Principle can by sympathetic reasoning be imputed to them. I therefore welcome Gordon's quoted passage from Smith and will give it brief mathematical formulation:

$$(1) \qquad dp/dt = k(D - S)$$

where k is a positive number that may be approximated by a constant and where D is the quantity demanded (as shown by the demand schedule) and S is the quantity supplied (as shown by the supply schedule). To parrot Gordon's words, "Very likely Adam Smith would be surprised to find that he talked in terms of differential equations as well as prose." But, of course, how we choose to describe the contents of his thought will not alter its content or be relevant to his terminology.

Granting equation (1), do we conclude that it supplants or contradicts the Correspondence Principle? Not at all. From (1) alone, Smith and Gordon cannot conclude anything about *comparative statics*. They can make the following *comparative dynamic statement*: "If price has been stationary, and if after time t_0 the demand curve shifts rightward (and remains there), then in the following time intervals we can expect price to rise from its initial level." That is all.

If now we want to make a comparative static statement, we must somehow add hypotheses. Thus, we might stipulate the empirical hypothesis that such a shift in demand will always be followed by an approach to a new stationary equilibrium. This is an hypothesis of dynamic stability: and with this hypothesis, we can infer from (1) that the comparative statical price change must be positive. But in so doing we are using — guess what? Of course, the Correspondence Principle.[4]

In conclusion, may I repeat my lack of confidence that I have correctly apprehended Professor Gordon's friendly criticisms.

PAUL A. SAMUELSON

[4]An even better case is provided by Gordon's earlier example of the simple multiplier model: $y_t = cy_{t-1} + I$, where all variables are measured in deviations from some equilibrium levels. Our primitive instinct is dynamic: a higher marginal propensity to consume c or I will raise money income. But if c is already greater than one, the comparative statical theorem tells us that a permanent rise in autonomous investment or consumption spending is compatible only with a *lower* level of income! Again, it is the Correspondence Principle that is involved, only this time on the pathological side.

129

COMMENT ON ERNEST NAGEL'S "ASSUMPTIONS IN ECONOMIC THEORY"

When Maxwell's Demon rank orders scientific disciplines by their "fruitfulness" and by their propensity to engage in methodological discussion, he finds a negative correlation and a strong inverse relationship. It is as if a science could lift itself by its own bootstraps: by maintaining a superlative silence on method, a science can become superlatively fruitful and accurate. Like many "as if" statements this is nonsense. It is more correct, albeit not very informative, to say that soft sciences spend time in talking about method because Satan finds tasks for idle hands to do. Nature does abhor a vacuum and hot air fills up more space than cold. When libertines lose the power to shock us, they take up moral pontification to bore us.

But, of course, I jest. Methodological discussion, like calisthenics and spinach, is good for us, and Dr. Nagel deserves our thanks for taking the time away from other sciences to help straighten us economists out. It is the Lord's work, and we are grateful.

As I understand his paper, Nagel comes to save Milton Friedman from himself. Nagel believes that "theory" does have an important role to play in economics and any discipline, but that Friedman's attempt in his essay on positive economics to vindicate the importance of abstract theory involves mistakes which might themselves be wrongly held against theory's establishable role.

I think Nagel's paper[1] is valuable in pointing out certain errors in

[1]Ernest Nagel, "Assumptions in Economic Theory," *American Economic Review*, May 1963 Proceedings, pp. 211–219.

the stated claims for theory. I think, within the limits imposed by his need for brevity, it performs the constructive function of sketching some valid arguments for the useful role of theories in an empirical science. But Professor Nagel is too polite. He has not, to my mind, vindicated against itself that which was special and distinctive in the Friedman[2] methodology; instead he seems to have jettisoned what might be called the special "Friedman Twist." And rightly so, I am afraid.

Let me first state some valid interpretations of the "as if" character of using theory to help organize our descriptions of empirical reality. Then point out some illegitimate interpretations.

When a writer on positive economics says that hypotheses or theories should be judged on their "consequences" — or their ability to describe well and organize well empirical observations — he is saying something valuable. Valuable, but perhaps not new. Pragmatists have long insisted that a theory's worth is measured by the consequences of believing it rather than something else or nothing else. Scientists and philosophers who never read Peirce, James, Dewey, Mach, Bridgman, or Carnap have enunciated this same view.

Heinrich Hertz said that a belief in Maxwell's theory of light meant nothing more and nothing less than that the observable measurements agreed with the partial differential equations of Maxwell. (With the advent of quantum mechanics and wave theory the situation became one of *reductio non ad absurdum:* physicists didn't know or much care what it was that was waving in Schrödinger's equation, a probability or what not, so long as the facts of refraction and emission could be described well by this mnemonic model.) Poincaré said that the whole content of classical dynamics was summed up in the hypothesis that certain sets of second-order differential equations exhibited solutions that to a good approximation duplicated the behavior of celestial bodies and terrestrial particles. Pascal made generous use of Occam's Razor in his "explanation" of why "nature abhors a vacuum [period or up to 30 inches of mercury and 30 feet of water]" was an inferior theory to one which assumes that there is an equilibrium balance reached between the "weight" of the unseen atmosphere and the seen mercury and water columns. When Newton wrote down his system of the world, he explicitly said what would have to be translated into modern terminology as "I don't care to speculate why n-bodies behave in accordance with the inverse-square law of gravity and acceleration; I am content to show what are the implications of this law in contrast to the implications of variant hypotheses, and to present my calculations demonstrating agreement with the observations of moons, apples, and planets."

So long as light rays continue to act so as to go from place to place by

[2]Milton Friedman, *Essays in Positive Economics* (Chicago: University of Chicago Press, 1953).

the paths of least time, except as a figure of speech no one insisted that they exercised conscious, self-conscious, deliberative will. At worst, some scientists who were Deists, or Sunday poets, said that God or Nature acted like a Great Economizer.

None of the above is banal or trite. As against other authorities who insisted on seeking "more ultimate explanations," these writers said what needed to be said and Professor Friedman is a welcome recruit to their camp. But what I and other readers believe is his new twist — which from now on I shall call the "F-Twist," avoiding his name because this may be, and I hope it is, a misinterpretation of his intention — is the following: A theory is vindicable if (some of) its consequences are empirically valid to a useful degree of approximation; the (empirical) unrealism of the theory "itself," or of its "assumptions," is quite irrelevant to its validity and worth.

At points, the F-Twist seems to go even farther and claim: It is a positive merit of a theory that (some of) its content and assumptions be unrealistic since only if it is not tailored closely to one small bit of reality can it give a useful fit to a wide spread of empirical situations. Unless we explain complex reality by something simpler than itself we have accomplished little (period or by theorizing).

The last part of this F-Twist is separable from its basic part. While I believe that this last part is misphrased and that its germ of truth should be stated in other terms, brevity forbids my discussing it here and forces me to concentrate on the basic F-Twist, which is fundamentally wrong in thinking that unrealism in the sense of factual inaccuracy even to a tolerable degree of approximation is anything but a demerit for a theory or hypothesis (or set of hypotheses). Some inaccuracies are worse than others, but that is only to say that some sins against empirical science are worse than others, not that a sin is a merit or that a small sin is equivalent to a zero sin.

To a philosopher or scientist, the F-Twist is of no great moment, and its discussion might perhaps be bypassed. To present-day economics — and I daresay to Professor Friedman — its validity would be of considerable moment. For, as Rotwein (*Q.J.E.*, 1959) and others have hinted, the nonpositivistic Milton Friedman has a strong effective demand which a valid F-Twist brand of positivism could supply. The motivation for the F-Twist, critics say, is to help the case for (1) the perfectly competitive laissez-faire model of economics, which has been under continuous attack from outside the profession for a century and from within since the monopolistic competition revolution of thirty years past; and (2), but of lesser moment, the "maximization-of-profit" hypothesis, that mixture of truism, truth, and untruth.

If Dr. Friedman tells us this was not so; if his psychoanalyst assures us that his testimony in this case is not vitiated by subconscious motivations; even if Maxwell's Demon and a Jury in Heaven concur — still it would seem a fair use of the F-Twist itself to say: "Our theory about the origin and purpose of the F-Twist may be 'unrealistic' (a euphemism for 'empirically dead wrong'), but what of that? The consequence of our theory agrees with the fact that Chicagoans use the methodology to explain away objections to their assertions."

This, however, is cheap humor. It is hard lines to hoist a man on his own petard, while at the same time arguing that there exists no such valid petard. I must be brief in explaining why the F-Twist lacks validity. Many of these arguments can actually be found in Friedman's essay, as Nagel has noted; but that may only indicate a noble inconsistency rather than invulnerability. Besides, I am discussing the F-Twist, not any person's views, and by any other name, such as the S-Twist, it would be just as bad.

1. Define a "theory" (call it B) as a set of axioms, postulates, or hypotheses that stipulate something about observable reality. (If no conceivable observation can even in principle refute, confirm, or touch or bear upon the axiom system taken as a whole, then B is not economics, astronomy, physics, biology, or anything properly called science. It might be a model of language, logic, mathematics, mathematical probability or geometry, or game-playing — but that is something different.)

2. A reader of Friedman might be forgiven for lapsing into thinking that the thing called B has consequences (call them C) that somehow come after it or are implied by it and that are somehow different from it.

3. That same reader might be forgiven for thinking that just as B has consequences C that come after it, it also has some things which are somehow antecedent to it called its "assumptions" (and which we can label A).

4. The F-Twist says that the empirical realism, at least up to some "tolerable degree of approximation," of C is important. If C is empirically valid (realistic), then B is important even if A — and for that matter B itself — is not empirically valid (is unrealistic in the sense of being empirically at variance with known or knowable facts, at any tolerable level of approximation).

5. If C is the complete set of consequences of B, it is identical with B. B implies itself and all the things that itself implies. There can be no factual correctness of C so defined that is not also enjoyed by B. The minimal set of assumptions that give rise to B are identical with B, and if A is given this interpretation, its realism cannot differ from that of the theory B and consequence C.

6. But now consider a proper subset of C, which contains some but not all of the implications of B and which we may call $C-$. And consider

a widened set of assumptions that includes A as a proper subset, so that it implies A (and B and C and $C-$) but is not fully implied by A. Call this $A+$.

In symbolic notation we can say

$$A + \supset A \equiv B \equiv C \supset C-$$

7. Now, suppose that C has complete (or satisfactory) empirical validity. Then bully for it. And bully for the theory B and for its assumption A.

8. We cannot say bully for $A+$ in the same sense — unless its full content, which we may call $A+ \equiv B+ \equiv C+$, also has empirical validity. If that part of $C+$ which is not in C is unrealistic in the sense of being empirically false at the required level of approximation, then $A+$ is definitely the worse for it. The invalidity of part of $A+$ is not irrelevant to its worth. If only the A subset of $A+$ is valid, then so much the worse for $(A+) - (A)$ and for $A+$.

If as often happens we do not have evidence on the factual inaccuracy or accuracy for $A+$, we simply reserve judgment about it, and keep saying bully for A. If no evidence can bear on $(A+) - (A)$, then we use Occam's Razor and concentrate on $A \equiv B \equiv C$ above, forgetting $A+$.

9. It should be unnecessary for me to explain why the empirical validity of $C-$ does not, of itself, import any luster to $A \equiv B \equiv C-$ unnecessary because this is the same logical case as I have just disposed of.

This completes my demonstration that the F-Twist is fallacious. I shall illustrate briefly with some examples, primarily economic.

Let B be maximizing ordinal utility (satisfying certain regularity conditions) subject to a budget constraint defined by given income and prices.

Let C be the Weak and Strong Axioms of revealed preference, which are stated in testable form involving $\sum P_j Q_j$, price-quantity data. My above arguments will show how misleading it is to think such tests are in any genuine sense "indirect" ones.

It happens that C implies B as well as being implied by it. It is nonsense to think that C could be realistic and B unrealistic, and nonsense to think that the unrealism of B could then arise and be irrelevant.

But suppose the Weak Axiom, $C-$, is valid and the Strong Axiom is definitely not. If the F-Twist means anything, it says, "Never mind that B is unrealistic; its consequence $C-$ is realistic, and that is all that counts."

Surely this is nonsense. B has been shown to be empirically false. That $C-$, one of its implications, is valid does not in any way atone for the fact that $(C) - (C-)$ is definitely false. Only that part of B

which is $C-$ has been vindicated by the validity of $C-$. That other part, $(B) - (B-)$, has been refuted. The only sensible thing to do, I mean the only thing to do, is jettison $(B) - (B-)$ and replace as your theory $B-$. If you say, "But $B-$ is a truncated fragment of the organic whole B, and it is odd to call $B-$ my theory," I simply reply: "How do you define organic wholes, and anyway I'd rather have the valid tail of a theory than have an invalid dog's body attached to that tail. What is required is not Occam's Razor so much as God's Hatchet."

Similar examples could be given where it is a question of maximizing profit and not utility. Let me add as an aside that I should be astonished to find a beast who consistently satisfied the Weak Axiom and consistently violated the Strong Axiom. That beast has a nonintegrable preference field. While I can see why a man with a mind should exercise it consistently, I fail to see why a beast with no mind should satisfy the Weak Axiom or even consistency of demand choices. I am here applying Samuelson's Razor, which, unlike Occam's which is primarily aesthetic, is based on a lifetime of sad experience: All economic regularities that have no common-sense core that you can explain to your wife will soon fail. This cannot be said of all that you can explain to her; so my statement is not an empty one. It is considerations like this which make me think that the Alchian doctrine of survival adds something to the maximization hypothesis.

Almost all the remarks about the $S = \dfrac{1}{2} gt^2$ law for falling bodies that Friedman thinks support his thesis seem to me misleading. They could as well, or poorly, apply to a purely empirical theory that says: The first terms in a Taylor's expansion for motion of a body at rest released at $S = 0$ are of the form $S = 0 + 0t + \dfrac{1}{2} gt^2 +$ remainder.

Galileo's simple theory, $S''(t) = + g$, has a subset of consequences that is in tolerable agreement with some facts; e.g., for t "small," $S''(t) = + g$. But it, B, is vastly inferior, as every parachute jumper, golfer, and schoolboy knows, to $B*$ which says $S'' = - f(S') + g$, $f(0) = 0$, $f'(S') > 0$ and which correctly predicts $S'''(t) \neq 0$ and, $t \overset{\text{lim}}{\rightarrow} \infty$ $S'(t) =$ a constant; etc., etc.

To reject, as I was taught to do in Chicago, monopolistic competition on the ground that it is not a "nice, simple, unified" theory like that of perfect competition is like insisting that $f(S') \equiv 0$ because that is simpler and more manageable. If perfect competition is the best simple theory in town, that is no excuse for saying we should regard it as a good theory if it is not a good theory. To use the F-Twist to minimize its imperfections or irrelevancies is, as I have argued, simply wrong.

We must not impose a regularity — or approximate regularity — in the complex facts which is not there. Good science discerns regularities and simplicities that are there in reality — I almost said "out there." Epicycles are more horrid than perfect circles, but the ancient astronomers were right to abandon perfect circles and not say, "Well, even if wrong or imperfect, they are the best wheels in town."

Post-Copernicans were also wrong to go to the stake for the belief that Keplerian ellipses, B, were a more correct theory than epicycles, B^*. Relativism should have told both sides that this was a nonsense issue. Actually, B^* is merely a representation of B and deductively $B \equiv B^*$. However, to imperfect human minds the B^* formulation "looks" simpler and has the great mnemonic virtues of "economical description" which Mach rightly recognizes as the essence of good science. Mach has few friends today: physicists who confuse the psychological process of arriving at notions with the validity of those notions find him sterile. I should record that my experience with economics led me to notions that seem much like Mach's.

There is a final point, which was perhaps not made explicitly by Nagel, Friedman, or Mach and yet which I feel I share with Einstein and practitioners of harder sciences.

Experience suggests that nature displays a mysterious simplicity if only we can discern it. This is a bonus and need not have been so. And unrealistic, abstract models often prove useful in the hunt for these regularities. (Sometimes they prove misleading to a whole generation of searchers.)

This psychological usefulness should not be confused with empirical validity. Black coffee may be useful to physicists, mathematicians, economists, and artists. But coffee is coffee. Such abstract models are like scaffolding used to build a structure; the structure must stand by itself. If the abstract models contain empirical falsities, we must jettison the models, not gloss over their inadequacies.

The empirical harm done by the F-Twist is this. In practice it leads to Humpty-Dumptiness. Lewis Carroll had Humpty-Dumpty use words any way he wanted to. I have in mind something different: Humpty-Dumpty uses the F-Twist to say, "What I choose to call an admissible amount of unrealism and empirical invalidity is the tolerable amount of unrealism."

The fact that nothing is perfectly accurate should not be an excuse to relax our standards of scrutiny of the empirical validity that the propositions of economics do or do not possess.

CONTENTS

Volume I

Contents

ACKNOWLEDGMENTS

The author, editor, and The M.I.T. Press wish to thank the publishers of the following essays for permission to reprint them here. The selections are arranged chronologically, with cross references in brackets to the chapter numbers used in this collection.

"A Note on Measurement of Utility," *The Review of Economic Studies*, Vol. IV, No. 2 (February 1937), pp. 155–161. [Chapter 20]

"Some Aspects of the Pure Theory of Capital," *The Quarterly Journal of Economics*, Vol. LI (May 1937), pp. 469–496. [Chapter 17]

"A Note on the Pure Theory of Consumer's Behaviour," *Economica*, Vol. V, No. 17 (February 1938), pp. 61–71. [Chapter 1]

"Welfare Economics and International Trade," *The American Economic Review*, Vol. XXVIII, No. 2 (June 1938), pp. 261–266. [Chapter 60]

"A Note on the Pure Theory of Consumer's Behaviour: An Addendum," *Economica*, Vol. V (August 1938), pp. 353–354. [Chapter 1]

"The Numerical Representation of Ordered Classifications and the Concept of Utility," *The Review of Economic Studies*, Vol. VI, No. 1 (October 1938), pp. 65–70. [Chapter 2]

"The Empirical Implications of Utility Analysis," *Econometrica*, Vol. 6, No. 4, (October 1938), pp. 344–356. [Chapter 3]

"The Rate of Interest under Ideal Conditions," *The Quarterly Journal of Economics*, Vol. LIII, No. 2 (February 1939), pp. 286–297. [Chapter 18]

"The End of Marginal Utility," *Economica*, Vol. VI (February 1939), pp. 86–87. [Chapter 4]

"The Gains from International Trade," *Canadian Journal of Economics and Political Science*, Vol. 5, No. 2 (May 1939), pp. 195–205. [Chapter 61]

"Interactions between the Multiplier Analysis and the Principle of Acceleration," *The Review of Economics and Statistics*, Vol. XXI, No. 2 (May 1939), pp. 75–78. Copyright 1939 by the President and Fellows of Harvard College. [Chapter 82]

Acknowledgments

"A Synthesis of the Principle of Acceleration and the Multiplier," *The Journal of Political Economy*, Vol. XLVII, No. 6 (December 1939), pp. 786–797. Copyright 1939 by the University of Chicago. [Chapter 83]

"The Theory of Pump-Priming Reëxamined," *The American Economic Review*, Vol. XXX, No. 3 (September 1940), pp. 492–506. [Chapter 85]

"Concerning Say's Law," abstract of a paper read to Econometric Society at New Orleans, December 1940, published in *Econometrica*, Vol. 9, No. 2 (April 1941), pp. 177–178. [Chapter 88]

"The Stability of Equilibrium: Comparative Statics and Dynamics," *Econometrica*, Vol. 9, No. 2 (April 1941), pp. 97–120. [Chapter 38]

"A Statistical Analysis of the Consumption Function," Appendix in A. H. Hansen, *Fiscal Policy and Business Cycles* (New York: W. W. Norton, 1941), pp. 250–260. [Chapter 87]

"Conditions that the Roots of a Polynomial Be Less than Unity in Absolute Value," *The Annals of Mathematical Statistics*, Vol. XXI, No. 3 (September 1941), pp. 360–364. [Chapter 45]

"Professor Pigou's Employment and Equilibrium," *The American Economic Review*, Vol. XXXI, No. 3 (September 1941), pp. 545–552. [Chapter 89]

With W. F. Stolper, "Protection and Real Wages," *The Review of Economic Studies*, Vol. IX, No. 1 (November 1941), pp. 58–73. [Chapter 66]

"A Note on Alternative Regressions," *Econometrica*, Vol. 10, No. 1 (January 1942), pp. 80–83. [Chapter 46]

"The Stability of Equilibrium: Linear and Nonlinear Systems," *Econometrica*, Vol. 10, No. 1 (January 1942), pp. 1–25. [Chapter 40]

"Constancy of the Marginal Utility of Income," in Lange *et al.*, eds., *Studies in Mathematical Economics and Econometrics, in Memory of Henry Schultz* (Chicago: University of Chicago Press, 1942), pp. 75–91. Copyright 1942 by the University of Chicago. [Chapter 5]

"Fiscal Policy and Income Determination," *The Quarterly Journal of Economics*, Vol. LVI, No. 4 (August 1942), pp. 575–605. [Chapter 86]

"The Business Cycle and Urban Development," in Guy Greer, ed., *The Problem of the Cities and Towns*, Conference on Urbanism, Harvard University, March 5–6, 1942, pp. 6–17. [Chapter 97]

"A Method of Determining Explicitly the Coefficients of the Characteristic Equation," *The Annals of Mathematical Statistics*, Vol. XIII, No. 4 (December 1942), pp. 424–429. [Chapter 47]

"Dynamics, Statics, and the Stationary States," essays in honor of Joseph Schumpeter, *The Review of Economics and Statistics*, Vol. XXV, No. 1 (February 1943), pp. 58–68. Copyright by the President and Fellows of Harvard College. [Chapter 19]

"Full Employment after the War," in S. E. Harris, ed., *Postwar Economic Problems* (New York: McGraw-Hill, 1943), pp. 27–53. Copyright 1943 by McGraw-Hill Book Co. [Chapter 108]

"Fitting General Gram-Charlier Series," *The Annals of Mathematical Statistics*, Vol. XIV, No. 2 (June 1943), pp. 179–187. [Chapter 48]

"A Fundamental Multiplier Identity," *Econometrica*, Vol. II, No. 3–4 (July–October 1943), pp. 221–226. [Chapter 90]

"Further Commentary on Welfare Economics," *The American Economic Review*, Vol. XXXIII, No. 3 (September 1943), pp. 605–607. [Chapter 76]

"A Simple Method of Interpolation," *Proceedings of the National Academy of Sciences*, Vol. 29, No. 11 (December 1943), pp. 397–401. [Chapter 49]

"Efficient Computation of the Latent Vectors of a Matrix," *Proceedings of the National Academy of Sciences*, Vol. 29, No. 11 (December 1943), pp. 393–397. [Chapter 50]

"The Relation between Hicksian Stability and True Dynamic Stability," *Econometrica*, Vol. 12, Nos. 3 and 4 (July–October 1944), pp. 256–257. [Chapter 39]

"The Effect of Interest Rate Increases on the Banking System," *The American Economic Review*, Vol. XXXV, No. 1 (March 1945), pp. 16–27. [Chapter 50]

"The Turn of the Screw," *American Economic Review*, Vol. XXXV, No. 4 (September 1945), pp. 674–676. [Chapter 96]

"A Convergent Iterative Process," *Journal of Mathematics and Physics*, Vol. XXIV, Nos. 3–4 (November 1945), pp. 131–134. [Chapter 51]

Book review of Jacob L. Mosak, *General Equilibrium Theory in International Trade* in *The American Economic Review*, Vol. XXXV, No. 5 (December 1945), pp. 943–945. [Chapter 63]

"Comparative Statics and the Logic of Economic Maximizing," *The Review of Economic Studies*, Vol. XIV (1), No. 35 (1946–1947), pp. 41–43. [Chapter 6]

"A Connection between the Bernoulli and Newton Iterative Processes," *Bulletin of the American Mathematical Society*, Vol. 52, No. 3 (March 1946), p. 239. [Chapter 54]

"Computation of Characteristic Vectors," *Bulletin of the American Mathematical Society*, Vol. 52, No. 3 (March 1946), pp. 239–240. [Chapter 53]

"Generalization of the Laplace Transform for Difference Equations," *Bulletin of the American Mathematical Society*, Vol. 52, No. 3 (March 1946), p. 240. [Chapter 52]

With C. C. Holt, "The Graphic Depiction of Elasticity of Demand," *The Journal of Political Economy*, Vol. LIV, No. 4 (August 1946), pp. 354–357. Copyright 1946 by the University of Chicago. [Chapter 7]

"A Generalized Newton Iteration," *Bulletin of the American Mathematical Society*, Vol. 53, No. 3 (March 1947), p. 283. [Chapter 56]

"Generalization of the Laplace Transform for Any Operator," *Bulletin of the American Mathematical Society*, Vol. 53, No. 3 (March 1947), pp. 283–284. [Chapter 55]

Acknowledgments

"Some Implications of 'Linearity'," *The Review of Economic Studies*, Vol. XV (2), No. 38 (1947–1948), pp. 88–90. [Chapter 8]

"The Simple Mathematics of Income Determination," in L. A. Metzler *et al.*, *Income, Employment and Public Policy: Essays in Honor of Alvin Hansen* (New York: W. W. Norton, 1948). [Chapter 91]

"Dynamic Process Analysis" for the American Economic Association's *A Survey of Contemporary Economics*, Vol. I, ed. by Howard Ellis (Philadelphia: Blakiston, 1948: Homewood, Illinois: Richard D. Irwin, 1952). [Chapter 41]

"Disparity in Postwar Exchange Rates," in Seymour Harris, ed., *Foreign Economic Policy for the United States* (Cambridge: Harvard University Press, 1948), pp. 397–412. Copyright 1948 by the President and Fellows of Harvard College. [Chapter 64]

"Exact Distribution of Continuous Variables in Sequential Analysis," *Econometrica*, Vol. 16, No. 2 (April 1948), pp. 191–198. [Chapter 57]

"International Trade and Equalisation of Factor Prices," *Economic Journal*, Vol. LVIII, No. 230 (June 1948), pp. 163–184. [Chapter 67]

"Consumption Theory in Terms of Revealed Preference," *Economica*, Vol. XV (November 1948), pp. 243–253. [Chapter 9]

"International Factor-Price Equalisation Once Again," *Economic Journal*, Vol. LIX, No. 234 (June 1949), pp. 181–197. [Chapter 68]

Book Review of Hla Myint, *Theories of Welfare Economics* in *Economica*, Vol. XVI (November 1949), pp. 371–374. [Chapter 79]

Market Mechanisms and Maximization, Part I: "The Theory of Comparative Advantage"; Part II: "The Cheapest-Adequate-Diet Problem"; and Part III: "Dynamics and Linear Programming"; published by the RAND Corporation, Parts I and II, March 28, 1949, and Part III, June 29, 1949. [Chapter 33]

"The Le Chatelier Principle in Linear Programming," published by the RAND Corporation, August 4, 1949. [Chapter 43]

"Evaluation of Real National Income," *Oxford Economic Papers* (New Series), Vol. II, No. 1 (Oxford, England: University Press, January 1950), pp. 1–29. [Chapter 77]

"Iterative Computation of Complex Roots," *Journal of Mathematics and Physics*, Vol. XXVII, No. 4 (January 1950), pp. 259–267. [Chapter 58]

"The Problem of Integrability in Utility Theory," *Economica*, Vol. XVII, No. 68 (November 1950), pp. 355–385. [Chapter 10]

"Probability and the Attempts to Measure Utility" (English and Japanese), *The Economic Review* (*Keizai Kenkyu*), Vol. 1 (Tokyo: Hitotsubashi University, July 1950), pp. 167–173. [Chapter 12]

"Principles and Rules in Modern Fiscal Policy: A Neo-Classical Reformulation," in *Money, Trade and Economic Growth: Essays in Honor of John Henry Williams* (New York: Macmillan, 1951), pp. 157–176. [Chapter 98]

"Abstract of a Theorem Concerning Substitutability in Open Leontief Models," Chapter VII in Cowles Commission for Research in Economics, *Activity Analysis of Production and Allocation,* ed. by T. C. Koopmans (New York: Wiley, 1951). [Chapter 36]

"Economic Theory and Wages," in David McCord Wright, ed., *The Impact of the Union: Eight Economic Theorists Evaluate the Labor Union Movement* (New York: Harcourt, Brace, 1951), pp. 312–342. [Chapter 117]

"Schumpeter as a Teacher and Economic Theorist," *The Review of Economics and Statistics,* Vol. XXXIII, No. 2 (May 1951), pp. 98–103. Copyright 1951 by the President and Fellows of Harvard College. [Chapter 116]

"Comment," in *A Survey in Contemporary Economics,* Vol. II, ed. by B. F. Haley (Homewood, Ill.: Richard D. Irwin, 1952). [Chapter 81]

"A Comment on Factor Price Equalisation," *The Review of Economic Studies,* Vol. XIX (2), No. 49 (February 1952), pp. 121–122. [Chapter 69]

"Economic Theory and Mathematics: An Appraisal," *The American Economic Review,* Vol. XLII, No. 2 (May 1952), pp. 56–66. [Chapter 126]

"Spatial Price Equilibrium and Linear Programming," *The American Economic Review,* Vol. XLII, No. 3 (June 1952), pp. 283–303. [Chapter 72]

"The Transfer Problem and Transport Costs: The Terms of Trade When Impediments Are Absent," *Economic Journal,* Vol. LXII, No. 246 (June 1952), pp. 278–304. [Chapter 74]

"Probability, Utility, and the Independence Axiom," *Econometrica,* Vol. 20, No. 4 (October 1952), pp. 670–678. [Chapter 14]

"Rapidly Converging Solutions to Integral Equations," *Journal of Mathematics and Physics,* Vol. XXXI, No. 4 (January 1953), pp. 276–286. [Chapter 59]

"Consumption Theorems in Terms of Overcompensation rather than Indifference Comparisons," *Economica,* New Series, Vol. XX, No. 77 (February 1953), pp. 1–9. [Chapter 11]

"Prices of Factors and Goods in General Equilibrium," *The Review of Economic Studies,* Vol. XXI (1), No. 54 (1953–1954), pp. 1–20. [Chapter 70]

"Full Employment versus Progress and Other Economic Goals," Chapter XII of Max Millikan, ed., *Income Stabilization for a Developing Economy* (New Haven: Yale University Press, 1953). [Chapter 99]

With R. M. Solow, "Balanced Growth under Constant Returns to Scale," *Econometrica,* Vol. XXI, No. 3 (July 1953), pp. 412–424. [Chapter 24]

"The Transfer Problem and Transport Costs, II: Analysis of Effects of Trade Impediments," *Economic Journal,* Vol. LXIV, No. 254 (June 1954), pp. 264–289. [Chapter 75]

"The Pure Theory of Public Expenditure," *The Review of Economics and Statistics,* Vol. XXXVI, No. 4 (November 1964), pp. 387–389. Copyright 1954 by the President and Fellows of Harvard College. [Chapter 92]

Acknowledgments

"Some Psychological Aspects of Mathematics and Economics," *The Review of Economics and Statistics*, Vol. XXXVI, No. 4 (November 1954), pp. 380–382. Copyright 1954 by the President and Fellows of Harvard College. [Chapter 127]

Comment on "Professor Samuelson on Operationalism in Economic Theory," by Donald F. Gordon, in *The Quarterly Journal of Economics*, Vol. LXIX (May 1955), pp. 310–314. [Chapter 128]

"Linear Programming and Economic Theory," *Proceedings of the Second Symposium in Linear Programming* (Washington, D. C., National Bureau of Standards and U. S. Air Force, January 27–29, 1955), Vol. 1, pp. 251–272. [Chapter 34]

"The New Look in Tax and Fiscal Policy," Joint Committee on the Economic Report, 84th Congress, 1st Session, *Federal Tax Policy for Economic Growth and Stability*, November 9, 1955 (Washington: U. S. Government Printing Office, 1956), pp. 229–234. [Chapter 100]

"Diagrammatic Exposition of a Theory of Public Expenditure," *The Review of Economics and Statistics*, Vol. XXXVII, No. 4 (November 1955), pp. 350–356. Copyright 1955 by the President and Fellows of Harvard College. [Chapter 93]

"Social Indifference Curves," *The Quarterly Journal of Economics*, Vol. LXX, No. 1 (February 1956), pp. 1–22. [Chapter 78]

"Economic Forecasting and National Policy" in *The Employment Act Past and Future: A Tenth Anniversary Symposium*, edited by Gerhard Colm (Washington: National Planning Association, Special Report No. 41 (February 1956), pp. 130–134. [Chapter 101]

"Recent American Monetary Controversy," *Three Banks Review*, March 1956, pp. 1–21. [Chapter 109]

With R. M. Solow, "A Complete Capital Model Involving Heterogeneous Capital Goods," *The Quarterly Journal of Economics*, Vol. LXX (November 1956), pp. 537–562. [Chapter 25]

"The Economics of Eisenhower: A Symposium," *The Review of Economics and Statistics*, Vol. XXXVIII, No. 4 (November 1956), pp. 371–373. Copyright 1956 by the President and Fellows of Harvard College. [Chapter 110]

"Wages and Interest: A Modern Dissection of Marxian Economic Models," *The American Economic Review*, Vol. XLVII, No. 6 (December 1957), pp. 884–912. [Chapter 29]

"Intertemporal Price Equilibrium: A Prologue to the Theory of Speculation," *Weltwirtschaftliches Archiv*, Band 79, Heft 2 (Hamburg: Hoffmann & Campe Verlag, December 1957), pp. 181–219. [Chapter 73]

Book review of J. de V. Graaff, *Theoretical Welfare Economics* in *The Economic Journal*, Vol. 68, No. 271 (September 1958), pp. 539–541. [Chapter 80]

"Aspects of Public Expenditure Theories," *The Review of Economics and Statistics*, Vol. XL, No. 4 (November 1958), pp. 332–338. Copyright 1958 by the President and Fellows of Harvard College. [Chapter 94]

"Frank Knight's Theorem in Linear Programming," *Zeitschrift Für National-ökonomie*, Band XVIII, Heft 3 (1958), pp. 310–317. [Chapter 35]

"An Exact Consumption-Loan Model of Interest with or without the Social Contrivance of Money," *The Journal of Political Economy*, Vol. LXVI, No. 6 (December 1958), pp. 467–482. Copyright 1958 by the University of Chicago. [Chapter 21]

Book review of Torsten Gårdlund, *The Life of Knut Wicksell* in *The Review of Economics and Statistics*, Vol. XLI, No. 1 (February 1959), pp. 81–83. Copyright 1959 by the President and Fellows of Harvard College. [Chapter 120]

"A Modern Treatment of the Ricardian Economy: I. The Pricing of Goods and of Labor and Land Services," *The Quarterly Journal of Economics*, Vol. LXXIII, No. 1 (February 1959), pp. 1–35. [Chapter 31]

"What Economists Know," Chapter 7 in Daniel Lerner, ed., *The Human Meaning of the Social Sciences* (New York: Meridian Books, 1959), pp. 183–213. © Copyright by Meridian Books, Inc., 1959. [Chapter 121]

"A Modern Treatment of the Ricardian Economy: II. Capital and Interest Aspects of the Pricing Process," *The Quarterly Journal of Economics*, Vol. LXXIII, No. 2 (May 1959), pp. 217–231. [Chapter 32]

"Alvin Hansen and the Interactions between the Multiplier Analysis and the Principle of Acceleration," *The Review of Economics and Statistics*, Vol. XLI, No. 2, Part I (May 1959), pp. 183–184. Copyright 1959 by the President and Fellows of Harvard College. [Chapter 84]

"Reply" (Abba P. Lerner, "Consumption-Loan Interest and Money"), *The Journal of Political Economy*, Vol. LXVII, No. 5 (October 1959), pp. 518–522. Copyright 1959 by the University of Chicago. [Chapter 22]

"The St. Petersburg Paradox as a Divergent Double Limit," *International Economic Review*, Vol. 1, No. 1 (January 1960), pp. 31–37. [Chapter 15]

"Infinity, Unanimity, and Singularity: A Reply," *The Journal of Political Economy*, Vol. LXVIII, No. 1 (February 1960), pp. 76–83. Copyright 1960 by the University of Chicago. [Chapter 23]

With R. M. Solow, "Analytical Aspects of Anti-Inflation Policy," *The American Economic Review*, Vol. L, No. 2 (May 1960), pp. 177–194. [Chapter 102]

"American Economics," in Ralph E. Freeman, ed., *Postwar Economic Trends in the U.S.* (New York: Harpers, 1960), pp. 31–50. [Chapter 122 includes pp. 44–50 only]

"Harold Hotelling as Mathematical Economist," *American Statistician*, Vol. XIV, No. 3 (June 1960), pp. 21–25. [Chapter 118]

"Structure of a Minimum Equilibrium System," in Ralph W. Pfouts, ed., *Essays in Economics and Econometrics: A Volume in Honor of Harold Hotelling* (Chapel Hill: University of North Carolina Press, 1960), pp. 1–33. [Chapter 44]

"An Extension of the LeChatelier Principle," *Econometrica*, Vol. 28, No. 2 (April 1960), pp. 368–379. [Chapter 42]

Acknowledgments

"Efficient Paths of Capital Accumulation in Terms of the Calculus of Variations," in Kenneth J. Arrow, Samuel Karlin, and Patrick Suppes, eds., *Mathematical Methods in the Social Sciences, 1959* (Stanford: Stanford University Press, 1960), pp. 77–88. [Chapter 26]

"Reflections on Monetary Policy," *The Review of Economics and Statistics*, Vol. XLII, No. 3, Part 1 (August 1960), pp. 263–269. Copyright 1960 by the President and Fellows of Harvard College. [Chapter 103]

"Wages and Interest — A Modern Dissection of Marxian Economic Models: Reply," *The American Economic Review*, Vol. L, No. 4 (September 1960), pp. 719–721. [Chapter 30]

"Prospects and Policies for the 1961 American Economy," a Report to President-Elect Kennedy, Thursday, January 6, 1961. Reprinted as Chapter 3, "Economic Frontiers," in M. B. Schnapper, ed., *New Frontiers of the Kennedy Administration* (Washington, D.C: Public Affairs Press, 1961). [Chapter 111]

"The Evaluation of 'Social Income': Capital Formation and Wealth," Chapter 3 in F. A. Lutz and D. C. Hague, eds., *The Theory of Capital* (London: Macmillan, 1961), pp. 32–57. [Chapter 27]

"A New Theorem on Nonsubstitution," in *Money, Growth, and Methodology*, published in honor of Johan Åkerman, Vol. 20, Lund Social Science Studies (Lund, Sweden: CWK Gleerup, March 1961), pp. 407–423. [Chapter 37]

"Problems of the American Economy: An Economist's View," Stamp Memorial Lecture, delivered before the University of London on November 9, 1961 (London: The Athlone Press, 1962), pp. 1–30. [Chapter 123]

"Economists and the History of Ideas," (Presidential Address), *The American Economic Review*, Vol. LII, No. 1 (March 1962), pp. 1–18. [Chapter 113]

"Economic Policy for 1962," *The Review of Economics and Statistics*, Vol. XLIV, No. 1 (February 1962), pp. 3–6. Copyright 1962 by the President and Fellows of Harvard College. [Chapter 112]

Memorandum for The Royal Commission on Banking and Finance, Ottawa, Canada, October 19, 1962. [Chapter 104]

"Parable and Realism in Capital Theory: The Surrogate Production Function," *The Review of Economic Studies*, Vol. XXIX, No. 3 (June 1962), pp. 193–206. [Chapter 28]

"The Gains from International Trade Once Again," *The Economic Journal*, Vol. LXXII (December 1962), pp. 820–829. [Chapter 62]

"Stability and Growth in the American Economy," Wicksell Lectures 1962 (Stockholm: Alqvist and Wiksell, December 1962). [Chapter 124]

"Comment on Ernest Nagel's 'Assumptions in Economic Theory,'" *Papers and Proceedings of the American Economic Association*, December 29, 1962, pp. 231–236. [Chapter 129]

"Fiscal and Financial Policies for Growth," *Proceedings — A Symposium of Economic Growth*, sponsored by The American Bankers Association, Monday, February 25, 1963, Washington, D.C., pp. 78–100. [Chapter 105]

"Risk and Uncertainty: A Fallacy of Large Numbers," *Scientia*, 6th Series, 57th year (April–May 1963). [Chapter 16]

"Economic Thought and the New Industrialism," in Arthur M. Schlesinger, Jr., and Morton White, eds., *Paths of American Thought* (Boston: Houghton Mifflin Company, 1963), pp. 219–237. [Chapter 125]

"Modern Economic Realities and Individualism," *The Texas Quarterly*, Summer 1963, pp. 128–139. [Chapter 106]

"The Economic Role of Private Activity," in *A Dialogue on the Proper Economic Role of the State*, discussion given at Swarthmore, early 1963; Selected Papers No. 7, University of Chicago Graduate School of Business. [Chapter 107]

"Reflections on Central Banking," *The National Banking Review*, Vol. 1, No. 1 (September 1963), pp. 15–28. [Chapter 104]

"D. H. Robertson (1890–1963)", *The Quarterly Journal of Economics*, Vol. LXXVII, No. 4 (November 1963), pp. 517–536. [Chapter 119]

"The General Theory," and "A Brief Survey of Post-Keynesian Developments" in Robert Lekachman, ed., *Keynes' General Theory: Reports of Three Decades* (New York: St. Martin's Press, 1964), pp. 315–347. [Chapters 114 and 115]

"Theoretical Notes on Trade Problems," *The Review of Economics and Statistics*, Vol. XLVI, No. 2 (May 1964), pp. 145–154. Copyright 1964 by the President and Fellows of Harvard College. [Chapter 65]

"Equalization by Trade of the Interest Rate Along with the Real Wage," in *Trade, Growth, and the Balance of Payments*, essays in honor of Gottfried Haberler (Chicago: Rand McNally & Co., 1965), pp. 35–52. [Chapter 71]

INDEX

Unemployed, reserve army of, 365, 382 n., 389, 1511, 1561 n.
Unemployment, 1183 ff.
  automation and, 1673
  disguised, 1260
  and inflation, 1341 ff.
  involuntary, 1182
  in large versus small cities, 1258–1259, 1263–1269
  rural versus urban, 1260–1263
  versus stable prices, 1477
Unemployment compensation, 1486–1487
Uniformity, the new, 1629–1630
Uniqueness of equilibrium, theorem of, 908
Uniqueness in the large, theorem of, 908
Unitary income elasticities, 1030–1031
Urban renewal programs, 1486
Urbanization
  as cause of unemployment, 1269–1270
  trends in, 1266–1269
U.S. Budget, *see* Budget, U.S.
U.S. Treasury, *see* Treasury, U.S.
Utility, 3 ff., 75 ff., 127 ff., 137 ff., 212–218
  Bernoulli theory, 119 ff., 127 ff.
  cardinal, 3, 15 ff., 38, 117 ff., 129, 137
  diminishing marginal, 21
  Friedman-Savage theory, 121
  Giffen's paradox, 23 n.
  history, 21
  integrable, 3, 10, 75 ff.
  marginal, 35–53, 1013 ff.
  marginal rate of substitution, 3, 4
  measurability, 3
  von Neumann-Morgenstern theory, 120
  ordinal, 15 ff., 117 ff., 137
  ordinality, 22, 776
  Weber-Fechner law, 21, 93
Utility feasibility function, 1062 ff.
Utility possibility frontier, 795 ff., 1079, 1228
  maximal, 1223
Utility-possibility function, 1049 ff.
Utility satiation, 273 ff.
Uzawa, H., 338

Valk, W. L., 497
Vandermonde-Cauchy matrix, 721
Vandermonde determinant, 721
Vandermonde matrix, 713, 715, 716, 717, 727
Van der Pol, B., *see* Pol, B. van der
Vanek, Jaroslav, 909 n., 922, 923 n.
Veblen, Thorstein, 1062 n., 1082, 1629, 1683, 1684, 1736, 1742, 1743, 1745, 1746

Vectors
  characteristic, 727–728
  latent, of a matrix, 718 ff.
Velocity of money, 1140, 1143, 1144, 1158 n., 1166 ff., 1358, 1604
  and the multiplier, 1140 ff., 1166 ff.
Verhulst-Pearl logistic, 378
Vickrey, W., 120 n.
Villard, H. H., 1140 n., 1169 n., 1170
Ville, 114
Viner, Jacob, 202 n., 381 n., 391 n., 535, 542 n., 790 n., 792, 803, 828, 832 n., 834, 843 n., 847 n., 851 n., 856 n., 864 n., 866 n., 886, 926 n., 945 n., 986 ff., 1028, 1030, 1036, 1037, 1076 n., 1355, 1415 n., 1603, 1650, 1738, 1743
Vinson, Fred M., 1256, 1257, 1467
Voltaire, 428, 1503
Volterra, Vito, 75, 217 n., 568 n., 748, 1194 n.
Volterra linear integral equations, 568 n.
Von Mises, L., *see* Mises, L. von
Von Mises, R., *see* Mises, R. von
Von Neumann, J., *see* Neumann, J. von
Von Stackelberg, H., *see* Stackelberg, H. von
Von Thünen, J. H., *see* Thünen, J. H. von
Von Wieser, F., *see* Wieser, F. von

Wage fund, 361, 1561–1565
Wage-price spiral, 1491–1492
Wages
  and economic theory, 1557–1587
  falling, 349
  indeterminacy of, 1565, 1567
  iron law of, 1559
  purchasing power theory of, 1577 ff.
  real, 831 ff.
    and employment, 1182
  theories on, 1558–1559
Wagner, C., 753, 754
Wald, Abraham, 495, 497, 499, 500, 505 n., 730, 732, 733, 735, 886, 1091 ff.
Wald statistical decision theory, 495
Walker, Francis, 1562, 1732, 1737
Wallich, H. C., 1204 n.
Walras, Léon, 21, 248, 364, 365, 380, 390, 403, 412, 495, 497, 505, 511, 512, 542, 545, 546, 551, 590, 802, 804, 866 n., 920, 988, 1074, 1084, 1091, 1099, 1187, 1189, 1271, 1336, 1411 n., 1501, 1502, 1513, 1521, 1556, 1566, 1572 n., 1576, 1588, 1611 n., 1614, 1682, 1686, 1687, 1688, 1689, 1738, 1753, 1754, 1756, 1758, 1760, 1766